Employment Law

ASPEN CASEBOOK SERIES

Employment Law

Private Ordering and Its Limitations

Fourth Edition

Timothy P. Glynn
Senior Associate Dean and
Andrea J. Catania Endowed Professor
Seton Hall Law School

Charles A. Sullivan
Professor of Law and
Senior Associate Dean of Finance and Faculty
Seton Hall Law School

Rachel S. Arnow-Richman
Chauncey Wilson Memorial Research Professor and
Director, Workplace Law Program
University of Denver Sturm College of Law

 Wolters Kluwer

Published by Wolters Kluwer in New York.

Wolters Kluwer Legal & Regulatory U.S. serves customers worldwide with CCH, Aspen Publishers, and Kluwer Law International products. (www.WKLegaledu.com)

To contact Customer Service, e-mail customer.service@wolterskluwer.com, call 1-800-234-1660, fax 1-800-901-9075, or mail correspondence to:

> Wolters Kluwer
> Attn: Order Department
> PO Box 990
> Frederick, MD 21705

Printed in the United States of America.

1 2 3 4 5 6 7 8 9 0

ISBN 978-1-5438-0106-4

Library of Congress Cataloging-in-Publication Data

Names: Glynn, Timothy P., 1967- author. | Sullivan, Charles A., author. | Arnow-Richman, Rachel, 1970- author.
Title: Employment law : private ordering and its limitations / Timothy P. Glynn, Senior Associate Dean and Andrea J. Catania Endowed Professor, Seton Hall Law School; Charles A. Sullivan, Professor of Law and Senior Associate Dean of Finance and Faculty, Seton Hall Law School; Rachel S. Arnow-Richman, Chauncey Wilson Memorial Research Professor and Director, Workplace Law Program, University of Denver, Sturm College of Law.
Description: Fourth edition. | New York : Wolters Kluwer, [2019] | Series: Aspen casebook series | Includes bibliographical references and index.
Identifiers: LCCN 2018056064
Subjects: LCSH: Labor laws and legislation—United States. | LCGFT: Casebooks (Law)
Classification: LCC KF3455 .G59 2019 | DDC 344.7301—dc23
LC record available at https://lccn.loc.gov/2018056064

About Wolters Kluwer Legal & Regulatory U.S.

Wolters Kluwer Legal & Regulatory U.S. delivers expert content and solutions in the areas of law, corporate compliance, health compliance, reimbursement, and legal education. Its practical solutions help customers successfully navigate the demands of a changing environment to drive their daily activities, enhance decision quality and inspire confident outcomes.

Serving customers worldwide, its legal and regulatory portfolio includes products under the Aspen Publishers, CCH Incorporated, Kluwer Law International, ftwilliam. com and MediRegs names. They are regarded as exceptional and trusted resources for general legal and practice-specific knowledge, compliance and risk management, dynamic workflow solutions, and expert commentary.

For My Parents
T.P.G.

For Jack Paul
C.A.S.

For My Students, Past, Present & Future
R.S.A.R.

Summary of Contents

Contents

Preface

Few institutions receive greater attention in Americans' private lives and in public policy debates than employment. Employment is everywhere: It is the means by which most Americans make their living; it is, for many, where they spend the majority of their waking hours and develop most of their interpersonal relationships; and it provides the primary economic input ("human capital") firms and government agencies rely on to produce their goods and services.

Because of its pervasiveness and importance, employment-related issues, such as outsourcing to foreign countries or whether to raise the minimum wage, receive significant public attention. More profoundly, many of the fundamental policy disputes of the day—immigration, health care, civil rights, environmental regulation, information privacy, globalization, social security, and tax policy—are either inherently entangled with employment or heavily influenced by employment-related considerations.

Thus, the institution of employment is paramount not just for individual workers and employing firms and government agencies, but also for society as a whole. Correspondingly, then, the legal rules governing the employment relationship have profound implications beyond the two parties to that relationship. This book will introduce you to the core aspects of this body of law and its implications.

As you work your way through the book, you will discover that the structure of employment law is complex and varied. It derives from multiple sources, including contract, tort, agency law, state and federal statutes, and, at least for government workers, federal and state constitutions. In addition, its application varies greatly depending upon a number of factors, including type of worker (e.g., employee v. nonemployee, unionized v. nonunionized, white collar v. blue collar, disabled v. nondisabled); type of employer (large v. small, public v. private); type of industry; and jurisdiction (state v. state). Moreover, because American employment law leaves fundamental aspects of the relationship largely for the parties to determine, the "law" governing the American workplace is subject to immense individual variation. Indeed, for many workers, the most important terms of their relationship—including wage levels, benefits, hours, job security, and privacy considerations—are far more likely to be determined by market forces than by externally imposed legal mandates. Finally, like the structure of the workplace itself, the law of employment is ever-changing.

Given its intricate and dynamic nature, employment law is challenging to understand and apply. This is what makes your study of it so critical. Workers and firms must rely heavily on counsel for advice on how to (1) structure working relationships to protect their interests and minimize their risks and (2) advocate on behalf of these interests when disputes arise. Similarly, employment policy makers need a solid understanding of the legal doctrines that govern employment, their implications and limitations, and how the varied aspects of the law interact with one another. This need for employment law expertise extends well beyond those engaged in employment-related work since employment and its legal rules have implications for a wide range of other areas and disciplines.

This text provides an accessible and comprehensive introduction into the study of employment law. Following the Introduction, the book contains seven parts with thirteen chapters exploring various employment law topics. You will be introduced immediately to our unifying theme of private ordering and its limitations—that is, the core tension in the law between the terms the parties themselves establish and publicly imposed mandates. In pursuing this theme through the various subtopics that make up our discipline, not only will you master (sometimes abstruse) doctrine but you will also be asked repeatedly to consider the law from transactional, counseling, litigation, and policy-making perspectives.

We have included standard cases to provide you with a solid background in each topic area. These are supplemented with more recent decisions addressing cutting-edge issues in the twenty-first century, including the growth of outsourcing and contingent (semi- or nonpermanent) work arrangements, the role of new whistleblower protections such as those in the Sarbanes-Oxley and Dodd-Frank laws, privacy in the workplace, new developments with regard to noncompetition agreements, important changes in antidiscrimination law, the law's role in facilitating the work/family balance, and the growth in various risk-management techniques by employers. We also provide extensive notes and commentary that offer further background and probe deeper into the compelling and difficult employment developments of the day. Finally, each chapter contains problems designed to expose you to the real-world challenges employment counsel face as both planners and litigators. If you want to sample even more recent developments in employment law, visit the casebook's website at http://law.shu.edu/private_ordering.

We believe this text offers a cohesive, thorough, and fascinating first look at employment-law theory and practice. We hope you enjoy it.

A Note on Editing

In cases and law review excerpts, all omissions are indicated by ellipses or brackets, except for footnotes and citations, many of which have been deleted or shortened to enhance readability. The footnotes that remain retain their original numbers.

Timothy P. Glynn
Charles A. Sullivan
Rachel S. Arnow-Richman

December 2018

Acknowledgments

Like all casebooks, Employment Law: Private Ordering and Its Limitations builds on the experiences of its authors in wrestling with the problems of employment law with their law students at Seton Hall and the University of Denver. At each of these law schools, colleagues provided important insights in the formation of our pedagogic approaches. In a more focused way, we are indebted to the late Mike Zimmer of Loyola Chicago (emeritus at Seton Hall) and Rebecca Hanner White, former Dean of Georgia, for their generosity in allowing us to abridge portions of Cases and Materials on Employment Discrimination (Aspen, 8th ed. 2012) and to Mike Zimmer and to Deborah Calloway of the University of Connecticut for permitting us to draw on a precursor to the present book, Cases and Materials on Employment Law (Aspen, 1993). Despite these deep intellectual debts, Private Ordering is a radical departure from earlier efforts, offering a new understanding of employment law as both a scholarly discipline and a vibrant field of practice.

This casebook would not have been possible without the support of Barbara Roth, Carol McGeehan, Richard Mixter, Troy Froebe, Kathy Langone, Sylvia Rebert, Dana Wilson, and Sarah Hains. Moreover, we all want to thank Mike Zimmer and Judd Sneirson, who were brave enough to teach out of the first edition as it was being written and provided us with invaluable feedback. Professor Arnow-Richman particularly acknowledges the support of Melissa Hart, Martin Katz, Nantiya Ruan, and Catherine Smith. We are also grateful to the unidentified professors who Aspen retained to review chapters as they emerged from the three authors. While we do not know who these reviewers are, they will see our responses to their critiques throughout this work.

Then there are the individuals who helped us turn this project into reality. They include Teresa Rizzo, Ana Santos, Silvia Cardoso, Beth Krauzlis, and Latisha Porter, Professors Sullivan's and Glynn's administrative assistants at Seton Hall, and the following Seton Hall research assistants for both Professors Sullivan and Glynn: Carmella Campisano and Andrew Raimondi, Seton Hall class of 2020; John Dumnich and Angela Raleigh, Seton Hall class of 2016; Michael Amalfe, Kelly Bradshaw, Mark Heftler, Temenouga R. Kolarova, Renee Levine, Steven Morris, and Caitlin Petry, class of 2012; Alison Andolena, class of 2011; Michele Austin, Christina Bae, Joseph Fanning, Robert Flanagan, Angela Kopolovich, Gregory Reid, and Allison Scaduto, class of '08; Lauren DeWitt, Rawan Hmoud, and Mohamed Shiliwala, class of '07; Julie Yoo, class of '06; and Monica Perrette, Shulamit Shvartsman, and Lauren Walter, class of '05. Professor Arnow-Richman would like to thank Melissa Brand, Lindsay Burleson, Keenan Jones, Crystal Littrell-Miller, Lindsay Noyce, Marlys Hartley Roehm, and Cristel Shepherd from the University of Denver; James Boyer and Ralph Powell from Temple Law School; and her fall 2005 Law of the Workplace students.

As the copious citations to scholarship indicate, we have benefited greatly from the many scholars who have focused their research on employment issues. We have collected the citations in a Table of Selected Secondary Authorities at page 1011, but we acknowledge more directly the following for permission to reprint parts of their work:

Price Fishback & Shawn Kantor, *The Adoption of Worker's Compensation in the United States, 1900–30*, 41 J.L. & Econ. 305, 315-19 (1998). Reprinted with permission.

Ethan Lipsig et al., Planning and Implementing Reductions in Force, C922 ALI-ABA 1165, 1231-36 (1994). Reprinted with permission.

Introduction

Private Ordering and Its Limitations

For most of its history, employment law in the United States has been a constant struggle between private ordering and government mandates. The term "private ordering" refers to the rules the parties themselves establish to govern their relationship. Such ordering may occur by the parties' express agreement, such as in a collective bargaining agreement or an individual employment contract. Absent formal agreement, such terms may be implied from the circumstances. In addition, private ordering may occur in absence of any express or implied agreement through a "default rule" establishing terms unless the parties "opt out" by an agreement to the contrary. As you will explore in later chapters, the most prominent default rule in American employment law is the notion that the relationship is "at will"—that is, that it may be terminated by either party at any time for any reason.

In contrast to a pure private-ordering regime, public mandates are government-imposed limitations that directly set terms and conditions of employment or affect such terms and conditions indirectly. Mandates range from flat commands—such as the requirement that employers pay a minimum wage, grant leave for certain family and medical needs, or provide compensation for workplace injuries—to rules creating procedural mechanisms to govern the workplace. Unionization and collective bargaining are the prime examples of the latter. Mandates are often negative: Employers must not discriminate on the basis of race, sex, or religion. But sometimes they are positive: Employers must reasonably accommodate disabilities if doing so would not cause an undue hardship. Mandates are often distinctive to employment law—such as the requirement that mass layoffs be conducted only with sufficient advance warning. However, they also come from more general sources of law; for instance, the U.S. Constitution provides federal and state government workers some protections that their private sector counterparts lack. A critical aspect of true mandates is the inability of workers to waive the substantive rights provided.

From the 30,000-foot level, the law governing the employment relationship has moved away from purely private ordering and toward greater government regulation. During much of the nineteenth century, laissez faire and "freedom of contract" prevailed in employment—with the striking exception of the law being largely constitutive of the subordination of African Americans and women (indeed, often removing both groups from "employment").

Thus, in the post-Civil War era, the law tended to view employers and employees as equals, whose participation in "market transactions" would result in employment contracts—often "at will"—that the courts would then neutrally enforce. The reality of this view was always dubious. Many scholars have pointed out that cases such as *Bradwell v. Illinois*, 83 U.S. 130 (1873) (upholding a state statute barring women from the practice of law), and the use of antitrust laws to repress unions showed that the law was far from a neutral arbiter and often placed a heavy thumb on the side of the scale favoring employers and the interests of capital. Nevertheless, the prevailing ideology during the nineteenth century and well into the twentieth was one of the supremacy of private ordering, reflected most dramatically by "*Lochner* Era" court decisions that struck down public mandates regulating work in the name of freedom of contract. *See, e.g., Lochner v. New York*, 198 U.S. 45 (1905) (regulation of bakers' working hours); *Coppage v. Kansas*, 235 U.S. 1 (1915) (prohibition on agreements barring employees from joining unions); *Adkins v. Children's Hospital*, 261 U.S. 525 (1923) (minimum wage mandate for female workers).

Even as *Lochner* was decided, however, change was in the air. In the next two decades, workers' compensation regimes would supplant the minimal protections tort law accorded to workers injured on the job. Perhaps critically, this statutory inroad for workers involved a trade-off of more certain liability for lower recoveries and therefore was also in the interests of employers who thereby avoided the risks of a developing tort regime. In any event, as the twentieth century proceeded, workers' rights became increasingly recognized in the law. The Great Depression brought the New Deal, and the New Deal brought, among other initiatives, the National Labor Relations Act ("NLRA"), 29 U.S.C. §§151-69 (2018), protecting the right to unionize and bargain collectively, and the Fair Labor Standards Act ("FLSA"), 29 U.S.C. §§201-19 (2018), establishing a federal minimum wage and regulating overtime and child labor practices. The demise of *Lochner* in the wake of President Roosevelt's court-packing proposal, *see West Coast Hotel Co. v. Parrish*, 300 U.S. 379 (1937), signaled for many the beginning of the end of private ordering.

Fast-forward 30 years, private ordering suffered another assault, beginning with a legislative response to the Civil Rights movement. Title VII of the Civil Rights Act of 1964, 42 U.S.C. §2000e-2000e-17 (2018), ushered in, for the first time on a national level, federal regulation effectively limiting employers' ability to hire and fire at will, by prohibiting discrimination on the basis of race, sex, national origin, and religion. That statute was followed within three years by the Age Discrimination in Employment Act ("ADEA"), 29 U.S.C. §§621-634 (2018), and, after two more decades, by the Americans with Disabilities Act ("ADA") of 1990, 42 U.S.C.A. §§12101-12213 (2018). As a result of these three laws, most employers no longer have free rein in their hiring and firing decisions, and states, even in what had been the Deep South, added their own legislation prohibiting discriminatory employment practices to reach many employers too small to be covered by the federal antidiscrimination laws.

The 1970s saw two further federal inroads on private ordering in employment, the Employee Retirement Income Security Act ("ERISA"), 29 U.S.C. §§1001-1381 (2018), and the Occupational Safety and Health Act ("OSHA"), 29 U.S.C. §§651-78 (2018). ERISA was a response to horror stories of employers firing workers to avoid paying their pensions or otherwise reneging on promises of long-term benefits. The statute was designed to provide both carrots and sticks to ensure an equitable private retirement system. OSHA, more directly command-and-control, was intended to be proactive in protecting worker safety. While the workers' compensation regimes enacted decades earlier ensured payment for injuries suffered, OSHA was designed to prevent injuries in the first place through a series of explicit administrative regulations and corresponding agency enforcement.

On top of these statutory limitations on private ordering, state courts were busy cutting back on what they viewed as the excesses of the at-will rule. This movement produced two major strands—one contractual, the other tort-based. First, drawing on general contract principles, the courts in most states expanded protections for job security beyond formal, written employment contracts to include oral agreements and terms implied from the circumstances. They also began to enforce job security provisions in personnel manuals and read individual agreements or circumstances to provide something more than at-will status. Second, drawing in part on the statutes that proscribe certain reasons as illegitimate bases for employment decisions, the courts began to formulate a tort-based "public policy" exception to the at-will doctrine. That is, while employers remained generally free to fire an employee for most reasons, there were certain reasons that the courts declared to be impermissible. Unlike earlier efforts in this direction that condemned specific reasons for termination (e.g., antiunion animus, race), the newer decisions were more open-ended. An actionable termination was one which offended "public policy," a term whose meaning depends upon judicial interpretation. While employers still did not need a "good" reason to fire someone, they could not act from "bad" reasons, and the list of bad reasons was no longer confined to statutory prohibitions like the antidiscrimination laws.

Thus, by the mid-1980s, public mandates appeared to be winning the day, and private ordering correspondingly seemed in eclipse. But this view was accurate, if at all, only at the 30,000-foot level. Closer to the ground, the picture was significantly different. The NLRA, for example, legalized unions and put the power of the federal government behind collective bargaining. But statutory amendments and court and National Labor Relations Board decisions limited the economic power of unions. In part as a result of these subsequent legal developments, union representation of the private-sector workforce has experienced a steady and dramatic decline over the past half century. Similarly, the FLSA provides for a minimum wage and overtime protection, but it has always contained significant exemptions, and the failure of Congress to increase minimum wage levels to keep pace with inflation means that the federal floor provides very limited, and arguably inadequate, protection. In the antidiscrimination arena, legislative expansion has been countered by judicial contraction, with judicially crafted doctrines and proof problems blunting the thrust of the antidiscrimination laws. This was particularly true of the ADA whose definition of "disability" was subject to such narrow interpretations by the Supreme Court that Congress reacted with the Americans with Disabilities Act Amendments Act of 2008 ("ADAAA"), Pub. L. 110-325, 122 Stat. 3553, to try to provide rights to workers with a broader range of physical and mental impairments. Finally, both OSHA and ERISA have been harshly criticized as ineffective. Indeed, ERISA has come to be seen as a barrier to workers' rights. An example is a decision striking down a Maryland law requiring very large employers, such as Wal-Mart, to provide health insurance for their workers. The court held that the law was preempted by ERISA, which regulates, but does not require, employers to provide any benefits to its workforce. *Retail Indus. Leaders Ass'n v. Fielder*, 435 F. Supp. 2d 481 (D. Md. 2006), *aff'd*, 475 F.3d 180 (4th Cir. 2007). In reality then, despite substantial federal regulation, many aspects of the most important terms of the employment relationship—job security, wages, and benefits—are left to private ordering between employers and employees.

In addition, in recent decades there has been a retreat from mandates and a corresponding increased commitment to private ordering at the state level. While the public policy tort for wrongful discharge has survived, its reach has been narrowed in many states. Further, progressive state contract-law decisions on employee handbooks have been largely negated by judicial approval of employer-drafted disclaimers of contractual liability. In the privacy area, state common-law protections that had emerged in the 1970s have largely disappeared as a practical matter, except where embodied in a few state statutes. Meaningful federal protections are scarce as well, contained only in a few discrete statutes like the Employee Polygraph Protection Act, 29 U.S.C. §§2001-2009 (2018), and the Genetic Information Nondiscrimination Act of 2008 ("GINA"), Pub. L. 110-233, 122 Stat. 881 (May 21, 2008) (codified in various sections of 26, 29, and 42 U.S.C. (2018)).

Other recent developments in employment-law mandates have been mixed as well. For example, in enacting the Family and Medical Leave Act ("FMLA") in 1993, 29 U.S.C. §§2601-54 (2018), Congress finally responded to the calls for protection for employees who want to balance work and family demands. Yet the protection provided is limited both in substance (eligible workers receive only unpaid leave) and scope (only larger employers are covered). Similarly, there has been a substantial growth in statutory whistleblower protections at the state and federal levels, the most prominent examples being the Sarbanes-Oxley Act of 2002 ("SOX"), Pub. L. No. 107-204, 116 Stat. 745, the health care reform law, Pub. L. 111-148, 124 Stat. 119, and the Dodd-Frank financial reform statute, Pub. L. 111-203, 124 Stat. 1376. All of these statutes provide whistleblower protections for employees who report behavior by their employers that violates the substantive provisions of those laws. But these protections, too, tend to be fairly narrowly drawn, leaving workers with perhaps less protection in reality than they might think.

Finally, employers are becoming increasingly creative in augmenting their baseline rights through contract. This can be seen in the widespread reliance on noncompetition clauses and other restrictive covenants. In addition, employers are developing robust forms of private ordering, including various liability and forum management provisions (e.g., arbitration clauses, severance agreements, and forum-selection provisions) that, despite meaningful limitations, fundamentally alter the law's control over private ordering, leaving employers freer to protect their interests and minimize their liability risks.

In short, employment law is a story of private ordering and its limitations. But today, more than ever, it is a complex story, and one in which neither private ordering nor government mandates have achieved unqualified primacy. Importantly, the tension between these competing conceptions generally plays out not at the 30,000-foot level but on the ground in particular employment law practices and disputes. Because the practice of law is largely done from a close-up perspective, it is important to understand what is left to private ordering and what is not and to recognize that today's sphere of free enterprise may be tomorrow's field of government regulation (or vice versa).

The Importance and Elusiveness of Employment Law

This struggle between private ordering and public mandates within American employment law occurs in the context of a universally important relationship. Almost every adult in the United States is or has been an employee. The employment relationship is not only the vehicle through which most Americans make their living, but the workplace is also the place where they spend most of their waking hours and develop many of their interpersonal relationships. For many, personal identity is bound up not only with what they do but with where they do it. Professor Paul Weiler summarized this reality:

> The job rather than the state has become the source of most of the social safety net on which people must rely when they are not employed—that is, when they are sick, disabled, or retired. And the plants and offices in which we work are the places where we spend much of our adult lives, where we develop important aspects of our personalities and our relationships, and where we may be exposed to a variety of physical and psychological traumas.

Paul Weiler, Governing the Workplace: The Future of Labor and Employment Law 3 (1990). The stakes today are perhaps even higher. The development of communications and other technologies has tended to push the "workplace" further into what was previously personal time and space, and aspects of the employment safety net have eroded, making access to "quality" employment (in terms of stability, flexibility, accommodations, wages, benefits, and prospects for intra- or inter-firm mobility, etc.) even more important to workers.

From the employer's perspective, the employment relationship is the means by which firms produce most of their value and government agencies provide most of their services. Indeed, in the modern economy, employers' success often depends more on the quality of their workers—their creativity, cooperation, adaptability, and productivity—than on other assets: "However rich its natural resources, however costly and sophisticated the capital technology, a firm or an economy which does not have a skilled or committed work force will not be able to transform those physical assets into efficient and productive enterprises." *Id.*

Thus, the institution of employment matters a great deal to individual workers, employing firms, government agencies, and society as a whole. Naturally then, the legal rules that govern this relationship have profound, wide-ranging implications.

Yet despite the overview laid out above, employment law is not easy to define or summarize. Even the threshold question of what constitutes "employment"—as opposed to one of several different kinds of relationships in which human beings work with and for others—is uncertain. Unlike other disciplines such as constitutional law, the law of employment does not flow from a single source, nor does it derive from a single doctrinal regime like contracts or torts. Rather, because employment law governs a relationship that is both pervasive and variable, it draws from many sources, for example, contract, tort, agency law, constitutional law, and federal and state statutes.

Just as the sources of employment law vary, so too do its rules. Different legal doctrines apply depending on the state in which an employee works, whether the workplace is unionized, and whether the employer is a public or private entity. Even federal statutes do not provide complete uniformity, but rather govern some employment relationships and not others. This is due to limitations on coverage (small employers are typically exempted, with "small" being defined differently in different statutes) and various codified exemptions (certain "professional" employees, for instance, are excluded from the maximum hours provisions of the FLSA and many agricultural and transportation workers are excluded from coverage completely). The governing law therefore depends on factors such as the type of occupation and the size of the employer. In application, it may also depend on more nebulous factors such as the autonomy and economic vulnerability of the worker, key considerations in determining whether a worker is an employee protected by federal employment statutes.

In addition, as suggested above, many of the terms governing a particular relationship may be established by, and therefore are unique to, the parties in that relationship. The "law" in the American workplace, as it is currently constituted, leaves ample—some would say, too much—room for individual variation in its most important terms, including wage levels, benefits, hours, job security, and privacy protections. All of these critical terms and conditions of employment are far more likely to be determined by the parties' reactions to market forces than by legal constraints. Again, for example, the federally mandated minimum wage is too low to have a direct effect on most workers' negotiating for compensation because both employers and workers start compensation discussions at a point far in excess of that wage. In light of its patchwork nature, understanding when and how the law constrains or promotes these terms, either directly or indirectly, is a formidable challenge.

Finally, the law of employment is dynamic because the workplace is ever-evolving; indeed, the pace of technological, organizational, and market-based changes that affect work and workers is accelerating. Tomorrow's workplace will be very different than today's, and so will tomorrow's law—a law you will help shape after you graduate. At best, then, we can say that employment law embodies the legal rules and standards that govern the employment relationship, but those legal rules and standards vary enormously in kind, substance, and application.

The breadth and variability of employment law poses significant challenges to workers and firms trying to understand their rights and obligations. There is in fact much misunderstanding regarding both, especially among workers. One particularly important example is that most workers believe that the law provides them with greater job security than it actually does, as you will explore in Chapter 2. This misperception can affect worker behavior, for instance, lulling them into thinking they need not seek greater protections, whether through unions, individual contracts, or otherwise. In addition, uncertainty in the law can inflict real costs on employers, not only ex post (litigation expenses and unexpected liabilities) but also ex ante (in terms of risk aversion and investments in planning and compliance).

The maze of employment-law doctrines also creates enormous difficulties for counsel seeking to advise parties on how to comply with the law, protect their interests, and avoid liability and other risks attendant to employment relationships. Given the increasing importance of human capital in our information- and technology-driven economy, a basic understanding of the law of the workplace and its implications is essential even for lawyers practicing in other areas. For example, employment law needs to be understood by attorneys in other fields—from corporate law to intellectual property to health law to privacy and cyber security. And social and cultural trends and conflicts almost always have direct implications for the law of the workplace—the #MeToo movement is the primary contemporary example. Indeed, surveys of corporate general counsel and other practitioners frequently show that, among legal areas, labor and employment litigation and risks rank at or near the top. *See e.g.,* Aebra Coe, *The Four Hottest Practice Areas for 2018*, Law360 (Jan. 1, 2018), available at https://www.law360.com/articles/992014/the-4-hottest-practice-areas-for-2018 (discussing how #MeToo and other phenomena make labor and employment law among the four hottest practice areas). This concern is especially pointed in tough economic times, like the Great Recession, when employers are more likely to lay off workers and terminated workers are less able to find replacement employment. The year 2010 saw the largest number of filings on record at the EEOC—nearly 100,000—although a variety of other factors besides the economy may explain this surge. *See* Nathan Koppel, *Claims Alleging Job Bias Rise with Layoffs,* WALL STREET JOURNAL, Sept. 24, 2010, at A6.

The nature and scope of employment law mean that a single course cannot cover every legal issue and doctrine that may govern or affect the workplace. Largely for this reason, most law schools offer other courses addressing areas of employment law, including courses in Employment Discrimination, Labor Law, Workers' Compensation, Employee Benefits, and even more particularized disciplines, such as Disability Discrimination and Labor and Employment Arbitration. In addition, some of these areas, most notably Labor Law (which governs unionization and collective bargaining), are sufficiently distinct doctrinally that they are best left to separate study, except to the extent they provide context for broader inquiries.

Private Ordering and Its Limitations as a Framework

So how should one approach learning employment law? Despite employment law's disparate sources and wide variability, there is, as we suggested at the outset, a theme common to the law of the workplace. Employment law is, at its core, a course about *private ordering and its limitations.* This description not only captures the core historical conflict over employment regulation but also provides a framework for analyzing the key pressure points in the various aspects of what we call "employment law" today. It is the lens through which we can not only begin to discuss what the law is and what it ought to be in a multitude of contexts but also explore various legal risks and incentives of the parties and the extent to which these may be altered by planning.

This tension between public ordering and private mandates is scarcely unique to employment law. Yet, because the employment relationship is consensual, pervasive, and of profound importance to individual stakeholders and society, this relationship is one of the primary contexts—both qualitatively and quantitatively—in which the law seeks to balance contractual freedoms and market forces with countervailing social interests. Indeed, this tension runs through each doctrinal area in employment, from formation (i.e., whether worker and firm have an "employment" relationship or some other kind of legal status or relationship defined purely by contract) to job security to issues of worker autonomy (e.g., privacy) to discrimination to accommodations for workers' personal needs to employment compensation to how and where employment disputes are resolved.

How to resolve this conflict is therefore a paramount issue in employment law. Unsurprisingly, it is the source of ongoing political, judicial, and scholarly controversy. Whether or not you have seen the term "private ordering" before, you undoubtedly have seen or heard of the conflict between private ordering and its limitations playing out in public policy debates. It is a central theme in the cyclical debates over whether to increase the minimum wage. It also appears frequently in discussions of the "hot" employment issues of the day, including whether to mandate certain types of employer health care coverage, whether to require employers to provide paid parental leave, the extent to which employees ought to be protected from intrusive employer monitoring or oversight, whether to expand whistleblower and other related protections for employees, and whether employers should be able to compel private arbitration of employment disputes.

Some scholars have argued that the various terms of employment should be almost exclusively the product of private ordering. They claim that leaving the terms of employment to individual bargaining ultimately will produce socially optimal arrangements, and that various market forces (such as workers' supposed ability to freely reject or abandon employment) will generally prevent abuse. Indeed, perhaps most famously (or infamously, depending on one's perspective), Professor Richard Epstein has urged that we ought to abandon antidiscrimination laws because market forces ultimately will do a better job of correcting the effects of status-based discrimination. *See generally* RICHARD A. EPSTEIN, FORBIDDEN GROUNDS: THE CASE AGAINST EMPLOYMENT DISCRIMINATION LAWS (1992).

Of course, the scholarly responses to these types of arguments have been legion. Private ordering raises two different sets of concerns. First, scholars have identified a number of "market failures" in labor markets, which they argue justify greater mandated protections for workers. Many have pointed out that individual workers, often due to economic and social vulnerabilities, lack the power and resources to bargain effectively on their own behalf. Other scholars have contended that, even when workers are not economically powerless to protect themselves, they may suffer from informational disadvantages and cognitive constraints in assessing proposed terms of employment. Still others argue for public mandates because, in their view, employer preferences often are based on factors or biases that are not rational in an economic sense, leading to inefficient, discriminatory, or otherwise problematic decisions about who to hire, retain, or promote, and under what terms and conditions. Some of these critiques of private ordering have marshaled empirical evidence to support their claims.

In addition, there is the question of the extent to which private ordering must be constrained because of the negative impact the parties' actions may have on third parties or society as a whole. Few would question whether the public has an interest in protecting itself from employee/employer conduct that inflicts direct and substantial social harm. Indeed, the NLRA was in large part a response to the economic (and sometimes physical) warfare between unions and management that impeded the flow of goods and services to the public. The current debate centers on when such harm exists, when it is sufficient to justify public intervention, how the law ought to intervene, and which decision makers ought to resolve these issues. Indeed, as you work your way through this book, you will see the potential tensions between the interests of worker, firm, and the public, as well as the differing views on when and how to address these competing interests, play out again and again.

This casebook will help you identify the role of private ordering and its limitations in each area and demonstrate how the law currently strikes a balance between them. You will be challenged to think critically about that balance and its effects on workplace incentives and risks from a policy perspective. At the same time, the focus on private ordering means that this casebook is designed to assist you in learning how to be an employment-law practitioner—someone whose decisions help create and structure, that is "order," work relationships. Of course, the lawyer's role includes understanding how to develop persuasive legal arguments in litigation and other employment disputes on behalf of both employees and employers. But, at least as importantly, it also includes assessing and managing risk. The defining aspect of private ordering is the ability of employees and employers to structure their work relationships to protect their interests and reduce legal risks—transactional skills that are becoming more and more dominant in the practice of employment law.

Employment Law in the Twenty-First Century

Now that you have been introduced to the challenges of learning and practicing employment law and the core tension that binds aspects of this discipline together, it is worth taking a moment to appreciate where the law is today. What we now think of as "employment law" in the United States reflects a relatively new development having its roots in the Industrial Revolution. Before that, "employment" in this country took a variety of forms, including indentured servitude, slavery, self-employment, personal service, and family work (primarily on farms). Employment as we know it was not the primary means of earning a living.

After the Civil War, the United States rapidly industrialized and agriculture became increasingly less important. The population of employees grew, including, for the first time, large numbers of women working outside the home/farm and domestic service. By the dawn of the twentieth century, industry became the rule rather than the exception, and employment typically became not merely another option but the only choice. As a result, workers became increasingly dependent on their ability to obtain and retain positions working for others in order to survive. While "contract" theoretically ordered the relationship between these workers and their employers, the increasing economic dependency of employees severely diminished their bargaining power, thus tending to erode their rights.

Although some workers obtained greater protection by virtue of individual employment contracts specifying the terms and conditions of their work, most employers refused to enter into such arrangements with most workers. Employers preferred to be free to hire and fire as they wished, and the common law accommodated this desire by characterizing employment relationships as "at will" unless the parties were especially specific in providing otherwise.

While facially neutral, the at-will rule generally favored employers since they could easily replace an employee who quit; in contrast, a fired employee's options in a period of limited geographic mobility were typically very limited and often very unpalatable. The unrestrained power of employers sometimes manifested itself in starvation wages, unsanitary and dangerous working conditions, long hours, child labor, and little or no job security for many employees.

As sketched above, these conditions led to attempts to deal with the problem of unrestricted industrial power in sweeping ways. In addition to federal approaches to curbing abuse of industrial power, such as antitrust laws, state legislatures made some early attempts to deal directly with the exercise of such power as it affected employment, such as laws regulating maximum hours of work. Again, prior to the New Deal, *Lochner* Era courts repeatedly found such regulation unconstitutional. Still, there were some early reform successes, most notably the widespread creation and adoption of workers' compensation regimes during the Progressive Era.

Also during this period, the American union movement began to make some headway in securing rights for employees despite organized employer resistance and government hostility. The rallying cry of unions was the plight of the workers who were subjected to the unbridled power of employers. The "union solution" was to create countervailing power through the aggregation of workers in the hope that the resultant conflict would produce a balance in the interests of both workers and employers. *See generally* JOHN KENNETH GALBRAITH, AMERICAN CAPITALISM: THE CONCEPT OF COUNTERVAILING POWER (1952).

Unions were concerned with compensation, hours, job safety, and job security. Job security served unions not only by protecting individual members but also as a means to other ends (e.g., eliminating competition between union members to avoid weakening unity and protecting against employer retaliation). As a result, unions typically tried to negotiate contracts with employers limiting the power to discharge individual workers to situations involving "just cause" and specifying how employees should be treated in economic reductions in force, typically by requiring that workers be selected for layoff in reverse order of seniority.

Other initiatives also worked to strengthen job security, albeit among particular subgroups of workers. One was the civil service movement in government employment, which preserved employment "during good behavior" for those who qualified. While civil service protections originated in the nineteenth century, the growth of government during the twentieth century resulted in these systems covering significantly more employees. In addition, advocates of academic tenure (and the job security it provides) were also likewise successful not only for the college and university professors for whom tenure was originally devised, but also for teachers in public elementary and secondary schools. From an economic perspective, both civil service and academic tenure were originally viewed as a tradeoff between lower compensation, on the one hand, and less pressure combined with greater job security on the other.

The Great Depression ushered in leaders more interested in expanding government power and addressing the plight of the common worker. The revised view of government power brought on by the Depression enabled federal and state legislation according employees' basic rights to survive constitutional attack. New Deal legislation was in two forms: first, statutes protecting and supporting employees' efforts to bargain collectively with their employers, and, second, legislation providing the first effective national regulation of some terms and conditions of employment.

Regarding the first category, the NLRA granted workers the right to engage in "concerted action" by protecting such action from employer retaliation. The statute also established a structure for the recognition of unions as "exclusive bargaining representatives" for workers and imposed on employers a duty to bargain with them. This federal labor legislation (and subsequent state efforts aimed at the public sector) did not impose any particular terms and conditions on employers. Rather, it dealt with workplace problems indirectly by establishing a procedure whereby such problems could be resolved by bargaining between the parties. Where unions were strongest, the result was collective bargaining agreements that provided detailed regulation not only of wages and hours, but of many other aspects of employment, including job safety and job security. In its most developed form, this regulation is implemented by a quasi-judicial system of arbitration of disputes between labor and management.

In the short run, unionization became a dominant mode of regulating the employment relationship. Prior to the NLRA, the unionized percentage of the American workforce was less than 15 percent. By the mid-1950s, the number had increased to nearly 40 percent. But, over the next several decades, especially in the 1980s, the union movement faltered. Unions now represent a smaller percentage of American workers—under 11 percent overall and less than 7 percent in the private sector—than before the NLRA was passed. The causes of the decline of the union movement are contested, although, as described previously, less favorable statutory, judicial, and agency treatment has certainly played a role. The merits of unions and collective bargaining remain disputed, but the decline in unionization is undeniable. Thus, for better or worse, although most employees enjoy protections for concerted actions under the NLRA, the vast majority are not employed under or governed by a collective bargaining regime.

The second form of regulation that emerged during the New Deal and thereafter directly regulated the terms and conditions of private employment. The FLSA, setting a minimum hourly wage, is one example. During this period, the federal government also regulated the terms and conditions of "unemployment" by fostering unemployment compensation.

Perhaps in part due to the notion that collective bargaining would address most problems, there was little new direct regulation of terms and conditions of employment for almost 40 years. The 1970s saw Congress enact both OSHA and ERISA: again, despite their differences—OSHA was designed to protect worker safety through a traditional New Deal-style command-and-control approach while ERISA embodied a carrot-and-stick approach to promoting and then protecting employee benefit plans—both regimes remain the subject of significant controversy and criticism. It is worth noting that ERISA was primarily intended to ensure pension benefits for workers, but it also addresses welfare benefits including employer-provided health insurance. It has been expanded over the years by some important amendments, and it now guarantees continuation of health coverage in most terminations of employment—assuming the temporary employee had health benefits to begin with and assuming she is able to bear the group-rate costs of the insurance. However, as discussed previously, this has come at a price since ERISA's preemptive effect has served as a barrier to state-level benefits reforms, most notably in the health care context.

None of these statutory regimes deals primarily or directly with job security; rather, they regulate various aspects of employment. Nevertheless, job security is implicated in most of these laws, at least to the extent that they contain provisions barring employers from retaliating against employees who exercise their statutory rights. A different approach to regulating employer abuses emerged most dramatically in the 1960s—beginning with Title VII and thereafter supplemented by the ADEA, the ADA, and other statutes. The centerpiece of these laws was not direct regulation of terms and conditions of employment; rather, they ruled out certain reasons for employer actions (race, sex, age, disability). Employers, at least in theory, remained free to hire and fire and structure their workplaces for any reason—good or bad— so long as these defined reasons did not influence their decisions. The states were also active during this period, enacting antidiscrimination laws that sometimes went beyond the protections provided by the federal government. One notable example is the numerous state laws prohibiting discrimination based on sexual orientation, which most courts still believe is not prohibited per se under Title VII or any other federal statute.

In sum, by the 1970s, a variety of different legal regimes addressed different aspects of the employment relationship. With respect to job security, individual employees with sufficient bargaining power could negotiate contractual protection. In addition, there were statutes encouraging "procedural" solutions for all workers (such as regulating unionism and the collective bargaining process) and statutes directly providing job security for civil servants and academics. Finally, there were statutes providing some degree of job security by prohibiting certain reasons for firing employees. With respect to terms and conditions of employment, workers were protected by the same set of laws, supplemented by additional statutes directly regulating certain matters (e.g., minimum wages, maximum hours) for private and public, unionized and nonunionized employees.

Although some may have thought this collection of protections adequate, others perceived more exceptions than rules. Certainly, the average worker (employed by a nonunionized, private, nonacademic employer) had relatively narrow protections. Such a person was unlikely to have a personal employment contract and thus was an "at will" employee. Beyond the floor protections provided by minimum wage laws, workers' compensation, OSHA, and prohibitions on status discrimination, a worker would have very little in the way of legal protections.

This reality triggered state common-law efforts to limit employer power and expand employee rights by carving away at the at-will principle through a more expansive view of contract protections and through the public policy tort. While some of these decisions have become a permanent part of the employment landscape, there has also been significant judicial retrenchment in these areas. Similarly, while new state statutory whistleblower and related protections have codified and even expanded the common law developments of the 1970s and 1980s, major new legislation seemed stalled until, in response to examples of corporate misfeasance, SOX provided employee protections, although admittedly not as an end in themselves but rather as a means to ensure an honest securities market. In the wake of the Great Recession, there has been a new spate of whistleblower protections on the federal level as part of the stimulus package and the comprehensive legislation dealing with health care and financial institution regulation. Like SOX, the goal of these provisions is not to protect employees per se but to encourage employees to report violations of the laws' substantive provisions.

Compounding the ferment in the law was a radical restructuring of the economy. As the twentieth century was coming to a close, changes in the nature of the American economy, the workforce, and the structure of the workplace brought new issues to the fore and, correspondingly, presaged new legal developments. For example, consistent with the growing number of households in which all employable adults work, there has been a growing awareness of the need for accommodation of workers' familial and personal needs. Legislative reforms along these lines have been modest, but they include the FMLA, which provides limited protections for employees' life needs in the form of mandated unpaid leave due to a personal medical condition or that of a family member. A very few states provide paid leave or more generous unpaid leave. Similarly, the ADA requires "reasonable accommodation" of disabled individuals in many circumstances and the enactment of the ADAAA promises to revive the significance of this requirement.

Moreover, as discussed previously, as the American economy has transformed into one dominated by services, information, and technology, the value of certain employees has increased. In significant sectors, firms are becoming more dependent on employee creativity, information, and innovation, resulting in a heightened concern among *employers* about protecting themselves. Some find it more than a little telling that a pure at-will regime is now being challenged not merely by advocates of employee interests but also by employers who find themselves increasingly at risk. There has been a rise in litigated conflicts between employers and (often former) employees in such areas as trade secrets, copyrights, and ownership of employee inventions, and claims to business good will, customer lists, and various types of confidential information. Because the default protections for employer interests—employee fiduciary duties and employer intellectual property and trade secrets protections—are limited and often difficult to enforce, there has been dramatic growth in the use of restrictive covenants in recent years. These covenants—including noncompetition, nondisclosure, nonsolicitation, and holdover agreements—are becoming more common, as are questions about the limits the law ought to place on them. Because the stakes on both sides are higher than in past decades, the validity and extent of such agreements are much more frequently litigated.

The governing employment law regime itself, market forces, and other factors have also wrought dramatic changes in the structure of the American workplace. Among the most important is the growth in the outsourcing—both domestic and foreign—of various aspects of production to independent firms or suppliers of labor and the rise of nontraditional working relationships, including growth in independent contracting and part-time work. Undoubtedly, firms take advantage of such non-traditional work structures to avoid some of the legal requirements of "employment" and reduce risks associated with having "employees." By avoiding "employment" relationships and opting instead for independent contractors or other work structures, firms can avoid most statutory protections—which apply only to "employees" and "employers"—along with other legal consequences of an employment relationship, including such things as respondeat superior liability and obligations under immigration laws. The corresponding rise in what some have called the "contingent work-force" may have significant social consequences because these workers, on average, are more likely to be both on the economic margins and less likely—for both legal and practical reasons—to be able to enforce whatever work-related rights they may have.

Yet another change in the workplace is the shift from a fairly hierarchical structure to less formal, more team-oriented workplaces. While hierarchy remains alive and well in many settings, the past decades have seen a flattening of hierarchies as tiers of management are replaced with more collaborative working arrangements. The result is, in one sense, fewer bosses and, in another, more bosses. Such structural changes pose a variety of challenges for the law, especially in areas like sexual harassment.

Finally, sweeping technological innovations are changing the workplace and, correspondingly, creating new legal issues and challenges. The rise of social media, for example, not only has altered the way workers and firms interact with one another, but also has raised new concerns about employer intrusions into worker interests in privacy and free expression. In addition, the deployment of new tools for utilizing data, big data and artificial intelligence are promising to enable enterprises to operate more efficiently, but methods of collection and, increasingly, utilization by managers and human resources professionals raise a host of potential legal concerns, from worker privacy to discrimination to fair wage and hour treatment.

All of these trends are being affected, in one way or another, by the Great Recession from which the country is slowly emerging. Unemployment has dropped to 4% but wage growth has remained remarkably stagnant despite a recent uptick. Although it is still too early to say precisely how economic conditions will affect employment going forward, one does not need a crystal ball to predict that, should we again have a large number of qualified unemployed or underemployed workers hanging over the market, there would be dramatic effects on employment practices.

In short, the law continues to struggle to address these fundamental changes, both as a matter of doctrine and of on-the-ground enforcement. Despite the growth of regulation, the law leaves many decisions regulated only in skeletal ways. Nevertheless, the intersection of various legislative regimes and common-law doctrines means that few employment-related decisions are entirely immune from legal challenge. This reality has produced one final, burgeoning area of employment law, counseling, and litigation. Recent years have seen the rise of "second-level" risk management techniques, usually used by employers, to control or minimize the risks of downstream employment-related conflicts or liabilities. These techniques include internal compliance practices such as the implementation of sexual harassment policies and internal investigations, mandatory pre-dispute arbitration agreements, a rise in substantial severance pay in exchange for releases of claims upon termination, and the inclusion of choice-of-law and choice-of-forum clauses in employment contracts. The substantive law governing these various approaches to risk management differs, as does their success in shifting risk from employers to employees. However, as long as the law of the employment relationship remains uncertain, risk management techniques and the legal rules that constrain them will continue to play a central role in the life of the employment lawyer.

As you can see from this short tour of employment law, the American legal approach to employment in the twenty-first century is a crazy quilt of regulation and laissez faire. For many employees and employers, this means market forces remain far more important than "law" in determining the most important terms of their relationship, including whether "employment" exists at all and how long such a relationship lasts. But there are some significant legal constraints that frame the parties' choices. Understanding this patchwork of laws governing workplace relationships—a combination of contract-law principles operating against a backdrop of tort law rules and general and employment-specific statutes and regulations—presents serious challenges for workers, firms, policy makers, legal counsel, and, of course, law students.

The Organization of This Book

This casebook is organized in 7 parts containing 13 chapters. Part I addresses issues of formation of an employment relationship; that is, whether there is an "employment" relationship at all—as opposed to some other type of relationship—and the consequences that flow from that determination. The 2 chapters in Part II then address how employment terms are set or limited by contract, particularly terms related to job security. They explore the contours of the at-will rule and its exceptions and the interpretation and enforcement of express agreements that vary from this rule and set other important terms of employment, such as compensation.

Part III then turns to tort-based protections for employees: Chapter 4 explores the public policy exception, state statutory antiretaliation and whistleblower provisions modeled on the public policy decisions, and federal approaches, focusing on SOX. Chapter 5 covers traditional workplace torts, including intentional interference with the employment relationship, defamation, intentional infliction of emotional distress, and fraud. The 2 chapters in Part IV then shift the focus to worker autonomy interests, that is, privacy and speech. In both of these contexts, the disparate sources of potential protection are considered (in both the public and the private employer settings) as well as the balance the law strikes between legitimate employer interests and the autonomy interests of workers.

Part V turns to workplace property rights and related interests of employers. Chapter 8 explores various legal safeguards for these interests, including those flowing from fiduciary duty, trade secrets, and intellectual property protections. It also addresses employers' attempts to supplement these legal protections through contract—for example, restrictive covenants such as noncompetition, nonsolicitation, and holdover agreements—and the limits the law places on the scope and enforcement of such provisions.

Part VI contains 4 chapters addressing the principal statutory regimes that govern directly or indirectly various terms and conditions of employment: Chapter 9 explores antidiscrimination mandates; Chapter 10 examines required accommodations for aspects of workers lives, including workers' disabilities, health, pregnancy, and family caregiving needs. Chapter 11 discusses regulation of employee wages, and Chapter 12 reviews legal regimes addressing workplace safety and health. These chapters cover not only the primary federal statutes addressing these matters—such as Title VII, the ADEA, the ADA, the FMLA, the FLSA, and OSHA—but also state workers' compensation regimes (Chapter 12) and state efforts to supplement federal antidiscrimination, accommodation, and wage protections and enforcement.

Finally, Part VII offers a fitting conclusion to the study of employment law by exploring various methods of managing the risks and costs of potential liabilities of employment—liabilities arising from the contractual, common-law, and statutory aspects of employment law you will have explored in earlier chapters. In other words, Chapter 13 addresses the second-level private ordering techniques that employers commonly utilize to control the risks and costs of employment disputes by minimizing liability exposure or choosing the forum within which such disputes are resolved. They include policies for preventing and correcting discriminatory harassment, internal investigations of misconduct, release and severance agreements, arbitration agreements, liquidated damages provisions, liability insurance, and bankruptcy protection. Of course, this survey discusses not only the content of these practices and contractual provisions but also the limitations the law imposes them.

Part One

THE BENEFITS AND BURDENS OF EMPLOYMENT

1

The Stakes of "Employment"

A useful starting point in the study of employment law is this fundamental question: Why does the existence of an "employment" relationship matter? Organizations, both governmental and private, structure their activities in a wide variety of ways, and the individuals who perform work or provide services for these institutions may have various kinds of legal relationships with them and with one another. For example, a person who works on a firm's behalf may be its sole proprietor, a partner, an employee, or an independent contractor. In addition, firms engage other firms to perform some of their activities, leaving to the second firm the task of engaging workers to perform these tasks. For instance, growing attention has been focused on outsourcing various services across international borders and, in the domestic context, on utilizing "contingent"—that is, temporary or nonpermanent—workers.

Distinguishing between employment and other types of relationships is important because each offers its own mix of risks and benefits, both legal and nonlegal—what we call the stakes of employment. For example, many well-known legal protections for workers apply only to "employees." While firms owe duties to employees that they do not owe to other workers, they may benefit from their employer status in various ways. The nature of the work relationship also has important consequences for third parties, who are far more likely to be able to hold firms or government entities liable for injuries caused by their employees than by independent contractors.

To understand the stakes of employment, you must have a basic grasp of the potential rights and obligations arising from the employment relationship and of how they differ from those arising from other relationships. Thus, in this chapter we explore the definitions of "employee" and "employer," the distinctions between employment and other types of legal relationships, and the consequences of employment for employees, employers, and third parties. Workers may prefer to be employees for some reasons and in some circumstances but not others; similarly, firms and government agencies may seek to avoid being employers for certain purposes but may benefit from employer status in other ways. And third parties and the public may have an independent interest in treating some workers as employees but not others.

As you work your way through these preferences and interests, think about the role private ordering should play—that is, the extent to which worker and firm ought to be able to define the nature of their relationship through contract. Should such agreements be enforceable and dispositive, or should the law limit parties' ability to decide whether theirs is an "employment" relationship?

Before reading the cases and notes in this chapter, take a moment to consider the following problem:

PROBLEM

1-1. Compliance Boom. Worldwide Compliance Education, LLC ("WCE"), is a small company that provides training and continuing education to compliance professionals in the financial services industry. WCE's founders and owners, Faith and Ethan Morales, historically have provided onsite, live training programs for compliance professionals within large enterprises, often tailored specifically to that client's needs. Through their efforts, WCE has become very successful and is known as an industry leader in compliance training. WCE now employees eight people (in addition to Faith and Ethan), including assistant trainers and support staff.

As a result of the strength of WCE's brand and the continuing increase in compliance risks, both domestically and abroad, Faith and Ethan have decided to expand the business. After consulting with their principal clients and a business adviser, and securing outside financing, they have decided to begin producing compliance and ethics training videos for sales, brokerage, and other noncompliance personnel working for financial services firms. In Phase I of the expansion, they plan to produce and market both client-specific training modules (tailored to a firm's particular compliance needs) and standard, off-the-shelf modules any company in the finance and insurance industries can purchase. Because they intend to deliver the videos through the web, as well as maintain assessment and interactive components, they will need to develop internet and human resources infrastructure for delivering and hosting the trainings. In Phase II, they intend to develop more advanced modules as well as modules focusing on new developments.

Until now, Faith and Ethan have directly overseen all aspects of WCE. With the new expansion, they will no longer be able to do so. They will have to devote significant time to developing the content of the videos, as well as continuing to serve their clients' live training needs. In addition, the video training venture will require IT, production, and marketing expertise they do not have. WCE will also be moving into a larger office space in a new building it just purchased.

Going forward, Faith and Ethan will continue to manage the entire operation, but they will need to utilize the services of the following people:

- An office manager
- A part-time accounting assistant to handle billing and accounts receivables
- A software engineer and/or information technology expert who will design the web-based system, and—whether the same person or not—an IT professional to maintain and expand the system once it is in operation
- A marketing expert to develop and implement a marketing plan for the videos

- A salesperson who will engage in customer relations and eventually take responsibility for most of WCE's video marketing and sales
- At least two production specialists to create the training videos in Phase I, and then, on the basis of need, a specialist to create and update videos in Phase II and beyond
- On a short-term or "need" basis, various other workers to assist in video production, including script writers, script readers, graphic designers, and editors
- One or more workers to provide maintenance and janitorial services for the new building

Consider this hypothetical from the following perspectives. First, why might WCE decide to treat these workers as employees or independent contractors, or, alternatively, to hire an independent firm to supply the labor or perform particular tasks? Second, why might some of the workers prefer employment with WCE while others may prefer a different relationship? Finally, might the public or third parties have a preference, and, if so, when should their interests override the interests of the parties? And, relatedly, to what extent should WCE's or a worker's expectations, or an agreement between WCE and a worker, determine the nature of the relationship? Continue to consider these questions as you read the material in this chapter.

A. DISTINGUISHING "EMPLOYEE" FROM "INDEPENDENT CONTRACTOR"

By far the most commonly litigated issue in defining the employment relationship is whether a worker is an employee or an independent contractor. This is true for three reasons. First, most workers—that is, participants in the production of firm goods and services—are either employees or independent contractors (as opposed to, inter alia, sole proprietors, corporate directors, or partners or some other type of co-owner).

Second, a host of legal consequences flow from the workers' status, often making this issue worth litigating. For example, most of the federal statutory protections for workers studied in this course cover only "employees." These include federal labor, wage, hour, and benefit protections, *see, e.g.*, Labor Management Relations Act of 1947, 29 U.S.C. §152(2)-(3) (2018); National Labor Relations Act, 29 U.S.C. §158(b)(4)(i) (2018); Employee Retirement and Income Security Act, 29 U.S.C. §1002 (5)-(6) (2018) ("ERISA"); Fair Labor Standards Act of 1938, 29 U.S.C. §201(2) (2018); Family Medical Leave Act of 1993, 29 U.S.C. §2611(3) (2018), as well as most federal prohibitions on status discrimination, *see, e.g.*, Age Discrimination in Employment Act of 1967, 29 U.S.C. §630(f) (2018); Civil Rights Act of 1964, Title VII, 42 U.S.C. §2000e(f) (2018); Americans with Disabilities Act of 1990, 42 U.S.C. §12111(4) (2018). They also include state employment law regimes, including workers compensation laws, and state wage and antidiscrimination protections. There are exceptions, including 42 U.S.C. §1981, which prohibits race and alienage discrimination in most contractual relations, *see Runyon v. McCrary*, 427 U.S. 160 (1976), and the various tort-based protections. But the vast majority of employment law protections—the bulk of those discussed in Chapters 4 through 13—cover only employees.

Third, distinguishing between employees and independent contractors is difficult. As the cases that follow will illustrate, drawing this line is a formidable challenge in terms of both factual and policy analysis. Governing legislation itself rarely offers much meaningful guidance. Indeed, in virtually all of the foregoing statutes, Congress failed to define meaningfully "employee" or "employer," offering only the unhelpful and circular statement that an "employee" is "an individual employed by an employer." Thus, in determining the meaning of "employee" and "employer" in these regimes, the Supreme Court has often held that Congress intended to describe the master-servant relationship as understood by common-law agency doctrine. *See, e.g., Nationwide Mut. Ins. Co. v. Darden*, 503 U.S. 318, 322-23 (1992) (ERISA); *Cmty. for Creative Non-Violence v. Reid*, 490 U.S. 730, 739-40 (1989) (Copyright Act). Regulatory definitions of "employee" from other areas, such as tax law, intellectual property law, and state laws likewise offer variations on the common-law definition.

As we will see in the first two cases, however, reliance on the common-law definition is highly controversial for various reasons. One is that the original purpose of the common-law definition was to determine liability under the doctrine of respondeat superior, which provides that an employer is vicariously (hence strictly) liable for torts committed by its employees within the scope of their employment; the definition was not designed to determine how far labor and employment regulations and protections ought to extend. Nevertheless, given its historical prominence and continued importance, the common-law definition is typically where the employee/independent contractor analysis begins.

As summarized in the Restatement (Second) of Agency, which continues to dominate court discussions despite the promulgration of the Third Restatement of Employment Law (discussed below), a "master" or employer is "a principal who employs an agent to perform service in his affairs and who controls or has the right to control the physical conduct of the other in the performance of the service." RESTATEMENT (SECOND) OF AGENCY, §2(1) (1958). Correspondingly, a servant or employee is "an agent employed by a master to perform service in his affairs whose physical conduct in the performance of the service is controlled or is subject to the right to control by the master." *Id.* §2(2). In contrast, an independent contractor is one "who contracts with another to do something for him but who is not controlled by the other nor subject to the other's right to control with respect to his physical conduct in the performance of the undertaking." *Id.* §2(3). The Restatement goes on to provide a more detailed definition of "servant," a term that has since been displaced by "employee," containing a nonexclusive list of factors for determining servant/employee status:

§ 220. Definition of Servant

(1) A servant is a person employed to perform services in the affairs of another and who with respect to the physical conduct in the performance of the services is subject to the other's control or right to control.

(2) In determining whether one acting for another is a servant or an independent contractor, the following matters of fact, among others, are considered:
>   (a) the extent of control which, by the agreement, the master may exercise over the details of the work;
>   (b) whether or not the one employed is engaged in a distinct occupation or business;
>   (c) the kind of occupation, with reference to whether, in the locality, the work is usually done under the direction of the employer or by a specialist without supervision;
>   (d) the skill required in the particular occupation;
>   (e) whether the employer or the workman supplies the instrumentalities, tools, and the place of work for the person doing the work;
>   (f) the length of time for which the person is employed;
>   (g) the method of payment, whether by the time or by the job;
>   (h) whether or not the work is a part of the regular business of the employer;
>   (i) whether or not the parties believe they are creating the relation of master and servant; and
>   (j) whether the principal is or is not in business.

See also RESTATEMENT (THIRD) OF AGENCY §7.07 (3)(a) (2006) (for purposes of employer vicarious liability, "an employee is an agent whose principal controls or has the right to control the manner and means of the agent's performance of work").

In contrast, the new Restatement of Employment Law, which is not primarily concerned with employer liability to third parties, frames the inquiry somewhat differently. It provides that an employment relationship exists whenever a worker acts, at least in part, to serve the interests of the employer; the employer consents to receive the services of the worker; and the worker is not rendering services as an independent business, which means that the worker does not exercise entrepreneurial control over the manner and means of the work. *See* RESTATEMENT (THIRD) OF EMPLOYMENT LAW §1.01 (2015). Although "control" remains central in this formulation, the test is framed in the negative: namely, that a worker is an employee *unless he or she exerts entrepreneurial control,* which means "control over important business decisions, including whether to hire and where to assign assistants, whether to purchase and where to deploy equipment, and whether and when to service other customers." *Id.* Keep in mind, however, that the ultimate impact of this new Restatement will remain unknown for some time. Although it has been approved by the American Law Institute ("ALI"), no jurisdiction has yet adopted it. Nevertheless, as you read the following cases, consider whether such a formulation is consistent with the analysis or outcome in any of the cases and, if so, whether it is better or worse than existing approaches.

≡ *FedEx Home Delivery v. NLRB*
563 F.3d 492 (D.C. Cir. 2009)

BROWN, *Circuit Judge*:

FedEx Ground Package System, Inc. ("FedEx"), a company that provides small package delivery throughout the country, seeks review of the determination of the National Labor Relations Board ("Board") that FedEx committed an unfair labor practice by refusing to bargain with the union certified as the collective bargaining representative of its Wilmington, Massachusetts drivers. The Board cross-applies for enforcement of its order. Because the drivers are independent contractors and not employees, we grant FedEx's petition, vacate the order, and deny the cross-application for enforcement.

I.

. . . FedEx Home delivers packages of up to 75 pounds, mostly to residential customers. The Wilmington terminals are part of FedEx Home, a network that operates 300 stand-alone terminals throughout the United States . . . . FedEx Home has independent contractor agreements with about 4,000 contractors nationwide with responsibility for over 5,000 routes.

In July 2006, the International Brotherhood of Teamsters, Local Union 25, filed two petitions with the NLRB seeking representation elections at the Jewel Drive and Ballardvale Street terminals in Wilmington, neither of which boasts many contractors. The Union won the elections . . . and was certified as the collective bargaining representative at both. FedEx refused to bargain with the Union[, disputing] the preliminary finding that its single-route drivers are "employees" within the meaning of Section 2(3) of the National Labor Relations Act, 29 U.S.C. §152(3). . . .

II.

To determine whether a worker should be classified as an employee or an independent contractor, the Board and this court apply the common-law agency test, a requirement that reflects clear congressional will. *See NLRB v. United Ins. Co.*, 390 U.S. 254 (1968). . . . While this seems simple enough, the Restatement's non-exhaustive ten-factor test is not especially amenable to any sort of bright-line rule, a long-recognized rub. Thus, "there is no shorthand formula or magic phrase that can be applied to find the answer, but all of the incidents of the relationship must be assessed and weighed with no one factor being decisive," *United Ins. Co.*, always bearing in mind the "legal distinction between 'employees' . . . and 'independent contractors' . . . is permeated at the fringes by conclusions drawn from the factual setting of the particular industrial dispute." *North Am. Van Lines, Inc. v. NLRB*, 869 F.2d 596, 599 (D.C. Cir. 1989) ("*NAVL*").

This potential uncertainty is particularly problematic because the line between worker and independent contractor is jurisdictional—the Board has no authority whatsoever over independent contractors. . .

For a time, when applying this common law test, we spoke in terms of an employer's right to exercise control, making the extent of actual supervision of the means and manner of the worker's performance a key consideration in the totality of the circumstances assessment. Though all the common law factors were considered, the meta-question, as it were, focused on the sorts of controls employers could use without transforming a contractor into an employee. . . . For example, "efforts to monitor, evaluate, and improve" a worker's performance were deemed compatible with independent contractor status. [*NAVL*, 869 F.2d at 599.] . . . "[E]vidence of unequal bargaining power" also did not establish "control." *Id.*

Gradually, however, a verbal formulation emerged that sought to identify the essential quantum of independence that separates a contractor from an employee, a process reflected in cases like *C.C. Eastern* [*Inc. v. NLRB*, 60 F.3d 855 (D.C. Cir. 1995)] and *NAVL* where we used words like control but struggled to articulate exactly what we meant by them. "Control," for instance, did not mean all kinds of controls, but only *certain* kinds. Even though we were sufficiently confident in our judgment that we reversed the Board, long portions of both opinions were dedicated to explaining why some controls were more equal than others. In other words, "control" was close to what we were trying to capture, but it wasn't a perfect concurrence. It was as if the sheet music just didn't quite match the tune.

In any event, the process that seems implicit in those cases became explicit—indeed, as explicit as words can be—in *Corporate Express Delivery Systems v. NLRB*, 292 F.3d 777 (D.C. Cir. 2002). In that case, both this court and the Board, while retaining all of the common law factors, "shift[ed the] emphasis" away from the unwieldy control inquiry in favor of a more accurate proxy: whether the "putative independent contractors have 'significant entrepreneurial opportunity for gain or loss.'" (quoting *Corp. Express Delivery Sys.*, 332 N.L.R.B. 1522, 332 N.L.R.B. No. 144, at 6 (Dec. 19, 2000)). This subtle refinement was done at the Board's urging in light of a comment to the Restatement that explains a "'full-time cook is regarded as a servant,'"—and not "an independent contractor"—"'although it is understood that the employer will exercise no control over the cooking.'" *Id.* (quoting RESTATEMENT (SECOND) OF AGENCY §220(1) cmt. d). Thus, while all the considerations at common law remain in play, an important animating principle by which to evaluate those factors in cases where some factors cut one way and some the other is whether the position presents the opportunities and risks inherent in entrepreneurialism. *Id.*

Although using this "emphasis" does not make applying the test purely mechanical, the line drawing is easier, or at least this court and the Board in *Corporate Express* seem to have so hoped. . . . In *C.C. Eastern*, for instance, we decided drivers for a cartage company who owned their own tractors, signed an independent contractor agreement, "retain[ed] the rights, as independent entrepreneurs, to hire their own employees" and could "use their tractors during non-business hours," and who were "paid by the job" and received no employee benefits, should be characterized as independent contractors. We also noted the company did not require "specific work hours" or dress codes, nor did it subject workers to conventional employee discipline. Conversely, in *Corporate Express*, emphasizing entrepreneurialism, we straightforwardly concluded that where the owner-operators "were not permitted to employ others to do the Company's work or to use their own vehicles for other jobs," they "lacked all entrepreneurial opportunity and consequently functioned as employees rather than as independent contractors." . . .

The record here shares many of the same characteristics of entrepreneurial potential. In the underlying representation decision, the Regional Director found the contractors sign a Standard Contractor Operating Agreement that specifies the contractor is not an employee of FedEx "for any purpose" and confirms the "manner and means of reaching mutual business objectives" is within the contractor's discretion, and FedEx "may not prescribe hours of work, whether or when the contractors take breaks, what routes they follow, or other details of performance"; "contractors are not subject to reprimands or other discipline"; contractors must provide their own vehicles, although the vehicles must be compliant with government regulations and other safety requirements; and "contractors are responsible for all the costs associated with operating and maintaining their vehicles." They may use the vehicles "for other commercial or personal purposes . . . so long as they remove or mask all FedEx Home logos and markings," and, even on this limited record, some do use them for personal uses like moving family members, and in the past "Alan Douglas[] used his FedEx truck for his 'Douglas Delivery' delivery service, in which he delivered items such as lawn mowers for a repair company." Contractors can independently incorporate, and at least two in Wilmington have done so. At least one contractor has negotiated with FedEx for higher fees.

Tellingly, contractors may contract to serve multiple routes or hire their own employees for their single routes; more than twenty-five percent of contractors have hired their own employees at some point. "The multiple route contractors have sole authority to hire and dismiss their drivers"; they are responsible for the "drivers' wages" and "all expenses associated with hiring drivers, such as the cost of training, physical exams, drug screening, employment taxes, and work accident insurance."... The drivers' pay and benefits, as well as responsibility for fuel costs and the like, are negotiated "between the contractors and their drivers." In addition, "both multiple and single route contractors may hire drivers" as "temporary" replacements on their own routes; though they can use FedEx's "Time Off Program" to find replacement drivers when they are ill or away, they need not use this program, and not all do. Thus, contrary to the dissent's depiction, contractors do not need to show up at work every day (or ever, for that matter); instead, at their discretion, they can take a day, a week, a month, or more off, so long as they hire another to be there. "FedEx [also] is not involved in a contractor's decision to hire or terminate a substitute driver, and contractors do not even have to tell FedEx [] they have hired a replacement driver, as long as the driver is 'qualified.'" "Contractors may also choose to hire helpers without notifying FedEx at all; at least six contractors in Wilmington have done so. This ability to hire "others to do the Company's work" is no small thing in evaluating "entrepreneurial opportunity." *Corp. Express.*

Another aspect of the Operating Agreement is significant, and is novel under our precedent. Contractors can assign at law their contractual rights to their routes, without FedEx's permission. The logical result is they can sell, trade, give, or even bequeath their routes, an unusual feature for an employer-employee relationship. In fact, the amount of consideration for the sale of a route is negotiated "strictly between the seller and the buyer," with no FedEx involvement at all other than the new route owner must also be "qualified" under the Operating Agreement, with "qualified" merely meaning the new owner of the route also satisfies Department of Transportation ("DOT") regulations. Although FedEx assigns routes without nominal charge, the record contains evidence, as the Regional Director expressly found, that at least two contractors were able to sell routes for a profit ranging from $3,000 to nearly $16,000.

In its argument to this court, the Board, echoed by the dissent, discounts this evidence of entrepreneurial opportunity by saying any so-called profit merely represents the value of the vehicles, which were sold along with the routes. But if a vehicle depreciates in value, it is not worth as much as it was before; that is tautological. Here, buyers paid more for a vehicle and route than just the depreciated value of the vehicle—in one instance more than $10,000 more. Therefore, as the Regional Director did, we find this value is profit. The *amount* of profit may be "murky," as it may be as high as $6,000 and $16,000 or as low as $3,000 or $11,000, respectively, but the profit is real. That this potential for profit exists is unsurprising: routes are geographically defined, and they likely have value dependent on those geographic specifics which some contractors can better exploit than others. For example, as people move into an area, the ability to profit from that migration varies; some contractors using more efficient methods can continue to serve the entire route, while others cannot.

It is similarly confused to conclude FedEx gives away routes for free. A contractor agrees to provide a service in return for compensation, i.e., both sides give consideration. If a contractor does not do what she says, FedEx suffers damages, just as she does if FedEx does not pay what is owed. Servicing a route is not cheap; one needs a truck (which the contractor pays for) and a driver (which the contractor also pays for, either directly or in kind). To say this is giving away a route is to say when one hires a contractor to build a house, one is just giving away a construction opportunity. All of this evidence thus supports finding these contractors to be independent.

The Regional Director, however, thought FedEx's business model distinguishable from those where the Board had concluded the drivers were independent contractors. For example, FedEx requires: contractors to wear a recognizable uniform and conform to grooming standards; vehicles of particular color (white) and within a specific size range; and vehicles to display FedEx's logo in a way larger than that required by DOT regulations. The company insists drivers complete a driving course (or have a year of commercial driving experience, which need not be with FedEx) and be insured, and it "conducts two customer service rides per year" to audit performance. FedEx provides incentive pay (as well as fuel reimbursements in limited instances) and vehicle availability allotments, and requires contractors have a vehicle and driver available for deliveries Tuesday through Saturday. Moreover, FedEx can reconfigure routes if a contractor cannot provide adequate service, though the contractor has five days to prove otherwise, and is entitled to monetary compensation for the diminished value of the route. These aspects of FedEx's operation are distinguishable from the business models in [two other NLRB decisions.]

But those distinctions, though not irrelevant, reflect differences in the type of service the contractors are providing rather than differences in the employment relationship. In other words, the distinctions are significant but not sufficient. FedEx Home's business model is somewhat unique. The service is delivering small packages, mostly to residential customers. Unlike some trucking companies, its drivers are not delivering goods that FedEx sells or manufacturers, nor does FedEx move freight for a limited number of large clients. Instead, it is an intermediary between a diffuse group of senders and a broadly diverse group of recipients. With this model comes certain customer demands, including safety. . . . And once a driver wears FedEx's logo, FedEx has an interest in making sure her conduct reflects favorably on that logo, for instance by her being a safe and insured driver—which is required by DOT regulations in any event. *See Representation Decision.* . . .

Likewise, "an incentive system designed 'to ensure that the drivers' overall performance meets the company standards' . . . is fully consistent with an independent contractor relationship." *C.C. Eastern* (quoting *NAVL*. At the same time, a contractual willingness to share a small part of the risk—for instance, by providing fuel reimbursements when prices jump sharply, or by guaranteeing a certain minimum amount of income for making a vehicle available—does not an employee make.

The Regional Director also emphasized that these "contractors perform a function that is a regular and essential part of FedEx Home's normal operations, the delivery of packages," and that few have seized any of the alleged entrepreneurial opportunities. While the essential nature of a worker's role is a legitimate consideration, it is not determinative in the face of more compelling countervailing factors, otherwise companies like FedEx could never hire delivery drivers who are independent contractors, a consequence contrary to precedent. . . . And both the Board and this court have found the failure to take advantage of an opportunity is beside the point. Instead, "it is the worker's retention of the right to engage in entrepreneurial activity rather than his regular exercise of that right that is most relevant for the purpose of determining whether he is an independent contractor." *C.C. Eastern.*

III.

Our dissenting colleague reads our precedent differently than we do, and thus reaches a different conclusion. . . .

The dissent, for instance, argues that emphasizing entrepreneurialism has only truly begun with this case, and suggests we are doing so here for reasons apart from allegiance to precedent. Lest any be confused, we again quote *Corporate Express*: "[W]e uphold as reasonable the Board's decision, at the urging of the General Counsel, to focus not upon the employer's control of the means and manner of the work but instead upon whether the putative independent contractors have a 'significant entrepreneurial opportunity for gain or loss.'" . . . We retained the common law test (as is required by the Court's decision in *United Insurance*), but merely "shift[ed our] emphasis to entrepreneurialism," using this "emphasis" to evaluate common law factors such as whether the contractor "supplies his own equipment," *id. Corporate Express* is thus doctrinally consistent with *United Insurance* and the Restatement. . . .

But even if *Corporate Express* never happened, the result here is unchanged. While on some points *C.C. Eastern* and *NAVL* are distinguishable . . . the overwhelming majority of factors favoring independent contractor status are the same, and, importantly, this case is particularly straightforward because only here can the contractors own and transfer the proprietary interest in their routes. Moreover, all contractors here own their vehicles, something that cannot be said in *NAVL*, where not even the *majority* did. True, these drivers—who need not be, and not always are, the same persons as the contractors—must wear uniforms and the like, but a rule based on concern for customer service does not create an employee relationship. . . .

IV.

We have considered all the common law factors, and, on balance, are compelled to conclude they favor independent contractor status. The ability to operate multiple routes, hire additional drivers (including drivers who substitute for the contractor) and helpers, and to sell routes without permission, as well as the parties' intent expressed in the contract, augurs strongly in favor of independent contractor status. Because the indicia favoring a finding the contractors are employees are clearly outweighed by evidence of entrepreneurial opportunity, the Board cannot be said to have made a choice between two fairly conflicting views. . . .

GARLAND, *Circuit Judge*, dissenting in part.

In *National Labor Relations Board v. United Insurance Co. of America*, the Supreme Court held that Congress intended "the Board and the courts" to "apply the common-law agency test . . . in distinguishing an employee from an independent contractor" under the National Labor Relations Act (NLRA). 390 U.S. 254 (1968). In this case, the National Labor Relations Board (NLRB) applied that multi-factor test and concluded that FedEx Home Delivery's drivers are the company's employees. My colleagues disagree, concluding that the drivers are independent contractors.

This is not merely a factual dispute. Underlying my colleagues' conclusion is their view that the common-law test has gradually evolved until one factor—"whether the position presents the opportunities and risks inherent in entrepreneurialism"—has become the focus of the test. Moreover, in their view, this factor can be satisfied by showing a few examples, or even a single instance, of a driver seizing an entrepreneurial opportunity.

. . . I detect no such evolution. To the contrary, the Board and the courts have continued to follow the Supreme Court's injunction that "there is no shorthand formula or magic phrase that can be applied to find the answer, but all of the incidents of the relationship must be assessed and weighed with no one factor being decisive." *United Ins.* The common-law test may well be "unwieldy," but a court of appeals may not " 'displace the Board's choice between two fairly conflicting views, even though the court would justifiably have made a different choice had the matter been before it *de novo*.' " *United Ins.* (quoting *Universal Camera Corp. v. NLRB*, 340 U.S. 474, 488 (1951)). While the NLRB may have authority to alter the focus of the common-law test, this court does not. . . . Accordingly, on the existing record, I cannot join in condemning the Board's determination. . . .

I.

A.

[The dissent recounted the common-law agency test and the Board's application of it over the years, noting that, in doing so, the Board has looked to the Restatement (Second) of Agency for the relevant factors.] . .

B.

My colleagues contend that "[g]radually," both this Court and the Board shifted away from "the unwieldy control inquiry in favor of a more accurate proxy: whether the 'putative independent contractors have significant entrepreneurial opportunity for gain or loss.' " . . . .

The cases, however, do not evidence this gradual evolution to a test that emphasizes entrepreneurial opportunity. [While *NAVL* and *C.C. Eastern* listed entrepreneurial opportunity as a relevant factor, even though "it is not expressly mentioned in either *United Insurance* or the Restatement (or in any comment to the Restatement. . . .)," both decisions "explicitly stated that entrepreneurial opportunity was only one of multiple factors to consider—and not the most important one."]

My colleagues cite only one case from this (or any) Circuit, our 2002 opinion in *Corporate Express*, for the proposition that entrepreneurial opportunity has "explicit[ly]" become the emphasis of the independent contractor test. . . . . But *Corporate Express* did not purport to overrule Supreme Court, Circuit, and Board precedent. Indeed, in affirming as reasonable the *Board's* determination that the owner-operator drivers in that case were *not* independent contractors, the court not only agreed that they lacked entrepreneurial opportunity, but also acknowledged that the Board may have correctly determined that the employer controlled the way in which they performed their jobs. *Corporate Express.* Hence, *Corporate Express* can also be read as merely holding that the Board was reasonable in determining that entrepreneurial opportunity tipped the balance in *that* case—a logical result given that the court thought the vector of the other common-law factors somewhat unclear, while finding that the "owner-operators lacked *all* entrepreneurial opportunity" (emphasis added). . . .

There was certainly nothing in the NLRB's opinion in *Corporate Express* to suggest that entrepreneurial opportunity had become the focus of the Board's own analysis. To the contrary, the Board simply followed its traditional approach of examining the common-law factors—including, inter alia, both entrepreneurial opportunity and employer control. After doing so, it concluded that, "*weighing all of the incidents of their relationship* with the Respondent, we find that the owner-operators are employees and not independent contractors" (emphasis added).

. . . . Until the Supreme Court or the Board tells us differently, we must continue to apply the multi-factor common-law test as set forth by the Supreme Court and applied by the Board.

II . . . .

A.

In a lengthy and considered opinion, the [NLRB's] Regional Director found the following facts to favor a determination that FedEx Home Delivery's drivers, whom the company calls "contractors," were employees:

> [A]ll the FedEx Home contractors perform a function that is a regular and essential part of FedEx Home's normal operations, the delivery of packages. . . . [A]ll contractors must do business in the name of FedEx Home[,] . . . wear[ ] FedEx Home-approved uniforms and badges, . . . [and] operate vehicles that must meet FedEx Home specifications and uniformly display the FedEx Home name, logo, and colors. . . . No prior delivery training or experience is required, and FedEx Home will train those with no experience. . . .
>
> . . . [C]ontractors are not permitted to use their vehicles for other purposes while providing service for FedEx Home. The contractors have a contractual right to use their FedEx Home trucks in business activity outside their relationship with FedEx Home during off-hours, provided they remove all FedEx Home markings, but only one former multiple route contractor . . . and no current contractors at either Wilmington terminal have ever done so. . . .
>
> . . . FedEx Home exercises substantial control over all the contractors' performance of their functions. FedEx Home offers what is essentially a take-it-or-leave-it agreement. . . . [It] retains the right to reconfigure the service area unilaterally. All contractors must furnish a FedEx Home-approved vehicle and FedEx Home-approved driver daily from Tuesday through Saturday; they do not have discretion not to provide delivery service on a given day. While all contractors control their starting times and take breaks when they wish, their control over their work schedule is by the requirement that all packages be delivered on the day of assignment. . . .

. . . FedEx Home provides support to all its contractors in various ways that are inconsistent with independent contractor status. . . . FedEx Home provides extensive support to contractors by offering the Business Support Package and arranging for the required insurance, thus providing an array of required goods and services that would be far more difficult for contractors to arrange on their own. . . .

FedEx Home also offers to arrange for approved substitute drivers for its contractors by virtue of the Time Off Program. FedEx Home provides contractors who maintain sufficient vehicle maintenance accounts with $100 per accounting period to help defray repair costs[, and] requires contractors to permit FedEx Home to pay certain vehicle-related taxes and fees on their behalf and to have the payments deducted from their settlement.

. . . My colleagues nonetheless reject the import of many of these facts, arguing that they merely "reflect differences in the type of service the contractors are providing rather than differences in the employment relationship." In particular, the court rejects the import of the following requirements imposed by FedEx: that drivers wear a recognizable uniform; that vehicles be of a particular color and size range; that trucks display the FedEx logo in a size larger than Department of Transportation regulations require; that drivers complete a driving course if they do not have prior training; that drivers submit to two customer service rides per year to audit their performance; and that a truck and driver be available for deliveries every Tuesday through Saturday. The courts and the Board, however, have repeatedly regarded the presence or absence of these very factors as important in determining whether a worker is an employee or independent contractor.

One factor that the Regional Director emphasized was that the drivers "perform a function that is a regular and essential part of FedEx Home's normal operations, the delivery of packages" to homes. Although my colleagues acknowledge that "the essential nature of a worker's role is a legitimate consideration," they minimize it as "not determinative." But that is true of every factor in the common-law test. Moreover, the cases have repeatedly cited this particular factor in concluding that workers are employees. . . .

B.

In accord with court and agency precedent, the Regional Director also considered whether FedEx Home Delivery's drivers have significant entrepreneurial opportunity for gain or loss. For the following reasons, she concluded that the evidence of entrepreneurial opportunity was weak:

The contractors' compensation package also supports employee status. With [one] exception . . ., FedEx Home unilaterally establishes the rates of compensation for all contractors. . . . [T]here is little room for the contractors to influence their income through their own efforts or ingenuity, as their terminal manager determines, for the most part, how many deliveries they will make each day. . . . A contractor's territory may be unilaterally reconfigured by FedEx Home. FedEx Home tries to insulate its contractors from loss to some degree by means of the vehicle availability payment, which they receive just for showing up, and the temporary core zone density payment, both of which payments guarantee contractors an income level predetermined by FedEx Home, irrespective of the contractors' personal initiative. FedEx Home also shields drivers from loss due to substantial increases in fuel prices by means of the fuel/mileage settlement.

Notwithstanding these findings, my colleagues perceive many "characteristics of entrepreneurial potential" in the drivers' relationship to FedEx. Some of the characteristics they cite, however, appear to have little to do with entrepreneurial opportunity. For example, the court's opinion notes that FedEx's Standard Contractor Operating Agreement "specifies the contractor is not an employee of FedEx for any purpose." But the label FedEx puts on its relationship with its workers does not affect whether they have entrepreneurial opportunity for gain or loss.

My colleagues also observe that FedEx "may not prescribe hours of work [or] whether or when the contractors take breaks," and that the drivers "are not subject to reprimands or other discipline," all of which go not to the workers' entrepreneurial opportunity but to the extent of the employer's control, a factor discussed in Part II.A above. In any event, although FedEx does not fix specific hours or break times, it does require its contractors to provide delivery services every day, Tuesday through Saturday, and to finish each day's deliveries by the end of the day. The insurance agents in *United Insurance* had neither fixed hours nor fixed break times, yet the Supreme Court affirmed the Board's determination that they were employees. . . . .

In addition, my colleagues state that "[a]t least one contractor has negotiated with FedEx for higher fees." Without agreeing that a worker's ability to negotiate his salary takes him out of the category of "employee," the Regional Director rightly regarded the only evidence on this point as quite weak: One former manager testified that one former driver "once requested some customer service rides to gauge if his core zone payment was set properly, and the payment was raised as a result, although [the manager] was not sure by how much. There is no evidence that any other contractors at the Wilmington facilities have negotiated a change in their core zone payment."

Closer to the mark on the issue of entrepreneurial opportunity is the court's observation that drivers "are responsible for all the costs associated with operating and maintaining their vehicles." But FedEx does much to limit the drivers' risk of loss. As the Regional Director found, the company "shields drivers from loss due to substantial increases in fuel prices by means of the fuel/mileage settlement" and guarantees them a significant amount of income "just for showing up." . . . .

My colleagues further note that, under the Operator Agreement, drivers "may use the vehicles for other commercial or personal purposes" when they are not in the service of FedEx, "so long as they remove or mask all FedEx Home logos and markings." But do the drivers actually use their trucks for other purposes? Not so much. Indeed, the most that can be said is that "some do use them for personal uses like moving family members," hardly an indicator of a "'significant entrepreneurial opportunity for gain or loss,'" (quoting *Corporate Express*). Although the drivers' use of their trucks to conduct business independent of FedEx could well be an indicator of entrepreneurialism, the Regional Director found that "no current contractors at either Wilmington terminal have ever done so." Nor would they have much time, even if they wanted to. The Operator Agreement states that the company "seek[s] to manage its business so that it can provide sufficient volume of packages to Contractor *to make full use* of Contractor's equipment." The contractor must provide daily service,[1] and "[w]hile the Equipment is in the service of [FedEx], it shall be used by Contractor exclusively for the carriage of the goods of [FedEx], and for no other purpose."

Based on these facts, the Regional Director found that the

> "lack of pursuit of outside business activity appears to be less a reflection of entrepreneurial choice by the . . . drivers and more a matter of the obstacles created by their relationship with [the Company.]" Thus, the contractors' contractual right to engage in outside business falls within the category of "entrepreneurial opportunities that they cannot realistically take," because the contractors' work schedules prevent them from taking on additional business during their off-hours during the workweek.

That is at least a fair conclusion, and consequently one that we may not displace. *See United Ins.*

Another indicator of entrepreneurialism to which my colleagues point is the fact that operators may hire drivers as temporary replacements and occasional helpers. . . . Once again, however, the record evidence on this issue was weak. The Regional Director found that "many contractors who hire substitute drivers use the FedEx Home 'temp' drivers," and that the record did not reveal how often contractors hired outside helpers. Nor was there any evidence that any operator at the terminals at issue in this case ever hired a substitute on a full-time basis.

My colleagues also note the fact that FedEx drivers "may contract to serve multiple routes," and that if they do so, they may hire other drivers to handle those routes. Although this, too, may indicate entrepreneurial opportunity, there were only 3 multiple-route drivers operating out of the Wilmington facilities. . . . Moreover, the Regional Director excluded multiple-route drivers from the bargaining unit on the ground that they were not employees but rather statutory supervisors.

My colleagues find particularly significant the fact that drivers have a contractual right to sell their routes, and that this could provide an opportunity for profit. That theoretical possibility, however, is tightly constrained. The drivers may sell only to those buyers whom FedEx accepts as qualified; the company gives out routes without charge,[2] as it did at the two Wilmington terminals; and FedEx can reconfigure a route, "in its sole discretion," at any time. These facts cannot help but limit (or eliminate) any opportunity for profit.

In light of these constraints, it is not surprising that, although there was evidence that drivers abandoned their routes without selling them, there was little evidence that any driver had ever materially profited from a sale. . . .

---

1. It is true that a driver could take on extra work on his weekends (although none do). But *C.C. Eastern* did not hold that this would make him an independent contractor—no more than taking on a second, weekend job would turn any full-time employee into an "entrepreneur."

2. There is nothing confused about saying that FedEx gives out routes without charge when it does not charge anything for routes. Of course, the driver agrees to provide delivery service on the route, and of course FedEx pays compensation for that service. But the fact that FedEx will give a new driver a route without charging for it, and can reconfigure any route that a driver purchases from a former driver, plainly constrains the value of the latter.

C.

. . . . In concluding that the indicia of entrepreneurial opportunity were weak, the Regional Director emphasized that few operators seized any of the opportunities that allegedly were available to them. Accordingly, she adhered to the NLRB's precedent . . . wherein the [Board concluded that evidence of a few sales is insufficient to find independent contractor status.]

My colleagues, by contrast, maintain that the failure to actually exercise theoretical opportunities is "beside the point" because " 'it is the worker's retention of the right to engage in entrepreneurial activity rather than his regular exercise of that right that is most relevant.' " But the proper emphasis in that quotation from our *C.C. Eastern* opinion is on the word "regular." It may not be necessary for workers to *regularly* exercise their right to engage in entrepreneurial activity for that factor to weigh in the balance, but "if a company offers its workers entrepreneurial opportunities that they cannot realistically take, then that does not add any weight to the Company's claim that the workers are independent contractors." *C.C. Eastern* . . . .

The import of my colleagues' suggestion that one or even a few examples of the exercise of contractual rights can be enough to decide the entrepreneurialism factor is magnified by their view that this factor is not just one element in a multi-factor test, but rather the test's "emphasis" —so that an insubstantial exercise may, in effect, tilt the entire outcome. . . .

Dynamex Operations West, Inc. v. Superior Court
416 P.3d 1 (Cal. 2018)

CANTIL-SAKAUYE, C. J.:

Under both California and federal law, the question whether an individual worker should properly be classified as an employee or, instead, as an independent contractor has considerable significance for workers, businesses, and the public generally. On the one hand, if a worker should properly be classified as an employee, the hiring business bears the responsibility of paying federal Social Security and payroll taxes, unemployment insurance taxes and state employment taxes, providing workers' compensation insurance, and, most relevant for the present case, complying with numerous state and federal statutes and regulations governing the wages, hours, and working conditions of employees. The worker then obtains the protection of the applicable labor laws and regulations. On the other hand, if a worker should properly be classified as an independent contractor, the business does not bear any of those costs or responsibilities, the worker obtains none of the numerous labor law benefits, and the public may be required under applicable laws to assume additional financial burdens with respect to such workers and their families.

Although in some circumstances classification as an independent contractor may be advantageous to workers as well as to businesses, the risk that workers who should be treated as employees may be improperly misclassified as independent contractors is significant in light of the potentially substantial economic incentives that a business may have in mischaracterizing some workers as independent contractors. Such incentives include the unfair competitive advantage the business may obtain over competitors that properly classify similar workers as employees and that thereby assume the fiscal and other responsibilities and burdens that an employer owes to its employees. In recent years, the relevant regulatory agencies of both the federal and state governments have declared that the misclassification of workers as independent contractors rather than employees is a very serious problem, depriving federal and state governments of billions of dollars in tax revenue and millions of workers of the labor law protections to which they are entitled.

. . . Here we must decide what standard applies, under California law, in determining whether workers should be classified as employees or as independent contractors *for purposes of California wage orders,* which impose obligations relating to the minimum wages, maximum hours, and a limited number of very basic working conditions (such as minimally required meal and rest breaks) of California employees.

In the underlying lawsuit in this matter, two individual delivery drivers, suing on their own behalf and on behalf of a class of allegedly similarly situated drivers, filed a complaint against Dynamex Operations West, Inc. (Dynamex), a nationwide package and document delivery company, alleging that Dynamex had misclassified its delivery drivers as independent contractors rather than employees. The drivers claimed that Dynamex's alleged misclassification of its drivers as independent contractors led to Dynamex's violation of the provisions of Industrial Welfare Commission wage order No. 9, the applicable state wage order governing the transportation industry, as well as various sections of the Labor Code, and, as a result, that Dynamex had engaged in unfair and unlawful business practices under Business and Professions Code section 17200.

Prior to 2004, Dynamex classified as employees drivers who allegedly performed similar pickup and delivery work as the current drivers perform. In 2004, however, Dynamex adopted a new policy and contractual arrangement under which all drivers are considered independent contractors rather than employees. Dynamex maintains that, in light of the current contractual arrangement, the drivers are properly classified as independent contractors.

[T]he trial court ultimately certified a class action embodying a class of Dynamex drivers who, during a pay period, did not themselves employ other drivers and did not do delivery work for other delivery businesses or for the drivers' own personal customers. [It] relied upon the three alternative definitions of "employ" and "employer" set forth in the applicable wage order as discussed in this court's then-recently decided opinion in *Martinez v. Combs,* [231 P.3d 259 (2010)] (*Martinez*)]. As described more fully below, *Martinez* held that "[t]o employ . . . under the [wage order], has three alternative definitions. It means: (a) to exercise control over the wages, hours or working conditions, *or* (b) to suffer or permit to work, *or* (c) to engage, thereby creating a common law employment relationship." The trial court rejected Dynamex's contention that in the wage order context, as in most other contexts, the multifactor standard set forth in this court's seminal decision in *S. G. Borello & Sons, Inc. v. Department of Industrial Relations,* [769 P.2d 399 (1989)] (*Borello*) is the only appropriate standard under California law for distinguishing employees and independent contractors.

[Dynamex argued "that two of the alternative wage order definitions of "employ" relied upon by the trial court do not apply to the employee or independent contractor issue. Dynamex contended, instead, that those wage order definitions are relevant only to the distinct joint employer question that was directly presented in this court's decision in *Martinez*—namely whether, when a worker is an admitted employee of a primary employer, another business or entity that has some relationship with the primary employer should properly be considered a joint employer of the worker and therefore also responsible, along with the primary employer, for the obligations imposed by the wage order. . . .

For the reasons discussed below, we agree with the Court of Appeal that the trial court did not err in concluding that the "suffer or permit to work" definition of "employ" contained in the wage order may be relied upon in evaluating whether a worker is an employee or, instead, an independent contractor for purposes of the obligations imposed by the wage order. . . .

[Further, we] conclude that in determining whether, under the suffer or permit to work definition, a worker is properly considered the type of independent contractor to whom the wage order does not apply, it is appropriate to look to a standard, commonly referred to as the "ABC" test, that is utilized in other jurisdictions in a variety of contexts to distinguish employees from independent contractors. Under this test, a worker is properly considered an independent contractor to whom a wage order does not apply only if the hiring entity establishes: (A) that the worker is free from the control and direction of the hirer in connection with the performance of the work, both under the contract for the performance of such work and in fact; (B) that the worker performs work that is outside the usual course of the hiring entity's business; and (C) that the worker is customarily engaged in an independently established trade, occupation, or business of the same nature as the work performed for the hiring entity. . . .

I. Facts and Proceedings Below. . . .

Dynamex is a nationwide same-day courier and delivery service that operates a number of business centers in California. Dynamex offers on-demand, same-day pickup and delivery services to the public generally and also has a number of large business customers—including Office Depot and Home Depot—for whom it delivers purchased goods and picks up returns on a regular basis. Prior to 2004, Dynamex classified its California drivers as employees and compensated them pursuant to this state's wage and hour laws. In 2004, Dynamex converted all of its drivers to independent contractors after management concluded that such a conversion would generate economic savings for the company. Under the current policy, all drivers are treated as independent contractors and are required to provide their own vehicles and pay for all of their transportation expenses, including fuel, tolls, vehicle maintenance, and vehicle liability insurance, as well as all taxes and workers' compensation insurance.

Dynamex obtains its own customers and sets the rates to be charged to those customers for its delivery services. It also negotiates the amount to be paid to drivers on an individual basis. For drivers who are assigned to a dedicated fleet or scheduled route by Dynamex, drivers are paid either a flat fee or an amount based on a percentage of the delivery fee Dynamex receives from the customer. For those who deliver on-demand, drivers are generally paid either a percentage of the delivery fee paid by the customer on a per delivery basis or a flat fee basis per item delivered.

Drivers are generally free to set their own schedule but must notify Dynamex of the days they intend to work for Dynamex. Drivers performing on-demand work are required to obtain and pay for a Nextel cellular telephone through which the drivers maintain contact with Dynamex. On-demand drivers are assigned deliveries by Dynamex dispatchers at Dynamex's sole discretion; drivers have no guarantee of the number or type of deliveries they will be offered. Although drivers are not required to make all of the deliveries they are assigned, they must promptly notify Dynamex if they intend to reject an offered delivery so that Dynamex can quickly contact another driver; drivers are liable for any loss Dynamex incurs if they fail to do so. Drivers make pickups and deliveries using their own vehicles, but are generally expected to wear Dynamex shirts and badges when making deliveries for Dynamex, and, pursuant to Dynamex's agreement with some customers, drivers are sometimes required to attach Dynamex and/or the customer's decals to their vehicles when making deliveries for the customer. Drivers purchase Dynamex shirts and other Dynamex items with their own funds.

In the absence of any special arrangement between Dynamex and a customer, drivers are generally free to choose the sequence in which they will make deliveries and the routes they will take, but are required to complete all assigned deliveries on the day of assignment. If a customer requests, however, drivers must comply with a customer's requirements regarding delivery times and sequence of stops.

Drivers hired by Dynamex are permitted to hire other persons to make deliveries assigned by Dynamex. Further, when they are not making pickups or deliveries for Dynamex, drivers are permitted to make deliveries for another delivery company, including the driver's own personal delivery business. Drivers are prohibited, however, from diverting any delivery order received through or on behalf of Dynamex to a competitive delivery service.

Drivers are ordinarily hired for an indefinite period of time but Dynamex retains the authority to terminate its agreement with any driver without cause, on three days' notice. And, as noted, Dynamex reserves the right, throughout the contract period, to control the number and nature of deliveries that it offers to its on-demand drivers. . . .

In essence, the underlying action rests on the claim that, since December 2004, Dynamex drivers have performed essentially the same tasks in the same manner as when its drivers were classified as employees, but Dynamex has improperly failed to comply with the requirements imposed by the Labor Code and wage orders for employees with respect to such drivers. . . .

[A class was certified based on information provided by drivers who returned questionnaire seeking information relevant to class membership. As finally certified,] the class consisted only of individual Dynamex drivers who had returned complete and timely questionnaires and who personally performed delivery services for Dynamex but did not employ other drivers or perform delivery services for another delivery company or for the driver's own delivery business. The trial court's certification order states that 278 drivers returned questionnaires and that from the questionnaire responses it appears that at least 184 drivers fall within the proposed class.

[The trial court certified the class after finding all prerequisites for a class action satisfied. As to "commonality," whether common issues predominate over individual issues, the trial court found that requirement satisfied because all of plaintiffs' causes of action rest on the contention that Dynamex misclassified the drivers as independent contractors when they should have been classified as employees.] . . . Thus, the facts that are relevant to that legal claim necessarily relate to the appropriate legal standard or test that is applicable in determining whether a worker should be considered an employee or an independent contractor.

[The parties disagreed as to the proper legal standard applicable in determining whether a worker is an employee or an independent contractor for purposes of plaintiffs' claims. Plaintiffs relied on *Martinez*, maintaining that the standards or tests for employment set forth in *Martinez* are applicable in the present context, and that the standard for determining the employee or independent contractor question set forth in this court's decision in *Borello* is not the sole applicable standard. Dynamex, by contrast, took the position that the alternative definitions of "employ" and "employer" discussed in *Martinez* are applicable only in determining whether an entity should be considered a joint employer of the employee, and *not* in deciding whether a worker is properly classified as an employee or an independent contractor.]

[The trial court not only agreed with plaintiffs that Martinez applied generally but also found that *Martinez*] represents "a redefinition of the employment relationship under a claim of unpaid wages as follows: 'To employ, then, under the IWC's [Industrial Welfare Commission's] definition, has three alternative definitions. It means (a) to exercise control over the wages, hours or working conditions, (b) to suffer or permit to work, or (c) to engage, thereby creating a common law employment relationship.'" (Quoting *Martinez*. . . .)

With regard to the "exercise control over wages, hours or working conditions" test, the trial court stated that "'control over wages' means that a person or entity has the power or authority to negotiate and set an employee's rate of pay" and that "[w]hether or not Dynamex had the authority to negotiate each driver's rate of pay can be answered by looking at its policies with regard to hiring drivers. . . . [I]ndividual inquiry is not required["]. . . .

With regard to the suffer or permit to work test, the trial court stated in full: "An employee is suffered or permitted to work if the work was performed with the knowledge of the employer. This includes work that was performed that the employer knew *or should have known* about. Again, this is a matter that can be addressed by looking at Defendant's policy for entering into agreements with drivers. Defendant is only liable to those drivers with whom it entered into an agreement (i.e., knew were providing delivery services to Dynamex customers). This can be determined through records, and does not require individual analysis."

With regard to the common law employment relationship test referred to in *Martinez*, the trial court stated that this test refers to the multifactor standard set forth in *Borello*. The trial court described the *Borello* test as involving the principal factor of "'whether the person to whom services [are] rendered has the right to control the manner and means of accomplishing the result desired'" as well as the following nine additional factors: "(1) right to discharge at will, without cause; (2) whether the one performing the services is engaged in a distinct occupation or business; (3) the kind of occupation, with reference to whether in the locality the work is usually done under the direction of the principal or by a specialist without supervision; (4) the skill required in the particular occupation; (5) whether the principal or the worker supplies the instrumentalities, tools, and the place of work for the person doing the work; (6) the length of time for which the services are to be performed; (7) method of payment, whether by the time or by the job; (8) whether or not the work is part of the regular business of the principal; and (9) whether or not the parties believe they are creating the relationship of employer-employee." As the trial court observed, *Borello* explained that "'the individual factors cannot be applied mechanically as separate tests; they are intertwined and their weight depends often on particular combinations.'"

[The trial court then discussed the various *Borello* factors, finding that most are subject to common proof and do not require individualized inquiry of the class members. "But the main factor in determining whether an employment agreement exists—control of the details—does require individualized inquiries due to the fact that there is no indication of a classwide policy that only defendants obtain new customers, only the defendants provide customer service and create the delivery schedules."]

With respect to the entire question of commonality, however, the trial court concluded: "Common questions predominate the inquiry into whether an employment relationship exists between Dynamex and the drivers. The first two alternative definitions of 'employer' can both be demonstrated through common proof, even if the common law test requires individualized inquiries."

Having found that common issues predominate, the trial court went on to conclude that "[a] class action is a superior means of conducting this litigation." . . .

II. Relevant Wage Order Provisions

[The wage order applicable to the transportation industry, Cal. Code Regs., tit. 8, §11090, reaches "all persons employed," with some exemptions not applicable here "Employ" is defined "to engage, suffer, or permit to work."

The order's substantive provisions "establish protections for workers or impose obligations on hiring entities relating to minimum wages, maximum hours, and specified basic working conditions (such as meal and rest breaks)." The order does not define "independent contractor," or otherwise specifically address "the potential distinction between workers who are employees covered by the terms of the wage order and workers who are independent contractors who are not entitled to the protections afforded by the wage order."]

III. Background of Relevant California Judicial Decisions

[The court provided a detailed history of the most relevant California judicial decisions, including *Martinez*, *Borello*, and *Ayala*. The key takeaways from this discussion are as follows: Courts in all jurisdictions have had difficulty in devising an acceptable general test or standard that properly distinguishes employees from independent contractors. It cited *Board v. Hearst Publications* 322 U.S. 111, 121 (1944) for the proposition that this difficulty began in the tort context, where the Restatement approach originated, and has spread to other areas, including coverage under employment laws.

Although *Borello*'s test appears similar to the common-law approach to distinguishing employees from independent contractors, *Borello* is better viewed as calling for resolution of the employee or independent contractor question by focusing on the intended purpose of the particular statutory provision at issue. *Borello* calls for application of a statutory purpose standard rather than adhering strictly to the common-law articulation as has been true of more recent federal wage law decisions.

The *Martinez* court concluded that the applicable wage order sets forth three alternative definitions of employment for purposes of the wage order: "(a) to exercise control over the wages, hours or working conditions, *or* (b) to suffer or permit to work, *or* (c) to engage, thereby creating a common law employment relationship."

IV . . .

. . . [W]e conclude that the suffer or permit to work standard [stated in *Martinez*] properly applies to the question whether a worker should be considered an employee or, instead, an independent contractor, and that under the suffer or permit to work standard, the trial court class certification order at issue here should be upheld. . . . Accordingly, we confine the discussion of Dynamex's argument to an analysis of the scope and meaning of the suffer or permit to work standard in California wage orders.

A. Does the Suffer or Permit to Work Definition Apply to the Employee/Independent Contractor Distinction?

[The court rejected Dynamex's contention that the suffer or permit to work standard applies only to the joint employer question, not to the question of whether an individual is an employee or independent contractor. In so finding, the court relied on the historical discussion and analysis in *Martinez*. The court rejected Dynamex's arguments, including that, because the *Borello* standard was adopted well after the suffer and permit to work test was articulated and has been utilized by California courts in many contexts, it is the exclusive test for determining worker status.]

[Dynamix also] argues that the suffer or permit to work standard cannot serve as the test for distinguishing employees from independent contractors because a literal application of that standard would characterize *all* individual workers who directly provide services to a business as employees. . . .

. . . [That the] literal language of the suffer or permit to work standard does not itself resolve the question whether a worker is properly considered a covered employee . . . does not mean that the suffer or permit to work standard has no substantial bearing on the determination whether an individual worker is properly considered an employee or independent contractor for purposes of a wage and hour statute or regulation. . . .

At the outset, it is important to recognize that over the years and throughout the country, a number of standards or tests have been adopted in legislative enactments, administrative regulations, and court decisions as the means for distinguishing between those workers who should be considered employees and those who should be considered independent contractors. The suffer or permit to work standard was proposed and adopted in 1937 as part of the FLSA, the principal federal wage and hour legislation. One of the authors of the legislation, then-Senator (later United States Supreme Court Justice) Hugo L. Black, described this standard as "the broadest definition" that has been devised for extending the coverage of a statute or regulation to the widest class of workers that reasonably fall within the reach of a social welfare statute. More recent cases, in referring to the suffer or permit to work standard, continue to describe the standard in just such broad, inclusive terms.

The adoption of the exceptionally broad suffer or permit to work standard in California wage orders finds its justification in the fundamental purposes and necessity of the minimum wage and maximum hour legislation in which the standard has traditionally been embodied. Wage and hour statutes and wage orders were adopted in recognition of the fact that individual workers generally possess less bargaining power than a hiring business and that workers' fundamental need to earn income for their families' survival may lead them to accept work for substandard wages or working conditions. The basic objective of wage and hour legislation and wage orders is to ensure that such workers are provided at least the minimal wages and working conditions that are necessary to enable them to obtain a subsistence standard of living and to protect the workers' health and welfare.

. . . . At the same time, California's *industry-wide* wage orders are also clearly intended for the benefit of those law-abiding businesses that comply with the obligations imposed by the wage orders, ensuring that such responsible companies are not hurt by unfair competition from competitor businesses that utilize substandard employment practices. Finally, the minimum employment standards imposed by wage orders are also for the benefit of the public at large, because if the wage orders' obligations are not fulfilled the public will often be left to assume responsibility for the ill effects to workers and their families resulting from substandard wages or unhealthy and unsafe working conditions.

[Given the intended expansive reach of the suffer or permit to work standard, the court concluded that it must be interpreted and applied broadly to include within the covered "employee" category *all* individual workers who can reasonably be viewed as "*working in [the hiring entity's] business*" (quoting *Martinez*).]

The federal courts, in applying the suffer or permit to work standard set forth in the FLSA, have recognized that the standard was intended to be broader and more inclusive than the preexisting common law test for distinguishing employees from independent contractors, but at the same time, does not purport to render every individual worker an employee rather than an independent contractor. [T]he federal courts have developed what is generally described as the "economic reality" test for determining whether a worker should be considered an employee or independent contractor for purposes of the FLSA—namely, whether, as a matter of economic reality, the worker is economically dependent upon and makes a living in another's business (in which case he or she is considered to be a covered employee) or, instead is in business for himself or herself (and may properly be considered an excluded independent contractor). In applying the economic reality test, federal courts have looked to a list of factors that is briefer than, but somewhat comparable to, the list of factors considered in [*Borello*]. . . .

A multifactor standard—like the economic reality standard or the *Borello* standard—that calls for consideration of all potentially relevant factual distinctions in different employment arrangements on a case-by-case, totality-of-the-circumstances basis has its advantages. A number of state courts, administrative agencies and academic commentators have observed, however, that such a wide-ranging and flexible test for evaluating whether a worker should be considered an employee or an independent contractor has significant disadvantages, particularly when applied in the wage and hour context.

First, these jurisdictions and commentators have pointed out that a multifactor, "all the circumstances" standard makes it difficult for both hiring businesses and workers to determine in advance how a particular category of workers will be classified, frequently leaving the ultimate employee or independent contractor determination to a subsequent and often considerably delayed judicial decision. . . .

Second, commentators have also pointed out that the use of a multifactor, all the circumstances standard affords a hiring business greater opportunity to evade its fundamental responsibilities under a wage and hour law by dividing its work force into disparate categories and varying the working conditions of individual workers within such categories with an eye to the many circumstances that may be relevant under the multifactor standard. . . .

As already noted, a number of jurisdictions have adopted a simpler, more structured test for distinguishing between employees and independent contractors—the so-called "ABC" test—that minimizes these disadvantages. The ABC test presumptively considers all workers to be employees, and permits workers to be classified as independent contractors only if the hiring business demonstrates that the worker in question satisfies *each* of three conditions.[3]

Unlike a number of our sister states that included the suffer or permit to work standard in their wage and hour laws or regulations *after* the FLSA had been enacted and had been interpreted to incorporate the economic reality test, California's adoption of the suffer or permit to work standard predated the enactment of the FLSA. Thus, as a matter of legislative intent, the IWC's adoption of the suffer or permit to work standard in California wage orders was not intended to embrace the federal economic reality test. . . .

We find merit in the concerns noted above regarding the disadvantages, particularly in the wage and hour context, inherent in relying upon a multifactor, all the circumstances standard for distinguishing between employees and independent contractors. As a consequence, we conclude it is appropriate, and most consistent with the history and purpose of the suffer or permit to work standard in California's wage orders, to interpret that standard as: (1) placing the burden on the hiring entity to establish that the worker is an independent contractor who was not intended to be included within the wage order's coverage; and (2) requiring the hiring entity, in order to meet this burden, to establish *each* of the three factors embodied in the ABC test—namely (A) that the worker is free from the control and direction of the hiring entity in connection with the performance of the work, both under the contract for the performance of the work and in fact; *and* (B) that the worker performs work that is outside the usual course of the hiring entity's business; *and* (C) that the worker is customarily engaged in an independently established trade, occupation, or business of the same nature as the work performed. . . .

We briefly discuss each part of the ABC test and its relationship to the suffer or permit to work definition.

---

3. The wording of the ABC test varies in some respects from jurisdiction to jurisdiction. The version we have set forth in text (and which we adopt hereafter) tracks the Massachusetts version of the ABC test. (See Mass. Gen. Laws, ch. 149, §148B; see also Del. Code Ann. tit. 19, §§3501(a)(7), 3503(c).) Unlike some other versions, which provide that a hiring entity may satisfy part B by establishing *either* (1) that the work provided is outside the usual course of the business for which the work is performed, *or* (2) that the work performed is outside all the places of business of the hiring entity (see, e.g., N.J. Stat. Ann. §43:21-19(i)(6)(A)–(C)), the Massachusetts version permits the hiring entity to satisfy part B only if it establishes that the work is outside the usual course of the business of the hiring entity. In light of contemporary work practices, in which many employees telecommute or work from their homes, we conclude the Massachusetts version of part B provides the alternative that is more consistent with the intended broad reach of the suffer or permit to work definition in California wage orders.

Many jurisdictions that have adopted the ABC test use the standard only in the unemployment insurance context, but other jurisdictions use the ABC test more generally in determining the employee or independent contractor question with respect to a variety of employee-protective labor statutes. (See, e.g., Mass. Gen. Laws ch. 149, §148B; Del. Code Ann. tit. 19, §§3501(a)(7), 3503(c); *Hargrove, supra,* 106 A.3d at pp. 462–465; see generally *ABC on the Books, supra,* 18 U. Pa. J.L. & Soc. Change, at pp. 65–72 [discussing numerous state statutes and judicial decisions].)

1. Part A: Is the worker free from the control and direction of the hiring entity in the performance of the work, both under the contract for the performance of the work and in fact?

. . . [T]he suffer or permit to work definition was intended to be broader and more inclusive than the common law test, under which a worker's freedom from the control of the hiring entity in the performance of the work, both under the contract for the performance of the work and in fact, was the principal factor in establishing that a worker was an independent contractor rather than an employee. Accordingly, because a worker who is subject, either as a matter of contractual right or in actual practice, to the type and degree of control a business typically exercises over employees would be considered an employee under the common law test, such a worker would, a fortiori, also properly be treated as an employee for purposes of the suffer or permit to work standard. Further, . . . depending on the nature of the work and overall arrangement between the parties, a business need not control the precise manner or details of the work in order to be found to have maintained the necessary control that an employer ordinarily possesses over its employees, but does not possess over a genuine independent contractor. The hiring entity must establish that the worker is free of such control to satisfy part A of the test.

2. Part B: Does the worker perform work that is outside the usual course of the hiring entity's business?

. . . [O]ne principal objective of the suffer or permit to work standard is to bring within the "employee" category *all* individuals who can reasonably be viewed as working "*in [the hiring entity's] business*" (see *Martinez,* italics added), that is, all individuals who are reasonably viewed as providing services to the business in a role comparable to that of an employee, rather than in a role comparable to that of a traditional independent contractor. Workers whose roles are most clearly comparable to those of employees include individuals whose services are provided within the usual course of the business of the entity for which the work is performed and thus who would ordinarily be viewed by others as working in the hiring entity's business and not as working, instead, in the worker's own independent business.

Thus, on the one hand, when a retail store hires an outside plumber to repair a leak in a bathroom on its premises or hires an outside electrician to install a new electrical line, the services of the plumber or electrician are not part of the store's usual course of business and the store would not reasonably be seen as having suffered or permitted the plumber or electrician to provide services to it as an employee. On the other hand, when a clothing manufacturing company hires work-at-home seamstresses to make dresses from cloth and patterns supplied by the company that will thereafter be sold by the company, or when a bakery hires cake decorators to work on a regular basis on its custom-designed cakes, the workers are part of the hiring entity's usual business operation and the hiring business can reasonably be viewed as having suffered or permitted the workers to provide services as employees. In the latter settings, the workers' role within the hiring entity's usual business operations is more like that of an employee than that of an independent contractor.

Treating all workers whose services are provided within the usual course of the hiring entity's business as employees is important to ensure that those workers who need and want the fundamental protections afforded by the wage order do not lose those protections. If the wage order's obligations could be avoided for workers who provide services in a role comparable to employees but who are willing to forgo the wage order's protections, other workers who provide similar services and are intended to be protected under the suffer or permit to work standard would frequently find themselves displaced by those willing to decline such coverage. . . .

[A] focus on the nature of the workers' role within a hiring entity's usual business operation also aligns with the additional purpose of wage orders to protect companies that in good faith comply with a wage order's obligations against those competitors in the same industry or line of business that resort to cost saving worker classifications that fail to provide the required minimum protections to similarly situated workers. A wage order's *industry-wide* minimum requirements are intended to create a level playing field among competing businesses in the same industry in order to prevent the type of "race to the bottom" that occurs when businesses implement new structures or policies that result in substandard wages and unhealthy conditions for workers. . . .

3. Part C: Is the worker customarily engaged in an independently established trade, occupation, or business of the same nature as the work performed for the hiring entity?

[T]he suffer or permit to work standard . . . is intended to preclude a business from evading the prohibitions or responsibilities embodied in the relevant wage orders directly or indirectly—through indifference, negligence, intentional subterfuge, or misclassification. It is well established, under all of the varied standards that have been utilized for distinguishing employees and independent contractors, that a business cannot unilaterally determine a worker's status simply by assigning the worker the label "independent contractor" or by requiring the worker, as a condition of hiring, to enter into a contract that designates the worker an independent contractor. . . .

As a matter of common usage, the term "independent contractor," when applied to an individual worker, ordinarily has been understood to refer to an individual who *independently* has made the decision to go into business for himself or herself. Such an individual generally takes the usual steps to establish and promote his or her independent business—for example, through incorporation, licensure, advertisements, routine offerings to provide the services of the independent business to the public or to a number of potential customers, and the like. When a worker has not independently decided to engage in an independently established business but instead is simply designated an independent contractor by the unilateral action of a hiring entity, there is a substantial risk that the hiring business is attempting to evade the demands of an applicable wage order through misclassification. A company that labels as independent contractors a class of workers who are not engaged in an independently established business in order to enable the company to obtain the economic advantages that flow from avoiding the financial obligations that a wage order imposes on employers unquestionably violates the fundamental purposes of the wage order. The fact that a company has not prohibited or prevented a worker from engaging in such a business is not sufficient to establish that the worker has independently made the decision to go into business for himself or herself.

Accordingly, in order to satisfy part C of the ABC test, the hiring entity must prove that the worker is customarily engaged in an independently established trade, occupation, or business.

. . . [I]n order to establish that a worker is an independent contractor under the ABC standard, the hiring entity is required to establish the existence of each of the three parts of the ABC standard. Furthermore, . . . a court is free to consider the separate parts of the ABC standard in whatever order it chooses. Because . . . it may be easier and clearer for a court to determine whether or not part B or part C of the ABC standard has been satisfied than for the court to resolve questions regarding the nature or degree of a worker's freedom from the hiring entity's control for purposes of part A of the standard, the significant advantages of the ABC standard—in terms of increased clarity and consistency—will often be best served by first considering one or both of the latter two parts of the standard in resolving the employee or independent contractor question. . . .

[The court affirmed the trial court's ultimate determination that there is a sufficient commonality of interest to support certification. It found sufficient commonality of interest with regard to Part B of the ABC test—the question whether the work provided by the delivery drivers within the certified class is outside the usual course of the hiring entity's business to permit plaintiffs' claim of misclassification to be resolved on a class basis, since Dynamex's entire business is that of a delivery service. While it found such commonality is enough, the court also concluded that there is sufficient commonality of interest under Part C.]

NOTES

1. *Similar Facts, Immense Stakes, Differing Outcomes.* In each of these cases, the drivers made deliveries for a company engaged in the parcel delivery business and were subject to a contract crafted by the company that purported to render them independent contractors (both explicitly and through a series of financial and other terms). Moreover, both cases were high stakes in that they each involved matters of great import to the parties and society: the right to unionize and the applicability of wage and hour protections. Indeed, workers who are not employees *cannot* unionize or engage in other work-related collective activity—that would run afoul of federal antitrust law. And, except in rare circumstances, nonemployees enjoy no minimum wage or overtime protection. These kinds of stakes, along with the other legal risks and obligations of employment, explain why both FedEx and Dynamex attempted to avoid employment relationships with their drivers.

Yet the courts reached very different conclusions: In rejecting the NLRB's approach, the majority's analysis in *FedEx* found that the drivers are independent contractors; the California Supreme Court's decision in *Dynamex* affirming class action treatment forges a clear path to a finding that the drivers are employees. Can these disparate conclusions be explained by factual distinctions? That is, are the relationships between the drivers and FedEx distinguishable from those between Dynamex and its drivers? If so, how? If not, then what explains the difference? One result of the courts' differing approaches is that "employment" for purposes of drivers unionizing under the NLRB is far narrower than for wage and hour protections under California law. Does that difference make sense?

2. *The Common-Law Approach.* Again, in the vast majority of circumstances, federal and state courts addressing the distinction between employees and independent contractors have applied some version of the common-law definition. All three opinions—the majority and dissent in *FedEx* and the decision in *Dynamex*—acknowledge the history and prominence of this approach. Yet they each take a very different view on applying it. The *FedEx* majority, while purporting to adhere to the common law, eschewed a multifactored balancing test for determining control and instead emphasized entrepreneurial opportunity for gain and loss as the touchstone for determining whether an employee had sufficient control or independence to be deemed an independent contractor. The dissent disagreed with the majority's focus on entrepreneurialism, as a matter both of precedent and of policy, arguing that a multifactored inquiry that included within it entrepreneurialism is the correct approach. The *Dynamex* court accepted a variant of the common-law approach (the *Borello* test) as one test for determining employee status, but it recognized the "ABC test" as an alternative. In practice in California, few minimum wage cases are likely to turn on the *Borello* test going forward.

The entrepreneurialism approach, at least as articulated and applied, is clearly the narrowest of the three. While it appears closely related to the alternative later articulated in the Third Restatement, some might argue that application of the Third Restatement test would not be as strict, in part because, by its framing, the Restatement implicitly places the burden on the firm to show that the worker exercises sufficient entrepreneurial control, and also because of the FedEx court's willingness to accept "entrepreneurial potential" (rather than actual exercise of entrepreneurial opportunities for gain or loss) as sufficient for finding independent contractor status. The dissent's articulation of the common-law multifactored approach adopted is broader, and the ABC test, which abandons the necessity for control and includes the sweeping "outside of the usual course" of business element, is broader still.

In thinking about which approach is best, consider the inquiries that emerge from each decisions' criticisms of other approaches: (1) Does the test lead to adequately predicable results? (2) Does the test define the scope of employment appropriately in light of the purpose of the underlying employment law doctrine at issue? (3) Is the test's application subject to party—usually employer—manipulation? Consider each decision's discussion of these issues. Which is the most persuasive? Going a step deeper, the *FedEx* dissent also criticized how the majority defined and applied its entrepreneurism approach, arguing that entrepreneurial potential (opportunity in theory but not in practice) should not be sufficient to demonstrate independent contractor status or negate employee status. Does this affect your view about whether the majority's approach is more predictable, appropriate as a policy matter, or manipulable? *See* Jeffrey M. Hirsch, *Employee or Entrepreneur?*, 68 WASH. & LEE L. REV. 353 (2011).

Note that these inquiries are also reflected in *Dynamex*'s consideration of "economic reality" test. As *Dynamex* discussed, courts have adopted this test when seeking to determine worker status for purposes of social welfare legislation, such as the Fair Labor Standards Act ("FLSA")—the principal federal law governing the minimum wage and overtime pay—and some state wage and workers' compensation laws. The idea is to serve the remedial purpose of the statute by expanding the common-law definition through, among other things, considering worker dependence on the firm. *See, e.g., Bartels v. Birmingham,* 332 U.S. 126, 130 (1947). As suggested in *Dynamex,* however, the economic realities test is similar to the common-law test both in structure (a multifactored inquiry) and substance (a focus on control). *See Bartels,* 332 U.S. at 130 ("[P]ermanency of the relation, the skill required, the investment in the facilities for work and opportunities for profit or loss from the activities were also factors that should enter into judicial determination as to the coverage of the Social Security Act."); RESTATEMENT OF EMPLOYMENT LAW, §1.01 cmt. a (suggesting that courts that have relied on the common-law and economic realities approaches have tended to utilize the same factors and reach the same results); *see also Oestman v. National Farmers Union Ins. Co.,* 958 F.2d 303, 305 (10th Cir. 1992) (suggesting a "hybrid" approach that considers both control and dependence). Indeed, some courts deny any substantive difference between the tests. *See, e.g., Murray v. Principal Fin. Group, Inc.,* 613 F.3d 943, 945 (9th Cir. 2010) (concluding that "there is no functional difference" between the tests of common-law control, economic realities, and a so-called hybrid of the two).

   3. *The Critique Continued.* The inquiries highlighted in the prior note—and the *FedEx* and *Dynamex* courts' attempts to grapple with them—reflect the broader debate over continued reliance on the common-law test. First, as the cases illustrate, the test and its variations are highly fact-intensive and therefore often create uncertainties regarding the relationship. These uncertainties may impose real costs on both workers and firms: They increase ex ante planning and risk management costs and ex post costs, including the costs of litigation. Indeed, this lack of predictability may be particularly problematic for workers who have legitimate expectations (e.g., of workers' compensation coverage for workplace injuries), which ultimately are defeated ex post.

   One should consider counterarguments, however: While bright-line rules offer greater predictability, there may be no bright line to draw, and thus, any such rule may suffer from over- or underinclusiveness. In addition, a clearer but less fact-intensive rule may have troublesome implications related to the second and third inquires. That is, unless it is well calibrated to serve the remedial or other purposes of the underlying employment doctrine, a clearer rule may defeat these purposes. For example, if employment status were determined by the parties' agreement or firm-worker intent alone, the rule would be clearer, but firms often would be able to avoid altogether the strictures of wage, antidiscrimination, and other employment laws. On the other end of the spectrum, the ABC test probably creates greater certainty (most long-term workers will be employees), but management-side advocates would argue that its sweep is too broad.

   The second, frequent criticism of the common-law test relates, again, to purpose. The test was originally intended to draw a distinction between employees and independent contractors only for determining whether the worker's principal is liable under the doctrine of respondeat superior to a third party harmed by the workers' tortious conduct. Indeed, this is why the level of control is so central in the analysis: Tort and agency law seek to link legal accountability with control. Yet other forms of employment regulation serve different ends. Because the regimes discussed in this book advance social policies separate and distinct from the ends that respondeat superior was designed to serve, the common-law definition is ill-suited to determine who is subject to such regulation. *See, e.g.,* Steven F. Befort, *Revisiting the Black Hole of Workplace Regulation: A Historical and Comparative Perspective of Contingent Work,* 24 BERKELEY J. EMP. & LAB. L. 153, 168 (2003); Dennis R. Nolan et al.,

Working Group on Chapter 1 of the Proposed Restatement of Employment Law: Existence of Employment Relationship, 13 EMP. RTS. & EMP. POL'Y 43 (2009).

Of course, *Dynamex*'s analysis reflects this critique. In a famous case in which the Seventh Circuit held that migrant agriculture workers hired to pick cucumbers were "employees" under the FLSA and, hence, entitled to minimum wage protection, Judge Easterbrook offered a similar appraisal:

> [The independent contractor doctrine] is a branch of tort law, designed to identify who is answerable for a wrong (and therefore, indirectly, to determine who must take care to prevent injuries). To say "X is an independent contractor" is to say that the chain of vicarious liability runs from X's employees to X but stops there. . . . All the details of the common law independent contractor doctrine having to do with the right to control the work are addressed to identifying the best monitor and precaution-taker. . . . The reasons for blocking vicarious liability at a particular point have nothing to do with the functions of the FLSA.

Secretary of Labor v. Lauritzen, 835 F.2d 1529, 1544-45 (7th Cir. 1987) (Easterbrook, J., concurring). Judge Easterbrook suggests that the test ought to reflect the purposes of the FLSA and that, thus, the statute should cover all workers (common-law "employees" or not) with few or no skills—those "who possess *only* dedication, honesty, and good health." *Id*. at 145. Is this approach more or less appropriate than the common law or related economic reality approach? How does it compare with the ABC test?

Turning then to another area of employment regulation, consider whether the court correctly determined in *Lerohl v. Friends of Minnesota Sinfonia*, 322 F.3d 486 (8th Cir. 2003), that two female musicians were independent contractors of the symphony for which they performed regularly (until they were terminated) and therefore were unable to claim sex and disability discrimination under Title VII and the ADA. In analyzing the workers' status, the court purported to apply the common-law factors. It recognized that the symphony's conductor exercised significant, almost exclusive, control over the work itself, namely, the production of music in rehearsals and concerts. Yet because the musicians were highly skilled professionals, required no on-the-job training, retained the discretion to play for others, could reject playing in particular performances (upon adequate notice), and were not treated as employees for tax and benefit purposes, the court found that they were not employees as a matter of law. Outcomes in other cases involving the employment status of musicians and other performers are mixed. *Compare Alberty-Velez v. Corporacion de P.R. para la Difusion Publica*, 361 F.3d 1 (1st Cir. 2004) (holding that the host and producer of a local television show was an independent contractor and thus could not sue the station for discrimination under Title VII), *with Jaclyn S. v. Buffalo Bills, Inc.*, 997 N.Y.S.2d 669 (N.Y. Sup. Ct. 2014) (denying a motion to dismiss cheerleaders' claims against the Buffalo Bills because, despite being recruited by two independent agencies and having signed agreements stating that they were independent contractors, allegations of the organization's minute control over the cheerleaders were enough to suggest they were employees). *Jackson v. Gaylord Entertainment Co.*, 2007 U.S. Dist. LEXIS 92514 (M.D. Tenn. Dec. 14, 2007) (finding sufficient facts to support the contention that a performer at the Grand Old Opry was an employee for statutory purposes and distinguishing *Lerohl* because of the terms of the written agreement in this case suggesting employment) and *Lancaster Symphony Orchestra*, 357 NLRB No. 152

(2011) (in finding that members of the orchestra were employees for federal labor law purposes, the National Labor Relations Board (NLRB) distinguished the facts in *Lerohl* as well as noted that *Lerohl* was decided under a different statutory regime).

Whether the outcome in *Lerohl* was correct even under the common-law approach is debatable. *See* Jeff Clement, Lerohl v. Friends of Minnesota Sinfonia: *An Out of Tune Definition of "Employee" Keeps Freelance Musicians from Being Covered by Title VII*, 3 DePaul Bus. & Com. L.J. 489 (2005). In any event, in the status discrimination context, it is not readily apparent why protection ought to hinge on such a balance of control and worker independence. *See generally* Lewis L. Maltby & David C. Yamada, *Beyond Economic Realities: The Case for Amending Federal Employment Discrimination Laws to Include Independent Contractors*, 38 B.C. L. Rev. 239, 241-42 (1997). Should workers who are somewhat less controlled by those for whom they work or who are less economically dependent because of their skills be unprotected from, say, sex discrimination? Or is there a more appropriate way to determine who ought to be free from discrimination in paid work?

4. *The Lengthy and Varied History of Litigation over FedEx Drivers Status.* The same determination of employment status at issue in the Wilmington FedEx location in the above case also arose in FedEx's Hartford location. *FedEx Home Delivery v. NLRB*, 849 F.3d 1123 (D.C. Cir. 2017). There, the NLRB decided that the single-route ground division drivers were employees. *Id.* at 1124. When this issue came before the D.C. Circuit in 2017, the court again determined the Hartford drivers were independent contractors. *Id.* Yet, in other litigation under other statutory regimes, FedEx delivery drivers have been found to be employees. For example, the Kansas Supreme Court, in certifying answers to the Seventh Circuit court hearing this case, found the FedEx workers were employees for the purpose of the Kansas Wage Payment Act. *Craig v. FedEx Ground Package Sys.*, 335 P.2d 66 (2014). Notably, the court focused on manipulation, emphasizing that FedEx had structured the agreement such that the drivers could be labeled independent contractors so that it could avoid additional costs associated with employees. *Id.* at 91. The court took a dim view of the fact that this was a "case by design, not happenstance." *Id.* at 73; *see also Alexander v. FedEx Ground Package Sys.*, 765 F.3d 981 (9th Cir. 2014) (finding that the drivers are employees as a matter of law for claims for employment expenses and unpaid wages under the California Labor Code). *But see* In re *FedEx Ground Package Sys., Inc. Employment Practices Litig.*, 2010 U.S. Dist. LEXIS 53733 (N.D. Ind. May 28, 2010) (holding that FedEx misclassified plaintiff driver as an independent contractor instead of an employee and noting that there were over 60 wage-related lawsuits pending against FedEx in other jurisdictions); *see generally* Todd D. Saveland, *FedEx's New "Employees": Their Disgruntled Independent Contractors*, 36 Transp. L. J. 95 (2009) (discussing the litigation).

The fact that FedEx's strategy with regard to the structure of the relationship with its workers has been met with mixed litigation success might seem puzzling at first blush; after all, if FedEx so desperately wants to avoid employment status, why hasn't it abandoned this structure and granted its drivers far more actual control over their routes, timing, finances, customers, and other aspects of the work? The likely answer, as discussed more fully following the next case, is that while FedEx wants to avoid the risks and costs of employment, it also wants to retain as much control over its enterprise as possible to ensure quality and customer satisfaction, protect its brand, and stabilize its financial risks and rewards. In other words, it wants to have its cake and eat it too.

5. *The ABC Test and the Gig Economy.* Not lost on close observers of the so-called "gig" economy—also sometimes described as the "on-demand" or "sharing" economy—are the enormous implications of *Dynamex*'s adoption of the ABC test. There has been much discussion, debate, and litigation over whether gig economy workers, including those working for ride-sharing services such as Uber and Lyft—or other types of services such as Handy, TaskRabbit, and Instacart—are employees or independent contractors. The rise of businesses like these that use online platforms to connect consumers with workers providing labor services has created new problems in employee classification. *See, e.g.,* Benjamin Means & Joseph Seiner, *Navigating the Uber Economy,* 29 U.C. DAVIS L. REV. 1511 (2016); Brishen Rogers, *Employment Rights in the Platform Economy: Getting Back to Basics,* 10 HARV. L. & POL'Y REV. 479 (2016). Both Uber and Lyft classify their drivers as independent contractors but exercise control over important aspects of the driver/customer interaction. Drivers around the country have brought suits against the companies alleging they are employees and, hence, entitled to various protections—including wages and hours—they have been denied.

In light of these many claims, courts have begun to grapple with the challenge of determining how to classify such workers, especially Uber and Lyft drivers. As the court said in *Cotter v. Lyft,* this kind of challenge is like being "handed a square peg and asked to choose between two round holes." *Cotter v. Lyft, Inc.,* 60 F. Supp. 3d 1067, 1081 (N.D. Cal. 2015). Still, few have reached definitive conclusions on the issue, in part because the companies have settled a number of the cases, often to avoid resolution of the employment status issue. *See, e.g.,* *O'Connor v. Uber Techs., Inc.,* 80 Cal. Comp. Cases 852 (N.D. Cal. Sept. 1, 2015); Mike Isaac & Noam Scheiber, *Uber Settles Cases with Concessions, but Drivers Stay Freelancers,* N.Y. TIMES, Apr. 22, 2016, at B1. Nevertheless, many suits that turn on the status question are still pending in courts around the country. *See, Doe v. Uber Technologies, Inc.,* 184 F. Supp. 3d 744 (N.D. Cal. May 4, 2016) (alleging vicarious liability for sexual assaults by Uber drivers); Heather Kelly, *Uber and Lyft Drivers in Austin Sue the Companies,* CNN MONEY (June 10, 2016, 5:54 P.M.), http://money.cnn.com/2016/06/10/technology/austin-lawsuits-uber-lyft (discussing suits alleging violations of the Worker Adjustment and Retraining Notification Act). State administrative agencies that have addressed the question of the drivers' status have reached differing conclusions. Mike Isaac & Natasha Singer, *California Says Uber Driver Is Employee, Not a Contractor,* N.Y. TIMES, June 18, 2016, at B1; Michael Auslen, *State Job Chief: Uber Drivers Are Contractors, Not Employees,* MIAMI HERALD (Dec. 3, 2015), http://www.miamiherald.com/news/business/article47843400.html.

The Uber and Lyft phenomenon has spawned various calls for modification of the common-law definition. *See generally* Keith Cunningham-Parmeter, *From Amazon to Uber: Defining Employment in the Modern Economy,* 96 BU L. Rev. 1673 (2016) (using the FLSA's original broad definition of "employment" as a lens to urge a refocused notion of control for it and other statutes to look not merely to daily, direct supervision but also to the numerous ways in which firms may control workers). *Cf.* Benjamin Means & Joseph A. Seiner, *Navigating the Uber Economy,* 49 U.C. DAVIS L. REV. 1511, 1515 (2016) (arguing for a test of employment that would look to "[h]ow much flexibility do individuals have in determining the time, place, price, manner, and frequency of the work they perform."); Richard R. Carlson, *Employment by Design: Employees, Independent Contractors and the Theory of the Firm,* https://ssrn.com/abstract=2919670 (proposing incorporating the theory of the firm in the rules for determining whether a worker is an employee or a non-employee seller of work, i.e., an independent contractor). But the ABC test sweeps more broadly. Aren't Uber and Lyft drivers pretty clearly employees under the ABC test? If so, then they are subject to California wage and hour and perhaps other laws. Are there viable counterarguments?

And the effects of *Dynamex* and the ABC test extend further, since the gig economy can no longer be viewed as merely a small corner of the labor market (or merely about ridesharing services). Estimates of its size vary widely, as do definitions of its scope. According to Intuit, for example, the gig economy accounts for approximately 34 percent of the current workforce and is expected to reach 43 percent by 2020 (Patrick Gillespie, *The Gig Economy May Be Bigger Than You Think*, CNN Money (May 24, 2017), http://money.cnn.com/2017/05/24/news/economy/gig-economy-intuit/). A 2017 Bureau of Labor Statistics Report, on the contrary, suggests such estimates may be far too high, at least as a measure of workers' primary jobs, *see* Bureau of Labor Statistics, Department of Labor, USDL-18-0942, Contingent and Alternative Employment Arrangements—May 2017 (June 7, 2018). Yet even the most conservative estimates (and narrowest definitions) indicate the sector is far from de minimis.

Nevertheless, how the law should address work relationships in this new sector remains a puzzle. *See, e.g.*, Miriam A. Cherry, *"Dependent Contractors" in the Gig Economy: A Comparative Approach*, 66 Am. U.L. Rev. 635 (2017) (discussing comparative approaches); *see also* Orly Lobel, *The Gig Economy & The Future of Employment and Labor Law*, 51 U.S.F. L. Rev. 51, 58-71 (2017) (discussing four proposals for reform beyond the traditional master-servant relationship); Brishen Rogers, *Employment Rights in the Platform Economy: Getting Back to Basics*, 10 Harv. L. & Pol'y Rev. 479 (2016) (arguing that there are powerful reasons for holding economy platform companies to employment duties, at least around basic economic conditions such as wages and reimbursements). Because the status of such workers under the common-law and other control-based approaches is debatable, and the ABC test is unlikely to be adopted as federal law, such gig economy workers face the prospect of a mixed status, subject to employee protections under some legal regimes but not others.

Still, even if gig economy workers enjoy greater protections in light of developments like *Dynamex*, enforcement of these rights remains a challenge. For example, arbitration agreements that preclude class or collective pursuit of work-related claims may deter such claims—a matter discussed in greater detail in Chapter 13; *see also* Charlotte Garden, *Disrupting Work Law: Arbitration in the Gig Economy*, 2017 U. Chi. Legal F. 205, 207 (2018). Other challenges gig economy and other low-paid workers face in enforcing their rights are discussed in the next section of this chapter.

6. *The Role of Private Ordering.* None of the tests for determining employee/independent contractor status discussed in this section treat the parties' view of their relationship or the express terms of the contract as dispositive. Thus, on this issue, private ordering has its limits. Nevertheless, the ability of the parties to structure their relationship can affect most factors in the common-law analysis, whether focused on entrepreneurialism or not. Again, this is tied to the manipulation critique of the common-law test—i.e., to serve the purposes of an underlying employment doctrine or protection, we ought to limit the ability of the employer to impose terms that affect the employment status analysis. Is this kind of argument convincing, or should the parties' intent or agreement play a significant role in the determination? To what extent do effects on third parties or the public as a whole matter in this analysis?

7. *Legal Advantages of Employment Relationships for Firms.* The doctrine of respondeat superior and the legal protections for employees discussed above may provide strong incentives for firms to contract with third parties for services and avoid direct employment relationships. Firms can also benefit from an employment relationship with workers, however. For example, workers' compensation law creates potentially conflicting incentives for firms. As discussed in Chapter 5, workers' compensation regimes are premised on the trade-off of greater coverage but lower benefits: Employers pay premiums into a disability fund or insurance program from which employees injured on the job—regardless of fault—receive a defined amount of compensation for medical expenses and for lost wages while they are disabled and unable to work; in exchange, the workers' compensation program is the employees' exclusive remedial scheme for workplace injuries, thereby shielding the employer from potentially more costly tort liability. LEX K. LARSON, WORKERS' COMPENSATION LAW §§1.01, 100.01 (Matthew Bender & Co., Inc., Rev. Ed. 2014). Thus, when a worker is injured on the job, firms generally have an incentive to claim that the worker is an employee to preclude possible greater tort liability. On the other hand, because workers' compensation coverage is no-fault and otherwise broader than tort liability, firms occasionally claim that a worker is an independent contractor and not entitled to coverage, particularly when the employee would have a weak tort claim against the firm. *See, e.g.,* Dean J. Haas, *Falling Down on the Job: Workers' Compensation Shifts from a No-Fault to a Worker-Fault Paradigm*, 79 N.D. L. REV. 203, 234 (2003). Furthermore, by classifying workers as independent contractors, the firm may avoid paying compensation insurance premiums for those individuals during their employment.

In addition, firms may prefer employment over other statuses because employees may owe the firm more demanding fiduciary duties. As will be discussed in Chapter 8, the reach and content of such duties are controversial. Nevertheless, they may be particularly important from the firm's perspective when it is vulnerable to worker attempts to usurp its opportunities or good will or otherwise compete with it for business. *See, e.g., Midwest Ink Co. v. Graphic Ink Systems*, No. 98 C 7822 2003 WL 360089 (N.D. Ill. Feb. 18, 2003) (holding that whether a company's former salesman owed the firm a duty not to compete during his tenure on the sales force depended on his status an employee or independent contractor). The next case offers another example of a circumstance in which a firm has a strong incentive to treat workers as employees, at least for certain purposes. Still, as you read, also consider why the firm did not structure the relationship differently at the outset to increase the probability of a favorable outcome on this issue. Consider also how a firm with a strong incentive to treat workers as employees for certain purposes might protect its interests even without assurance of a judicial finding of an employment relationship.

≡ *Natkin v. Winfrey*
≡ *111 F. Supp. 2d 1003 (N.D. Ill. 2000)*

CASTILLO, District Judge.

This case is about eleven photographs of Oprah Winfrey taken by Plaintiffs Paul Natkin and Stephen Green on the set of her (rather) well-known television show. The photographs were subsequently published in Winfrey's book *Make the Connection*, co-authored with Bob Greene and published in 1996 by Buena Vista Books under the name Hyperion, without [Natkin's or Green's] permission. That publication resulted in this copyright infringement action and various other causes of action under the Lanham Act and Illinois state law. The defendants counterclaim seeking a declaration of rights.

. . . At base, we must decide whether either side has definitively established ownership of the copyrights to the photographs: To succeed on their motion, Natkin and Green must show that they own the copyrights to the exclusion of the defendants. . . . For the reasons that follow, we conclude that there is no genuine issue that the defendants authored the photographs, either solely or jointly, but that a triable issue exists as to whether the defendants used the pictures pursuant to a valid license. . . .

Background

Natkin and Green are both professional "live event" photographers. Natkin owns (and owned during the relevant times) a private photography studio, Photo Reserve, Inc., and throughout the relevant time period he photographed concerts, live television broadcasts, movie sets, rock video productions, and album/CD covers. Green, since 1982, has been employed by the Chicago Cubs baseball organization, but also engages in freelance photography for others, such as the organizers of the World Series and NBA playoff games.

Natkin photographed *The Oprah Winfrey Show* between 1986 and 1993; Green worked on the show from 1989 to 1996. The photos at issue here were taken between 1988 and 1995. Natkin and Green primarily shot pictures of the show while it was being taped live in the Chicago studio. On occasion, however, when the show was broadcast from another location, they traveled with the show to take pictures. Additionally, Natkin and Green took posed photographs of Winfrey, usually with her more famous guests, either at the show's studio or their own studios. Both men used their own camera equipment and lenses, brought additional equipment (such as lights and backdrops) when taking posed shots, chose the appropriate film, and usually processed the film themselves. The record contains conflicting evidence about who arranged to process the film when Natkin and Green did not perform that task, which company processed the film, and in all cases who stored the negatives.

When photographing the live show, Natkin and Green had no control over the position or appearance of their subjects (i.e., Winfrey and her guests, the audience, etc.), the layout and design of the sets, or even the lighting of the set—Harpo [Winfrey's production firm and one of the defendants in the case] prohibited Natkin and Green from using flash bulbs or any other light source not provided by the studio. Additionally, during live taping of the show, Natkin and Green were restricted to certain locations—they were allowed to move freely about the set only during commercial breaks. But, as to creating the photographs, Natkin and Green had complete discretion over the technical aspects of the shoot: They chose which cameras, lenses, and film to use; the appropriate shutter speed, aperture settings, and timing for the shots; and how to frame the images.

During the relevant times, neither Natkin nor Green worked pursuant to a written agreement. Both men billed Harpo Productions a flat fee for each show they photographed and for any related expenses, including such items as parking and film. Harpo never withheld federal income taxes, FICA, or state income taxes from their payments to Natkin and Green and reported those payments to the IRS on 1099 forms (rather than W-2 forms) as "nonemployee compensation." Additionally, Harpo did not provide health or life insurance, pension benefits, or paid vacation to either Natkin or Green, and both men purchased the insurance for their equipment. Neither photographer was ever given a copy of the Harpo employee manual, but both received paid parking, access to the company cafeteria, Harpo security, and invitations to Harpo staff functions. Additionally, both were referred to, and referred to themselves as, staff photographers for the show. When Natkin or Green was unable to photograph a show due to other commitments, they hired the substitute photographer and billed Harpo.

Green's invoices each contained the following provision: "*Terms/Conditions:* One time, non-exclusive reproduction rights to the photographs listed above, solely for the uses and specifications indicated. . . . Acceptance of this submission constitutes acceptance of these terms." . . . Natkin's invoices explicitly reserved his copyright to the invoiced photos: "All photos remain the property of, and copyrights remain with, Photo Reserve, Inc." Natkin and Green contend that they were freelance photographers that were hired by Harpo and Winfrey as independent contractors to take pictures for publicity purposes only. They claim they are the sole authors of the photographs and, having never transferred their copyrights, are the sole owners of the rights to the pictures. Additionally, Natkin and Green maintain that the only possible license Harpo or Winfrey could have obtained was an oral, non-exclusive license to use the photos for publicity purposes. Thus, according to Natkin and Green, publication of the photos in *Make the Connection* infringed their copyrights.

The defendants, on the other hand, contend that Harpo and Winfrey are the authors of the pictures and thus own the copyrights to them. The defendants assert that Natkin and Green were employees of Harpo and that the pictures were taken within the scope of their employment. Alternatively, they argue that Harpo and Winfrey are joint authors of the photographs because they controlled the vast majority of the picture elements. Finally, as to the infringement claim, the defendants allege that their publication of the pictures in the book was pursuant to a valid license. . . .

I. Copyright Infringement Claims

To establish copyright infringement, Natkin and Green must demonstrate that they own the copyrights to the photographs. Under the Copyright Act, ownership of a copyright "vests initially in the author or authors of the work." Usually, the author of a work is "the person who translates an idea into a fixed, tangible expression entitled to copyright protection." *Community for Creative Non-Violence v. Reid*, 490 U.S. 730, 737 (1989). Under normal circumstances, a photographer is the author of his or her photographs. But, as with any general rule, exceptions exist. Two specific exceptions are relevant to this case: the "work made for hire" and "joint work" exceptions.

A. Works Made for Hire

Works made for hire are "authored" by the hiring party, and the "initial owner of the copyright is not the creator of the work but the employer or the party that commissioned the work." A work made for hire is "(1) a work prepared by an employee within the scope of his or her employment; or (2) a work specially ordered or commissioned . . . if the parties expressly agree in a written instrument signed by them that the work shall be considered a work made for hire." 17 U.S.C. §101. The defendants concede that they do not have a written "work made for hire" agreement with either Natkin or Green covering the eleven photographs. Instead, they argue that Natkin and Green were Harpo employees, as opposed to independent contractors, when they took the pictures.

The Supreme Court has set forth a nonexhaustive, thirteen-factor test for determining whether a creator is an employee within the meaning of the Copyright Act's work made for hire provision. The *Reid* factors are

> the hiring party's right to control the manner and means by which the product is accomplished[;] . . . the skill required; the source of the instrumentalities and tools; the location of the work; the duration of the relationship between the parties; whether the hiring party has the right to assign additional projects to the hired party; the extent of the hired party's discretion over when and how long to work; the method of payments; the hired party's role in hiring and paying assistants; whether the work is part of the regular business of the hiring party; whether the hiring party is in business; the provision of employee benefits; and the tax treatment of the hired party.

Additionally, *Reid* instructs courts to use general common law agency principles to analyze whether the author of a work for hire is an independent contractor or an employee.

Applying the *Reid* factors to our circumstances demonstrates that Natkin and Green were not Harpo employees. Both men were highly skilled professionals specializing in live-action photography; both used (and insured) their own equipment; and both exercised discretion in hiring substitute photographers when they themselves were unavailable and paid those substitutes. Most importantly, neither photographer was ever treated like an employee in terms of compensation, benefits, and taxes: Natkin and Green, via their companies, billed Harpo for their services and expenses, they did not receive regular paychecks or salary; they received none of the employee benefits traditionally associated with employee status, such as health insurance, life insurance, and paid vacation;[4] and Harpo never withheld any payroll taxes on behalf of the photographers.

Further, Harpo's IRS reports describe the payments to Green and Natkin as "nonemployee compensation." We believe this factor alone would outweigh those few factors, discussed below, that favor the defendants' position. Harpo may not obtain the benefits associated with hiring an independent contractor and, at the same time, enjoy the advantages of treating that person as an employee; it must choose.

---

4. The defendants' argument that staff parking, security on the set, and invitations to Harpo staff functions are employee benefits provided to Natkin and Green that weigh in favor of their employee status is unavailing, particularly in the face of the utter lack of any employee benefit normally associated with one's status as an employee.

Here, as to Natkin and Green, Harpo chose the independent contractor route and cannot now change its position to reap a different benefit it probably had not considered when making its choice (i.e., ownership of the photographs).

The only factors clearly favoring the defendants are that the defendants are engaged in business and the duration of the parties' relationship. That Harpo is a business and that Green and Natkin worked for Harpo over an extended period of time (seven years each) doesn't come close to overriding the impact of the factors favoring the photographers' status as independent contractors. Moreover, that Natkin and Green were referred to as "staff photographers" carries very little weight.

The remaining factors are either inconclusive or add insignificant weight in favor of either party's position. For example, all of the parties exercised control over the manner and means of production to some extent: Harpo controlled the appearance of Winfrey and her guests, the sets, and the lighting, while Natkin and Green controlled the technical aspects of taking the photographs (i.e., lenses, film speed, etc.) and, ultimately, the image on the photographs. However, because the task was to create photographs, this factor weighs slightly in favor of independent contractor status. In any event, Harpo's control of the product here resembles the defendants' control over the statue at issue in *Reid*, where the Supreme Court concluded the artist was an independent contractor. . . .

Finally, the parties vigorously contest whether "the work is part of [Harpo's] regular business." Natkin and Green contend that the defendants are in the business of producing a television show, not taking pictures of the show, whereas the defendants maintain that they are in the business of promoting Oprah Winfrey, which includes taking photographs of her on the show. Even assuming this factor weighs in favor of the defendants' position, Harpo's treatment of Natkin and Green as independent contractors in terms of pay, taxes, and benefits; the photographers' use of their own equipment, judgment, and expertise; and that the relationship was technically between Harpo and the photographers' companies definitively establishes that Natkin and Green were independent contractors.

On the basis of the record before us, we conclude there is no genuine issue that Natkin and Green were ever Harpo employees. They were not. Harpo hired Natkin and Green as independent contractors, and they continued in that capacity during their tenures with the show. Thus, Harpo must produce a written work made for hire agreement signed by both sides to successfully claim exclusive ownership of the copyrights to these photographs. Harpo does not have such a document. Consequently, we grant Natkin and Green's motion for partial summary judgment on the work made for hire issue.

[The court went on to grant summary judgment denying defendants' claim that the photographs were a "joint work" of them and Natkin and Green but denied summary judgment on defendants' claim that they had a license to publish the photographs.]

NOTES

1. *Conflicting Legal Incentives and Trying to Have It Both Ways.* You will learn more about the growing implications of employment on intellectual property rights (including copyrights) and other workplace intangibles in Chapter 8. Nevertheless, by now you have seen some of the considerations that influence a firm's decision to hire

employees versus independent contractors, as well as the benefits and disadvantages of these two relationships for workers. These incentives may conflict depending on the context. Of course, decisions about the structure of a relationship are typically made at the point of hire, before the circumstances that might give rise to a dispute are known. Does this give firms a reason to be intentionally vague about the status of their workforce? *Natkin* suggests that one must take the bitter with the sweet: "Harpo may not obtain the benefits associated with hiring an independent contractor and, at the same time, enjoy the advantages of treating that person as an employee; it must choose." Other courts, however, have been willing to look beyond such an express disclaimer of an employer-employee relationship. *See, e.g., Fitzgerald v. Mobil Oil Corp.*, 827 F. Supp. 1301 (E.D. Mich. 2003) (finding a truck driver to be an employee of Mobil under Michigan's workers' compensation law even though their contract expressly disclaimed employment status).

And at least some workers have similarly conflicting incentives. In a famous case litigated in the 1990s, workers originally hired by Microsoft Corporation to perform various technical services—including editing, proofreading, and testing—claimed that they were employees entitled to take advantage (retroactively) of the firm's lucrative profit-sharing plans, even though they had signed agreements expressly stating that they were "independent contractors" not entitled to participate. *See Vizcaino v. Microsoft Corporation*, 120 F.3d 1006 (9th Cir. 1997) (en banc). Of course, Microsoft had incentives to classify the workers originally as independent contractors, including avoiding a number of tax obligations. But the workers also arguably benefited from this arrangement since they did not have taxes and other amounts withheld from their paychecks. Indeed, the workers did not complain about their status or their exclusion from the plans until after the Internal Revenue Service determined, applying its own variation of the common-law test in a separate dispute with Microsoft, that they were employees for tax purposes. After a long series of twists and turns, the workers achieved a partial victory, and Microsoft agreed to pay the class $97 million. *See Employee Benefits—Contingent Workforce: Microsoft to Pay $97 Million to Settle Temporary Workers' Class Action Lawsuits*, 69 U.S.L.W. 2363 (Dec. 19, 2000).

The parties in *Microsoft* wanted to have it both ways: Microsoft wanted to exercise fairly exacting control over workers, but it wanted them treated as independent contractors for various reasons; the workers seemingly benefited in some ways from this arrangement, but later wanted to be treated as employees for other purposes. Despite this, the parties had not left the relationship ambiguous. On the contrary, they had expressly agreed up front that the workers were independent contractors. Should the workers have been held to the terms to which they initially agreed, just as Harpo Productions was in *Natkin*? What might justify the different outcome? Note that, whether or not the terms to which the parties had initially agreed were enforced, the prevailing party in *Microsoft* would succeed in having it both ways.

Still, some benefits that workers receive from initial misclassification might constitute a setoff against damages in some circumstances. For example, this has been an issue in the recent wave of wage and hour litigation involving exotic dancers, who frequently sign contracts with clubs stating that they are independent contractors and will retain a substantial portion of the performance fees they receive from customers. Courts have differed on whether and when these fees can constitute an offset against unpaid wages (under an unjust enrichment theory or otherwise) if the dancers are found to be employees. *Compare Doe v. Cin-Lan, Inc.*, No. 08-cv-12719, 2010 WL 726710 (E.D. Mich. Feb. 24, 2010) (refusing to dismiss breach of contract and unjust enrichment counterclaims brought by a strip club for return of dance fees as an offset in an exotic dancer's wage and hour suit) *with Hart v. Rick's Cabaret Intern., Inc.*, 967 F. Supp. 2d 901 (S.D.N.Y. 2014) (refusing to recognize the club's unjust enrichment theory because the fees were not mandatory and because, the club assumed the risk by misclassifying its dancers).

2. *Contracting to Have It Both Ways.* The last question addresses again the core issue of what role contract or party intent or expectations should play in defining the relationship between worker and firm. Now take this inquiry one step further. Suppose that an agreement provides unambiguously that a worker is an employee for purposes of workers' compensation and intellectual property laws, but an independent contractor for all other purposes. Should a court enforce the agreement, or should the law not permit the parties to define their relationship in this way? To what extent do the stakes—that is, what and whose interest(s) the underlying legal doctrine is designed to protect—matter, if at all? In answering that question, note that, even absent an agreement, a particular worker can be an employee under one statute and an independent contractor under another. What would be the status of Green and Natkin for minimum wage purposes if the ABC test applied?

3. *Protecting Interests Despite Employee/Independent Contractor Status.* Although there are limits on firms' ability to disclaim employment status, parties can contract to avoid the default consequences of that relationship. For example, assuming the workers in *Natkin* were independent contractors, how might the firm have still protected its interests? If Harpo Productions could have protected its rights in the photographs, then is this case simply an example of poor planning?

But not all consequences of relationship status can be altered or eliminated by contract. For example, an independent contractor cannot bargain for protection under federal antidiscrimination laws. The worker may contract for some similar protections, for example, a just-cause term that prohibits termination based on age, race, or sex, but that would not enable her to sue under the federal statutes. Likewise, once a firm is found to be a covered employer, it cannot bargain its way out of federal prohibitions on status discrimination. *See* Chapters 9 and 10. Nor can employers or employees waive the wage and hour requirements of the FLSA, via contract or otherwise. *See* Chapter 11. And, obviously, third parties (including tort victims) will have no opportunity to contract around the legal implications of a worker's employment status. Thus, although private ordering can virtually eliminate the legal consequences of employment status in some contexts and ameliorate them in others, the status of the relationship still has enormous implications.

4. *Worker Status and Socioeconomic Considerations.* Distinctions that reflect the socioeconomic class of workers—skilled and unskilled, managerial and nonmanagerial, white collar and blue collar, permanent and temporary—pervade employment law and policy discussions. Consider the differences between the delivery drivers in *FedEx* and *Dynamex* as compared to *Natkin*, and how the benefits and costs of employment status align with the workers' socioeconomic status in those cases. On balance, most workers, and particularly lower-skilled workers, probably would choose employee status over being an independent contractor or a worker hired through an independent supplier of labor. This is not simply because of the legal protections described above but also because regular employees tend to have greater job, hour, and wage stability and better benefits. On the other hand, workers with skills or knowledge in high demand may benefit (personally, professionally, and economically) from the greater control and flexibility independent contractor status may afford.

Indeed, workers with creative skills like the photographers in *Natkin* and those with established customer relationships, such as sales people or those providing professional services directly to customers, may have incentives to retain as much independence as possible. The workers in *Microsoft* might fall somewhere in the middle, since they have technical skills but not highly valuable talents or customer connections.

Independent contracting has recently been made more attractive for some by a new provision in the tax code allowing such individuals to deduct 20 percent of their revenue from their taxable income. Noam Scheiber, *Tax Law Offers a Carrot to Gig Workers. But It May Have Costs.*, N.Y. TIMES, Dec. 31, 2017, https://www.nytimes.com/2017/12/31/business/economy/tax-work.html. Whether this tax break outweighs the loss of fringe benefits, greater stability, and legal protections that traditional employment provides will depend on a worker's circumstances.

5. *Other Costs of Employment for Potential Employers.* Firm avoidance of tax obligations through "misclassification" of workers as independent contractors costs federal and state governments billions of dollars in tax revenue each year and has led to enhanced enforcement efforts as well as some high-profile disputes. *See* Steven Greenhouse, *U.S. Cracks Down on "Contractors" as a Tax Dodge*, N.Y. TIMES, Feb. 17, 2010, at A1. And women and minorities may be disproportionately harmed by misclassification, given their overrepresentation in occupations at high risk. *See* Charlotte S. Alexander, *Misclassification and Antidiscrimination: An Empirical Analysis,* 101 MINN. L. REV. 907, 910-11 (2017) ("[W]omen and/or people of color are overrepresented in seven of the eight occupations at highest risk for misclassification, suggesting that misclassification may be removing Title VII protection from workers who most need antidiscrimination rights").

As *Dynamex* exemplifies, California is a leader in more aggressively seeking to prevent misclassification. In 2011, it enacted legislation imposing significant penalties ($5,000 to $25,000 per violation) on employers that willfully misclassify workers as independent contractors. *See* CAL. LAB. CODE §226.8 (West 2018). Other states have teamed with the Department of Labor to enhance enforcement and reduce misclassification. *See* Department of Labor, News Release, *US Labor Department Signs Agreements with NY Labor Department and NY Attorney General's Office to Reduce Misclassification of Employees,* November 18, 2013, http://www.dol.gov/opa/media/press/whd/WHD20132180.htm.

Misclassification raises special problems in the immigration context, where the Immigration Reform and Control Act of 1986 ("IRCA"), 8 U.S.C. §§1324a et seq. (2018), prohibits employers from knowingly hiring or retaining workers who are "unauthorized aliens." It also requires employers to examine specific documents that establish worker identity and authorization to work in the United States. By outsourcing to a labor contractor, a firm can reduce the risk of violating IRCA (it remains liable only if it knows a worker is unauthorized), avoid compliance costs, and, often at the same time, reduce labor costs. Workers who are in the country illegally or at least are not authorized to work here have strong incentives to participate in this arrangement when, as is often the case in certain industries, the subcontracting firm is less likely to demand or scrutinize documentation. *See, e.g.*, John A. Pearce II, *The Dangerous Intersection of Independent Contractor Law and the Immigration Reform and Control Act: The Impact of the Wal-Mart Settlement*, 10 LEWIS & CLARK L. REV. 597 (2006); Steven Greenhouse, *Wal-Mart Raids by U.S. Aimed at Illegal Aliens*, N.Y. TIMES, Oct. 24, 2003, at A1. Not surprisingly, given a vulnerable workforce, such subcontracting firms are also less likely to comply with other legal mandates, including wage and hour laws, since undocumented workers may be functionally unable to vindicate their rights. *See* Steven Greenhouse, *Among Janitors, Labor Violations Go with the Job*, N.Y. Times, July 13, 2005, at A1.

6. *Why Are There Still So Many Employees?* Despite the many forgoing disincentives, firms and government agencies have nonlegal incentives to hire workers as employees. Among these are worker preferences for employment, which matter in competitive markets for labor; economies of scale and other efficiencies; the productivity-enhancing or synergistic effects of intrafirm interaction; greater retention of sensitive or valuable information or techniques; and worker morale and a heightened sense of ownership over firm objectives.

But perhaps the most important reason for choosing to employ workers rather than outsource or contract with independents is to exercise greater control over worker activities. Control over the enterprise—over the various aspects of the creation, production, marketing, sale, and/or distribution of the goods, services, and information the firm or agency provides—has enormous value. When control over work details or daily activities is less valuable, for example, where the work requires few skills or particularized training or where quality can be maintained without close supervision, outsourcing to independent workers or firms may be an attractive option. Yet when the exercise of more exacting control is necessary to maintain quality or content, preserve confidentiality, retain good will, ensure coordination between components of the enterprise, or reduce business or legal risks, hiring workers as employees may be preferable.

7. *Control and the Limits of Planning.* The centrality of control in the stakes of employment should now be apparent. Recall the cases we have seen so far: Although each articulates a different test or standard for determining whether a worker is an employee or independent contractor, all except the ABC test emphasize the level of firm control. Each test includes one or more factors that mention control explicitly, and most other factors address aspects of control, including supervisory authority, the power to terminate, and dominion over tools, tasks, the workspace, etc. This means that party expectations regarding the nature of the relationship, whether embodied in an agreement or not, often will be subordinated to countervailing facts about who exercises control over the worker's performance. Again, the *Microsoft* case provides an example. Microsoft and the workers expressly agreed that the workers were independent contractors; yet, in practice, Microsoft treated them much like its ordinary employees—that is, it integrated them into its regular workforce and exercised significant control over their work, resulting in them being treated as "employees" for legal purposes. *See Vizcaino*, 120 F.3d, at 1008-10. As the cases suggest, this tension between firm incentives to exercise control and incentives to avoid the legal consequences of employment creates difficult planning challenges. It also accounts for many of the thousands of cases addressing independent contractor/employee status.

8. *"Covered Employees."* Not all employees fall within the coverage of every employment regulation. Limitations on the "protected class" in certain antidiscrimination statutes provide an obvious example. *See, e.g.*, ADEA, 29 U.S.C. §631(a) (2018) (defining "age" to include only those 40 years of age or older); ADA, 42 U.S.C. §12112(b)(5) (2018) (protection limited to "qualified individuals with a disability"). In addition, the FMLA excludes new employees and part-time workers, *see* Chapter 10, and the FLSA exempts many professional employees from its minimum wage and overtime protections, *see* Chapter 11. Domestic workers—including various kinds of cleaners and caregivers—have been frequently excluded from various employment law protections. In recent years, however, some states have extended

protections to these workers. For example, in 2017, Illinois enacted the Domestic Workers' Bill of Rights Act, extending minimum wage and state human rights protections to various domestic workers, including housekeepers, nannies, and other caregivers. *See* ILL. PUB. ACT 099-0758 (2017).

Note on the Rise of Work at (or Beyond) the Edges of Employment

Among the most debated topics in employment law is whether and how to address the precipitous growth of work relationships that do not fit the traditional conception of employment. Although this discussion focuses on what we characterize as the edges of employment, it should not be viewed as unimportant since it implicates tens of millions of workers and tens of thousands of workplaces.

The Contingent Workforce

Much of the conversation centers on so-called contingent workers. This term encompasses a range of workers in different industries who, for one reason or another, have a less permanent relationship with the firm or government agency for which they work than the "typical" employee. It is, therefore, merely descriptive, having no uniform definition, and one's status as a contingent worker has no independent legal significance. These workers may be short-term employees or independent contractors of the primary firm, or may work (again, as employees or independent contractors) for another firm—a temporary help agency, labor subcontractor, or some other kind of intermediary—that performs services for the primary firm. Indeed, each of the workers at issue in the three cases in the last section, many workers in the on-demand economy, and the workers at issue in the next case involving a labor contractor could be viewed as "contingent workers."

Although the parameters of contingent work are far from clear, the growth and plight of contingent workers as a class has been the subject of intense scholarly interest. *See, e.g.*, DAVID WEIL, THE FISSURED WORKPLACE 271-74 (2014); Seth D. Harris & Alan B. Krueger, *A Proposal for Modernizing Labor Laws for Twenty-First Century Work: The "Independent Worker,"* THE HAMILTON PROJECT (2015), http://www.hamiltonproject.org/assets/files/modernizing_labor_laws_for_twenty_first_century_work_krueger_harris.pdf. As we saw earlier with regard to the scope and size of the gig economy, there is disagreement over how large the contingent workforce is, although there is broad agreement that the contingent workforce has grown faster than the overall workforce in the last several decades. WEIL, *supra*, at 271-73 (suggesting that contingent workers account for 30% of the workforce) *with* BUREAU OF LABOR STATISTICS, DEPARTMENT OF LABOR, USDL-18-0942, CONTINGENT AND ALTERNATIVE EMPLOYMENT ARRANGEMENTS—May 2017 (June 7, 2018) (suggesting the number of workers in various categories that might be described as contingent is significantly smaller than this).

For the same reasons that firms may prefer contingent workers, many workers' interests may be harmed by such relationships. For example, on average, contingent workers receive lower wages and fewer benefits—vacation, disability insurance, medical coverage, etc.—than ordinary employees and have less wage stability than their counterparts in more traditional employment relationships. *See* Arindrajit Dube & Ethan Kaplan, *Does Outsourcing Reduce Wages in the Low-Wage Service Occupations? Evidence from Janitors and Guards*, 63 INDUS. & LAB. REL. REV. 287 (2010) (finding that outsourcing reduces wages and benefits for janitors and security guards). Given all of this and the fact that members of this group tend to have lower skills, they are more likely to be on the economic margins. They are also disproportionately female and African American. *See, e.g.*, Michelle A. Travis, *Telecommuting: The Escher Stairway of Work/Family Conflict*, 55 ME. L. REV. 261 (2003) (discussing how one form of contingent work—telecommuting—is producing greater gender inequalities). While the law does not treat these workers as a distinct group, recent litigation in a few areas of employment law addresses issues facing many contingent working relationships. One involves the wage and overtime protections—*Dynamex* and the next case, *Ansoumana v. Gristede's Operating Corp.*, 255 F. Supp. 2d 184 (S.D.N.Y. 2003), are good examples. But the vexing question is whether and how employment law ought to be reformed to confront more holistically the policy issues raised by the tremendous growth of these kinds of work arrangements.

The Treatment of Volunteers and Students

A related phenomenon that has received much recent attention is the employment status of workers who are not paid wages for the services they provide, including volunteers, student interns, and scholarship athletes. The Restatement of Employment Law takes the position that an individual is a volunteer and *not* an employee "if the individual renders uncoerced services without being offered a material inducement." RESTATEMENT OF EMPLOYMENT LAW §1.02. For example, under the antidiscrimination laws, remuneration is at least a factor in determining whether a worker is an employee, although volunteers who receive no wage or salary can still be employees if they receive other types of benefits—e.g., workers' compensation, insurance or pension benefits, or certification. *See, e.g., Bryson v. Middlefield Volunteer Fire Dept., Inc.*, 656 F.3d 348 (6th Cir. 2011). *But see Juino v. Livingston Parish Fire Dist. No. 5*, 717 F.3d 431 (5th Cir. 2013) (remuneration is not merely a factor in deciding whether an individual is an employee but rather a threshold requirement). *See generally* Mitchell H. Rubinstein, *Our Nation's Forgotten Workers: The Unprotected Volunteers*, 9 U. PA. J. LAB. & EMP. L. 147 (2006).

Another issue is the extent to which unpaid internships, purportedly for educational purposes, violate wage and hour laws. Controversy over such internships in for-profit firms has received growing media attention in recent years. In 2010, the Department of Labor issued new guidance on when unpaid internships in the for-profit private sector constitute an exception to the Fair Labor Standards Act's wage and hour requirements. *See* DOL, Wage and Hour Division, *Fact Sheet #71, Internship Programs Under the Fair Labor Standards Act* (April 2010), http://www.dol.gov/whd/regs/compliance/whdfs71.htm. The guidance provides a six-factor test, focused largely on whether the internship is genuinely educational and whether the intern, as opposed to the firm, is the primary beneficiary. If the internship displaces work otherwise performed by employees in the firm's operations or is used as a trial period for employment with the firm, it is unlikely to survive scrutiny. The DOL emphasized that, because unpaid internships are an exception to the FLSA's mandates, their scope should be construed narrowly; thus, a firm can demonstrate it is not an employer of an intern only if all of the factors listed are met. *See id.; compare* Stephanie A. Pisko, *Comment, Great Expectations, Grim Reality: Unpaid Interns and the Dubious Benefits of the DOL Pro Bono Exception*, 45 Seton Hall L. Rev. 613 (2015).

In contrast, however, the Department of Labor (DOL), in a letter to the American Bar Association, approved internships in law firms so long as the students worked on pro bono matters and some safeguards were in place; http://www.americanbar.org/content/dam/aba/images/news/PDF/ MPS_Letter_reFLSA_091213. pdf. Moreover, at least one circuit court refused to adopt this kind of onerous test in the context of determining whether a student was an employee or "trainee" of a boarding school he attended (which had mandated he perform various work tasks), opting instead for a more flexible "primary beneficiary" analysis that focuses on whether the student or the entity is the primary beneficiary of the internship. *See Solis v. Laurelbrook Sanitarium & Sch., Inc.*, 642 F.3d 518, 524 (6th Cir. 2011).

Nevertheless, a growing number of current and former interns are filing lawsuits alleging employee status and seeking unpaid wages for work performed during the internship. A well-publicized example in the entertainment industry—which is among the industries known for having large numbers of unpaid interns—involves claims brought by interns who worked on production and post-production of the movie *Black Swan*. Although prevailing in the district court, the interns lost before the Second Circuit. *Glatt v. Fox Searchlight Pictures, Inc.*, 811 F.3d 528 (2d Cir. 2015), declined to follow the DOL guidance and instead adopted a three-factor test to determine whether the intern or the employer is the "primary beneficiary" of the relationship: (1) what the intern receives in exchange for his work, (2) the economic reality between the intern and employer, and (3) the intern's expectation of receiving educational or vocational benefits not expected with all forms of employment. *Id.* at 536. The Eleventh Circuit has recently adopted a similar test. *See Schumann v. Collier Anesthesia, P.A.*, 803 F.3d 1199, 1209-10 (11th Cir. 2015).

In contrast with these decisions, a few states have enacted laws providing nonemployee interns with some employee-like protections. While these statutes obviously do not mandate wages or wage levels, they do provide employment-like antidiscrimination and antiretaliation protections. *See, e.g.*, 2014 N.Y. Sess. Laws Ch. 97 (McKinney); Or. Rev. Stat. §659A.350 (2018). *But see Masri v. State of Wisconsin Lab. and Indus. Rev. Comm'n*, 850 N.W.2d 298 (2014) (holding that an unpaid intern cannot state a claim under a Wisconsin whistleblower statute because she received no compensation or tangible benefits and therefore was not an employee).

A further area of controversy is the employment status of scholarship college athletes, particularly in revenue-generating sports (usually football and basketball). Of course, unlike volunteers and unpaid interns, such athletes receive a financial benefit for their participation in the form of scholarship grants. Nevertheless, the issue remains whether such participation constitutes employment. This question made front-page headlines when, in response to a petition by the College Athletes Players Association (CAPA), the NLRB's regional director in Chicago held that students who were on athletic scholarships to play football for Northwestern University were employees within the meaning of the Act. Northwestern University, 2014-15 NLRB Dec. P15781 (March 26, 2014). In reaching this conclusion, the director noted that these players received significant sums for playing and the university received a substantial economic benefit from their services—tens of millions of dollars over the prior decade. In addition, the players devoted a considerable amount of time to their athletic training and performance, at times much more than they devoted to their academic work. Moreover, the players were subject to strict and extensive control by the coaching staff, who also wielded the authority to terminate their scholarships. *See* Steven Willborn, *College Athletes as Employees: An Overflowing Quiver*, 69 U. MIAMI L. REV. 65 (2014). However, the full NLRB unanimously punted (pun intended) by declining to assert jurisdiction in the matter. The board reasoned that ruling on the employment status of a single team would not promote the stability of the NCAA and the Big Ten. *Northwestern University and College Athletes Players Association*, 362 N.L.R.B. No.167 (2015).

Elsewhere, the treatment of student athletes has varied. The Seventh Circuit affirmed a lower court decision holding that track-and-field athletes at the University of Pennsylvania are not employees under the Fair Labor Standards Act. *Berger v. NCAA*, 843 F.3d 285 (7th Cir. 2016). In *O'Bannon v. NCAA*, 802 F.3d 1049 (2015), the Ninth Circuit upheld a lower court's determination that NCAA rules restrained trade in relation to using players' names, images, and likenesses in violation of antitrust laws, although it overturned the portion of the remedy imposed by the lower court involving cash payments to the players.

Outside the athletic context, in *Columbia University*, 364 N.L.R.B. No. 40 (2016), the NLRB held that graduate assistants who have a common-law employment relationship with their university are statutory employees within the meaning of the Labor Act. In so doing, it overturned its prior, contrary precedent in *Brown University*, 342 N.L.R.B. 483 (2004). The broader effects of the decision remain to be seen, in part because it is unclear how a newly constituted Trump NLRB might address this issue. In the interim, however, the decision has had obvious implications for organizing campaigns at other private universities, which appear to be on the rise.

Prison Work

Generally speaking, prisoners who are required to do work in a correctional facility for purposes of punishment or rehabilitation are viewed as not being in an employment relationship with the facility. Thus, prisoners are not generally treated as employees of the correctional institution, despite the exercise of control by the facility. Work for third parties as part of work release or other related programs, as well as work in other custodial contexts, is more likely to be treated as employment. *See, e.g.*, RESTATEMENT OF EMPLOYMENT LAW, *supra*, §1.02 cmt. c. For a history and critique of the treatment of prisoners' employee status, *see* Noah D. Zatz, *Working at the Boundaries of Markets: Prison Labor and the Economic Dimension of Employment Relationships*, 61 VAND. L. REV. 857 (2008).

PROBLEM

1-2. Suppose you have been retained as employment counsel by Microsoft. The firm plans to launch a number of new software products over the next several years. As in earlier years, it will need a large number of code and text reviewers—proofreaders, testers, and editors—to assist in final stages of production. If possible, the firm would prefer to hire these workers as independent contractors for various reasons, including flexibility; the fact that the workers' services will be needed only for discrete projects; its belief that many skilled reviewers might prefer such an arrangement; and the avoidance of various legal obligations to the workers. The firm does not know how long it might retain these workers—that will depend on how well the software products perform and how robust sales are. It concedes that it will need to maintain quality control, which will require monitoring and reviewing the workers' performance, although it does not need to oversee their work on a daily basis.

Microsoft asks you to offer your advice as to how to structure the relationships to reduce the probability that the workers might be found to be its "employees" for one or more regulatory purposes. Obviously, the firm's earlier problems with the IRS and the benefits litigation that followed loom large, and the firm wants to avoid any similar problems in the future. With that in mind, here are some additional facts—"hints"—from that case. The Ninth Circuit described the circumstances regarding the workers' tenure at Microsoft as follows:

> At various times before 1990, Microsoft hired the Workers to perform services for it. They did perform those services over a continuous period, often exceeding two years. They were hired to work on specific projects and performed a number of different functions, such as production editing, proofreading, formatting, indexing, and testing. "Microsoft fully integrated [the Workers] into its workforce: They often worked on teams along with regular employees, sharing the same supervisors, performing identical functions, and working the same core hours. Because Microsoft required that they work on site, they received admittance card keys, office equipment and supplies from the company."
>
> Microsoft did not withhold income or Federal Insurance Contribution Act taxes from the Workers' wages, and did not pay the employer's share of the FICA taxes. Moreover, Microsoft did not allow the Workers to participate in the [firm's profit-sharing benefit plans]. The Workers did not complain about those arrangements at that time.

Vizcaino v. Microsoft Corporation, 120 F.3d 1006, 1008 (9th Cir. 1997) (en banc). However, the workers were treated differently in other ways:

> They had different color employee badges, different e-mail addresses, and were not invited to company parties and functions. Instead of receiving a regular paycheck from Microsoft's Payroll department (like Microsoft's regular employees), [these workers] submitted invoices for their services to the Accounts Payable department.

Id. at 1019 (O'Scannlain, concurring in part and dissenting in part). In addition, the workers signed contracts that provided, among other things, the following terms:

> CONTRACTOR is an independent contractor for [Microsoft]. Nothing in this Agreement shall be construed as creating an employer-employee relationship, or as a guarantee of a future offer of employment. CONTRACTOR further agrees to be responsible for all federal and state taxes, withholding, social security, insurance and other benefits. . . .
>
> [A]s an Independent Contractor to Microsoft, you are self-employed and are responsible to pay all your own insurance and benefits.

Id.

What would you recommend the firm do if, in fact, it is serious about hiring "real" independent contractors to do software editing and testing? Specifically, what language and provisions should it include in its contracts with the workers, and how should it structure its interactions (e.g., pay, training, oversight, allocation of risk, and provision of office space and resources) with the workers? How confident would you be in your advice—that is, in your ability to ensure that the firm avoids its earlier fate?

B. THE FLIP SIDE: WHO IS AN "EMPLOYER"?

The prior section introduced you to the realities of the modern business enterprise. For example, fewer and fewer workers and firms are engaged in what was traditionally thought of as the standard employment relationship—that is, a (long-term) relationship in which the managers of a single firm exert exclusive control over their workers' day-to-day activities in the production of the firm's goods or services. These changes have created challenges for parties, regulators, and courts as more and more workers and entities fit less neatly into the traditional categories of independent contractor, employee, and employer. Indeed, whether they were correctly decided or not, none of the principal cases in the last section (*Fedex, Dynamex,* and *Natkin*) involved what an observer from the middle of the last century would view as a typical employee-employer relationship.

While that section focused primarily on the distinction between employees and independent contractors, this section explores the obviously related questions of who is an "employer" and how to distinguish employers both from nonemployer firms and from "employees." Given the structure of the modern business enterprises, two commonly litigated issues surrounding the definition of employer are (1) to whom to extend employer status and (2) the status of firm owners—manager-owners and parent corporations.

1. "Employer" Status and Accountability for Violations in Disaggregated Enterprises

Business enterprises are now frequently splintered into smaller, independent parts. These arrangements typically involve a large, end-user firm contracting with smaller, independent firms to perform certain tasks within the enterprise, and these smaller firms then retaining workers (employees or independent contractors) to provide labor. Although there are other reasons for end-user firms to outsource services and production, as you are now aware, limitations on liability for work-law violations invite these arrangements. Once limited to the margins, these kinds of structures now are present in most large enterprises, capturing many millions of workers.

Such disaggregation may create significant enforcement obstacles for workers' vindicating their work-related rights, particularly at the low end of the labor market.

Smaller operations are less visible, so detection of violations by regulators and others who might offer assistance to vulnerable workers is more difficult. Moreover, workers may be left to seek remedies against an undercapitalized labor supplier, which is likely to lead to unpaid judgments, heavily discounted settlements, or unprosecuted claims. Outsourcing therefore may do more than shift legal responsibility from one firm to others: It may allow end-user firms to avoid noncompliance risks while benefitting from labor at a price discounted by the low probability of enforcement of employment-law mandates. For a detailed exploration of the disaggregation phenomenon in many sectors of the economy, as well as its legal, economic, and social consequences, *see generally* DAVID WEIL, THE FISSURED WORKPLACE (2014).

A frequently litigated question then is whether and when "employer" status—that is, legal responsibility for employment law violations—can be extended beyond the third-party labor supplier that retained the workers. As foreshadowed in the note about contingent workers, this issue now often arises in FLSA litigation.

As discussed in the prior section, the FLSA requires nonexempt "employees" to be paid a minimum hourly wage and receive overtime compensation at one and one half their "regular rate of pay" for hours worked in excess of 40 hours per week. The minimum wage, set by Congress, currently is $7.25 per hour, although, as discussed in Chapter 11, many states and municipalities have their own laws that set a higher minimum wage.

In most circumstances, the substantive requirements of the FLSA are straightforward; in other words, when they apply, the FLSA's wage and hour requirements are mandatory and fairly simple. Thus, FLSA litigation often focuses on the statute's coverage. The next case addresses who—that is, *which* firms and firm managers—are potentially accountable as "employers" or "joint employers" for unpaid wages.

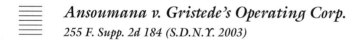

Ansoumana v. Gristede's Operating Corp.
255 F. Supp. 2d 184 (S.D.N.Y. 2003)

HELLERSTEIN, District Judge.

Plaintiffs Faty Ansoumana et al., and the class they represent, were delivery workers for supermarkets and drugstore chains, including stores owned and operated by Duane Reade, Inc., a defendant. The delivery workers were hired by the Hudson/Chelsea group of defendants[5] and assigned to Duane Reade stores to make deliveries to customers and to provide general in-store services, as directed by the store supervisors. I am asked to decide, on these cross-motions for summary judgment, whether, as to the Hudson/Chelsea defendants, the plaintiffs were independent contractors or employees entitled to be paid a minimum wage and time-and-a-half for overtime and, if plaintiffs were employees, whether Duane Reade was a "joint employer," jointly obligated with the Hudson/Chelsea defendants to pay minimum wages and overtime. I will be applying, in determining the issues put to me, the Fair Labor Standards

---

5. The group is made up of Scott Weinstein, Steven Pilavin, Hudson Delivery Service, Inc., and Chelsea Trucking, Inc. Hudson Delivery Service, Inc. is owned and operated by Weinstein, and Chelsea Trucking, Inc. is owned and operated by Pilavin, Weinstein's brother-in-law. The opinion will refer to these defendants as "the Hudson/Chelsea defendants."

Act ("FLSA"), 29 U.S.C. §§201-219 (2002), and the New York Minimum Wage Act, N.Y. Lab. Law §§650-665 (2002).

The defendant, Duane Reade, Inc. is a large retail drugstore chain in the New York metropolitan area. Duane Reade outsourced its requirements for delivery workers by engaging the Hudson/Chelsea defendants to provide delivery workers to the Duane Reade stores, at the rate of $250 to $300 per week, per worker. The Hudson/Chelsea defendants, in turn, paid the delivery workers whom they assigned $20–$30 per day, characterizing them as independent contractors in order to avoid the minimum wage and overtime provisions of federal and New York law.

I hold in this decision that those delivery workers who were assigned to work in Duane Reade stores and made deliveries on foot were not independent contractors, that the Hudson/Chelsea defendants are liable to them for violations of the FLSA and the New York Labor law, and that Duane Reade and the Hudson/Chelsea defendants were joint employers within the meaning of those laws and were jointly and severally obligated to pay minimum wages and overtime to the delivery workers. . . .

I. Background

Plaintiffs filed this action on January 13, 2000 against three large chains of New York supermarkets and drugstores, and several companies and individuals who hired employees to work as deliverymen in such chains. Plaintiffs alleged that the defendants were operating in violation of the FLSA and the New York Minimum Wage Law. They claimed that the defendants, who had hired the delivery workers, and the chains to which they were assigned and in which they worked were jointly and severally liable to them. In May 2001, I certified a class of delivery workers and dispatchers who had worked for defendants between January 13, 1994 and May 24, 2001 and who had not been paid the minimum wage or overtime required under New York law. More than 500 delivery workers have filed consents and are participating in this lawsuit pursuant to the collective action provisions of the FLSA.

The delivery workers involved in the motion before me were hired by the Hudson/Chelsea defendants and were assigned to and worked for Duane Reade stores in Manhattan. The workers are mainly unskilled immigrants, mostly from West Africa. They provided services in the stores and made deliveries from the stores, and, despite working eight to eleven hours a day, six days a week, were paid a flat rate of between $20–$30 per day, well below minimum wage requirements.

The record developed in discovery shows that the Hudson/Chelsea defendants hired the delivery workers for 45 to 60 of the 200 Duane Reade stores located in Manhattan and the boroughs. By oral agreement between Duane Reade and the Hudson/Chelsea defendants, Duane Reade has depended on the Hudson/Chelsea defendants exclusively, since 1994, to supply its stores with delivery workers and has been paying the Hudson/Chelsea defendants a flat weekly rate of $250–$300 per worker. The Hudson/Chelsea defendants hired their workers essentially without advertising, from recommendations by one worker to another, and provided them with uniforms and delivery carts. Since 1989, the Hudson/Chelsea defendants have regarded their delivery workers as independent contractors, not employees, and have required some of the workers to sign statements so acknowledging. The Hudson/Chelsea defendants have not withheld federal, state, or local taxes, nor made FICA or other statutory required withholdings from the payments to the workers, and have given them IRS Forms 1099 rather than W-2s to reflect their compensation. The Hudson/Chelsea defendants did not maintain a system for tracking the delivery workers' hours or pay and did not keep records of any tips the delivery workers received.

In March 2000, the Hudson/Chelsea defendants entered into a collective bargaining agreement with those of its delivery workers who had joined Local 338, Retail, Wholesale and Department Store Workers Union, AFL-CIO. That agreement required that all employees hired by the Hudson/Chelsea defendants earn at least $5.15 an hour and time and a half for overtime. Employees assigned to drug stores are allowed $1.65 of the wage to be credited as tip allowance. Since the agreement was signed, the Hudson/Chelsea defendants have been issuing IRS Forms W-2 to their delivery workers.

The delivery workers assigned to Duane Reade stores reported to the Duane Reade store to which they had been assigned and received directions from Duane Reade personnel in that store. Generally, they were assigned to the pharmacy departments and made deliveries of pharmaceutical items to customers. Duane Reade personnel provided the pharmaceutical stickers, issued the delivery instructions and, if payment was to be collected, instructed the delivery workers how much money to bring back from the customer. The Duane Reade stores maintained logs at the stores, and the delivery workers signed in and out of the logs upon each delivery, recording deliveries and receipts. In their spare time, the delivery workers were often asked to help customers with heavy items, provided bagging services at check-out registers, helped with security, stocked shelves, and moved products from one Duane Reade store to another. If a delivery worker was unsatisfactory, the Duane Reade manager asked Hudson/Chelsea to reassign the worker and provide another to replace him. Thus, the delivery worker, although not hired or paid by Duane Reade, was directed by Duane Reade managers and supervisors and provided services essentially similar to other Duane Reade employees.

II. Legal Framework

A. The Fair Labor Standards Act

. . . The FLSA defines an "employee," with certain exceptions not relevant here, as "any individual employed by an employer." *Id*. §203(e)(1). The statute in turn defines "employ" as "to suffer or permit to work," *id*. §203(g), and "employer" to include "any person acting directly or indirectly in the interest of an employer." *Id*. §203(d). The terms are to be expansively defined, with "striking breadth," in such a way as to "stretch . . . the meaning of 'employee' to cover some parties who might not qualify as such under a strict application of traditional agency law principles." *Nationwide Mut. Ins. Co. v. Darden*, 503 U.S. 318, 326 (1992). As the Second Circuit has ruled, the FLSA, in accordance with its remedial purpose, has been written in the "broadest possible terms," *Carter v. Dutchess Cmty. Coll.*, 735 F.2d 8, 12 (2d Cir. 1984), and is to be construed broadly, for it would run "counter to the breadth of the statute and to the Congressional intent to impose a qualification which permits an employer who exercises substantial control over a worker . . . to escape compliance with the Act."

The regulations implementing the FLSA contemplate that an employee may have more than one employer. 29 C.F.R. §791.2(a) ("a single individual may stand in the relation of an employee to two or more employers at the same time" under the FLSA). Such "joint employment" arises when the employee "performs work which simultaneously benefits two or more employers" and "one employer is acting directly or indirectly in the interest of the other employer (or employers) in relation to the employee." 29 C.F.R. §791.2(b). This question of joint employment of plaintiffs, by Duane Reade and by the Hudson/Chelsea defendants, is a central issue in these cross motions.

[The New York Minimum Wage Act largely tracks the FLSA, although at times it has required a higher wage than did the federal statute.]

III. Plaintiffs Are Employees of the Hudson/Chelsea Defendants

There is no dispute that the plaintiffs were hired by one or the other of Scott Weinstein, Hudson Delivery Service, Inc., Steven Pilavin, and Chelsea Trucking, Inc. (also known as Hudson York)—the defendants to whom I have been referring as "the Hudson/Chelsea defendants." These defendants also do not dispute that they may be treated interchangeably. Thus, if one corporate entity is held liable, that finding may extend to the others. There is also no dispute that the Hudson/Chelsea defendants regarded the plaintiffs as independent contractors, not employees, and until the collective bargaining agreement with Local 338, which became effective March 26, 2000, the Hudson/Chelsea defendants did not keep the records mandated for employees by the FLSA and the New York Minimum Wage Act, did not pay minimum wages or overtime, did not withhold taxes or FICA from payroll, and issued IRS Forms 1099, rather than W-2s.

An employer's characterization of an employee is not controlling, however, for otherwise there could be no enforcement of any minimum wage or overtime law. There would be nothing to prevent old-fashioned labor contractors from rounding up workers willing to sell their labor cheaply, and assigning them to perform outsourced work, without complying with minimum wage requirements. Thus, not the characterization of a hiring hall, but the test of "economic reality," governs how a relationship of employment is to be characterized in relation to the FLSA.

In *Brock v. Superior Care, Inc.*, 840 F.2d 1054, 1059 (2d Cir. 1988), the Court set out an "economic reality" test to distinguish between employees and independent contractors. The test considers five factors: (1) the degree of control exercised by the employer over the workers; (2) the workers' opportunity for profit or loss and their investment in the business; (3) the degree of skill and independent initiative required to perform the work; (4) the permanence or duration of the working relationship; and (5) the extent to which the work is an integral part of the employer's business. *Brock; United States v. Silk*, 331 U.S. 704 (1947). No one factor is dispositive; the "ultimate concern" is "whether, as a matter of economic reality, the workers depend upon someone else's business for the opportunity to render service or are in business for themselves." *Brock*.

Normally, the existence and degree of each factor is a question of fact, and the legal conclusion to be drawn from those facts is a question of law. *Id*. Here, however, as the discussion below makes clear, there is no genuine issue of material fact as to plaintiffs' proper status as employees.

The Hudson/Chelsea defendants argue that they merely "placed" workers with the Duane Reade stores, and it was the store managers and supervisors, not the Hudson/Chelsea defendants, who exercised control. However, the Hudson/Chelsea defendants were more than a placement agency. Hudson/Chelsea, not Duane Reade, paid the delivery workers, and controlled their hiring, firing, transfer and pay. If a worker assigned to a Duane Reade store met with disfavor, the store manager asked the Hudson/Chelsea defendants to transfer him out and assign someone else. Moreover, the Hudson/Chelsea defendants never offered proof of any license as an employment agency, and did not function, vis-à-vis Duane Reade, in the manner of an employment agency, receiving a commission based on several weeks or months of earnings.

The Hudson/Chelsea defendants' relationship with plaintiffs satisfies the first of the *Brock* considerations, showing a substantial degree of control over the workers. As *Brock* made clear, "[a]n employer does not need to look over his workers' shoulders every day in order to exercise control." . . . The fact that the Hudson/Chelsea defendants hired, fired, transferred and paid the delivery workers weighs substantially in favor of finding an employment relationship between the Hudson/Chelsea defendants and plaintiffs.

The second consideration of *Brock*—opportunity for investment, and profit or loss—also weighs heavily in favor of an employment relationship. As defendants conceded, plaintiffs' investment in the business was negligible. Plaintiffs are not asked to invest in Duane Reade, Hudson/Chelsea, or their own jobs. Hudson/Chelsea provided the delivery workers with delivery carts that they could rent and uniforms that they could purchase; the workers did not have to make an up-front investment in such things in order to be hired or assigned to a Duane Reade store.

Hudson/Chelsea argues that delivery services require plaintiffs to exercise "skill and independent initiative," the third consideration of *Brock*, but clearly this is not so in any objective sense. The Duane Reade stores are located throughout Manhattan and the boroughs, and customers typically reside within a neighborhood of a few blocks. Little "skill" or "initiative" is needed to find one's way from a Duane Reade store to a customer's residence.

The fourth consideration, the permanence and duration of the plaintiffs' working relationship with the Hudson/Chelsea defendants, is disputed. Plaintiffs claim that most delivery workers have been working for the Hudson/Chelsea defendants for years, but offer testimony of only four deliverymen, of approximately 500 delivery workers who opted into the lawsuit, to support their claim, and even these four had only a three-year working relationship with the Hudson/Chelsea defendants. Nevertheless, the transience of the work force here says less about the status of the worker than about the nature of the job. Many delivery workers do not endure for long periods of time in this line of work due to the long hours, the low pay, the dangers of the streets, and the vagaries of the weather inherent in delivery work. Any transience of the work force therefore reflects "the nature of [the] profession and not [the workers'] success in marketing their skills independently." *Brock*.

The fifth consideration looks at the extent to which the work is integral to the business, and it also weighs heavily in favor of an employment relationship. The Hudson/Chelsea defendants concede that they are engaged primarily in the business of providing delivery services to retail establishments and that plaintiffs perform the actual delivery work. Thus, plaintiffs' services constitute an integral part of the Hudson/Chelsea defendants' business.

It is clear, from the "economic reality" and the totality of circumstances, that the delivery workers depend upon the Hudson/Chelsea defendants for the opportunity to sell their labor and are not in any real sense in business for themselves. . . . The delivery workers, as a matter of law, are employees, not independent contractors, and are entitled to summary judgment against the Hudson/Chelsea defendants. . . .

IV. Defendants Weinstein and Pilavin Are Individually Liable as Employers

Plaintiffs argue that, along with their companies Hudson Delivery Service, Inc. and Chelsea Trucking, Inc., Scott Weinstein and Steven Pilavin are "employers," and are therefore individually liable under the FLSA for underpayments of minimum wages and overtime. Plaintiffs are correct.

Officers and owners of corporations may be deemed employers under the FLSA where "the individual has overall operational control of the corporation, possesses an ownership interest in it, controls significant functions of the business, or determines the employees' salaries and makes hiring decisions." *Lopez v. Silverman*, 14 F. Supp. 2d 405, 412 (S.D.N.Y. 1998). In *Herman v. RSR Security Services, Ltd.*, 172 F.3d 132 (2d Cir. 1999), the Second Circuit found that a shareholder and member of the board was an "employer" under the FLSA where he had the authority to hire managerial staff, occasionally supervised and controlled employee work schedules, and had the authority to sign payroll checks. The Court emphasized that "the overarching concern is whether the alleged employer possessed the power to control the workers in question," and looked at the "totality of the circumstances" in determining whether defendant had "operational control." Thus, it did not matter that the putative employer did not directly hire workers, but only managerial staff, and that he did not have direct control over the workers in question; instead, the Court looked at whether he had "operational control" over the business.

Weinstein and Pilavin argue that they should not be held individually liable for underpayments because they did not directly control the delivery workers. Clearly, however, Weinstein and Pilavin exercised operational management of Hudson Delivery and Chelsea Trucking, and that is sufficient under the law to satisfy the broad statutory definition of "employer." *See* 29 U.S.C. §203(d). Weinstein and Pilavin are the founders, owners, and sole shareholders of Hudson Delivery Service and Chelsea Trucking, and together they personally oversee and operate the companies and their agents on a daily basis. Thus, under *Herman*, each is an "employer" under the FLSA, and can be held individually liable for failure to pay minimum wages to their employees.

Weinstein and Pilavin argue that they could not be said to exercise control over the delivery workers if Duane Reade exercised such control. This argument misses the point; as I discuss below, the FLSA recognizes joint employment, meaning that more than one employer can be responsible for FLSA obligations. Because Weinstein and Pilavin had operational control over Hudson Delivery Service and Chelsea Trucking, they are individually liable under the FLSA for any underpayments in plaintiffs' salaries. Thus, plaintiffs are entitled to summary judgment against Weinstein and Pilavin, as well as against Hudson Delivery Services, Inc. and Chelsea Trucking, Inc.

V. Duane Reade Is a Joint Employer

The FLSA contemplates that more than one employer may be responsible for underpayments of minimum wages and overtime. 29 C.F.R. §791.2(a)-(b). Duane Reade may be liable to plaintiffs for such underpayments, jointly and severally with the Hudson/Chelsea defendants, if Duane Reade was also their "employer" under the FLSA. The issue is determined by an "economic reality" test, which takes into account the real economic relationship between the employer who uses and benefits from the services of workers and the party that hires or assigns the workers to that employer.

In *Rutherford Food Corporation v. McComb*, 331 U.S. 722 (1947), meat boners who worked on the premises of a slaughterhouse were hired by another employer under contract with the slaughterhouse, much as the delivery workers for Duane Reade were hired to work there by the Hudson/Chelsea defendants. The issue in *Rutherford* was whether the slaughterhouse should be considered the employer of the meat boners when there already was an employer, the head boner who had hired the workers, and also managed and paid them.

The Supreme Court held that the slaughterhouse was a joint employer with the head meat boner for the purpose of minimum wage obligations under the FLSA. The Supreme Court considered that the boners' work was "part of the integrated unit of production," and that the workers did a "specialty" job on the production line, integral to the entire operation of the line. It was the boners themselves, not their company, functioning like piece-workers on a production line, who used the premises and equipment of the slaughterhouse to do their work, rather than shifting from one slaughterhouse to another as "an enterprise that actually depended for success upon the initiative, judgment or foresight of the typical independent contractor."

In *Carter v. Dutchess Community College*, 735 F.2d 8, 12 (2d Cir. 1984), the Second Circuit considered a work-release program of the New York State Department of Correctional Services ("DOCS"), which assigned inmates to work at sites of private employers. The plaintiff was a prison inmate and, under a DOCS program for college graduates, was assigned to work as a teaching assistant at Dutchess County Community College ("DCC"). DOCS paid plaintiff a stipulated allotment, less than the minimum wage, and plaintiff sued under the FLSA for back wages, punitive damages, and an injunction requiring defendants to pay all tutors, including inmate tutors, the same compensation.

The Second Circuit set out a four-part set of criteria to help determine whether DOCS, or DCC, or both, were "employers" required to pay minimum wages, examining who hired and fired the workers; who supervised and controlled their work schedules and conditions of employment; who determined the rate and method of payment; and who was to maintain employment records. Applying the criteria, the Court of Appeals found that it was DCC that had initially proposed to employ prisoners and suggested the wage to pay them; that DCC had established the standards to decide who would be eligible to be a teaching assistant and had identified several inmates whom it proposed to accept; that DCC reserved the right to refuse those inmates whom it did not want; and that DCC had decided for how many sessions and for how long an inmate would be permitted to tutor. On this record, the Court of Appeals held that there were questions of fact whether DCC had exercised sufficient control over the prison inmates to make DCC an "employer" required to pay minimum wages and overtime under the FLSA. Nevertheless, even taking into account the plaintiff's status as a prisoner, the Court did not rule out the possibility that he had FLSA claims against DCC as an employer, stating that the record, while not perhaps reflecting "the full panoply of an employer's prerogatives," may be sufficient to warrant FLSA coverage.

In *Torres-Lopez v. May*, 111 F.3d 633, 642-44 (9th Cir. 1997), farm laborers were procured through a labor agent, who hired them and assigned them to a farm. The Ninth Circuit Court of Appeals found that because these laborers constituted an integral part of the farm's business and because the farm exercised indirect control over them by supervising them and controlling the harvest schedule and the number of workers it needed for harvesting, the farm was a joint employer, along with the labor agent who hired them.

Like the meat boners in *Rutherford*, [and] the farm workers in *Torres-Lopez*..., the delivery workers assigned to Duane Reade performed an integral service for the stores in which they worked, enabling Duane Reade to compete more effectively with mail order fulfillment companies and other drug stores by offering drug deliveries to its customers. The delivery workers worked from the premises of the Duane Reade stores, and assisted other workers in those stores with bagging items at check-out counters, stocking shelves, providing security, and making inter-store deliveries.

Duane Reade offers an analogy to Federal Express, United Parcel, and other delivery services, but the analogy is misplaced. Duane Reade's delivery workers worked out of the Duane Reade stores, and not from a central depot; deliveries were made directly from the pharmacy counters to customers' homes, and not via a central facility; and control was exercised throughout by Duane Reade, and not by some independent service. Duane Reade used the delivery workers to extend its shelves and counters to the homes of customers, allowing them the convenience of shopping from home instead of having to come physically into a store. Duane Reade managers and supervisors directed the delivery workers in their tasks, instructing them what to pick up, where to make deliveries, how to log their deliveries, and how much to receive in payment. The delivery workers worked as individuals, and not as a group shifting from store to store according to seasonal and hourly needs. Indeed, it was not until they were organized by Local 338, in March 2000, that they even had a bargaining representative to negotiate for them as a collective. Clearly, the economic reality of the relationship between Duane Reade and the delivery workers reveals that Duane Reade was an employer of the delivery workers, responsible for assuring that they were paid the wages required by the FLSA and the New York Minimum Wage Act as a condition of their employment.

Additionally, the relationship between Duane Reade and the Hudson/Chelsea defendants establishes joint employment. That relationship was "so extensive and regular as to approach exclusive agency." The Hudson/Chelsea defendants acted directly in the interest of Duane Reade in relation to the delivery workers, 29 C.F.R. §791.2, and Duane Reade used the Hudson/Chelsea defendants' services almost exclusively, for a lengthy period of years, since 1994, showing consistent dependence on them for delivery services.

I therefore hold, looking at the "circumstances of the whole activity," that plaintiffs were economically dependent on both the Hudson/Chelsea defendants and Duane Reade, and that both were their "employers" under the FLSA and the New York Minimum Wage Act. . . .

VII. Conclusion

Duane Reade had the right to "outsource" its requirement for delivery services to an independent contractor, here the Hudson/Chelsea defendants, and seek, by such outsourcing, an extra measure of efficiency and economy in providing an important and competitive service. But it did not have the right to use the practice as a way to evade its obligations under the FLSA and the New York Minimum Wage Act. Both Duane Reade and the Hudson/Chelsea defendants were the "employers" of the plaintiffs under these laws, jointly and severally obligated for underpayments of minimum wage and overtime during the period between January 13, 1994 and March 26, 2000. . . .

NOTES

1. *The FLSA and Contingent Workers.* Duane Reade's use of independent suppliers of laborers reflects the common practice of contracting out low-skilled work by large corporations and other end-user firms. *See, e.g.,* Cynthia Estlund, *Who Mops the Floors at the Fortune 500? Corporate Self-Regulation and the Low-Wage Workplace,* 12 Lewis & Clark L. Rev. 671, 685 (2008). Avoidance of the FLSA's requirements (and corresponding liability risks) is among the most cited and controversial reasons for such outsourcing. *See, e.g.,* Stephen F. Befort, *Labor and Employment Law at the Millennium: A Historical Review and Critical Assessment,* 43 B.C. L. Rev. 351, 367–71 (2002); Richard R. Carlson, *Why the Law Still Can't Tell an Employee When It Sees One and How It Ought to Stop Trying,* 22 Berkeley J. Emp. & Lab. L. 295, 360 (2001); Katherine V.W. Stone, *Legal Protections for Atypical Employees: Employment Law for Workers Without Workplaces and Employees Without Employers,* 27 Berkeley J. Emp. & Lab. L. 251 (2006); Alan Hyde, *Who Speaks for the Working Poor?: A Preliminary Look at the Emerging Tetralogy of Representation of Low-Wage Service Workers,* 13 Cornell J. L. & Pub. Pol'y 599 (2004).

Although many violations go unchallenged, this phenomenon has resulted in a significant number of FLSA and state-law wage and hour suits. As exemplified by *Dynamex* and *Ansoumana,* these disputes implicate the employee/independent contractor distinction, the definition of employer and joint employer, or both. Most of these challenges have arisen in areas commonly known to be rife with wage and other employment-law violations, including delivery services, garment work, light manufacturing, janitorial services, light construction, and landscaping. Some have led to high-profile wage and hour litigation, including the claims by janitorial workers against Wal-Mart, *see e.g., Zavala v. Wal-Mart Stores, Inc.,* 393 F. Supp. 2d 295 (D.N.J. 2005), and the numerous suits by drivers against FedEx, *see* page 33. Note, however, that wage and hour claims also have emerged in unexpected contexts, such as the recent wave of claims brought by exotic dancers. *See, e.g., McFeeley v. Jackson St. Entm't, LLC,* 825 F.3d 235 (4th Cir. 2016) (applying "economic realities" test to determine that exotic dancers were employees of the clubs in which they performed).

2. *Individual Liability.* The *Ansoumana* court found that Defendants Weinstein and Pilavin were "employers" under the FLSA, along with the entities they owned, because they had direct managerial control over the firms. Note that operational control, not mere ownership, is the touchstone, which means that, even in small or closely held entities, holding owners liable will depend on such control. *Compare Gray v. Powers*, 673 F.3d 352 (5th Cir. 2012) (holding an owner/member of a limited liability company was not an "employer" under the FLSA because, although he had an ownership interest in the employing firm, he did not exercise operational or active control over the employees) *with Irizarry v. Catsimatidis*, 722 F.3d 99 (2d Cir. 2013) (finding that the owner of a chain of supermarkets was an "employer" despite the size of the business and his lack of personal responsibility for the FLSA violations and the business entity because of his "active exercise of overall control over the company, his ultimate responsibility for the plaintiffs' wages, his supervision of managerial employees, and his actions in individual stores.").

There are a few other situations outside the wage-and-hour context in which individual owners and supervisors may be held individually liable for employment-law violations. Employees may have personal liability to a discrimination victim under §1981. *See, e.g., Smith v. Bray*, 681 F.3d 888 (7th Cir. 2012); *Jemmott v. Coughlin*, 85 F.3d 61 (2d Cir. 1996). Likewise, those who engage or assist in violations of the FMLA may be subject to aiding and abetting liability or FLSA-like supervisory liability. *See* Chapter 10; *see also* 29 C.F.R. §825.104(d) ("As under the FLSA, individuals such as corporate officers 'acting in the interest of an employer' are individually liable for any violations of the requirements of FMLA."). Individual officers and directors also are potentially liable for violations of Sarbanes-Oxley's whistleblower protections (discussed in Chapter 4). *See* 18 U.S.C. §1514A(a) (2018). Moreover, individual employees may be liable as tortfeasors for the commonly litigated workplace torts not involving personal injury—intentional interference with contract/business advantage, defamation, intentional infliction of emotional distress, and fraud (discussed in Chapter 5). Finally, a few states have enacted narrow "veil piercing" statutes providing that certain shareholders can be held personally liable for unpaid wages. *See* N.Y. Bus. Corp. Law §103 (McKinney 2018); Wis. Stat. Ann. §180.0622 (West 2017).

However, under most common-law and statutory schemes, only the entity (whether a partnership, limited liability company, corporation, or government agency) is the "employer." Thus, manager-owners, supervisors, and other employees within the entity generally are not subject to liability. For example, federal circuit courts are in agreement that supervisory or controlling persons are not subject to liability as employers under Title VII, the ADEA, or the ADA. *See, e.g., Butler v. City of Prairie Village*, 172 F.3d 736 (10th Cir. 1999) (ADA); *Miller v. Maxwell's Int'l, Inc.*, 991 F.2d 583 (9th Cir. 1993) (Title VII and ADEA).

What purposes does individual liability serve in circumstances like *Ansoumana*? Are such purposes unique to the FLSA and small number of other regimes that provide for individual liability? Or are there similar reasons to hold firm managers and controlling personnel liable for other firm torts and statutory violations? Consider how the risk of individual liability might alter firm incentives and affect choices regarding how to structure firm activities and manage liability risk. *See generally* Timothy P. Glynn, *Beyond "Unlimiting" Shareholder Liability: Vicarious Tort Liability for Corporate Officers*, 57 Vand. L. Rev. 329 (2004).

3. *"Joint Employer" Liability.* The court also held that Duane Reade is subject to FLSA liability as a "joint employer" because of Duane Reade's direct supervision of the plaintiffs, plaintiffs' economic dependence on it, and Duane Reade's relationship with the Hudson/Chelsea defendants. The joint employer doctrine is recognized in other contexts as well. *See, e.g.,* EEOC Compliance Manual, Section 2: Threshold Issues, No. 915.003, section 2-III.B.1.a.iii.b (discussing application of the joint employer doctrine under antidiscrimination laws); *see also* RESTATEMENT OF EMPLOYMENT LAW §1.04 (2015) (recognizing that workers can be employees of two or more employers at the same time). *Compare Service Employees Intern. Union v. N.L.R.B.*, 647 F.3d 435 (2nd Cir. 2011) (applying the joint employer doctrine under the National Labor Relations Act, but affirming the NLRB's finding that the secondary firm in this case did not exercise sufficient control over how the workers performed their work to constitute a joint employer).

In a sense, *Ansoumana* was an "easy"—or at least conventional—joint employer case, since the plaintiffs interacted directly with (and were directly supervised by) Duane Reade personnel at Duane Reade stores. But enforcement agencies and private plaintiffs have also sought to extend accountability for employment law violations in other types of enterprise arrangements in which significant control by a second entity is alleged, but there is not this kind of direct interaction with the workers. Courts and enforcement agencies continue to struggle with this question, articulating and applying various tests. *See, e.g., Salinas v. Commercial Interiors, Inc.*, 848 F.3d 125 (4th Cir. 2017) (stating that the core inquiry under the FLSA is whether two or more persons or entities are "not completely disassociated" with respect to a worker such that they share, agree to allocate responsibility for, or otherwise codetermine—formally or informally, directly or indirectly—the essential terms and conditions of the worker's employment).

A high-profile example of a long-running dispute over indirect control is the enforcement activity against McDonald's Corporation for labor violations at its franchised stores. McDonald's owns a very small percentage of its restaurants; the vast bulk are owned independently by franchisees, and McDonald's does not directly supervise the workers at those locations. Yet, through its franchise agreements and monitoring, McDonald's protects its brand by imposing strict requirements on franchisees with regard to food, equipment, cleanliness, some employment practices, and various other matters. In 2014, the NLRB's general counsel announced that he would be pursuing unfair labor practices against McDonald's for alleged labor violations occurring at some of its franchises, and the Board itself called for briefing on the scope of the joint employer doctrine in *Browning-Ferris*, discussed below. *See* Press Release, NLRB Office of Public Affairs, *NLRB Office of the General Counsel Authorizes Complaints Against McDonald's Franchisees and Determines McDonald's, USA, LLC Is a Joint Employer* (June 29, 2014); NLRB, Notice and Invitation to File Briefs, *Browning-Ferris Indus.*, 32-RC-109684 (May 12, 2014). Moreover, McDonald's has been named as a defendant in a number of wage and hour suits brought by employees working at franchised McDonald's restaurants, *see* Stephen Greenhouse, *McDonald's Workers File Wage Suits in 3 States*, NY TIMES, May 14, 2014, at B8. Although, most claims against restaurant franchisors have failed for various reasons, the potential franchisor liability for unpaid wages has been recognized in a handful of other recent decisions, *see, e.g., Cano v. DPNY, Inc.*, 287 F.R.D. 251, 258-59 (S.D.N.Y. 2012) (refusing to dismiss allegations of franchisor's joint employment status); *Orozco v. Plackis*, No. A11–CV–703, 2012 WL 2577522, at *8 (W.D. Tex. July 3, 2012) (same).

While the McDonald's matter was being litigated, the Board issued its decision in *Browning-Ferris Indus of Cal., Inc.*, 362 N.L.R.B. No. 186 (2015), rearticulated its test for determining whether two or more entities are joint employers:

> Two or more entities are joint employers of a single work force if [(1)] they are both employers within the meaning of the common law, and [(2)] if they share or codetermine

those matters governing the essential terms and conditions of employment. In evaluating the allocation and exercise of control in the workplace, we will consider the various ways in which joint employers may "share" control over terms and conditions of employment or "codetermine" them.

In 2017, however, the newly constituted Board overturned *Browning-Ferris* and returned to the prior requirement for joint employer status of actual control that is direct and immediate. *Hy-Brand Industrial Contractors, Ltd.*, 365 NLRB No. 156 (2017). *Hy-Brand* proved to be short lived, as the decision was vacated in early 2018 due to ethics concerns over the participation in that decision of a member whose former law firm was involved in the underlying litigation. This means a return to the *Browning-Ferris* standard, at least temporarily. Since then, the Board has voiced its intention of engaging in rule-making for a joint-employment test. Thus, the status of the joint-employment test is very much up in the air. Meanwhile, as of the date this book went to press, the McDonald's matter remains unresolved.

The pendulum swing on the NLRB and twists and turns in the McDonald's litigation reflect the increasingly politicized nature of employment status disputes. For example, shortly after the change in administration, the Trump Department of Labor withdrew two Obama-era guidelines that had taken expansive approaches to employment status: one addressing the "economic realities" and the other confronting joint employment status. *See* U.S. Dep't of Labor, News Release, *US Secretary of Labor Withdraws Joint Employment, Independent Contractor Informal Guidance* (June 7, 2017), https://www.dol.gov/newsroom/releases/opa/opa20170607; *see also* U.S. Dep't of Labor, Wage & Hour Div., Administrator's Interpretation No. 2015-1 (2015) (economic realities); U.S. Dep't of Labor, Wage & Hour Div., Administrator's Interpretation No. 2016-01 (2016) (joint employment).

And the policy debate over whether the joint employer doctrine is socially beneficial (and how far should it extend) remains robust. On the positive side, how might it enhance compliance? Note that one study found that wage and hour violations are much more likely to occur at franchised restaurants than at those owned and operated by the branded company, suggesting that the franchise enterprise structure itself may induce noncompliance for a host of reasons—financial, reputational, and otherwise. *See* Min Woong Ji and David Weil, *Does Ownership Structure Influence Regulatory Behavior? The Impact of Franchising on Labor Standards Compliance* (2010), http://fortunedotcom.files.wordpress.com/2014/05/franchising_and_compliance_20100716_ji_weil.pdf. On the other hand, might this kind of enterprise liability also create incentives for firms to change their operations in ways that actually harm the interests of at least some kinds of contingent workers? Relatedly, how might firms such as Duane Reade and McDonald's seek to avoid "joint employer" status?

4. *Beyond "Employer" and "Joint Employer" Liability.* Despite the significant amount of litigation discussed in Note 1 and the FLSA's reach in terms of potentially accountable "employers" and "joint employers," enforcement of wage and hour laws at the low end of the labor market remains rare and is, according to many commentators and employee rights advocates, inadequate. There are many reasons for this, including the socioeconomic vulnerability of low-wage workers; regulatory agencies' limited enforcement resources; often insufficient economic incentives for plaintiffs' attorneys to bring suit; and, as suggested above, the fact that down-enterprise labor suppliers often operate below the radar and are judgment-proof. *See generally* WEIL, *supra*, at 15-20, 215-22; Cynthia Estlund, *Rebuilding the Law of the Workplace in* *an Era of Self-Regulation*, 105 COLUM. L. REV. 319 (2005); Craig Becker & Paul Strauss, *Representing Low-Wage Workers in the Absence of a Class: The Peculiar Case of Section 16 of the Fair Labor Standards Act and the Underenforcement of Minimum Labor Standards*, 92 MINN. L. REV. 1317 (2006); Nanitya Ruan, *Same Law, Different Day: A Survey of the Last Thirty Years of Wage Litigation and Its Impact on Low-Wage Workers*, 30 HOFSTRA LAB. & EMP. L.J. 355 (2013); Noah Zatz, *Working Beyond the Reach or Grasp of Employment Law*, in THE GLOVES-OFF ECONOMY: WORKPLACE STANDARDS AT THE BOTTOM OF AMERICA'S LABOR MARKET 31 (Annette Bernhardt et al. eds., Cornell University Press 2008). But another reason is that the reach of employer and joint employer liability, although arguably more expansive under the FLSA than elsewhere, remains limited to firms exercising fairly detailed control over the work. *See, e.g., Martinez v. Combs*, 231 P.3d 259 (Cal. 2010) (finding produce merchants did not exercise enough control over seasonal agricultural workers hired by an insolvent farmer to constitute "employers" liable for unpaid wage violations under California law, despite some financial and operational integration between the merchants and the farmer).

While these concerns have resulted in various calls for regulatory and doctrinal reform, one potentially promising approach involves expanding liability beyond controlling persons and firms—that is, beyond those who exercise sufficient control to be deemed "employers" or "joint employers." The central idea is to counteract the powerful incentives for end-user (or top-of-the-enterprise) firms to undercut the market by purchasing labor services over which they need not exercise exacting control from labor suppliers that maintain low prices by violating wage laws. Although such reform has not emerged at the federal level, there is movement in this direction at the state level. For one thing, application of the ABC test to the joint employer inquiry (as discussed in *Dynamex*) gets part of the way there, although it would not capture the outsourcing of activities not in the usual course of business by end-user firms as long as they do not exercise control over those activities. In addition, a number of states have enacted statutory provisions that extend liability for wage violations beyond its traditional limits. *See* CAL. LAB. CODE §2810(a) (Deering 2018) (holding firms in certain low-skill industries responsible for labor violations committed by subcontractors where such violations were reasonably foreseeable from the terms of the contract); 820 ILL. COMP. STATS. §175/85 (2018) (extending responsibility for staffing agency violations in certain industries to firms purchasing such agencies' services). In addition, commentators have proposed extending liability beyond firms and persons with direct control over workers. *See generally* WEIL, *supra*, at 184–214 (discussing various strategies for extending legal responsibility in "fissured" enterprises); Timothy P. Glynn, *Taking the Employer Out of Employment Law? Accountability for Wage and Hour Violations in an Age of Enterprise Disaggregation*, 15 EMP. RTS. & EMP. POL'Y J. 201 (2011) (arguing that commercial actors should be held strictly liable for wage and hour violations in the production of any goods and services they purchase, sell, or distribute, whether directly or through intermediaries); Brishen Rogers, *Toward Third-Party Liability for Wage Theft*, 11 BERKELEY J. EMPL. & LAB. L. 1 (2010) (proposing a third-party negligence regime under which firms would be held to a duty of reasonable care to prevent wage and hour violations within their domestic supply chains); Zatz, *supra*, at 31-32, 50-56 (offering a number of proposals to expand responsibility beyond employers). *See also* Matthew T. Bodie, *Participation as a Theory of Employment*, 89 NOTRE DAME L. REV. 661 (2014).

5. *Immigration, Wages, and Wage Protections.* As the court noted, many of the plaintiffs in *Ansoumana* were immigrants. Although the plaintiffs' immigrant status was not central to this case, immigration and wage protection issues often are closely linked. For example, a recurring issue in the contemporary immigration reform debate is the effect of both documented and undocumented immigration on wages, given that immigration has provided a steady supply of low-skilled workers, and whether that effect (combined with other benefits and costs of immigration) is good or bad for the country. *See,* generally NATIONAL ACADEMIES OF SCIENCES, ENGINEERING, AND MEDICINE, THE ECONOMIC AND FISCAL CONSEQUENCES OF IMMIGRATION (2017), https://www.nap.edu/catalog/23550/the-economic-and-fiscal-consequences-of-immigration (analyzing the evidence for and against various positions on immigration, including its effects on wages and employment rates); Thomas B. Edsall, *What Does Immigration Actually Cost Us?*, NY TIMES, September 29, 2016, https://www.nytimes.com/2016/09/29/opinion/campaign-stops/what-does-immigration-actually-cost-us.html (discussing arguments and evidence regarding the costs and benefits of immigration).

Another concern is the plight of immigrant workers, since undocumented workers in particular are highly vulnerable to work and wage abuses. As a group, immigrants (both documented and undocumented) constitute a significant portion of the low wage workforce. *See, e.g.,* Octavio Bianco, *Immigrant Workers Are More Likely to Have These Jobs*, CNN MONEY, March 16, 2017, https://money.cnn.com/2017/03/16/news/economy/immigrant-workers-jobs/index.html (discussing the proportion of immigrants in various job categories and industries). Thus, in *Ansoumana* and many similar FLSA minimum wage cases—and particularly those also involving the outsourcing of low-skilled work to subcontracting firms—the plaintiff workers are immigrants. *See, e.g.,* Scott L. Cummings, *Hemmed In: Legal Mobilization in the Los Angeles Anti-Sweatshop Movement*, 30 BERKELEY J. EMP. & LAB. L. 1 (2009).

Whether and when undocumented workers may take advantage of federal labor and employment protections remains unresolved. For example, in *Hoffman Plastic Compounds, Inc. v. NLRB*, 535 U.S. 137 (2002), the Court held that federal immigration policy, as expressed by Congress in the Immigration Reform and Control Act of 1986, foreclosed the NLRB from awarding back pay to an undocumented alien after the employer terminated the worker for engaging in union organizing activities. However, *Hoffman* and its reasoning may not extend to other contexts. Most notably, decisions have generally held that undocumented workers are entitled to full FLSA protections. *See, e.g., Solis v. SCA Rest. Corp.*, 938 F. Supp. 2d 380, 401 (E.D.N.Y. 2013) ("the Court found the overwhelming weight of authority persuasive and holds that *Hoffman* does not preclude an award of backpay to undocumented worker" in FLSA cases). Yet even though such workers have wage protections in theory, they often cannot take advantage of them. Immigrants present or working in the country illegally face various risks, including deportation, if they seek enforcement of these protections. These workers' heightened fear of deportation under Trump Administration policies has made agency enforcement of employment protections more difficult, increasing the risk of exploitation. *See* Sam Levin, *Immigration Crackdown Enables Worker Exploitation, Labor Department Staff Say*, THE GUARDIAN, March 30, 2017, https://www.theguardian.com/us-news/2017/mar/30/undocumented-workers-deportation-fears-trump-administration-department-labor.

Although there may be other reasons for hiring undocumented workers, avoiding wage and hour mandates is one obvious and problematic incentive. This moral hazard raises important policy and enforcement questions in both the employment and immigration areas. *See generally*, Leticia M. Saucedo, *A New "U": Organizing Victims and Protecting Immigrant Workers*, 42 U. RICH. L. REV. 891 (2008); Lori A. Nessel, *Undocumented Immigrants in the Workplace: The Fallacy of Labor Protection and the Need for Reform*, 36 HARV. C.R.-C.L. L. REV. 345 (2001).

In recent years, several states have enacted legislation seeking to address undocumented workers through employment-based enforcement measures. These mandates have produced a significant amount of litigation over the limits of state authority regarding immigration matters, culminating in two Supreme Court decisions. First, in *Chamber of Commerce v. Whiting*, 563 U.S. 582 (2011), the Court upheld an Arizona law imposing sanctions on employers who knowingly hire undocumented workers or fail to confirm workers' status. The Court's conclusion that the Arizona mandate is not preempted by the IRCA—because it falls within that statute's preemption savings clause allowing for enforcement through licensing laws—was seen as potentially opening the door to a broad range of state-level employment-based approaches to addressing unlawful immigration. *See, e.g.*, Marisa S. Cianciarulo, *The "Arizonification" of Immigration Law: Implications of* Chamber of Commerce v. Whiting *for State and Local Immigration Legislation*, 15 HARV. LATINO L. REV. 85 (2012); Lauren Gilbert, *Immigrant Laws, Obstacle Preemption and the Lost Legacy of* McCulloch, 33 BERK. J. EMP. & L. LAW 153 (2012). The following term, however, the Court held in *Arizona v. United States*, 567 U.S. 387 (2012), that federal law preempts three other provisions of Arizona law, including one that criminalized the conduct of undocumented employees (thereby going far beyond the civil sanctions for undocumented workers under the IRCA). The Arizona decision thus limits the potential reach of state immigration-related employment regulation, at least to the extent such regulation seeks to impose sanctions on undocumented workers beyond those contained in the IRCA. How *Arizona* and *Whiting* might be interpreted and applied to future workplace laws remains uncertain. *See generally* Stella Burch Elias, *The New Immigration Federalism*, 74 OHIO ST. L. REV. 703 (2013); Note, *Developments in the Law—State and Local Regulation of Unauthorized Immigrant Employment*, 126 HARV. L. REV. 1608 (2013). Moreover, enhanced immigration enforcement at by the Trump Administration may reduce their practical effect. In fact, many of the policy and legal debates regarding the role of states and municipalities in the immigration have flipped, such as with the rise of "sanctuary cities" and other state and local initiatives seeking to protect immigrants.

6. *FLSA Enforcement and the Role of Unions.* The workers in *Ansoumana* got exceedingly lucky. First, although it is not mentioned in the opinion, they had the support of the National Employment Law Project and state authorities. The local retail union also successfully organized these workers into a union before the resolution of the case. Unionization of such workers is rare since there are practical and statutory impediments to organizing contingent workers (which you will study if you take Labor Law). And without such unionization and the rights and resources that result, this segment of the workforce has little protection at all— no access to the courts and no collective bargaining.

7. *"Professional" Workers as Contingent Laborers.* The discussion in this section has focused primarily on low-skilled workers. Recall, however, that higher-skilled workers—such as the photographers in *Natkin* and the technical workers in

Microsoft—also can be described as contingent laborers. There are obvious differences between such workers and those at issue in *Ansoumana* as well as differences between what was at stake in the underlying cases. Such high-skilled workers may benefit from their contingent status. Indeed, in his dissent in the *Microsoft* case, Judge O'Scannlain speculated that the plaintiffs may have enjoyed higher wages as independent contractors than they would have if they had been hired as standard employees. *See Vizcaino*, 120 F.3d at 1021. Moreover, these workers may not fit within the category of "involuntary, impermanent" contingent workers for whom commentators express the most concern. On the other hand, just because a worker is skilled does not ensure that he or she will be treated fairly or will have the power or sophistication to bargain for alternative protections. What is to prevent an employer who saves money by hiring contract workers or through temporary staffing agencies from pocketing the difference rather than passing along a portion of that benefit to its workers in the form of higher pay? Should differences in the professional status of workers matter in determining who is an employee or how far to extend accountability of employment-law violations?

8. *Is Enterprise Disaggregation and Contingent Work Too Socially Costly?* In light of what you have learned thus far in this chapter, consider some of the bigger questions arising from increasing enterprise disaggregation and the growth of contingent work arrangements. These phenomena are likely to have various social effects—perhaps both good and bad. Think about possible effects both within and outside the firm. Might increased reliance on contingent or third-party supplied labor harm firms' long-term productivity? Consider the court's observation in *Microsoft* that the benefits associated with employment status "guarantee a competent and happy workforce." As for the interests of the public, we have already discussed how worker misclassification may reduce tax revenues and how disaggregation may lead to greater noncompliance with employment law standards in certain sectors. Does a firm's ability to externalize certain costs by outsourcing or engaging independent contractors harm society in other ways? Consider, for instance, how our society manages the costs of a nonnegligent personal injury sustained on the job by a worker not covered by workers' compensation or the company health plan. While we might expect firms to strike the optimal balance on contingent/permanent labor with respect to their productivity and morale, they have little incentive to take account of costs borne by society, as in the personal injury example. Do such costs justify legal reform? If so, what kind?

2. Determining the Status of Firm Owners

As *Ansoumana* demonstrates, high-ranking supervisory personnel, including owner-managers, may be liable as "employers" under the FLSA and in a few other contexts, and independently chartered firms exercising sufficient control over workers employed by another entity, may be liable as "joint employers." Elsewhere, however, firm owners rarely are considered "employers" for liability purposes.

Nevertheless, unresolved questions regarding the status of firm owners remain. The most frequently litigated issue relates to individual owners: Since they usually are not employers for liability purposes, when, if ever, are owner-managers considered "employees"? The next two cases address this issue. A note at the end of this section addresses a second question: When, if ever, may an employee of a subsidiary "pierce the corporate veil" to hold a parent corporation liable as an "employer" for the subsidiary's employment law violations?

As originally conceived, the common-law test was designed to distinguish employees from independent contractors. It does not purport to distinguish employees from others who perform services for a firm but are more akin to firm owners than employees (e.g., partners, stakeholders in professional corporations, members of limited liability companies, and shareholders in closely held corporations). Determining the status of such workers has been the subject of intense litigation in the federal employment discrimination area. Whether owners are treated as employees rather than employers (or vice versa) matters for two reasons. First, the number of statutory employees often determines whether a particular firm meets the threshold for coverage under the various employment statutes that might be invoked in a suit by an employee. Workers who are deemed to be employers are not counted for these purposes. Second, if the worker is considered an employer, rather than employee, then, like independent contractors, he or she will not be protected by applicable employment statutes.

≡ *Clackamas Gastroenterology Associates v. Wells*
≡ 538 U.S. 440 (2003)

STEVENS, J.

The Americans with Disabilities Act of 1990 ("ADA" or "Act"), 42 U.S.C. §12101 *et seq.*, like other federal antidiscrimination legislation,[6] is inapplicable to very small businesses. Under the ADA an "employer" is not covered unless its workforce includes "15 or more employees for each working day in each of 20 or more calendar weeks in the current or preceding calendar year." §12111(5). The question in this case is whether four physicians actively engaged in medical practice as shareholders and directors of a professional corporation should be counted as "employees."

I.

Petitioner, Clackamas Gastroenterology Associates, P.C., is a medical clinic in Oregon. It employed respondent, Deborah Anne Wells, as a bookkeeper from 1986 until 1997. After her termination, she brought this action against the clinic alleging unlawful discrimination on the basis of disability under Title I of the ADA. Petitioner denied that it was covered by the Act and moved for summary judgment, asserting that it did not have 15 or more employees for the 20 weeks required by the statute. It is undisputed that the accuracy of that assertion depends on whether the four physician-shareholders who own the professional corporation and constitute its board of directors are counted as employees.

[The district court relied on an economic realities test and concluded that the four doctors were "more analogous to partners in a partnership than to shareholders

---

6. *See, e.g.*, 29 U.S.C. §630(b) (setting forth a 20-employee threshold for coverage under the Age Discrimination in Employment Act of 1967 (ADEA)); 42 U.S.C. §2000e(b) (establishing a 15-employee threshold for coverage under Title VII of the Civil Rights Act of 1964).

in a general corporation" and therefore were "not employees for purposes of the federal antidiscrimination laws." The Ninth Circuit reversed. It saw "no reason to permit a professional corporation to secure the 'best of both possible worlds' by allowing it both to assert its corporate status in order to reap the tax and civil liability advantages and to argue that it is like a partnership in order to avoid liability for unlawful employment discrimination."]

II

"We have often been asked to construe the meaning of 'employee' where the statute containing the term does not helpfully define it." *Nationwide Mut. Ins. Co. v. Darden*, 503 U.S. 318, 322 (1992). The definition of the term in the ADA simply states that an "employee" is "an individual employed by an employer." 42 U.S.C. §12111(4). That surely qualifies as a mere "nominal definition" that is "completely circular and explains nothing." *Darden*. As we explained in *Darden*, our cases construing similar language give us guidance on how best to fill the gap in the statutory text.

In *Darden* we were faced with the question whether an insurance salesman was an independent contractor or an "employee" covered by the Employee Retirement Income Security Act of 1974 (ERISA). Because ERISA's definition of "employee" was "completely circular," we followed the same general approach that we had previously used in deciding whether a sculptor was an "employee" within the meaning of the Copyright Act of 1976, *see Community for Creative Non-Violence v. Reid*, 490 U.S. 730 (1989), and we adopted a common-law test for determining who qualifies as an "employee" under ERISA. Quoting *Reid*, we explained that "when Congress has used the term 'employee' without defining it, we have concluded that Congress intended to describe the conventional master-servant relationship as understood by common law agency doctrine."

Rather than looking to the common law, petitioner argues that courts should determine whether a shareholder-director of a professional corporation is an "employee" by asking whether the shareholder-director is, in reality, a "partner." The question whether a shareholder-director is an employee, however, cannot be answered by asking whether the shareholder-director appears to be the functional equivalent of a partner. Today there are partnerships that include hundreds of members, some of whom may well qualify as "employees" because control is concentrated in a small number of managing partners. Thus, asking whether shareholder-directors are partners—rather than asking whether they are employees—simply begs the question.

Nor does the approach adopted by the Court of Appeals in this case fare any better. The majority's approach, which paid particular attention to "the broad purpose of the ADA," is consistent with the statutory purpose of ridding the Nation of the evil of discrimination. *See* 42 U.S.C. §12101(b).[7] Nevertheless, two countervailing

---

7. The meaning of the term "employee" comes into play when determining whether an individual is an "employee" who may invoke the ADA's protections against discrimination in "hiring, advancement, or discharge," 42 U.S.C. §12112(a), as well as when determining whether an individual is an "employee" for purposes of the 15-employee threshold. *See* §12111(5)(A). Consequently, a broad reading of the term "employee" would—consistent with the statutory purpose of ridding the Nation of discrimination—tend

considerations must be weighed in the balance. First, . . . the congressional decision to limit the coverage of the legislation to firms with 15 or more employees has its own justification that must be respected—namely, easing entry into the market and preserving the competitive position of smaller firms. Second, as *Darden* reminds us, congressional silence often reflects an expectation that courts will look to the common law to fill gaps in statutory text, particularly when an undefined term has a settled meaning at common law. . . .

Perhaps the Court of Appeals' and the parties' failure to look to the common law for guidance in this case stems from the fact that we are dealing with a new type of business entity that has no exact precedent in the common law. State statutes now permit incorporation for the purpose of practicing a profession, but in the past "the so-called learned professions were not permitted to organize as corporate entities." 1A W. Fletcher, Cyclopedia of the Law of Private Corporations §112.10 (rev. ed. 1997-2002). Thus, professional corporations are relatively young participants in the market, and their features vary from State to State.

Nonetheless, the common law's definition of the master-servant relationship does provide helpful guidance. At common law the relevant factors defining the master-servant relationship focus on the master's control over the servant. The general definition of the term "servant" in the RESTATEMENT (SECOND) OF AGENCY §2(2) (1958), for example, refers to a person whose work is "controlled or is subject to the right to control by the master." *See also id.* §220(1). In addition, the Restatement's more specific definition of the term "servant" lists factors to be considered when distinguishing between servants and independent contractors, the first of which is "the extent of control" that one may exercise over the details of the work of the other. *Id.* §220(2)(a). We think that the common-law element of control is the principal guidepost that should be followed in this case.

This is the position that is advocated by the Equal Employment Opportunity Commission (EEOC), the agency that has special enforcement responsibilities under the ADA and other federal statutes containing similar threshold issues for determining coverage. It argues that a court should examine "whether shareholder-directors operate independently and manage the business or instead are subject to the firm's control.". . .

We are persuaded by the EEOC's focus on the common law touchstone of control . . . and specifically by its submission that each of the following six factors is relevant to the inquiry whether a shareholder-director is an employee:

1) Whether the organization can hire or fire the individual or set the rules and regulations of the individual's work
2) Whether and, if so, to what extent the organization supervises the individual's work
3) Whether the individual reports to someone higher in the organization
4) Whether and, if so, to what extent the individual is able to influence the organization
5) Whether the parties intended that the individual be an employee, as expressed in written agreements or contracts

---

to expand the coverage of the ADA by enlarging the number of employees entitled to protection and by reducing the number of firms entitled to exemption.

10) Whether the individual shares in the profits, losses, and liabilities of the organization.[8]

As the EEOC's standard reflects, an employer is the person, or group of persons, who owns and manages the enterprise. The employer can hire and fire employees, can assign tasks to employees and supervise their performance, and can decide how the profits and losses of the business are to be distributed. The mere fact that a person has a particular title—such as partner, director, or vice president—should not necessarily be used to determine whether he or she is an employee or a proprietor. *See ibid.* ("An individual's title . . . does not determine whether the individual is a partner, officer, member of a board of directors, or major shareholder, as opposed to an employee"). Nor should the mere existence of a document styled "employment agreement" lead inexorably to the conclusion that either party is an employee. *See ibid.* (looking to whether "the parties intended that the individual be an employee, as expressed in written agreements or contracts"). Rather, as was true in applying common law rules to the independent-contractor-versus-employee issue confronted in *Darden*, the answer to whether a shareholder-director is an employee depends on " 'all of the incidents of the relationship . . . with no one factor being decisive.' "

III

Some of the District Court's findings—when considered in light of the EEOC's standard—appear to weigh in favor of a conclusion that the four director-shareholder physicians in this case are not employees of the clinic. For example, they apparently control the operation of their clinic, they share the profits, and they are personally liable for malpractice claims. There may, however, be evidence in the record that would contradict those findings or support a contrary conclusion under the EEOC's standard that we endorse today. Accordingly, as we did in *Darden*, we reverse the judgment of the Court of Appeals and remand the case to that court for further proceedings consistent with this opinion. . . .

GINSBURG, J., with whom BREYER, J. joins, dissenting.

"There is nothing inherently inconsistent between the coexistence of a proprietary and an employment relationship." *Goldberg v. Whitaker House Cooperative, Inc.*, 366 U.S. 28, 32 (1961). As doctors performing the everyday work of petitioner Clackamas Gastroenterology Associates, P.C., the physician-shareholders function in several respects as common-law employees, a designation they embrace for various purposes under federal and state law. Classifying as employees all doctors daily engaged as caregivers on Clackamas' premises, moreover, serves the animating purpose of the [ADA]. Seeing no cause to shelter Clackamas from the governance of the ADA, I would affirm the judgment of the Court of Appeals.

An "employee," the ADA provides, is "an individual employed by an employer." 42 U.S.C. §12111(4). Where, as here, a federal statute uses the word "employee" without explaining the term's intended scope, we ordinarily presume "Congress intended to describe the conventional master-servant relationship as understood by

---

8. The EEOC asserts that these six factors need not necessarily be treated as "exhaustive." We agree. . . .

common-law agency doctrine." *Nationwide Mut. Ins. Co. v. Darden*. The Court today selects one of the common-law indicia of a master-servant relationship—control over the work of others engaged in the business of the enterprise—and accords that factor overriding significance. I would not so shrink the inquiry.

Are the physician-shareholders "servants" of Clackamas for the purpose relevant here? The Restatement defines "servant" to mean "an agent employed by a master to perform service in his affairs whose physical conduct in the performance of the service is controlled or is subject to the right to control by the master." RESTATEMENT (SECOND) OF AGENCY §2(2) (1958) (hereinafter Restatement). When acting as clinic doctors, the physician-shareholders appear to fit the Restatement definition. The doctors provide services on behalf of the corporation, in whose name the practice is conducted. . . .The doctors have employment contracts with Clackamas, under which they receive salaries and yearly bonuses, and they work at facilities owned or leased by the corporation. In performing their duties, the doctors must "compl[y] with . . . standards [the organization has] established."

The physician-shareholders, it bears emphasis, invite the designation "employee" for various purposes under federal and state law. The Employee Retirement Income Security Act of 1974 (ERISA), much like the ADA, defines "employee" as "any individual employed by an employer." 29 U.S.C. §1002(6). Clackamas readily acknowledges that the physician-shareholders are "employees" for ERISA purposes. Indeed, gaining qualification as "employees" under ERISA was the prime reason the physician-shareholders chose the corporate form instead of a partnership. Further, Clackamas agrees, the physician-shareholders are covered by Oregon's workers' compensation law. . . . Finally, by electing to organize their practice as a corporation, the physician-shareholders created an entity separate and distinct from themselves, one that would afford them limited liability for the debts of the enterprise. I see no reason to allow the doctors to escape from their choice of corporate form when the question becomes whether they are employees for purposes of federal antidiscrimination statutes.

Nothing in or about the ADA counsels otherwise. As the Court observes, the reason for exempting businesses with fewer than 15 employees from the Act, was "to spare very small firms from the potentially crushing expense of mastering the intricacies of the antidiscrimination laws, establishing procedures to assure compliance, and defending against suits when efforts at compliance fail." The inquiry the Court endorses to determine the physician-shareholders' qualification as employees asks whether they "ac[t] independently and participat[e] in managing the organization, or . . . [are] subject to the organization's control." Under the Court's approach, a firm's coverage by the ADA might sometimes turn on variations in ownership structure unrelated to the magnitude of the company's business or its capacity for complying with federal prescriptions.

This case is illustrative. In 1996, Clackamas had 4 physician-shareholders and at least 14 other employees for 28 full weeks; in 1997, it had 4 physician-shareholders and at least 14 other employees for 37 full weeks. Beyond question, the corporation would have been covered by the ADA had one of the physician-shareholders sold his stake in the business and become a "mere" employee. Yet such a change in ownership arrangements would not alter the magnitude of Clackamas' operation: In both circumstances, the corporation would have had at least 18 people on site doing the everyday work of the clinic for the requisite number of weeks.

The Equal Employment Opportunity Commission's approach, which the Court endorses, it is true, "excludes from protection those who are most able to control the firm's practices and who, as a consequence, are least vulnerable to the discriminatory treatment prohibited by the Act." As this dispute demonstrates, however, the determination whether the physician-shareholders are employees of Clackamas affects not only whether they may sue under the ADA, but also—and of far greater practical import—whether employees like bookkeeper Deborah Anne Wells are covered by the Act. Because the character of the relationship between Clackamas and the doctors supplies no justification for withholding from clerical worker Wells federal protection against discrimination in the workplace, I would affirm the judgment of the Court of Appeals.

NOTES

1. *Employer vs. Employee Muddle?* The issue in *Clackamas* is *not* the plaintiff's employment status, but that of her bosses. Only if the physicians are counted as employees can the defendant be a covered employer meeting the 15-employee threshold. Given this very different question, why is the common-law test—originally fashioned to distinguish employees from independent contractors for purposes of respondeat superior liability—given such prominence in the *Clackamas* analysis? The dissent argues that, given the remedial purposes of the ADA, its coverage should be interpreted broadly in terms of who is an employee and, therefore, who is a covered employer.

Should "employee" mean different things even within the same statute depending on what issue the court is seeking to address? For example, should "employee" mean one thing when, as here, the issue is whether the firm is large enough to be covered, but something else when the issue is whether the alleged victim(s) of unlawful discrimination are employees, as would be the case had one of the four doctors sued? A well-known case in which "owners" alleged unlawful discrimination against the firm is *EEOC v. Sidley Austin Brown & Wood*, 315 F.3d 696 (7th Cir. 2002). The underlying claim in *Sidley* was that a law firm mandatory retirement policy resulting in the demotion of 32 partners violated the ADEA. The parties disputed whether the partners affected by the policy were "employees" in light of the firm's management and control structure. The court did not resolve the issue, and the case ultimately settled, with the firm's agreeing to pay $27.5 million to the partners. Judge Posner's majority opinion and Judge Easterbrook's concurrence provide a useful survey of the difficult issues raised in this context and the considerable differences—within and between courts prior to *Clackamas*—in analyzing the proper status given to workers with ownership interests. *See also* Leonard Bierman & Rafael Gely, *So, You Want to Be a Partner at Sidley & Austin?*, 40 HOUS. L. REV. 969, 990 (2003); Donald J. Labriola, *But I'm Denny Crane! Age Discrimination in the Legal Profession After* Sidley, 72 ALB. L. REV. 367, 368 (2009); Ann C. McGinley, *Functionality or Formalism? Partners and Shareholders as "Employees" Under the Anti-Discrimination Laws*, 57 SMU L. REV. 3 (2004).

Despite the lingering disputes over the proper analytical framework for determining the employment status of workers who have an ownership interest, the new Restatement of Employment Law essentially adopts the *Clackamas* formulation, albeit offering a bit more guidance through its illustrations and making clear that minority ownership interests generating little or no effective control are insufficient to support "employer" status. *See* RESTATEMENT OF EMPLOYMENT LAW §1.03 (and corresponding illustrations). It is also worth noting that, although it remains unresolved whether *Clackamas* might be extended to sweep in other managerial personnel who are not owners, the one circuit court that has addressed the issue in detail held that high placed workers lacking an ownership interest (or director status) are employees under federal antidiscrimination laws. *See Smith v. Castaways Family Diner*, 453 F.3d 971 (7th Cir. 2006).

2. *Significance of the Corporate Form.* The majority in *Clackamas* downplayed the significance of the physicians' choice to organize their practice as a professional corporation, indicating that it would look beyond mere formalities and titles and focus instead on the substantive question of whether the physicians exercised employer-like control over the enterprise. The Court did so in part because it seemed to assume that individuals who are "employers" or, at least, exercise employer-like control, cannot also be "employees." Is this a correct assumption? Aren't firm owners also frequently employed by the corporations, LLCs, and partnerships for which they work? *See generally* Frank Menetrez, *Employee Status and the Concept of Control in Federal Employment Discrimination Law*, 63 SMU L. Rev. 137 (2010) (arguing that applying the common law control test should often, perhaps usually, result in owners of the enterprise also being employees).

Indeed, why did the physicians organize their practice as a corporation in the first place? Recall that the physicians had classified themselves as shareholders, directors, *and* supervisory employees. As the dissent mentioned, the physicians incorporated in order to gain employee status for ERISA and workers' compensation purposes. It also appears likely that the corporate form was used to take advantage of the legal fiction that the corporation itself, and not its physician-owners, is the employer. That would limit individual exposure of each physician to malpractice (and other third-party liability) for the acts of the other physicians. Indeed, it seems ironic that the majority suggested that the physicians may be akin to employers under the common-law test, given that the original purpose of that test was to determine when a controlling party is liable under the doctrine of respondeat superior, and the physicians incorporated their practice to *avoid* such liability (and other forms of liability) by shifting employer status to the corporation. Undoubtedly, if the practice had been slightly larger— 15 undisputed employees—and plaintiff's discrimination claim therefore had been viable, the physicians would have argued that, despite their control of the enterprise, the corporation is the only "employer" subject to potential liability in this case. And, as discussed in Note 1 following *Ansoumana*, page 59, they almost certainly would have won this argument.

3. *Different Inquiry, Same Problems and Policy Issues?* Recall some of the recurring themes in the previous cases in the chapter: (1) private ordering's role in determining employment status, (2) whether a firm or worker "can have it both ways" in terms of such status, (3) the importance of the case's posture and the underlying interests at stake, and (4) the central role that control plays when determining if an employment relationship exists. How do these themes play out in *Clackamas?* Should the questions raised be answered differently when the court is not assessing the status of the plaintiff herself but rather the status of others on whom her right to relief depends?

In addition, how successful is the opinion in avoiding or addressing the other two concerns discussed throughout this chapter, namely, the costs of uncertainty and the disconnect between the test for determining employee/employer status and the aims of the underlying employment doctrine? In thinking about this question, put yourself in the shoes of corporate counsel. In light of the Court's analysis, how might you structure a small business to minimize the likelihood of being subject to the ADA's obligations? How confident are you that such structuring would achieve its purposes?

4. *"Covered Employers."* Like the ADA, many other federal employment statutes limit the definition of employer based on the number of employees. Title VII, for example, has a 15-employee floor, *see* 42 U.S.C. §2000e(b) (2018), and the ADEA applies only to employers with 20 or more employees, *see* 29 U.S.C. §630(b) (2018). The Family and Medical Leave Act ("FMLA") applies only to employers with 50 or more employees, and only to employees employed at a worksite where the employer employs at least 50 employees within a 75-mile radius. *See* 29 U.S.C. §2611(2)(B) (ii), (4)(A)(i) (2018). Federal employment statutes also contain other exceptions to employer status; for example, religious entities are exempted from Title VII's prohibition of discrimination on the basis of religion. *See* 42 U.S.C. §2000e-1(a). Thus, the issue presented in *Clackamas* will be relevant any time a small business is sued by an employee raising claims under any number of employment protection statutes.

Whether an employer is public or private also affects statutory coverage or remedies. Some federal labor statutes, including the Labor Management Relations Act and National Labor Relations Act, do not apply to public employers, *see* 29 U.S.C. §152(2) (2018), although the federal government has its own regime for federal employees and states frequently have their own statutes governing state and local public-sector labor relations. On the other hand, federal constitutional protections—including constitutional rights to speech, association, religious freedom, and due process—apply only in public workplaces. Moreover, federal, state, and local government employees often enjoy substantive protections pursuant to civil service codes that are unavailable in the private sector.

5. *A Different Approach.* The year after it decided *Clackamas* the Supreme Court held in *Yates v. Hendon*, 541 U.S. 1 (2004), that a working owner (also a doctor), in common with other employees, qualifies for the protections ERISA affords plan participants and is governed by the rights and remedies ERISA specifies. In so ruling, the court rejected the position, that a business owner may be only an "employer" and not also as an "employee" for purposes of ERISA plan participation. Even more notable than the difference in outcomes between *Clackamas* and *Yates* is the stark contrast between the Court's analytical approach in each. The *Yates* majority explicitly avoided analyzing the doctor's employment status under the common-law framework that dominated the *Clackamas* decision, opting instead to focus on only the language of ERISA and its predecessors and the purposes behind the statutory scheme. It was also far more willing, in this case, to consider formalistic distinctions relating to a working owner's status and role. The explanation for the differences in these two opinions may be distinctions between the statutory schemes at issue. Or perhaps it really does reflect a shift in analytical approach. It is worth noting that Justice Ginsburg, after writing the dissent in *Clackamas*, wrote the unanimous opinion in *Yates*.

Note on Parent Corporation Liability for Employment-Law Violations

Clackamas introduced you to the role of the corporate form—limiting owners' liability for the debts and other obligations of the enterprise. Indeed, limited liability is the *primary reason* why business owners incorporate or charter an alternative limited liability entity, such as an LLC or limited partnership. Keep in mind, however, that business entities also are often owners (e.g., shareholders) of other entities—that is, their subsidiaries. Although there are a number of reasons why firm managers might separately assign aspects of their enterprise's operations into parent and subsidiary firms, avoiding liability exposure for the larger enterprise (from the obligations of one or more of its subdivisions) is central among them. Akin to the rise of outsourcing, the splintering of enterprises into separately chartered entities has proliferated in recent years.

Such formal intraenterprise distinctions may matter a great deal in the employment context. As an initial matter, at least in some circumstances, corporate formalities themselves may define the limits of employment-related protections. For example, until the Dodd-Frank Wall Street Reform and Financial Protection Act extended coverage, *see* 111 Pub. L. 203, §922, 124 Stat. 1376, §922, amending 18 U.S.C.A. §1514A (2010), employees of privately held subsidiaries of publicly traded firms who reported possible securities violations were found to be outside of the scope of the Sarbanes-Oxley's whistleblower protections, *see* Richard E. Moberly, *Unfulfilled Expectations: An Empirical Analysis of Why Sarbanes-Oxley Whistleblowers Rarely Win*, 49 WM. & MARY L. REV. 65, 71, 109, 134 (2007).

More broadly, where this kind of structure exists, a question of growing importance in the employment context is whether and when an employee of a subsidiary can hold the parent liable for employment-law violations. Given what you already have learned, you can deduce what might be at stake. Like the fly-by-night labor contractors discussed in the FLSA context, a subsidiary may lack the capital or insurance to cover its employment-related legal obligations or liabilities. Or it may be that, similar to *Clackamas*, a subsidiary alone has too few employees to be a covered employer under various statutory protections, even though it is part of a large enterprise. In addition, the ability of the plaintiff to reach the parent may affect other matters, such as the extent to which evidence of practices and violations elsewhere in the enterprise might be relevant and discoverable.

If the subsidiary's corporate veil could never be pierced to hold the parent accountable for the subsidiary's employment-law violations, one can imagine the compliance-avoidance techniques that firms might implement. While parent corporations do not enjoy such absolute protection, the law on when parents are accountable for subsidiaries' employment-law violations is far from clear. This is not surprising, since the more generalized "veil piercing" and "enterprise-entity liability" doctrines governing the liability of corporate parents in other contexts are in conceptual disarray. *See generally* Timothy P. Glynn, *Beyond "Unlimiting" Shareholder Liability: Vicarious Tort Liability for Corporate Officers*, 57 VAND. L. REV. 329 (2004); Stephen M. Bainbridge, *Abolishing Veil Piercing*, 43 CORP. PRAC. COMMENTATOR 517 (2001). Under these theories, a plaintiff typically must show, at the very least, significant control by the parent over the subsidiary's activities and some failure to maintain formal distinctions between the two entities, but application varies wildly. *See* Glynn, *supra*, at 353–56. This kind of traditional veil-piercing analysis may also apply to employment-law claims brought against parent corporations. *See, e.g., Corrigan v. U.S. Steel Corp.*, 478 F.3d 718 (6th Cir. 2007) (applying a traditional piercing framework and granting summary judgment on state-law claims brought against a parent by a subsidiary's employees because plaintiffs failed to show that the parent exercised "complete control" over the subsidiary such that the firms were fundamentally indistinguishable).

In addition, the Supreme Court has adopted a framework for determining whether two or more related but formally distinct (e.g., separately chartered) entities constitute a "single employer" under the National Labor Relations Act. *See Radio & Television Broadcast Technicians Local Union 1264 v. Broadcast Service of Mobile, Inc.*, 380 U.S. 255, 256 (1965) (per curiam). This four-part test examines the "interrelation of operations, common management, centralized control of labor relations and common ownership." *Id.* This issue continues to arise with some frequency in labor disputes before the NLRB and reviewing courts, and outcomes vary in light of the contextual nature of the four factors. For a recent example, *see Carnival Carting, Inc. v. NLRB*, 455 F. App'x 20 (2d Cir. 2012) (upholding the NLRB's determination that two commonly owned and managed corporate entities constitute a "single employer" under this framework). *But see Bridge v. New Holland Logansport, Inc.*, 815 F.3d 356, 366 (7th Cir. 2016) (declining to extend the NLRB test to the ADEA).

Although there is no broadly applicable statutory treatment of this question under federal or state employment laws, in a 1984 amendment to the ADEA and the 1991 Civil Rights Act (abrogating *EEOC v. Arabian American Oil Co.*, 499 U.S. 244 (1991)), Congress addressed a related issue when it extended the reach of antidiscrimination laws to American employees working in foreign countries for U.S. employers or their subsidiaries. *See* 29 U.S.C. §623(h) (2018) (ADEA); 42 U.S.C. §2000e-1(c) (2018) (Title VII); 42 U.S.C. §12112(c)(2) (2018) (ADA). Title VII and the ADA now provide that if "an employer controls a corporation whose place of incorporation is a foreign country, any [violation] . . . engaged in by such corporation shall be presumed to be engaged in by such employer." The determination of whether an employer controls a corporation is based on the following factors:

- The interrelation of operations
- The common management
- The centralized control of labor relations
- The common ownership or financial control of the employer and the corporation

See 42 U.S.C. §2000e-1(c) (2018); 42 U.S.C. §12112(c)(2) (2018).

On occasion, courts confront the issue of holding parents accountable for employment-law violations by subsidiaries in the domestic context, and a number of circuit courts have now addressed the question in the antidiscrimination cases. There are similarities in the courts' approaches; for example, each of the circuit courts and the EEOC has adopted a framework focused on the level of parent-corporation control and operational entanglement that is similar to or mirroring the four-factor test Congress adopted in the foreign entity context. *See Sandoval v. American Bldg. Maintenance Indus., Inc.*, 578 F.3d 787 (8th Cir. 2009); *Frank v. U.S. West, Inc.*, 3 F.3d 1357 (10th Cir. 1993); *Johnson v. Flowers Indus., Inc.*, 814 F.2d 978 (4th Cir. 1987); EEOC COMPLIANCE MANUAL, Section 2: Threshold Issues, No. 915.003, section 2-III.B.1.a.iii.a (addressing "integrated enterprises" in the context of determining whether an employer has a sufficient number of employees to be subject to antidiscrimination laws).

But there are also important differences. Contrary to Congress's approach to the treatment of foreign entities, most of the circuit courts have stated that, in light of the doctrine of limited liability, there is a "strong presumption" against finding a parent corporation liable to subsidiary's employees. *See Johnson*, 814 F.2d at 980-81; *Frank*, 3 F.3d at 1362 (suggesting that such an extension of accountability beyond the employing subsidiary should occur only in extraordinary circumstances). However, the Eighth Circuit adopted—consistent with EEOC guidance—an approach less hostile to finding that a parent and subsidiary form an integrated enterprise. *Sandavol*, 578 F.3d at 792-96; EEOC COMPLIANCE MANUAL, *supra* (focusing on control and articulating no presumption against a finding of sufficient integration).

Like the common-law and related approaches to determining "employee" status, as well as the "joint employer" doctrine and the test adopted in *Clackamas*, such a fact-specific, multifactored test focused on control is destined to produce variations in outcomes over time, unless a "strong presumption" against extension of liability to the parent corporation sets the bar prohibitively high. It also raises the kinds of planning, litigation, and policy challenges we have discussed throughout the chapter. How should we balance the benefits for shareholder limited liability against the moral hazard—the incentive to utilize corporate formalities to slice up the enterprise into undercapitalized or otherwise unaccountable subparts—that may result from adhering to strictly the formal distinctions between parents and subsidiaries? How might a rule be crafted to reflect this balance?

PROBLEM

1-3. A Second Look at "Compliance Boom." Building on what you have learned in this chapter, return again to the Compliance Boom hypothetical on page 4.

Assume first that you represent WCE. In light of what you have now learned about the stakes of employment and the scope of the employment relationship, what legal advice would you give regarding how WCE ought to structure its relationships with the various types of workers? What arrangements—contract provisions, management structures, corporate formalities, use of third-party labor suppliers, provision of resources (tools, equipment, vehicles)—might assist in achieving the desired outcome? And think about the types of additional information you would need or want from Faith and Ethan before offering such advice. For example, with regard to both the video production and office maintenance tasks, how might the need for detailed oversight matter? How might your advice regarding software/IT workers be affected by the fact that the video training platform to be developed would be so firm-specific that it likely would be of limited use to others in the industry? With regard to the assistants and salesperson, would it make a difference if there were significant barriers to entry into the compliance training market, such as high start-up costs, special equipment needs, and a limited number of potential clients? Would your advice with regard to one or more categories of workers depend on how close to having 15 workers the firm is (or will become)? Finally, how confident are you that, once you are satisfied that you have all of the client information you need, your advice will produce optimal results for your client?

Now assume you represent each of the workers. What expectations do you believe each worker may have regarding his or her employment status? How likely is it that each worker will be able to bargain for protections that meet these expectations? If a worker is in a position to bargain, what kind of relationship and additional protections should he or she seek? What kinds of contractual provisions are most likely to achieve these ends? How confident are you that the result of the bargaining would be accepted by a court?

Finally, consider whether and when the public has an interest in determining the type of relationship that exists between WCE and each of its workers. When, if ever, should the public interest or the interests of third parties trump the interests of the firm and worker? And, relatedly, when and to what extent should WCE's or a worker's intent, or an agreement between the two, determine the nature of the relationship?

Part Two

PRIVATE ORDERING AND DEFAULT TERMS

2

The "At-Will" Default Rule and Its Limits

In contrast to most European countries, employment in the United States is "at will," meaning that both the employer and the employee may terminate the relationship at any time and for any reason in the absence of some exception. The rule is considered a "default" rule because it may be varied by the parties. The employer and employee may agree, for instance, that their relationship will endure for a certain number of years, or until the employer has just cause to terminate the worker. Barring such a contract, however, the law deems the relationship to be terminable at will.

Most employees implicitly understand part of this equation. They know that they can quit their job any time they want without providing an explanation. Indeed, popular culture is replete with images of workers who, fed up with the daily grind, spontaneously decide to walk off the job, usually following a final snide remark to the boss.

What many employees do not appreciate is that at will is a two-way street. The default rules of the workplace allow employers to terminate workers at any time, with or without reason. If asked the right question, employees may acknowledge that they are at will. But with surprising illogic, empirical studies of employee perceptions of workplace law reveal that most workers simultaneously, and mistakenly, believe that they can be fired only for cause, and they believe, again wrongly, that they are entitled to advance notice of termination.

What accounts for this disconnect? It may be due in part to the fact that employer practices tend to be in accord more with employee expectations of how employers should act than with what the law allows employers to do. Most employers do not terminate employees unless there is a business-related reason, such as poor performance or economic necessity. After all, employers benefit from a consistent, high-quality workforce. They also benefit from good workforce morale, which job security occasions. That said, most employers do not promise most employees job security. That is, they rarely contractually bind themselves to terminate only for cause, except for contracts with a few high-level employees or collectively bargained agreements. They prefer to give more than the law requires without changing the rules of the game. Indeed, employers often go to great lengths to try to ensure that the at-will rule remains the default position for their employees.

This raises several questions. What is the function of the at-will default rule in the modern employment regime in light of basic managerial practices? How does this legal principle intersect with nonlegal (or, at least, "unlawyered") aspects of the employment relationship? Should the expectations of employees or the implicit commitments they make to their jobs have any bearing on their legal entitlements? Should the actions of the employer—its past practices, its procedures for discipline and termination, and its promises to its workers—affect at-will status? When, if ever, should courts imply some type of job security absent an explicit negotiated agreement between the parties?

This chapter explores such questions. It begins with a description of employment at will and the historical approach to deviations from the default principle. It then considers the erosion of the traditional at-will approach through contract and related common law doctrines that courts have adopted in responding to inequitable terminations.

A. JOB SECURITY AND THE PRINCIPLE OF AT-WILL EMPLOYMENT

Hanson v. Central Show Printing Co., Inc.
130 N.W.2d 654 (Iowa 1964)

THOMPSON, J.

. . . The case as made by the plaintiff's evidence is that he was a skilled pressman, and had been in the employ of the defendant corporation at Mason City for many years prior to 1959. In the autumn of that year he had an opportunity to obtain a steady job with the Stoyles Printing Company, also of Mason City. He knew that the defendant's business was often slack in the winter, and contacted G. C. Venz, the president of defendant, to learn whether he would have steady work with it. This resulted, after some negotiations, in an arrangement expressed in a letter from Venz to the plaintiff, which is set out:

Oct. 21, 1959
Mr. Harry Hanson,

Starting today Oct. 21, I will guarantee you 40 hours work per week thru out the entire year each year until you retire of your own choosing.

/s/ G. C. Venz, Pres.

The plaintiff thereupon elected to remain in the employ of the defendant, and did so until October 21, 1961, when he was discharged, without cause. His hourly rate of pay was $2.77 1/2. He asks "damages in the past and in the future at the rate of $2.77 1/2 per hour for 40 hours per week throughout the entire year for each year and until he retires, all according to the terms of the employment contract," and for costs. At the close of his evidence the trial court granted the defendant's motion for a directed verdict. . . .

The question before us is essentially a simple one, and has been before the courts of the various jurisdictions many times. The rule which has been generally followed is thus set forth:

> [I]n the absence of additional express or implied stipulation as to the duration of the employment or of a good consideration additional to the services contracted to be rendered, a contract for permanent employment, for life employment, for as long as the employee chooses, or for other terms purporting permanent employment, is no more than an indefinite general hiring terminable at the will of either party.

Issue

This rule fits the situation before us, where the employment was to be "until you retire of your own choosing." . . .

The defendant urges here lack of mutuality; that is, it contends the plaintiff was not bound to any specific or enforceable term of employment. This is true; but lack of mutuality is not always proof of want of consideration. We have said: "If the lack of mutuality amounts to a lack of consideration, then the contract is invalid. But mere lack of mutuality in and of itself does not render a contract invalid. Though consideration is essential to the validity of a contract, it is not essential that such consideration consist of a mutual promise." *Standard Oil Co. v. Veland*, 224 N.W. 467, 469 [(Iowa 1929)].

So the lack of mutuality in itself is not fatal to plaintiff's case, if there is other consideration. He contends that he gave up the opportunity to take other employment; that this was a detriment to him, and so furnished consideration for the agreement. But it has been repeatedly held that this is not sufficient in contracts for permanent employment, or, as the plaintiff contends here, until he should "retire of your own choosing."

consideration

. . . The question was extensively considered in *Skagerberg v. Blandin Paper Co.*, 266 N.W. 872 (Minn. 1936). The plaintiff's case showed that he was a consulting engineer, specializing in the field of heating, ventilating, and air conditioning. While he was employed by the defendant, he received an offer from Purdue University for employment at a yearly salary. . . . He communicated this offer to the defendant, which promised, if he would refuse the Purdue offer, it would give him permanent employment. . . .

With reference to plaintiff's contention that consideration passed from him to the defendant, the court said: [The plaintiff] "merely abandoned other activities and interests to enter into the service of defendant—a thing almost every desirable servant does upon entering a new service, but which, of course, cannot be regarded as constituting any additional consideration to the master."

. . . In *Faulkner v. Des Moines Drug Co.*, 90 N.W. 585 (Iowa 1902), . . . the plaintiff claimed a contract for employment "until mutually agreed void." Much of [this Court's] discussion pertained to the indefiniteness of the contract, as to amount of prospective earnings, and the length of time the damages should be computed. We said: . . . "if it be said that the profits earned before the breach of the contract furnish a basis for estimating future returns, then for what length of time shall they be computed? Shall it be for one month, one year, ten years, or for the entire period of the plaintiff's expectancy of life? Who can place any reasonable estimate upon the period which would probably elapse before the parties 'mutually agree' that the contract between them shall be considered 'void'?" If we substitute for the "mutually agree" the words "until you retire of your own choosing," an equally uncertain happening, we have the identical case. . . . How would the trier of the facts have any guide as to how many years it might be "until he chose to retire"; or how much his loss might be mitigated by other employment which he might secure? . . .

There is a class of cases in which sufficient consideration to uphold a contract for permanent, or life, employment, or employment so long as the employee chooses, has been found. These are cases in which the servant has been found to have paid something for the promise of the employment, in addition to his agreement to render services. A majority of them are cases in which the employer, faced with a claim for damages, agreed to give the claimant permanent employment in consideration of the release of his claim. A case involving a different but also valid consideration is *Carning v. Carr*, 46 N.E. 117 (Mass. 1897), [in which the] plaintiff had been engaged in a competing business with the defendant, and had accepted permanent employment which involved the abandonment of his own enterprise. The defendant thereby received the benefit of removal of competition. . . .

We think the real basis for the majority rule is that there is in fact no binding contract for life employment when the employee has not agreed to it; that is, when he is free to abandon it at any time. So in the instant case, the plaintiff was bound only so long as he chose to work. It does not help to say that a contract for life employment, or permanent employment, may be binding if it is fully agreed upon, even though the only consideration furnished by the employee is his agreement to serve. The fact is he has not agreed to serve for life, or permanently; but only so long as he does not elect to "retire of his own choosing." What the rule might be if he had bound himself to work for life, or so long as he was able, we have no occasion to determine. These observations go to the lack of mutuality and would not be important if there was other consideration. Many difficulties would arise even if such a contract had been made and upheld, in the way of determining the damages because of uncertainty of type of employment, or rate of pay, or how much his loss might be mitigated, in the event of wrongful discharge, by other employment which he might find. But we have no occasion to go further into those questions here. . . .

NOTES

1. *The "Additional Consideration" Requirement.* The *Hanson* court articulates the traditional rule that, absent an express term of employment or "additional" consideration to the employer, a contract of employment is deemed terminable at will. What does the court mean by "additional" consideration? Additional to what?

2. *The Express Term Exception.* Is the additional consideration requirement even relevant here? The court says that additional consideration is necessary where the parties do not agree to a fixed term of employment. Look at the employer's letter. It promises Hanson 40 hours per week each week of every year until his retirement. Isn't that an express provision as to the duration of employment? Surprisingly, no: Courts traditionally have treated indefinite time periods like this—as well as promises of "lifetime employment," "permanent employment," or "long-term employment"—as expressing nothing more than an ordinary at-will relationship. *See, e.g., Turner*

v. Newsom, 3 So. 3d 913, 915 (Ala. App. 2008); *Henkel v. Educ. Research Council*, 344 N.E.2d 118, 121-22 (Ohio 1976); *Forrer v. Sears, Roebuck & Co.*, 153 N.W.2d 587, 589-90 (Wis. 1967). Why? Don't these phrases suggest intent to provide job security, albeit for an indefinite term?

To be clear then, *Hanson* and these other decisions treat at-will status as more than a typical default rule. It is a presumption or, as one scholar has put it, a "sticky default" rule; that is, one that is difficult to contract out from under. *See* Matthew T. Bodie, *The Best Way Out Is Always Through: Changing the Employment At-Will Default to Protect Personal Autonomy*, 2017 U. ILL. L. REV. 223. As you will see, identifying what evidence is sufficient to overcome this presumption dominates the litigation over whether a binding job security term exists, and the modern treatment of at will can be characterized as largely maintaining the presumption but loosening its strictures. *See, e.g., Burford v. Accounting Practice Sales, Inc.*, 786 F.3d 582 (7th Cir. 2015) (while Illinois law generally finds a contract for an indefinite term to be terminable at will and a perpetually renewing agreement would so qualify, a clause in the agreement that permitted the employer to terminate upon the employee's violation of its provisions provided the necessary clear statement that took the agreement out of that category).

3. *Proof of Additional Consideration.* What would Hanson have had to prove to show additional consideration? Why isn't it sufficient that Hanson turned down a "steady job" at another printing company? In *Skagerberg v. Blandin Paper Co.*, 266 N.W. 872 (Minn. 1936), described in *Hanson*, the Minnesota Supreme Court rejected the plaintiff's argument that he had supplied sufficient additional consideration upon accepting the defendant's offer of "permanent" employment by forgoing a faculty position at Purdue University. Compare these facts (and the facts in *Hanson* itself) to the two precedents cited in the opinion in which the courts found proof of additional consideration. Those cases involved the settlement of a claim against the employer and the surrender of a competitive business. Do you see the distinction between these cases and *Hanson*? Can you think of other factual scenarios in which a plaintiff might be able to establish additional consideration as understood by these courts? *See, e.g., Kabe's Rest. v. Kinter*, 538 N.W.2d 281, 284 (Iowa 1995) (finding fact that employee personally invested in employer's business to be evidence of additional consideration sufficient to submit breach of contract claim to a jury). Are there any circumstances under which simply rejecting alternative employment should constitute additional consideration? Does it matter whether the plaintiff is a new employee choosing between competing offers (as in *Skagerberg*) or an existing employee who is contemplating leaving (as in *Hanson*)?

4. *The Uncertain Damages Rationale.* The court talks about the difficulty of calculating damages where the duration of employment is uncertain. Do you find this a convincing rationale for the additional consideration requirement? Consider that courts routinely calculate lost earnings as damages in commercial cases involving a going concern in which it is uncertain how long the business would have endured. They also calculate lost wages in cases involving breach of a fixed-term contract (as where the employer promises continued employment for a set number of years), although the employee could have departed before the expiration of the term. Suppose that Hanson is 50 years old at the time of the letter agreement. Can you think of a fair way to calculate his damages had the court found an enforceable contract for job security? What proof would you expect each side to submit on this issue?

5. *A Historical View of at Will.* The wide adoption of the at-will presumption by American jurisdictions is generally attributed to an 1877 treatise on "master and servant" law by attorney Horace Gray Wood. In it, Wood famously stated that, unlike the British system,

> [w]ith us the rule is inflexible, that a general or indefinite hiring is *prima facie* a hiring at will, and if the servant seeks to make it out a yearly hiring, the burden is upon him to establish it by proof. . . . [I]t is an indefinite hiring and is determinable at the will of either party.

HORACE G. WOOD, MASTER AND SERVANT §134 (1877).

Some modern scholars have cast doubt on the accuracy of Wood's statement as a reflection of the law of his time. *See, e.g.,* Jay Feinman, *The Development of the Employment at Will Rule,* 20 AM. J. LEGAL HIST. 118, 126-27 (1976) (noting that the cases cited by Wood did not support his conclusion and that he incorrectly stated that no American court had adopted the British rule that an indefinite hiring is presumed to endure one year). Nonetheless, "Wood's rule" has not only become black letter doctrine, it is arguably the centerpiece of all of American employment law.

What accounts for the vast appeal of the at-will presumption? Professor Feinman has suggested that the rule reflected the development of American capitalism in the late nineteenth century. He traces the development of industry from owner-managed businesses to more complex organizations and the resultant effort by mid-level managers to gain more of a voice. The courts rejected their attempt and "instead announced the new principle of employment at will," which is founded on "the class division fundamental to the capitalist system: the distinction between owners and non-owners of capital." He summarizes:

> Employment at will is the ultimate guarantee of the capitalist's authority over the worker. The rule transformed long-term and semi-permanent relationships into non-binding terminable at will. If employees could be dismissed on a moment's notice, obviously they could not claim a voice in the determination of the conditions of work or the use of the product of their labor. Indeed, such a fleeting relationship is hardly a contract at all. . . .

Id. at 132.

6. *Other Bases for the At-Will Rule?* If you are not convinced by the rationales put forth by the *Hanson* court in support of the historical presumption of at-will employment, can you think of other justifications for the rule? Consider the arguments put forth in the next case, decided some 20 years later.

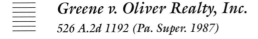

Greene v. Oliver Realty, Inc.

526 A.2d 1192 (Pa. Super. 1987)

CIRILLO, President Judge.

. . . Appellant, William Greene[,] began working for Grant Building, Inc. in 1959. Greene allegedly agreed to work at a pay rate below union scale in exchange for a promise that Grant would employ him "for life." In 1975, appellee Oliver Realty, Inc. took over management of Grant Building but Oliver's president assured former Grant employees that existing employment contracts would be honored. During that same year Greene explained the terms of his agreement to an Oliver Realty supervisor. The supervisor stated that he would look into the matter but never got back to Greene. . . . In 1983, Greene was laid off and he brought this action for breach of contract. The trial court ruled that under Pennsylvania law a contract "for life" is a contract at will. The court also held that a contract at will may become a contract for a reasonable time if it is supported by sufficient additional consideration other than the employee's services. The court stated that there was no such consideration in this case. . . . [T]he court granted Oliver's motion for summary judgment. . . .

Contemporary contract law generally provides that a contract is enforceable when the parties reach mutual agreement, exchange consideration and have outlined the terms of their bargain with sufficient clarity. An agreement is sufficiently definite if the parties intended to make a contract and there is a reasonably certain basis upon which a court can provide an appropriate remedy. . . .

However, there is one area of contract law which is strikingly idiosyncratic. That is the law of employment contracts. It has developed contrary to all of the standard, modern contract principles discussed above. If the parties to an employment contract do not specify the duration of the contract, a court will not imply a reasonable duration. The contract is considered terminable at will. If the parties contract for "lifetime" employment, many courts will refuse to enforce their bargain even if their intentions are clear. Even if the agreement is oral, courts refuse to consider the surrounding circumstances. Though mutuality of obligation is a discredited notion, it is often required in the employment context, even when the employment agreement is a unilateral contract. Also, courts routinely refuse to enforce employment contracts if they entail a single promise made in exchange for several promises. In reaching these results, courts rely on anachronistic theories which they would never apply in other fields of contract law. The strong resistance of employment law to modern contract doctrine is a testament to the influence of a uniquely American legal tradition: the at-will presumption. . . .

[T]here are five policies underlying the presumption: (1) The policy of freedom of contract; (2) the need for mutuality of obligation; (3) common experience that it usually effectuates the intent of the parties; (4) as a procedural protection against meritless but vexatious lawsuits; and (5) fairness and equity. . . .

[F]reedom of contract implies that the parties are free to determine the terms of their relationship. The at-will presumption was supposedly based upon this principle. Yet, courts [have] formalistically enforced the rule, allowing it to become a substantive limitation upon the parties' freedom to contract. . . . If two parties desire to contract "for life," courts should be encouraged to enforce their agreement. Of course, the at-will presumption may still be a sound legal rule. It is only when it is allowed to conclusively foreclose proof of the parties['] intent that it becomes an obstacle to freedom of contract. . . .

One rationale for the rule which is illogical and undeserving of perpetuation is that of mutuality of obligation. Courts have often held that mutuality of obligation is lacking in the employment context, particularly in regard to contracts for permanent employment. . . .

However, consideration may be any bargained for benefit or detriment. An employer is free to promise lifetime employment to someone in exchange for that person coming to work for the employer. Once that person accepts and starts work, the employer has received exactly what he bargained for. The employee has performed the desired act. That act is the consideration for the employer's promise and their agreement is a unilateral contract. It is irrelevant that the employee's services are also consideration for his salary. Modern contract law recognizes that consideration may be a single act exchanged for several promises. *See* RESTATEMENT CONTRACTS (SECOND) §79. Therefore, an employee is free to sell his services in exchange for wages *and* a promise of lifetime employment.

Once the employee begins work, the employer may be the only party obligated, but that is standard in situations involving a unilateral contract. The promisor has requested a performance as the price of his promise. Once he receives that performance, it would defy all notions of equity to allow him to avoid his obligation by claiming that the promisee is no longer obligated. He is no longer obligated because he has already performed the agreed upon acts. . . .

The at-will presumption, like most other legal presumptions, is also based upon common experience. In the vast majority of employer-employee relationships, both sides are silent about the expected duration of the employment agreement. The employee usually feels free to leave and take another job if it presents a more desirable opportunity. Similarly, the employer generally feels free to discharge the employee if he no longer wants his services. The at-will presumption is simply a legal recognition of the parties' normal expectations. . . . It is a waste of time and resources to require parties to re-prove time and again that which experience shows is normally true. It is much more efficient . . . [to] require the parties to demonstrate if exceptional circumstances are present. . . .

The at-will presumption also provides another important procedural protection. If there were no such rule, any dismissed employee could file suit based on an alleged oral contract. The ensuing lawsuit would then hinge solely on credibility. We note that a jury is much more likely to be composed of employees as opposed to employers. We hope that it does not exhibit too cynical a view of humanity for us to be concerned that this might affect more than an occasional verdict. The law is replete with procedural rules designed to guard against the danger of prejudicial jury verdicts. The at-will presumption . . . can be rebutted by clear evidence that the parties intended a contrary result. This is a sufficient safeguard. It balances the need to protect against prejudicial verdicts with the legal system's obligation to enforce the individual parties['] expectations. . . . A contract for life is a heavy burden to impose upon an employer. Courts should be careful that when such a burden is imposed it is because that is what was contracted for. . . . The parties may have used the words "permanently" or "for life" in an off-hand manner. These words are much too ambiguous to provide the sole basis for a jury's imposition of such a tremendous obligation. Courts must look to the surrounding circumstances to determine the parties['] intent. . . .

Another policy supporting continued recognition of the at-will presumption is that of simple fairness. . . .

[W]here the employer and employee both agree that the employment relation is to last for a definite period[, b]oth parties are then bound for that period. If the employer fires the employee, he can sue his former boss and recover damages. However, if the employee quits before the agreed upon period of time has expired, what recourse is available to the employer? If he sues the employee, he will have difficulty proving damages. He will need to show that the loss of this one employee caused his business to lose money. Even if the employer wins a judgment he would then have to enforce it. The old adage that you cannot get blood from a stone is particularly apt in this situation. Most individuals do not have the resources to satisfy anything but the most meager judgment. Therefore, an aggrieved employee will probably have a legal remedy, but an aggrieved employer will not. . . .

The at-will presumption is a partial response to this quandary. . . . The presumption may make it slightly more difficult for the employee to recover if he brings an action. But this merely serves as a partial redress of the unfair situation which would otherwise occur. . . .

Therefore, our review of the applicable policies demonstrates that the at-will presumption remains a sound legal rule. It provides a sensible balance of the relevant concerns. . . . But, courts must remain flexible and not allow the presumption to foreclose proof of the parties' intent. . . .

[I]n cases involving lifetime employment contracts, many courts ignore the parties' desires. In some jurisdictions, lifetime employment contracts are terminable at will unless the[r]e is proof of "sufficient additional consideration." . . . In these jurisdictions, the presumption will not be rebutted even by strong, independent evidence that the parties intended the contract to last for life. . . .

However, other courts utilize a more flexible approach. These courts view the presence of such consideration as proof that the parties intended the employment relation to be more binding than the standard terminable at will agreement. These courts view additional consideration as a factor to consider in determining the parties['] intent but not as a rigid requirement. . . .

If the parties exchanged "extra" consideration, it is logical that they expected their relationship to be more lasting than the usual employment agreement. However, it is very possible that the parties so intended but did not exchange additional consideration. The surrounding circumstances and the parties' own expressions may still provide clear evidence of that intent. . . .

We agree with [this] reasoning. The at-will presumption may only be rebutted by clear evidence that the parties contracted for a definite period. . . . A promise of permanent or lifetime employment may be nothing more than a casual aside. Or, it may be purely aspirational. The employer may be expressing his hope that a valued employee will stay with him forever. However, he may not have intended to create a binding agreement. These dangers are sufficiently real that courts must look to the circumstances surrounding the parties' agreement. . . . The presence of additional consideration is only a single factor, albeit an important one, which a court must consider to ascertain that intent. When the court is certain of the parties' intent, it must enforce that intent, irrespective of whether additional consideration is present. . . .

In the instant case, Oliver Realty impliedly adopted Grant Building's promise to Greene of lifetime employment. In exchange for that promise, Greene alleges that he worked for twenty-four years at a pay rate below union scale. . . . The [trial] court concluded that Greene worked at sub-union rates in exchange for a promise that he would not be laid off and not in exchange for a lifetime contract. This is an inappropriate conclusion. . . . Greene's belief that he had been promised lifetime employment was sufficiently strong that he explained his position to a supervisor after Oliver took over Grant Building. The court must allow the jury to consider Greene's alleged "additional consideration" as well as all the circumstances surrounding the agreement. A jury might reasonably . . . conclude that Greene has clearly rebutted the at-will presumption. . . .

NOTES

1. *Policy Support for at Will?* *Greene* provides a more considered analysis of the validity of the at-will presumption than *Hanson*. The court rejects the doctrinal arguments grounded in notions of mutuality and criticizes precedents invoking the additional consideration requirement. Yet the court ultimately comes out in favor of the at-will presumption based largely on pragmatic concerns. Are they convincing?

2. *Employer and Employee Expectations.* The *Greene* court suggests that treating at will as a presumption is administratively efficient because it accords with what most parties want. If at will is in fact a "legal recognition of the parties' normal expectations," then using the presumption reduces costs that litigating this issue would entail. Do most "parties" really desire an at-will relationship? Some commentators say yes, citing the prevalence of at-will relationships. Given that parties can contract out of at will, the fact that they generally do not, attests to their preference for at-will relationships. *See, e.g.*, Richard A. Epstein, *In Defense of the Contract at Will*, 51 U. Chi. L. Rev. 947, 951-52 (1984); J. Hoult Verkerke, *An Empirical Perspective on Indefinite Term Employment Contracts: Resolving the Just Cause Debate*, 1995 Wis. L. Rev. 837. Other commentators see the predominance of at-will relationships as a reflection of employee vulnerability and suggest that a rule favoring continued employment more closely approximates employee expectations and preferences. *See, e.g.*, Lawrence E. Blades, *Employment at Will vs. Individual Freedom: On Limiting the Abusive Exercise of Employer Power*, 67 Colum. L. Rev. 1404, 1404-05 (1967); Clyde W. Summers, *The Contract of Employment and the Rights of Individual Employees: Fair Representation and Employment at Will*, 52 Fordham L. Rev. 1082, 1105-06 (1984). Which position do you find more persuasive?

Do employees even think in terms of negotiating for job security? In her studies of workers' perceptions of employment rights, Professor Pauline Kim found that a majority of respondents erroneously believed that the law protected them from certain types of arbitrary discharge. *See* Pauline T. Kim, *Bargaining with Imperfect Information: A Study of Worker Perceptions of Legal Protection in an At-Will World*, 83 Cornell L. Rev. 105, 133-36 (1997); *see also* Larry A. Dimatteo, Robert C. Bird, & Jason A. Colquitt, Justice, *Employment, and the Psychological Contract*, 90 Or. L. Rev. 449, 513 (2011) (empirical study showing that "scenarios involving procedural or substantive unfairness were positively correlated with increased propensities [of employees] to retaliate and litigate").

Stories about seemingly arbitrary terminations occasionally spark headlines. One prominent example was the firing of car salesman John Stone for wearing a Green Bay Packers tie to work at a Chicago car dealership—and then refusing to remove it—the day after the Packers defeated the Chicago Bears in the 2011 NFC Championship Game. Stone claimed he wore the tie to support the team and to honor his late grandmother, a life-long Packers fan who passed away before the big victory. Stone's manager fired him after repeatedly telling Stone to remove the tie. The manager admitted firing Stone for failure to remove necktie, contending that it was inconsistent with the dealership's promotions associated with the Bears and might be off-putting to customers. *See* posting of Jeffery M. Hirsch to Workplace Prof Blog, *Apparently Someone Isn't a Packers Fan* (Jan. 26, 2011). Does the outrage or criticism that usually follows such an arbitrary termination tell us something about worker expectations regarding the legality of such discharges? Or does it simply reflect moral disapproval of how the employer "conducts business"?

If most employees do not fully understand the at-will regime, is it possible to draw conclusions about their contractual preferences? Does the prevalence of misinformation and the risk of employer overreaching suggest a need to rethink at will as a default rule? *See* Cynthia Estlund, *How Wrong Are Employees About Their Rights?*, 77 N.Y.U. L. Rev. 21-27 (2002) (suggesting that erroneous beliefs held by employers that they are overly vulnerable to litigation and those of employees—that they can only be fired for just cause—justify a need for a law requiring an explicit waiver of just cause protection). *See generally* Rachel Arnow-Richman, *Mainstreaming Employment Contract Law: The Common Law Case for Reasonable Notice of Termination*, 66 Fla. L. Rev. 1513 (2014); Jeffrey M. Hirsch, *The Law of Termination: Doing More with Less*, 68 Md. L. Rev. 89 (2008); Nicole B. Porter, *The Perfect Compromise: Bridging the Gap Between At-Will Employment and Just Cause*, 87 Neb. L. Rev. 62, 84 (2008).

3. *Who Is the Employer?* What does it mean to talk about the interests of the "employer"? Since the employer is usually an entity, not a person, actions or decisions of its individual representatives—its managers, supervisors, and executives—may not be consistent. Note that in *Greene* the employer that made the alleged lifetime employment commitment was Grant Building; the defendant in the case was Oliver Realty, a successor company. Unionized employees generally have provisions in their collective bargaining agreements dealing with the possibility of a change of control, but unrepresented workers without written contracts may be at the mercy of the new employer. Similar problems can arise in the context of ordinary managerial turnover. What one supervisor tells a subordinate may not be acceptable to his or her replacement in subsequent years, or even to that supervisor's own immediate supervisor who may be unaware of the assurances being made. Does the risk of managerial turnover suggest the need for greater job security for the workers? Or does it underscore the need for the flexibility the at-will presumption provides?

4. *The Role of the Jury.* What do you make of the court's concern about jury sympathies? Does this reflect an elitist view of the intellectual capabilities and emotional susceptibility of ordinary people? Or do you think there are legitimate reasons to distrust juries in employment cases? Is this kind of dispute different from other cases involving a single individual suing a business or commercial entity?

5. *Mutuality of Obligation.* Both *Hanson* and *Greene* allude to "mutuality of obligation," a notion historically invoked by courts as a justification for the additional consideration requirement. Mutuality is the idea that, where there is an exchange of promises, both parties must be bound for the court to recognize a contract. Mutuality does not, however, require equivalency of obligation. So viewed, it is just another term for consideration. *See Avion Syst. v. Thompson*, 666 S.E.2d 464, 467 (Ga. App. 2008) ("[Where] the employer offers employment and agrees to pay definite compensation, this consideration is adequate to sustain the contract, and '[t]he fact that the employee agrees to further restrictions and warranties not placed upon the employer does not divest the contract of mutuality.'"); *Worley v. Wyoming Bottling Co.*, 1 P.3d 615, 623 (Wyo. 2000) ("The demand for mutuality of obligation, although appealing in its symmetry, is simply a species of the forbidden inquiry into the adequacy of consideration."). The *Hanson* court seems to acknowledge this, noting that "lack of mutuality in itself is not fatal to the plaintiff's case" if the consideration requirement is satisfied. But the court ultimately finds against the plaintiff, concluding "that there is in fact no binding contract for life employment when the employee has not agreed to it; that is, when he is free to abandon it at any time." Similarly, although

Greene disclaims the relevance of mutuality of obligation, it expresses concern that the employer and employee do not have equal ability to enforce their contractual rights. That is, in a situation where the employer and employee both agree to be bound for a set period of time, it can be difficult for the employer to obtain relief if the employee breaches the agreement. Don't such statements cast doubt on the courts' assertions that mutuality, in the sense of equivalency of obligation, is a dead letter? Are the concerns raised by *Greene* with respect to remedies relevant in a case where no one is alleging a fixed commitment by the employee? Or is the court just bringing mutuality of obligation in through the back door?

6. *Employment and Unilateral Contract Theory.* A further criticism of the mutuality rationale draws on the distinction between unilateral and bilateral contracts. Recall your first-year Contracts class. Bilateral contracts involve two promises, made in exchange for each other, which each party is obligated to perform. The presence of a promise on each side creates mutuality. Unilateral contracts involve a single promise made in exchange for a performance, which obligates the promisor only if the offeree renders the requested performance. *See generally Cook v. Johnson*, 221 P.2d 525, 527 (Wash. 1950). In a unilateral contract there is no mutuality, nor is mutuality required, because the contract is formed following performance, at which point only the promisor is bound. Historically, employment has been viewed as unilateral: The employer promises to pay wages if the employee performs the job. However, the employee is not obligated to work; he or she may quit at any point. Do you agree with this characterization of the relationship? Does the employee make any return promises to the employer? If so, do they make the relationship bilateral? If the relationship is unilateral, as courts suggest, mutuality should not pose an obstacle to claims for job security. On the other hand, there may be reasons why treating the relationship as bilateral can benefit employees, for instance, in cases involving implied contracts for job security based on employer policies, which will be discussed later in this chapter.

7. *Understanding the Significance of a Presumption.* What is the status of the at-will presumption in Pennsylvania following *Greene*? What factors are relevant in determining whether a contract for job security exists? Does *Greene*'s refinement of the additional consideration requirement alter the traditional at-will presumption articulated in Wood's treatise? Or does it represent a return to the true meaning of presumption as a vehicle for determining intent? Consider Professor Clyde Summers's view of the additional consideration requirement as traditionally applied by courts:

> [A]s any first semester law student knows, however, one performance can be consideration to support two or even twenty promises. The work performed could be consideration for both the wages paid and the promise of future employment. The requirement of additional consideration was but a device for converting [the at-will] presumption into a substantive rule so that even an express promise of permanent employment would not bind the employer.

Clyde W. Summers, *The Contract of Employment and the Rights of Individual Employees: Fair Representation and Employment At Will*, 52 FORDHAM L. REV. 1082, 1098 (1984). Some modern defenders of Wood have suggested that he has been unfairly dissed. "[T]here is nothing 'rigid' or inflexible about Wood's formulation," since a plaintiff may always "prove that the parties intended that the employment relationship would last for a certain length of time." Mayer G. Freed & Daniel D. Polsby, *The Doubtful Provenance of "Wood's Rule" Revisited*, 22 ARIZ. ST. L.J. 551, 553 (1990). Maybe that's true after *Greene*; it seems strained in light of cases like *Hansen*. *See also* Arnow-Richman, *supra* (arguing that the ability of at-will parties to terminate the relationship without notice "is neither historically supported nor legally correct"; instead, "reasonable notice" should be required).

8. *Are the Bad Old Days Still Here?* Don't necessarily believe that *Greene* marks a sea change in judicial approach to the question. Even in Pennsylvania, courts can find repeated references to "permanent employment" insufficient to provide job security and the employee's agreement to assign any inventions to the employer not to constitute additional consideration for such rights. *Scott v. Extracorporeal*, 545 A.2d 334 (Pa. Super. Ct. 1988). And some modern courts continue to hold fast to the historical version of the rule set out in *Hanson*. *See, e.g., Edwards v. Geisinger Clinic*, 459 F. App'x 125 (3d Cir. 2012) (holding that the parties did not enter into an express employment contract for a definite term when the clinic agreed to sponsor the physician's three-year H-1B visa or by virtue of the clinic's statements to the American Board of Radiology that the plaintiff was participating in four-year certification program); *Turner v. Newsome*, 3 So. 3d 913, 922 (Ala. App. 2008) (concluding that the written promise to employ plaintiff "until the retirement of the President" was an indefinite contract and employee accepting additional responsibilities and work hours, putting educational opportunities on hold, and not revealing employer's "immoral conduct" were not sufficient consideration to support an "extraordinary" contract for lifetime employment).

9. *Just Cause and Legislative Reform.* One U.S. jurisdiction has statutorily rejected the employment at will presumption. The Montana Wrongful Discharge from Employment Act of 1987 ("WDEA") creates a statutory cause of action for employees terminated without "good cause" subsequent to their completion of the employer's designated probationary period. *See* MONT. CODE ANN. §39-2-904(2) (2017). Similarly, under the proposed Model Employment Termination Act of 1991 ("META"), an employer could not terminate without good cause unless the parties mutually agree to waive the good cause requirement in a written agreement. *See* META §§3(a), 4(c). These approaches essentially reverse the at-will presumption, making job security the default rule. In exchange for this benefit, they place certain limits on damages that protect employers. *See, e.g.,* MONT. CODE ANN. §39-2-905 (2013) (capping damages at four years of wages and disallowing other forms of compensatory damages). No state has adopted META or followed Montana's lead. Why do you think that is?

History suggests a possible answer. The movement to adopt unjust dismissal legislation came about in the 1980s following the issuance of a number of pro-plaintiff decisions, several of which you will read in the subsequent sections. Many perceived these decisions as heralding judicial adoption of a broad rule requiring just cause for termination. In such an environment, employers were willing to support unjust dismissal legislation that offered increased predictability over common law expansion of employee rights and created an opportunity for employer interest groups to exact some pro-business concessions in the legislative drafting process. Indeed, both the WDEA and META were widely viewed as compromise proposals, and employers played a significant role in securing adoption of the Montana law. *See* Alan B. Krueger, *The Evolution of Unjust-Dismissal Legislation in the United States*, 44 INDUS. & LAB. REL. REV. 644 (1990–91); Daniel J. Libenson, *Leasing Human*

Capital: Toward A New Foundation for Employment Termination Law, 27 Berkeley J. Emp. & Lab. L. 111 (2006).

As the previous note suggests, however, fears of a full-scale retreat from employment at will proved unfounded. In fact, contemporary developments have led some to speculate that the law is moving in the opposite direction, toward a revived presumption of employment at will. Perhaps the most dramatic example is the rule's enshrinement in the new Restatement of Employment Law (ALI 2015). *See* §2.01 cmt. B ("The high courts in 49 states and the District of Columbia recognize as the default rule the principle that employment is presumptively an at-will relationship."). *See also* Rachel Arnow-Richman, *Employment as Transaction*, 39 Seton Hall L. Rev. 447 (2009); Jonathan Fineman, *The Inevitable Demise of the Implied Employment Contract*, 29 Berkeley J. Emp. & Lab. L. 345 (2008). Therefore, it is scarcely unsurprising that employer support for legal reform (and consequently the ability to pass unjust dismissal legislation) ultimately dwindled.

PROBLEM

2-1. Suppose that William Greene hires you to serve as his trial attorney on remand following the Superior Court's decision. What litigation strategy would you pursue? Would you try to demonstrate additional consideration? Can you? What other evidence, if any, can Greene use to establish the parties' intention to create a lifetime employment contract? Who would you rather have as a client given the rules articulated by the Superior Court—Greene or Hanson?

B. ORAL AND IMPLIED CONTRACT RIGHTS TO JOB SECURITY

As you can see from *Greene*, despite the entrenched idea of employment at will, modern courts have questioned the justifications for the rule and the inflexible manner in which it has traditionally been applied. Indeed, in the last several decades, courts have recognized a variety of exceptions grounded in contract and related common law principles that have significantly weakened the at-will presumption. No one reason explains this trend. Depending on the case and the court, judicial resistance to the at-will presumption may reflect disenchantment with the rule on policy grounds, doctrinal objections to its application as a presumption, sympathy for individual plaintiffs in particular cases, or a desire to make the law conform more closely to the real expectations of parties in a complex relationship.

As you read, keep these possible explanations in mind. In each case, consider whether courts are correctly applying contract doctrine, whether the result they reach is fair under the particular facts, and what policy implications flow from the decision. Is it fair to say that the contract rules surrounding at-will employment are in disarray, as some commentators have suggested, or can you see any unifying themes in the exceptions?

1. Reliance on Offers of Employment

The ability to terminate employment at will can have harsh effects on neophyte employees who may quit an existing job, relocate, or turn down other job offers in order to accept a new position. Should the law provide any recourse for at-will employees terminated shortly after accepting work?

≡≡≡ *Goff-Hamel v. Obstetricians & Gynecologists*
      588 N.W.2d 798 (Neb. 1999)

WRIGHT, J.

[Julie] Goff-Hamel worked for Hastings Family Planning for 11 years. Prior to leaving Hastings Family Planning, Goff-Hamel was earning $24,000 plus [benefits].

In July 1993, Goff-Hamel met with representatives of Obstetricians regarding the possibility of employment. Present at the meeting were [Dr. George Adam, a part owner of Obstetricians] and Larry Draper, a consultant of Obstetricians involved in personnel decisions. Adam had approached Goff-Hamel in June 1993 about working for him as a patient relations and outreach coordinator. [She initially declined the offer.] Adam spoke to her one month later, asking her to reconsider and whether she was ready to "jump ship and come work for him." Goff-Hamel told Adam she would be interested in hearing some details, and an interview was set for July 27 at Adam's office.

At the meeting, Adam represented to Goff-Hamel that the position would be full time and would start at a salary of $10 per hour and that she would be provided 2 weeks' paid vacation, three or four paid holidays, uniforms, and an educational stipend. A retirement plan would start after the end of the second year, retroactive to the end of the first year. The job would not provide health insurance.

Goff-Hamel was offered a job with Obstetricians during the July 27, 1993, meeting, and she accepted the job offer at that time. . . . [I]t was agreed that she would start her employment on October 4. Goff-Hamel gave notice to Hastings Family Planning in August. . . .

Subsequently, Goff-Hamel was provided with uniforms for her job. She was given a copy of her schedule for the first week of work. . . .

On October 3, 1993, Goff-Hamel was told by Draper that she should not report to work the next morning as had been planned. Draper told her that Janel Foote, the wife of a part owner of Obstetricians, Dr. Terry Foote, opposed the hiring of Goff-Hamel.

. . . Goff-Hamel sought replacement employment, but was unable to obtain employment until April 1995, when she was employed part time at the rate of $11 per hour.

The trial court concluded that since Goff-Hamel was to be employed at will, her employment could be terminated at any time, including before she began working. The court concluded that under either contract law or promissory estoppel, Obstetricians was entitled to a judgment as a matter of law. . . .

We have consistently held that when employment is not for a definite term and there are no contractual, statutory, or constitutional restrictions upon the right of discharge, an employer may lawfully discharge an employee whenever and for whatever cause it chooses. Therefore, the trial court correctly determined as a matter of law that Goff-Hamel could not bring a claim for breach of an employment contract.

Goff-Hamel's second cause of action was based upon promissory estoppel. "[T]he development of the law of promissory estoppel 'is an attempt by the courts to keep remedies abreast of increased moral consciousness of honesty and fair representations in all business dealings.'" *Rosnick v. Dinsmore*, 457 N.W.2d 793, 801 (Neb. 1990).

Promissory estoppel provides for damages as justice requires and does not attempt to provide the plaintiff damages based upon the benefit of the bargain. It requires only that reliance be reasonable and foreseeable. It does not impose the requirement that the promise giving rise to the cause of action must be so comprehensive in scope as to meet the requirements of an offer that would ripen into a contract if accepted by the promisee.

We have not specifically addressed whether promissory estoppel may be asserted as the basis for a cause of action for detrimental reliance upon a promise of at-will employment. . . .

Other jurisdictions which have addressed the question of whether a cause of action for promissory estoppel can be stated in the context of a prospective at-will employee are split on the issue. Some have held that an employee can recover damages incurred as a result of resigning from the former at-will employment in reliance on a promise of other at-will employment. They have determined that when a prospective employer knows or should know that a promise of employment will induce an employee to leave his or her current job, such employer shall be liable for the reliant's damages. Recognizing that both the prospective new employer and the prior employer could have fired the employee without cause at any time, they have concluded that the employee would have continued to work in his or her prior employment if it were not for the offer by the prospective employer. Although damages have not been allowed for wages lost from the prospective at-will employment, damages have been allowed based upon wages from the prior employment and other damages incurred in reliance on the job offer.

In contrast, other jurisdictions have held as a matter of law that a prospective employee cannot recover damages incurred in reliance on an unfulfilled promise of at-will employment, concluding that reliance on a promise consisting solely of at-will employment is unreasonable as a matter of law because the employee should know that the promised employment could be terminated by the employer at any time for any reason without liability. These courts have stated that an anomalous result occurs when recovery is allowed for an employee who has not begun work, when the same employee's job could be terminated without liability 1 day after beginning work. . . .

In *Grouse v. Group Health Plan, Inc.*, 306 N.W.2d 114 (Minn. 1981), a pharmacist working at a drugstore desired employment with a hospital or clinic. He accepted employment with a clinic and gave 2 weeks' notice to the drugstore. During this period, he declined a job with a hospital because he had accepted employment with the clinic. Upon reporting to work, he was told that someone else had been hired because the pharmacist did not satisfy certain hiring requirements of the clinic. He had difficulty obtaining other full-time employment and suffered wage loss as a result.

. . . The court stated:

> [A]ppellant had a right to assume he would be given a good faith opportunity to perform his duties to the satisfaction of respondent once he was on the job. He was not only

denied that opportunity but resigned the position he already held in reliance on the firm offer which respondent tendered him.

Id. at 116.

The court also recognized that under appropriate circumstances, promissory estoppel could apply even if the employee was fired after he had commenced employment, thus concluding that its ruling would not necessarily create an anomalous result.

[The court went on to summarize additional cases from other jurisdictions.]

Having reviewed and considered decisions from other jurisdictions, we conclude under the facts of this case that promissory estoppel can be asserted in connection with the offer for at-will employment and that the trial court erred in granting Obstetricians summary judgment. A cause of action for promissory estoppel is based upon a promise which the promisor should reasonably expect to induce action or forbearance on the part of the promisee which does in fact induce such an action or forbearance. Here, promissory estoppel is appropriate where Goff-Hamel acted to her detriment in order to avail herself of the promised employment. . . .

STEPHAN, J., dissenting.

I respectfully dissent. In my opinion, the district court correctly determined as a matter of law that Goff-Hamel could not proceed under either a breach of contract or a promissory estoppel theory of recovery. I cannot reconcile the result reached by the majority or its rationale with our firmly established legal principles governing at-will employment. As succinctly and, in my view, correctly stated by the district court: "Since plaintiff could have been terminated after one day's employment without the defendant incurring liability, logic dictates she could also be terminated before the employment started."

The majority relies in part on *Grouse v. Group Health Plan, Inc.*, which concluded that the principles of promissory estoppel set forth in the RESTATEMENT OF CONTRACTS §90 (1932) could apply to a termination of at-will employment which occurred before the employee actually started working because "under appropriate circumstances we believe [Restatement of Contracts] section 90 would apply even after employment has begun." However, we held in *Merrick v. Thomas*, 522 N.W.2d 402 (Neb. 1994), that an at-will employee who was discharged a short time after she began working could not, as a matter of law, assert a promissory estoppel claim for damages resulting from resignation of her previous employment. Thus, this essential premise of the holding in *Grouse* is directly contrary to our law. Another basis for the decision in *Grouse*, as quoted in the majority opinion, is that one who is offered employment has "a right to assume he would be given a good faith opportunity to perform his duties to the satisfaction" of the employer. This concept is foreign to our law and entirely inconsistent with the established principle, acknowledged by the majority, that in the absence of contractual, statutory, or constitutional restrictions, an employer may discharge an at-will employee "whenever and for whatever cause it chooses." *Myers v. Nebraska Equal Opp. Comm.*, 582 N.W.2d 362 (Neb. 1998). Thus, whether an at-will employee performs in a satisfactory manner is immaterial to the employer's right to discharge, and there is no basis under our law for an assumption that satisfactory performance by such an employee would create an entitlement to continued employment. . . .

The conflict between the court's decision today and the law of at-will employment is further demonstrated by the manner in which the majority addresses the issue of damages. Goff-Hamel's damage claim is based entirely upon her allegation that after learning on October 3, 1993, that appellee had withdrawn its offer of employment, she was unable to find "comparable" full-time employment until May 15, 1995. The majority acknowledges that under the theory of recovery which it recognizes in this case, damages cannot be "based upon the wages the employee would have earned in the prospective employment because the employment was terminable at will." Following the same logic, damages based upon wage loss during any *interval* between withdrawal of a promise of at-will employment and the securing of "comparable" employment would not be recoverable, because the promised employment could have been terminated by either party at any time after it had begun. . . .

I would follow what I consider to be the better reasoned view, that promissory estoppel may not be utilized to remedy an unfulfilled promise of at-will employment. I acknowledge that this reasoning would produce a seemingly harsh result from the perspective of Goff-Hamel under the facts of this case, but to some degree, this is inherent in the concept of at-will employment. [For example,] an employer which has made a significant expenditure in training an at-will employee may feel harshly treated if, upon completing the training, the employee immediately utilizes his or her newly acquired skills to secure more remunerative employment with a competitor. If the law of at-will employment were regularly bent to circumvent what some may consider a harsh result in a particular case, its path would soon become hopelessly circuitous and impossible to follow.

Employment for a specific duration imposes certain benefits and burdens upon each party to the relationship. Under our established law, parties wishing to create such a relationship must do so by contract. Where, as in this case, the parties have not chosen to impose contractual obligations upon themselves, it is my view that a court should not utilize the principle of promissory estoppel to impose the subjective expectations of either party upon the other. . . .

NOTES

1. *Promissory Estoppel, Employment at Will, and Newly Hired Employees.* In recognizing the plaintiff's promissory estoppel claim, *Goff-Hamel* cites *Grouse v. Group Health Plan* for the proposition that an employee is entitled to a good faith opportunity to perform to the employer's satisfaction. The dissent criticizes this premise as "directly contrary" to employment at will. Which opinion do you find more convincing? In practice, many employers designate starting employees as "probationary," reinforcing the idea that the employee has no job security during the first few months of employment. Does this point to a logical flaw in the courts' analyses in *Goff-Hamel* and *Grouse*? Or is it still possible to reconcile promissory estoppel protection with the at-will presumption?

2. *The One-Day Worker.* A Minnesota court directly addressed the *Goff-Hamel* and *Grouse* scenario of the one-day-hired, one-day-fired employee. In *Gorham v. Benson Optical*, 539 N.W.2d 798 (Minn. Ct. App. 1995), Gorham accepted a job offer as a regional manager with the defendant. After confirming the position, he gave notice to his current employer, who tried to entice him to stay by offering him a raise, which he declined. Prior to starting his new job, however, the company officer who had hired Gorham left, and Gorham was terminated on his first day at work. In addressing his subsequent promissory estoppel claim, the court saw "no relevant difference between Gorham, who reported to the national sales meeting on his first day of employment,

and Grouse, who was denied even one day on the job." Both relied to their detriment on the promise of a new job and "had a 'good faith opportunity to perform his duties.'" *Id.* at 801. Gorham was fired the very day he showed up for work. How much more time would have constituted a "good faith opportunity" to perform his duties? Two weeks? A month? A 90-day "probationary" period?

3. *Reasonableness of Reliance.* Courts rejecting the applicability of promissory estoppel often do so on the grounds that, while the worker does in fact rely, the reliance is not reasonable if the offer is for at-will employment. *See, e.g., White v. Roche Biomedical Labs., Inc.,* 807 F. Supp. 1212 (D.S.C. 1992). Pushed to its logical conclusion, this argument would seem to foreclose promissory estoppel liability entirely since, by definition, there is no promise of continued employment and any reliance to the contrary would be ipso facto unreasonable.

Do you agree? Can it be reasonable (as a practical matter) for an employee to rely on a job offer even if there is no legal commitment to continued employment? If you said yes, does your answer change if the employer is more explicit about the plaintiff's at-will status? In an episode that garnered much media attention, the University of Illinois rescinded an offer of employment to a professor who had apparently quit his prior tenured position and moved to Champaign-Urbana to begin teaching there. Although the facts are debated and much of the discussion has focused on First Amendment and academic freedom issues, there is an interesting contract overlay. Reportedly, the "offer" was subject to the approval of the University's Board of Trustees and therefore (despite the fact that such approval may have been routine), there was no offer at all. Even if that were true, does it follow that promissory estoppel would not apply because it would be unreasonable to rely on a nonoffer? Or is that the exact gap in contract law that promissory estoppel is supposed to fill? The contrasting views are on full display at http://www.concurringopinions.com/archives/2014/08/steven-salaitas-promissory-estoppel-claim-is-weak.html; see also http://www.concurringopinions.com/archives/2014/08/does-salaita-have-a-contract-claim.html#more-90272 (discussing whether there was an "offer" at all).

4. *Remedy.* The majority in *Goff-Hamel* is careful to point out the limited nature of the promissory estoppel remedy. Understand the difference between the amount of damages for promissory estoppel with the damages available had the plaintiffs been able to establish breach of a contract for job security. Suppose, for instance, that Goff-Hamel earned $1,500 per month in her old job and was promised $1,600 per month by the defendant. After being terminated, she searches unsuccessfully for alternate employment for two months before accepting a position at $1,400 per month. How should the court calculate her damages, assuming she prevails on remand? Now suppose instead that following her termination Goff-Hamel's former employer happily takes her back at the same salary she had earned prior to giving notice. Is she entitled to anything?

Damages in promissory estoppel cases are often calculated based on the plaintiff's *prior* employment—the loss of that is his "reliance" interest. But what if that position was itself at will? Should that limit recovery, or should the plaintiff be able to recover his "expectation" interest—the amount he would have earned in the new position? And even as to the reliance interest, there is no guarantee that the plaintiff would have remained in the prior job. The employer in *Toscano v. Greene Music,* 21 Cal. Rptr. 3d 732 (Ct. App. 2004), made such an argument in seeking to limit the plaintiff's damages to wages lost between resigning his prior employment and the anticipated start date of the promised job. The court rejected the limitation, holding that lost future wages with a prior employer are recoverable under a promissory estoppel theory, provided they are not "speculative, remote, contingent or merely possible." *Id.* at 738. It went on, however, to hold that the trial court's award of lost wages until plaintiff's retirement was improper under this standard because it was based solely on the fact that Toscano had a history of remaining with his current employer until offered new employment.

Do results like this diminish the significance to employees of courts' recognition of the promissory estoppel cause of action? Or do such limitations strike an appropriate balance in light of the at-will presumption? Given the result in *Toscano*, how would you go about helping a future plaintiff overcome such hurdles to establishing damages? *Cf. Helmer v. Bingham Toyota Isuzu*, 29 Cal. Rptr. 3d 136 (Ct. App. 2005) (affirming award of damages of lost future wages with prior employer from time of resignation through retirement on plaintiff's promissory fraud claim where prior supervisor testified that plaintiff was a reliable employee and would have been rehired but for a strict no-rehire policy).

5. *Proof of Reliance.* What constitutes detrimental reliance for purposes of promissory estoppel? The most convincing cases are those involving employees who relocate or incur significant expense in preparing for their new job. *See, e.g., Sheppard v. Morgan Keegan & Co.*, 266 Cal. Rptr. 784, 787 (Ct. App. 1990) ("[A]n employer cannot expect a new employee to sever his former employment and move across the country only to be terminated before the ink dries on his new lease[.]"). *Goff-Hamel* suggests giving up one's current job alone is sufficient to state a promissory estoppel claim. In *Grouse*, the employee gave up his job and turned down a second offer. What if the employee simply refrains from applying for other jobs based on the assurances of his or her current employer? *See Hanly v. Riverside Methodist Hosps.*, 603 N.E.2d 1126, 1131 (Ohio Ct. App. 1991) (no promissory estoppel claim where plaintiff neither looked for nor turned down other employment nor was expressly dissuaded by employer from seeking outside opportunities). Is the problem less the reliance than the absence of proof other than the employee's "bare assertion" of foregoing a job search? Or maybe proof that the reliance was detrimental? *See Fregara v. Jet Aviation Business Jets*, 764 F. Supp. 940, 949 (D.N.J. 1991) (no promissory estoppel claim where plaintiff was unemployed at time of job offer and therefore did not forgo anything of value in accepting position). If so, would it be enough to show that more lucrative alternative positions were available?

6. *Promises, Offers, and Representations.* Difficulties in proving reliance are not the only potential pitfalls for plaintiffs pursuing promissory estoppel claims. The way in which courts interpret and apply other elements often makes establishing promissory estoppel difficult. An example is found in *Schoff v. Combined Insurance Company of America*, 604 N.W.2d 43 (Iowa 1999), where plaintiff accurately answered "no" on the application form to the question of whether he had ever been convicted of a felony but disclosed to the interviewer that he had been convicted of only misdemeanors. He was assured at least twice that there would be "no problem" with his criminal record. When the employer's bonding company discovered that the misdemeanor convictions had stemmed from what were originally felony charges, Schoff was discharged. The court rejected his estoppel claim based on the assurances that Schoff's criminal record would not affect his employment and that only felony convictions were relevant to employment and bonding decisions. It reasoned:

> Initially, we conclude that any statements made by Hageman that only felony convictions were important do not constitute an assertion that Combined would forbear a certain specific act, namely, discharging Schoff because of his felony charges and/or his failure to be bonded. These statements by Hageman more clearly fall within the common definition of a representation: "a statement . . . made to convey a particular view or impression of something with the intention of influencing opinion or action." Statements that only felony convictions are relevant to employment and bonding decisions are not the equivalent of a declaration that Combined would not fire Schoff because of his felony record. Hageman's statements merely conveyed his *impression* or *understanding* of a certain fact—that only felony convictions were relevant; as a matter of law, these statements do not constitute a promise.

Id. at 51. As to the second statement made by Hageman—that Schoff's criminal record would not be a problem, even if the statement constituted a promise—it was not clear and definite:

> [A]ny statement that Schoff's "criminal record" would not affect his employment is subject to some ambiguity in that the parties did not have the same knowledge with respect to the nature and extent of Schoff's criminal record. This ambiguity is crucial because Schoff was not fired because of his criminal record in general; he was fired because he could not be bonded. Similarly, he was not denied a bond due to his criminal record in general; rather he was not bonded because he had been charged with felonies and/or had not revealed his criminal record on his bond application. As a matter of law, any "promises" that Schoff's criminal record would not be a problem simply do not clearly and definitely encompass a promise that Schoff's felony charges would not be a problem or that his failure to be bonded would not be a problem. . . .

Id.

The court goes to some length to distinguish between the "representations" made by Hageman and the type of definitive promise required for promissory estoppel. Do you understand the distinction the court is drawing? In promissory estoppel claims outside of the employment context courts have held that the plaintiff need not demonstrate a definite offer to contract in order to show the defendant made a promise justifying reliance. *See, e.g., Hoffman v. Red Owl Stores, Inc.*, 133 N.W.2d 267, 276 (Wis. 1965) (noting in suit over promise to provide a store franchise that §90 "does not impose the requirement that the promise . . . be so comprehensive in scope as to meet the requirements of an offer that would ripen into a contract if accepted"). Yet the court in *Schoff*, as well as courts in other employment cases, often construe the elements of a promissory estoppel claim more strictly. *See, e.g., Dumas v. Infinity Broadcasting Corp,* 416 F.3d 671, 677 (7th Cir. 2005) (suggesting that disc jockey who gave up previous job based on negotiations for employment that failed to come to fruition could not sustain a claim for promissory estoppel unless capable of establishing all of the elements of a valid contract other than consideration); *Ruud v. Great Plains Supply, Inc.*, 526 N.W.2d 369, 372 (Minn. 1995) (finding statements that "good employees would be taken care of" and plaintiff would be offered a "similar" position if things did not work out after he accepted relocation to management position at unprofitable store insufficiently definite to give rise to promissory estoppel claim). *But see Brueck v. John Maneely Co., Inc.*, 131 F. Supp. 3d 774 (N.D. Ind. 2015) (finding prospective employee alleged valid promissory estoppel claim by relying on several representations that could be interpreted as a definite promise of employment, even though offer was rescinded based on falsehoods in job application). Does the employment context require a different interpretation of the doctrine than in other failed contract scenarios?

2.   Assurances Made During Employment

The last section involved promises made to newly hired employees, some of whom had not even begun working for the employer. This section addresses the extent to which employees who have been working for some length of time for the employer are protected when relying on assurances of obtaining a certain position or of continued employment. The discussion begins where it left off above, with promissory estoppel. It then turns to various contract theories.

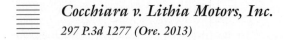

Cocchiara v. Lithia Motors, Inc.
297 P.3d 1277 (Ore. 2013)

BALMER, C.J.

In this employment case we must determine whether a prospective employee may bring a promissory estoppel claim or a fraudulent misrepresentation claim based on an employer's representations regarding a job that is terminable at will. Plaintiff worked as a salesperson for defendant for nearly eight years before he had a heart attack that required him to seek a less stressful job. In reliance on his manager's promise that plaintiff had been given a new "corporate" job with defendant that would meet his health needs, plaintiff turned down a job with a different employer. Ultimately, defendant did not hire plaintiff for the corporate job, and plaintiff subsequently had to take jobs that paid less than the corporate job with defendant or less than the position that he had turned down. Plaintiff brought this action against defendant claiming [*inter alia* promissory estoppel and fraudulent misrepresentation].

Facts

We state the facts in the light most favorable to plaintiff because the trial court granted defendant's motion for partial summary judgment. Plaintiff worked as a salesperson at a Lithia Dodge dealership from 1997 to October 2005. Following a major heart attack in 2004, plaintiff's doctors recommended that he find a less stressful job that would allow him to work shorter hours and avoid working on the weekends. Plaintiff discussed those needs with Summers, his General Sales Manager at the dealership, but he also pursued other employment because his sales job could not meet his health needs.

Plaintiff received an offer to be a sales representative for the Medford Mail Tribune, a position that satisfied his health requirements. Plaintiff went to Summers to tell him that he planned to take the Medford Mail Tribune job, and he told Summers that that job would be less stressful and would provide compensation that was comparable to his current position. Summers responded that plaintiff should not accept the Medford Mail Tribune position because he was "too valuable" to defendant. Summers then told plaintiff that there was a new "corporate" job available with defendant that would meet his health needs.

After placing a call to defendant's corporate offices, Summers advised plaintiff that he had been given the corporate position and that he would be contacted the next day to come in to finalize the paperwork. Plaintiff then asked Summers to confirm that the offer was definite, given plaintiff's outstanding offer from the Medford Mail Tribune. Summers confirmed that plaintiff had been given the job and that the meeting the next day was a "mere formality." Plaintiff acknowledges that there was no discussion as to whether or not the corporate job would be terminable at will. After his discussion with Summers, plaintiff told the Medford Mail Tribune that he had decided not to accept its offer because he had received another job with defendant.

. . . Ultimately, defendant did not hire plaintiff for that job. When plaintiff then tried to accept the Medford Mail Tribune's prior job offer, that job had been filled. Plaintiff later accepted a different sales representative job with the Medford Mail Tribune, but the job paid less than the previously offered job at the Medford Mail Tribune. Plaintiff subsequently accepted yet another job that paid less than the promised corporate job with defendant.

. . . As part of his claim for damages, plaintiff sought economic damages for the income that he would have earned in the corporate job with defendant. Defendant filed a motion for partial summary judgment, arguing that, because the corporate job was an at-will position that defendant could have fired plaintiff from at any time, plaintiff had no reasonable basis to rely on the corporate job offer, as required for both the promissory estoppel and fraudulent misrepresentation claims. Moreover, defendant argued, it would be illogical to hold defendant liable for damages that plaintiff would have been unable to recover had he been terminated on his first day. The trial court granted summary judgment on the promissory estoppel and fraudulent misrepresentation claims, noting that, even if plaintiff had relied on all the statements that Summers allegedly had made, plaintiff would lose

> [b]ecause they didn't tell him you got a job for the rest of your life here. * * * He didn't rely on having a job for more tha[n] a day because * * * nobody said to him, and you're going to have this job for X amount of days, months, or years. * * * [H]e couldn't rely on something that was never said to him.

[The Court of Appeals affirmed, relying on its prior decision in *Slate v. Saxon, Marquoit, Bertoni & Todd,* 999 P.2d 1152 (2000), which had held that a law clerk at the defendant law firm had no cause of action when the firm reneged on its offer of an associate attorney position. Given the nature of at-will employment, there was no reasonable basis for reliance since "the plaintiff could not *reasonably* have understood that the promised employment would last for any particular length of time"; further, "the plaintiff would have experienced the same losses if the defendants had hired him, but had 'discharged [him] immediately after he came to work rather than before.'" The Oregon Supreme Court had affirmed *Slate.*

Plaintiff argued that *Slate* was incorrectly decided "because it ignored the reality that prospective employees often rely on offers of at-will employment and that employers expect prospective employees to rely on those offers." Defendant responded that recognition of such a rule would essentially render the at-will rule meaningless. Holding that a prospective employee could recover for reasonable reliance on an offer of at-will employment "would create an unworkable rule regarding how long an employer would have to employ new hires."]

At-Will Employment Doctrine

Both parties agree that, in Oregon, "the general rule is that an employer may discharge an employee at any time and for any reason, absent a contractual, statutory, or constitutional requirement to the contrary." . . .

Perhaps because the at-will employment doctrine focuses on termination, courts have disagreed regarding the significance of the at-will nature of employment before employment begins. In particular, courts have disagreed whether it is reasonable to rely on an offer of at-will employment, which in turn affects whether an employer's termination of an at-will employment agreement before the employee begins working is actionable under a theory of promissory estoppel or fraudulent misrepresentation.

Promissory Estoppel

[Oregon has adopted §90 of the RESTATEMENT (SECOND) of CONTRACTS (ALI 2013)] and [n]othing in our case law or the RESTATEMENT (SECOND) suggests that a promisee's reliance is *per se* unreasonable if the underlying promise is for a contract that is terminable at will. . . . Far from foreclosing such a claim, the RESTATEMENT (SECOND) provides the following illustration in the section on promissory estoppel:

> A applies to B, a distributor of radios manufactured by C, for a "dealer franchise" to sell C's products. Such franchises are revocable at will. B erroneously informs A that C has accepted the application and will soon award the franchise, that A can proceed to employ salesmen and solicit orders, and that A will receive an initial delivery of at least 30 radios. A expends $1,150 in preparing to do business, but does not receive the franchise or any radios. B is liable to A for the $1,150 but not for the lost profit on 30 radios.

RESTATEMENT (SECOND) §90 comment d, illustration 8. Similarly to that illustration, in this case, Summers erroneously informed plaintiff that he had been given a job (that was terminable at will) and told him that he should turn down the position with the Medford Mail Tribune. The RESTATEMENT (SECOND) illustration indicates that the at-will nature of an underlying promise of employment does not bar a claim based on promissory estoppel, even if it might limit the nature of the damages available in some cases.

The RESTATEMENT (SECOND) approach is sound. An employer's legal right to fire an employee at any time and for any reason absent contrary contractual, statutory, or constitutional requirements does not carry with it a conclusive presumption that the employer will exercise that right. *See Tadsen v. Praegitzer Industries, Inc.,* 928 P.2d 980 (Ore. 1996) (rejecting the premise in a wrongful discharge case that "an employer should enjoy a conclusive presumption that, had it not discharged the employee illegally, it would have discharged him or her lawfully at any time after it in fact did so unlawfully"). Absent that presumption, it may be reasonable for an employee to rely on a promise of employment, because the employee may have reason to believe that the employer's right to terminate at will not be exercised before the employee begins work. Particularly where, as here, the employee has had a lengthy employment relationship with his employer, and the employer asserts the employee's value to the company, it may be reasonable for the employee to rely on the promise of employment, even though the job is terminable at will. We caution, however, that reasonableness is an issue for the jury, considering all the relevant circumstances.

[The court rejected the argument in *Slate* that no injustice would be avoided by allowing a party to recover for revocation of a promise of employment when the same party would not be entitled to recover for the "termination of the consummated contract."] Although an employer has a right to fire an at-will employee—though not for an unlawful reason—without liability, the fact that the employer has that right does not mean that a prospective employee can never reasonably rely on a promise of at-will employment. And if a prospective employee does reasonably rely on such a promise, a remedy may be necessary to avoid injustice.

[As for whether the plaintiff can recover damages for failure to be awarded the corporate job, the court stressed that defendant did not argue] that, in general, damages associated with the corporate job could not be recovered in an action for promissory estoppel (or fraudulent misrepresentation). Instead, both defendant and the Court of Appeals relied on *Slate* for the proposition that the at-will nature of the corporate job precluded plaintiff from recovering lost wages for that job. However, this court has rejected a similar proposition in a wrongful discharge case. In *Tadsen* a jury awarded front pay to an at-will employee who had alleged unlawful employment practices, including wrongful discharge, and this court affirmed the trial court's denial of a motion to strike the claim for front pay. In that case, the employer had argued that an at-will employee cannot recover front pay because the employee has no "'right' to, or assurance of" future employment. *Tadsen*. This court rejected that argument[, stating that while at-will employment may be a factor that bears on whether the proof is sufficient, "the right to terminate someone's employment does not establish as a matter of law that an employee cannot prove the existence of front pay damages."]

Similarly, in this case, the fact that the corporate job was terminable at will, standing alone, does not create a conclusive presumption that plaintiff cannot prove damages related to the loss of that job. Instead, as in *Tadsen*, plaintiff may seek to prove what he would have earned in the corporate job and how long he likely would have remained in that job had he been hired as promised and allowed to start work. Although it may be easier for a plaintiff to prove the likely duration of employment in a wrongful discharge case, where the employee has a history of employment with the employer, a plaintiff is entitled to attempt to make such a showing outside the wrongful discharge context. Of course, if an employer lawfully fires an employee after the employee has started work, which could include firing the employee for no reason at all under the at-will employment doctrine, the employee will not be able to show that the job would have continued beyond that point. In this case, however, plaintiff was not allowed to start the corporate job; indeed, the employer told him that he had never actually been hired for that job, making it difficult for the employer to argue that plaintiff was lawfully fired. Thus, the general principle from *Tadsen* applies in this case: The at-will nature of the employment does not foreclose plaintiff from attempting to prove the likely duration of employment had he been hired as promised and allowed to start work, although "[a]t-will employment may be a factor that bears on whether the proof is sufficient in a particular case [.]" *Id*. Whether plaintiff is ultimately entitled to recover damages associated with not being hired for the corporate job, and in what amount, is not before this court. Nonetheless, defendant is not entitled to judgment as a matter of law solely because the corporate job was terminable at will.

We recognize that allowing a prospective employee to bring a promissory estoppel claim raises practical concerns that the Court of Appeals articulated in *Slate:* "It would serve the interests of no one—least of all new professional persons in search of work—to discourage putative employers from discharging them earlier rather than later, under circumstances where there is no possibility that an actual employment relationship will ever exist." On the other hand, as the Eighth Circuit has recognized:

> [I]f damages sustained in reasonable reliance on an employer promise were not available, the effect of such a rule would be to allow the employer to take advantage of whatever benefits might accrue to him by his inducing a potential employee to leave behind home and/or steady employment while at the same time being completely free of any obligation to keep his word.

Bower v. AT & T, Technologies, Inc., 852 F.2d 361, 364 (8th Cir.1988). Moreover, a rule barring a promissory estoppel (or fraudulent misrepresentation) claim would allow an employer to abuse its ability to induce the reliance of prospective employees. For example, an employer could promise an at-will job to multiple people to keep them available while the employer continued to vet them or to prevent them from accepting a position with a competitor. Acknowledging the possibility of reasonable reliance "encourages employers [and employees] to take [their] promises seriously," *id.,* and, more importantly, is consistent with the law of promissory estoppel. . . .

[The portion of the opinion dealing with plaintiff's fraud claim is reproduced at page 305.]

NOTES

1. *Comparing and Contrasting New Hire and Mid-Term Employee Promissory Estoppel Claims.* Note that the same conceptual issues that courts struggle with in the new hire context regarding promissory estoppel animate the discussion of the viability of the theory in a mid-term employment case like *Cocchiara.* In both contexts, courts continue to disagree on the extent to which promissory estoppel is simply inconsistent with at-will employment; whether a worker can reasonably rely on promises of employment in an at-will relationship; how definite the assurances must be; and whether damages exist and how they can be calculated. But are there distinctions between the two contexts that might make a difference, legally or factually? For example, is reliance on assurances by a current employee of a better position or continued employment more likely to be found reasonable than an assurance of employment to one being hired, when the employment itself is at will?

2. *Why Not Breach of Contract?* Cocchiara either did not plead breach of contract or abandoned the claim by the time the case was appealed. Why? After all, assuming Summer's promise was sufficiently definite, wasn't it in exchange for valuable consideration—namely, Cocchiara's turning down his other job offer—and, hence, a unilateral contract? Furthermore, wouldn't the forbearance of an existing job offer elsewhere be enough to show "additional consideration," and, thus, satisfy any evidentiary burden required to overcome the at-will or other presumption?

One answer might be concern about the statute of frauds. In cases based on oral promises, employees frequently face challenges based on the statute of frauds, a rule of contract law that requires particular classes of contracts to be evidenced by a signed written instrument. In most jurisdictions, the requirements of the statute of frauds apply to contracts "not capable of performance within a year from the time of their formation." RESTATEMENT (SECOND) OF CONTRACTS §178(1) (ALI 1981). This rule may provide employers with a valid defense, at least in cases involving oral promises guaranteeing a fixed term of employment, such as employment for three years.

Employers sometimes argue that "lifetime" or "permanent" employment contracts similarly cannot be completed within a year and therefore must be established through written evidence. A majority of courts have rejected this argument, however, noting that such contracts *could* be fully performed within one year, for example, where the employee dies or quits or the employer has cause to terminate the employee within a year of her hiring. *See, e.g., Foley v. Interactive Data Corp.*, 765 P.2d 373 (Cal. 1988); *see also Kalmus v. Oliver*, 390 S.W.3d 586, 593 (Tex. App. 2012). While some judges have criticized such legal gymnastics, the rejection of the statute-of-frauds defense in cases involving oral employment contracts is consistent with the general contract law trend limiting the application of the statute of frauds to situations where completion within one year is truly impossible. *See generally* Daniel P. O'Gorman, *The Statute of Frauds and Oral Promises of Job Security: The Tenuous Distinction Between Performance and Excusable Nonperformance*, 40 SETON HALL L. REV. 1023 (2010).

A more likely explanation is that courts are reluctant to find that oral assurances create any kind of binding job security terms—lifetime employment, employment for a definite term, or otherwise—when the promise is only for employment itself (in the new hire cases) or only for a better position within the company (such as in *Cocchiara*). Put another way, in oral promise cases involving assurances making no reference to job security or length of term, courts resist finding that the relationship is anything other than at will, and hence, that the assurance produced some other kind of binding contract. In such cases then, promissory estoppel is the worker's only recourse. *See Peters v. Gilead*, 533 F.3d 594 (7th Cir. 2008) (after the employer confirmed in writing that an employee was entitled to leave to undergo surgery pursuant to terms in the employer's handbook, the court found that the employer's failure to abide by these assurances, while not necessarily establishing that a binding contract had been created, gave rise to a valid promissory estoppel claim).

3. *Assurances of Continued Employment Enforceable in Contract.* In contrast, when oral assurances provide something more, courts may find them to be promises enforceable in contract. For example, in *Shebar v. Sanyo Business Systems Corp.*, 544 A.2d 377 (N.J. 1988), as in *Cocchiara*, the plaintiff (Shebar) turned down a position at another company after his current employer (Sanyo) made oral assurances. The assurances in *Shebar*, however, included references to job security and the long-term nature of the relationship. The court described the circumstances as follows:

> The critical events allegedly occurred on October 1, 1984, when plaintiff accepted the Sony offer and tendered his written resignation to Sanyo. According to Shebar's certification, Sanyo's president, Mr. Yamazaki, called him into his office after he received plaintiff's letter of resignation. When plaintiff went into Mr. Yamazaki's office, Mr. Yamashita, executive vice president of Sanyo, was also present. According to plaintiff, Mr. Yamashita told him that he was personally insulted by his resignation, that his performance was exceptionally good, that plaintiff should have brought any problems or dissatisfaction to

his attention, and that the company did not want plaintiff to resign, but rather wanted to eliminate any problems that existed. Yamazaki apparently agreed with Yamashita. Yamazaki held the resignation letter, ripped it to shreds, and said "I will not accept your resignation. We will solve your problems."

Plaintiff claims that Yamazaki and Yamashita expressly stated to him that Sanyo does not fire its managers. They told him, plaintiff contends, that he had a job for the rest of his life, and that Sanyo had never fired, and never intended to fire, a corporate employee whose rank was manager or above. Plaintiff acknowledges that they did not discuss money at this meeting, but maintains that they assured him that he would receive a substantial raise in March 1985.

As a result of this meeting and in reliance on the assurances made to him there, plaintiff revoked his acceptance of Sony's offer. Thereafter, he informed Mr. Yamashita that he had rejected the Sony offer. According to plaintiff, Yamashita congratulated him on a wise decision, and again assured him that he was "married" to Sanyo and no divorce was allowed.

Id. at 379-30.

When Sanyo terminated Shebar four months later, Shebar sued, alleging breach of oral contract. The court held that Shebar had produced sufficient evidence to go to trial on whether a contract existed between him and Sanyo, and whether it had been breached. Interestingly, the court characterized the potential contract not as one guaranteeing lifetime employment, but rather as for an indefinite term terminable only for cause, which "protects the employee only from arbitrary termination." *Id.* at 382. The court then went on to describe why Shebar's evidence could establish the elements of such a contract claim:

> We find that plaintiff has presented a material issue of fact concerning whether his employer orally promised to discharge him only for cause. Plaintiff's superiors specifically represented to him that he would have continued employment at the company. Those representations were obviously intended to induce plaintiff to remain with Sanyo as Sanyo's computer sales manager and revoke his acceptance of Sony's employment offer. Plaintiff acted in reliance on the alleged promise by forgoing the job opportunity he had secured at Sony. . . . Furthermore, we hold that a factfinder could conclude that plaintiff gave valuable consideration for Sanyo's promise of continued employment with termination only for cause. The essential requirement of consideration is a bargained-for exchange of promises or performance that may consist of an act, a forbearance, or the creation, modification, or destruction of a legal relation. . . .
>
> Taking plaintiff's allegations as true, he agreed to relinquish his new position at Sony in exchange for job security at Sanyo. Sanyo, in turn, agreed to relinquish its right to terminate plaintiff's employment at will in exchange for the retention of a valued employee. Such bargained-for and exchanged promises furnish ample consideration for an enforceable contract. . . .
>
> Additionally, in order to be enforceable the terms of such a contract must be sufficiently clear and capable of judicial interpretation. We find that as a matter of law, the purported contract at issue is not so vague and indefinite that it cannot be enforced. . . .

Id. at 383-84.

4. *The Nature of the Promise.* In characterizing Sanyo's promise as one of protection from arbitrary termination, *Shebar* distinguished *Savarese v. Pyrene Manufacturing Co.*, 89 A.2d 237 (N.J. 1952), which had articulated the traditional rule that "permanent" or "lifetime" employment is considered at will absent additional consideration. In *Savarese*, an employee's supervisors induced him to play on the company baseball team, despite his fear of being injured, by allegedly stating that "If you get hurt I will take care of you. You will have a foreman's job the rest of your life." Plaintiff alleges that the supervisor specified the job as " 'the one I had, the one I earned.' " The plaintiff in fact sustained an injury while playing baseball, but returned to the company and continued to work there for 21 years, at which point the company terminated his employment. Afterwards, Savarese sued, contending that the company breached his contract of lifetime employment. Do you see a meaningful factual difference between the promises in the two cases? If not, one might argue that the court should have simply overruled *Savarese*.

Still, the distinction the *Shebar* court draws is potentially significant. First, as the opinion itself suggests reconceptualization of the nature of the assurance(s) is important because courts remain reluctant to recognize lifetime employment contracts. Second, what constitutes "cause" to terminate an employee may vary by type of employment contract. For example, because lifetime and definite term contracts purport to protect the employment from uncertainties such as changing circumstances, courts often find that economic downtown does not constitute cause to terminate under such contracts. In contrast, "cause" protections in indefinite term contracts may be less robust. *See, e.g.*, RESTATEMENT OF EMPLOYMENT LAW §2.04 (distinguishing between definite and indefinite term contracts, and stating that significant changes in the employer's economic circumstances constitute cause only with regard to the latter type of contract). You will see an example of this in the next case and confront such distinctions again in Chapter 3.

5. *Proof on Remand*. One historical justification for the statute of frauds was that evidence of oral contracts is likely to be factually unreliable, yet highly persuasive to juries. An interested plaintiff has a strong incentive to testify untruthfully about past promises or, absent bad faith, to misremember the defendant's precise statements. How will Cocchiara and Shebar prove their claims on remand? Absent corroboration of some kind (e.g., something in writing or third-party testimony regarding what was said), is it just their word against that of their respective employers? Is this a good reason to insist on a writing in cases like *Shebar*?

6. *"Married" to the Company*. Assuming Shebar's rendition of his employer's statements is true, long-term employment among high-level employees was the norm at Sanyo. As anyone who has worked more than one job knows, organizations differ widely in their treatment and expectations of their workers. These differences may result from a combination of factors, including the employer's corporate philosophy, the management styles of key personnel, the nature of the work itself, industry standards, and the personality of the company's clientele and workforce. The organizational culture of a particular workplace can create shared understandings about the way work relationships will progress and under what circumstances they may be terminated. Thus, employees may feel deeply wronged when denied regular raises and promotions, long-term employment absent poor performance, and other benefits and rewards commonly bestowed within the organization. Such shared understandings are sometimes referred to as "psychological" or "implicit" contracts of employment. *See, e.g.*, Katherine V. W. Stone, *The New Psychological Contract: Implications of the Changing Workplace for Labor and Employment Law*, 48 UCLA L. REV. 519, 549-50 (2001). To what extent should employer practices, mid-term worker expectations, and organizational culture affect the existence of legally recognized job security rights?

Pugh v. See's Candies, Inc.
171 Cal. Rptr. 917 (Ct. App. 1981)

GRODIN, J.

After 32 years of employment with See's Candies, Inc., in which he worked his way up the corporate ladder from dishwasher to vice president in charge of production and member of the board of directors, Wayne Pugh was fired. [Asserting that he had been fired in breach of contract, he sued his former employer for wrongful termination. The trial court granted defendants' motions for nonsuit, and this appeal followed.]

Pugh began working for See's at its Bay Area plant (then in San Francisco) in January 1941 washing pots and pans. From there he was promoted to candy maker, and held that position until the early part of 1942, when he entered the Air Corps. Upon his discharge in 1946 he returned to See's and his former position. After a year he was promoted to the position of production manager in charge of personnel, ordering raw materials, and supervising the production of candy. When, in 1950, See's moved into a larger plant in San Francisco, Pugh had responsibility for laying out the design of the plant, taking bids, and assisting in the construction. While working at this plant, Pugh sought to increase his value to the company by taking three years of night classes in plant layout, economics, and business law. When See's moved its San Francisco plant to its present location in South San Francisco in 1957, Pugh was given responsibilities for the new location similar to those which he undertook in 1950. By this time See's business and its number of production employees had increased substantially, and a new position of assistant production manager was created under Pugh's supervision.

In 1971 Pugh was again promoted, this time as vice president in charge of production and was placed upon the board of directors of See's northern California subsidiary, "in recognition of his accomplishments." In 1972 he received a gold watch from See's "in appreciation of 31 years of loyal service."

In May 1973 Pugh traveled with Charles Huggins, then president of See's, and their respective families to Europe on a business trip to visit candy manufacturers and to inspect new equipment. Mr. Huggins returned in early June to attend a board of director's meeting while Pugh and his family remained in Europe on a planned vacation.

Upon Pugh's return from Europe on Sunday, June 25, 1973, he received a message directing him to fly to Los Angeles the next day and meet with Mr. Huggins.

Pugh went to Los Angeles expecting to be told of another promotion. The preceding Christmas season had been the most successful in See's history, the Valentine's Day holiday of 1973 set a new sales record for See's, and the March 1973 edition of See's Newsletter, containing two pictures of Pugh, carried congratulations on the increased production.

Instead, upon Pugh's arrival at Mr. Huggins' office, the latter said, "Wayne, come in and sit down. We might as well get right to the point. I have decided your services are no longer required by See's Candies. Read this and sign it." Huggins handed him a letter confirming his termination and directing him to remove that day "only personal papers and possessions from your office," but "absolutely no records, formulas or other material"; and to turn in and account for "all keys, credit cards, et cetera." The letter advised that Pugh would receive unpaid salary, bonuses and accrued vacation through that date, and the full amount of his profit-sharing account, but "No severance pay will be granted." Finally, Pugh was directed "not to visit or contact Production Department employees while they are on the job."

The letter contained no reason for Pugh's termination. When Pugh asked Huggins for a reason, he was told only that he should "look deep within [him]self" to find the answer, that "Things were said by people in the trade that have come back to us." Pugh's termination was subsequently announced to the industry in a letter which, again, stated no reasons.

When Pugh first went to work for See's, Ed Peck, then president and general manager, frequently told him: "if you are loyal to [See's] and do a good job, your future is secure." Laurance See, who became president of the company in 1951 and served in that capacity until his death in 1969, had a practice of not terminating administrative personnel except for good cause, and this practice was carried on by his brother, Charles B. See, who succeeded Laurance as president.

During the entire period of his employment, there had been no formal or written criticism of Pugh's work.[1] No complaints were ever raised at the annual meetings which preceded each holiday season, and he was never denied a raise or bonus. He received no notice that there was a problem which needed correction, nor any warning that any disciplinary action was being contemplated.

Pugh's theory as to why he was terminated relates to a contract which See's at that time had with the defendant union. . . .

In 1968 [See's supplemental union contract] contained a new rate classification which permitted See's to pay its seasonal employees at a lower rate. At a company meeting prior to the 1968 negotiations, Pugh had objected to the proposed new seasonal classification on the grounds that it might make it more difficult to recruit seasonal workers and create unrest among See's regular seasonal workers who had worked previously for other manufacturers at higher rates. Huggins overruled Pugh's objection and (unknown to Pugh) recommended his termination for "lack of cooperation" as to which Pugh's objection formed "part of the reason." His recommendation was not accepted. . . .

In April of that year, Huggins asked Pugh to be part of the negotiating team for the new union contract. Pugh responded that he would like to, but he was bothered by the possibility that See's had a "sweetheart contract" with the union. In response, someone banged on the table and said, "You don't know what the hell you are talking about." Pugh said, "Well, I think I know what I am talking about. I don't know whether you have a sweetheart contract, but I am telling you if you do, I don't want to be involved because they are immoral, illegal and not in the best interests of my employees." At the trial, Pugh explained that to him a "sweetheart contract" was "a contract whereby one employer would get an unfair competitive advantage over a competitor by getting a lower wage rate, would be one version of it." He also felt, he testified, that "if they in fact had a sweetheart contract that it wouldn't be fair to my

---

1. Huggins testified that in 1953 there was some personality conflict between Pugh and Huggins's assistant, a Mr. Forrest, on account of which Huggins recommended to Laurance See that Pugh be terminated, but See declined. Huggins again recommended Pugh's termination in 1968, under circumstances to be described in this opinion, and again See declined. It does not appear that Huggins's actions in this regard, or the criticism of Pugh which they implied, were made known to Pugh.

female employees to be getting less money than someone would get working in the same industry under the same manager." . . .

The presumption that an employment contract is intended to be terminable at will is subject, like any presumption, to contrary evidence. This may take the form of an agreement, express or implied, that the relationship will continue for some fixed period of time. Or, and of greater relevance here, it may take the form of an agreement that the employment relationship will continue indefinitely, pending the occurrence of some event such as the employer's dissatisfaction with the employee's services or the existence of some "cause" for termination. Sometimes this latter type of agreement is characterized as a contract for "permanent" employment, but that characterization may be misleading. In one of the earliest California cases on this subject, the Supreme Court interpreted a contract for permanent employment as meaning "that plaintiffs' employment . . . was to continue indefinitely, and until one or the other of the parties wish, *for some good reason*, to sever the relation."

A contract which limits the power of the employer with respect to the reasons for termination is no less enforceable because it places no equivalent limits upon the power of the employee to quit his employment. "If the requirement of consideration is met, there is no additional requirement of . . .equivalence in the values exchanged, or 'mutuality of obligation.'" Rest. 2d Contracts §81.

Moreover, while it has sometimes been said that a promise for continued employment subject to limitation upon the employer's power of termination must be supported by some "independent consideration," i.e., consideration other than the services to be rendered, such a rule is contrary to the general contract principle that courts should not inquire into the adequacy of consideration. "A single and undivided consideration may be bargained for and given as the agreed equivalent of one promise or of two promises or of many promises." 1 Corbin on Contracts §125 (1963). Thus there is no analytical reason why an employee's promise to render services, or his actual rendition of services over time, may not support an employer's promise both to pay a particular wage (for example) and to refrain from arbitrary dismissal.

The most likely explanation for the "independent consideration" requirement is that it serves an evidentiary function: it is more probable that the parties intended a continuing relationship, with limitations upon the employer's dismissal authority, when the employee has provided some benefit to the employer, or suffers some detriment, beyond the usual rendition of service. . . .

In determining whether there exists an implied-in-fact promise for some form of continued employment courts have considered a variety of factors in addition to the existence of independent consideration. These have included, for example, the personnel policies or practices of the employer, the employee's longevity of service, actions or communications by the employer reflecting assurances of continued employment, and the practices of the industry in which the employee is engaged. . . .

[In this case] there were facts in evidence from which the jury could determine the existence of such an implied promise: the duration of appellant's employment, the commendations and promotions he received, the apparent lack of any direct criticism of his work, the assurances he was given, and the employer's acknowledged policies. While oblique language will not, standing alone, be sufficient to establish agreement, it is appropriate to consider the totality of the parties' relationship: Agreement may be " 'shown by the acts and conduct of the parties, interpreted in the light of the subject matter and of the surrounding circumstances.'" ' We therefore conclude that it was error to grant respondents' motions for nonsuit as to See's.

Since this litigation may proceed toward yet uncharted waters, we consider it appropriate to provide some guidance as to the questions which the trial court may confront on remand. We have held that appellant has demonstrated a prima facie case of wrongful termination in violation of his contract of employment. The burden of coming forward with evidence as to the reason for appellant's termination now shifts to the employer. Appellant may attack the employer's offered explanation either on the ground that it is pretextual (and that the real reason is one prohibited by contract or public policy), or on the ground that it is insufficient to meet the employer's obligations under contract or applicable legal principles. Appellant bears, however, the ultimate burden of proving that he was terminated wrongfully. *Cf. McDonnell Douglas Corp. v. Green* (1973) 411 U.S. 792.

By what standard that burden is to be measured will depend, in part, upon what conclusions the jury draws as to the nature of the contract between the parties. The terms "just cause" and "good cause," "as used in a variety of contexts . . . have been found to be difficult to define with precision and to be largely relative in their connotation, depending upon the particular circumstances of each case." Essentially, they connote "a fair and honest cause or reason, regulated by good faith on the part of the party exercising the power." Care must be taken, however, not to interfere with the legitimate exercise of managerial discretion. "Good cause" in this context is quite different from the standard applicable in determining the propriety of an employee's termination under a contract for a specified term. And where, as here, the employee occupies a sensitive managerial or confidential position, the employer must of necessity be allowed substantial scope for the exercise of subjective judgment. . . .

NOTES

1. *Cause on Remand.* At the end of the opinion, the court sets out the procedural steps for determining whether See's had cause to terminate Pugh's employment. When employees allege implied contracts for job security, demonstrating the existence of such a contract is only half the battle; the plaintiff must then show that the employer is in breach. As *Pugh* cautions, in determining whether a termination was justified, courts must not interfere with subjective managerial decision making. The burden of proof, coupled with this deference to management, can make it difficult for an employee to ultimately prevail. Indeed, Pugh himself did not succeed. On retrial, the jury returned a verdict for the defendant, crediting Huggins's testimony that Pugh was "rude, argumentative, belligerent, and uncooperative" on their trip to Europe and testimony of other See's employees that Pugh was "disrespectful to his superiors and subordinates, disloyal to the company, and uncooperative with other administrative staff." *See Pugh v. See's Candies, Inc.* (*Pugh II*), 250 Cal. Rptr. 195, 214 (Ct. App. 1988) (affirming judgment for defendant).

2. *Terminations That Offend Public Policy.* Pugh believed he was terminated for objecting to corruption in his employer's negotiations with union representatives. In an omitted portion of the opinion, he alleged that he had been tortiously discharged in violation of public policy, in addition to claiming breach of an implied contract. Pugh's tort argument was rejected. In Chapter 4, you will take up public policy torts. When you do, try to figure out why Pugh lost on this count.

3. *Implied-in-Fact Theory.* An implied-in-fact contract is one in which an agreement to be legally bound is implied from the circumstances, albeit without any clear oral or written communication between the parties. A classic example is getting a haircut or styling. When you sit down, you agree to pay the posted charge (or perhaps a reasonable charge in the absence of a pricelist) and the stylist agrees to cut your hair, although none of this is explicitly stated. How does this theory of liability compare to the others you have seen so far—oral contract and promissory estoppel? Does the idea of an implied-in-fact contract better reflect the realities of workplace relationships? Or does it seem a contrived (or result-oriented) way of doing justice under the circumstances?

4. *Hard Facts?* There is an adage that hard facts make bad law. *Pugh* is a rags-to-riches tale in which the employer seemingly takes advantage of the industry and dedication of a long-term employee. From the first sentence of the opinion it is clear which way the court will hold. Was the court unduly influenced by sympathy for the employee, or is there a broader justification for the decision?

Dean Stewart Schwab suggests there is. Under the "efficiency-wage" theory of long-term employment relationships, employers set wages to rise steadily over the course of employment in order to motivate employees throughout the relationship. *See* Stewart J. Schwab, *Life-Cycle Justice: Accommodating Just Cause and Employment at Will*, 92 MICH. L. REV. 8, 39 (1993). As a result, new employees may be underpaid relative to the value they produce while senior employees may actually earn more than their marginal work product (because wages continue to rise when productivity reaches its zenith). *Id.* at 16-17. While the difference balances out if the employment relationship is allowed to run its full course, senior employees may be at risk of "opportunistic" firings, at which point the employer has already reaped the benefits of the arrangement. As Dean Schwab explains:

> [E]mployees invest heavily as they pursue a career with a single employer. First, they obtain training that is more useful for their own employer than it would be elsewhere—what economists term job-specific human capital. Second, they join the company's career path [which] ties pay, promotions, and benefits to seniority and generally forbids lateral entry. A major cost of pursuing a career with one firm is that one forgoes other ladders and must start over at the bottom if one leaves the firm. Additionally, as they plan for a lifetime with an employer, workers put down roots, establish networks of friends in the workplace and the community, buy homes within commuting distance of the job, and build emotional ties to the community. . . .
>
> [T]hese investments, roots, and ties are sunk costs that trap the worker in his current firm, inhibiting him from departing voluntarily. Even if the career does not proceed as anticipated, the employee is reluctant to quit because the job remains preferable to alternative jobs. Such trapped workers are vulnerable to opportunism. The employer might pay them less than the implicit contract requires or work them harder, knowing they cannot easily quit. . . .
>
> Court scrutiny of opportunistic firings may offer [one] method of policing long-term contracts. . . . The danger, of course, is that court intervention will diminish the employer's flexibility in firing [shirkers]. The question is whether court intervention can be limited to opportunistic firings, rather than to a broader supervision against unfair firings in general.

Id. at 24-28. Can courts craft an administrable rule that will identify only opportunistic firings? Does the multi-factored test articulated in *Pugh* succeed?

Guz v. Bechtel National, Inc.
8 P.3d 1089 (Cal. 2000)

BAXTER, J.

This case presents questions about the law governing claims of wrongful discharge from employment as it applies to an employer's motion for summary judgment. Plaintiff John Guz, a longtime employee of Bechtel National, Inc. (BNI), was released [when his work unit was eliminated and its tasks transferred to another office]. Guz sued BNI and its parent [(collectively Bechtel) alleging] breach of an implied contract to be terminated only for good cause and breach of the implied covenant of good faith and fair dealing. The trial court granted Bechtel's motion for summary judgment. [T]he Court of Appeal reversed, . . .

BNI, a division of Bechtel Corporation, is an engineering, construction, and environmental remediation company that focuses on federal government programs, principally for the Departments of Energy and Defense. . . .

[Guz was hired by Bechel in 1971 and by 1986 was working for BNI's six staff member Management Information Group. He had generally favorable performance reviews.] In 1992, at age 49, he was employed as a financial reports supervisor. . . .

During this time, Bechtel maintained Personnel Policy 1101, dated June 1991, on the subject of termination of employment (Policy 1101). Policy 1101 stated that "Bechtel employees have no employment agreements guaranteeing continuous service and may resign at their option or be terminated at the option of Bechtel."

Policy 1101 also described several "Categories of Termination," including "Layoff" and "Unsatisfactory Performance." With respect to Unsatisfactory Performance, the policy stated that "[e]mployees who fail to perform their jobs in a satisfactory manner may be terminated, provided the employees have been advised of the specific shortcomings and given an opportunity to improve their performance." A layoff was defined as "a Bechtel-initiated termination [] of employees caused by a reduction in workload, reorganizations, changes in job requirements, or other circumstances. . . ." Under the Layoff policy, employees subject to termination for this reason "may be placed on 'holding status' if there is a possible Bechtel assignment within the following 3-month period." Guz understood that Policy 1101 applied to him.

[In 1992, Robert Johnstone became president of BNI and soon became unhappy with the size, cost, and performance of BNI-MI. In April 1992, he advised BNI's manager of government services, Edward Dewey, Guz's manager, Ronald Goldstein, and Guz that BNI-MI's work could be done by three people.] . . .

On December 9, 1992, Goldstein informed Guz that BNI-MI was being disbanded, that its work would be done by another unit of Bechtel, SFRO-MI (San Francisco Regional Office Management Information Group), and that Guz was being laid off. Goldstein told Guz the reason he had been selected for layoff was to reduce costs. . . .

[Two members of BNI-MI, were transferred to SFRO-MI, while all the remaining BNI-MI employees, like Guz, were laid off. During early 1993, while Guz was on holding status, three other positions became available in SFRO-MI, partly because of that unit's expanded responsibilities for BNI-MI. Two of these positions were filled by SFRO-MI employees and one was filled by a newcomer.]

Guz sought to furnish evidence that the cost reduction and workload downturn reasons given him for the elimination of BNI-MI, and his own consequent layoff, were arbitrary, false, and pretextual. To rebut the implication that a general business slowdown required BNI to lay off workers, Guz submitted an excerpt from Bechtel Corporation's 1992 Annual Report. There, Bechtel Corporation's president stated that the "Bechtel team had an exceptional year," and that the company as a whole had achieved healthy gains in both revenue from current projects and new work booked. In his own declaration, Goldstein stated that BNI-MI's 1992 and projected 1993 workload was high, . . . [and that] the net savings from elimination of BNI-MI were only a small fraction of its budget.

Guz also submitted . . . Bechtel's 1989 Reduction-in-Force Guidelines (RIF Guidelines) and Bechtel's Personnel Policy 302 (Policy 302).

Policy 302 described a system of employee ranking . . . based on the fair, objective, and consistent evaluation of employees' comparative job-relevant skills and perform-ance. . . .

The RIF Guidelines specified that when choosing among employees to be retained and released during a reduction in force, the formal ranking system set forth in Policy 302 was to be employed. . . .

The RIF Guidelines also explained the term "holding status" and its benefits [which included] "[t]ransfer and [p]lacement [a]ssistance." . . . In his deposition, BNI president Johnstone agreed that Bechtel's practice was to place an employee on holding status prior to termination, to attempt to reassign the employee during this period, and to "continue to look for positions even after the employee has been laid off."

In their declarations, Goldstein and Guz insisted Guz was qualified for each of the several vacant positions in SFRO-MI, as well as for several other positions that became available within Bechtel. . . .

The trial court granted summary judgment. The court reasoned that "[Guz] was an at-will employee and has not introduced any evidence that he was ever told at any time that he had permanent employment or that he would be retained as long as he was doing a good job. [The Court of Appeal reversed, reasoning that, under *Foley v. Interactive Data*, 765 P.2d 373 (Cal. 1988)], Guz's longevity, promotions, raises, and favorable performance reviews, together with Bechtel's written progressive dis-cipline policy and Bechtel officials' statements of company practices, raised a triable issue that Guz had an implied-in-fact contract to be dismissed only for good cause. There was evidence that Bechtel breached this term by eliminating BNI-MI, on the false ground that workload was declining, as a pretext to weed out poor performers without applying the company's progressive discipline procedures.

II. Implied contract claim . . .

While the statutory presumption of at-will employment is strong, it is subject to several limitations. . . .

One example of a contractual departure from at-will status is an agreement that the employee will be terminated only for "good cause." . . .

The contractual understanding need not be express, but may be implied in fact, arising from the parties' conduct evidencing their actual mutual intent to create such enforceable limitations. In *Foley* we identified several factors, apart from express terms, that may bear upon "the existence and content of an . . . [implied-in-fact] agreement" placing limits on the employer's right to discharge an employee. These factors might include "'the personnel policies or practices of the employer, the employee's longevity of service, actions or communications by the employer reflecting assurances of continued employment, and the practices of the industry in which the employee is engaged.'" *Id*. (quoting *Pugh* . . .).

Foley asserted that "the totality of the circumstances" must be examined to determine whether the parties' conduct, considered in the context of surrounding circumstances, gave rise to an implied-in-fact contract limiting the employer's termination rights. We did not suggest, however, that every vague combination of *Foley* factors, shaken together in a bag, necessarily allows a finding that the employee had a right to be discharged only for good cause, as determined in court.

On the contrary, "courts seek to enforce the actual understanding" of the parties to an employment agreement. Whether that understanding arises from express mutual words of agreement, or from the parties' conduct evidencing a similar meeting of minds, the exact terms to which the parties have assented deserve equally precise scrutiny. . . .

Every case thus turns on its own facts. Where there is no express agreement, the issue is whether other evidence of the parties' conduct has a "tendency in reason" to demonstrate the existence of an actual mutual understanding on particular terms and conditions of employment. . . .

Guz alleges he had an agreement with Bechtel that he would be employed so long as he was performing satisfactorily and would be discharged only for good cause. Guz claims no express understanding to this effect. However, he asserts that such an agreement can be inferred by combining evidence of several *Foley* factors, including (1) his long service; (2) assurances of continued employment in the form of raises, promotions, and good performance reviews; (3) Bechtel's written personnel policies, which suggested that termination for poor performance would be preceded by progressive discipline, that layoffs during a work force reduction would be based on objective criteria, including formal ranking, and that persons laid off would receive placement and reassignment assistance; and (4) testimony by a Bechtel executive that company practice was to terminate employees for a good reason and to reassign, if possible, a laid-off employee who was performing satisfactorily.

Guz further urges there is evidence his termination was without good cause in two respects. First, he insists, the evidence suggests Bechtel had no good cause to eliminate BNI-MI, because the cost reduction and workload downturn reasons Bechtel gave for that decision (1) were not justified by the facts, and (2) were a pretext to terminate him and other individual BNI-MI employees for poor performance without following the company's progressive discipline rules. Second, Guz asserts, even if there was good cause to eliminate his work unit, his termination nonetheless lacked good cause because Bechtel failed to accord him fair layoff rights set forth in its written personnel rules, including (1) use of objective force ranking to determine which unit members deserved retention, and (2) fair consideration for other available positions while he was in holding status.

As we shall explain, we find triable evidence that Bechtel's written personnel documents set forth implied contractual limits on the circumstances under which Guz, and other Bechtel workers, would be terminated. On the other hand, we see no triable evidence of an implied agreement between Guz and Bechtel on additional, different, or broader terms of employment security. . . .

At the outset, Bechtel insists that the existence of implied contractual limitations on its termination rights is negated because Bechtel expressly disclaimed all such agreements. Bechtel suggests the at-will presumption was conclusively reinforced by language Bechtel inserted in Policy 1101, which specified that the company's employees "have no . . . agreements guaranteeing continuous service and may be terminated at [Bechtel's] option." . . .

[N]either the disclaimer nor the statutory presumption necessarily foreclosed Guz from proving the existence and breach of [an agreement limiting Bechtel's termination rights]. Cases in California and elsewhere have held that at-will provisions in personnel handbooks, manuals, or memoranda do not bar, or necessarily overcome, other evidence of the employer's contrary intent. [But even if a handbook disclaimer is not controlling, such language must be taken into account, along with all other pertinent evidence, in ascertaining the terms on which a worker was employed.]

At the outset, it is undisputed that Guz received no individual promises or representations that Bechtel would retain him except for good cause, or upon other specified circumstances. Nor does Guz seriously claim that the practice in Bechtel's industry was to provide secure employment. Indeed, the undisputed evidence suggested that because Bechtel, like other members of its industry, operated by competitive bidding from project to project, its work force fluctuated widely and, in terms of raw numbers, was in general decline.

However, Guz insists his own undisputed long and successful service at Bechtel constitutes strong evidence of an implied contract for permanent employment except upon good cause. . . .

A number of post-*Foley* California decisions have suggested that long duration of service, regular promotions, favorable performance reviews, praise from supervisors, and salary increases do not, without more, imply an employer's contractual intent to relinquish its at-will rights. These decisions reason that such events are but natural consequences of a well-functioning employment relationship. . . .

We agree that an employee's mere passage of time in the employer's service, even where marked with tangible indicia that the employer approves the employee's work, cannot alone form an implied-in-fact contract that the employee is no longer at will. Absent other evidence of the employer's intent, longevity, raises and promotions are their own rewards for the employee's continuing valued service. . . .

On the other hand, long and successful service is not necessarily irrelevant to the existence of such a contract. Over the period of an employee's tenure, the employer can certainly communicate, by its written and unwritten policies and practices, or by informal assurances, that seniority and longevity do create rights against termination at will. The issue is whether the employer's words or conduct, on which an employee reasonably relied, gave rise to that specific understanding. . . .

Insofar as *Foley* applied the long service factor to its own facts, it did so consistent with the principles of implied-in-fact contracts. In *Foley*, the employer claimed the employee's six years and nine months of service was too short a period to evidence an implied agreement not to discharge at will. We answered that "[l]ength of employment [was] a relevant consideration" and the plaintiff's length of service was "sufficient time for conduct to occur on which a trier of fact could find the existence of an implied contract." Prominent among the conduct alleged by the *Foley* plaintiff was "repeated oral assurances of job security."

. . . Guz claims no particular " 'actions or communications by [Bechtel]' " and no industry customs, practices, or policies which suggest that by virtue of his successful longevity in Bechtel's employ, he had earned a contractual right against future termination at will.

If anything, Bechtel had communicated otherwise. The company's Policy 1101 stated that Bechtel employees had no contracts guaranteeing their continuous employment and could be terminated at Bechtel's option. Nothing in this language suggested any exception for senior workers, or for those who had received regular raises and promotions. While occasional references to seniority appear in other sections of Bechtel's personnel documents, the narrow context of these references undermines an inference that Bechtel additionally intended, or employees had reason to expect, special immunities from termination based on their extended or successful service.

Finally, Guz asserts there is evidence that, industry custom and written company personnel policies aside, Bechtel had an unwritten "polic[y] or practice[]" to release its employees only for cause. As the sole evidence of this policy, Guz points to the deposition testimony of Johnstone, BNI's president, who stated his understanding that Bechtel terminated workers only with "good reason" or for "lack of [available] work." But there is no evidence that Bechtel employees were aware of such an unwritten policy, and it flies in the face of Bechtel's general disclaimer. This brief and vague statement, by a single Bechtel official, that Bechtel sought to avoid arbitrary firings is insufficient as a matter of law to permit a finding that the company, by an unwritten practice or policy on which employees reasonably relied, had contracted away its right to discharge Guz at will.

In sum, if there is any significant evidence that Guz had an implied contract against termination at will, that evidence flows exclusively from Bechtel's written personnel documents. . . .

The parties do not dispute that certain of these provisions, expressly denominated "Policies" . . . were disseminated to employees and were intended by Bechtel to inform workers of rules applicable to their employment. There seems little doubt, and we conclude, a triable issue exists that the specific provisions of these Policies did become an implicit part of the employment contracts of the Bechtel employees they covered, including Guz.

As Bechtel stresses, Policy 1101 itself purported to disclaim any employment security rights. However, Bechtel had inserted other language, not only in Policy 1101 itself, but in other written personnel documents, which described detailed rules and procedures for the termination of employees under particular circumstances. Moreover, the specific language of Bechtel's disclaimer, stating that employees had no contracts "guaranteeing . . . continuous service" (italics added) and were terminable at Bechtel's "option," did not foreclose an understanding between Bechtel and all its workers that Bechtel would make its termination decisions within the limits of its written personnel rules. Given these ambiguities, a fact finder could rationally determine that despite its general disclaimer, Bechtel had bound itself to the specific provisions of these documents. . . .

The Court of Appeal did not address Guz's second theory, i.e., that Bechtel also breached its implied contract by failing, during and after the reorganization, to provide him personally with the fair layoff protections, including force ranking and reassignment help, which are set forth in its Policies and RIF Guidelines. This theory raises difficult questions, including what the proper remedy, if any, should be if Guz ultimately shows that Bechtel breached a contractual obligation to follow certain procedural policies in the termination process. . . . On remand, the Court of Appeal should confront this issue and should determine whether Guz has raised a triable issue on this theory.

III.   Implied covenant claim . . .

Guz urges that even if his contract was for employment at will, the implied covenant of good faith and fair dealing precluded Bechtel from "unfairly" denying him the contract's benefits by failing to follow its own termination policies.

Thus, Guz argues, in effect, that the implied covenant can impose substantive terms and conditions beyond those to which the contract parties actually agreed. [However, the] covenant of good faith and fair dealing, implied by law in every contract, exists merely to prevent one contracting party from unfairly frustrating the other party's right to receive the benefits of the agreement actually made. . . . It cannot impose substantive duties or limits on the contracting parties beyond those incorporated in the specific terms of their agreement.

[The presumption is] that an employer may terminate its employees at will, for any or no reason. A fortiori, the employer may act peremptorily, arbitrarily, or inconsistently, without providing specific protections such as prior warning, fair procedures, objective evaluation, or preferential reassignment. Because the employment relationship is "fundamentally contractual," limitations on these employer prerogatives are a matter of the parties' specific agreement, express or implied in fact. The mere existence of an employment relationship affords no expectation, protectible by law, that employment will continue, or will end only on certain conditions, unless the parties have actually adopted such terms. Thus if the employer's termination decisions, however arbitrary, do not breach such a substantive contract provision, they are not precluded by the covenant.

This logic led us to emphasize in *Foley* that "breach of the implied covenant cannot logically be based on a claim that [the] discharge [of an at-will employee] was made without good cause." As we noted [in *Foley*], "[b]ecause the implied covenant protects only the parties' right to receive the benefit of their agreement, and, in an at-will relationship there is no agreement to terminate only for good cause, the implied covenant standing alone cannot be read to impose such a duty."

The same reasoning applies to any case where an employee argues that even if his employment was at will, his arbitrary dismissal frustrated his contract benefits and thus violated the implied covenant of good faith and fair dealing. Precisely because employment at will allows the employer freedom to terminate the relationship as it chooses, the employer does not frustrate the employee's contractual rights merely by doing so. . . .

Similarly at odds with *Foley* are suggestions that independent recovery for breach of the implied covenant may be available if the employer terminated the employee in "bad faith" or "without probable cause," i.e., without determining "honestly and in good faith that good cause for discharge existed." Where the employment contract itself allows the employer to terminate at will, its motive and lack of care in doing so are, in most cases at least, irrelevant.

Of course, as we have indicated above, the employer's personnel policies and practices may become implied-in-fact terms of the contract between employer and employee. If that has occurred, the employer's failure to follow such policies when terminating an employee is a breach of the contract itself.

A breach of the contract may also constitute a breach of the implied covenant of good faith and fair dealing. But insofar as the employer's acts are directly actionable as a breach of an implied-in-fact contract term, a claim that merely realleges that breach as a violation of the covenant is superfluous. This is because, as we explained at length in *Foley*, the remedy for breach of an employment agreement, including the covenant of good faith and fair dealing implied by law therein, is solely contractual. In the employment context, an implied covenant theory affords no separate measure of recovery, such as tort damages. Allegations that the breach was wrongful, in bad faith, arbitrary, and unfair are unavailing; there is no tort of "bad faith breach" of an employment contract.

We adhere to these principles here. To the extent Guz's implied covenant cause of action seeks to impose limits on Bechtel's termination rights beyond those to which the parties actually agreed, the claim is invalid. To the extent the implied covenant claim seeks simply to invoke terms to which the parties did agree, it is superfluous. Guz's remedy, if any, for Bechtel's alleged violation of its personnel policies depends on proof that they were contract terms to which the parties actually agreed. The trial court thus properly dismissed the implied covenant cause of action.

NOTES

1. Pugh *Claims Post*-Pugh. What does *Guz* suggest about the significance of *Pugh* in the twenty-first century? Seven years after *Pugh*, the California Supreme Court reaffirmed its holding in *Foley v. Interactive Data Corp.*, 765 P.2d 373 (Cal. 1988), discussed at length in *Guz*. Foley worked for six years as a product manager, during which time he received steady salary increases, promotions, bonuses and positive performance evaluations, before being terminated, allegedly for reporting that his supervisor was under FBI investigation for embezzlement. Like Pugh, Foley alleged he received repeated assurances that his job was secure so long as his performance remained adequate. In allowing the claim to go forward, the court declined the defendant's invitation to distinguish *Pugh* based on the fact that Foley had worked for the defendant only six years. *See id.* at 387-88. It also explicitly disagreed that employment security agreements are "inherently harmful or unfair to employers," finding that "[o]n the contrary, employers may benefit from the increased loyalty and productivity that such agreements may inspire." *Id.* at 387.

However, the California Supreme Court's subsequent decision in *Guz* offers a much narrower view of the kinds of employer conduct that will give rise to an implied-in-fact promise. In light of *Guz*, can you articulate evidence that would create a prima facie case of breach of an implied contract in California? Can you identify the evidence that might preclude such a claim? How concerned do contemporary employers need to be about the costs associated with implied-in-fact rights? Professor Jonathan Fineman argues that companies have little to fear as long as they keep their house in order. *See The Inevitable Demise of the Implied Employment Contract*, 29 BERKELEY J. EMP. & LAB. L. 345 (2008). He argues that, in the wake of decisions expanding employee contractual rights, employers "began restructuring their employment documents, policies and practices to avoid liability," thus effectively immunizing themselves against implied contract claims. "[E]mployers today have little fear of implied contract lawsuits. As a result, many employees are arguably now worse off than they were in the 1970s." Fineman contends that this was also inevitable: Since any contract claim depends on the agreement of the parties, careful employer drafting an effectively extinguish potential rights to job security or even particular procedures:

> Conceptualizing the employment relationship as one of private contract, the terms of which as a practical matter are established by employers, means that we will always end up with employment contracts that benefit employers. As long as individual employers are able to define the scope of their own obligations, efforts to instill more structured, effective and binding workplace norms through the doctrine of implied contracts will be unsuccessful.

Id. at 349-50. Do you agree with this critique, or is Professor Fineman overly pessimistic about the viability of employee claims? If you represented an employer, would you feel confident that with careful planning you could fully eliminate the risk of a successful employee claim in a situation where your client did not intend to provide job security?

   2. *The Decline of Long-Term Employment. Pugh* and *Guz* together suggest that longevity and consistent advancement may be necessary although not sufficient facts from which a court can discern an implied-in-fact contract. How typical is it for workers to have 20- to 30-year employment records like the plaintiffs in those cases? In the contemporary economy, long-term employment with a single company is in decline, as are clear promotional hierarchies within individual firms. Instead, many employees have what Professor Katherine Stone describes as "boundaryless careers." She explains:

> A boundaryless career is a career that does not depend upon traditional notions of advancement within a single hierarchical organization. It includes an employee who moves frequently across the borders of different employers, such as a Silicon Valley technician, or one whose career draws its validation and marketability from sources outside the present employer, such as professional and extraorganizational networks. It also refers to changes within organizations, in which individuals are expected to move laterally, without constraint from traditional hierarchical career lattices. . . .
>
>   The concept of a boundaryless career, like that of the new psychological contract, reflects the shift in job structures away from [early twentieth century] internal labor markets. Instead of job ladders along which employees advance within stable, long-term employment settings, there are possibilities for lateral mobility between and within firms, with no set path, no established expectations, and no tacit promises of job security. As [writer Peter] Drucker says, "there is no such thing as 'lifetime employment' anymore. . . ."

Katherine V. W. Stone, *The New Psychological Contract: Implications of the Changing Workplace for Labor and Employment Law*, 48 UCLA L. REV. 519, 554-55 (2001). As a result, Professor Stone suggests that parties no longer share an implicit expectation of long-term employment. Rather, employers reward loyal work by enhancing their employees' marketability, by providing skills training, networking opportunities, and externally competitive pay. *Id.* at 568-72. Does this trend suggest that the utility of implied-in-fact contract theory is diminishing? Or might implied-in-fact theory be adapted to redress other types of opportunistic employer behavior that violate what Professor Stone calls the "new psychological contract" of employment?

Professor Arnow-Richman has suggested as much. She argues that, rather than implying job security rights, the law should enforce the contemporary psychological contract by imposing an obligation on employers to provide advance notice (or its equivalent in pay) to terminated workers. *Just Notice: Re-Reforming Employment At-Will*, 58 UCLA L. Rev. 1 (2010). She explains:

[T]he distinguishing feature of the new social contract of employment is the increased expectation of possible job loss. If employers no longer implicitly offer workers long-term job security, and employees no longer expect to remain in the same job for their lifetime, the guiding theory of worker protection should focus on enabling continued labor market participation rather than on preserving particular jobs.

[This] could take the form of a legislative "pay-or-play" obligation upon termination. Under such a system, employers would be obligated to provide workers advance notice of termination or, at the employer's election, continued pay and benefits for the duration of the notice period. This system would allow employees a degree of income continuity, enabling them to search for new employment or, in the event the employer elects severance pay, to invest in training.

Just cause reform, with its focus on the reason for termination and its goal of job preservation, would do [little to help workers in the contemporary economy]. In contrast, pay-or-play reform would advance an entirely different set of goals and expectations. [W]hereas just cause would foster job retention, pay-or-play would ease employment transitions, . . . giving legal force to employers' implicit promise of long-term employ*ability*. . . . Whereas just cause protection would oblige employers to justify termination, in effect to defend their deviation from the norm of continued employment, a pay-or-play system would translate the implicit promise of marketability into a legal obligation to directly underwrite the costs of re-employment.

Id. at 38-41; *see also* Rachel Arnow-Richman, *Modifying At-Will Employment Contracts*, 57 B.C. L. Rev. 427 (2016) (arguing that modifications of employment contracts should be subject to a universal reasonable notice rule for enforceability that provides "amount of time necessary for the employee to assess the significance of the change and consider alternatives"); Rachel Arnow-Richman, *Mainstreaming Employment Contract Law: The Common Law Case for Reasonable Notice of Termination*, 66 Fla. L. Rev. 1513 (2014). *But see Johnston v. William E. Wood & Assocs.*, 787 S.E.2d 103 (Va. 2016) (finding no duty to give a terminated employee "reasonable notice" and stating that such a requirement would be inconsistent with the at-will doctrine). Recall the discussion in Note 9, page 93 of the history of unjust dismissal in Montana or elsewhere. How viable is Professor Arnow-Richman's alternative reform strategy? Would "pay or play" reform be appealing only to employees or might employers support it as well? What are the limitations of such an approach?

3. *Policies as Contracts. Pugh* identified the "policies and practices" of the employer as an important factor in determining the existence of an implied contract. It involved an employer that allegedly made a *practice* of retaining workers long term. In contrast, *Guz* involves employer *policies*, written materials that set forth the formal rules and procedures of the company. Such documents are increasingly common in large companies, and, as *Guz* describes, they offer advantages to both employers and employees. A frequent source of employer policies is the company's personnel manual or handbook, a collection of materials usually provided to employees upon hire. Courts can treat polices and handbooks in at least two ways: as evidence of an implied-in-fact contract or as a contract in and of themselves (generally analyzed as a unilateral contract). How does *Guz* use Bechtel's policies in determining the plaintiff's rights? Does the existence of the policies help Guz's case? Hurt it? Both? The role of personnel manuals, and in particular language in such documents that disclaim employee rights, will be explored in greater detail in the next section.

4. *The Implied Duty of Good Faith.* In addition to his implied contract claim, Guz proceeded under the theory that the employer had breached an implied duty of good faith. As you may recall from your first year, every contract contains an implicit promise that the parties will do nothing to interfere with the other's ability to reap the fruits of the agreement. *See* RESTATEMENT (SECOND) OF CONTRACTS §205. An important limitation on the implied duty, however, is that it may not be used to alter express terms of the parties' agreement. For this reason, at-will employees have generally fared poorly in using the good faith duty to challenge the reason for their termination. *See, e.g., Murphy v. American Home Prod. Corp.* 448 N.E.2d 86 (N.Y. 1983) (rejecting breach of implied duty of good faith claim by at-will accountant allegedly terminated for revealing internal financial irregularities, noting that "parties may by express agreement limit or restrict the employer's right of discharge, but to imply such a limitation from the existence of an unrestricted right would be internally inconsistent") There are two exceptions, however. Some early cases allowed breach of the implied duty of good faith claims in situations where the plaintiff's termination violated public policy. In *Monge v. Beebe Rubber Co.*, 316 A.2d 549, 552 (N.H. 1974), for instance, the court sanctioned the good faith claim of a woman who was terminated for refusing to date her foreman. Today such cases would be pursued on statutory grounds (for instance, as sex discrimination) or as claims of wrongful discharge violating public policy, topics that will be explored in later chapters. The other situation in which plaintiffs have succeeded is where the termination resulted in the plaintiff losing vested compensation or benefits. *See, e.g., Fortune v. National Cash Register*, 364 N.E.2d 1251 (Mass. 1977) (recognizing limited cause of action for lost commission where plaintiff was terminated after consummation of large sale but prior to merchandise delivery date upon which final installment of earned commissions were to be paid). We will pick up this theory in Chapter 3 when we turn to compensation.

PROBLEMS

2-2. James Pert worked for 15 years at Thistletown Race Track, a family-run horse track in Ohio. He started his employment as a stable boy and worked his way up to being a track manager and judge. Pert had no written contract of employment. Throughout his employment he received positive evaluations and consistent salary increases. At one point during Pert's tenure, the track fell on hard times, and Pert asked the president of the race track, Edward DeBart, if he should consider looking for other work. DeBart responded, "There's no need. You have been one of our best employees. Whatever happens, your future is secure."

Recently, Pert's wife received a desirable job offer in Florida. The couple had always wanted to live in a warmer climate, but they knew they could not afford to move without Pert's salary. The national market for track judges tends to be tight because there are relatively few jobs and limited turnover in the position. Pert met with DeBart and asked him if it would be possible for him to keep his job working part-time from Florida and flying back to Ohio at his own expense for the four races per year that the track sponsored. DeBart agreed to this proposal. "We are more than willing to accommodate you," he said, "and if things don't work out in Florida, your job is always open here."

Pert and DeBart shook hands to seal the long-distance arrangement, but they did not draft any written document. Pert and his wife sold their house, bought a house in Florida, and moved their belongings. One year later, Ed DeBart passed away and his daughter, Donna York, assumed responsibility for the track. Several months later, Pert received a notice of termination from York, stating that the company had decided to eliminate the "part-time manager position." Pert subsequently learned that he had been replaced by a full-time manager on location in Ohio.

Suppose that you are hired to represent Pert in an action against Thistletown. Do you think Pert can establish an implied-in-fact contract? Are any other theories of recovery that you have studied in this chapter relevant to his situation? What further information would you need to know to answer these questions? *See generally Pertz v. Edward J. DeBartolo Corp.*, 188 F.3d 508 (6th Cir. 1999).

2-3.   Christine Montell had been working as a student loan account representative for the Huntington Corporation for ten years, when she received a competing offer for a position with the Student Loan Fund ("SLF"). SLF offered her an annual salary of $50,000, a 5 percent increase above her current salary with Huntington, an annual 3 to 6 percent bonus based on performance, and moving expenses. Montell needed the extra cash, but she was reluctant to leave her current employment because she had a good relationship with her boss, Keith Berner, had always received good feedback and training, and was reluctant to relocate. Before responding to the offer, she e-mailed Berner and asked whether Huntington would be able to match SLS's offer.

(a)   Suppose that prior to answering Montell's e-mail, Berner contacts his own boss, Janis Goodman, who has the foresight to contact you, the company's legal counsel. Goodman would like to do everything possible to retain Montell, including matching SLF's salary and offering Montell a promotion, but she does not want to put the company at risk of long-term liability. What do you recommend she do? Is there anything in particular that Goodman or Berner should avoid saying or doing in responding to Montell's e-mail?

(b)   Suppose instead that Montell does not send an e-mail, but rather meets with Berner over lunch to discuss her competing offer. Upon hearing the offer, Berner immediately promises to meet SLF's salary. Berner also tells Montell, "You are a valuable member of our team, and the only one with the technical expertise to run student loans. Losing you would really hurt the company. If you stay, I promise Huntington will take care of you for the long run." As in-house counsel, you learn about this exchange only after you come across the paperwork altering Montell's title and pay, and you contact Berner to inquire about it. What concerns might you have at this point about the statements Berner made to Montell? Is there anything you recommend doing now that could reduce the risk of any long-term obligation on the part of the company?

3. Written Employment Manuals or Handbooks and Employee Contract Rights

As you saw in *Guz*, the written documents prepared by an employer and distributed in the workplace can in some cases be a source of employee rights. Depending on what the documents say, they can also be a means by which employers constrict rights or reinforce the idea that employment is at will. Thus, from the lawyer's perspective, reviewing employment documents is a critical component of assessing the viability of an employee claim or, on the employer's side, in preventing claims and avoiding liability. This section looks at two recurring situations in which a plaintiff's success in challenging termination turns on the documentation provided by the employer: situations in which employer documentation seeks to disclaim the existence of contractual rights and situations in which employers try to alter existing employment policies.

In both situations, the analysis begins with what today is a relatively uncontroversial principle—that employment manuals and other written policies can be contractually binding. That idea was first established in two influential 1980s decisions, *Woolley v. Hoffmann-LaRoche, Inc.* 491 A.2d 1257 (N.J. 1985), and *Toussaint v. Blue Cross & Blue Shield*, 292 N.W.2d 880 (Mich. 1980). In *Woolley,* the employer distributed a "Personnel Policy Manual" to all its employees, including the plaintiff, who received it shortly after he began employment. The self-described purpose of the manual was to offer "a practical operating tool in the equitable and efficient administration of our employee relations program." The New Jersey Supreme Court summarized the provisions related to termination:

> [The manual] defines "the types of termination" as "layoff," "discharge due to performance," "discharge, disciplinary," "retirement," and "resignation." As one might expect, layoff is a termination caused by lack of work, retirement a termination caused by age, resignation a termination on the initiative of the employee, and discharge due to performance and discharge, disciplinary, are both terminations for cause. There is no category set forth for discharge without cause. The termination section includes "Guidelines for discharge due to performance," consisting of a fairly detailed procedure to be used before an employee may be fired for cause. Preceding these definitions of the five categories of termination is a section on "Policy," the first sentence of which provides: "It is the policy of Hoffmann-La Roche to retain, to the extent consistent with company requirements, the services of all employees who perform their duties efficiently and effectively."

491 A.2d at 1258. Rejecting the defendant's contention that the manual was "simply an expression of the company's 'philosophy,'" the court found a jury question as to whether it contained an enforceable implied promise that termination would occur only for cause. The court concluded first that the manual could constitute a contractual offer:

> In determining the manual's meaning and effect, we must consider the probable context in which it was disseminated and the environment surrounding its continued existence. The manual, though apparently not distributed to all employees, [covers all of them. It] represents the most reliable statement of the terms of their employment. At oral argument counsel conceded that it is rare for any employee [to have an individual contract]. Having been employed, like hundreds of his co-employees, without any individual

employment contract, by an employer whose good reputation made it so attractive, the employee is given this one document that purports to set forth the terms and conditions of his employment, a document obviously carefully prepared by the company with all of the appearances of corporate legitimacy that one could imagine. If there were any doubt about it (and there would be none in the mind of most employees), the name of the manual dispels it, for it is nothing short of the official policy of the company, it is the Personnel Policy Manual. As every employee knows, when superiors tell you "it's company policy," they mean business.

The [Manual's] changeability—the uncontroverted ability of management to change its terms—is argued as supporting its non-binding quality, but one might as easily conclude that, given its importance, the employer wanted to keep it up to date, especially to make certain, given this employer's good reputation in labor relations, that the benefits conferred were sufficiently competitive with those available from other employers, including benefits found in collective bargaining agreements. The record suggests that the changes actually made almost always favored the employees.

Given that background, then, unless the language contained in the manual were such that no one could reasonably have thought it was intended to create legally binding obligations, the termination provisions of the policy manual would have to be regarded as an obligation undertaken by the employer. It will not do now for the company to say it did not mean the things it said in its manual to be binding . . . no matter how sincere its belief that they are not enforceable.

[margin note: what makes a contract]

Job security is the assurance that one's livelihood, one's family's future, will not be destroyed arbitrarily; it can be cut off only "for good cause," fairly determined. Hoffmann-La Roche's commitment here was to what working men and women regard as their most basic advance. It was a commitment that gave workers protection against arbitrary termination.

Many of these workers undoubtedly know little about contracts, and many probably would be unable to analyze the language and terms of the manual. Whatever Hoffmann-La Roche may have intended, that which was read by its employees was a promise not to fire them except for cause.

Id. at 1265-66.

The court went on to consider whether this offer had been accepted by Hoffmann-La Roche's employees:

> In most of the cases involving an employer's personnel policy manual, the document is prepared without any negotiations and is voluntarily distributed to the workforce by the employer. It seeks no return promise from the employees. It is reasonable to interpret it as seeking continued work from the employees, who, in most cases, are free to quit since they are almost always employees at will, not simply in the sense that the employer can fire them without cause, but in the sense that they can quit without breaching any obligation. Thus analyzed, the manual is an offer that seeks the formation of a unilateral contract—the employees' bargained-for action needed to make the offer binding being their continued work when they have no obligation to continue.

Id. at 1267. The court noted that its analysis was "perfectly adequate for that employee who was aware of the manual and who continued to work intending that continuation to be the action in exchange for the employer's promise; it is even more helpful in support of that conclusion if, but for the employer's policy manual, the employee would have quit." *Id*. Absent such evidence, however, the court suggested that reliance on the manual should be presumed. It drew on *Toussaint*, in which the Michigan court analyzed the legal effect of a personnel manual containing similar statements. In discussing workers' reliance on the manual, *Toussaint* noted:

> While an employer need not establish personnel policies or practices, where an employer chooses to establish such policies and practices and makes them known to its employees, the employment relationship is presumably enhanced. The employer secures an orderly, cooperative and loyal work force, and the employee the peace of mind associated with job security and the conviction that he will be treated fairly. No pre-employment negotiations need take place and the parties' minds need not meet on the subject; nor does it matter that the employee knows nothing of the particulars of the employer's policies and practices or that the employer may change them unilaterally. It is enough that the employer chooses, presumably in its own interest, to create an environment in which the employee believes that, whatever, the personnel policies and practices, they are established and official at any given time, purport to be fair, and are applied consistently and uniformly to each employee. The employer has then created a situation "instinct with an obligation."

Toussaint, 292 N.W.2d at 892.

Woolley went on the address possible concerns of employers. Seemingly undermining its plaintiff-friendly holding, the final paragraphs of the decision offer employers a way to avoid contractual liability for the promises made in their manuals:

> Our opinion need not make employers reluctant to prepare and distribute company policy manuals. Such manuals can be very helpful tools in labor relations, helpful both to employer and employees, and we would regret it if the consequence of this decision were that the constructive aspects of these manuals were in any way diminished. We do not believe that they will, or at least we certainly do not believe that that constructive aspect should be diminished as a result of this opinion.
>
> All that this opinion requires of an employer is that it be fair. It would be unfair to allow an employer to distribute a policy manual that makes the workforce believe that certain promises have been made and then to allow the employer to renege on those promises. What is sought here is basic honesty: If the employer, for whatever reason, does not want the manual to be capable of being construed by the court as a binding contract, there are simple ways to attain that goal. All that need be done is the inclusion in a very prominent position of an appropriate statement that there is no promise of any kind by the employer contained in the manual; that regardless of what the manual says or provides, the employer promises nothing and remains free to change wages and all other working conditions without having to consult anyone and without anyone's agreement; and that the employer continues to have the absolute power to fire anyone with or without good cause.

491 A.2d at 1271.

Woolley is important for several reasons. Like *Pugh* and *Guz*, it stands for the proposition that in the workplace contractual rights are determined by an examination of factual circumstances, including the reasonable expectations of employees inculcated by management policy and practice. *Woolley* is also notable for its use of unilateral contract principles in assessing the legal enforceability of Hoffmann-La Roche's manual. For better or worse, this approach has been espoused by most courts dealing with disputes over manuals and written policies. *See, e.g., Hackney v. Lincoln Nat'l Fire Ins. Co.*, 657 F. App'x 563 (6th Cir. 2016) (holding employer's salary continuation plan enforceable despite the absence of employee contributions because plaintiff's continued employment constituted consideration for the promises in the Plan).

How convincing do you find *Woolley*'s analysis of offer and acceptance? Consider one commentator's view:

> [U]nilateral contract analysis fits uneasily into the handbook context. Except for the communication prerequisite, all of [the] unilateral contract elements are implied by the court rather than intended by the parties. [M]ost employers have no intention of extending a contractual offer when issuing an employee handbook. Similarly, the court infers the employee's acceptance and consideration from conduct that, in reality, could occur regardless of the handbook's existence.
>
> The notion of a bargained-for exchange in this setting is a fiction, but the fiction is convenient and understandable. These advantages have induced courts to stretch unilateral contract theory in order to achieve a desirable policy result: the enforcement of handbook promises that benefit employers by creating legitimate expectations among the work force.

Stephen F. Befort, *Employee Handbooks and the Legal Effect of Disclaimers*, 13 INDUS. REL. L. J. 326, 342-43 (1991/1992). In the cases that follow, consider whether unilateral contract theory offers an accurate description of the parties' relationship. Consider also the degree to which this theory allows courts to achieve particular policy goals.

Finally, *Woolley* is important because of its particular facts and its concluding dicta, which together create uncertainty about the extent to which any particular manual will be held enforceable. A critical fact in the case is the strength of the assurances in the company's manual. Does it surprise you that Hoffmann-La Roche was willing to make such an explicit commitment to job security? How common is it for modern employers to make such statements, let alone in writing? *Cf. Green v. Vermont Country Store*, 191 F. Supp. 2d 476, 481 (D. Vt. 2002) ("value statement" in employer handbook espousing equal treatment contained only general statements of policy and did not constitute a definitive promise for a specific course of treatment). An even more important limitation is the final paragraph permitting employers to disclaim the contractual significance of their handbooks. As you will see, this final paragraph is the source of a great deal of case law limiting the enforceability of written manuals and polices in the contemporary workplace.

Conner v. City of Forest Acres
560 S.E.2d 606 (S.C. 2002)

WALLER, Justice.

. . . Respondent Evelyn Conner worked for the City of Forest Acres ("the City") as a police dispatcher. She was hired in July 1984 and was terminated in October 1993. At the time of her termination, J.C. Rowe was the Chief of Police, and Corporal Lewis Langley was her immediate supervisor. Beginning in November 1992, Conner received numerous reprimands for such things as violating the dress code, tardiness, performing poor work, leaving work without permission, and using abusive language. In July 1993, Conner was evaluated as unsatisfactory and placed on a 90-day probation. She was reprimanded twice in August 1993, and her October 1993 evaluation showed only slight improvement; therefore, the City terminated her on October 7, 1993.

Conner filed a grievance, and at the hearing before the grievance committee, she disputed many of the reprimands. The grievance committee voted 2-1 to reinstate

Conner. The City Council, however, rejected the grievance committee's decision and voted to uphold Conner's termination.

During her employment, Conner received two employee handbooks. After receiving each one, Conner signed an acknowledgment form. The 1993 acknowledgment stated as follows:

> I acknowledge that I have received a copy of the City of Forest Acres Personnel Policy and Procedures Manual (Adopted July 1, 1993). I understand that I am responsible for reading, understanding, and abiding by the contents of these policies and procedures. I further understand that all the policies contained herein are subject to change as the need arises. I further understand that nothing in these policies and procedures creates a contract of employment for any term, that I am an employee at-will and nothing herein limits the City of Forest Acres's rights for dismissal.

On page 1 of the handbook, entitled INTRODUCTION, there is the following language:

Important Notice

> MANY OF THE POLICIES CONTAINED IN THIS HANDBOOK ARE BASED ON LEGAL PROVISIONS, INTERPRETATIONS OF LAW, AND EMPLOYEE RELATIONS PRINCIPLES, ALL OF WHICH ARE SUBJECT TO CHANGE. FOR THIS REASON, THIS HANDBOOK IS CONSIDERED TO BE A GUIDELINE AND IS SUBJECT TO CHANGE WITH LITTLE NOTICE. THE HANDBOOK DOES NOT CONSTITUTE A CONTRACT OF EMPLOYMENT FOR ANY TERM. NOTHING IN THIS HANDBOOK SHALL BE CONSTRUED TO CONSTITUTE A CONTRACT. THE CITY HAS THE RIGHT, AT ITS DISCRETION, TO MODIFY THIS HANDBOOK AT ANY TIME. NOTHING HEREIN LIMITS THE CITY'S RIGHTS TO TERMINATE EMPLOYMENT. ALL EMPLOYEES OF THE CITY ARE AT-WILL EMPLOYEES. NO ONE EXCEPT THE CITY ADMINISTRATOR HAS THE AUTHORITY TO WAIVE ANY OF THE PROVISIONS OF THIS HANDBOOK, OR MAKE REPRESENTATIONS CONTRARY TO THE PROVISIONS OF THIS HANDBOOK.

This same language appears on the last page of the handbook.

The handbook contained a section entitled "Code of Conduct." In this section, the handbook states that conduct "reflecting unfavorably upon the reputation of the City, the Department, or the employee will not be tolerated." Furthermore, this section advises that:

> This code of conduct is designed to guide all employees in their relationship with the City.
>
> The following is a non-exclusive list of acts which are considered a violation of the Code of Conduct expected of a City employee, and such conduct will be disciplined in accords with its seriousness, recurrence, and circumstances. Degrees of discipline are given under the section entitled "Discipline" in this manual.

The list enumerates 23 different acts.

The Disciplinary Procedures section of the handbook states that it is the "duty of all employees to comply with, and to assist in carrying into effect [t]he provisions of the personnel policy and procedures." Additionally, the handbook states the following:

Ordinarily, discipline shall be of an increasingly progressive nature, the step of progression being (1) oral or written reprimand, (2) suspension, and (3) dismissal. Discipline should correspond to the offense and therefore NO REQUIREMENT EXISTS FOR DISCIPLINE TO BE PROGRESSIVE. FIRST VIOLATIONS CAN RESULT IN IMMEDIATE DISMISSAL WITHOUT REPRIMAND OR SUSPENSION.

Furthermore, this section states that violations of the code of conduct "*are declared*" to be grounds for discipline and that discipline "*will be used* to enforce the City's Code of Conduct." (Emphasis added.) Finally, the grievance procedure is outlined in detail. In this section, the handbook states "[i]t is the policy of the City of Forest Acres that all employees shall be treated fairly and consistently in all matters related to their employment."

[Conner brought suit against the City alleging breach of contract. The trial court granted the defendants' motions for summary judgment, but the Court of Appeals reversed.]

The City argues there was no contract created by the handbook because: (1) the procedures in the employee handbook did not alter Conner's at-will status, (2) the disclaimers in the handbook were conspicuous and therefore effective, and (3) Conner signed acknowledgments of her at-will status. Additionally, the City contends that even if the handbook did create a contract, it did not breach the contract because it followed the prescribed procedures.

The general rule is that termination of an at-will employee normally does not give rise to a cause of action for breach of contract. However, where the at-will status of the employee is altered by the terms of an employee handbook, an employer's discharge of an employee may give rise to a cause of action for wrongful discharge. Because an employee handbook may create a contract, the issue of the existence of an employment contract is proper for a jury when its existence is questioned and the evidence is either conflicting or admits of more than one inference.

The Court in *Small* [*v. Springs*, 357 S.E.2d 452, 455 (S.C. 1987)] stated that "[i]t is patently unjust to allow an employer to couch a handbook, bulletin, or other similar material in mandatory terms and then allow him to ignore these very policies as 'a gratuitous, nonbinding statement of general policy' whenever it works to his disadvantage." The *Small* Court instructed that if an employer wishes to issue written policies, but intends to continue at-will employment, the employer must insert a conspicuous disclaimer into the handbook. However, in *Fleming v. Borden*, 450 S.E.2d 589 (S.C. 1994), the Court indicated that whether the disclaimer is conspicuous is generally a question for the jury. Specifically, the *Fleming* Court stated that "[i]n most instances, summary judgment is inappropriate when the handbook contains both a disclaimer and promises."

Relying primarily on *Fleming*, the Court of Appeals in the instant case found that summary judgment was inappropriate. We agree. While the City argues that its handbook contained disclaimers which were effective as a matter of law and that Conner signed acknowledgments of her at-will status, the fact remains that the handbook outlines numerous procedures concerning progressive discipline, discharge, and subsequent grievance. The language in the handbook is mandatory in nature[4] and

---

4. For example, the handbook states that: (1) "violations of the Code of Conduct *will be* disciplined," (2) "discipline *shall be* of an increasingly progressive nature," and (3) "all employees *shall be* treated fairly and consistently in all matters related to their employment." (Emphasis added.)

therefore a genuine issue of material fact exists as to whether Conner's at-will status was modified by the policies in the handbook.

The City also argues that if a contract exists, then as a matter of law, it did not breach the contract because it followed the procedures outlined in the handbook. The Court of Appeals found that because "Conner disputes the City's version of the events resulting in her reprimands and subsequent termination," summary judgment was not proper "on the issue of whether Conner was fired for cause."

Although this is a closer question, we agree with the Court of Appeals that there is a genuine issue of material fact as to whether Conner was wrongfully terminated. The appropriate test on the issue of breach is as follows: "If the fact finder finds a contract to terminate only for cause, he must determine whether the employer had *a reasonable good faith belief* that sufficient cause existed for termination."[5] We note that the fact finder must not focus on whether the employee actually committed misconduct; instead, the focus must be on whether the employer reasonably determined it had cause to terminate.

Conner's basic argument is there was no just cause for her termination. Although it appears that the City followed its handbook procedures in effectuating Conner's termination, the grievance committee voted to reinstate Conner; i.e., the committee found no just cause for Conner's firing. Subsequently, the City Council overturned the committee's decision. While the committee and City Council both could have reached their respective conclusions reasonably and in good faith, it nonetheless appears that reasonable minds can differ as to whether just cause existed to support Conner's termination. Thus, there remains the ultimate question of whether the City had a reasonable good faith belief that sufficient cause existed for termination. This is a question that generally should not be resolved on summary judgment, and therefore, the Court of Appeals correctly reversed the trial court's grant of summary judgment in favor of the City. . . .

NOTES

1. *Putting* Woolley *and* Conner *Together.* Why did the city of Forest Acres lose this case? Didn't its manual contain the requisite *Woolley* disclaimers in abundance? What exactly is the outstanding factual issue on the enforceability of the manual that requires a remand?

2. *Clarity and Conspicuousness.* One reason that plaintiffs sometimes prevail despite the presence of at-will language in a handbook or other document is because the clause is not clear or conspicuous. *See Evenson v. Colorado Farm Bureau Mut. Ins. Co.,* 879 P.2d 402, 409 (Colo. Ct. App. 1993) (jury question presented on whether handbook formed contract where language disclaiming contractual significance was clear, but not "emphasized"); *Nicosia v. Wakefern Food Corp.,* 643 A.2d 554, 560 (N.J. 1994) (disclaimer ineffective under *Woolley* because it contained "legalese" such as "not contractual," "consideration," and "subject to . . . interpretation"); *Sanchez v. Life Care Ctrs. of Amer., Inc.,* 855 P.2d 1256, 1259 (Wyo. 1993) (reversing summary judgment for employer where disclaimer language was "not bold lettered," was "buried

---

5. The Court in *Small* noted that where the jury found that a handbook created an employment contract, it was for the jury to decide whether the employer "reasonably could have determined that Small's actions" warranted immediate discharge as a "serious offense." Therefore, it is generally a jury question as to whether the employer acted reasonably pursuant to the employment contract.

in introductory paragraphs," was "not designed to attract attention," and was "stated in language that does not tell the employee what he needs to know"). *See also Becker v. Fred Meyer Stores, Inc.*, 335 P.3d 1110 (Alaska 2014) (given the sheer level of detail, disclaiming language would have to be very prominent to be effective). From what you can tell, was the disclaimer in *Conner* prominently placed? Was the text emphasized in any way? Assuming it was noted and read, was it understandable to an employee?

3. *Judicial Deference to Employer Disclaimer Language. Conner* represents one extreme in judicial treatment of employer disclaimers. Not all courts parse so closely the language of the manual or recognize possible inconsistencies of the type that led to a plaintiff victory in *Conner.* Recall *Guz,* for instance, in which the California Supreme Court rejected the employee's claim, based in part on the at-will provision of the employer's manual, notwithstanding other provisions and policies that made promises about the method by which workers would be selected for termination. In contrast to *Conner,* many courts treat disclaimer language as dispositive of employee contract rights, routinely awarding summary judgment to employers in such cases. *See, e.g., Sidlo v. Millercoors, LLC,* 718 F. App'x 718, 730 (10th Cir, 2018); *Finch v. Farmers Co-op Oil Co. of Sheridan,* 109 P.3d 537, 541-42 (Wyo. 2005); *Grossman v. Computer Curriculum Corp.,* 131 F. Supp. 2d 299, 305-06 (D. Conn. 2000). Some scholars believe that a judicial tendency to "rubberstamp" employer disclaimer language may be on the rise. *See* Arnow-Richman, *Employment as Transaction, supra,* at 468-71 (linking judicial treatment of disclaimers to larger trend of increasing deference to private ordering in employment relationships); Fineman, *The Inevitable Demise, supra,* at 365-77 (tracing increasing judicial deference to disclaimer language in California as employers refined their drafting techniques to avoid liability).

4. *Disclaimers and Oral Assurances.* The effectiveness of written disclaimers is a recurring theme in all types of employment contract disputes, not just those centered on manuals. In part as a result of cases like *Woolley,* employers frequently place recitals of at-will status in a variety of personnel materials, including employment applications, offer letters, and reimbursement forms. Often these are standardized documents that are distributed as a matter of course to all personnel. The effect of these statements in the face of other evidence suggesting a contract for job security depends both on the facts and the court. The contrary evidence may be treated as inadmissible parol statements, evidence of a modification, or simply additional evidence to be submitted to a fact finder who will determine the contractual status of the employee under the circumstances. Not surprisingly, the outcomes of such cases tend to be highly fact-dependent. For example, oral assurance-based contract claims sometimes prevail, despite the presence of clear written disclaimers. *See, e.g., Worley v. Wyoming Bottling Co.,* 1 P.3d 615 (Wyo. 2000) (holding plaintiff may proceed with breach of contract and promissory estoppel claims based on express assurances of job security by supervisor despite at-will disclaimers contained in job application and employee handbook). In many other cases, however, courts reject claims that express, written waivers can be overcome by oral assurances or other surrounding circumstances. *See, e.g., Edwards v. Geisinger Clinic,* 459 F. App'x 125 (3d Cir. 2012) (holding physician who signed a practice agreement acknowledging that his employment with the clinic was "at will" had no breach of contract claim when his employment was terminated earlier despite recruitment discussions and an offer letter proposing a four-to-six-year relationship); *Scott v. Merck & Co., Inc.,* 497 F. App'x 331, 335-36 (4th Cir. 2012) (concluding that a statement in plaintiff's employment application acknowledging that Merck had the right to terminate at will, together with Manager's Policies to the same effect, barred any suit based on subsequent assurance of nonretaliation for reporting objectionable business practices).

5. *Grievance Procedures.* Note that the handbook in *Conner* set forth a grievance procedure to be followed when an employee allegedly violated Forest Acre's policies. Whether the city was bound to follow these procedures was not in dispute here, since it in fact followed them. Handbook representations regarding processes or procedures for employee discipline can be found to be binding assurances as well, however. *See, e.g., Langenkamp v. Olson*, 628 F. App'x 50 (2d Cir. 2015) (finding employee stated a claim for breach of contract where she alleged termination procedures were set forth in the employer's handbook, the employer's offer of employment required employee to agree to abide by employer's policies as a condition of employment, and the employer did not follow those procedures).

6. *Turnabout Is Fair Play.* Most cases turning on the significance of disclaimer language involve suits by employees who, like Conner, claim their employer breached a promise of job security. Employers occasionally have found themselves in the uncomfortable position of having to circumvent their own language in trying to enforce promises made by employees, however. Such cases can arise when the employer has placed an arbitration policy or a prohibition on post-employment competition in its handbook. When an employee subsequently engages in prohibited behavior, the company is at pains to explain why the employee's commitment should be enforced when the handbook in which it was found expressly disclaims its contractual significance. *See, e.g., Heurtebise v. Reliable Bus. Computers*, 550 N.W.2d 243 (Mich. 1996) (policy in handbook did not constitute enforceable arbitration agreement where handbook's opening statement disclaimed an intent to be bound); *Snow v. BE & K Const. Co.*, 126 F. Supp. 2d 5 (D. Maine 2001) (refusing to enforce arbitration clause because employer was "trying to have it both ways" by including disclaiming language in handbook to avoid being bound while, at the same time, seeking to enforce its terms against employees). Unfortunately for employees, such victories are short-lived. Employers are able to correct the problem easily by removing such commitments from the general personnel handbook and placing them in formal contract documents separately signed by the employee. *See, e.g., Currier, McCabe & Assocs. v. Maher*, 906 N.Y.S.2d 129, 131 (N.Y. App. 2010) (defendant-employee bound by handbook's tuition repayment policy despite disclaimer where employee's separately executed employment agreement provided the he had "read the EMPLOYEE HANDBOOK and agrees to [its] terms and conditions"). If you find yourself representing management, you would do well to remember these examples.

PROBLEM

2-4. Imagine that, following *Woolley*, the Human Resources director at Hoffmann-La Roche contacts you about revising the company's personnel manual. The HR director feels that the manual is good for employee morale and would like to continue using it, but she hopes to alter the language so as to protect the company from future contractual liability. Look at footnote 2 of *Woolley*, which contains the key language that gave rise to Woolley's claim. How would you redraft this? What might you add? Will the revision you create satisfy the company's goals?

Demasse v. ITT Corp.
984 P.2d 1138 (Ariz. 1999)

FELDMAN, Justice.

The United States Court of Appeals for the Ninth Circuit certified to us [the following question] of Arizona law. . . .

1. Once a policy that an employee will not be laid off ahead of less senior employees becomes part of the employment contract . . . as a result of the employee's legitimate expectations and reliance on the employer's handbook, may the employer thereafter unilaterally change the handbook policy so as to permit the employer to layoff employees without regard to seniority? . . .

ITT hired Roger Demasse, Maria A. Garcia, Billy W. Jones, Viola Munguia, Greg Palmer, and Socorro Soza (collectively "Demasse employees") as hourly workers at various times between 1960 and 1979. Although it is unclear when ITT first issued an employee handbook, evidently there have been five editions, the most recent in 1989. . . .

The issues presented focus on the 1989 handbook, which included two new provisions. First, a disclaimer added to the first page "Welcome" statement provided that "nothing contained herein shall be construed as a guarantee of continued employment. . . . ITT Cannon does not guarantee continued employment to employees and retains the right to terminate or layoff employees." Second, this Welcome statement included a new modification provision, which read:

> Within the limits allowed by law, ITT Cannon reserves the right to amend, modify or cancel this handbook, as well as any or all of the various policies, rules, procedures and programs outlined in it. Any amendment or modification will be communicated to affected employees, and while the handbook provisions are in effect, will be consistently applied.

. . .When the 1989 handbook was distributed, ITT employees signed an acknowledgment that they had received, understood, and would comply with the revised handbook.

Four years passed before ITT notified its hourly employees that effective April 19, 1993, its layoff guidelines for hourly employees would not be based on seniority but on each employee's "abilities and documentation of performance." Demasse, Soza, and Palmer were laid off ten days after the new policy went into effect, Munguia five days later, and Jones and Garcia almost nine months later. All were laid off before less senior employees but in accordance with the 1993 policy modification.

The Demasse employees brought an action in federal district court alleging they were laid off in breach of an implied-in-fact contract created by the pre-1989 handbook provisions requiring that ITT lay off its employees according to seniority. [The court granted summary judgment for the employer finding that the employer had validly modified its layoff policy in the 1993 handbook.]

A. The Implied-in-Fact Contract . . .

At-will employment contracts are unilateral and typically start with an employer's offer of a wage in exchange for work performed; subsequent performance by the employee provides consideration to create the contract. Thus, before performance is rendered, the offer can be modified by the employer's unilateral withdrawal of the old offer and substitution of a new one: The employer makes a new offer with different terms and the employee again accepts the new offer by performance (such as continued employment). Thus a new unilateral contract is formed—a day's work for a day's wages. . . .

While employment contracts without express terms are presumptively at will, an employee can overcome this presumption by establishing a contract term that is either expressed or inferred from the words or conduct of the parties. . . .

When employment circumstances offer a term of job security to an employee who might otherwise be dischargeable at will and the employee acts in response to that promise, the employment relationship is *no longer at will* but is instead governed by the terms of the contract. . . .

This, of course, does not mean that all handbook terms create contractual promises. A statement is contractual only if it discloses "a promissory intent or [is] one that the employee could reasonably conclude constituted a commitment by the employer. If the statement is merely a description of the employer's present policies . . . it is neither a promise nor a statement that could reasonably be relied upon as a commitment." *Soderlun v. Public Serv. Co.*, 944 P.2d 616, 620 (Colo. App. 1997). An implied-in-fact contract term is formed when "a reasonable person could conclude that both parties intended that the employer's (or the employee's) right to terminate the employment relationship at-will had been limited." *Metcalf v. Intermountain Gas Co.*, 778 P.2d 744, 746 (Idaho 1989).

When an employer chooses to include a handbook statement "that the employer should reasonably have expected the employee to consider as a commitment from the employer," that term becomes an offer to form an implied-in-fact contract and is accepted by the employee's acceptance of employment. . . .

B.   Modification

ITT argues that it had the legal power to unilaterally modify the contract by simply publishing a new handbook. But as with other contracts, an implied-in-fact contract term cannot be modified unilaterally. . . .[3]

[T]o effectively modify a contract, whether implied-in-fact or express, there must be: (1) an offer to modify the contract, (2) assent to or acceptance of that offer, and (3) consideration.

The 1989 handbook, published with terms that purportedly modified or permitted modification of pre-existing contractual provisions, was therefore no more than an offer to modify the existing contract. Even if the 1989 handbook constituted a valid offer, questions remain whether the Demasse employees accepted that offer and whether there was consideration for the changes ITT sought to effect.

---

3. In the unilateral or at-will context, once the offer is accepted by commencement of performance, the terms cannot be changed. RESTATEMENT (SECOND) OF CONTRACTS §45. Thus, if an employer offers a day's pay for a day's work, the employer cannot, after employee performance, reduce the offer of pay that induced the performance.

1. Continued Employment Alone Does Not Constitute Consideration for Modification

. . .Consideration will be found when an employer and its employees have made a "bargained for exchange to support [the employees'] . . . relinquishment of the protections they are entitled to under the existing contract."

The cases ITT cites hold that continued work alone both manifested the Demasse employees' assent to the modification and constituted consideration for it. We disagree with both contentions and the cases that support them. Separate consideration, beyond continued employment, is necessary to effect a modification.

. . .Any other result brings us to an absurdity: The employer's threat to breach its promise of job security provides consideration for its rescission of that promise.

2. Acceptance

Continued employment after issuance of a new handbook does not constitute acceptance, otherwise the "illusion (and the irony) is apparent: To preserve their right under the [existing contract] . . . plaintiffs would be forced to quit." *Doyle* [*v. Holy Cross*, 708 N.E.2d 1140 (Ill. 1999)]. It is "too much to require an employee to preserve his or her rights under the original employment contract by quitting working." *Brodie* [*v. General Chem. Corp.*, 934 P.2d 1263, 1268 (Wyo. 1997)]. Thus, the employee does not manifest consent to an offer modifying an existing contract without taking affirmative steps, beyond continued performance, to accept. . . . If passive silence constituted acceptance, the employee "could not remain silent and continue to work. Instead [he] would have to give specific notice of rejection to the employer to avoid having his actions construed as acceptance. Requiring an offeree to take affirmative steps to reject an offer . . . is inconsistent with general contract law." The burden is on the employer to show that the employee assented with knowledge of the attempted modification and understanding of its impact on the underlying contract.

To manifest consent, the employee must first have legally adequate notice of the modification. Legally adequate notice is more than the employee's awareness of or receipt of the newest handbook. An employee must be informed of any new term, aware of its impact on the pre-existing contract, and affirmatively consent to it to accept the offered modification.

When ITT distributed the 1989 handbook containing the provisions permitting unilateral modification or cancellation, it did not bargain with those pre-1989 employees who had seniority rights under the old handbooks, did not ask for or obtain their assent, and did not provide consideration other than continued employment. The employees signed a receipt for the "1989 handbook stating that they had received the handbook[,] understood that it was their responsibility to read it, comply with its contents, and contact Personnel if they had any questions concerning the contents." The Demasse employees were not informed that continued employment— showing up for work the next day—would manifest assent, constitute consideration, and permit cancellation of any employment rights to which they were contractually entitled. Thus, even if we were to agree that continued employment could provide consideration for rescission of the job security term, that consideration would not have been bargained for and would not support modification. . . .

C . . .

If a contractual job security provision can be eliminated by unilateral modification, an employer can essentially terminate the employee at any time, thus abrogating any protection provided the employee. For example, an employer could terminate an employee who has a job security provision simply by saying, "I revoke that term and, as of today, you're dismissed"—no different from the full at-will scenario in which the employer only need say, "You're fired." This, of course, makes the original promise illusory. . . .

To those who believe our conclusion will destroy an employer's ability to update and modernize its handbook, we can only reply that the great majority of handbook terms are certainly non-contractual and can be revised, that the existence of contractual terms can be disclaimed in the handbook in effect at the time of hiring and, if not, permission to modify can always be obtained by mutual agreement and for consideration. In all other instances, the contract rule is and has always been that one should keep one's promises.

JONES, Vice Chief Judge, concurring in part and dissenting in part:

I respectfully dissent. . . . The [majority's] response undermines legitimate employer expectations in a remarkable departure from traditional at-will employment principles. It transforms the conventional employer-employee contract from one that is *unilateral* (performance of an act in exchange for a promise to pay) to one that is *bilateral* (a promise for a promise). The decision is unsupported by Arizona precedent and unwarranted as a matter of law.

The majority exacts from the certified question the premise that the employment relationship between the Demasse plaintiffs and ITT is "no longer at-will." I disagree. A single contract term in a policy manual may, while it exists, become an enforceable condition of employment, but it does not alter the essential character of the relationship. In my view, ITT, as the party unilaterally responsible for inserting it into the manual may, on reasonable notice, exercise an equal right to remove it.

For purposes of this discussion, it is assumed the reverse-seniority layoff provision became part of the "employment contract" years earlier when ITT initially placed it into the policy manual and that it remained a part of the "contract" as long as it remained a part of the manual. The simple question put to us is whether ITT may unilaterally bring about its removal and thereafter be free of any prospective reverse-seniority obligation in the event of a layoff. That question does not catapult the case beyond the reach of at-will employment principles.

. . . ITT added a contract disclaimer to its 1989 handbook: "[N]othing contained herein shall be construed as a guarantee of continued employment." In the same handbook, ITT expressly reserved "the right to amend, modify, or cancel this handbook, as well as any or all of the various policies, rules, procedures, and programs outlined within it." Each of the Demasse plaintiffs signed a certification acknowledging that the new policy had been received and reviewed.

The "at-will" status of the Demasse-ITT contract both before and after the 1989 amendments is confirmed by at least two factors: (1) the contract was always one of indefinite duration, and (2) the Demasse employees had the absolute right to quit at any time. . . .

The right to quit in opposition to changed policies, despite the majority's view, is properly characterized as a right. It is an inherent feature of at-will employment. . . .

When ITT modified its policy manual in 1989 by adding the contract disclaimer and the power to amend, and offered continuing employment to employees having received notice and having signed the acknowledgment, the employees effectively gave their acceptance to the amendment by continuing to work. Moreover, in 1993, when ITT revised its layoff policy, the employees had known for four years that such change could occur.

[handwritten: how to modify]

The majority overlooks another point. Just as at-will employees are unilaterally free to quit at any time, employers may be unilaterally forced by economic circumstance to curtail or shut down an operation, something employers have the absolute right to do. When the employer chooses in good faith, in pursuit of legitimate business objectives, to eliminate an employee policy as an alternative to curtailment or total shutdown, there has been forbearance by the employer. Such forbearance constitutes a benefit to the employee in the form of an offer of continuing employment. The employer who provides continuing employment, albeit under newly modified contract terms, also provides consideration to support the amended policy manual. . . .

The majority imposes a bilateral principle on the at-will relationship by holding that in order for ITT to eliminate the reverse-seniority layoff policy, some form of new consideration, in addition to an offer of continuing employment, is necessary to support each individual employee's assent to the amended manual. The majority's approach effectively mandates that ITT, in order to free itself of future reverse-seniority obligations, would be required to give a wage increase, a one-time bonus, or some other new benefit to the employees with the explicit understanding that such benefit was given in exchange for the amendment to the policy manual. This becomes artificial because it is foreign to the unilateral at-will relationship and, as a practical matter, it leaves the employer unable, at least in part, to manage its business. I disagree with the proposition that "new" consideration is necessary.

The majority further asserts that ITT's exercise of the unilateral right to amend the handbook renders the employer's original reverse-seniority promise illusory. Once again, I disagree. An illusory promise is one which by its own terms makes performance optional with the promisor whatever may happen, or whatever course of conduct he may pursue. The reverse-seniority promise was not illusory because it was not optional with ITT as long as it remained a part of ITT's handbook policy. During the years of its existence, it was fully enforceable. . . .

The majority opinion produces the net result that the reverse-seniority layoff policy, as a permanent term of the "employment contract" with respect to any employee who at any time worked under it, gains parity with a negotiated collective bargaining agreement having a definite term, usually three years. In fact, the ITT policy would have force and effect even greater than a collective agreement because its existence, as to the Demasse plaintiffs and others similarly situated, becomes perpetual. This result grants preferential treatment to every employee who worked under the policy but denies such treatment to employees hired after its removal. A collective bargaining agreement is bilateral, and to impose a bilateral relationship on simple at-will employment is, in my view, an attempt to place a square peg in a round hole. Inevitably, this will impair essential managerial flexibility in the workplace. It will also cause undue deterioration of traditional at-will principles. . . .

Principles of equity and pragmatic reason have also governed the employer's unilateral right to change an implied-in-fact term in a handbook. The federal district court, applying Arizona law in *Bedow* [*v. Valley National Bank*, 5 BNA IER CAS

1678 (D. Ariz. 1988)], correctly asserted that the last-distributed handbook controls employment conditions and trumps prior inconsistent handbook terms:

> *Any other conclusion would create chaos for employers who would have different contracts of employment for different employees depending upon the particular personnel manual in force when the employee was hired.* Such a result would effectively discourage employers from either issuing employment manuals or subsequently upgrading or modifying personnel policies.

(Emphasis added.) . . .

The majority's answer to the certified question will frustrate the legitimate expectations of both employers and employees. The notion that one term in an employee handbook—a reverse-seniority layoff term—can be perpetually binding as to some but not all employees will effectively undermine [cases] on which employers have relied for years. The opinion unduly punishes ITT and other employers similarly situated. We said [previously] that employers should place contract disclaimer language in their handbooks to preserve the at-will relationship. ITT responded by inserting such language. We should leave it at that.

NOTES

1. *"Separate" Consideration.* The majority rejects the idea that continued employment can be consideration for the change in ITT's layoff policy, insisting on "separate" consideration for the modification. What is "separate" consideration? Is it any different from the discredited notion of "additional" consideration used by courts to defeat plaintiffs' claims to "permanent" or "lifetime" employment? Recall from your first-year contracts class the general common law rule that contract modifications require consideration to be binding. A corollary to this rule is that a "pre-existing legal duty" does not constitute consideration. *See* RESTATEMENT (SECOND) OF CONTRACTS §370. Does the pre-existing legal duty concept help you distinguish between the "permanent" employment and handbook modification scenarios? Or is *Demasse* simply co-opting the additional consideration doctrine in order to turn the tables on employers?

2. *The Fiction of Assent.* The majority suggests that even if continued employment constituted consideration it could not suffice as an acceptance because it was not given knowingly. If tacit acceptance worked in *Woolley* to establish contractual rights based on a handbook, why doesn't it work here? Are *Demasse* and *Woolley* inconsistent? Which court's treatment of assent is more in keeping with basic contract law? Must parties actually negotiate terms in order to be contractually bound? Must they at least know what the terms are?

3. *Advising the Employer.* The law of personnel manual modification is currently evolving; not every jurisdiction has addressed the issue, nor has there been agreement among those that have. *Compare Boswell v. Panera Bread Co.*, 879 F.3d 296, 302 (8th Cir. 2018) (holding under Missouri law that employees' continuing to work after announcement of a cap on a previously promised bonus did not constitute a waiver or assent to the formation of a new contract) and *Torosyan v. Boehringer Ingelheim Pharmaceuticals, Inc.*, 662 A.2d 89, 98-99 (Conn. 1995) (employee continuing work does not constitute acceptance of a modified handbook that "substantially interferes with [the] employee's legitimate expectations") *with Asmus v. Pac. Bell*, 999 P.2d 71, 78 (Cal. 2000) (unilaterally conferred contract rights may be reduced or eliminated unilaterally).

This uncertainty can pose difficulties for employers. Assuming the law in your jurisdiction is undecided, how would you advise an employer seeking to modify the terms of a pre-existing handbook? Would you recommend trying to comply with the majority opinion in *Demasse*? If yes, by what means would you recommend obtaining employee assent? Would it be enough to amend the signature receipts to include an explanation of the modifications? Now consider what you might provide as "separate" consideration. Would a one-time bonus of $1,000 suffice? How about a one-time bonus of $10? Does the employer have to provide something that is distinct from the usual adjustments made regularly to employee salaries? For instance, what about making the modification coincident with an annual cost-of-living adjustment? Might these examples offer ways to avoid the "chaos" envisioned by the dissent of different manuals applying to different employees depending on their date of hire? *See generally* Rachel S. Arnow-Richman, *Modifying At-Will Employment Contracts*, 57 B.C. L. Rev. 427 (2016) (calling for enforcement of mid-term modifications only where worker received reasonable advance notice of the change); Stephen F. Befort, *Employee Handbooks and Policy Statements: From Gratuities to Contracts and Back Again*, 12 Empl. Rts & Empl. Pol'y J. 307 (2017) (critiquing the Restatement of Employment Law's approach to employee handbooks and disclaimers).

4. *Square Peg in a Round Hole?* Consider the various objections raised by the dissent. Chief among them is a disagreement with the majority's premise that, upon the employer's adoption of the original personnel manual, the parties' relationship changed from a unilateral at-will relationship to a bilateral relationship with job security. Who is right? In commercial settings, it is not uncommon for parties to have long-term sales or service contracts that are terminable at will but bind both parties to a variety of terms during the life of the agreement. Generally, such contracts provide that a designated amount of notice must be given prior to termination. Does the commercial context offer a viable analogy for handbook modifications?

The Restatement of Employment Law adopts a comparable approach. It rejects efforts to apply contract principles to employer handbooks as "analytically unsatisfying" and permits the employer to "modify or revoke an obligation established pursuant to a unilateral statement" by providing "reasonable notice" of the change. *See* Restatement of Employment Law §2.06. If notice is the touchstone for enforceable unilateral modifications, how much time is reasonable? In *Demasse*, four years passed between ITT's change in policy and the lay-offs in question. Would four months suffice? Four days? *See, e.g., Asmus v. Pac. Bell*, 999 P.2d at 78 (sanctioning unilateral modification made two years after notice to employees that job security program might be eliminated); *Bankey v. Storer Broad. Co.*, 443 N.W.2d 112, 117-20 (Mich. 1989) (denying breach of contract claim by employee discharged two months after unilateral modification of employer's policy digest in recognition of employer's need for managerial flexibility). What is the point of notice? To allow employees who are unhappy to seek another job? If so, does that help determine the proper length of notice?

PROBLEM

2-5.   During the mid-1990s, Pacific Telecom was facing competitive pressure from the burgeoning technology industry in California and lost several key employees to startup ventures offering stock option deals. In response, the company disseminated a new "Management Employment Security Policy" to all management personnel. The document provided, "It will be our policy to offer all management employees who continue to meet our changing business expectations employment security through reassignment to and retraining for other management positions, even if their present jobs are eliminated."

Five years later, following a crash in the tech sector, Pacific Bell realized it could not afford to maintain its employment security policy and needed to institute a reduction in force. It announced to all management personnel that the Employment Security Policy had been terminated and was being replaced with a new Management Force Reduction Program under which designated employees would be offered enhanced pension and severance benefits in exchange for their voluntary resignations. Craig Astor was a technical manager at Pacific Telecom who received both documents. He declined to resign under Pacific's Reduction Program. Six months later he was involuntarily terminated.

(a)   Suppose Astor sues for breach of an implied contract for job security under the original Security Policy. Is he likely to succeed? Are there any other legal theories he might be able to pursue?

(b)   How would it affect your analysis if Pacific Telecom had sent a notice to all managers one year prior to announcing its Management Force Reduction Program, alerting them to the fact that it would shortly be altering its Security Policy?

(c)   What if the original Security Policy contained the following additional sentence: "This Policy will remain in effect unless and until changing market conditions necessitate its revocation"?

3

Written Contracts and Expressly Negotiated Terms of Employment

As discussed in the previous chapter, the at-will presumption is merely a default rule; the words, actions, and practices of the employer can confer greater contractual rights to job security. While Chapter 2 dealt primarily with oral and implied promises, this chapter looks at situations where the employer and an individual employee explicitly discussed particular terms of employment—issues such as job duration, bases for termination, and methods of compensation—and then took the time to reduce those terms to writing, sometimes with the help of a lawyer.

Employers and employees who opt for a written contract do so for the same reasons that parties choose written contracts in other contexts. They hope to memorialize their understanding in a fixed form so that it will not be forgotten or challenged in the future by competing understandings. An employer may use a writing to make clear that the employment relationship is at will in order to avoid subsequent claims to job security based on oral assurances or workplace practices like those explored in the last chapter. In contrast, employees will desire written contracts mostly to lock in employment and its benefits.

Employers are increasingly using narrowly focused agreements, like an acknowledgment of at-will status or arbitration agreements, even with rank and file employees. Thus, written contracts are increasingly used but agreements providing for any kind of job security remain the exception in the American workplace since employers, who generally control whether a written contract will be executed, remain protected by the ability to terminate at will. Nevertheless, written contracts guaranteeing some variety of job security continue to exist, primarily where the employee has sufficient bargaining power. These include the collective bargaining context where unionized employees (through their union representatives) negotiate a written "collective bargaining agreement," a process generally studied in a separate course on Labor Law. These "CBAs" govern all workers in the relevant "bargaining unit" and are often very detailed, covering various terms and conditions of employment including job security. Individual written contracts, by contrast, are used most frequently with high-level employees, such as executives and upper-level managers. Individual written contracts are also used with some regularity among sales employees and other workers whose compensation fluctuates based on performance. In those instances, the writing rarely guarantees any length of employment; instead, it usually serves the employer's practical need to document a complex commission or bonus structure.

While written contracts will resolve some uncertainties, they can create others. Planning and drafting are imperfect processes that can result in a document that is ambiguous, vague, or simply incomplete. And since employment is sometimes long term, the parties' expectations can change, sometimes dramatically, over the course of the relationship. Think how hard it would be to capture every obligation of the employer and employee in a particular work relationship in a single written document. And then think of the changes that might occur over five or even two years. As a result, parties often find that their written employment contracts are silent as to a particular issue or even inconsistent with the way the relationship has developed.

This chapter explores written contracts in the context of a dynamic employment relationship. Section A begins by looking at situations where the written contract is ambiguous as to job security and then covers how written provisions conferring job security apply in the context of termination, as where an employee's performance is substandard or an employer fails to comply with specific obligations. Section B tackles problems related to compensation arrangements, such as commissions and profit sharing. Consider whether and how parties might have avoided litigation by drafting their agreement differently and what the resulting decisions say about the value and efficacy of written employment contracts.

A. JOB SECURITY TERMS

1. Identifying and Interpreting Job Security Provisions

Tropicana Hotel Corporation v. Speer
692 P.2d 499 (Nev. 1985)

GUNDERSON, Justice.

This appeal arises out of the brief association of Donald Speer with Tropicana Hotel. In July 1975 Mitzi Stauffer Briggs acquired a controlling interest in the Tropicana Hotel Corporation . . . [and] looked for a competent general manager who could restore the hotel to its former prosperity. She offered the position to Donald Speer, general manager at the Desert Inn.

Speer indicated that he would accept the position only if, in addition to a generous salary, he could have equity in the Tropicana Hotel Corporation. After some preliminary discussions, Briggs invited Speer, his counsel and her counsel to her home in Atherton, California, in the hope of concluding an agreement. It is undisputed that agreement was reached on the terms of the employment contract; the parties could not agree, however, on how the stock should be transferred.

After Speer returned to Las Vegas, he left his position at the Desert Inn and began working as general manager at the Tropicana Hotel. Two months later Briggs signed an employment agreement prepared by her attorneys according to drafts of the Atherton discussions, and forwarded it to Speer. Speer never signed the agreement. He testified at trial that his counsel advised him not to sign it until a satisfactory stock option agreement was prepared and signed by Briggs.

In March 1976 a culinary strike forced the hotel to close. Disagreements over hotel management developed between Speer and Briggs, and after two of Speer's trusted subordinates were fired by the executive committee, Speer left the hotel. The parties disagreed at trial over whether Speer had resigned or whether he had been terminated. Speer filed suit [alleging breach of an oral employment contract reached at Atherton by his termination without cause.... The district court, sitting without a jury, found that binding oral agreements existed, and that Tropicana had breached the employment contract. . . . [H]owever, it found that the statute of frauds rendered the stock option agreement unenforceable.

We turn first to the stock option transfer. . . . We need not decide here whether [the statute of frauds] applies to stock option agreements executed in connection with employment contracts, because our examination of the record compels us to conclude that no agreement on the transfer of stock was ever reached.

The record shows that at Atherton the parties merely agreed that Speer would receive $100,000 worth of points, or approximately 3.2% of Briggs's holding. The parties could not agree on the precise form of the transfer, because Speer wished to be left with $100,000 after the payment of his capital gains tax, and counsel could not work out the tax consequences to their satisfaction. Even after the meeting at Atherton, numerous drafts of proposed agreements circulated between counsel but were never satisfactory to both parties. When important terms remain unresolved, a binding agreement cannot exist.

We next turn to Speer['s claim of] breach of his oral employment contract. . . .

The record shows that during their negotiations the parties contemplated that any agreement concerning Speer's employment would become effective only when reduced to writing and signed by the parties.[3]

At trial Speer as well as Briggs admitted that the terms of the proposed written agreement corresponded to the terms agreed on at Atherton. Nevertheless, on advice of counsel Speer decided not to sign the draft until Briggs signed a satisfactory stock option agreement. Clearly, Speer withheld his signature to pressure Briggs to consummate the stock option transfer, and his conduct is inconsistent with his assertion that the oral agreement reached at Atherton was intended to be immediately binding. Had the proposed written agreement been merely a memorialization of a binding oral contract, Speer's signature would not have been of sufficient legal significance to exert any influence on Briggs. We have previously stated that since some measure of agreement must usually be reached before a written draft is prepared, the evidence that the parties intended to be presently bound must be convincing and subject to no other reasonable interpretation. . . .

A similar situation confronted us in *Loma Linda Univ. v. Eckenweiler,* 469 P.2d 54 (Nev. 1970). Negotiations regarding plaintiff's employment contract continued during his employment by the University. A written agreement was prepared but rejected

---

3. This is shown by the testimony of Speer himself.

    COUNSEL FOR TROPICANA: Mr. Speer, when you left the Atherton meeting, was it your understanding that a written contract embodying the terms of your employment contract as well as the points would be drawn up and signed by the parties?

    SPEER: I did.

    COUNSEL FOR TROPICANA: Mr. Speer, it was always your intention, was it not, both pre-Atherton, at Atherton and post-Atherton that you would have a written contract or that you would be protected as far as your position as general manager at the Tropicana Hotel; is that true?

    SPEER: That's true.

by the plaintiff. Neither party signed the agreement. After plaintiff's employment was terminated, he attempted to enforce an alleged oral agreement regarding severance pay. We held that even accepting the district court's view that the parties had reached a meeting of the minds on the issue of severance pay, judgment for plaintiff had to be reversed. The proposed written agreement was an offer by the University which plaintiff had declined to accept. Important terms remained unresolved and the oral agreement was incomplete; moreover, the parties had contemplated consummation by written agreement and plaintiff himself had rejected the written contract. Similarly, since Speer refused to sign the written draft and clearly demonstrated his intent not to be immediately bound, no contract arose between the parties.

Speer contends that the fact that he commenced his employment at the Tropicana Hotel before a written contract was even prepared shows that he regarded the oral employment agreement as binding. Generally, performance by a party after agreement has been reached but before a writing has been prepared is regarded as some evidence that the writing was only a memorial of a binding agreement. However, where the evidence clearly shows that the party performing did not consider the agreement to be binding, the fact that he began performance does not compel a contrary conclusion.

Moreover, even assuming *arguendo* that a binding agreement existed, Speer has not demonstrated that it was breached. The district court determined that the termination of two of Speer's trusted associates by Briggs and the executive committee so undermined Speer's ability to perform his duties that it amounted to a constructive discharge. We do not find this theory persuasive. In spite of protracted negotiations, the continued employment of members of Speer's "team" was never suggested as a term of any proposed agreement. In the absence of such an understanding, the termination of the two men over Speer's objections cannot be regarded as an invasion of Speer's authority sufficient to amount to a constructive discharge. . . .

NOTES

1. *Significance of an Unsigned Writing.* Understand the difference between drafting a written contract and memorializing an oral one. When parties draft a written document, they generally expect their execution of that document (i.e., their signatures on the page) to consummate the deal. Their discussions, including oral commitments, that led up to that point are viewed as part of the negotiation process. It is this assumption that undergirds core contracts principles, such as the parol evidence rule, which (you may be disappointed to learn) we will be revisiting shortly.

However, parties may intend to reach an agreement orally and use a subsequent writing merely to capture after the fact what they have already committed to. In these situations, there is the intent to be bound requisite to contract enforcement from the moment of the oral agreement. *See Kolchins v. Evolution Mkts., Inc.*, 96 N.E.3d 784 (N.Y. 2018) (even though a formal document was contemplated and never executed, email communications between the parties could be found sufficient to renew a prior contract since the parties apparently agreed on all material terms). Which of these two scenarios describes what happened in *Speer*? How does the court know?

2. *Intent of the Parties.* Consider the role of party intent in your response to the preceding note. Based in part on the testimony set out in footnote 3, the court concludes that Speer and Tropicana "contemplated that any agreement concerning

Speer's employment would become effective only when reduced to writing and signed by the parties." Does it necessarily follow that there was no binding contract? Even if, at that point in time, no contract existed, Speer worked for roughly a year, so he had to be subject to some employment agreement. Might the parties have impliedly agreed to those terms by their conduct? What were the terms of the parties' oral or implied contract if not those agreed to in the writing? The opinion does not indicate Speer's salary. Suppose, however, that during his one year of employment he was paid the exact salary that the parties had agreed to in the unsigned contract. How would this affect your understanding of what happened? *Cf. Hendricks v. Smartvideo Techs. Inc.*, 511 F. Supp. 2d 1219, 1228 (M.D. Fla. 2007) (finding question of fact whether parties entered into contract notwithstanding plaintiff's failure to sign written agreement where plaintiff was employed for several months and "Smartvideo also partially performed, paying Hendricks a salary pursuant to the alleged agreement").

3. *The Stock Option Agreement.* It appears that the only written term on which the parties could not agree was the stock options provision. Would it have been a better litigation strategy for Speer to concede he had no stock rights and seek to enforce only the other terms of employment? The court suggests that Speer withheld his signature from the final written document in order to pressure Tropicana into conceding to his stock demands. If so, the court arguably should not allow Speer to have his cake and eat it too—that is, to have the benefit of terms he deliberately chose to reject in order to secure a bargaining advantage. If that is what happened, perhaps Speer got his just deserts. On the other hand, is this view of the facts consistent with Speer accepting employment absent an executed agreement? What bargaining advantage could he gain at that point by refusing the written document?

4. *Restitution.* Another way to conceptualize this arrangement is as a failed contract—the parties never agreed to final terms of employment but began performance nonetheless. If so, should Speer be entitled to the reasonable value of his services under a restitution theory? *See generally* RESTATEMENT (SECOND) OF CONTRACTS §370 (ALI 1981). The employer would be credited for whatever wages it paid Speer, but that does not necessarily reflect the reasonable value of his services, especially given the discussion of stock options.

5. *Constructive Discharge.* Understand the significance of the penultimate paragraph in the opinion. Speer does not contend that Tropicana formally terminated him, but rather that it "constructively discharged" him by breaching its contractual obligations. The concept of constructive discharge is important in many areas of employment law. Although employees often resign voluntarily, employees sometimes claim that their quitting was in some sense coerced, thus constituting a constructive discharge. Absent such a doctrine, employers would be able to avoid liability for unlawful termination by creating working conditions so intolerable as to force the employee to resign. In the context of status discrimination, constructive discharge analysis can be used, for example, to hold employers liable for damages that result when an employee reasonably quits in response to workplace harassment based on a protected characteristic such as race or gender. *See* Chapter 9. The challenge with any allegation of constructive discharge is figuring out whether the employer's conduct was sufficiently severe to justify the employee's resignation. Otherwise, the law deems the employee's departure voluntary. Indeed, such a departure can be a breach of contract by the employee if she is bound by the contract to a longer term.

Under discrimination law, adverse employment actions amounting to a constructive discharge include "a humiliating demotion, extreme cut in pay, or transfer to a position [involving] unbearable working conditions." *Pa. State Police v. Suders*, 542 U.S. 129, 134 (2004). Claims of constructive discharge in cases involving a contract for job security have had mixed success. *Compare Guiliano v. Cleo, Inc.*, 995 S.W.2d 88 (Tenn. 1999) (finding constructive discharge where vice president of marketing was stripped of responsibilities, reassigned to his home, and told to await future assignments, which never came), *with Rubin v. Household Comm. Fin. Servs., Inc.*, 746 N.E.2d 1018, 1028 (Mass. App. Ct. 2001) (no constructive discharge of plaintiff-CEO where management circumvented plaintiff on some financial issues but he retained title and position and management continued to rely on his plaintiff's expertise). Often the determination turns on whether the employer's behavior was itself in breach of the parties' employment agreement. In what way does Speer claim Tropicana breached its contract? How critical is the fact that there were no specific terms in the proposed written agreement dealing with Speer's staff?

Tropicana, of course, was a case in which no document was finally executed. But legal problems can arise even when the parties have signed what purports to be an employment agreement. The next case dramatically illustrates the point while at the same time introducing us to a variety of employment contracts.

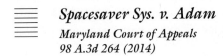

Spacesaver Sys. v. Adam
Maryland Court of Appeals
98 A.3d 264 (2014)

Adkins, J.

Oil and water naturally resist each other. No matter how much one tries, the two cannot be mixed together successfully. As this case demonstrates, the same is often true of family and business. Following a dispute between sibling business partners, we are asked to re-examine the contours of the firmly established doctrine of at-will employment. We do so in order to determine if a written contract containing a for-cause provision, but no definite term of employment, exists as an at-will contract, a lifetime contract, or something else.

Facts and Legal Proceedings

Petitioner, Spacesaver Systems, Inc. ("SSI"), was incorporated in the District of Columbia in 1973 by Jack and Alyce Schmidt. SSI sells and installs mobile storage equipment, including tracked shelving systems, to businesses and governmental organizations with large storage needs. In the 1990's, the Schmidts began transferring ownership of the business to their three children: Carla Adam ("Respondent"), Amy Hamilton ("Hamilton"), and David Craig ("Craig"). As the Schmidts eased out of the business and moved to Florida, the three siblings assumed greater responsibility in the company.

[The governing employment agreements for all three siblings contained a termination for cause provision:]

> 4.2 Termination by the Company For Cause. The Company may, at any time and without notice, terminate the Employee for "cause." Termination by the Company of the Employee for "cause" shall include but not be limited to termination based on any of the following grounds: (a) insubordination or refusal to perform duties of employee's

position as directed by the President of Company and affirmed by a majority vote of the Directors; (b) fraud, misappropriation, embezzlement or acts of similar dishonesty; (c) conviction of a felony involving moral turpitude; (d) illegal use of drugs or excessive use of alcohol in the workplace; (e) intentional and willful misconduct that may subject the Company to criminal or civil liability; (f) breach of the Employee's duty of loyalty, including the diversion or usurpation of corporate opportunities properly belonging to the Company; (g) willful disregard of Company policies and procedures; (h) material breach of any of the terms herein; and (i) material nonperformance or negligence in Employee's performance of her duties.

[The siblings also executed a Stock Purchase Agreement which would compel an employee terminated by SSI to sell her stock to the other shareholders.] Articles 3 and 5 of the Stock Purchase Agreement provide that SSI will redeem the stock in the event of disability or death of a shareholder. Article 4 provides that shareholders can be forced to sell their shares if they engage in "Prohibited Acts." These "Prohibited Acts" generally mirror the for-cause provisions listed in the Employment Agreement.

On October 19, 2006, Adam, Craig, and Hamilton each signed the individual executive employment agreements and stock purchase agreements drafted by Ellentuck. Shortly after the employment agreements were executed, Craig resigned as President and Director of SSI. Pursuant to Adam's Stock Purchase Agreement, Craig's stock was sold equally to Adam and Hamilton, who consequently each held a 50% interest in SSI.

Despite Craig's departure, sibling harmony did not last long, as Hamilton and Adam began to have disputes about their respective job responsibilities and compensation. According to Hamilton, Adam's sales performance was "not very good." Consequently, Adam was removed from the sales force.

On May 28, 2009, Hamilton wrote Adam expressing her intent to acquire Adam's SSI stock, and concluding that Adam's employment was terminated. The conflict reached its apex when, on January 28, 2010, SSI sent Adam a letter terminating her employment. [Adam sued, claiming she was terminated without cause in violation of the agreement.]

Adam filed a Motion for Partial Summary Judgment, contending that the Employment Agreement established that she could only be terminated for cause. SSI [opposed the motion and itself cross-moved for summary judgment], denying that the Employment Agreement guaranteed Adam lifetime employment and asserting that even if the Employment Agreement were so construed, Adam had failed to give "additional consideration" for a lifetime contract.

Following a hearing, the motions court denied both motions for summary judgment on August 19, 2011. The hearing judge found the contract ambiguous, ruling that "extraneous evidence of what the parties intended may be admitted to assist the court in determining the agreement of the parties." After three days of testimony, the trial court ultimately concluded that the Employment Agreement transformed what had previously been an "at-will relationship" to a "lifetime contract," such that Adam could only be terminated for cause, death, or disability. Crucial to the trial court's analysis was that the for-cause provision would be rendered superfluous if the Employment Agreement were construed as at-will. The trial judge rhetorically asked, "why in the world would you have to worry about [cause] if you had an at-will contract?" The trial judge found a breach of the Employment Agreement, and awarded Adam $255,868.20, representing lost salary and commission.

SSI appealed to the Court of Special Appeals [which affirmed in part and reversed in part, and this court granted certiorari] to answer the following questions:

1. Is there any difference between lifetime and "continuous for-cause" contracts?
2. Did the Court of Special Appeals err in applying dicta from *Towson University v. Conte*, 862 A.2d 941 (2004), which suggests that a "just cause" provision transforms at-will employment into lifetime employment terminable only for cause?
3. Does the presence of a for-cause provision, which does not state employment is terminable only for cause, transform at-will employment to lifetime employment terminable only for cause?

As to the second question, we affirm the judgment of the Court of Special Appeals. The first and third questions we shall answer in the course of explaining why this written employment contract is distinct from the alleged "lifetime employment contracts" that we have historically held to be unenforceable.

Standard of Review

"The interpretation of a contract, including the determination of whether a contract is ambiguous, is a question of law, subject to de novo review." Conte. Maryland law dictates the objective interpretation of contracts, which [means that it is "not what the parties to the contract intended it to mean, but what a reasonable person in the position of the parties would have thought it meant."]

Discussion

Petitioner attacks the opinion of the Court of Special Appeals on several grounds. First, Petitioner maintains that when the Employment Agreement is read in conjunction with SSI's Employee Handbook, it is clear that the contract could be terminated with or without cause. SSI highlights that the Employment Agreement's for-cause provision says that SSI "may" terminate for cause. The provision did not say that Adam can "only" be terminated for cause. . . .

Petitioner's most significant argument concerns the distinction that the intermediate appellate court drew between "continuous for-cause" and lifetime contracts. In Petitioner's view, there is no distinction between the two. SSI contends that both are terminable by the employer only for cause and terminable by the employee without cause. SSI alleges that the Court of Special Appeals described Adam's employment with the novel moniker of "continuous for-cause" to escape the requirements to establish a lifetime employment contract.

Expanding on this theme, Petitioner leans on the major presumption under Maryland law that an employment relationship is presumptively at-will unless the parties clearly and expressly set forth their agreement that the contract is to last for a specific period of time. In SSI's view, the lower court failed to apply the heightened standard applicable to lifetime contracts, making no finding that SSI's intent to provide lifetime employment was specific, definite, and unequivocal. Moreover, Petitioner argues that Adam failed to provide the "special consideration" required to support such a contract. In sum, Petitioner contends that, instead of addressing the various issues surrounding lifetime employment contracts, the Court of Specials Appeals simply created an "evil twin" and said "it is a for-cause contract that is of continuous duration, but it is not a lifetime contract."

Finally, and in a similar vein, Petitioner argues that the Court of Special Appeals ignored a strong precept of Maryland law that the at-will doctrine invariably applies when an employment contract is of an indefinite duration. Specifically, SSI posits that the intermediate appellate court has wrongly elevated dicta to law by holding that under *Conte*, the inclusion of a for-cause provision transforms an at-will contract to a for-cause contract. In SSI's view, this directly contravenes our previous holding in *Suburban Hospital, Inc. v. Dwiggins*, 596 A.2d 1069 (Md. 1991), that an employment contract of indefinite duration is employment at-will, even if it states some bases giving the employer cause for termination. In this respect, SSI contends that this holding erodes the doctrine of lifetime employment.

In reply, Respondent urges us to affirm the Court of Special Appeals. Rather than responding directly to each of Petitioner's arguments, Respondent lays out a number of propositions that, in her view, compel the affirmance of the Court of Special Appeals. First, Respondent alleges that the Employment Agreement is not an unambiguous at-will contract. She underscores that two lower courts have rejected the contract as unambiguously at-will based on the rationale that a for-cause provision is inconsistent with an at-will contract. In her view, the very terms of the Employment Agreement establish that it is not an at-will agreement. Similarly, Respondent rejects any applicability of the SSI Employee Handbook, observing that the Employment Agreement itself explicitly states that it will trump the provisions of the Handbook.

Respondent similarly rejects the relevance of "special consideration." Respondent states that no Maryland authority supports the position that "special consideration" is necessary to establish a contract such as this one. Adam avers that, although some jurisdictions require that lifetime contracts be supported by "special consideration," we are dealing with a "continuous for-cause" contract, not a lifetime contract. . . .

Presumption of At-Will Employment

We begin by laying out the fundamentals of Maryland employment law. Our starting place is one of our most venerated common law precepts, the employment at-will doctrine. . . . [The court traced the at-will rule in Maryland precedents, stressing that it "reflects the courts' concern with promoting freedom of contract and fundamental fairness." It quoted SAMUEL WILLISTON & RICHARD A. LORD, A TREATISE ON THE LAW OF CONTRACTS, §54:39 (4th ed. 2001):]

> [T]he courts have shown a marked reluctance to enforce contracts for life employment. In large part, this stems from the realization that such contracts frequently are, in practical effect, unilateral undertakings by the employer to provide a job for so long as the employee wishes to continue in it but impose no corresponding obligation upon the employee. When this is the case, the burden of performance is unequal, as the employer appears to be bound to the terms of the contract, while the employee is free to terminate it at will. Accordingly, it has been said:

> An employee is never presumed to engage his services permanently, thereby cutting himself off from all chances of improving his condition; indeed, in this land of opportunity it would be against public policy and the spirit of our institutions that any man should thus handicap himself; and the law will presume . . . that he did not so intend. And if the contract of employment be not binding on the employee for the whole term of such employment, then it cannot be binding upon the employer; there would be lack of "mutuality"

Yet we observe that presumptions can only act as an aid to interpreting a contract, not as a substantive limit on parties' ability to contract. . . .

Indeed the presumption of at-will employment can be defeated through the inclusion of a just-cause requirement, or by specifying a duration of employment:

> While the language of the contract itself may express a just cause requirement, a contractual delineation of the length of the employment period will also create a just cause employment relationship because by specifying the length or term of employment, the employer usually is considered to have surrendered its ability to terminate the employee at its discretion.

Conte.

One type of for-cause employment is lifetime employment. We discussed lifetime employment at length in *Chesapeake & Potomac Telephone Co. of Baltimore City v. Murray*, 84 A.2d 870 (1951). "[A] contract for permanent or life employment is valid and continues to operate as long as the employer remains in the business and has work for the employee and the employee is able and willing to do his work satisfactorily and does not give good cause for his discharge." We declared, however, that those claiming a lifetime employment contract faced an uphill climb.

First, the law protects stockholders' ability to alter a corporation's management by electing boards of directors. Recognizing that the directors' authority would be hollow if corporate officers were able to grant "persons of their selection employment for life," we stated that one hurdle to lifetime contacts is "proof that there was definite authority, by by-law, action by the board of directors, or otherwise, to make such a contract."

Second, a lifetime employment contract must be supported by consideration beyond that incident to accepting the position. *See id; see also Page v. Carolina Coach Co.*, 667 F.2d 1156, 1158 (4th Cir. 1982) (holding that relinquishing a job and benefits to assume a new position was not sufficient consideration for lifetime employment).

Third, a lifetime employment contract must clearly stipulate the "terms as to work and salary" in order to be enforceable. *Murray; see also Balt. & Ohio R. Co. v. King*, 176 A. 626, 628 (Md. 1935) (holding that lifetime contracts "at least should be specific and definite, with little or no room for misunderstanding, even if they are not required to be in writing"); *Yost v. Early*, 589 A.2d 1291, 1300-01 (Md. App. 1991) (reaffirming that an alleged oral lifetime employment contract was only employment at-will because there was no showing that it clearly expressed the specific terms of the agreement, including duties, wages, and performance guidelines).

Before evaluating the Employment Agreement, we observe that our primary inquiry concerns whether the contract created at-will or for-cause employment. For our purposes here, employment contracts can be broken into three categories, those with: (i) specific temporal duration, terminable before the expiration only for cause; (ii) no specified temporal duration, but containing a clear for-cause termination provision; and (iii) no temporal duration, and no for-cause termination provision, which are terminable at will. Placing the Employment Agreement in one of these three categories will determine the resolution of this controversy, as Adam has no cause of action sounding in breach of her employment contract if she fits in the third category, at-will employment.

Nature of the Employment Agreement

"Our analysis begins, as it should, with the language of the employment contract at issue." *Conte.* Under the objective interpretation of contracts, we focus upon whether a reasonable person, in the parties' position, would have thought that the contract provided any measure of job security. "Under the objective view, a written contract is ambiguous if, when read by a reasonably prudent person, it is susceptible of more than one meaning." *Calomiris* [*v. Woods*, 727 A.2d 358, 363 (Md. 1999)] (citation omitted). . . .

Although the Employment Agreement is silent as to its duration, which can signify at-will employment, it also contains a for-cause provision, which negates an at-will employment contract. *Conte* is instructive on this point. After evaluating Dr. Conte's employment contract, which had a for-cause provision similar to Adam's and a definite durational term, we held that the contract "makes clear that Dr. Conte was not an 'at-will' employee." *Conte.* We also held that the university could not avail itself of the protections afforded employers who terminate at-will employees. *Id.*

Of special import here, the *Conte* Court also opined that either a for-cause provision or "a contractual delineation of the length of the employment period" will *independently* establish that an employee was not at-will. *Id.* Petitioner characterizes this pronouncement as dicta that is at odds with *Dwiggins.* We agree that it was dicta, but feel secure in embracing it here. Indeed, *Conte* finds support from a number of other jurisdictions that have adopted a similar rule. *See Gladden v. Ark. Children's Hosp.*, 728 S.W.2d 501, 505 (Ark. 1987) ("[W]e reject as outmoded and untenable [the view] that the at will rule applies even where the employment agreement contains a provision that the employee will not be discharged except for cause, unless it is for a definite term."); *Dillman v. N.H. College*, 838 A.2d 1274, 1276 (N.H. 2003) ("Where, however, an employment agreement specifies a definite term, it is generally implied that the employee can be discharged only for cause.").

We disagree with Petitioner's claim that the rule from *Conte* that we embrace here is in any way contradicted by *Dwiggins.* In *Dwiggins*, an employee was suspended for violating rules set by his employer. He was reinstated but placed on probation and required to sign a document with very specific performance conditions. After violating the terms of this probation, he was terminated, but then brought suit claiming that he was no longer an at-will employee. The Court held that the reinstatement agreement that the parties signed to resolve the employee's disciplinary action and govern his probationary status would not convert an at-will employment agreement into a for-cause agreement. Thus, *Dwiggins* involved performance conditions with which an employee must comply to maintain satisfactory probationary status under a *reinstatement agreement.* This is fundamentally distinct from an employee who, free from probationary status, contracts the terms under which her employer will have cause to terminate her employment in an *employment agreement*. Thus, we find no reason to hesitate in relying on the dictum in *Conte* to support our conclusion that the for-cause termination clause in the Employment Agreement removed it from the category of at-will employment.

This conclusion is consonant with the position of the parties at the time that the contract was executed. We emphasize that each of the three siblings owned one-third of SSI and also served as a high-level executive. Moreover, they each signed a Stock Purchase Agreement allowing the corporation to acquire their shares at a reduced value if their employment were terminated. A reasonable person in that position could only have thought that the language of the for-cause provision would be operative and provide for the job security stated by its terms. Thus, the only legitimate interpretation of the plain language of the Employment Agreement is that the parties reasonably expected and mutually assented to some degree of job security. This is in contrast to other situations in which the employee has no reasonable expectation of job security.

Yet the conclusion that Adam's Employment Agreement was for-cause, on its own, would leave one key issue unaddressed. As described above, Adam's Employment Agreement did not provide a specific term of employment. Significantly, Section 2.1 of the Employment Agreement referenced an "Exhibit A" that would set forth Adam's salary "for years beyond the first year" of employment, but this exhibit was never created. In other words, SSI had the option of setting a definite term for Adam's employment but chose not to. Thus, the Court is presented with a for-cause contract with an indefinite durational term. Petitioner argues that such a contract must be characterized as providing for lifetime employment and, consequently, tested against the three requirements for a lifetime contract. We move to this contention now.

"Continuous For-Cause" v. Lifetime Contracts . . .

The Court of Special Appeals then described these contracts as "essentially continuous for-cause contracts that remain in effect until the employee is removed for cause, or until the employee is no longer 'competent to discharge the duties of the office or efficient in the performance of them.'" *Spacesaver*. In this sense, the intermediate appellate court held "continuous for-cause" contracts to be distinct from at-will, satisfaction,[10] and lifetime employment contracts. . . .

---

10. A "satisfaction contract" is one "in which the employer, notwithstanding the inclusion of a durational term of employment, expressly reserves the right to terminate if it deems the employee's performance unsatisfactory." *Conte*. As we explained in *Ferris v. Polansky*:

> In a contract where the employer agrees to employ another as long as the services are satisfactory, the employer has the right to terminate the contract and discharge the employee, whenever he, the employer, acting in good faith is actually dissatisfied with the employee's work. This applies, even though the parties to the employment contract have stipulated that the contract shall be operative during a definite term, if it provides that the services are to be performed to the satisfaction of the employer.

59 A.2d 749, 752 (Md. 1948). We agree with the Court of Special Appeals' observation that a satisfaction contract without a durational term of employment is distinct from a lifetime employment contract terminable for cause. In our view, the intermediate appellate court properly stated that under Maryland law, a trial court will evaluate an employer's objective motivation for termination of a lifetime contract, whereas under a satisfaction contract, the jury must focus on the employer's subjective motivation for termination.

As both a legal and terminological matter, "continuous for-cause" better describes the nature of Adam's Employment Agreement than the term, "lifetime contract." This Court has previously expressed its assumption that even a so-called "lifetime contract" only "continues to operate as long as the employer remains in the business and has work for the employee and the employee is able and willing to do his work satisfactorily and does not give good cause for his discharge." *Murray.* The same is true of Adam's contract. Surely, Adam's continued employment depended on, in addition to her compliance with the for-cause provisions listed in the Employment Agreement, the continued success of SSI's current business and its resulting need for Adam's services.[11] We see that, to some extent, the so-called "lifetime contract" and "continuous for-cause" contract are similar, and do overlap.

Yet in significant respects, Adam's Employment Agreement is distinct from the alleged "lifetime employment" that was generally rejected by this Court.[12] The cases in which this Court has wrestled with alleged lifetime employment have arisen from lower-level employees' allegations that someone higher up in a company had given an oral representation that they would have a job "for life." *See, e.g., Pullman Co. v. Ray*, 94 A.2d 266, 267 (Md. 1953) (alleged oral promise of lifetime employment in exchange for forbearance from suit); *Murray* (alleged oral promise of lifetime employment in exchange for refraining from selling to previous customers for commissions). These cases support the proposition that alleged oral contracts for continued employment stand on weaker ground than written contracts. Indeed, although a Maryland appellate case has expressly contemplated the potential that oral representations could support a "lifetime contract," we have found no Maryland cases actually upholding such alleged oral contracts. . . .

[Because such promises may be "nothing more than a casual aside" or "purely aspirational,"] we have held allegations of lifetime employment subject to a requirement of definiteness.

But unlike those cases involving alleged lifetime agreements, in which the lack of definiteness and "verifiability" inherent in oral representations justified a court's skepticism, Adam's Employment Agreement contained an express for-cause provision *in writing*. This provision, in concert with SSI's failure to specify a term of employment on "Exhibit A," cannot but be read to imply a continued period of employment. The Agreement's operative terms are expressed—or in the case of the employment's durational term, omitted—definitively. Therefore, the concerns over its accuracy, probability, and provenance are not present. The contract is clear, as is the fact that the parties assented to it. In this context, we refrain from imposing the additional requirement of special consideration, which evolved from a line of lifetime employment cases, to contracts of a "continuous for-cause" nature.[15]

---

11. Surely SSI could change the nature of its business in a way that rendered Adam's services superfluous, and therefore her employment would end. This would have to be done in good faith, for a legitimate business reason, and not with the motivating intent to rid the company of her services.

12. Testimony at the trial court indicated that at least two of the siblings envisioned a lifetime tenure when they signed the Employment Agreement. Under the objective interpretation of contracts, the court will only look at extrinsic evidence if the contract is found to be ambiguous, a finding that, as we discuss *infra*, we disclaim here. *See Sy-Lene of Wash., Inc. v. Starwood Urban Retail II, LLC*, 829 A.2d 540, 544 (Md. 2003).

15. [In some cases, such contracts may raise "concerns over corporate authority to execute" such a contact, but that "concern is not present here" given that all shareholders and directors consented.]

In drawing a distinction between lifetime and "continuous for-cause" contracts, we follow a path laid by other courts. . . . In so holding, we signal no retreat from our recognition and veneration of the employment at-will doctrine. This judgment in no way erodes that doctrine, as the presumption for at-will employment persists and is only defeated when the parties explicitly negotiate and provide for a definite term of employment or a clear for-cause provision. We emphasize that in this case, SSI's corporate attorney could easily have kept Adam's employment at-will by inserting an at-will provision in the Employment Agreement, or making sure that no for-cause provision made its way into the contract.

We also reject any contention that the Employee Handbook should change our decision. The Employment Agreement states that SSI's Employee Handbook governs "to the extent not described in this Employment Agreement[.]" It further states that "[i]n the event of a conflict between this Employment Agreement and the employees' handbook or existing practices, the terms of this agreement shall govern." We reject any argument that the two documents, read together, make clear that the contract could be terminated *either* with or without cause. It would defy the plain language of the Employment Agreement to hold otherwise.

The same can be said for Petitioner's argument that if the for-cause provision were meant to carry so much weight, the Employment Agreement would have authorized termination "only" for cause. The parties do not cite, and the Court has not found, any case holding that the inclusion of "may" in a for-cause provision defeats the purpose of that provision. This argument logically fails, and the trial court was right to reject it. . . .

NOTES

1. *At-Will and Satisfaction Contracts.* The *Spacesaver* court identifies and discusses a bewildering number of potential employment contracts. Least protective of employees is the at-will arrangement, which we've met before. But, at the risk of repetition, note that these are not just one kind of employment contract: They are *the* presumptive agreement unless sufficiently clear language creates something stronger.

Slightly more protective of employees are "satisfaction" agreements. Courts vary in their interpretation of such agreements, but they are generally understood to provide less job security than a just-cause agreement. *See, e.g., Silvestri v. Optus Software, Inc.*, 814 A.2d 602, 607-08 (N.J. 2003) (subjective assessment of employer satisfaction applies where contract preserved right to terminate). According to footnote 10, in Maryland at least, an agreement providing for job security as long as the employer is "satisfied" with the employee's performance allows for review of "the employer's *subjective* motivation" for termination rather than the objective basis. However, unlike the *Spacesaver* court's focus on subjective motivation, some contracts speak of "reasonable satisfaction." *See, e.g., McKnight v. Simpson's Beauty Supply, Inc.*, 358 S.E.2d 107 (N.C. Ct. App. 1987) ("reasonable satisfaction" provision not satisfied by unreasonable or capricious demands, but only for not performing in a reasonably diligent and effective manner).

2. *Durational or Term Contracts.* From the employee's perspective, a satisfaction contract is better than at-will, but maybe not by much. If you represented an employee, what's the next stage of protection? That's not so clear. You could try to negotiate what *Spacesaver* calls a durational contract, sometimes called a contract for a term. That provides great protection but only for the specified duration since, as the court suggests, it is generally understood that an employee with a fixed-term contract can only be terminated for "just cause." *See, e.g., Sarvis v. Vermont State Colleges,* 772 A.2d 494, 497 (Vt. 2001). This is consistent with the contract principle of material breach: If an individual does not perform at all or performs so poorly that she is in material breach of her duties as an employee, then the employer is excused from performing its end of the bargain and may terminate the agreement. In the next section, we will take up the question what constitutes "just cause" or performance sufficient to constitute material breach. For now, it is important to know that even a fixed-term contract is not an absolute guarantee of employment, but the protection it provides during the term is fairly robust.

3. *How Long a Duration?* Employees have strong protection during the term of a durational contract, but the length of the term is obviously critical. So a ten-year contract is very protective; a ten-week one not so much. This reality gives rise to an oddity to the uninitiated: contracts that describe themselves as, say, five-year employment contracts but which provide either party the right to terminate on, say, a month's notice. In any meaningful sense, these are one-month durational contracts. *See Cave Hill Corporation v. Hiers,* 570 S.E.2d 790 (Va. 2002). The remedy for an employer's discharge without giving the specified notice is damages equal to the compensation that would have been paid during the notice period. *See, e.g., Shivers v. John H. Harland Co.,* 423 S.E.2d 105, 107 (S.C. 1992).

4. *Rate-of-Pay Recitals.* A recurring question is whether the inclusion of a compensation period, such as an annual salary term, in an offer letter or other document indicates an intention that employment will endure for at least the length of the pay period. According to the traditional British rule, a hiring at a stated price per week, month, or year is presumed to be a hiring for the named time period. Under the modern American rule, however, a stated term of compensation does not in itself defeat the presumption that employment is at will. *See, e.g., Thomas v. Ballou-Latimer Drug Co.,* 442 P.2d 747, 751 (Idaho 1968). (*But see* GA. CODE ANN. §34-7-1 (2017) ("If a contract of employment provides that wages are payable at a stipulated period, the presumption shall arise that the hiring is for such period.") Of course, that presumption, like the at-will presumption itself, can always be rebutted. *See, e.g., Carriker v. Am. Postal Workers Union,* No. 13900, 1993 WL 385807 (Ohio Ct. App. Sept. 30, 1993) (finding that, while contract containing annual pay rate is presumed to be at will, such a term coupled with a provision for periodic pay increases created ambiguity as to duration of contract to justify admission of additional evidence regarding parties' intent).

5. *Just Cause and Lifetime Contracts.* Even more protective than durational contracts are contracts guaranteeing a position unless there is just cause to discharge (and the contract might define just cause very narrowly to maximize protection). Look at the language in Spacesaver's Employment Agreement. The qualifying conduct is pretty extreme. Does that mean that an employee has a right to lifetime employment (absent just cause)? *Spacesaver* says no: Continuous for-cause contracts are not contracts for lifetime employment, terminable for cause." But that's not because an employer's business might not change "in a way that rendered Adam's services superfluous." *See* footnote 11. That might happen and be a legitimate reason for termination—which would be true under either a lifetime contract or a "continuous for-cause" contract. And while Ms. Adam has a continuous for-cause agreement, she doesn't have a lifetime contract. Why isn't that the same thing? The answer for the court seems to lie in the unreliability of most alleged agreements for lifetime employment. The *Spacesaver* court worries about the informality of the usual claim and thus requires definiteness and, maybe, additional consideration. Recall that we ran into the additional consideration question before. *See* Chapter 2 at pages 84-85.

By the way, continuous for-cause contracts, like the one found in *Spacesaver,* are not as uncommon as you might think. Academic tenure in private educational institutions can be viewed as exactly that. Such arrangements, though sometimes described as such, are not promises of lifetime employment, because the teacher can typically be discharged not only for performance problems but also for programmatic reasons. Tenure in public schools and public colleges and universities is more often a creature of statute but tends to adopt the same type of approach.

6. *The Parol Evidence Rule.* There was a trial in *Spacesaver* because the contract was ambiguous as to job security. That seems questionable. As the trial judge said, "Why in the world would you have to worry about [cause] if you had an at-will contract?" But the finding of ambiguity created the necessity for a trial to determine the meaning of the agreement: If the contract is susceptible of only one meaning, the court should so interpret it. When a contract is ambiguous, however, a court can look to "extrinsic evidence" to decide the correct interpretation. That's exactly what happened here, with extensive testimony as to what the parties thought the contract meant. But consideration of such evidence for interpretive purposes is permissible *only* when the contract is ambiguous. *See also Cruz v. Visual Perceptions, LLC,* 84 A.3d 828, 835 (Conn. 2014) (since letter agreement "reasonably may be interpreted as evincing either an intent to create a definite term of employment or an intent to set the terms and conditions of an at-will employment contract," parol evidence should be admitted at trial to resolve the ambiguity). *Cf. Dore v. Arnold Worldwide,* 139 P.3d 56, 58 (Cal. 2006) (provision that "your employment with Arnold Communications, Inc. is at will. This simply means that Arnold Communications has the right to terminate your employment at any time . . ." was not ambiguous, despite separate clause speaking of a 90-day assessment period). *Accord Cave Hill Corporation v. Hiers,* 570 S.E.2d 790 (Va. 2002) (a contract not ambiguous when, despite a stated term of five years, it also expressly provided that either party could terminate it upon 30-days' notice).

You'll recall from your first-year Contracts class that evidence of prior or contemporaneous oral or even written negotiations is inadmissible to alter, contradict, or explain the terms of a written instrument provided the document is complete, unambiguous, and unconditional. *Id.* at 794. But one of the subtler aspects of parol evidence is that courts must determine whether a written agreement is fully or partially "integrated" (that is, final) before deciding what, if any, parol evidence can be admitted. If an agreement is "completely integrated," no parol evidence may be admitted other than for interpretation; but if the agreement is only "partially integrated," evidence may be admitted to supplement the agreement. In no case, however, may parol evidence be used to contradict the written terms. *See generally* RESTATEMENT (SECOND) OF CONTRACTS §213 (ALI 1981). We will explore the contours of the parol evidence rule again in the next case.

7. *Individual Contracts and Employee Handbooks.* We met employee handbooks as possible contracts in Chapter 2. As you might guess, whatever contractual rights such handbooks might or might not create tend to be trumped by individual contracts, and that was true in *Spacesaver.* Note particularly its Employee Handbook, which indicates that employment with Spacesaver is at will; that is, it has no effect. In the case itself that is because the handbook had a disclaimer of contractual effects. And note the court's skepticism about such sources of rights to begin with. *See* footnote 16. But even if it were framed to contractually make all employees at will, wouldn't it be trumped by a subsequent individual contract? But what if such a disclaimer were signed *after* the individual contract? In thinking about these questions, recall again from your Contracts class that parol evidence is admissible to establish a later modification of a contractual relationship, even if the original agreement was fully integrated at the time at which it was entered.

≡ *Hinkel v. Sataria Distrib. & Packaging, Inc.*
920 N.E.2d 766 (Ind. Ct. App. 2010)

VAIDIK, J:

The appellant, Mark Hinkel, was hired to work for the appellee, Sataria Distribution and Packaging, Inc. ("Sataria"). Hinkel was allegedly promised a year's worth of salary and insurance coverage if he were ever terminated involuntarily, but his written employment contract did not provide for severance pay or post-employment benefits. Hinkel was soon terminated, and he did not receive the severance package he says he was promised. Hinkel sued for breach of contract and/or promissory estoppel. The trial court entered summary judgment in favor of Sataria. We hold that (1) Hinkel's written employment contract is a completely integrated agreement which precludes consideration of any prior or contemporaneous oral promises, (2) to the extent the severance agreements were made after the execution of the written contract, they were not supported by additional consideration, and (3) Hinkel is unable to sustain his claim of promissory estoppel. We affirm.

Facts and Procedural History

Hinkel was employed by Refractory Engineers, Inc. and Ceramic Technology, Inc. John Jacobs was the owner of Sataria. In late August or September 2005, Hinkel and Jacobs met to discuss working together. Jacobs offered Hinkel a job at Sataria. Hinkel had reservations. Jacobs told him, "Mark, are you worried that I'll f*** you? If so, and things don't work, I'll pay you one (1) year's salary and cover your insurance for the one (1) year as well. But let me make it clear, should you decide this is not for you, and you terminate your own employment, then the agreement is off." Jacobs later sent Hinkel the following written job offer:

Dear Mark,
This is written as an offer of employment. The terms are as described below:

1.	Annual Compensation:	$120,000
2.	Work Location:	Belmont Facility
3.	Initial Position:	Supervisor Receiving Team
4.	Start Date:	08/19/2005
5.	Paid Vacation:	To be determined
6.	Health Insurance:	Coverage begins 09/01/2005 pending proper Enrollment submission

Please sign and return.

Hinkel signed the offer and resigned from his other employers. He began working at Sataria in September 2005. According to Hinkel, Jacobs reiterated the severance promise again in November 2005 and December 2005.

Sataria terminated Hinkel's employment involuntarily on January 23, 2006. Sataria paid Hinkel six weeks of severance thereafter. Hinkel brought this action for breach of contract and/or promissory estoppel against Sataria. He claimed that Sataria owed him the severance package that Jacobs promised. Sataria moved for summary judgment. The trial court granted Sataria's motion. Hinkel now appeals. . . .

I. Breach of Contract Claim

According to Hinkel, Jacobs orally promised him a year's salary and insurance coverage if he were ever involuntarily terminated. Sataria argues that any alleged oral promises are barred from consideration by the parol evidence rule.

The parol evidence rule provides that "[w]hen two parties have made a contract and have expressed it in a writing to which they have both assented as the complete and accurate integration of that contract, evidence . . . of antecedent understandings and negotiations will not be admitted for the purpose of varying or contradicting the writing." *Dicen v. New Sesco, Inc.*, 839 N.E.2d 684, 688 (Ind. 2005) (quoting 6 Arthur Linton Corbin, Corbin on Contracts §573 (2002 reprint)) (emphasis removed). This rule "effectuates a presumption that a subsequent written contract is of a higher nature than earlier statements, negotiations, or oral agreements by deeming those earlier expressions to be merged in to or superseded by the written document." 11 Richard A. Lord, Williston on Contracts §33:1 (4th ed. 1999) (footnote omitted).

The first step when applying the parol evidence rule is determining whether the parties' written contract represents a complete or partial integration of their agreement. *See* Restatement (Second) of Contracts §§209, 210 (1981). If the contract is completely integrated, constituting a final and complete expression of all the parties' agreements, then evidence of prior or contemporaneous written or oral statements and negotiations cannot operate to either add to or contradict the written contract. *Franklin v. White*, 493 N.E.2d 161, 167 (Ind. 1986). The preliminary question of integration, either complete or partial, requires the court to hear all relevant evidence, parol or written. *Id.* "Whether a writing has been adopted as an integrated agreement is a question of fact to be determined in accordance with all relevant evidence." Restatement (Second) of Contracts §§209 cmt. c. Nevertheless, what is ordinarily a question of fact may become a question of law "where the facts are undisputed and only a single inference can be drawn from those facts." *Jones v. Ind. Bell Tel. Co.*, 864 N.E.2d 1125, 1127 (Ind. Ct. App. 2007) (breach of duty). "[T]he absence of an integration clause is not conclusive as to whether parties intend a writing to be completely integrated." *Sees v. Bank One, Ind., N.A.*, 839 N.E.2d 154, 163 n.7 (Ind. 2005) (Boehm, J., concurring and dissenting) (citing Restatement (Second) of Contracts §209 cmt. b).

In addition,

> The test of [parol evidence] admissibility is much affected by the inherent likelihood that parties who contract under the circumstances in question would simultaneously make both the agreement in writing which is before the court, and also the alleged

parol agreement. The point is not merely whether the court is convinced that the parties before it did in fact do this, but whether reasonable parties so situated naturally would or might obviously or normally do so. . . . The vast majority of courts assessing the admissibility of parol evidence at common law apply this test. . . .

11 *Williston on Contracts* §33:25 (footnotes omitted).

Here, Jacobs and Hinkel negotiated the terms of Hinkel's employment before completing their written contract. Jacobs allegedly promised Hinkel that he would receive one year of salary and benefits if he were ever terminated involuntarily. The parties then executed their written agreement. The written employment offer specified Hinkel's compensation, work location, title, start date, and the date on which his insurance coverage would begin. It did not provide that Hinkel would receive severance pay or benefits following termination. Hinkel signed the letter and began working at Sataria. In light of all the relevant evidence, we find as a matter of law that Hinkel's contract represented a complete integration of the parties' employment agreement. Jacobs allegedly promised Hinkel a severance package, but the written contract enumerates both compensation and insurance coverage while saying nothing of post-employment salary and/or benefits. The offer leaves one term to be decided—paid vacation—but the contract imports on its face to be a complete expression with respect to salary and insurance. And since a lucrative severance provision would "naturally and normally" be included in an employment contract, its glaring omission here further supports the conclusion that Hinkel's written contract superseded any alleged prior oral promises. We hold that the written contract constituted a final representation of the parties' agreement, and any contemporaneous oral agreements that the parties made as to severance are not subject to interpretation.

To the extent Jacobs may have promised Hinkel a severance package after their written contract was executed, an additional question is whether Jacobs's promise could have constituted a valid contract modification. "The modification of a contract, since it is also a contract, requires all the requisite elements of a contract." *Hamlin v. Steward*, 622 N.E.2d 535, 539 (Ind. Ct. App. 1993). "A written agreement may be changed by a subsequent one orally made, upon a sufficient consideration." *Id.* . . .

Here, if Jacobs promised Hinkel a severance package after the written employment contract was executed, there is no evidence that Hinkel provided additional consideration in exchange for the promise. Hinkel argues that he had to agree "to continue working for Sataria" and "to not *voluntarily* resign his employment." But Hinkel had assumed those duties and employment obligations as consideration for the original agreement. Any subsequent promise by Jacobs respecting severance was not supported by an independent, bargained-for exchange. Accordingly, Jacobs's alleged oral promises could not have constituted valid modifications of Hinkel's employment contract. . . .

II. Promissory Estoppel Claim

[The court rejected any promissory estoppel claim because, even if Hinkel gave up his prior employment, he "was provided with a period of employment at Sataria, a substantial salary, and six weeks of severance. Hinkel has not shown an injury so independent and severe that injustice could only be avoided by enforcement of Jacobs's alleged promise."]

RILEY, J., concurs.

CRONE, Judge, dissenting.

I respectfully dissent because I disagree with the majority's conclusion that Jacobs's oral promise to Hinkel regarding a severance package is "barred from consideration by the parol evidence rule." I do so for two reasons. First, I believe that a genuine issue of material fact exists regarding whether the parties intended for Jacobs's written job offer to Hinkel to be completely integrated, i.e., a "final and complete expression of *all* the parties' agreements[.]" (Emphasis added.)[1] Although not conclusive, the offer—a one-page document with six bullet points for a position paying $120,000 per year—does not contain an integration clause. More persuasive is its statement that Hinkel's vacation terms were yet to be determined, which indicates to me that the parties had not yet reached agreement on that issue. Based on the foregoing, a factfinder reasonably could conclude that the offer is more akin to a memorandum of understanding and represents only a partial integration of the parties' agreements, and that therefore the parol evidence rule would not apply to bar consideration of Jacobs's oral promise regarding the severance package.

Second, the terms of the severance package do not vary from or contradict the terms of the written offer, but merely cover that which was not covered in the offer. As such, even assuming that the offer is completely integrated, the terms of the severance package would not be barred by the parol evidence rule. *See Malo v. Gilman*, 379 N.E.2d 554, 557 and note 5 (Ind. App. 1978) ("[P]arol evidence may be admitted to supply an omission in the terms of the contract. . . . Using parol evidence to supply an omission will not modify the written agreement, but merely adds to it."). Therefore, I would reverse the trial court's grant of summary judgment in favor of Sataria and remand for further proceedings.

NOTES

1. *Complete vs. Partial Integration.* Students are often confused as to what it means for a term (or a contract) to be "integrated." The answer is almost tautological: It means that the parties have agreed that the writing reflects their final agreement—on that term (if partial) or the entire contract (if complete). The *Hinkel* court is certainly correct that, if the contract is a complete integration, no parol evidence can be admitted to add to it. If it is a partial integration, parol evidence may supplement but not contradict the writing; in other words, the alleged agreement must be "consistent" with the writing. As we have seen, in either case parol evidence may be introduced to clarify an ambiguity—once the court determines that the writing is ambiguous.

The trick, of course, is how to figure out whether a writing is integrated. Does it make any sense to think that the document in *Hinkel* is completely integrated? Aren't there a hundred things the parties might have agreed to that are not reflected in the sketchy offer? For example, work hours, work week, office, expense account, 401(k)?

---

1. The majority concedes that the offer "leaves one term to be decided" but paradoxically concludes that it "constituted a final representation of the parties' agreement[.]" I fail to see how a contract can be completely integrated if it expressly defers agreement on a particular issue.

Some courts have been much more sympathetic to claims that contracts are at most partially integrated. *See Esbensen v. Userware International, Inc.,* 14 Cal. Rptr. 2d 93 (Ct. App. 1992) (the written document was only a partial integration in light both of the absence of either a merger clause or any provision for termination).

2. *Consistent Collateral Agreement.* Having decided that the contract was a complete integration, the *Hinkel* majority's work was basically done: No parol evidence was admissible even to supplement the writing. In *Esbensen,* by contrast, having found the agreement was not completely integrated, the court had to go on to decide whether the oral agreement was consistent with the partial integration. Again, that is because an oral agreement that contradicts even a partially integrated writing is not admissible, and the defendant argued that a promise of renewal was inconsistent with the provision for a one-year term. The court disagreed since the promise of renewal could be interpreted to mean that the parties were "obligated to negotiate in good faith at the end of each year toward the goal of renewal on mutually acceptable terms." 14 Cal. Rptr. 2d at 98. Such a promise would not contradict the one-year term. Do you agree? Or is this stretching to avoid finding an inconsistency?

3. *The "Naturally Excluded" Test.* Finding the relevant document to be a complete integration often will be outcome determinative. Most, but not all, courts use the same test, asking whether the oral understanding sought to be admitted might "naturally" have been excluded from the written contract. This approach, sometimes referred to as the "modern" or "California" approach to parol evidence, tends to favor the admission of extrinsic evidence that stricter approaches would exclude. It is to be contrasted with the "four corners" test, under which a court looks to see if the writing *appears* to be complete. *See Kay v. Prolix Packaging, Inc.,* 993 N.E.2d 39, 52 (Ill. App. 2013) ("Looking at the four corners of the instrument reveals whether or not it is fully integrated."). As *Hinkel* makes clear, however, even the more liberal test is not a slam dunk for the party seeking to have the court consider parol evidence.

4. *An Integration Clause to the Rescue?* The more detailed the contract, the more likely that an omitted term will be found to be inconsistent with one or more provisions. But asking that every employment contract reduce almost everything to writing may be asking too much. An obvious safeguard is for the parties to include an integration clause (sometimes called a merger clause) to the effect that the written document supersedes all other understandings. While such clauses do not necessarily preclude parol evidence, they are usually effective in doing so.

5. *Prior or Contemporaneous Evidence.* An important limitation on the parol evidence rule is that it bars evidence only of agreements or actions prior to or contemporaneous with the execution of the written contract. It has no application to subsequent agreements, which are admissible to show the parties modified their written agreement. That's why the *Hinkel* court had to consider the significance of promises supposedly made after the contract had been signed. As that decision indicates, however, while subsequent statements are not barred by the parol evidence rule, employees face a separate set of obstacles when trying to prove that such a statement modified a written contract. For instance, as in *Hinkel,* contract formation rules generally require that modifications be supported by consideration. Further, the statute of frauds may apply to modified agreements not capable of being performed within one year.

6. *Backfiring Integration Clauses.* As discussed in Chapter 2, employers often place disclaimers of contractual rights or recitals of employees' at-will status in the personnel documents they use in the workplace. Such documents are frequently effective to foreclose suits based on prior oral assurances about job security or other terms of employment. This is a pretty straightforward operation of the parol evidence rule. While such documents have obvious disadvantages for employees who lose the benefit of any bargain struck orally, such provisions have sometimes backfired on employers. For example, employers often require applicants for employment to agree to arbitration should a dispute arise. While that agreement might be perfectly enforceable when signed, a later agreement that doesn't mention arbitration and has an integration clause may well negate it. *See Grey v. American Management Services*, 139 Cal. Rptr. 3d 210, 214 (Cal. App. 2012). *But see Pelletier v. Yellow Transportation, Inc.*, 549 F.3d 578 (1st Cir. 2008) (finding an arbitration agreement signed at the same time as an employment application with a merger clause barring "contemporaneous agreements" to nevertheless be consistent). *See also MAPEI Corp. v. Prosser*, 761 S.E.2d 500 (Ga. Ct. App. 2014) (a second agreement omitting a non-compete clause superseded an agreement containing such a clause signed only a week earlier when it had a merger clause so providing). *See generally* Charles A. Sullivan, *Man Bites Dog: The Parol Evidence Rule as the Employee's Friend?*, http://lawprofessors.typepad.com/laborprof_blog/2009/02/sullivan-on-the.html.

7. *The Value of an Imperfect Writing.* Many employment agreements are pretty sketchy (maybe in both senses of the term!). Perhaps most often, this reflects the absence of an attorney. But even where the contract has been "lawyered," there are often gaps. These can, of course, result from failure to anticipate issues or carelessness in drafting. Other times, particularly in heavily negotiated contracts, gaps mean that the parties were unable to come to agreement on those points. Contract drafters sometimes "punt" on hard issues, using vague terms to paper over their disagreement. An integration clause can preclude parol evidence to fill such gaps—but the court will still have to interpret the written terms of the contract to resolve the problem.

PROBLEMS

3-1. Paula Adams, a travel agent, is employed by Evan's Vacation, Inc. under a written contract that sets out Adams's salary and benefits and contains a noncompete agreement. The contract includes the following language:

> 5. **Term.** The "Term of Employment," as used herein, shall mean a period commencing January 1, 2018, and ending on the third anniversary of such date (the "Ending Date"); provided, however, that the occurrence of any of the following prior to the Ending Date shall result in the immediate termination of the Term of Employment, but shall not result in the termination of this Agreement:
>
> i. the termination by the Employer of the Term of Employment for any reason, including, but not limited to, the commission by the Employee of any act constituting a dishonest or other act of material breach or a fraudulent act or a felony under the laws of any state or of the United States to which the Employer or Employee is subject; or
> ii. the death of the Employee; or
> iii. the failure of the Employee to perform her duties hereunder.

Suppose that in January 2019, Evan's Vacation decides to reduce its staff due to a downturn in business and selects Adams for layoff. Prior to informing

Adams, the company consults you. What would you advise the company about its legal obligations under this agreement? Can you make a plausible argument that would support the employer's decision if it goes through with the termination? Would it matter if the contract contained the following additional language?

> Employee shall be on a probationary employment period ("Probationary Period") of ninety (90) days during which Employer has the sole right to terminate Employee without cause.

What would your ultimate recommendation be with respect to whether the employer should terminate Adams under each of these scenarios? Is there any other information you would like to know before deciding? Regardless of your ultimate conclusion, can you think of a better way for the company to draft this agreement in the future? *See generally Evan's World Travel, Inc. v. Adams*, 978 S.W.2d 225 (Tex. App. 1998).

3-2. Irving Sliff was hired as general counsel of Condec Corp. At the time, Sliff was 55 years old and had been employed for 20 years as general counsel at Shell Corp., where he was fully vested in his employer's pension plan. During his negotiations with the president of Condec, Sliff made clear that he was not interested in the new position unless he was guaranteed employment until such time as he would fully vest in Condec's pension plan, which would require a minimum employment term of 10 years. The president orally assured him that this would be the case, and Sliff accepted the position. Several years later, as a result of changes in the management, Sliff became concerned that he had nothing in writing to confirm his oral understanding with the company. He prepared the following memo for execution by the president:

> This will confirm our discussions, both prior and subsequent to my employment, relating to my completion of sufficient years of service during my employment as General Counsel of Condec Corporation to qualify for 100% vesting in each of the employee benefit plans currently offered, as they now exist or may be modified or amended in the future, and any such plans which may hereafter be adopted. It is agreed that I shall be employed by Condec Corporation at a competitive and adequate compensation for at least such period of years as is required to accomplish 100% vesting in the employee benefit plans referred to above, unless discharged for due cause, i.e., dishonesty, or criminal conduct injurious to Condec.

Suppose that the president refuses to sign the memo asserting that it is "too specific." One year later, Sliff is terminated for unsatisfactory performance. When asked for an explanation, he is told by the president that he "hasn't grown with the job."

Does Sliff have a viable claim for breach of contract? Of what significance, if any, is the unsigned memo? If Sliff has a contract for a fixed term equaling the number of years until he is 100% vested in the company pension plans, can he be fired prior to that time nonetheless? On what grounds? *See generally Slifkin v. Condec Corp.*, 538 A.2d 231 (Conn. App. Ct. 1988).

2. Defining "Just Cause" to Terminate

In assessing whether a terminated worker has a legitimate breach of contract claim, analyzing whether the contract contemplates a fixed term of employment or contains some other type of job security term is just the beginning of the inquiry. Assuming a contractual right to job security exists, either based on clear language in the contract or through the resolution of ambiguous circumstances in favor of the employee, the court must then determine whether the employee's right has been violated. In other words, did the employer breach the job security provision of the contract in terminating the employee?

This question raises a number of related legal issues. As we saw in *Hinkel*, this often means asking whether the employer had "just cause" to terminate the employee. Some employment contracts expressly define that term, some do not. If the contract defines cause, the question becomes one of interpretation: Does the conduct at issue meet the definition the parties adopted in their agreement? Even where a contract defines such terms, it may not do so clearly. *See Hackney v. Lincoln Nat'l Fire Ins. Co.*, 657 F. App'x 563, 574-75 (6th Cir. 2016) (term in contract providing for severance except for "job abandonment" was ambiguous as to whether an employee's resignation for health reasons counted as abandonment, requiring the admission of extrinsic evidence). And what happens if the employee commits misconduct that does not fall within the contractual definition? Is the employer still liable to the employee, or can it argue that the employee materially breached his or her duties to the employer? On the other hand, what happens if the contract fails to define cause? As a practical matter, this is frequently the case even in expressly negotiated written instruments. What standard should be used to determine if the termination was justified in such a case? And who gets to decide whether that standard was satisfied—the judge or the jury?

A variety of factual issues also are implicated in breach of contract inquiries. For obvious reasons, employees generally do not admit to engaging in misconduct. Suppose the employer argues that it terminated an employee for embezzling funds from the company. The employee will no doubt deny the charge, creating a factual issue as to whether the embezzlement occurred. Who bears the burden of proof on this issue, the employer or the employee? Is it necessary even to establish that the misconduct occurred, or is it enough that the employer believed it occurred? If the latter, must that belief be objectively reasonable, reached in good faith, or both? *See Sanders v. Kettering Univ.*, 411 F. App'x 771, 778 (6th Cir. 2010) (employer's honest belief that employee's actions constituted just cause was no sufficient because a jury could conclude otherwise). Remember *Hinkel's* discussion of the difference between "satisfaction" contracts and cause! Finally, regardless of whether the misconduct actually occurred, to what extent should courts inquire into the honesty of the employer's asserted reason for termination? It is entirely possible for an employer to fire an employee for a reason prohibited under the contract, but justify its decision based on a reason permitted under the contract. How should breach of contract be resolved where the employer's motive is in doubt?

These questions have yet to be fully resolved by courts. Indeed, most breach of employment contract cases will raise only a small subset of these issues, and it is not always clear which ones are implicated or what standards courts are using to address them.

Benson v. AJR, Inc.
599 S.E.2d 747 (W. Va. 2004)

PER CURIAM:

Danny L. Benson appeals from [a grant of summary judgment to AJR, Inc. in connection with his claim of breach of employment contract]. [W]e determine that there is a genuine issue of material fact concerning the basis for [defendant's] decision to terminate Mr. Benson's employment with AJR. Accordingly, the grant of summary judgment was improper. . . .

I.   Factual and Procedural Background

AJR is a small heavy manufacturing business engaged in the manufacture and welding of truck beds. At the time when Appellant was first employed by AJR as a general welder in 1990, the company was owned by three individuals: Jackie L. Benson; Robert W. Benson; and Patricia Benson. Appellant is the son of Jackie Benson. On May 1, 1997, Appellant was promoted to supervisor and was assigned primary responsibility over three aspects of the company's operations, one of which was safety. In his supervisory position, Appellant was charged with the responsibility for directing and leading the company's safety programs and ensuring that AJR's safety rules were both observed and enforced.

During the summer of 1997, the three AJR shareholders decided to sell the company to an employee, Appellee John M. Rhodes. As part of the sales transaction, Mr. Rhodes agreed to enter into an employment agreement with Appellant whereby Mr. Benson would be guaranteed employment for a period of eight years beginning on August 29, 1997. While AJR had the right to terminate appellant with only one day's written notice under this agreement, it was required to continue paying Mr. Benson his salary for the balance of the eight-year term of employment in the absence of three specified conditions. Those conditions were: (a) dishonesty; (b) conviction of a felony; and (c) voluntary termination of the agreement by Appellant.

Within less than a month after the execution of the employment agreement, Appellant acknowledged in writing his receipt of an employee manual which specified certain acts that were grounds for termination. Those grounds included the sale, possession, or use of controlled substances while on the job, during working hours, or while on company business. At the end of September 1997, concurrent with his receipt of the employee manual, Appellant signed a consent form permitting his employer to conduct random controlled substance tests.

On March 2, 1998, a drug test was administered to the employees of AJR. The results of the drug testing revealed that Appellant had more than three times the limit utilized by the United States Department of Transportation ("DOT") to establish drug use and impairment. Between the time when the drug test was administered and the results were made available, Mr. Rhodes conducted meetings with various AJR personnel during which he inquired of those in attendance whether anyone was aware of an employee who was using illegal drugs or who was arriving at work with illegal drugs or alcohol in their system. Appellant attended one of those meetings and admits that he did not respond to this question despite personal knowledge that his drug test would come back positive.

Along with eleven other employees who also tested positive for drug use, Appellant was terminated from the employ of AJR on March 6, 1998. AJR prepared two different termination forms in connection with Appellant's dismissal from the company. The first of the two forms indicated that Mr. Benson had resigned from his employment.[7] The second of the two termination forms lists a different reason for termination—"controlled substance testing" and "tested positive for cocaine." . . .

Discussion

A. *Breach of Employment Contract*

At the center of this dispute is whether AJR is required to comply with the salary payment obligation contained in the employment agreement. Under the terms of the agreement, in the event AJR decided to terminate Mr. Benson, the company was required to pay Appellant the salary that was in effect on August 29, 1997, absent a dismissal that was based on dishonesty, conviction of a felony, or if Mr. Benson voluntarily terminated the employment agreement. Appellant contends that the lower court erred in its determination that the basis for AJR's termination of Mr. Benson was dishonesty. . . .

To resolve the critical question of whether Appellant's positive drug test fell within the parameters of "dishonest" conduct, the trial court defined the term "dishonesty" by referring to entries in Webster's Dictionary and Black's Law Dictionary.[9] Relying on these generalized definitions, the lower court concluded that Appellant's "actions in failing a drug test and arriving at work with drugs in his system demonstrates a lack of integrity, probity, or adherence to a code of moral values." Rather than limiting its analysis to just the definition of "dishonesty," however, the circuit court included a listing of various definitions of "integrity" and found that "[a]ctions which lack integrity are, by definition, dishonest." After weighing these two definitions in essentially *pari materia,* the trial court ruled that "[p]laintiff's positive drug test, in light of all the facts and circumstances of the case, demonstrates dishonesty and a lack of integrity."[10]

In marked contrast to the trial court's willingness to define the term "dishonesty" within the meaning of the employment contract at issue, we recognize the futility of attempting to fashion a "one size fits all" definition for such term. Dishonesty, like any term that has significance in a given contract, must be defined based on the subject matter of the contract and the intent of the document's drafters. We note, however, that it has been observed that "[d]ishonesty, unlike embezzlement or larceny,

---

7. While Appellant was given the opportunity to resign from AJR, he did not choose to resign his employment.

9. The trial court cited a definition in Webster's, which described dishonesty as "a lack of honesty or integrity; a disposition to defraud or deceive." As defined by the legal dictionary, dishonesty included a "[d]isposition to lie, cheat, deceive, or defraud; untrustworthiness; lack of integrity."

10. One of the circumstances relied upon by the trial court was Mr. Benson's admission that he had been dishonest in failing to answer Mr. Rhodes' question regarding knowledge of drug use in the work place when he "knew to an absolute certainty that he had used illegal drugs and had them in his system when asked the question." Additional evidence cited by the trial court to support its conclusion regarding Appellant's dishonesty was the fact that "[p]laintiff admitted that he used cocaine and does not challenge the drug test."

is not a term of art." More often than not, the issue of whether conduct qualifies as dishonest is determined to be a question best resolved by a jury.

In this case, the record evidences Mr. Benson's admission that he was dishonest in connection with his failure to truthfully answer the question posed by Mr. Rhodes with regard to his awareness of drug use by any AJR employees. Given Appellant's clear admission of dishonesty, we proceed to determine what impact, if any, this admission of dishonesty has on the case at hand.

The lower court appears to have assumed that upon finding conduct that qualified as dishonest, this case could be resolved solely on legal grounds without requiring the assistance of a jury. The trial court reasoned that "[n]o reasonable jury could find that Plaintiff's failing of the drug test, under all the circumstances present herein, was not dishonest behavior." Critically, however, a factual issue that must be determined for purposes of ascertaining whether AJR was required under the terms of the contract to pay Appellant his salary for the remainder of the eight-year contractual period is the *reason* upon which AJR relied in terminating Mr. Benson's employment. Under the employment contract at issue, the determining factor that controls the issue of continued salary payment is whether the basis for the termination was "dishonesty" or "conviction of a felony," or, alternatively, whether there was a "voluntary termination of . . . [the] agreement."

The record in this case is unclear as to whether AJR dismissed Mr. Benson from its employ for drug use or for dishonesty. As Appellant emphasizes in his argument, nowhere on either of the two termination forms that were introduced below is there any indication that he was dismissed for dishonesty. We are unwilling to make the leap that the trial court did to broadly encompass testing positive for drug use within the meaning of the term "dishonesty." Consequently, we conclude that Appellant is entitled to have a jury determine the basis for AJR's decision to terminate Mr. Benson from its employ. If the jury determines that drug use, rather than dishonesty, was the basis for the dismissal, then the provisions of the employment contract with regard to continued payment of Appellant's salary for the duration of the contractual term are applicable. If, however, the jury determines that Mr. Benson was in fact terminated for being dishonest, then AJR is not required to pay his salary under the terms of the employment contract. . . .

MAYNARD, C.J., concurring, in part, and dissenting, in part.

What a terrible message this case sends to small West Virginia employers and businesses! This Court tells this company that it should not have fired an employee who:

1. admitted that he used cocaine;
2. reported to work with cocaine in his system;
3. failed a drug test in which he tested positive for cocaine;
4. misrepresented his drug use by failing to truthfully answer management's inquiries about drug use;
5. worked in a plant where steel fabrication involving constant welding occurs;
6. continually worked around large quantities of explosives and highly volatile gases and liquids including acetylene, oxygen tanks, thinner paint, and other explosive substances; and, here is the icing on the cake;
7. was the SAFETY DIRECTOR of the company!! Appalling!

This Court now says that AJR was wrong to fire a deceitful, coke-head safety director in a plant where tanks of acetylene, oxygen, and other explosives are everywhere! The irony is that if there had been some explosion or other accident which killed or seriously injured another employee, the victim of that accident could have successfully sued under our workers' compensation deliberate intent statute and obtained a large verdict. This Court doubtless would have upheld the large verdict based on the fact that the company allowed a cocaine user to be its safety director.

In distinguishing between dishonesty and drug use under the specific facts of this case, the majority opinion does one of the finest jobs of legalistic hairsplitting in the history of American jurisprudence. The undisputed facts show that if Appellant was terminated for dishonesty, AJR was not obligated to pay Appellant his salary for the balance of the employment agreement. Appellant was responsible for safety at AJR's facility including enforcing AJR's drug-free workplace policy. Appellant received a copy of AJR's employee manual which states, in part, that employees may be terminated for the sale, possession, or use of controlled substances while on the job, during work hours, or while on company business. After Appellant failed a drug test, he admitted that he used cocaine the Saturday immediately prior to the Monday drug test. Finally, he also admitted that he was dishonest with management when he failed to answer management's questions regarding possible drug use in the workplace because he knew to an absolute certainty that he had used illegal drugs and had them in his system when asked the question.

Given these facts, I must disagree with the majority that a jury could determine that drug use rather than dishonesty was the basis for Appellant's dismissal. This is a distinction without a difference. Appellant's drug use, established by the positive drug test, demonstrates dishonesty. Specifically, Appellant, who was responsible for enforcing a drug-free workplace, knowingly violated his employer's drug-free workplace policy by coming to work with cocaine in his system. This is dishonest conduct. Actually testing positive for the drug use is evidence of this dishonest conduct. Therefore, it is irrelevant whether the official reason for Appellant's dismissal was dishonesty or drug use.

Finally, troubling also is the majority opinion's failure to address AJR's argument that Appellant's decision to appear for work under the influence of cocaine was tantamount to a willful quit; substantial public policy against rewarding a person for his or her dishonesty; and the impact of Appellant's admission of dishonesty. The plain fact is that any of these matters would have been sufficient for this Court to affirm the summary judgment on behalf of AJR. . . .

STARCHER, J., concurring.

I write separately to emphasize what the majority's opinion really says, and what it does not say.

This case is all about the power of a contract. The defendant-employer, AJR, Inc., entered into a written contract in 1997 with plaintiff-employee Danny L. Benson that guaranteed Mr. Benson employment until August 2005. Nobody disputes the clarity of this part of the agreement.

However, nowhere does the contract say that Mr. Benson cannot be fired. The contract did allow the defendant-employer to show Mr. Benson the door with pink slip in hand any time it chose to do so. But the contract also contained a clear, black-and-white penalty clause which said that if the defendant-employer let Mr. Benson go, then the defendant-employer would still be required to pay Mr. Benson his remaining wages through August 2005. Again, none of the parties disputes the clarity of this penalty clause built into the agreement.

The fuzzy area in this case is a loophole for the defendant-employer that was built into the contract which allowed the defendant-employer to escape the penalty clause if Mr. Benson was fired because of "dishonesty." The contract does not define "dishonesty." So, when Mr. Benson's drug use was discovered, and the defendant-employer fired him, the question was raised whether Mr. Benson's firing was motivated by Mr. Benson's dishonesty, or for some other reason.

The defendant-employer vigorously asserts that it fired Mr. Benson because the owner of the company conducted meetings with company employees that included Mr. Benson, at which time the owner asked if anyone was aware of an employee who was using illegal drugs or was arriving for work with illegal drugs in his or her system; Mr. Benson said nothing when asked the question. The defendant-employer now asserts that Mr. Benson was fired when the cocaine test results were returned because his dishonesty—in the form of not responding to the question—was revealed. The defendant-employer therefore asserts that it does not have to pay Mr. Benson his remaining wages in compliance with the penalty clause.

The problem with the employer's argument is the written documentation surrounding Mr. Benson's firing. When Mr. Benson was fired, the employer completed a form indicating he was fired in accordance with the employees' manual (which mandated automatic termination for drug usage) for "controlled substance testing" and "tested positive for cocaine." This position was reiterated in writing several times by the company's owner and the company's counsel. The contractual "dishonesty" loophole was not raised by the employer until sometime later, when Mr. Benson asserted his contractual right to his remaining years of wages.

The competing positions taken by the employer raise, beyond a doubt, is a question of fact for jury resolution as to the true motivating factor behind Mr. Benson's termination. . . . That said, let's get straight what this case is *not* about. This case is not—as my dissenting colleague suggests—a case that says a small employer cannot fire an employee who uses drugs. The employer in this case was fully within its rights to fire Mr. Benson—but it had to be willing to pay the price if that firing breached the employment contract. A contract is a promise, and a breach of that promise carries consequences. I disagree with my dissenting colleague's implicit suggestion that because of bad facts, this Court should make bad law, throw hundreds of years of contract law to the wind, and find that because Mr. Benson's actions are less-than-palatable, the contract should be ignored.

If anything, this case says that small employers should not give their employees open-ended contracts guaranteeing them employment. The defendant-employer in this case could have easily put in the contract a clause allowing Mr. Benson to be fired, without penalty to the defendant-employer, for using illicit substances on the job. . . .

NOTES

1. *Clarifying the Issue.* The various opinions in this case express very different views about what is at stake. What is the majority trying to accomplish by remanding, given that Benson has admitted to both drug use and dishonesty? Do you see, as the majority does, a meaningful distinction between the possible grounds for termination

under these facts? Or, to use the dissent's term, is this just "legalistic hairsplitting"? In any event, how do you think the jury will receive Benson's argument? (Stay tuned for the answer to this question.)

2. *The Meaning of Dishonesty.* Suppose Benson did not admit to dishonesty, just drug use. After all, he never affirmatively lied, he just kept quiet when asked an incriminating question. Does this seem like dishonesty to you? If you answered no, or if you are unsure, then perhaps Benson made a tactical error in conceding this point. Certainly the employer appears to have erred in carving out a "dishonesty" exception without defining that term. Or might there be a reason why it chose to leave "dishonesty" vague?

3. *Pretext Analysis.* As the majority suggests, the key factual issue in this case is the employer's motive for terminating Benson. How does a party prove motive, and who bears the burden of proof on this issue? Motive issues arise with great frequency in status discrimination cases where the employee alleges that the employer based its decision to terminate on a protected characteristic such as gender or race. The employer typically responds by asserting a legitimate personnel-based reason for its decision. In discrimination cases, the plaintiff bears the ultimate burden of proving that discrimination was at least a motivating factor in the employer's decision. *See* Chapter 9. By contrast, in the typical express contract case, once the employee has established a contractual right to job security, the employer typically has the burden of proving that cause to terminate existed (e.g., was the employee late, insubordinate, a poor performer?). As we will see in *Uintah Basin Med. Ctr. v. Hardy*, page 177, courts apply several different standards in determining the first issue. But this is a different inquiry from that in *Benson*, where factual cause existed but the question was what cause motivated the decision to terminate. Who has the burden of persuasion on that issue? Are there policy arguments that can be made in support of allocation to one party over the other? Is the allocation of proof likely to have an impact on the outcome in this case?

4. *Contractual Definitions of Cause.* *Benson* makes clear that the meaning of cause depends on the terms of the agreement. For this reason, attention to drafting is extremely important when hiring an employee whose termination rights will turn on the presence or absence of cause. Courts often construe a contract against its drafter, and *Benson* is just one example of cases where employers lost due to the narrowness of their own clauses. Another, dramatic example is a case in which a panel of arbitrators found that the CEO of Massachusetts Mutual Life Insurance was not properly fired for cause despite the fact that he had affairs with two female employees, made millions in profits by trading using the previous day's closing price, and misused the company's aircraft. None of this conduct, the panel concluded, constituted "willful gross misconduct" resulting in "material harm" to the company, as required under the executive's contract. Julie Creswell, *Firing Chief Was Wrong, Panel Says*, N.Y. TIMES, Oct. 21, 2006, at C1.

In response to this problem, drafters have taken different approaches, some insisting on significant detail and formality and others opting for more general language. Compare, for instance, the handwritten "Termination Agreement" of the plaintiff-vice president in *Chard v. Iowa Machinery & Supply Co.*, 446 N.W.2d 81, 83 (Iowa Ct. App. 1989), which defined cause as "no performance, violation of company policy, insubordination, etc.," to the following language in the contract of an executive assistant in *Ten Cate Enbi, Inc. v. Metz*, 802 N.E.2d 977, 979 (Ind. Ct. App. 2004):

Cause shall mean (i) a reasonable certainty exists establishing that [Metz] has engaged in embezzlement, theft, misappropriation or conversion of any assets of [Enbi]; (ii) a material breach by [Metz] of a provision of this agreement or the Basic Business Regulations unless cured by [Metz] within ten days after [Enbi] gives [Metz] written notice thereof excepting that no notice need be given by [Enbi] in the event of a second material breach by [Metz] of the same provision; and (iii) [Metz's] failure or refusal to follow standard policies of [Enbi] or the reasonable directions of and guidelines established by the Board of Directors unless cured by [Metz] within ten days after [Enbi] gives [Metz] written notice thereof excepting that no notice need be given by [Enbi] in the event of a second material failure or refusal by [Metz] of the same policy, direction or guideline.

Which contract provision would you prefer as an employer? If you were the employee?

5. *Managing Risk upon Termination.* Another lesson from *Benson* is that employers should carefully review an employee's contract before making a personnel decision. The concurrence thought Benson survived summary judgment simply because the reason for termination contained in his separation notice (drug use) differed from the reason the employer advanced in the litigation (dishonesty). A similar inconsistency resulted in a jury verdict for the employee in *Ainsworth v. Franklin County Cheese Corp.*, 592 A.2d 871 (Vt. 1991). There the plaintiff was a plant manager whose contract provided for severance upon termination without cause. The employer requested the plaintiff's resignation, providing no explanation for its decision. The plaintiff acquiesced and went about training a replacement and winding down his work. It was only a month later that he received a letter stating that he had been terminated for cause and therefore he was not entitled to severance. Affirming a verdict for plaintiff, the Vermont Supreme Court held that, even assuming cause for termination existed, the jury could reasonably have concluded that the employer terminated the plaintiff pursuant to the no cause provision of his contract and was therefore obligated to pay severance.

From the employer's perspective, both *Ainsworth* and *Benson* illustrate the risks of poorly planned terminations. Had the employers examined the contracts at issue and consulted with counsel before acting, liability might have been avoided. The employee likewise can benefit from a better understanding of his or her agreement. In *Benson*, wouldn't it have been better for the plaintiff to have admitted his drug use when asked since the contract permitted discharge for dishonesty, but not for drug use? Of course, there are obvious downsides to admitting addictions, and perhaps he was not in a condition to make such decisions.

6. *Forms of Job Security in Written Contracts.* Durational contracts are perhaps the most common agreements providing employees with some kind of job security. But such contracts are not a guarantee of employment so much as a guarantee of pay. Of course, either party to any contract can decide to breach the agreement and pay damages rather than perform. Since an employee cannot be ordered to specifically perform, it would be a rare case in which an employer were required, as a matter of contract law, to either reinstate the employee or pay damages in excess of the agreed compensation. In the employment context, many agreements providing job security are expressly structured to ensure this result, using entitlement to severance pay to discouraging arbitrary or opportunistic firings while at the same time limiting employer liability to the compensation specified. A typical executive employee contract, for instance, will, like *Benson*, provide for both termination for cause and termination without cause, granting the employee different rights depending on which provision of the agreement the employer invokes. Under the "for cause" provision, the terminated executive will get little or no compensation or benefits, compared to what is generally a very lucrative payout under the "no cause" provision. *See generally* Stewart Schwab & Randall Thomas, *An Empirical Analysis of CEO Employment Contracts: What Do Top Executives Bargain For?* 63 WASH. & LEE L. REV. 231 (2006). Of course, voluntary quitting does not usually involve severance, but disputes can arise as to how voluntary a departure was. *See Alexander v. Agilysys Inc.*, 696 F. App'x 487 (11th Cir. 2017) (jury question as to whether plaintiff voluntarily left his employment and thus lost his right to severance pay when his company was acquired, and he left to work for the buyer). That said, the universe of possible job security provisions is broad. For important positions, contracts may be extremely complex and highly idiosyncratic. Consider the following provision in the 2005 "offer letter" provided by Microsoft to its chief operating officer, Kevin Turner. Recognizing the loss of "accumulated equity compensation" when he left his current employer, Microsoft promised an "on-hire payment of $7,000,000" but also required Turner to repay it on a sliding scale if he left voluntarily or was terminated for cause in fewer than three years. The letter carefully defined "for cause" (requiring only "a good faith determination" by the company of nonperformance or misconduct) but also allowed Microsoft to discharge him without cause, although in that case Turner got to keep his $7 million. In short, and in contrast to *Benson*, the Microsoft offer calls for a return of money to the company in the event of a "for cause" termination or voluntary departure as well as a payout in the event of a termination without cause. Why might parties prefer this arrangement instead of the simpler cause/no cause structure for severance? Does the prospect of the employee paying the company, rather than the reverse, change the parties' incentives? Are there other interests in play here besides concerns about permissible bases for an employer-initiated termination?

7. *Severance as Liquidated Damages.* Along these lines, can severance be thought of as a type of liquidated damages clause specifying the amount to be paid to the employee in the event that the employer terminates the relationship in breach of contract? It is generally difficult at the outset of a contract to predict an employee damages for an unlawful termination, as they will depend on various factors outside the parties' control, such as the future market for the employee's services. This makes job security contracts good candidates for a liquidated damage provision. Note, however, that while liquidated damages clauses are presumptively valid under contract law, they will not be enforced if they provide for damages that are disproportionate to actual or foreseeable loss. *See* RESTATEMENT (SECOND) OF CONTRACTS §356 (1981). Can an employer avoid its obligation to pay an employee upon termination by arguing that the amount of pay provided for in the contract is excessive? *See Guiliano v. Cleo, Inc.*, 995 S.W.2d 88, 101 (Tenn. 1999) (upholding contractual severance in excess of $90,000 for terminated employee who found immediate reemployment at higher salary because, at the time of contract formation, it appeared the employee "might suffer damages that would be difficult to prove, including loss of professional status, prestige, and advancement opportunities"). We will discuss liquidated damages again in Chapter 8, but notice that typically the duty to pay severance is not framed as damages for breach in the first place, but rather as simply what is owed to the employee upon termination.

8. *The Right to Fire?* The concurring justice in *Benson* emphasizes that the court's decision does not constrain the employer's ability to fire at will but merely

enforces the continuation of the salary provision the parties adopted in their agreement. The dissent, in contrast, believes the court's decision saddles the employer with an irresponsible and potentially dangerous worker who is effectively immune from termination. Which justice gets it right?

9. *Choosing Between Cause and No Cause.* In *Benson*, AJR could have fired Benson for any reason and paid his salary or fired him for an enumerated reason (dishonesty) and avoided further liability. While it may seem like an obvious choice, employers often elect to fire high-level employees under no-cause provisions despite the financial disincentives to doing so. Sometimes this choice reflects an unwillingness to risk legal exposure or simply a desire to avoid conflict or publicity. In cases involving more obscure or less serious performance deficiencies than *Benson*, terminating without cause allows the executive and the company to part amicably, preserving key relationships in the small world of big business.

Yet there are disadvantages to the strategy as well. By making sizeable and seemingly unwarranted payouts to departing executives, firm directors may put themselves at risk of shareholder derivative suits and, in some circumstances, intense public criticism that may be even more damaging than legal action. In a highly publicized example, shareholders of the Walt Disney Company sued the company's board of directors for breach of fiduciary duty based on its 1996 decision to terminate former CEO Michael Ovitz without cause. Ovitz left his position with Disney after a turbulent 14 months of employment, with a severance package estimated at $140 million. Employers' decisions as to whether and on what grounds to terminate an executive are usually insulated by the business judgment rule, and the Disney plaintiffs ultimately lost on the merits following a bench trial. *Brehm v. Eisner*, 906 A.2d 27 (Del. 2006). But the fact that the class was successful in getting to trial, however, was widely seen as a cautionary tale in the business community about the growing reluctance of the public (and the judiciary) to give companies free rein on rewarding their own. *See Brehm v. Eisner*, 746 A.2d 244, 249 (Del. 2000) (noting that "the sheer size of the payout to Ovitz . . . pushes the envelope of judicial respect for the business judgment of directors in making compensation decisions").

10. *Material Breach Analysis.* An employer's argument that it had "just cause" to terminate is sometimes framed in terms of the employee committing a "material breach" of the employment agreement that relieves the employer of its contractual obligations. See RESTATEMENT (SECOND) OF CONTRACTS §237. For example, in *Prozinski v. Northeast Real Estate Services, Inc.*, 797 N.E.2d 415, 423-24 (Mass. App. 2003), the employee was the chief operating and financial officer. He was fired during the contract term, but the court held the alleged behavior giving rise to Prozinski's termination—financial misconduct and sexual harassment—might have excused the employer's duty to pay. A material breach of the employee's duties would excuse any employer reciprocal duties, and there were triable questions as to whether Prozinski violated his "duties of loyalty, utmost good faith, and of protecting Northeast's interests." *But see Balles v. Babcock Power Inc.*, 70 N.E.3d 905, 913 (2017) (favoritism in advancing a female intern with whom an executive was having a consensual affair was not a "for cause" basis for dismissal within a shareholder agreement).

"For cause" is at issue in a high profile #MeToo setting, as CBS and Les Moonves maneuver over whether his alleged conduct is sufficient to deny him a multimillion-dollar payout. James B. Stewart, *Why Les Moonves Might Still Get $120 Million From CBS*, NY TIMES, 9/22, 2018, B1 ("For most people, the allegations against Mr. Moonves would be more than enough cause. But in the strange world of chief executive contracts, they may not be."). Ironically, it may be less the alleged misconduct that denies Moonves his severance (some of the most serious allegations predate his arrival at CBS) than his failure to be forthcoming in CBS's investigation, a requirement of his contract.

Suppose an employment agreement contains the following language: "If Employer terminates employee for any reason, including a material breach of this agreement by Employee, Employer shall pay Employee's salary for the balance of the contract period." Would the *Prozinski* court enforce this clause? Should it? *See Fields v. Thompson Printing Co.*, 363 F.3d 259, 269 (3d Cir. 2004) (finding in favor of employee denied benefits and pay upon termination for sexual harassment because "[the contract] requires [the employer] to pay certain sums if they terminated Fields, ostensibly for any reason, including improper and offensive conduct. Had [the employer] intended to avoid this result, [it] could have bargained for a limiting provision.").

11. *Material vs. Immaterial Performance Deficiencies.* In your first-year Contracts course, you probably learned that a material breach is one that goes to the essence of the contract. Engaging in sexual harassment and stealing from the company are likely to be found material breaches by any court, but what about less egregious conduct? *See, e.g., Shah v. Cover-It, Inc.*, 859 A.2d 959, 963 (Conn. 2004) (manager materially breached employment contract where he overstayed vacation, did not report to work for weeks upon return, and spent long time periods at work visiting web sites unrelated to his job); *Central Alaska Broadcasting, Inc. v. Bracale*, 637 P.2d 711, 712 (Alaska 1981) (finding employee's refusal to obey order of board of directors to terminate subordinate a material breach where employee's contract granted him personnel management authority but subject to the supervision and control of the Board); *see also Gilman v. Marsh & McLennan Cos.*, 826 F.3d 69, 74 (2d Cir. 2016) (an employer had good cause to discharge employees for refusal to cooperate with an internal investigation when they "had been implicated in an alleged criminal conspiracy" imperiling the company even though they were in the "tough position of choosing between employment and [possible] incrimination").

What about drug use like that at issue in *Benson*? In the ordinary case, the answer depends on the severity of the employee's conduct. Off-duty behavior that does not affect job performance will rarely if ever constitute a material breach. Thus, the analysis would turn on such things as whether Benson actually showed up to work impaired, how often, and whether, if there were only isolated instances of impairment, special circumstances (like access to or use of hazardous materials or equipment) justified a finding of material breach.

If Benson's drug use did rise to this level, the question would be whether the material breach could excuse the employer's payment obligation given the termination provision in the contract. Indeed, this question brought Benson's case back before the West Virginia Supreme Court six years after the remand ordered in the opinion you just read. *See Benson v. AJR*, 698 S.E.2d 638 (W. Va. 2010) (*Benson II*). At trial, AJR argued both that dishonesty (not drug use) motivated its termination decision and that Benson's drug use was a material breach relieving it of contractual liability. The jury returned a general verdict stating that plaintiff had materially breached but, on special interrogatories, answered that drug use, not dishonesty, had motivated the employer's decision. The judge awarded Benson his lost wages, and the West Virginia Supreme Court affirmed because "Mr. Benson's material breach of the Employment Agreement is not an enumerated reason that would relieve AJR of the duty to pay him his salary under the remainder of the contract period." *Id*. at 649.

Benson II suggests that a contractual definition of cause can preclude a generic material breach argument. Given the availability of material breach analysis under ordinary contract law, why would an employer ever choose to enumerate causes for termination in an employment agreement? A concurring justice in *Benson II* concluded that the parties' "amazingly narrow" agreement indicated that "[F]rom a business sense, the eight years of employment was . . . factored into the purchase price of AJR." *Id*. at *15. Does this description shed some light on the question?

≡≡≡ **Uintah Basin Medical Center v. Hardy**
≡≡≡ *110 P.3d 168 (Utah Ct. App. 2005)*
≡≡≡

JACKSON, J.:

. . . Background

Dr. Hardy is a board-certified pathologist. On November 29, 1994, he executed an employment agreement [to provide pathology services for Uintah Basin Medical Center.] Under the Agreement, which consists of only two pages taken almost verbatim from that of Dr. Hardy's predecessor, UBMC was to refer certain types of laboratory work to Dr. Hardy and pay a $400 monthly laboratory director's fee. In return, Dr. Hardy would work as the director of UBMC's laboratory and provide related services, which included weekly visits to the hospital. The Agreement does not include a fixed termination date; rather, it would "continue to bind parties . . . until terminated after ninety (90) days written notice for just cause of termination by either party or by mutual consent of the parties to a shorter notice period." The Agreement does not define "just cause" or otherwise clarify what grounds would justify termination.

On July 29, 1996, UBMC sent Dr. Hardy notice of termination and later hired Dr. Thomas Allred in his place. [UBMC brought a suit for declaratory judgment to establish that its termination of the Agreement with Dr. Hardy was for "just cause," and Dr. Hardy counterclaimed for breach of contract. The trial court granted UBMC summary judgment, finding the Agreement unreasonable in duration based on Dr. Hardy's deposition testimony that he understood the agreement to be terminable only upon his death or incapacity, or the hospital's discontinuance of pathology services.]

Analysis

I. Interpretation of the Just Cause Provision

The key question in this case is what the "just cause" provision in the Agreement means. Once this question is answered, we may gauge . . . whether UBMC had just cause to terminate Dr. Hardy.

To interpret the "just cause" provision, the trial court relied primarily on extrinsic evidence, namely Dr. Hardy's deposition testimony regarding his understanding of the term. . . .

Although both parties here have ascribed different meanings to the "just cause" provision, we cannot conclude that the term is ambiguous. UBMC has taken the position that it has "just cause" to terminate Dr. Hardy's employment when the business exigencies of the hospital and the interests of the patients warrant a change in personnel. In contrast, Dr. Hardy testified in his post-remand affidavit that he understood the "just cause" provision to allow UBMC to terminate the Agreement only under specific circumstances:

> In essence, UBMC would have just cause to terminate my Agreement if I failed to perform or something substantial changed as to the need of UBMC for pathology services (e.g., hospital closure) which may be caused by financial concerns. Those financial concerns, however, could not include merely getting a lower price for the pathology services or histology lab supervision.

Hardy also asserts that he understood "just cause" to imply that

> [i]f UBMC perceived a need for changes in scope or manner of the provided pathology services, I expected them to approach me regarding such a need, and if jointly agreed upon, I would have adjusted accordingly. If I could not accommodate these changes, then UBMC would be free to terminate the Agreement.

Dr. Hardy's interpretation is ultimately untenable for two reasons. First, the evidence on record does not indicate that the parties understood the "just cause" provision to have a unique meaning particular to the Agreement, much less the detailed meaning understood by Dr. Hardy. The parties have stipulated that the Agreement is, for all practical purposes, identical to that of Dr. Hardy's predecessor, Dr. Joseph Sannella. The "just cause" termination provision was copied from the Sannella contract and included in the Agreement without any substantial negotiation. The parties did not incorporate other documents, such as the UBMC bylaws, to define when either party would have cause to terminate the Agreement. Thus, we must conclude that any particular meaning of "just cause" as understood or intended by Dr. Hardy is unique to himself and is, as he concedes in his brief, irrelevant to its interpretation.

Second, Dr. Hardy's interpretation of "just cause" is at odds with the ordinary meaning of the term. Unlike an at-will employment agreement, which allows an employer to discharge an employee for any, or no, reason, termination for just cause is widely understood to permit discharge only for "a fair and honest cause or reason, regulated by good faith . . . as opposed to one that is trivial, capricious, unrelated to business needs or goals, or pretextual." *Guz v. Bechtel Nat'l, Inc.*, 8 P.3d 1089, 1100 (Cal. 2000). This broad definition of just cause allows an employer to discharge an employee not only for misconduct or poor performance but also for other legitimate economic reasons.[4] Courts have recognized that "'[i]n deciding whether [just]

---

4. *See also Zoerb v. Chugach Elec. Ass'n*, 798 P.2d 1258, 1262-63 (Alaska 1990) ("A reduction in work force compelled by legitimate and sufficient business reasons may constitute 'good cause' to terminate an employee."); *Havill v. Woodstock Soapstone Co.*, 783 A.2d 423, 428 (Vt. 2001) ("Economic circumstances that necessitate employer layoffs constitute good cause for termination." (Quotations, citation, and alteration omitted.)).

cause exists, there must be a balance between the employer's interest in operating its business efficiently and profitably and the employee's interest in continued employment. . . . Care must be exercised so as not to interfere with the employer's legitimate exercise of managerial discretion." ' *Cotran v. Rollins Hudig Hall Int'l, Inc.*, 948 P.2d 412, 417 (Cal. 1998).

In sum, absent evidence that the parties intended a meaning of "just cause" unique to this particular agreement, we must conclude that the parties intended the term to have its ordinary meaning. Accordingly, we hold that the "just cause" provision is unambiguous and is ordinarily understood to provide employers with power to terminate an employee for legitimate business reasons and in the interest of improving client services as long as the justification is not a mere pretext for a capricious, bad faith, or illegal termination. . . .

III. UBMC's Just Cause to Terminate

The only remaining issue is whether the Board discharged Dr. Hardy for just cause. Because the trial court did not reach this issue in its summary judgment ruling, we remand for the trial court to determine whether the Board terminated Dr. Hardy for legitimate business reasons or whether the termination was capricious, in bad faith, or illegal.

However, we address here the question of what an employer must show to prove it terminated an employee for just cause, a matter of first impression for Utah courts. There appear to be three different approaches to this question. Some courts seem to give deference to the justifications stated by the employer. *See e.g., Gaudio v. Griffin Health Servs. Corp.*, 733 A.2d 197, 208 (Conn. 1999) ("[A]n employer who wishes to terminate an employee for cause must do nothing more rigorous than 'proffer a proper reason for dismissal.'"). A few other courts have taken the opposite approach and required the employer to prove that the conditions necessitating termination actually existed. *See, e.g., Toussaint v. Blue Cross & Blue Shield of Mich.*, 292 N.W.2d 880, 895 (Mich. 1980) ("[W]here an employer has agreed to discharge an employee for cause only, its declaration that the employee was discharged for unsatisfactory work is subject to judicial review. The jury as trier of fact decides whether the employee was, in fact, discharged for unsatisfactory work.").

A far greater number of states have adopted a more balanced approach that requires an employer to justify termination with an objective good faith reason supported by facts reasonably believed to be true by the employer. *See, e.g., Towson Univ. v. Conte*, 862 A.2d 941, 950-51, 954 (Md. App. 2004) ("[I]n the just cause employment context, a jury's role is to determine the objective reasonableness of the employer's decision to discharge, which means that the employer act in objective good faith and base its decision on a reasoned conclusion and facts reasonably believed to be true by the employer.") These courts recognize that an employer's justification for discharging an employee should not be taken at face value but also recognize that a judge or jury should not be called upon to second-guess an employer's business decisions.

We agree with the majority of courts and adopt the objective reasonableness approach. Accordingly, in order to establish just cause on remand, UBMC need not prove that the Board's assumptions in terminating Dr. Hardy were true or that the benefits it expected were actually realized. Rather, UBMC need only show that the

Board acted in good faith by adequately considering the facts it reasonably believed to be true at the time it made the decision.

NOTES

1. *Cause in the Absence of a Contractual Definition.* UBMC deals with the problem of determining whether termination of a contractually protected employee was based on "cause" where the parties' agreement fails to define the term. In answering that question, a court has essentially two choices: Either it can try to ascertain the parties' intended definition of cause in the particular agreement or it can apply a general definition or standard of cause. The former requires finding some ambiguity in the meaning of the term (nor a hard task, as you've seen in this chapter!). *See Joy v. Hay Group, Inc.*, 403 F.3d 875 (7th Cir. 2005) (allowing an employee to testify that she was told that "cause" meant "serious misconduct" as to her understanding that meaning of "cause" when she had been terminated without severance pay for failure to meet a billing quota). Nevertheless, in *UBMC*, the court opts for the latter approach, concluding that "cause" is an unambiguous term subject to a generally understood meaning.

2. *Cause Not Attributable to Performance.* Having found a generally applicable definition of cause, the court finds it necessary to explore which of three approaches to defining cause is applicable. Maybe the meaning is not so generally understood! In other words, what does that definition encompass? In *UBMC*, the employer offered an economic reason for its decision to terminate Dr. Hardy: By hiring a replacement, it could obtain pathology services more cost-effectively. In finding in favor of the employer, the court asserts that a business reason of this sort fits within the "widely understood" meaning of cause, despite the fact that it is unrelated to the employee's performance. Does this statement of the legal definition of cause surprise you? Is it consistent with your own understanding of what constitutes just cause for termination?

Collective bargaining agreements almost always distinguish between terminations (which can only be for just cause related to performance) and "layoffs," which can be for economic reasons and are usually done on the basis of seniority—last in, first out. *See* Roger I. Abrams & Dennis R. Nolan, *Toward a Theory of "Just Cause" in Employee Discipline Cases*, 1985 DUKE L.J. 594-95. A similar distinction exists in both academic tenure and civil service. In the latter situation, the source of just cause protection is frequently statutory rather than contractual, but the focus is on the conduct of the particular employee, and economic concerns are addressed under a different rubric. *See, e.g., Yoder v. Town of Middleton*, 876 A.2d 216, 218 (N.H. 2005) (cause for removal of police chief pursuant to state statute requires demonstration of unfitness or incapacity to perform job duties).

In cases like those we have been studying involving individual private sector employment contracts, whether economic bases for termination constitute cause is a question that often turns on the form and context of the parties' agreement. Consistent with *UMBC*, courts generally interpret cause as encompassing legitimate, non-performance-based reasons for termination in indefinite just-cause contracts like Dr. Hardy's, that is, contracts promising protection against arbitrary dismissal but guaranteeing no particular term of employment.

On the other hand, under a contract providing for a fixed term of employment, courts usually treat cause as meaning a reason for termination related to the employee's conduct or performance. The RESTATEMENT OF EMPLOYMENT LAW (ALI 2015) captures this by defining cause for termination of agreements "for a definite term" to include material breach, "including by persistent neglect of duties; by engaging in misconduct or other malfeasance, including gross negligence" or being unable to perform because of "long-term disability." §2.04(a). Where the contract is for an indefinite term, however, "cause" also includes "a significant change in the employer's economic circumstances [such that] the employer no longer has a business need" for the employee's services." §2.04(b).

3. *Termination Based on Poor Results.* Once it is clear that an employee's contract requires a performance-based reason for termination (either by its express terms or as interpreted by a court), the question remains how serious the employee's performance problems must be to constitute cause. The Restatement seems to require serious problems (for example, negligence is apparently not sufficient since it speaks in terms of "gross negligence"). On the other hand, no moral shortcoming is required— long-term disability will suffice. Not all courts are so demanding. *See Cole v. Valley Ice Garden, L.L.C.*, 113 P.3d 275, 280 (Mont. 2005) (firing ice hockey coach based on team's poor win-loss record constituted termination for cause despite his good faith efforts and the fact that contract did not contain performance goals).

4. *Actual Cause vs. Reasonable Decision Making.* A related factual question is whether the grounds asserted by the employer in support of termination are true. What happens, for instance, if an employer terminates a worker for embezzlement— something that everyone would agree constitutes cause—but the employer was mistaken about the employee's culpability? As previously discussed, courts generally agree that the employer bears the burden of proof where cause is disputed, at least with respect to express contracts, but they disagree about what exactly the employer needs to prove. The last part of *UMBC* describes a number of approaches that courts take, ranging from significant deference to the employer's proffered reason to requiring the employer to establish that cause in fact existed. Which approach discussed in *UBMC* makes the most sense as a policy matter? Consider the following rationale for applying a reasonable good faith test like that adopted in *UBMC*:

> The decision to terminate an employee for misconduct is one that not uncommonly implicates organizational judgment and may turn on intractable factual uncertainties, even where the grounds for dismissal are fact specific. If an employer is required to have in hand a signed confession or an eyewitness account of the alleged misconduct before it can act, the workplace will be transformed into an adjudicatory arena and effective decisionmaking will be thwarted. Although these features do not justify a rule permitting employees to be dismissed arbitrarily, they do mean that asking a civil jury to reexamine in all its factual detail the triggering cause of the decision to dismiss—including the retrospective accuracy of the employer's comprehension of that event—months or even years later, in a context distant from the imperatives of the workplace, is at odds with an axiom underlying the jurisprudence of wrongful termination.

Cotran v. Rollins Hudig Hall Int'l, Inc., 948 P.2d 412, 421 (Cal. 1998). Does this approach amount to allowing some employers to get away with breach? After all, if there really was no cause, there was no contractually legitimate basis for the termination. In contrast, consider a typical commercial contract involving a sale of goods.

Clearly a buyer could not reject a shipment under contract merely because he or she reasonably and in good faith, but mistakenly, thought the goods were defective. Is there a reason why a lower standard should govern employment?

One consideration may be the type of contract involved. *Cotran* was based on an implied just cause agreement rather than a written job security contract. Should the source of protection, express versus implied agreement, matter at all? *See Towson Univ. v. Conte*, 862 A.2d 941 (Md. App. 2004) (no difference); *Khajavi v. Feather River Anesthesia Med. Group*, 100 Cal. Rptr. 2d 627 (Ct. App. 2000) (holding that, unlike wrongful discharge based on an implied contract, employment for a specified term may not be terminated prior to the term's expiration based upon employer's honest but mistaken belief of misconduct).

5. *Procedural Aspects of Just Cause.* In *UBMC*, Dr. Hardy argued not only that there was no cause for termination but also that the employer should have consulted with him first about its desire to reduce costs. Some courts incorporate a procedural component in the obligation to dismiss only for cause. *See Nadeau v. Imtec, Inc.*, 670 A.2d 841, 844 (Vt. 1995) ("To be upheld, a discharge for just cause must meet two criteria: first, that the employee's conduct was egregious enough that the discharge was reasonable, and second, that the employee had fair notice, express or implied, that such conduct could result in discharge."); *Cotran*, 948 P.2d at 422 (Good cause means "fair and honest reasons . . . supported by substantial evidence gathered through an adequate investigation that includes notice of the claimed misconduct and a chance for the employee to respond."). *But see New England Stone v. Conte*, 962 A.2d 30, 33 (R.I. 2009) (declining to impose any "due-process mandates" on the employer where a contract enumerated grounds for cause and provided "that cause 'shall be determined by the [c]ompany in good faith'"). Why should procedure matter, at least if the employer can ultimately prove cause? If a procedural component exists and is breached, what should the remedy be? What could a court award Dr. Hardy if his contract required the hospital to consult with him about costs?

6. *It Isn't Over 'Til It's Over.* Dr. Hardy lost the first round of litigation but subsequently defeated UBMC's motion for summary judgment on the issue of cause. On remand, UBMC filed for summary judgment arguing that there was no material factual issue in dispute about the reason for termination given its various business-related reasons for replacing Dr. Hardy with Dr. Allred. The trial court granted the motion, but the Utah Supreme Court reversed, finding that the facts could support a finding that UBMC's reasons were pretextual. *UBMC v. Hardy (UBMC II)*, 179 P.3d 786, 790-91 (Utah 2008). It explained:

> First, UBMC did not give Dr. Hardy any contemporaneous reason for the termination of his Agreement. UBMC simply thanked Dr. Hardy for his service and told him that he had been replaced. And UBMC's administrator, Brad LeBaron, admitted in his deposition that he told Dr. Hardy after the termination that he would need to look and see what kind of potential issues could be raised to defend UBMC's decision. In addition, even though UBMC now relies on its desire for an on-site pathologist as a justification for the termination decision, this desire was never expressed to Dr. Hardy before his Agreement was terminated, and Dr. Hardy was given no opportunity to cure or address any demonstrated need or desire of UBMC for an on-site pathologist. Indeed, UBMC undertook no investigation into the actual need or the financial impact of hiring an on-site pathologist before it terminated Dr. Hardy's Agreement. This lack of investigation before the termination suggests that UBMC's stated need for an on-site pathologist was merely pretextual. The facts also establish that UBMC failed to conduct a comprehensive investigation of Dr. Allred prior to hiring him. . . . Finally, UBMC did not terminate

Dr. Hardy for poor performance, misconduct, breach of the Agreement, or failure to fulfill his obligations.

Does this victory for the employee surprise you given the very deferential standard adopted by the court in *UBMC I*? Results like this perhaps explain why employers often vehemently dispute the existence of contractual job security protection even when they have a plausible reason for terminating.

PROBLEM

3-3. Bonnie Blackwell was hired by the board of directors of a television merchandising company for the position of general manager. During Blackwell's employment there was significant conflict on the board of directors involving accusations by the board chair and company president that two other board members were improperly documenting withdrawals of company funds. The chair on several occasions asked Blackwell informally to look into this problem. Blackwell, reluctant to get involved in an internal matter between board members, repeatedly resisted this request, explaining that it was outside her authority. One year into her employment, Blackwell submitted a request for a two-week unpaid leave of absence for health reasons, a benefit available to all employees per company policy. Upon receiving the request, the president called Blackwell to his office and informed her that it was "a very bad time to plan a vacation." He cited the recent loss of a cable affiliate and an upcoming meeting with a possible new affiliate and stated that it was a "critical time" for the company. Blackwell responded that her request was not for vacation and that the meeting could be handled by her subordinates. Blackwell did not appear at work for the next two weeks, although she conferenced into the meeting with the potential affiliate by telephone. When she returned to work, she was terminated, effective immediately, and given no severance pay. During her one year of employment, Blackwell received only one performance evaluation, which was positive, and the company met all of its sales and budgetary goals under her leadership.

Assess whether Blackwell has any claim against the company under each of the following scenarios:

A. Blackwell's contract provides: "This agreement shall run for two years from the date of hire unless terminated earlier on the basis of just cause. Just cause means gross misconduct, dishonesty, commission of a crime, or other conduct that seriously jeopardizes the company."

B. Blackwell's contract provides: "This agreement shall run for two years from the date of hire. In the event that the company terminates Blackwell prior to that date, Blackwell shall receive her full salary for the remainder of the contract term." never going to see this

C. Blackwell's contract provides: "This agreement can only be terminated on the basis of just cause and upon one month's notice."

See generally Video Catalog Channel v. Blackwelder, No. 03A01-9705-CH-00155, 1997 Tenn. App. LEXIS 636 (Tenn. Ct. App. Sept. 19, 1997).

B. COMPENSATION TERMS

Job security and cause for discharge are not the only contractual issues fueling litigation in sophisticated employment relationships. The main reason job security is important to workers, after all, is that it ensures a steady flow of income. For high-level employees especially, compensation can mean much more than base wages. You have already seen that written contracts frequently promise exit pay or other separation benefits upon termination. High-level employees are often paid during the course of their relationship pursuant to complex compensation schemes that include incentive pay.

"Incentive pay" generally refers to compensation that is tied to performance, such as bonuses, stock options, profit sharing or other arrangements under which the amount of compensation varies depending on the success of the employee or the company as a whole. Where compensation structures are properly aligned with performance indicators and the health and success of the firm, they can be extremely beneficial to both parties. From the perspective of the employer, such arrangements not only encourage superior performance, they help retain good workers who might otherwise defect to competitors (the so-called golden handcuffs effect). For employees, incentive pay arrangements offer a degree of control over their earning capacity and create the potential for high payoffs. Indeed, for some employees, incentive pay greatly exceeds their base salary.

Many believe, however, that this is not the way incentive compensation works in practice. A wide body of literature has criticized the current system for rewarding executives for moderate or even poor firm performance. *See generally* Lucian Arye Bebchuk et al., *Managerial Power and Rent Extraction in the Design of Executive Compensation,* 69 U. Chi. L. Rev. 751, 761-83 (2002) (describing and critiquing the "optimal contract approach" to executive compensation). It suggests that outsize pay packages result not from legitimate market forces but rather from cozy relationships between corporate managers and directors and arrangements that encourage executives to place short-term management interests ahead of larger corporate goals. Professors Lucian Bebchuk and Jesse Fried explain some of these concerns:

> According to the "official" view of executive compensation, corporate boards setting pay arrangements are guided solely by shareholder interests and operate at arm's-length from the executives whose pay they set. [This] view serves as the practical basis for legal rules and public policy. . . .
>
> The official arm's-length story is neat, tractable, and reassuring. But it fails to account for the realities of executive compensation. . . .
>
> Directors have had and continue to have various economic incentives to support, or at least go along with, arrangements that favor the company's top executives. A variety of social and psychological factors—collegiality, team spirit, a natural desire to avoid conflict within the board, friendship and loyalty, and cognitive dissonance—exert additional pull in that direction. Although many directors own some stock in their companies, their ownership positions are too small to give them a financial incentive to take the personally costly, or at the very least unpleasant, route of resisting compensation arrangements sought by executives. In addition, limitations on time and resources have made it difficult for even well-intentioned directors to do their pay-setting job properly. Finally, the market constraints within which directors operate are far from tight and do not prevent deviations from arm's-length contracting outcomes in favor of executives. . . .

The same factors that limit the usefulness of the arm's-length model in explaining executive compensation suggest that executives have had substantial influence over their own pay. Compensation arrangements have often deviated from arm's-length contracting because directors have been influenced by management, insufficiently motivated to insist on shareholder-serving compensation, or simply ineffectual. Executives' influence over directors has enabled them to obtain "rents," benefits greater than those obtainable under true arm's-length contracting.

Pay Without Performance: Overview of the Issues, 30 J. CORP. L. 647, 653-59 (2005). The debate continues both in the law reviews and the mainstream media, often these days in terms of the corrosive effects of income inequality on the social fabric. *See, e.g.,* Paul Krugman, *Iron Men of Wall Street,* NY TIMES, Feb. 16, 2014.

It is important to remember, however, that not all recipients of incentive compensation are high-level executives able to secure lucrative pay packages and other favorable terms of employment. Many sales workers, for instance, are compensated primarily through commissions, a structure that can create hardships for workers struggling to generate revenue in difficult economic times. In addition, incentive compensation is often deferred, meaning that under the employer's policy a worker may not realize payment until a future date, possibly after the entitlement has "accrued." We have seen that high-level employees generally negotiate contractual protection against termination. For mainstream workers, however, the employer's unfettered ability to terminate can jeopardize the realization of incentive compensation. Thus, the interplay between employment at will and contractual bonus and commission schemes is important in evaluating employee compensation rights.

For all of these reasons, alleged failures to pay compensation that has been in some sense earned are a common source of employment litigation. These disputes raise issues similar to those that arise with respect to job security or any other contractual term of employment, such as whether the employer's promise is binding and whether it has been breached.

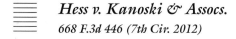

Hess v. Kanoski & Assocs.
668 F.3d 446 (7th Cir. 2012)

WOOD, Circuit Judge.

This case involves a spat over attorneys' fees—in particular, the fees that the firm of Kanoski & Associates allegedly owes to its former associate, Lawrence Hess. After some five years at the firm, Hess was abruptly dismissed. Afterwards, the firm settled several of the cases on which Hess had been working and refused to pay Hess bonuses or fees based on those settlements. Hess believes that he is entitled to some of that money. . . .

I.

Kanoski & Associates bills itself as the "largest personal injury law firm in central Illinois." The firm hired Hess on May 9, 2001, to work primarily on medical malpractice cases. His employment was governed by an agreement that set out his salary and bonus pay. At first Hess apparently performed well for the firm and obtained several favorable settlements. But by 2007, things had gone south; on February 14 of that year, Ronald Kanoski [the firm's president] fired Hess. In the wake of that action, the firm transferred several of Hess's cases to Kennith Blan, Jr., a lawyer working as an independent contractor for the firm. Over the course of the next year and a half, the firm—largely through Blan's efforts—settled many of these cases. For example, in June 2008, one case settled for $1.25 million.

Hess believed that Blan and the firm had pushed him out in order to settle his cases without sharing with him the generous compensation that accompanied the settlements. . . .

At its essence, this case boils down to a single question of contract interpretation: Was Hess entitled under his employment agreement to compensation arising out of any of the post-termination settlements? . . .

II.

A.

We begin with the two counts in Hess's complaint that rest most directly on his employment agreement: Count I, the claim under the [Illinois Wage Payment and Collection Act]; and Count IV, the claim for breach of contract. . . .

To succeed on his breach of contract claim, Hess must show "(1) the existence of a valid and enforceable contract; (2) performance by the plaintiff; (3) breach of contract by the defendant; and (4) resultant injury to the plaintiff." *Henderson-Smith & Assocs. v. Nahamani Family Serv. Ctr.*, 752 N.E.2d 33, 43 (Ill. App. Ct. 2001). To prevail on his IWPCA claim, Hess must first show that he had a valid contract or employment agreement. Illinois courts have explained that an agreement under the IWPCA is "broader than a contract." *Zabinsky v. Gelber Group, Inc.*, 807 N.E.2d 666, 671 (Ill. App. Ct. 2004) (the IWPCA "requires only a manifestation of mutual assent on the part of two or more persons; parties may enter into an 'agreement' without the formalities and accompanying legal protections of a contract"). The IWPCA requires an employer to pay an employee any final compensation due under that contract or agreement at the time of separation; it defines final compensation to include "wages, salaries, earned commissions, earned bonuses, . . . and any other compensation owed by the employer pursuant to an employment contract or agreement between the two parties." 820 ILCS 115/2 (2006).

The parties do not dispute that Hess had a valid contract with the firm (his "employment agreement," not to be confused with "agreement" as it is used by the IWPCA) and that, until his termination, he adequately performed as an employee under that contract. The dispute is solely over whether Hess's employment agreement entitled him to bonuses on settlements that were collected after he left the firm. The employment agreement originally provided that Hess would receive "15% of all fees generated over the base salary (or $5,000 per month) with a guarantee of One Hundred and Twenty-Five Thousand ($125,000). Bonus shall increase to 25% of all fees received annually in excess of $750,000.00." The firm later modified Hess's compensation on June 21, 2002, increasing his base salary and changing the bonus structure to "40% of all fee revenue generated" (with some exceptions). . . .

No court has ever resolved the question whether this contract requires the firm to pay Hess bonuses from post-termination settlements. The language of the contract is not clear because the contract does not define when fees are "generated." Fees might be "generated" when work is performed on a case, because the work ultimately leads to the settlement. This does not seem odd if one considers the scenario in which an attorney works on a case until it is nearly ready for settlement, is fired, and then the next day the firm accepts a settlement without her. If, on the other hand, fees are "generated" only when received by the firm, Hess would not be entitled to the post-termination settlement earnings.

Under Illinois law, undefined terms are generally given their "plain, ordinary, and popular meaning" as found in dictionary definitions. *Outboard Marine Corp. v. Liberty Mut. Ins. Co.*, 607 N.E.2d 1204, 1215 (Ill. 1993). Resort to dictionary definitions often, however, does not settle the question; that is the case here. The infinitive "to generate" means (among other things) "to bring into existence" or "to be the cause of." Merriam-Webster Dictionary Online. . . . Work performed before a settlement is obtained in some sense produces or brings that settlement into existence. On the other hand, it is possible that the parties intended "generated" to be limited to the final act of bringing a fee into existence, i.e., actually obtaining the cash in hand. Where language in a contract appears to be "susceptible to more than one meaning," Illinois courts will "consider extrinsic evidence to determine the parties' intent." *Thompson v. Gordon*, 948 N.E.2d 39, 47 (Ill. 2011).

Even if the district court concludes that Hess's interpretation is too broad and thus the contract does not entitle Hess to bonuses on *all* of the post-termination settlements, Hess has a good argument that he is entitled at least to the fees related to settlements obtained within the 30-day period after he was fired. The contract required the firm to give Hess 30 days' notice before it ended his employment, but it did not do so. A 30-day provision is consistent with an at-will contract, *H. Vincent Allen & Associates, Inc. v. Weis*, 379 N.E.2d 765, 771-72 (Ill. App. Ct. 1978), but breach of the 30-day provision requires the firm to pay Hess whatever compensation he was due during that time. *See, e.g., Equity Ins. Managers of Ill., LLC v. McNichols*, 755 N.E.2d 75, 81 (Ill. App. Ct. 2001). At least one of the settlements Hess has identified—the Hoelscher settlement—was obtained within that 30-day period. He is entitled to press his argument that the contract gave him the right to bonuses in connection with that settlement, no matter what the parties meant by the term "generated." . . .

[The court remanded for the district court "to interpret the contract and consider the merits of Hess's theories under Counts I and IV."]

Weiss v. DHL Express, Inc.
718 F.3d 39 (1st Cir. 2013)

HOWARD, Circuit Judge.

Jeremy Weiss was a rising star at DHL Express, Inc. ("DHL") until his termination in September 2009, ostensibly for his failure to properly investigate, document, and ameliorate the misconduct of an employee under his supervision. The termination occurred just months before Weiss was to receive a $60,000 bonus. Weiss filed suit in Massachusetts state court to recover the bonus on the grounds that he was terminated without good cause, which under the terms of the bonus plan entitled him to a full payout. He asserted breach of the implied covenant of good faith and fair dealing, detrimental reliance, unjust enrichment, and violation of the Massachusetts Wage Act. DHL removed the case to federal court on diversity grounds. The court allowed a single cause of action to go to the jury—a "straight-forward" breach-of-contract claim. The jury found for Weiss. DHL's main claim on appeal is that the court erroneously allowed the jury to independently determine whether good cause existed for Weiss's termination because the bonus plan reserved this determination for a committee of the company. In his cross-appeal, Weiss challenges the grant of summary judgment to DHL on his Wage Act claim and the denial of his attorney's fees. We reverse the jury verdict and affirm the summary judgment order.

I.

The relevant facts are undisputed. In 2004, DHL, an international express mail services company, acquired Airborne Express, a package delivery company operating in the United States. Weiss, who had been employed at Airborne Express since 1996, continued his employment at DHL as District Sales Manager for downtown Boston. He was promoted within a year to the post of Regional Sales Director in charge of overseeing a number of sales districts in the Northeast, including Brooklyn, New York. The following year, DHL named him "Regional Sales Director of the Year." Weiss was then elevated to the position of Director of National Accounts in August 2007. He remained in that position until his termination two years later.

A. The Bonus Plan

In December 2007, DHL informed Weiss that it had selected him to participate in the company's "Commitment to Success Bonus Plan" (the "Plan"). Under the Plan, Weiss became eligible for a $60,000 service-based bonus if he remained with the company through the end of 2009, and a $20,000 bonus if DHL met its performance objectives in 2009. The Employment Benefits Committee (the "Committee") of the company was given broad authority to administer the Plan:

> The Committee shall have full power and discretionary authority to interpret the Plan, make factual determinations, and to prescribe, amend and rescind any rules . . . and to make any other determinations and take such other actions as the Committee deems necessary or advisable in carrying out its duties under the Plan. Any action required of the Committee under the Plan shall be made in the Committee's sole discretion and not in a fiduciary capacity and need not be uniform as to similarly situated individuals. The Committee's administration of the Plan, including all such rules and regulations, interpretations, selections, determinations, approvals, decisions, delegations, amendments, terminations and other actions, shall be final, conclusive and binding on the Company, the Participant, and any other persons having or claiming an interest hereunder. The Committee could delegate its functions to a subcommittee or to one or more individuals. It also reserved the right to amend or terminate the Plan.

In October 2008, Weiss received notice that "some adjustments to the Plan" were made "in order to better reflect our changing work environment." Under the amended Plan, Weiss was still eligible to receive $80,000, but no portion of it was tied to the company's performance. Instead, the entire bonus was now contingent on continued employment through the end of 2009, with Weiss's performance remaining "in good standing." The first installation of $20,000 was payable in January 2009 and the remaining $60,000 in January 2010. In the event that DHL terminated him "without cause" and eliminated his position, Weiss would receive the full payout upon termination. If he voluntarily left DHL or if terminated for "good cause" prior to the payment dates, he would be ineligible for the bonus.

DHL paid Weiss the first installment of the bonus in January 2009. When he was terminated in September 2009, DHL refused to pay the remaining $60,000 on the basis that his termination was for good cause.

B. *The Termination*

[Recurrent problems arose involving Sergio Garcia, a sales representative in Brooklyn, who was the subject of questions about the rates used on customer accounts on several occasions. Although not his direct supervisor, Weiss was involved in an initial verbal warning to Garcia that his conduct could result in disciplinary action, including termination. The company's manager handbook provided that such verbal warnings must be documented, but Weiss was not aware of the policy and did not document the warning or inform the human resources department. Another problem occurred a few months later involving Garcia and other sales representatives; while three resigned, Garcia received only a three-day suspension and was transferred to another district. Weiss was not involved in dealing with this problem. A third incident several months later resulted in an internal investigation that revealed that the scheme had resulted in a multimillion-dollar loss to DHL. The earlier verbal warning by Weiss was discovered, but Garcia still did not lose his job, even though he refused to cooperate with the investigation. Ultimately, Weiss received a customer complaint alleging that Garcia was asking customers to pay kickbacks in exchange for receiving preferential shipping rates. He immediately forwarded the complaint to his superiors, and Garcia resigned.]

DHL responded to the allegation by retaining attorney Kenneth Thompson to conduct an investigation. In addition to confirming the kickbacks allegation, Thompson also found that Garcia and several other representatives in Brooklyn had engaged in various improper sales practices during the preceding years, including while Weiss was in charge of the district. Specifically, Thompson reported that the billing issue that precipitated Weiss's verbal warning to Garcia involved an unauthorized shipping rate extension. Thompson informed DHL of Weiss's "management failures" relating to his oversight of Garcia, including his failure to properly discipline Garcia in 2007, to document the 2007 verbal warning, to consult the human resources and security departments about the verbal warning, and to further investigate Garcia's conduct to determine of the scope of the misconduct.

At the conclusion of the investigation, Michael Berger, Weiss's supervisor at the time, informed Weiss that DHL was terminating his employment. The termination letter stated that Weiss was terminated for "just cause" because the results of the Thompson investigation "present[ed] a picture of significant management failures" while Weiss was Regional Sales Director in charge of the Brooklyn district "and thereafter." Berger was unaware of those failures until the Thompson investigation. When Weiss asked who made the decision to fire him, Berger told him, "it's above me."

Upon termination, Weiss did not receive the $60,000 bonus that he was set to receive in four months. DHL's General Counsel John Olin, who was the head of the Committee in charge of administering the Plan, testified that this was because Weiss was terminated for "good cause," which under the terms of the Plan made him ineligible for the bonus.

C. The Court Proceedings

Weiss sued DHL over the unpaid bonus, alleging that he was entitled to payment because his termination was without good cause. He asserted four claims for relief: [but the court allowed only the "straightforward" breach-of-contract claim to go to the jury. None of the other issues were raised on appeal.]

The court instructed the jury that the key issue was whether Weiss was terminated without "good cause" because, if so, DHL breached the Plan by not paying him the bonus. DHL objected on the ground that the Plan reserved the good cause determination for the Committee. The court acknowledged that the Plan "has the language in it" reserving for the Committee decisions "about performance and the like." But because the Plan uses the words "good cause," the court explained, it was for the jury to decide whether the termination was without good cause, regardless of the Committee's nomenclature. So instructed, the jury found for Weiss. After the court denied DHL's motion for judgment as a matter of law without comment, DHL filed this timely appeal.

II.

A. The Breach-of-Contract Claim

DHL maintains that the Plan gives the Committee the sole and exclusive authority to determine whether good cause existed for a participant's termination, and that in this instance the Committee so determined. Accordingly, DHL argues, it is entitled to judgment as a matter of law because there could be no breach of contract under the undisputed facts. Weiss retorts that it was for the jury to decide whether Weiss's termination was for good cause because the Plan is ambiguous as to whether the Committee retained such authority. . . .

We begin by reviewing long-standing principles of contract law Interpretation of a contract is ordinarily a question of law for the court. *Seaco Ins. Co. v. Barbosa*, 761 N.E.2d 946, 951 (Mass. 2002). "[W]hen several writings evidence a single contract or comprise constituent parts of a single transaction, they will be read together." *FDIC v. Singh*, 977 F.2d 18, 21 (1st Cir. 1992). Absent an ambiguity, the court interprets a contract "according to its plain terms," *Den Norske Bank AS v. First Nat'l Bank of Bos.*, 75 F.3d 49, 52 (1st Cir. 1996), in a manner that gives reasonable effect to each of its provisions, *J.A. Sullivan Corp. v. Commonwealth*, 494 N.E.2d 374, 378 (Mass. 1986).

"A contract is not ambiguous simply because litigants disagree about its proper interpretation." *Singh.* Ambiguity arises only if the language "is susceptible of more than one meaning and reasonably intelligent persons would differ as to which meaning is the proper one." *S. Union Co. v. Dep't of Pub. Utils.*, 941 N.E.2d 633, 640 (Mass. 2011) (internal quotation marks omitted). There is no ambiguity in the instant contract.

The plain language of the Plan designates the Committee as the sole arbiter of whether a Plan participant is terminated for good cause. The original Plan document makes clear that it is for the Committee to determine bonus eligibility and to construe the Plan's terms. The Plan specifies that the Committee "shall have full power and discretionary authority" to make determinations under the Plan and that its decisions regarding "rules and regulations, interpretations, selections, determinations, approvals, decisions, delegations, amendments, terminations and other actions, shall be final, conclusive and binding." In short, as the Plan administrator, the Committee was given broad discretionary authority to determine all matters pertaining to the Plan, including whether a participant qualified for payment.

The amendment to the Plan neither trumps the Committee's sweeping authority nor creates an ambiguity in this regard. By its express terms, the amendment only made "some adjustments" to the Plan, namely to provide that the bonus was no longer tied to the company's performance but only to continued service and to permit a participant terminated without good cause to receive the payout. The amendment did not purport to modify the Committee's role in any way. . . . Interpreting the original Plan document and the amendment as a single agreement, as we must, it becomes plain that the contract is susceptible only to one plausible construction: whether Weiss was terminated without good cause and thus remained eligible for the bonus was a decision within the ambit of the Committee's sole and final decision-making authority.

Weiss argues that the Plan is ambiguous because the amendment provides for the good cause determination but is silent about who decides, whereas the original Plan document addresses the Committee's decision-making authority but not the good cause protection. According to Weiss, this "tension" between the two documents could plausibly suggest that the employer and not the Committee is to determine whether a participant is terminated for good cause, in which case the jury could review the employer's decision. We disagree. The provision designating the Committee as the sole and final authority on decisions of this type is broad enough to encompass the good cause determination. And nothing in the amendment suggests that someone other than the Committee would make such decisions. Hence, the two documents are not incongruous. The only plausible construction of the Plan as a whole that gives reasonable effect to the provisions in both writings is that the Committee's decision-making authority extends to this eligibility determination.

Simply put, under the Plan, the Committee was free to deny Weiss the bonus if, in its sole judgment, his employment was terminated for good cause. Cf. *Nolan v. CN8*, 656 F.3d 71, 82 (1st Cir. 2011) (Selya, J., concurring) (where the employment agreement designated the employer as "the sole arbiter of whether the plaintiff's actions reflected unfavorably on [the employer's] interests or reputation (and, thus, warranted termination)," the plaintiff's contractual right to continued employment was extinguished when the employer exercised its prerogative). Neither we nor the district court can rewrite the contract to take away the Committee's discretion and empower the jury to decide whether Weiss was terminated for good cause.

The only relevant question regarding Weiss's breach-of-contract claim, then, is whether the Committee determined that Weiss was terminated for good cause. There is no room to doubt that it did so. Olin, the head of the Committee, testified unrebutted that, as permitted under the Plan, the Committee delegated to DHL's management its authority to determine whether good cause existed for a Plan participant's termination. DHL's executives testified, again unrebutted, that they decided to terminate Weiss because of his management failures in overseeing Garcia.

That effectively ends the matter. The Committee's determination that Weiss was terminated for good cause made him ineligible for the bonus, precluding his breach-of-contract claim. Accordingly, we reverse the judgment against DHL.

This outcome is not unfair, as Weiss urges. Weiss was a handsomely compensated employee in a significant position at DHL. He accepted the terms of the Plan that gave the Committee unfettered discretion in matters such as the eligibility decision at issue here. The preclusion of his breach-of-contract claim, moreover, does not mean that Weiss had no recourse but to bow his head and accept the Committee's decision. As Weiss recognized early in the game, Massachusetts law implies in every contract a covenant of good faith and fair dealing. *Ayash v. Dana-Farber Cancer Inst.*, 822 N.E.2d 667, 683 (Mass. 2005). A party may breach the covenant without breaching any express term of the contract. *See Fortune v. Nat'l Cash Register Co.*, 364 N.E.2d 1251, 1255-56 (Mass. 1977). In his complaint, Weiss asserted a claim for breach of the covenant. We pass no judgment on the viability of the claim, however, because it is not before us. When the district court discarded the good faith and fair dealing claim, leaving only a "straightforward" breach-of-contract claim, Weiss did not object. And he does not argue on appeal that the covenant claim remains. We therefore have no choice but to conclude that Weiss has abandoned the claim. *See United States v. Zannino*, 895 F.2d 1, 17 (1st Cir. 1990).

[The court also rejected Weiss's claim under the Massachusetts Wage Act, Mass. Gen. Laws ch. 149, §148, which generally "requires prompt payment of 'wages earned' on pain of civil and criminal penalties, treble damages, and attorney's fees." That Act did not reach Weiss's bonus because, given his termination and the defendant's determination of "good cause," it was never "earned."]

NOTES

1. *A Bird's Eye View.* The two principal cases are a study in contrasts, not least because the employee prevails on appeal in *Hess* and loses in *Weiss*, although on remand in *Hess*, the employee also lost. *Hess v. Kanoski & Assocs.*, 2014 U.S. Dist. LEXIS 42584 (C.D. Ill. Mar. 28, 2014); *aff'd, Hess v. Bresney*, 784 F.3d 1154 (7th Cir. 2015). Beyond that, however, each involves a different kind of incentive pay: Hess reflects an arrangement structured to encourage performance. In contrast, all Weiss had to do was stick around (and not give DHL good cause to fire him): This latter kind of arrangement is frequently described as a "retention bonus" and is often used when a firm is being acquired in order to help ensure that the target firm's employees remain in place. *See Uphoff v. Wachovia Securities*, 2009 U.S. Dist. LEXIS 116679, *2 (S.D. Fla. 2009) ("It is a standard practice in the brokerage/securities business to pay retention bonuses to current brokers and financial advisors when institutional sales and mergers are announced in order to reduce the attrition of established brokers and financial advisors who would otherwise be lured by bonus and compensation promises of competitors."). But the two categories are not mutually exclusive: Incentive bonuses often get paid at the end of the calendar year, which provides an incentive for employees contemplating departure to remain employed until after the bonus is paid. *See, e.g., Pick v. Norfolk Anesthesia*, 755 N.E.2d 382,

387-88 (Neb. 2008) (distinguishing between retention bonuses and those designed to improve productivity in holding that nurses who left employment prior to the end of December were not entitled to profit-based bonus awarded annually at firm holiday party).

Yet another distinction between the two cases is that the DHL bonus plan is heavily "lawyered" while the arrangement in *Hess*—despite being between a law firm and one of its attorneys—has a "back of the envelope" feel to it. It's probably not an accident that the employee prevailed in the latter case—at least on the first round—and lost in the former.

2. *Legal Entitlement or Something Less?* A threshold issue in any dispute over incentive pay is whether the employee has a legal entitlement as opposed to a contingent right or a mere expectation of compensation based on employer practices. Where a bonus system gives the employer discretion in determining whether to compensate and how much, courts generally treat the bonuses as gratuities. *See, e.g., Jensen v. International Business Machines Corp.*, 454 F.3d 382, 388 (4th Cir. 2006); *Arby's, Inc. v. Cooper*, 454 S.E.2d 488 (Ga. 1995). In *Weiss*, the employer seemed to go further and actually promise a particular amount. However, the "good cause" provision, especially because it reserved the absolute power to determine good cause, renders that promise illusory. Do you think that Weiss understood that his retention bonus was dependent on the whim of DHL? Or is that too strong a statement for the court's result? *Cf. Schaffart v. ONEOK, Inc.*, 686 F.3d 461 (8th Cir. 2012) (employees had right to *pro rata* recovery under a stock incentive plan when they retired; the decision that certain conditions were not met was not entitled to deference when not made by the designated agent for the plan).

3. *More Employee Victories. Hess* is not the only case finding an employer potentially liable for a bonus. In a remarkably similar scenario, *Guggenheimer v. Bernstein Litowitz & Grossman, L.L.P.*, 810 N.Y.S.2d 880 (Sup. Ct. 2006), plaintiff, an associate at a law firm specializing in class action litigation, was told upon hire that she would be eligible for bonuses for bringing successful cases to the firm. There was no written bonus policy, but it was commonly understood that the associate could receive up to 10 percent of the legal fees awarded to the firm. The plaintiff subsequently brought in and developed several high-profile cases. While they were pending, she wrote a memo to a supervising partner detailing her work and was orally assured that she would receive her bonus. The partner later circulated an e-mail message, titled "Special Bonuses for Business Referrals," stating that fees awarded to associates would be capped at $250,000. Following this message, the partner e-mailed Guggenheimer that the cap would not apply to cases referred to the firm prior to the institution of the new policy.

Ultimately the firm received fees of $1.35 million and $900,000 in two of her cases. When it balked at giving her 10 percent, she sued. The firm moved to dismiss on the ground that it retained discretion not to award bonus compensation. The court denied that motion because, whether the disputed amount was a discretionary "bonus" or "earned wages" was an issue of fact given the plaintiff's testimony about the oral agreement. Further, the fact that the exact amount of the bonus was not specified was not fatal to plaintiff's claim so long as "there exist sufficiently definite guidelines to enable a court to supply a bonus figure is a factual issue and survives a motion to dismiss." *Id.* at 885-86. In a number of other recent cases plaintiffs successfully sought recovery of bonuses. *See Ryan v. Kellogg Partners Institutional Servs.*, 967 N.E.2d 947 (N.Y. 2012) (plaintiff entitled to a guaranteed, nondiscretionary bonus of $175,000 orally promised by the managing partner; since the bonus constituted "wages" within the meaning of the Labor Law, failure to pay it entitled the employee to an award of attorney's fees); *Fishoff v. Coty Inc.*, 634 F.3d 647 (2d Cir. 2011) (once the CFO optionee validly exercised his rights, the employer was obligated to pay him the fair market value of the optioned shares and could not arbitrarily and retroactively revalue those shares); *Lewitton v. ITA Software, Inc.*, 585 F.3d 377, 381 (7th Cir. 2009) (rejecting the argument that a stock option incentive system resulted in a windfall to plaintiff above and beyond the value of his contributions to the company; the contract had mechanisms to strip the employee of vested shares, but the employer did not rely on any of them during plaintiff's employment).

4. *Was There Good Cause to Terminate Weiss?* The jury found for Weiss, although that verdict was overturned on appeal. Had it been appropriate to review the employer's decision, was the jury correct? Garcia seems to have been a real bad apple, but Weiss's sin might boil down to simple failure to record in writing a verbal warning of what at the time seemed a pretty mild offense. Weiss claimed not to have known that DHL policy was to make such a record. Considering that it was a "verbal" warning to begin with, is that so surprising or so egregious? Further, the Garcia saga, both at the time of Weiss's interactions with him and thereafter, involved a number of high-level officials who also failed to discipline Garcia. There is no indication that disciplinary action was taken against them. On the other hand, perhaps had Weiss been more proactive, Garcia's misconduct would have come to light earlier.

5. *Promissory Estoppel and Incentive Pay.* In *Uphoff v. Wachovia Securities*, 2009 U.S. Dist. LEXIS 116679 (S.D. Fla. 2009), the plaintiffs alleged that Wachovia orally promised to pay retention bonuses to its 14,600 financial advisors and brokers in order to retain their services and client base in the wake of an October 2008 announcement that it would be purchased by Wells Fargo. While no exact amount was promised, the plaintiffs cited an industry custom that justified each broker reasonably anticipating a minimum of $100,000. The court rejected the contract claim because there was no allegation of either an amount actually promised or a method for determining that amount. "Custom in a particular industry . . . cannot change the requirement of contract law that the parties mutually agree on the essential term of price." *Id.* at 8.

However, the plaintiffs also asserted a promissory estoppel claim and alleged that class members had chosen not to pursue alternative employment on the basis of Wachovia's promise. On that claim, the court found the promise of a bonus sufficiently clear to support suit—although the question of whether it was reasonable to rely on that promise in the circumstances of the financial industry at the time would have to be resolved at trial. Why did the court reject the brokers' contract claim but permit their promissory estoppel claim to proceed? Is it because the remedy—compensating the plaintiffs' reliance interest—seems fairer? How likely was it that the plaintiffs could have found other jobs in the midst of a financial meltdown? In any event, promissory estoppel is no panacea. *See Geras v. IBM*, 638 F.3d 1311 (10th Cir. 2011) (although the employer's records reflected an accrued commission of $156,072 for plaintiff, the employer owed him neither that sum nor separation pay since its plan did not constitute an enforceable promise because it disclaimed any contractual obligation and therefore could not be reasonably relied on by an employee).

6. *Bonuses and Public Outrage.* History tells us why Wachovia retracted the promised bonuses: The decision came in the midst of the economic crisis of 2008 and shortly after billions of dollars in federal bailout funds were handed over to private

financial firms through the Troubled Asset Relief Program (TARP). Public controversy over the federal bailout program grew to a fever pitch in 2009, when several
TARP recipients announced millions of dollars in bonuses to employees. Wells Fargo,
which bought Wachovia, was a TARP fund recipient. Yielding to public pressure,
Wachovia rescinded the bonuses.

In contrast to Wachovia, insurance giant AIG, which received $170 billion in
bailout funds, went forward with paying $165 million in promised bonuses one
month after Wachovia opted to forgo them. The company was skewered by Congress
and the media for the payments. *See* Liam Pleven et al., *AIG Faces Growing Wrath
Over Payouts*, WALL ST. J., March 19, 2009, at A1. AIG defended its decision to pay
out, stating that their lawyers had concluded that the bonuses were "legal, binding
obligations" of the company. *See id.*

While the public outcry was driven mostly by the perception that the bonuses
were rewards for financial failure, another sore point for many was the belief that,
in the middle of a financial crisis, none of the firms had to pay retention bonuses in
order to keep their workforces in place. Given the massive blow to Wall Street, there
were probably very few opportunities for reemployment even for the best workers.
Whichever view you find more persuasive, consider the position of the AIG employees
who had been promised the pay.

7. *Reforming Executive Pay.* Calls to end outlandish pay for corporate executives
are nothing new, but the recession of 2008 heightened interest in reform. Whereas
past calls had focused on the need to protect shareholders, the events of 2008 and
2009 exposed how poorly structured compensation could incent unduly risky behavior
with detrimental consequences to the economy as a whole. As a condition of receiving
federal bailout funds, firms were obligated to comply with Treasury Department
"guidelines" that set limits on executive compensation but did not address bonuses.
Subsequently, Congress imposed executive pay requirements on all publicly traded
companies in its financial overhaul legislation, the Dodd-Frank Wall Street Reform
and Consumer Protection Act of 2010. While the law does not put any substantive
limits on the amounts companies may pay, it requires that pay packages, including
"golden parachute" compensation, be put to a shareholder vote, and that executive
compensation committee members, as well as their advisors, be independent decision
makers. *See* 15 U.S.C.A. §§78n-1, 78j-3 (2018). In addition, the law creates new
disclosure rules and requires companies to develop a mechanism to "clawback" erroneously awarded compensation. *See* 15 U.S.C.A. §78j-4 (2018); 17 C.F.R. 229.402
(2018). *See generally* Jesse Fried & Nitzan Shilon, *Excess-Pay Clawbacks*, 36 IOWA
J. CORP. L. 721 (2011).

8. *Wage Payment Laws.* The plaintiff in *Weiss* also asserted a claim under the
state's Wage Act, although it was unsuccessful. Such laws are common in the United
States, generally prohibiting the willful failure to pay earned wages and enhancing
the remedies that would otherwise be available. *See, e.g.*, N.Y. LAB. LAW §198(1-a)
(McKinney 2018) (providing for 25 percent penalty on wages wrongfully withheld
and attorney's fees). However, the viability of such claims in incentive compensation
scenarios rests on the plaintiff's ability to show that the bonus is in fact an "earned"
wage. As a result, such statutes serve principally to enhance damages for workers
who can demonstrate the existence of a vested benefit and would consequently have
succeeded under common law. They generally are unavailing for plaintiffs alleging
entitlement to discretionary or non-performance-based bonuses, such as those based
on retention or firm performance. *See Geysen v. Securitas Sec. Servs. USA, Inc.*, 142

A.3d 227 (Conn. 2016) (Wage Act does not bar employer from specifying by contract when wages were considered earned). *But see Kolchins v. Evolution Mkts., Inc.,* 96 N.E.3d 784, 790-91 (N.Y. 2018) (contractual bonus based on plaintiff's performance could constitute nonforfeitable "wages" under New York law, in which case, a contract provision denying such payment after they were "earned" would be void as against public policy).

* * *

You may have noticed that Weiss asserted a claim that his employer violated the duty of good faith and fair dealing implied in every contract, although the court did not address that issue. After you've read the next principal case, ask yourself whether Weiss had a good claim under that theory.

Geysen v. Securitas Sec. Servs. USA, Inc.
142 A.3d 227 (Conn. 2016)

ROGERS, C. J.

This consolidated appeal presents the question of whether an at-will employment agreement, providing that an employee's commissions will not be paid unless the employer has invoiced commissionable amounts to the client prior to the employee's termination, is contrary to public policy and a violation of General Statutes (Supp. 2016) §31-72. [On the employer's appeal on this issue, the court held no. Addressing the plaintiff's cross appeal for the dismissal of his count alleging breach of the implied covenant of good faith and fair dealing, the court reversed.]

The following procedural history and facts are relevant to this appeal. The defendant is a security services company that provides various protection services to industrial and commercial clients. These services are marketed through employees hired as business development managers (managers) who solicit new business from prospective and existing customers. [Plaintiff was hired in 2005 under a compensation arrangement that included a weekly base salary and commissions on contracts he procured. The incentive plan was subsequently amended to provide that commissions were due only after work was performed and invoiced to the client. The employment apparently went smoothly until May 22, 2008, at which point] Thomas R. Fagan, the defendant's regional vice president for human resources, hand delivered a memorandum to the plaintiff terminating his employment. The memorandum explained that the defendant had conducted an investigation into improper business activities that had resulted in significant risk exposure to the defendant and, as a result of the investigation findings, the defendant was terminating the plaintiff's employment effective May 22, 2008. . . .

I.

[The court first found the commission provision not void on public policy grounds because it did not act to negate §31-72. That statute "does not embody substantive standards to determine the amount of wages that are payable but provides penalties in order to deter employers from deferring wage payments once they have accrued." In other words, the Connecticut wage statutes do not define the wages due but merely require that the wages agreed to will not be withheld for any reason. Prior cases had allowed deductions from commissions otherwise due for returned goods, and therefore effectively rejected any rule that an employee's right to wages necessarily accrued at the time of sale. In the case at bar, the contract's clear language that commissions were not due until the customer was invoiced made that action a condition precedent to earning the commission, and that act had to be completed before plaintiff's termination for the commissions to be "due" within the meaning of the statute.]

II . . .

A.

We analyze first the plaintiff's cross appeal seeking reinstatement of the breach of the implied covenant of good faith and fair dealing count. "[I]t is axiomatic that the . . . duty of good faith and fair dealing is a covenant implied into a contract or a contractual relationship. . . . In other words, every contract carries an implied duty requiring that neither party do anything that will injure the right of the other to receive the benefits of the agreement. . . . The covenant of good faith and fair dealing presupposes that the terms and purpose of the contract are agreed upon by the parties and that what is in dispute is a party's discretionary application or interpretation of a contract term."[11] *De La Concha of Hartford, Inc. v. Aetna Life Ins. Co.*, 849 A.2d 382 (2004).

"To constitute a breach of [the implied covenant of good faith and fair dealing], the acts by which a defendant allegedly impedes the plaintiff's right to receive benefits that he or she reasonably expected to receive under the contract must have been taken in bad faith. . . . Bad faith in general implies . . . actual or constructive fraud, or a design to mislead or deceive another, or a neglect or refusal to fulfill some duty or some contractual obligation, not prompted by an honest mistake as to one's rights or duties, but by some interested or sinister motive. . . . Bad faith means more than mere negligence; it involves a dishonest purpose." (Citation omitted; internal quotation marks omitted.) *De La Concha of Hartford, Inc. v. Aetna Life Ins. Co.* "[B]ad faith may be overt or may consist of inaction, and it may include evasion of the spirit of the bargain . . . . *Elm Street Builders, Inc. v. Enterprise Park Condominium Assn., Inc.*, 778 A.2d 237 (2001), quoting 2 RESTATEMENT (SECOND), CONTRACTS §205, comment (d) (1981); see also 23 S. Williston, Contracts (4th Ed. Lord 2002) §63:22, p. 508 (a party who evades the spirit of the contract . . . may be liable for breach of the implied covenant of good faith and fair dealing . . .)." (Internal quotation marks omitted.)

In *Magnan v. Anaconda Industries, Inc.*, 479 A.2d 781 (1984), this court addressed the implied covenant of good faith and fair dealing in employment contracts. The plaintiff in that case contended that the good faith principle was applicable

11. "Essentially [the implied covenant of good faith and fair dealing] is a rule of construction designed to fulfill the reasonable expectations of the contracting parties as they presumably intended. The principle, therefore, cannot be applied to achieve a result contrary to the clearly expressed terms of a contract, unless, possibly, those terms are contrary to public policy." *Magnan v. Anaconda Industries, Inc.*, 479 A.2d 781 (1984).

and subjected the employer to liability whenever an employee is discharged without just cause. For guidance, the court looked to Massachusetts cases applying the implied covenant of good faith and fair dealing in the employment context. While the court recognized the applicability of the covenant of good faith to employment contracts, it concluded that a breach of such an implied covenant cannot be predicated simply upon the absence of good cause for discharge. The court specifically declined the plaintiff's invitation "to transform the requirement of good faith into an implied condition that an employee may be dismissed only for good cause." In *Magnan*, the court left for another day the determination of the applicability of the covenant of good faith and fair dealing to a discharge that was motivated by an intent to deprive an employee of clearly identifiable compensation related to past services. As such, the court acknowledged, but did not fully consider, the Massachusetts case of *Fortune v. National Cash Register Co.*, 364 N.E.2d 1251 (1977).

Fortune is particularly illustrative in our present case. In *Fortune*, under the express terms of an at-will employment contract, the plaintiff employee had received all the bonus commissions to which he was entitled when his employment with the defendant was terminated. The court acknowledged that "an employer is entitled to be motivated by and to serve its own legitimate business interests; that an employer must have wide latitude in deciding whom it will employ in the face of the uncertainties of the business world; and that an employer needs flexibility in the face of changing circumstances." Nevertheless, the Massachusetts Supreme Judicial Court held that the employer's written contract contained an implied covenant of good faith and fair dealing and that, in a situation where commissions are to be paid for work performed by the employee, a bad faith termination constituted a breach of that contract.[12]

The court in *Fortune* further stated that "[w]here the principal seeks to deprive the agent of all compensation by terminating the contractual relationship when the agent is on the brink of successfully completing the sale, the principal has acted in bad faith and the ensuing transaction between the principal and the buyer is to be regarded as having been accomplished by the agent. . . . The same result obtains where the principal attempts to deprive the agent of any portion of a commission due the agent. Courts have often applied this rule to prevent overreaching by employers and the forfeiture by employees of benefits almost earned by the rendering of substantial services." (Citation omitted.)

Thus, although an employer may terminate the employee at will, the employer may not act in bad faith to prevent paying the employee commissions he reasonably expected to receive for services rendered under the contract. . . .

To be clear, an employer does not act in bad faith solely by refusing to pay commissions on sales invoiced after an employee's termination if that obligation is an express contract term. An employer's action or inaction that attempts to avoid the spirit of the bargain or which evinces a dishonest purpose, however, would violate the implied covenant of good faith and fair dealing as it relates to the contractual provision for payment of commissions.

---

12. [*Fortune*] noted that while some other courts had fashioned a remedy in tort to avoid the rigidity of the "at will" rule, it believed that there was a remedy based on the contract. The Massachusetts Supreme Judicial Court subsequently stated that the employer's predatory motivation in *Fortune* could be classified as a reason contrary to public policy. See *Cort v. Bristol-Myers Co.*, 431 N.E.2d 908 (1982).

In the present case, the trial court considered the plaintiff's claim that the covenant was breached to be essentially the same as a wrongful discharge claim. A breach of the implied covenant of good faith and fair dealing contract claim, however, is different than a wrongful termination claim because the former focuses on the fulfillment of the parties' reasonable expectations rather than on a violation of public policy.[13] As articulated in *Wakefield v. Northern Telecom, Inc.*, [769 F.2d 109, 112 (2d Cir. 1985)], while an at-will employee may not be able to "recover for his termination per se . . . the contract for payment of commissions creates rights distinct from the employment relation, and . . . obligations derived from the covenant of good faith implicit in the commission contract may survive the termination of the employment relationship. Implied contractual obligations may coexist with express provisions which seemingly negate them where common expectations or the relationship of the parties as structured by the contract so dictate. . . . A covenant of good faith should not be implied as a modification of an employer's right to terminate an at-will employee because even a whimsical termination does not deprive the employee of benefits expected in return for the employee's performance. This is so because performance and the distribution of benefits occur simultaneously, and neither party is left high and dry by the termination.

"Where, however, a covenant of good faith is necessary to enable one party to receive the benefits promised for performance, it is implied by the law as necessary to effectuate the intent of the parties. . . . *[A contract] cannot be read to enable the defendant to terminate an employee for the purpose of avoiding the payment of commissions which are otherwise owed.* Such an interpretation would make the performance by one party the cause of the other party's [nonperformance]." (Emphasis added; citations omitted.) Accord *Arbeeny v. Kennedy Executive Search, Inc.*, 893 N.Y.S.2d 39 (2010) ("[a]lthough an at-will employee such as [the] plaintiff would not be able to sue for wrongful termination of the contract [under New York law], he should nonetheless be able to state a claim that the employer's termination action was specifically designed to cut off commissions that were coming due to the employee").[14]

We find the reasoning in *Fortune*, *Wakefield* and *Arbeeny* persuasive, and therefore, recognize the availability of a breach of the implied covenant of good faith and fair dealing contract claim when the termination of an employee was done with the intent to avoid the payment of commissions.

Turning to the allegations of the plaintiff's complaint in the present case, the plaintiff claims in relevant part that the defendant had "failed to pay commissions due to [the] [p]laintiff on certain sales made" and as such, the "[d]efendant's aforementioned conduct violated the implied covenant of good faith and fair dealing by failing to comply with [the] [p]laintiff's reasonable expectation that the [d]efendant would pay commissions earned by the [p]laintiff." These allegations focus on damages suffered due to the violation of the plaintiff's reasonable expectation regarding

---

13. Under such a claim, termination is incidental, or a means, to accomplish the breach of the implied covenant of good faith and fair dealing. . . .

14. In *Wakefield v. Northern Telecom, Inc.*, in analyzing New Jersey and New York law, the Second Circuit Court of Appeals held that the jury could have awarded damages if it found that the employer discharged the employee in order to avoid paying him commissions earned on sales that were completed but for formalities. In *Arbeeny v. Kennedy Executive Search, Inc.*, the court held that an at-will employee could state a claim for breach of contract to recover unpaid earned commissions.

the payment of commissions.[15] If an employer can be shown to have interfered in bad faith with an employee's ability to secure his commissions, this would violate the reasonable expectation that his employer would not inhibit his ability to earn commissions he worked for under the contract. Accordingly, on the basis of the allegations in the complaint, the plaintiff has stated a legally sufficient claim for breach of the implied covenant of good faith and fair dealing.

NOTES

1. *The Duty of Good Faith—Again.* Recall the discussion of the implied duty in *Guz v. Bechtel* in Chapter 2. There the court rejected the employee's claim that by terminating him unfairly the employer breached the duty of good faith, concluding that such an interpretation ran counter to employment at will, which specifically allows arbitrary and unfair terminations. *Geysen* is certainly consistent with that. However, plaintiffs have often been successful in using the implied duty to challenge refusals to pay earned wages or benefits as opposed to challenging the termination itself. The seminal case is *Fortune v. National Cash Register*, 364 N.E.2d 1251 (Mass. 1977), upon which *Geysen* heavily relies. There, the employer had a policy provided that employees would receive some commissions on sales only on delivery of the goods to customer. Fortune was terminated a few days after closing on a record-breaking sale but prior to delivery on that order. On his suit for those commissions, the Supreme Court of Massachusetts held that, while there was no breach under the express terms of the contract, it was reasonable for the jury to find bad faith in breach of the implied duty, and that the express terms of the contract were no impediment since the duty of good faith was designed to remedy situations where the challenged conduct, while not in breach of any specific term, undermined the counterparty's reasonable expectations.

2. *The Meaning of the Duty.* Are *Geysen* and *Fortune* consistent with the court's rejection of the implied duty claim in *Guz*? The latter case focused on whether an employer's right to fire an at-will employee was limited by good faith, holding no. Neither *Geysen* nor *Fortune* infringe this employer right directly—they merely refuse to allow an employer to use the expedient of discharge to deny benefits that would have earned but for the discharge. In other words, an employee suing on the covenant can't recover damages for being discharged; she can merely recover the otherwise earned benefits. *See also Kmak v. Am. Century Cos.*, 754 F.3d 513 (8th Cir. 2014) (looking to Missouri's public policy to find that Kmak breached the implied covenant by retaliating against plaintiff for testifying in an arbitration proceeding: American Century may have had the right to call Kmak's shares "at any time," but it did not have the right to call those shares for any reason, if doing so would violate public policy).

---

15. The defendant claims that "the plaintiff did not allege that [he was fired] in order to deprive him of commissions that he might have earned at some unknown time in the future" due to the plaintiff's numerous assertions that the alleged commissions were "earned" and "due to him." Reading the complaint broadly, as we must, we find this argument unpersuasive. We believe that, although the plaintiff had not "earned" the commissions under the wage statutes, he may yet be able to demonstrate that he was nevertheless "owed" them because he was prevented from earning them due to the employer's breach of the implied covenant of good faith and fair dealing. In the present case, the plaintiff did allege that the defendant's "reasons for [his] termination were false and a pretext for nonpayment of *owed* commissions." (Emphasis added.)

See also Beidel v. Sideline Software, Inc., 811 N.W.2d 856 (Wis. 2013) (recognizing a former employee's action for specific performance of stock repurchase agreement for violation of duty of good faith when he alleged that he was discharged without cause in order to limit his recovery to a lesser appraised value of shares).

While not all jurisdictions recognize the doctrine's limit on employer power, *see, e.g., Cramer v. Fairfield Med. Ctr.*, 914 N.E.2d 447, 455 (Ohio App. 2009) ("Ohio law does not recognize a good faith and fair dealing requirement in employment-at-will relationships."), the Restatement of Employment Law does recognize a contractual "non-waivable duty of good faith and fair dealing" between employer and employee, "which includes an agreement by each not to hinder the other's performance under, or deprive the other of the benefit of, the contract," §2.07(a). Tracking the distinction between *Geysen/Fortune* and *Guz*, it cautions that that duty "must be read in a manner consistent with the essential nature of an at-will relationship." §2.07(b). More specifically, the section goes on to provide that the implied covenant "includes the duty not to terminate . . . the employment relationship for the purpose of . . . preventing the vesting or accrual of an employee right or benefit." §2.07(c)(1). Illustration 1 is essentially *Fortune*.

Perhaps more radically, the proposed Restatement also invokes the duty to bar an employer from "retaliating against the employee for performing the employee's obligations under the employment contract or law." §2.07(c)(2). Illustration 2 hypothesizes an accounting manager under a contractual duty to certify his employer's financial statements as consistent with applicable professional standards. According to the Illustration, "termination of E for performing this contractual obligation violates the duty of good faith and fair dealing." The Reporters' Notes state that the Illustration is "based on the facts, while rejecting the holding" of *Sabetay v. Sterling Drug Co.*, 514 N.Y.S.2d 209 (N.Y. 1983). *See generally* Lea VanderVelde, *Where Is the Concept of Good Faith in the Restatement of Employment?*, 21 EMPL. RTS. & EMPL. POL'Y J. 335 (2108).

3. *Proving Bad Faith.* Presumably, any violation of the duty of good faith is dependent on proof that the termination was intended to prevent the payment of the earned benefit. How does a plaintiff convince the factfinder that his or her employer had the requisite intent? Not surprisingly, employers are unlikely to admit it, and the employee often must rely on circumstantial evidence, such as the timing of the termination relative to the anticipated payment and the length and history of the employment relationship. *Fortune* is the poster boy for this kind of proof. At least one case has seemingly loosened the intent requirement, finding it sufficient that a termination without cause deprived an employee of anticipated commissions. In *Gram v. Liberty Mutual Insurance Co.*, 429 N.E.2d 21 (Mass. 1981), an insurance salesman, the most productive seller in his office, was terminated after a disagreement over a letter sent to clients. As a result, he lost out on potential commissions from policy renewals. The court determined that the termination was without cause, but that the evidence did not support a finding that the employer had considered Gram's accrual of commissions in making its decision. It nonetheless allowed Gram's claim of breach of an implied duty of good faith. Despite the absence of evidence of bad intent, the court noted that "the fact remains that Gram lost reasonably ascertainable future compensation based on his past services." Given his "reasonable expectancy of some renewal commissions," the court believed the duty of good faith "requires that the employer be liable for the loss of compensation that is so clearly related to an employee's past service, when the employee is discharged without good cause." *Id.* at 28-29.

The dissent accused the court of "restructur[ing] an at-will employment agreement to reflect an imposed condition never heretofore recognized by this court and one of doubtful legitimacy." *Id*. at 30. Re-read the proposed Restatement rule. Isn't it clear from the "purpose" language that *Gram* goes further than the ALI? Would the *Geysen* court agree with *Gram*?

4. *Vested Benefits Versus Anticipated Earnings.* In *Geysen*, the court clearly rejected the claim that the commissions at issue were in any sense "due"; had the defendant owed them to plaintiff, the Connecticut wage statute would have been implicated. While the courts tend to agree that plaintiffs cannot recover future wages under a duty of good faith claim, as would be available under breach of an implied or express contract for job security, they do allow the recovery of compensation that would have been earned but for the breach. Does this make sense? In any event, punitive damages are not available, despite the cause of action's close relationship to tort. *See Foley v. Interactive Data Corp.*, 765 P.2d 373 (Cal. 1988). These restrictions place a critical limitation on the cause of action as a vehicle for challenging at-will terminations.

5. *"Earned," "Accrued," and Non-Waivable.* The theory of good faith and fair dealing is said by the Restatement to be "non-waivable," which is consistent with the general approach to that duty in the law of contracts. But the duty is also generally recognized to be a gap-filler, which means that it cannot trump an explicit provision of the contract. In cases like *Geysen* and *Fortune,* the governing contract required continued employment in order for the benefit to be paid, but it did not expressly allow the employer to fire the employees in order to forestall the compensation. That created a "gap" that the duty of good faith and fair dealing could then fill: The employer was allowed to fire the employee but not for the purpose of preventing the accrual of the benefit.

You won't be surprised to learn that employers are now drafting their contracts to close the gap: While the duty of good faith remains unwaivable, it has no role absent a gap in the express agreement of the parties. To see this, suppose the agreements in *Geysen* and *Fortune* provided something like: "Employee must remain with the company in order to receive the designated compensation, and employer reserves the right to discharge her in order to prevent her from receiving said compensation"?

6. *Back to* Weiss. In light of what you've learned, what do you think of Weiss's claim of breach of the duty of good faith and fair dealing? Given the facts alleged, is it a good claim? Is there something else he would have to assert to make it viable? In *Geysen*, what kind of proof will plaintiff need to adduce in order to prevail? Would it be enough to show that he was not guilty of the offenses alleged? Would he also have to prove that his employer did not believe him to be guilty?

PROBLEMS

(3-4.) Roseland Property Company, a real estate development firm, entered into an agreement with Carol Naderny to serve as the main developer in its new Boston office. The relevant parts of her contract provided:

> 8.   You will be entitled to a participation interest in all new projects which originate out of Roseland's Boston office during the period of your employment.

Your participation interest in each applicable project will be equal to 15 percent of the cash distributed to the Roseland Entity after the Roseland Entity has received cash distributions equal to the Roseland Entity's capital contributions plus an 8 percent return on such contributions for such project. Your interest in such new projects will vest at the same time that the Roseland Entity's interests vest. Your participation percentage is subject to review each year. . . .

14. Roseland will have and retain sole ownership and control of all new business developed by you while at Roseland and all Roseland business will remain with Roseland following termination of our relationship for any reason.

15. The relationship between you and Roseland is and at all times will be strictly an "at will" relationship, and either you or Roseland may terminate your employment and this relationship at any time with or without cause, for any reason or no reason, and with or without notice.

Three years later, Roseland and Naderny amicably parted ways as a result of differences in their business philosophy. During her employment, Naderny had initiated four projects but none had closed or begun construction as of the date of her departure. As a result, Roseland did not pay her a "participation interest." One year later, however, Roseland succeeded in closing on one of Naderny's projects and received a sizeable sum. Naderny has since sent Roseland a demand letter requesting my "15 percent interest now that the project has vested."

> (a) Suppose you represent Roseland. How would you respond to Naderny's letter?
> (b) Suppose you had represented Roseland during the negotiation of Naderny's contract. How would you have drafted it to prevent future liabilities to terminated employees?
> (c) Suppose you represented Naderny during the negotiation of her contract. How would you have drafted it to ensure that she received her cut on all projects she initiated?
> (d) Returning to part (a), suppose that as a result of your efforts on behalf of Roseland, the parties reach a settlement, resolve their differences, and decide they want to work together again. In order to avoid any possible future disputes, they would like to enter into a revised contract that clarifies any points of ambiguity. Consider the competing versions of the contract you have created in response to parts (b) and (c). Can you think of ways in which the parties might compromise their positions to achieve an agreement? What would it look like in writing?

3-5. Don Broadbent was employed by Westport Inc. as a Senior Vice President in charge of operations. He was hired under a five-year written contract containing the following provisions related to termination:

> **Termination without cause.** If the Executive is involuntarily terminated without cause, the Executive will receive severance equaling two years' salary and 25,000 shares of common stock.
> **Termination for cause.** If the Executive is involuntarily terminated for cause, the Executive forfeits rights to further payment and all obligations of the Company under this contract will cease.
> **Termination following a change in control.** If the Executive is involuntarily terminated within six months of a sale of substantially all of the Company's assets, or a merger in which the Company is not the surviving entity, the Executive

will receive severance equal to one year's salary and 25,000 shares of the common stock of the purchasing or surviving entity.

Three years after hiring Broadbent, Westport experiences legitimate and sustained financial difficulties. It begins discussions with Motoport Co., a successful competitor, about the possibility of Motoport buying the company. In order to make itself more marketable, Westport undertakes a corporate restructuring and lays off a significant percentage of its workforce, including Broadbent, who is paid pursuant to the "termination without cause" provision of his contract. Five months later, Motoport purchases Westport, and Motoport's stock rises significantly as a result of the acquisition.

Broadbent subsequently reads about Motoport's purchase and stock rise in the newspaper. He pulls out a copy of his contract, does the math, and realizes that, due to the dramatic increase in stock price, he would have come out with a lot more money had he been terminated under the "change in control" provision of his contract, despite the lesser amount of severance he would have received. Might he have a viable breach of contract claim?

Part Three

TORT-BASED PROTECTIONS FOR WORKERS

4

The Public Policy Exception to the At-Will Rule

When is the firing of an employee tortious under the common law? Prior to the 1970s, the conventional answer to this question would have been never. Actions taken *in connection with* a discharge could be tortious, even if the discharge itself were not. For example, an employee who was coercively interrogated in connection with employer investigation of a theft might have a cause of action for false imprisonment, or one who was publicly slandered in connection with his discharge could have sued in defamation. While such torts continue to constrain employer conduct (*see* Chapter 5), it was not until the late 1970s that some discharges themselves became tortious and employees were no longer limited to claims based on contract or statutory law.

Currently, most jurisdictions recognize the termination of an employee as actionable, although they often differ on the circumstances in which the tort will lie. This new law encompasses several theories; some are expansive of older theories and others are true innovations. Perhaps the most developed approach is "the public policy exception" to the at-will rule, often referred to as "wrongful discharge." Although some courts view the doctrine as partially contractual, the more widely held view is that discharging an employee for a reason that offends public policy constitutes a tort. It is this tort that will be the subject of section A of this chapter.

A natural outgrowth of the common law public policy exception was legislation codifying protection for employees who engage in conduct required or permitted by public policy. Statutes have long provided protection ancillary to the main thrust of the law itself. For example, Title VII of the Civil Rights Act of 1964 bars discrimination on account of race, sex, religion, and national origin, but it also bars retaliation against employees who file charges of discrimination or otherwise oppose unlawful employment practices under the statute. *See* Chapter 9. There are numerous federal and state laws with such statute-specific provisions aimed at protecting employees from reprisal for engaging in particular activities. But increasingly more general statutes, often described as "whistleblower" laws, protect employees who engage in a wide range of activities furthering public policy. This topic is the subject of Section B.

A. THE COMMON LAW PUBLIC POLICY EXCEPTION

The emergence of a public policy exception to the at-will rule has been one of the most important developments in employment law. Not only has it provided employees with an important new source of rights, but it has also forced employers to reconsider their entire approach to termination. While relatively few discharges, in the final analysis, implicate public policy, employers are well advised to ensure that all terminations are reviewed carefully given the financial and reputational consequences of a misstep.

The paradigm public policy case arises when an employee claims that she has been discharged for engaging in conduct that has been mandated, or at least encouraged, by some public policy not directly connected with employment. For example, an employee may claim that she has been fired because she testified truthfully before a legislative body or court. When such testimony adversely affects the employer, it is easy to see the motivation for discharge. Originally, the common law recognized no legal bar to discharging an at-will employee in these circumstances, however reprehensible it might seem and however perverse from a societal perspective. But courts have moved away from that position. An early case recognizing a cause of action in such circumstances was *Petermann v. International Brotherhood of Teamsters*, 344 P.2d 25 (Cal. App. 1959), which upheld an employee's suit when he was fired for refusing to perjure himself before the California legislature. This tort was at first very limited—*Petermann* stressed that the employee had been fired for refusing to commit a felonious act—but it gradually expanded. By 1975, for example, a court recognized that discharge of an employee for serving on a jury was actionable, even absent a statute according such protection. *See Nees v. Hocks*, 536 P.2d 512 (Or. 1975).

As cases accumulated where courts encountered actions by employers that tended to frustrate public policy, the downside of pure private ordering became apparent. Even if it was appropriate to leave to private ordering questions that affected the employer and its employees alone, a different set of considerations developed when the relationship between the two affected third parties—such as legislative investigation in *Petermann* or the availability of qualified jurors in *Nees*. Thus, there gradually developed what came to be called the wrongful discharge or public policy tort: Where public policy is sufficiently implicated, a discharge in contravention of that policy is actionable as a tort. Understanding this tort requires considering a number of related questions. The initial one—whether the courts (as opposed to the legislature) should recognize such a cause of action—has been generally resolved in favor of court action although some jurisdictions have rejected the tort entirely. *See Murphy v. Am. Home Prods. Corp.*, 448 N.E.2d 86, 89 (N.Y. 1983) ("[S]uch a significant change in our law is best left to the Legislature.").

Others have applied the tort sparingly as a kind of gap filler where the state had announced a policy in a statute but did not legislate directly with respect to the employment setting. For example, some workers' compensation schemes failed to explicitly provide a cause of action for employees discharged for filing a claim. In such instances, states often vindicated the policy underlying workers' compensation by protecting those who filed claims. *See, e.g., Freas v. Archer Servs., Inc.*, 716 A.2d 998 (D.C. 1998). The view of tort as a gap filler is reinforced by those courts that have refused to apply the tort when predicate legislation provides its own remedial scheme.

For example, most courts have been unwilling to find a public policy tort based on sex discrimination. While there is obviously a strong public policy against such conduct, it is expressed in statutes that provide their own enforcement schemes, and these courts have held that there is therefore no need to recognize a separate tort. *See, e.g., Makovi v. Sherwin-Williams Co.*, 561 A.2d 179 (Md. 1989) (sex discrimination); *Sands Regent v. Valgardson*, 777 P.2d 898 (Nev. 1989) (age discrimination). *See generally* Jarod Spencer González, *State Anti-Discrimination Statutes and Implied Preemption of Common Law Torts: Valuing the Common Law*, 59 S. CAR. L. REV. 115 (2007).

When a court accepts the premise of the public policy tort, what should count as "public policy"? In its narrowest formulation, the tort might bar employers only from discharging employees for doing what the law requires or for not doing what the law forbids. For instance, in *Petermann*, a state statute required truthful testimony in response to a subpoena, and permitting an employer to discharge someone for providing such testimony would discourage this conduct. At the other extreme, the public policy tort could bar employers from terminating workers for activities that the judiciary views as "socially useful." For instance, education is generally viewed as a social good, but is it appropriate to bar employers from terminating someone for enrolling in law school? *See Scroghan v. Kraftco Corp.*, 551 S.W.2d 811 (Ky. App. 1977) (no). As might be expected, the cases are strung along this spectrum, with conflicting views of the scope of the tort competing for attention. *See Sherrill v. Farmers Ins. Exch.*, 374 P.3d 723 (N.M. Ct. App. 2016) (insurer's duty to deal with insureds in good faith provided a sufficient public policy basis for an employee's claim of wrongful discharge for objecting to claims-processing procedures incentivizing adjustors to coerce claimants to settle for unreasonably low amounts); *Swindol v. Aurora Flight Scis. Corp.*, 194 So. 3d 847 (Miss. 2016) (public policy bars employers from discharging a worker for having a firearm inside his locked vehicle on company property); *Moore v. Warr Acres Nursing Ctr., LLC*, 376 P.3d 894 (Okla. 2016) (terminating a licensed practical nurse for missing work in a nursing center when sick with influenza would violate public policy due to public health concerns). *But see Robinson v. Salvation Army*, 791 S.E.2d 577 (Va. 2016) (no violation of Virginia public policy when an employee is terminated for refusing demands for private sexual activity).

One recent attempt to bring coherence to the cases is the American Law Institute's ("ALI") Restatement of Employment Law (2015), which provides:

§ 5.02 Employer Discipline in Violation of Public Policy: Protected Activities

An employer is subject to liability in tort under §5.01 for discharging an employee because the employee, acting in a reasonable manner,

(a) refuses to commit an act that the employee reasonably and in good faith believes violates a law or other well-established public policy, such as a professional or occupational code of conduct protective of the public interest;

(b) performs a public duty or obligation that the employee reasonably and in good faith believes the law imposes;

(c) files a charge or claims a benefit under an employment statute or law, whether or not the charge or claim is meritorious;

(d) refuses to waive a nonnegotiable or nonwaivable right where the employer's insistence on the waiver as a condition of employment or the court's enforcement of the waiver would violate well-established public policy;

(e) reports or inquires about conduct that the employee reasonably and in good faith believes violates a law or an established principle of a professional or occupational code of conduct protective of the public interest; or

(f) engages in other activity directly furthering a well-established public policy.

As you work through this chapter, consider whether this proposal is an accurate "restatement" of the law as it has evolved or as it should be formulated in the future.

But note what is *not* protected by this formulation of the public policy tort: an employee's conscientious performance of his duties to his employer. The seminal case for this proposition is *Foley v. Interactive Data Corp.*, 765 P.2d 373, 380 (Cal. 1988), where plaintiff claimed he had been discharged for reporting internally that a supervisor was being investigated for embezzlement from another company. The court rejected the public policy tort:

> Whether or not there is a statutory duty requiring an employee to report [to his own employer] information relevant to his employer's interest, we do not find a substantial public policy prohibiting an employer from discharging an employee for performing that duty. Past decisions recognizing a tort action for discharge in violation of public policy seek to protect the public, by protecting the employee who refuses to commit a crime . . . or who discloses other illegal, unethical, or unsafe practices. . . . No equivalent public interest bars the discharge of the present plaintiff. When the duty of an employee to disclose information to his employer serves only the private interest of the employer, the rationale underlying the [public policy] cause of action is not implicated.

Id. This limitation is consistent with the idea that a public policy must concern the public interest, not just a private matter between a worker and employer. Another way to say this is that third parties must be potentially affected. In an extreme example of this, one court rejected a public policy claim when a female employee was fired because of an incident in which she was the victim of an assault and rape. *Green v. Bryant*, 887 F. Supp. 798 (E.D. Pa. 1995).

While some legal commentators and many would-be plaintiffs are not happy with the result, it reflects the law's line-drawing between private ordering and its limitations. The employer is free to structure its internal operations and reward (or punish) those who serve its private interests. When, however, actions taken against employees have effects on third parties, it is appropriate to constrain the employer's freedom of action.

Fitzgerald v. Salsbury Chemical, Inc.
613 N.W.2d 275 (Iowa 2000)

CADY, Justice.

Tom Fitzgerald was employed by Salsbury Chemical, Inc. at its production plant in Charles City. Salsbury manufactures chemicals and pharmaceutical bulk actives. Fitzgerald was employed as a production foreman at the plant.

Fitzgerald was terminated from his employment with Salsbury on September 19, 1995. The termination followed an incident on August 30, 1995, involving a production worker named Richard Koresh. Koresh failed to properly monitor the temperature and pressure of a tank used to mix a chemical compound. His conduct created a potentially dangerous condition.

Koresh was suspended from his employment on September 4, 1995, after Salsbury conducted a preliminary investigation into the incident. He was ultimately terminated on September 19, 1995, a few hours prior to the time Fitzgerald was terminated. Fitzgerald was responsible for supervising Koresh on the date of the incident.

Salsbury asserted Fitzgerald was terminated for failing to properly supervise Koresh and to prevent the potentially dangerous incident. Fitzgerald, however, believed he was discharged because he did not support Salsbury's decision to discharge Koresh and Salsbury officials feared he would provide testimony in support of Koresh in the course of threatened legal action by Koresh.

The events supporting this claim extend back to August 15, 1995, when Koresh gave deposition testimony in a wrongful discharge action against Salsbury by a former employee named John Kelly. Kelly was terminated several years earlier, one day prior to his scheduled deposition in a wrongful death action against Salsbury by the estate of a former employee. The former employee died after a chemical compound he was mixing at the plant overheated and exploded. Salsbury claimed Kelly was terminated because his unsafe conduct caused the explosion. Kelly claimed he was terminated by Salsbury in an effort to cover up its culpability in the incident. During the deposition on August 15, 1995, Koresh contradicted earlier deposition testimony by two Salsbury management officials concerning the internal investigation of the work practices of Kelly. Koresh also testified he believed Kelly was a safe operator. Following the deposition, Koresh felt shunned by Salsbury management. He was also told by a foreman the company was going to find a way to fire him. After Koresh was suspended on September 4, 1995, he told a Salsbury official that he had hired an attorney and was "not going to be another John Kelly."

Fitzgerald engaged in a conversation with the plant operations manager on September 19, 1995, a few hours prior to the time he was told of his termination. The manager asked Fitzgerald what discipline he believed should result to Koresh because of the incident on August 30. Fitzgerald responded he did not believe it was fair to fire Koresh over a single mistake. Fitzgerald also indicated he did not believe Koresh should be fired in light of his long years of service to the company. The manager then informed Fitzgerald he needed to begin to think like a foreman if he was going to be one, and he needed to find out which side he was on. Fitzgerald was also informed the matter may result in a lawsuit. Fitzgerald does not claim he responded to the statements.

Fitzgerald instituted this wrongful discharge action against Salsbury. He alleged his termination violated a public policy of this state to protect workers who oppose the unlawful termination of a co-worker. Additionally, he claimed he was terminated because he intended to provide testimony in Koresh's future wrongful termination lawsuit that would be unfavorable to Salsbury and the company wanted to discredit his potential testimony as a disgruntled former employee. Fitzgerald claims Salsbury's motivation to terminate him violated the public policy of this state to provide truthful testimony in court proceedings.

[The trial court dismissed the action.]

III. The Employer-Employee Relationship . . .

B. *The Public Policy Exception*

We have identified the elements of an action to recover damages for discharge in violation of public policy to require the employee to establish (1) engagement in a protected activity; (2) discharge; and (3) a causal connection between the conduct and the discharge. *Teachout v. Forest City Community Sch. Dist.*, 584 N.W.2d 296 (Iowa 1998). These elements properly identify the tort of wrongful discharge when a protected activity has been recognized through the existence of an underlying public policy which is undermined when an employee is discharged from employment for engaging in the activity. However, when we have not previously identified a particular public policy to support an action, the employee must first identify a clear public policy which would be adversely impacted if dismissal resulted from the conduct engaged in by the employee.[2] *See Yockey v. State*, 540 N.W.2d 418 (Iowa 1995) (the public policy in favor of permitting employees to seek workers' compensation benefits not jeopardized by termination from employment for missing work following injury); *Borschel v. City of Perry*, 512 N.W.2d 565 (Iowa 1994) (no public policy in favor of presumption of innocence in work place to give rise to an action for wrongful discharge for conduct which resulted in criminal charges).

1. Determining Public Policy

In first recognizing the public policy exception to the at-will employment doctrine, we were careful to limit the tort action for wrongful discharge to cases involving only a well-recognized and clear public policy. This requirement has been incorporated in our subsequent cases. This important element sets the foundation for the tort and it is necessary to overcome the employer's interest in operating its business in the manner it sees fit. It also helps ensure that employers have notice that their dismissal decisions will give rise to liability.

In determining whether a clear, well-recognized public policy exists for purposes of a cause of action, we have primarily looked to our statutes but have also indicated our Constitution to be an additional source. We have not been asked to extend our

[margin note: I. need to show public policy]

---

2. Some courts are beginning to articulate the elements of a cause of action for wrongful discharge as:

1. The existence of a clear public policy (the clarity element).
2. Dismissal of employee under circumstances alleged in the case would jeopardize public policy (the jeopardy element).
3. The plaintiff engaged in public policy conduct and this conduct was the reason for the dismissal (the causation element).
4. Employer lacked an overriding business justification for the dismissal (the absence of justification element).

Gardner v. Loomis Armored, Inc., 913 P.2d 377 (Wash. 1996); *Collins v. Rizkana*, 652 N.E.2d 653 (Ohio 1995).

This approach is derived from the methodology proposed by Dean and Law Professor Henry H. Perritt, Jr. *See generally* Henry H. Perritt, Jr., *The Future of Wrongful Dismissal Claims: Where Does Employer Self-Interest Lie?*, 58 U. CIN. L. REV. 397 (1989). This four-part structure of proof is now detailed in Professor Perrit's multi-volume treatise on the subject. EMPLOYEE DISMISSAL LAW AND PRACTICE [now in its 5th edition, 2006]. . . .

sources of public policy beyond our statutes and Constitution, but recognize other states have used additional sources such as judicial decisions and administrative rules.

Some statutes articulate public policy by specifically prohibiting employers from discharging employees for engaging in certain conduct or other circumstances.[3] Yet, we do not limit the public policy exception to specific statutes which mandate protection for employees. *Teachout.* Instead, we look to other statutes which not only define clear public policy but imply a prohibition against termination from employment to avoid undermining that policy. *See Borschel.*

Our insistence on using only clear and well-recognized public policy to serve as the basis for the wrongful discharge tort emphasizes our continuing general adherence to the at-will employment doctrine and the need to carefully balance the competing interests of the employee, employer, and society. An employer's right to terminate an employee at any time only gives way under the wrongful discharge tort when the reason for the discharge offends clear public policy.

The need for clarity in public policy is similarly recognized in our reluctance to search too far beyond our legislative pronouncements and constitution to find public policy to support an action. . . . Any effort to evaluate the public policy exception with generalized concepts of fairness and justice will result in an elimination of the at-will doctrine itself. Moreover, it could unwittingly transform the public policy exception into a "good faith and fair dealing" exception, a standard we have repeatedly rejected.

2. Determining Jeopardy to Public Policy

Once a clear public policy is identified, the employee must further show the dismissal for engaging in the conduct jeopardizes or undermines the public policy. Thus, this element requires the employee to show the conduct engaged in not only furthered the public policy, but dismissal would have a chilling effect on the public policy by discouraging the conduct. . . . Thus, when the conduct of the employee furthers public policy or the threat of dismissal discourages the conduct, public policy is implicated. On the other hand, if a public policy exists, but is not jeopardized by the discharge, the cause of action must fail. *See Yockey; French* [*v. Foods, Inc.*, 495 N.W.2d 768 (Iowa 1993)] (public policy against suborning perjury not implicated if employer terminates the employee after using coercive and high-handed tactics to obtain confession). This element guarantees an employer's personnel management decisions will not be challenged unless the public policy is genuinely threatened.

[handwritten margin note: 2. need to show that dismissal of conduct undermines public policy]

3. Claim of Public Policy to Oppose Wrongful Termination of Co-Employee

Fitzgerald first claims there is a public policy in this state which protects an employee from discharge by an employer for opposing the wrongful termination of a co-employee. He claims this public policy in favor of opposing the unlawful termination of a co-employee is derived from [state and federal antidiscrimination

---

3. *See* Iowa Code §§29A.43 (2005) (absences for membership in military reserves protected); 49.109-.110 (absence for voting protected); 70A.2 (employee may take medical leave of absence upon recommendation of physician without retaliation). . . .

statutes]. While those laws prohibit retaliation only where the employee is opposing a discriminatory practice as defined by the legislation, plaintiff argues that such statutes "reveal a broad public policy for employees to oppose all unlawful employment practices including the termination of a co-employee which is contrary to public policy."[4] Fitzgerald claims the termination of Koresh was contrary to public policy of this state to provide truthful testimony and he should be afforded the same protection as the law provides Koresh.

We are reluctant to infer a broad public policy from a statute which is limited in its scope to specific discriminatory practices. Instead, we continue to adhere to our guiding principle to only declare public policy which is clearly articulated by a statute or other appropriate source. The statutes identified by Fitzgerald clearly do not expressly protect his conduct. . . .

We also observe Fitzgerald has failed to show how any public policy in favor of opposing the claimed unlawful termination of a co-employee would be jeopardized by his dismissal. Fitzgerald offered no evidence that he expressed opposition to the discharge of a co-worker because it was unlawful. Instead, Fitzgerald admits the only objection he voiced to his employer over the termination of Koresh was the length of his employment service and the lack of prior infractions. He offered no evidence he objected to the termination of Koresh for providing truthful deposition testimony. The conduct of Fitzgerald, therefore, did not promote the claimed public policy, and his actions were not necessary to enforce any public policy. Fitzgerald failed to tie his conduct with his claim of public policy.

4. Claim of Public Policy to Provide Truthful Testimony in a Legal Proceeding

We next address the claim by Fitzgerald that he was terminated because he intended to provide truthful testimony, adverse to his employer, in a threatened future lawsuit of a co-employee against Salsbury. Our first task is to decide whether a public policy exists in this state against discharge of an employee for giving or intending to give truthful testimony in a legal proceeding.

Before considering our statutes, we observe other jurisdictions have recognized a public policy against firing an employee for giving testimony in court proceedings. [Here the court cited *Petermann*, which first recognized a cause of action for wrongful discharge when an employee was terminated for refusing to perjure himself at his employer's request.]

This same reasoning has appealed to other courts when faced with actions by employees who were discharged either for refusing to perjure themselves or for testifying truthfully against their employers. Similarly, we find ample statutory support for a public policy in Iowa in favor of refusing to commit perjury. Our statutes make

---

4. It is not necessary for us to specifically decide if the public policy to support the tort of wrongful discharge in Iowa can be derived from a federal statute. There is a split of authority among the states. *See, e.g., Faulkner v. United Techs. Corp.*, 693 A.2d 293, 297-98 (Conn. 1997) (a federal law can be a source of public policy); *Griffin v. Mullinix*, 947 P.2d 177 (Okla. 1997) (federal statute cannot serve as a basis for state public policy); *see also* Perritt §7.13, at 31-32. The issue gives rise to a host of considerations, including potential federal preemption issues. *See* 1 HENRY H. PERRITT, JR., EMPLOYEE DISMISSAL LAW AND PRACTICE §§2.39-.46, at 168-91 (4th ed. 1998).

it a crime to commit perjury, suborn perjury, or tamper with a witness. Moreover, this public policy is not simply confined to the refusal to commit perjury but clearly embraces a broader public policy to provide truthful testimony in legal proceedings. *Page v. Columbia Natural Resources, Inc.*, 480 S.E.2d 817 (W. Va. 1996). A policy in favor of refusing to commit perjury necessarily implies an inverse corresponding public policy to provide truthful testimony. Additionally, the integrity of the judicial system, its fundamental ability to dispense justice, depends upon truthful testimony. This principle forms the basis for our perjury and related statutes. Furthermore, a reasonable employer should be aware that attempts to interfere with the process of obtaining truthful testimony, whether through intimidation or retaliation, is a violation of this public policy. Thus, we conclude the public policy derived from our statutes against perjury and suborning perjury also supports a public policy to provide truthful testimony. We next consider whether this public policy is undermined when an employee is discharged from employment for engaging in the conduct claimed by Fitzgerald.

[Defendant argued that this public policy was inapplicable because "Fitzgerald never testified in a legal proceeding, was never requested to testify in a legal proceeding, and never expressed an intent to testify."]

We agree a dismissed employee must engage in conduct related to public policy before the discharge can undermine that public policy. However, we view the good faith intent to engage in a protected activity the same as performing the protected activity. This is because employees would be discouraged from engaging in the public policy if they were discharged for their intent to engage in the public policy the same as if they actually engaged in the conduct. Thus, Fitzgerald must only show he had a good faith intent to truthfully testify.

An essential element of proof to establish the discharge undermines or jeopardizes the public policy necessarily involves a showing the dismissed employee engaged in conduct covered by the public policy. Although proof the employee engaged in the conduct is also a part of the causation element of the tort, we must review Fitzgerald's conduct in this case to determine if it sufficiently matched the public policy of providing truthful testimony.[5]

Fitzgerald did not directly express an intention to testify truthfully in the lawsuit threatened by Koresh. Furthermore, he never told any company officials he possessed any particular damaging information about the threatened lawsuit. These facts suggest Fitzgerald did not contemplate testifying in a threatened lawsuit by Koresh prior to his discharge. Thus, we must review the summary judgment record to determine if a reasonable inference can be drawn that Fitzgerald maintained a good faith intent to testify truthfully in a lawsuit action prior to the discharge. . . .

The conduct engaged in by Fitzgerald prior to his discharge amounted to internal opposition to the termination of a co-employee [which would not generally support an inference the employee intended to give truthful testimony in future litigation]. However, there are additional facts which must be considered in our analysis at this stage of the proceedings.

This case is not simply about Fitzgerald expressing support for Koresh. Salsbury not only admonished Fitzgerald for failing to support his employer, but warned him

---

5. No jeopardy can be shown if the plaintiff fails to match the conduct with the public policy. Causation, however, also involves proof of conduct. With this element, the plaintiff must show the dismissal resulted from the protected conduct, and not for some other reason.

that the matter could result in litigation and he must decide which side he would support. Thus, Salsbury placed Fitzgerald's support for Koresh in the context of litigation and transformed the conversation into choosing sides in a lawsuit. There was no evidence to suggest Fitzgerald backed down from his support for Koresh after the conversation turned to litigation. These facts permit a reasonable inference to be drawn that Fitzgerald, prior to his discharge, developed an intent to testify in threatened future litigation against his employer.

There are, of course, other inferences that could be drawn from the evidence. However, at this stage we are required to draw those reasonable inferences in favor of Fitzgerald as the nonmoving party to the summary judgment proceedings. In light of these inferences, we conclude that there is evidence to support the claim Fitzgerald engaged in policy-based conduct.

Nevertheless, Salsbury argues the jeopardy element of the tort cannot be satisfied as a matter of law because it never requested Fitzgerald to testify inconsistent with the public policy. . . .

Some jurisdictions require the employer to actually make a request to the employee to commit perjury before finding the public policy against perjury is implicated. *Bushko v. Miller Brewing Co.*, 396 N.W.2d 167 (Wis. 1986). Thus, a discharge based on an employer's concern that the employee will testify truthfully if asked to testify or that the employee intends to testify contrary to the interests of the employer is insufficient to support a cause of action under the public policy exception. *See Daniel v. Carolina Sunrock Corp.*, 436 S.E.2d 835 (N.C. 1993) (statement by employer reminding employee for whom she worked and to say as little as possible prior to providing testimony was insufficient to implicate the public policy against the perjury).

We believe the dismissal of an employee can jeopardize public policy when the employee has engaged in conduct consistent with public policy without a request by the employer to violate public policy just as it can when the employee refuses to engage in conduct which is inconsistent with public policy when requested by the employer. The focus is on the adverse actions of the employer in response to the protected actions of the employee, not the actions of the employer which may give rise to the protected actions of the employee. Furthermore, in considering whether the dismissal undermines public policy, we not only look to the impact of the discharge on the dismissed employee, but the impact of the dismissal on other employees as well. Public policy applies to all employees. If the dismissal of one employee for engaging in public policy conduct will discourage other employees from engaging in the public policy conduct, public policy is undermined.

In this case, if Salsbury was motivated to dismiss Fitzgerald because he intended to testify truthfully in a future lawsuit, a dismissal would have a chilling effect on other employees by discouraging them from engaging in similar conduct. Thus, it makes no difference that a dismissal in this particular case may give the employee an enhanced incentive to testify after a dismissal. The action by the employer could inhibit other employees from truthfully testifying in the future out of fear of dismissal.

Salsbury further argues that interpreting the tort to include conduct alleged by Fitzgerald will open the flood gates to litigation for wrongful discharge on public policy grounds whenever an employee internally expresses reservations over the termination of a co-employee and then is later dismissed for some valid reason unrelated to the prior termination of the co-employee. This argument, however, can be made to practically every public policy claim which serves as the basis for a wrongful discharge action. We simply recognize a tort for discharge in violation of a public policy to provide truthful testimony, and leave it to the jury to determine if the facts support the claim. The action in this case is based in part upon an internal complaint by the employee, but is enough to withstand summary judgment because the context of the internal complaint justifies an inference of an intent to testify against the employer which may have caused the employer to dismiss the employee.

5. Causation Element

We next consider if the evidence is sufficient to support a causal connection between the conduct engaged in by Fitzgerald and the discharge. The protected conduct must be the determinative factor in the decision to terminate the employee. Of course, if the employer has no knowledge the employee engaged in the protected activity, causation cannot be established. Similarly, the existence of other legal reasons or motives for the termination are relevant in considering causation.

The causation standard is high, and requires us to determine if a reasonable fact finder would conclude Fitzgerald's intent to testify truthfully was the determinative factor in the decision to discharge him. Generally, causation presents a question of fact. Thus, if there is a dispute over the conduct or the reasonable inferences to be drawn from the conduct, the jury must resolve the dispute. Additionally, any dispute over the employer's knowledge of the conduct is generally for the jury, as well as the existence of other justifiable reasons for the termination. . . .

In this case, the different inferences to be drawn from the evidence precludes [sic] summary judgment. After a recommendation was made to Salsbury to terminate Koresh, Salsbury wanted to know if Fitzgerald supported Koresh. Moreover, Salsbury gathered this information in the context of a potential lawsuit threatened by Koresh. In light of these inferences, summary judgment was improper. . . .

NOTES

1. *Recognition of the Public Policy Tort.* As reflected in the *Fitzgerald* decision, Iowa is one of the vast majority of jurisdictions that recognize some version of what is now generally called the public policy tort. There are, however, states where the tort is still not recognized. For example, New York has continued to adhere to a strict version of the at-will rule: No matter the degree to which public policy may be implicated, a firing is not actionable unless there is a statute expressly according such a right to an employee. *See Murphy v. Am. Home Prods. Corp.*, 448 N.E.2d 86, 87 (N.Y. 1983). In that case, plaintiff asserted that he was fired in retaliation for reporting to his employer's officers and directors that "he had uncovered at least $50 million in illegal account manipulations of secret pension reserves which improperly inflated the company's growth in income and allowed high-ranking officers to reap unwarranted bonuses from a management incentive plan." Although this conduct might currently be actionable for a publicly traded company under the Sarbanes-Oxley Act, *see* page 249, there was no New York or federal statute providing a cause of action for an employee at that time.

For the New York Court of Appeals, this was a sufficient basis to deny plaintiff's claim since "such a significant change in our law is best left to the Legislature," which

[handwritten margin note: NY: no public policy tort against wrongful discharge]

was better equipped to answer not only the fundamental question of whether such liability should be recognized but also to craft the appropriate solution:

> The Legislature has infinitely greater resources and procedural means to discern the public will, to examine the variety of pertinent considerations, to elicit the views of the various segments of the community that would be directly affected and in any event critically interested, and to investigate and anticipate the impact of imposition of such liability. Standards should doubtless be established applicable to the multifarious types of employment and the various circumstances of discharge. If the rule of nonliability for termination of at-will employment is to be tempered, it should be accomplished through a principled statutory scheme, adopted after opportunity for public ventilation, rather than in consequence of judicial resolution of the partisan arguments of individual adversarial litigants.

Id. at 79-80. Does this make sense to you, given that the at-will rule is a judicial innovation to begin with? Or is the point less separation of powers than institutional competence? In other words, that common law development over a wide variety of settings may be seen as an inefficient method of furthering the public interest.

Most states follow some version of Iowa's approach, not New York's. *See generally* RESTATEMENT OF EMPLOYMENT LAW §5.01, Reporters Notes, cmt. a (ALI 2015) (listing seven states rejecting the public policy tort). This is true even in states with statutes providing protection in varying situations. Indeed, Iowa has a grab bag of statutes protecting employees in a variety of settings, but *Fitzgerald* did not view that as a reason to stay the judicial hand. Nevertheless, the diversity of rules emerging in the jurisdictions adopting the tort suggests that there is something to be said for a statutory solution. Indeed, several states have enacted comprehensive laws, sometimes called whistleblowing statutes, to address the problem. In New York itself, there has been an outpouring of special-purpose statutes focusing on what *Murphy* called "the various circumstances of discharge." Nevertheless, New York remains largely true to *Murphy. See Sullivan v. Harnisch*, 969 N.E.2d 758, 761 (N.Y. 2012) (denying public policy protection to a hedge fund's compliance officer). *But see Wieder v. Skala*, 609 N.E.2d 105 (N.Y. 1992), discussed in Note on Attorneys and the Public Policy Tort, page 222.

2. *Specificity of the Public Policy.* Some courts have been hesitant to limit employer freedom when the predicate public policy is too general. *Fitzgerald* is obviously not one of those cases since it allows a very generic policy (truthful testimony) to be the predicate for the tort. Can you imagine public policies that are too diffuse to justify a restriction on the employer's right to discharge a worker? *See Turner v. Mem'l Med. Ctr.*, 911 N.E.2d 369 (Ill. 2009) (discharge for a respiratory therapist's reporting his hospital's deviation from an electronic patient-charting accreditation standard not actionable; although providing good medical care is in the public interest, the court required a more focused public policy*); see also* RESTATEMENT §5.03 cmt. d ("Broad, vague, or highly abstract language in judicial decisions, however, may not provide a sufficiently defined source of public policy to support the wrongful-discharge tort."). *But see Feliciano v. 7-Eleven, Inc.*, 559 S.E.2d 713 (W. Va. 2001) (discharge because of exercise of right of self-defense in response to lethal imminent danger may violate state's public policy).

3. *The Jeopardy Element.* The principal case notes that an employee must not only identify a clear public policy but "must further show the dismissal for engaging in the conduct jeopardizes or undermines the public policy," which requires "the employee to show the conduct engaged in not only furthered the public policy, but dismissal would have a chilling effect on the public policy by discouraging the conduct." The Washington Supreme Court addressed the jeopardy question in *Cudney v. ALSCO, Inc.*, 259 P.3d 244 (Wash. 2011) (en banc), giving a decidedly plaintiff-unfriendly answer. A former employee challenged his discharge for reporting violations of drunk driving laws by other workers at the company. The court, however, found the "jeopardy" element not satisfied because the tort "should be precluded unless the public policy is inadequately promoted through other means and thereby maintaining only a narrow exception to the underlying doctrine of at-will employment." *Id.* at 247. For the plaintiff to sue "the criminal laws, enforcement mechanism, and penalties all have to be inadequate to protect the public from drunk driving. . . . Police and state troopers patrol our roads and highways looking for signs of driving under the influence. There is a huge legal and police machinery around our state designed to address this very problem. It is very hard to believe that the 'only available adequate means' to protect the public from drunk driving was for Cudney to tell his manager about Bartich's drunk driving." *Id.* at 250. *See also Weiss v. Lonnquist*, 293 P.3d 1264, 1271 (Wash. App. 2013) (jury verdict for attorney reversed when she was discharged for refusing to engage in unethical conduct because the disciplinary rules of the state bar offered an adequate means of protecting that public policy at issue by her reporting to the authorities; the inability of the state bar to offer redress to plaintiff was irrelevant). *But see Becker v. Cmty. Health Sys., Inc.*, 332 P.3d 1085, 1087 (Wash. Ct. App. 2014) (refusing to dismiss a wrongful discharge complaint despite "a myriad of statutes and regulations adequately promot[ing] the public policy of honesty in corporate financial reporting, rendering a private common law tort remedy superfluous.").

4. *The Predicate Policy Must Protect the "Public." Fitzgerald* suggests that opposition to unwise or unfair employment decisions or policies (as opposed to illegal ones) is not a basis for tort protection. As we have seen, this is consistent with allowing private ordering full rein except when the public interest is implicated. Recall *Foley v. Interactive Data Corp.*, 765 P.2d 373 (Cal. 1988), where plaintiff claimed that he was discharged after he informed management that his new supervisor was under criminal investigation for embezzlement. California had previously recognized a public policy tort, but the court cautioned: "[W]e must still inquire whether the discharge is against public policy and affects a duty which inures to the benefit of the public at large rather than to a particular employer or employee." *Id.* at 379. The fact that the employee may have owed his employer a duty to report such information (*see* Chapter 8) was irrelevant: "[W]e do not find a substantial public policy prohibiting an employer from discharging an employee for performing that duty." 765 P.2d at 380. Justice Mosk's dissent in *Foley* stressed the intolerable choice facing the plaintiff: remaining silent, and abandoning his duty to his employer, or speaking up and risking discharge. But isn't that the essence of the at-will rule: good reason, bad reason, or no reason?

Many courts agree with the *Foley* point, that the thrust of the tort is to protect third parties and society as a whole, *see* RESTATEMENT §5.01, cmt. a, but the distinction between public and private has shifted over time. Recall *Murphy*, in which the plaintiff claimed that his employer fired him for opposing its accounting improprieties. The New York court rejected limiting the at-will rule, essentially because it viewed the matter as affecting only the rights of employer and employee. Where only two parties are concerned, private ordering is normally appropriate.

But were the facts of *Murphy* to arise today, the dispute would be viewed very differently: After the enactment of Sarbanes-Oxley ("SOX"), which is discussed in more detail at page 249, this scenario might be seen as implicating a public interest precisely because "third parties"—shareholders and the securities market generally—would now be seen as affected. American Home Products was publicly traded, and Murphy raised serious questions about financial mismanagement or worse. Of course, since *Murphy* rejects a public policy tort entirely, a New York employee's only resort might be SOX itself.

The critical point is that courts must see some adverse consequences on some person *outside* the employment relationship in order for the public policy tort to have traction. Thus, even today, after SOX, *Foley* itself would still be within the private sphere because the plaintiff was questioning the wisdom of employing an embezzler, not claiming that he was embezzling. And, of course, even a claim of embezzlement from the employer would not trigger federal protection if the employer were a closely held, rather than a publicly traded, company. In short, the public/private distinction remains operative, even if the borders are in flux.

5. *Wrongful Discipline?* The public policy tort arose in the context of discharges, and most cases have considered employees who are challenging terminations. As with employment discrimination, however, the public policy tort has been applied to constructive discharge cases, *e.g., Colores v. Bd. of Trustees*, 130 Cal. Rptr. 2d 347 (App. 2003), and even adverse employment actions that fall short of either actual or constructive discharge. *See, e.g., Trosper v. Bag'N Save*, 734 N.W.2d 704 (Neb. 2007) (recognizing cause of action for retaliatory demotion); *Brigham v. Dillon Cos.*, 935 P.2d 1054 (Kan. 1997) (wrongful demotion). *But see Touchstone Television Productions v. Superior Court*, 145 Cal. Rptr. 766 (Cal. App. 2012) (no public policy claim when the only adverse action was failure to renew a contract after it expired, which is not actionable in tort); *Mintz v. Bell Atl. Leasing Sys. Int'l*, 909 P.2d 559 (Ariz. App. 1995) (no cause of action for wrongful failure to promote). The Restatement of Employment Law originally extended the tort beyond discharge, but the final version will take no position on the issue. §5.01 cmt. c. Would allowing employers to punish workers so long as they don't (constructively) discharge them be consistent with the rationale for the tort in the first place?

6. *Judge and Jury Functions.* Who decides what is public policy? In an omitted portion of its opinion, the *Fitzgerald* court wrote: "It is generally recognized that the existence of a public policy, as well as the issue whether that policy is undermined by a discharge from employment, presents questions of law for the court to resolve. . . . On the other hand, the elements of causation and motive are factual in nature and generally more suitable for resolution by the finder of fact." 613 N.W.2d at 282. This is the general approach. *See, e.g., Turner v. Mem'l Med. Ctr.*, 911 N.E.2d 369 (Ill. 2009); RESTATEMENT §5.03 cmt. a. If the question is protecting the public interest, shouldn't the jury be allowed to decide whether a public policy qualifies for the tort?

7. *Tort or Contract? Fitzgerald* takes the majority view that the public policy cause of action sounds only in tort, and some jurisdictions carry this principle so far as to impose individual liability on those supervisors who participate in the wrongful conduct. *VanBuren v. Grubb*, 733 S.E.2d 919, 920 (Va. 2012); *Jasper v. H. Nizam, Inc.*, 764 N.W.2d 751 (Iowa 2009). *Contra Farrow v. St. Francis Med. Ctr.*, 407 S.W.3d 579, 595 (Mo. 2013). However, a few jurisdictions define it as contract-based and not tortious, generally looking to the implied duty of good faith. *See, e.g., Knight v. Am. Guard & Alert, Inc.*, 714 P.2d 788 (Alaska 1986); *Brockmeyer v. Dun*

& Bradstreet, 335 N.W.2d 834 (Wis. 1983). Viewing the cause of action as contractual limits plaintiff's recovery to economic damages and would seem to foreclose individual liability, while tort law permits recovery for mental distress, *see, e.g., Wendeln v. Beatrice Manor, Inc.*, 712 N.W.2d 226 (Neb. 2006), and only in torts may punitive damages be awarded. *See* RESTATEMENT §9.5(a) (recoverable tort damages "include past and reasonably certain future economic loss, noneconomic loss, the expenses of reasonable efforts to mitigate damages, and reasonably foreseeable consequential damages. An employee may also recover punitive damages if the employer was sufficiently culpable, or nominal damages if no actual damages are proven."). However, statutes of limitations are typically longer for contracts than torts, so a time-barred tort suit might be "cured" by a timely contract action.

🌿8. *Reasonable or Right?* Should protection depend on the employee being correct or just reasonable in the perception that he or she is acting in the public interest? Suppose the employee believes, for example, that the company's actions violate the law. Would an employee be protected if she "blew the whistle" to state agencies even if her charges were incorrect, as long as she reasonably and/or in good faith believed the company was violating a criminal statute? Several of the categories of protection in Restatement §5.02 on page 209 require the employee to act "reasonably and in good faith," which seems to require both subjective and objective reasonableness. But other categories in §5.02 require only good faith or have no intent requirement. Do you see why?

There is, however, a kicker in the section: To be protected, the employee must not only have the requisite basis for acting but also must be "acting in a reasonable manner." The notion that the employee has to be reasonable in both what she is protesting and how she goes about doing it generally reflects what the courts are doing with the public policy tort and parallels the general rule with respect to retaliation for opposing discrimination. *See* Chapter 9, page 671. That means that, no matter how clear the public policy, the plaintiff may not recover unless he is reasonable in believing that the employer is contravening it. *See Fine v. Ryan Int'l Airlines*, 305 F.3d 746 (7th Cir. 2002) (in determining whether employer is acting unlawfully, a reasonable employee might rely on what she learns from co-workers). Further, no matter how clear the public policy and the employee's reasonableness in believing it to be jeopardized, an employee may not be protected if the manner of his protest is viewed as unreasonable.

🌿9. *Advising the Employee.* Suppose an employee in Mr. Fitzgerald's situation comes to you for advice. That is, she has previously been in hot water for backing another employee suit, and she now believes that her supervisor is sending signals that she had better "cooperate" with respect to the discharge of another worker. *Fitzgerald* states the law, but isn't the real problem proof? Do you advise your client to elicit less ambiguous orders that she commit perjury? Do you advise her to secretly tape record any conversations in order to have proof later? How would she do this and what are the risks?

Of course, before you consider the latter course, you should ascertain whether secret taping is criminal in the jurisdiction. In most jurisdictions, the secret taping of a conversation by one of the parties (as opposed to a third party) is *not* criminal. A few states are to the contrary. For example, California criminalizes taping a "confidential" conversation without the consent of all parties. *Cal. Penal Code* §632 (2014). There is also a private cause of action for any person injured as a result of such a taping. *See Coulter v. Bank of Am.*, 33 Cal. Rptr. 2d 766 (1994) (upholding counterclaims in sexual harassment suit for plaintiff's taping of conversations with her supervisor and coworkers). Even absent criminal repercussions, there have been ethical concerns for attorneys when tape recording or advising clients to tape record conversations, although those concerns are reduced by American Bar Association's Formal Opinion 01-422, which concludes that undisclosed taping is not necessarily prohibited. If it is not unethical for you to tape or advise your client to tape, are there still reasons to be wary of it?

🖋 **10.** *Advising the Employer.* Suppose you represent an employer in a setting saturated in public policy issues—say, a pharmaceutical company whose manufacturing is subject to detailed regulation by the Food and Drug Administration. Maybe virtually everything you do has public policy implications. Management is ready to fire a compliance officer because, although he is very good at his job, he is a perfectionist whose demands make it impossible to work with the team. What advice do you have for your client?

Note on Attorneys and the Public Policy Tort

In footnote 2, the *Fitzgerald* court suggested that an element for a public policy case is that "[e]mployer lacked an overriding business justification for the dismissal (the absence of justification element)." Since it is hard to imagine a justification for perjury, *Fitzgerald* itself never pursued that element, and Iowa later made clear that justification was a defense. *Rivera v. Woodward Res. Ctr.*, 865 N.W.2d 887, 898 (Iowa 2015) ("the lack of legitimate business justification is not an element of the claim that the plaintiff must prove. Plaintiffs are rarely required to prove a negative."). But justifications for some dismissals implicating public policy are possible, typically those in which there is a countervailing public policy. One such scenario is when an attorney blows the whistle on his client. Client confidentiality requirements generally bar such disclosure, although there are situations in which it is permitted or even required. *See* MODEL RULES OF PROF'L CONDUCT R. 1.6 (2003). Isn't it clear that a law firm can discharge an attorney who reports a client's violation to public authorities, at least where the reporting violates state ethics rules? In that case, one public policy (confidentiality) cancels out the other. *See, e.g.*, Alex Long, *Whistleblowing Attorneys and Ethical Infrastructures*, 68 MD. L. REV. 786 (2009).

Suppose instead that the attorney is discharged for refusing to perform an illegal act. Is the public policy tort available now? Even New York, which is generally hostile to the public policy tort, has recognized something akin to that tort in this situation. *Wieder v. Skala*, 609 N.E.2d 105 (N.Y. 1992), involved an associate in a law firm who claimed to have been discharged because he insisted that the firm report another associate's misconduct to the Disciplinary Committee, as required by the state's Code of Professional Responsibility. While reaffirming that New York did not recognize a general public policy tort, the Court of Appeals found a cause of action in contract stated. Wieder's role in providing legal services to the firm's clients as a member of the Bar "was at the very core and, indeed, the only purpose of his association" with the law firm, and his "responsibilities as a lawyer and as an associate of the firm" are "incapable of separation." *Id.* at 635. Further, the ethical rule at issue was indispensable to attorney self-regulation, and Wieder's failure to comply with it would have put him at risk of serious discipline. The unique characteristics of the legal profession made the relation of an associate to a law firm employer "intrinsically different" from such relationships as financial manager to corporate employers as in *Murphy*. The court also stressed that both Wieder and the firm were bound to follow the ethical rule in question. MODEL CODE OF PROF'L RESPONSIBILITY DR 1-103 (A).

Other courts have found that the special role that lawyers play in our society makes the public policy tort inappropriate precisely because lawyers are governed by the rules of ethics. *Balla v. Gambro Inc.*, 584 N.E.2d 104 (Ill. 1991) (no cause of action because attorneys already have a duty to abide by rules of professional ethics); *see also Tartaglia v. UBS PaineWebber, Inc.*, 961 A.2d 1167 (N.J. 2008) (holding that, in order to prevail on a common law public policy tort claim, plaintiff must "demonstrate that the employer's behavior about which she complained actually violated [the Rules of Professional Conduct]. Any lesser standard of proof . . . would inappropriately intrude on the role of our disciplinary authorities."). Courts have been reluctant to impose liability even where the governing state whistleblower law does not explicitly except attorneys. *See Kidwell v. Sybaritic*, Inc., 784 N.W.2d 220 (Minn. 2010) (an attorney would be protected under the state whistleblower law if he was acting to expose illegal conduct rather than simply seeking to bring his client into compliance with legal requirements); *cf. Trzaska v. L'Oreal USA, Inc.*, 865 F.3d 155, 162 (3d Cir. 2017) (attorney stated a claim for violation of whistleblower statute by alleging he was discharged for objecting to his employer's quota for patent filings, which he alleged could be met only by violating the Rules of Professional Conduct by submitting applications for inventions that were not patentable); *see generally* Ernest F. Lidge III, *Wrongfully Discharged In-House Counsel: A Proposal to Give The Employer a Veto Over Reinstatement While Giving the Terminated Lawyer Front Pay*, 52 WAKE FOREST L. REV. 649 (2017).

Rackley v. Fairview Care Centers, Inc.
23 P.3d 1022 (Utah 2001)

HOWE, J. . . .

[In] 1993, plaintiff Cathleen L. Rackley began working as an at-will employee for defendant Fairview Care Centers, Inc., as the administrator of a nursing home known as Fairview West.

Sometime in February 1994, Karleen Merkley, the manager responsible for resident funds at Fairview West, informed most of the members of the staff that a check for $720 from the Veteran's Administration was expected to arrive for resident Ms. Mellen, and that Ms. Mellen was not to be notified when it came. Plaintiff was not informed of that prohibition. Sharon Mellen, Ms. Mellen's daughter-in-law who had been aiding Ms. Mellen in managing her financial affairs for many years, had requested that Ms. Mellen not be told about the money because she feared Ms. Mellen would try to use it to move out of Fairview West and attempt to live on her own. Sharon wanted to inform Ms. Mellen of the check's arrival personally and to convince her to use the money to purchase a new wheelchair.

In the latter part of February, upon notification that the check had arrived, Sharon went to Fairview West, signed an authorization form in the presence of a witness, and took the check and deposited it in Ms. Mellen's personal bank account. Soon thereafter, plaintiff became aware that the check had arrived and had been picked up by Sharon. She notified Ms. Mellen of that fact. Ms. Mellen was upset that she had not been informed of the check's arrival or subsequent deposit and consequently requested that plaintiff contact Sharon on her behalf.

There is some dispute about the content of the phone call to Sharon. Plaintiff contends that she simply told Sharon she had notified Ms. Mellen of the arrival of the check and expressed concern about the impropriety of keeping the information from Ms. Mellen. Plaintiff asserts that Sharon "screamed" at her for telling Ms. Mellen about the money because "she was promised that nobody would find out about the money, that Karleen had talked to her and nobody should find out about it." Sharon contends that plaintiff called her at her place of work, yelled at her over the phone, and accused her of dishonesty and improper conduct. She stated, "all she did was kept telling me, you're stealing Ms. Mellen's money, you can't do that, you need to turn it—return the money to Fairview West. . . . She was very unprofessional. She had me in tears." Plaintiff did not then notify Joseph Peterson, owner and general manager of Fairview, of what had transpired or request investigation by any outside authority.

[However, Sharon later contacted Peterson and told him her version of what had happened. Peterson ultimately reprimanded Merkley, and Sallie Maroney, the manager of Fairview East, for failing to tell Ms. Mellen about the check. A new policy was promulgated requiring that residents be informed of their incoming funds. Plaintiff, however, was reprimanded for calling Sharon at work and later terminated.]

The parties dispute the precise issue before us. Fairview contends that the key issue is whether notification to care center residents of the arrival of their personal funds is a clear and substantial public policy. . . . We agree with plaintiff that if we were to require the law to be so specifically tailored, the public policy exception would be meaningless. Thus, we hold that the proper issue before us is whether a care facility resident's right to manage her own funds constitutes a clear and substantial public policy.

[To succeed on a public policy wrongful discharge claim], plaintiff must satisfy a four-pronged test. Plaintiff must prove that (1) her employment was terminated; (2) a clear and substantial public policy existed; (3) the plaintiff's conduct implicated that clear and substantial public policy; and (4) the termination and conduct in furtherance of the public policy are causally connected. Because Fairview concedes for purposes of this case that plaintiff was terminated, we move directly to the second prong.

I. Clear and Substantial Public Policy

The public policy exception to the employment at-will presumption is much narrower than traditional notions of public policy. Only "clear and substantial public policies will support a claim of wrongful discharge in violation of public policy." . . .

We have stated that a public policy is "clear" if it is plainly defined by one of three sources: (1) legislative enactments; (2) constitutional standards; or (3) judicial decisions. *See Dixon v. Pro Image Inc.*, 987 P.2d 48 (Utah 1999). For example, we have held that the enforcement of a state's criminal code that reflects Utah policy constitutes a clear and substantial public policy. *See Peterson* [*v. Browning*, 832 P.2d 1280 (Utah 1992)] (holding that employer who fired employee for refusing to feloniously provide false information on tax forms could be held liable for wrongful termination).

We have also held that a public policy is "substantial" if it is of "overreaching importance to the public, as opposed to the parties only." *Ryan* [*v. Dan's Food Stores, Inc.*, 972 P.2d 395 (Utah 1998)]. "We must . . . inquire whether the discharge is against public policy and affects a duty which inures to the benefit of the public at large rather than to a particular employer or employee." *Foley v. Interactive Data Corp.*, 765 P.2d 373 (Cal. 1988); *see, e.g., Fox* [*v. MCI Commun. Corp.*, 931 P.2d 857 (Utah 1997)] (holding that retaliatory termination for reporting possible criminal conduct of co-workers to employer does not give rise to a violation of substantial public policy). Statutes that simply regulate conduct between private individuals or impose requirements whose fulfillment does not implicate fundamental public policy concerns are not sufficient to require an exception to the at-will presumption. . . .

[The court stressed that "not every employment termination that has the effect of violating some public policy is actionable." Rather, the scope of the public policy exception must be kept narrow "to avoid unreasonably eliminating employer discretion in discharging employees."]

Plaintiff first asserts that two provisions in the Utah Constitution form the basis of a clear public policy. Article I, section 1 of the Utah Constitution provides in pertinent part that "all men have the inherent and inalienable right to . . . acquire, possess and protect property. . . ." Article I, section 27 provides that "frequent recurrence to fundamental principles is essential to the security of individual rights and the perpetuity of free government." While these two provisions do protect the right to acquire, possess, and protect property, they do not enunciate the narrow type of policy envisioned by our case law creating the public policy exception. The right of a care facility resident to manage her own funds is not "plainly defined by . . . [these] constitutional standards." . . .

Next, plaintiff contends that 42 U.S.C. §§3058g(a)(3) and (5), and sections 62A-3-201 to 208 of the Utah Code also plainly define such a public policy.[5] Plaintiff specifically points to subsections (a)(3) and (a)(5) in support of her position. However, subsections (a)(3) and (a)(5) are devoid of any language relating to a resident's right to manage her funds. While these provisions broadly discuss the duty of the ombudsman to monitor and protect the rights of care facility residents, they in no way state a narrow and clear public policy necessary for an exception to the at-will rule. This statute governs the duties and functions of the office of the ombudsman and its representatives and entities, and in no way enunciates rights of care facility residents.

Similarly, we find sections 62A-3-201 and -202 of the Utah Code unavailing. The stated purpose of these provisions "is to establish within the division [of Aging and Adult Services] the [Utah] long-term care ombudsman program for the aging . . . and identify duties and responsibilities of that program . . . in order to address problems relating to long-term care." In pertinent part, the ombudsman is to address the difficulties of the aging citizens of the state by assisting in asserting their civil and human rights as residents of care facilities through legal means. We similarly find this language too broad to constitute a clear and substantial specific public policy. . . .

5. In general, 42 U.S.C. §3058g provides that in order to receive federal funding for state long-term care ombudsman programs, states must meet certain requirements, including appointing an ombudsman and establishing an official office of the ombudsman. *See* 42 U.S.C. §3058g(a)(1), (2).

[As for 42 U.S.C. §1396r(c)(6),] which governs the requirements care facilities must meet to obtain grants for medical assistance programs, provides that "the nursing facility . . . may not require residents to deposit their personal funds with the facility." Subsection (c)(6) includes guidelines for how care facilities are to manage resident funds when management of such funds has been authorized by the resident. Although not clearly stated, this section could imply that care facility residents have the right to manage their own financial affairs. In the past we have held that we may look beyond the provision in question to determine whether the motivating policy behind it constitutes a clear and substantial public policy. However, we conclude that a mere hint to such an underlying policy, as is the case here, is insufficient to constitute the type of clear and substantial policy necessary to establish an exception to the employment-at-will doctrine. Thus, we hold that 42 U.S.C. §1396r(c)(6) does not rise to the level of a clear public policy.

Rule 432-150-4.400 of the Utah Administrative Code provides that "the resident has the right to maintain his financial affairs and the facility may not require a resident to deposit his personal funds with the facility." Both of these sections plainly state that care facility residents have the right to manage their own finances.

Additionally, 42 C.F.R. §483.10, governing resident rights that must be recognized by long-term care facilities, provides the most detailed and applicable provision. It states:

> The resident has a right to a dignified existence, self-determination, and communication with and access to persons and services inside and outside the facility. A facility must protect and promote the rights of each resident, including . . . the right to manage his or her financial affairs, and the facility may not require residents to deposit their personal funds with the facility.

This regulation explicitly states that care facility residents have the right to manage their own funds.

However, we have earlier pointed out that a clear public policy must be found in our statutes or constitutions, or judicial decisions. The provision in 42 C.F.R. §483.10 is an executive agency regulation that governs practice and procedure before federal administrative agencies. Similarly, R432-150-4.400 is a provision in the Utah Administrative Code.

Administrative regulations by their very nature are not "substantial" under our case law. The character of the public policy exception is that it furthers policies that "protect the public or promote public interest." Agency regulations are created by the agencies themselves and are tailored to govern specific agency needs. The public policy exception must be "narrow enough in its scope and application to be no threat to employers who operate within the mandates of the law and clearly established public policy as set out in the duly adopted laws." Thus, we hold that while 42 C.F.R. §483.10 and R432-150-4.400 of the Utah Administrative Code expressly state that care facility residents have the right to manage their own funds, our case law does not allow for administrative regulations alone to constitute expressions of clear public policy.[8]

In so holding, we recognize that care facility residents are often at the mercy of the facilities in which they reside. Residents face many challenges as their mobility decreases and their ability to take care of themselves physically, mentally, and

---

8. We do not hold that an administrative regulation may not provide support to a legislatively or judicially created public policy.

emotionally deteriorates. However, while we agree with plaintiff that "the rights of nursing home residents, especially with the increasing longevity of Utah residents and the growth of Utah's population, are a matter of most significant public concern," we also recognize the reality that many residents, while remaining in control of their funds, voluntarily seek the assistance of family members or friends with their banking and spending decisions. That appears to have been the situation in the instant case. Such efforts by honest and helpful advisors should be encouraged and not discouraged by rigid, government-imposed requirements. . . .

DURHAM, Justice, dissenting:

I respectfully dissent. There is, I believe, abundant support for the proposition that a long-term care facility resident's right to manage her own funds is a matter of clear and substantial public policy. We are dealing here with one of our system's most fundamental and well-understood rights: the right of a legally competent person to control her property and manage her financial affairs. . . .

This court is now faced with the question of whether to recognize a public policy exception protecting the right of a legally competent long-term care facility resident to manage her own financial affairs. I believe that the majority's view of the legitimacy of the public policy in question is mistaken. We can, and should, recognize administrative regulations as a valid source of Utah public policy for exceptions to the at-will employment doctrine; the regulatory process occurs through legislative delegation and under legislative oversight. It is undertaken by persons and entities with considerable expertise and knowledge regarding legislative intent. Furthermore, there is clear and substantial public policy supporting a long-term care facility resident's right to manage her funds in related federal regulations identical to those adopted by this state, in the Utah Probate and Criminal Code, in Utah case law, and in the Utah Constitution. . . .

[The dissent, in reviewing other sources of public policy, cited *In re Guardianship of Valentine*, 294 P.2d 696 (Utah 1956), a case involving the appointment of a guardian for the property of an alleged incompetent; *Valentine* held that "the right of every individual to handle his own affairs even at the expense of dissipating his fortune is a right jealous[l]y guarded and one which will not be taken away except in extreme cases." It interpreted Sharon Mellen's request to Ms. Merkley, the Fairview employee in charge of residents' funds, not to inform Ms. Mellen of the arrival of a check as an effort to manage Ms. Mellen's affairs for her.] It is impossible for one to manage one's financial affairs if one is purposefully deprived of the knowledge of relevant information, such as the arrival or deposit of a personal check. . . .

It is important to note that Ms. Merkley and Ms. Maroney received written reprimands from Fairview for failing to tell Ms. Mellen about her check. In fact, a new policy was instituted by Fairview after this incident requiring that residents be informed of all their incoming funds, regardless of who assists them with their financial affairs. This change was, I submit, an acknowledgment by Fairview of what the laws and public policy of Utah require. . . .

NOTES

1. *Sources of Public Policy.* In states recognizing the public policy tort, the first question is what policies count, that is, what sources may a court look to? *Fitzgerald* and *Rackley* both deal with the sources of public policy that will support a tort suit. *Fitzgerald* writes that the state constitution and state statutes will suffice, but it does not decide whether administrative regulations will do so. What about *Rackley*? Is the court too grudging in its analysis of applicable public policies? Even assuming that the Utah constitutional provisions relating to owning property are too generalized, don't the federal and state laws requiring ombudsmen to protect residents of nursing homes nevertheless indicate a strong public interest in maintaining the integrity and autonomy of such persons? If there is any doubt about this, isn't it resolved by the federal and state laws related to safeguarding the property of nursing home residents?

Other states have gone further and recognized judicially created public policies, *see Feliciano v. 7-Eleven, Inc.* 559 S.E.2d 713 (W. Va. 2001) (judicially recognized policy favoring self-defense could trump the at-will rule where store employee violated company policy to disarm a robber). Perhaps the most far-reaching decision in terms of sources of public policy is *Pierce v. Ortho Pharm. Corp.*, 417 A.2d 505 (N.J. 1980), which holds that even a professional code of ethics might be a source of public policy.

The new Restatement concurs on this point and is generally sweeping, allowing courts to look to "(a) federal and state constitutions; (b) federal, state, and local statutes, ordinances, and decisional law; (c) federal, state, and local administrative regulations, decisions, and orders; and (d) well-established principles in a professional or occupational code of conduct protective of the public interest."

2. *Administrative Regulations.* The *Rackley* court recognizes that administrative regulations directly address a patient's right to manage her own financial affairs. But it refuses to accord "public policy" status to such regulations. Are you persuaded by the court's analysis? Isn't it true, at least on the federal level, that courts view (valid) administrative regulations as an exercise of congressional law-making authority delegated to the agency? *See Chevron U.S.A. Inc. v. Nat. Resources Def. Council, Inc.*, 467 U.S. 837 (1984); *United States v. Mead Corp.*, 533 U.S. 218 (2001). Why should such laws be insufficient predicates for the public policy tort? Is it because regulations may be too detailed and technical? Even so, aren't regulated industries expected to obey governing regulations? The dissent in *Rackley* stressed that other states recognized regulations as an appropriate source of public policy. *See also Jasper v. H. Nizam, Inc.*, 764 N.W.2d 751, 764-65 (Iowa 2009); *cf. Yuan v. Johns Hopkins Univ.*, 157 A.3d 254 (Md. 2017) (federal regulations, which direct federally funded institutions to investigate allegations of research misconduct and address retaliation for reporting it, do not provide a clear public policy to support a wrongful termination claim). In one sense, *Rackley* may seem divorced from much of employment law because it involves a set of statutes and administrative regulations focused on one particular setting—the nursing home. But it is common in our highly regulated society for particular segments of the economy to be subject to detailed administrative controls. *Rackley* involved only one aspect of the highly regulated health care industry where public policy concerns are pervasive. Other highly regulated industries include transportation and energy. An attorney advising employees or employers in these settings must be alert to the potential of the public policy tort limiting the employer's discretion to terminate, a matter that would otherwise be left to private ordering.

Notice the Catch-22* that *Rackley* creates for employees. Constitutional and statutory provisions are likely to be too general to address a particular question.

___

* There was only one catch and that was Catch-22, which specified that a concern for one's own safety in the face of dangers that were real and immediate was the process of a rational mind. Orr was crazy

Precisely for that reason, Congress and state legislatures authorize agencies to provide more specific rules through regulations. However, the very regulations that are specific enough to satisfy the court in this respect are not of sufficient authority to state public policy. Reread footnote 8. Is the court suggesting that in some cases regulations may make general policy statements sufficiently concrete to support the tort? If so, why was this not true in *Rackley* itself?

3. *Federal Law Supporting State Public Policy Torts.* In a system with an enormous amount of federal regulation, the relationship between the state public policy tort and federal law is critical. In a footnote, *Fitzgerald* avoided deciding whether federal law could have provided the underlying public policy for a tort action in Iowa. Other cases have looked to federal law as a source of state public policy. As *Fitzgerald*'s footnote 4 indicates, this has raised the question whether the federal statute preempts even consistent state law, perhaps by occupying the field. While a few decisions have found preemption by particular federal laws, *see, e.g., Fasano v. FRB*, 457 F.3d 274 (3d Cir. 2006) (federal reserve banks not subject to state employment laws); *Chrisman v. Philips Indus., Inc.*, 751 P.2d 140 (Kan. 1988) (state tort action for discharge for refusing to approve defective nuclear products preempted by federal energy law), most have not. *See, e.g., Sargent v. Cent. Natl. Bank & Trust Co.*, 809 P.2d 1298 (Okla. 1991) (no National Bank Act preemption); *Fragassi v. Neiburger*, 646 N.E.2d 315 (Ill. App. 1995) (no OSHA preemption). *See generally* Nancy Modesitt, *Wrongful Discharge: The Use of Federal Law as a Source of Public Policy*, 8 U. PA. J. LAB. & EMP. L. 623 (2006).

4. *Plaintiff's Conduct.* Suppose the dissent had prevailed as to the requisite public policies. Did plaintiff's call to Sharon further those policies? Even if it did, would Fairview have been within its rights to discharge Ms. Rackley for the *manner* in which she made the call—calling Sharon at work and screaming at her? Of course, plaintiff denied she screamed, but would that matter if Fairview thought (reasonably?) that she had? *See Curlee v. Kootenai County Fire & Rescue*, 224 P.3d 458 (Idaho 2008) (an employee terminated for documenting her co-workers' time-wasting activities had a triable claim under the Idaho whistleblowing statute, which protects one who "communicates in good faith the existence of any waste of public funds, property or manpower").

Reviewing the Public Policy Exception

We saw earlier that §5.02 of the Restatement of Employment Law identifies six categories under the public policy exception. There is considerable debate both as to whether these categories are too restrictive and whether the formulation of the categories accurately captures the decisions in the area, but understanding the various possible headings for the tort is important.

Refusing to Commit an Illegal Act Perhaps the most obviously justifiable instance of protection is where the employee is discharged for refusing to perform

---

and could be grounded. All he had to do was ask; and as soon as he did, he would no longer be crazy and would have to fly more missions. . . . If he flew them he was crazy and didn't have to; but if he didn't want to he was sane and had to. . . .

JOSEPH HELLER, Catch-22, 46 (1961).

an illegal act, or violate a code of professional conduct or other occupational code. The employee must only reasonably and in good faith believe the conduct to be illegal or a violation. *See McGarrity v. Berlin Metals Inc.*, 774 N.E.2d 71 (Ind. App. 2002) (refusal to be a party to an illegal tax underreporting scheme for the purpose of defrauding the state and creditors). The principle has been applied to protect employees who testified against their employer's wishes in legal proceedings. *Reust v. Alaska Petroleum Contrs., Inc.*, 127 P.3d 807 (Alaska 2005). *But see Harney v. Meadowbrook Nursing Ctr.*, 784 S.W.2d 921 (Tenn. 1990) (termination of nurse who testified at a co-worker's compensation hearing did not implicate public policy tort if the employer had a good faith belief that her testimony was perjured).

Whistleblowing The Restatement also protects an employee who "reports or inquires about employer conduct that the employee reasonably and in good faith believes violates a law or established principle of a professional or occupational code of conduct protective of the public interest." §5.02(e). Many believe that, after protecting employees for refusing to violate the law, the next most compelling case for protection is when the employee reports a serious violation of law. Unlike instances where employees testify under court process, citizens generally do not have any affirmative duty to make such reports. It, therefore, cannot be said that the employer who discharges a worker for reporting a violation forces her to choose between retaining her job and violating the law; an employee who did not volunteer information would be acting perfectly legally. Nevertheless, it is certainly in the public interest for individuals to report violations; indeed, statutes such as the federal False Claims Act, *see* note on pages 269-272, essentially offer bounties for pursuing fraud where federal funds are involved. And, as *Fitzgerald* indicated, all states bar interference with witnesses. Accordingly, a great number of cases have recognized a public policy suit where the employee alleges that she was discharged for reporting violations to appropriate public authorities. *See, e.g., Kanagy v. Fiesta Salons, Inc.*, 541 S.E.2d 616 (W. Va. 2000) (reporting violations to the state Board of Barbers and Cosmetologists); *Prince v. Rescorp Realty*, 940 F.2d 1104 (7th Cir. 1991) (reporting faulty fire safety equipment to town).

But many courts sharply distinguish between reports to public authorities and internal reports, with only the latter being protected—presumably because of the absence of effects beyond the two parties to the employment relationship. *See, e.g., Bielser v. Prof'l Sys. Corp.*, 177 F. App'x 655 (9th Cir. 2006). While an external reporting requirement limits the tort in terms of what conduct is protected, isn't it a perverse rule even from an employer's perspective insofar as it tends to require employees to wash their company's dirty laundry in public rather than seek to remedy problems internally? The Restatement protects reports made internally, *see* 5.03, Ill. 18, but counterbalances that by seeming to require an internal report before going outside, at least to the newspapers. Ill. 20.

Performing a Public Duty As framed by the Restatement, employees are also protected when "perform[ing] a public duty or obligation that the employee reasonably and in good faith believes the law imposes." The cases dealing with refusals to commit perjury could be so described. The other major "public duty" category is jury service. *Nees v. Hock*, 536 P.2d 512 (Or. 1975). The Restatement views this as a narrow category: The obligation must be a public one, "not merely a personal, familial, or moral obligation." §5.03, cmt. c.

But the line between the two is not always so bright. Illustration 10 of §5.02 would protect an employee who is late to work because the police "require" him to fill out a witness report about an accident he observed, but suppose the employee is late because the police *request* him to comfort an injured family member until the EMTs arrive? *See Gaspar v. Peshastin Hi-Up Growers*, 128 P.3d 627 (Wash. Ct. App. 2006) (recognizing a public policy encouraging cooperation with police and prosecutors in criminal investigations). *But see Brennan v. Cephalon, Inc.*, 298 F. App'x 147 (3d Cir. 2008) (a "statutorily imposed duty" claim failed because the statutes in question, while requiring the disclosure of certain "compliance indicators," did not impose an affirmative duty on the employee to report his audit findings to the Food and Drug Administration).

Claiming a Benefit Still another category of protection under the Restatement is "fil[ing] a charge or claim[ing] a benefit in good faith under an employment statute or law whether or not the charge or claim is meritorious." §5.03(c). Some of the court cases spoke in terms of "the exercise of a public right," with the prototype being decisions recognizing a cause of action for filing a workers' compensation claim. *See, e.g., Springer v. Weeks & Leo Co.*, 429 N.W.2d 558 (Iowa 1988). But even the public right cases take a more limited view of the rights that are protected than might first appear. For example, a number of cases rejected claims by employees who were fired for doing what, in normal speech, we would say they had a right to do. *See, e.g., Beam v. IPCO*, 838 F.2d 242 (7th Cir. 1988) (hiring an attorney not protected); *Scroghan v. Kraftco Corp.*, 551 S.W.2d 811 (Ky. Ct. App. 1977) (discharge of an employee for attending law school permitted). *See also Hoven v. Walgreen Co.*, 751 F.3d 778 (6th Cir. 2014) (finding no public policy basis when a pharmacist was fired by his employer for shooting at armed robbers since self-defense statutes applied only to criminal laws). The Restatement shifts the focus from "right" in the abstract to rights accorded by "an employment statute or law." It would, however, protect workers who act in "good faith," cmt. d, thus avoiding any objective reasonableness requirement for those claiming a benefit.

Waiving a Nonwaivable Right The Restatement also recognizes a public policy tort for an employee who "refuses to waive a nonnegotiable or nonwaivable right where the employer's insistence on the waiver as a condition of employment or the court's enforcement of the waiver would violate well-established public policy." §5.03(d). It relies on *Edwards v. Arthur Andersen LLP*, 1b89 P.3d 285, 289 (Cal. 2008), which recognized that firing an employee for refusing to waive his statutory rights to compete with, and to be indemnified by, his employer would be actionable. That court, however, tempered the decision by reading the indemnity waiver not to violate this principle. The waiver was framed in terms of "any and all" claims, including "claims that in any way arise from or out of, are based upon or relate to Employee's employment by, association with or compensation from" the employer. Nevertheless, the court found this not specific enough to include the nonwaivable right of indemnification.

The Catchall? Although hotly debated, the Restatement retains a catchall category, inserted because of concerns that limiting the public policy tort to the other categories would tend to freeze the law and not permit appropriate judicial responses to situations that might arise in the future. Accordingly, §5.03(f) protects an employee from discipline for "engag[ing] in other activity directly furthering a well-established public policy." Illustration 24, based on *Gardner v. Loomis Armored Inc.*, 913 P.2d 377 (Wash. 1996), involves an armored car driver who, in violation of company policy, left his vehicle to rescue a hostage during a bank robbery. Is *Danny v. Laidlaw Transit Services, Inc.*, 193 P.3d 128, 138 (Wash. 2008), another example? There, the court recognized "a clear public policy of protecting domestic violence survivors and their children and holding domestic violence perpetrators accountable." The result would be to preclude the employer from firing the plaintiff for absences due to her dealing with domestic violence, at least if such absences were unavoidable.

* * *

The public policy exception necessarily means that the right of an employee to blow the whistle trumps any employer expectation that the employee's duty of loyalty forbids such disclosure. *See* Chapter 8. *See generally* Orly Lobel, *Lawyering Loyalties: Speech Rights and Duties Within Twenty-First Century New Governance*, 77 FORDHAM L. REV. 1245 (2010). But the relationship between the two conflicting obligations is ill defined. The problem may be illustrated by the employee who is approached by the FBI investigating the employer—say, in a False Claims Act case. *See* page 269. The employee doesn't believe the employer has done anything wrong, so she doesn't fit within §5.03(e). The law does not require her to cooperate with the FBI, so it's not a "public duty or obligation," which raises questions about §5.03(b) (although maybe she would "reasonably believe" that the law required her to respond). There might be a "public right" to cooperate with a criminal government investigation, but the Restatement is limited to claiming benefits connected to employment. Is the catchall provision the solution? Cooperating with the government has to be protected, doesn't it? And it can't violate the duty of loyalty, can it?

Note on Free Speech and the Public Policy Tort

Many of the public policies we have examined implicate speech rights, but the First Amendment articulates a policy only against *state* repression of speech. Under that view, public policy concerns do not reach beyond state action. *See Grinzi v. San Diego Hospice Corp.*, 14 Cal. Rptr. 3d 893 (Ct. App. 2004) (First Amendment free speech not a basis for a public policy claim against a private employer); *Edmondson v. Shearer Lumber Products*, 75 P.3d 733 (Idaho 2003) (free speech is not a sufficiently strong public policy to sustain a wrongful discharge cause of action). A few courts, however, have found private coercion of political activity to be actionable even if restrictions on free speech, as such, are not. *See Chavez v. Manville Products. Corp.*, 777 P.2d 371 (N.M. 1989) (dismissal for refusal to participate in company's lobbying efforts actionable). Even in the public sector, which is treated in more detail in Chapter 7, much employee speech is unprotected: (1) The matter must be one of "public concern," (2) the matter must not be part of the employee's official duties, and (3) the employee's speech must not be too disruptive. *See Garcetti v. Ceballos*, 547 U.S. 410 (2006), reproduced at page 411.

One state generally protects speech against private interference. Connecticut's Free Speech Act, CONN. GEN. STAT. §31-51q (2018), bars adverse action against an employee "on account of the exercise of rights under the first amendment of the

United States Constitution" or under the corollary provisions of the Connecticut constitution. This prohibition is subject to the condition that the employee's "activity does not substantially or materially interfere with the employee's bona fide performance or the working relationship between the employee and the employer. . . ." A few other states have limited laws prohibiting discrimination on the basis of political affiliation or have statutes guaranteeing the right to run for office or to vote. *See, e.g.,* CAL. LABOR L. §1101 (2018). *See generally* Eugene Volokh, *Private Employees' Speech and Political Activity: Statutory Protection Against Employer Retaliation*, 16 TEX. REV. LAW & POL. 295 (2012).

Would a public employee who spoke out as Fitzgerald or Rackley did be protected from discharge by the First Amendment? Did either of them speak on matters of public concern? What about under the Connecticut statute?

PROBLEMS

4-1. Lauren Lopez was a fifth-year associate at one of the top defense firms in Gotham. In the course of representing Dr. Sidley in a medical malpractice case, Lopez became suspicious that her client used cocaine. Sidley was a surgeon, and the case involved a claim by a woman who was left paralyzed after back surgery. The basis for Lopez's suspicions of Sidley's drug use included a constantly irritated nose, occasional "high" states, and extreme mood swings during the course of the two-year representation. As the case neared trial, Lopez became increasingly convinced that Sidley had a drug addiction problem. She received what she believed to be confirmation of this when she interviewed one of the prospective witnesses, an operating room nurse, who told her, "off the record," that Sidley "had had a cocaine problem but was really working on it."

Lopez took her concerns to the partner supervising her section, L. L. Cohen. He downplayed her worries, telling her she was no expert on symptoms of drug abuse, and she shouldn't believe the nurse's "hearsay." He concluded, "Just forget about it." She was still worried about the matter a week later when Cohen called her into his office on another case and, as she was leaving, said, "Oh, by the way, we've settled that claim against Sidley." Lopez was surprised, since she would normally have been involved in the settlement negotiations. When she asked what the settlement was, Cohen named a figure that was several hundred thousand dollars higher than what Cohen had previously said Sidley's malpractice carrier would be willing to pay.

Rather than lay her concerns to rest, this settlement actually increased Lopez's distress. After wrestling with her conscience, Lopez decided that she had to report her concerns to the state licensing authorities. She wrote a letter to them, copying both Sidley and Cohen and setting forth the bases for her concern.

A day after the letter was sent, Cohen came into Lopez's office and said, "I got your letter. You know I don't agree with you, but I guess we all have to do what we all have to do." He never mentioned the matter again.

You are managing partner of the firm. Both Cohen and Lopez separately speak with you about these events. Lopez is scheduled to be considered for partnership next year. The general sentiment before this episode was that she was unlikely to make partner, although no formal action has been taken. What, if anything, should you do?

4-2. Now imagine you represent Lopez, who is concerned about these events and her consideration for partnership. What advice would you give her? Would it be a good idea to contact the firm before the partnership decision? If so, what would you say or write? If you decide to do nothing, and she is turned down for partnership, what course of action would you advise?

B. STATUTES CREATING PUBLIC POLICY CAUSES OF ACTION

The early public policy cases looked to preexisting statutes for the public policy they discerned. But as the courts began to expand the public policy tort, some legislatures responded by enacting laws designed to protect employees. Such statutes create their own causes of action. The materials that follow explore these statutes and their relationship to the public policy tort created by the courts.

Of course, these general "whistleblower" laws had precursors; it was common for statutes providing substantive protections to employees to also bar employers from retaliating against workers for initiating or participating in enforcement proceedings. For example, the Fair Labor Standards Act bars retaliation for seeking enforcement of that statute's minimum wage and maximum hour provisions. 29 U.S.C.S. §215(a)(3) (2018). Another example is the retaliation provisions of the antidiscrimination laws, which we will encounter in Chapter 9. Less directly related to employment are whistleblowing provisions in federal statutes regulating such areas as nuclear energy, *see* Energy Reorganization Act of 1974, 42 U.S.C. §5851(a) (2018); transportation, *see* Surface Transport Assistance Act, 49 U.S.C. §2305(a) (2018); and heath care, *see* Patient Protection and Affordable Care Act, §1150B(d) (2018) (penalizing long-term care facilities for retaliation against an employee who engaged in lawful acts).

While these and similar state laws could be viewed as whistleblowing statutes, that term is often reserved for more open-ended enactments that create civil remedies for employees who are discharged or otherwise adversely treated by their employees because they disclose violations of the law or engage in other conduct in which there is a legitimate public concern. Prior to 1980 there were no general statutes, at either the state or federal level, that broadly protected private whistleblowers. Indeed, in the absence of such statutes led so many courts to recognize a public policy suit for discharges of employees who reported violations of the law to relevant authorities. In the wake of such decisions, however, several states enacted whistleblower statutes—that is, laws providing a measure of protection to employees, whether in the public or private sector, for conduct the legislature deemed to be worthy of protection. At the federal level, there is still no comprehensive statute, but a new wave of protection has taken hold this century, starting with the Sarbanes-Oxley Act. *See* page 249.

1.   State Approaches

State statutes have varying substantive provisions, but an appreciation of the problems faced in drafting and applying these laws may be gained by comparing two state statutes in detail.

Conscientious Employee Protection Act ("CEPA")
N.J. Stat. Ann. §34:19-1 (2018)

§ 34:19-3. Retaliatory action prohibited

An employer shall not take any retaliatory action against an employee because the employee does any of the following:

a. Discloses, or threatens to disclose to a supervisor or to a public body an activity, policy or practice of the employer, or another employer, with whom there is a business relationship, that the employee reasonably believes:

(1) is in violation of a law, or a rule or regulation promulgated pursuant to law, including any violation involving deception of, or misrepresentation to any shareholder, investor, client, patient, customer, employer, former employee, retiree or pensioner of the employer or any governmental entity, or, in the case of an employee who is a licensed or certified health care professional, reasonably believes constitutes improper quality of patient care; or

(2) is fraudulent or criminal, including any activity, policy or practice of deception or misrepresentation which the employee reasonably believes may defraud any shareholder, investor, client, patient, customer, employee, former employee, retiree or pensioner of the employer or any governmental entity;

b. Provides information to, or testifies before, any public body conducting an investigation, hearing or inquiry into any violation of law, or a rule or regulation promulgated pursuant to law by the employer, or another employer, with whom there is a business relationship, including any violation involving deception of, or misrepresentation to, any shareholder, investor, client, patient, customer, employee, former employee, retiree or pensioner of the employer or any governmental entity, or, in the case of an employee who is a licensed or certified health care professional, provides information to, or testifies before, any public body conducting an investigation, hearing or inquiry into the quality of patient care; or

c. Objects to, or refuses to participate in any activity, policy or practice which the employee reasonably believes:

(1) is in violation of a law, or a rule or regulation promulgated pursuant to law, including any violation involving deception of, or misrepresentation to, any shareholder, investor, client, patient, customer, employee, former employee, retiree or pensioner of the employer or any governmental

entity, or, if the employee is a licensed or certified health care professional, constitutes improper quality of patient care;

(2) is fraudulent or criminal, including any activity, policy or practice of deception or misrepresentation which the employee reasonably believes may defraud any shareholder, investor, client, patient, customer, employee, former employee, retiree or pensioner of the employer or any governmental entity; or

(3) is incompatible with a clear mandate of public policy concerning the public health, safety or welfare or protection of the environment.

CEPA goes on to provide for a one-year statute of limitations and a jury trial. §34:19-5. Remedies include legal or equitable relief, including punitive damages, attorneys' fees, and a civil fine, although punitive damages can be awarded only if "upper management" is implicated and the violation is "especially egregious." *Longo v. Pleasure Prods., Inc.,* 71 A.3d 775 (N.J. 2013). In an unusual provision, §34:19-6 allows reasonable attorneys' fees and court costs to the *employer* if an employee's suit is "without basis in law or in fact."

Minn. Stat. §181.932 (2018)

Disclosure of Information by Employees

1. Prohibited action.

An employer shall not discharge, discipline, threaten, otherwise discriminate against, or penalize an employee regarding the employee's compensation, terms, conditions, location, or privileges of employment because:

(1) the employee, or a person acting on behalf of an employee, in good faith, reports a violation, suspected violation, or planned violation of any federal or state law or common law or rule adopted pursuant to law to an employer or to any governmental body or law enforcement official;

(2) the employee is requested by a public body or office to participate in an investigation, hearing, inquiry;

(3) the employee refuses an employer's order to perform an action that the employee has an objective basis in fact to believe violates any state or federal law or rule or regulation adopted pursuant to law, and the employee informs the employer that the order is being refused for that reason;

(4) the employee, in good faith, reports a situation in which the quality of health care services provided by a health care facility, organization, or health care provider violates a standard established by federal or state law or a professionally recognized national clinical or ethical standard and potentially places the public at risk of harm;

(5) a public employee communicates the findings of a scientific or technical study that the employee, in good faith, believes to be truthful and accurate, including reports to a governmental body or law enforcement official; or

(6) an employee in the classified service of state government communicates information that the employee, in good faith, believes to be truthful and

accurate, and that relates to state services, including the financing of state services, to:

> (i) a legislator or the legislative auditor; or
> (ii) a constitutional officer.

The disclosures protected pursuant to this section do not authorize the disclosure of data otherwise protected by law.

The Minnesota statute bars not only discharge but also "penalizing" employees for protected conduct, with that term being defined to mean "conduct that might dissuade a reasonable employee from making or supporting a report." §181.931. Although the statute was originally interpreted to require that a whistleblower act with the purpose of exposing an illegality in order to be protected, an amendment in 2013—defining "good faith" to exclude knowing falsehoods or reckless disregard of the truth—was interpreted to dispense with any such requirement. *Friedlander v. Edwards Lifesciences, LLC*, 900 N.W.2d 162 (Minn. 2017). The statute authorizes a civil suit for "all damages recoverable at law" in addition to reasonable attorney's fees and appropriate equitable relief. It explicitly authorizes "reinstatement, back pay, restoration of lost service credit, if appropriate, compensatory damages, and the expungement of any adverse records of an employee who was the subject of the alleged acts of misconduct." §181.935. The six-year statute of limitations for causes of action under a statute applied to a whistleblower action, rather than the two-year period for torts resulting in personal injury, because the claim was created by statute before it was recognized at common law. *Ford v. Minneapolis Pub. Sch.*, 857 N.W.2d 725 (Minn. Ct. App. 2014).

Both the New Jersey and Minnesota statutes, like others of their kind, speak in terms of "employees," which may mean that it is permissible for an employer to refuse to hire an applicant who blew the whistle on a prior employer. *See* Leora F. Eisenstadt & Jennifer Pacella, *Whistleblowers Need Not Apply*, AM. BUS. L. J. (forthcoming 2018).

NOTES

1. *Applying the Statutes.* Suppose CEPA had been in effect in Utah. Would Rackley have fared better? Section 3 protects disclosures, inter alia, to "supervisors" of "an activity, policy or practice of the employer that the employee reasonably believes is in violation of a law. . . ." Did Rackley satisfy this standard? What about applying CEPA in Iowa—would it have affected Fitzgerald's suit? Would he have won under CEPA? Read §3 carefully. Now apply the Minnesota analysis to the facts of the two cases. Rackley's conduct might or might not be protected, depending in part on whether it relates to the "quality of health care services" the home provided.

2. *"Exhaustion."* CEPA's §34:19-4 limits protection for disclosures to a "public body" to an employee who has first brought the problem "to the attention of [her] supervisor . . . *by written notice*" (emphasis added). This departs from the common-law cases, which have not generally imposed any duty of "exhaustion of internal remedies," much less required a writing. Indeed, to the extent that many states do not extend public policy tort protection to internal complaints, it is a radical departure.

The Minnesota statute requires notice (but does not require that it be in writing) only when the employee "refuses an employer's order to perform an action that the employee has an objective basis in fact to believe violates any state or federal law or rule or regulation adopted pursuant to law." In such cases, protection depends on the employee's informing the employer that the order is being refused for that reason. §181.932(1)(c). If your jurisdiction were considering a statute along the lines of the CEPA or the Minnesota law, would you recommend any requirement of resort to internal remedies? If so, when?

3. *Reasonable Belief.* How certain must an employee be that his employer is violating public policy in order to receive statutory protection? Neither state requires the employee to be correct. CEPA speaks in terms of the employee's "reasonable belief," but the Minnesota statute is even more protective. It protects "good faith" reports of violations, §181.932(1)(c), and the statute essentially defines good faith to mean no knowing or reckless falsehoods. §181.931(4). However, when the employee refuses to perform what he views as an illegal act, he must have an "objective basis in fact" for believing that the performance would violate the law. §181.932(1)(c); *see also Koch Foods, Inc. v. Sec'y, U.S. Dep't of Labor*, 712 F.3d 476, 484 (11th Cir. 2013) (Surface Transportation Assistance Act requires an employee to be correct about the existence of a violation before he can refuse to work). An "objective basis in fact" appears to be something akin to a "reasonable belief." Why do you suppose the Minnesota legislature decided to include different standards in subparts (a) and (c)?

In contrast to the expansive approaches of Minnesota and New Jersey, a few other states take more restrictive views, such as an "at the employee's peril" approach to protection. For example, *Pooler v. Maine Coal Products*, 532 A.2d 1026 (Me. 1987), applied that state's narrow law protecting employees who refuse to follow an employer order that violates a law and would put anyone's health and safety at risk. It held that an employee who refused to drive an allegedly unsafe truck must prove an actual safety violation. Which of these three approaches is preferable? *See also Webb-Weber v. Community Action for Human Servs., Inc.*, 15 N.E.3d 1172 (N.Y. 2014) (while Labor Law §740(2) prohibits employers from retaliation against employee for disclosing employer practices violating laws related to public health or healthcare fraud, it requires plaintiff to prove an actual violation that creates a substantial and specific danger to the public health or safety). Suppose the employee has a reasonable belief in a public policy violation but is motivated by self-interest, not public spiritedness? *Whitman v. City of Burton*, 831 N.W.2d 223, 225-26 (Mich. 2013), applying the Michigan Whistleblower Protection Act, held it immaterial that the plaintiff "acted to advance own financial interests, not to inform public on matter of public concern," since the state statute did not require a public-minded "primary motivation." The federal Whistleblower Protection Act was amended to make irrelevant "the employee's or applicant's motive for making [a protected] disclosure." 5 U.S.C. §2302(f)(1)(C) (2018).

4. *Complaint Box or 1-800 Number?* Section 7 of CEPA requires an employer to designate "the persons . . . to receive written notifications pursuant to section 4 of this act." Would you consider retaining individuals who are required to keep the name of the notifying employee confidential from others within the company? Such an approach, if effective, would tend to immunize complainers from retaliation and thereby tend to protect you from suit. How could you make the confidentiality provision credible? Name an ombudsman? Choose an outside professional such as an attorney? Ironically, in *Estate of Roach v. TRW, Inc.*, 754 A.2d 544 (N.J. 2000), the employer set up a hotline staffed by its attorneys, but the plaintiff's call "fell through the cracks."

5. *Scope of Public Policy.* CEPA and the Minnesota statute seem to be both broader and narrower than the common law. For example, neither protects an employee from reprisal for "claiming a benefit arising from employment." On the other hand, CEPA's catch-all language—protecting an employee who refuses to participate in an activity she reasonably believes to be "incompatible with a clear mandate of public policy concerning the public health, safety, or welfare or protection of the environment," 3(c)(3)—seems to go far beyond a refusal to participate in activities that are "illegal." And Minnesota protects communicating "the findings of a scientific or technical study," which does not require any nexus to public policy. Again, imagine you are drafting a statute for your jurisdiction. How would you frame the substantive protections in terms of the scope of public policy?

6. *Limitations on Whistleblowing. Fitzgerald* recognized that an employer's retaliation might be justified if the employee's whistleblowing were somehow inappropriate, and we saw in the Note on Attorneys and the Public Policy Tort on page 222 that professional ethics might bar disclosure of client confidences and therefore justify actions against an attorney who violated those confidences. CEPA contains no explicit exceptions to its protection, but the Minnesota statute expressly excludes from its general protection (1) most disclosures of "the identity of any employee making a report to a governmental body or law enforcement official"; (2) false disclosures—that is, "statements or disclosures [made by an employee] knowing that they are false or that they are in reckless disregard of the truth"; and (3) and disclosure of "confidential information"—that is, "disclosures that would violate federal or state law or diminish or impair the rights of any person to the continued protection of confidentiality of communications provided by common law." §181.932 (2), (3), (5). If you were drafting a statute, would you include any exceptions? If so, do the Minnesota ones make sense? Do you understand what the last one is driving at?

The new Defend Trade Secrets Law of 2016 addresses aspects of this problem. 18 U.S.C. §1833(b)(1) (2018) immunizes from criminal or civil liability under "any Federal or State trade secret law" the disclosure of a trade secret to a government official "solely for the purpose of reporting or investigating a suspected violation of law" or in a court filing under seal. Similarly, §1833(b)(2), while not speaking in terms of immunity, allows disclosure of a trade secret by a whistleblowing plaintiff to her attorney and its use in a subsequent court proceeding if the document containing the secret is filed under seal and not otherwise disclosed (except pursuant to court order). Employers are supposed to provide employees with notice of these rights in their nondisclosure agreements, §1833(b)(3), but the remedy is merely the denial of exemplary damages and attorneys' fees in a successful trade secret suit

What about a more general limitation on the public policy tort? Suppose the plaintiff was herself implicated in the violation of public policy? Should she nevertheless be permitted to bring suit? *Galle v. Isle of Capri Casinos, Inc.,* 180 So. 3d 619, 620 (Miss. 2015) (plaintiff who willingly participated in the allegedly illegal activity may not bring a public policy claim). The issue has also arisen under federal bounty programs. See pages 262-263. Relatedly, Miriam H. Baer, *Reconceptualizing the Whistleblower's Dilemma,* 50 U.C. Davis L. Rev. 2215 (2017), argues that the absence of immunity provisions in whistleblowing laws blunts financial incentives to report violations for individuals who may be complicit in them.

7. *A Job Duties Exception?* When we reach Chapter 7, we will discover that First Amendment protection does not extend to public employees whose actions fall within their job duties. Does such an exception operate under the Minnesota or New Jersey laws? In *Kidwell v. Sybaritic, Inc.*, 784 N.W.2d 220 (Minn. 2010), Minnesota rejected such an exception under that state's statute, largely because it was inconsistent with the broad statutory language. The court limited its holding, however, by suggesting that a protected employee must be motivated by a desire to expose an illegality, which might not be the case when the action taken was within an employee's job duties. A subsequent statutory amendment to the definition of "good faith," however, seems to have negated this limitation, since employees are now protected unless their reports are knowingly or recklessly false. *Friedlander v. Edwards Lifesciences, LLC*, 900 N.W.2d 162 (Minn. 2017). After some uncertainty, New Jersey seems to have resolved the issue by finding "watchdog" employees protected by CEPA. *Lippman v. Ethicon, Inc.*, 119 A.3d 215 (N.J. 2015), (employees whose job duties entail securing compliance with a relevant standard of care may invoke CEPA's whistleblower protections and are not subject to any special requirement of exhaustion of internal avenues to seek compliance); *cf. Pippin v. Blvd. Motel Corp.*, 835 F.3d 180, 186 (1st Cir. 2016) (while there was no general "job duties" exception to Maine laws, an employee's conduct must be motivated by opposition to illegal activities in order to be protected).

Similarly, the federal Whistleblower Protection Act, 5 U.S.C. §2302(b)(8) (2018), was originally interpreted restrictively to include a "job duties" exception. However, the statute was amended to broaden its protection. Thus, it now provides that conduct is protected from reprisal even if "made during the normal course of duties" of an employee. §2302(f)(2). *See generally* Nancy Modesitt, *The* Garcetti *Virus*, 80 U. CIN. L. REV. 137 (2011).

PROBLEMS

4-3. Review Problem 4-1. How would you resolve it under the New Jersey and Minnesota statutes?

4-4. Review Problem 4-2. How would you resolve it under the New Jersey and Minnesota statutes?

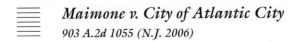

Maimone v. City of Atlantic City
903 A.2d 1055 (N.J. 2006)

SKILLMAN, J.

This appeal involves a claim under the [CEPA] by a police officer who alleges he was transferred from detective to patrolman in retaliation for his objections to the Chief of Police's decision to terminate enforcement of provisions of the Code of Criminal Justice prohibiting promotion of prostitution and restricting the location of sexually-oriented businesses.

I.

Plaintiff Angelo Maimone has been a member of the Atlantic City Police Department since 1988. He was transferred in 1991 from a patrolman position to detective in the Special Investigations Unit. As a result, plaintiff became contractually entitled after one year to receive an additional 3% of his base salary. Beginning in 1993, plaintiff was assigned to conduct investigations of prostitution and other sexually-related offenses, which he continued to do until early 2001.

In May 2000, defendant Arthur C. Snellbaker was appointed Chief of the Atlantic City Police Department. According to plaintiff, around eight months after Snellbaker's appointment, Captain William Glass told him at a staff meeting that he could not initiate any new promotion of prostitution investigations unless they "directly impacted the citizens of Atlantic City." Shortly thereafter, plaintiff's immediate supervisor, Sergeant Glenn Abrams, directed him to terminate all pending investigations into the promotion of prostitution and to conduct only narcotics investigations. Plaintiff alleges that Abrams told him that "they," referring to prostitution investigations, "don't exist." Plaintiff, who at that point was the only detective still actively involved in promotion of prostitution investigations, understood this directive to apply not only to him but also to all other officers in the Special Investigations Unit.

Around the same time Abrams gave plaintiff this directive, the files plaintiff had maintained regarding persons involved in the promotion of prostitution were removed from a filing cabinet under his control, and thereafter, plaintiff's access to those files was restricted. When plaintiff complained to Abrams about his loss of access to these files, Abrams allegedly told him: "You're never going to see the files again."

[In April 2001, plaintiff sent a memorandum to Sergeant Abrams complaining about his inability to access those files. It noted that he routinely updated files "on Escort and Massage services working in Atlantic City," and referred to "at least seven new services operating this month alone." The memorandum complained about the absence of file space for new files and the absence of any means of cross-referencing these files against current files. It asked for Chief Snellbaker's response.]

According to plaintiff, after Abrams read this memorandum, he shook his head and said to plaintiff: "You're asking for it."

In 2001, Maimone also complained about Atlantic City's failure to enforce *N.J.S.A.* 2C:34-7, which makes it a fourth-degree offense for a sexually-oriented business to operate within 1,000 feet of a church or school. After the county prosecutor decided that *N.J.S.A.* 2C:34-7 should be enforced by the revocation of the mercantile licenses of offenders rather than by criminal prosecution, plaintiff wrote letters to the municipal solicitor requesting the initiation of proceedings to revoke the licenses of sexually-oriented businesses that were operating in violation of this prohibition. When the city solicitor failed to take any action, plaintiff sent a memorandum to Abrams, dated May 26, 2001, which stated in part:

> I am respectfully asking, that this Office request that the mercantile license of AC News and Video be revoked, due to the fact that this location is clearly in violation of 2C:34-7. This location is clearly a detriment to the neighborhood. There is a Covenant House for juveniles on the same block as well as an elementary school and Synagogue being nearby. As you are aware, it has been and continues to be the practice of the Atlantic County Prosecutor's Office, not to prosecute this statute. It is their contention that civil remedies (IE: Removal of Mercantile license) would be sufficient and thus relieving the Prosecutors Office from utilizing their limited resources in prosecution.
>
> If the city chooses not to enforce this statute in this matter, all future prosecutions will be jeopardized.

Within days after he sent this memorandum, Captain Glass said to plaintiff: "You're out of here, you're going to patrol." Effective June 10, 2001, plaintiff was transferred from his detective position in the Special Investigations Unit to patrol officer. Plaintiff was told that the reason for his transfer was an April 17, 2001 newspaper story that disclosed he had attended the wedding of a daughter of a suspected organized crime figure.

II.

[The trial court granted summary judgment to the defendants because plaintiff could not create a genuine issue of material fact that he reasonably believed Atlantic City's decision to cease enforcing the provisions of the Code relating to promotion of prostitution and restricting the location of sexually oriented businesses "violat[ed] . . . a clear mandate of public policy." The Appellate Division reversed, and Supreme Court granted defendants' petition for certification.]

III.

Plaintiff's CEPA claim is based on *N.J.S.A.* 34:19-3c, which provides:

> An employer shall not take any retaliatory action against an employee because the employee does any of the following. . . .
> c. Objects to, or refuses to participate in any activity, policy or practice which the employee reasonably believes:

[T]he Court held in *Dzwonar* [*v. McDevitt*, 828 A.2d 893 (N.J. 2003)] that a plaintiff who brings an action under this section must demonstrate that:

> (1) he or she reasonably believed that his or her employer's conduct was violating either a law, rule, or regulation promulgated pursuant to law, or a clear mandate of public policy; (2) he or she performed a "whistle-blowing" activity described in *N.J.S.A.* 34:19-3c; (3) an adverse employment action was taken against him or her; and (4) a causal connection exists between the whistle-blowing activity and the adverse employment action.

These requirements must be liberally construed to effectuate CEPA's important social goals.

Defendants do not dispute that plaintiffs' objections to Atlantic City's alleged policy decision to cease enforcement of the provisions of the Code that prohibit promotion of prostitution and restrict the location of sexually-oriented businesses constituted a "whistle-blowing" activity, thus satisfying the second requirement of a claim under *N.J.S.A.* 34:19-3c identified in *Dzwonar*. However, defendants argue that the evidence plaintiff presented in opposition to their motion for summary judgment was insufficient to establish the other three requirements of a claim under this section. We address those requirements in the order set forth in *Dzwonar*.

A.

Plaintiff rests his claim solely on subsection (3) of *N.J.S.A.* 34:19-3c. At the outset, it is appropriate to compare the elements of a claim under this subsection with a claim under c(1). While an employee who proceeds under c(1) must show that he or she reasonably believed that the employer's activity, policy or practice "violat[ed]" a law, rule, or regulation, an employee who proceeds under c(3) is only required to show that the employer's activity, policy, or practice is "incompatible" with a clear mandate of public policy. To "violate" a law, a person must commit "[a]n infraction or breach of the law," BLACK'S LAW DICTIONARY 1564 (7th ed.1999), but a person's conduct may be found "incompatible" with a law based solely on a showing that the conduct is "irreconcilable" with that law, *id.* at 768. Moreover, since the recognized sources of public policy within the intent of c(3) include state laws, rules and regulations, *Mehlman v. Mobil Oil Corp.*, 707 A.2d 1000 (N.J. 1998), a plaintiff who pursues a CEPA claim under this subsection may rely upon the same laws, rules and regulations that may be the subject of a claim under c(1). Consequently, it is easier for an employee who proceeds under c(3) to prove that he or she reasonably believed the employer's conduct was "incompatible" with a clear mandate of public policy expressed in a law, rule or regulation than to show, as required by c(1), a reasonable belief that the employer's conduct "violated" a law, rule or regulation.

However, an employee who proceeds under c(3) must establish an additional element that is not required to prove a claim under c(1). Although an employee may pursue an action under c(1) based on objections to employer conduct that he or she reasonably believes violated any law, rule or regulation, an employee who proceeds under c(3) must make the additional showing that the "clear mandate of public policy" he or she reasonably believes the employer's policy to be incompatible with is one that "concern[s] the public health, safety or welfare or protection of the environment." *See Estate of Roach v. TRW, Inc.*, 754 A.2d 544 (N.J. 2000). This requirement is "unique" to c(3). *Id.*

The significance of this additional element of a claim under c(3) is illustrated by *Maw v. Advanced Clinical Commc'ns*, 846 A.2d 604 (N.J. 2004), in which an employee brought a CEPA claim challenging her termination for refusing to execute an employment agreement containing what the employee believed to be an overly expansive do-not-compete clause. This Court concluded that case law which allows a no-compete provision only if it is reasonable does not constitute "a clear mandate of public policy" within the intent of c(3) because an employer's attempt to impose an unreasonable no-competition agreement impacts solely upon the individual employee and does not "implicate the public interest." *Maw.*

Unlike in *Maw* the provisions of the Code of Criminal Justice that prohibit promotion of prostitution and restrict the location of sexually-oriented businesses constitute "a clear mandate of public policy concerning the public health, safety or welfare[.]" The Code makes promotion of prostitution either a third or fourth-degree offense, depending on the circumstances, *see N.J.S.A.* 2C:34-1b(2) and *N.J.S.A.* 2C:34-1c(3), and it makes the operation of a sexually-oriented business within 1,000 feet of a school or church a fourth-degree offense, *N.J.S.A.* 2C:34-7. These provisions reflect a legislative recognition that the promotion of prostitution and other commercial sexual activities are a source of "venereal disease, . . . profit and power for criminal groups who commonly combine it with illicit trade in drugs and liquor, illegal gambling and even robbery and extortion[,] . . . [and] corrupt influence on government and law enforcement machinery." II *The New Jersey Penal Code, Final Report of the N.J. Criminal Law Revision Commission*, 301-2-cmt. 1 on NJSA §2C:34-2 (1971).

To prevail on a CEPA claim under c(3), plaintiff is not required to show that defendants' alleged policy decision to cease enforcement of the provisions of the Code prohibiting the promotion of prostitution and restricting the location of sexually-oriented businesses actually violated or was incompatible with a statute, rule or other clear mandate of public policy. *See Dzwonar.* Plaintiff only has to show that he had an "objectively reasonable belief" in the existence of such a violation or incompatibility. Plaintiff may carry this burden by demonstrating that "there is a substantial nexus between the complained-of conduct"—the cessation of investigations of promotion of prostitution and failure to enforce laws relating to the location of sexually-oriented businesses—and "[the] law or public policy identified by . . . plaintiff"—in this case the provisions of the Code proscribing such criminal conduct.

We conclude that plaintiff's proofs met this burden. Viewing the evidence in the light most favorable to plaintiff, as required on a motion for summary judgment, it could support a finding that he had an objectively reasonable belief that defendants made a policy decision to cease all investigation and enforcement of the Code provisions prohibiting the promotion of prostitution and restricting the location of sexually-oriented businesses. Plaintiff testified that Captain Glass told him at a staff meeting in January 2001 not to initiate any new prostitution investigations unless they directly impacted the citizens of Atlantic City, and shortly thereafter, Sergeant Abrams issued a directive to terminate all pending promotion of prostitution investigations. Around the same time Sergeant Abrams issued this directive, the files plaintiff had maintained regarding persons involved in the promotion of prostitution were removed from a filing cabinet under his control, and thereafter, his access to those files was severely restricted. Since plaintiff was the only detective still actively involved in promotion of prostitution investigations at that time, he could reasonably have believed that the intent of Sergeant Abrams' directive and the removal of his investigation files was to terminate all such investigations in Atlantic City.

In addition, when plaintiff sent a memorandum requesting his superiors' assistance in persuading the municipal solicitor to initiate proceedings to revoke the mercantile licenses of sexually-oriented businesses operating in violation of *N.J.S.A.* 2C:34-7, the only response he received was Captain Glass' comment: "You're out of here, you're going to patrol." Plaintiff further testified that the City never took any action to revoke the licenses of sexually-oriented businesses that were operating in violation of *N.J.S.A.* 2C:34-7. Therefore, a trier of fact could find that plaintiff had an objectively reasonable belief that Atlantic City had made a policy decision not to enforce this statutory prohibition.

[Unlike an earlier case in which plaintiff had alleged that his employer had failed to follow his recommendations regarding two petitions of exclusion from casinos, Maimone's] claim is not simply that defendants decided to assign a "lower degree of priority" to investigations of violations of the Code provisions prohibiting promotion of prostitution and restricting the location of sexually-oriented businesses, but rather that they made a policy decision to terminate all enforcement of these criminal laws. Plaintiff was not told, and had no other reason to believe, that this alleged policy decision was due to budgetary constraints or an administrative determination that there was a need to assign additional officers to the investigation of more serious crimes. Therefore, a trier of fact could find that plaintiff had an objectively reasonable belief that defendants made a policy decision that was incompatible with a clear mandate of public policy concerning the public health, safety and welfare.

B.

We next consider defendants' argument that plaintiff failed to present sufficient evidence to support a jury finding that "an adverse employment action" was taken against him.

CEPA prohibits an employer from taking "retaliatory action" against an employee for protected conduct. *N.J.S.A.* 34:19-3. "Retaliatory action" is defined by CEPA to mean "the discharge, suspension or demotion of an employee, or *other adverse employment action* taken against an employee *in the terms and conditions of employment*." *N.J.S.A.* 34:19-2(e) (emphasis added). Under this definition, any reduction in an employee's compensation is considered to be an "adverse . . . action . . . in the terms and conditions of employment." Moreover, even without any reduction in compensation, a withdrawal of benefits formerly provided to an employee may be found in some circumstances to constitute an adverse employment action.

Plaintiff presented sufficient evidence that his transfer from a detective position to patrol duty resulted in both a reduction in his compensation and a loss of other benefits to satisfy this element of a cause of action under *N.J.S.A.* 34:19-3. Although plaintiff's transfer to patrol duty was not considered a demotion in rank, it resulted in a 3% reduction in his compensation. . . . In addition, plaintiff testified that detectives have an opportunity to earn substantially more overtime than officers assigned to patrol duty, that the 3% salary differential is reflected in the calculation of a retiring police officer's pension, and that detectives are assigned unmarked police cars that they can use to commute back and forth to work. We conclude that this alleged reduction in compensation and loss of other benefits as a result of plaintiff's transfer from his detective position to patrol duty could support a finding that he suffered an "adverse employment action."

C.

The requirement that an employee who brings a CEPA claim under *N.J.S.A.* 34:19-3 must show "a causal connection exists between the whistle-blowing activity and the adverse employment action[,]" *Dzwonar*, can be satisfied by inferences that the trier of fact may reasonably draw based on circumstances surrounding the employment action, *Roach v. TRW, Inc.* The temporal proximity of employee conduct protected by CEPA and an adverse employment action is one circumstance that may support an inference of a causal connection. . . .

Furthermore, there is evidence that would support a finding that the reason defendants gave for plaintiff's transfer to patrol was pretextual. On April 17, 2001, during the period plaintiff was complaining to Sergeant Abrams about the City's alleged non-enforcement of the laws relating to the promotion of prostitution, Chief Snellbaker requested the Internal Affairs Bureau to conduct an investigation into plaintiff's attendance at the 1998 wedding of the daughter of a suspected organized crime figure. On May 25, 2001, the Internal Affairs Bureau issued a report that concluded plaintiff's superiors had authorized his attendance at the wedding for the purpose of "gathering intelligence information," and that plaintiff had submitted an intelligence report after the wedding describing what he had observed and heard. Consequently, the Internal Affairs Bureau concluded plaintiff's attendance at the wedding was "justified, legal and proper." Although the Internal Affairs Bureau exonerated plaintiff of any wrongdoing in connection with his attendance at the wedding, plaintiff was told that this was the reason for his transfer to patrol duty. The implausibility of this explanation for plaintiff's transfer is an additional circumstance that could support a finding that the real reason for this adverse employment action was plaintiff's complaints about defendants' alleged failure to enforce the laws relating to promotion of prostitution and the location of sexually-oriented businesses. . . .

IV.

The dissent charges that our opinion "appears to graft a new limitation on the discretionary governance prerogatives of an employer[.]" However, there is nothing novel in the proposition that a statute—in this instance the Code of Criminal Justice—constitutes a "clear mandate of public policy" within the intent of CEPA. Plaintiff does not seek, as the dissent asserts, "to determine law enforcement policy for [the] entire [Atlantic City Police Department]." He only seeks to avail himself of the judicial remedies provided by CEPA for the adverse employment action taken against him for objecting to the police department's alleged policy decision to cease enforcement of the Code provisions prohibiting promotion of prostitution and restricting the location of sexually-oriented businesses. Plaintiff's claim does not rest simply on his personal disagreement with this policy decision, but on an objectively reasonable belief that it "is incompatible with a clear mandate of public policy concerning the public health, safety or welfare[.]" *N.J.S.A.* 34:19-3c(3). Therefore, our recognition of plaintiff's right to pursue this claim before a jury is mandated by the State legislative policy expressed in CEPA to protect employee whistle-blowing activity. . . .

RIVERA-SOTO, Justice, dissenting. . . .

[The trial court's decision was correct in viewing plaintiff's claim as "an unsupportable extension" of CEPA "to afford to every police officer the ability, under the authority of a CEPA claim, to hold his or her department accountable to the officer for any discretionary determinations of resource allocation and law enforcement priorities solely because those determinations differed from the officer's views." Further, "[i]t would be manifestly inappropriate to substitute, for the City's judgment, [plaintiff's] view or that of a court or jury with regard to the appropriate priorities for applying the law enforcement resources available to the City."]

NOTES

1. *"Whistleblowing Activity."* New Jersey has made clear that, to invoke paragraph (c), the plaintiff must "identify a statute, regulation, rule, or public policy that closely relates to the complained-of conduct." *Dzwonar v. McDevitt*, 828 A.2d 893, 901 (2003). Assuming he can do that, what does the plaintiff have to do to trigger CEPA protections? The *Maimone* court described him as engaged in a "whistleblowing activity, but the plaintiff did not, even metaphorically, blow a whistle—he just stood up to his bosses. Paragraph (c), however, reaches "objecting to" employer conduct, and Maimone's actions were apparently enough to count as "objecting." The Supreme Court has similarly broadly construed Title VII's antiretaliation provision, which in part protects individuals who "oppose" unlawful employment practices.

Crawford v. Metropolitan Government of Nashville & Davidson County, 555 U.S. Ct. 271 (2009).

Whatever the reach of paragraph (c), paragraphs (a) and (b) describe yet additional kinds of protected conduct, some of which are more intuitively whistleblowing. But *Maimone* quickly determines that (a) does not apply—to be protected under that prong, the employee must reasonably believe that the "activity, policy, or practice" being disclosed "is in violation of a law." According to the court, there was no way a police officer could reasonably believe a shift in law enforcement priorities was illegal. What if plaintiff believed that the new policy was the result of a payoff to Snellbaker? That would be in violation of law, but, absent more information, would Maimone have had a basis to "reasonably believe" (as opposed to suspect) that that was the explanation?

Thus, as interpreted by the court, (c) is broader than (a). The employee must, again, reasonably believe that what he objects to occurs, but the policy or practice does not have to violate any law or regulation. *See also Estate of Frank L. Roach v. TRW, Inc.*, 754 A.2d. 544, 551 (N.J. 2000) (Paragraph (c)(3) "evidences a legislative recognition that certain forms of conduct might be harmful to the public although technically not a violation of a specific statute or regulation."). Doesn't the structure of (3) clearly justify this conclusion? After all, if an employee objects to what she reasonably believes is a violation of law, she is already protected by paragraph (c)(1). But the result is a sweeping law that cuts the statutory protection loose from any particular statute. Can you identify why, exactly, the court felt Maimone's conduct was protected?

2. *Patent Absurdity?* The dissent speaks of the majority "allowing a rank-and-file police officer to determine law enforcement policy for an entire department." Surely, that's an overstatement. The question isn't whether the department must follow Maimone's views of proper enforcement priorities; rather, it's whether the department can retaliate against Maimone for objecting to the new priorities. But note that paragraph (c)(1) protects employees not only for objecting to activities but also for "refusing to participate" in them. Might the dissent have been concerned that, had Maimone continued to pursue sex-based violations, he couldn't have been demoted for insubordination?

3. *Reasonable Belief.* The *Maimone* decision stresses that plaintiff need not be correct about the activity in question violating a law or a clear mandate of public policy; he or she need only be reasonable. This is a consistent theme in the New Jersey cases. *See FOP v. City of Camden*, 842 F.3d 231, 240-41 (3d Cir. 2016) (police officers were reasonable, if not correct, in reporting a policy regarding enforcement as violating a state antidiscrimination quota law, although law barred only quotas for arrests and citations, not for "encounters"); *Mehlman v. Mobil Oil Corp*, 707 A.2d 1000, 1015-16 (N.J. 1998) ("The object of CEPA is not to make lawyers out of conscientious employees but rather to prevent retaliation against those employees who object to . . . . conduct that they reasonably believe to be unlawful or indisputably dangerous to the public health, safety or welfare."). But the court has suggested some limitations. In *Estate of Roach v. TRW, Inc.*, 754 A.2d 544, 552 (N.J. 2000), for example, plaintiff claimed to have been terminated because he reported two of his co-workers for conflicts of interest and for false expense reports and time cards. It wrote:

Although the term "reasonably believes" in sections 3c.(1) and 3c.(2) provides ample justification to sustain the jury's verdict in the present case, we caution that in future cases that language may prove fatal to an employee's claim. For instance, if an employee were to complain about a co-employee who takes an extended lunch break or makes a personal telephone call to a spouse or friend, we would be hard pressed to conclude that the complaining employee could have "reasonably believed" that such minor infractions represented unlawful conduct as contemplated by CEPA. CEPA is intended to protect those employees whose disclosures fall sensibly within the statute; it is not intended to spawn litigation concerning the most trivial or benign employee complaints.

See also Battaglia v. United Parcel Serv., Inc., 70 A.3d 602 (N.J. 2013) (vague comments about inappropriate use of credit cards and employees going out for liquid lunches did not suggest fraudulent activity). In *McMillin v. Ted Russell Ford, Inc.*, 2014 Tenn. App. LEXIS 450 (Tenn. Ct. App. July 31, 2014), the court found no significant public concern implicated by plaintiff's refusal to take potential buyers on test drives in cars without dealer plates or proof of insurance.

    4. *Adverse Employment Action.* In most of the cases we have seen so far, the claim is for "wrongful dismissal," but plaintiff in *Maimone* wasn't discharged—he was demoted with relatively minor economic consequences. The court, nevertheless, found that the requisite adversity for a violation of CEPA. *See also Donelson v. DuPont Chambers Works*, 20 A.3d 384 (N.J. 2011) (not necessary to show constructive discharge in order to recover lost wages under CEPA). This is an important point of distinction between statutory claims and common-law claims. While some courts have applied the common-law tort to less severe actions than dismissal, *see* Note 5, page 220, whistleblower statutes tend to be framed to reach at least any actions with economic consequences. This is generally true even under the more restrictive federal decisions requiring an "adverse employment action" in the discrimination context. *See* Chapter 9.

    5. *Notifying the Employer.* CEPA protects employees for actions directed at their employer. Thus, paragraph (a) reaches disclosures to a supervisor and paragraph (c) protects the kind of objection Maimone made. But CEPA also protects disclosure to a public body, paragraph (a), as well as participating in a public hearing or investigation. Paragraph (b). However, in the latter case, CEPA requires the employee to bring the matter "to the attention of a supervisor of the employee by written notice." §34:19-4. Had Maimone later taken his concerns to the state attorney general, his memorandum presumably would have satisfied this requirement. The written notice requirement is *not* applicable where the employee "is reasonably certain that the activity, policy, or practice is known to one or more supervisors." *Id.* Isn't this likely to almost always be true? The notice requirement is also inapplicable "where the employee reasonably fears physical harm as a result of the disclosure." *Id.*

    6. *Relationship of CEPA to the Public Policy Tort and Other Causes of Action.* Section 34:19-8 preserves an employee's rights under other laws, including any "federal or State law or regulation or under any collective bargaining agreement or employment contract," but simultaneously provides that the institution of a CEPA action "shall be deemed a waiver of the rights and remedies available under any other contract, collective bargaining agreement, state law, rule or regulation, or under the common law." This is evidently intended to preserve claims of employment discrimination as well as breach of just cause provisions in individual contracts and collective bargaining agreements. But it also seems to require the employee to elect between pursuing CEPA claims and the other causes of action. *Young v. Schering Corp.*, 660 A.2d 1153 (N.J. 1995), however, held that this provision does not require dismissal of tort and contract claims because they are sufficiently distinct from the CEPA claim. Rejecting a literal reading, the court wrote, "we are thoroughly convinced the Legislature did not intend to penalize former employees by forcing them to choose between a CEPA claim and other legitimate claims that are substantially, if not totally, independent of the retaliatory discharge claim." *Id.* at 25. Prior to CEPA, however, New Jersey had recognized a common-law public policy tort. *Pierce v. Ortho Pharm. Corp.*, 417 A.2d 505 (N.J. 1980). Presumably, such tort claims would not be "independent of the retaliatory discharge claim" and an employee would have to elect between them and the statute. In making that decision, CEPA has the advantage of a possible award of attorneys' fees, but the CEPA statute of limitations is only one year, while tort suits in New Jersey are normally subject to a two-year limitation. *See McGrogan v. Till*, 771 A.2d 1187 (N.J. 2001). Other states have confronted the question of whether the public policy tort can be deployed by workers with other sources of job security protection. *See Ackerman v. State*, 901 N.W.2d 837 (Iowa 2017) (a contract employee may challenge a discharge in violation of public policy; the claim is not limited to employees at will).

2. Federal Whistleblower Protection

While statutory protection is increasingly common in the states, the federal government has long had statutes providing protection for specific disclosures. Generally speaking, however, these were intended to bulwark particular regulatory regimes, such as nuclear energy or transportation or the antidiscrimination laws. As a result of Enron and other corporate meltdowns, Congress enacted the most sweeping federal statute providing whistleblower protections in the form of the Sarbanes-Oxley Act ("SOX") of 2002. While SOX is not a true general whistleblower statute, in the sense that it does not provide protection for conduct furthering a wide range of public policies, it is the first wide-angle federal enactment that broadly reaches the private sector. Further, it turned out to be the prototype for more aggressive uses of whistleblower protections in federal legislation. As we will see, the Obama administration's stimulus package, health care reform legislation, and financial reform law all have whistleblowing provisions, all of which are variations on the SOX theme.

Professor Miriam Cherry summarized the origins of SOX:

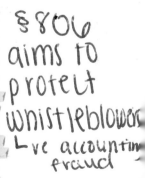

> As the accounting scandals surrounding Enron and WorldCom dominated the headlines and business ethics became increasingly suspect, two whistleblowers became symbols of integrity to the American public. Indeed, Sherron Watkins and Cynthia Cooper were among "The Whistleblowers" named as *Time* magazine's "Persons of the Year" for 2002. At significant risk to their careers, financial well-being, and mental health, Cooper and Watkins alerted high-level executives at their respective companies to accounting fraud. Unfortunately, most whistleblowers take all these risks when they report illegal activities occurring within their organizations. The magnitude of these recent frauds is startling and, unfortunately, appears to be indicative of a widespread problem. . . . In response to the corporate scandals of 2002, Congress enacted the Sarbanes-Oxley Act (the Act) to prevent future corporate corruption and securities fraud. The Act contains a provision, §806, that aims to protect whistleblowers such as Cooper and Watkins who report accounting fraud. [The Act covers] all workers at publicly traded companies who "blow the whistle" on suspect accounting practices, whether that whistleblowing is done within the organization, to government agencies, or as part of a shareholder lawsuit. . . .

Miriam A. Cherry, *Whistling in the Dark? Corporate Fraud, Whistleblowers, and the Implications of the Sarbanes-Oxley Act for Employment Law*, 79 WASH. L. REV. 1029, 1031–33, 1063-64 (2004). *See also* Elizabeth C. Tippett, *The Promise of Compelled Whistleblowing: What the Corporate Governance Provisions of Sarbanes-Oxley Mean for Employment Law*, 11 EMPL. RTS. & EMPLOY. POL'Y J. 1 (2007). There is some reason to believe that these efforts have had success. Gretchen Morgenson, *Whistle-Blowers Spur Companies to Change Their Ways*, N.Y. TIMES, BU1, Dec. 16, 2016 (reporting a study showing that financial wrongdoing dropped at companies that were subject to investigations).

The anti-retaliation provision of Sarbanes-Oxley, 18 U.S.C. §1514A, provides, in relevant part that no publicly traded company or any agent thereof,

> may discharge, demote, suspend, threaten, harass, or in any other manner discriminate against an employee in the terms and conditions of employment because of any lawful act done by the employee—
>
> (1) to provide information, cause information to be provided, or otherwise assist in an investigation regarding any conduct which the employee reasonably believes constitutes a violation of . . . [a list of mail and wire-fraud statutes, including 18 U.S.C. §§1341, 1343, 1344, or 1348], any rule or regulation of the Securities and Exchange Commission, or any provision of Federal law relating to fraud against shareholders, when the information or assistance is provided to or the investigation is conducted by— (A) a Federal regulatory or law enforcement agency; (B) any Member of Congress or any committee of Congress; or (C) a person with supervisory authority over the employee (or such other person working for the employer who has the authority to investigate, discover, or terminate misconduct); or
>
> (2) to file, cause to be filed, testify, participate in, or otherwise assist in a proceeding filed or about to be filed (with any knowledge of the employer) relating to an alleged violation of [the same provisions].

Genberg v. Porter
882 F.3d 12 (10th Cir. 2018)

BACHARACH, Circuit Judge.

This appeal grew out of the firing of Mr. Carl Genberg, an executive for Ceragenix Corporation. Mr. Genberg allegedly suspected misconduct by Ceragenix's Board of Directors. When he acted on these alleged suspicions, he was fired.

[Genberg sued Ceragenix's Chief Executive Officer, Steven Porter, for retaliation under the Sarbanes-Oxley Act of 2002 and defamation under Nevada law. The district court granted summary judgment on both claims, but the appeals court reverse as to SOX. The portion of the opinion affirming as to the defamation claim is omitted.]

In 2005, Mr. Porter and Mr. Genberg worked for a company that merged into Ceragenix. This merger entitled shareholders of the old company to shares in Ceragenix. With the merger, the shares went into escrow and the Ceragenix Board obtained a proxy to exercise voting rights for the escrowed shares. The new shareholders, including Mr. Genberg, believed that the shares would soon be distributed. But Board members continued to use the proxy for roughly five years, reelecting themselves and increasing their own compensation. . . .

Objecting to continued use of the proxy, Mr. Genberg drafted an email under the name of one of Ceragenix's largest shareholders. The email urged the Ceragenix

Board to abandon the proxy and allow the shareholders to exercise their own voting rights. When Mr. Genberg drafted this email, the shareholder was part of a group trying to take control of Ceragenix, a move opposed by the Ceragenix Board. The shareholder sent Mr. Genberg's email to the Ceragenix Board on March 2, 2010. . . .

On March 3, the Board met to address the email and suspicion about Mr. Genberg's role. At this meeting, Mr. Porter told the Board that the email had been written by Mr. Genberg to aid another company's attempt to buy Ceragenix. Mr. Porter viewed Mr. Genberg as disloyal, suspecting him of helping the group to seize control of Ceragenix. Similar suspicions led other Board members to suggest that Mr. Genberg be fired. But Mr. Porter thought that the firing would need to wait because Mr. Genberg was actively engaged in fundraising efforts. In the meantime, the Board demanded that Mr. Genberg stop communicating with the shareholder who had sent the March 2 email. . . .

On March 4, Mr. Genberg sent an email to a Board member, accusing Mr. Porter of insider trading. In response, the Board hired an attorney to investigate

- the allegations of insider trading and
- Mr. Genberg's relationship with the group attempting to acquire Ceragenix.

Though the attorney found no evidence of insider trading, he did confirm that Mr. Genberg had been involved in the effort to acquire Ceragenix. . . .

In response, the Board fired Mr. Genberg for cause. Afterward, Mr. Porter reported the firing to a public-relations consultant and two Ceragenix lenders. In these reports, Mr. Porter made four statements about Mr. Genberg that he regards as defamatory. . . .

III.   The Sarbanes-Oxley Claim

Congress passed the Sarbanes-Oxley Act to "protect investors by improving the accuracy and reliability of corporate disclosures." Sarbanes-Oxley Act of 2002, Pub. L. No. 107-204, 116 Stat. 745, 745. To further this goal, the Act protects whistle-blowing employees of publicly traded companies who tell superiors about a violation of federal securities law. 18 U.S.C. §1514A. The Act supplies this protection by allowing suit against a publicly traded company or its officers for retaliation. *Id.*

For a prima facie case of retaliation, a plaintiff must show that

- he or she engaged in protected activity,
- the employer knew of the protected activity,
- the plaintiff suffered an unfavorable employment action, and
- the protected activity was a factor that contributed to the unfavorable employment action.

Lockheed Martin Corp. v. Admin. Review Bd., U.S. Dep't of Labor, 717 F.3d 1121, 1129 (10th Cir. 2013). If a prima facie case is shown, the defendant can assert a statutory defense known as the "same-action defense." This defense requires proof by "clear and convincing evidence" that the same action would have been taken even without the protected activity. *Id.*

Mr. Genberg's statutory claim is premised on two separate acts of protected activity: (1) ghostwriting the March 2 email about proxies and (2) writing the March 4 email that accused Mr. Porter of insider trading. Mr. Porter admits that writing the March 4 email constituted protected activity, but he argues that

- the March 2 email did not involve protected activity,
- Mr. Genberg's protected activity did not contribute to his firing, and
- the same-action defense applies.

A reasonable factfinder could view both of Mr. Genberg's emails as protected under Sarbanes-Oxley. Thus, we need not parse which email led to his firing: It is enough under the statute and the summary-judgment standard that a reasonable factfinder could regard either email as a factor contributing to the firing. In addition, Mr. Porter forfeited the same-action defense, and a reasonable factfinder could conclude that Mr. Porter had not shown that the Board would have fired Mr. Genberg in the absence of protected activities. These conclusions lead us to reverse the grant of summary judgment to Mr. Porter on the Sarbanes-Oxley claim.

A. *A factfinder could reasonably regard the writing of both emails as protected activity.*

. . . The March 4 email accused Mr. Porter of giving inside information to a stockholder to rig the price of Ceragenix shares. Mr. Porter admits that writing this email constituted protected activity under Sarbanes-Oxley.

. . . The March 2 email demanded that the Ceragenix Board transfer proxy voting rights to the shareholders. The Board had come to control the proxy rights in November 2005. When receiving the email, the Board had controlled the proxy rights for roughly five years. The email stated that it was "neither fair, just [n]or equitable" for the Ceragenix Board to "retain the voting power over these shares for [five] years and use such power to re-elect the members of the Board of Directors without any consideration for the interests of investors." This retention of voting power, the email argued, clashed with SEC policies of "sound corporate governance and shareholder accountability."

The district court concluded that writing the March 2 email was not protected activity, reasoning that the email had not " 'definitively and substantively' " related to a violation of law. In drawing this conclusion, the court pointed out that the March 2 email had not cited a specific SEC rule. This omission led the district court to conclude that the email had not involved protected activity.

The district court applied the wrong standard to determine whether the March 2 email had involved protected activity. Under the proper standard, a factfinder could reasonably characterize writing the March 2 email as protected activity.

1. The district court's "definitive and specific" standard is no longer applicable.

The district court stated that the March 2 email was protected only if Mr. Genberg had specifically identified the rule being violated. This statement of the burden was incorrect, for the Administrative Review Board of the Department of Labor has "explicitly disavowed the 'definitive and specific' evidentiary standard." *Lockheed Martin Corp. v. Admin. Review Bd., U.S. Dep't of Labor*, 717 F.3d 1121, 1132 n.7 (10th Cir. 2013). And the Administrative Review Board's interpretation of Sarbanes-Oxley is subject to *Chevron* deference. . . .

Mr. Porter admits that the "definitive and specific" test no longer applies. But he contends that the district court applied the correct standard. We disagree. The district court noted that Mr. Genberg's allegations in the email had not been specific and had failed to "specifically refer to any of the six enumerated laws" in the Sarbanes-Oxley Act. This lack of specificity led the district court to conclude that Mr. Genberg had no "reasonable belief that any *specific* SEC rule or regulation was being violated." (Emphasis added.) In light of this conclusion and the rationale, we conclude that the district court used the obsolete "definitive and specific" standard.

2. Applying the correct standard, a factfinder could reasonably conclude that writing the March 2 email had entailed a protected activity.

In *Sylvester v. Parexel International*, the Administrative Review Board stated the correct standard for a protected activity: "[T]he [plaintiff] need only show that he or she 'reasonably believes' that the conduct complained of constitutes a violation of the laws listed" in the Sarbanes-Oxley Act. No. 07-123, 2011 DOLSOX LEXIS 39, 2011 WL 2517148, at *11 (Admin. Rev. Bd., U.S. Dep't of Labor May 25, 2011). As noted above, we accord *Chevron* deference to the Administrative Review Board's interpretation of the statutory standard. *See Lockheed Martin.* In light of the need for deference, the only four circuits to address the issue have followed *Sylvester*'s articulation of the standard. . . . And here, Mr. Porter has not questioned the need to defer to the Administrative Review Board's articulation of the standard.

The *Sylvester* standard contains subjective and objective components. Under the subjective component, the employee "must actually believe" that the conduct raised in the communication is unlawful. *Lockheed.* Under the objective component, the email would constitute a protected activity if

- Mr. Genberg had actually believed that the Board's retention of the proxy "constituted a violation of relevant law" and
- a reasonable person might adhere to the same belief.

Mr. Porter's appeal brief mentions both the objective and subjective components of the *Sylvester* standard. But his arguments challenge only the subjective component (Mr. Genberg's actual belief that the Board violated an SEC rule by retaining the proxy); Mr. Porter makes no meaningful arguments regarding whether such a belief would have been reasonable. Thus, we focus on the subjective component.

The March 2 email

- accused the Board of holding onto the proxy for "years longer than was ever contemplated" and
- argued that the Board had "deprived [the shareholders] of any voice in the management of Ceragenix."

Mr. Genberg defends this accusation based in part on SEC Rule 14a-4(d)(2). This rule states that "[n]o proxy shall confer authority . . . [t]o vote at any annual meeting other than the next annual meeting . . . ." 17 C.F.R. §240.14a-4(d)(2).

Mr. Genberg stated under oath that he had believed that the Ceragenix Board was violating SEC Rule 14 by continuing to rely on the initial proxy. Though Mr. Porter challenges the truth of Mr. Genberg's sworn statement, the credibility of the statement cannot be resolved on summary judgment. A reasonable factfinder could conclude that Mr. Genberg was telling the truth when he stated under oath that he had regarded retention of the proxy as a violation of Rule 14. The reasonableness of that factual finding prevents summary judgment on the subjective requirement.

subjective ✓ (margin note)

Mr. Porter points out that the email acknowledged that the Board was not violating a particular SEC rule. But a reasonable factfinder could conclude that this part of the email was discussing a different issue. There Mr. Genberg was apparently addressing the purpose of SEC Rule 452, which governed proxy voting rules for shares held in street names voted by brokers. The requirements in Rule 452 are distinct from those in Rule 14.

The district court relied not only on the discussion apparently involving Rule 452 but also on Mr. Genberg's sophistication in the industry, suggesting that Mr. Genberg didn't truly believe that the Board was violating a particular SEC rule. Otherwise, why wouldn't he have referred to SEC Rule 14 in the email?

But a factfinder might reasonably conclude that there was little need for Mr. Genberg to name the rule, for it seems to clearly bar use of a proxy for shareholder votes after the next annual meeting. 17 C.F.R. §240.14a- 4(d)(2). In light of Rule 14, a factfinder might reasonably conclude that Mr. Genberg believed that the Board was violating the SEC rule.

* * *

This conclusion would require the court to consider the writing of the March 2 email as a protected activity. As noted above, Mr. Porter does not question satisfaction of the objective requirement (the reasonableness of Mr. Genberg's belief). And a factfinder could reasonably conclude that Mr. Genberg had believed that continued use of the proxy would violate SEC Rule 14.

B. A genuine factual dispute existed on whether the emails had contributed to the firing.

emails contributed to the firing (margin note)

Mr. Porter contends that neither email had contributed to Mr. Genberg's termination. In our view, however, a reasonable factfinder could conclude that both emails had contributed to the termination.

The fourth element of the statutory claim is that the protected activity contributed to Mr. Genberg's termination. *Lockheed Martin Corp.* This element is "broad and forgiving," requiring the plaintiff to point to "'any factor'" that "'tends to affect *in any way* the outcome of the decision.'" *Id.* (emphasis in original) (quoting *Klopfenstein v. PCC Flow Techs.*, No. 04-149, 2006 DOL Ad. Rev. Bd. LEXIS 50, 2006 WL 3246904, at *13 (Admin. Rev. Bd., U.S. Dep't of Labor May 31, 2006)). The contributing factor need not be "'significant, motivating, substantial, or predominant.'" *Id.* (internal quotation marks omitted) (quoting *Klopfenstein*).

1. A reasonable factfinder could conclude that the March 2 email had contributed to Mr. Genberg's termination.

The sequence of events supports Mr. Genberg's argument that the March 2 email contributed to his termination. Reacting to the email, the Board took less than a month to begin an investigation, finish it, and fire Mr. Genberg. *See Lockheed* ("Temporal proximity between the protected activity and adverse employment action may alone be sufficient to satisfy the contributing factor test.").

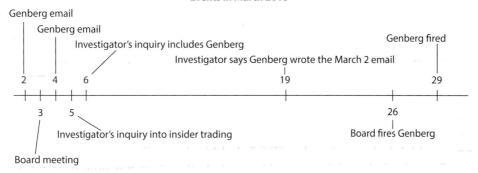

Events in March 2010

In fact, Mr. Porter argues that the Board decided to fire Mr. Genberg on March 3, only one day after receiving Mr. Genberg's email: "The undisputed evidence establishes that the Board decided on March 3 that they needed to fire Genberg, but wanted to temporarily delay his firing until Ceragenix secured the capital it needed to survive."

Mr. Porter argues that the Board fired Mr. Genberg in part because he had concealed his role in the March 2 email. According to Mr. Porter, the Board did not act because of anything that Mr. Genberg had said in the email, pointing out that Mr. Genberg had raised similar concerns in February 2010. But the factfinder had no obligation to credit Mr. Porter's focus on "concealment" or Mr. Genberg's prior expression of concern. The factfinder could reasonably conclude that Mr. Genberg had been fired because of what he had said. After all, Mr. Porter does not suggest that Mr. Genberg had lied about his role in drafting the email. And Mr. Genberg had expressed concern in February 2010 to a different Board member (Mr. Jeff Sperber), not Mr. Porter. Thus, Mr. Porter's alternative explanations for the firing do not justify summary judgment.

2. Mr. Porter cannot avoid liability based on a "legitimate intervening event."

On March 4, Mr. Genberg also sent a second email to a Board member, alleging that Mr. Porter had leaked inside information to a stockholder to aid efforts to rig the price of Ceragenix stock. Mr. Porter admits (for purposes of summary judgment) that this email constituted protected activity. But he denies that this email contributed to the termination. Instead, Mr. Porter attributes the firing to a legitimate intervening event: the investigator's determination that Mr. Genberg had breached a fiduciary duty to Ceragenix. *See Feldman v. Law Enforcement Assocs.*, 752 F.3d 339, 348-49 (4th Cir. 2014) (discussing how an intervening event can prevent consideration of protected activity as a significant cause of the termination). We disagree.

To rely on a legitimate intervening event, the adverse action cannot be inextricably intertwined with the protected activity; therefore, Mr. Porter needed to explain Mr. Genberg's termination "without reference to [his] protected activity." *Palmer v. Canadian Nat'l Ry./Ill. Cent. R.R.*, No. 16-035, 2016 DOL Ad. Rev. Bd. LEXIS 60, 2016 WL 5868560, at *34 (Admin. Rev. Bd., U.S. Dep't of Labor Sept. 30, 2016). Mr. Porter did not satisfy this burden. Ceragenix began to investigate Mr. Genberg only after he had written the two emails, and we have already held that a reasonable factfinder could regard the writing of both emails as protected activity.

If we take away both emails, Ceragenix would never have had a reason to investigate Mr. Genberg. Therefore, a reasonable factfinder could conclude that Mr. Genberg's protected activities on March 2 and 4 were inextricably intertwined with his termination. *See* 2016 DOL Ad. Rev. Bd. LEXIS 60, [WL] at *34-35 (stating that if the protected activity had led the employer to investigate a possible rule violation and then fired the employee for violating the rule, "the protected activity . . . would be 'inextricably intertwined' with the adverse action"). And if the investigation was inextricably intertwined with protected activities, we could not regard the investigation as an "independent" cause for the termination. *See id.* Thus, Mr. Porter cannot avoid liability based on a legitimate intervening event.

3. A reasonable factfinder could conclude that Mr. Genberg would not have been fired in the absence of a protected activity.

Mr. Porter also invokes the same-action defense. This defense allows the defendant to prevail by submitting clear and convincing evidence that the employee would have been fired even without the protected conduct. *Lockheed Martin Corp.* Mr. Porter forfeited this defense, and it would not justify summary judgment even if the issue had been preserved.

Mr. Porter did not assert this defense either in his Answer or in his summary-judgment briefs. Mr. Porter points out that he argued that Mr. Genberg's protected activity had not contributed to his termination and asserts that this argument was sufficient to preserve his same-action defense. We disagree. The "contributing factor" inquiry considers everything that took place and requires the employee to prove that the protected activity was taken into account as a reason for the firing. In contrast, the same-action defense requires the employer to show that it would have taken the same action even if there had never been a protected activity.

Application of the two tests would entail different inquiries. Under the "contributing factor" inquiry, the question is whether the content of Mr. Genberg's communications had been a factor in his termination. But under the same-action defense, the court would consider what would have happened if Mr. Genberg had never written either email: No one would have been investigating Mr. Genberg, so the Board would never have known that Mr. Genberg had done anything wrong. Thus, Mr. Porter's challenge in district court on the "contributing factor" element did not preserve reliance on the same-action defense.

But let's assume, for the sake of argument, that this defense was preserved. Even with this assumption, Mr. Porter could not justify the award of summary judgment. To prevail on this defense, Mr. Porter needed to show that Mr. Genberg would have been fired even if he had not written either email. Mr. Genberg might have been fired even if he had not written either the March 2 or March 4 email. But that possibility does not entitle Mr. Porter to summary judgment on the Sarbanes-Oxley claim.

On this issue, a reasonable factfinder could have gone either way. The March 2 email led the Board to conclude that Mr. Genberg could be terminated "for cause," and Mr. Porter acknowledges that the Board decided to fire Mr. Genberg on March 3 based on his email one day earlier. In addition, the March 4 email led the Board to order an investigation that ultimately confirmed Mr. Genberg's role in the March 2 email. The Board purported to rely on this confirmation to fire Mr. Genberg. Thus, it is unclear whether the Board would have fired Mr. Genberg absent the March 2 and March 4 emails. In light of this uncertainty, Mr. Porter could not obtain summary judgment even if he had preserved the same-action defense. . . .

[The court affirmed summary judgment for defendant on plaintiff's defamation claim based on statements to a Ceragenix consultant, Ceragenix lenders, and the SEC. Nevada law recognizes a common-interest privilege for defamation, and a reasonable jury could not find that Porter abused the privilege.]

***

[Circuit Judge Harris Hartz dissented as to the majority's reversing summary judgment on the SOX claim because "no reasonable juror could infer that Mr. Genberg subjectively believed that the March 2, 2010 email to the board . . . was reporting a past, or even potential, violation of federal securities law." Genberg was "a lawyer sophisticated in securities law, the email never states that any conduct by anyone had violated or would violate federal securities law. And the email's references to the proxy, which the panel opinion suggests may have violated an SEC regulation, complain about the proxy only in terms of bad policy or corporate management."]

NOTES

1. *Protected Conduct Under SOX.* As the language of the statute suggests, the conduct at issue must be of a certain nature to come within SOX protection. First, the employee must "provide information or otherwise assist in an investigation." Not all "whistleblowing" qualifies. *See Tides v. Boeing Co.*, 644 F.3d 809 (9th Cir. 2011) (finding SOX did not protect internal auditors who reported problems with compliance to a newspaper since the law protected only employees' disclosures to federal regulatory and law enforcement agencies, Congress, and employee supervisors). *Cf. Digital. Realty Trust, Inc. v. Somers*, 138 S. Ct. 767 (2018) (Dodd-Frank protects whistleblowers only if they complain to the SEC).

Second, SOX reaches only "a publicly traded company," thus exempting other employers from potential liability. However, the Supreme Court has held that statute's language reaching "any officer, employee, contractor, subcontractor, or agent" of such a company reaches retaliation by contractors against their own employees (not merely against employees of the public company itself). *Lawson v. FMR LLC*, 114 S. Ct. 1158 (2014). Since the publicly traded defendant in that case, a mutual fund, was structured (like all mutual funds) to have no employees, the decision essentially prevented SOX from being entirely inapplicable in that part of the financial sector.

Further, "gatekeeper" firms, such as law firms and accounting firms, were effectively swept within SOX's protection throughout the financial industry.

Third, the employee's action must be taken with respect to "conduct which the employee reasonably believes" constitutes a violation of six identified federal statutes. These include mail fraud, 18 U.S.C. §1341, wire fraud, §1343, bank fraud, §1344, or securities fraud, §1348, or "any [SEC] rule or regulation . . . or any provision of Federal law relating to fraud against shareholders, when the information or assistance is provided to . . . a person with supervisory authority over the employee . . . ." 18 U.S.C. §1514A(a)(1). *Lockheed Martin Corp. v. Admin. Review Bd.*, 717 F.3d 1121, 1131 (10th Cir. 2013), rejected a frontal assault on the statute, concluding that it was not limited to violations of such laws resulting in loss of shareholder value.

The requisite nexus to other federal laws raises issues of the scope of those statutes, however. *See, e.g., Flake v. United States DOL*, 248 F. App'x 287 (2007) (alternative holding that ARB decision not clearly erroneous in finding that SOX did not apply when there were fewer than 300 holders of the employer's securities, and the employer therefore had no duty to file certain reports); *see also Verfuerth v. Orion Energy Sys.*, 879 F.3d 789, 793-94 (7th Cir. 2018) (former CEO had no claim under Sarbanes-Oxley both because his differences with the employer's Board did not involve "fraud" within the meaning of the statute and because an "executive who advises board members to disclose a fact that the board already knows about has not 'provide[d] information' about fraud.")

2. *Objectively and Subjectively Reasonable.* As *Genberg* states, the employee's belief must be both objectively and subjectively reasonable. While the plaintiff's protected communication need not be specific as to what law is implicated, he must himself believe that there is illegality under at least one of those laws and such a belief must be reasonable. Further, a successful SOX retaliation suit must identify a predicate law and establish the relationship between that law and the allegedly protected conduct. *See Rhinehimer v. U.S. Bancorp Invs., Inc.*, 787 F.3d 797, 811 (6th Cir. 2015) ("Objective reasonableness is evaluated based on the knowledge available to a reasonable person in the same factual circumstances with the same training and experience as the aggrieved employee"; *Nielsen v. AECOM Tech. Corp.*, 762 F.3d 214 (2d Cir. 2014)("The objective prong of the reasonable belief test focuses on the 'basis of knowledge available to a reasonable person in the circumstances with the employee's training and experience.'"); *Wiest v. Lynch*, 710 F.3d 121, 135 (3d Cir. 2013) (plaintiff sufficiently plead a qualifying belief when he foresaw a potentially fraudulent tax deduction and accounting misstatement when the employer reported as "advertising expenses" costs that were more appropriately characterized as employee income); *see also Harp v. Charter Communs., Inc.*, 558 F.3d 722, 725 (7th Cir. 2009) ("If the specific conduct reported was violative of federal law, the report would be sufficient to trigger Sarbanes-Oxley protection even if the employee did not identify the appropriate federal law by name.").

A number of plaintiffs have had their claims dismissed because they could not reasonably believe the laws they identified had in fact been violated. *See, e.g., Beacom v. Oracle Am., Inc.*, 825 F.3d 376 (8th Cir. 2016) (given "the predictive nature of revenue projections," a minor discrepancy of $10 million for a company that annually generates billions of dollars made plaintiff's belief objectively unreasonable); *Day v. Staples, Inc.*, 555 F.3d 42 (1st Cir. 2009) (inefficient business practices, even if they might lead to a short-term reduction in profits, could not support an objectively reasonable belief that they were "shareholder fraud"); *Livingston v. Wyeth, Inc.*, 520

F.3d 344, 355 (4th Cir. 2008) (even if Wyeth made the false statements to compliance auditors and the FDA, none would be a material statement necessary to violate Rule 10b-5).

3. *Adverse Employment Action*. SOX bars covered employers from taking certain actions—to "discharge, demote, suspend, threaten, harass, or in any other manner discriminate"—against an employee for engaging in protected conduct. In addition, *Lockheed Martin*, 717 F.3d at 1133, held that a plaintiff would be protected absent these actions if her treatment constituted a constructive discharge, and viewed this as "when an employer unlawfully creates working conditions so intolerable that a reasonable person in the employee's position would feel forced to resign. . . . The standard is objective: the employer's subjective intent and the employee's subjective views on the situation are irrelevant." *See also Smith v. LHC Grp., Inc.*, No. 17-5850, 727 F. App'x 100 (6th Cir. 2018) (in a False Claims Act suit, a "jury may find that the employer's alleged fraudulent behavior plus the employee's moral conscience and reasonable fear of being accused of participating in the employer's fraud is enough to justify quitting."). Absent constructive discharge, whether alleged harm is cognizable is often addressed by looking to *Burlington N. & Santa Fe Ry. Co. v. White*, 548 U.S. 53, 57 (2006), a Title VII retaliation cases, *see* page 671, and asking whether the retaliatory actions were of the kind that would dissuade a reasonable employee from reporting violations. *See Halliburton, Inc. v. Admin. Review Bd.*, 596 F. App'x 340 (5th Cir. 2014) (applying *Burlington* standard to uphold ARB's conclusion that the employer's disclosure of plaintiff's identity as the whistleblower was a "materially adverse" action).

4. *Proof of a Contributing Factor*. Unlike most other regimes, SOX does not require the complaining party to prove that her protected conduct actually resulted in her discharge—sometimes called "but for" causation or "determinative factor" causation. Rather, she must show by a preponderance of the evidence only that the protected conduct was a "contributing factor" to the challenged employment action. 49 U.S.C. §42121 (2018) (incorporated by reference in 18 U.S.C. §1514A). *See Wiest v. Tyco Elecs. Corp.*, 812 F.3d 319, 330 (3d Cir. 2016) (under SOX, a contributing factor is "any factor, which alone or in combination with other factors, tends to affect in any way the outcome of the decision" and may be proven by either direct or circumstantial evidence).

If the plaintiff does so, the employer can still avoid liability by proving that it would have made the same decision in any event, but it must do so by "clear and convincing evidence." *Bechtel v. Admin. Review Bd., U.S. Dep't of Labor*, 710 F.3d 443, 448-49 (2d Cir. 2013) (if plaintiff proved contributing factor, "the burden would then have shifted to CTI to prove, by clear and convincing evidence, that it would have taken the same action absent Bechtel's protected activity"). But the difficulties in carrying that burden are apparent in *Genberg*: apparently even good cause for discharge is irrelevant if it was discovered as a result of an investigation of protected conduct.

Some courts have suggested considerations applicable to how an employer carries its burden of proving that it would have made the same decision in any event. *Miller v. DOJ*, 842 F.3d 1252, 1257 (Fed. Cir. 2016) (under the Whistleblower Protection Act, a court should look to three nonexclusive factors, including: (1) the strength of the agency's evidence in support of its personnel action; (2) the existence and strength of any motive to retaliate on the part of the agency officials who were involved in the decision; and (3) evidence that the agency takes similar actions against similarly situated employees who are not whistleblowers); *see also Smith v. DOL*, 674 F. App'x 309, 315 (4th Cir. 2017) ("In evaluating a 'same action' or 'same decision' affirmative defense, an ALJ must consider three non-dispositive factors . . . (1) whether the evidence is 'clear' and 'convincing' regarding the independent significance of the non-protected activity; (2) the extent of the evidence showing whether the employer would have made the same adverse decision; and (3) any facts that would have changed had the protected activity not occurred."); *see generally* Nancy M. Modesitt, *Causation in Whistleblowing Claims*, 50 U. Rich. L. Rev. 1193 (2016).

But the first step is for plaintiff to prove a contributing factor. And the initial question is what that means. By definition, the protected conduct doesn't have to actually cause the adverse employment action, which implies that it is enough if the conduct tended to cause the action. While the issue is explored in more detail in Chapter 9, antidiscrimination law originally used but-for causation, requiring a showing that discriminatory intent was a "determinative factor" for the decision in question. That standard still operates under most antidiscrimination laws, where it means that the plaintiff can prevail only if she can show that, but for the intent to discriminate, the adverse employment action would not have occurred. Since the 1991 Amendments reduced the level of causation required to "motivating factor," however, a lower standard applies for Title VII status discrimination cases. As a result, discriminatory intent can be a "motivating factor," and therefore violate Title VII, even if the trier of fact ultimately concludes that the employer would have made the "same decision" even had it not been motivated by the prohibited consideration. *See generally* Martin J. Katz, *The Fundamental Incoherence of Title VII: Making Sense of Causation in Disparate Treatment Law*, 94 Geo. L. J. 489 (2006).

"Motivating factor" as used in Title VII is scarcely self-explanatory in the confused world of causation. Further, Congress's use of "contributing factor" in Sarbanes-Oxley suggests the same or perhaps even a lower level of causation. Presumably, it is the slightest degree that can still be said to "play a role" in the termination decision. That must be true since the defendant can still prevail by proving that it would have made the same decision even had the plaintiff not engaged in protected conduct. This necessarily means that the plaintiff's proof can be less than but-for causation, since the defendant's affirmative defense of "same decision anyway" amounts to establishing the absence of "but for" causation. While the plaintiff's proof of "contributing factor" must be something less than "but for," how much less is not clear. Note also that the field is not level. The plaintiff must prove a "contributing factor" only by a preponderance of the evidence, while the defendant must establish that it "would have taken the same unfavorable personnel action in the absence of [the protected] behavior" by "clear and convincing evidence."

This proof structure makes the question of what suffices for proof of a contributing factor critical. "Temporal proximity" can help, as in *Genberg*, but the protected conduct and the adverse action need not be very close in time in order for plaintiff to prevail. *See Lockheed Martin*.

5. *Administrative Procedure for SOX Claims.* Sarbanes-Oxley has complicated enforcement procedures. In this it borrows from AIR 21 (the Wendell H. Ford Aviation Investment and Reform Act for the 21st Century), now codified at 49 U.S.C. §42121 (2018), which requires resort to the Department of Labor's Occupational Safety and Health Administration ("OSHA") within 180 days of the violation. OSHA, in turn, processes the complaint in a quasi-judicial setting, which involves a hearing before an administrative law judge, an administrative appeal, and judicial review in the

appropriate circuit court. Such review gives deference to the agency's reasonable construction of the Act and overturns administrative factual determinations only when
not supported by "substantial evidence." *Lockheed Martin*, 717 F.3d at 1129.

There is, however, an alternative procedure. To guard against agency delay, the
statute provides that if there is no agency final decision within 180 days of the filing
of the complaint and no bad faith delay by the claimant, the claimant may bring suit
in federal district court. 18 U.S.C.A. §1514A(b). The regulations also provide, however, that a plaintiff must file a notice of her intent to file a complaint in federal court
15 days in advance of doing so. 29 C.F.R. §1980.114(b). Filing this notice of intent
to sue presumably gives the agency a last chance to complete its proceedings. Where
the agency fails to do so, suit may be brought in federal court; *see Collins v. Beazer
Homes USA, Inc.*, 334 F. Supp. 2d 1365 (N.D. Ga. 2004), where the action is heard
de novo. That means that, even if the agency later rules on the complaint, its decision is not in any way preclusive, although such a decision may be introduced in
evidence in the civil suit. *See Chandler v. Roudebush*, 425 U.S. 840, 864 (1976). *See*
Fed. Rule Evid. 803(8)(c). In addition to satisfying the time limitations for filing with
OSHA, SOX retaliation suits must be brought within four years of the violation. *Jones
v. Southpeak Interactive Corp.*, 777 F.3d 668 (4th Cir. 2015).

Where the circuit courts review agency actions, the resulting deference to agency
findings can cut either for or against employees. OSHA decisions have historically
been mostly adverse to employees. Richard Moberly, *Unfulfilled Expectations: An
Empirical Analysis of Why Sarbanes-Oxley Whistleblowers Rarely Win*, 49 Wm. & Mary
L. Rev. 65 (2007); *see also* Terry Morehead Dworkin, *SOX and Whistleblowing*, 105
Mich. L. Rev. 1757, 1764 (2007); Nancy M. Modesitt, *Why Whistleblowers Lose: An
Empirical and Qualitative Analysis of State Court Cases*, 62 U. Kan. L. Rev. 165, 194
(2013). *But see* Richard Moberly, *Sarbanes-Oxley's Whistleblower Provisions: Ten Years
Later*, 64 S.C. L. Rev. 1 (2012); Richard E. Moberly, *Sarbanes-Oxley's Structural
Model to Encourage Corporate Whistleblowers*, 2006 BYU. L. Rev. 1107, 1109.

6. *State Claims.* Suppose that *Genberg* arose in New Jersey or Minnesota. Would
plaintiff have a cause of action under those state statutes? If so, would such an action
arise only because of the public policy evinced in SOX itself, or would the claim have
been actionable even before SOX as a means of vindicating federal policies regarding
proxies? Was that policy definite enough? If you conclude that an adverse employment action would have been actionable under either or both state laws only because
SOX created a right to be free of reprisal for engaging in this conduct, is there a
problem with states creating a cause of action that duplicates the federal one? Before
you answer no too quickly, wouldn't a state claim allow an employee to end-run
the requirement of filing with OSHA? Sarbanes-Oxley provides that "[n]othing in
this section shall be deemed to diminish the rights, privileges, or remedies of any
employee under any Federal or State law, or under any collective bargaining agreement." 18 U.S.C. §1514A. But if a state were to predicate a public policy tort on
SOX itself, would this language apply?

7. *Employer Reaction.* As the debate between the majority and the dissent indicates, it will not always be clear whether an employee's actions are within the umbrella
of SOX protections. Ironically, the defendant's reactions to the plaintiff's allegations
may lead a court to conclude that the conduct is protected. *See Collins v. Beazer Homes
USA, Inc.*, 334 F. Supp. 2d 1365 (N.D. Ga. 2004). In that case, although the plaintiff also complained about inefficient business practices, her supervisor's description
of the plaintiff's complaint as a "serious allegation" and the supervisor's recognition

that "there was something that may be criminal, against the law or against company policy, including violations of the company's Standards of Corporate Conduct" were factors in the court's finding the plaintiff's conduct protected.

8. *Remedies.* SOX provides for "all relief necessary to make the employee whole, including "reinstatement with the same seniority status" and "back pay, with interest." 18 U.S.C. §1514A. This has been interpreted to include emotional distress damages. *Jones v. Southpeak Interactive Corp.*, 777 F.3d 668 (4th Cir. 2015); *Halliburton, Inc. v. Admin. Review Bd.*, 771 F.3d 254, 266 (5th Cir. 2014). Punitive damages are not available but "compensation for any special damages sustained as a result of the discrimination, including litigation costs, expert witness fees, and reasonable attorney fees" is to be awarded. *Id.* The Dodd-Frank Wall Street Reform and Financial Protection Act amended SOX to make clear that there is a right to a jury trial in any court suit. 18 U.S.C.A. §1514A(b)(2)(e). That statute also amended SOX to bar mandatory arbitration. §1514(e). The parties can still agree to arbitrate, but only after a dispute has arisen.

9. *A New Wave of Federal Protection.* SOX was just the first in a new wave of federal laws containing antiretaliation provisions that may help workers, including the Affordable Care Act of 2010, 111 P.L. 148, 124 Stat. 119 Most importantly, the Dodd-Frank Wall Street Reform and Consumer Protection Act, Pub. L. 111-203, §922, 124 Stat. 2129, created three new whistleblower protections related to the Commodities Futures Trading Commission ("CFTC"), the Securities and Exchange Commission ("SEC"), and the newly established Consumer Financial Protection Bureau ("CFPB"). With respect to both the CFTC and SEC, the statute creates both a bounty system and an antiretaliation provision.

This Dodd-Frank retaliation protection, while overlapping considerably in terms of the predicate public policies, differs from SOX in a number of respects. Most obviously, the protection is much narrower since Dodd-Frank's explicit definition of "whistleblower" protects employees only for disclosures made to the SEC and thus, unlike SOX, does not reach disclosures to other governmental bodies or internal disclosures. *Dig. Realty Tr., Inc. v. Somers*, 138 S. Ct. 767 (2018) (limitation of whistleblower protection consistent with Congress's effort to encourage reporting to the SEC through the statute's bounty program). In other words, the two statutes reflect dramatically different policies: SOX encourages before-the-violation compliance by incentivizing internal reports; Dodd-Frank favors after-the-fact punishment by incentivizing reports to the SEC.

Where Dodd-Frank operates however, it has advantages over SOX in its enforcement proceedings, both because rights are vindicated through court suit, not an administrative procedure, U.S.C. §78u-6(h)(1)(B)(i), (iii)(I)(aa) (2018), and because of enhanced remedies. Indeed, in addition to the possibility of a bounty, double back-pay is available. §78u-6(h)(1)(C)(ii). Dodd-Frank, however, lacks SOX's provision for "compensation for any special damages sustained as a result of the discrimination." §1514A(c)(1), (2)(C).

As for protection of disclosures related to the new CFPB, Dodd-Frank's coverage reaches a broad array of entities dealing with financial products, and it protects disclosures not only to the Board itself but also to other governmental agencies and internally. *Dig. Realty Tr.*, 138 S. Ct. at 777. This protection, however, is enforced through an administrative filing although, like SOX, de novo suit may be brought if the Department of Labor does not act quickly enough. 12 U.S.C. §1558 (2018). Like SOX, the burden-shifting provisions are plaintiff-friendly.

Perhaps not surprisingly, some firms have sought to blunt these incentives by contractual provisions. Jennifer M. Pacella, *Silencing Whistleblowers by Contract*, 55 AM. BUS. L.J. 261 (2018) (analyzing contracts that seek to prevent employees from benefiting from Dodd-Frank whistleblower bounty awards). It seems unlikely that such agreements will be found enforceable, since to do so would substantially blunt the incentives Congress provided for reporting suspected violations.

10. *Justifying Punishing Whistleblowers?* At several points in these materials, particularly the Note on Attorneys and the Public Policy Tort, on p. 222, we have seen a clash between the right to blow the whistle and considerations of confidentiality. We will encounter that issue again and, more generally, when we reach Chapter 8 and consider the employee's duty of loyalty, which would often bar disclosure of employers' confidential information. The Restatement of Employment Law, not so very helpfully, requires such a duty to be consistent with other employee rights. *See* p. 473, Note 8, *Whistleblowing*. In the following case, the Supreme Court encountered a conflict between federal whistleblower protections and plausible potential harm to national security posed by the disclosures in question. You might be surprised to know that the right to disclose won out!

Department of Homeland Security v. Maclean
135 S. Ct. 913 (2015)

Chief Justice ROBERTS delivered the opinion of the Court.

Federal law generally provides whistleblower protections to an employee who discloses information revealing "any violation of any law, rule, or regulation," or "a substantial and specific danger to public health or safety." 5 U.S.C. §2302(b)(8)(A). An exception exists, however, for disclosures that are "specifically prohibited by law." *Ibid*. Here, a federal air marshal publicly disclosed that the Transportation Security Administration (TSA) had decided to cut costs by removing air marshals from certain long-distance flights. The question presented is whether that disclosure was "specifically prohibited by law."

I.

A.

In 2002, Congress enacted the Homeland Security Act. As relevant here, that Act provides that the TSA "shall prescribe regulations prohibiting the disclosure of information obtained or developed in carrying out security . . . if the Under Secretary decides that disclosing the information would . . . be detrimental to the security of transportation." 49 U.S.C. §114(r)(1)(C).

Around the same time, the TSA promulgated regulations prohibiting the unauthorized disclosure of what it called "sensitive security information." The regulations described 18 categories of sensitive security information, including "[s]pecific details of aviation security measures . . . [such as] information concerning specific numbers of Federal Air Marshals, deployments or missions, and the methods involved in such operations." 49 CFR §1520.7(j) (2002). Sensitive security information is not classified, so the TSA can share it with individuals who do not have a security clearance, such as airport employees.

B.

Robert J. MacLean became a federal air marshal for the TSA in 2001. In that role, MacLean was assigned to protect passenger flights from potential hijackings.

On July 26, 2003, the Department of Homeland Security (DHS) issued a confidential advisory about a potential hijacking plot. The advisory said that members of the terrorist group al Qaeda were planning to attack passenger flights, and that they "considered suicide hijackings and bombings as the most promising methods to destroy aircraft in flight, as well as to strike ground targets." The advisory identified a number of potential targets, including the United Kingdom, Italy, Australia, and the east coast of the United States. Finally, the advisory warned that at least one of the attacks "could be executed by the end of the summer 2003."

The TSA soon summoned all air marshals (including MacLean) for face-to-face briefings about the hijacking plot. During MacLean's briefing, a TSA official told him that the hijackers were planning to "smuggle weapons in camera equipment or children's toys through foreign security," and then "fly into the United States . . . into an airport that didn't require them to be screened." The hijackers would then board U.S. flights, "overpower the crew or the Air Marshals and . . . fly the planes into East Coast targets."

A few days after the briefing, MacLean received from the TSA a text message cancelling all overnight missions from Las Vegas until early August. MacLean, who was stationed in Las Vegas, believed that cancelling those missions during a hijacking alert was dangerous. He also believed that the cancellations were illegal, given that federal law required the TSA to put an air marshal on every flight that "present[s] high security risks," 49 U.S.C. §44917(a)(2), and provided that "nonstop, long distance flights, such as those targeted on September 11, 2001, should be a priority," §44917(b).

MacLean therefore asked a supervisor why the TSA had canceled the missions. The supervisor responded that the TSA wanted "to save money on hotel costs because there was no more money in the budget." MacLean also called the DHS Inspector General's Office to report the cancellations. But a special agent in that office told him there was "nothing that could be done."

Unwilling to accept those responses, MacLean contacted an MSNBC reporter and told him about the canceled missions. In turn, the reporter published a story about the TSA's decision, titled "Air Marshals pulled from key flights." The story reported that air marshals would "no longer be covering cross-country or international flights" because the agency did not want them "to incur the expense of staying overnight in hotels." The story also reported that the cancellations were "particularly disturbing to some" because they "coincide[d] with a new high-level hijacking threat issued by the Department of Homeland Security."

After MSNBC published the story, several Members of Congress criticized the cancellations. Within 24 hours, the TSA reversed its decision and put air marshals back on the flights.

[When the TSA discovered that MacLean was the source, it fired him for disclosing sensitive security information without authorization. The Merit Systems

Protection Board found that MacLean did not qualify for protection under 5 U.S.C §2302(b)(8)(A) because his disclosure was "specifically prohibited by law."

The Federal Circuit vacated the Board's decision.] The parties had agreed that, in order for MacLean's disclosure to be "specifically prohibited *by law*," it must have been "prohibited by a statute rather than by a regulation." (Emphasis added.) Thus, the issue before the court was whether the statute authorizing the TSA's regulations— now codified at 49 U.S.C. §114(r)(1)—"specifically prohibited" MacLean's disclosure. [The circuit court first held that Section 114(r)(1) did not itself expressly prohibit employee disclosures but only authorized the TSA to do so. Further, were Section 114(r)(1) to be treated as a prohibition, it was not "sufficiently specific."]

II.

Section 2302(b)(8) provides, in relevant part, that a federal agency may not take

> a personnel action with respect to any employee or applicant for employment because of
> (A) any disclosure of information by an employee or applicant which the employee or applicant reasonably believes evidences
>   (i) any violation of any law, rule, or regulation, or
>   (ii) gross mismanagement, a gross waste of funds, an abuse of authority, or a substantial and specific danger to public health or safety,
> if such disclosure is not specifically prohibited by law and if such information is not specifically required by Executive order to be kept secret in the interest of national defense or the conduct of foreign affairs.

The Government argues that this whistleblower statute does not protect MacLean because his disclosure regarding the canceled missions was "specifically prohibited by law" in two ways. First, the Government argues that the disclosure was specifically prohibited by the TSA's regulations on sensitive security information: 49 CFR §§1520.5(a)-(b), 1520.7(j) (2003). Second, the Government argues that the disclosure was specifically prohibited by 49 U.S.C. §114(r)(1), which authorized the TSA to promulgate those regulations. We address each argument in turn.

A.

1

In 2003, the TSA's regulations prohibited the disclosure of "[s]pecific details of aviation security measures . . . [such as] information concerning specific numbers of Federal Air Marshals, deployments or missions, and the methods involved in such operations." 49 CFR §1520.7(j). MacLean does not dispute before this Court that the TSA's regulations prohibited his disclosure regarding the canceled missions. Thus, the question here is whether a disclosure that is specifically prohibited by regulation is also "specifically prohibited *by law*" under Section 2302(b)(8)(A). (Emphasis added.)

The answer is no. Throughout Section 2302, Congress repeatedly used the phrase "law, rule, or regulation." . . . In contrast, Congress did not use the phrase "law, rule, or regulation" in the statutory language at issue here; it used the word "law" standing alone. That is significant because Congress generally acts intentionally when it uses particular language in one section of a statute but omits it in another. *Russello v. United States,* 464 U.S. 16, 23 (1983). Thus, Congress's choice to say "specifically prohibited by law" rather than "specifically prohibited by law, rule, or regulation" suggests that Congress meant to exclude rules and regulations.

The interpretive canon that Congress acts intentionally when it omits language included elsewhere applies with particular force here for two reasons. First, Congress used "law" and "law, rule, or regulation" in close proximity—indeed, in the same sentence. §2302(b)(8)(A) (protecting the disclosure of "any violation of any law, rule, or regulation ... if such disclosure is not specifically prohibited by law"). Second, Congress used the broader phrase "law, rule, or regulation" repeatedly—nine times in Section 2302 alone. Those two aspects of the whistleblower statute make Congress's choice to use the narrower word "law" seem quite deliberate. . . .

In addition, a broad interpretation of the word "law" could defeat the purpose of the whistleblower statute. If "law" included agency rules and regulations, then an agency could insulate itself from the scope of Section 2302(b)(8)(A) merely by promulgating a regulation that "specifically prohibited" whistleblowing. But Congress passed the whistleblower statute precisely because it did not trust agencies to regulate whistleblowers within their ranks. Thus, it is unlikely that Congress meant to include rules and regulations within the word "law."

2

[The Court rejected the Government's argument that, although some regulations are not "law" under Section 2302(b)(8)(A), "law" includes "all regulations that have the 'force and effect of law' (*i.e.,* legislative regulations), while excluding those that do not (*e.g.,* interpretive rules)." While that may sometimes be true, "Congress's use of the word 'law' in close connection with the phrase 'law, rule, or regulation,' provides the necessary 'clear showing' that 'law' does not include regulations."]

In sum, when Congress used the phrase "specifically prohibited by law" instead of "specifically prohibited by law, rule, or regulation," it meant to exclude rules and regulations. We therefore hold that the TSA's regulations do not qualify as "law" for purposes of Section 2302(b)(8)(A).

B.

We next consider whether MacLean's disclosure regarding the canceled missions was "specifically prohibited" by 49 U.S.C. §114(r)(1) itself. As relevant here, that statute provides that the TSA "shall prescribe regulations prohibiting the disclosure of information obtained or developed in carrying out security . . . if the Under Secretary decides that disclosing the information would . . . be detrimental to the security of transportation." §114(r)(1)(C).

This statute does not prohibit anything. On the contrary, it *authorizes* something—it authorizes the Under Secretary to "prescribe regulations." Thus, by its terms Section 114(r)(1) did not prohibit the disclosure at issue here.

The Government responds that Section 114(r)(1) did prohibit MacLean's disclosure by imposing a "legislative mandate" on the TSA to promulgate regulations to that effect. *See* SOTOMAYOR, J., dissenting. But the Government pushes the statute too far. Section 114(r)(1) says that the TSA shall prohibit disclosures only *"if the Under Secretary decides* that disclosing the information would . . . be detrimental to the security of transportation" (emphasis added). That language affords substantial discretion to the TSA in deciding whether to prohibit any particular disclosure.

The dissent tries to downplay the scope of that discretion, viewing it as the almost ministerial task of *"identifying* whether a particular piece of information falls within the scope of Congress' command." But determining which documents meet the statutory standard of "detrimental to the security of transportation" requires the exercise of considerable judgment. For example, the Government says that Section 114(r)(1) requires the Under Secretary to prohibit disclosures like MacLean's. The Government also says, however, that the statute does not require the Under Secretary to prohibit an employee from disclosing that "federal air marshals will be absent from important flights, but declining to specify which flights." That fine-grained distinction comes not from Section 114(r)(1) itself, but from the Under Secretary's exercise of discretion. It is the TSA's regulations—not the statute—that prohibited MacLean's disclosure. And as the dissent agrees, a regulation does not count as "law" under the whistleblower statute. . . .

III

Finally, the Government warns that providing whistleblower protection to individuals like MacLean would "gravely endanger public safety." That protection, the Government argues, would make the confidentiality of sensitive security information depend on the idiosyncratic judgment of each of the TSA's 60,000 employees. And those employees will "most likely lack access to all of the information that led the TSA to make particular security decisions." Thus, the Government says, we should conclude that Congress did not intend for Section 2302(b)(8)(A) to cover disclosures like MacLean's.

Those concerns are legitimate. But they are concerns that must be addressed by Congress or the President, rather than by this Court. Congress could, for example, amend Section 114(r)(1) so that the TSA's prohibitions on disclosure override the whistleblower protections in Section 2302(b)(8)(A). . . . *See* §114(r)(1) (authorizing the TSA to prohibit disclosures "[n]otwithstanding section 552 of title 5"); *see also* 10 U.S.C. §2640(h) ("the Secretary of Defense may (notwithstanding any other provision of law) withhold from public disclosure safety-related information that is provided to the Secretary voluntarily by an air carrier for the purposes of this section"). Congress could also exempt the TSA from the requirements of Section 2302(b)(8)(A) entirely, as Congress has already done for the Federal Bureau of Investigation, the Central Intelligence Agency, the Defense Intelligence Agency, the National Geospatial–Intelligence Agency, the National Security Agency, the Office of the Director of National Intelligence, and the National Reconnaissance Office. *See* 5 U.S.C. §2302(a)(2)(C)(ii)(I).

Likewise, the President could prohibit the disclosure of sensitive security information by Executive order. Indeed, the Government suggested at oral argument that the President could "entirely duplicate" the regulations that the TSA has issued under Section 114(r)(1). Such an action would undoubtedly create an exception to the whistleblower protections found in Section 2302(b)(8)(A).

Although Congress and the President each has the power to address the Government's concerns, neither has done so. It is not our role to do so for them. . . .

[Justice SOTOMAYOR, with whom Justice KENNEDY joined, dissented.]

NOTES

1. *Right Result?* Before plunging into the Court's analysis, is this a case of all's well that ends well? MacLean's disclosures resulted in a quick reversal of the TSA policy, which meant that flights had air marshals, apparently consistent with what Congress required in the statute. Under that view, MacLean's disclosure brought about compliance with the law, not to mention improved passenger safety. But is this too much of a "just so" story? The disclosures could have failed to achieve this goal and alerted terrorists that security was looser than they might have expected. And if MacLean really wanted to force compliance with his view of the law, why didn't he just call his congressional representatives rather than the media?

2. *Textual Analysis.* Of course, none of this matters in terms of the Court's opinion, which is a straightforward textualist analysis of where MacLean's conduct fell in terms of the balance struck by the Whistleblower Protection Act between generally permitted disclosures and those that are "specifically prohibited by law." The decision turned on whether an administrative regulation, which did prohibit MacLean's conduct, was a "law" within the meaning of the statute. While the Court's rather technical analysis may make sense on its own terms, might not a more purposive approach have been more consistent with congressional intent in drafting the statute in the first place? Should Congress amend the WPA to state "specifically prohibited by law or regulation"? Or is the Court onto something, given the repeated use of "rule or regulation" in the statute? And from a policy perspective, maybe Congress shouldn't allow agencies to silence their employees – arguably a classic case of not putting the fox in charge of the henhouse.

3. *A Statutory Prohibition?* The Court went on to consider whether the statute authorizing the regulation in question was itself a prohibition, and it had no difficulty concluding that it does not prohibit anything. But if Congress wanted to avoid having the fox guard the henhouse, why would it have authorized it to issue such regulations? Is that the point of the dissent?

4. *Corrective Action?* The Court pointed out a number of ways to protect the country from perhaps well-meant but dangerous disclosures. None of them seems to have been taken. What do you make of that?

5. *Absence of Justification?* Whatever the problems of the federal Whistleblower Protection Act, it at least recognized that not all conduct that could be described as whistleblowing should be protected. Some other public policy protections seem to envision some such limitations (recall the "absence of justification" prong in Iowa), but others don't. *See* CEPA, *supra.* Do you think that most situations could present some countervailing public policy override? *MacLean* did not, but that was presumably because Congress itself had drawn the boundaries of the cause of action.

The False Claims Act

The False Claims Act ("FCA"), 31 U.S.C. §3730(b) (2018), functions as a very powerful source of employee rights in a wide range of situations. Its general thrust is to empower any citizen to bring a claim, often referred to as a qui tam suit, in the name of the United States against any entity that submits "a false or fraudulent claim for payment" to the federal government. Because of the federal government's huge expenditures on Medicare and Medicaid reimbursement, much FCA litigation has centered on the health care industry, but claims may arise against any corporation that does business with the government. 18 U.S.C.A. §1514A.

Although the FCA traces its origins back to the Civil War, a series of recent amendments designed to make it more effective show Congress's continued commitment to using a bounty system to protect the federal fisc. *See* Anthony J. Casey & Anthony Niblett, *Noise Reduction: The Screening Value of Qui Tam*, 91 Wash. L. Rev. 1169 (2014).

The bounty provisions of the False Claims actions are very attractive from the plaintiff's perspective since the statute authorizes award of from 15 to 30 percent of any recovery to the private plaintiff. 31 U.S.C. §3730(d). *See generally* Marsha J. Ferziger & Daniel G. Currell, *Snitching for Dollars: The Economics and Public Policy of Federal Civil Bounty Programs*, 1999 U. Ill. L. Rev. 1141 (1999). Fraud, especially health care fraud, is big business, and the government often recovers billions of dollars, with significant recoveries by "relators." *See* Katie Thomas & Michael S. Schmidt, *Glaxo Agrees to Pay $3 Billion in Fraud Settlement*, N.Y. Times, July 2, 2012, A1. Beyond the health care industry, both military procurement and disaster relief offer large opportunities for employees who believe their employer is seeking compensation from the federal government to which it is not entitled.

While anyone can be a relator under the FCA, employees are typically in the best position to know when a company may be submitting false claims for reimbursement. Thus, employees or former employees are typically the relators in qui tam actions. But the FCA does not limit its remedies to qui tam recoveries. The statute has a section explicitly providing that any employee "discharged, demoted, suspended, threatened, harassed, or in any other manner discriminated against in the terms and conditions of employment" for furthering FCA actions is "entitled to all relief necessary to make the employee whole," including "2 times the amount of back pay" due. 31 U.S.C. §3730(h).

Retaliation suits under this section can be brought together with or separate from qui tam claims, but they are not subject to the limitations of qui tam actions. *See, e.g., United States ex rel. Carson v. Manor Care, Inc.*, 851 F.3d 293, 306 (4th Cir. 2017) (the FCA's first-to-file rule limitation on relator bounty recovery has no application to claims of retaliation under that statute). These suits typically raise the same issues we have explored elsewhere in this chapter. For example, there can be issues about reasonableness of the employee's belief that a violation has occurred. *See United States ex rel. Campie v. Gilead Scis.*, 862 F.3d 890, 908 (9th Cir. 2017) (an employee is protected under the FCA when his actions are motivated by a good faith and reasonable belief that the employer "is possibly committing fraud against the government"). Likewise, there may be issues as to whether the adverse employment action was caused by the protected conduct. *See DiFiore v. CSL Behring, LLC*, 879 F.3d 71, 78 (3d Cir. 2018) (plaintiff must prove that the retaliation was the but-for cause of an adverse employment action); *Thompson v. Quorum Health Res., LLC*, 485 F. App'x 783 (6th Cir. 2012) (jury reasonably could have found that the employer's proffered reason for terminating the employee was pretextual when it did not suspend him for violating its code of conduct until a month after learning of his FCA suit); *see also United States v. Solvay Pharm., Inc.*, 871 F.3d 318, 334 (5th Cir. 2017) (plaintiffs could not prove retaliation when they admitted serious violations of the employer's marketing policies).

FCA relator suits can also fall afoul of pleading requirements. Because such claims necessarily involve fraud, the heightened pleading requirements of Rule 9 of the Federal Rules of Civil Procedure apply, and requiring that fraud be pled "with particularity" has proven to be a serious barrier. *See, e.g., U.S. ex rel. Ge v. Takeda Pharm. Co. Ltd.*, 737 F.3d 116, 124 (1st Cir. 2013). *But see Foglia, ex rel. U.S. v. Renal Ventures Management, LLC*, 754 F.3d 153 (3d Cir. 2014) (adopting the "nuanced" approach of several circuits to pleading False Claims Act complaints).

Qui tam suits under the False Claims Act are subject to a number of limitations and somewhat unusual procedures. As described by David Freeman Engstrom,

> Not anyone can initiate a qui tam suit. The FCA contains several provisions designed to minimize wasteful private enforcement efforts, including: (i) a "first-to-file" provision precluding claims that mirror a previously filed qui tam suit; (ii) a bar on claims related to an already existing government enforcement proceeding; and (iii) a bar on claims that were previously "publicly disclosed" except where the relator is an "original source"— that is, has direct, firsthand knowledge—of the information underlying the fraud claim. Together, these provisions are designed, as the Supreme Court has noted, to achieve "the golden mean between adequate incentives for whistle-blowing insiders . . . and discouragement of opportunistic plaintiffs who have no significant information to contribute of their own."
>
> [One] set of FCA provisions vests the Attorney General . . . with substantial authority to oversee and control qui tam litigation. For instance, DOJ may dismiss or settle a qui tam case out from under a private relator, subject only to a basic fairness hearing, or veto private dismissals or settlements. . . .
>
> Perhaps the most significant form of oversight authority is DOJ's ability to intervene in qui tam suits. By statute, a qui tam relator files her complaint with the court under seal, serving it only on the government. A statutory sixty-day period (often subject to extensions) follows, during which DOJ investigates the allegations and decides whether to terminate or settle the case out from under the relator, intervene and take "primary responsibility" for the litigation of the case, or decline to intervene and allow the relator to proceed alone. Importantly, the amount of the bounty paid to a successful relator turns, at least in part, on DOJ's case-election decision: where DOJ declines intervention, a successful relator earns 25% to 30% of any recovery; if DOJ intervenes, a relator keeps only 15% to 25%. During legislative debates leading up to the FCA's 1986 revival, this tiered system of payoffs was seen as essential to incentivize relators to go it alone where a politicized bureaucracy refused to enforce.

Public Regulation of Private Enforcement: Empirical Analysis of DOJ Oversight of Qui Tam Litigation Under the False Claims Act, 107 Nw. U. L. Rev. 1689 (2013); *see also* David Freeman Engstrom, *Harnessing the Private Attorney General: Evidence from Qui Tam Litigation*, 112 Colum. L. Rev. 1244 (2012).

The FCA statute of limitations is normally six years, 31 U.S.C. §3731(b)(1) (2018), although it may be reduced or expanded in certain circumstances, §3731(b)(2). The Supreme Court recently held that the Wartime Suspension of Limitations

Act did not toll that statute since the Suspension Act applies only to criminal cases. *Kellogg Brown & Root Servs. v. United States ex rel. Carter*, 135 S. Ct. 1970 (2015).

Further, it is not clear whether employee arbitration agreements would reach an FCA qui tam action brought in the name of the United States. *Cf. United States ex rel. Welch v. My Left Foot Children's Therapy, LLC*, 871 F.3d 791, 794 (9th Cir. 2017) (not deciding whether an employee can agree to arbitrate relator claims but holding employer cannot compel arbitration of employee's qui tam claim when the arbitration agreement was limited to claims of the employee, not all disputes).

In a qui tam suit, the plaintiff must establish that the defendant submitted a false claim within the meaning of the statute. As the Engstrom extract indicates, one important exclusion from the FCA is the ban of suits brought where there has been "public disclosure" in (1) criminal, civil, or administrative hearings; (2) congressional or administrative reports or investigations; or (3) the news media, "unless . . . the person bringing the action is an original source of the information." §3730(e)(4) (A). *See Schindler Elevator Corp. v. U.S. ex rel. Kirk*, 563 U.S. 401 (2011) (government Freedom of Information Act responses were "reports" subject to FCA's public disclosure bar). The FCA also has a bar on suits brought while another suit is "pending." *But see Kellogg Brown & Root Servs. v. United States ex rel. Carter*, 135 S. Ct. 1970 (2015) (the first-to-file bar, which precludes a qui tam suit based on the same facts as a "pending" action, does not bar a second suit when the earlier one has been dismissed).

As with other whistleblower causes of action, FCA claims pose special problems for attorneys. In *United States ex rel. Fair Laboratory Practices Associates v. Quest Diagnostics, Inc.*, 734 F.3d 154 (2d Cir. 2013), the Second Circuit affirmed dismissal of a qui tam suit brought in essence by the employer's former general counsel. The court determined that the general counsel had violated his ethical obligations under the New York Rules of Professional Conduct. The court stressed "the tension between an attorney's ethical duty of confidentiality and the federal interest in encouraging 'whistleblowers' to disclose unlawful conduct harmful to the government." *Id.* at 157. While not disqualifying attorneys per se from a role in qui tam litigation, the court found that the counsel had violated Rule 1.9(c)'s duty of client confidentiality. Rule 1.6(b) permits a lawyer to "reveal or use confidential information to the extent that the lawyer reasonably believes necessary . . . to prevent the client from committing a crime," but the general counsel was found to have revealing more than was "necessary." Although the FCA does require relators to make "written disclosure of substantially all material evidence and information the person possesses" to the government, "the confidential information [the general counsel] revealed was greater than reasonably necessary to prevent any alleged ongoing fraudulent scheme." In part that was because there were other relators whose information would have justified the suit and in part because the general counsel "could have made limited disclosures." *Id.* at 165.

Quest is not the first instance we've seen where whistleblower protections are dramatically reduced when attorneys are involved. *See* Note on Attorneys and the Public Policy Tort, page 222. One difference, however, between *Quest* and the previous other cases is that *Quest* involved a federal statute, and there was at least an argument that state rules of professional responsibility were trumped by the FCA. The court gave short shrift to that contention. *See generally* Kathleen Clark & Nancy J. Moore, *Buying Voice: Financial Rewards for Whistleblowing Lawyers*, 56 B.C. L. Rev. 1697 (2015); Kathleen M. Boozang, *The New Relators: In-House Counsel and Compliance*

Officers, 6 J. HEALTH & LIFE SCIENCES L. 16 (2010). Central to the *Quest* opinion was that the plaintiffs could have prosecuted their FCA suit without the general counsel's disclosure of confidential information. Does that mean that an employee-attorney will rarely be able to make any disclosure unless that disclosure is truly critical to the case? *See* Posting of Charles A. Sullivan to Workplace Prof Blog, *Balancing Away Qui Tam Actions*, Nov. 25, 2013, http://lawprofessors.typepad.com/laborprof_blog/2013/11/balancing-away-qui-tam-actions.html.

5

Traditional Torts in the Employment Relationship

The history of tort law's approach to the employment relationship starts with the struggle during the latter part of the nineteenth century over injuries sustained in the workplace. At the time, tort law theoretically offered redress for workplace injuries. In fact, however, employees seeking compensation for negligence were often frustrated by three doctrines—contributory negligence, assumption of risk, and the fellow servant rule—that together rendered it difficult or impossible for employees to recover from their employers. In large measure, then, tort law left workplace safety to private ordering. Rather than abolishing these restrictive doctrines while operating within the traditional tort system, populist reformers advanced workers' compensation laws as the means of reform. The system, which won universal acceptance, was a compromise between full compensation for employees and the hit-or-miss cause of action for negligence. Workers' compensation laws replaced the common law tort of negligence with an administrative system of strict liability for work-related injuries and diseases, providing more certain recovery but restricting the amounts recovered. *See generally* LEX K. LARSON, LARSON'S WORKERS' COMPENSATION LAW (Matthew Bender and Co., Inc. 2018); Price Fishback & Shawn Everett Kantor, *The Adoption of Workers' Compensation in the United States*, 1900-1930, 41 J.L. & ECON. 305 (1998). The trade-off of lower amounts for more certain recovery required that workers' compensation be the exclusive remedy against the employer for physical injuries to employees in accidents arising out of their employment. Thus, tort law as a means to redress employee injuries largely disappeared during the twentieth century.

We will explore the parameters of workers' compensation exclusivity and the system as a whole at the end of this chapter. For now, it is enough to know that workers' compensation systems typically left intentional torts actionable. Employee suits for intentional torts against their employers or individual supervisors or co-workers are therefore possible, but they remain more the exception than the rule in employment law. A few torts play an occasional role. For example, employees sometimes claim assault and battery for physical altercations, *Kelly v. County of Monmouth*, 883

A.2d 411 (N.J. App. Div. 2005) (suit against co-worker who grabbed plaintiff's genitals when hand-shaking contest escalated into a "testosterone type thing"), and occasionally allege false imprisonment, most often in the context of too-enthusiastic interrogation during employer investigations of employee dishonesty. *Levin v. Canon Bus. Solutions, Inc.*, 2010 WL 731645 (Cal. Ct. App. Mar. 4, 2010) (false imprisonment verdict upheld when employer investigators required plaintiff to ride in their car to his home under threat of criminal charges). Malicious prosecution claims are also sometimes brought against employers who report suspected theft to the police without an adequate basis. *See Bennett v. R & L Carriers Shared Servs.*, LLC, 492 F. App'x 315 (4th Cir. 2012) (upholding jury verdict for malicious prosecution stemming from a "brief and ham-handed" internal investigation). These kinds of intentional torts are also commonly deployed as ancillary causes of action to other claims. For example, in the sexual harassment context, the tort of assault may allow suit against the individual harasser, who might otherwise not be personally liable since discrimination statutes typically apply only to the corporate employer. *See* Chapter 9. Even here, however, some courts have found tort suits for sexual assault to be barred by workers' compensation exclusivity. *See* Chapter 12.

Of somewhat more general application are four other intentional torts that are treated in this chapter, and privacy torts, which are treated in Chapter 6. Of these, only one—intentional interference with contract or prospective advantage—is primarily used to seek compensation for lost employment per se. For that reason, intentional interference is treated first in Section A. The other three torts focus more on terms and conditions of employment than on job security and are only incidentally concerned with discharge. They are treated here in declining order of their importance in the employment law landscape. Defamation, taken up in Section B, and intentional infliction of emotional distress, treated in Section C, both focus on the employee's right to be treated with dignity. Although both may be implicated in terminations, that is not their primary focus, and both offer relatively weak protection in this context. Finally, fraud or misrepresentation is typically raised in the context of inducement to enter employment or with respect to compensation or other benefits, but it may also be raised in connection with termination. Discussed in Section D, it is a very powerful tool when applicable, but is so narrowly confined as to be rarely useful for employees.

This chapter concludes with Section E, which considers two important limitations on the use of tort doctrines. First, there is some question as to the extent to which the exclusivity provisions of state workers' compensation laws we have noted bar tort suit. Second, the increased recognition of tort actions for employee termination under state law has led to questions about whether such state causes of action are preempted by federal law.

A. INTENTIONAL INTERFERENCE WITH THE EMPLOYMENT RELATIONSHIP

Tort law has long protected parties to a contract from third parties intentionally interfering with their relationship. In the employment field, this tort has traditionally been asserted by employers seeking to prevent other employers from "pirating" their workers or seeking compensation for the loss of key employees. *See* Chapter 8. But employees can also use this tort. The employment relationship between company and worker may be viewed as the contract (or at least the "prospective advantage") interfered with, and, if so, the question becomes whether a third party has unjustifiably interfered with that relationship. *See generally* Alex Long, *Tortious Interference with Business Relations: "The Other White Meat" of Employment Law*, 84 Minn. L. Rev. 863 (2000).

The Restatement of Employment Law states the general rule:

> An employer wrongfully interferes with an employee's employment or prospective employment with another employer when the employer, by improper means or without a legitimate business interest, intentionally causes another employer (i) to terminate the employment of the employee; or (ii) not to enter into an employment relationship with the employee.

§6.03(a) (ALI 2015). This tort is, however, subject to a qualified privilege, *see* §6.02, which permits the publication of statements to, inter alia, other employers, unless the employer "either (i) knows [the statement] is false or acts with reckless disregard of its truth or falsity, or (ii) knows or should know that neither the employer nor the recipient has a legitimate interest in the recipient receiving the statement."

A threshold question is whether the tort applies to at-will employment. As the Restatement inclusion of "prospective employment" reflects, most courts have found at-will contracts still to be contracts and so within the tort, and, in any event, the intentional interference tort reaches not only contracts but also interference with "prospective advantage." *See, e.g., Stanek v. Greco*, 323 F.3d 476, 480 (6th Cir. 2003); *Hensen v. Truman Med. Ctr., Inc.*, 62 S.W.3d 549, 553 (Mo. Ct. App. 2001). *But see Stanton v. Tulane Univ.*, 777 So. 2d 1242 (La. Ct. App. 2001) (at-will employee could not assert the tort); *McManus v. MCI Comm. Corp.*, 748 A.2d 949 (D.C. 2000) (same); *see generally* Alex Long, *The Disconnect Between At-Will Employment and Tortious Interference with Business Relations: Rethinking Tortious Interference Claims in the Employment Context*, 33 Ariz. St. L.J. 491 (2001). However, the scope of the privilege to interfere is broader when the employment is at will. *See CRST Van Expedited, Inc. v. Werner Enters.*, 479 F.3d 1099, 1106-07 (9th Cir. 2007) ("independently wrongful act" necessary when at-will workers are induced to leave their employment).

A more difficult problem arises when the interference is by someone who is, in some sense, the employer itself. The Employment Restatement speaks in terms of liability when an employer "causes *another employer* not to enter into or to discontinue an employment relationship" (emphasis added). This means that the employer cannot be liable for the tort when it terminates its own employee. *See also* §766 Restatement (Second) of Torts (ALI 1965). But jurisdictions have taken inconsistent approaches to whether an officer or director of an employer or a co-worker can be a third party with respect to the plaintiff's contract or business relationship with the employer. One view is that a supervisor is not a "third party" since the supervisor has an absolute privilege to interfere with the employment relationship. *See, e.g., Halvorsen v. Aramark Unif. Servs., Inc.*, 77 Cal. Rptr. 2d 383, 390 (Ct. App. 1998). Under this approach, a co-worker may be liable since his interference will not normally be within the scope of his employment, but a supervisor will not be.

In most jurisdictions, the answer turns on whether the defendant is acting within the scope of his or her employment. *E.g., Gruhlke v. Sioux Empire Fed. Credit Union, Inc.,* 756 N.W.2d 399, 408 (S.D. 2008) ("when corporate officers act within the scope of employment, even if those actions are only partially motivated to serve their employer's interests," the officers cannot be viewed as third parties capable of interfering with the employment contract); *Trail v. Boys & Girls Clubs of Northwest Ind.,* 845 N.E.2d 130, 138 (Ind. 2006) (same).

However, according to §228 of the Restatement (Second) of Agency (ALI 1957), acting within the scope of employment requires that the supervisor be motivated, at least in part, by a desire to serve the principal. *See also* RESTATEMENT (THIRD) OF AGENCY §7.07 (ALI 2006). Thus, a supervisor will be liable only when his actions are intended to further only "some individual or private purpose not related to the interests of the employer." *Huff v. Swartz,* 606 N.W.2d 461, 467 (Neb. 2000). As one court framed it, "[w]hile a party to a contract may breach it, it is logically impossible for a party to interfere tortiously with its own contract. However, if the agent's sole purpose is one that is *not* for the benefit of the corporation, the agent is not acting within the scope of employment and may be liable." *Kaelon v. USF Reddaway, Inc.,* 42 P.3d 344 (Ore. Ct. App. 2002). Think about the desirability of these various approaches as you consider the next case.

≡≡ ### *Kumpf v. Steinhaus*
≡≡ *779 F.2d 1323 (7th Cir. 1985)*

EASTERBROOK, Circuit Judge.

From 1973 until August 1983 William A. Kumpf was the president and chief executive officer of Lincoln National Sales Corp. of Wisconsin (Lincoln Wisconsin). He owned 20% of Lincoln Wisconsin's stock. Lincoln National Sales Corp. (Lincoln Sales) owned the other 80% of the stock, and two of the three members of Lincoln Wisconsin's board of directors were employees of Lincoln Sales. Lincoln Sales is in turn a subsidiary of Lincoln National Life Insurance Co. (Lincoln Life). Lincoln Sales is the marketing arm of Lincoln Life; Lincoln Wisconsin was the Wisconsin agency of Lincoln Sales.

In April 1981 Orin A. Steinhaus became an executive vice-president of Lincoln Life, leaving a post as head of Lincoln's sales agency in Columbus, Ohio. The president of Lincoln Life gave Steinhaus and other employees the task of revising the firm's sales structure, which was losing money. Lincoln Life closed 25 sales agencies and decided to consolidate others. In August 1983 Steinhaus decided to consolidate five Midwestern sales agencies into a single agency. (Doubtless other officers of Lincoln Life concurred in these decisions, but for simplicity we write as if Steinhaus made all decisions himself.) He instructed Lincoln Sales's directors on the board of Lincoln Wisconsin to approve a merger of Lincoln Wisconsin into Lincoln Chicago Corp. (Lincoln Chicago); Lincoln Wisconsin's board approved the merger by a vote of two to one, over Kumpf's dissent. Lincoln Wisconsin disappeared, and so did Kumpf's job. This litigation is the residue.

The district court dismissed most of Kumpf's claims for relief but sent to the jury a claim that Steinhaus and the Lincoln corporations tortiously interfered with the employment contract between Kumpf and Lincoln Wisconsin. Kumpf was an employee at will, but even at-will employment is contractual and therefore potentially the basis of a tort action. *Mendelson v. Blatz Brewing Co.*, 101 N.W.2d 805 (Wis. 1960). Kumpf was fired by Lincoln Wisconsin, and Lincoln Wisconsin cannot "interfere" with its own employment relations. But because Lincoln Sales owned only 80% of Lincoln Wisconsin's stock, Kumpf argued that other participants in the Lincoln family of firms could not intervene.

The defendants maintain that their interference with Kumpf's contract was privileged because it took place in the course of business. Kumpf replied that it was not privileged because it was done with an improper motive. After the reorganization, Steinhaus became president of Lincoln Chicago. In the insurance business the head of an agency receives a percentage of the agency's revenue. Income that used to go to Kumpf now went to Steinhaus, and the reorganization increased Steinhaus's total income. Kumpf argued that Steinhaus engineered the reorganization to advance his personal interests, and that this defeats the claim of privilege.

Kumpf asked the judge to instruct the jury that if the defendants' acts were "based—even in part—upon personal considerations, malice or ill will" then their acts were not privileged. Kumpf later proposed an instruction that would make privilege turn on "predominant" motivation. The district court, however, told the jury that "if you find that the actions of the defendants were motivated solely by a desire for revenge, ill will or malice, or in the case of the defendant Orin Steinhaus, solely by personal considerations, then you may find their actions improper." The jury returned a verdict for the defendants, and Kumpf attacks the "sole motive" instruction. . . .

Malice, ill will, and the like mean, in Wisconsin, an intent to act without justification. *Mendelson*. So the initial question is whether Kumpf has identified an unsupportable consideration that led to his dismissal. The only one Kumpf presses on us is Steinhaus's self-interest (Kumpf calls it "greed"). . . .

The basis of the privilege in question is the economic relations among the Lincoln family of corporations. The managers of the firm at the apex of the structure have an obligation to manage the whole structure in the interests of investors. Kumpf and Lincoln Wisconsin knew that when they started—when Kumpf took the risks associated with owning 20% of the stock, and holding one of three seats on the board, in a subsidiary of Lincoln Life. The superior managers in such a structure try to serve the interests of investors and other participants as a whole, and these interests will not always be congruent with the interests of managers of subsidiaries. Corporate reorganizations may reduce the costs of operation and put the structure in the hands of better managers, though this may be costly to existing managers.

If Kumpf had directly challenged the wisdom of a business decision of the managers of Lincoln Life, he would have been rebuffed with a reference to the business judgment doctrine—a rule of law that insulates business decisions from most forms of review. Courts recognize that managers have both better information and better incentives than they. The press of market forces—managers at Lincoln Life must continually attract new employees and capital, which they cannot do if they exploit existing participants or perform poorly—will more effectively serve the interests of all participants than will an error-prone judicial process. *See* Daniel R. Fischel, *The Business Judgment Rule and the Trans-Union Case*, 40 Bus. Law. 1437, 1439-43 (1985).

The privilege to manage corporate affairs is reinforced by the rationale of employment at will. Kumpf had no tenure of office. The lack of job security gave him a keen motive to do well. Security of position may diminish that incentive. *See* Richard A. Epstein, *In Defense of the Contract at Will*, 51 U. Chi. L. Rev. 947 (1984).

Employment at will, like the business judgment doctrine, also keeps debates about business matters out of the hands of courts. People who enter a contract without a fixed term know there is some prospect that their business partners may try to take advantage of them or simply make a blunder in deciding whether to continue the relationship. Yet people's concern for their reputation and their ability to make other advantageous contracts in the future leads them to try to avoid both mistakes and opportunistic conduct. Contracting parties may sensibly decide that it is better to tolerate the risk of error—to leave correction to private arrangements—than to create a contractual right to stay in office in the absence of a "good" reason. The reason for a business decision may be hard to prove, and the costs of proof plus the risk of mistaken findings of breach may reduce the productivity of the employment relation.

Many people have concluded otherwise; contracts terminable only for cause are common. But in Wisconsin, courts enforce whichever solution the parties select. A contract at will may be terminated for any reason (including bad faith) or no reason, without judicial review; the only exception is a termination that violates "a fundamental and well-defined public policy as evidenced by existing law." *Brockmeyer v. Dun & Bradstreet*, 335 N.W.2d 834 (Wis. 1983). Greed—the motive Kumpf attributes to Steinhaus—does not violate a "fundamental and well-defined public policy" of Wisconsin. Greed is the foundation of much economic activity, and Adam Smith told us that each person's pursuit of his own interests drives the economic system to produce more and better goods and services for all. "It is not from the benevolence of the butcher, the brewer, or the baker, that we expect our dinner, but from their regard to their own interest. We address ourselves, not to their humanity but to their self-love, and never talk to them of our own necessities but of their advantages." THE WEALTH OF NATIONS 14 (1776; Modern Library ed.).

The reasons that led Wisconsin to hold in *Brockmeyer* that it is "unnecessary and unwarranted for the courts to become arbiters of any termination that may have a tinge of bad faith attached" also establish that greed is not the sort of prohibited motive that will support Kumpf's tort action. In *Mendelson* the court stated that majority shareholders possess a privilege "to take whatever action they deem[] advisable to further the interests of the corporation." The court then quoted with approval from a text stating that a person enjoys no privilege "if his object is to put pressure upon the plaintiff and coerce him into complying with the defendant's wishes in some collateral matter."

If Steinhaus got rid of Kumpf because Kumpf would not marry Steinhaus's daughter, that would have been pressure in a "collateral matter." It is quite another thing to say that a jury must determine whether Steinhaus installed himself as head of Lincoln Chicago "predominantly" because he thought that would be good for Lincoln Life or "predominantly" because Steinhaus would enjoy the extra income. The decision to consolidate agencies and change managers is not "collateral" to the business of Lincoln Life, and the rationale of the business judgment rule interdicts any attempt to look behind the decision to determine whether Steinhaus is an astute manager.

Often corporations choose to align the interests of investors and managers by giving the managers a share of the firm's revenue or profits. Commissions, the ownership of stock or options, and bonuses all make managers and investors do well or poorly together. Lincoln Life chose to give managers a financial stake in each agency's revenues. Steinhaus was privileged to act with that incentive in mind. Suppose a major auto manufacturer decides to pay its chief executive officer $1 per year plus a percentage of the firm's profit. The officer then closes an unprofitable subsidiary (owned 80% by the firm), discharging its employees. Under Kumpf's theory any of the employees would be entitled to recover from the executive if the jury should estimate that in the executive's mind making money for himself predominated over making money for the firm. Yet since the two are the same thing, that would be a bootless investigation, and one with great potential to stifle the executive's vigorous pursuit of the firm's best interests. We do not think this is the law in Wisconsin or anywhere else.

Kumpf presents one last argument. He asked the judge to charge the jury that it should consider "recognized ethical codes or standards for a particular area of business activity" and "concepts of fair play" in deciding whether the defendants' acts were privileged. This "business ethics" instruction, Kumpf contends, would have allowed the jury to supplement the rules of tort and contract with "the rules of the game" in business. Although language of this sort appears in the Restatement (Second) of Torts §767 comment j (1979), it was not designed to be given to a jury. It would leave the jury at sea, free to impose a brand of ethics for which people may not have bargained. No case in Wisconsin has required an instruction even remotely like this one. . . .

The contention that businesses should be more considerate of their officers should be addressed to the businesses and to legislatures. Some firms will develop reputations for kind treatment of executives, some will be ruthless. Some will seek to treat executives well but find that the exigencies of competition frustrate their plans. The rule of this game is that Kumpf was an employee at will and had no right to stay on if his board wanted him gone. His board was dominated by people who answered to Lincoln Sales, which answered to Lincoln Life. Kumpf did not bargain for legal rights against Lincoln Life, and the judge properly declined to allow the jury to convert moral and ethical claims into legal duties.

NOTES

1. *Proper and Improper Motives.* In the movie *Wall Street* (1987) (the original, not the much later sequel, *Wall Street: Money Never Sleeps* (2010)), Gordon Gekko, played by Michael Douglas, celebrates the virtues of greed:

> The point is, ladies and gentlemen, that greed, for lack of a better word, is good; greed is right; greed works; greed clarifies, cuts through, and captures the essence of the evolutionary spirit; greed in all its forms: greed for life, for money, for love, knowledge, has marked the upward surge of mankind, and greed—you mark my words—will not only save Teldar Paper but that other malfunctioning corporation called the U.S.A.

(20th Century Fox 1987); *see also* M. Todd Henderson & James C. Spindler, *Corporate Heroin: A Defense of Perks, Executive Loans, and Conspicuous Consumption*, 93 Geo. L. J. 1835 (2005). *But see* Eric A. Posner, *The Jurisprudence of Greed*, 151 U. Pa. L. Rev. 1097 (2003). Is this the point of Judge Easterbrook's defense of Steinhaus's conduct? Because *Kumpf* finds that greed is not an improper motive, it need not address whether liability would be appropriate if the termination decision was based only in part on that motive. Had greed counted as an improper motive, how should the mixed-motive question have been decided? We encountered this question in Chapter 4 in connection with Sarbanes-Oxley liability for whistleblowers, and we will meet it again in Chapter 9 in connection with the antidiscrimination laws, but it is not clear that these statutory questions will influence the common law on issues such as intentional interference.

2. *A Detour into Judgecraft.* Judge Easterbrook is associated with the Chicago School of economic analysis of the law. One of the chief thrusts of the Chicago School is that "economic efficiency" ought to inform legal rules, frequently displacing (or at least modifying) notions of ethics and morals, and Easterbrook gives short shrift to the plaintiff's "business ethics" argument. Further, as Easterbrook's citation indicates, Professor Epstein is a strong defender of the economic efficiency of the at-will rule. As a federal judge deciding a diversity case like *Kumpf*, Easterbrook is supposed to be applying Wisconsin law, not the theories of the Chicago School. *See Erie R.R. v. Tompkins*, 304 U.S. 64 (1938). Do you think that he is faithful to *Erie*?

3. *More on Motives.* Kumpf argued that pursuit of self-interest by Steinhaus, as distinct from pursuit of corporate interests, suffices to make the interference actionable. What's wrong with that argument? Judge Easterbrook appeals to the business-judgment analogy, which ordinarily insulates corporate directors from liability for their decisions. But business-judgment protection may be lost if one or more directors are interested in the transaction. *See* R. Clark, Corporate Law §3.4 (1986).

In addition, reading Easterbrook's opinion, one might forget that the business judgment rule applies to protect decisions of *directors* of a corporation, acting in their capacity as board members, not all of its "managers." Indeed, Easterbrook's language elides this distinction and effectively extends the business judgment rule to "managers" without benefit of any citation. But is he right on what the law should be? Does Easterbrook's auto manufacturer hypothetical help you? He may be correct that the CEO should not be subject to suit by ex-employees if he closes an unprofitable subsidiary. But suppose the CEO's only motive was to increase his personal profits, regardless of whether his corporation lost or made money. Should this be actionable under the intentional interference tort?

One way to avoid this entire problem would be doctrinal—holding that Steinhaus is absolutely privileged to take the actions he did. While some states take this approach, Wisconsin is not one of those jurisdictions, leaving Judge Easterbrook to struggle with the question of what motives taint a decision. If greed does not count as an improper motive in Wisconsin, what motives will? Easterbrook suggests that Kumpf would have had a good claim if Steinhaus had persuaded his firm to fire Kumpf because Kumpf refused to marry Steinhaus's daughter. But in a subsequent Seventh Circuit case, Judge Posner rejected an interference claim based on the defendant having fired him to advance his lover. He worried about a rash of suits by disgruntled former employees given that "[f]ew are the employees whose actions are motivated solely by a selfless devotion to the employer's interests." Posner would require that a plaintiff "prove both that the employer did not benefit from the defendant's act and that the act was independently tortious, for example as fraud or defamation." *Preston v. Wis. Health Fund*, 397 F.3d 539, 543-44 (7th Cir. 2005).

4. *Personal Enough?* In *Kaelon v. USF Reddaway, Inc.*, 42 P.3d 344 (Ore. Ct. App. 2002), the plaintiff claimed that an executive had "openly carried on a romantic affair with another female employee and gave preferential employment treatment to this employee," and that he believed (incorrectly) that the plaintiff had gossiped about the affair. She claimed that, in retaliation, he had denied her promotion and belittled and humiliated her to force her to leave her employment. Contrary to *Preston*, the court found such conduct would be actionable:

> [A] reasonable juror could find that defendant, in humiliating plaintiff in the workplace, in denying her promotions, and in causing her to leave her employment, was retaliating

against plaintiff for complaining about his romantic relationship with Hiepler. Under several of our prior cases, such a finding by the jury would support the further finding that defendant acted solely for his own benefit, and not at all for the benefit of Reddaway.

Id. at 348. At trial, the dispute would be whether the defendant acted solely from that motive or instead (or also) from a desire to advance his employer's interests. *See also Stanek v. Greco*, 323 F.3d 476 (6th Cir. 2003) (discharge by president because plaintiff had reported his misuse of funds actionable); *Sides v. Duke Hospital*, 328 S.E.2d 818 (N.C. App. 1985) (doctors who induced a hospital to discharge plaintiff, a nurse, because her deposition in a malpractice suit was damaging to them were acting for improper or strictly personal motives).

5. *Terminology.* The threshold question of whether the defendant is a "third party" tends to merge with the question of justification for his conduct or privilege, although note that the defendant need only be motivated "partially" by an intent to serve the employer. Thus, some courts recognize that the supervisor is not the employer but nevertheless is privileged to cause the employer to breach its contract. As we have seen, some jurisdictions see the privilege as absolute, *Halvorsen v. Aramark Unif. Servs., Inc.*, 77 Cal. Rptr. 2d 383 (Ct. App. 1998) (recognizing an absolute "manager's privilege" to interfere), but most courts view it as qualified, requiring reasonable, good faith pursuit of the employer's business and no predominant motive of malice or spite. *See, e.g., Luketich v. Goedecke*, 835 S.W.2d 504, 508 (Mo. Ct. App. 1992); *Nordling v. N. States Power Co.*, 478 N.W.2d 498, 506 (Minn. 1991). The Employment Restatement opts for a qualified privilege. §6.02.

6. *Reputational Constraints.* The court in *Steinhaus* suggests that the law need not provide a remedy to deter harms like the one inflicted on the plaintiff because the market is generally self-correcting: "[P]eople's concern for their reputation and their ability to make other advantageous contracts in the future leads them to try to avoid both mistakes and opportunistic conduct." Obviously, such a "remedy" provides little solace for individual plaintiffs, but are you convinced that reputational consequences sufficiently reduce mistakes and opportunism? Summarizing the literature, Professor Sam Estreicher describes reputation as "a late-appearing deus ex machina explaining why opportunistic behavior by employers . . . is likely to be relatively unimportant," and questions whether it is likely to have this effect in employment markets. *Employer Reputation at Work*, 27 HOFSTRA LAB. & EMP. L. J. 1 (2009); Gillian Lester, *Restrictive Covenants, Employee Training, and the Limits of Transaction-Cost Analysis*, 76 IND. L. J. 49, 64 (2001) (explaining why there is ample room for opportunism with respect to restrictive covenants despite potential reputational consequences).

PROBLEM

5-1. Marco Ramirez, the president of Free Market Enterprises, Inc., called Ashley Appleton into his office at salary review time near the end of the year. He congratulated her on a superlative job that year and told her that she would receive a 15 percent raise. Appleton was very happy until, at the end of the meeting, Ramirez told her that he was sure she would "show her gratitude with a small gift, say of 5 percent of her salary, in cash—small bills only, please."

Appleton comes to you for help. She had heard rumors from co-workers of required kickbacks, but this is the first time that she has been asked for money. Free Market Enterprises is a publicly held company, although your client believes that Ramirez, its founder, holds about 20 percent of the stock and is generally thought to have a controlling interest. Next, suppose Appleton does not make a gift and the following year, Ramirez selects her for termination in a company-wide layoff. Advise her.

B. DEFAMATION

A cause of action for defamation arises when statements made in writing (libel) or orally (slander) "harm the reputation of another so as to lower him in the estimation of the community or to deter third persons from association or dealing with him." RESTATEMENT (SECOND) OF TORTS §558 (ALI 1977). The Restatement establishes four elements of the tort: "(a) a false and defamatory statement concerning another; (b) an unprivileged publication to a third party; (c) fault amounting at least to negligence on the part of the publisher; and (d) either actionability of the statement irrespective of special harm or the existence of special harm caused by the publication." *See also* RESTATEMENT OF EMPLOYMENT LAW §6.01(a) ("[A]n employer publishing a false and defamatory statement about an employee is subject to liability for the harm the publication causes.").

When judges enforce the law of defamation, however, they impose restrictions on speech, restrictions that may interfere with the constitutional free speech interests of defamation defendants. Much of the modern law of defamation, therefore, focuses on balancing the conflicting interests of reputation and freedom of speech inherent in every defamation case. The weight accorded to speech interests varies, however, with the identity of the parties to the suit. When public officials or public figures sue the media for defamation, the media's free speech interests predominate and constitutional standards play a large role in the case. *New York Times v. Sullivan*, 376 U.S. 254 (1964). At the other extreme, when a private individual sues a nonmedia defendant, the individual's interest in reputation predominates and the constitution plays a far lesser role in limiting the common law of defamation. *Dun and Bradstreet v. Greenmoss Builders*, 472 U.S. 749 (1985). Because defamation in the context of employment almost always involves the latter situation, this section will concentrate on traditional common law issues that dominate employment-related defamation law, including the meaning of "publication," when a statement can be characterized as defamatory, and when defamation is privileged. We will also consider the fault element of defamation in the employment context.

≡≡≡ *Cockram v. Genesco, Inc.*
≡≡≡ *680 F.3d 1046 (8th Cir. 2012)*

GRUENDER, Circuit Judge.

Jessica Cockram sued her former employer, Genesco, Inc., after the company made public statements about Cockram's involvement in an incident in which a pernicious racial slur appeared on a return receipt that Cockram handed to a customer. The district court dismissed Cockram's claim for false light invasion of privacy and granted summary judgment in favor of Genesco on her defamation claim. Cockram now appeals, and we affirm the dismissal of the false light claim and reverse and remand the defamation claim.

I. Background

On October 17, 2008, in the course of her duties at a Journeys retail store owned by Genesco, Cockram assisted Keith Slater, an African-American, with a merchandise return. For efficiency in processing the return, Cockram entered a generic phone number, (913) 555–5555, into the store register. Unbeknownst to Cockram, Richard Hamill, a former employee whom Journeys had fired prior to this incident, had inserted into a store-level database a racial slur as one of the names associated with the phone number Cockram entered. Cockram unwittingly selected the entry with the racial slur from the list of names associated with the phone number. She then printed a return receipt that included the racial slur, signed it without reading it, and handed it to Slater.

The next day, Slater, accompanied by members of his family, returned to Journeys with the return receipt. Slater's sister demanded Cockram's name, and Cockram complied. Slater and his family were outraged about the incident and told people in and near Journeys about what had happened, resulting in what Cockram described as a "riot."

On October 20, Genesco fired Cockram. In response to inquiries about the incident, Genesco provided a statement ("first statement") on October 21, 2008, reading:

> While we are continuing to investigate this incident, it now appears that an employee in one of our stores entered highly inappropriate statements in a form used to process a merchandise return. Needless to say, such an act was not authorized by Journeys, and will not be tolerated. This employee has been terminated.
>
> At Journeys, we pride ourselves on valuing and respecting every customer. We are shocked and sickened that a former associate could be responsible for an act so out of keeping with our culture and our values. We profoundly regret this incident.

Multiple news stories regarding the incident quoted the first statement, and some people posting comments to the online versions of those stories labeled as racist the involved employee. Additionally, after Genesco released the statement, Cockram received numerous messages and calls from people who called her a racist, blamed her for the racial slur, and threatened her. These accusations and threats made Cockram fearful, and she moved out of her apartment and temporarily placed her young child with her parents.

Cockram sued Genesco for defamation and false light invasion of privacy based on the content of the first statement . . . .

II. Discussion

Our jurisdiction in this case is based on diversity of citizenship, and the parties agree that Missouri law governs. . . .

A. Defamation

In a defamation action, a plaintiff must establish: "1) publication, 2) of a defamatory statement, 3) that identifies the plaintiff, 4) that is false, 5) that is published with the requisite degree of fault, and 6) damages the plaintiff's reputation." *Missouri ex rel. BP Prods. N. Am. Inc. v. Ross*, 163 S.W.3d 922, 929 (Mo. 2005). In seeking summary judgment, Genesco argued that Cockram could not establish that the statements were false, that Genesco published them with the requisite degree of fault, and that Cockram's reputation was damaged. . . .

1. Falsity of the Statements

We must determine whether the "gist" or "sting" of the statements was false. *See Turnbull v. Herald Co.*, 459 S.W.2d 516, 519 (Mo. Ct. App. 1970). Under Missouri law, a statement is not considered "false" for purposes of defamation simply because it contains an erroneous fact. *Thurston v. Ballinger*, 884 S.W.2d 22, 26 (Mo. Ct. App. 1994). Rather, if a statement is essentially true, such that its divergence from the truth "would have no different effect on the reader's mind than that produced by the literal truth," the statement is not actionable in defamation. *See id.*

As a preliminary matter, we note that counsel for Genesco conceded at oral argument that the first statement could be read as referring to Cockram and that Genesco knew prior to issuing the first statement that Cockram's name had appeared in news reports. Moreover, Roger Sisson, an officer at Genesco, agreed during his deposition that the words "[t]his employee has been terminated" in the first statement referred to Cockram. Thus, there is no real dispute that the reference to an "employee" in the first statement could be interpreted as referring to Cockram.

Genesco argues that the first statement was truthful as a matter of law because (1) Cockram did enter a racial slur into a form by selecting it from a list of names, and (2) her action was not authorized because she used a generic phone number, rather than entering Slater's actual information into the register as required by Genesco policy. We are not persuaded. When the entirety of the first statement is considered in the light most favorable to Cockram, it can be read as asserting that Cockram intentionally directed a racial slur at Slater, not just that she violated company policy requiring the entry of a customer's actual phone number to generate a return receipt. In other words, the first statement did not necessarily assert that Cockram was terminated merely because she violated company policy by entering a generic phone number into the register and generating a return receipt containing a racial slur without being conscious of the offensive output. It is not "[n]eedless to say" that Genesco would not authorize entering a generic phone number and blindly selecting a name entry in order to expedite a customer's return. And a reasonable jury may not consider such a practice by itself to be so out of line with Genesco's culture and values as to make Genesco "shocked and sickened." Instead, the use of these phrases in Genesco's statement reasonably could be read to imply that Cockram intentionally communicated the racial slur. Because Cockram denies that she intentionally produced a return receipt with a racial slur, and produced evidence supporting this assertion, a genuine issue of material fact exists as to whether the gist of the first statement was true. Thus, the district court erred by determining as a matter of law that the first statement was substantially true. . . .[3]

2. Requisite Degree of Fault

Genesco argues that Cockram did not present sufficient evidence that Genesco published the relevant statements with actual malice, "that is, with knowledge that the statements were false, or with a reckless disregard as to whether they were true or false," which is the applicable standard if Cockram was a limited-purpose public figure. *See Warner v. Kan. City Star Co.,* 726 S.W.2d 384, 385 (Mo. Ct. App. 1987). However, if Cockram was simply a private figure, she only needs to show negligence on the part of Genesco, even if Genesco's statement is considered to relate to an issue of "public concern or interest." *See Englezos v. Newspress & Gazette Co.,* 980 S.W.2d 25, 30-31 (Mo. Ct. App. 1998). Thus, we must decide whether Cockram was a limited-purpose public figure or, as Cockram contends, a private figure.

In explaining the rationale for the differing burdens borne by public figures and private figures in defamation suits, the Supreme Court noted that public figures are more likely to have access to the media to minimize a defamatory statement's "adverse impact on reputation," and, more importantly, public figures typically "thrust themselves to the forefront of particular public controversies in order to influence the resolution of the issues involved," thus "invit[ing] attention and comment." *Gertz v. Robert Welch, Inc.,* 418 U.S. 323, 344-45 (1974). The Court did state, however, that, "[h]ypothetically, it may be possible for someone to become a public figure through no purposeful action of his own, but the instances of truly involuntary public figures must be exceedingly rare." A limited-purpose public figure "is defined as one who 'voluntarily injects himself or is drawn into a particular public controversy and thereby becomes a public figure for a limited range of issues.'" *Stepnes v. Ritschel,* 663 F.3d 952, 963 (8th Cir. 2011) (quoting *Gertz*). . . . Here, Cockram entered a generic phone number into the register that resulted in a racial slur appearing on a return receipt and found herself in the middle of a public controversy. She did not "voluntarily inject" herself into a preexisting controversy, nor did she knowingly produce the racial slur that initiated the controversy. It was only after the controversy arose and Genesco blamed Cockram for the racial slur by issuing the first statement that Cockram responded to media inquiries in an attempt to salvage her reputation. *See Hutchinson v. Proxmire,* 443 U.S. 111, 134-35 (1979) (stating that the defendant's argument that the plaintiff was a limited-purpose public figure based on the plaintiff's access to the media was unavailing where, *inter alia,* the plaintiff's access to the media occurred after the alleged libel). When Cockram ultimately did agree to be interviewed, she insisted that her name not be used, thus indicating an intent to defend her reputation among those who knew that she was the subject of the reports while avoiding any additional exposure among those unaware of her involvement in the

---

3. Because of our conclusion that there is a genuine issue of material fact as to whether Genesco's statements were false, we do not address "whether 'truth' is an affirmative defense to be proved by defendant, or 'falsity' is an element of the cause of action to be proved by plaintiff." *See Kenney v. Wal–Mart Stores, Inc.,* 100 S.W.3d 809, 814 n.2 (Mo. 2003).

incident, And, even though Cockram succeeded in gaining some access to the media, the more important point is that she did not voluntarily place herself at the center of controversy, but merely found herself there. Thus, we conclude that Cockram was a private figure, not a limited purpose public figure. Because private figures need only show negligence to recover for defamation, and Genesco does not argue that Cockram failed to produce sufficient evidence of negligence, Genesco's argument for affirmance based on the "requisite degree of fault" element fails,

3. Damages to Cockram's reputation

Under Missouri law, "proof of actual reputational harm is an absolute prerequisite in a defamation action." *Kenney v. Wal–Mart Stores, Inc.*, 100 S.W.3d 809, 817 (Mo. 2003). Because "rules of *per se* and *per quod*" defamation do not apply in Missouri, a plaintiff must always prove actual damages. *Id.* "To demonstrate actual damages [in Missouri], plaintiffs must show that defamatory statements caused a quantifiable professional or personal injury, such as interference with job performance, psychological or emotional distress, or depression." *Arthaud v. Mut. of Omaha Ins. Co.*, 170 F.3d 860, 862 (8th Cir.1999). . . .

Genesco argues that it is entitled to summary judgment because Cockram "failed to present any evidence that Genesco's statements caused her reputational damage and cannot differentiate between damages that she allegedly sustained as a result of Genesco's statements and damages resulting from the media's coverage of the receipt incident before Genesco published any statements." When the facts are viewed in the light most favorable to Cockram and all reasonable inferences are made in her favor, the evidence is sufficient to allow a reasonable jury to find actual reputational harm flowing from Genesco's statements.

Cockram argues that there are multiple pieces of evidence indicating that her reputation was harmed by Genesco's statements. She stated that "[p]eople posting comments to media stories carrying Genesco's statement would call me racist." For example, one person writing a comment in response to an online article containing Genesco's first statement said that a "racist teenager entered the words on their [sic] own" and was "rightfully fired." Cockram also received numerous messages containing threats and accusations of racism after Genesco released the first statement. Cockram claims that these "accusations and threats made [her] afraid and [she] moved out of [her] apartment and placed [her] child with [her] parents temporarily." Cockram's father confirmed that Cockram was so concerned about the threats that she asked him to allow her daughter to live with him for a period. Furthermore, Cockram's father stated that his family's friends and acquaintances contacted him and questioned whether Cockram was racist after the stories with Genesco's statements appeared. Thus, we cannot say as a matter of law that Cockram cannot show actual reputational harm.[4] . . .

[As for the argument that Cockram cannot differentiate the reputational harm caused by her employer as compared to other news source,] comments to online news stories containing portions of Genesco's first statement provide evidence that some

---

4. Although we do not assume damages, one certainly can suffer severe reputational harm if accused of a racist act.

readers viewed Cockram as a racist after reading Genesco's statement. Additionally, . . . Cockram did not suggest that Genesco's statements placing blame on her inflicted the "same kind of injury" as the generic news stories covering the incident. Indeed, a news story that includes Genesco's statement placing blame on Cockram is likely to cause a greater degree of harm to reputation than one simply providing general information about the incident. Finally, Cockram's receipt of personal threats and messages accusing her of racism *after* Genesco released its statements (where Genesco points to no instances in the record of Cockram receiving such personal messages before Genesco's first statement despite three prior days of news coverage) also supports her causation argument. Under these circumstances, a reasonable jury could conclude that at least some of the reputational harm Cockram suffered resulted from Genesco's statements blaming her for using the racial slur as opposed to news stories that did not mention Genesco's statements. Accordingly, we cannot say that a properly instructed jury will be unable to address reasonably the question of causation. Therefore, we decline to affirm on this ground.

In sum, Cockram is a private figure and a reasonable jury could conclude that Genesco's statements were false, that they harmed Cockram's reputation, and that this harm was distinguishable from any harm flowing from the generic news stories. Hence, the district court erred by granting summary judgment to Genesco on Cockram's defamation claim.

NOTES

1. *The Meaning of "Defamatory."* The court has little problem with finding the "gist" or "sting" of the defendant's statements to be that plaintiff was a racist and that such an accusation would be defamatory. But not every negative false statement concerning an individual gives rise to a defamation claim. "Defamation" requires something more serious. Statements accusing the plaintiff of a crime are obviously defamatory. *See Forster v. W. Dakota Veterinary Clinic, Inc.*, 689 N.W.2d 366 (N.D. 2004). But what of other derogatory statements? In the employment context, much less damning comments may also be actionable. *See Government Micro Resources, Inc. v. Jackson*, 624 S.E.2d 63 (Va. 2006) (holding that statements suggesting that plaintiff's incompetence had caused his employer to lose millions of dollars was defamatory).

Even vaguer statements challenging an employee's competence have been found to be defamatory. In *Falls v. Sporting News Publishing Co.*, 834 F.2d 611, 613-15 (6th Cir. 1987), plaintiff was a columnist for a newspaper. He successfully established defamation based on his editor's comment, made in response to a reader's inquiry about the discontinuance of plaintiff's column: "I know Joe brightened a lot of hearts with his column through the years but we felt it was time to make a change, with more energetic columnists who attend more events and are closer to today's sports scene." Similarly defamatory was a statement by another Sporting News official: "Those who seem to have reached maturity and are on the downswing are giving way to up-and-coming young writers who we think deserve a chance."

The test of whether a statement is defamatory, according to section 559 of the Restatement (Second) of Torts, is whether it "tends so to harm the reputation of another as to lower him in the estimation of the community or to deter third persons from associating or dealing with him." The "community" includes any "substantial and respectable minority of members of the community." It is not enough, however, if the statement "offends some individual or individuals with views sufficiently peculiar to regard as derogatory what the vast majority of persons regard as innocent." §559 cmt. e. Who was the "community" in *Falls*? In the employment context, would not any statement explaining a former employee's deficiencies in the job risk being sufficiently defamatory to be actionable? *See Hogan v. Winder*, 762 F.3d 1096 (10th Cir. 2014) (a vague reference to "performance issues" is "simply too nonspecific to sustain a defamatory meaning").

2. *Fact versus Opinion*. Whether the statement is "fact" or "opinion" will determine whether a defamatory statement is actionable. As the Employment Restatement says, "[a]n opinion or prediction alone cannot be actionable. Neither is subject to verification when made." §6.01 cmt. e. How, then, did the *Falls* court find the at-issue statements actionable? Consistent with the Restatement, which says that "[a]n employer's opinion . . . may be actionable if it false implies that there is a factual basis but does not disclose it," *id*. *Falls* explained:

> [Looking at the phrase "reached maturity and on the downswing,"] whether "a person has 'reached maturity' may be a statement of fact, and insofar as plaintiff is concerned [57 years old], it could not be false." It also might be viewed as a derogatory opinion, a mild form of ridicule, but it reasonably could not be regarded as defamatory. However, the statement that plaintiff was "on the downswing" is capable of bearing a defamatory meaning since a jury could reasonably find that it implied that Waters knew undisclosed facts that would justify such an opinion—for example, that plaintiff's writing and reasoning abilities had deteriorated, or that the quality of his work had declined to the point that others had to rewrite or cover for him. . . .
>
> Similarly, Barnidge's [the editor] letter can be construed, by negative implication, as an expression of opinion that plaintiff was inferior to his replacements because he was less energetic than other columnists, attended fewer events, and was not as close as they to the current sports scene. This comment creates a reasonable inference that it is justified by the existence of undisclosed facts, such as, for example, that plaintiff did not work hard or he was prevented by his physical condition from exerting himself; that he did not frequently attend sports events to obtain first-hand knowledge of the events reported in his sports columns; and that he was out-of-touch with current sports personalities, an outsider who lacked good "sources." Obviously, these kinds of undisclosed facts could be defamatory.

834 F.2d at 616. Courts have had great difficulty formulating standards for distinguishing fact from opinion. Are you satisfied with the *Falls* resolution? *See also Thomas v. United Steelworkers Local 1938*, 743 F.3d 1134, 1142-43 (8th Cir. 2014) (holding that, while statement such as "Thomas is a prick" merely expressed the speaker's subjective opinion, other statements about the number of complaints supposedly received about plaintiff's harassing behavior were capable of being proven false even if they included adjectives rather than specific acts). *See generally* John Bruce Lewis & Gregory V. Mersol, *Opinion and Rhetorical Hyperbole in Workplace Defamation Actions: The Continuing Quest for Meaningful Standards*, 52 DePaul L. Rev. 19 (2002).

3. *Truth as a Defense*. Defamation is sometimes confused with falsehood. The Restatement of Employment Law speaks in terms of actionable statements "being false and defamatory." §6.01. In other words, a statement can be both defamatory and true, although there can be no liability for true statements. A plaintiff was traditionally not required to prove that a defamatory statement was false, but merely to allege falsity, in order to make out a prima facie case of defamation. The burden then fell on the defendant to establish the truth of the statement. While many states continue to so allocate the burdens, Supreme Court decisions raise questions about the constitutionality of this approach. The argument is that the First Amendment requires, as a prerequisite to liability, proof that the defendant is at fault with respect to the falsity of a communication. *See Philadelphia Newspapers, Inc. v. Hepps*, 475 U.S. 767, 776 (1986); *BE&K Construction Co. v. NLRB*, 536 U.S. 516 (2002). *See generally* RESTATEMENT (SECOND) OF TORTS §581A cmts. a, b (1977). Note the *Cockram* court's dodging this issue in footnote 3.

   Cockram also makes clear that what might be called "technical truth" will not necessarily avoid liability. Although the statements made by the defendant may have been technically true, the message they conveyed—that plaintiff knowingly printed a racist receipt—were not. Illustration 10 of the new Restatement makes the point by positing a statement that a worker was discharged for "gross insubordination." It explains: "It is true that M charged E with "gross insubordination" at the time of his discharge. If the implied underlying false fact—that E was grossly insubordinate— damages E's reputation, the true statement that M charged E with gross insubordination is not a defense."

   4. *Publication and Self-Publication.* "Publication" is a term of art in defamation. It consists merely of "communication [of defamatory matter] intentionally or by a negligent act to one other than the person defamed." RESTATEMENT (SECOND) OF TORTS §577 (1977). In *Cockram* there was no dispute about publication. In *Falls*, some of the defamation was published in the more intuitive meaning of the word: It had been printed in a newspaper.

   Suppose, however, that someone in Genesco had made similar statements about Cockram to another Genesco employee, perhaps the director of Human Resources. Comment i of Restatement §577 states that "[t]he communication within the scope of his employment by one agent to another agent of the same principal" is a publication. Thus, intracorporate communications will constitute publication under the Restatement of Torts. *See also* RESTATEMENT OF EMPLOYMENT LAW §6.01(b)(2) (liability for publication "within the employer's organization"); *Trail v. Boys & Girls Clubs of Northwest Ind.*, 845 N.E.2d 130, 136 (Ind. 2006) (employee evaluations communicated intracompany to management personnel are published for purposes of defamation); *Taggart v. Drake Univ.*, 549 N.W.2d 796 (Iowa 1996) (communications between corporate supervisors may be subject to a qualified privilege, but they are published). *But see Halsell v. Kimberly-Clark Corp.*, 683 F.2d 285, 288-89 (8th Cir. 1982) ("Until the defamatory statement is communicated outside the corporate sphere or internal organization, it has not been published.").

   A few courts have even found the defendant responsible when the plaintiff himself republishes the defamation under the "compulsory self-publication" doctrine. *See, e.g., Lewis v. Equitable Life Assurance Soc'y*, 389 N.W.2d 876 (Minn. 1986). *But see Emery v. Northeast Ill. Reg'l Commuter R.R. Corp.*, 880 N.E.2d 1002, 1011-12 (Ill. App. Ct. 2007) (rejecting the compulsory self-publication doctrine as a minority rule in only four states). Where this doctrine exists, an employee's revealing the reasons for his former employer's adverse action against him in order, say, to obtain a new position, may satisfy the publication requirement. *See generally* Markita D. Cooper, *Between a Rock and a Hard Case: Time for a New Doctrine of Compelled Self-Publication*, 72 NOTRE DAME L. REV. 373 (1997). The Restatement of Employment Law would recognize a modified version of the doctrine, which would apply only if the employer either tells the worker that it "intends to communicate substantially the same message to third parties" or, refuses an employee's request for a promise that it will not be so communicated. §6.01. cmt. d.

5. *Actions as Statements.* A few cases have considered whether actions can be treated as statements for defamation purposes, which is especially important in the employment context. For example, in *Tyler v. Macks Stores of N.C. Inc.*, 272 S.E.2d 633 (S.C. 1980), an employee was required to take a polygraph and soon afterward was discharged. He argued that this led other employees and others to believe that his discharge was based on some wrongful activity and that "this insinuation and inference of wrongdoing can amount to the publication of defamatory matter." The court agreed. Defamation may be "by actions or conduct as well as by word" and "need not be accomplished in a direct manner. To render the defamatory statement actionable, it is not necessary that the false charge be made in a direct, open and positive manner. A mere insinuation is as actionable as a positive assertion if it is false and malicious and the meaning is plain." *Id.* at 634. However, mere silence has been held not actionable even when it was alleged that the natural inference was defamatory. *See Trail v. Boys & Girls Clubs of Northwest Ind.*, 845 N.E.2d 130, 137 (Ind. 2006) If defamation may be accomplished through actions as well as through words, is the act of sending security guards to escort a fired employee from the building defamatory? Does it matter whether this is standard practice in cases of suspension or discharge? *See Phelan v. May Dep't Stores Co.* 819 N.E.2d 550 (Mass. 2004) (employer's conduct during investigation of potential theft too ambiguous to be actionable by employee). The Employment Restatement agrees §6.01, cmt. f., Ills. 11 and 12.

6. *Employer Fault.* The *Cockram* court makes clear that there are varying degrees of fault necessary for actionable defamation. The lowest standard is for "private figures," who need prove only negligence. Public figures, even "limited purpose public figures," have to prove the defendant published the defamation with "knowledge that the statements were false, or with a reckless disregard as to whether they were true or false." In the principal case, the court concluded that Cockram was a private figure, which was probably crucial to her success. Note that, as we will discuss below, overcoming one of the various "qualified privilege" protections ordinarily will require plaintiffs who are private figures to prove some kind of fault greater than negligence. In other words, these privilege protections heighten the fault standard.

7. *Counseling the Employer.* What can an employer do to protect against defamation actions? Obviously, care should be taken to ensure that discharges are based on proven violations. Truth will avoid liability. Even after careful investigation, however, erroneous judgments will sometimes be made. Would you advise an employer not to tell employees the reason they are being discharged? Informing only the employee would not usually be actionable because of the publication requirement—but recall the compelled self-publication doctrine. One commentator recommends regularly scheduled, objective evaluations, accessible only by those with a need to see them, and investigation of possible employee misconduct, preferably by a designated person to ensure consistency. When discharge is necessary, information should be released only to those with a "need to know." Reference inquiries from prospective new employers should be directed to a central office, such as human resources, and the information disclosed should be limited to "dates of employment, positions held, and wage/salary information," or "other verifiable and objective facts. Avoid giving subjective or emotional evaluations." Thomas A. Jacobson, *Avoiding Claims of Defamation in the*

Workplace, 72 N. DAK. L. REV. 247, 264-65 (1996). What do you think of this advice? Might adopting such practices create other legal risks or costs for the employer?

8. *Mishandling Matters.* For a good example of how *not* to handle a reference request, consider *Matthews v. Wis. Energy Corp.*, 534 F.3d 547, 553-54 (7th Cir. 2008), which is all the more striking because a lawyer caused the problem. The case arose from settlement of a discrimination suit. The employer's in-house attorney, English, recited the terms regarding references in open court, which required the company to follow its policy of limited disclosure, "what you call name, rank, and serial number." That is, the company would "confirm people worked there, the dates of employment, and their position or at least their last position." Later, Matthews hired Schwartz to help him find employment, and Schwartz ended up talking to English on the phone. In that conversation, she discussed far more than name, rank, and serial number, and, according to Schwartz, disclosed his litigation history and displayed an "obvious sense of distrust" of Matthews. The Seventh Circuit found the attorney's comments actionable as a breach of the settlement agreement. Because this was not a defamation suit, the plaintiff would be limited to contract damages rather than the lucrative damages available under tort law.

9. *Overly Positive Recommendations.* Another reason for an employer to adopt a policy limiting the information that will be provided about present or former employees is to limit liability to third parties when an employment reference is too favorable. This can arise when the employee subsequently engages in misconduct upon being hired by the new employer. While liability in such situations is rare, it is not unknown and is most common in cases involving affirmative misrepresentations, rather than mere nondisclosure. *See, e.g., Kadlec Med. Ctr. v. Lakeview Anesthesia Assocs.*, 527 F.3d 412 (5th Cir. 2008) (no duty for a hospital to disclose doctor's narcotic addiction to another hospital when its letter merely confirmed dates of work; however, glowing letters from a practice group to second hospital were actionable because they were misleading); *Randi W. v. Muroc Joint Unified School Dist.*, 929 P.2d 582, 584 (Cal. 1997) (although failing to disclose negative information is not usually actionable, liability may be imposed if the recommendation letter "amounts to an *affirmative* misrepresentation presenting a foreseeable and substantial risk of physical harm to a third person"). In an era of #MeToo, employers might often be well advised to avoid such misleading statements where serious misconduct has occurred.

10. *Libel and Slander.* To this point, we have spoken of "defamation" without distinguishing the old common-law categories of libel and slander. For most purposes, these categories are no longer important, but they retain some vitality in some jurisdictions. Libel is a defamation embodied in a permanent form, such as a letter or a newspaper article, or on the Internet. According to the Restatement (Second) of Torts §568A, libel in the modern world also includes "[b]roadcasting of defamatory matter by means of radio or television . . . whether or not it is read from a manuscript." The "downswing" statement in *Falls* was libel. Slander is characterized by impermanence and includes, therefore, unrecorded spoken words as well as gestures. The significance of the distinction lies in whether the plaintiff must prove "special damages"—actual provable damages such as loss of employment—in order to sustain an action. *See* RESTATEMENT (SECOND) OF TORTS §75 cmt. b (1977). Libel, because its permanence rendered it more dangerous, was traditionally actionable without such proof. However, certain kinds of slander (slander "per se") could also be established without showing special damages. And such per se slander included that relating to a person's trade or profession. *See Wilcox v. Newark Val. Cent. School Dist.*, 904

N.Y.S.2d 523, 527 (3d Dep't 2010). As a result, the distinction between libel and slander will not often be significant in defamation cases in the employment setting, even if it retains some significance in other contexts in some jurisdictions.

11. *Reconsidering Perverse Incentives.* Potential liability for defamation discourages providing references to prospective employers. As Note 7 suggests, many employers have adopted policies regarding employment references, under which supervisors and Human Resources officers provide minimal information. Adherence to such policies will limit defamation exposure and the possible liability for overly positive recommendations. Of course, it also limits the extent to which any potential employer can be sure about the work history and habits of an applicant. In extreme cases, the failure to provide information may result in the hiring of a sexual predator or a thief. For that reason, there have been repeated calls for statutory immunity for employment references, and most states have enacted job reference immunity statutes, although the provisions vary widely, and scholars do not believe that such laws have meaningfully changed employer unwillingness to provide references. *See generally* Matthew W. Finkin & Kenneth G. Dau-Schmidt, *Solving the Employee Reference Problem: Lessons from the German Experience*, 57 Am. J. Comp. L. 387 (2009); Markita D. Cooper, *Job Reference Immunity Statutes: Prevalent But Irrelevant*, 11 Cornell J.L. & Pub. Pol'y 1 (2001); J. Hoult Verkerke, *Legal Regulation of Employment Reference Practices*, 65 U. Chi. L. Rev. 115, 199 (1998). Reconsider the need for such statutes after you have read the next principal case, which explores the concept of privilege. Recently, hiring firms have been using technology to avoid the problems posed by the refusals of most employers to provide references. Using a service called "Reference Search" on LinkedIn (available only to premium account holders) to identify former co-workers, the employers have been contacting such persons to obtain information about applicants. Natasha Singer, *Funny, They Don't Look Like My References*, N.Y. Times, Nov. 9, 2014, p. BU4. Think about the legal implications of that practice.

12. *Consenting to Being Defamed.* Employers seem to be increasingly asking applicants for consent to inquire of former employees and presumably using such consent to obtain information that might not otherwise be provided. The extent to which consent may operate to absolve a speaker of liability is unclear. *See* Alex B. Long, *The Forgotten Role of Consent in Defamation and Employment Reference Cases*, 66 Fla. L. Rev. 719 (2014).

13. *And Then There's False Light.* The *Cockram* court rejected the plaintiff's "false light" claim: The Missouri cases did not recognize that tort where the essence of the allegation was defamation. As this suggests, defamation and false light liability overlap, but in theory at least, the two torts protect different interests: Defamation protects reputation, while false light protects privacy, although the viability of this tort is questionable. *See* Chapter 6.

≡≡≡ *Shannon v. Taylor AMC/Jeep, Inc.*
≡≡≡ *425 N.W.2d 165 (Mich. Ct. App. 1988)*

McDonald, J.

. . . Plaintiff worked for Taylor for approximately twelve years, the last eight years as parts manager. Plaintiff's employment was terminated in June, 1982, for his alleged involvement with stolen parts.

During his employment as parts manager, one of the employees under plaintiff's supervision was Laurie Cherup. Around the beginning of 1982, plaintiff had to discipline Cherup and eventually fire her. Rick Howard, the AMC branch manager responsible for Taylor AMC, reinstated Cherup and told plaintiff to leave her alone. Howard and Cherup were involved in a physical relationship in late 1981 or early 1982. Following plaintiff's termination, Cherup became the new parts manager. Cherup was overheard on several occasions telling customers over the phone that plaintiff was no longer parts manager because plaintiff had "gotten caught stealing," and that plaintiff was fired "for being involved in theft of parts."

Plaintiff testified that he was not involved with stolen parts for profit or personal gain, but was working with Taylor Police Officer James Black in an attempt to set up persons attempting to sell stolen parts to Taylor. On June 15, 1982, plaintiff was contacted on the phone and asked if he wanted to buy a Jeep hardtop. The phone call made plaintiff suspicious that the hardtop was stolen, so plaintiff called Black, a personal friend, for advice. Black advised plaintiff that the police would need "hard evidence" such as names and driver's license numbers of the suspects. Plaintiff purchased two hardtops which he suspected to be stolen, and placed them in the back of the parts department. When another Taylor employee indicated that a customer was interested in purchasing one of the hardtops, plaintiff responded that they were not for sale as he had reason to believe the hardtops were stolen. Plaintiff was fired the same day Black was allegedly going to write up a report on the stolen goods. . . .

[This appeal questions the propriety of the verdict of no cause of action on the slander claim. The court held that the trial judge erred in instructing the jury on qualified privilege and actual malice.]

A communication is defamatory if it tends to lower an individual's reputation in the community or deter third persons from associating or dealing with him. *Swenson-Davis v. Martel*, 354 N.W.2d 288 (Mich. App. 1984). Slander per se is found where the words spoken are false and malicious and are injurious to a person in his or her profession or employment. *Swenson-Davis.*

Here, the trial court found that Cherup's statements about plaintiff to defendant's customers were protected from action by a qualified privilege. . . . [I]n order to have a qualified privilege, the communication must be: (1) bona fide; (2) made by a party who has an interest, or a duty to communicate the subject matter; and (3) made to a party who has a corresponding interest or duty.

Although in the instant case neither party addresses the first prerequisite, the "bona fide" nature of the communication, we question whether Cherup's statements were bona fide. Not only had plaintiff previously fired Cherup, but there was testimony indicating that another employee overheard a conversation between Cherup, Howard and two others regarding possible ways in which to "get rid of" plaintiff, and wherein Howard allegedly suggested that they "link" plaintiff with some stolen parts.

Nonetheless, even if the statements were bona fide, we find that they do not meet the remaining two requirements. The problem with determining if a qualified privilege applies is that privilege varies with the situation; it is not a constant. Defendant Taylor contends that the particular facts of this situation call for the application of qualified privilege, arguing that it had a duty to inform customers that the parts manager (plaintiff) had been fired for purchasing stolen parts. Taylor asserts that if the customers were not presently told and found out years later that stolen parts were purchased from Taylor, they would cease to do business with the dealership. In

Taylor's opinion, the potential detrimental effect on customer relations justifies the application of qualified privilege to the statements. We disagree.

For defendant's argument to have merit, and before defendant could acquire an interest in telling customers why plaintiff was fired, a determination should have been made as to whether stolen goods were actually sold to customers. Taylor knew that plaintiff had possession of the Jeep hardtops. There was no reason to believe that any stolen goods ended up in customers' hands. Therefore, there was no qualified privilege to tell customers that plaintiff was fired because he dealt with stolen parts. Thus, absent evidence that stolen parts had been passed along to customers, plaintiff's good name should have been protected by not allowing an employee to tell customers why plaintiff was fired. . . .

Furthermore, we find no corresponding interest or duty to hear the communication on the part of the customers. In *Merritt v. Detroit Memorial Hospital*, 265 N.W.2d 124 (Mich. App. 1978), this Court stated that an employer has a qualified privilege to tell those of its employees responsible for hiring and firing of accusations of employee misconduct. However, an employer cannot tell all employees why someone was fired in order to quiet rumors or restore morale. *Sias v. General Motors Corp.*, 127 N.W.2d 357 (Mich. 1964). In the instant case Taylor does not allege or offer proof that any customer received stolen goods purchased from plaintiff. If Taylor had a good faith belief that stolen auto parts had been sold to a particular customer, the customer may have had an interest, but that is not the situation in the instant case. Here, the customer's interest is like the employees' interest in *Sias*: just a general interest or curiosity in finding out why a former employee was fired.

The trial court erred in instructing the jury that a qualified privilege existed. Absent the existence of a qualified privilege, plaintiff would not have been required to prove actual malice. We cannot say that the instructional error was harmless beyond a reasonable doubt and therefore reverse for a new trial.

NOTES

1. *Underpinnings of the Privilege.* As *Shannon* indicates, defamatory information communicated in the ordinary course of the employment relationship frequently will be subject to a qualified privilege. The law recognizes a public policy interest in frank and open communication when the speaker has a duty to speak or an interest in speaking. In the employment context, this includes employment references and communications between employers and employees, employees complaining to supervisors, supervisors evaluating and reviewing employees' work product, and employers informing employees of the reason for disciplinary action. It may also include customers of the business. *See* RESTATEMENT (SECOND) OF TORTS §§594-96 (1977).

In *Shannon*, the court found that no privilege existed to inform customers: The customers had no interest in the matter because there was no claim plaintiff had been selling stolen goods to them. In contrast, *Grice v. FedEx Ground Package Sys.*, 925 So. 2d 907, 912 (Miss. Ct. App. 2006), dealt with statements to co-workers and contractors that plaintiff had tuberculosis. These were qualifiedly privileged because the individuals informed "had a genuine interest in knowing whether a co-worker with whom they were in frequent contact had a highly contagious disease." Even if there were no privilege to tell customers in *Shannon*, there may have been a privilege as to internal communications. This suggests the highly contextual nature of conditional privileges.

2. *Qualified vs. Absolute Privileges.* Privileges may be absolute or qualified. An absolute privilege confers immunity from liability regardless of motive. For example, while communication of a reason for discharge to courts or agencies, such as an unemployment compensation board, clearly constitutes publication, that communication serves the needs of a judicial or quasi-judicial process and therefore is absolutely privileged. In *Fulghum v. United Parcel Service, Inc.*, 378 N.W.2d 472 (Mich. 1985), the court held that accusations of dishonesty made during the course of the grievance procedure under a collective bargaining agreement are accorded an absolute privilege because potential defamation liability would "directly and severely impair the functioning of the agreed-upon grievance procedure. . . ." *See also Rosenberg v. Metlife, Inc.*, 866 N.E.2d 439 (N.Y. 2007) (statements made in brokerage's U-5 filing with NASD were absolutely privileged). *But see Galarneau v. Merrill Lynch, Pierce, Fenner & Smith Inc.*, 504 F.3d 189 (1st Cir. 2007) (U-5 filings were only conditionally privileged).

Most privileges, however, are not absolute, but rather are qualified in that false statements made with actual malice are not privileged even if made in what ordinarily would be a privileged context. A qualified privilege obviously reflects a lower public interest in free communication. The burden lies with the defendant to establish that the defamation is subject to a qualified privilege, but such a privilege may be lost (i.e., exceeded) in a variety of ways. For example, §6.02(a) of the Restatement of Employment Law provides:

> [A]n employer has a privilege to publish statements about an employee to
> (1) prospective employers and employment agencies,
> (2) public or private regulatory or licensing authorities, and
> (3) the employer's own employees and agents.

However, §6.02(b) is "denie[s]" the privilege when the employer "either (i) knows [the statement] is false or acts with reckless disregard of its truth or falsity, or (ii) knows or should know that neither the employer nor the recipient has a legitimate interest in the recipient receiving the statement."

3. *Malice and the Privilege.* The first prong of abuse of privilege requires showing that the employer made the defamatory statements with knowledge of their falsity or without regard to whether they were true. This is sometimes referred to as "actual malice." Recall that, as in *Cockram*, defamation may ordinarily be established by demonstrating mere negligence, but actual malice requires knowledge of falsity or at least recklessness. Some courts also find malice when the speaker was actuated by improper motives, regardless of whether she believed her statements to be true. Is that what the *Shannon* court had in mind when it questioned whether Cherup's statements were "bona fide"? What else could it have meant? *See Gambardella v. Apple Health Care, Inc.*, 969 A.2d 736 (Conn. 2009) (qualified privilege may be lost when there is "'malice in fact,' namely, the publication of a false statement with bad faith or improper motive"). In general, the privilege seeks to balance interests in communicating against the possible damage to the plaintiff's reputation by permitting the defendant to speak if she honestly and reasonably believes the information is true, but not if she knows the information is false or is reckless as to that possibility.

In *Soto-Lebron v. Fed. Express Corp.*, 538 F.3d 45 (1st Cir. 2008), the court found that circulation of written statements within the corporation to the effect that plaintiff had shipped cocaine were actionable. The statements were published, although only circulated internally, and the conditional privilege was properly found to have been exceeded: "[O]nce FedEx was on notice that the drug allegations were questionable, it was obligated to either stop repeating them or adequately investigate them. It did neither." 538 F.3d at 64; *cf. Dugan v. Mittal Steel USA, Inc.*, 929 N.E.2d 184, 189 (Ind. 2010) (qualified privilege for intracompany communications about theft of company property applies not only to statements made on personal knowledge but also to reporting information received from others).

4. *Exceeding the Privilege.* The other way to "abuse" the privilege is for the employer to make the defamatory statements to a wider audience than necessary. How these doctrines interact can be seen by revisiting *Cockram*. As made, the statements would not have been subject to the Restatement's formulation of a qualified privilege because they were made to the broader community, not merely to coworkers. But had similar statements been made to Genesco's own employees, a qualified privilege would attach. At that point the plaintiff would have to show that the defendant abused the privilege. It could have done so by showing knowing falsity or reckless disregard (not just the negligence proved in the case itself). Failing that, the plaintiff could have prevailed only by showing that some of the employees to whom it was made had no legitimate interest in the information. *See also Thomas v. United Steelworkers Local 1938*, 743 F.3d 1134, 1144 (8th Cir. 2014) (no qualified privilege where the statements were not "based upon reasonable or probable cause" because of a failure to investigate supposed complaints).

5. *Damages.* Prevailing plaintiffs in defamation actions are entitled to compensatory damages, damages for emotional distress, and potentially punitive damages. The latter forms of damages are important because it may be difficult for an at-will employee to prove compensatory damages. In both *Falls* and *Shannon*, for example, the loss of the plaintiffs' jobs was separate from the defamation—and therefore lost salary and benefits were not caused by the defamation. In *Soto-Lebron*, the court vacated the damages award because plaintiff's testimony as to his emotional distress and his inability to get other jobs was not linked to the libelous statements, as opposed to the fact that he had been terminated. 538 F.3d at 67.

As for punitive damages, they are available when "the defendants' conduct is shown to be motivated by evil motive or intent, or when it involves reckless or callous indifference to the federally protected rights of others." *Smith v. Wade*, 461 U.S. 30, 56 (1983). Some courts will not award punitive damages unless there have been actual damages as well, while others require a showing of actual malice as a prerequisite to recovery in defamation actions. *See Senna v. Florimont*, 958 A.2d 427 (N.J. 2008).

PROBLEMS

5-2. Tina Kim is a carpenter. Until recently, she worked for Cozy Cabinets, a small company producing custom-built furniture. Tina was responsible for completing the finish work on some of the more elaborate designs. Last week, Mr. Gregory, the vice president in charge of production at Cozy Cabinets, discharged Tina. Gregory told Tina that she was fired. His explanation was that Jim Mineta, Tina's supervisor, had evaluated her finish work as "just not up to Cozy's standards." Tina has come to you for advice. She is afraid to apply for any carpentry jobs because she doesn't know what Cozy will say about her discharge, and she is certain that she won't get another job if she explains why Cozy let her go. She tells you that she thinks Mineta "had it in for her" because, a few weeks ago, she complained to Gregory that Mineta had failed to provide her with adequate supplies to complete a job on time. Tina worked for Cozy for two years, and all of her previous evaluations were good. She is an at-will employee. Tina is terribly upset because she is afraid that she will never get another carpentry job. She wants to know if there is any way to get her job back or if she has any other remedies.

   5-3. Suppose you represent Cozy Cabinets. Gregory received a voice mail from an old friend in the industry who is considering hiring Kim but wants to know "the scoop" on her. Gregory would like to be honest because the two exchange favors all the time. Should he return the call? If so, what should he say?

C. INTENTIONAL INFLICTION OF EMOTIONAL DISTRESS

≡≡≡ *Subbe-Hirt v. Baccigalupi*
≡≡≡ *94 F.3d 111 (3d Cir. 1996)*

NYGAARD, Circuit Judge.

   [Elaine Subbe-Hirt was a salesperson for Prudential Insurance Company, and brought suit against Prudential, her former employer] and Robert Baccigalupi, her former supervisor at Prudential, presenting several claims arising out of her employment with Prudential. The district court granted summary judgment in favor of the defendants on Subbe-Hirt's claim for intentional infliction of emotional distress. It held alternatively that her claim was barred by the exclusive remedy provided by the New Jersey Worker's Compensation Act. . . . Subbe-Hirt appeals from that ruling, [but did not appeal from the adverse resolution of her other claims, including sex discrimination claims. The appeals court first reversed the district court finding that workers' compensation exclusivity barred plaintiff's tort suit and then turned to the tort claim.]

III

   Subbe-Hirt contends that the district court also committed legal error by basing its summary judgment on a conclusion that defendants' conduct was not sufficiently outrageous to support a claim for intentional infliction of emotional distress. On this allegation of error we have but two issues to decide: 1) whether Robert Baccigalupi intended to inflict emotional distress upon Elaine Subbe-Hirt; and 2) whether the evidence supports appellant's contention that Baccigalupi succeeded in inflicting that distress. We answer both questions in the affirmative and hold that the record in this case exceeds a threshold showing of outrageous behavior sufficient to preclude summary judgment.

A

The present record, when viewed in the light most favorable to Subbe-Hirt, shows that Robert Baccigalupi unquestionably intended to inflict emotional distress upon Elaine Subbe-Hirt. According to sales manager Mark Parisi, Baccigalupi "would berate [Subbe-Hirt] or talk about getting her." Indeed, Baccigalupi stated, "I'm going to get her."

Moreover, according to the deposition testimony of Parisi and sales manager Robert LaNicca, Baccigalupi stated, in the presence of other managers and on more than one occasion, that he "was going to trim her bush";[1] a blatantly sexist metaphor to brag of how Baccigalupi would handle females in general and Subbe-Hirt in particular. According to sales manager David Meyer, "when it was brought to R. Baccigalupi's attention that [Subbe-Hirt] was soon going to be returning from disability, R. Baccigalupi quickly remarked, 'Well, don't worry about her. I'm going to trim her bush.'" When asked by counsel to explain what he understood Baccigalupi's remark to mean, Meyer testified, "I understood it that he was going to lay into her quite hard and put her in her place." LaNicca said that on another occasion Baccigalupi stated, "Let's bring Elaine in here on Friday and we'll trim her bush." Parisi understood that phrase to mean:

> That he was going to come down on her, whatever his particular style was, forcing her to either go out on disability or leave the company or to cease the union activity. . . . [This] is, unfortunately with Prudential, is an avenue that agents take when they can't take the—you know, when management pressure goes up, and that's what [Baccigalupi] might use that for.

Likewise, Robert King, a district agent, said:

> There came a point in time where it was almost embarrassing for many of us to watch a woman being— . . . it was pretty much obvious that Elaine wouldn't and couldn't bear up under the general atmosphere . . . —her time was expiring. . . . We talked amongst ourselves that, you know, this was a critical stage. . . . There was a persecution going of myself and Elaine, and Elaine in particular. . . . [Baccigalupi said] more or less than [sic] she was history and that if I intended to continue that I would—I should leave things go as they are going.

Baccigalupi's intent to inflict emotional distress can be further seen in his total lack of any vestige of compassion for any woman in the office. On one occasion Meyer told Baccigalupi that he "couldn't continue performing 'root canal'[2] on women agents on his staff because they broke down in tears." At that point, Baccigalupi simply selected a woman agent to abuse as a demonstration, saying "Well, don't worry. I'll show you how to handle it." Appellant describes this contrived encounter as follows:

> He then called one of the women agents in for a review, and started the "root canal" and the intimidation on her until she broke down and started crying. R. Baccigalupi kept

---

1. I.e., pubic hair. Sales manager David Meyer testified, "Well, he wasn't going to go out and trim her azalea bush at home. It was a sexist remark."
2. "Root canal" is a term coined by Baccigalupi to describe intense and emotionally painful sessions in which he would berate and demean disfavored agents with the purpose of forcing them out of the company.

tearing and pressing into her and when it was over and she had left the office, he was holding out his suspender straps as if to say, "this is how you handle it; don't let their emotions get in your way."

Indeed, Baccigalupi admitted his intent when he said to Subbe-Hirt, "do you know who Joan of Arc is, read between the lines, do you know why I'm looking at your work so closely, do you think I do this to everyone?"

We have no difficulty in concluding that a reasonable jury could find from this evidence that Baccigalupi intended that his conduct subject Elaine Subbe-Hirt to emotional distress, and will turn next to whether Baccigalupi's conduct had its intended effect, and whether that effect was sufficient as a matter of law to state a claim of intentional infliction.

B

1

The district court erred when it held that Subbe-Hirt did not allege, nor did the record on summary judgment show, conduct sufficiently outrageous to state a claim that Baccigalupi had intentionally inflicted emotional distress upon her. In *Buckley v. Trenton Sav. Fund Soc'y*, 544 A.2d 857 (N.J. 1988), the New Jersey Supreme Court applied the view of the Restatement (Second) of Torts §46 to the tort of intentional infliction. The district court was therefore correct that, under New Jersey law, intentional infliction of emotional distress comprehends conduct "so outrageous in character, and so extreme in degree, as to go beyond all possible bounds of decency, and to be regarded as atrocious, and utterly intolerable in a civilized community." [C]omment d. We disagree, however, with the district court's conclusion that Baccigalupi's conduct was not sufficiently outrageous, and are led inexorably to the conclusion that summary judgment should have been denied.

2 . . .

Baccigalupi created a predatory tactic he descriptively termed "root canal," which he used to control older agents such as Subbe-Hirt. Baccigalupi instructed his sales managers how to perform this verbal attack "operation." According to sales manager Meyer, Baccigalupi "came up with the concept of root canal as a way to intimidate and basically destroy these people to the point of submission or of just getting the hell out of the business." Meyer related at his deposition that Baccigalupi picked the term "root canal" specifically because it was made to be a very uncomfortable, pain-producing, anxiety-producing procedure that you would keep going deeper and deeper until you struck a nerve, which would either end up in the agent submitting, or reaching the point of anxiety where they just couldn't stand any job any longer.

According to Meyer, at Thursday management meetings, sales managers would role play with each other how to deal with "problem agents [such as Subbe-Hirt]." LaNicca's deposition indicates that Subbe-Hirt was "brought in more often than others for performance reviews," which was Baccigalupi's opportunity for using his root canal procedure on her. According to Subbe-Hirt, Baccigalupi "held [her] in the office twice as long as anyone else."

Baccigalupi was relentless in his contumely against Subbe-Hirt. To begin with, according to Meyer and Parisi, Baccigalupi replaced females' given names, and other polite nouns such as "lady" and "woman," with the term "cunt," to depersonalize and deride the women in the office. He would also taunt Subbe-Hirt by asking if she "knew the word heretic" and threaten her "by asking if she knew who Joan of Arc was." Moreover, he would ask Subbe-Hirt for her resignation almost every time she was in the office. Baccigalupi even went so far as to have an unsigned resignation on his desk; we would then ask Subbe-Hirt "why don't you sign it; if you don't want to sign it, go on disability."

In his meetings with Subbe-Hirt, Baccigalupi would "grill" her on work she submitted, asking "why did you do this, what did you do here, what was said here?" If he was not "satisfied" with her answer, he would call Subbe-Hirt's clients in front of her and say "Elaine says this; what do you say?"

Baccigalupi's conduct had a devastating consequence. After one meeting with Baccigalupi, Subbe-Hirt "literally blacked out behind the wheel and hit a tractor trailer just from stress and emotion[,]" suffering severe injuries that required eight days of hospitalization. This incident forced Subbe-Hirt to take temporary disability leave; indeed, her treating psychiatrist has opined that she remains totally disabled with post traumatic stress disorder triggered by Baccigalupi's badgering and intimidation.

Baccigalupi was on notice that such an incident was a distinct possibility. Before the collision, Subbe-Hirt had consulted with her family doctor because of stress. The doctor wrote a letter which Subbe-Hirt showed to Baccigalupi before the incident, asking that it be placed in her personnel file. [It stated that she should not be subjected] "to any undue stress or work load at this time." When Subbe-Hirt requested that the letter be placed in her personnel file, Baccigalupi refused, his exact words being: "I'll decide what goes in your personnel file." According to the evidence, "Mr. Baccigalupi handed it back to [her] and said he didn't see that letter, and he never wanted to see it again and he wouldn't put it in [her] file." From this evidence, a jury could well conclude that, in his attempt to drive Subbe-Hirt out of Prudential, Baccigalupi targeted her now-documented weakness, of which he was fully cognizant. Such specific targeting of an individual's weak point is itself a classic form of "outrageous" conduct under Restatement §46, comment f, which provides:

> The extreme and outrageous character of the conduct may arise from the actor's knowledge that the other is peculiarly susceptible to emotional distress, by reason of some physical and mental condition or peculiarity. The conduct may be heartless, flagrant, and outrageous when the actor proceeds in the face of such knowledge, where it would not be so if he did not know.

We conclude that the record is sufficient to support a finding that Baccigalupi essentially set out to put Subbe-Hirt under unnecessary stress to force her out of the company, all the while knowing that her physician had stated specifically that her condition required her to avoid such stress. . . .

COWEN, Circuit Judge, dissenting.

[The dissent thought that the district court should be upheld both on grounds of workers' compensation exclusivity and because] the facts of the case as alleged by the plaintiff fall short of the New Jersey cause of action of intentional infliction of emotional distress. The New Jersey Supreme Court has defined this tort as requiring conduct "so outrageous in character and so extreme in degree as to go beyond all possible bounds of decency, and to be regarded as atrocious and utterly intolerable in a civilized community." *Buckley* [*v. Trenton Sav. Fund Soc'y*, 544 A.2d 857, 863 (N.J. 1988)]. The conduct of the perpetrator of such a tort must be by its nature "so severe that no reasonable man could be expected to endure it."

[New Jersey courts have rarely found conduct to meet this extremely high level of uncivilized conduct, and when they have, it has involved instances such as "a doctor knowingly and untruthfully advising parents that their child had cancer, *Hume v. Bayer*, 428 A.2d 966 (Law Div. 1981)." Further, the] New Jersey Supreme Court has made it abundantly clear in *Buckley*, that when a claim is made for intentional infliction of emotional distress, the trial court must clearly exercise a gatekeeping role: "the court decides whether as a matter of law such emotional distress can be found" and the jury decides whether it has in fact been proved. . . .

The district court correctly performed its function by determining that under New Jersey law the facts alleged as a matter of law failed to reach the elevated and high standard required for the cause of action of intentional infliction of emotional distress. The district court recognized that Baccigalupi's statements, if credited, were "inexcusable" and "offensive," but did not rise to the level of outrageous and unacceptable in a civilized society. Plaintiff's claims boil down to an assertion that her supervisor's choice of words required her to put up with "more than the normal pressure of a job." Being subject to "more than normal pressure" at work is a long distance from conduct that is "so outrageous in character and so extreme in degree as to go beyond all possible bounds of decency, and to be regarded as atrocious, and utterly intolerable in a civilized community." Even plaintiff had a difficult time labeling Baccigalupi's actions as anything beyond harmless threats, intimidation, and ridicule. Admittedly, the words allegedly spoken by Baccigalupi were strong and even harsh at times, but they were merely words. There is no proof, nor even an allegation, that Baccigalupi even touched her or that he set in motion any physical or other instrumentality to bring about an injury or illness.

III

The majority is to be lauded in its desire to upgrade the repartee of the workplace and to be offended by language which it deems inappropriate. But the workplace is not the dance of a minuet and employers are not nursemaids. As judges we will rue the day we sat in judgment of the propriety of speech which should transpire in the workplace between an employer and his employee. I respectfully dissent.

NOTES

1. *Outrageous or Merely Offensive?* The majority and dissent seem to basically agree on the legal standard for an intentional infliction of emotional distress claim—also known as the tort of "outrage." Their agreement is not surprising since

New Jersey, like most jurisdictions, looks to the Restatement's definition of the tort. Current Section 46(1) of the Restatement (Third) of Torts, Liability for Physical and Emotional Harm, largely tracks the earlier Restatement on which *Baccigalupi* relied: "An actor who by extreme and outrageous conduct intentionally or recklessly causes severe emotional harm to another is subject to liability for that emotional harm . . . ." To limit the tort from reaching garden-variety emotional harms, the action must be "extreme and outrageous." §46 cmt. d.

The problem, of course, is that the tort turns on whether the conduct challenged is "outrageous," which is less a standard than an epithet. It is not surprising that some, like the majority, will be outraged and others, like the dissent, merely offended. But the dissent would uphold the district court judgment because reasonable minds could *not* differ over whether this was too extreme. Is that possible? You might be surprised to learn that the dissent is more typical of traditional intentional infliction cases than is the majority. Indeed, the situations in which courts have found egregious conduct not sufficiently outrageous to be actionable are legion. *See, e.g., Island v. Buena Vista Resort*, 103 S.W.3d 671, 681 (Ark. 2003) (an employer's sexual advances not sufficiently outrageous because plaintiff "failed to offer proof that she suffered damages or emotional distress so severe that no reasonable person could be expected to endure it" since she endured the advances for several years without protesting).

Baccigalupi, however, indicates that the theory may sometimes be fruitful, and there are some other successful claims in the employment setting. *See, e.g., Durham v. McDonald's Restaurants of Oklahoma, Inc.*, 256 P.3d 64, 66 (Okla. 2011) (manager's denial of three requests by 16-year-old plaintiff to take prescription anti-seizure medication and calling plaintiff a "f***ing retard" in denying the last request created a triable issue of outrage); *Archer v. Farmer Bros. Co.*, 70 P.3d 495 (Colo. App. 2002) (worker fired by his supervisors who came to his home to do so while he was in bed recovering from a heart attack). Note that *Baccigalupi* stressed the abuser's knowledge of plaintiff's particular susceptibility, quoting the Second Restatement. The Third Restatement also imposes liability where the actor knows of the victim's "special vulnerability." §46, cmt. j.

2. *How Is the Workplace Different?* One might take the view that employees are particularly vulnerable to abuse and therefore entitled to heightened protection against infliction of emotional distress. The paucity of successful claims, however, suggests the opposite—that most judges believe the demands of many workplaces require managerial practices that would be unacceptable in other settings. Look at Judge Cowen's dissent, who essentially argues that employers are justified in pressuring and disciplining employees in ways that may be inappropriate elsewhere. Further, victims can always quit if they want to avoid further abuse. Look at the last paragraph of the dissent. Is it equivalent to saying that emotional abuse is "standard operating procedure," at least in some workplaces? *See also* RESTATEMENT OF EMPLOYMENT LAW, §4.06, cmt. f, Ill. 6-9.

3. *That's Life.* Several years before Judge Cowen wrote his opinion, Professor Regina Austin critiqued such an approach:

> It is generally assumed that employers and employees alike agree that some amount of such abuse is a perfectly natural, necessary, and defensible prerogative of superior rank. It assures obedience to command. . . . Workers for their part are expected to respond to psychologically painful supervision with passivity, not insubordination and resistance.

They must and do develop stamina and resilience. If the supervision is intolerable, they should quit and move on to another job.

In sum, there is little reason for workers to take undue umbrage at the treatment they receive at work. The pain, insults, and indignities they suffer at the hands of employers and supervisors should be met with acquiescence and endurance. That's life. Who believes this?

Regina Austin, *Employer Abuse, Worker Resistance, and the Tort of Intentional Infliction of Emotional Distress*, 41 STAN. L. REV. 1 (1988); *see also* Dennis P. Duffy, *Intentional Infliction of Emotional Distress and Employment at Will: The Case Against "Tortification" of Labor and Employment Law*, 74 B.U. L. REV. 387 (1994).

   4. *Workplace Bullying.* The limitations of the intentional infliction tort have led some commentators to urge legislation to deal with serious emotional and psychological abuse of workers that may, nevertheless, not be sufficiently "outrageous" to be actionable under current tort law. *See, e.g.*, David C. Yamada, *Crafting a Legislative Response to Workplace Bullying*, 8 EMPL. RTS. & EMPLOY. POL'Y J. 475 (2004); David C. Yamada, *The Phenomenon of "Workplace Bullying" and the Need for Status-Blind Hostile Work Environment Protection*, 88 GEO. L. J. 475 (2000). While legislative efforts addressing bullying have been successful in the school context, no workplace antibullying legislation has yet been passed in this country. Might rising concerns about civility and/or the #MeToo movement change this in the near future?

   5. *Other Claims.* Because the plaintiff in *Baccigalupi* did not or was unable to raise her other claims on appeal, the Third Circuit did not consider them. One that jumps out is sex discrimination, particularly sexual or gender harassment. This topic is discussed in Chapter 9. *See generally* Kerri Lynn Stone, *From Queen Bees and Wannabes to Worker Bees: Why Gender Considerations Should Inform the Emerging Law of Workplace Bullying*, 65 N.Y.U. ANN. SURV. AM. L. 35 (2009). Is it clear that Baccigalupi was discriminating against plaintiff because she was a woman? In other words, might he have been an "equal opportunity harasser" who abused both men and women alike? The "root canal" strategy was not gender-specific, and a male co-worker, Robert King, also claimed to be a target of such abuse. However, Baccigalupi's crude anatomical references certainly suggest a discrimination claim, and the opinion seems to imply he was targeting plaintiff for especially severe abuse because she was a woman. Claims of racial or ethnic slurs have also been held actionable under the outrage tort, *see, e.g.*, *Woods v. Graphic Communs.*, 925 F.2d 1195 (9th Cir. 1991), either as the sole cause of action or as supplementary to a racial discrimination claim. *See also Pollard v. E.I. DuPont de Nemours, Inc.*, 412 F.3d 657, 664-65 (6th Cir. 2005) (applying Tennessee law as the sole cause of action); *Wal-Mart, Inc. v. Stewart*, 990 P.2d 626, 634-36 (Alaska 1999) (race discrimination).

   While Title VII expressly allows for supplementary tort claims, 42 U.S.C. §2000e-7 (2018), state civil rights statutes sometimes preempt tort claims and sometimes permit overlap. For example, some courts hold that intentional infliction of emotional distress cannot be brought where "the gravamen of the complaint is really another tort." *Hoffman-La Roche, Inc. v. Zeltwanger*, 144 S.W.3d 438, 447-48 (Tex. 2004); *see also Haubry v. Snow*, 31 P.3d 1186, 1193 (Wash. Ct. App. 2001) ("employee may recover damages of emotional distress . . . but only if the factual basis for the claim is distinct from the factual basis for the discrimination claim"). *See generally* Martha Chamallas, *Discrimination and Outrage: The Migration from Civil Rights to*

Tort Law, 48 Wm. & Mary L. Rev. 2115, 2115-16 (2007) ("The dominant approach views tort claims as mere "gap fillers" that should come into play only in rare cases that do not fit comfortably under other recognized theories of redress"). Even where a discrimination claim is viable, a tort cause of action may be helpful in fixing liability on the individual tortfeasor or in end-running statutory caps on discrimination remedies. *See* Chapter 9 at pages 722-23.

PROBLEM

5-4. Wilma is a vegan who had no on-the-job problems with her dietary practices until a new manager was hired. Once he learned that Wilma was a vegan, he continually made negative comments about her eating. They have occurred two or three times a week for the past year, usually when she is leaving for lunch. During the past few weeks, the comments have gotten more extreme. At two recent company social events, the manager sat down next to Wilma, ordered a hamburger ("extra rare, I want to see the blood"), and offered Wilma a bite. Wilma believes that this pattern of abuse is undercutting her ability to interact with co-workers, who are beginning to avoid her. The manager has taken to calling Wilma "Veg." She has experienced stress, nervousness, and difficulty sleeping as a result of the name-calling and other comments. The supervisor also "picks on" other co-workers for a variety of personal traits. Wilma does not view her veganism as "religious." Does she have a case under tort law?

D. FRAUD AND OTHER MISREPRESENTATION

In the law, "fraud" is often used broadly to encompass intentional misrepresentation, negligent misrepresentation, and even failure to disclose when there is a duty to do so. It is easiest to establish when used as a shield—that is, when used as a defense to a contract claim, or in other words, to "avoid" a contract. For example, an employee under a contract for a term of years might seek to escape liability for breach by arguing misrepresentation or failure to disclosure material facts. To void a contract, a misrepresentation must be either "fraudulent" or "material." Restatement (Second) of Contracts §164 (ALI 1981). Voiding a contract for nondisclosure is more difficult, but it is possible in a variety of circumstances that may arise in entering an employment relation. *Id.* at §161.

As a sword, however—that is, as a tort cause of action for damages suffered in reliance on false statements—fraud is most often used when an employee is discharged after being recently hired and typically after being recruited from another position and/or relocating to the new job. The employee then claims that, although she was admittedly employed at will, statements made in the hiring process were false and led her to accept the position. California, in fact, has a statute dealing with this scenario. Cal. Lab. Code § 970 (2018) prohibits false inducing anyone to relocate by means of "knowingly false representations" about a variety of matters, including the kind of work, the term of employment, and the compensation to be paid; it provides "double damages" for violations. A variation on this scenario occurs when an employer makes false statements in order to retain an employee who is considering a competing offer. What if the employer promises job security to the employee but has no intent to provide such security? An employee who is a victim of such misrepresentation and who subsequently is discharged may have a remedy in tort.

The Restatement of Employment Law §6.05 provides that

> An employer is subject to liability for intentionally inducing a current or prospective employee, through a knowingly false representation of fact, current intent, opinion, or law:
> (a) to enter into, maintain, or leave an employment relationship with the employer; or
> (b) to refrain from entering into or maintaining an employment relationship with another employer.

See also §6.06 (dealing with negligent misrepresentations). In the employment setting, the following case is a classic application of the doctrine.

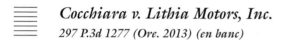

Cocchiara v. Lithia Motors, Inc.
297 P.3d 1277 (Ore. 2013) (en banc)

BALMER, C.J.

[The facts of this case are reproduced in Chapter 2, at page 102. In the portion of the opinion there, the Supreme Court dealt with the promissory estoppel claim; in this section, the court deals with the plaintiff's claim of fraud.]

Fraudulent Misrepresentation

This court has previously articulated the elements of a common law fraud claim, also known as an action in deceit, in more than one way, which is not surprising because "fraud" is " 'a term so vague that it requires definition in nearly every case.'" *Riley Hill General Contractor v. Tandy Corp.*, 737 P.2d 595 (1987) (quoting W. PAGE KEETON, ET AL., PROSSER AND KEETON ON THE LAW OF TORTS §105, 727 (W. Page Keeton ed., 5th ed. 1984)). For purposes of this case, two elements that are consistently required for a fraud claim are relevant: justifiable reliance and damages. *See Riley Hill General Contractor* (listing five elements of action in deceit, including " '[j]ustifiable reliance upon the representation'" and " '[d]amage to the plaintiff, resulting from such reliance'" (quoting KEETON, PROSSER AND KEETON ON THE LAW OF TORTS §105 at 728)); *U.S. National Bank v. Fought*, 630 P.2d 337 (1981) (listing nine elements of an action in deceit, including " 'reliance on [the misrepresentation's] truth,'" a " 'right to rely thereon,'" and " 'consequent and proximate injury'").

[W]e disagree with the Court of Appeals that, for purposes of his fraud claim, plaintiff could not reasonably rely on defendant's statement that plaintiff had definitely been given the corporate job. In a fraud claim, "[t]he principal argument in support of some such requirement as justifiability of reliance would seem to be that of providing some objective corroboration to plaintiff's claim that he did rely. . . . [T]he foolish nature of the plaintiff's conduct if he did rely is relevant primarily because of the likelihood that he did not rely." KEETON, PROSSER AND KEETON ON THE LAW OF TORTS §108 at 749-50. In this case, a jury could find that plaintiff reasonably relied on defendant's promise, because a jury could find that he was planning to accept the job with the Medford Mail Tribune—as evidenced by plaintiff notifying Summers that he planned to take that job—until defendant offered him the corporate job.

Moreover, the standard for reasonable or justifiable reliance in the context of fraud is both subjective and objective:

> If he is a person of normal intelligence, experience and education, he may not put faith in representations which any such normal person would recognize at once as preposterous . . . or which are shown by facts within his observation to be so patently and obviously false that he must have closed his eyes to avoid discovery of the truth, and still compel the defendant to be responsible for his loss. . . .
> [T]he matter seems to turn upon an individual standard of the plaintiff's own capacity and the knowledge which he has, or which may fairly be charged against him from the facts within his observation in the light of his individual case[.]

KEETON, PROSSER AND KEETON ON THE LAW OF TORTS §108 at 750-51 (footnote omitted). "Normal" people rely on offers of at-will employment every day, or at least a jury would be entitled to so find, based on the facts in a particular case. Here, a jury could find that plaintiff's reliance was not "preposterous" or based on plaintiff ignoring an obviously false statement, particularly given Summers' assertion about plaintiff's value to the company and his recommendation that plaintiff turn down the Medford Mail Tribune job.

In addition, allowing fraud claims in the context of at-will employment serves the purpose behind allowing fraud claims: "The type of interest protected by the law of deceit is the interest in formulating business judgments without being misled by others—in short, in not being cheated." *Riley Hill General Contractor*. If employers could make misleading statements to prospective at-will employees without liability, business judgments regarding employment would not be protected from deceit. Business judgments regarding at-will employment inherently involve some risk, and a prospective employee (or employer) should be able to evaluate that risk without the interference of fraud.

Although a prospective employee can bring a fraudulent misrepresentation claim in the context of at-will employment, we emphasize that there are limitations on those claims. Most notably, a plaintiff will have to prove damages to bring a successful claim. *See, e.g., Riley Hill General Contractor* (listing damage to the plaintiff as an element of a fraud claim). Nonetheless, plaintiff's decision to plead only damages associated with the loss of the corporate job—rather than damages associated with turning down the Medford Mail Tribune job—does not defeat his fraud claim, as the Court of Appeals suggested. As noted, the at-will nature of employment does not create a conclusive presumption barring a plaintiff from recovering future lost pay where the employee has been unlawfully terminated from the job, *Tadsen [v. Praegitzer Industries, Inc.*, 928 P.2d 980 (Ore, 1996)], or, as in this case, where plaintiff was never hired as promised or allowed to start work. Because this case was decided on a motion for summary judgment, however, whether plaintiff can sufficiently prove his damages associated with not being hired for the corporate job is not now before this court.

For those reasons, the Court of Appeals erred in determining that, as a matter of law, plaintiff could not reasonably rely on defendant's representations and could not recover future lost wages solely because of the at-will nature of the corporate job. We emphasize that our holding goes no further, and we express no view as to whether plaintiff's reliance was in fact reasonable, whether plaintiff can satisfy the other elements of his promissory estoppel and fraudulent misrepresentation claims, or whether plaintiff is entitled to recover his claimed damages. . . .

NOTES

1. *Fraud versus Contract.* In Chapter 2, we saw that Lithia Motors's alleged promises stated a cause of action in promissory estoppel. In this extract, we see that the same promise was also the basis for a fraud claim, but there was, of course, a twist. A mere failure to perform a promise can be actionable in contract but not in tort. For such a failure to be tortious, the defendant must have intended at the time it made the promise not to perform. The theory behind this requirement is that a promisor who makes a promise by that very act implies that he intends to perform that promise when the time for performance arrives. If the promisor lacks that intent, he has made a misrepresentation of fact (his state of mind), which satisfies one element of fraud. *See, e.g., Clement-Rowe v. Michigan Health Care Corp.*, 538 N.W.2d 20, 23 (Mich. Ct. App. 1995) (evidence suggests that the employer knew that the statement about funding for the position "was untrue or made it without any knowledge of its truth" in order to "allay plaintiff's hesitancy to accept the job because of concern about the financial health of the company"); *Neco, Inc. v. Larry Price & Assocs., Inc.*, 597 N.W.2d 602, 607 (Neb. 1999) (fraud may be predicated on a representation about a future event in control of the maker if the representation is known to be false when made or is made in reckless disregard as to its truthfulness); *see generally* RESTATEMENT (THIRD) OF TORTS: LIABILITY FOR ECONOMIC HARM §9; Frank J. Cavico, *Fraudulent, Negligent, and Innocent Misrepresentation in the Employment Context: The Deceitful, Careless, and Thoughtless Employer*, 20 CAMPBELL L. REV. 1 (2007).

An earlier, similar case arose out of New Jersey, with the claim being that, in order to retain a current employee, the employer promised him a job for life. *Shebar v. Sanyo Business Systems Corp.*, 544 A.2d 377 (N.J. 1988). Like *Cocchiara*, the plaintiff in *Shebar* asserted both contract and fraud claims. The fraud claim was predicated on evidence that, at the time Sanyo promised to continue plaintiff's employment, it did not intend to perform. The court thought that a jury could find that to be true in the very extreme circumstances at bar—the executive recruiter who had arranged the Sony offer informed plaintiff that Sanyo was searching for his replacement. Further, when Shebar confronted his supervisor with this information, he denied it. Since Sanyo was in fact seeking a replacement after just having promised plaintiff lifetime employment, and lied about whether it was doing so, a jury could find that the promise of lifetime employment was itself fraudulent when made in that Sanyo did not intend to perform it at that time. Absent such unusual circumstances, proving fraudulent misrepresentation is very difficult

2. *A Different View.* Not every court allows claims such as Cocchiara's. *Smalley v. Dreyfus Corp.*, 882 N.E.2d 882 (N.Y. 2008), rejected this approach entirely in the at-will context. Several employees had accepted positions with the defendant in reliance on its promise that there were no merger talks that would eliminate those positions. Although the Court of Appeals did not seem to question that the elements of fraud were alleged, the court found any misrepresentation not actionable precisely because it occurred in the context of at-will employment:

> [P]laintiffs alleged no injury separate and distinct from termination of their at-will employment. In that the length of employment is not a material term of at-will employment, a party cannot be injured merely by the termination of the contract—neither party can be said to have reasonably relied upon the other's promise not to terminate the contract. Absent injury independent of termination, plaintiffs cannot recover damages for what is at bottom an alleged breach of contract in the guise of a tort.

882 N.E.2d at 884-85. Presumably, *Smalley* would have rejected *Cocchiara's* claim because he was an at-will employee. *See also Sawyer v. E. I. du Pont de Nemours & Co.*, 430 S.W.3d 396 (Tex. 2014) (plaintiff cannot sue an employer for fraud when the fraudulent representation related to prospective employment since such a promise would be illusory in any event); *Mackenzie v. Miller Brewing Co.*, 623 N.W.2d 739 (Wis. 2001) (no cause of action for intentional misrepresentation to induce continued employment). However, the Restatement of Employment Law opts for liability in such situations.

3. *Negligent Misrepresentation.* Some jurisdictions recognize a tort of negligent misrepresentation, in which case it is, of course, unnecessary to prove intent to deceive. In *D'Ulisse-Cupo v. Board of Directors of Notre Dame H.S.*, 520 A.2d 217 (Conn. 1987), for instance, the court held that statements made by the high school principal assuring her that "there would be no problem" with plaintiff teaching the following year and that "everything looked fine for rehire" may have negligently led her to reasonably believe she would be employed for the next year. *See also Berger v. Security Pac. Info. Sys.*, 795 P.2d 1380 (Colo. Ct. App. 1990) (statements about the company's glowing prospects to a prospective employee created a duty to disclose serious problems). The Restatement of Employment Law would impose on employers "a duty to a current or prospective employee to exercise reasonable care not to provide false information on a topic about which the employer has special knowledge and that the employee may reasonably rely on in deciding whether to enter into or maintain an employment relationship." §6.06(a).

4. *Reliance.* In addition to a misrepresentation and the requisite fault, a plaintiff claiming fraud must show detrimental reliance. *See Coffel v. Stryker Corp.*, 284 F.3d 625, 637 (5th Cir. 2002) (jury could find that plaintiff, in giving up his rights under a prior bonus plan, relied on Stryker's representations that a new bonus plan would adequately compensate him and that this reliance was justified because of Stryker's past practice and assurances). This element may be hard to establish, especially in cases involving current employees who were hired before the allegedly fraudulent statement and who likely cannot show that they abandoned other opportunities because of it. Further, any reliance that the employee can establish must also be reasonable. *See Shelby v. Zayre Corp.*, 474 So. 2d 1069 (Ala. 1985) (reliance on promise of permanent employment unreasonable in face of signed application form that employment was at will).

5. *The Specificity of the Representation.* Some employees have tried to predicate tort claims on more amorphous employer statements than the ones we have seen to this point. In Chapter 2, we considered when an employer's failure to follow its policies might be actionable as a breach of contract under some version of the employee handbook doctrine. But occasionally an employee also asserts a tort claim in that situation.

For example, *Daley v. Aetna Life & Casualty Company*, 734 A.2d 112 (Conn. 1999), involved a plaintiff who was repeatedly denied requested accommodations when she became a mother. When she was finally discharged, she claimed, among other things, negligent misrepresentation by Aetna because of numerous statements it had made indicating that it was family-friendly. The court upheld a jury verdict against her, agreeing with Aetna that it "never represented to Daley that a work-at-home arrangement was an entitlement, nor that an employee who relentlessly pursued such an arrangement would not be discharged." *Id.* at 127-28. Thus, *Daley* strongly suggests that general policies will rarely support a claim for negligent misrepresentation and, of course, it would be even harder to pitch an intentional misrepresentation claim on such policies. We will revisit the accommodation issue in Chapter 10, but you might note that the court also upheld a directed verdict for Aetna on Daley's public policy tort claim: There was no "important public policy that requires employers to provide flexible work schedules for working parents, and that prohibits employers from discriminating against individuals who pursue such arrangements." *Id.* at 130.

E. LIMITATIONS ON TORT ACTIONS

There are two potentially important limitations on tort suits against employers. Although we have previously touched on both workers' compensation and preemption, a more detailed consideration of both follows.

1. Workers' Compensation

As described earlier in the chapter, workers' compensation statutes embody a fairly explicit trade-off: Employers are strictly liable for on-the-job injuries, but the amount of recovery for employees is much more limited than under traditional tort law. "A predicate of workers' compensation laws is that the compensation system is the exclusive remedy" for covered injuries. *See, e.g.,* N.J. STAT. ANN. §34:15-8 (West 2018), which clearly precludes tort suits in what was the paradigmatic situation for which workers' compensation was designed: negligently caused personal injury on the job. Ironically, employees originally preferred to be within workers' compensation regimes because of the hostility of the tort system. But, a century later, employees sometimes seek higher damages by claiming that their injuries are not covered by workers' compensation. Concomitantly, employers now frequently seek to defeat tort suits by arguing workers' compensation exclusivity.

The dispute typically centers on the meaning of "except for intentional wrong" or a similar exception in states' workers' compensation laws. This may not be as obvious an exclusion as one might think. Recall that in *Subbe-Hirt v. Baccigalupi*, page 297, the majority and dissent disagreed not only on whether the conduct was sufficiently outrageous to be actionable but also as to whether plaintiff's tort claim was barred by the New Jersey workers' compensation exclusivity. There was no doubt that plaintiff had pled an "intentional tort" but some question as to what that meant. Although that portion of the opinions is not reproduced, the majority reasoned that the conduct was actionable if "a plaintiff show[s] *deliberate intention* to avoid the exclusive remedy provided by the Compensation Act," *Baccigalupi*, 94 F.3d at 112-13 (emphasis in original), while the dissent read state workers compensation law as making such conduct actionable in tort only if it was substantially certain to cause the harm pled. *Id*. at 116.

Another example of the uncertain line separating torts that are actionable and those that are preempted by workers' compensation is *Ford v. Revlon, Inc.*, 734 P.2d 580 (Ariz. 1987), in which an employee charged that her supervisor, Karl Braun, sexually harassed her. His conduct included demanding sex from her, threatening reprisals when she rejected him, and physical molestation. Ford unsuccessfully tried to get Revlon management to address her complaints, during which time she experienced severe symptoms of emotional stress and ultimately attempted suicide. Her suit charged both Braun and Revlon with assault and battery and intentional infliction of emotional distress. One of Revlon's defenses was the exclusivity of Arizona's workers' compensation law, which covered employees "injured by accident arising out of and in the course of employment." ARIZ. REV. STAT. ANN. §23-1021(B). Further, §23-1043.01(B) specifically provided that "mental injury" was not "a personal injury by accident" unless "unexpected, unusual or extraordinary stress . . . or some physical injury . . . was a substantial contributing cause." The Arizona Supreme Court held against Revlon, noting that Ford's emotional distress was neither caused by an "accident" nor was it "unexpected." Since the injury was not within the workers' compensation scheme, plaintiff's tort suit remained viable. A concurrence disagreed as to the rationale but concluded that the case involved "one of those torts outside the purpose and intent of the workers' compensation scheme," 743 P.2d at 588, because "the wrong is one not ordinarily resulting from an inherent risk or danger of the employment" and "the essence of the tort action ordinarily is non-physical." *Id*. at 590-91.

The *Revlon* majority's distinction between an "accident" and "intent" is a common approach to the problem. This distinction finds support in the language of many workers' compensation statutes, which define compensable injuries in terms of "accidents" and frequently have an express exclusion for "intentional" harm. *See Lichtman v. Knouf*, 445 S.E.2d 114 (Va. 1994) (sexual harassment action not barred by workers' compensation because injury was not an "injury by accident" since it was gradually incurred and not the result of an identifiable incident). Nevertheless, the concurrence's alternative approach, which looks to the purposes of the workers' compensation statute, also has support. *See Cole v. Chandler*, 752 A.2d 1189, 1195 (Me. 2000) ("We have refused to carve out an exception [to worker's compensation exclusivity] for intentional torts" since doing so would counteract the purpose of the workers' compensation exclusivity provision and since the legislature would have provided an exception for intentional torts if they had intended to do so.).

Is the argument persuasive that sexual harassment is not the kind of injury intended to be within the statute? *See Cox v. Chino Mines/Phelps Dodge*, 850 P.2d 1038 (1993) (workers' compensation does not provide an adequate remedy for sexually harassed workers; such claims are better pursued under other causes of action). *Contra Doe v. Purity Supreme*, 664 N.E.2d 815 (Mass. 1996) (exclusivity provision of workers' compensation precludes an action against an employer for intentional infliction of emotional distress arising out of sexual harassment and even for injuries resulting from a rape or other sexual assault). Isn't association with co-workers an inherent risk of being employed? In a "post-industrial" economy, isn't bureaucratic incompetence a more likely cause of injury than "machinery breaking, objects falling, explosives exploding, tractors tipping, fingers getting caught in gears, excavations caving in," *Revlon*, 734 P.2d at 590, which the concurrence cited as the original focus of workers' compensation laws? *See generally* Jane Byeff Korn, *The Fungible Woman and Other Myths of Sexual Harassment*, 67 TUL. L. REV. 1363, 1384-89 (1993).

Even if sexual harassment is outside workers' compensation under this view, what about some of the other types of claims we have examined, such as intentional infliction of emotional distress? *See Gantt v. Sec., USA, Inc.*, 356 F.3d 547 (4th Cir. 2004) (intentional infliction claims not actionable under Maryland law, unless the employer had a deliberate intent to injure); *Driscoll v. General Nutrition Corp.*, 752 A.2d 1069, 1076 (Conn. 2000) (although plaintiff limited her tort action to recovery only for emotional distress and emotional injury, the workers' compensation law could not be "unbundled" for pleading purposes simply to escape the exclusivity provision). *Contra Coates v. Wal-Mart Stores, Inc.*, 976 P.2d 999 (N.M. 1999) (outrage claim not barred). How about an interference case? *Vacanti v. State Comp. Ins. Fund*, 14 P.3d 234, 243-44 (Cal. 2001) (tortious interference claim not barred). What about defamation? *Nassa v. Hook-SupeRx, Inc.*, 790 A.2d 368 (R.I. 2002) ("The prevalent view throughout the nation, however, is that the exclusive-remedy provisions of workers' compensation laws do not bar employment-related defamation claims.").

2. Federal Preemption

The law we have studied in this chapter is largely state law and, as such, is vulnerable to being overridden by federal enactments. Indeed, the checkered pattern of federal and state regulation of employment has resulted in frequent preemption issues. For example, in *Ingersoll-Rand Co. v. McLendon*, 498 U.S. 133 (1990), the Court held that a Texas decision recognizing a public policy cause of action for discharge to avoid employer contributions to a pension plan was preempted by the Employee Retirement Income Security Act ("ERISA"), a federal statute regulating pensions and other benefit plans, such as health insurance. *See also Aetna Health Inc. v. Davila*, 542 U.S. 200, 209 (2004) (rejecting any state cause of action that "duplicates, supplements, or supplants the ERISA civil enforcement remedy"). On the other hand, *English v. General Elec.*, 496 U.S. 72 (1990), found that the Energy Reorganization Act did not preempt a state-law claim for intentional infliction of distress in retaliation for nuclear safety complaints. *See also Schweiss v. Chrysler Motors*, 922 F.2d 473 (8th Cir. 1990) (Occupational Safety and Health Act does not preempt public policy tort for worker terminated for reporting alleged employer violations); *Parten v. Consolidated Freightways*, 923 F.2d 580 (8th Cir. 1991) (Surface Transportation Act did not preempt state public policy tort).

Federal statutes such as ERISA may, of course, specify their own preemptive effects, but, absent that, preemption can be found either because there is a conflict between federal and state law or because federal law is pervasive enough to preempt an entire field of activity. In either case, the Supremacy Clause mandates that federal law trumps state law. For conflict preemption, the court must determine that state law in some sense frustrates the purposes of federal law, and that analysis can be complicated. Even with the broader "field preemption," courts must mark out the precise field that Congress has occupied. For example, the defendant in *English v. General Electric* claimed that the Energy Reorganization Act preempted the entire field of nuclear safety. It therefore argued that a state tort claim for retaliation for nuclear safety complaints was barred. The Court, however, defined the field of exclusive federal authority very narrowly—radiological safety—and, even there, federal law preempted only those state laws that had a "direct and substantial effect" on such safety.

While preemption can arise in a variety of contexts, one of the most important areas for employment law purposes is just-cause discharge under collective bargaining agreements. On its face, §301 of the National Labor Relations Act, codified at 29 U.S.C. §185(a) (2006), merely provides a cause of action and federal court jurisdiction over suits for violation of collective bargaining agreements. Nevertheless, it has been interpreted to broadly preempt state law. *See, e.g., Local 174, Teamsters, Chauffeurs, Warehousemen & Helpers of Am. v. Lucas Flour Co.*, 369 U.S. 95 (1962). While §301 and other labor law preemption doctrines do not apply outside the collective bargaining arena, employers have frequently resisted suits by unionized employees on the basis that federal labor law preempts state remedies. Although it will not be explored in detail here, §301 has been the basis for a very elaborate jurisprudence on the respective roles of state and federal law in the employment arena predicated on a few relatively straightforward principles. First, the law to be applied by both state and federal courts is federal law, a common law to be developed setting uniform standards for the entire country. Second, the touchstone for §301 preemption is whether the state law in question requires interpreting a collective bargaining agreement.

For example, *Allis-Chalmers Corp. v. Lueck*, 471 U.S. 202 (1985), involved a suit by an employee against both his employer and the insurance company for a nonoccupational back injury. Plaintiff claimed that the defendants "intentionally, contemptuously, and repeatedly failed" to make disability payments under a company-provided disability plan, in breach of their duty "to act in good faith and deal fairly with his disability claims." *Id.* at 206. The Supreme Court found his state law claim preempted because the Wisconsin tort action for breach of the duty of good faith was "inextricably intertwined" with the terms of the labor contract. Since any attempt to assess liability would inevitably involve contract interpretation, the Court held that the claim must either be treated as a §301 claim or dismissed as preempted by federal labor-contract law.

In contrast to *Lueck*, the Court in *Lingle v. Norge Division of Magic Chef, Inc.*, 486 U.S. 399 (1988), found no preemption. Plaintiff had been fired for allegedly filing a false workers' compensation claim. Although she was protected by a union and in fact filed a grievance under the governing collective bargaining agreement, her tort suit alleged she had been discharged in retaliation for exercising her rights under Illinois's workers' compensation laws. A retaliatory discharge claim did not require interpretation of the collective-bargaining agreement, nor did the defense of such a suit turn on the meaning of the agreement. Since the state-law remedy was "independent" of the collective-bargaining agreement, there was no §301 preemption. *Id.* at 407. *See also Hawaiian Airlines v. Norris*, 512 U.S. 246, 263 (1994) (holding that claims for discharge in violation of public policy and the Hawaii Whistleblower Protection Act are not preempted by the Railway Labor Act).

In short, the Court has held that an application of state law is preempted by §301 of the Labor Management Relations Act of 1947 only if such application requires the interpretation of a collective-bargaining agreement. However, the question of whether an interpretation is necessary is more complicated than would appear on its face. This is reflected in varying results in the lower courts as to preemption of various state law tort claims. *See generally* William R. Corbett, *The Narrowing of the National Labor Relations Act: Maintaining Workplace Decorum and Avoiding Liability*, 27 BERKELEY J. EMP. & LAB. L. 23 (2006); Rebecca Hanner White, *Section 301's Preemption of State Law Claims: A Model for Analysis*, 41 ALA. L. REV. 377 (1990); Richard A. Bales, *The Discord Between Collective Bargaining and Individual Employment Rights: Theoretical Origins and a Proposed Reconciliation*, 77 B.U. L. REV. 687 (1997); Jane Byeff Korn, *Collective Rights and Individual Remedies: Rebalancing the Balance After* Lingle v. Norge Div., 41 HASTINGS L.J. 1149 (1990).

Part Four

PROTECTING WORKER AUTONOMY

6

Workplace Privacy Protections

The protection of privacy in the workplace is but one aspect of a much larger, burgeoning inquiry into the public policy implications of the recognition and protection of privacy interests. *See, e.g.*, DANIEL J. SOLOVE & PAUL M. SCHWARTZ, INFORMATION PRIVACY LAW (6th ed. 2018). This broader debate is reflected in the controversy surrounding federal government's mass surveillance programs—including those revealed in recent years by Edward Snowden—and intrusive investigative techniques and the collection, utilization, and sale of consumer and other information by private entities and other governments. But these issues also pervade the workplace: Although employers have always used a variety of means to keep tabs on their workers, employee privacy interests have become increasingly salient due to technological advances in testing, monitoring, and data collection and analytics, which allow for far more effective and searching oversight than previously. *See, e.g.*, Steve Lohr, *Unblinking Eyes Track Employees*, N.Y. TIMES, June 21, 2014, at A1 (discussing employers' increasingly sophisticated and detailed methods of data collection and monitoring of employees at work); *see also* Matthew T. Bodie, et al., *The Law and Policy of People Analytics*, 88 U. COLO. L. REV. 961 (2017) (discussing privacy implications of using new technologies to collect and use data for "people analytics").

In addition, with the rise of smartphones, social media, and other forms of electronic communications, how employees interact and communicate has undergone tremendous transformation in recent years. These profound changes have blurred the lines between work and nonwork. They also coincide with increasing employer concerns about what used to be viewed as the "private lives" of employees, in part because of growing stakes involving everything from seeking to hire the best employees to protecting employer property to avoiding legal and reputational risks. Indeed, recent studies have found that most major employers in the United States monitor employee communications and activities. Some employers also test some or all employees for drugs. Still others require physical exams or engage in other potentially intrusive activities upon hiring workers.

Privacy law in the employment context involves interests that are strongly contested. Not only is the workplace considerably more public than some protected areas, such as the home, but there also are strong countervailing considerations to personal privacy. After all, while at work, employees are not simply pursuing their own goals but are primarily engaged in furthering their employers' ends. Some commentators go so far as to suggest the law should have close to no role in protecting employee privacy in the workplace. *See, e.g.*, Michael Selmi, *Privacy for the Working Class: Public Work and Private Lives*, 66 LA. L. REV. 1035, 1042-49 (2006) (arguing for conceding the workplace is the employers' domain but for strict limits on employer encroachments elsewhere). Even among those arguing for greater privacy protections, there is little agreement on the scope of the right.

Ultimately, an employee's interest in privacy must be balanced against the employer's legitimate business and risk-management reasons for intruding. *See, e.g.*, Jessica Fink, *In Defense of Snooping Employers*, 16 U. PA. J. BUS. LAW 101 (2013) (identifying various employer interests for monitoring, surveillance, and other practices implicating employee privacy). It is therefore not surprising that this area of law is far from settled, offering significant challenges for employees, firms, policy makers, and, of course, counsel. And recent statutory developments, particularly at the state level, suggest continued changes in the law going forward.

Workplace privacy issues arise in a variety of circumstances. As an initial matter, "privacy" involves several related but distinct employee interests. The new Restatement of Employment Law, for example, identifies three: the interest in the employee's person and in employer-provided physical and electronic work locations in which the employee has a reasonable expectation of privacy; the interest in the employee's private information of a personal nature; and the interest in the employee's private information disclosed in confidence to the employer. RESTATEMENT OF EMPLOYMENT LAW (ALI 2015) §§7.02-7.05. Further, the Restatement recognizes additional employee "autonomy" interests, including engaging in lawful conduct away from work, adhering to religious and other beliefs, and participating in lawful associations. *See id.* at §7.08. These interests implicate many different laws and legal theories. For a discussion of these laws and theories, *see generally* MATTHEW W. FINKIN, PRIVACY IN EMPLOYMENT LAW 3 (4th ed. 2013 and 2017 Cumulative Supp.)

Nevertheless, despite the seemingly endless array of workplace privacy disputes, the vast majority of the litigated cases in this area fall into one of the following, sometimes overlapping, categories:

1. *Physical and Psychological Testing.* Many employers subject job applicants or employees to intrusive tests. Among these, the most commonly litigated is drug and alcohol testing. *National Treasury Employees Union v. Von Raab*, 489 U.S. 656 (1989), reproduced at page 356, and *Borse v. Piece Goods Shop, Inc.*, 963 F.2d 611 (3d Cir. 1992), reproduced at page 337, address such testing disputes, the former involving a public employer and the latter a private one. Recently, however, other kinds of testing, including physical examinations, psychological examinations, "honesty" testing, polygraphs, and genetic testing, have received growing judicial and legislative attention. Although some employers contend such tests provide important information relevant to applicant and employee qualifications and future job performance (including skills, potential safety concerns, health risks, and compatibility), workers often consider these procedures to be highly intrusive, intimidating, and overreaching. Indeed, as discussed below, privacy concerns have resulted in legislation specifically limiting the use of polygraph, physical examinations, and genetic testing by employers.

2. *Investigatory Interrogations and Searches of Persons and Spaces.* After receiving reports of misconduct in the workplace, employers sometimes interrogate workers and search their possessions and work spaces, with or without what might be called reasonable suspicion. Interrogations, which may include polygraph examinations, sometimes delve into personal issues or otherwise implicate worker privacy interests. Investigatory searches frequently include electronic and cyber searches of worker computer files, e-mail, and Internet activities. *Stengart v. Loving Care Agency, Inc.*, 990 A.2d 650 (N.J. 2010), reproduced at page 389, involves such an electronic search.

3. *Monitoring and Surveillance.* Employers engage in various forms of monitoring and surveillance to promote productivity, provide security, and prevent, discover, and remedy worker misconduct. Such monitoring historically had been limited to physical oversight by supervisors and other personnel and standard audits of activity in the workplace, such as the review of employee timesheets and telephone records. However, recent advances in communications and surveillance technology have dramatically increased the opportunities, effectiveness, and sometimes incentives for greater employee monitoring. The use of video and other surveillance technologies in the workplace and the monitoring of employee computer use, electronic communications, and Internet activities have received much attention in recent years. Thus, it is no surprise that there has been significant litigation in this area recently. A prominent example is the first case in this chapter, *City of Ontario v. Quon*, 560 U.S. 746 (2010).

4. *Inquiries into or Prohibitions of Off-Site Conduct.* Another sphere of employee activity with privacy implications is an employee's off-site or after-hours conduct and associations. Employees and applicants typically view their activities away from work as beyond their employer's legitimate concern, absent some direct impact on workplace performance. Workers may view some of these activities—including the pursuit of personal interests, intimate relationships, password-protected Internet communications, and religious and political preferences—as very private matters. This includes both "privacy" in the sense of protection from disclosure of private activities and more "public" activities viewed as "private" in the autonomy sense—they are simply none of the employer's business. Nevertheless, employers sometimes have legitimate reasons (e.g., protecting good will, avoiding public relations problems, ensuring loyalty, and preserving morale) to inquire into employees' or applicants' activities away from work and either regulate or take disciplinary action for such conduct. A number of note materials throughout the chapter explore this tension.

5. *Revelations of Private Matters.* A final type of employer conduct implicating employee privacy interests involves challenges to employer-compelled revelations by employees of private matters or employer publication of employee confidential information. The employer may define as a job requirement (or a supervisor may demand that an employee reveal) something the employee considers very personal. Sometimes these obligations involve physical revelations, such as commands that an employee undress or perform some otherwise-revealing physical act. Such demands or requirements have been challenged occasionally, including in *Feminist Women's Health Center v. Superior Court*, 61 Cal. Rptr. 2d 187 (Ct. App. 1997), reproduced at page 381. Other times, employees have challenged required revelations about information, involving intimate thoughts or beliefs, embarrassing facts, or matters of personal history the employee prefers not to share. In still other situations, an employee challenges not the employer's initial mandate to disclose or reveal information to it, but, rather, the employer's publication or sharing of this information with others.

This chapter is structured around three themes that dominate the inquiry regardless of the circumstances—the five situations discussed above—in which employee privacy interests are implicated. These are (1) the search for sources of protection, (2) the balance between worker and employer interests, and (3) private ordering and the limits of employee consent. To begin thinking about these themes and the various issues they raise, consider the following problem.

PROBLEM

6-1. Data Enterprises, Inc. ("DEI") provides each of its office employees with desktop computers linked to DEI's network, access to DEI's e-mail system, and access to the Internet. DEI has included in its employee guidelines a "Computer Use and Electronic Communications Policy," which provides as follows:

> Employees may use office computers to engage in electronic communications for authorized purposes only. As a general matter, an authorized purpose includes work-related activities and communications. However, authorized use also includes limited personal use by employees during non-work time *provided* such use does not interfere with or disrupt DEI's business in any way, involves minimal additional expense, and does not otherwise harm DEI's interests.
>
> To ensure compliance with this policy and to protect DEI from harm and disruption, DEI may at any time audit, inspect, and/or monitor employee's electronic communications and review, audit, and inspect employee computers and information stored therein.

Amy Smith is an at-will employee working in DEI's main office. She frequently accesses the Internet from her desktop computer during her lunch hour, and, among other things, checks messages and sends e-mails to friends through her personal Gmail account. One evening after Smith left the office, her supervisor, with whom she has had some personality conflicts, decided to review her computer and Internet activities. He, along with an IT staff member, noticed Smith's frequent visits to her Gmail Internet page and, after guessing her password (her birthday), accessed her account. The two discovered a number of e-mails sent by Smith to friends who are not co-workers in which she criticizes the supervisor and makes derogatory comments about him and several other employees. All of these messages were sent by Smith on days she was at work and from her work computer, but always during her lunch break. When Smith arrived at the office the next morning, the supervisor terminated her.

As you read the materials in this chapter, consider the following. First, think about whether and in what circumstances Smith might have a cognizable privacy-based claim against DEI. Second, if there is any risk of such liability to DEI, consider how DEI, through better planning, might have reduced this risk. Finally, think like a policy maker and consider whether electronic communications like the e-mails at issue in this situation ought to receive additional protection and, if so, to what extent.

A. SOURCES OF PRIVACY PROTECTION

1. Constitutional Protections

≣ *City of Ontario v. Quon*
    560 U.S. 746 (2010)

KENNEDY, Justice, delivered the opinion of the Court.

This case involves the assertion by a government employer of the right, in circumstances to be described, to read text messages sent and received on a pager the employer owned and issued to an employee. The employee contends that the privacy of the messages is protected by the ban on "unreasonable searches and seizures" found in the Fourth Amendment to the United States Constitution, made applicable to the States by the Due Process Clause of the Fourteenth Amendment. *Mapp v. Ohio,* 367 U.S. 643 (1961). Though the case touches issues of far-reaching significance, the Court concludes it can be resolved by settled principles determining when a search is reasonable.

I

A

The City of Ontario (City) is a political subdivision of the State of California. The case arose out of incidents in 2001 and 2002 when respondent Jeff Quon was employed by the Ontario Police Department (OPD). He was a police sergeant and member of OPD's Special Weapons and Tactics (SWAT) Team. The City, OPD, and OPD's Chief, Lloyd Scharf, are petitioners here. In October 2001, the City acquired 20 alphanumeric pagers capable of sending and receiving text messages. Arch Wireless Operating Company provided wireless service for the pagers. Under the City's service contract with Arch Wireless, each pager was allotted a limited number of characters sent or received each month. Usage in excess of that amount would result in an additional fee. The City issued pagers to Quon and other SWAT Team members in order to help the SWAT Team mobilize and respond to emergency situations.

Before acquiring the pagers, the City announced a "Computer Usage, Internet and E-Mail Policy" (Computer Policy) that applied to all employees. Among other provisions, it specified that the City "reserves the right to monitor and log all network activity including e-mail and Internet use, with or without notice. Users should have no expectation of privacy or confidentiality when using these resources." In March 2000, Quon signed a statement acknowledging that he had read and understood the Computer Policy.

The Computer Policy did not apply, on its face, to text messaging. Text messages share similarities with e-mails, but the two differ in an important way. In this case, for instance, an e-mail sent on a City computer was transmitted through the City's own data servers, but a text message sent on one of the City's pagers was transmitted using wireless radio frequencies from an individual pager to a receiving station owned by Arch Wireless. It was routed through Arch Wireless' computer network, where it remained until the recipient's pager or cellular telephone was ready to receive the message, at which point Arch Wireless transmitted the message from the transmitting station nearest to the recipient. After delivery, Arch Wireless retained a copy on its computer servers. The message did not pass through computers owned by the City.

Although the Computer Policy did not cover text messages by its explicit terms, the City made clear to employees, including Quon, that the City would treat text messages the same way as it treated e-mails. At an April 18, 2002, staff meeting at which Quon was present, Lieutenant Steven Duke, the OPD officer responsible for the City's contract with Arch Wireless, told officers that messages sent on the pagers "are considered e-mail messages. This means that [text] messages would fall under the City's policy as public information and [would be] eligible for auditing." Duke's comments were put in writing in a memorandum sent on April 29, 2002, by Chief Scharf to Quon and other City personnel.

Within the first or second billing cycle after the pagers were distributed, Quon exceeded his monthly text message character allotment. Duke told Quon about the overage, and reminded him that messages sent on the pagers were "considered e-mail and could be audited." Duke said, however, that "it was not his intent to audit [an] employee's text messages to see if the overage [was] due to work related transmissions." Duke suggested that Quon could reimburse the City for the overage fee rather than have Duke audit the messages. Quon wrote a check to the City for the overage. Duke offered the same arrangement to other employees who incurred overage fees.

Over the next few months, Quon exceeded his character limit three or four times. Each time he reimbursed the City. Quon and another officer again incurred overage fees for their pager usage in August 2002. At a meeting in October, Duke told Scharf that he had become "'tired of being a bill collector.'" Scharf decided to determine whether the existing character limit was too low—that is, whether officers such as Quon were having to pay fees for sending work-related messages—or if the overages were for personal messages. Scharf told Duke to request transcripts of text messages sent in August and September by Quon and the other employee who had exceeded the character allowance.

[At Duke's request,] Arch Wireless provided the desired transcripts. Duke reviewed the transcripts and discovered that many of the messages sent and received on Quon's pager were not work related, and some were sexually explicit. Duke reported his findings to Scharf, who, along with Quon's immediate supervisor, reviewed the transcripts himself. After his review, Scharf referred the matter to OPD's internal affairs division for an investigation into whether Quon was violating OPD rules by pursuing personal matters while on duty.

The officer in charge of the internal affairs review was Sergeant Patrick McMahon. Before conducting a review, McMahon used Quon's work schedule to redact the transcripts in order to eliminate any messages Quon sent while off duty. He then reviewed the content of the messages Quon sent during work hours. McMahon's report noted that Quon sent or received 456 messages during work hours in the month of August 2002, of which no more than 57 were work related; he sent as many as 80 messages during a single day at work; and on an average workday, Quon sent or received 28 messages, of which only 3 were related to police business. The report concluded that Quon had violated OPD rules. Quon was allegedly disciplined.

B

[Quon filed suit in federal court claiming that, by obtaining and reviewing the transcript of Quon's pager messages, the City violated his Fourth Amendment rights, the Stored Communications Act (SCA), 18 U.S.C. §2701 et seq., and California law. Quon was joined by the recipients of his text messages: Jerilyn Quon, Jeff Quon's then-wife, from whom he was separated; April Florio, an OPD employee with whom Jeff Quon was romantically involved; and Steve Trujillo, another member of the OPD SWAT Team. The complaint also named Arch Wireless as a defendant, alleging it violated the SCA by turning over the transcript to the City.

[Both the district court and the Ninth Circuit held that Quon had a reasonable expectation of privacy in the content of his text messages. The district court would have made liability turn on whether the purpose of the audit was to determine whether Quon was wasting time (impermissible) or assessing the appropriateness of the existing character limits (permissible). The Ninth Circuit reversed in part, holding that even though the search was conducted for "a legitimate work-related rationale," it was not reasonable in scope. The court found that there was a "host of simple ways" for the OPD to achieve its legitimate goals that were less intrusive than the audit.] The Court of Appeals further concluded that Arch Wireless had violated the SCA by turning over the transcript to the City. . . .

II

The Fourth Amendment states: "The right of the people to be secure in their persons, houses, papers, and effects, against unreasonable searches and seizures, shall not be violated. . . ." It is well settled that the Fourth Amendment's protection extends beyond the sphere of criminal investigations. . . . The Fourth Amendment applies as well when the Government acts in its capacity as an employer. *Treasury Employees v. Von Raab*, 489 U.S. 656, 665 (1989).

The Court discussed this principle in [*O'Connor v. Ortega*, 480 U.S. 709 (1987)]. There a physician employed by a state hospital alleged that hospital officials investigating workplace misconduct had violated his Fourth Amendment rights by searching his office and seizing personal items from his desk and filing cabinet. All Members of the Court agreed with the general principle that "[i]ndividuals do not lose Fourth Amendment rights merely because they work for the government instead of a private employer." A majority of the Court further agreed that "'special needs, beyond the normal need for law enforcement,'" make the warrant and probable-cause requirement impracticable for government employers (plurality opinion) (quoting *New Jersey v. T. L. O.*, 469 U.S. 325, 351 (1985) (Blackmun, J., concurring)); *O'Connor* (opinion of Scalia, J.) (quoting same).

The *O'Connor* Court did disagree on the proper analytical framework for Fourth Amendment claims against government employers. A four-Justice plurality concluded that the correct analysis has two steps. First, because "some government offices may be so open to fellow employees or the public that no expectation of privacy is reasonable," a court must consider "[t]he operational realities of the workplace" in order to determine whether an employee's Fourth Amendment rights are implicated. On this view, "the question whether an employee has a reasonable expectation of privacy must be addressed on a case-by-case basis." Next, where an employee has a legitimate privacy expectation, an employer's intrusion on that expectation "for non-investigatory, work-related purposes, as well as for investigations of work-related misconduct, should be judged by the standard of reasonableness under all the circumstances."

Justice Scalia, concurring in the judgment, outlined a different approach. His opinion would have dispensed with an inquiry into "operational realities" and would conclude "that the offices of government employees . . . are covered by Fourth Amendment protections as a general matter." But he would also have held "that government searches to retrieve work-related materials or to investigate violations of workplace rules—searches of the sort that are regarded as reasonable and normal in the private-employer context—do not violate the Fourth Amendment."

Later, in the *Von Raab* decision, the Court explained that "operational realities" could diminish an employee's privacy expectations, and that this diminution could be taken into consideration when assessing the reasonableness of a workplace search. In the two decades since *O'Connor*, however, the threshold test for determining the scope of an employee's Fourth Amendment rights has not been clarified further. Here, though they disagree on whether Quon had a reasonable expectation of privacy, both petitioners and respondents start from the premise that the *O'Connor* plurality controls. It is not necessary to resolve whether that premise is correct. The case can be decided by determining that the search was reasonable even assuming Quon had a reasonable expectation of privacy. The two *O'Connor* approaches—the plurality's and Justice Scalia's—therefore lead to the same result here.

III

A

. . . [The record establishes that OPD made clear at the outset that pager messages were not considered private.] The City's Computer Policy stated that "[u]sers should have no expectation of privacy or confidentiality when using" City computers. Chief Scharf's memo and Duke's statements made clear that this official policy extended to text messaging. The disagreement . . . is over whether Duke's later statements overrode the official policy. Respondents contend that because Duke told Quon that an audit would be unnecessary if Quon paid for the overage, Quon reasonably could expect that the contents of his messages would remain private.

At this point, were we to assume that inquiry into "operational realities" were called for, it would be necessary to ask whether Duke's statements could be taken as announcing a change in OPD policy, and if so, whether he had, in fact or appearance, the authority to make such a change and to guarantee the privacy of text messaging. It would also be necessary to consider whether a review of messages sent on police pagers, particularly those sent while officers are on duty, might be justified for other reasons, including performance evaluations, litigation concerning the lawfulness of police actions, and perhaps compliance with state open records laws. These matters would all bear on the legitimacy of an employee's privacy expectation.

The Court must proceed with care when considering the whole concept of privacy expectations in communications made on electronic equipment owned by a government employer. The judiciary risks error by elaborating too fully on the

Fourth Amendment implications of emerging technology before its role in society has become clear. *See, e.g., Olmstead v. United States,* 277 U.S. 438 (1928), overruled by *Katz v. United States,* 389 U.S. 347, 353 (1967). In *Katz,* the Court relied on its own knowledge and experience to conclude that there is a reasonable expectation of privacy in a telephone booth. It is not so clear that courts at present are on so sure a ground. Prudence counsels caution before the facts in the instant case are used to establish far-reaching premises that define the existence, and extent, of privacy expectations enjoyed by employees when using employer-provided communication devices.

Rapid changes in the dynamics of communication and information transmission are evident not just in the technology itself but in what society accepts as proper behavior. As one *amici* brief notes, many employers expect or at least tolerate personal use of such equipment by employees because it often increases worker efficiency. Another *amicus* points out that the law is beginning to respond to these developments, as some States have recently passed statutes requiring employers to notify employees when monitoring their electronic communications [(citing DEL. CODE ANN., tit. 19, §705 (2005)); CONN. GEN. STAT. ANN. §31-48d (West 2003)]. At present, it is uncertain how workplace norms, and the law's treatment of them, will evolve.

Even if the Court were certain that the *O'Connor* plurality's approach were the right one, the Court would have difficulty predicting how employees' privacy expectations will be shaped by those changes or the degree to which society will be prepared to recognize those expectations as reasonable. Cell phone and text message communications are so pervasive that some persons may consider them to be essential means or necessary instruments for self-expression, even self-identification. That might strengthen the case for an expectation of privacy. On the other hand, the ubiquity of those devices has made them generally affordable, so one could counter that employees who need cell phones or similar devices for personal matters can purchase and pay for their own. And employer policies concerning communications will of course shape the reasonable expectations of their employees, especially to the extent that such policies are clearly communicated.

A broad holding concerning employees' privacy expectations vis-á-vis employer-provided technological equipment might have implications for future cases that cannot be predicted. It is preferable to dispose of this case on narrower grounds. For present purposes we assume several propositions *arguendo:* First, Quon had a reasonable expectation of privacy in the text messages sent on the pager provided to him by the City; second, petitioners' review of the transcript constituted a search within the meaning of the Fourth Amendment; and third, the principles applicable to a government employer's search of an employee's physical office apply with at least the same force when the employer intrudes on the employee's privacy in the electronic sphere.

B

Even if Quon had a reasonable expectation of privacy in his text messages, petitioners did not necessarily violate the Fourth Amendment by obtaining and reviewing the transcripts. Although as a general matter, warrantless searches "are *per se*

unreasonable under the Fourth Amendment," there are "a few specifically established and well-delineated exceptions" to that general rule. *Katz.* The Court has held
that the "'special needs'" of the workplace justify one such exception. *O'Connor;*
Von Raab.

Under the approach of the *O'Connor* plurality, when conducted for a "noninvestigatory, work-related purpos[e]" or for the "investigatio[n] of work-related misconduct," a government employer's warrantless search is reasonable if it is "'justified at
its inception"' and if "'the measures adopted are reasonably related to the objectives
of the search and not excessively intrusive in light of"' the circumstances giving rise to
the search. *O'Connor.* The search here satisfied the standard of the *O'Connor* plurality
and was reasonable under that approach.

The search was justified at its inception because there were "reasonable grounds
for suspecting that the search [was] necessary for a noninvestigatory work-related
purpose." As a jury found, Chief Scharf ordered the search in order to determine
whether the character limit on the City's contract with Arch Wireless was sufficient
to meet the City's needs. This was, as the Ninth Circuit noted, a "legitimate work-
related rationale." The City and OPD had a legitimate interest in ensuring that
employees were not being forced to pay out of their own pockets for work-related
expenses, or on the other hand that the City was not paying for extensive personal
communications.

As for the scope of the search, reviewing the transcripts was reasonable because
it was an efficient and expedient way to determine whether Quon's overages were the
result of work-related messaging or personal use. The review was also not "'excessively intrusive.'" *O'Connor* (plurality opinion). Although Quon had gone over his
monthly allotment a number of times, OPD requested transcripts for only the months
of August and September 2002. While it may have been reasonable as well for OPD
to review transcripts of all the months in which Quon exceeded his allowance, it
was certainly reasonable for OPD to review messages for just two months in order
to obtain a large enough sample to decide whether the character limits were efficacious. And it is worth noting that during his internal affairs investigation, McMahon
redacted all messages Quon sent while off duty, a measure which reduced the intrusiveness of any further review of the transcripts.

Furthermore, and again on the assumption that Quon had a reasonable expectation of privacy in the contents of his messages, the extent of an expectation is relevant to assessing whether the search was too intrusive. *See Von Raab.* Even if he could
assume some level of privacy would inhere in his messages, it would not have been
reasonable for Quon to conclude that his messages were in all circumstances immune
from scrutiny. Quon was told that his messages were subject to auditing. As a law
enforcement officer, he would or should have known that his actions were likely to
come under legal scrutiny, and that this might entail an analysis of his on-the-job
communications. Under the circumstances, a reasonable employee would be aware
that sound management principles might require the audit of messages to determine
whether the pager was being appropriately used. Given that the City issued the pagers to Quon and other SWAT Team members in order to help them more quickly
respond to crises—and given that Quon had received no assurances of privacy—Quon
could have anticipated that it might be necessary for the City to audit pager messages
to assess the SWAT Team's performance in particular emergency situations.

From OPD's perspective, the fact that Quon likely had only a limited privacy
expectation, with boundaries that we need not here explore, lessened the risk that

the review would intrude on highly private details of Quon's life. OPD's audit of messages on Quon's employer-provided pager was not nearly as intrusive as a search of his personal e-mail account or pager, or a wiretap on his home phone line, would have been. That the search did reveal intimate details of Quon's life does not make it unreasonable, for under the circumstances a reasonable employer would not expect that such a review would intrude on such matters. The search was permissible in its scope.

The Court of Appeals erred in finding the search unreasonable. It pointed to a "host of simple ways to verify the efficacy of the 25,000-character limit . . . without intruding on [respondents'] Fourth Amendment rights." The panel suggested that Scharf "could have warned Quon that for the month of September he was forbidden from using his pager for personal communications, and that the contents of all his messages would be reviewed to ensure the pager was used only for work-related purposes during that time frame. Alternatively, if [OPD] wanted to review past usage, it could have asked Quon to count the characters himself, or asked him to redact personal messages and grant permission to [OPD] to review the redacted transcript."

This approach was inconsistent with controlling precedents. This Court has "repeatedly refused to declare that only the 'least intrusive' search practicable can be reasonable under the Fourth Amendment." That rationale "could raise insuperable barriers to the exercise of virtually all search-and-seizure powers," because "judges engaged in *post hoc* evaluations of government conduct can almost always imagine some alternative means by which the objectives of the government might have been accomplished." The analytic errors of the Court of Appeals in this case illustrate the necessity of this principle. Even assuming there were ways that OPD could have performed the search that would have been less intrusive, it does not follow that the search as conducted was unreasonable.

Respondents argue that the search was *per se* unreasonable in light of the Court of Appeals' conclusion that Arch Wireless violated the SCA by giving the City the transcripts of Quon's text messages. The merits of the SCA claim are not before us. But even if the Court of Appeals was correct to conclude that the SCA forbade Arch Wireless from turning over the transcripts, it does not follow that petitioners' actions were unreasonable. Respondents point to no authority for the proposition that the existence of statutory protection renders a search *per se* unreasonable under the Fourth Amendment. And the precedents counsel otherwise. *See Virginia v. Moore*, 553 U.S. 164, 168 (2008) (search incident to an arrest that was illegal under state law was reasonable); *California v. Greenwood*, 486 U.S. 35, 43 (1988) (rejecting argument that if state law forbade police search of individual's garbage the search would violate the Fourth Amendment). Furthermore, respondents do not maintain that any OPD employee either violated the law him- or herself or knew or should have known that Arch Wireless, by turning over the transcript, would have violated the law. The otherwise reasonable search by OPD is not rendered unreasonable by the assumption that Arch Wireless violated the SCA by turning over the transcripts.

Because the search was motivated by a legitimate work-related purpose, and because it was not excessive in scope, the search was reasonable under the approach of the *O'Connor* plurality. For these same reasons—that the employer had a legitimate reason for the search, and that the search was not excessively intrusive in light of that justification—the Court also concludes that the search would be "regarded as reasonable and normal in the private-employer context" and would satisfy the approach of Justice Scalia's concurrence. The search was reasonable, and the Court of

Appeals erred by holding to the contrary. Petitioners did not violate Quon's Fourth Amendment rights.

C

[The litigation posture of the case permitted the Court to avoid deciding whether the search might have violated the Fourth Amendment rights of Jerilyn Quon, Florio, and Trujillo, including the issue of "whether a sender of a text message can have a reasonable expectation of privacy in a message he knowingly sends to someone's employer-provided pager."]

[Justice STEVENS concurred.] . . .

SCALIA, Justice, concurring in part and concurring in the judgment.

I join the Court's opinion except for Part III-A. I continue to believe that the "operational realities" rubric for determining the Fourth Amendment's application to public employees invented by the plurality in *O'Connor v. Ortega* is standardless and unsupported. In this case, the proper threshold inquiry should be not whether the Fourth Amendment applies to messages on *public* employees' employer-issued pagers, but whether it applies *in general* to such messages on employer-issued pagers.

. . . [He criticized the majority for its digression into an unnecessary discussion of the threshold question of whether there was an expectation of privacy to begin with, since it found that the search was reasonable anyway.]

Worse still, the digression is self-defeating. . . . [L]ower courts will likely read the Court's self-described "instructive" expatiation on how the *O'Connor* plurality's approach would apply here (if it applied) as a heavy-handed hint about how *they* should proceed. Litigants will do likewise, using the threshold question whether the Fourth Amendment is even implicated as a basis for bombarding lower courts with arguments about employer policies, how they were communicated, and whether they were authorized, as well as the latest trends in employees' use of electronic media. In short, in saying why it is not saying more, the Court says much more than it should.

The Court's inadvertent boosting of the *O'Connor* plurality's standard is all the more ironic because, in fleshing out its fears that applying that test to new technologies will be too hard, the Court underscores the unworkability of that standard. Any rule that requires evaluating whether a given gadget is a "necessary instrumen[t] for self-expression, even self-identification," on top of assessing the degree to which "the law's treatment of [workplace norms has] evolve[d]," is (to put it mildly) unlikely to yield objective answers.

I concur in the Court's judgment.

NOTES

1. *The Fourth Amendment and the Basic Framework. Quon* is important because the Court applies the Fourth Amendment to electronic communications on employer-provided equipment, a context rife with litigation and controversy. However, much of the legal doctrine in *Quon* simply reaffirms the analysis set forth in *O'Connor v. Ortega*, 480 U.S. 709 (1987). In that case, which involved the search of a public

employee's office space and file drawers, the Court initially recognized that, pursuant to its prohibition on unreasonable searches and seizures, government workers enjoy some Fourth Amendment protection while at work. This recognition alone was significant: There are more than 23 million government (federal, state, and local) employees in the United States, and, at least as a default matter, they have some claim to privacy while at work.

The *Quon* decision goes on to apply the operative framework set forth in *O'Connor* for determining whether there has been a violation of a public employee's Fourth Amendment rights. It provides a two-step inquiry. First, in order to enjoy any Fourth Amendment protection, the employee must have had a "reasonable expectation of privacy" in the area or thing (physical or virtual) intruded upon or searched. Second, if the employee had such an expectation, then it must be determined whether the employer's intrusion into this area or thing was "reasonable." In *Quon*, the Court found it unnecessary to resolve the first inquiry, since it determined that the resulting search was reasonable at its inception. Nevertheless, the Court's arguably gratuitous discussion of the subject—as well as Justice Scalia's scolding response in his concurrence—offers some new guidance and plenty of fodder for debate.

2. *The First Prong: Reasonable Expectation of Privacy.* The Court assumes arguendo that Quon had a reasonable expectation of privacy in the content of the pager messages. Thus, it initially states that it need not resolve definitively which approach—the *O'Connor* plurality's "operational realities" standard or Justice Scalia's categorical approach—governs the determination of whether an employee had a reasonable expectation of privacy. Nevertheless, the majority goes on to discuss in some detail why it cannot and should not adopt a "broad holding concerning employees' privacy expectations vis-á-vis employer-provided technological equipment." Justice Scalia contended that, in so doing, the majority endorsed an operational realities approach. Do you agree?

To appreciate what is at stake, take a moment to consider the policy and practical implications that are at the heart of the dispute. The *O'Connor* plurality justified its case-by-case approach to determining the reasonableness of an employee's expectation of privacy (regarding physical spaces in the workplace) this way:

> Individuals do not lose Fourth Amendment rights merely because they work for the government instead of a private employer. The operational realities of the workplace, however, may make *some* employees' expectations of privacy unreasonable when an intrusion is by a supervisor rather than a law enforcement official. Public employees' expectations of privacy in their offices, desks, and file cabinets, like similar expectations of employees in the private sector, may be reduced by virtue of actual office practices and procedures, or by legitimate regulation. . . . The employee's expectation of privacy must be assessed in the context of the employment relation. An office is seldom a private enclave free from entry by supervisors, other employees, and business and personal invitees. Instead, in many cases offices are continually entered by fellow employees and other visitors during the workday for conferences, consultations, and other work-related visits. Simply put, it is the nature of government offices that others—such as fellow employees, supervisors, consensual visitors, and the general public—may have frequent access to an individual's office. We agree with Justice Scalia that "[constitutional] protection against *unreasonable* searches by the government does not disappear merely because the government has the right to make reasonable intrusions in its capacity as employer," but some government offices may be so open to fellow employees or the public that no expectation of privacy is reasonable. Given the great variety of work environments in the

public sector, the question whether an employee has a reasonable expectation of privacy must be addressed on a case-by-case basis.

O'Connor, 480 U.S. at 718.

Like the *O'Connor* plurality, Justice Scalia concluded in that case that Ortega had a reasonable expectation of privacy in his office spaces, desk, and office drawers. But, in arriving at this conclusion, he criticized the plurality's case-by-case methodology because it is "so devoid of content that it produces rather than eliminates uncertainty." 480 U.S. at 729-30. Further, a categorical approach to determining whether the employee had a privacy interest in the space or area is also more consistent with existing Fourth Amendment jurisprudence:

> Whatever the plurality's standard means, however, it must be wrong if it leads to the conclusion on the present facts that if Hospital officials had extensive "work-related reasons to enter Dr. Ortega's office" no Fourth Amendment protection existed. It is privacy that is protected by the Fourth Amendment, not solitude. A man enjoys Fourth Amendment protection in his home, for example, even though his wife and children have the run of the place—and indeed, even though his landlord has the right to conduct unannounced inspections at any time. Similarly, in my view, one's personal office is constitutionally protected against warrantless intrusions by the police, even though employer and co-workers are not excluded. Constitutional protection against *unreasonable* searches by the government does not disappear merely because the government has the right to make reasonable intrusions in its capacity as employer. . . .

Id. at 730-32. Which opinion do you find more convincing? Is one approach more likely to provide public employees with meaningful privacy protections than the other? Should that matter? Had the Court had to decide the threshold issue of a reasonable expectation of privacy in *Quon*, which test should it have used? Is your conclusion affected at all by the nature of the privacy interest at stake—that is, text messages on an employer-provided communications device—rather than physical spaces in employer-provided offices?

Courts addressing employee Fourth Amendment claims after *O'Connor* (but before *Quon*) usually adopted the plurality's contextual approach although, as a practical matter, the application of this standard has been categorical with regard to certain types of searches or intrusions. For example, for searches and testing involving an employee's person or bodily fluids, including drug testing, the Supreme Court and other courts have virtually always assumed or found some reasonable expectation of privacy. *See, e.g., Nat'l Treasury Employees Union v. Von Raab*, 489 U.S. 656 (1989) (drug testing) (reproduced at page 356); *Skinner v. Railway Labor Executives' Ass'n*, 489 U.S. 602 (1989) (same). In addition, in the wake of *Carpenter v. United States*, 138 S. Ct. 2206 (2018), in which the Court held in a criminal case that one has a reasonable expectation of privacy in cell-site location information from a personal cellphone, a public sector employee likely enjoys Fourth Amendment protection for data on his or her own electronic device, absent some kind of waiver or sharing of the data beyond the employee's wireless carrier. Yet in cases involving intrusions into spheres in which employee privacy expectations are less obvious—for example, physical work spaces like those at issue in *Ortega* and, as more commonly litigated today, electronic files and communications on employer-provided devices like those at issue in *Quon*—the results are mixed, often hinging on the specific areas of alleged privacy involved and workplace practices and policies. Importantly, then, whether an employee enjoys any Fourth Amendment protection at all will depend on both the nature of the intrusion and the particulars of the workplace.

3. *An Invitation to Regulate Privacy out of Existence? Quon* assumes a reasonable expectation of privacy in the underlying communications, but did plaintiff have one? On a purely technical level, one might ask whether the oral assurance overrode the written policy, which might require an inquiry into agency law. Or is a "reasonable expectation" less a question of what documents say than what most employees in the situation might expect?

Those favoring privacy protections for workers might view *Quon* as a partial victory, given that the Ninth Circuit—applying the *O'Connor* plurality's approach—did find that Quon had a reasonable expectation of privacy in the content of his communications on equipment provided by the City, *see Quon v. Arch Wireless Operating Co., Inc.*, 554 F.3d 769, 772 (9th Cir. 2009) (Wardlaw, J. concurring in denial of *en banc* review), and the Supreme Court expressly left open the question. But because particular workplace practices and circumstances will affect whether such an expectation exists (at least under the contextual approach), the partial victory for the plaintiffs in this case likely was more a function of employer missteps than an expansion of employee privacy interests in electronic communications or otherwise. What are the lessons here for employers who want discretion to review the content of employee electronic communications? What mistakes did the Department make and what steps could an employer take to prevent them? In other words, can a public employer effectively negate any reasonable expectation of privacy by establishing and abiding by clear policies and procedures regarding employee communications and work spaces?

Courts analyzing constitutional and other kinds of workplace privacy claims often find that employees have no reasonable expectation of privacy in electronic communications or files on employer-provided devices where the employer has a sufficiently broad policy that clearly states that employee communications and files may be monitored. *See, e.g., Biby v. Bd. of Regents*, 419 F.3d 845 (8th Cir. 2005); *United States v. Simons*, 206 F.3d 392 (4th Cir. 2000); *Holmes v. Petrovich Development Co.*, 119 Cal. Rptr. 3d 878 (Cal. Ct. App. 2011); *see also State v. M.A.*, 954 A.2d 503 (N.J. App. Div. 2008) (concluding employee lacked reasonable expectation of privacy in the personal information stored in his employer-provided computer where employee was advised that computers were company property and that the firm and co-workers had access to it). Indeed, the Restatement of Employment Law's limitations on an employee's "reasonable expectation of privacy" for a physical or virtual location are consistent with this treatment of employer monitoring and use policies:

> (b) An employee has a reasonable expectation in the privacy of a physical or electronic work location provided by the employer if:
>> (1) the employer has provided notice that the location or aspects of the location are private for employees; or
>> (2) the employer has acted in a manner that treats the location or aspects of the location as private for employees, the type of location is customarily treated as private for employees, and the employee has made reasonable efforts to keep the employee's activities in that location private.

RESTATEMENT OF EMPLOYMENT LAW §7.03.

Still, the existence of such a policy is not necessarily enough; as the Restatement articulation suggests, employer treatment and practices are what matters. Thus, when employees are able to establish a reasonable expectation of privacy, it tends to be because the employer did not adhere to the policy (as in *Quon*) or the policy was, for one reason or another, insufficiently clear or broad to cover the particular communications or electronic files in question. *See United States v. Ziegler*, 474 F.3d 1184, 1189-90 (9th Cir. 2007) (holding that an employee possessed a reasonable expectation of privacy in a computer in a locked office despite a company policy that computer usage would be monitored); *Pure Power Boot Camp, Inc. v. Warrior Fitness Boot Camp, LLC*, 587 F. Supp. 2d 548, 560 (S.D.N.Y. 2008) (finding that an employee had a reasonable privacy expectation in personal Hotmail account that he accessed on his employer-provided work computer because the company's e-mail policy did not state that e-mails stored on third-party providers and not within the employer's e-mail system could be subject to inspection); *see also Stengart v. Loving Care Agency, Inc.*, 990 A.2d 650 (N.J. 2010), reproduced at page 389 (stating that an employer policy regarding access to employee e-mail could not trump the employee's attorney-client privilege). It might be that the seemingly idiosyncratic *Quon* facts are more typical than they appear. Employers usually have "appropriate use" policies on paper, but there are many reasons why workplace norms could vary significantly from written policies. Even before *Quon*, if an employer really wished to forestall any expectations of privacy, it was advisable to frequently monitor worker communications—and let them know that's being done. But can you see why employers, whatever documents their attorneys draft, might be reluctant to do so?

Nevertheless, if employer monitoring and review of employee electronic communications is or becomes the standard practice, doesn't this cut against the legitimacy of an expectation that such communications are private? Wouldn't these practices help to form the norms and societal expectations to which the majority refers? Such expectation-reducing actions by employers would have a similar effect under Justice Scalia's categorical approach although, the reasonableness of an employee's expectation of privacy would not hinge on the particulars of given workplace practices or structures. But what is the likely treatment of the category—electronic communications on employer-provided devices—in a world in which employer monitoring and review are standard practice? In light of these lessons, *Quon* might lead many (most?) employers to act in ways that, as a practical matter, reduce the amount of privacy or autonomy employees enjoy at work or while using employer-provided communications devices. Or are there reasons to be more optimistic?

4. *The Second Prong: The Reasonableness of the Search or Intrusion. Quon*'s central holding was on the second prong of the inquiry: After assuming Quon had a reasonable expectation of privacy in the content of the text messages, the Court concluded that the department's review of the text message transcripts was "reasonable." In *O'Connor*, the Court had determined that the need to balance the legitimate interests of the government employer against the privacy interests of its employees justified exempting work-related searches from the usual Fourth Amendment requirement of obtaining a warrant. Such a requirement would be "unduly burdensome," especially in workplaces unfamiliar with the criminal justice system. "[T]he imposition of a warrant requirement would conflict with 'the common-sense realization that government offices could not function if every employment decision became a constitutional matter.'" *O'Connor*, 480 U.S. at 721-22 (quoting *Connick v. Myers*, 461 U.S.

138, 143 (1983)). The Court also rejected a warrantless "probable cause" standard as impracticable:

> The governmental interest justifying work-related intrusions by public employers is the efficient and proper operation of the workplace. Government agencies provide myriad services to the public, and the work of these agencies would suffer if employers were required to have probable cause before they entered an employee's desk for the purpose of finding a file or piece of office correspondence. Indeed, it is difficult to give the concept of probable cause, rooted as it is in the criminal investigatory context, much meaning when the purpose of a search is to retrieve a file for work-related reasons. Similarly, the concept of probable cause has little meaning for a routine inventory conducted by public employers for the purpose of securing state property. To ensure the efficient and proper operation of the agency, therefore, public employers must be given wide latitude to enter employee offices for work-related, noninvestigatory reasons.
>
> . . . Public employers have an interest in ensuring that their agencies operate in an effective and efficient manner, and the work of these agencies inevitably suffers from the inefficiency, incompetence, mismanagement, or other work-related misfeasance of its employees. Indeed, in many cases, public employees are entrusted with tremendous responsibility, and the consequences of their misconduct or incompetence to both the agency and the public interest can be severe. In contrast to law enforcement officials, therefore, public employers are not enforcers of the criminal law; instead, public employers have a direct and overriding interest in ensuring that the work of the agency is conducted in a proper and efficient manner. In our view, therefore, a probable cause requirement for searches of the type at issue here would impose intolerable burdens on public employers. The delay in correcting the employee misconduct caused by the need for probable cause rather than reasonable suspicion will be translated into tangible and often irreparable damage to the agency's work, and ultimately to the public interest. . . . [Additionally, it] is simply unrealistic to expect supervisors in most government agencies to learn the subtleties of the probable cause standard. . . .

Id. at 723-24.

Instead, the *O'Connor* Court adopted a much less searching "reasonableness" standard for determining the validity of the intrusion. This inquiry addresses the reasonableness of both the inception and scope of the intrusion:

> Ordinarily, a search of an employee's office by a supervisor will be "justified at its inception" when there are reasonable grounds for suspecting that the search will turn up evidence that the employee is guilty of work-related misconduct, or that the search is necessary for a noninvestigatory work-related purpose such as to retrieve a needed file. . . .
>
> [A] search will be permissible in its scope when "the measures adopted are reasonably related to the objectives of the search and not excessively intrusive in light of . . . the nature of the [misconduct]."

Id. at 726.

Applying this standard, *Quon* held that the department's review of the text messages was justified at its inception by a legitimate, noninvestigatory work-related rationale and found the level of intrusiveness to be reasonable. Perhaps the most significant doctrinal takeaway from the Court's analysis was its rejection of the Ninth Circuit's finding that the search was unreasonable in scope because the department had less intrusive means at its disposal for achieving the same work-related end. Thus, to survive scrutiny with regard to the extensiveness of the intrusion, a government employer need not utilize the "least intrusive" search practicable. Do you agree with the Court's reasoning? It's hard to imagine a "reasonableness" test that doesn't consider alternatives. Is the Court saying that alternatives are irrelevant or only that the employer doesn't have to use the less intrusive one? If the latter, how unnecessarily intrusive can a search be and still be "reasonable"?

5. *Reasonableness, Deference, and Uncertainty.* As you may have noticed already, deference to government employers' interests plays a crucial role in the Fourth Amendment analysis. For example, the need for some deference to government employers' decision making and practical constraints were central to the *O'Connor* Court's adoption of a reasonableness inquiry instead of imposing the traditional warrant and probable cause requirements. The perceived necessity to give employers some leeway also informed *Quon*'s rejection of a more onerous "least intrusive means" requirement.

Moreover, outcomes in individual cases may hinge on the level of deference courts accord government employers' justifications for their intrusions and the means they utilize to serve these ends. If, as Justice Scalia suggests, the *O'Connor* plurality's approach to the "expectation of privacy" inquiry may lead to uncertainty, the same undoubtedly can be said of the second prong's reasonableness standard as articulated in *O'Connor* and *Quon*. This standard is more deferential to the employer than a probable cause or strict scrutiny requirement would be, but how much deference is to be accorded to the government's articulated justification and chosen means remains unclear. For example, is an intrusion valid as long as an employer is able to articulate (truthfully) some workplace productivity, security, or efficiency justification and the intrusion is not greater than that needed to serve this end? The extent to which the level of scrutiny varies by circumstance or by the nature of intrusion likewise remains unresolved. The *Quon* majority states that "the extent of an expectation is relevant to assessing whether the search was too intrusive," but how this seemingly sliding scale is to be applied in other cases is unclear.

6. *Due Process Protections for Public Sector Employees.* In addition to the protection accorded by the Fourth Amendment, public employees may enjoy other privacy protections. The Fifth and Fourteenth Amendments' due process clauses protect employees' "liberty interests," including privacy interests, and these interests may be enforceable under 42 U.S.C. §1983 or directly against federal officials under *Bivens v. Six Unknown Named Agents*, 403 U.S. 388 (1971). For example, in *Whalen v. Roe*, 429 U.S. 589 (1977), the Supreme Court recognized constitutional privacy interests in "avoiding disclosure of personal matters" and in "independence in making certain kinds of important decisions." *See also Nixon v. Administrator of General Services*, 433 U.S. 425 (1977) ("[P]ublic officials, including the President, are not wholly without constitutionally protected privacy rights in matters of personal life unrelated to any acts done by them in their public capacity."). Although this right to "information privacy" is widely recognized in the circuits, its contours are not well defined.

In *National Aeronautics and Space Administration v. Nelson*, 562 U.S. 134 (2011), the Supreme Court confronted privacy-based challenges to the National Aeronautics and Space Administration's (NASA) background checks for employees in nonsensitive or low-risk positions. Among other things, NASA required these employees to submit to in-depth background investigations and answer questions about private matters including "adverse information" about financial issues, alcohol and drug abuse, and mental and emotional stability. *See id.* at 141-42. However, the Court found no violation while avoiding the constitutional question:

We assume, without deciding, that the Constitution protects a privacy right of the sort mentioned in *Whalen* and *Nixon*. We hold, however, that the challenged portions of the Government's background check do not violate this right in the present case. The Government's interests as employer and proprietor in managing its internal operations, combined with the protections against public dissemination provided by the Privacy Act of 1974 satisfy any "interest in avoiding disclosure" that may "arguably ha[ve] its roots in the Constitution."

Id. at 138. Concurring, Justice Scalia (joined by Justice Thomas) would have found no such right exists. *See id.* at 159-68.

With regard to other types of claims based on "substantive due process" rights, protection depends largely on whether the privacy interest at stake has been identified as "fundamental." Where it has not, the government employer's action must simply be rational or nonarbitrary, and employees invariably lose such challenges. Where, however, the interest has been deemed fundamental—for example, involving marriage or other intimate relations, procreation, abortion, child rearing, or perhaps intimate personal information—the alleged infringement of these rights will be subjected to more searching scrutiny, and courts have found violations in various contexts. *See, e.g., Perez v. City of Roseville*, 882 F.3d 843 (9th Cir. 2018) (holding that termination of a probationary police officer on basis of her extramarital affair with a fellow officer violated her constitutional rights to privacy and intimate association, where affair did not have meaningful effect upon her job performance and violated only the standardless rule against "conduct unbecoming an officer," rather than narrowly tailored department regulation); *Barrett v. Steubenville City Schs.*, 388 F.3d 967 (6th Cir. 2004) (finding an employee stated a claim of violation of constitutional right to rear a child after school district denied her permanent position because she removed her child from the public schools); *Barrow v. Greenville Indep. Sch. Dist.*, 332 F.3d 844 (5th Cir. 2003) (recognizing the same right). However, courts have often rejected such claims, finding either no fundamental right or a legitimate employment-related justification for the action, or that the agency's action survives strict scrutiny. *See, e.g., Seegmiller v. Laverkin City*, 528 F.3d 762 (10th Cir. 2008) (holding that a police officer did not have fundamental liberty interest to engage in private act of consensual sex, and that, under rational basis review, the city reasonably reprimanded officer under its code of ethics); *Sylvester v. Fogley*, 465 F.3d 851 (8th Cir. 2006) (holding that an investigation into whether a police officer had sexual relations with victim of crime he was investigating did not violate officer's right to privacy because the police investigation was narrowly tailored to serve a compelling interest).

7. *State Constitutions.* Many state constitutions also protect privacy rights of government workers. For example, the plaintiffs in *Quon* claimed violations of Article I, Section 1 of the California Constitution, which provides that all people have inalienable rights, including life, liberty, and "privacy." *See also* AK. CONST. art. I, §22 ("The right of the people to privacy is recognized and shall not be infringed."); WASH. CONST. art. I, §7 ("No person shall be disturbed in his private affairs, or his home invaded, without authority of law.").

8. *Statutory Protections for Public Sector Employees.* While there is no comprehensive workplace privacy statute or statutory scheme protecting federal workers' privacy, federal employees have some additional protections from intrusions. For example, under the Civil Service Reform Act, 5 U.S.C. §2302 (2018), civil service workers are protected against termination for conduct that does not adversely affect their employment performance or the performance of others. Also, federal employees may enjoy protection against the government collecting, using, and disclosing some kinds of personal information under the Privacy Act of 1974, 5 U.S.C. §552a (2018). State protections for public workers vary, but many have civil service regimes akin to the one under federal law. Many other state statutory protections apply to both public and private sectors.

9. *Spillovers Between the Public and Private Workplace.* Although *Quon* involves a public employer, two of plaintiffs' three primary legal theories—the Stored Communications Act, 18 U.S.C. §§2702-2711 (2018), discussed in more detail on page 349, and California constitutional claims—could also be available in the private employer context. Indeed, while most state constitutional protections, like their federal counterparts, are limited to government intrusions, California's privacy provision applies to private actors, including private employers. *See Hernandez v. Hillsides, Inc.,* 211 P.3d 1063 (Cal. 2009); *Soroka v. Dayton Hudson Corp.,* 1 Cal. Rptr. 2d 77 (Ct. App. 1991); *cf. Hennessey v. Coastal Eagle Point Oil Co.,* 609 A.2d 11 (N.J. 1992) (holding that the right to privacy in the New Jersey Constitution does not apply to private actors directly but can form part of the basis for a clear mandate of public policy supporting a wrongful discharge claim). Nevertheless, since federal constitutional, most state constitutional, and other statutory protections (like those discussed in Note 8) are available only to government workers, the public/private sector distinction is a potentially dispositive one in the privacy context.

Still, there are a number of other ways in which privacy claims in public and private workplace converge. First, Justice Scalia's concurrence in *O'Connor* suggests that private sector norms and practices may be relevant to the reasonableness inquiry. *See O'Connor,* 480 U.S. at 732 (stating that "searches of the sort that are regarded as reasonable and normal in the private-employer context" do not violate the Fourth Amendment). Reliance on private sector norms and practices might seem odd, given that worker expectations about when the government can intrude upon certain spaces and communications may vary greatly (and legitimately) from their views of when private employers may intrude. Indeed, isn't it likely that the background constitutional and statutory constraints themselves shape public sector employees' expectations differently than those in the private sector? For criticism of the suggestion in *Quon* that private sector norms might influence expectations of privacy for public sector workers, see Paul M. Secunda, *Privatizing Workplace Privacy,* 88 NOTRE DAME L. REV. 277 (2012).

On the flip side, Fourth Amendment cases like *O'Connor* have proven highly influential beyond the public workplace as courts analyzing private sector claims borrow heavily from the legal framework developed in the Fourth Amendment cases. As we will see, the analytical framework set forth in *O'Connor* is similar to those adopted by courts addressing privacy claims based on statutory, state constitutional, and tort theories. For example, as the Ninth Circuit's panel decision in *Quon* stated, the analysis under the California Constitution tracks the Fourth Amendment. *See* 529 F.3d 892, 903 (9th Cir. 2008). Moreover, the new Restatement, which seeks to provide guidance on common law principles (recall the discussion in Chapter 1), expressly relies on the reasoning in the government sector cases because they have been influential in shaping the analysis in the private sector context. *See* RESTATEMENT OF EMPLOYMENT LAW (2015) §7.01 cmt. g ("Although decisions involving government workers generally do not apply to workers in private firms because of the absence of constitutional and civil-service protections in the private sector, principles developed in these decisions help shape common-law rulings in the private sector as well as the public sector.).

2. Tort-Based Protections

Borse v. Piece Goods Shop, Inc.
963 F.2d 611 (3d Cir. 1992)

BECKER, Circuit Judge.

Plaintiff Sarah Borse brought suit against her former employer, Piece Goods Shop, Inc. ("the Shop"), in the district court for the Eastern District of Pennsylvania. She claimed that, by dismissing her when she refused to submit to urinalysis screening and personal property searches (conducted by her employer at the workplace pursuant to its drug and alcohol policy), the Shop violated a public policy that precludes employers from engaging in activities that violate their employees' rights to privacy and to freedom from unreasonable searches. . . . This appeal requires us to decide whether an at-will employee who is discharged for refusing to consent to urinalysis screening for drug use and to searches of her personal property states a claim for wrongful discharge under Pennsylvania law.

Because we predict that, under certain circumstances, discharging a private-sector, at-will employee for refusal to consent to drug testing and to personal property searches may violate the public policy embodied in the Pennsylvania cases recognizing a cause of action for tortious invasion of privacy, and because the allegations of Borse's complaint are not sufficient for us to determine whether the facts of this case support such a claim, we will vacate the district court's [dismissal for failure to state a claim] and remand with directions to grant leave to amend.

I. The Allegations of the Complaint . . .

Borse was employed as a sales clerk by the Piece Goods Shop for almost fifteen years. In January 1990, the Shop adopted a drug and alcohol policy which required its employees to sign a form giving their consent to urinalysis screening for drug use and to searches of their personal property located on the Shop's premises.

Borse refused to sign the consent form. On more than one occasion, she asserted that the drug and alcohol policy violated her right to privacy and her right to be free from unreasonable searches and seizures as guaranteed by the United States Constitution. The Shop continued to insist that she sign the form and threatened to discharge her unless she did. On February 9, 1990, the Shop terminated Borse's employment.

The complaint alleges that Borse was discharged in retaliation for her refusal to sign the consent form and for protesting the Shop's drug and alcohol policy. It asserts that her discharge violated a public policy, embodied in the First and Fourth Amendments to the United States Constitution, which precludes employers from engaging in activities that violate their employees' rights to privacy and to freedom from unreasonable searches of their persons and property. Plaintiff seeks compensatory damages for emotional distress, injury to reputation, loss of earnings, and diminished earning capacity. She also alleges that the discharge was willful and malicious and, accordingly, seeks punitive damages.

II. Overview of the Public Policy Exception to the Employment-at-Will Doctrine in Pennsylvania

[The Court recognized that, as a federal court sitting in diversity, it must apply Pennsylvania tort law in this case. In so doing, it was obliged to predict how the Pennsylvania Supreme Court would resolve the question of whether discharging an at-will employee who refuses to consent to urinalysis and to searches of his or her personal property located on the employer's premises violates public policy. It concluded that Pennsylvania law continues to recognize a claim for wrongful discharge when dismissal of an at-will employee violates a clear mandate of public policy.]

III. Sources of Public Policy

In order to evaluate Borse's claim, we must attempt to "discern whether any public policy is threatened" by her discharge. As evidence of a public policy that precludes employers from discharging employees who refuse to consent to the practices at issue, Borse primarily relies upon the First and Fourth Amendments to the United States Constitution and the right to privacy included in the Pennsylvania Constitution. As will be seen, we reject her reliance on these constitutional provisions, concluding instead that, to the extent that her discharge implicates public policy, the source of that policy lies in Pennsylvania common law.

A. Constitutional Provisions

1. The United States Constitution

Although the Supreme Court has made clear that the Constitution proscribes only the *government* from violating the individual's right to privacy, and to freedom from unreasonable searches, *Skinner v. Railway Labor Executives Association,* 489 U.S. 602 (1989) (Fourth Amendment does not apply to searches by private party), Borse argues that our decision in *Novosel v. Nationwide Insurance Co.,* 721 F.2d 894 (3d Cir. 1983), permits us to consider the public policies embodied in the First and Fourth Amendments despite the lack of state action. In *Novosel,* defendant Nationwide instructed its employees to participate in its effort to lobby the Pennsylvania House of Representatives, which was then considering an insurance reform act. Specifically, Nationwide directed its employees to clip, copy, and obtain signatures on coupons bearing the insignia of the Pennsylvania Committee for No-Fault Reform. Novosel alleged that he was discharged for refusing to participate in the lobbying effort and for privately stating opposition to his employer's political stand.

In response to Novosel's claim, Nationwide argued that a wrongful discharge action depends upon the violation of a *statutorily* recognized public policy. We disagreed. After noting that the public policy exception applies only in the absence of statutory remedies, we reasoned:

> Given that there are no statutory remedies available in the present case and taking into consideration the importance of the political and associational freedoms of the federal and state Constitutions, the absence of a statutory declaration of public policy would appear to be no bar to the existence of a cause of action. Accordingly, a cognizable expression of public policy may be derived in this case from either the First Amendment of the United States Constitution or Article I, Section 7 of the Pennsylvania Constitution.[5]

[While the district court's opinion erred insofar as it suggested that a constitutional provision may never serve as a source of public policy in Pennsylvania], it correctly refused to extend *Novosel* to Borse's claim. As the district court observed, the Superior Court has refused to extend constitutional provisions designed to restrict governmental conduct in the absence of state action. . . .

The Pennsylvania Supreme Court has not considered the propriety of applying constitutional principles to wrongful discharge actions against private employers. Its most recent decisions regarding the cause of action admonish us, however, that the public policy exception applies "only in the most limited of circumstances," *Paul* [*v. Lankenau Hospital*, 569 A.2d 346, 348 Pa. (1990)]. . . .

Novosel's holding (i.e., that using the power of discharge to coerce employees' political activity violates public policy) is not at issue here and thus we need not decide whether the recent Pennsylvania cases constitute such "persuasive evidence of a change in Pennsylvania law" that we are free to disregard it. Instead, we need only decide whether to *extend* the approach taken in *Novosel*. In light of the narrowness of the public policy exception and of the Pennsylvania courts' continuing insistence upon the state action requirement, we predict that if faced with the issue, the Pennsylvania Supreme Court would not look to the First and Fourth Amendments as sources of public policy when there is no state action. Accordingly, we decline to extend the approach taken in *Novosel* to this case.

2. The Pennsylvania Constitution

[The court predicted that the Pennsylvania Supreme Court would find that the state constitution does not encompass privacy invasions by private actors and would not look to that constitution's right to privacy as a source of public policy in a wrongful discharge action.]

B. *Pennsylvania Common Law*

Although we have rejected Borse's reliance upon constitutional provisions as evidence of a public policy allegedly violated by the Piece Goods Shop's drug and

---

5. Article I, section 7 states in pertinent part:

The free communication of thoughts and opinions is one of the invaluable rights of man, and every citizen may freely speak, write and print on any subject, being responsible for the abuse of that liberty.

alcohol program, our review of Pennsylvania law reveals other evidence of a public policy that may, under certain circumstances, give rise to a wrongful discharge action related to urinalysis or to personal property searches. Specifically, we refer to the Pennsylvania common law regarding tortious invasion of privacy.

Pennsylvania recognizes a cause of action for tortious "intrusion upon seclusion." *Marks v. Bell Telephone Co.*, 331 A.2d 424, 430 (Pa. 1975). The Restatement defines the tort as follows:

> One who intentionally intrudes, physically or otherwise, upon the solitude or seclusion of another or his private affairs or concerns, is subject to liability to the other for invasion of his privacy, if the intrusion would be highly offensive to a reasonable person.

RESTATEMENT (SECOND) OF TORTS §652B.[8]

Unlike the other forms of tortious invasion of privacy,[9] an action based on intrusion upon seclusion does not require publication as an element of the tort. *Harris by Harris v. Easton Publishing Co.*, 483 A.2d 1377, 1383 (1984). The tort may occur by (1) physical intrusion into a place where the plaintiff has secluded himself or herself; (2) use of the defendant's senses to oversee or overhear the plaintiff's private affairs; or (3) some other form of investigation or examination into plaintiff's private concerns. Liability attaches only when the intrusion is substantial and would be highly offensive to "the ordinary reasonable person."

We can envision at least two ways in which an employer's urinalysis program might intrude upon an employee's seclusion. First, the particular manner in which the program is conducted might constitute an intrusion upon seclusion as defined by Pennsylvania law. The process of collecting the urine sample to be tested clearly implicates "expectations of privacy that society has long recognized as reasonable," *Skinner v. Railway Labor Executives Association*, 489 U.S. 602, 617 (1989).[10] In addition, many urinalysis programs monitor the collection of the urine specimen to ensure that the employee does not adulterate it or substitute a sample from another person. Monitoring collection of the urine sample appears to fall within the definition of an intrusion upon seclusion because it involves the use of one's senses to oversee the private activities of another. RESTATEMENT (SECOND) OF TORTS §652B, comment b. *See also Harris.* . . .

Second, urinalysis "can reveal a host of private medical facts about an employee, including whether she is epileptic, pregnant, or diabetic." *Skinner*. A reasonable person might well conclude that submitting urine samples to tests designed to ascertain these types of information constitutes a substantial and highly offensive intrusion upon seclusion.

---

8. In *Vogel v. W.T. Grant Co.*, 327 A.2d 133 (Pa. 1974), the Pennsylvania Supreme Court adopted the definition of tortious invasion of privacy as stated in a tentative draft of the RESTATEMENT (SECOND) OF TORTS §652 (Tent Draft Nov. 13, 1967). Although the Pennsylvania Supreme Court has not expressly adopted the final version of section 652, our analysis of Pennsylvania law in *O'Donnell v. United States*, 891 F.2d 1079 (3d Cir. 1989), led us to predict that it would do so if presented with the issue. *See also Vernars v. Young*, 539 F.2d 966 (3d Cir. 1976) (upholding invasion of privacy claim under Pennsylvania law when corporate officer opened and read personal mail addressed to fellow employee).

9. The action for invasion of privacy encompasses four analytically distinct torts. In addition to intrusion upon seclusion, the tort also includes: (1) appropriation of name or likeness; (2) publicity given to private life; and (3) publicity placing a person in a false light. *See Marks.*

10. [W]e caution against the wholesale application to private employers of the limitations imposed on public employers by the Fourth Amendment. We find the cases involving government employers helpful, however, in defining the individual privacy interest implicated by urinalysis.

The same principles apply to an employer's search of an employee's personal property. If the search is not conducted in a discreet manner or if it is done in such a way as to reveal personal matters unrelated to the workplace, the search might well constitute a tortious invasion of the employee's privacy. *See, for example, K-Mart Corp. Store No. 7441 v. Trotti*, 677 S.W.2d 632 (Tex. App. 1984) (search of employee's locker). *See also Bodewig v. K-Mart, Inc.*, 635 P.2d 657 (1981) (subjecting cashier accused of stealing to strip search).

The Pennsylvania courts have not had occasion to consider whether a discharge related to an employer's tortious invasion of an employee's privacy violates public policy. . . .

[W]e believe that when an employee alleges that his or her discharge was related to an employer's invasion of his or her privacy, the Pennsylvania Supreme Court would examine the facts and circumstances surrounding the alleged invasion of privacy. If the court determined that the discharge was related to a substantial and highly offensive invasion of the employee's privacy, we believe that it would conclude that the discharge violated public policy.[11] Indeed, the following language in [*Geary v. United States Steel Corp.*, 319 A.2d 174 (Pa. 1974)] might well be considered to presage such an approach:

> It may be granted that there are areas of an employee's life in which his employer has no legitimate interest. An intrusion into one of these areas by virtue of the employer's power of discharge might plausibly give rise to a cause of action, particularly where some recognized facet of public policy is threatened. . . .

Only a handful of other jurisdictions have considered urinalysis programs implemented by private employers.[12] The majority of these decisions balance the employee's privacy interest against the employer's interests in order to determine whether to uphold the programs. *See,* for example, *Luedtke v. Nabors Alaska Drilling, Inc.*, 768 P.2d 1123 (Alaska 1989). In *Luedtke*, two employees challenged their employer's urinalysis program, alleging violation of their state constitutional right of privacy, common-law invasion of privacy, wrongful discharge, and breach of the covenant of good faith and fair dealing. (Under Alaska law, the public policy exception to the employment-at-will doctrine is "largely encompassed within the implied covenant of good faith and fair dealing.") After determining that the relevant provision of the Alaska constitution did not apply to private action, the Alaska Supreme Court concluded that a public policy protecting an employee's right to withhold private information from his employer exists in Alaska and that violation of that policy "may rise to the level of a breach of the implied covenant of good faith and fair dealing."

---

11. The Sixth Circuit recently rejected an invasion of privacy claim challenging an employer's urinalysis program. *Baggs v. Eagle-Picher Industries, Inc.*, 957 F.2d 268 (6th Cir. 1992) (applying Michigan law). Michigan law permits an employer to use "intrusive and even objectionable means to obtain employment-related information about an employee." In contrast, Pennsylvania has not exempted employers from the principles ordinarily applied in actions for tortious invasion of privacy.

12. Several of these cases are inapposite because they involve state law that differs significantly from Pennsylvania's. For example, some state constitutions include a right of privacy that applies to private action. Our discussion in the text focuses on selected cases typifying the various approaches taken in the remaining cases. We are unaware of any case considering whether the dismissal of an at-will employee who refuses to consent to personal property searches violates public policy.

As evidence of public policy, the court looked to the state's statutes,[13] Constitution,[14] and common law.[15] The court concluded:

> Thus, the citizens' rights to be protected against unwarranted intrusions into their private lives has been recognized in the law of Alaska. The constitution protects against governmental intrusion, statutes protect against employer intrusion, and the common law protects against intrusions by other private persons. As a result, there is sufficient evidence to support the conclusion that there exists a public policy protecting spheres of employee conduct into which employers may not intrude.

The court then turned to the question "whether employer monitoring of employee drug use outside the work place is such a prohibited intrusion." The Court reasoned that the boundaries of the employee's right of privacy "are determined by balancing [that right] against other public policies, such as 'the health, safety, rights and privileges of others.'" Because the *Luedtke* plaintiffs performed safety-sensitive jobs, the court concluded that the public policy supporting the protection of the health and safety of other workers justified their employer's urinalysis program.

[The West Virginia Supreme Court also applied a balancing test in *Twigg v. Hercules Corp.*, 406 S.E.2d 52 (W. Va. 1990), reasoning that its holding that requiring employees to submit to polygraph examinations violated public policy should be extended to requiring an employee to submit to drug testing. West Virginia, however, recognized two exceptions: when the urinalysis is based on "reasonable good faith objective suspicion" of an employee's drug use or when the employee's job involves public safety or the safety of others. Not all other jurisdictions have applied a balancing test to urinalysis programs, but the balancing test is more consistent with Pennsylvania law.]
. . . Pennsylvania's intermediate appellate courts have recognized a public policy exception to the employment-at-will doctrine on three occasions and have emphasized the need to examine all the circumstances in a wrongful discharge action. . . . More importantly, under Pennsylvania law an employee's consent to a violation of public policy is no defense to a wrongful discharge action when that consent is obtained by the threat of dismissal.[18]

13. The court observed that a statute prohibiting employers from requiring employees to take polygraph tests as a condition of employment supports "the policy that there are private sectors of employees' lives not subject to direct scrutiny by their employers." The court also noted that a statute prohibiting employment discrimination on the basis of, among other things, marital status, changes in marital status, pregnancy or parenthood, demonstrates "that in Alaska certain subjects are placed outside the consideration of employers in their relations with employees."

14. The court reasoned that although Alaska's constitutional right of privacy does not proscribe private action, the inclusion of a specific clause protecting the right "supports the contention that this right 'strike[s] as the heart of a citizen's social rights.'"

15. The court observed that the action for tortious intrusion upon seclusion evidences the existence of a common-law right of privacy.

18. In *Leibowitz v. H.A. Winston Co.*, 493 A.2d 111 (Pa. Super. 1985), plaintiff was fired after a polygraph test indicated that he lied about stealing money from his employer. Because plaintiff had signed a release prior to taking the polygraph test, however, his employer argued that he could not maintain a cause of action for wrongful discharge. The court disagreed. It noted that Pennsylvania law prohibits employers from requiring polygraph tests as a condition of employment and that discharging an employee for refusing to submit to a polygraph test violates public policy, *see Perks v. Firestone Tire & Rubber Co.*, 611 F.2d 1363 (3d Cir. 1979) (upholding wrongful discharge action of employee fired for refusing to take polygraph test). The court then reasoned that although "mere economic or financial pressure [usually] does not suffice to invalidate a release," that rule does not apply when an employer requires an employee to sign a release as a condition of continued employment. Under those circumstances, the release is invalid. *Accord Polsky v.*

In view of the foregoing analysis, we predict that the Pennsylvania Supreme Court would apply a balancing test to determine whether the Shop's drug and alcohol program (consisting of urinalysis and personal property searches) invaded Borse's privacy. Indeed, determining whether an alleged invasion of privacy is substantial and highly offensive to the reasonable person necessitates the use of a balancing test. The test we believe that Pennsylvania would adopt balances the employee's privacy interest against the employer's interest in maintaining a drug-free workplace in order to determine whether a reasonable person would find the employer's program highly offensive.

We recognize that other jurisdictions have considered individualized suspicion and concern for safety as factors to be considered in striking the balance, see, for example, *Twigg* (allowing urinalysis based on individualized suspicion or when employee's job implicates safety concerns). We do not doubt that, in an appropriate case, Pennsylvania would include these factors in the balance, but we do not believe that the Pennsylvania Supreme Court would require private employers to *limit* urinalysis programs or personal property searches to employees suspected of drug use or to those performing safety-sensitive jobs.

This precautionary note springs from two sources. First, these limitations originated in cases applying constitutional principles to urinalysis programs conducted by government employers. *See Skinner; Von Raab.* We do not believe that the Pennsylvania courts would transfer the jurisprudence of the cases involving government employers to actions against private employers because the standard applied in cases involving government employers differs significantly from that applied in the tortious invasion of privacy cases. In the cases involving government employers, courts have asked whether the urinalysis program is reasonable under Fourth Amendment principles. In contrast, in order for an invasion of privacy to be tortious, it must be both substantial and highly offensive to the reasonable person. Therefore, even though [we reason] that if a private employer's drug and alcohol program tortiously invaded its employees' privacy the Pennsylvania Supreme Court would hold that discharges related to that program violated public policy, we do not believe that the Pennsylvania Supreme Court would simply transpose Fourth Amendment limitations on public employers to urinalysis programs or personal property searches conducted by private employers.

Second, the case law concerning the public policy exception reflects "a pattern of favoring the employer's interest in running its business," and a willingness to define that interest broadly. . . . Given this backdrop, we find it unlikely that Pennsylvania would impose the strict limitations of the Fourth Amendment cases.

In sum, based on our prediction of Pennsylvania law, we hold that dismissing an employee who refused to consent to urinalysis testing and to personal property searches would violate public policy if the testing tortiously invaded the employee's privacy. [Borse should be accorded leave to amend her complaint to specify how her privacy was invaded.]

Radio Shack, 666 F.2d 824 (3d Cir. 1981) (applying Pennsylvania law). *See* Stephen M. Fogel, Gerri L. Kornblut & Newton P. Porter, *Survey of the Law on Employee Drug Testing,* 42 U. Miami L. Rev. 553, 669 (1988) (criticizing contrary result as creating Catch-22 for employee).

NOTES

1. *The Search for a Cause of Action.* Why did the plaintiff have to rely on the public policy exception in this case? An obvious answer is that there was no statutory protection on point and, because the employer in this case is a private employer, federal and state constitutional protections do not apply directly. Thus, as is often the case, the plaintiff here was engaged in a search for a source of protection. Yet, this is not a complete explanation; after all, in its analysis of public policy, the court notes that Pennsylvania courts have recognized the tort of intrusion upon seclusion, which gives employees a cause of action against private employers. In answering this question, consider how the claim here (as well as the remedy sought) is distinguishable from a stand-alone intrusion upon seclusion claim.

2. *The Public Policy Exception.* The *Borse* court concludes that Pennsylvania is likely to recognize a cause of action under the public policy doctrine in this case if the testing tortiously invaded the employee's privacy. To reach this result, the court explicitly rejects reliance on constitutional sources, relying instead on common-law tort. Some courts in other jurisdictions have recognized public policy claims in the employee drug-testing context, based on state constitutional, statutory, or common-law sources of public policy. In addition to the sources cited in *Borse, see, e.g., Hennessey v. Coastal Eagle Point Oil Co.*, 609 A.2d 11 (N.J. 1992) (finding public policy embodied in constitutional privacy protections). Other courts have been less amenable to recognition of these claims.

The Restatement of Employment Law likewise recognizes a claim for discharge for retaliation for refusing a privacy invasion: "An employer who discharges an employee for refusing to consent to a wrongful employer intrusion upon a protected employee privacy interest under this Chapter is subject to liability for wrongful discharge in violation of well-established public policy under Chapter 5 [of the Restatement]." §7.07. The reporter's comments to this section make clear that, in order to prevail on this claim, the employee would have to establish that the intrusion to which the consent was sought would violate §7.06, discussed in the next note. *See id.*, §7.07 cmt. c.

3. *Intrusion upon Seclusion. Borse* discusses the tort of intrusion upon seclusion, the most widely recognized common-law privacy claim in the employment context. As *Borse* indicates, the tort requires (1) an intentional intrusion (2) into an area of solitude or seclusion (3) that would be highly offensive to the reasonable person. Note the similarity between this articulation and the Fourth Amendment analysis in *O'Connor* and *Quon.* As in a Fourth Amendment case, much hinges on whether the intrusion was into an area (spatial or otherwise) in which the employee has a reasonable expectation of privacy. This is satisfied in the drug and medical testing and other bodily intrusion contexts since courts agree that one has a reasonable expectation of privacy in his or her person. But whether such an expectation exists with regard to employee work spaces or communications is a more difficult issue that depends on the particulars of the job and workplace. *Compare Fischer v. Mt. Olive Lutheran Church*, 207 F. Supp. 2d 914 (W.D. Wis. 2002) (finding that employee had reasonable expectation in the e-mails in his personal Hotmail account); *Hernandez v. Hillsides, Inc.*, 211 P.3d 1063 (Cal. 2009) (concluding that employees had reasonable expectation that office that could be locked would not be secretly videotaped); *Koeppel v. Speirs*, 808 N.W.2d 177 (Iowa 2011) (finding a genuine issue of material fact as to whether a security camera that the employer had surreptitiously installed in a workplace bathroom, though inoperable when discovered, could have potentially transmitted images of the employee, thereby intentionally intruding into a matter in which the employee had a right to expect privacy); *with Holmes v. Petrovich Development Co.*, 119 Cal. Rptr. 3d 878 (Cal. Ct. App. 2011) (holding employee's belief that her emails were private was unreasonable because she was warned that the company would monitor email to ensure employees were complying with office policy and she was told that she had no expectation of privacy in any messages she sent from the company computer) and *Thygeson v. U.S. Bancorp*, 2004 U.S. Dist. LEXIS 18863 (D. Or. Sept. 15, 2004) (suggesting an employee has no reasonable expectation of privacy in e-mails on employer's e-mail system).

If there is such an intrusion by the employer, the next inquiry is whether it was objectively offensive. Oddly enough, whether the intrusion is offensive is not measured by how subjectively offensive it is to the employee but rather whether it is justified by a legitimate employer interest and appropriately tailored to serving that interest. Indeed, this is stated expressly in the new Restatement of Employment Law's version of the tort:

> §7.06. Wrongful Employer Intrusions
> (a) An employer is subject to liability for a wrongful intrusion upon an employee's protected privacy interest (see §§7.03-7.05) if the intrusion would be highly offensive to a reasonable person under the circumstances.
> (b) An intrusion is highly offensive under subsection (a) if the nature, manner, and scope of the intrusion upon the employee's protected privacy interest are clearly unreasonable when judged against the employer's legitimate business interests or the public's interests in intruding.

In short, a reasonable employee should not be offended by a justifiable intrusion. As in the Fourth Amendment context, resolution of this inquiry often depends on the leeway courts are willing to give employers' articulated ends and the means for achieving them. *Compare Speer v. Ohio Dep't of Rehab. and Corr.*, 624 N.E.2d 251 (Ohio Ct. App. 1993) (finding that a supervisor's hiding in the ceiling of a staff rest room to monitor an employee suspected of misconduct was unreasonable) *with Saldana v. Kelsey-Hayes*, 443 N.W.2d 382 (Mich. Ct. App. 1989) (upholding an employer's surveillance of an employee's home because the employer had a legitimate right to investigate the employee's claim of workplace injury); *see generally* Daniel P. O'Gorman, *Looking Out for Your Employer: Employers' Surreptitious Physical Surveillance of Employees and the Tort of Invasion of Privacy*, 85 Neb. L. Rev. 212 (2006).

4. *Other Privacy Torts.* Other privacy torts are litigated occasionally in the workplace context. For example, Restatement (Second) of Torts (ALI 1979) §652D recognizes the tort of public disclosure of private facts, which creates a cause of action when one publicly discloses a private matter that is "highly offensive" to the reasonable person and as to which the public has no legitimate concern. Employers typically have access to private information about employees (e.g., disabilities or more general health information), and thus, their disclosure of such information to the public or third parties without justification may give rise to liability. *See, e.g., Miller v. Motorola, Inc.*, 560 N.E.2d 900 (Ill. App. Ct. 1990). However, the sharing of such information with workplace personnel may not give rise to liability, either because such a sharing is not sufficiently "public" to satisfy the public disclosure element, or because a legitimate business justification may render such disclosure "reasonable." *See, e.g., Bratt v. Int'l Bus. Machines*, 785 F.2d 352 (1st Cir. 1986) (finding no liability for the sharing of information about an employee's psychological condition with other managerial personnel); *see generally* Jonathan B. Mintz, *The Remains of Privacy's Disclosure Tort: An Exploration of the Private Domain*, 55 MD. L. REV. 425 (1996). Another theory that may provide protection in certain workplace contexts is the tort of false light, that is, where the employer discloses a matter about the employee that places the employee in a "false light" that is "highly offensive" to a reasonable person. *See* RESTATEMENT (SECOND) OF TORTS §652C (1977).

Despite the theoretical applicability of these tort causes of action, the statutory protections discussed in the next subsection are more likely to provide meaningful protection for the workplace privacy interests implicated. However, other workplace tort theories that implicate privacy or related dignitary interests are more likely to be pursued, including defamation, discussed in Chapter 5, and intentional infliction of emotional distress, discussed below.

5. *Intentional Infliction of Emotional Distress.* The means by which an employer may seek to monitor employee activities or gain information from an employee may give rise to an intentional infliction of emotional distress claim. As discussed in this chapter, the Restatement (Second) of Torts provides that such a cause of action exists when "one who by extreme and outrageous conduct intentionally or recklessly causes severe emotional distress to another." In most cases, the key inquiry is whether the employers' conduct—in this context, intrusive actions—is sufficiently "extreme and outrageous" to justify liability. Courts occasionally have found that employers' methods reach this level. *Rulon-Miller v. Int'l Bus. Machines Corp.*, 208 Cal. Rptr. 524 (Ct. App. 1984) (discussed at page 355). *See also Bodewig v. K-Mart, Inc.*, 635 P.2d 657 (Or. Ct. App. 1981) (recognizing a claim for intentional infliction of emotional distress after the employer required an employee to disrobe in front of a customer who claimed the employee had taken her money).

6. *The Request for Consent "Catch-22."* Numerous courts have found consent (or, at least, fully informed consent) to an alleged privacy intrusion to be a near-absolute defense to common-law privacy claims. *See, e.g., Stewart v. Pantry, Inc.*, 715 F. Supp. 1361 (W.D. Ky. 1988) (holding consent is a complete defense to an intrusion claim involving polygraph tests); *Jennings v. Minco Tech. Labs, Inc.*, 765 S.W.2d 497 (Tex. Ct. App. 1989) (same in drug-testing context); *cf. Baggs v. Eagle-Picher Indus., Inc.*, 750 F. Supp. 264 (W.D. Mich. 1990) (finding no expectation of privacy because employees were on notice of possible drug testing); *TBG Ins. Services Corp. v. Superior Court*, 117 Cal. Rptr. 2d 155 (Cal. App. 2002) (finding, in the context of a discovery dispute, that employee had no reasonable expectation of privacy in files on an employer-provided home computer because he had agreed in writing to employer's policy that computer use would be monitored). Should an employee's agreement to be tested, searched, or monitored, in response to an employer's request (or insistence) be a defense to a public policy claim? Similarly, should such agreement preclude recovery under an intrusion upon seclusion theory, either because consent destroys any reasonable expectation of privacy or because consent makes the intrusion not objectively offensive? On the other hand, if the employee refuses to agree to the intrusion, and no intrusion thereby occurs (i.e., no drug test, no intrusive questioning, no requested search of spaces or communications), some courts have held that that there is no intrusion upon seclusion claim. *See, e.g., Rushing v. Hershey Chocolate-Memphis,*

2000 WL 1597849 (6th Cir. 2000); *Baggs, supra* (holding that those who did not participate in the drug-testing program cannot recover because there was no intrusion); *Luedtke v. Nabors Alaska Drilling, Inc.*, 768 P.2d 1123 (Alaska 1989) ("[N]o cause of action for invasion of privacy arises where the intrusion is prevented from taking place").

And here lies the Catch-22: If the employee agrees to the test, search, or other intrusion, she has consented to it; if she refuses (and loses her job as a result), there is no intrusion. Either way, she has no claim. Under this framework then, an employer can shield itself from liability by always asking for the employee's agreement or waiver before any intrusion occurs because any response by the employee will bar the claim. Obviously, not all courts have taken this view, and some courts, including *Borse* and *Luedtke*, as well as §7.07 of the Restatement, have recognized that a public policy claim arising out of the employee's termination might exist even if an intrusion upon seclusion claim fails. Nevertheless, the potential waiver of rights and remedies when employers seek consent to otherwise actionable intrusions creates a further incentive for employers to make the demand for consent (to monitoring, surveillance, workplace searches, etc.) standard practice, and employees are then in a very difficult position when deciding how to respond.

3.   Statutory Protections

a.   *Federal Law*

While, unlike the European Union's General Data Privacy Rule, see p. 354, there is no comprehensive federal statutory scheme governing privacy rights in the private workplace, a number of federal statutory regimes protect privacy interests of private sector employees. Some protect such interests incidentally or as part of a larger scheme addressing other regulatory objectives. For example, antidiscrimination statutes provide indirect protection from certain forms of invasive employer activity or inquiries. While the Americans with Disabilities Act ("ADA") explicitly prohibits inquiry into its protected category, all antidiscrimination laws prohibit employers from altering the terms and conditions of employment based on an employee's protected status, which means that employers should steer clear of inquiries that might implicate such status—such as one's religion, age, or pregnancy status. *See, e.g., Norman-Bloodshaw v. Lawrence Berkeley Lab.*, 135 F.3d 1260 (9th Cir. 1998) (holding that challenges to employer's medical and genetic testing program raised cognizable discrimination claims because they revealed sex- and race-linked traits or conditions). In addition, offensive intrusions into private matters by supervisors or co-workers may contribute to a discriminatory harassment claim if the conduct is linked to the victim's protected status (e.g., sex or religion). Various employment screening procedures—testing, medical screening, questioning, and so forth—also may violate antidiscrimination statutes if they have a disparate impact on a protected class and cannot be justified by business necessity. *See* Chapter 9.

In the past several decades, however, a number of statutory developments have focused directly on privacy interests. A high-profile example is the 2008 Genetic Information Nondiscrimination Act ("GINA"), 42 U.S.C. §2000ff et seq. (2018), which is discussed at the end of this subsection. These statutory regimes offer meaningful protections, but, as you will see, they are sometimes qualified or limited in important respects.

Earlier federal enactments tended to focus on intrusive interrogation techniques and employee surveillance and monitoring. For example, the Employee Polygraph Protection Act of 1988 ("EPPA"), 29 U.S.C. §§2001-09 (2018), bans the use of a polygraph for pre-employment screening for post-employment purposes it delineates both the circumstances in which polygraphs may be used in employer investigations following a theft of property and the procedures for such use. The EPPA applies to most private employees; however, government employees and employees working in various defense and security contexts are exempted.

In addition, the federal wiretapping statute, now embodied in the Electronic Communications Privacy Act of 1986 ("ECPA"), 18 U.S.C. §§2510-22 (2018), protects against various kinds of electronic surveillance and interception of communications by public and private actors, including private employers. It declares unlawful the intentional interception of oral wire communications, other oral communications, and electronic communications (all non-oral wire communications). While this act may appear to provide robust protections for electronic communications, including e-mails and Internet activity, three exemptions from its prohibitions limit protection for employee communications: (1) interceptions by a service provider (often the employer) to protect the rights or property of the provider, (2) interception by certain devices of communications made in the "ordinary course of business," and (3) interceptions when one party to the communication consents. Moreover, courts have construed "interception" narrowly in various contexts. *See, e.g., Konop v. Hawaiian Airlines, Inc.*, 302 F.3d 868 (9th Cir. 2002) (construing "interception" to cover only communications acquired during transmission); *see also McCann v. Iroquois Mem'l Hosp.*, 622 F.3d. 745 (7th Cir. 2010) (granting summary judgment to individual hospital managers on ECPA claims for allegedly retaliating against two workers based on a conversation that had been recorded by another worker; there was no evidence the managers knew that the recording had been illegally made); Ariana Levinson, *Toward a Cohesive Interpretation of the Electronic Communications Privacy Act for the Electronic Monitoring of Employees*, 114 W. VA. L. REV. 461 (2012). On the other hand, the exceptions also have been interpreted narrowly. *See, e.g., Deal v. Spears*, 980 F.2d 1153 (8th Cir. 1992) (ordinary course of business exception); *Burrow v. Sybaris Clubs International, Inc.*, 2013 WL 5967333 (N.D. Ill., Nov. 08, 2013) (refusing to find secret recordings of employees' personal and business telephone conversations on a separate computer protected by the ordinary course of business exception). The increased use of "cloud-based" or third-party hosting services to facilitate electronic communications has raised new questions of interpretation as to when an employer is a "service provider." *See, e.g., Brown Jordan Int'l, Inc. v. Carmicle* 846 F.3d 1167 (11th Cir. 2017) (cloud-based service Microsoft 365 is an electronic communication "facility"); *Brooks Grp. & Assocs. v. LeVigne*, No. 12-2922, 2014 U.S. Dist. LEXIS 52479 (E.D. Pa. Apr. 15, 2014) (holding that the ECPA claim would turn on whether the emails in question were stored on employer's servers); *Joseph v. Carnes* 108 F. Supp. 3d 613 (N.D. Ill. 2015) (stating that an employer who retrieved emails through third-party archival service was not a "service provider"). Nevertheless, these carve-outs significantly limit protections for most workers.

The Stored Communications Act ("SCA"), 18 U.S.C. §§2702-11 (2018), provides similar protections against unauthorized access to stored electronic communications, although it too is subject to the limitations of the ECPA. Recall that in *Quon* the SCA was one of theories underlying the claims brought against Arch Wireless by Quon and his co-plaintiffs. It therefore is a potential source of protection for employees against third parties; indeed, Quon's claims against Arch Wireless as a remote computing service for its unauthorized release of the transcripts of the text messages were successful. For a detailed discussion of the SCA claims in *Quon*, see the underlying panel opinion, *Quon v. Arch Wireless Operating Co., Inc.*, 529 F.3d 892 (9th Cir. 2008). In addition, despite the limited protections against employer monitoring of electronic communications in the workplace, the ECPA and SCA are potential sources of protection from unauthorized employer intrusions into employee communications and other electronic activities outside of work. *See, e.g., Pietrylo v. Hillstone Rest. Group*, No. 06-5754 (FSH), 2009 WL 3128420 (D.N.J. Sept. 25, 2009) (upholding a jury verdict finding that employees' managers violated the SCA by knowingly accessing a chat group on MySpace without authorization)*; Maremont v. Susan Fredman Design Grp., Ltd.*, No. 10 C 7811, 2014 U.S. Dist. LEXIS 26557 (N.D. Ill. Mar. 3, 2014) (finding a viable SCA claim where a social media manager's private Facebook and Twitter accounts were accessed in her absence and social media posts promoting her employer were made on her behalf).

With the rise of smart phones and other technologies, employees' secret recordings of conversations with co-workers and supervisors have become more common. Because the recording party consents to the communications being recorded, protection under federal and state law is limited. For a discussion of this phenomenon and potential legal and practical implications, *see* David Koeppel, *More People Are Using Smartphones to Secretly Record Office Conversations*, BUSINESS INSIDER (Jul. 28, 2011), http://www.businessinsider.com/smartphones-spying-devices-2011-7. *But see Senderra Rx Partners, LLC v. Loftin*, No. 15-13761, 2016 U.S. Dist. LEXIS 173203, *10-11 (E.D. Mich. Dec. 8, 2016) (concluding that, despite a former employee's automatically forwarding emails to her personal email account even after she was terminated, the user exception of the SCA applied, precluding liability, because only the person the emails were originally intended for was receiving the emails).

In addition, the Computer Fraud and Abuse Act, 18 U.S.C. § 1030 (2018) ("CFAA"), originally aimed at computer "hacking," prohibits access to a computer that is either unauthorized or in excess of authorization. Thus, an employer may run afoul of CFAA if it seeks to gain unauthorized access to an employee-owned computer. Because access to a computer is not limited to physical access, employers also may violate CFAA if they gain unauthorized access to an employee's private email or the password-protected portions of an employee's social media account. But the shoe can be on the other foot: Employers sometimes bring CFAA claims against employees or former employees who gain unauthorized access to the employers' computers or data. See pages 531-32.

In recent years, Congress has increasingly focused on privacy interests involving health, medical, and personal financial information. For example, the ADA, 42 U.S.C. §12112 (2018), prohibits employers from inquiring about or asking applicants whether such applicant has a disability. The ADA permits an employer to make pre-employment inquiries into the applicant's ability to perform job-related functions and to require all entering employees to undergo a medical examination *after* an initial offer of employment has been made. But the statute also prohibits employers from requiring current employees to undergo medical examinations unless they are job-related and "consistent with business necessity." *See* §12112(d)(4); *see also Karraker v. Rent-a-Center, Inc.*, 411 F.3d 831 (7th Cir. 2005) (finding that the administering of a psychological test to job applicants as part of a regime of exams violated the ADA because the test, as administered and applied, could be used to reveal a mental disorder); *Horgan v. Simmons* 704 F. Supp. 2d 814 (N.D. Ill. 2010) (upholding a claim by HIV-positive employee who allegedly was compelled to respond to supervisor inquiries regarding his medical condition); *see also Kroll v. White Lake Ambulance Auth.*, 691 F.3d 809 (6th Cir. 2012) (psychological counseling required of employee was a medical examination because it was designed to reveal a mental health impairment). The ADA also requires employers to treat certain information confidentially, but not all health information an employer obtains from its workers is protected. *See EEOC v. Thrivent Fin. for Lutherans*, 700 F.3d 1044 (7th Cir. 2012) (holding that an inquiry into the reasons for an employee's absence was not a "medical inquiry" within the meaning of §12112(d)(4)(B) and thus the employer had no need to treat the response, which revealed a history of migraine headaches, as a confidential medical record).

In addition, the Health Insurance Portability and Accountability Act ("HIPAA"), 42 U.S.C. §300gg (2018), imposes certain conditions on the release of medical records by health care providers. Thus, an employer's requirement that an applicant release medical information often must conform to these requirements. Since employers potentially have great access to this kind of employee information because they frequently provide health insurance, HIPAA has had a significant impact on medical record keeping and confidentiality practices. *See* Sharona Hoffman, *Employing E-Health: The Impact of Electronic Health Records on the Workplace,* 19 Kan. J. L. & Pub. Pol'y 409 (2010).

Another federal statute that provides procedural protections for personal information regarding employees and employment applicants is the Fair Credit Reporting Act, 15 U.S.C. §§1681-1681x (2018). It requires an employer to notify employees or applicants if it intends to obtain a consumer report on the individual prepared by a consumer reporting agency, obtain written authorization to review such a report, and notify the person promptly if information in the report may result in a negative employment decision (e.g., a decision not to hire or promote). In addition, the FCRA prohibits use or dissemination of the information for any purpose other than those listed in the act. *See Doe v. Saftig*, No. 09-C-1176, 2011 WL 1792967 (E.D. Wis. 2011) (holding that the plaintiff raised a triable issue of fact on the question of whether a co-worker and employer who had obtained financial information from the plaintiff as part of the application process had shared the information with co-workers for purposes not permitted under the FCRA). Employees have had mixed success in seeking to vindicate alleged rights under the FCRA. *Compare Dutta v. State Farm Mut. Auto. Ins. Co.*, 895 F.3d 1166, 1175-76 (9th Cir. 2018) (plaintiff, who, in violation of the FCRA, had been rejected for a job without an opportunity to correct errors on his credit report, nevertheless had no standing to sue since the basis of the denial was not an error and plaintiff therefore suffered no concrete injury from the violation), *with Robertson v. Allied Sols., LLC,* No. 17-3196, 2018 U.S. App. LEXIS 24563, at *12-13, 902 F.3D 690, 696 (7th Cir. 2018) (a plaintiff denied a job because of information in a background check had standing to press an FCRA case when the alleged violation of her right to a copy of the report and a chance to respond deprived her of the opportunity to "review the reason for any adverse decision and to respond"; these rights are "independent of any underlying factual disputes" since a plaintiff might want to provide context to put apparent blemishes in a better light).

Finally, Congress enacted GINA in 2008, marking the first direct and comprehensive federal response to the discriminatory use of genetic information by insurers and employers. At first blush, Congress's concern about this issue might seem puzzling, since few employers have actually engaged in this practice, and there have been only a handful of cases addressing it. Nevertheless, concerns about such testing had already produced significant regulatory and legislative responses. A majority of states had imposed some kind of restriction on genetic testing by employers, *see* http://www.ncsl.org/programs/health/genetics/ndiscrim.htm, and commentators had also expressed grave concerns about the future of such testing, its potential discriminatory effects, and its implications for employee privacy. *See, e.g.*, Pauline T. Kim, *Genetic Discrimination, Genetic Privacy: Rethinking Employee Protections for a Brave New Workplace*, 96 Nw. U. L. Rev. 1497 (2002); Paul M. Schwartz, *Privacy and the Economics of Personal Health Care Information*, 76 Tex. L. Rev. 1 (1997).

What is troubling to many about such testing is precisely what makes it potentially appealing to employers; that is, genetic testing could potentially provide them with otherwise hidden, but highly valuable information about employees or applicants. Thus, GINA addresses the widespread concern that genetic testing might be utilized to make preemptive insurance and employment decisions, including screening out those who are genetically predisposed to developing diseases or other medical conditions. But it is also designed to promote genetic testing by ensuring that patients are not deterred from such testing for medical purposes out of fear that the data might be utilized to their detriment by health insurers and employers. Interestingly, unlike most other kinds of testing addressed in this chapter, legal decision makers have almost uniformly favored the privacy or autonomy interests at stake over employers' interests in gathering useful information.

Title I of the Act addresses genetic discrimination in health insurance. Of particular note is §101, which generally prohibits health plans from requesting or requiring an individual or family members of an individual to undergo genetic testing and requesting, requiring, or purchasing genetic information about an individual or family member. *See* 29 U.S.C §§1132, 1182, 1191 (2018). It also prohibits use of genetic information to establish eligibility for health coverage. *See* 42 U.S.C. §300gg-52. The term "genetic information" is defined as information about an individual's genetic tests, the genetic tests of family members of such individual, and the manifestation of a disease or disorder in family members of such individual. The term "genetic test" means "an analysis of human DNA, RNA, chromosomes, proteins, or metabolites that detects genotypes, mutations, or chromosomal changes." 26 U.S.C. §9832; 42 U.S.C. §2000ff.

Title II prohibits employment discrimination based on genetic information. Among other things, it provides that it is unlawful to discriminate against an employee (or applicant) in the terms and conditions of employment because of genetic information with respect to the employee or to limit or classify employees in any way that would deprive them of employment opportunities or adversely affect their status because of their genetic information. Employers are also prohibited from requesting, requiring, or purchasing genetic information with respect to an employee or a family member of the employee, except in certain specified circumstances. These include where the collection of such information is necessary to comply with other federal laws; is for certain law enforcement purposes; is pursuant to health or genetic services offered by the employer (with consent and pursuant to confidentiality measures and other limitations); or is to be used for genetic monitoring of the biological effects of toxic substances in the workplace, but only if various notice, disclosure, and other requirements are satisfied. *See* 42 U.S.C. §2000ff.

Title II further requires employers possessing any genetic information about an employee to treat such information as a confidential medical record and prohibits disclosure of genetic information except to the employee or in other narrowly defined circumstances. *See* 42 U.S.C. §2000ff-5. In large part, the coverage, remedies, and procedures are applicable under Title VII. The statute does, however, expressly state that disparate impact on the basis of genetic information does not establish a cause of action. *See* 42 U.S.C. §2000ff-7. Finally, GINA prohibits retaliation against anyone who has opposed any act or practice made unlawful under the act or because such individual made a charge, testified, assisted, or participated in any manner in an investigation or proceeding under the statute. *See* 42 U.S.C. §2000ff-6.

The near-unanimous support for GINA in Congress is noteworthy in an age of bitter disagreements over the federal government's role in regulating the workplace. But since its enactment, GINA has been the subject of significant criticism regarding its scope and other limitations, as well as doubts about its effectiveness. *See, e.g.,* Bradley A. Areheart, *GINA, Privacy, and Antisubordination*, 46 Ga. L. Rev. 705 (2012); Pauline T. Kim, *Regulating the Use of Genetic Information: Perspectives from the U.S. Experience*, 31 Comp. Lab. L. & Pol'y J. 693 (2010); Jessica L. Roberts, *The Genetic Information Nondiscrimination Act as an Antidiscrimination Law*, 86 Notre Dame L. Rev. 597 (2011). For example, Professors Bradley Areheart and Jessica Roberts, in *The Future of Genetic Privacy*, 128 Yale L.J (forthcoming 2019), *available at* https://ssrn.com/abstract=3214163, report that the law has not served its purpose of promoting genetic testing among patients; that it has been construed and applied narrowly in various contexts; and, most surprisingly, that there is not a single reported case in which discrimination is alleged on the basis of genetic test results. Moreover, they note that Title I of GINA was rendered largely useless by the Affordable Care Act's much more sweeping protections against collection of medical information by health insurers. On the other hand, Areheart and Roberts discuss numerous examples of successful employee claims against employers seeking genetic data, particularly in the form of family medical history. They therefore conclude that, while GINA has been a disappointment in some ways, it has provided meaningful protection for employees from intrusive employer data requests, arguably offering a model for future statutory protections for employee data privacy.

b. State Law

No state has a statutory scheme generally governing privacy in the workplace, but some states have enacted laws that provide specific protections for workers. These laws and the protections they provide vary greatly. As stated above, prior to the passage of GINA, most states had restricted employers from testing employees or prospective employees for genetic traits.

Many states also have their own statutory protections for communications and surveillance, some of which extend beyond federal protections. *See, e.g.,* Conn. Gen. Stat. §31-48B (2018) (prohibiting use of certain electronic surveillance devices). Some states also impose restrictions on other medical inquiries, such as HIV testing, *see, e.g.,* Wis. Stat. §103.15(2) (2017), and commitments to medical treatment facilities, *see, e.g.*, Mass. Gen. Laws. ch. 151B §4(9) (2018), or existing or past medical or psychological conditions, *see, e.g.*, Md. Code Ann. Lab. & Empl. §3-701 (2014); *see also Doe v. Walgreens Co.*, 2010 WL 4823212 (Tenn. Ct. App. Nov. 24, 2010) (concluding employee and her husband stated a claim for relief under Tennessee statutes protecting confidential health records and in tort based on allegations that the employee's co-worker unlawfully accessed Walgreen's database and shared confidential information regarding her HIV status with other co-workers, causing the employee to resign due to humiliation).

A number of states have enacted statutes either limiting drug testing or regulating the means by which drug testing is implemented. *See, e.g.*, Conn. Gen. Stat. §31-51x (2018) (requiring a safety-related interest in drug testing); Minn. Stat. §181.951(4) (2018) (same). Some state statutes also prohibit employers from asking job applicants questions or making inquiries concerning certain other private matters. *See, e.g.*, Neb. Rev. Stat. §81-1932 (2018) (prohibiting inquiries into sexual practices or marital relationships); Or. Rev. Stat. §659A.885 (2018) (prohibiting inquiries into and use of employees' credit history for employment purposes except in narrowly defined circumstances). Finally, state antidiscrimination laws serve the same intrusion-deterrence function as federal antidiscrimination statutes, and thus protect workers against additional forms of discrimination that implicate private matters, such as discrimination based on sexual orientation, political affiliation, marital status, or physical or psychological conditions not covered under the ADA. The recent legislative activity involving protections for employee and applicant social media accounts and limiting inquiries into criminal and arrest histories is discussed in the next section.

As discussed elsewhere in the chapter, states frequently respond before the federal government to changes in technology that have privacy implications for workers. For example, in the years since GINA, a developing area of state legislation addresses employer collection and usage of employee biometric data. Of particular concern is employers' use of emerging technologies—such as types of eye, hand, and facial scans. Biometric data privacy statutes generally require that employers provide written notice as to the collection of data and its purpose and require protection of that data using the standard of care in the employer's industry. However, these statutory protections typically are limited in various ways, including in the breadth of their protections (e.g., what types of biometric identifiers are covered) and the availability of private rights of action. *See, e.g.*, 740 Ill. Comp. Stat. Ann. 14/15 (West 2018) (covering various forms of biometric information but excluding many others); Tex. Bus. & Com. Code § 503.001 (2017) (consent does not need to be in writing, violations can be enforced only by Attorney General); Wash. Rev. Code Ann. § 40.26.020 (West 2018) (applies only to biometric data which is stored in a commercial database and provides for enforcement only by the Attorney General); *see also Rosenbach v. Six Flags Entm't Corp.*, 2017 IL App (2d) 170317 (technical violations of Illinois statute are not enough for a cause of action, some actual injury or adverse effect must be proven), *petition of leave to app. granted*, 98 N.E.3d 36 (Ill. 2018).

c. Foreign Law: The Implications of the General Data Protection Regulation

Legal developments elsewhere can have an impact on workplace privacy in the United States. The most important of these developments is the European Union's adoption of the General Data Protection Regulation (GDPR) in 2016. The GDPR applies to "controllers" and "processors" of electronic data established in the EU that offer "goods or services" to EU based individuals or that might monitor the behaviors of EU citizens. Thus, companies and other organizations in the United States with operations in the EU or that employ EU citizens are covered by the regulation. In brief, the GDPR includes mandates on storage and protection of covered personally identifiable data and grants certain rights to employees and customers to access, delete, and otherwise control such data, including limiting employer data collection and use.

While non–EU citizens working in the United States will not directly enjoy GDPR protections, they ultimately may benefit from the greater care taken by employers subject to the regulation in designing data storage systems and handling personal data. Moreover, US states are looking to the GDPR as a model for data protection. Indeed, in June of 2018, California enacted the Consumer Privacy Act (CPA), which, like the GDPR, provides consumers with notice and access rights regarding the collection and use of their personal data, although without GDPR's robust consent mandates. The act also creates a private right of action for up to $750 per violation, and authorizes the state's attorney general to bring suit for "intentional violation[s] of privacy." CAL CIV CODE § 1798.125 (West Ann. 2018) (effective Jan. 1, 2020). Although the CPA does not expressly include employees, consumers are defined broadly (all "residents" of California), which many assume will be interpreted to cover employees. Moreover, many expect that the California legislature will clarify that the law covers employees before it becomes effective in 2020.

4. Contractual Privacy Protections

As with many other terms and conditions of employment, employees may bargain for specific privacy rights. These may come in the form of particular guarantees not to intrude or monitor, accommodations that may implicate privacy interests, or limits on the scope of employment or employer oversight authority that shield certain employee activities or spaces from employer scrutiny. Yet such express terms are rare in individual employment contracts for various reasons, among them limited bargaining power and the failure to foresee privacy-related "problems" at the outset of the relationship. In addition, there is an inevitable tension in a prospective employee demanding greater than normal privacy—the very demand might reveal information the employee would prefer to keep private. Moreover, some of the most common employer requirements that implicate privacy—various forms of testing, disclosures, and intrusive questioning—occur at the application stage, before an employee has a meaningful ability to bargain. And, ironically, some workers who have the incentives and are in a position to bargain for significant freedom from firm intrusions may end up attaining independent contractor rather than employee status. Indeed, as will be discussed below, express terms generally reduce rather than expand privacy protections: It is far more common for employers to demand that employees consent to various kinds of intrusions and monitoring as a condition of employment and for employees to agree to such conditions to secure the job.

Thus, contract-based protections for employees typically come in several other forms. The first is collective bargaining agreements. One high-profile example of addressing privacy interests through collective bargaining involves the limitations on the use of on steroid testing in Major League Baseball: In response to mounting public pressure, the players' union agreed to a strict testing regimen and stiff penalties after years of protecting the players' privacy interest in avoiding testing. These kinds of terms and related procedures are often addressed in the bargaining process and in labor arbitration thereafter. *See generally* Ariana R. Levinson, *Industrial Justice: Privacy Protection for the Employed*: 18 CORNELL J. L. & PUB. POL'Y 609 (2009).

A second kind of contractual protection, albeit a less direct one, flows from the just-cause provisions contained in some employment contracts. Although a just-cause termination provision would not protect against employer intrusions directly, it would provide a remedy for unjustified adverse employment actions resulting from such intrusions. An employer could not, for instance, terminate an employee simply because it does not like the employee's off-site associations or activities. On the other hand, just-cause provisions may create an incentive for an employer to monitor its employees' activities more closely, since, to take adverse actions against them, the employer would need evidence showing employee misconduct or some other legitimate business reason for so acting.

A further kind of contractual privacy protection is implied-in-fact. Perhaps the most famous example of a successful implied-in-fact claim can be found in *Rulon-Miller v. International Business Machines Corp.*, 208 Cal. Rptr. 524 (Ct. App. 1985), which upheld a verdict in favor of an employee who had been terminated for engaging in a romantic relationship with the manager of a rival office. Her claim was based on employer policies indicating that IBM was not concerned about off-site employee conduct that did not affect on-the-job performance and emphasizing respect for employees' personal privacy. *Rulon-Miller* was a victory for the particular plaintiff, but the long-term effects may be far less favorable for employees generally. If you were counsel for an employer in the wake of this case, what would you advise your client to do to avoid liability? Would your advice be similar to the advice you would give to avoid the types of implied-in-fact contract claims discussed in Chapter 2? What other practices would you advocate your clients adopt to avoid liability for implied-in-fact privacy claims? If employers were to follow such advice, would employees be better off?

Note parallels between such potential unintended consequences and those that might flow from the Supreme Court's discussion of the reasonable expectation of privacy issue in *Quon*. Indeed, today, successful implied-in-fact claims are rare, although employees occasionally find success in utilizing this theory. See, e.g., *Enslin v. Coca-Cola Co.*, 136 F. Supp. 3d 654 (E.D. Pa. 2015) (concluding employee stated a viable implied contract claim against employer who promised to protect employees' personal information, but failed to prevent losses employee incurred from identify theft); *Shepherd v. Kohl's Dep't Stores,* No. 1:14-cv-01901-DAD-BAM, 2016 U.S. Dist. LEXIS 101279 (E.D. Cal. Aug. 2, 2016) (holding plaintiff has a viable claim for breach of implied contract where his termination following a positive drug test for marijuana when the company had a policy that "no person will be discriminated against in hiring, termination . . . or otherwise be penalized" for being a registered medical marijuana cardholder).

B. "BALANCING" EMPLOYEE AND EMPLOYER INTERESTS

If there is a potential source of protection—constitutional, statutory, tort, or contractual—available, and the employer has intruded upon or compromised an employee's privacy interest, the analysis usually focuses next on whether the employer's alleged intrusion and resulting actions were justified. Regardless of the theory, courts often describe this inquiry as one of "balancing" the employer's interests with the privacy interests of the employee. How is this concept recognized or applied in the cases discussed above? Now, consider how the Supreme Court engages in this inquiry in the following case.

≡ *National Treasury Employees Union v. Von Raab*
≡ *489 U.S. 656 (1989)*

KENNEDY, J., with REHNQUIST, C.J. and WHITE, BLACKMUN, and O'CONNOR, JJ. joined.

We granted certiorari to decide whether it violates the Fourth Amendment for the United States Customs Service to require a urinalysis test from employees who seek transfer or promotion to certain positions.

I

A

The United States Customs Service, a bureau of the Department of the Treasury, is the federal agency responsible for processing persons, carriers, cargo, and mail into the United States, collecting revenue from imports, and enforcing customs and related laws. An important responsibility of the Service is the interdiction and seizure of contraband, including illegal drugs. In 1987 alone, Customs agents seized drugs with a retail value of nearly $9 billion. In the routine discharge of their duties, many Customs employees have direct contact with those who traffic in drugs for profit. Drug import operations, often directed by sophisticated criminal syndicates, may be effected by violence or its threat. As a necessary response, many Customs operatives carry and use firearms in connection with their official duties.

In December 1985, respondent, the Commissioner of Customs, established a Drug Screening Task Force to explore the possibility of implementing a drug-screening program within the Service. After extensive research and consultation with experts in the field, the task force concluded that "drug screening through urinalysis is technologically reliable, valid and accurate." Citing this conclusion, the Commissioner announced his intention to require drug tests of employees who applied for, or occupied, certain positions within the Service. The Commissioner stated his belief that "Customs is largely drug-free," but noted also that "unfortunately no segment of society is immune from the threat of illegal drug use." Drug interdiction has become the agency's primary enforcement mission, and the Commissioner stressed that "there is no room in the Customs Service for those who break the laws prohibiting the possession and use of illegal drugs."

In May 1986, the Commissioner announced the implementation of the drug-testing program. Drug tests were made a condition of placement or employment for positions that meet one or more of three criteria. The first is direct involvement in drug interdiction or enforcement of related laws, an activity the Commissioner deemed fraught with obvious dangers to the mission of the agency and the lives of Customs agents. The second criterion is a requirement that the incumbent carry firearms, as the Commissioner concluded that "[p]ublic safety demands that employees who carry deadly arms and are prepared to make instant life or death decisions be drug free." The third criterion is a requirement for the incumbent to handle "classified" material, which the Commissioner determined might fall into the hands of smugglers if accessible to employees who, by reason of their own illegal drug use, are susceptible to bribery or blackmail.

After an employee qualifies for a position covered by the Customs testing program, the Service advises him by letter that his final selection is contingent upon successful completion of drug screening. An independent contractor contacts the employee to fix the time and place for collecting the sample. On reporting for the test, the employee must produce photographic identification and remove any outer garments, such as a coat or a jacket, and personal belongings. The employee may produce the sample behind a partition, or in the privacy of a bathroom stall if he so chooses. To ensure against adulteration of the specimen, or substitution of a sample from another person, a monitor of the same sex as the employee remains close at hand to listen for the normal sounds of urination. Dye is added to the toilet water to prevent the employee from using the water to adulterate the sample.

[There are specified requirements for processing the sample, which is ultimately tested in a laboratory] for the presence of marijuana, cocaine, opiates, amphetamines, and phencyclidine. Two tests are used. An initial screening test uses the enzyme-multiplied-immunoassay technique (EMIT). Any specimen that is identified as positive on this initial test must then be confirmed using gas chromatography/mass spectrometry (GC/MS). Confirmed positive results are reported to a "Medical Review Officer," "[a] licensed physician . . . who has knowledge of substance abuse disorders and has appropriate medical training to interpret and evaluate an individual's positive test result together with his or her medical history and any other relevant biomedical information." HHS Reg. §1.2, 53 Fed. Reg. 11980 (1988); HHS Reg. §2.4(g), 53 Fed. Reg. at 11983. After verifying the positive result, the Medical Review Officer transmits it to the agency.

Customs employees who test positive for drugs and who can offer no satisfactory explanation are subject to dismissal from the Service. Test results may not, however, be turned over to any other agency, including criminal prosecutors, without the employee's written consent.

B

[A union of federal employees and a union official filed suit on behalf of current Customs Service employees who sought covered positions claiming that the drug-testing program violated, inter alia, the Fourth Amendment. The District Court enjoined the program. The Fifth Circuit, although holding that requiring an employee to produce a urine sample for chemical testing is a Fourth Amendment search, found the searches at issue to be reasonable under that Amendment. While the Supreme Court affirmed the Fifth Circuit in upholding testing of employees directly involved in drug interdiction or required to carry firearms, it vacated the judgment approving testing of applicants for positions requiring handling of classified materials.]

II

In *Skinner v. Railway Labor Executives' Assn.*, 489 U.S. 602, decided today, we held that federal regulations requiring employees of private railroads to produce urine samples for chemical testing implicate the Fourth Amendment, as those tests invade reasonable expectations of privacy. Our earlier cases have settled that the Fourth Amendment protects individuals from unreasonable searches conducted by the Government, even when the Government acts as an employer, *O'Connor v. Ortega*, and, in view of our holding in *Railway Labor Executives* that urine tests are searches, it follows that the Customs Service's drug-testing program must meet the reasonableness requirement of the Fourth Amendment.

While we have often emphasized, and reiterate today, that a search must be supported, as a general matter, by a warrant issued upon probable cause, our decision in *Railway Labor Executives* reaffirms the longstanding principle that neither a warrant nor probable cause, nor, indeed, any measure of individualized suspicion, is an indispensable component of reasonableness in every circumstance. As we note in *Railway Labor Executives*, our cases establish that where a Fourth Amendment intrusion serves special governmental needs, beyond the normal need for law enforcement, it is necessary to balance the individual's privacy expectations against the Government's interests to determine whether it is impractical to require a warrant or some level of individualized suspicion in the particular context.

It is clear that the Customs Service's drug-testing program is not designed to serve the ordinary needs of law enforcement. Test results may not be used in a criminal prosecution of the employee without the employee's consent. The purposes of the program are to deter drug use among those eligible for promotion to sensitive positions within the Service and to prevent the promotion of drug users to those positions. These substantial interests, no less than the Government's concern for safe rail transportation at issue in *Railway Labor Executives*, present a special need that may justify departure from the ordinary warrant and probable-cause requirements. . . .

B

Even where it is reasonable to dispense with the warrant requirement in the particular circumstances, a search ordinarily must be based on probable cause. Our cases teach, however, that the probable-cause standard " 'is peculiarly related to criminal investigations.' " In particular, the traditional probable-cause standard may be unhelpful in analyzing the reasonableness of routine administrative functions, especially where the Government seeks to *prevent* the development of hazardous conditions or to detect violations that rarely generate articulable grounds for searching any particular place or person. Our precedents have settled that, in certain limited circumstances, the Government's need to discover such latent or hidden conditions, or to prevent their development, is sufficiently compelling to justify the intrusion on privacy entailed by conducting such searches without any measure of individualized suspicion. We think the Government's need to conduct the suspicionless searches required by the Customs program outweighs the privacy interests of employees engaged directly in drug interdiction, and of those who otherwise are required to carry firearms.

The Customs Service is our Nation's first line of defense against one of the greatest problems affecting the health and welfare of our population. . . .

Many of the Service's employees are often exposed to this criminal element and to the controlled substances it seeks to smuggle into the country. The physical safety of these employees may be threatened, and many may be tempted not only by bribes from the traffickers with whom they deal, but also by their own access to vast sources of valuable contraband seized and controlled by the Service. The Commissioner indicated below that "Customs [o]fficers have been shot, stabbed, run over, dragged by automobiles, and assaulted with blunt objects while performing their duties." At least nine officers have died in the line of duty since 1974. He also noted that Customs officers have been the targets of bribery by drug smugglers on numerous occasions, and several have been removed from the Service for accepting bribes and for other integrity violations.

It is readily apparent that the Government has a compelling interest in ensuring that front-line interdiction personnel are physically fit, and have unimpeachable integrity and judgment. Indeed, the Government's interest here is at least as important as its interest in searching travelers entering the country. . . . This national interest in self-protection could be irreparably damaged if those charged with safeguarding it were, because of their own drug use, unsympathetic to their mission of interdicting narcotics. A drug user's indifference to the Service's basic mission or, even worse, his active complicity with the malefactors, can facilitate importation of sizable drug shipments or block apprehension of dangerous criminals. The public interest demands effective measures to bar drug users from positions directly involving the interdiction of illegal drugs.

The public interest likewise demands effective measures to prevent the promotion of drug users to positions that require the incumbent to carry a firearm, even if the incumbent is not engaged directly in the interdiction of drugs. Customs employees who may use deadly force plainly "discharge duties fraught with such risks of injury to others that even a momentary lapse of attention can have disastrous consequences." We agree with the Government that the public should not bear the risk that employees who may suffer from impaired perception and judgment will be promoted to positions where they may need to employ deadly force. Indeed, ensuring against the creation of this dangerous risk will itself further Fourth Amendment values, as the use of deadly force may violate the Fourth Amendment in certain circumstances.

Against these valid public interests we must weigh the interference with individual liberty that results from requiring these classes of employees to undergo a urine test. The interference with individual privacy that results from the collection of a urine sample for subsequent chemical analysis could be substantial in some circumstances. We have recognized, however, that the "operational realities of the workplace" may render entirely reasonable certain work-related intrusions by supervisors and co-workers that might be viewed as unreasonable in other contexts.

See O'Connor v. Ortega. While these operational realities will rarely affect an employee's expectations of privacy with respect to searches of his person, or of personal effects that the employee may bring to the workplace, it is plain that certain forms of public employment may diminish privacy expectations even with respect to such personal searches. Employees of the United States Mint, for example, should expect to be subject to certain routine personal searches when they leave the workplace every day. Similarly, those who join our military or intelligence services may not only be required to give what in other contexts might be viewed as extraordinary assurances of trustworthiness and probity, but also may expect intrusive inquiries into their physical fitness for those special positions.

We think Customs employees who are directly involved in the interdiction of illegal drugs or who are required to carry firearms in the line of duty likewise have a diminished expectation of privacy in respect to the intrusions occasioned by a urine test. Unlike most private citizens or government employees in general, employees involved in drug interdiction reasonably should expect effective inquiry into their fitness and probity. Much the same is true of employees who are required to carry firearms. Because successful performance of their duties depends uniquely on their judgment and dexterity, these employees cannot reasonably expect to keep from the Service personal information that bears directly on their fitness. While reasonable tests designed to elicit this information doubtless infringe some privacy expectations, we do not believe these expectations outweigh the Government's compelling interests in safety and in the integrity of our borders.[2]

Without disparaging the importance of the governmental interests that support the suspicionless searches of these employees, petitioners nevertheless contend that the Service's drug-testing program is unreasonable in two particulars. First, [it was not based on any perceived drug problem among Customs employees, and has not led to the discovery of a significant number of drug users—] no more than 5 employees out of 3,600 have tested positive for drugs. Second, . . . illegal drug users can avoid detection with ease by temporary abstinence or by surreptitious adulteration of their urine specimens. These contentions are unpersuasive.

Petitioners' first contention evinces an unduly narrow view of the context in which the Service's testing program was implemented. Petitioners do not dispute, nor can there be doubt, that drug abuse is one of the most serious problems confronting our society today. There is little reason to believe that American workplaces

---

2. The procedures prescribed by the Customs Service for the collection and analysis of the requisite samples do not carry the grave potential for "arbitrary and oppressive interference with the privacy and personal security of individuals," *United States v. Martinez-Fuerte*, 428 U.S. 543, 554 (1976), that the Fourth Amendment was designed to prevent. Indeed, these procedures significantly minimize the program's intrusion on privacy interests. Only employees who have been tentatively accepted for promotion or transfer to one of the three categories of covered positions are tested, and applicants know at the outset that a drug test is a requirement of those positions. Employees are also notified in advance of the scheduled sample collection, thus reducing to a minimum any "unsettling show of authority," *Delaware v. Prouse*, 440 U.S. 648, 657 (1979), that may be associated with unexpected intrusions on privacy. There is no direct observation of the act of urination, as the employee may provide a specimen in the privacy of a stall.

Further, urine samples may be examined only for the specified drugs. The use of samples to test for any other substances is prohibited. And, as the Court of Appeals noted, the combination of EMIT and GC/MS tests required by the Service is highly accurate, assuming proper storage, handling, and measurement techniques. Finally, an employee need not disclose personal medical information to the Government unless his test result is positive, and even then any such information is reported to a licensed physician. Taken together, these procedures significantly minimize the intrusiveness of the Service's drug-screening program.

are immune from this pervasive social problem, as is amply illustrated by our decision in *Railway Labor Executives*. Detecting drug impairment on the part of employees can be a difficult task, especially where, as here, it is not feasible to subject employees and their work product to the kind of day-to-day scrutiny that is the norm in more traditional office environments. Indeed, the almost unique mission of the Service gives the Government a compelling interest in ensuring that many of these covered employees do not use drugs even off duty, for such use creates risks of bribery and blackmail against which the Government is entitled to guard. In light of the extraordinary safety and national security hazards that would attend the promotion of drug users to positions that require the carrying of firearms or the interdiction of controlled substances, the Service's policy of deterring drug users from seeking such promotions cannot be deemed unreasonable.

The mere circumstance that all but a few of the employees tested are entirely innocent of wrongdoing does not impugn the program's validity. The same is likely to be true of householders who are required to submit to suspicionless housing code inspections, *see Camara v. Municipal Court of San Francisco*, 387 U.S. 523 (1967), and of motorists who are stopped at the checkpoints we approved in *United States v. Martinez-Fuerte*, 428 U.S. 543 (1976). The Service's program is designed to prevent the promotion of drug users to sensitive positions as much as it is designed to detect those employees who use drugs. Where, as here, the possible harm against which the Government seeks to guard is substantial, the need to prevent its occurrence furnishes an ample justification for reasonable searches calculated to advance the Government's goal.

We think petitioners' second argument—that the Service's testing program is ineffective because employees may attempt to deceive the test by a brief abstention before the test date, or by adulterating their urine specimens—overstates the case. As the Court of Appeals noted, addicts may be unable to abstain even for a limited period of time, or may be unaware of the "fade-away effect" of certain drugs. More importantly, the avoidance techniques suggested by petitioners are fraught with uncertainty and risks for those employees who venture to attempt them. A particular employee's pattern of elimination for a given drug cannot be predicted with perfect accuracy, and, in any event, this information is not likely to be known or available to the employee. Petitioners' own expert indicated below that the time it takes for particular drugs to become undetectable in urine can vary widely depending on the individual, and may extend for as long as 22 days. Thus, contrary to petitioners' suggestion, no employee reasonably can expect to deceive the test by the simple expedient of abstaining after the test date is assigned. Nor can he expect attempts at adulteration to succeed, in view of the precautions taken by the sample collector to ensure the integrity of the sample. In all the circumstances, we are persuaded that the program bears a close and substantial relation to the Service's goal of deterring drug users from seeking promotion to sensitive positions.[4]

In sum, we believe the Government has demonstrated that its compelling interests in safeguarding our borders and the public safety outweigh the privacy

---

4. Indeed, petitioners' objection is based on those features of the Service's program—the provision of advance notice and the failure of the sample collector to observe directly the act of urination—that contribute significantly to diminish the program's intrusion on privacy. Thus, under petitioners' view, "the testing program would be more likely to be constitutional if it were more pervasive and more invasive of privacy."

expectations of employees who seek to be promoted to positions that directly involve the interdiction of illegal drugs or that require the incumbent to carry a firearm. We hold that the testing of these employees is reasonable under the Fourth Amendment.

C

We are unable, on the present record, to assess the reasonableness of the Government's testing program insofar as it covers employees who are required "to handle classified material." We readily agree that the Government has a compelling interest in protecting truly sensitive information from those who, "under compulsion of circumstances or for other reasons, . . . might compromise [such] information." We also agree that employees who seek promotions to positions where they would handle sensitive information can be required to submit to a urine test under the Service's screening program, especially if the positions covered under this category require background investigations, medical examinations, or other intrusions that may be expected to diminish their expectations of privacy in respect of a urinalysis test. . . .

It is not clear, however, whether the category defined by the Service's testing directive encompasses only those Customs employees likely to gain access to sensitive information. Employees who are tested under the Service's scheme include those holding such diverse positions as "Accountant," "Accounting Technician," "Animal Caretaker," "Attorney (All)," "Baggage Clerk," "Co-op Student (All)," "Electric Equipment Repairer," "Mail Clerk/Assistant," and "Messenger." We assume these positions were selected for coverage under the Service's testing program by reason of the incumbent's access to "classified" information, as it is not clear that they would fall under either of the two categories we have already considered. Yet it is not evident that those occupying these positions are likely to gain access to sensitive information, and this apparent discrepancy raises in our minds the question whether the Service has defined this category of employees more broadly than is necessary to meet the purposes of the Commissioner's directive.

We cannot resolve this ambiguity on the basis of the record before us, and we think it is appropriate to remand the case. . . . [T]he Court of Appeals should examine the criteria used by the Service in determining what materials are classified and in deciding whom to test under this rubric. [T]he court should also consider pertinent information bearing upon the employees' privacy expectations, as well as the supervision to which these employees are already subject.

Justice SCALIA, with whom Justice STEVENS joins, dissenting.

The issue in this case is not whether Customs Service employees can constitutionally be denied promotion, or even dismissed, for a single instance of unlawful drug use, at home or at work. They assuredly can. The issue here is what steps can constitutionally be taken to *detect* such drug use. The Government asserts it can demand that employees perform "an excretory function traditionally shielded by great privacy," *Skinner v. Railway Labor Executives' Ass'n*, while "a monitor of the same sex . . . remains close at hand to listen for the normal sounds," and that the excretion thus produced be turned over to the Government for chemical analysis. The Court agrees that this constitutes a search for purposes of the Fourth Amendment—and I think it obvious that it is a type of search particularly destructive of privacy and offensive to personal dignity.

[While I joined the opinion in *Skinner* allowing "a less intrusive bodily search of railroad employees involved in train accidents," I did so] because the demonstrated frequency of drug and alcohol use by the targeted class of employees, and the demonstrated connection between such use and grave harm, rendered the search a reasonable means of protecting society. I decline to join the Court's opinion in the present case because neither frequency of use nor connection to harm is demonstrated or even likely. In my view the Customs Service rules are a kind of immolation of privacy and human dignity in symbolic opposition to drug use.

The Court's opinion in the present case . . . will be searched in vain for real evidence of a real problem that will be solved by urine testing of Customs Service employees. Instead, there are assurances that "[t]he Customs Service is our Nation's first line of defense against one of the greatest problems affecting the health and welfare of our population"; that "[m]any of the Service's employees are often exposed to [drug smugglers] and to the controlled substances [they seek] to smuggle into the country"; that "Customs officers have been the targets of bribery by drug smugglers on numerous occasions, and several have been removed from the Service for accepting bribes and other integrity violations"; that "the Government has a compelling interest in ensuring that front-line interdiction personnel are physically fit, and have unimpeachable integrity and judgment"; that the "national interest in self-protection could be irreparably damaged if those charged with safeguarding it were, because of their own drug use, unsympathetic to their mission of interdicting narcotics"; and that "the public should not bear the risk that employees who may suffer from impaired perception and judgment will be promoted to positions where they may need to employ deadly force." To paraphrase Churchill, all this contains much that is obviously true, and much that is relevant; unfortunately, what is obviously true is not relevant, and what is relevant is not obviously true. The only pertinent points, it seems to me, are supported by nothing but speculation, and not very plausible speculation at that. It is not apparent to me that a Customs Service employee who uses drugs is significantly more likely to be bribed by a drug smuggler, any more than a Customs Service employee who wears diamonds is significantly more likely to be bribed by a diamond smuggler—unless, perhaps, the addiction to drugs is so severe, and requires so much money to maintain, that it would be detectable even without benefit of a urine test. Nor is it apparent to me that Customs officers who use drugs will be appreciably less "sympathetic" to their drug-interdiction mission, any more than police officers who exceed the speed limit in their private cars are appreciably less sympathetic to their mission of enforcing the traffic laws. (The only difference is that the Customs officer's individual efforts, if they are irreplaceable, can theoretically affect the availability of his own drug supply—a prospect so remote as to be an absurd basis of motivation.) Nor, finally, is it apparent to me that urine tests will be even marginally more effective in preventing gun-carrying agents from risking "impaired perception and judgment" than is their current knowledge that, if impaired, they may be shot dead in unequal combat with unimpaired smugglers—unless, again, their addiction is so severe that no urine test is needed for detection.

What is absent in the Government's justifications—notably absent, revealingly absent, and as far as I am concerned dispositively absent—is the recitation of *even a single instance* in which any of the speculated horribles actually occurred: an instance, that is, in which the cause of bribe-taking, or of poor aim, or of unsympathetic law enforcement, or of compromise of classified information, was drug use. Although the Court points out that several employees have in the past been removed from the Service for accepting bribes and other integrity violations, and that at least nine officers have died in the line of duty since 1974, there is no indication whatever that these incidents were related to drug use by Service employees. Perhaps concrete evidence of the severity of a problem is unnecessary when it is so well known that courts can almost take judicial notice of it; but that is surely not the case here. . . .

The Court's response to this lack of evidence is that "[t]here is little reason to believe that American workplaces are immune from [the] pervasive social problem" of drug abuse. Perhaps such a generalization would suffice if the workplace at issue could produce such catastrophic social harm that no risk whatever is tolerable—the secured areas of a nuclear power plant, for example, *see Rushton v. Nebraska Pub. Power District*, 844 F.2d 562 (CA8 1988). But if such a generalization suffices to justify demeaning bodily searches, without particularized suspicion, to guard against the bribing or blackmailing of a law enforcement agent, or the careless use of a firearm, then the Fourth Amendment has become frail protection indeed. . . .

[I]n extending approval of drug testing to that category consisting of employees who carry firearms, the Court exposes vast numbers of public employees to this needless indignity. Logically, of course, if those who carry guns can be treated in this fashion, so can all others whose work, if performed under the influence of drugs, may endanger others—automobile drivers, operators of other potentially dangerous equipment, construction workers, school crossing guards. A similarly broad scope attaches to the Court's approval of drug testing for those with access to "sensitive information." Since this category is not limited to Service employees with drug interdiction duties, nor to "sensitive information" specifically relating to drug traffic, today's holding apparently approves drug testing for all federal employees with security clearances—or, indeed, for all federal employees with valuable confidential information to impart. Since drug use is not a particular problem in the Customs Service, employees throughout the Government are no less likely to violate the public trust by taking bribes to feed their drug habit, or by yielding to blackmail. Moreover, there is no reason why this super-protection against harms arising from drug use must be limited to public employees; a law requiring similar testing of private citizens who use dangerous instruments such as guns or cars, or who have access to classified information, would also be constitutional.

[Justice Scalia further argued that the real "driving force" behind policy was Commissioner's stated desire to " 'set an important example in our country's struggle with this most serious threat to our national health and security.' "] I think it obvious that this justification is unacceptable; that the impairment of individual liberties cannot be the means of making a point; that symbolism, even symbolism for so worthy a cause as the abolition of unlawful drugs, cannot validate an otherwise unreasonable search. . . .

NOTES

1. *Sources of Protection.* Since *Von Raab* involves a public employer the Fourth Amendment provided the source of privacy protection. Again, however, as *Borse* suggested, the public policy and intrusion upon seclusion torts provide possible theories of liability for drug testing. Statutory protections also exist in some states. And, as described elsewhere in this chapter, other invasive procedures and inquiries utilized in screening applicants or existing employees run afoul of statutory protections, including genetic testing, some medical testing, and polygraph examinations.

Still other intrusive screening procedures have resulted in liability. One that has been the subject of a large number of legal challenges in the last century is (paper and pencil) psychological testing. Although not physically invasive like drug or other types of physical testing, psychological testing arguably is intrusive because it tends to include questions about intimate matters, including religious beliefs and sexual desires and preferences. In *Soroka v. Dayton Hudson Corp.*, 1 Cal. Rptr. 2d 77 (Ct. App. 1991), the court found in favor of a group of applicants for security guard jobs at Target who challenged a testing program on state constitutional grounds and pursuant to state statutes protecting against discrimination based on religious beliefs and political affiliations. Although these bases for private-sector protection are California specific, a small number of other states directly restrict employer use of paper and pencil honesty testing, *see, e.g.*, MASS. GEN. LAWS ch. 149, §19B (2018) and R.I. GEN. LAWS §28-6.1-1 (2018). However, there may be other more indirect forms of protection; for example, referring back to the possible sources of privacy protection already discussed in this chapter, might claimants today have other potential theories of liability against Target in these circumstances? *See, e.g., Karraker v. Rent-a-Center, Inc.*, 411 F.3d 831 (7th Cir. 2005) (finding that the administering of a psychological test to job applicants as part of a regime of exams violated the ADA because the test, as administered and applied, could be used to reveal a mental disorder); *see generally* Scott P. Kramer, *Why Is the Company Asking About My Fear of Spiders? A New Look at Evaluating Whether an Employer-Provided Personality Test Constitutes a Medical Examination Under the ADA*, 2007 U. ILL. L. REV. 1279 (2007). *See also* Susan J. Stabile, *The Use of Personality Tests as a Hiring Tool: Is the Benefit Worth the Cost?*, 4 U. PA. J. LAB. & EMP. L. 279 (2002) (critiquing the use of personality tests as a screening tool).

2. *Comparing* Von Raab *with* O'Connor *and* Quon. The *Von Raab* court relies on *O'Connor* and finds that neither a warrant nor probable cause is needed for the government's drug-testing program. Yet *Von Raab*'s "reasonableness" inquiry may not be consistent with the standards *O'Connor* describes. While *O'Connor* suggested that the employer must merely demonstrate the reasonableness of its privacy intrusion in terms of ends and means, the *Von Raab* court uses language such as "compelling interest" in upholding most aspects of the drug-testing program, although suggesting that one portion of the program may be broader than "necessary." Such language suggests that some more rigorous level of scrutiny is in play, although the Court never expressly says as much. And isn't this inconsistent with the deferential approach apparent in *Quon*, especially that Court's rejection of the "least intrusive means" inquiry?

One explanation, consistent with at least some of the language in *Quon* (*see* Note 5, page 419), is that the reasonableness inquiry itself involves a balancing of the interests at stake. In other words, whether the employer's actions are reasonable is determined by using a sliding scale: The more serious the intrusion into an employee's privacy, the more compelling the employer's justification must be. Thus, to be "reasonable," searches involving bodily fluids, including urine testing, must be justified by more substantial governmental interests than other, less serious intrusions. This may also explain why the *Von Raab* majority went out of its way to emphasize that the urine testing in this circumstance was a somewhat less serious intrusion (involving a "dimin-ished" expectation of privacy) than such testing might be in other contexts. Is there a countervailing suggestion in *Quon* that the intrusion at issue there—the review of the text messages—was a less serious one? Would you rather have your bodily fluids tested or have your supervisor rummage through your employer-provided computer?

Of course, Justice Scalia might find all of this particularly ironic, since, in his view, the government failed to demonstrate *any* pressing need for such a testing program. His objections bring us back yet again to issues of deference; it may matter less what level of scrutiny is articulated than how willing the courts are to accept the govern-ment's proffered reasons for acting. In your view, was the *Von Raab* majority correct to accept the interests on which the government relied?

3. *Deference to the Employer's Interest.* What are the interests articulated by the government in *Von Raab*? As Scalia's dissent hints, perceived importance alone may be dispositive. In other words, even though courts may suggest that they are "balancing" the employer interest against the interest of the employee to be free from intrusions into his or her sphere of privacy, if the employer is able to *articulate* (not necessarily demonstrate with evidence) a sufficiently compelling justification, the court is likely to uphold all but the most severe intrusions. For example, drug-testing programs involving employees engaged in inherently dangerous work or work that puts third parties at risk of physical harm are almost always upheld, regardless of whether the policy arises in the public or private context and regardless of the nature of the under-lying claim. *See, e.g., Von Raab; Skinner v. Ry. Labor Executives' Ass'n*, 489 U.S. 602 (1989) (upholding drug testing of railroad employees who had been involved in an accident after detailing just how intrusive urinalysis testing is); *Krieg v. Seybold*, 481 F.3d 512 (7th Cir. 2007) (upholding random drug testing of city sanitation worker who operated large vehicles and equipment); *Luedtke v. Nabors Alaska Drilling, Inc.*, 768 P.2d 1123 (Alaska 1989) (upholding drug testing for oil rig workers). Similarly, when the employer has well-founded, particularized suspicion that an employee has engaged in unlawful or otherwise harmful conduct, courts almost always uphold resulting searches and the monitoring of work spaces and communications. *See, e.g., United States v. Slanina*, 283 F.3d 670 (5th Cir. 2002) (upholding employer's and law enforcement's searches of employee's computers after employer discovered links to Web sites containing child pornography). And in many settings, the degree of def-erence the court gives to the employer's assertions regarding the importance of the interests to be served will be dispositive.

When courts perceive the articulated reasons as less compelling, they are more likely to scrutinize closely the employer's methods and show concern for the employee interests. The interests articulated in the *Soroka* case discussed above—a preference for hiring people with "good judgment and emotional stability" to be unarmed store security guards, 1 Cal. Rptr. 2d at 79—and perhaps the one underlying the testing in *Borse* may be examples of this. Indeed, proffered employer justifications lie along a continuum. Such justifications may include, for example, protecting public health and safety, protecting worker health and safety, addressing known criminal conduct, preventing criminal conduct, protecting employer tangible and intangible property, preventing other types of employee misconduct or shirking, determining who is bet-ter qualified for a job or promotion, protecting the employer's public image, and improving workplace morale or efficiency. How would you order the interests in this listing to reflect a continuum from more to less compelling?

4. *Negligent Hiring and Retention.* Another interest employers sometimes advance is the avoidance of civil liability. In a variety of contexts, employers may be liable for failing to prevent employee conduct that causes harm to third parties or other employees. *See, e.g., Doe v. XYC Corp.*, 887 A.2d 1156 (N.J. App. Div. 2005) (holding an employer potentially liable to daughter of employee who posted nude photographs of her on the Internet after employer was placed on notice that employee was viewing graphic forms of pornography—although not necessarily child pornography—on his workplace computer; there was a triable claim that the employer failed to exercise reasonable care to report and/or take effective action to stop employee's Internet activities). These matters arguably have taken on greater prominence in recent years, in light of the rise of legal incentives (sticks and carrots) for organizations in highly regulated industries to prevent wrongdoing through robust compliance programs, and the growing reputational and legal consequences in this #MeToo era of failing to discover and prevent various forms of harassment. While these topics will receive greater attention in Chapters 9 and 13, avoiding such harms sometimes may require greater monitoring of employee conduct or intrusions into private or intimate matters.

Along these lines, in recent years there has been growth in the number of negligent hiring, supervision, and retention claims brought against employers by third parties (including co-workers) injured by the employer's workers. Although the elements of negligence theories vary, most are based on section 213 of the RESTATEMENT (SECOND) OF AGENCY (ALI 1957), which provides that an employer is liable if it is negligent or reckless:

> (b) in the employment of improper persons or instrumentalities in work involving risk of harm to others;
> (c) in the supervision of the activity; or
> (d) in permitting, or failing to prevent, negligent or other tortious conduct by persons, whether or not his servants or agents, upon premises or with instrumentalities under his control.

See also RESTATEMENT (SECOND) OF TORTS §317 (providing for a negligent supervision claim where the employer fails to exercise reasonable care to prevent an employee from intentionally harming others on the employer's premises or in other circumstances in which the employer can exercise control). Liability under these theories is often difficult to establish. For example, to prevail on a negligent hiring where a third party is harmed by an employee's criminal act, the plaintiff normally must establish not only that the employer failed to exercise ordinary care in selecting the employee— that is, failed to perform an adequate background check—but also that the exercise of such care would have made the type of crime the employee later committed reasonably foreseeable. *See, e.g., McCafferty v. Preiss Enterprises, Inc.*, 534 F. App'x 726 (10th Cir. 2013) (holding that plaintiff failed to establish a negligent supervision claim because, for activities such as sexual misconduct that fall outside the scope of his employment, the employer is liable only if the conduct occurs on its premises or through use of its chattels); *Monroe v. Universal Health Servs., Inc.*, 596 S.E.2d 604 (Ga. 2004) (finding that, although the mental health assistant who sexually assaulted plaintiff—a patient of employer—had provided incomplete or inaccurate information during his application process, employer did not breach its duty of care because the application and background investigation process had not revealed a risk of violent or criminal activity).

Nevertheless, these sources of potential liability create strong incentives for employers to engage in robust background screening and testing of applicants, establish intrusive techniques for monitoring current employees, and conduct very thorough investigations of employees alleged to have engaged in tortious or wrongful conduct. *See, e.g., Saine v. Comcast Cablevision of Arkansas, Inc.*, 126 S.W.3d 339, 343-45 (Ark. 2003) (while adequate background check precluded negligent hiring claim, there were material issues of fact with regard to negligent supervision and retention claims because employer had notice of complaints of inappropriate conduct of employee toward another female cable customer prior to his rape of plaintiff); *see also Wada v. Aloha King, LLC*, 154 F. Supp. 3d 981 (D. Haw. 2015) (holding renter of a storage unit and his daughter stated viable negligence claims against subcontractor that failed to disclose that the facility manager was a registered sex offender).

5. *The Employee's Interest.* As discussed in each of the cases in this chapter, in order for an employee or applicant to have a cognizable breach of privacy claim (of any kind), he or she must have a legitimate or reasonable expectation of privacy in the sphere upon which the employer intruded. Without such an expectation, there is nothing to "balance" against the employer's interest. As discussed above, establishing the existence of such an expectation may often be the employee's most difficult hurdle.

Assuming the worker can establish such an expectation, however, the value the court places on the interest, and hence, the scrutiny the court will apply, may vary by the perceived intrusiveness of the employer's conduct. *See, e.g., Anchorage Police Dep't Empls. Ass'n v. Municipality of Anchorage*, 24 P.3d 547 (Alaska 2001) (upholding portions of drug-testing program linked to hiring, promotion, and investigating accidents but striking down random drug testing in part because it is more intrusive); *Robinson v. City of Seattle*, 10 P.3d 452 (Wash. Ct. App. 2000) (stating that government intrusions into certain personal information or confidentiality interests receive rational basis scrutiny while infringements of the right to autonomy warrant strict scrutiny). As *Von Raab* suggests, intrusions involving bodily functions or integrity— drug and medical testing, polygraph testing, strip searches, video surveillance of locker rooms or restrooms—may be subjected to the most rigorous scrutiny. *See, e.g., Carter v. County of Los Angeles*, 770 F. Supp. 2d 1042 (C.D. Cal. 2011) (holding public works department's covert video surveillance of its dispatch room—locked and inaccessible to the public—violated employees' Fourth Amendment and California constitutional rights despite the fact that the department installed the camera in response to alleged employee misconduct)*; see also Gustafson v. Adkins*, 803 F.3d 883 (7th Cir. 2015) (affirming denial of summary judgment on a Fourth Amendment claim arising from the installation of covert video surveillance equipment in office used by female officers as a changing area).

Slightly less intrusive conduct, such as questioning applicants about intimate matters, monitoring personal communications at work, audio surveillance, and searches of personal work spaces and stored data, may receive somewhat less scrutiny. Still less intrusive practices, such as overt video surveillance of less personal work areas, periodically auditing work-related communications (as in *Quon*), and monitoring or searches of less personal spaces and data compilations, often receive the least scrutiny.

Even if there is general agreement about which employer activities are more or less intrusive, and thus, which should receive greater scrutiny, "balancing" such intrusions against employer interests remains elusive. Despite common references to that term, courts and other lawmakers avoid the unwieldy task of attempting to weigh and then balance these competing interests in particular contexts. For example, although genetic and polygraph tests could produce a number of efficiencies for employers, protect employees themselves from various risks, and even benefit the public in some circumstances, legislative enactments addressing these forms of testing often include outright prohibitions across categories of employment, rather than provide for any type of balancing of interests in particular cases.

With the rise of new data technologies and techniques, human resources professionals in particular and employers in general are beginning to rely on data-driven strategies to evaluate and improve employee performance, enhance productivity, etc. Because some of these strategies involve collection of data via employee monitoring and other arguably intrusive techniques, they potentially raise employee privacy concerns. *See generally* Matthew T. Bodie, et al., *The Law and Policy of People Analytics*, 88 U. Colo. L. Rev. 961 (2017) (discussing privacy implications of using new technologies to collect and use data for "people analytics"). Some employers also seek to lower healthcare costs by incentivizing employees to exercise and utilizing technology such as Fitbit or apps installed in smartphones to monitor such activity. While, again, such monitoring has privacy implications, employees may have few protections against such programs, particularly if they consent on the front end to participation. *See* Elizabeth A. Brown, *The Fitbit Fault Line: Two Proposals to Protect Health and Fitness Data at Work*, 16 Yale J. Health Pol'y L. & Ethics 1 (2016); Elizabeth A. Brown, *Workplace Wellness: Social Injustice*, 20 N.Y.U. J. Legis. & Pub. Pol'y 191 (2017); *see also* Emily J. Tewes, *#Privatesphere: Can Privacy Law Adequately Protect Employees Amidst the Complexities of the Modern Employment Relationship?*, 57 Santa Clara L. Rev. 287, 312 (2017) (contending that employers usually can defeat invasion of privacy claims by careful planning and adherence to industry standards).

6. *The "Nexus" Requirement.* Once it is determined that there are both legitimate employer and employee privacy interests at stake, courts—including the *Von Raab* and *Soroka* courts—often focus on the nexus between the articulated interest and the nature of the intrusion. While *Quon* used different terminology, it too acknowledged that reasonableness of the intrusion is measured not just by the work-related purpose of the search, but also by the relationship between that purpose and the means utilized (i.e., the scope of the search). Thus, under the analytical framework provided in each of these cases, intrusions justified for reasons of equal importance may not receive equal treatment by the courts because the means chosen in one context might be more closely tailored to serve the end than in the other context. However, some decisions diverge on how closely the means must be tied to the purpose. Recall that *Quon* rejected arguments that the employer must utilize the least intrusive means, holding that the review of the text messages was reasonable despite the availability of less intrusive alternatives. Contrast that analysis with *Soroka*, in which the court stated that the employer "must demonstrate a compelling interest and must establish that the test serves a job-related purpose" and then found that the employer had made no showing—nothing beyond generalized assertions—that the intrusive questions in the psychological test had any bearing on the emotional stability or on the ability of a security guard to fulfill the job's responsibilities. *See Soroka*, 1 Cal. Rptr. 2d at 86. Thus, *Soroka* suggested that intrusions may be held unlawful when they are unnecessarily broad—that is, when the same legitimate employer interest may be served as effectively by less intrusive means. Still, much may depend on the deference courts

are willing to give employers when it comes to this nexus; that is, courts may vary in how demanding they may be in requiring narrow tailoring. Ultimately, how much deference should the employer's chosen means be given?

7. *The Limits on Drug Testing.* On the same day the Supreme Court decided *Von Raab*, it decided *Skinner v. Ry. Labor Executives' Ass'n*, 489 U.S. 602 (1989), which upheld as permissible under the Fourth Amendment mandatory blood and urine tests, for alcohol and drugs, of railroad employees who have been involved in railroad accidents. In both cases, the majority focused on the safety-sensitive or high-risk nature of the positions. Since these two cases were decided, lower courts have routinely upheld mandatory drug-testing programs (random or otherwise) in safety- or security-sensitive positions in public workplaces and pursuant to regulatory requirements in some private workplaces.

However, in *Chandler v. Miller*, 520 U.S. 305 (1997), the Supreme Court struck down a Georgia law that required candidates for some state offices to take a drug test to qualify for election. In so doing, the Court distinguished *Von Raab* and *Skinner*, noting that Georgia had presented no evidence that the state's elected officials performed the kinds of high-risk or safety-sensitive tasks that the employees in the previous cases performed. The Court then rejected the symbolic value—that is, commitment to the fight against drug abuse—of such a testing program as being sufficiently important to justify the intrusion. Recall Justice Scalia's opinion in *Von Raab. See also National Federation of Federal Employees v. Vilsack*, 681 F.3d 483 (D.C. Cir. 2012) (concluding that the secretary of agriculture had not shown a genuine safety concern or record of drug use that demonstrated the "special needs" necessary to justify random drug testing of all Forest Service Job Corps Center employees); *Lewis v. Dist. of Columbia.*, 282 F. Supp. 3d 169 (D.D.C. 2017) (stating random, warrantless drug tests are "inherently suspect" in holding that the Office of Medical Examiner did not show why periodic testing of all employees was warranted); *Ass'n of Indep. Sch. of Greater Wash. v. District of Columbia*, 311 F. Supp. 3d 262 (D.D.C.2018) (finding that, in random drug testing of incumbent nursery school teachers, child safety interests do not overcome "robust" privacy interest of public employees); *Wilson v. Jones,* No. 4:16-cv-04025-SLD-JEH, 2018 U.S. Dist. LEXIS 78878 (C.D. Ill. May 10, 2018) (rejecting contention that drug testing for municipal clerical worker was permissible via balancing test).

Courts recognizing breach of privacy claims for drug testing in the private employer context have likewise tended to focus on the nature of the employee's job and, hence, the importance of the testing program. *See, e.g., Luedtke*, 768 P.2d at 1123; *Hennessey v. Coastal Eagle Point Oil Co.*, 609 A.2d 11 (N.J. 1992). Occasionally, however, the methods or procedures utilized in drug testing have been invalidated even in safety-sensitive contexts. *See, e.g., Anchorage Police Dep't Empls. Ass'n*, 24 P.3d at 557-60 (striking down only random portion of drug-testing program); *AFGE v. Sullivan*, 744 F. Supp. 294 (D.D.C. 1990) (enjoining testing regulations in part because government articulated insufficient reasons for requiring urine samples be provided under direct visual observation); *see generally* John Gilliom, Surveillance, Privacy and the Law: Employee Drug Testing and the Politics of Social Control (1994); Pauline T. Kim, *Collective and Individual Approaches to Protecting Employee Privacy: The Experience with Workplace Drug Testing*, 66 La. L. Rev. 1009 (2006); Lindsay J. Taylor, *Congressional Attempts to "Strike Out" Steroids: Constitutional Concerns About the Clean Sports Act*, 49 Ariz. L. Rev (2007). In light of this backdrop, and assuming testing procedures themselves are reasonable, what classes of employees are unlikely to prevail in challenges against mandatory drug-testing requirements? Any employee with access to a firearm? Any employee working with hazardous materials or chemicals? Any employee who drives a motor vehicle? Any teacher? Changing approaches to drug laws and enforcement—such as the legalization of marijuana use in some states—may complicate the drug-testing analysis. For a discussion of the social benefits and costs of workplace drug testing in changing regulatory environments, see Jeremy Kidd, *The Economics of Workplace Drug Testing,* 50 U.C. Davis L. Rev. 707 (2016) (arguing that maximizing profits for a business will balance the cost of infringing upon employee privacy).

8. *Applicant vs. Employee.* Some statutory and common-law privacy protections draw a distinction between applicants for employment and employees—protecting the latter to a greater extent than the former. *Soroka* recognizes, but ultimately rejects, the possible distinction between employees and applicants. Are there good reasons to protect employees to a greater extent than applicants? Are there ways in which employees are more vulnerable than the applicants? How about vice versa?

Even if breach of privacy claims are equally available to applicants, establishing such a breach may be more difficult for them. *See generally* Mary Madden, et al., *Privacy, Policy, and Big Data: A Matrix of Vulnerabilities for Poor Americans,* 95 Wash U. L. Rev. 53 (2017) (detailing the increased usage of "applicant tracking systems," which analyze data in screening applicants, their privacy implications, and the difficulties of enforcing privacy violations related to these systems under laws such as the FCRA and Title VII). In addition, an applicant may not have the same expectation of privacy as current employees. It is also highly unlikely that an applicant could establish a contract-based privacy claim, since, at the application stage, no express or implied contract will have been formed. Moreover, the "Catch-22" described in Note 6 on page 347 is even more pronounced for applicants than for employees, because applicants must consent even to be considered for the job but such consent may bar his or her claims.

Note on Off-Site Activities, Including Associational Preferences and Internet Use

A broad array of off-site activities or lifestyle choices—from political and religious affiliations, to intimate relationships, to hobbies and leisure activities, to consumption choices (food, alcohol, tobacco, etc.) might conflict with employer preferences and affect their hiring, retention, and promotion decisions. Although there is no single legal doctrine or approach to addressing when employers can and cannot regulate such off-site conduct, a number of specific legal theories and protections have emerged in recent years. Much depends on the context, including whether the workplace is public or private, the nature of the off-site conduct, and the ability of the employer to articulate a business-related justification for regulating or prohibiting the conduct.

Public Sector Workers

As discussed in the last section, public sector workers enjoy some, albeit limited, constitutional and statutory protections in this context. And there have been a few new developments that suggest their robustness. For example, utilizing monitoring devices to track employee activity away from work has garnered recent attention. Indeed, in the wake of *United States v. Jones*, 565 U.S. 400 (2012), in which the Supreme Court held that placing a global positioning (GPS) device on a vehicle constitutes a search for Fourth Amendment purposes, the New York Court of Appeals suppressed the evidence in a disciplinary hearing of a state employee because it was collected by placing such a device on the employee's automobile. *See Cunningham v. New York State Dept. of Labor*, 997 N.E.2d 468 (N.Y. 2013). Because the device tracked much activity with which the state had no legitimate concern, including the employee's activities on weekends and evenings, the court found that its attachment to the vehicle was excessively intrusive and, hence, an unreasonable search under the Fourth Amendment. *See id*. at 473-74.

Furthermore, a few years ago, the Food and Drug Administration came under heavy criticism in the media and in Congress for engaging in surveillance of several of its scientists' communications regarding certain medical devices, including the interception of thousands of e-mails and other documents. *See, e.g.*, Eric Lichtblau, *Vast F.D.A. Effort Tracked E-Mails of Its Scientists*, N.Y. TIMES, July 14, 2012, at A1; Eric Lichtblau, *Investigation Sought of Extensive F.D.A. Surveillance*, N.Y. TIMES, June 16, 2012, at A14. Along with Edward Snowden's revelations regarding the federal agencies' much broader domestic and international surveillance programs, the FDA controversy illustrates society's ambivalence towards mass electronic surveillance by government employers. *See, e.g.*, Jennifer Stisa Granick & Christopher Jon Sprigman, *The Criminal N.S.A.*, N.Y. TIMES, June 27, 2013, *available at* http://www.nytimes.com/2013/06/28/opinion/the-criminal-nsa.html?pagewanted=all (discussing the twin revelations that telecom carriers have been secretly giving the National Security Agency information about Americans' phone calls, and that the N.S.A. has been capturing e-mail and other private communications from Internet companies as part of a secret program).

Private Sector Workers

Although these Fourth Amendment decisions and background concerns regarding excessive government surveillance do not apply to the private sector workplace, as discussed earlier in the chapter, we have seen that the reasoning in Fourth Amendment cases may influence courts in determining whether private sector employees who have been monitored away from work in this or similar ways may have viable intrusion upon seclusion or public policy claims. Nevertheless, in private, at-will employment, employees historically have enjoyed few protections from employer retaliation for such activities, choices, or associations. *See, e.g., Brunner v. Al Attar*, 786 S.W.2d 784 (Tex. Ct. App. 1990) (dismissing an employee's claim alleging breach of privacy after being terminated for volunteering for the AIDS Foundation). Many such off-site conduct and associational claims are unsuccessful, often because they do not fit neatly within statutory or common-law tort theories such as the public policy doctrine, intrusion upon seclusion, and intentional infliction of emotional distress. *See, e.g., Curay-Cramer v. The Ursuline Acad. of Wilmington*, 450 F.3d 130 (3d Cir. 2006) (rejecting employee's Title VII retaliation theory in circumstances in which employee was terminated from her position as a teacher at a Catholic school after allowing her name to be included in a prochoice advertisement in the local newspaper and admitting her association with a prochoice organization); *Edmondson v. Shearer*

Lumber Prods., 75 P.3d 733 (Idaho 2003) (refusing to recognize a public policy claim for a worker terminated for participating in a local government task force).

Can you see why establishing liability in cases involving conduct or associations away from work that are not secret or protected (say, by a password or limited to secluded locations such as the home) might be very difficult? And, looking back at *Borse*, why might a public policy claim moored to constitutional notions of "freedom of association" or "fundamental rights" be unlikely to succeed?

While there are no existing tort theories that easily fit this kind of circumstance, the new Restatement endorses such a theory. Section 7.08 recognizes protected employee autonomy interests in lawful conduct, adherence to religious and other personal beliefs, and belonging to or participating in associations, provided these activities and beliefs do not reference or involve the employer or its business. This section then goes on to provide:

> (b) Unless the employer and employee agree otherwise, an employer is subject to liability for intruding upon an employee's personal autonomy interests if the employer discharges the employee because of the employee's exercise of a personal autonomy interest under §7.08(a).
>
> (c) The employer is not liable under §7.08(b) if it can prove that it had a reasonable and good-faith belief that the employee's exercise of an autonomy interest interfered with the employer's legitimate business interests, including its orderly operations and reputation in the marketplace.

See RESTATEMENT OF EMPLOYMENT LAW (2015) §7.08; *see also* Matthew T. Bodie, *The Best Way Out Is Always Through: Changing the Employment At-Will Default to Protect Personal Autonomy*, 2017 U. ILL. L. REV. 223 (arguing for modifying the at-will rule to prevent employers from looking to employee actions outside the employment relation as a basis for discharge). Still, at least in work settings with heavily lawyered employment agreements, the Restatement's "unless the employer and employee agree otherwise" caveat very well could be the contracted term that swallows the tort—something we will address again in Part C of this chapter. And notice that the Restatement does not require the employer to be correct that the employee's activities interfered with its legitimate interests: It merely needs to have a "reasonable and good-faith belief" to that effect. Moreover, "orderly operations and reputation in the marketplace" is potentially quite broad. Indeed, might it sweep in an employee's participation in a political rally (on the right or left) that causes embarrassment or boycott threats to the employer? *Compare* §7.08, illus. 11 (allowing employer to terminate employee who had distributed Nazi paraphernalia outside of work). If so, then how meaningful is the protection? We turn to these issues again in Chapter 7.

Moreover, as *Rulon-Miller* and the *Soroka* decisions (discussed in the notes above) suggest, there is some protection from employer interference with or repercussions from some such activities and choices. When available, such protection often hinges on whether the employer can articulate a sufficient business-related reason for its actions. For example, in both *Soroka* and *Rulon-Miller*, the employer was found to have breached worker privacy rights, at least in part because it inquired into such private matters outside the workplace and acted upon those inquiries without sufficient justification.

And the law in this area is changing, mostly, but not exclusively, as a result of state-level legislative reforms. For instance, a growing number of state legislatures are protecting workers against adverse employment actions caused by a worker's political and other affiliations, recreational activities, or other kinds of legal off-site conduct where employers do not have a sufficiently compelling reason for taking such action. *See, e.g.,* CAL. LAB. CODE §§96(k), 98.6 (West Ann. 2018) (prohibiting adverse employment actions in response to lawful employee conduct occurring during nonworking hours away from the employer's premises); COL. REV. STAT. §24-34-402.5 (2018) (prohibiting employers from terminating employees for lawful off-site activities absent job relatedness); MINN. STAT. §181.938 (2018) (prohibiting employers from taking adverse actions against employees or applicants because the applicant or employee uses or enjoys lawful consumable products—including food, alcohol, and tobacco products—if the use or enjoyment takes place off the employer's premises during nonworking hours, unless the employer can demonstrate a bona fide occupational requirement for doing so or the need to avoid a conflict of interest); N.Y. LAB. LAW §201-d (McKinney 2018) (prohibiting employers in most circumstances from taking adverse actions against employees based on employee political affiliations, legal use of consumable products, recreational activities, or union membership); *see also* Eugene Volokh, *Private Employees' Speech and Political Activity: Statutory Protection Against Employer Retaliation,* 16 TEX. REV. L. & POL. 295 (2012) (providing a comprehensive survey of state statutes protecting various forms of speech and political activity). Of course, whether these statutes will provide meaningful protection for employees' off-site activities and associations depends on judicial interpretation. *See, e.g., McCavitt v. Swiss Reins. Am. Corp.* 237 F.3d 166 (2001) (finding "romantic dating" of a co-worker not to be a protected recreational activity under the New York statute). For further discussion of the burgeoning workplace conflicts over such activities and choices, and the range of legal issues raised regarding employer prohibitions or other responses, *see, e.g.,* Rafael Gely & Leonard Biermanm, *Workplace Blogs and Workers' Privacy,* 66 LA. L. REV. 1079 (2006); James A. Sonne, *Monitoring for Quality Assurance: Employer Regulation of Off-Duty Behavior,* 43 GA. L. REV. 133 (2008); Stephen D. Sugarman, *"Lifestyle" Discrimination in Employment,* 24 BERKELEY J. EMP. & LAB. L. 377 (2003). In contrast, courts sometimes have construed statutory protections broadly. *See Smith v. Millville Rescue Squad,* 139 A.3d 1 (N.J. 2016) (state prohibition of discrimination based on marital status not limited merely to the state of being single or married but also bars discrimination against those who were separated or in the process of divorcing).

Internet Activities

Another area of potential employer-employee conflict is Internet activities. As we have seen, employers may have significant interests in regulating employee Internet use at work or on employer time, networks, or equipment. As the discussion in Note 3 following *Quon* suggested, *see* page 331, employers often prevail in such Internet monitoring and computer search cases. *See also Thygeson v. U.S. Bancorp,* 2004 U.S. Dist. LEXIS 18863 (D. Or. Sept. 15, 2004) (rejecting breach of privacy claims after employer monitored website addresses employee accessed and searched e-mail files). *But see Fischer v. Mt. Olive Lutheran Church, Inc.,* 207 F. Supp. 2d 914 (W.D. Wis. 2002) (finding that employee had reasonable expectation of privacy in e-mails in his Web-based e-mail account, which employer searched after guessing employee's password, for intrusion upon seclusion claim).

But what about employee Internet activities—including maintaining personal websites, social networking, participation in interactive websites or chat rooms, or basic surfing—that occur off-site, during nonwork hours, and without using employer equipment? Many employers have adopted "blogging" policies, warning workers about potential adverse consequences if employee blogging or other web-based activities harm the employer. And, unsurprisingly, employees are terminated for such activities, particularly when they make online statements critical of their employers. *But see* posting of Nathan Koppel to Wall Street Journal Law Blog, *High School Principal Harshly Criticizes Teacher/Blogger Natalie Munroe* (Aug. 3, 2011, 2:59 p.m. EDT), http://blogs.wsj.com/law/2011/08/03/high-school-principal-harshly-criticizes-teacherblogger-natalie-munroe/ (discussing the reinstatement of high school teacher Natalie Munroe after she was suspended for harshly criticizing her students in blog posts). Case law on the subject remains sparse, although litigation over such issues appears to be growing. *See, e.g., Pietrylo v. Hillstone Rest. Group*, No. 06-5754 (FSH), 2009 WL 3128420 (D.N.J. Sept. 25, 2009) (upholding a jury verdict finding that employees' managers violated the Stored Communications Act (SCA) by knowingly accessing a chat group on a social networking website without authorization); *see also Dible v. City of Chandler*, reproduced at page 430 (upholding summary judgment on police officer's speech, privacy, and other claims arising out of his termination by the City for maintaining sexually explicit website featuring him and his wife). The increased blurring of the line between work and home also may have implications for employee privacy as it pertains to online activities and communications. *See generally* Paul M. Secunda, *The Employee Right to Disconnect*, 8 NOTRE DAME J. INT'L & COMP. L. (2018) (arguing for modifications under OSHA to protect employees from employee intrusions outside of the workplace). *See also* Robert Sprague, *Employee Electronic Communications in a Boundaryless World*, 53 U. LOUISVILLE L. REV. 433 (2016); Stuart S. Waxman & Frank G. Barile, *"Eye in the Sky": Employee Surveillance in the Public Sector*, 79 ALB. L. REV. 131 (2016).

In recent years, there also has been much attention focused on employer access to, and demands for access to, electronic communications on personal devices or in password-protected social media and other accounts, both at the application stage and during employment. As an initial matter, employers occasionally face trouble, legal or otherwise, for overly aggressive off-site surveillance or investigatory activities to flush out anonymous posters or leakers. One high-profile example is the scandal surrounding Hewlett-Packard's use of highly aggressive spying techniques and deceptive tactics to discover the identity of a leaker (who turned out to be on its board of directors). The controversy that followed resulted in a number of directors and officers in the company resigning. *See, e.g.*, Damon Darlin, *H.P., Red-Faced but Still Selling*, N.Y. TIMES, Oct. 1, 2006, at 31. Criminal charges against the chair of Hewlett-Packard's board of directors ultimately were dismissed, although one of its investigators did plead guilty to theft and conspiracy. *See* Matt Richtel, *Charges Dismissed in Hewlett-Packard Spying Case*, N.Y. TIMES, Mar. 15, 2007, *available at* http://www.nytimes.com/2007/03/15/technology/15dunn.html?_r=1&ref= patricia_c_dun. In addition, Hewlett-Packard ultimately agreed to pay $14.5 million to settle a civil suit brought by the California attorney general. *See* Damon Darlin, *H.P. Will Pay $14.5 Million to Settle Suit*, N.Y. TIMES, Dec. 8, 2006, *available at* http://www.nytimes.com/2006/12/08/technology/08hewlett.html.

The Illinois Supreme Court upheld a jury verdict in favor of a former employee on her intrusion upon seclusion claim against her former employer for the "pretexting" activities of a third-party private investigator the employer had retained. *Lawlor v. North American Corp. of Illinois*, 983 N.E.2d 414 (Ill. 2012). The jury found that the investigator had engaged in pretexting to obtain the employee's phone records as part of the former employer's efforts to determine whether she had violated the terms of a noncompetition agreement. *See also Ehling v. Monmouth-Ocean Hosp. Service Corp.*, 872 F. Supp. 2d 369 (D.N.J. 2012) (finding an employee's allegations that her postings to a Facebook page accessible only by those invited by the employee sufficient to plead a reasonable expectation of privacy in her page, when the supervisor compelled another employee with access to the page to view it in front of the supervisor).

Furthermore, since 2012, there has been a burst of state legislation barring or restricting employers from demanding access to applicants' and employees' personal e-mail and social media passwords, which will quickly and profoundly alter hiring practices in certain contexts. To date, at least twenty-five states have adopted such statutes. The National Conference of State Legislatures tracks these developments at http://www.ncsl.org/research/telecommunications-and-information-technology/employer-access-to-social-media-passwords-2013.aspx; *see also* Ariana R. Levinson, *Social Media, Privacy, and the Employment Relationship: The American Experience*, SPANISH LAB. L. AND EMPL. REL. J., Vol. 2, No. 1 (2013) (discussing statutory and common law developments); Charles J. Stiegler, *Developments in Employment Law and Social Media*, 71 BUS. LAW. 321 (2016) (same).

But these prohibitions vary, and some expressly allow such requests in investigations involving present employees. For example, New Jersey's statute generally prohibits employers from retaliating or discriminating against employees for refusing to provide access to social media accounts, but it also provides the following exclusion:

> Nothing in this act shall prevent an employer from conducting an investigation:
>
> (1) for the purpose of ensuring compliance with applicable laws, regulatory requirements or prohibitions against work-related employee misconduct based on the receipt of specific information about activity on a personal account by an employee; or
> (2) of an employee's actions based on the receipt of specific information about the unauthorized transfer of an employer's proprietary information, confidential information or financial data to a personal account by an employee.

N.J. STAT. ANN. 34:6B-6 (2018). Still, this investigation exception is quite narrow. There must be more than a generalized suspicion of wrongdoing or other "reasonable justification" for seeking access; the employer must also have "specific information" to believe the suspected offense involved use of the particular account.

These protections have other limitations as well; for example, most statutes, including New Jersey's, impose only minor administrative fines for violations and do not provide for a private right of action. Yet some of these statutes nevertheless provide fairly robust remedies. *See, e.g.*, CONN. GEN. STAT. § 31-40x (2018) (beyond small fines, additional appropriate relief may include rehiring or reinstatement and payment of back wages); *see also* MD. CODE, LABOR AND EMP. LAW § 3-712 (2018) (providing for possible suit by the Attorney General on behalf of the applicant or employee for injunctive relief, damages, or other relief). Nebraska's statute, in contrast, creates a private right of action with a one-year statute of limitations, and the aggrieved party may be awarded appropriate relief in the form of temporary or permanent injunction, general and special damages, and reasonable attorney fees and costs. NEB. REV. STAT. § 48-3511 (2017).

In addition, if workers utilize social networking or other electronic means to discuss work-related conditions with one another, their communications may be protected as "concerted activity" under the National Labor Relations Act. *See* 29 U.S.C. §157 (2018); *see also* page 448, *infra* (discussing protection for concerted activity). Indeed, the National Labor Relations Board and its general counsel have addressed the issue of concerted activity and employer social media policies a number of times. The Board found, for example, that Facebook postings by two employees expressing concern about working late at night in an unsafe neighborhood were protected activity. *Design Technology Group, LLC,* 359 NLRB No. 96 (2013). To the extent such postings are protected concerted activity, employers are prohibited from disciplining employees for them and cannot promulgate social media policies that might have a chilling effect on such activity. *See, e.g., Three D, LLC v. N.L.R.B.,* 629 F. App'x 33 (2d Cir. 2015) (holding endorsement of former employee's claim on social networking website that employer had erred in tax withholding was concerted activity protected by NLRA); Operations Management Memorandum 1259 from Ann Purcell, Assoc. Gen. Counsel, to all Reg'l Dirs., Officers in Charge, and Resident Officers, "Report of the Acting General Counsel Concerning Social Media Cases" (May 30, 2012), available at http://www.nlrb.gov/reports-guidance/operations-management-memos?memo_number=OM%5C+12 (discussing employer social media policies and rules that violate Sections 7 and 8(a)(1)); *see also* Pauline T. Kim, *Electronic Privacy and Employee Speech,* 87 CHI.-KENT L. REV. 901 (2012) (discussing the interaction between employee privacy interests in electronic communications and protections for socially valuable speech, including concerted activity); Ann C. McGinley & Ryan P. McGinley-Stempel, *Beyond the Water Cooler: Speech and the Workplace in an Era of Social Media,* 30 HOFSTRA LAB. & EMP. L.J. 75 (2012) (discussing social media and speech in the private workplace context and the implications of the NLRB's recent concerted-activity decisions). It is worth noting, however, that the Trump Administration's NLRB is likely to take a narrower view of the extent to which employer regulation of employee social media activity interferes with employee rights to concerted activity.

At this point, and despite some calls for legislative action by the blogger community and others, the potential sources of protection for publicly accessible Internet activities are limited. As will be discussed in the next chapter, public employee speech on the Internet enjoys qualified First Amendment protection. *See, e.g., City of San Diego v. Roe,* 543 U.S. 77, 80 (2004); *United States v. Nat'l Treasury Employees,* 513 U.S. 454, 465 (1995). Also, in the private employment context, Internet activities that touch on other protected spheres, such as religious or political affiliations, may receive some protection under federal antidiscrimination law, state associational protections, or, conceivably, the public policy exception.

It is unlikely, however, that most intrusion upon seclusion or other breach of privacy claims relating to Internet activity will succeed since rarely will one have a reasonable expectation of privacy in postings or other activities on the Internet. And, of course, unless protected as "concerted activity," the more closely the content of the Internet activity or speech relates to areas of employer concern—for example, complaints about the employer or co-workers, statements that may embarrass or otherwise harm the employer or co-workers, revelations of confidential or proprietary interests, and so forth—the less likely the conduct is to be protected. *See, e.g., Roe, supra* (finding no constitutional violation where city terminated employee after employee made clear references to his status as a police officer in sexually explicit videos he sold on an online auction site); *see also* Helen Norton, *Constraining Public Employee Speech: Government's Control of Its Workers' Speech to Protect Its Own Expression*, 59 DUKE L.J. 1 (2009) (discussing how courts are increasingly concluding that off-duty/off-site conduct by government workers—including Internet activities—affect employer interests).

As a practical matter then, at-will employees and job applicants ought to assume that they have little protection against adverse employment actions resulting from things they say or see on non-password-protected areas of the Internet. Indeed, workers, and job applicants in particular, would be well advised to assume that anything they say or post in publicly accessible areas of the Internet will become known to potential employers, since many employers now conduct Internet searches for information on prospective employees. *See, e.g.,* Microsoft Online Reputation Data Study, *Online Reputation in a Connected World* (Jan. 2010) *available at* http://www.microsoft.com/privacy/dpd/research.aspx (finding that 70 percent of employers in the United States have rejected employees because of information discovered online, and that nearly all employers believe it is appropriate to consider prospective employees' online reputation). Although anonymous participation may provide greater protections, maintaining such anonymity forever may be both difficult and costly (in the sense that one cannot take credit for his or her postings), and examples of repercussions upon an employer's discovery of the true identity of a blogger or poster now abound.

Background Inquiries

Finally, there is the related issue regarding the extent to which employers can inquire into employees' past or present unlawful conduct. Drug testing (including for illicit drug use) is addressed above, as are psychological test questions that may probe into such matters. But another concern is employer inquiries and searches regarding applicants' criminal backgrounds. A number of states have statutes prohibiting employers from considering an applicant's criminal and/or arrest records absent job-relatedness. *See, e.g.,* HAW. REV. STAT. §378-2.5(a) (2018) (an employer may inquire about and consider an applicant's criminal conviction record if it bears "a rational relationship to the duties and responsibilities of the position); MASS. GEN. LAWS ANN. ch. 151B, §4(9) (2018) (prohibiting employer or its agent from requesting information regarding, inter alia, "an arrest . . . in which no conviction resulted" or any conviction of a misdemeanor which occurred five years prior to date of employee's application); N.Y. CORRECT. LAW §752 (McKinney2018) (prohibiting denial of employment based on previous conviction of applicant unless there is "a direct relationship" between the offenses and the specific license or position or where accepting the applicant would involve "an unreasonable risk" to property or public safety). Other states impose such limitations only on public employers. *See, e.g.,* CONN. GEN. STAT. §46a-80 (2018). And the so-called Ban-the-Box movement—pressing cities and counties to stop screening out those with criminal records at the application stage—has had some significant successes. *See, e.g.,* National Employment Law Project, *Ban the Box: Major U.S. Cities and Counties Adopt Fair Hiring Policies to Remove Unfair Barriers to Employment of People with Criminal Records* (July 2014), available at http://www.nelp.org/page/-/sclp/2011/cityandcountyhiringinitiatives.pdf?nocdn=1. Such laws, however, generally still permit an inquiry at an interview. *See generally* Dallan F. Flake, *Do Ban-the-Box Laws Really Work?*, 104 Iowa L. Rev. (forthcoming 2019) (detailing recent developments in "ban-the-box" legislation and arguing for their effectiveness in increasing employment opportunities for prior criminal offenders).

Although explored more in connection with antidiscrimination laws, there is also a possibility that denying applicants jobs based on prior offenses is actionable "disparate impact" race discrimination. *See El v. Southeastern Pennsylvania Transportation Authority*, 479 F.3d 232 (3d Cir. 2007). *See also* EEOC Enforcement Guidance on the Consideration of Arrest and Conviction Records in Employment Decisions Under Title VII of the Civil Rights Act of 1964, April 25, 2012, http://www.eeoc.gov/laws/guidance/arrest_conviction.cfm. The EEOC has filed several suits that challenge such use. *See generally* Tammy R. Pettinato, *Employment Discrimination Against Ex-Offenders: The Promise and Limits of Title VII Disparate Impact Theory*, 98 Marq. L. Rev. 831(2014).

Laws prohibiting discrimination based on criminal history serve various social goals, ensuring fairness to the individual worker and helping to facilitate ex-convicts' reentry into the mainstream economy, a key factor in preventing recidivism. For their part, employers often legitimately fear damage or loss to their property or business as well as possible tort liability to other employees or third parties in the event that the worker commits another offense. For instance, where an employer knows (or should know) of a worker's criminal history and that individual subsequently injures or assaults a co-worker, the employer may be found to have engaged in a negligent hiring. Do the statutory examples provided above offer a way of striking a balance between employers' risk-management concerns and other societal interests? Should an employer faced with a negligent hiring claim be able to use such a statute as a defense to liability? Note too that, even if warranted, these kinds of laws are difficult to enforce: an ordinary Internet search can turn up information about criminal background, and it may be difficult to prove reliance on information from such a search in litigation in the unlikely event that someone denied employment is willing to bring suit in the first instance.

Driven in part by pay equity concerns, there is also a growing movement to prohibit prospective employers from inquiring about or screening for salary/pay history. California, Delaware, and Massachusetts have enacted such legislation, with Oregon to follow in January 2019. *See* Cal. Lab. Code § 432.3 (West Ann. 2018); Del. Code Ann. tit. 19, § 709B (West 2018); Mass. Gen. Laws Ann. ch. 149, § 105A (2018); Or. Rel. Stat. §652.220 (2018). *Compare Rizo v. Yovino*, 854 F.3d 1161, 1166 (9th Cir. 2017) (holding that pay differentials between female and male employees based on county's use of prior salary to determine starting salary was not per se violation of the Equal Pay Act and remanding the case for a determination of whether stated business reasons for use of prior salary were factors other than sex under the Act).

Note on Employee Dress and Appearance

Choices about dress and grooming are also often expressions of individual autonomy and dignitary interests. For this reason, disputes over employee appearance in the workplace may be conceptualized as matters of worker privacy. Despite significant scholarly and public attention in recent years, there are few protections for worker preferences with regard to their appearance, and challenges to employer policies and practices in this area rarely succeed. Statutory protections that address dress and grooming choices directly are rare, and, where they exist, they may be subject to significant limitations. *See, e.g.* D.C. CODE §2-1402.11 (2014) (prohibiting discrimination based on "personal appearance" but expressly exempting various policies, including those that relate to cleanliness, health or safety, and uniform requirements that apply across a class of employees). In the absence of free speech or free exercise implications, public employees' challenges to dress and grooming policies on substantive due process grounds are unlikely to be successful since they are subject only to rational basis review. *See, e.g., Kelley v. Johnson*, 425 U.S. 238 (1976) (rejecting a challenge to hair-grooming standards for members of a police force).

Perhaps the most important sources of potential protection in this area are those that prohibit status-based discrimination, including antidiscrimination statutes and the First Amendment's Free Exercise Clause. Employees have had some success challenging some such policies as discriminatory. *See, e.g., E.E.O.C. v. R.G. & G.R. Harris Funeral Homes, Inc.*, 100 F. Supp. 3d 594 (E.D. Mich. 2015) (denying the employer's motion to dismiss an EEOC claim alleging that an employer violated Title VII's prohibition on sex discrimination by terminating an employee who intended to dress in women's business attire while transitioning from male to female); *Frank v. United Airlines*, 216 F.3d 845 (9th Cir. 2000) (striking down the airline's disparate weight standards for male and female flight attendants as facially discriminatory); *FOP Newark Lodge No. 12 v. City of Newark*, 170 F.3d 359 (3d Cir. 1999) (holding the city's refusal to accommodate officers whose religion required them to wear beards violated the free exercise clause), However, other such challenges have failed, including claims addressing gender-specific differences in dress and grooming codes, and the disparate effects of such codes on women and religious and other minorities. *See, e.g., Webb v. City of Philadelphia*, 562 F.3d 256 (3d Cir. 2009); *Jespersen v. Harrah's Operating Co.*, 444 F.3d 1104 (9th Cir. 2006) (en banc); *Harper v. Blockbuster Entm't Corp.*, 139 F.3d 1385 (11th Cir. 1998). Courts afford employers substantial deference in making decisions about the appearance of their workers even when the result is to reinforce gender-conformity norms. The limiting principle is that no particular protected group may be singled out or subjected to far greater burdens. There may also be legal restrictions on dress requirements that increase the risk that women will be subjected to sexual harassment from customers or co-workers. Despite the limits of current law, many commentators have focused attention on the discriminatory effect of such policies and other sources of pressure to conform to "majority" expectations with regard to appearance, habits, and demeanor while at work. *See, e.g.,* Katharine T. Bartlett, *Only Girls Wear Barrettes: Dress and Appearance Standards, Community Norms and Workplace Equality*, 92 MICH. L. REV. 2541, 2543-46 (1994); Mary Anne C. Case, *Disaggregating Gender from Sex and Sexual Orientation: The Effeminate Man in the Law and Feminist Jurisprudence*, 105 YALE L. J. 1, 68-69 (1995); Catherine L. Fisk, *Privacy, Power, and Humiliation at Work: Re-Examining Appearance Regulation as an Invasion of Privacy*, 66 LA. L. REV. 1111 (2006); Roberto J. Gonzalez, *Cultural Rights and the Immutability Requirement in Disparate Impact Doctrine*, 55 STAN. L. REV. 2195, 2227 (2003); Tristin K. Green, *Work Culture and Discrimination*, 93 CAL. L. REV. 623 (2005); Karl E. Klare, *Power/Dressing: Regulation of Employee Appearance*, 26 NEW ENG. L. REV. 1395 (1992); Gowri Ramachandran, *Intersectionality as "Catch-22": Why Identity Performance Demands Are Neither Harmless nor Reasonable*, 69 ALB. L. REV. 299

(2005); Camille Gear Rich, *Performing Racial and Ethnic Identity: Discrimination by Proxy and the Future of Title VII*, 79 N.Y.U. L. Rev. 1134 (2004); Kenji Yoshino, *Covering*, 111 Yale L. J. 769 (2002); *see generally* Symposium, *Makeup, Identity Performance & Discrimination*, 14 Duke J. Gender L. & Pol'y 1 (2007).

C. PRIVATE ORDERING: ARE THERE ANY LIMITS TO CONSENT?

The first part of this chapter discussed contract as a possible source of privacy rights. One might say, from the employee perspective, that the use of contract to create or expand the sphere of employee privacy protection is the "positive" side of private ordering. On the "negative" side is the use of contract, workplace guidelines and practices, and employee consent to eliminate or reduce the legally cognizable sphere of privacy that otherwise might exist.

In light of this, and employers' increasing use of employment "privacy" policies and waiver forms, whether otherwise cognizable privacy rights may be limited or eliminated through such private ordering may be the most important question in this area today. And it raises critical, ultimate questions: Are there and should there be any limitations on employers' ability to extract employee consent to intrusions or, more broadly, eliminate spheres of expected privacy? If so, what kinds? Consider these questions as you read the next case.

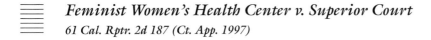 *Feminist Women's Health Center v. Superior Court*
61 Cal. Rptr. 2d 187 (Ct. App. 1997)

Puglia, P.J., with Sparks, J., and Nicholson, J., concurring.

The issue presented by this petition is whether a female health center employee who agrees voluntarily to demonstrate a cervical self-examination to female clients and employees at the health center may sue the health center (and several of its supervisory employees) because the self-examination violates her constitutional right to privacy.

Respondent superior court granted summary adjudication of all of plaintiff Claudia Jenkins's claims except the one alleging she was wrongfully terminated from employment in violation of her right to privacy. The defendants—Feminist Women's Health Center ("Center") and several of its employees—filed the instant petition seeking a writ to compel the superior court to adjudicate this remaining claim in their favor. We shall order the writ to issue. . . .

Plaintiff alleged: She was hired by defendants as a health worker pursuant to an oral contract entered in August 1993; defendants mandated that all female employees disrobe and display their vaginas to the employee defendants and various other employees; those who refused were advised that they either would be fired or would not receive promotions or raises; plaintiff refused to disrobe and was transferred to an intake clerk position before being terminated from employment on January 6, 1994; defendants' policy violated plaintiff's right to privacy and her right freely to maintain and practice religious and cultural beliefs as they pertained to the treatment and care of her body. . . .

Defendant Dido Hasper, executive director of the Center, declared that the Center was founded as a nonprofit corporation in Chico in 1974. The Center was created because unmarried women found it difficult to obtain abortion and mid-wifery services as well as information regarding birth control, adoption, and repro-duction. The Center was inspired by the existence of similar centers in Los Angeles and Oakland. The Chico Center began offering services in 1975, including abortion services, pregnancy screening, well-woman gynecology, family planning, and a speak-ers' bureau on women's health topics. The Center expanded and presently has four clinics, located in Chico, Sacramento, Santa Rosa, and Redding.

Hasper's declaration discussed self-help groups at which cervical self-examination was demonstrated. Hasper defined a self-help group as a gathering of women who want to learn more about their bodies and reproductive health care. She declared: "The goal is to give women the opportunity to talk to each other, share experiences, learn from each other, and learn about their own bodies. A common realization of par-ticipants in self-help groups is that women's bodies and their normal reproductive functions have been medicalized and remain a mystery to them. The goal of self-help is to demystify and redefine the normal functions of a woman's body. Our unique and effective, although not strictly necessary tool to accomplish this is for women to visu-alize their own cervixes and vaginas, which are not usually seen with the naked eye without the use of a vaginal speculum. In many, but not necessarily all, self-help clinic sessions, women are given the opportunity to learn how to use a plastic speculum. . . . The Health Center offers self-help 'clinics' as a community education service to other women's groups, high school and college classes, and makes self-help group facili-tators available for any appropriate gathering of interested women. . . . When self-examination occurs in a self-help group, two customs are observed. A woman does self-examination only if and when she feels comfortable doing so, and she looks at her own cervix first before any of the other participants in the self-help group."

Hasper declared that the position of "feminist health worker" (for which plain-tiff was hired) was a unique one, requiring, at a minimum, "a great deal of empathy and training, strict absence of judgmentalism, a sophistication to react to a variety of clients' circumstances in a calm, respectful manner, and the ability to think on one's feet and appropriately respond to the needs of Health Center clients."

Hasper further declared that an element of the health worker's training process was an orientation to the self-help educational process. A senior health worker or director presides over the orientation, which includes a slide show about the his-tory of the women's self-help movement and self-examination. Self-examination of the cervix thereafter is demonstrated for those attendees who express an interest. A plastic speculum is used to observe the cervix, and attendees are given the oppor-tunity to take one home to examine themselves. Hasper concluded: "It is not the goal of self-help or of the Health Center, nor is it possible, to compel or require any woman to do self-examination of her own cervix. . . . Many senior health workers become facilitators for self-help clinics, although this too is not a job requirement. It has been the Center's experience that those health workers who are genuinely enthu-siastic about the concept of self-help, if they possess the other qualities stated above, become outstanding staff members, embracing the goals of their organization. . . . A health worker cannot perform as a woman's advocate during the abortion process at the Health Center's standard if she has a strong aversion to the self-help concept."

Defendant Lisa Williams, the clinic manager for the Center's Sacramento office in August 1993, submitted a declaration detailing the circumstances of plaintiff's employment. Williams declared that plaintiff was hired as a health worker at the Center's Sacramento branch in August 1993. Williams interviewed plaintiff and explained the role of the health worker in the abortion clinic. She gave plaintiff a copy of the health worker job description, which plaintiff read and acknowledged reading. Williams detailed the training program for health workers. She explained the self-help philosophy of the clinic and that health workers, as part of their training, would be oriented to self-help and invited to participate in a self-help clinic. In October 1993, several months after plaintiff had been hired, plaintiff applied for a vacant position of intake clerk. Williams explained to plaintiff that she would have to undergo a new interview process for the intake clerk position, since a different supervisor was involved. Williams declared that plaintiff never expressed dissatisfaction with self-help, even though she had many opportunities to do so at regularly scheduled staff meetings where dissent was encouraged. Williams declared that she did not participate in the decision to hire or fire plaintiff from the intake worker position.

Appended to Williams's declaration is a hiring interview form, signed by plaintiff, which states in part: "I have read and understand the job description for the position I am being hired. [sic] [¶] I have read and understand the Personnel Policies of the Feminist Women's Health Center."

The health worker job description which plaintiff reviewed also was appended. Under "qualifications" for the health worker position, two of the qualifications emphasize self-help:

1. Must attend Orientation and Self-Help demonstration
    . . .
1. Must have an interest in women's healthcare and Self-Help

Under the heading "responsibilities and duties" in the health worker job description, participation in self-help clinics and the demonstration of the self-cervical exam at those clinics is explicitly stated:

1. Attends and conducts self-help clinics as assigned.
    . . .
1. Is a Healthworker for drop-in pregnancy screening and pregnancy screening groups as scheduled:
    a. Facilitates pregnancy screening groups.
    b. Demonstrates self cervical exam to pregnancy screening groups.
    c. Counsels clients about pregnancy screening.
    d. Makes appropriate referrals for clients.
    e. Performs UCG pregnancy test or early urine pregnancy tests for clients.
    f. Acts as an advocate during exams by the medical professional as needed.

Defendants argued that their evidence establishes that plaintiff's wrongful termination cause of action lacks merit because plaintiff, as an at-will employee, was subject to reasonable conditions of employment, of which cervical self-examination was one.

In order to rebut defendants' showing that plaintiff understood and expressly agreed to demonstrate cervical self-examination, plaintiff's opposition papers explain the circumstances surrounding self-help and how she was pressured into demonstrating it. Plaintiff declared that during her employment interview "I was not told it was mandatory to disrobe and insert a speculum in my vagina in front of a group of health workers." At a September 1993 self-help session (one month after she was hired), plaintiff was instructed by defendant Eileen Schnitger to disrobe and insert a speculum in her vagina. Plaintiff refused. After further refusals, defendant Lisa Williams instructed plaintiff that she was required to participate in self-help. In October 1993, plaintiff applied for an intake clerk position because it was her understanding that it would not require participation in self-help, although she wasn't sure. Plaintiff became an intake worker on November 1, 1993, at the same rate of pay she had received as a health worker. Tensions were high at this time due to the self-help controversy. Plaintiff and fellow employee Kimya Lambert tried to defuse the problem by suggesting less personally intrusive methods such as using mannequins or privately inserting the speculum and then discussing results in the group sessions. Defendant Eileen Schnitger steadfastly refused these alternatives.

In December 1993, at the insistence of plaintiff and others, volunteer nurse Maggie Gunn wrote [an anonymous letter requesting that the Center "stop pressuring people to do the self-help"]. Gunn and another employee, Shirley Anderson, quit soon thereafter because of the self-help mandate. Plaintiff and Kimya Lambert were fired because of their work performance. Plaintiff's declaration concluded: "I believe and continue to believe 'self-help' in general has no relation to my position as a health worker because as a health worker I did not counsel clients about 'self-help.' I merely assisted in the abortion process. In fact, many of the movies we viewed at 'self-help' meetings featured issues such as how to climax and I know for certain I was not going to discuss this with any abortion client. I had a very difficult time sitting through these movies about climaxing but did so to preserve my job. I had to draw the line, although, at the request to disrobe in front of a group of people."

Shirley Anderson, employed as a nurse and health worker at the Center from May 1993 to January 1994, submitted a declaration in which she declared that she was not informed that she would have to disrobe in front of people as part of self-help. It was only after a few sessions that Eileen Schnitger clarified that self-examination was a job requirement. Lisa Williams told her she would receive no raises or promotions unless she participated in self-examination.

[The trial court granted summary judgment as to all claims except the one for wrongful termination in violation of public policy, and as to that, "limited [it] to the exception with regard to a contention of discharge in invasion of the right of privacy."]

Defendants argue there can be no liability of the Center or its employees for terminating an employee who, having been hired as a health worker whose duties included the demonstration of cervical self-examination before groups of women, objected to and refused to perform that job duty. Defendants argue it was undisputed that the written job description for the health worker position for which plaintiff was hired expressly states that cervical self-examination is a job duty of the health worker. In defendants' view, the trial court ignored this express agreement and also failed to engage in the balancing analysis required in cases involving an alleged violation of the constitutional right to privacy. Defendants posit that the court's denial, pro tanto, of their summary adjudication motion cripples the Center's health education program and threatens the Center's existence by giving every health worker the right to sue for damages for violation of privacy rights.

Plaintiff responds that these arguments are specious as the superior court's order "does not prohibit or eliminate anything nor declare anything illegal." Plaintiff contends that summary adjudication was properly denied based on the existence of a number of disputed issues, namely: whether there was a self-help program in effect during plaintiff's employment; whether such a program included cervical self-examination; whether cervical self-examination was a vital part of the self-help program; whether the cervical self-examination required employees to disrobe in front of other females; whether an employee had the right to refuse to perform cervical self-examination; and whether the Center's interest outweighed plaintiff's right to privacy.

[After reviewing the relevant case law, the court concluded that California's constitutional right to privacy forms a sufficient touchstone of public policy to serve as a basis for plaintiff's wrongful termination claim. The defendants did not dispute the existence of such a cause of action, but argued instead that there is no material factual dispute whether plaintiff's right to privacy was violated.]

The principal case discussing the elements of a violation under California's constitutional privacy provision is *Hill v. National Collegiate Athletic Ass'n*, [865 P.2d 633 (Cal. 1994),] involving university students' action against the National Collegiate Athletic Association ("NCAA") to enjoin the NCAA's drug testing program for student athletes. The Supreme Court held that] the drug testing program did not violate the California Constitution's right to privacy.

The court summarized the elements of a privacy claim and defenses thereto as follows:

> [W]e hold that a plaintiff alleging an invasion of privacy in violation of the state constitutional right to privacy must establish each of the following: (1) a legally protected privacy interest; (2) a reasonable expectation of privacy in the circumstances; and (3) conduct by defendant constituting a serious invasion of privacy.
>
> Whether a legally recognized privacy interest is present in a given case is a question of law to be decided by the court. Whether plaintiff has a reasonable expectation of privacy in the circumstances and whether defendant's conduct constitutes a serious invasion of privacy are mixed questions of law and fact. If the undisputed material facts show no reasonable expectation of privacy or an insubstantial impact on privacy interests, the question of invasion may be adjudicated as a matter of law.
>
> A defendant may prevail in a state constitutional privacy case by negating any of the three elements just discussed or by pleading and proving, as an affirmative defense, that the invasion of privacy is justified because it substantially furthers one or more countervailing interests. The plaintiff, in turn, may rebut a defendant's assertion of countervailing interests by showing there are feasible and effective alternatives to defendant's conduct which have a lesser impact on privacy interests. Of course, a defendant may also plead and prove other available defenses, e.g., consent, unclean hands, etc., that may be appropriate in view of the nature of the claim and the relief requested.
>
> The existence of a sufficient countervailing interest or an alternative course of conduct present threshold questions of law for the court. The relative strength of countervailing interests and the feasibility of alternatives present mixed questions of law and fact. Again, in cases where material facts are undisputed, adjudication as a matter of law may be appropriate.

In *Hill*, the court accepted as given that the NCAA's policy of observing athletes urinate into vials impinged on a legally protected privacy interest. The court further concluded, though, that student athletes had diminished expectations of privacy by reason of their participation in intercollegiate athletic activities and advance notice of the drug testing. Notwithstanding the diminished expectation of privacy resulting therefrom, the court evaluated the competing interests at stake due to the seriousness of the privacy invasion. The court ultimately concluded that "[t]he NCAA's information-gathering procedure (i.e., drug testing through urinalysis) is a method reasonably calculated to further its interests in enforcing a ban on the ingestion of specified substances in order to secure fair competition and the health and safety of athletes participating in its programs."

Applying the analytical framework of *Hill*, we agree with plaintiff that the observation of the insertion of a speculum into plaintiff's vagina by fellow employees and female clients of the Center infringes a legally protected privacy interest. This invasion is at least as serious as observing urination, and we do not question plaintiff's assertions that it was contrary to her religious and cultural beliefs.

The reasonableness of plaintiff's expectation of privacy is no greater than in the *Hill* case, however. In *Hill*, the student athletes had diminished expectations of privacy by reason of occasional communal undress and the sharing of information regarding physical fitness and bodily condition. Two elements of the NCAA's drug testing program further diminished the student athlete's reasonable expectation of privacy: advance notice and the opportunity to consent to testing. The court acknowledged that participation in athletic contests was conditioned on consent to testing, but that this did not render the consent involuntary, since the students did not have a right to participate in such competitions.

In the present case, the evidence established that plaintiff agreed to demonstrate cervical self-examination as a job requirement. She signed a form which manifested her understanding of and agreement to fulfill certain job duties. Those duties included participating in self-help and demonstrating cervical self-examinations to pregnancy screening groups.

Plaintiff did not dispute that she had agreed to these employment terms. Her dispute, rather, centered on the meaning of the phrase "demonstrates self-cervical exam to pregnancy screening groups." According to plaintiff's declaration, "I was not told it was mandatory to disrobe and insert a speculum in my vagina in front of a group of health workers." Assuming this statement to be true, it still fails to undermine her agreement to demonstrate cervical self-examinations. Disrobing and inserting a speculum in the vagina is a means by which cervical self-examination is demonstrated. Plaintiff's professed ignorance of the particulars of cervical self-examination does not vitiate her agreement to perform it.

The real issue is whether this type of cervical self-examination may reasonably be required of the Center's employees. In other words, the seriousness of the privacy invasion leads us to the third part of the *Hill* test: consideration of the Center's countervailing interests and the feasibility of the alternatives proposed by plaintiff.

[The court repeated Executive Director Hasper's statement about the reasons for the Center's use of cervical self-examination.] It is true, as plaintiff notes, that Hasper's declaration reveals that the job requirement of cervical self-examination varies with the circumstances. These variations give rise to an inference that self-help is not an inflexible part of the Center's self-examination orientation sessions or demonstrations to interested groups.

But the declaration also makes clear that cervical self-examination is important in advancing the Center's fundamental goal of educating women about the function and health of their reproductive systems. Other parts of Hasper's declaration also show that the ability to demonstrate self-examination properly and without reservation identified employees who would be outstanding health care workers and potential group leaders. The declaration implied that the identification and retention of such employees was critical to the continued success of the Center. Considering the Center's expansion since its inception some 20 years ago, it was not unreasonable for Hasper to infer that new clients were drawn to the candid knowledge and intimacy imparted by the Center's unique methods, of which cervical self-examination was one.

The Center also could reasonably conclude that the alternative methods of self-examination proposed by plaintiff would have stifled such candor. These alternatives, such as the use of mannequins, or the private use of the speculum followed by discussion, are pale imitations of uninhibited group cervical self-examination.

It goes without saying that certain individuals would have an aversion to cervical self-examination or other aspects of self-help which were used to advance the Center's goal of shared experiences and learning. Plaintiff, for one, acknowledges that her religious and cultural background was not well suited to the practices of the Center.

In balancing these competing interests, we return to plaintiff's consent to demonstrate cervical self-examination as part of her employment agreement with the Center. The Center was not obligated to hire plaintiff, and consent remains a viable defense even in cases of serious privacy invasions. (*Hill.*) Therefore, we believe the facts as disclosed in the trial court give rise to the following inferences only: the requirement that health workers perform cervical self-examinations in front of other females is a reasonable condition of employment and does not violate the health worker's right to privacy where the plaintiff's written employment agreement evidences her knowledge of this condition and agreement to be bound by it. Where the employee thereafter refuses to abide by the agreement, the employee's wrongful termination claim based on a violation of the right to privacy is rendered infirm. Such is the case under the facts presented, and the superior court should have granted summary adjudication of this claim. . . .

NOTES

1. Quon *and* FWHC: *Disparate Facts, Common Themes.* In some ways, *Quon* and *Feminist Women's Health Center* ("*FWHC*")—are very different. First, the claims involve different types of employers, one public, one private, and therefore derive from different sources of law. In addition, *Quon* involves a fairly typical challenge to employer monitoring of electronic communications. *FWHC* addresses a unique set of circumstances, involving an employee challenge to a highly unusual job requirement tied to the employer's particular mission. Indeed, the controversy underlying *FWHC* and the resulting litigation over privacy rights seem ironic, given that a core component of the employer's mission is to further women's autonomy.

Yet consider what these cases have in common. As we have seen throughout this chapter, although the factual circumstances and articulations of the legal standards may differ, the courts tend to ask the same questions: whether the employee has a legitimate expectation of privacy, whether the employer has articulated a workplace-related interest to justify the alleged intrusion, the strength or importance of this employer interest, the nexus between the employer interest and the intrusion, and the extent to which the employee consented to or was on prior notice of the intrusion(s).

2. *The Role of Consent.* As a formal matter, there are two different ways in which explicit or implicit employee consent to particular intrusions defeat privacy claims. The employer electronic communications and computer use policy cases mentioned above provide an example of the first. These claims frequently fail because the employee's consent to monitoring and oversight eliminates any reasonable expectation of privacy in the underlying communications or files. Now consider why the *FWHC* analysis is different. Ask yourself, does plaintiff in *FWHC* have a reasonable expectation of privacy even though she consented? If yes, then how does consent operate to defeat her claim?

Given these potential effects of consent, and the growing sophistication of employers in crafting employment policies and waivers, the more courts accept private ordering in the workplace, the less privacy protection will exist for workers. The fact that *FWHC* is a California decision may be particularly troubling to workplace privacy advocates since California is one of the few jurisdictions that recognizes a state constitutional right to privacy in the private workplace and is considered among the *most* amenable to employee privacy claims. And recall that employees may fare no better even if they are in a position to challenge ex ante employer demands for consent because of the "Request for Consent Catch-22." Thus, the employer's request for consent itself may effectively preclude many privacy claims. Could plaintiff in *FWHC* have sued if she had been denied a job when she first applied because of the job description?

3. *The Limits of Consent.* Some of the particular statutory protections discussed in this chapter—for example, prohibitions on polygraph, genetic, and forms of medical testing as well as the new state laws protecting social media accounts—cannot be waived by employees, even by express consent. Also, in the public employer context, employees cannot be compelled to shed their constitutional rights at the workplace door, *see Pickering v. Board of Educ.*, 391 U.S. 563 (1968), although, as *Quon* and the *O'Connor* plurality's framework suggest, implicit consent to workplace monitoring, surveillance, testing, and other intrusive activities may limit or destroy an employee's legitimate expectation of privacy, and hence, any real hope of establishing a Fourth Amendment or due process violation.

Should there be other limits to the immunizing effect of consent? As we have seen in other contexts, one reason to curtail private ordering between worker and firm is to protect the public or third parties. Is the public interest implicated in the privacy context? If so, when, how, and to what extent? *Cf. Cramer v. Consol. Freightways, Inc.*, 255 F.3d 683 (9th Cir. 2001) (en banc) (holding that, even if collective bargaining agreement expressly contemplated employer's video surveillance of employee restrooms, the term would be unenforceable because such surveillance violated a California criminal statute).

Should there be further substantive or procedural limitations? For example, in *Quon* the possibility that the employees had a reasonable expectation of privacy in the text messages despite the employers' fairly clear use policy suggests that inconsistent employer practices or representations can defeat apparent expectation-eliminating language in written policies or waivers. But, assuming no such inconsistency, how clear must a workplace policy or practice be before a court should find that it immunizes the employer from liability? Was the disclosure in *FWHC* sufficiently clear as to what plaintiff was expected to do? Should consent be limited at all by the importance of the employer interest to be served or the "nexus" between that interest and the particular intrusion to which the employee has consented? Should consent obtained at the start of employment be treated differently than consent obtained or notice provided after the employee has started work? *See generally* Steven L. Willborn, *Consenting Employees: Workplace Privacy and the Role of Consent*, 66 LA. L. REV. 975 (2006); *see also* James A. Sonne, *Monitoring for Quality Assurance: Employer Regulation of Off-Duty Behavior*, 43 GA. L. REV. 133, 166 (2008).

Are there other reasons for discounting even clear and unequivocal forms of express consent to employer intrusions? Consider the next case.

═══ *Stengart v. Loving Care Agency, Inc.*
═══ *990 A.2d 650 (N.J. 2010)*

CHIEF JUSTICE RABNER delivered the Opinion of the Court.

In the past twenty years, businesses and private citizens alike have embraced the use of computers, electronic communication devices, the Internet, and e-mail. As those and other forms of technology evolve, the line separating business from personal activities can easily blur.

In the modern workplace, for example, occasional, personal use of the Internet is commonplace. Yet that simple act can raise complex issues about an employer's monitoring of the workplace and an employee's reasonable expectation of privacy.

This case presents novel questions about the extent to which an employee can expect privacy and confidentiality in personal e-mails with her attorney, which she accessed on a computer belonging to her employer. Marina Stengart used her company-issued laptop to exchange e-mails with her lawyer through her personal, password-protected, web-based e-mail account. She later filed an employment discrimination lawsuit against her employer, Loving Care Agency, Inc. (Loving Care), and others.

In anticipation of discovery, Loving Care hired a computer forensic expert to recover all files stored on the laptop including the e-mails, which had been automatically saved on the hard drive. Loving Care's attorneys reviewed the e-mails and used information culled from them in the course of discovery. In response, Stengart's lawyer demanded that communications between him and Stengart, which he considered privileged, be identified and returned. Opposing counsel disclosed the documents but maintained that the company had the right to review them. Stengart then sought relief in court. . . .

We hold that, under the circumstances, Stengart could reasonably expect that e-mail communications with her lawyer through her personal account would remain private, and that sending and receiving them via a company laptop did not eliminate the attorney-client privilege that protected them. By reading e-mails that were at least arguably privileged and failing to notify Stengart promptly about them, Loving Care's counsel breached *RPC* 4.4(b). We therefore modify and affirm the judgment of the Appellate Division and remand to the trial court to determine what, if any, sanctions should be imposed on counsel for Loving Care.

I . . .

Loving Care provides home-care nursing and health services. Stengart began working for Loving Care in 1994 and, over time, was promoted to Executive Director of Nursing. The company provided her with a laptop computer to conduct company business. From that laptop, Stengart could send e-mails using her company e-mail address; she could also access the Internet and visit websites through Loving Care's server. Unbeknownst to Stengart, certain browser software in place automatically made a copy of each web page she viewed, which was then saved on the computer's hard drive in a "cache" folder of temporary Internet files. Unless deleted and over-written with new data, those temporary Internet files remained on the hard drive.

On several days in December 2007, Stengart used her laptop to access a personal, password-protected e-mail account on Yahoo's website, through which she communicated with her attorney about her situation at work. She never saved her Yahoo ID or password on the company laptop.

Not long after, Stengart left her employment with Loving Care and returned the laptop. On February 7, 2008, she filed the pending complaint [alleging constructive discharge because of a hostile work environment, retaliation, and harassment based on gender, religion, and national origin].

In an effort to preserve electronic evidence for discovery, in or around April 2008, Loving Care hired experts to create a forensic image of the laptop's hard drive. Among the items retrieved were temporary Internet files containing the contents of seven or eight e-mails Stengart had exchanged with her lawyer via her Yahoo account.[1] Stengart's lawyers represented at oral argument that one e-mail was simply a communication he sent to her, to which she did not respond.

A legend appears at the bottom of the e-mails that Stengart's lawyer sent. It warns readers that

> THE INFORMATION CONTAINED IN THIS EMAIL COMMUNICATION IS INTENDED ONLY FOR THE PERSONAL AND CONFIDENTIAL USE OF THE DESIGNATED RECIPIENT NAMED ABOVE. This message may be an Attorney-Client communication, and as such is privileged and confidential. If the reader of this message is not the intended recipient, you are hereby notified that you have received this communication in error, and that your review, dissemination, distribution, or copying of the message is strictly prohibited. If you have received this transmission in error, please destroy this transmission and notify us immediately by telephone and/or reply email.

At least two attorneys from the law firm representing Loving Care, Sills Cummis (the "Firm"), reviewed the e-mail communications between Stengart and her attorney. The Firm did not advise opposing counsel about the e-mails until months later. In its October 21, 2008, reply to Stengart's first set of interrogatories, the Firm stated that it had obtained certain information from "e-mail correspondence"—between Stengart and her lawyer—from Stengart's "office computer on December 12, 2007 at 2:25 p.m." In response, Stengart's attorney sent a letter demanding that the Firm identify and return all "attorney-client privileged communications" in its possession. The Firm identified and disclosed the e-mails but asserted that Stengart had no reasonable expectation of privacy in files on a company-owned computer in light of the company's policy on electronic communications.

---

1. The record does not specify how many of the e-mails were sent or received during work hours. Loving Care asserts that the e-mails in question were exchanged during work hours through the company's server. However, counsel for Stengart represented at oral argument that four of the e-mails were transmitted or accessed during non-work hours—three on a weekend and one on a holiday. It is unclear, and ultimately not relevant, whether Stengart was at the office when she sent or reviewed them.

[The court assumed that the employer's Electronic Communication policy applied to Stengart, even though she was a senior company official. That Policy provides:]

> The company reserves and will exercise the right to review, audit, intercept, access, and disclose all matters on the company's media systems and services at any time, with or without notice. . . .
>
> E-mail and voice mail messages, internet use and communication and computer files are considered part of the company's business and client records. Such communications are not to be considered private or personal to any individual employee.
>
> The principal purpose of electronic mail (*e-mail*) is for company business communications. Occasional personal use is permitted; however, the system should not be used to solicit for outside business ventures, charitable organizations, or for any political or religious purpose, unless authorized by the Director of Human Resources.

The Policy also specifically prohibits "[c]ertain uses of the e-mail system" including sending inappropriate sexual, discriminatory, or harassing messages, chain letters, "[m]essages in violation of government laws," or messages relating to job searches, business activities unrelated to Loving Care, or political activities. The Policy concludes with the following warning: "Abuse of the electronic communications system may result in disciplinary action up to and including separation of employment."

Stengart's attorney applied for an order to show cause seeking return of the e-mails and other relief. The trial court concluded that the Firm did not breach the attorney-client privilege because the company's Policy placed Stengart on sufficient notice that her e-mails would be considered company property. Stengart's request to disqualify the Firm was therefore denied.

The Appellate Division . . . reversed the trial court order and directed the Firm to turn over all copies of the e-mails and delete any record of them. Assuming that the Policy applied to Stengart, the panel found that "[a]n objective reader could reasonably conclude . . . that not all personal e-mails are necessarily company property." In other words, an employee could "retain an expectation of privacy" in personal e-mails sent on a company computer given the language of the Policy.

II.

Loving Care argues that its employees have no expectation of privacy in their use of company computers based on the company's Policy. In its briefs before this Court, the company also asserts that by accessing e-mails on a personal account through Loving Care's computer and server, Stengart either prevented any attorney-client privilege from attaching or waived the privilege by voluntarily subjecting her e-mails to company scrutiny. Finally, Loving Care maintains that its counsel did not violate *RPC* 4.4(b) because the e-mails were left behind on Stengart's company computer— not "inadvertently sent," as per the *Rule*—and the Firm acted in the good faith belief that any privilege had been waived.

Stengart argues that she intended the e-mails with her lawyer to be confidential and that the Policy, even if it applied to her, failed to provide adequate warning that Loving Care would save on a hard drive, or monitor the contents of, e-mails sent from a personal account. Stengart also maintains that the communications with her lawyer were privileged. When the Firm encountered the arguably protected e-mails, Stengart contends it should have immediately returned them or sought judicial review as to whether the attorney-client privilege applied. . . .

III.

Our analysis draws on two principal areas: the adequacy of the notice provided by the Policy and the important public policy concerns raised by the attorney-client privilege. Both inform the reasonableness of an employee's expectation of privacy in this matter. We address each area in turn.

A.

We start by examining the meaning and scope of the Policy itself. The Policy specifically reserves to Loving Care the right to review and access "all matters on the company's media systems and services at any time." In addition, e-mail messages are plainly "considered part of the company's business . . . records."

It is not clear from that language whether the use of personal, password-protected, web-based e-mail accounts via company equipment is covered. The Policy uses general language to refer to its "media systems and services" but does not define those terms. Elsewhere, the Policy prohibits certain uses of "the e-mail system," which appears to be a reference to company e-mail accounts. The Policy does not address personal accounts at all. In other words, employees do not have express notice that messages sent or received on a personal, web-based e-mail account are subject to monitoring if company equipment is used to access the account.

The Policy also does not warn employees that the contents of such e-mails are stored on a hard drive and can be forensically retrieved and read by Loving Care.

The Policy goes on to declare that e-mails "are not to be considered private or personal to any individual employee." In the very next point, the Policy acknowledges that "[o]ccasional personal use [of e-mail] is permitted." As written, the Policy creates ambiguity about whether personal e-mail use is company or private property.

The scope of the written Policy, therefore, is not entirely clear.

B.

[The policies underlying the attorney-client privilege further animate this discussion. The primary purpose of the privilege is to encourage free and full disclosure of information between client and attorney. E-mail exchanges are covered by the privilege.]

The e-mail communications between Stengart and her lawyers contain a standard warning that their contents are personal and confidential and may constitute attorney-client communications. The subject matter of those messages appears to relate to Stengart's working conditions and anticipated lawsuit against Loving Care.

IV.

Under the particular circumstances presented, how should a court evaluate whether Stengart had a reasonable expectation of privacy in the e-mails she exchanged with her attorney?

A.

Preliminarily, we note that the reasonable-expectation-of-privacy standard used by the parties derives from the common law and the Search and Seizure Clauses of both the Fourth Amendment and Article I, paragraph 7 of the New Jersey Constitution. The latter sources do not apply in this case, which involves conduct by private parties only.

The common law source is the tort of "intrusion on seclusion," which can be found in the RESTATEMENT (SECOND) OF TORTS §652B (1977). That section provides that "[o]ne who intentionally intrudes, physically or otherwise, upon the solitude or seclusion of another or his private affairs or concerns, is subject to liability to the other for invasion of his privacy, if the intrusion would be highly offensive to a reasonable person." RESTATEMENT, *supra*, §652B. A high threshold must be cleared to assert a cause of action based on that tort. A plaintiff must establish that the intrusion "would be highly offensive to the ordinary reasonable man, as the result of conduct to which the reasonable man would strongly object." RESTATEMENT, *supra*, §652B cmt. d.

As is true in Fourth Amendment cases, the reasonableness of a claim for intrusion on seclusion has both a subjective and objective component. . . . Moreover, whether an employee has a reasonable expectation of privacy in her particular work setting "must be addressed on a case-by-case basis." *O'Connor v. Ortega*, 480 U.S. 709, 718 (1987) (plurality opinion) (reviewing public sector employment).

B.

[While no reported decisions in New Jersey offer direct guidance for the facts of this case, courts in other jurisdictions have recognized a lesser expectation of privacy when employees communicate with attorneys using a company e-mail system and have found the existence of a clear company policy banning personal e-mails to also diminish the reasonableness of an employee's claim to privacy in e-mail messages with his or her attorney. The location of the company's computer may also be relevant.]

V.

A.

Applying the above considerations to the facts before us, we find that Stengart had a reasonable expectation of privacy in the e-mails she exchanged with her attorney on Loving Care's laptop.

Stengart plainly took steps to protect the privacy of those e-mails and shield them from her employer. She used a personal, password-protected e-mail account instead of her company e-mail address and did not save the account's password on her computer. In other words, she had a subjective expectation of privacy in messages to and from her lawyer discussing the subject of a future lawsuit.

In light of the language of the Policy and the attorney-client nature of the communications, her expectation of privacy was also objectively reasonable. As noted earlier, the Policy does not address the use of personal, web-based e-mail accounts accessed through company equipment. It does not address personal accounts at all. Nor does it warn employees that the contents of e-mails sent via personal accounts can be forensically retrieved and read by the company. Indeed, in acknowledging that occasional personal use of e-mail is permitted, the Policy created doubt about whether those e-mails are company or private property.

Moreover, the e-mails are not illegal or inappropriate material stored on Loving Care's equipment, which might harm the company in some way. They are conversations between a lawyer and client about confidential legal matters, which are historically cloaked in privacy. Our system strives to keep private the very type of conversations that took place here in order to foster probing and honest exchanges.

In addition, the e-mails bear a standard hallmark of attorney-client messages. They warn the reader directly that the e-mails are personal, confidential, and may be attorney-client communications. . . .

Under all of the circumstances, we find that Stengart could reasonably expect that e-mails she exchanged with her attorney on her personal, password-protected, web-based e-mail account, accessed on a company laptop, would remain private.

It follows that the attorney-client privilege protects those e-mails. In reaching that conclusion, we necessarily reject Loving Care's claim that the attorney-client privilege either did not attach or was waived. In its reply brief and at oral argument, Loving Care argued that the manner in which the e-mails were sent prevented the privilege from attaching. Specifically, Loving Care contends that Stengart effectively brought a third person into the conversation from the start—watching over her shoulder—and thereby forfeited any claim to confidentiality in her communications. We disagree.

Stengart has the right to prevent disclosures by third persons who learn of her communications "in a manner not reasonably to be anticipated." *See* N.J.R.E. 504(1)(c)(ii). That is what occurred here. The Policy did not give Stengart, or a reasonable person in her position, cause to anticipate that Loving Care would be peering over her shoulder as she opened e-mails from her lawyer on her personal, password-protected Yahoo account. The language of the Policy, the method of transmittal that Stengart selected, and the warning on the e-mails themselves all support that conclusion.

Loving Care also argued in earlier submissions that Stengart waived the attorney-client privilege. For similar reasons, we again disagree.

A person waives the privilege if she, "without coercion and with knowledge of [her] right or privilege, made disclosure of any part of the privileged matter or consented to such a disclosure made by anyone." N.J.R.E. 530 (codifying N.J.S.A. 2A:84A–29). Because consent is not applicable here, we look to whether Stengart either knowingly disclosed the information contained in the e-mails or failed to "take reasonable steps to insure and maintain their confidentiality." [*Trilogy Communications, Inc. v. Excom Realty, Inc.* 652 A.2d 1273 (N.J. Super. 1994).]

As discussed previously, Stengart took reasonable steps to keep discussions with her attorney confidential: she elected not to use the company e-mail system and relied on a personal, password-protected, web-based account instead. She also did not save the password on her laptop or share it in some other way with Loving Care.

As to whether Stengart knowingly disclosed the e-mails, she certified that she is unsophisticated in the use of computers and did not know that Loving Care could read communications sent on her Yahoo account. Use of a company laptop alone does not establish that knowledge. Nor does the Policy fill in that gap. Under the circumstances, we do not find either a knowing or reckless waiver.

B.

Our conclusion that Stengart had an expectation of privacy in e-mails with her lawyer does not mean that employers cannot monitor or regulate the use of workplace computers. Companies can adopt lawful policies relating to computer use to protect the assets, reputation, and productivity of a business and to ensure compliance with legitimate corporate policies. And employers can enforce such policies. They may discipline employees and, when appropriate, terminate them, for violating proper workplace rules that are not inconsistent with a clear mandate of public policy. . . . For example, an employee who spends long stretches of the workday getting personal, confidential legal advice from a private lawyer may be disciplined for violating a policy permitting only occasional personal use of the Internet. But employers have no need or basis to read the specific *contents* of personal, privileged, attorney-client communications in order to enforce corporate policy. Because of the important public policy concerns underlying the attorney-client privilege, even a more clearly written company manual—that is, a policy that banned all personal computer use and provided unambiguous notice that an employer could retrieve and read an employee's attorney-client communications, if accessed on a personal, password-protected e-mail account using the company's computer system—would not be enforceable.

VI.

[The Court went on to hold the defendant's law firm's review and use of the privileged e-mails violated RPC 4.4(b), which provides that "[a] lawyer who receives a document and has reasonable cause to believe that the document was inadvertently sent shall not read the document or, if he or she has begun to do so, shall stop reading the document, promptly notify the sender, and return the document to the sender." Although the firm did not act in bad faith, the court found that its review fell within the rule and that the firm erred in] not setting aside the arguably privileged messages once it realized they were attorney-client communications, and failing either to notify its adversary or seek court permission before reading further. . . . [T]he Firm should have promptly notified opposing counsel when it discovered the nature of the e-mails.

[The Court then agreed with the Appellate Division's decision to remand to the trial court to determine the appropriate remedy, including what sanctions, if any, to impose.]

We leave to the trial court to decide whether disqualification of the Firm, screening of attorneys, the imposition of costs, or some other remedy is appropriate. . . .

NOTES

1. Stengart *and Electronic Communications.* With regard to whether Stengart had a reasonable expectation of privacy in e-mails to her attorney on the employer's computer, the court's holding boils down to two key (although arguably alternative) conclusions: (1) the employer's ambiguous company policy did not put an employee on notice that personal e-mail was company property and, hence, Stengart had a reasonable expectation of her privacy in those e-mails; and (2) because of the important public policy concerns underlying the attorney-client privilege, even a clearer policy— one that banned all use for personal reasons and provided unambiguous notice that an employer could retrieve and read an employee's attorney-client communications, if accessed on a personal, password-protected e-mail account using the company's computer system—would not be enforceable.

The court's first conclusion is not particularly novel, although its narrow reading of the policy (construing it against the drafter, the employer) might not be emulated by all courts. And, as the note materials following *Quon* emphasize, even a clearer policy may not immunize the employer, since underlying, inconsistent practices have been found to support a reasonable expectation of privacy. The court's second conclusion, however, is potentially much more groundbreaking. While at least one court has expressly rejected *Stengart*'s reasoning, *see Aventa Learning, Inc. v. K12, Inc.*, 830 F. Supp. 2d 1083 (W.D. Wash. 2011), it remains to be seen whether other courts will reach a similar conclusion, at least with regard to electronic files reflecting attorney-client privileged communications in an employee's personal e-mail account.

2. *Uncertain Implications.* A straightforward takeaway from *Stengart* is that, at least once identified as communications between an attorney and client, there is likely to be little justification or excuse for delving into the content. Note that this is true even though such communications are likely to be *highly relevant* (i.e., very helpful) to the employer in an investigatory or litigation context. However, even in New Jersey, it is unclear how far *Stengart*'s reasoning and protection might extend. First, we do not know whether *Stengart*'s conclusion extends to attorney-client privileged communications contained in company e-mail. *Compare Holmes v. Petrovich Development Co.*, 119 Cal. Rptr. 3d 878 (Ct. App. 2011) (distinguishing *Stengart* because the attorney-client communications in this case were on the company's email system). Indeed, one could argue that such attorney-client communications are not even privileged in the first place, since the privilege requires reasonable efforts to maintain confidentiality, and communicating through someone else's e-mail system falls short. Second, because this was a case about attorney conduct and sanctions, not potential privacy-based liability brought by the employee, it is not clear whether the decision will be extended to support such a claim, although the court's public policy-based reasoning would seem to suggest as much. Finally, given the court's emphasis on the particular policies underlying the attorney-client privilege, e-mails containing highly confidential and personal, but not privileged, communications might or might not be protected. In other words, it is unclear whether even the New Jersey courts would extend *Stengart*'s reasoning to protect communications in personal e-mail accounts that might reveal, for example, familial interactions, medical or health-related information, sensitive financial issues, or other intimate or otherwise confidential matters.

3. *Risk Management Implications.* This discussion offers a number of lessons for employers, employees, and counsel. First, with regard to employer monitoring and accessing employee electronic communications, the employer's policies need to be both clear and sufficiently broad to cover all anticipated uses. And, as repeated throughout this chapter, employers should ensure that employees read these policies and that workplace norms do not stray from these written provisions. Forestalling any expectations of privacy may require frequently monitoring worker communications— and letting employees know that is being done. But you can imagine why employers and individual supervisors, regardless of whatever documents their attorneys' have drafted, might be reluctant to do that. So immunizing the workplace from potential privacy claims arising out of such communications is an ongoing and far more complex endeavor than it might first appear.

Second, at the auditing, investigation, or post-termination stages, *Stengart* counsels great care reviewing employee/former employee files. No one should assume that the content of files backing up electronic communications are the employer's property simply because the computer or other device is owned by the employer. Again, the state-level statutory developments with regard to protecting employee social media accounts press in the same direction. Those conducting the investigation or review therefore ought to know that there are potential pitfalls in reviewing the content of files apparently containing employees' personal communications on nonemployer provided e-mail systems or other media. Moreover, even employer-provided communication systems (such as the messaging system in *Quon*) might contain content that is prima facie protected, if, for example, the employers' policy or practices have not been airtight. All of this suggests that monitoring and audits should be overseen by counsel or others who are cognizant of the risks and aware of potential steps that may have to be taken with regard to certain types of information.

On the flip side, given the uncertain reach of *Stengart*'s reasoning, and the fact that it has not been adopted in other jurisdictions, attorneys representing employees should counsel them to avoid attorney-client communications not only through employer-provided e-mail, but also on work time and through employer-provided equipment—computers, smart-phones, etc. Indeed, warning employees away from such forms of communications ought to be standard practice, since employees themselves frequently will not understand the larger risks, much less the nuanced distinctions discussed here.

4. FWHC, Stengart, *and Consent Reconsidered*. Having read both *FWHC* and *Stengart*, do you think both were correctly decided? If so, why? Certainly, it cannot be that the privacy interest at stake was greater in *Stengart* than *FWHC*, at least not in an abstract sense. Maybe it is the lack of clarity of the policy in the former, although again, one could argue the job requirements as described at the outset in *FWHC* were not entirely unambiguous. Nor can it be said, at a level of generality, that the intrusion in *FWHC* was employment related while the one in *Stengart* was not—again, the employer had a powerful interest/incentive in reviewing the attorney-client communications, since it was preparing for anticipated litigation with the employee! So why else? Does it turn on close nexus considerations—that is, the *necessity* of the intrusion in *FWHC* and its absence in *Stengart*? If so, then the conversation circles back to whether the cervical self-examination was really necessary and how much deference courts should accord employer assertions of such need.

If you think *Stengart* was wrongly decided, why? If it is because workplace policies or consent ought to trump privacy interests (including the privilege), then, for all practical purposes, there is no privacy in the workplace. If so, are you comfortable with that result? Or is this an overstatement? If you think *FWHC* was wrongly decided, then how would you draw the line between appropriate and inappropriate job-related intrusions or commands?

All of this, of course, simply leads back to the discussion at the beginning of this chapter: Grappling with the contours of privacy in the workplace is challenging because the interests at stake and appropriate role of private ordering are contestable, and the workplace and technology are constantly changing. This assures that, at minimum, there will continue to be new legal developments in this area as well as ongoing debate.

PROBLEM

6-2. Return now to the facts in Problem 6-1 set forth at the outset of this chapter. If DEI is a private sector employer, what potential claims might be available to Smith, the terminated employee? Obviously, given the nature of the intrusion, the Stored Communications Act might provide a starting point, but what limitations discussed above might preclude recovery under this theory? Assuming there is no liability under the Act, what other theories might be available? What barriers might there be to recovery? What other kinds of information would you need to assess the possibilities? Would your answer change if DEI is a public sector employer?

Now turn to counseling the employer. To the extent DEI faces potential liability, what could it have done differently to prevent or reduce the risk of this liability? Again, what additional information would be useful in providing advice? As a general matter, how confident are you in your assessments?

Finally, think about these circumstances from a policy perspective. Should Smith's communications be protected? Why or why not?

7

Workplace Speech and Association Protections

Another area where employee and employer prerogatives and preferences often collide is employee expression, whether in the form of speech or association. The employee interests at stake in this area often differ from the interests underlying privacy claims. Speech rights protect one's ability to express or "share" through words (and sometimes conduct) one's views or beliefs and to associate with those who have common views. Privacy rights, on the other hand, usually shield one from having to share; that is, these rights allow the exclusion of others from one's "space" (literal or metaphorical).

Despite their differences, speech and privacy in the workplace have much in common. First, speech and privacy rights both protect aspects of autonomy, and, in fact, some autonomy interests could be characterized as implicating both spheres. For example, as discussed in Chapter 6, one could conceptualize various expressive activities at work—such as dress and grooming—and conduct away from work—including associational, leisure, and internet activities—as either "speech" or "private" activities. *See* Chapter 6 at page 371. Accordingly, various protections for worker expressive activities and off-site conduct could be viewed as preserving either speech or privacy rights.

Moreover, because worker speech and privacy protections both involve a clash between worker autonomy and employer prerogatives, the themes dominating the public policy debates and legal inquiry are often similar. For instance, as with privacy, public employees enjoy qualified constitutional protections for speech and association, while employees in the private sector may lack a "source" of such protection. Indeed, in the speech context, the divide between public and private employment is even greater, with public employees enjoying at least limited protection for certain kinds of speech and association and private employees left largely unprotected. In addition, where a potential source of protection exists, the courts often focus on the balance between employee and employer interests, and, as in the privacy cases, the level of deference a court accords the employer's justification for its speech-related restriction or actions is often dispositive. Finally, private ordering may alter the rights and obligations of employee and employer.

Workplace speech cases tend to fall into three broad categories. The first, exemplified by *Connick v. Myers*, 461 U.S. 138 (1983) and *Garcetti v. Ceballos*, 547 U.S. 410 (2006), reproduced at pages 400 and 411, respectively, involves disputes arising out of adverse employment actions resulting from public employee speech or expressive activity at or related to work. The second concerns employer regulation or coercion of or retaliation for an employee's political, religious, or other associational preferences or affiliations. *Edmondson v. Shearer Lumber Products*, 75 P.3d 733 (Idaho 2003), reproduced at page 449, is an example of such litigation in the private employer context. Finally, the third category, addressed in *Dible v. City of Chandler*, 515 F.3d 918 (2008), reproduced at page 430, includes disputes over employer attempts to control employee speech and expression outside of work.

Although these three types of claims raise distinct issues, the public/private employer divide is by far the most important in terms of assessing the potential scope of protection for employee speech or association. This chapter explores potential rights and claims in each of these settings. Most of this chapter is devoted to the public context for the simple reason that, while public employees often enjoy limited protections for their speech and association, protections in the private context are even weaker.

A.   THE PUBLIC WORKPLACE

≡ *Connick v. Myers*
≡ *461 U.S. 138 (1983)*

WHITE, J.

In *Pickering v. Board of Education*, 391 U.S. 563 (1968), we stated that a public employee does not relinquish First Amendment rights to comment on matters of public interest by virtue of government employment. We also recognized that the State's interests as an employer in regulating the speech of its employees "differ significantly from those it possesses in connection with regulation of the speech of the citizenry in general." The problem, we thought, was arriving "at a balance between the interests of the [employee], as a citizen, in commenting upon matters of public concern and the interest of the State, as an employer, in promoting the efficiency of the public services it performs through its employees." We return to this problem today and consider whether the First and Fourteenth Amendments prevent the discharge of a state employee for circulating a questionnaire concerning internal office affairs.

I

The respondent, Sheila Myers, was employed as an Assistant District Attorney in New Orleans for five and a half years. She served at the pleasure of petitioner Harry Connick, the District Attorney for Orleans Parish. During this period, Myers competently performed her responsibilities of trying criminal cases.

In the early part of October 1980, Myers was informed that she would be transferred to prosecute cases in a different section of the criminal court. Myers was strongly opposed to the proposed transfer[1] and expressed her view to several of her supervisors, including Connick. Despite her objections, on October 6, Myers was notified that she was being transferred. Myers again spoke with Dennis Waldron, one of the First Assistant District Attorneys, expressing her reluctance to accept the transfer. A number of other office matters were discussed and Myers later testified that, in response to Waldron's suggestion that her concerns were not shared by others in the office, she informed him that she would do some research on the matter.

That night Myers prepared a questionnaire soliciting the views of her fellow staff members concerning office transfer policy, office morale, the need for a grievance committee, the level of confidence in supervisors, and whether employees felt pressured to work in political campaigns. Early the following morning, Myers typed and copied the questionnaire. She also met with Connick who urged her to accept the transfer. She said she would "consider" it. Connick then left the office. Myers then distributed the questionnaire to 15 Assistant District Attorneys. Shortly after noon, Dennis Waldron learned that Myers was distributing the survey. He immediately phoned Connick and informed him that Myers was creating a "mini-insurrection" within the office. Connick returned to the office and told Myers that she was being terminated because of her refusal to accept the transfer. She was also told that her distribution of the questionnaire was considered an act of insubordination. Connick particularly objected to the question which inquired whether employees "had confidence in and would rely on the word" of various superiors in the office, and to a question concerning pressure to work in political campaigns which he felt would be damaging if discovered by the press. . . .

II

. . . Our task, as we defined it in *Pickering*, is to seek "a balance between the interests of the [employee], as a citizen, in commenting upon matters of public concern and the interest of the State, as an employer, in promoting the efficiency of the public services it performs through its employees." . . .

A

. . . Connick contends at the outset that no balancing of interests is required in this case because Myers' questionnaire concerned only internal office matters and that such speech is not upon a matter of "public concern," as the term was used in *Pickering*. Although we do not agree that Myers' communication in this case was wholly without First Amendment protection, there is much force to Connick's submission. The repeated emphasis in *Pickering* on the right of a public employee "as a citizen, in commenting upon matters of public concern," was not accidental. This

---

1. Myers' opposition was at least partially attributable to her concern that a conflict of interest would have been created by the transfer because of her participation in a counseling program for convicted defendants released on probation in the section of the criminal court to which she was to be assigned.

language, reiterated in all of *Pickering*'s progeny, reflects both the historical evolvement of the rights of public employees, and the common-sense realization that government offices could not function if every employment decision became a constitutional matter.

For most of this century, the unchallenged dogma was that a public employee had no right to object to conditions placed upon the terms of employment—including those which restricted the exercise of constitutional rights. The classic formulation of this position was that of Justice Holmes, who, when sitting on the Supreme Judicial Court of Massachusetts, observed: "[A policeman] may have a constitutional right to talk politics, but he has no constitutional right to be a policeman." *McAuliffe v. Mayor of New Bedford*, 29 N.E. 517, 517 (Mass. 1892). For many years, Holmes' epigram expressed this Court's law.

The Court cast new light on the matter in a series of cases arising from the widespread efforts in the 1950's and early 1960's to require public employees, particularly teachers, to swear oaths of loyalty to the State and reveal the groups with which they associated. In *Wiemann v. Updegraff*, 344 U.S. 183 (1952), the Court held that a State could not require its employees to establish their loyalty by extracting an oath denying past affiliation with Communists. In *Cafeteria Workers v. McElroy*, 367 U.S. 886 (1961), the Court recognized that the government could not deny employment because of previous membership in a particular party. . . .

In all of these cases, the precedents in which *Pickering* is rooted, the invalidated statutes and actions sought to suppress the rights of public employees to participate in public affairs. The issue was whether government employees could be prevented or "chilled" by the fear of discharge from joining political parties and other associations that certain public officials might find "subversive." The explanation for the Constitution's special concern with threats to the right of citizens to participate in political affairs is no mystery. The First Amendment "was fashioned to assure unfettered interchange of ideas for the bringing about of political and social changes desired by the people." *Roth v. United States*, 354 U.S. 476, 484 (1957); *New York Times Co. v. Sullivan*, 376 U.S. 254, 269 (1964). "[Speech] concerning public affairs is more than self-expression; it is the essence of self-government." *Garrison v. Louisiana*, 379 U.S. 64, 74-75 (1964). Accordingly, the Court has frequently reaffirmed that speech on public issues occupies the "'highest rung of the hierarchy of First Amendment values,'" and is entitled to special protection.

Pickering v. Board of Education followed from this understanding of the First Amendment. In *Pickering*, the Court held impermissible under the First Amendment the dismissal of a high school teacher for openly criticizing the Board of Education on its allocation of school funds between athletics and education and its methods of informing taxpayers about the need for additional revenue. *Pickering*'s subject was "a matter of legitimate public concern" upon which "free and open debate is vital to informed decisionmaking by the electorate."

Our cases following *Pickering* also involved safeguarding speech on matters of public concern. . . . Most recently, in *Givhan v. Western Line Consolidated School District*, 439 U.S. 410 (1979), we held that First Amendment protection applies when a public employee arranges to communicate privately with his employer rather than to express his views publicly. . . .

Pickering, its antecedents, and its progeny lead us to conclude that if Myers' questionnaire cannot be fairly characterized as constituting speech on a matter of public concern, it is unnecessary for us to scrutinize the reasons for her discharge.

When employee expression cannot be fairly considered as relating to any matter of political, social, or other concern to the community, government officials should enjoy wide latitude in managing their offices, without intrusive oversight by the judiciary in the name of the First Amendment. Perhaps the government employer's dismissal of the worker may not be fair, but ordinary dismissals from government service which violate no fixed tenure or applicable statute or regulation are not subject to judicial review even if the reasons for the dismissal are alleged to be mistaken or unreasonable. . . .

Whether an employee's speech addresses a matter of public concern must be determined by the content, form, and context of a given statement, as revealed by the whole record.[7] In this case, with but one exception, the questions posed by Myers to her co-workers do not fall under the rubric of matters of "public concern." We view the questions pertaining to the confidence and trust that Myers' co-workers possess in various supervisors, the level of office morale, and the need for a grievance committee as mere extensions of Myers' dispute over her transfer to another section of the criminal court. . . . [W]e do not believe these questions are of public import in evaluating the performance of the District Attorney as an elected official. Myers did not seek to inform the public that the District Attorney's Office was not discharging its governmental responsibilities in the investigation and prosecution of criminal cases. Nor did Myers seek to bring to light actual or potential wrongdoing or breach of public trust on the part of Connick and others. Indeed, the questionnaire, if released to the public, would convey no information at all other than the fact that a single employee is upset with the status quo. While discipline and morale in the workplace are related to an agency's efficient performance of its duties, the focus of Myers' questions is not to evaluate the performance of the office but rather to gather ammunition for another round of controversy with her superiors. These questions reflect one employee's dissatisfaction with a transfer and an attempt to turn that displeasure into a cause célèbre.[8]

To presume that all matters which transpire within a government office are of public concern would mean that virtually every remark—and certainly every criticism directed at a public official—would plant the seed of a constitutional case. While as a matter of good judgment, public officials should be receptive to constructive criticism offered by their employees, the First Amendment does not require a public office to be run as a roundtable for employee complaints over internal office affairs.

One question in Myers' questionnaire, however, does touch upon a matter of public concern. Question 11 inquires if assistant district attorneys "ever feel pressured to work in political campaigns on behalf of office supported candidates." We have recently noted that official pressure upon employees to work for political candidates not of the worker's own choice constitutes a coercion of belief in violation of fundamental constitutional rights. *Branti v. Finkel*, [445 U.S. 507, 515-16 (1980)]; *Elrod*

---

7. The inquiry into the protected status of speech is one of law, not fact.

8. This is not a case like *Givhan*, where an employee speaks out as a citizen on a matter of general concern, not tied to a personal employment dispute, but arranges to do so privately. Mrs. Givhan's right to protest racial discrimination—a matter inherently of public concern—is not forfeited by her choice of a private forum. Here, however, a questionnaire not otherwise of public concern does not attain that status because its subject matter could, in different circumstances, have been the topic of a communication to the public that might be of general interest. The dissent's analysis of whether discussions of office morale and discipline could be matters of public concern is beside the point—it does not answer whether *this* questionnaire is such speech.

v. Burns, 427 U.S. 347 (1976). . . . [W]e believe it apparent that the issue of whether assistant district attorneys are pressured to work in political campaigns is a matter of interest to the community upon which it is essential that public employees be able to speak out freely without fear of retaliatory dismissal.

B

Because one of the questions in Myers' survey touched upon a matter of public concern and contributed to her discharge, we must determine whether Connick was justified in discharging Myers. Here the District Court again erred in imposing an unduly onerous burden on the State to justify Myers' discharge. The District Court viewed the issue of whether Myers' speech was upon a matter of "public concern" as a threshold inquiry, after which it became the government's burden to "clearly demonstrate" that the speech involved "substantially interfered" with official responsibilities. Yet *Pickering* unmistakably states . . . that the State's burden in justifying a particular discharge varies depending upon the nature of the employee's expression. Although such particularized balancing is difficult, the courts must reach the most appropriate possible balance of the competing interests.

C

The *Pickering* balance requires full consideration of the government's interest in the effective and efficient fulfillment of its responsibilities to the public. . . . *Ex parte Curtis*, [106 U.S. 371, 373 (1882)]. As Justice Powell explained in his separate opinion in *Arnett v. Kennedy*, 416 U.S. 134, 168 (1974):

> To this end, the Government, as an employer, must have wide discretion and control over the management of its personnel and internal affairs. This includes the prerogative to remove employees whose conduct hinders efficient operation and to do so with dispatch. Prolonged retention of a disruptive or otherwise unsatisfactory employee can adversely affect discipline and morale in the work place, foster disharmony, and ultimately impair the efficiency of an office or agency.

We agree with the District Court that there is no demonstration here that the questionnaire impeded Myers' ability to perform her responsibilities. The District Court was also correct to recognize that "it is important to the efficient and successful operation of the District Attorney's office for Assistants to maintain close working relationships with their superiors." Connick's judgment, and apparently also that of his first assistant Dennis Waldron, who characterized Myers' actions as causing a "mini-insurrection," was that Myers' questionnaire was an act of insubordination which interfered with working relationships. When close working relationships are essential to fulfilling public responsibilities, a wide degree of deference to the employer's judgment is appropriate. Furthermore, we do not see the necessity for an employer to allow events to unfold to the extent that the disruption of the office and the destruction of working relationships is manifest before taking action. We caution that a stronger showing may be necessary if the employee's speech more substantially involved matters of public concern.

. . . Questions, no less than forcefully stated opinions and facts, carry messages and it requires no unusual insight to conclude that the purpose, if not the likely result, of the questionnaire is to seek to precipitate a vote of no confidence in Connick and his supervisors. Thus, Question 10, which asked whether or not the Assistants had confidence in and relied on the word of five named supervisors, is a statement that carries the clear potential for undermining office relations.

Also relevant is the manner, time, and place in which the questionnaire was distributed. . . . Here the questionnaire was prepared and distributed at the office; the manner of distribution required not only Myers to leave her work but others to do the same in order that the questionnaire be completed.[13] Although some latitude in when official work is performed is to be allowed when professional employees are involved, and Myers did not violate announced office policy, the fact that Myers, unlike Pickering, exercised her rights to speech at the office supports Connick's fears that the functioning of his office was endangered.

Finally, the context in which the dispute arose is also significant. This is not a case where an employee, out of purely academic interest, circulated a questionnaire so as to obtain useful research. Myers acknowledges that it is no coincidence that the questionnaire followed upon the heels of the transfer notice. When employee speech concerning office policy arises from an employment dispute concerning the very application of that policy to the speaker, additional weight must be given to the supervisor's view that the employee has threatened the authority of the employer to run the office. . . .

III

Myers' questionnaire touched upon matters of public concern in only a most limited sense; her survey, in our view, is most accurately characterized as an employee grievance concerning internal office policy. The limited First Amendment interest involved here does not require that Connick tolerate action which he reasonably believed would disrupt the office, undermine his authority, and destroy close working relationships. Myers' discharge therefore did not offend the First Amendment. We reiterate, however, the caveat we expressed in *Pickering:* "Because of the enormous variety of fact situations in which critical statements by . . . public employees may be thought by their superiors . . . to furnish grounds for dismissal, we do not deem it either appropriate or feasible to attempt to lay down a general standard against which all such statements may be judged."

Our holding today is grounded in our longstanding recognition that the First Amendment's primary aim is the full protection of speech upon issues of public concern, as well as the practical realities involved in the administration of a government office. Although today the balance is struck for the government, this is no defeat for the First Amendment. For it would indeed be a Pyrrhic victory for the great principles of free expression if the Amendment's safeguarding of a public employee's right, as a citizen, to participate in discussions concerning public affairs were confused with the

---

13. The record indicates that some, though not all, of the copies of the questionnaire were distributed during lunch. Employee speech which transpires entirely on the employee's own time, and in non-work areas of the office, bring different factors into the *Pickering* calculus, and might lead to a different conclusion.

attempt to constitutionalize the employee grievance that we see presented here. The judgment of the Court of Appeals is *Reversed.*[*]

NOTES

1. *The* Pickering/Connick *Balancing Test.* In determining whether Myers's termination violated her First and Fourteenth Amendment speech rights, the Court applied an analytical framework that has come to be known as the *"Pickering/Connick* balancing test." For speech in or related to the workplace, the employee must first establish that the expression addresses a matter of public concern. As *Connick* demonstrates, aspects of the employee's speech that do not address matters of public concern receive no First Amendment protection. If the speech or portions of it do address matters of public concern, the court then "balances" the employee's interest in speaking on matters of public concern with the employer's interest in promoting workplace efficiency. Finally, even if the employee's interest in free expression prevails in the balance, the employee must also demonstrate causation; that is, the employer disciplined or dismissed the employee because of the employee's speech. This issue was not reached in *Connick*, given the Court's conclusion on the application of the balancing test; had the dissenting opinion been the majority, a remand would likely have been necessary to determine whether the district attorney fired Myers because of the protected aspect of her questionnaire or, as the district attorney's office alleged, because of her refusal to accept the transfer.

2. *"A Matter of Public Concern."* Why does the Court limit employee protection against speech-related adverse employment actions to matters of public concern? Obviously, the distinction is critical to any constitutional protection. *Connick* provides guidance as to what is *not* a matter of public concern: "When employee expression cannot be fairly considered as relating to any matter of political, social, or other concern to the community." Moreover, the *Connick* majority views speech addressing the internal affairs of the agency and not rising above mere dissatisfaction or displeasure with one's supervisors as not implicating public concern. In other words, mere personal concerns or interests, as opposed to those of the employee as a citizen, are not matters of public concern. *See, e.g., Alves v. Bd. of Regents of the Univ. Sys. of Georgia*, 804 F.3d 1149 (11th Cir. 2015) (holding that clinical psychologists employed by state university did not speak about a matter of public concern when

* *Editor's Note: Employment Law Trivia.* The defendant in *Connick v. Myers* was Harry Connick, Sr., district attorney for Orleans Parish. You may have heard of his son, musician Harry Connick, Jr. The father became district attorney by beating a famous (or infamous) predecessor in the post, Jim Garrison, who played a role in investigating the Kennedy assassination and, depending on whom you believe, either (1) uncovered the true conspiracy only to be foiled by the FBI, (2) bungled a potentially effective investigation, or (3) went on a wild goose chase. Coincidentally, *Garrison v. Louisiana*, cited by the Supreme Court in *Connick* as one of the foundational free speech cases, involved Jim Garrison, who had been found guilty of "criminal defamation"—when he claimed that the large backlog of pending criminal cases was due to the laziness of the judges and that failures of law enforcement were due to their failure to authorize funds for the district attorney. 379 U.S. at 66. The Supreme Court reversed Garrison's conviction. Undoubtedly, Ms. Myers relied heavily on her boss's predecessor's claims of free-speech rights in pursuing her suit against Connick. In the aftermath, Connick, Sr. continued on as New Orleans District Attorney until 2002, Dennis Waldron became a judge in the Criminal Court, and Sheila Myers is a well-respected criminal defense attorney who litigates frequently against her former employer. Myers's biggest regret, though, is that the decision "is cited as the case against public employees." http://www.freedomforum.org/templates/.

they complained of poor leadership and mismanagement by the director of a center, despite vague references to student safety).

On the flip side, *Connick* makes clear that employee expression need not be shared with the public to address a matter of public concern. In other words, it may be purely internal, although the fact that it is not shared with the public may affect the analysis of whether it implicates a public concern. *See also Rankin v. McPherson*, 483 U.S. 378 (1987) (finding one worker's statement to a co-worker, after finding out that President Reagan had been shot, that "[i]f they go after him again, I hope they get him" addressed a matter of public concern). In terms of content, speech relating to broad public policy issues and improprieties in the agency, as well as public statements questioning the effectiveness of the agency have been recognized as matters of public concern. *See, e.g., Pickering*, 391 U.S. at 571-73; *Boulton v. Swanson*, 795 F.3d 526 (6th Cir. 2015) (finding sergeant's speech at a union meeting was on matter of public concern where sergeant made specific statements regarding the need for proper training to protect detainees). In addition, statements about current political events or high-ranking public officials are matters of public concern. *See, e.g., Rankin*, 483 U.S. at 386-87; *Bland v. Roberts*, 730 F.3d 368 (4th Cir. 2013) (finding deputy sheriff's stated preferences about county sheriff candidates to be protected speech). Moreover, issues or information regarding the functioning, decisions, or initiatives of the department or agency have been found to be matters of public concern where the larger community has shown interest. *See, e.g., Kennedy v. Tangipahoa Parish Library Bd. of Control*, 224 F.3d 359, 373 (5th Cir. 2000) (asserting that "speech made against the backdrop of ongoing commentary and debate in the press involves the public concern"); *Burnham v. Ianni*, 119 F.3d 668 (8th Cir. 1997) (en banc) (holding a display in a public university's history department containing pictures of professors with props associated with their areas of expertise that sparked controversy was a matter of public concern because of the public interest in it). And, as the majority's citation of *Givhan* indicates, courts have usually found that allegations of discrimination raise matters of public concern. *See, e.g., Fender v. Delaware Div. of Revenue*, 628 F. App'x 95 (3d Cir. 2015) (finding female employee's complaint that her request for transfer was denied while similar request of a similarly situation male employee was granted, addressed gender discrimination, a matter of public concern); *Love-Lane v. Martin*, 355 F.3d 766 (4th Cir. 2004) (finding concerns regarding discriminatory practices in school system to be matter of public concern).

In *Janus v. AFSME*, 138 S. Ct. 2448 (2018), the Supreme Court held in a 5-4 decision that an Illinois statute authorizing public-sector unions to assess "agency fees" from non-member public employees on whose behalf the union negotiated, violates the First Amendment. Agency fees are mandated charges for the proportionate share of union dues attributable to activities germane to the union's duties as collective-bargaining representative. In holding such requirements unconstitutional, the Court's majority first stated that the *Pickering/Connick* analysis does not apply to such a blanket policy compelling employee speech. Nevertheless, it went on to state in the alternative that, if this framework were to apply, public-sector union speech in collective bargaining, including speech about wages and benefits, as well as speech during union grievance procedures, involve matters of great public concern. In the majority's view, such speech affects how public money is spent and other important matters, such as education, child welfare, healthcare, and minority rights. In a nutshell then, this means that collective employee speech—speech by unions or about unions—involves matters of public concern, even if, as *Connick* suggests, speech by individual employees (in the nonunion context) about the terms or conditions of employment may not involve matters of public concern. There is, of course, great debate on the Court itself and in commentary about whether the *Janus* majority's central holding and its treatment of *Pickering/Connick* are correct.

In *Snyder v. Phelps*, 562 U.S. 443 (2011), a nonemployment case, the Supreme Court offered some additional guidance on the contours of the public concern inquiry. In this decision, it held that the First Amendment shielded the Westboro Baptist Church and its members from tort liability for picketing outside of the funeral of Matthew Snyder, a soldier killed in the line of duty in the Iraq War. Because the Court determined that First Amendment protection depended on whether the speech involved matters of public concern, it explored that concept in some detail. In so doing, it quoted liberally from the government employee speech decisions—*Pickering, Connick, Rankin,* and *San Diego v. Roe* (discussed in the notes below). *See id.* at 444.

Although *Snyder* did not delve deeply into how to distinguish matters of public concern from those that are private in nature, it did confirm that the inquiry is contextual, requiring an examination of the "content, form, and context" of the speech as revealed by the whole record. *Id.* at 453-54. Despite being deeply offensive to many, Westboro's signs plainly related to public matters—the political and moral conduct of the United States and its citizens, the fate of the nation, homosexuality in the military, and scandals involving the Catholic clergy—and were designed to reach a broad public audience even though some of the messages related to a particular individual. *Id.* at 455. Additionally, while the picketing coincided with Snyder's funeral, it did not disrupt the ceremony because it occurred in a peaceful manner, 1,000 feet away in a public park, and Snyder's family was unaware of the context of the signs until they saw the display on the news later that evening. *Id.* at 457. Thus, the Court concluded that the connection of the picketing with Snyder's funeral did not transform the nature of the speech, even though Westboro's selection of Snyder's funeral may have been particularly hurtful to his family. *Id.* at 458-59.

Still, it remains unclear whether other matters of public interest not necessarily involving salient political issues, government policies, or government officials constitute matters of public concern. For example, although a resulting adverse action against a public employee may seem unlikely in this context, what about obnoxious statements regarding a celebrity, a sports team or famous athlete, or well-known entertainment event? Don't employee comments in support of or opposition to the NFL player protests involving the National Anthem implicate matters of public concern, given the nature of protests and their entry into the political discourse? So might speech criticizing or supporting Nike's use of Colin Kaepernick in its marketing. But what about other kinds of criticisms of celebrities or movies that are not as directly related to partisan politics or ongoing public policy or religious debates? Something involving the Kardashians? In other words, does "public concern" simply mean something that has captured the public's interest, or is something more required? *See generally* Randy J. Kozel, *Free Speech and Parity: A Theory of Public Employee Rights,* 53 Wm. & Mary L. Rev. 1985 (2012); Cynthia L. Estlund, *Speech on Matters of Public Concern: The Perils of an Emerging First Amendment Category,* 59 Geo. Wash. L. Rev. 1 (1990); *see also* George Rutherglen, *Public Employee Speech in Remedial Perspective,* 24 J. L. & Politics 129, 130 (2008) (questioning whether the "public concern" test is appropriate in light of its uncertain application).

3. *"Balancing" the Interests.* In balancing the employee's interest against the employer's, the Supreme Court has likewise provided less-than-clear guidance. The Court was unwilling in either *Pickering* or *Connick* to lay down clear parameters for how to engage in the balancing inquiry. *See, e.g., Pickering,* 391 U.S. at 569. Rather than weighing the competing interests, both opinions focused on the employer's interest in efficiency, exploring whether the employee's statements might have actually disrupted the workplace. Indeed, in *Pickering,* the Court's balancing analysis consisted entirely of the following discussion, after which the Court found in favor of the employee:

> The [teacher's] statements are in no way directed towards any person with whom appellant would normally be in contact in the course of his daily work as a teacher. Thus no question of maintaining either discipline by immediate superiors or harmony among coworkers is presented here. Appellant's employment relationships with the Board and, to a somewhat lesser extent, with the superintendent are not the kind of close working relationships for which it can persuasively be claimed that personal loyalty and confidence are necessary to their proper functioning.

Id. at 569-70; *see also Rankin,* 483 U.S. at 388-89 (finding employee's interests outweighed employer's in the case involving a deputy constable's comments about attempted presidential assassination after rejecting the employer's claims of disruption, public relations problems, and loss in efficiency).

Thus, once the employee has made his or her threshold showing, so-called "balancing" in the speech-in-the-workplace context—as in the privacy-in-the-workplace context—tends instead to be an inquiry into the strength of the employer's proffered justification for taking action against the employee. Occasionally, however, as hinted in *Connick,* courts have recognized that the importance of the content of the speech increases the burden on the government to show that efficiency concerns ought to prevail. *See, e.g., Love-Lane,* 355 F.3d at 785 (stating that because race discrimination in schools involves a substantial issue of public concern, the government's burden is heightened). Other efficiency interests recognized by the courts include preserving confidentiality and protecting the public, and, where it is necessary, ensuring loyalty. *See, e.g., Sheppard v. Beerman,* 317 F.3d 351 (2d Cir. 2003) (finding no constitutional violation after the judge terminated a law clerk who directed an obscene epithet at him because of the potential disruptiveness of retaining a disloyal and disrespectful clerk in the extremely close and confidential work setting).

The Supreme Court has also indicated that the employer bears the burden of establishing the objective good faith of its proffered efficiency concerns. In other words, it is the employer's obligation to demonstrate that its action was in good faith (not pretextual) and based on a reasonable assessment of the circumstances in terms of whether the speech actually occurred and the extent to which it is likely to lead to disruption or harm efficiency. *See Waters v. Churchill,* 511 U.S. 661, 677-78 (1994); *see also Munroe v. Cent. Bucks Sch. Dist.,* 805 F.3d 454 (3d Cir. 2015) (finding school district's interest in avoiding workplace disruption outweighed teacher's interest in speech after teacher used an "inappropriate tone of speech" while making derogatory comments about her students on her blog and to the media); *Heller v. Bedford Cent. Sch. Dist.,* 144 F. Supp. 3d 596 (S.D.N.Y. 2015) (finding public school teacher's private conversations stating a desire to kill people was not protected speech because those conversations would have disrupted the school and caused alarm if they became public).

4. Pickering/Connick *Applied*. Unsurprisingly, this framework has produced mixed results in the lower federal courts, although the defending government institution usually prevails. *Compare Nichols v. Dancer*, 657 F.3d 929 (9th Cir. 2011) (stating that the employer cannot prevail in *Pickering* balancing test merely because of speculation that the employee's show of support for her former boss at a school board meeting would cause some workplace disruption), *and Love-Lane*, 355 F.3d at 785 (indicating that "some disharmony" caused by employee's criticisms of allegedly discriminatory practices is not enough to justify adverse employment action), *with Vanderpuye v. Cohen*, 94 F. App'x 3 (2d Cir. 2004) (finding that, although city employee's speech regarding conflicts of interest was a matter of public concern, it was outweighed by potential for disruption in functioning of department), *and Sheppard*, 317 F.3d at 355 (upholding constitutionality of termination of judicial clerk after outbursts).

Public employers tend to prevail in cases in which the speech is offensive, threatening, or harassing to protected groups, including women and minorities, although courts are often unwilling to find vague or indirect statements, even if hyperbolic, to be threatening or harassing. *Compare Pappas v. Giuliani*, 290 F.3d 143 (2d Cir. 2002) (upholding municipality's right to terminate police officer after his anonymous dissemination of racist and anti-Semitic materials), *with Bauer v. Sampson*, 261 F.3d 775 (9th Cir. 2001) (rejecting defendant college's contention that professor's scathing and hyperbolic criticisms of new administrator were threatening or discriminatory and thus sufficiently disruptive to warrant discipline). To the extent that the employee's speech might itself violate the law, such as constituting racial or sexual harassment of co-workers until Title VII, *see* Chapter 9, Title XI (protecting against sex discrimination and harassment in education), or state law, the employer will obviously have a greater interest in acting. *See, e.g.*, J.M. Balkin, *Free Speech and Hostile Environments*, 99 COLUM. L. REV. 2295 (1999); Cynthia L. Estlund, *Freedom of Expression in the Workplace and the Problem of Discriminatory Harassment*, 75 TEX. L. REV. 687 (1997); Eugene Volokh, *What Speech Does "Hostile Work Environment" Harassment Law Restrict?*, 85 GEO. L. J. 627 (1997). Although there is not much case law on point yet, it will be interesting to see how courts will treat employer "no tolerance" or other robust antiharassment measures in the wake of the #MeToo movement.

5. *The Petition Clause and Workplace Speech*. In *Borough of Duryea v. Guarnieri*, 564 U.S. 369 (2011), the Court addressed a public employee's claims under the Petition Clause of the First Amendment. After Charles Guarnieri was terminated as the police chief of Duryea, he filed a union grievance and was reinstated to his position. When the borough council later issued directives instructing Guarnieri how to perform his duties, he filed suit, alleging that the directives were issued in retaliation for the filing of his first grievance, violating his First Amendment right to petition the government for a redress. He later amended his complaint to allege that the council also violated the Petition Clause by denying his request for overtime pay in retaliation for his having filed the suit. The Court held that a government employer's retaliatory actions against an employee do not give rise to liability under the Petition Clause unless the employee's petition relates to a matter of public concern. The Court reasoned that, although the Speech and Petition Clauses should not be treated identically, petitions, like speech, can "interfere with the efficient and effective operation of government." *Id.* at 389. Because public employers have a substantial interest in controlling petitions that can "bring the mission of the employer and professionalism of its officers into serious disrepute," employees should not be able to circumvent the limitations applicable to speech claims by simply labeling their grievance as a "petition." *Id.* at 390.

Turning to the question of whether an employee's petition relates to a matter of public concern, resolution depends on "the content, form, and context" of the petition, as revealed by the whole record. *Id.* at 398. The Court then noted, citing *Snyder, supra,* that the forum in which a petition is lodged will be relevant to determining whether the petition relates to a matter of public concern. It went on to state that "[a] petition filed with an employer using an internal grievance procedure in many cases will not seek to communicate to the public or to advance a political or social point of view beyond the employment context." *Id.*

In *Guarnieri*'s wake, it is doubtful whether the Petition Clause affords public employees much meaningful protection. The Court's treatment of the public concern test suggests that statements made by employees in internal grievance procedures are unlikely to be protected. Yet the Court also emphasized that external petitions, such as lawsuits (although more likely to implicate matters of public concern), may be highly disruptive to the public employer, and, hence, may not survive *Pickering/Connick* balancing. Moreover, post-*Guarnieri*, courts generally have applied the same analysis to claims brought under Petition Clause as those brought under the Free Speech Clause. *See, e.g., Devlin v. Kalm,* 630 F. App'x 534, 540 (6th Cir. 2015).

6. *Speech and Employee Duties.* What if employee speech on a matter of public concern is not only in the workplace, but also in the context of the employee performing his or her particular job duties? The Court took up this issue in the next case.

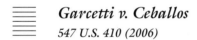

Garcetti v. Ceballos
547 U.S. 410 (2006)

Justice KENNEDY delivered the opinion of the Court.

It is well settled that "a State cannot condition public employment on a basis that infringes the employee's constitutionally protected interest in freedom of expression." *Connick v. Myers.* The question presented by the instant case is whether the First Amendment protects a government employee from discipline based on speech made pursuant to the employee's official duties.

I

Respondent Richard Ceballos has been employed since 1989 as a deputy district attorney for the Los Angeles County District Attorney's Office. During the period relevant to this case, Ceballos was a calendar deputy in the office's Pomona branch, and in this capacity he exercised certain supervisory responsibilities over other lawyers. In February 2000, a defense attorney contacted Ceballos about a pending criminal case. The defense attorney said there were inaccuracies in an affidavit used to obtain a critical search warrant. The attorney informed Ceballos that he had filed a motion to traverse, or challenge, the warrant, but he also wanted Ceballos to review the case.

According to Ceballos, it was not unusual for defense attorneys to ask calendar deputies to investigate aspects of pending cases.

After examining the affidavit and visiting the location it described, Ceballos determined the affidavit contained serious misrepresentations. The affidavit called a long driveway what Ceballos thought should have been referred to as a separate roadway. Ceballos also questioned the affidavit's statement that tire tracks led from a stripped-down truck to the premises covered by the warrant. His doubts arose from his conclusion that the roadway's composition in some places made it difficult or impossible to leave visible tire tracks.

Ceballos spoke on the telephone to the warrant affiant, a deputy sheriff from the Los Angeles County Sheriff's Department, but he did not receive a satisfactory explanation for the perceived inaccuracies. He relayed his findings to his supervisors, petitioners Carol Najera and Frank Sundstedt, and followed up by preparing a disposition memorandum. The memo explained Ceballos' concerns and recommended dismissal of the case. On March 2, 2000, Ceballos submitted the memo to Sundstedt for his review. A few days later, Ceballos presented Sundstedt with another memo, this one describing a second telephone conversation between Ceballos and the warrant affiant.

Based on Ceballos' statements, a meeting was held to discuss the affidavit. Attendees included Ceballos, Sundstedt, and Najera, as well as the warrant affiant and other employees from the sheriff's department. The meeting allegedly became heated, with one lieutenant sharply criticizing Ceballos for his handling of the case.

Despite Ceballos' concerns, Sundstedt decided to proceed with the prosecution, pending disposition of the defense motion to traverse. The trial court held a hearing on the motion. Ceballos was called by the defense and recounted his observations about the affidavit, but the trial court rejected the challenge to the warrant.

[Ceballos sued, claiming that he was subjected to a series of retaliatory employment actions for his March 2 memo. The district court granted defendants summary judgment, but the Ninth Circuit reversed, holding that "Ceballos's allegations of wrongdoing in the memorandum constitute protected speech under the First Amendment."]

II

As the Court's decisions have noted, for many years "the unchallenged dogma was that a public employee had no right to object to conditions placed upon the terms of employment—including those which restricted the exercise of constitutional rights." *Connick*. That dogma has been qualified in important respects. *See id.* The Court has made clear that public employees do not surrender all their First Amendment rights by reason of their employment. Rather, the First Amendment protects a public employee's right, in certain circumstances, to speak as a citizen addressing matters of public concern. *See, e.g.,* [*Pickering; Connick; Rankin v. McPherson*, 483 U.S. 378, 384 (1987); *United States v. Treasury Employees*, 513 U.S. 454, 466 (1995)]. . . .

[The Court outlined the *Pickering/Connick* balancing test.] A government entity has broader discretion to restrict speech when it acts in its role as employer, but the restrictions it imposes must be directed at speech that has some potential to affect the entity's operations. . . .

. . . When a citizen enters government service, the citizen by necessity must accept certain limitations on his or her freedom. Government employers, like private employers, need a significant degree of control over their employees' words and actions; without it, there would be little chance for the efficient provision of public services. *Cf. Connick* ("[G]overnment offices could not function if every employment decision became a constitutional matter"). Public employees, moreover, often occupy trusted positions in society. When they speak out, they can express views that contravene governmental policies or impair the proper performance of governmental functions.

At the same time, the Court has recognized that a citizen who works for the government is nonetheless a citizen. The First Amendment limits the ability of a public employer to leverage the employment relationship to restrict, incidentally or intentionally, the liberties employees enjoy in their capacities as private citizens. *See Perry v. Sindermann*, 408 U.S. 593, 597 (1972). So long as employees are speaking as citizens about matters of public concern, they must face only those speech restrictions that are necessary for their employers to operate efficiently and effectively. *See, e.g., Connick.*

The Court's employee-speech jurisprudence protects, of course, the constitutional rights of public employees. Yet the First Amendment interests at stake extend beyond the individual speaker. The Court has acknowledged the importance of promoting the public's interest in receiving the well-informed views of government employees engaging in civic discussion. *Pickering* again provides an instructive example. The Court characterized its holding as rejecting the attempt of school administrators to "limi[t] teachers' opportunities to contribute to public debate." It also noted that teachers are "the members of a community most likely to have informed and definite opinions" about school expenditures. The Court's approach acknowledged the necessity for informed, vibrant dialogue in a democratic society. It suggested, in addition, that widespread costs may arise when dialogue is repressed. The Court's more recent cases have expressed similar concerns. *See, e.g., San Diego v. Roe*, 543 U.S. 77, 82 (2004) *(per curiam)* ("Were [public employees] not able to speak on [the operation of their employers], the community would be deprived of informed opinions on important public issues. The interest at stake is as much the public's interest in receiving informed opinion as it is the employee's own right to disseminate it" (citation omitted)).

The Court's decisions, then, have sought both to promote the individual and societal interests that are served when employees speak as citizens on matters of public concern and to respect the needs of government employers attempting to perform their important public functions. Underlying our cases has been the premise that while the First Amendment invests public employees with certain rights, it does not empower them to "constitutionalize the employee grievance." *Connick.*

III

With these principles in mind we turn to the instant case. Respondent Ceballos believed the affidavit used to obtain a search warrant contained serious misrepresentations. He conveyed his opinion and recommendation in a memo to his supervisor. That Ceballos expressed his views inside his office, rather than publicly, is not dispositive. Employees in some cases may receive First Amendment protection for expressions made at work. *See, e.g., Givhan v. Western Line Consol. School Dist.*, 439 U.S. 410, 414 (1979). Many citizens do much of their talking inside their respective workplaces, and it would not serve the goal of treating public employees like "any member of the general public," *Pickering*, to hold that all speech within the office is automatically exposed to restriction.

The memo concerned the subject matter of Ceballos' employment, but this, too, is nondispositive. The First Amendment protects some expressions related to the speaker's job. As the Court noted in *Pickering*: "Teachers are, as a class, the members of a community most likely to have informed and definite opinions as to how funds allotted to the operation of the schools should be spent. Accordingly, it is essential that they be able to speak out freely on such questions without fear of retaliatory dismissal." The same is true of many other categories of public employees.

 The controlling factor in Ceballos' case is that his expressions were made pursuant to his duties as a calendar deputy. That consideration—the fact that Ceballos spoke as a prosecutor fulfilling a responsibility to advise his supervisor about how best to proceed with a pending case—distinguishes Ceballos' case from those in which the First Amendment provides protection against discipline. We hold that when public employees make statements pursuant to their official duties, the employees are not speaking as citizens for First Amendment purposes, and the Constitution does not insulate their communications from employer discipline.

Ceballos wrote his disposition memo because that is part of what he, as a calendar deputy, was employed to do. It is immaterial whether he experienced some personal gratification from writing the memo; his First Amendment rights do not depend on his job satisfaction. The significant point is that the memo was written pursuant to Ceballos' official duties. Restricting speech that owes its existence to a public employee's professional responsibilities does not infringe any liberties the employee might have enjoyed as a private citizen. It simply reflects the exercise of employer control over what the employer itself has commissioned or created. *Cf. Rosenberger v. Rector and Visitors of Univ. of Va.*, 515 U.S. 819, 833 (1995) ("[W]hen the government appropriates public funds to promote a particular policy of its own it is entitled to say what it wishes"). Contrast, for example, the expressions made by the speaker in *Pickering*, whose letter to the newspaper had no official significance and bore similarities to letters submitted by numerous citizens every day.

Ceballos did not act as a citizen when he went about conducting his daily professional activities, such as supervising attorneys, investigating charges, and preparing filings. In the same way he did not speak as a citizen by writing a memo that addressed the proper disposition of a pending criminal case. When he went to work and performed the tasks he was paid to perform, Ceballos acted as a government employee. The fact that his duties sometimes required him to speak or write does not mean his supervisors were prohibited from evaluating his performance.

This result is consistent with our precedents' attention to the potential societal value of employee speech. Refusing to recognize First Amendment claims based on government employees' work product does not prevent them from participating in public debate. The employees retain the prospect of constitutional protection for their contributions to the civic discourse. This prospect of protection, however, does not invest them with a right to perform their jobs however they see fit.

Our holding likewise is supported by the emphasis of our precedents on affording government employers sufficient discretion to manage their operations. Employers have heightened interests in controlling speech made by an employee in his or her professional capacity. Official communications have official consequences, creating a need for substantive consistency and clarity. Supervisors must ensure that their employees' official communications are accurate, demonstrate sound judgment, and promote the employer's mission. Ceballos' memo is illustrative. It demanded the attention of his supervisors and led to a heated meeting with employees from the sheriff's department. If Ceballos' superiors thought his memo was inflammatory or misguided, they had the authority to take proper corrective action.

Ceballos' proposed contrary rule, adopted by the Court of Appeals, would commit state and federal courts to a new, permanent, and intrusive role, mandating judicial oversight of communications between and among government employees and their superiors in the course of official business. This displacement of managerial discretion by judicial supervision finds no support in our precedents. When an employee speaks as a citizen addressing a matter of public concern, the First Amendment requires a delicate balancing of the competing interests surrounding the speech and its consequences. When, however, the employee is simply performing his or her job duties, there is no warrant for a similar degree of scrutiny. To hold otherwise would be to demand permanent judicial intervention in the conduct of governmental operations to a degree inconsistent with sound principles of federalism and the separation of powers.

The Court of Appeals based its holding in part on what it perceived as a doctrinal anomaly. The court suggested it would be inconsistent to compel public employers to tolerate certain employee speech made publicly but not speech made pursuant to an employee's assigned duties. This objection misconceives the theoretical underpinnings of our decisions. Employees who make public statements outside the course of performing their official duties retain some possibility of First Amendment protection because that is the kind of activity engaged in by citizens who do not work for the government. The same goes for writing a letter to a local newspaper, see *Pickering*, or discussing politics with a co-worker, *see Rankin*. When a public employee speaks pursuant to employment responsibilities, however, there is no relevant analogue to speech by citizens who are not government employees.

The Court of Appeals' concern also is unfounded as a practical matter. The perceived anomaly, it should be noted, is limited in scope: It relates only to the expressions an employee makes pursuant to his or her official responsibilities, not to statements or complaints (such as those at issue in cases like *Pickering* and *Connick*) that are made outside the duties of employment. If, moreover, a government employer is troubled by the perceived anomaly, it has the means at hand to avoid it. A public employer that wishes to encourage its employees to voice concerns privately retains the option of instituting internal policies and procedures that are receptive to employee criticism. Giving employees an internal forum for their speech will discourage them from concluding that the safest avenue of expression is to state their views in public.

Proper application of our precedents thus leads to the conclusion that the First Amendment does not prohibit managerial discipline based on an employee's expressions made pursuant to official responsibilities. Because Ceballos' memo falls into this category, his allegation of unconstitutional retaliation must fail.

Two final points warrant mentioning. First, as indicated above, the parties in this case do not dispute that Ceballos wrote his disposition memo pursuant to his employment duties. We thus have no occasion to articulate a comprehensive framework for defining the scope of an employee's duties in cases where there is room for serious debate. We reject, however, the suggestion that employers can restrict employees' rights by creating excessively broad job descriptions. The proper inquiry is a practical one. Formal job descriptions often bear little resemblance to the duties an employee actually is expected to perform, and the listing of a given task in an employee's written job description is neither necessary nor sufficient to demonstrate that conducting the task is within the scope of the employee's professional duties for First Amendment purposes.

Second, Justice Souter suggests today's decision may have important ramifications for academic freedom, at least as a constitutional value. There is some argument that expression related to academic scholarship or classroom instruction implicates additional constitutional interests that are not fully accounted for by this Court's customary employee-speech jurisprudence. We need not, and for that reason do not, decide whether the analysis we conduct today would apply in the same manner to a case involving speech related to scholarship or teaching. . . .

IV

Exposing governmental inefficiency and misconduct is a matter of considerable significance. As the Court noted in *Connick*, public employers should, "as a matter of good judgment," be "receptive to constructive criticism offered by their employees." The dictates of sound judgment are reinforced by the powerful network of legislative enactments—such as whistle-blower protection laws and labor codes—available to those who seek to expose wrongdoing. Cases involving government attorneys implicate additional safeguards in the form of, for example, rules of conduct and constitutional obligations apart from the First Amendment. *See, e.g.*, Cal. Rule Prof. Conduct 5-110 (2005) ("A member in government service shall not institute or cause to be instituted criminal charges when the member knows or should know that the charges are not supported by probable cause"); *Brady v. Maryland*, 373 U.S. 83 (1963). These imperatives, as well as obligations arising from any other applicable constitutional provisions and mandates of the criminal and civil laws, protect employees and provide checks on supervisors who would order unlawful or otherwise inappropriate actions.

We reject, however, the notion that the First Amendment shields from discipline the expressions employees make pursuant to their professional duties. Our precedents do not support the existence of a constitutional cause of action behind every statement a public employee makes in the course of doing his or her job. . . .

Justice SOUTER, with whom Justice STEVENS and Justice GINSBURG join, dissenting.

. . . I agree with the majority that a government employer has substantial interests in effectuating its chosen policy and objectives, and in demanding competence, honesty, and judgment from employees who speak for it in doing their work. But I would hold that private and public interests in addressing official wrongdoing and threats to health and safety can outweigh the government's stake in the efficient implementation of policy, and when they do public employees who speak on these matters in the course of their duties should be eligible to claim First Amendment protection.

I

Open speech by a private citizen on a matter of public importance lies at the heart of expression subject to protection by the First Amendment. At the other extreme, a statement by a government employee complaining about nothing beyond treatment under personnel rules raises no greater claim to constitutional protection against retaliatory response than the remarks of a private employee. *See Connick v. Myers.* In between these points lies a public employee's speech unwelcome to the government but on a significant public issue. Such an employee speaking as a citizen, that is, with a citizen's interest, is protected from reprisal unless the statements are too damaging to the government's capacity to conduct public business to be justified by any individual or public benefit thought to flow from the statements. *Pickering.* Entitlement to protection is thus not absolute.

This significant, albeit qualified, protection of public employees who irritate the government is understood to flow from the First Amendment, in part, because a government paycheck does nothing to eliminate the value to an individual of speaking on public matters, and there is no good reason for categorically discounting a speaker's interest in commenting on a matter of public concern just because the government employs him. Still, the First Amendment safeguard rests on something more, being the value to the public of receiving the opinions and information that a public employee may disclose. "Government employees are often in the best position to know what ails the agencies for which they work." *Waters v. Churchill,* 511 U.S. 661, 674 (1994).

The reason that protection of employee speech is qualified is that it can distract co-workers and supervisors from their tasks at hand and thwart the implementation of legitimate policy, the risks of which grow greater the closer the employee's speech gets to commenting on his own workplace and responsibilities. It is one thing for an office clerk to say there is waste in government and quite another to charge that his own department pays full-time salaries to part-time workers. Even so, we have regarded eligibility for protection by *Pickering* balancing as the proper approach when an employee speaks critically about the administration of his own government employer. In *Givhan v. Western Line Consol. School Dist.* we followed *Pickering* when a teacher was fired for complaining to a superior about the racial composition of the school's administrative, cafeteria, and library staffs . . ., and the same point was clear in *Madison Joint School Dist. No. 8 v. Wisconsin.* [T]he Court realized that a public employee can wear a citizen's hat when speaking on subjects closely tied to the employee's own job, and *Givhan* stands for the same conclusion even when the speech is not addressed to the public at large.

The difference between a case like *Givhan* and this one is that the subject of Ceballos's speech fell within the scope of his job responsibilities, whereas choosing personnel was not what the teacher was hired to do. The effect of the majority's constitutional line between these two cases, then, is that a *Givhan* schoolteacher is protected when complaining to the principal about hiring policy, but a school personnel officer would not be if he protested that the principal disapproved of hiring minority job applicants. This is an odd place to draw a distinction,[1] and while necessary judicial line-drawing sometimes looks arbitrary, any distinction obliges a court to justify its choice. Here, there is no adequate justification for the majority's line categorically denying *Pickering* protection to any speech uttered "pursuant to . . . official duties."

1. It seems stranger still in light of the majority's concession of some First Amendment protection when a public employee repeats statements made pursuant to his duties but in a separate, public forum or in a letter to a newspaper.

As all agree, the qualified speech protection embodied in *Pickering* balancing resolves the tension between individual and public interests in the speech, on the one hand, and the government's interest in operating efficiently without distraction or embarrassment by talkative or headline-grabbing employees. The need for a balance hardly disappears when an employee speaks on matters his job requires him to address; rather, it seems obvious that the individual and public value of such speech is no less, and may well be greater, when the employee speaks pursuant to his duties in addressing a subject he knows intimately for the very reason that it falls within his duties.[2]

The majority's response, that the enquiry to determine duties is a "practical one," does not alleviate this concern. It sets out a standard that will not discourage government employers from setting duties expansively, but will engender litigation to decide which stated duties were actual and which were merely formal.

As for the importance of such speech to the individual, it stands to reason that a citizen may well place a very high value on a right to speak on the public issues he decides to make the subject of his work day after day. Would anyone doubt that a school principal evaluating the performance of teachers for promotion or pay adjustment retains a citizen's interest in addressing the quality of teaching in the schools? (Still, the majority indicates he could be fired without First Amendment recourse for fair but unfavorable comment when the teacher under review is the superintendent's daughter.) Would anyone deny that a prosecutor like Richard Ceballos may claim the interest of any citizen in speaking out against a rogue law enforcement officer, simply because his job requires him to express a judgment about the officer's performance? (But the majority says the First Amendment gives Ceballos no protection, even if his judgment in this case was sound and appropriately expressed.) . . .

Indeed, the very idea of categorically separating the citizen's interest from the employee's interest ignores the fact that the ranks of public service include those who share the poet's "object . . .to unite [m]y avocation and my vocation";[3] these citizen servants are the ones whose civic interest rises highest when they speak pursuant to their duties, and these are exactly the ones government employers most want to attract. . . .

Nor is there any reason to raise the counterintuitive question whether the public interest in hearing informed employees evaporates when they speak as required on some subject at the core of their jobs. Two terms ago, we recalled the public value that the *Pickering* Court perceived in the speech of public employees as a class: "Underlying the decision in *Pickering* is the recognition that public employees are often the members of the community who are likely to have informed opinions as to the operations of their public employers, operations which are of substantial concern to the public.

---

2. I do not say the value of speech "pursuant to . . . duties" will always be greater, because I am pessimistic enough to expect that one response to the Court's holding will be moves by government employers to expand stated job descriptions to include more official duties and so exclude even some currently protectable speech from First Amendment purview. Now that the government can freely penalize the school personnel officer for criticizing the principal because speech on the subject falls within the personnel officer's job responsibilities, the government may well try to limit the English teacher's options by the simple expedient of defining teachers' job responsibilities expansively, investing them with a general obligation to ensure sound administration of the school. Hence today's rule presents the regrettable prospect that protection under *Pickering* may be diminished by expansive statements of employment duties.

3. R. FROST, TWO TRAMPS IN MUD TIME, COLLECTED POEMS, PROSE, & PLAYS 251, 252 (R. Poirier & M. Richardson eds., 1995).

Were they not able to speak on these matters, the community would be deprived of informed opinions on important public issues. The interest at stake is as much the public's interest in receiving informed opinion as it is the employee's own right to disseminate it." *San Diego v. Roe* (citation omitted). This is not a whit less true when an employee's job duties require him to speak about such things: when, for example, a public auditor speaks on his discovery of embezzlement of public funds, when a building inspector makes an obligatory report of an attempt to bribe him, or when a law enforcement officer expressly balks at a superior's order to violate constitutional rights he is sworn to protect. (The majority, however, places all these speakers beyond the reach of First Amendment protection against retaliation.)

Nothing, then, accountable on the individual and public side of the *Pickering* balance changes when an employee speaks "pursuant" to public duties. On the side of the government employer, however, something is different, and to this extent, I agree with the majority of the Court. The majority is rightly concerned that the employee who speaks out on matters subject to comment in doing his own work has the greater leverage to create office uproars and fracture the government's authority to set policy to be carried out coherently through the ranks. . . .

But why do the majority's concerns, which we all share, require categorical exclusion of First Amendment protection against any official retaliation for things said on the job? Is it not possible to respect the unchallenged individual and public interests in the speech through a *Pickering* balance without drawing the strange line I mentioned before[?] . . . It is thus no adequate justification for the suppression of potentially valuable information simply to recognize that the government has a huge interest in managing its employees and preventing the occasionally irresponsible one from turning his job into a bully pulpit. Even there, the lesson of *Pickering* (and the object of most constitutional adjudication) is still to the point: when constitutionally significant interests clash, resist the demand for winner-take-all; try to make adjustments that serve all of the values at stake.

Two reasons in particular make me think an adjustment using the basic *Pickering* balancing scheme is perfectly feasible here. First, the extent of the government's legitimate authority over subjects of speech required by a public job can be recognized in advance by setting in effect a minimum heft for comments with any claim to outweigh it. Thus, the risks to the government are great enough for us to hold from the outset that an employee commenting on subjects in the course of duties should not prevail on balance unless he speaks on a matter of unusual importance and satisfies high standards of responsibility in the way he does it. The examples I have already given indicate the eligible subject matter, and it is fair to say that only comment on official dishonesty, deliberately unconstitutional action, other serious wrongdoing, or threats to health and safety can weigh out in an employee's favor. . . .

My second reason for adapting *Pickering* to the circumstances at hand is the experience in Circuits that have recognized claims like Ceballos's here. First Amendment protection less circumscribed than what I would recognize has been available in the Ninth Circuit for over 17 years, and neither there nor in other Circuits that accept claims like this one has there been a debilitating flood of litigation. . . .

For that matter, the majority's position comes with no guarantee against fact-bound litigation over whether a public employee's statements were made "pursuant to . . . official duties." In fact, the majority invites such litigation by describing the inquiry as a "practical one," apparently based on the totality of employment circumstances. *See* n.2. Are prosecutors' discretionary statements about cases addressed to the press on the courthouse steps made "pursuant to their official duties"? Are government nuclear scientists' complaints to their supervisors about a colleague's improper handling of radioactive materials made "pursuant" to duties?

II

The majority seeks support in two lines of argument extraneous to *Pickering* doctrine. The one turns on a fallacious reading of cases on government speech, the other on a mistaken assessment of protection available under whistle-blower statutes.

A

The majority accepts the fallacy propounded by the county petitioners and the Federal Government as *amicus* that any statement made within the scope of public employment is (or should be treated as) the government's own speech, and should thus be differentiated as a matter of law from the personal statements the First Amendment protects. . . . Some public employees are hired to "promote a particular policy" by broadcasting a particular message set by the government, but not everyone working for the government, after all, is hired to speak from a government manifesto. There is no claim or indication that Ceballos was hired to perform such a speaking assignment. . . .

It is not, of course, that the district attorney lacked interest of a high order in what Ceballos might say. If his speech undercut effective, lawful prosecution, there would have been every reason to rein him in or fire him; a statement that created needless tension among law enforcement agencies would be a fair subject of concern, and the same would be true of inaccurate statements or false ones made in the course of doing his work. But these interests on the government's part are entirely distinct from any claim that Ceballos's speech was government speech with a preset or proscribed content. . . .

This ostensible domain beyond the pale of the First Amendment is spacious enough to include even the teaching of a public university professor, and I have to hope that today's majority does not mean to imperil First Amendment protection of academic freedom in public colleges and universities, whose teachers necessarily speak and write "pursuant to official duties."

B

The majority's second argument for its disputed limitation of *Pickering* doctrine is that the First Amendment has little or no work to do here owing to an assertedly comprehensive complement of state and national statutes protecting government whistle-blowers from vindictive bosses. [That is because much speech that should be protected is not classic whistleblowing and because] the combined variants of statutory whistle-blower definitions and protections add up to a patchwork, not a showing that worries may be remitted to legislatures for relief. [Indeed,] individuals doing the same sorts of governmental jobs and saying the same sorts of things addressed to civic concerns will get different protection depending on the local, state, or federal jurisdictions that happened to employ them.

III

[The opinion recounted in some detail the plaintiff's claims of retaliation not only for his written reports but also for his spoken statements to his supervisors, testimony at the hearing in the pending criminal case, and his speech at a meeting of the Mexican-American Bar Association about misconduct of the Sheriff's Department in the criminal case and the failure of the District Attorney's Office to handle allegations of police misconduct.]

Upon remand, it will be open to the Court of Appeals to consider the application of *Pickering* to any retaliation shown for other statements; not all of those statements would have been made pursuant to official duties in any obvious sense, and the claim relating to truthful testimony in court must surely be analyzed independently to protect the integrity of the judicial process.

NOTES

1. *Almost Eroded Away? Connick* was viewed at the time as substantially chipping away at speech protections for employees in the workplace, both because of its narrower definition of "matters of public concern," and its deferential approach to management's prerogatives in the balancing analysis. Now, in the wake of *Garcetti*, how much genuine protection for public employee speech is left? Not only is there no protection for speech that does not address a matter of public concern, but *all* speech falling within the scope of an employee's official duties appeared to be unprotected, although we will see a limited retreat from such an absolutist position shortly. Moreover, even where workplace speech does address a matter of public concern and does not fall within the scope of an employee's official duties, it will still be subjected to a balancing of interests and, hence, may be unprotected if it is disruptive or otherwise threatens efficient operation of the agency. Perhaps employees can rest assured that truly nondisruptive speech—that is, speech within the workplace about matters of public concern unrelated to work or the employee's duties—is still safe, but employees engaging in other types of workplace speech or public speech about work must do so at their peril. If this statement is accurate, does the First Amendment afford much protection to government workers? Should it? *Connick* and both *Garcetti* opinions emphasize the important civic interests First Amendment speech protections are supposed to foster. Does the protection actually afforded in the wake of these decisions match this rhetoric?

2. *Deference, Balancing, and Categorical Rules.* As we saw in the privacy context, the focus of the "balancing" inquiry on the employer's interest means that the outcome of a case often hinges on the extent to which the Court is willing to defer to the employer's justification. Indeed, the level of deference was the primary dispute between the majority and the omitted dissent of Justice Brennan in *Connick*. Are the disagreements in *Garcetti* driven by much the same thing? Put another way, although the dispute between the majority and dissent in *Garcetti* involves whether there ought to be a categorical rule governing speech within the scope of an employee's official duties, isn't this disagreement largely about how much deference to the public employer is warranted? Can you identify language in the opinion suggesting that the majority's concern about the practical implications of judicial interference with employer prerogatives makes *no* interference the only option? What is the dissent's response to such concerns? Which approach strikes the right balance?

3. *Private Ordering. Connick* and *Garcetti* both state that employees do not waive their constitutional speech and association protections when accepting government work. Although, as discussed in Chapter 6, government employees also cannot be required to prospectively jettison their Fourth Amendment rights, one could contend, at least prior to *Garcetti*, that the Constitution provides more robust protection for speech than for privacy rights. That is because privacy rights may be diminished or eliminated by workplace structures and policies that curtail reasonable expectations of privacy. Speech rights are not "bounded" by any such reasonable expectation requirement. *See* Renee Newman Knake, *Lawyer Speech in the Regulatory State*, 84 FORDHAM L. REV. 2099 (2016).

Post-*Garcetti*, however, job duties of any position may result in the substantial narrowing of one's freedom of expression, at least at work. In fact, the *Garcetti* dissenters express concern that the majority's categorical approach may prompt government employers to manipulate job definitions and duties to capture as much employee speech as possible. *See* Elizabeth M. Ellis, Garcetti v. Ceballos: *Public Employees Left to Decide "Your Conscience or Your Job,"* 41 IND. L. REV. 187 (2008) (arguing that *Garcetti's* threshold "official duties" test should be applied narrowly to prevent employers from broadly defining job descriptions). Is this danger real, or, as the majority suggests, is it overstated? Suppose a government agency decides to require all employees to "report to their supervisor any acts or omissions by other government employees or officials the employee believes in good faith to be in violation of state or federal law or agency policy or regulations." Failure to do so "may result in suspension, termination, or other disciplinary action." Are all such reports now per se unprotected by the First Amendment? Is the majority's assurance that what matters is not formal policies but actual job practices a sufficient response? *Cf. D'Olimpio v. Crisafi*, 462 F. App'x 79 (2d Cir. 2012) (holding that a state employee's complaints to the inspector general regarding alleged official misconduct by his supervisor were made in the performance of employee's duties, and thus any retaliation did not violate employee's free speech rights). Many universities, including public institutions, designate most professional employees as "mandated reporters" of sexual misconduct. Doesn't that mean that they can now be fired for reporting potential Title IX violations, at least as far as the First Amendment is concerned?

Of course, if an employee reports misconduct elsewhere—outside the agency or to the public—the First Amendment may be implicated, but then the speech is more likely to be disruptive by straining office morale and working relationships. Also, a need for confidentiality may sometimes limit external whistleblowing. Moreover, some government positions may require a public appearance of "neutrality" or the avoidance of conflicts of interest; speech contrary to these demands is unlikely to be protected. Thus, when an employee chooses to "go public," the government's countervailing interest in this area is more likely to trump the worker's interest in expression.

4. *Whither the Whistleblower?* As the prior note suggests, a paramount concern surrounding *Garcetti* is the plight of government whistleblowers. Indeed, Ceballos was a whistleblower, and his claim is premised on alleged retaliation for both his internal report of illegal activity and for certain external steps he took—that's the point of the dissent's argument as to what should happen on remand. The dissent also fears a chilling effect on government employees coming forward to report perceived misconduct, while the majority downplays this concern. The dissent and majority further contest whether *Garcetti* will create a perverse incentive for employees to go public with their concerns (report them externally) rather than report them internally up the chain of command within the agency.

Moreover, the dissent suggests that independent whistleblower and antiretaliation protections are inadequate to protect employees attempting to further the public's interest in good government. Recall the discussion in Chapter 4 of whistleblowing and the public policy tort more generally. As this casebook illustrates, the dissent is surely correct that such protections are a patchwork, but might some of the activities Ceballos alleged support state law public policy claims? In any event, is the lack of comprehensive statutory or common law regimes an argument for enhancing *constitutional* protections for employees?

Also note that many of the same themes that framed the public policy tort discussion in Chapter 4 are present in *Garcetti*—for example, separation of powers, the conflict between social benefits and employer prerogatives, calibrating employer and employee incentives, and floodgates and litigation cost concerns. Similarly, much of the discussion in Chapter 4 involved the balancing of employer, employee, and public interests. Naturally, one aspect of this discussion is how this balance might differ by type of employer—that is, public versus private. Does *Garcetti* shed any light on this? In other words, in the whistleblower context, are there reasons to strike the balance between the interests of employees, employers, and the public differently in the public employer context?

5. *The Aftermath.* Unsurprisingly, public employee free speech claims now commonly fail on the basis of *Garcetti*—many of which, like Ceballos's claim, might be characterized as involving whistleblowing. *See, e.g.*, *FOP v. City of Camden*, 842 F.3d 231 (3rd Cir. 2016) (affirming the District Court's decision to dismiss officers' First Amendment claims because they were not speaking as private citizens when they complained about a department's quota policy); *Coomes v. Edmonds Sch. Dist. No. 15*, 816 F.3d 1255 (9th Cir. 2016) (finding teacher's communication with parents concerning school district failures to provide certain programs was not made as a citizen, despite fact that teacher operated outside the district's chain-of-command); *Alves v. Bd. of Regents of the Univ. Sys. of Georgia*, 804 F.3d 1149 (11th Cir. 2015) (finding clinical psychologists employed by state university spoke as employees when drafting a memorandum alleging poor leadership by director of counseling and testing center); *Holub v. Gdowski*, 802 F.3d 1149 (10th Cir. 2015) (finding school district's internal auditor acted as an employee even though she took the uncustomary step of informing two school board members of alleged unlawful budgeting practices by the district); *Weintraub v. Bd. of Educ. of the City of New York*, 593 F.3d 196 (2d Cir. 2010) (holding that a public school teacher's filing of a grievance with the union after the school administrator had refused to discipline a student who had thrown books at him was pursuant to official duties). Even when a claim overcomes the barriers *Garcetti* imposes, employee speech claims often fail for other reasons. *See, e.g.*, *Bowers v. Scurry*, 276 F. App'x 278 (4th Cir. 2008) (holding that a state university's interest in providing effective services to the public strongly outweighed a human resources employee's interest in using her university e-mail to disseminate information regarding the potential impact on university employees of pending salary restructuring).

The post-*Garcetti* claims involving speech related to the public employee's job that have survived typically involve reports or complaints to the public or other government bodies falling clearly outside of the employee's chain of command. *See, e.g., Hardesty v. Cochran*, 621 F. App'x 771 (5th Cir. 2015) (finding genuine issue of material fact on whether employee informed waterworks district customers of district annexation plan as a citizen or as part of his job duties); *see also Ricciuti v. Gyzenis*, 834 F.3d 162, 170 (2nd Cir. 2016) (concluding that an employee's creation of an "overtime matrix" to expose supervisors for assigning themselves unnecessary overtime to "pad their pensions" did not fall under the meaning of "'pursuant to' official duties" under *Garcetti* merely because the speech owes its existence to the employees job); *Boulton v. Swanson*, 795 F.3d 526 (6th Cir. 2015) (finding sergeant spoke as a citizen in speech at union meeting because his job duties did not include acting in capacity of union member).

Scholarly criticisms of the majority opinion in *Garcetti*—as a matter of First Amendment doctrine and in terms of its practical implications for government whistle-blowers and others—are legion. *See, e.g.,* Cynthia Estlund, *Free Speech Rights That Work at Work: From the First Amendment to Due Process*, 54 UCLA L. REV. 1463 (2007); Orly Lobel, *Citizenship, Organizational Citizenship, and the Laws of Overlapping Obligations*, 97 CALIF. L. REV. 433 (2009); Scott A. Moss, *Students and Workers and Prisoners—Oh, My! A Cautionary Note About Excessive Institutional Tailoring of First Amendment Doctrine*, 54 UCLA L. REV. 1635 (2007); Helen Norton, *Constraining Public Employee Speech: Government's Control of Its Workers' Speech to Protect Its Own Expression*, 59 DUKE L.J. 1 (2009); Paul M. Secunda, Garcetti*'s Impact on the First Amendment Speech Rights of Federal Employees*, 7 FIRST AMEND. L. REV. 117, 118 (2008); Terry Smith, *Speaking Against Norms: Public Discourse and the Economy of Racialization in the Workplace*, 57 AM. U. L. REV. 523 (2008); Paul M. Secunda, *The Solomon Amendment, Expressive Associations, and Public Employment*, 54 UCLA L. REV. 1767 (2007). *But see* Lawrence Rosenthal, *The Emerging First Amendment Law of Managerial Prerogative*, 77 FORDHAM L. REV. 33 (2008) (defending *Garcetti* as consistent with First Amendment principles).

6. Lane v. Franks *and the Unresolved Contours of "Ordinary Job Duties."* In *Lane v. Franks*, 134 S. Ct. 2369 (2014), the Supreme Court's first decision addressing work-related speech following *Garcetti*, it held that the First Amendment protects a public employee who provided truthful sworn testimony, compelled by subpoena, outside the course of his ordinary job responsibilities. The case marks an important limitation on *Garcetti*: A public employee's compelled truthful testimony—that "relates to his public employment or concerns information learned during that employment" does not necessarily fall within the employee's "ordinary" job duties. And the decisive way in which the Court unanimously said so, at least with regard to sworn testimony, rejects the more aggressive approaches to extending the sweep of "ordinary job duties" some lower courts had adopted.

Nevertheless, *Lane*'s effect on the ground itself may be limited. First, the Court expressly avoided deciding whether a public employee's truthful sworn testimony would constitute citizen speech under *Garcetti* when given as part of the employee's job responsibilities. As the concurrence also notes, testifying is a routine part of job duties for the broad swath of public employees involved in investigatory and enforcement work, including police officers. Thus, whether testimony in such circumstances will receive First Amendment protection remains an open question.

Perhaps more importantly, however, the *Lane* Court did not need to address how "ordinary" job duties are determined because it was undisputed that Lane's testimony fell outside of his ordinary responsibilities. This means that the questions raised in Note 3 above remain open; whether and in what circumstances public employers, through private ordering, will be able to sweep otherwise potentially protected speech into the sphere of ordinary job responsibilities. Indeed, what if, as part of Lane's job responsibilities, he had been required to report—to appropriate government authorities or *through testifying in court proceedings*—activities within the agency that he reasonably believed to be unlawful, fraudulent, corrupt, etc.? The point is that public employers may still be able to reduce substantially potential First Amendment protections by crafting job duties and practices to encompass additional types of workplace speech, including, testimony and cooperation with other government officials. *Cf. Hurst v. Lee County*, 764 F.3d 480 (5th Cir. 2014) (holding that, in contrast to the speech in *Lane*, a correction officer's statements to the media were not protected because department policy permitted officers to speak to media if granted permission, and the officer's failure to seek permission did not convert his comments into citizen speech—that is, to speech outside of his job duties).

Turning to *Pickering*, the *Lane* Court found the balancing prong to be easy since the employer had failed to articulate any legitimate interest in efficiency to balance against Lane's interest in providing truthful testimony. But the Court also suggested that, in other contexts, such as nonobligatory statements to officials in other government agencies and nontestimonial public statements, the balance might come out differently. Once again, how much deference courts will accord articulated governmental interests remains an open question.

7. *Freedom of Association*. Beyond the First Amendment's protection for speech is freedom of association. Public sector workers enjoy qualified protections with regard to their political preferences and affiliations, and the Supreme Court has struck down various government requirements that infringe upon such rights. *See, e.g., Rutan v. Republican Party*, 497 U.S. 62 (1990) (holding unconstitutional promotion, transfer, recall, and hiring decisions involving low-level public employees based on political party affiliation and support); *Elrod v. Burns*, 427 U.S. 367 (1976) (holding that a public-sector employee who is not a policy-level decision maker may not be denied employment based on political affiliation); *Cafeteria & Rest. Workers Union v. McElroy*, 367 U.S. 886 (1961) (recognizing that the government could not deny employment because of previous membership in a particular party); *Shelton v. Tucker*, 364 U.S. 479 (1960) (finding unconstitutional an Arkansas requirement that public school teachers file annually an affidavit listing each organization to which they have contributed for five preceding years). Although these employee association cases are 30 or more years old, more recent court decisions upholding the right to expressive association suggest they have continued vitality. *See, e.g., Heffernan v. City of Paterson*, 136 S. Ct. 1412 (2016) (reaffirming that public employees may not be disciplined for protected associational activity (in this case political activity) absent a showing of adverse effects on the efficiency of the agency; the fact that the employee's supervisors were mistaken about his involvement in the political campaign at issue did not bar his claim); *Boy Scouts of America v. Dale*, 530 U.S. 640 (2000); *Wagner v. Jones*, 664 F.3d 259 (8th Cir. 2011) (finding applicant for legal writing instructor position at the University of Iowa Law School offered sufficient evidence for a factfinder to infer that the dean's repeated decisions not to hire the applicant were in part motivated by her constitutionally protected First Amendment rights of political belief and association);

see generally Paul M. Secunda, *The Solomon Amendment, Expressive Associations, and Public Employment*, 54 UCLA L. REV. 1767 (2007).

A few courts have also held that employees may not be dismissed because of other personal or familial associations. *See, e.g., Sowards v. Loundon County*, 203 F.3d 426 (6th Cir. 2000) (upholding law enforcement employee's right to political and intimate association in context in which she supported her husband's campaign for sheriff); *see also Roberts v. United States Jaycees*, 468 U.S. 609, 617-18 (1984) (stating that one type of protected freedom of association is the right to maintain certain intimate relationships because of the role such relationships have in safeguarding individual freedom). *But see Shahar v. Bowers*, 114 F.3d 1097 (11th Cir. 1997) (even assuming an attorney had a constitutionally protected right to participate in a marriage ceremony when same-sex marriages were not recognized as legal, Georgia's attorney general did not violate her right of association by withdrawing job offer because the employer's efficiency interests would be jeopardized given the policy-making nature of the position and working relationships within the department).

As in the speech context, employee association rights may be limited when there is a substantial governmental interest for doing so. In *Rutan*, 497 U.S. at 74, the Court struck down an Illinois executive order that established a *de facto* political patronage system ensuring that government agencies would promote and hire only Republican Party members. In so holding, the Court recognized the government's interest in ensuring employee effectiveness and efficiency but found that this interest could be served through the less drastic means of disciplining or discharging staff members whose work is inadequate. *See id.* However, the Court limited strong protection—that is, strict scrutiny—to the treatment of lower-level employees, reaffirming the prerogative of elected officials to fill policy-making positions with like-minded appointees. *See id.; see also Elrod*, 427 U.S. at 366-67.

8. *Worker Rank and Status.* In both the speech and association cases, the worker's rank and status often determine the outcome of the case. Indeed, in both contexts, lower-level employees appear to enjoy greater protection than higher-level workers. At the extreme, the president or a governor or mayor can choose members of his or her own party for his cabinet, and probably for most "policy making" positions. Beyond this, the greater protection for lower-level employees is a product not of their vulnerabilities, but rather, of the fact that the actions of higher-level employees are more likely to threaten the efficient functioning of the government employer, and thus more likely to justify employer intrusions or prohibitions. Do you think that an assistant district attorney's circulation of a survey on personnel issues (*Connick*) would be more disruptive to the workplace than a deputy's comments to her co-worker expressing a wish that the president had been killed (*Rankin*)? *See also Pickering*, 391 U.S. at 571-72 (noting that because the speaker was a teacher rather than a higher-ranking school district employee, incorrect assertions in his public statements could be easily corrected by the district and any harm done thereby alleviated). Also, consider whether the outcome in *Lane* might have been different if Lane had revealed his reasons for firing Schmitz to the media rather than recounting it in sworn testimony. Might the employer's interest in maintaining confidentiality with regard to personnel matters outweigh his interest in such revelations?

In addition to rank, the nature of the employee's work may affect the analysis. For example, as discussed below, courts seem to accord more deference to employer regulation of employee speech for certain types of workers, including law enforcement officials who interact with the public and teachers. In an omitted separate dissent, Justice Breyer found Ceballos's attorney status to be dispositive in his determination that the speech ought to protected:

> [T]he speech at issue is professional speech—the speech of a lawyer. Such speech is subject to independent regulation by canons of the profession. Those canons provide an obligation to speak in certain instances. And where that is so, the government's own interest in forbidding that speech is diminished. The objective specificity and public availability of the profession's canons also help to diminish the risk that the courts will improperly interfere with the government's necessary authority to manage its work.

547 U.S. at 447. Recall the unique treatment of attorneys in the context of the public policy tort in Chapter 4. Are there similar strands of thought running through the *Garcetti* opinions?

Note on *Garcetti* and Academic Freedom

One group of workers who may be treated differently with respect to speech rights is academics. Both the majority and dissent in *Garcetti* acknowledge the potential implications for academic freedom, recognizing that speech—expressed through scholarship, commentary, and classroom instruction—is at the center of an academic's work. Previously, the Court had recognized that the preservation of academic freedom is an important First Amendment concern. *See, e.g.*, *Keyishian v. Bd. of Regents*, 385 U.S. 589, 603 (1967) ("The vigilant protection of constitutional freedoms is nowhere more vital than in the community of American schools." (quoting *Shelton v. Tucker*, 364 U.S. 479, 487 (1960)); *see also Rodriguez v. Maricopa County Cmty. Coll. Dist.*, 605 F.3d 703 (9th Cir. 2009) (stating that a college is entitled to substantial deference in choosing not to discipline a professor whose racially charged e-mail offended some employees and expressing doubt that a professor's speech on a matter of public concern directed at the college community could ever form the basis of a hostile work environment claim under Title VII). Given the nature of their work and the social functions educational institutions serve, should academics employed by public colleges or universities receive special constitutional protection? What would be the rationale for such a distinction consistent with the text of the First Amendment? If you believe academic speech should not receive such heightened protection, how do you respond to the claim that, without such safeguards, academics will be chilled from engaging in socially useful but controversial or unpopular work, research, or commentary?

Despite the *Garcetti* Court's acknowledgment that academic freedom may raise unique First Amendment issues, some have expressed concern that its analysis may weaken protections for such speech. *See, e.g.*, Sheldon H. Nahmod, *Public Employee Speech, Categorical Balancing and §1983: A Critique of* Garcetti v. Ceballos, 42 U. RICH. L. REV. 561 (2008) (asserting that *Garcetti*'s modification of the prior "public concern" test significantly undermines the historical protection afforded to academic freedom). Issues surrounding academic freedom are taken up again in Note 8 at page 457. Moreover, the availability of a First Amendment claim does not always translate into meaningful protection for professors who make highly unpopular or controversial statements in the course of their work. Consider University of Colorado

Professor Ward Churchill, whose controversial essay likening 9/11 victims to Nazis caused an uproar and sparked calls for reevaluating the tenure system. The university ultimately terminated Churchill, purportedly for unrelated research misconduct (plagiarism). Churchill then sued, claiming that the university violated his First Amendment rights. At trial, the jury found in Churchill's favor, concluding that the content of the essay was the university's real reason for terminating him. This victory was a hollow one, however, since the jury awarded only $1.00 in compensatory damages and the judge later determined that Churchill was not entitled to reinstatement. *See, e.g.*, Kirk Johnson & Katherine Seelye, *Jury Says Professor Was Wrongly Fired*, N.Y. TIMES, Apr. 2, 2009; Tom McGhee, *No Job, No Money for Churchill*, DENVER POST, July 7, 2009; *see also* Archive of Postings to The Race to the Bottom Blog, http://www.theracetothe bottom.org/ward-churchill/ (containing archive of blog posts on the Churchill trial and its aftermath, and links to court documents and commentary).

Nevertheless, expression-based claims in the academic context have had mixed success since *Garcetti*. In what is perhaps the leading case, *Adams v. Trustees of the University of North Carolina-Wilmington*, 640 F.3d 550, 554 (4th Cir. 2011), the Fourth Circuit upheld such a claim. Michael Adams, an associate professor in criminology and prominent conservative commentator, filed suit against the university for failing to promote him to the rank of full professor. Adams alleged that UNCW did not promote him because of his speeches, articles, and books related to his outspoken Christian, conservative views. *Id*. The district court relied on *Garcetti* in dismissing Adams's speech claim, holding that the speeches, articles, and books were sufficiently related to Adams's professional capacity (as a professor) to fall within his official duties. In reversing, the Fourth Circuit noted that *Garcetti* itself had reserved the question of its rule's application to academic teaching and writing, and further suggested that the scholarship and other speech upon which Adams based his claim extended well beyond the specific, baseline duties demanded by the university:

> There may be instances in which a public university faculty member's assigned duties include a specific role in declaring or administering university policy, as opposed to scholarship or teaching. In that circumstance, *Garcetti* may apply to the specific instances of the faculty member's speech carrying out those duties. However, that is clearly not the circumstance in the case at bar. Defendants agree Adams' speech involves scholarship and teaching; indeed, as we discuss below, that is one of the reasons they say *Garcetti* should apply—because UNCW paid Adams to be a scholar and a teacher regardless of the setting for his work. But the scholarship and teaching in this case, Adams' speech, was intended for and directed at a national or international audience on issues of public importance unrelated to any of Adams' assigned teaching duties at UNCW or any other terms of his employment found in the record. Defendants concede none of Adams' speech was undertaken at the direction of UNCW, paid for by UNCW, or had any direct application to his UNCW duties.
>
> Applying *Garcetti* to the academic work of a public university faculty member under the facts of this case could place beyond the reach of First Amendment protection many forms of public speech or service a professor engaged in during his employment. That would not appear to be what *Garcetti* intended, nor is it consistent with our longstanding recognition that no individual loses his ability to speak as a private citizen by virtue of public employment. In light of the above factors, we will not apply *Garcetti* to the circumstances of this case.
>
> The Defendants nonetheless contend that because Adams was employed as an associate professor, and his position required him to engage in scholarship, research, and service to the community, Adams' speech constituted "statements made pursuant to

[his] official duties." *Cf., Garcetti.* In other words, the Defendants argue Adams was employed to undertake his speech. This argument underscores the problem recognized by both the majority and the dissent in *Garcetti,* that "implicates additional constitutional interests that are not fully accounted for" when it comes to "expression related to academic scholarship or classroom instruction.". . . Put simply, Adams' speech was not tied to any more specific or direct employee duty than the general concept that professors will engage in writing, public appearances, and service within their respective fields. For all the reasons discussed above, that thin thread is insufficient to render Adams' speech "pursuant to [his] official duties" as intended by *Garcetti.*

Id. at 563-64; *see also Demers v. Austin,* 746 F.3d 402 (9th Cir. 2014) (holding that the *Garcetti* test does not apply to speech related to scholarship or teaching—such speech is governed by *Pickering* test). Although *Adams* is protective of professor speech, it might simply mean that speech a professor engages in *outside* of his or her official duties as a professor is protected, meaning that there might not be protected "academic freedom" within such duties (however defined). *See generally* Edward J. Schoen, *Completing Government Speech's Unfinished Business: Clipping* Garcetti's *Wings and Addressing Scholarship and Teaching,* 43 HASTINGS CONST. L.Q. 537 (2016); Matthew Jay Hertzog, *The Misapplication of* Garcetti *in Higher Education,* 2015 BYU EDUC. & L.J. 203 (2015); Scott R. Bauries, *Individual Academic Freedom: An Ordinary Concern of the First Amendment,* 83 MISS. L.J. 677 (2014). Suppose Adams had expressed his views in the classroom? If so, would it make any difference whether those views were directly relevant to the subjects he taught?

Thus, while the *Adams* opinion does offer some insights into how courts might grapple with the *Garcetti* majority's seeming reluctance to extend an expansive official duties rule to the academic context, much remains uncertain. *See also Keating v. Univ. of South Dakota,* 569 F. App'x 469 (8th Cir. 2014) (finding university's civility policy, pursuant to which tenure-track professor was terminated, was not impermissibly vague under the Due Process Clause of the Fourteenth Amendment). *Adams* and other court decisions in the wake of *Garcetti* also may signal that instructor and professor speech in the university setting will be treated differently than class or instruction-related speech in primary or secondary schools. *See* Strasser, *supra,* at 671-73 (reviewing cases); *see also Evans-Marshall v. Bd. of Educ. of Tipp City Exempted Vill. Sch. Dist.,* 624 F.3d 332 (6th Cir. 2010) (upholding the dismissal of a high school teacher's free speech claim premised on her curricular and pedagogical choices in the classroom because these choices were made pursuant to her official duties and therefore were unprotected speech under *Garcetti*).

* * *

The final broad category of speech claims involves speech or other forms of expression away from work and, unlike *Lane, not* primarily about work or directed at work-related issues. The key question in this context is often whether the government employer has a sufficiently substantial interest to justify regulating or prohibiting such off-site speech. In *United States v. National Treasury Employees Union,* 513 U.S. 454 (1995) ("*NTEU*"), the Supreme Court struck down a federal statute banning certain honoraria for expressive activities including published works and presentations by broad classes of federal employees, among them activities that bore no direct relation to the nature of the employees' government work. In so doing, the Court found the government's interest in protecting integrity and ethics in government insufficient to support such a broad ban, stating that the "speculative benefits the honoraria ban may provide the Government are not sufficient to justify this crudely crafted burden on respondents' freedom to engage in expressive activities." *See id.* at 477.

The Supreme Court again addressed off-site expressive activity in *City of San Diego v. Roe*, 543 U.S. 77 (2004) (per curiam). In this case, the Court upheld the San Diego Police Department's termination of an officer after discovering that in the adults-only section of eBay he had sold a video of himself stripping off a police uniform and performing a sex act and had also sold police equipment and uniforms. *Id.* at 78. Relying on *NTEU*, the *Roe* Court stated that, first, it must be determined whether there is a relationship between the expression and the workplace, and then, if there is such a relationship, the *Pickering/Connick* analysis applies. Under this approach, the case was easy: Because Roe chose to tie his Internet activities to his status as a police officer and to his department, his expression related to the workplace; the Court thus applied the *Pickering/Connick* analysis, and the City prevailed because Roe's expressive conduct did not address a matter of public concern. *See Roe*, 543 U.S. at 80-82.

In reaching this conclusion, the Court was able to avoid a number of more difficult questions. For example, it did not address whether, in order to receive *any* protection, the off-site expressive conduct must address a matter of public concern. *NTEU* likewise had not addressed this because much of the prohibited expressive activity in that case *did* address matters of public concern. *See* 513 U.S. at 466. Also, the *Roe* Court did not clarify how close the nexus must be between the expressive activity and the person's employment to trigger the *Pickering/Connick* analysis. Moreover, the Court never reached the question of what governmental interest would justify regulation of employees' expressive activities entirely unrelated to the workplace. *NTEU* had held that, where the prohibited expressive activity does not relate directly to the workplace, and involves speech beyond that of highly ranked officials, the government must make some kind of evidentiary showing that the activity actually has a disruptive effect on the workplace. *See* 513 U.S. at 468-74. Again, however, *NTEU* involved a sweeping prohibition on honoraria for entire classes of workers (including workers at lower levels); it did not address an adverse employment action with regard to an individual worker. Finally, in reaching its conclusion that the officer's expression in this case did not address a matter of public concern, the *Roe* Court offered another specific example of speech that fails the test while providing little useful guidance for other cases. Each of these issues emerges again in the next case.

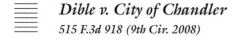

Dible v. City of Chandler

515 F.3d 918 (9th Cir. 2008)

Judge FERNANDEZ delivered the opinion of the Court.

I

Ronald and Megan Dible appeal from the district court's grant of summary judgment against them in their action against the City of Chandler, Arizona, the Chandler Police Department, and the Chandler Police Chief Bobby Joe Harris (collectively "the City"). Principally, the Dibles assert that Ronald Dible was a police officer whose rights under the First Amendment to the United States Constitution were violated when he was terminated for participating in (performing in, recording and purveying) a sexually explicit website with his wife. We affirm.

II

In January of 2002, the Chandler Police Department learned that one of its officers, Ronald Dible, was running a website featuring sexually explicit photographs and videos of his wife. After initially placing Ronald Dible on administrative leave and conducting an internal investigation into his involvement with the website, the City terminated his employment as a police officer.

Ronald Dible and his wife Megan Dible began running the website in September of 2000, after Megan Dible signed a contract with CDM Networks, which operated the website. The Dibles then posted pictures of Megan Dible on the website, under the pseudonym "Katelynn." Those photographs portrayed Megan Dible in various sexual poses and activities with Ronald Dible, another woman, and inanimate objects. The Dibles also posted, among other things, a videotape of Megan Dible masturbating that had been filmed by Ronald Dible. The Dibles did not intend to express any kind of message or engage in social or political commentary through the material they posted on their website. They participated in those activities to make money; it was as simple as that.

. . . Any computer user with internet capability could access the website's home page without charge. The home page featured partially nude pictures of Megan Dible in order to entice customers. If the user wanted to view more pictures of Megan Dible, a fee was required, but before the pictures could be reviewed, the user had to enter into a purported contract with CDM Networks. Once the user accepted the terms of the contract and paid the fee, he was free to view the website's sexually explicit photographs and videos.

The Dibles also offered a CD-ROM for sale on the website. . . . Although the photographs on the website and the CD-ROM generally did not show Ronald Dible's face, one of the photographs did.

The Dibles also promoted their website by attending "barmeets." The purpose of the barmeets was to have fans of the website meet Megan Dible, although Ronald Dible also attended. The barmeets, which took place at local bars, were open to the public, and attendees were free to take photographs. They did, and sometimes posted those on their own websites. Although some attendees knew Megan Dible only as Katelynn, others knew her true identity. At those barmeets, both Megan Dible and Ronald Dible posed in sexually suggestive ways with each other and with other people, some of whom were partially nude. The Dibles' photographs from the barmeets were compiled on a CD-ROM and were then sold through their website.

Ronald Dible believed, indeed most likely knew, that his position in the disreputable sexually explicit website business was not compatible with his position as a police officer and risked violating the City and Police Department rule against engaging "in conduct which might bring discredit to the City service." So he took steps to cover up his participation, and in so doing violated the rule that he could not engage in outside employment unless he first filled out and filed a request to engage in employment outside the department. He did not inform any Department officials about it. He did, however, tell a few people about it, including a fellow police officer, whom he urged to start his own website. The officer eventually did.

Sometime in the later part of 2001, rumors about the Dibles' website began circulating among members of the department, and eventually the news of the website filtered up to department officials. Upon learning about it, the police chief on January 25, 2002, ordered Ronald Dible to cease all activity with the website and placed him on administrative leave. The chief then opened an investigation into Ronald Dible's involvement with the website. The investigators questioned Ronald Dible about it, and, in response, he provided several misleading answers. After establishing that he was, in fact, involved in the website, the investigators questioned him about, among other things, whether he and Megan Dible had earned money from the site, and asked to see the contract between Megan Dible and CDM Networks.

By January 25, 2002, the press had also learned about the website and began reporting on it in an unflattering manner. The press reported that the website was run by the Dibles and that he was employed as a city police officer. The record contains no evidence identifying the person who alerted the press to the website's existence or to the Dibles' involvement in it, but, of course, a lot of people already knew. The result of that publicity was disquieting to say the least. A police lieutenant assigned to look into the situation spoke to a large number of officers and others, found that it had severely impacted their working situation, and declared that police officer morale "really hit bottom."

In due course, Ronald Dible's supervisor recommended his dismissal. The supervisor found that Ronald Dible had violated the department's regulation prohibiting its officers from bringing discredit to the city service, and that Ronald Dible had provided false answers to district investigators in the course of their investigation. Chief Harris approved Ronald Dible's dismissal.

Ronald Dible then appealed that decision to the City's Merit Board, which conducted an evidentiary hearing. At the hearing, several officers testified that they had been questioned and ridiculed about the website. A female officer, Amy Hedges, testified that she was called a "porn whore" by an individual she was attempting to arrest. She further testified that she was subjected to derogatory remarks while responding to a bar fight. Specifically, when she arrived at the bar, a patron began gyrating, told her to take off her clothes, and harassed her about the website. Officer Hedges testified that the patron's comments added to the instability of an already fluid field situation and confrontation. Another officer testified to the disrespect that he was shown after the website became publicly known. An investigating officer, who had interviewed many other officers, as well as other people, also testified to the impact of the Dibles' activity on the department. In addition, potential police recruits questioned an officer about the website on each of the five separate recruitment trips that she had conducted after the existence of the site became widely known to members of the public. Assistant Chief Joseph Gaylord testified that he believed the scandal involving Ronald Dible's participation in the sexually explicit website would negatively impact the department's efforts to recruit female officers for years to come. Ultimately, on April 3, 2002, the Merits Board issued a recommendation affirming the decision to discharge Ronald Dible.

IV

The major issue before us [in reviewing the district court's grant of summary judgment] is whether Ronald Dible's First Amendment right to freedom of speech was violated when he was terminated for maintaining and participating in a sexually explicit website with his wife, Megan Dible. In fact, for all practical purposes, the other issues in this case hinge on the decision of that issue. We will, therefore, consider it first and consider the other issues raised by the Dibles thereafter.

Freedom of Speech

[The court discussed *City of San Diego v. Roe*, 543 U.S. 77 (2004) as setting forth an analytical framework for consideration of First Amendment rights of governmental employees.] The Court first recognized that "[a] government employee does not relinquish all First Amendment rights otherwise enjoyed by citizens just by reason of his or her employment." That said, when a government employee's speech is under consideration, there are two paths of analysis, depending on whether the speech is related or unrelated to the person's employment. As the Court put it:

> [A] governmental employer may impose certain restraints on the speech of its employees, restraints that would be unconstitutional if applied to the general public. The Court has recognized the right of employees to speak on matters of public concern, typically matters concerning government policies that are of interest to the public at large, a subject on which public employees are uniquely qualified to comment. *See* [*Connick v. Myers; Pickering v. Bd. of Ed.*]. Outside of this category, the Court has held that when government employees speak or write on their own time on topics unrelated to their employment, the speech can have First Amendment protection, absent some governmental justification "far stronger than mere speculation" in regulating it. *United States v. Treasury Employees* (*NTEU*). We have little difficulty in concluding that the City was not barred from terminating Roe under either line of cases.

The Court then went on to consider whether Roe's speech activities were related or unrelated to his position as a police officer with the city. It determined that Roe's indecent activity, indeed, related to his employment. In so doing, the Court observed that in *NTEU* the speech in question was not only unrelated but also "had no effect on the mission and purpose of the employer." The Court also emphasized that in *NTEU* "none of the speech at issue 'even arguably [had] any adverse impact' on the employer." It finally pointed out that the City of San Diego had conceded that Roe's activities were unrelated in the sense that they were not concerned with the "workings or functioning" of the police department, but, it concluded:

> It is quite a different question whether the speech was detrimental to the SDPD. On that score the City's consistent position has been that the speech is contrary to its regulations and harmful to the proper functioning of the police force. The present case falls outside the protection afforded in *NTEU*. The authorities that instead control, and which are considered below, are this Court's decisions in *Pickering*, *Connick*, and the decisions which follow them.

Of course, as the Court noted, Roe had gone out of his way to identify himself with police work. Perhaps that alone would have sufficed to make his activity related to his employment. If that were the case, it must be said that Ronald Dible did not do what Roe did. Ronald Dible took some pains to keep the police out of the pictures, but because of other clues and information, it became publicly known that he was involved and that he was a police officer. In any event, Ronald Dible's attempts to conceal his activity came to nought and do not distinguish the underlying situation in *Roe*. Many a rule breaker does so clandestinely in the hope that his violations will not come to light and have untoward consequences. When that hope is dashed, the results and consequences for him are the same as they would have been if he had broken the rules overtly. Roe overtly broke his employer's rules (outside employment and immoral conduct) and he properly suffered the consequences by losing his job. Ronald Dible's discovered clandestine activity also broke his employer's rules (outside employment and conduct that brought disrepute) and he properly suffered the consequences by losing his job. In addition, it can be seriously asked whether a police officer can ever disassociate himself from his powerful public position sufficiently to make his speech (and other activities) entirely unrelated to that position in the eyes of the public and his superiors. Whether overt or temporarily hidden, Ronald Dible's activity had the same practical effect—it "brought the mission of the employer and the professionalism of its officers into serious disrepute."

That said, the Court has never explicitly defined what is or is not related, and we need not do so here. As in *Roe*, the result would be the same "under either line of cases." The Dibles cannot prevail. We will explain.

(1) *Related Speech*. If we determined that Ronald Dible's activities were related to his public employment, we would necessarily approach his First Amendment claim as did the Supreme Court in *Roe* [which quoted the *Pickering* balancing test. However, as] the Court explained, before an employee is even entitled to have the balancing test applied, the "speech must touch on a matter of 'public concern.'" The Court further pointed out: "*Connick* held that a public employee's speech is entitled to *Pickering* balancing only when the employee speaks 'as a citizen upon matters of public concern' rather than 'as an employee upon matters only of personal interest.'" And, while the borders of the territory of public concern are not entirely defined, they do encompass matters that are "of legitimate news interest; that is, a subject of general interest and of value and concern to the public at the time of publication," and even some private comments in the proper circumstances. So, for example, the Court has said that an employee's quiet statement to a fellow employee at a county constable's office, that she hoped that a future attempt at assassination of the President would succeed, touched on a matter of public concern. *See Rankin v. McPherson.*

No matter. Whatever a periplus of the outer limits of public concern might show, it was pellucid that Roe's vulgar behavior would be discovered to be outside of those borders. As the Court said, "there is no difficulty in concluding that Roe's expression does not qualify as a matter of public concern under any view of the public concern test. He fails the threshold test and *Pickering* balancing does not come into play." *Roe.*

The same is true of Ronald Dible's activities in this case. They did not give the public any information about the operations, mission or function of the police department, and were not even close to the kind of private remarks that the Court has countenanced. His activities were simply vulgar and indecent. They did not contribute speech on a matter of public concern. The Dibles could not prevail if Ronald Dible's speech is deemed to have been related to his employment.

(2) *Unrelated Speech.* If we determined that Ronald Dible's activities were unrelated to his public employment, we would also have to apply a balancing test. Interestingly enough, it is not entirely clear whether the public concern concept would be a necessary threshold to that balancing. In *Roe* the Supreme Court did not exactly say that the public concern concept must be considered, but it also did not expressly hold that the Court of Appeals' determination that public concern was part of the test was incorrect. And in *NTEU*, the Court pointed out that:

> Respondents' expressive activities in this case fall within the protected category of citizen comment on matters of public concern rather than employee comment on matters related to personal status in the workplace. The speeches and articles for which they received compensation in the past were addressed to a public audience, were made outside the workplace, and involved content largely unrelated to their government employment.

Moreover, in *Rankin*, the Court did indicate that a comment about the President was a matter of public concern, but *Rankin* dealt with an unrelated comment made at the workplace itself. We, however, need not resolve whether the public concern test must be satisfied in this instance. *See Locurto v. Giuliani*, 447 F.3d 159, 175 (2d Cir. 2006).

If a statement must be one of public concern when it consists of unrelated activity away from the workplace, Ronald Dible's conduct was no more protected than it would be if the activity were related, and the Dibles' claim would fail on that account. But, suppose passing the public concern test is not required when unrelated expressive activity takes place away from the work setting. What then? Again, we must balance the asserted First Amendment right against the government's justification. *See Roe.* The Dibles' First Amendment claim cannot survive that balance either.

We first note that a number of Supreme Court justices have expressed some dubiety about the strength of the protection offered to activities that can be said to be of the same ilk as those we deal with here, or, perhaps, of an even less indecent ilk. *See City of Erie v. Pap's A.M.*, 529 U.S. 277, 289 (2000) (plurality opinion) (stating that public nude dancing is "only within the outer ambit of the First Amendment protection"). . . . However, this court has said that plurality decisions of the Supreme Court do not make law and that "the degree of protection the first amendment affords speech does not vary with the social value ascribed to that speech by the courts." *Kev, Inc. v. Kitsap County*, 793 F.2d 1053, 1058 (9th Cir. 1986). None of those cases is exactly like the one at hand. We are not dealing with the rights of an ordinary citizen vis-à-vis the government; we are dealing with the rights of a governmental employee (a police officer at that) vis-à-vis his employer. In this context, the reflections of the Justices about the weight of the right to engage in public indecent activity commend themselves to our consideration. As *Roe* suggests, it is a bit difficult to give that activity the same weight as the right to engage in political debate [as in *City of Erie*] or to lecture on religion and black history or to write articles about the environment [as in *NTEU*]. Especially is that true where, as here, the employee admits that he was not interested in conveying any message whatsoever and was engaged in the indecent public activity solely for profit.

In any event, the interest of the City in maintaining the effective and efficient operation of the police department is particularly strong. It would not seem to require an astute moral philosopher or a brilliant social scientist to discern the fact that Ronald

Dible's activities, when known to the public, would be "detrimental to the mission and functions of the employer." *Roe*. And although the government's justification cannot be mere speculation, it is entitled to rely on "reasonable predictions of disruption." *Waters v. Churchill*, 511 U.S. 661 (1994) (plurality opinion).

Police departments, and those who work for them, are engaged in a dangerous calling and have significant powers. The public expects officers to behave with a high level of propriety, and, unsurprisingly, is outraged when they do not do so. The law and their own safety demands that they be given a degree of respect, and the sleazy activities of Ronald and Megan Dible could not help but undermine that respect. Nor is this mere speculation.

Almost as soon as Ronald Dible's indecent public activities became widely known, officers in the department began suffering denigration from members of the public, and potential recruits questioned officers about the Dibles' website. Moreover, the department feared that the recruiting of female officers would be affected because of what it seemed to say about the climate at the department. That is not rank speculation. In a similar case involving police officers' public sexual activities, the Eleventh Circuit Court of Appeals noted that this kind of activity by officers, once known, could not help but interfere with the functions and mission of the police department because "it reflected on [deputies'] fitness as deputies and undermined public confidence" in the department. *Thaeter v. Palm Beach County Sheriff's Office*, 449 F.3d 1342, 1356 (11th Cir. 2006). Just so.

We are not gallied by the Dibles' claim that Ronald Dible is being subjected to some kind of heckler's veto. Worries about a heckler's veto have generally dealt with the restriction of a citizen's speech based upon the anticipated disorderly reaction by members of an audience. *See Rosenbaum v. City and County of San Francisco*, 484 F.3d 1142, 1158-59 (9th Cir. 2007). Those worries do not directly relate to the wholly separate area of employee activities that affect the public's view of a governmental agency in a negative fashion, and, thereby, affect the agency's mission. The Dibles' argument ignores the fact that the public can form a negative view of a person due to his particular mode of expression—there is nothing unconstitutional about that. It also ignores the unique and sensitive position of a police department and its necessary and constant interactions with the public. . . .

As the Second Circuit Court of Appeals has pointed out, even where the unrelated expression is a matter of public concern—there a comment on race relations—police officers "are quintessentially public servants" and "part of their job is to safeguard the public's opinion of them." *Locurto*. Thus, said the court, the actions of the police department were not due to a heckler's veto, but rather an example of the government's accounting for the public's perception of the officers' actions when it considered the potential for disruption of the department's functions. *See also Rankin* (taking particular note of the fact that a clerical employee's comments were not made public and, therefore, did not discredit the constable's office).[7]

---

7. We have not overlooked *Flanagan v. Munger*, 890 F.2d 1557, 1566-67 (10th Cir. 1989) and *Berger v. Battaglia*, 779 F.2d 992, 1000-01 (4th Cir. 1985). However, to the extent that they minimize the potential for an actual effect on the efficiency and efficacy of police department functions arising from public perceptions of the inappropriate activities of police officers, they are severely undermined by *Roe*, and we decline to follow them.

In fine, whether Ronald Dible's activities were related to his employment or not, the City could discipline him for those activities without violating his First Amendment rights. Thus, the Dibles' claim to the contrary must be rejected.

[The court also rejected the Dibles' claim that their First Amendment rights to privacy and freedom of association were violated by the City. It recognized that the First Amendment implicates a right of privacy, which includes a right to make personal decisions and a right to keep personal matters private, and contains a right to the freedom of intimate expression and to associate with others in activities otherwise protected by the First Amendment. Nevertheless, the court found that, because the City had not released any information that connected the Dibles to the website, it could not have violated their right to privacy and intimate association by giving them unwanted publicity. The court went on to reject the association claim for the same reasons that it had rejected the speech claim, stating that "a governmental employee cannot avoid the strictures of the balancing tests that we have heretofore described by attempting to resurrect fallen speech claims as privacy and associational claims." It also affirmed the district court's grant of summary judgment on the Dibles' state law right to privacy, intentional infliction of emotional distress, and wrongful termination claims.]

CANBY, Circuit Judge, concurring in the judgment:

I

With all due respect, I am unable to join the majority opinion because I disagree with its resolution of Dible's First Amendment speech claim. Under the facts of this case and the existing precedent, the police department could not discharge Dible for his website expression without violating the First Amendment.

I have no quarrel with some of the majority's analysis. I agree that, if Dible's expressive website activity were properly characterized as employment-related, then his First Amendment claim would fail because his expression, while protected, was not of public concern. The majority opinion correctly reasons that this point is established by [*City of San Diego v. Roe*].

Dible's website activity was not employment-related, however. As the majority opinion points out, Dible was careful not to identify himself or his website with the police department or with police status at all. That fact differentiates his case from *Roe*. Certainly nothing in the activity Dible portrayed suggested a connection with the police. I am unwilling to conclude, for reasons I will set forth below, that such unrelated expression becomes related to Dible's employment simply because people who disapprove of his expression find out that he is a policeman and make their disapproval or disdain known to the police department in ways that could affect its work.

As the majority opinion points out, the Supreme Court has not, in *Roe* or its antecedents, made perfectly clear whether a governmental employee's expression unrelated to the employment must be of public concern to be protected. In my view it makes little sense to impose the public concern requirement for the protection of unrelated speech. The requirement of public concern comes from *Pickering*. Its usefulness is in making an exception to the right of a public employer to control the expression of employees in matters relating to their employment. One way of limiting the rule to its context, which I would follow, is to hold that there is no requirement that an employee's speech that is unrelated to his employment be of public concern in order to merit First Amendment protection. The Tenth Circuit adopted that rule in *Flanagan v. Munger*, 890 F.2d 1557, 1562-64 (1989). Another way of reaching the same result is to hold, as we did in *Roe v. City of San Diego*, 356 F.3d 1108, 1119 (9th Cir.), *rev'd*, 543 U.S. 77 (2004), that *any* speech by a government employee that is not about his employer, that occurs outside the workplace, and is directed to a segment of the general public, qualifies *ipso facto* as a matter of public concern. As the majority opinion here recognizes, the Supreme Court did not say this approach was incorrect when it reversed *Roe*. Similarly, in *Berger v. Battaglia*, 779 F.2d 992, 998 (4th Cir. 1985), the Fourth Circuit held, in a case of unrelated expression, that *all* such expression was of public concern unless it constituted a private personnel grievance. Either way—whether the public concern requirement is simply dispensed with for expression unrelated to employment, as I prefer, or whether the public concern requirement for unrelated speech is broadened to include virtually the universe of unrelated speech—the outcome is the same. Public concern should not be a hurdle depriving employee speech of First Amendment protection when that speech is unrelated to the employment.

Now, I recognize that pornography, although apparently popular, is not a very respected subject of First Amendment protection in many quarters. The majority opinion here reflects that distaste, variously characterizing Dible's expressive activities as "vulgar," "indecent," "sleazy," and "disreputable." But vigorous enforcement of the free speech guarantee of the First Amendment often requires that we protect speech that many, even a majority, find offensive. Pornography, and sexual expression in general, is protected by the First Amendment when it does not constitute obscenity (and there is no showing that Dible's expression meets that extreme standard). We should accept that fact and accord Dible's expression the constitutional protection to which it is entitled. The majority opinion here falls short of the First Amendment standard in two major respects.

Because Dible's expressive activity was not employment-related, the police department must demonstrate that the alleged harm caused by his expression was " 'real, not merely conjectural.' " *NTEU*. The evidence of harm in this case is so insubstantial that it can be characterized as "conjectural." An officer testified that he feared the effect on recruitment of female officers, but no such effect was demonstrated. At least three officers testified that they had been verbally harassed in a manner attributable to the website, but there was no testimony that this seriously interfered with the performance of their duties. In sum, the findings of interference with the mission of the police department are based on the conjecture that Dible's expressive activities might cause some persons to think less well of the police department and that this disfavor might in some ways lead to disruption of police activities. The evidence simply does not meet the *Treasury Employees* standard. It does not outweigh Dible's interest in expression, which is his "interest in engaging in free speech, not the value of the speech itself." *Flanagan*.[1]

A second flaw in the majority's analysis is that it enshrines the "heckler's veto" with respect to *all* conduct of a public employee, or at least of a police department

---

1. I place no significance at all on Dible's statement that he did not intend to convey any message in his expressive activity. His website constituted expression, and he has raised a First Amendment defense to his termination because of his website activity. It is equally irrelevant to his First Amendment protection that he sought to make money from his expression, as many speakers or writers do. *See, e.g., Smith v. California*, 361 U.S. 147, 150 (1959).

employee. Nothing that Dible did or said in relation to his website activities in itself caused any disruption to police department functions. The alleged (and minimal) disruption was caused by other persons' disapproval of Dible's activities once it became known that he was an officer of the police department. The rule to be drawn from the majority's analysis, apparently, is that police officers may be fired for engaging in expressive activities, unrelated to their employment, when numbers of the public disapprove of the expression vigorously and possibly disruptively. That rule empowers the heckler to veto the speech, and is inconsistent with the First Amendment. *See Terminiello v. Chicago*, 337 U.S. 1, 4-5 (1949). In such a situation, it is the duty of the police department to prevent the disruption by those opposed to the speech, not to suppress or punish the speech. [*See Cohen v. California*, 403 U.S. 15, 23 (1971).]

The heckler's veto applied to sexually expressive activities has disturbing potential for expansive application. A measurable segment of the population, for example, is vigorously antagonistic to homosexual activity and expression; it could easily be encouraged to mobilize were a police officer discovered to have engaged, off duty and unidentified by his activity, in a Gay Pride parade, or expressive cross-dressing, or any number of other expressive activities that might fan the embers of antagonism smoldering in a part of the population. For this reason, it is far better to adopt a rule that protects off-duty speech unrelated to employment when the speech itself causes no *internal* problems, and the only disruption is in the external relations between the police department and the public unhappy with the police officer's expression. The Tenth Circuit adopted just such a rule. *See Flanagan.* The Fourth Circuit avoided adopting an inflexible rule, but held that a police department could not prohibit off-duty, unrelated speech by an officer under circumstances parallel to those in Dible's case: "[N]ot only was the perceived threat of disruption only to external operations and relationships, it was caused not by the speech itself but by threatened reaction to it by offended segments of the public." *Berger.* This public reaction in *Berger* was not inconsequential; it threatened to disrupt the tenuous relationship between the police department and the black community. Even so, "this sort of threatened disruption by others reacting to public employee speech simply may not be allowed to serve as justification for public employer disciplinary action directed at that speech."

The majority opinion states that to the extent that *Flanagan* and *Berger* "minimize the potential for an actual effect on the efficiency and efficacy of police department functions arising from public perceptions of the inappropriate activities of police officers, they are severely undermined by *Roe.*" The rationale of *Flanagan* and *Berger*, however, was not that disruption was minimal, but that as part of the heckler's veto it could not support discipline of the employee. It is true that *Roe* permitted discipline of an officer because of public reaction to his expressive conduct, but that expressive conduct was purposely employment-related. The head of a governmental agency is entitled to control the speech of members of the agency with regard to agency-related matters, unless that speech is a matter of public concern. *Pickering.* But that rule is an exception to the general First Amendment protection of speech. *See NTEU.* To apply the same restriction to off-duty expression by a public employee, unrelated to his employment, is to reject the established principle that public employees may not be required to surrender their constitutional right of free speech as a condition of their employment. *Roe* did not extend to off-duty conduct unrelated to employment, and accordingly it did not undermine *Flanagan* and *Berger.* . . .

II

I concur in the judgment, however, because the record demonstrates that any rational trier of fact would find that Dible would have been discharged for making false statements to police department investigators, had he not been discharged for his website activity. *See Mt. Healthy City Sch. Dist. Bd. of Educ. v. Doyle*, 429 U.S. 274, 287 (1977). . . . Dible contends, however, that his false statements cannot be a ground for discharge because the entire investigation was instituted because of his First Amendment protected activity. [However, the] investigation by the police department in the present case was not illegitimate in its inception. The department was entitled to inquire into Dible's off-duty activity to see whether it was employment-related, which would bring it within the unprotected scope of *Roe*. In addition, the department had a policy requiring police officers to obtain prior approval before engaging in any outside employment, because certain jobs were deemed compromising. The department was entitled to inquire whether this policy had been violated. Nothing in the nature of the investigation entitled Dible to lie. . . .

NOTES

1. *Unresolved Issues Surrounding Off-Site Expression.* Recall the issues left unresolved in *NTEU* and *Roe*: (1) Must off-site expression be a matter of public concern to receive *any* protection? (2) How close must the nexus be between the expressive activity and the person's employment to trigger *Pickering/Connick* balancing? (3) What government interests are sufficient to justify regulation of employee expressive activity that is entirely unrelated to work? The *Dible* majority works hard to avoid answering the first two questions, but, in so doing, must answer the third—at least as necessary to support its alternative holding, which assumed the speech was unrelated to work. But does broad deference to the government's view of the importance of its interests mean that the answers to the first two questions are often irrelevant? Put another way, how likely is it that *any* expressive conduct by a police officer will be protected if it embarrasses the department?

Now compare this to how the concurring judge would resolve these three matters and how each resolution would affect the analysis of whether the speech is protected. For Judge Canby, the relatedness inquiry becomes paramount. Under this alternative framework, how likely is it that off-site expression related to work will be protected? But how about unrelated expression, whether involving a "matter of public concern" or not? What must the department show in order to regulate such unrelated expression? In making the determination that the speech in this case, unlike that in *Roe*, was unrelated to work, Judge Canby does not provide much analysis, but his focus appears to be on the extent to which the police officer made some reference to police work, the department, or his status as an officer. Other matters, including the content of the speech (i.e., how repugnant or embarrassing it might be) and how disruptive it is, are left to the second part of the inquiry, namely whether the department can demonstrate that the speech caused "real" harm. This approach offers a nice, clean analytical framework, but does it serve to protect any speech if one accepts the view that, given the nature of their work, police officers are representatives of the department and city 24/7?

The vast differences between the approaches to analyzing off-site expression claims reflected in the majority and concurring opinions are not merely a matter of academic interest. As their competing citations to other circuits make clear, federal courts are split on these matters. For a host of reasons, defendant police departments and individual supervisors prevail more often than not in these cases, but the *Flanagan* and *Berger* decisions are important counterexamples. *See generally* Mary-Rose Papandrea, *The Free Speech Rights of Off-Duty Government Employees*, 2010 BYU L. Rev. 2117 (2010) (arguing that off-duty, non-work-related speech by government employees should be entitled to presumptive protection because it is never possible to entirely separate the citizen from the employee).

2. *Even More Difficult Facts? Dible* was a more difficult case than *Roe* because Dible had made no reference to his position as a police officer or his police department on his website, although neither Ronald nor Megan Dible made much of an effort to keep their activities secret. Suppose Ronald had taken more pains to hide his identity from the beginning (to avoid having the public draw the connection with his police work) or to limit access to the site to a more selective group, but the public and his department ultimately found out anyway. Would the outcome on the First Amendment question have been different? If no, does that mean that a police department may prohibit *all otherwise legal*, sexually explicit expressive activity by its police officers? If yes, should a police officer's First Amendment right to expression depend on his or her ability or efforts to remain anonymous or unknown?

3. *Type of Speech.* In *Roe*, the Supreme Court had held that the sexually explicit video at issue in that case did not address a matter of public concern. The Court defined such a matter as "something that is a subject of legitimate news interest; that is, a subject of general interest and of value and concern to the public at the time of publication." 543 U.S. at 83-84. This standard may not provide much guidance for courts assessing very different kinds of speech (*see* the examples in Note 2 on page 406), thus requiring the periplus around its boundaries so feared by the *Dible* majority. But the speech at issue in *Roe* is similar enough to the expressive activity in *Dible* that the majority had no problem finding that Dible's Web site did not address a matter of public concern. Whether this conclusion is correct or not, are you gallied by the irony—that is, the sexually explicit expression at issue is deemed to be not a matter of public concern even though the principal reason the government employer wishes to regulate it is because it is a matter of significant concern to the public?

The *Dible* majority emphasized that certain forms of sexually explicit expression enjoy minimal First Amendment protection, Indeed, the majority went out of its way to make clear not only its distaste for such expression, but also the limited social value of sexually explicit materials distributed for profit. But, as the concurrence notes, much expression that may be deemed sexual in nature is still protected by the First Amendment. Can a police department's prohibition on "conduct which might bring discredit to the City service," "conduct unbecoming of an officer," and "immoral conduct" bar all such expression, consistent with the Constitution? How about the (legal) publication of semi-nude photos on an officer's Facebook page, for example, or sexual jokes or banter in off-site conversations, at a comedy club, or in an Internet chat room? Courts tend to side with police departments in off-site speech and association cases. *See, e.g., Piscottano v. Murphy*, 511 F.3d 247 (2d Cir. 2007) (holding that the Department of Corrections established that the conduct of several officers, expressing their approval of the Outlaws Motorcycle Club, had the potential to reflect negatively on its operations, and that its interest in "maintaining the efficiency, security, and integrity of its operations outweighed the associational interests" of the officers); see also *Anzaldua v. Ne. Ambulance & Fire Prot. Dist.*, 793 F.3d 822 (8th Cir. 2015) (holding fire department has greater interest in regulating speech than typical government employer to promote efficiency, loyalty, obedience, morale, and public confidence). But should they?

4. *Beyond Law Enforcement Officers.* Whatever you might think of the deference courts tend to accord to law enforcement agencies, how free should other types of government employers be in determining what off-site conduct is unbecoming or immoral, or, for that matter, sufficiently embarrassing or scandalous to justify regulation? Certainly, attempts by a government agency to regulate off-site expressive conduct or associations that implicate fundamental rights—religious freedom, intimate relationships, etc.—will be subject to some scrutiny. *See, e.g., Cameron v. Grainger County*, 274 F. App'x 437 (6th Cir. 2008) (denying summary judgment because a reasonable jury could find that former deputy county clerk's decision to marry into a family that was politically opposed to reelection of her employer was a motivating factor in the employer's decision to fire her); *cf. Flaskamp v. Dearborn Pub. Schs.*, 385 F.3d 935 (6th Cir. 2004) (upholding a school board's decision to disallow tenure to a teacher who had an intimate relationship with a former student). But what about other expressive conduct? Would your answer depend on the type of public employee who engages in the conduct of, for example, teachers, attorneys, public health workers, regulatory inspectors, clerical staff, or janitors? Does the mission of the agency matter, or whether the particular employee is supposed to be a "role model"? Also, would your answer depend as well on the viewpoint or opinions expressed? *See, e.g., Wales v. Bd. of Educ.*, 120 F.3d 82, 85 (7th Cir. 1997) (asserting that "[a] school district is entitled to put in its classrooms teachers who share its educational philosophy"). Should the fact that the speech or association is highly offensive to the community the agency serves be enough to justify the employer's adverse employment action? *See Melzer v. Bd. of Educ.*, 336 F.3d 185 (2d Cir. 2003) (upholding the termination of a teacher after it became known that he was a member of the North American Man/Boy Love Association in part because teachers must respect the views of parents in the community); see also Mary-Rose Papandrea, *Social Networks and the Law: Social Media, Public School Teachers, and the First Amendment*, 90 N.C. L. Rev. 1597 (2012).

5. *Hate Speech.* Should a government agency have greater discretion to regulate off-site, legal expression that might be characterized as "hate speech"—for example, the publication of racist or sexist statements or jokes, anti-Semitic caricatures, or cartoon depictions deeply offensive to Muslims—than expressive conduct that is "merely" irreverent or offensive to some but not within the foregoing categories? *See, e.g., Pappas v. Giuliani*, 290 F.3d 143, 147 (2d Cir. 2002) (noting the importance of maintaining legitimacy in the community in upholding the termination of a police officer who disseminated racist and anti-Semitic writings). In an age in which hate or other offensive speech (whether in person or in various media) appears to be on the rise in the political discourse and so unlikely to remain hidden from an employer, this issue has taken on new salience. For example, following the 2017 protests by white nationalists in Charlottesville, Virginia, pictures of protesters posted online led to their identification by employers. *See, e.g.*, Maura Judkis, *Charlottesville White Nationalist Demonstrator Loses Job at Libertarian Hot Dog Shop*, THE WASHINGTON POST (Aug. 14, 2017 https://www.washingtonpost.com/news/food/wp/2017/08/14/charlottesville-white-nationalist-demonstrator-fired-from-libertarian-hot-dog-shop/?utm_term=.4d052886da01). As we will explore in the next section, a protestor working for a private employer likely has no protection from termination as a result of the protest. But what if the employer were a public entity? Is the resulting offense or dissension by other employees or the public enough to justify termination? *See Grutzmacher v. Howard Cnty.*, 851 F.3d 332 (4th Cir. 2017) (upholding a fire department's termination of a paramedic responsible for supervising other first responders in part because his social media posts with perceived racist undertones interfered with the employer's interest in provision of services, outweighing the employee's interest in speaking on the matter).

Note that much of this expression is likely to address matters of public concern; *see* Note 2, page 406. Although again, the extent to which this matters for off-site conduct unrelated to work is unresolved. Recall that the fact that the particular expression would be unacceptable or offensive to most people does not preclude constitutional protection, even if the expression is at work. *See Rankin*, 483 U.S. at 390. So why is "hate speech" and certain other forms of "highly offensive" speech distinguishable? Is greater deference to the employer justified because, at least in some contexts (e.g., employment discrimination), the speech itself might be illegal? If employers did not have broad discretion to regulate such speech might there be troublesome downstream consequences for them, at least in some contexts?

6. *Private Ordering and Deference.* As in Chapter 6, the overarching themes of private ordering and the appropriate level of deference to employer prerogatives are also central to the off-site conduct inquiry. While public employees cannot be required to "waive" prospectively their First Amendment rights, *Roe* and *Dible* demonstrate how a public employer's framing of job responsibilities and conditions, and, accordingly, a worker's decision to accept the position so defined, may limit the freedom the employee has in off-site expression and conduct. Indeed, law enforcement departments may apply the motto that "you are a police officer twenty-four hours a day, seven days a week" more or less aggressively, and this may ultimately determine the scope of the employee's speech rights. Moreover, as a practical matter, an employee begins litigation in a far weaker position if he or she must concede knowledge of an agreement to department guidelines and practices with regard to off-site and after-hours conduct, whether classified as "unbecoming," "immoral," offensive, or otherwise. Deference also plays a role if, ultimately, the court seeks to balance the employee's interest in off-site expression against the employer's interest in avoiding harm to its mission or disruption of its operations. Note how the majority and concurring opinions in *Dible* differ on this question. *See generally* Heidi Kitrosser, *The Special Value of Public Employee Speech*, 2015 Sup. Ct. Rev. 301(2015); Pauline T. Kim, *Market Norms and Constitutional Values in the Government Workplace*, 94 N.C.L. Rev. 601, 647 (2016).

7. *Blogging and Other Web-Based Activities.* This discussion brings us back to the high-profile issue of employee blogging and other Web-based activities, discussed more fully at page 371 in Chapter 6. Under the framework in *NTEU* and *Roe*, public employee Internet activity that has a nexus with the workplace—either occurs at work or has work-related content—may have First Amendment protection but will be subject to the *Pickering/Connick* analysis. Internet activity that bears no relationship to work may be more likely to receive protection, although much remains unclear and seemingly depends on the nature of the expression, the worker's position, the role or mission of the agency, and, again, the level of deference courts may be willing to accord the government's justification for its actions. *See e.g.,* Paul M. Secunda, *Blogging While (Publicly) Employed: Some First Amendment*

Implications, 47 U. LOUISVILLE L. REV. 679 (2009); *see also Grutzmacher v. Howard Cnty.*, 851 F.3d 332 (4th Cir. 2017) (see Note 5 above). *But see Liverman v. City of Petersburg*, 844 F.3d 400 (4th Cir. 2016) (holding that a complete prohibition on social media posts that would discredit the city's police department was unconstitutional because the "speculative ills" the policy targeted were not sufficient to justify such broad restrictions).

8. *Other Protections for Public Employees.* Public employees may also enjoy certain additional protections for their speech or associational activities. Government restrictions on employee speech and expressive activity may run afoul of the Free Exercise, Equal Protection, and Due Process clauses of the Constitution. Thus, as discussed in Chapter 6, a government employer could not discipline or discharge an employee because of the employee's bona fide religious associations, *see Shrum v. City of Coweta*, 449 F.3d 1132 (10th Cir. 2006), or off-site associations that implicate fundamental rights, including intimate associations, unless the action is the result of a generally applicable policy that is justified by some governmental interest. *See* Chapter 6, at page 335. Similarly, statutory prohibitions on discrimination will limit a government agency's ability to regulate or prohibit both workplace and off-site conduct. *See id.*

Also, civil service codes and other statutes governing the public workplace often contain prohibitions against termination absent just cause, "good behavior," and other terms that restrict public employers' discretion in—and limit the reasons for—disciplining or terminating their employees. For example, federal law limits employee dismissals for misconduct to situations in which the agency can demonstrate that the misconduct impairs the efficiency of the service it provides and, hence, that a dismissal would promote efficiency. *See* 5 U.S.C. §§1101-5 (2018); 5 U.S.C. §7513(a) (2018). However, this greater substantive protection also has a procedural price: The Supreme Court has held that employees covered by the federal government's comprehensive civil service regime may seek remedies—even for constitutional violations—only within that scheme. *See Bush v. Lucas*, 462 U.S. 367 (1983). State civil service codes do not preclude federal constitutional claims brought under 42 U.S.C. §1983, but employee remedies for constitutional violations may nevertheless be limited by qualified immunity and other employer defenses. *See generally* Paul M. Secunda, *Whither the* Pickering *Rights of Federal Employees?* 79 U. COLO. L. REV. 1101 (2007).

In addition, collective bargaining agreements governing some government workers may carve out additional areas of protection and offer additional procedural constraints on agency discretion. Moreover, government agencies certainly may otherwise grant to their employees—unilaterally or by agreement—more protection than the First Amendment affords. *See, e.g., Waters v. Churchill*, 511 U.S. 661, 674 (1994) ("[T]he government may certainly choose to give additional protections to its employees beyond what is mandated by the First Amendment. . . .").

9. *Statutory Restrictions on Political Activity.* The Hatch Act, 5 U.S.C. §§7321-7326 (2018), and parallel state statutes, place restrictions on political activities by covered government employees, but also preserve certain freedoms. The Act and comparable state regimes were passed to prevent corruption and undue influence and, hence, impose significant restrictions on the partisan political activities of government workers. Many of these restrictions have been upheld in the face of First Amendment challenges. *See, e.g., United States Civil Serv. Comm'n v. Ass'n of Letter Carriers*, 413 U.S. 548 (1973); *Broadrick v. Oklahoma*, 413 U.S. 601 (1973) (upholding Oklahoma's version of the statute). However, amendments to the Hatch Act in 1993, *see* Pub. L. No. 103-94, 107 Stat. 1001 (1993), and exceptions in state statutes now provide limited rights for employees to take part in campaigns and other political activities while off-duty. Other activities are still banned, including the use of one's position for political influence, soliciting contributions from parties with business before the employee's agency, or engaging in political activities while on duty.

PROBLEMS

7-1. Michael Rasmusson is employed by the City Department of Health Services ("DHS") as a chemist's aide. In late May, DHS's Director of Workplace Diversity ("the Director") alerted all of its employees that June would be designated "Gay, Lesbian, Bisexual, and Transgender ("GLBT") Pride Month."

On June 2, another employee sent an e-mail to all co-workers, including Rasmusson, outlining the history of the gay and lesbian movement in the United States. Rasmusson e-mailed a reply to all recipients, which stated in part:

> I will not participate in gay celebrations because the Bible teaches that homosexuality is a horrible sin and those who practice it will not inherit the Kingdom of God. It is just as wrong for homosexuals to cause civil disorder today as it was in 1969 [the year the movement was founded], and they shouldn't have any more rights today than they did then.

The other employee then complained to the Director, as did other employees. The Director and a human resources officer then informed Rasmusson that sexual orientation is a protected status under state law and that it is unlawful to discriminate against individuals based on this status. He was further informed at the meeting that the DHS considered his e-mail messages to be in violation of this law.

On June 10, Rasmusson sent an e-mail message to one of DHS's high-ranking officials, in which he objected to the display of homosexual literature in the lobby of DHS's building and stated that homosexuality is an unhealthy lifestyle that should not be promoted.

On June 17, Rasmusson received an e-mail from another employee inviting members of the department to a voluntary Ellen DeGeneres "coming out" party (at which they would watch together the famous 1997 television episode of *Ellen*, now on DVD). Rasmusson sent the following e-mail in response to this message:

> How could a program such as this where Ellen "comes out" and tells everyone she is a lesbian be humorous? This is nothing for her to be proud of and we should not encourage her in this. Should we also have a party when a man "comes out" and tells everyone he is a child molester?

DHS contends that the employee who sent the invitation, and hence, the recipient of Rasmusson's responsive e-mail, is a lesbian.

Shortly thereafter, Rasmusson was advised by his supervisor that he should not send out any further messages expressing his views on homosexuality. The supervisor further told Rasmusson that, although he is entitled to his personal views, his actions could constitute harassment as defined by DHS's harassment policy. In response, Rasmusson told the supervisor that he should be able to express his opinion on these matters like any other employee and that he intends to do so in response to any further DHS e-mails or activities endorsing homosexuality. At that point, the supervisor terminated Rasmusson.

Assume for purposes of this problem that the relevant state law prohibits employment discrimination based on sexual orientation. Also, assume that Rasmusson has no claim under the Free Exercise Clause or for religious discrimination.

Does Rasmusson have a free speech claim? What are Rasmusson's best arguments? How about DHS's? How likely is Rasmusson to prevail? What additional information, if any, would help you assess the likelihood of success? *See Brown v. Minnesota Dep't of Health*, Civ. No. 98-63 (JRT/RLE) (D. Minn. 1998).

If DHS asks for your advice on how it should structure or restructure GLBT Pride Month to reduce the risk of liability (to Rasmusson or others) in the future, what advice would you give? Does this kind of initiative create inherent liability risks, or can it be organized in a way that no speech-related liability is possible?

7-2. Assume the same facts as in 7-1 except, instead of sending the messages described above, Rasmusson was terminated or disciplined by DHS after he responded to GLBT Pride Month in one of the following three ways:

a. Posting information about and criticisms of the event on a socially conservative blog.
b. Criticizing what he called the "perverse gay and lesbian lifestyle" on the blog, but never referring to his employer or the Pride Month event in his postings.
c. Publicly supporting a local campaign pursuing a ballot initiative to repeal the state statute prohibiting discrimination based on sexual orientation and posting campaign flyers in his work cubicle.

Would the change in the facts in each of these three scenarios affect your analysis? If so, how?

7-3. In a well-publicized incident, Derek Fenton, a New Jersey Transit Authority employee, was fired from his job after he burned pages of the Koran on the ninth anniversary of the September 11 terrorist attacks on the United States to protest the proposed Islamic center near Ground Zero. The ACLU filed suit on behalf of Fenton against the Authority, alleging that his termination violated his First Amendment rights. Eventually, the case settled, and NJ Transit reinstated Fenton without requiring him to recant or disavow his actions. For further discussion of the facts of the case and its ultimate resolution, *see* http://www.npr.org/blogs/thetwo-way/2011/04/22/135635324/new-jersey-to-rehire-transit-worker-fired-for-burning-quran/; http://www.nj.com/news/index.ssf/2010/11/nj_aclu_to_sue_nj_transit_for.html.

If this case had not settled, what would Fenton have had to prove? What defenses would have been available to the New Jersey Transit Authority? In light of the facts and the law as set forth in this chapter, how likely is it that Fenton would have prevailed? What other reasons might have led the Authority to settle the matter?

B.   THE PRIVATE WORKPLACE

In the private workplace, where neither civil service codes nor constitutional protections for expressive activity protect workers from employer actions, the sources of protection for employee speech and associational preferences are very limited. *See* David C. Yamada, *Voices from the Cubicle: Protecting and Encouraging Private Employee Speech in the Post-Industrial Workplace*, 19 Berkeley J. Emp. & Lab. L. 1 (1998). Indeed, unlike privacy, there are *no* traditional common-law torts that protect employee speech directly. The more recently developed public policy tort may provide some protection, but only in very narrow situations such as speech protected as whistleblowing. And, as discussed in Chapter 6, although the new Restatement of Employment Law (ALI 2015) would provide some limited protections for associational activities, it has yet to be adopted by the courts. *See* Chapter 6 at page 373 (discussing Restatement §7.08). Thus, as a general matter, employees in the private sector are left with a limited number of statutory protections for speech. These protections tend to apply only to certain types or categories of speech or association.

First, various statutory protections discussed elsewhere in this text may protect employee speech and expression directly or indirectly. For example, as discussed in Chapter 4, employee statements may be protected due to their content under federal and state statutes that prohibit employer retaliation against whistleblowers and those who testify in judicial or administrative proceedings. Also, as discussed in Chapter 6, federal and state antidiscrimination laws may protect employees from adverse treatment for certain associations, including religious affiliations and interracial intimate relationships, and occasional expressive conduct associated with other protected classifications. Moreover, some of the privacy protections discussed in that chapter, including the federal wiretapping statute, protect employees from highly intrusive or secret monitoring of their communications, which has the effect of protecting the content of these communications.

In addition, as also discussed in Chapter 6, a number of states have enacted statutes that protect both public- and private-sector employees from adverse employment actions resulting from legal, off-site conduct and personal and political associations. *See, e.g.*, Cal. Lab. Code §§96(k), 98.6 (2018); Col. Rev. Stat. §24-34-402.5 (2018) (prohibiting employers from terminating employees for lawful off-site activities absent job relatedness); Minn. Stat. §181.938 (2018) (same); N.Y. Lab. Law §201-d (McKinney 2018); Wash. Rev. Code § 42.17A.495(2) (2018) ("No employer or labor organization may discriminate against an officer or employee in the terms or conditions of employment for (a) the failure to contribute to, (b) the failure in any way to support or oppose, or (c) in any way supporting or opposing a candidate, ballot proposition, political party, or political committee."). In a 2012 article, Professor Eugene Volokh found that about half of the states have statutes addressing these matters, although their protections vary widely. *See generally* Eugene Volokh, *Private Employees' Speech and Political Activity: Statutory Protection Against Employer Retaliation*, 16 Tex. Rev. L. & Pol. 295 (2012); *see also* Restatement of Employment Law §7.08, Reporters Notes, cmt. b (citing state statutes). Of course, none of these statutes provides absolute protections: Each allows, explicitly or implicitly, employers to defend their actions by showing that they are necessary to serve a legitimate business purpose.

On its face, the most sweeping state protection is a Connecticut statute that makes an employer liable for discharging or disciplining an employee on account of the employee's exercise of rights guaranteed in the First Amendment or parallel portions of the state constitution, provided that such exercise does not "materially interfere with the employee's bona fide job performance or the working relationship between the employee and employer." Conn. Gen. Stat. §31-51q (2018). The Connecticut Supreme Court confirmed that the statute was intended to apply the free speech guarantees of the federal and state constitutions directly to private employers. *See Cotto v. United Technologies Corp.*, 738 A.2d 623 (Conn. 1999). The statute therefore provides potentially broad protection for public and private employee speech and association. However, given the qualifying language in the statute and, as you have now seen, the qualified nature of employee speech rights under the Constitution, it is not clear how meaningful the protection is. Indeed, in *Cotto* itself, the court found that an employee allegedly terminated for refusing to display at his workstation an American flag distributed by his employer did not state a claim under the statute. The court reasoned that no First Amendment–type interest was implicated because the employer's flag display directive did not require the employee to do or say anything related to his own political beliefs, did not compel him to "assume the risk that others might attribute to him any political beliefs about the flag that he did not share," and, hence, did not constitute coercion of expression or belief. *Id.* at 633-34. More recently, in *Shumann v. Dianon Systems, Inc.*, 43 A.3d 111 (Conn. 2012), the Connecticut Supreme Court rejected the argument that protections under the act are broader than those guaranteed under the Constitution, holding that *Garcetti* official duties limitation applies to claims under the statute.

Federal labor law provides another potentially important, albeit limited protection for employee expressive activities regarding workplace terms and conditions, even in the nonunionized context. Section 8(a)(1) of the National Labor Relations Act ("NLRA"), 29 U.S.C. §158(a)(1) (2018), protects an employee's expressive conduct in two important respects. First, it prohibits discharging an employee for organizing workers. Beyond this, however, it protects all workers in their right under §7 of the NLRA to "concerted activities for the purpose of . . . mutual aid or protection," even apart from the formation of a union. *See* 29 U.S.C. §157 (2014) ("Employees shall have the right to . . . engage in other concerted activities for the purpose of collective bargaining or other mutual aid or protection, and shall also have the right to refrain from any or all such activities. . . ."). In order to qualify for this protection, the employee activity must be "concerted"—that is, it must involve or be in preparation for group activity and involve a matter of potential common concern among employees, rather than merely activity by the worker solely on his or her own behalf. It must also involve "mutual aid and protection," which requires that it be reasonably work-related, addressing the conditions or terms of employment. Note that while other sources of speech and association rights tend to accord the greatest protection to off-site expressive activities unrelated to work, the "mutual aid and protection" requirement means that the protection under the NLRA applies *only* to work-related expression, whether it occurs on or off-site. For updates on the NLRB's social media-related actions, *see* Chapter 6, page 377. Finally, even if the conduct is concerted and has a work-related object, it is protected only if it constitutes "protected activity," a term of art in labor law. Activity is unprotected if it is unlawful, violent, or unduly disruptive to the workplace, but even peaceful but "disloyal" conduct can be unprotected. *See, e.g., NLRB v. Fansteel Metallurgical Corp.*, 306 U.S. 240 (1939) (finding prolonged sit-down strike resulting in seizure of employer's plant and destruction of some of its property to be concerted but unprotected activity); Charlotte Garden, *Citizens, United, and* Citizens United*: The Future of Labor Speech Rights?*, 53 Wm. & Mary L. Rev. 1 (2011) (discussing and critiquing various limits on protected concerted activity). However, mere offensiveness or harshness of the speech is not enough to make it unprotected. *See, e.g., Cooper Tire & Rubber Co. v. NLRB*, 866 F.3d 885 (8th Cir. 2017) (upholding the NLRB's finding that the employee could not be terminated for racist comments he made towards strikebreakers crossing the picket line because they were made as part of the picket and not persistent, threatening, or intimidating to a specific employee).

Consider how this protection for concerted activity might protect employee speech in a now familiar fact pattern: *Connick*. Although Myers would have had no concerted activity claim under the NLRA because the Act does not apply to public employers, a number of state labor statutes—which may apply to some classes of state and municipal employees—provide parallel protections for such activities. *See, e.g.,* William A. Herbert, *Can't Escape from the Memory: Social Media and Public Sector Labor Law*, 40 N. Ky. L. Rev. 427, 455-82 (2013) (discussing concerted activity protections under a number of state labor statutes). Suppose Myers had been working as a prosecutor in one of these states and was covered under the state's statute. If she had circulated a similar questionnaire in her office, might her speech have been entitled to protection? Or was it not "concerted"?

Beyond these provisions, the two other potential, albeit rarely available sources of protection for employees in the private sector are the public policy tort and contract.

Edmondson v. Shearer Lumber Products
75 P.3d 733 (Idaho 2003)

Walters, Justice.

This is a wrongful termination of employment case. The employee appeals from the district court's dismissal of the action upon the employer's motion for summary judgment [and denial of his motion to amend his complaint]. We affirm.

Facts

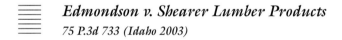
Michael Edmondson was employed by Shearer Lumber Products for twenty-two years at the company's Elk City mill. In 1999, he became a salaried employee and on his most recent performance review, he received a rating of "very good."

However, on February 15, 2000, the plant manager, David Paisley, following directions from his superiors fired Edmondson, by reading a statement that informed Edmondson: "Because of your continued involvement in activities that are harmful to the long-term interests of Shearer Lumber Products, we are terminating your employment immediately."

It was well known at Shearer Lumber that Edmondson was extensively involved in the community and regularly attended public meetings concerning matters of public interest and concern, such that he was recognized with the Idaho GEM Citizen Award by then Governor Batt. In January of 2000, Edmondson attended a public meeting of a group known as Save Elk City. One of the leaders of the group was the resource manager at Shearer Lumber, Dick Wilhite, who at the group meetings encouraged public support for the proposal that Save Elk City had submitted to the Federal Lands Task Force Working Group for consideration as to how best to manage the Nez Perce National Forest. Edmondson attended the group meetings, but he made no comments on the group's proposal. Nor did he discuss his opinions regarding the Save Elk City proposal at work with other employees.

Shearer Lumber did not openly campaign for the Save Elk City proposal, but Edmondson later learned from Wilhite that the proposal submitted in the name of Save Elk City was the project of Shearer Lumber's owner, Dick Bennett. At that time, Wilhite and Edmondson discussed the various outstanding proposals that might be competing for the Task Force's recommendation to the State Land Board, but Edmondson did not declare a preference for any of the proposals.

Shearer Lumber obtained information that Edmondson had attended meetings of the Task Force, had contacted someone in the administration of the Task Force, and was opposed to the collaborative project that Shearer had sponsored and submitted on behalf of the Save Elk City group. Edmondson was twice called into meetings at Shearer Lumber, where he claimed he was subjected to intimidation and pressure from Wilhite, Paisley, and John Bennett, Shearer's general manager. It was made clear that Edmondson was *not* to form any opinions on or make any statements to the Federal Lands Task Force. In effect, Edmondson was warned that any opposition to the collaborative project that was contrary to Shearer's interest would lead to serious consequences. Edmondson was informed at the February 2, 2000, meeting that Shearer Lumber wanted all of its employees to support the projects the mill was involved in, if they wanted to avoid serious consequences that would result if the project was derailed or negatively impacted.

John Bennett testified in his deposition that the reason Edmondson was terminated was that Edmondson was opposing the project that Shearer Lumber Products supported, in direct conflict with the company's goals that could ultimately jeopardize a Task Force decision favorable to Shearer's interests. Bennett also attributed to Edmondson contact with the Task Force administration, although it was Edmondson's wife, Jamie, who had made inquiries to the Task Force. . . .

* * *

[Edmondson sued Shearer Lumber for wrongful termination of employment, but the lower court awarded summary judgment to Shearer because Edmondson's allegations did not fall within Idaho's limited public policy exception.]

Discussion

I . . .

A. The district court did not err in granting summary judgment on the claim of breach of public policy exception to the at-will doctrine.

In Idaho, the only general exception to the employment at-will doctrine is that an employer may be liable for wrongful discharge when the motivation for discharge contravenes public policy. *MacNeil v. Minidoka Memorial Hosp.*, [701 P.2d 208 (Idaho 1985)]. . . . The purpose of the exception is to balance the competing interests of society, the employer, and the employee in light of modern business experience. *Crea v. FMC Corp.*, 16 P.3d 272. 275 (Idaho 2000). The public policy exception has been held to protect employees who refuse to commit unlawful acts, who perform important public obligations, or who exercise certain legal rights or privileges. *Sorensen v. Comm Tek, Inc.*, 799 P.2d 70, 74 (Idaho 1990). Public policy of the state is found in the constitution and statutes. *Boise-Payette Lumber Co. v. Challis Indep. Sch. Dist. No. 1*, 268 P. 26 (Idaho 1928). "In the absence of case law or statutory language . . ., the Court finds no basis for expanding the Idaho law that defines the public policy exception to the at-will doctrine." *Lord v. Swire Pacific Holdings, Inc.*, 203 F. Supp. 2d 1175, 1180 (D. Idaho 2002).

Courts have recognized that public policy expressed in the constitution and the statutes of the state may serve as a basis for finding an exception to the employment at-will doctrine. *See generally* 82 AM. JUR. 2d *Wrongful Discharge* §19, at 692 (1992). The First Amendment prohibits the government from restraining or abridging freedom of speech and assembly. Article I, §9 of the Idaho Constitution also guarantees the right of free speech: "Every person may freely speak, write and publish on all subjects, being responsible for the abuse of that liberty." Article I, §10 of the Idaho Constitution guarantees the right of freedom of association: "The people shall have the right to assemble in a peaceful manner, to consult for their common good; to instruct their representatives, and to petition the legislature for the redress of grievances." The First Amendment and Article I, §§9 and 10 of the Idaho Constitution do not apply to alleged restrictions imposed by private parties, however. . . .

Edmondson maintains that he was wrongfully terminated because he exercised his constitutionally protected rights of free speech and association. He argues that the public policy at issue prohibits restrictions on free speech and association. [But the cases he relies on] all deal with governmental restrictions on free speech and associative rights of employees of public agencies, which are inapplicable in the private employment context in which Edmondson worked. The prevailing view among those courts addressing the issue in the private sector is that state or federal constitutional free speech cannot, in the absence of state action, be the basis of a public policy exception in wrongful discharge claims. *See Tiernan v. Charleston Area Med. Ctr., Inc.*, 506 S.E. 578, 589-90 (W. Va. 1998), and cases cited therein.

Edmondson argues that I.C. §18-7901[1] expresses a public policy extending constitutional free speech protection to relationships between private employers and its employees. The district court did not make a finding specifically addressing I.C. §18-7901, but even if it had, the facts alleged by Edmondson regarding his termination fall far short of describing conduct that was harassing, intimidating or threatening and based upon the descriptive list set forth in the statute.[2]

Finally, Edmondson urges that public policy is implicated wherever the power to hire and fire is utilized to dictate the terms of an employee's political activities and associations, relying on *Novosel v. Nationwide Ins. Co.*, 721 F.2d 894, 900 (3d Cir. 1983). There the court held that an important public policy was at stake and that Novosel's allegations that the employer coerced political activity stated a wrongful discharge claim. *Id.* However, the public policy adopted in *Novosel* has not been endorsed by any other court, not even the Pennsylvania state courts within the federal district of the Circuit that issued *Novosel.* We likewise decline to extend Idaho's public policy exception through the adoption of *Novosel.*

Accordingly, we hold that an employee does not have a cause of action against a private sector employer who terminates the employee because of the exercise of the employee's constitutional right of free speech. The district court's dismissal of the claim of breach of public policy exception to the at-will doctrine is affirmed. . . .

III.

The district court did not err in denying Edmondson's motion to amend.

Following the decision of the district court on summary judgment, Edmondson filed a motion to amend his complaint to assert a breach of contract claim and a breach of the covenant of good faith and fair dealing. The district court denied the motion after a hearing, holding that the record did not support a claim for breach of an implied-in-fact contract. The district court also held that the record failed to show that the at-will relationship was somehow modified or did not apply to Edmondson.

. . . A limitation of an at-will employment will be implied when, from all the circumstances surrounding the relationship, a reasonable person could conclude that both parties intended that either's party's right to terminate the relationship was limited by the implied-in-fact agreement. *Mitchell v. Zilog, Inc.*, 874 P.2d 520, 523 (Idaho 1994). A plaintiff's subjective understanding is insufficient to establish an express or implied agreement limiting at-will employment. *Arnold v. Diet Center, Inc.*, 746 P.2d 1040 (Idaho Ct. App. 1987). Edmondson's personal belief that the company would not terminate him for attending public meetings, which the company allowed him to attend, or, would not terminate him without good cause, does not create limitations on Shearer's right to terminate him at will. . . .

---

1. I.C. §18-7901 provides as follows: The legislature finds and declares that it is the right of every person regardless of race, color, ancestry, religion or national origin, to be secure and protected from fear, intimidation, harassment, and physical harm caused by the activities of groups and individuals.

2. We do not suggest that the legislature's descriptive list should be deemed to exclude other well-recognized protected classes such as age, gender, or persons with mental or physical disabilities.

Justice KIDWELL, dissenting.

I wholeheartedly support the presumption that employment in Idaho is "at-will" unless otherwise provided. Unlike the majority, however, I would hold that there is a narrow, but important, public policy exception to the at-will presumption for certain exercises of one's first amendment rights. Therefore, I respectfully dissent. . . .

As the majority has stated, public policy may be imbedded in statutes. *See, e.g., Watson v. Idaho Falls Consol. Hosps., Inc.*, 720 P.2d 632 (Idaho 1986). I believe that statutes are not the only place in which one may find public policy. Indeed, one may find the most significant public policies in this state and our nation in the Idaho Constitution and the Constitution of the United States. Thus, I would hold that certain constitutional public policies deserve protection and vindication through the public policy exception to at-will employment even in the absence of a statutory enactment.

One such policy that deserves protection in the at-will employment context is the policy of encouraging participation and debate regarding issues of public concern. The Idaho Constitution makes clear that "[a]ll political power is inherent in the people. Government is instituted for their benefit, and they have the right to alter, reform, or abolish the same whenever they may deem it necessary. . . ." ID. CONST. Art. 1, §2. In order to exercise the political power inherent in the people, the Idaho and United States constitutions endow individuals with the liberty to speak freely and participate in vigorous public debate. U.S. CONST. Amend. 1; ID. CONST. Art. 1, §9. Allowing employers to terminate employment based on an individual's association and speech regarding public issues that may have little or nothing in connection with the employer's business, invites employers to squelch the association, speech, and debate so necessary to our system of government. This is particularly true in the context of the myriad of small Idaho communities with only one or two prominent employers. Thus, I would hold it against public policy to discharge an employee for constitutionally-protected political speech or activities regarding a matter of public concern, provided that such speech or activity does not interfere with the employee's job performance or the business of the employer.

The majority cites to *Tiernan v. Charleston Area Med. Ctr.*, for the proposition that absent a state action, the constitutional exercise of free speech is not a public policy exception to at will employment. It is my opinion that even absent a state action, a very narrowly drawn public policy exception to the employment at-will doctrine should apply. That narrowly drawn exception would require a two-step analysis. First, did the at-will employee's speech impact the employer's business in *any* manner? If so, was the employee terminated because of his or her speech? The free speech public policy exception would apply to at-will employment in the case where the employee's speech does not impact the employer's business and the employee was terminated for the speech. In *Tiernan* the plaintiff was fired because she wrote a letter to the editor criticizing her employer. Under this proposed public policy exception, the plaintiff's speech clearly impacted her employer and her termination was lawful.

In this case, the evidence in the record clearly creates genuine issues of material fact regarding whether Edmondson was terminated for political speech or activities regarding a matter of public concern. Further, the record shows genuine issues regarding whether Edmondson's speech and activities interfered with his job performance or the business of his employer. On these grounds, I would vacate summary judgment and remand this matter for further proceedings.

NOTES

1. *Freedom of Expression and the Public Policy Tort.* Which is more persuasive, the majority opinion or Justice Kidwell's dissent? Both opinions cited *Novosel v. Nationwide Insurance Co.*, 721 F.2d 894 (3d Cir. 1983), undoubtedly the leading case in which a court has found that state and federal constitutional protections for political expression and association are important public policies that can form the basis of an employee's wrongful discharge claim. In that case, a federal circuit panel sitting in diversity held that Novosel stated a claim under Pennsylvania law where he alleged that he was discharged for refusing to participate in his employer's lobbying effort and privately expressing opposition to the company's political stand:

> Although Novosel is not a government employee, the public employee cases do not confine themselves to the narrow question of state action. Rather, these cases suggest that an important public policy is in fact implicated wherever the power to hire and fire is utilized to dictate the terms of employee political activities. In dealing with public employees, the cause of action arises directly from the Constitution rather than from common law developments. The protection of important political freedoms, however, goes well beyond the question whether the threat comes from state or private bodies. The inquiry before us is whether the concern for the rights of political expression and association which animated the public employee cases is sufficient to state a public policy under Pennsylvania law. While there are no Pennsylvania cases squarely on this point, we believe that the clear direction of the opinions promulgated by the state's courts suggests that this question be answered in the affirmative.
>
> Having concluded thereby that an important public policy is at stake, we now hold that Novosel's allegations state a claim [under Pennsylvania law] in that Novosel's complaint discloses no plausible and legitimate reason for terminating his employment, and his discharge violates a clear mandate of public policy.

Id. at 900. Compare this reasoning with that of the majority and dissent in *Edmondson*. Thinking back to the discussion of the public policy tort in Chapter 4, which approach is more consistent with the contours of the theory outlined in that chapter? Which approach is more convincing?

2. *State of the Law on Public Policy Speech Claims.* The *Novosel* decision has generated an enormous amount of attention, often negative. Indeed, Judge Becker of the Third Circuit dissented from the full Third Circuit's denial of an *en banc* rehearing of this decision because, in his view, the panel greatly overreached:

> First, the opinion ignores the state action requirement of first amendment jurisprudence, particularly by its repeated, and, in my view, inappropriate citation of public employee cases, and by its implicit assumption that a public policy against government interference with free speech may be readily extended to private actors in voluntary association with another. Second, the opinion could be read to suggest that an explicit contractual provision authorizing an employer to dismiss a lobbyist for failure to undertake lobbying might be unenforceable or subject to a balancing test. Third, the opinion fails to consider other public policy interests, such as the economic interests of the public in efficient corporate performance, the first amendment interests of corporations, and the legitimate interests of a corporation in commanding the loyalty of its employees to pursue its economic well being.

721 F.2d at 903. There are a few other published cases in which courts have recognized speech or association-based claims under the public policy doctrine. *See, e.g., Chavez v. Manville Prods. Corp.*, 777 P.2d 371 (N.M. 1989). Yet, as *Edmondson* suggests, the courts that have rejected *Novosel*'s reasoning are legion, and, absent a statute, the vast majority of courts have refused to recognize a public policy claim for employee political, social, or associational choices in private workplaces. *See, e.g., Dixon v. Coburg Dairy, Inc.*, 330 F.3d 250 (4th Cir. 2003) (refusing to extend South Carolina's public policy doctrine to cover termination for the placement of Confederate flag stickers on a tool box); *Grinzi v. San Diego Hospice Corp.*, 14 Cal. Rptr. 3d 893 (Cal. App. 2004) (rejecting *Novosel*'s reasoning and citing to numerous decisions where other courts have done the same); *Tiernan v. Charleston Area Med. Ctr., Inc.*, 506 S.E.2d 578 (W. Va. 1998) (same).

   3. *Should There Be Stronger Protection for Private-Sector Employees?* Despite the criticism and widespread rejection of *Novosel*'s extension of the public policy doctrine, the power of the court's critique of the employer's conduct ensures its continuing relevance in the debate. Are the *Novosel* court and the dissent in *Edmondson* on to something when they suggest that coerced political activity by a private employer is potentially problematic? *Novosel* was handed down more than 30 years ago. Are private enterprises today more or less powerful economically and politically? How about employees, individually or collectively? Given that most employees work in the private sector, are the dangers associated with employer conduct like that in *Novosel* and *Edmondson* significant? Indeed, the conduct in *Novosel* and *Edmondson* might be particularly troublesome since the employer in each of these cases sought not only to prohibit employee activities but also to coerce employees into affirmatively participating in political activity on its behalf. If employer-coerced political activity is widespread, did *Novosel* correctly identify a danger to the functioning and legitimacy of our political system? Doesn't even the prospect of coercion threaten aspects of autonomy we view as so fundamental in democratic society such that we ought to recognize that such behavior violates public policy?

   Justice Kidwell seems deeply troubled by this, noting that the lack of protection for employees "invites employers to squelch the association, speech, and debate so necessary to our system of government[,]" and expressing particular concern "in the context of the myriad of small Idaho communities with only one or two prominent employers." Might this be even more true now in the wake of *Citizens United v. Federal Election Commission*, 558 U.S. 310 (2010), in which the Supreme Court held that independent political expenditures by for-profit corporations are protected by the First Amendment and therefore cannot be prohibited? Put another way, now that firms—that is, private employers—have robust protections accompanying their significant resources to influence the political process, perhaps we should be even more concerned about their coercing their employees to support or at least not oppose their policy preferences.

   If so, what is the response to Judge Becker's claim that the *Novosel* panel's approach might threaten an employer's ability to terminate a lobbyist? Would there be a workable way to limit such protection such that it would not inhibit, for example, a public relations firm's ability to terminate an employee who refused to speak out against state legislation harmful to the tobacco industry even though he was hired to improve the image and advocate on behalf of clients engaged in cigarette manufacturing? Does Kidwell's formulation deal with this problem?

4. *A Defense of or Threat to the Legislative Process?* As discussed in Chapter 4, a core objection to an expansive common-law public policy tort is that it violates separation of powers principles—that is, the legislature and not the courts ought to decide state public policy and, as importantly, which breaches of such policies should give rise to a private right of action. Even if one generally accepts this proposition, is the argument in favor of the legislative prerogative less strong here, where the concern is the distortion of the political process itself? In other words, should the protection at issue in *Novosel* and *Edmondson* be left to the political process when the public policy supporting the protection is to ensure the legitimacy of that process?

Nevertheless, if, as the *Edmondson* majority and most other courts have concluded, *Novosel* nevertheless went too far, perhaps the employer activity the opinion addresses and the dangers it identifies should be, at minimum, a call for legislative reform to protect both workers and the integrity of the political process. If you agree with this proposition, consider what kind of legislated protections would be appropriate. As discussed above, a few states have enacted statutes that may protect employee political activities and associations, although, interestingly, under some of the statutory regimes, off-site political conduct would receive protection while compelled political participation at work, of the type at issue in *Novosel*, would not. Again, the Connecticut statute, as interpreted by the Connecticut Supreme Court in *Cotto*, *see* page 448, probably would protect employees from such employer demands because it applies constitutional associational protections against private employers, and thereby likely prohibits affirmative coercive measures such as compelled political patronage. Is the Connecticut approach the correct one, or does it also go too far?

5. *Nonpolitical Speech in and Outside the Workplace.* Both *Novosel* and *Edmondson* involve political speech and association. If you believe such activity ought to receive some protection in the private workplace, would you extend the protection to nonpolitical speech addressing a matter of public interest—for example, recent world events, community activities, or entertainment and sports news? Similarly, would you extend associational protections to nonpolitical activities, such as participation in social clubs, corporate boards, nondenominational charities, volunteer organizations, and self-help groups? If so, why? What public policies are served by protecting nonpolitical speech? Finally, which of these activities, if any, are worth the costs—for example, litigation costs, counseling and administrative costs, hesitation to fire underperforming workers, the costs of uncertainty—additional restrictions invariably impose on employers?

6. *The Restatement Approach.* Chapter 5 of the Restatement addresses the tort of wrongful discharge in violation of public policy. *See* RESTATEMENT OF EMPLOYMENT LAW §5.01-5.03. Advocates of employee speech rights will be disappointed to learn that this draft contains no *Novosel*-like protection for employee speech or association. The draft does contain a "catch-all" provision, *see* §5.02(f) (protecting an employee who "engages in other activity directly furthering a substantial public policy"), but there is no suggestion that this would support a *Novosel*-like claim. Indeed, the Reporters Notes following this section recognize that courts generally have disfavored such claims. *See* §5.02 Reporters Notes cmt. d. Moreover, the Illustration 12 following section 7.08 (which provides limited autonomy protections) adopts the reasoning in *Edmondson*. *See* §7.08 Ill. 12 and cmt. g.

7. *Private Ordering and Employee Expression.* In addition to rejecting Edmondson's public policy claim, the court also rejected his contract theories, finding no express or implicit promise on the part of Shearer that Edmondson's employment was anything but at will. However, other courts have found that contract-based theories are available to employees terminated for speech and associational activities. For instance, in *Rulon-Miller*, discussed in Chapter 6 on page 355, the court upheld an implied-in-fact contract claim arising out of an employee's associational preferences—in that case, involving an employee's intimate association. Given the fairly wide acceptance of the theory of implied-in-fact contractual modifications to the at-will relationship, this is a potentially viable theory for employees claiming some right to expression.

Nevertheless, implied just-cause/good-cause terms (such as those alleged in *Edmondson* and *Novosel*) differ from the terms in *Rulon-Miller* in important respects. The terms enforced against the employer in *Rulon-Miller* addressed the employee's autonomy interests directly; that is, IBM had instituted a general policy of not interfering with its employees' off-site associations and activities. Implied just-cause/good-cause terms do not purport to protect associational rights in particular. In many speech and association cases, such a term may be of limited assistance to employees because it would be fairly easy for employers to articulate a legitimate business reason for terminating employees for their expression or associations. For example, assuming that the employer demands in *Novosel* and *Edmondson* violated no state law, didn't the employers in those cases have just cause/good cause to terminate the employees? Suppose, for instance, that the employer was lobbying for a government contract, which the employee opposed as not in the public interest. Wouldn't the employer be able to terminate the employee without breaching the contract? Indeed, the *Rulon-Miller* court cautioned, "We have concern with an employee's off-the-job behavior only when it reduces his ability to perform regular job assignments, interferes with the job performance of other employees, or if his outside behavior affects the reputation of the company in a major way."

8. *Express Contractual Speech and Association Rights.* In addition to the implied-in-fact contract theory, a few common forms of express contractual provisions protect individual employee expression. Collective bargaining agreements, for example, may include not only just cause provisions, but also specific protections for employee unionizing activity, political activity, and other forms of expression. In addition, high-level workers or those who are in high demand, including entertainers, sports figures, and executives, may negotiate for terms that give them significant expressive freedom. Such negotiated terms may include the ability to moonlight, the right to engage in philanthropic activities and social causes of one's choosing, and "for cause only" termination, defined so as to shield a great deal of expressive conduct from employer retaliation.

Consider those workers who are hired to express their opinions—for example, editorial writers, political commentators, cartoonists, certain performing artists, and, more and more frequently, bloggers. Obviously, these workers have incentives to negotiate for protections that provide them with sufficient "space" to express their opinions without fear of retribution. But given the many business and legal risks that might arise from such expression, what limitations are their employers likely to demand? These issues have garnered significant attention at different times, for example in the wake of National Public Radio's termination of news analyst Juan Williams (for his remarks regarding Muslims made on Fox News) and MSNBC's short suspension of host Keith Olbermann (for his failure to disclose political contributions as required by network policy).

The group of employees enjoying perhaps the most robust speech protections is tenured faculty members in academic institutions. The primary policy supporting tenure is academic freedom, although it is intended to serve other values as well, including economic security. *See, e.g.*, American Association of University Professors, *1940 Statement of Principles on Academic Freedom and Tenure*, in AAUP Policy Documents and Reports (1995), *available at* http://www.aaup.org/statements/ Redbook/1940stat.pdf. Academic tenure provides protected faculty with guaranteed employment subject to termination only for cause, and, because the aim is to preserve academic freedom, cause generally does not include the views expressed by the faculty member. As discussed above, in the public education context, academic freedom has been recognized as a potentially important First Amendment concern. Academic tenure has generally held strong in both the public and private context. There are, however, economic and political pressures to the contrary, as well as the occasional "spike" in anti-tenure sentiment, *see supra* Note 3, page 99 (discussing the controversy over the University of Illinois's refusal to follow through on its appointment of Steven Salaita for tweets concerning Israel's attacks in Gaza); Note on *Garcetti* and Academic Freedom, page 427 (discussing the uproar that followed Ward Churchill's statements about 9/11 victims); *see also* James J. Fishman, *Tenure: Endangered or Evolutionary Species*, 38 Akron L. Rev. 771 (2005) (addressing some of the current challenges to tenure).

There are relatively few litigated cases regarding "de-tenuring" or the discharge of tenured employees. Indeed, dismissal of tenured university faculty is relatively rare. *See, e.g.*, James J. Fishman, *Tenure and Its Discontents: The Worst Form of Employment Relationship Save All of the Others*, 21 Pace L. Rev. 159, 172-73 (2000). However, in a controversial recent decision, the Sixth Circuit held, under Michigan law, that a former law professor was due only the employment protection and process specified in her employment contract with the law school, despite references to "tenure" in the professor's contract and in school policies. *Branham v. Thomas M. Cooley Law School*, 689 F.3d 558 (6th Cir. 2012). The court concluded that such references, which did not define tenure as right to continuous employment, created no obligation of employment beyond the single year term to which the contract referred. *See id.* at 562-63. According to the court, the professor had tenure in the sense that she had academic freedom, but nothing in her contract or documents incorporated by reference therein provided for a term of employment greater than one year. *See id.* The ultimate impact of *Branham* outside of the Sixth Circuit (and, indeed, the facts of the case itself) remains unclear, but it calls into question the extent to which academic tenure provides robust job security in private educational institutions.

The most likely expression-related cause for dismissal of a tenured faculty member is sexual or other forms of harassment. *See* Fishman at 200-01 (stating that the other most frequent causes are other illegal activities, incompetence, and the institution's financial exigency). Another is plagiarism and related forms of research misconduct. Tenure, however, does not typically protect faculty members with regard to administrative positions they also hold, such as deanships and department chairs. *See, e.g., Jeffries v. Harleston*, 52 F.3d 9 (2d Cir. 1995) (holding right to academic freedom does not prevent removal of professor as chair of department). For further discussion of academic tenure, *see generally* Matthew W. Finkin, *"A Higher Order of Liberty in the Workplace": Academic Freedom and Tenure in the Vortex of Employment Practices and Law*, 53 Law & Contemp. Probs. 357 (1990).

Most other workers (i.e., nonunionized, non–high-level, non–civil service, and nontenured) have neither the bargaining power nor inclination at the outset of their employment to negotiate for terms that protect their speech and association prerogatives, and raising such issues at the formation stage may raise unwanted red flags. Such provisions, therefore, are rare and, as a result, the typical nonunionized worker enjoys no express contractual protection for expressive activities. This, combined with the limited availability of other common-law or statutory protections, means that most expressive and associational activity by private-sector employees has no legal protection.

9. *Contractual "Suppression" of Employee Speech.* For most employees, the far more likely kinds of contractual provisions are those designed to suppress or restrict employee speech. A typical example is an employee agreeing as a condition of employment or promotion, not to disclose broad categories of confidential and other work- or employer-related information to third parties during and after his or her term of employment. The enforceability of such provisions—or at least those that purport to limit expression beyond trade secrets, privileged communications, and other traditionally recognized forms of proprietary information—is controversial. One high-profile example is the confidentiality agreement between Jeffrey Wigand and his former employer, Brown & Williamson Tobacco Company ("B & W"), which purported to prohibit Wigand from discussing anything about B & W's business, products, or practices that was not generally known during and after termination of his employment relationship. B & W's attempts to enforce this agreement against Wigand and to prevent the CBS show *60 Minutes* from airing interviews with him received significant public attention and were ultimately the subject of the movie *The Insider.*

Another type of agreement that suppresses speech is a nondisclosure agreement associated with severance or a civil settlement. Such nondisclosure agreements have received much critical attention recently, both in the context of "hush money" agreements with various women—Stephanie Clifford (stage name Stormy Daniels) and others—who had alleged affairs or relationships with President Trump and as a result of scrutiny in light of the #MeToo movement. As for the latter, the concern is that confidential settlements containing nondisclosure agreements allow those who have engaged in sexual harassment to keep their jobs and repeat this behavior, since they are not held to account publicly.

The criticism of nondisclosure agreements—either at the outset or at the end of employment—is reflected in state-level legislative activity; indeed, at least sixteen states have proposed statutes limiting in various ways the enforceability of such agreements in either employment contracts or settlements of certain sexual assault or harassment claims, and a number, including California and Washington, have enacted such provisions. *See* National Conference of State Legislatures, *Addressing Sexual Harassment in the Workplace* (May 2018), http://www.ncsl.org/research/labor-and-employment/addressing-sexual-harassment-in-the-workplace.aspx. Most such laws would not impose a complete bar on nondisclosure agreements in settlements, and many victims' advocates oppose them; they contend that such provisions incentivize employers to resolve claims more favorably for victims and can benefit the victim by not revealing to potential future employers that she brought legal action against a former employer. Are there compelling counterarguments? Or is this one of those cases where we have to weigh the good of the many against the good of the few?

10. *Should There Be a Qualified Right to Free Expression in the Private Workplace?* A number of commentators have argued that there ought to be protection for various kinds of employee expression and association in the private workplace. *See, e.g.,* Cynthia L. Estlund, *Free Speech and Due Process in the Workplace*, 71 IND. L.J. 101 (1995); Joseph R. Grodin, *Constitutional Values in the Private Sector Workplace*, 13 INDUS. REL. L.J. 1 (1991); David C. Yamada, *Voices from the Cubicle: Protecting and Encouraging Private Employee Speech in the Post-Industrial Workplace*, 19 BERKELEY J. EMP. & LAB. L. 1 (1998). Now that you are familiar with the entire legal landscape (statutory, tort, and private ordering) and the practical realities for most workers, does the law treat employee expression appropriately? What reforms, if any, would you advocate?

PROBLEMS

7-4. Look back at Problems 7-1 and 7-2. This time, however, assume that the employer is not a city agency, but rather the health services department of a private, nonsectarian university, and that Rasmusson is a nontenured employee of the university. Assume all other facts and circumstances remain the same. What are the possible legal theories on which Rasmusson may pursue a claim against his employer for his termination under any of the scenarios described? How probable is it that he will prevail? If there is a risk of liability, how could the university reduce such risk in the future?

7-5. Patricia Patterson was employed by DollarSave Stores, Inc. ("DSI"), where she had been an accountant working at a large distribution facility for a dozen years. DSI is a large food wholesaler and retailer. Patterson had no written employment contract, although her superiors had always given her very positive work reviews and indicated to her that she had a bright future with DSI. Her job duties required no contact with the public.

After she experienced serious health problems several years ago, Patterson was diagnosed as highly allergic to certain synthetic hormones. These hormones are common in domestic nonorganic beef, poultry, and pork. They also are present in meat byproducts, including stocks, bullions, and lard. To avoid recurring health problems, Patterson's physicians imposed a no–nonorganic meat/ meat byproduct dietary restriction on her. As a result, Patterson became a semi-observant vegetarian, read food labels carefully, and purchased organic foods whenever possible. She also became an avid reader of health and organic food journals and a frequent participant in various online discussion groups supporting vegetarianism and organic lifestyles.

Recently, a food-labeling bill began to work its way through the state legislature. This bill would mandate detailed disclosures of both the origins of meat products and byproducts and the hormones and antibiotics used in their production. DSI sells a substantial amount of domestic meat products and other foods containing meat-based ingredients and byproducts, none of which is organic. It therefore opposed further food labeling. DSI informed its workers about its lobbying efforts in a monthly newsletter for employees, but it never asked its own employees to take any action.

On the eve of a legislative hearing on the bill, Patterson was contacted by one of her friends and asked if she could give a statement supporting food labeling. She agreed. At the hearing, she described her health problems, the difficulty she had in determining which foods contained meat byproducts containing hormones, and the corresponding need for better labeling. She never mentioned in her statement that she was employed by DSI. To her surprise, when she arrived at work the next morning, her supervisor terminated her.

First, consider whether Patterson has a cause of action against DSI sounding in tort or contract. What theories may be available to her, and how likely would she be to succeed on such claims? Next, consider whether she would have a viable claim under state statutes like those described at pages 447-48. What barriers to establishing liability might she face? Finally, in your view, should Patterson enjoy any legal protection in this context? Why or why not?

Part Five

WORKPLACE PROPERTY RIGHTS AND RELATED INTERESTS

8

Competition, Employee Loyalty, and the Allocation of Workplace Property Interests

This chapter moves dramatically from most of what we have studied thus far. It is not concerned with the rights of employees who have been fired, but rather with the rights of employers to prevent harm to their business interests by current and former employees. Thus, in the cases that follow, it is typically the employer who is the plaintiff and the employee who is the defendant.

Usually an employer sues a former employee because it believes she threatens its business position through competitive behavior. The employee may have left to work for a rival company and may have enticed other employees to join the competitor. The employee's new position might use her past work experience to create a competitive advantage for the rival. The employee may rely on knowledge of the former employer's product or business model, or she may solicit customers or clients previously serviced by the employer. And employers sometimes sue former employees for strategic reasons, for example, to deter other employees from leaving.

One of the rationales for the at-will regime in the United States is that, in theory, it gives employees the freedom to move between jobs. That ability would be compromised if the employee cannot use her knowledge and skills, including industry-specific ones, upon departure. Moreover, society benefits from healthy competition between multiple providers of goods and services. On the other hand, many employers spend significant time and money developing their customer base, intellectual property, and other business assets. They may also invest in training their employees. In his seminal article on noncompete agreements, Professor Harlan Blake explained the competing policy considerations:

> From the point of view of the employer, postemployment restraints are regarded as perhaps the only effective method of preventing unscrupulous competitors or employees from appropriating valuable trade information and customer relationships for their own benefit. Without the protection afforded by such covenants, it is argued, business[es] could not afford to stimulate research and improvement of business methods to a desirably high level, nor could they achieve the degree of freedom of communication within a company that is necessary for efficient operation.

The opposite view is that postemployment restraints reduce both the economic mobility of employees and their personal freedom to follow their own interests. These restraints also diminish competition by intimidating potential competitors and by slowing down the dissemination of ideas, processes, and methods. They unfairly weaken the individual employee's bargaining position vis-à-vis his employer and, from the social point of view, clog the market's channeling of [labor] to employments in which its productivity is greatest.

Harlan M. Blake, *Employee Agreements Not to Compete*, 73 HARV. L. REV. 625, 627 (1960).

Recognizing these conflicting impulses, the law accords the employer strong protection against worker competition during the course of the employment relationship but only limited protection against competition upon termination. This chapter looks specifically at three areas: worker recruitment and training; trade secrets and confidential information; and access to customers, clients, and co-workers. Both public law and private ordering play a role in allocating rights in each of these contexts. The rights and obligations of workers who wish to compete are governed by the tort duty of loyalty and statutory protection against the misappropriation of trade secrets, but employers often seek to expand these protections through contract.

Throughout the chapter, keep in mind the inherent conflict between freedom of competition for the employee and protection of employer property interests and investments. How do these competing concerns influence court decisions? Do courts strike a fair balance between employer and employee rights? If not, how can the situation be improved? Do we need clearer rules? More private ordering? A legislative solution?

A. FIDUCIARY DUTIES OF CURRENT EMPLOYEES

≡ *Scanwell Freight Express STL, Inc. v. Chan*
≡ *162 S.W.3d 477 (Mo. 2005)*

LIMBAUGH, Jr., J.

Scanwell Freight Express STL, Inc., sued Stevie Chan for breach of fiduciary duty and Dimerco Express (U.S.A.) Corp. for conspiracy to breach fiduciary duty. Following a jury trial, Scanwell was awarded $54,000 in damages from Chan and $254,000 from Dimerco. . . . The judgment is reversed, and the case is remanded.

I . . .

Scanwell, a freight forwarding business, hired Chan in April 1996 to be the general manager of its St. Louis Office. Chan was an at-will employee, and she was not required to sign a noncompete agreement. While serving as Scanwell's general manager, Chan made arrangements with Dimerco, Scanwell's direct competitor, to open a Dimerco office in St. Louis. At Dimerco's request, Chan created a "business proposal" for this purpose. She also arranged for Dimerco to take over the lease of Scanwell's St. Louis office upon its expiration. Chan resigned from Scanwell effective March 1, 2001, and approximately one month later, Dimerco opened its St. Louis office with Chan as its general manager. Dimerco operated in the same premises that Scanwell previously occupied, employed most of the same employees as Scanwell, and for a while even used the same telephone number. Dimerco also acquired a number of Scanwell's customers. . . .

II . . .

In the employer-employee relationship, this Court, drawing on the Restatement (2d) of Agency, has implicitly recognized a separate cause of action for breach of the duty of loyalty, *Nat'l Rejectors, Inc. v. Trieman*, 409 S.W.2d 1, 41 (Mo. 1966). . . .

Under *Trieman*, the seminal case on which both sides rely, . . . certain at-will employees were accused of misappropriating trade secrets from their employer in a scheme to compete with the employer. The factual context of the case is especially important because it involves the most common manifestation of the duty of loyalty, and the essence of Scanwell's claim here, which is that an employee has a duty not to compete with his or her employer concerning the subject matter of the employment. This Court described the duty of loyalty in the broad and general terms of section 387 of the Restatement (2d) of Agency, stating, "[an employee] must not, while employed, act contrary to the employer's interests." However, in addressing the corresponding duty not to compete, the Court held, nonetheless, that employees are allowed to "agree among themselves to compete with their then employer upon termination of their employment," and "[t]hey may plan and prepare for their competing enterprises while still employed." Admittedly, the mere decision to enter into competition is "contrary to the employer's interests," but the Court saw the need to balance the duty not to compete with the interest of promoting free competition. As some courts have put it, the law allows employees the privilege to plan and prepare for competition in recognition of the "competing interests of allowing an employee some latitude in switching jobs and at the same time preserving some degree of loyalty owed to the employer." *Cudahy Co. v. Am. Lab., Inc.*, 313 F. Supp. 1339, 1346 (D. Neb. 1970).

Although the *Trieman* Court did not elaborate on the conduct that would constitute a breach of the duty, it necessarily follows that a breach arises when the employee goes beyond the mere planning and preparation and actually engages in direct competition, which, by definition, is to gain advantage over a competitor. The Restatement (2d) of Agency, sec. 393, cmt. e, which this Court cited with favor in *Trieman*, plays on the same idea, further describing the kinds of activities that can constitute a breach of the duty of loyalty. That comment, in pertinent part, states:

> After termination of his agency, in the absence of a restrictive agreement, the agent can properly compete with his principal as to matters for which he has been employed. Even before the termination of the agency, he is entitled to make arrangements to compete,

except that he cannot properly use confidential information peculiar to his employer's business and acquired therein, Thus, before the end of his employment, he can properly purchase a rival business and upon termination of employment immediately compete. He is not, however, entitled to solicit customers for such rival business before the end of his employment nor can he properly do other similar acts in direct competition with the employer's business.

III

Applying these standards, this Court concludes that Scanwell presented a submissible case that Chan breached her duty of loyalty. Chan's actions were clearly contrary to Scanwell's interests, and . . . went beyond mere planning and preparation to compete. . . .

First, Chan gave Dimerco confidential information about Scanwell's operations and customers. This included general information on Scanwell's customer base and detailed information on a few of Scanwell's customers. Most of the evidence centered on the fact that Chan gave Dimerco a customer profile of one of Scanwell's largest customers, which included contact information, special handling requirements, rate structure, billing instructions, and other information. At trial, Chan admitted that the customer profile was confidential "[to] some degree" and that it would be helpful to a competitor in soliciting the business of the customer. Dennis Choy, Scanwell's president, also testified that this information was confidential and that, in fact, customer profiles were "the most vital pieces of information for any company to keep within [itself]." Although Chan and Dimerco argue that some of the information in the profile was not confidential because it could be obtained from other sources such as the customers themselves, at least some of the information in the profile, such as Scanwell's air freight rates, was entirely unavailable. Regardless of the extent of the disclosure of confidential information, as other courts have aptly noted, even "slight assistance to a direct competitor can constitute a breach of the employee's duty of loyalty." *Cameco, Inc. v. Gedicke*, 724 A.2d 783, 521-22 (N.J. 1999).

A second and more egregious activity was that Chan, while still employed by Scanwell, secured Scanwell's leased premises—Scanwell's business office—for Dimerco. The key testimony on the matter was uncontroverted. [Chan, as office manager, had signed an amended, renewable lease for Scanwell. She forwarded these documents to headquarters, but as the December 1, 2000, renewal deadline approached,] Chan, who was by then preparing to leave Scanwell and open the Dimerco office, took no action to renew the lease for Scanwell and did not notify Scanwell's home office that the renewal deadline was approaching.

Then in early February 2001, while still employed by Scanwell and at a time the Scanwell's premises still could have been relet to Scanwell, Chan, with Dimerco's approval, negotiated and signed a lease of the same premises for Dimerco. Although Chan signed the lease on February 15, 2001, it was on February 20, 2001, that Chan first informed Scanwell that she planned to resign. That same day, she sent a letter to her supervisor at Scanwell, M.B. Hassan, stating, "[t]he new rental lease has been turned back to the landlor[d] and will not be renewed. You can contact [the landlord's agent] if you have [a] different arrangement. Otherwise the lease will end[] [in] March."

While Chan and Dimerco claim that there are no cases holding that an employee owes a "duty to remind" his employer of its legal rights and obligations, they miss the larger issue. Chan did not merely fail to remind Scanwell of the renewal deadline, she arranged for Scanwell's direct competitor to take over the premises, and, in doing so, prevented Scanwell from being able to re-lease the premises after the renewal deadline had passed. As a result of her actions, Scanwell lost its business office, and Scanwell customers who thereafter called or visited the office talked with Dimerco representatives.

IV

Despite this Court's conclusion, [an instructional error requires reversal].

Where, as here, an allegation of breach of the duty of loyalty is presented in the context of an employee acting in competition with his or her employer, a proper definitional instruction of the duty of loyalty, consistent with the foregoing analysis, must set out the following elements: 1) In general, an employee must not, while employed, act contrary to the employer's interest; 2) however, an employee may agree with others to compete upon termination of the employment and may plan and prepare for their competing enterprise while still employed; and 3) but an employee may not, while still employed, go beyond mere planning and preparation and act in direct competition with the employer. *See Trieman*; Rest. (2d) Agency, sec. 393, cmt. e. In the absence of such a definitional instruction, the jury was unaware of the conduct that the law prohibits, and prejudice resulted because the jury was allowed to conclude that even mere planning and preparation for competition breached the duty.

[The court also criticized a jury instruction for as "fatally defective" because it "made actionable the aggregate of all of Chan's conduct in making those arrangements, even those arrangements that involved mere 'planning and preparation.' The jury was not limited to the allegations relating to the lease and the dissemination of confidential information."]

NOTES

1. *The Scope of the Duty of Loyalty.* Cases in which employers pursue breach of loyalty claims against employees for pre-departure activities typically involve one of several recurring fact patterns: while still employed, the employee solicits customers and/or co-workers and opens a competitive business; the employee aids a competitor or discloses information to a competitor, usually planning to join the competitor down the road; or the employee usurps a corporate opportunity. *See* RESTATEMENT OF EMPLOYMENT LAW §8.01(b) (ALI 2015). If you're wondering, there's no corresponding duty of loyalty running from the employer to the employee. *But see* Matthew T. Bodie, *Employment as Fiduciary Relationship*, 105 GEO. L.J. 819 (2017) (arguing for such a duty). With regard to the duty workers owe their employers, there are some exceptions. The Restatement would allow "moonlighting" at a competitor in limited situations—mostly of low-level workers whose performance is more or less fungible. §8.04(c) & cmt. b. And the *Scanwell* privilege to make *preparations* for departure is generally recognized, §8.04(b) ("competition . . . does not include reasonable preparation by an employee or group of employees to compete with the employer."), and it will sometimes insulate the employee from liability for this type of conduct. When did Chan cross the line from preparation to competition? How would you have advised her had she consulted you about how to transition to Dimerco without running afoul of the law?

2. *Fiduciary Duties of High-Level Employees.* The application and extent of any duty of loyalty is the threshold question and sometimes a difficult one. The Restatement provides that employees "in a position of trust and confidence" owe a fiduciary duty of loyalty and, further, that "[o]ther employees may depending on their position," owe a "contractual duty of loyalty." §8.0(a). These duties normally expire at the end of the relationship, but the Restatement would extend the duty to preserve trade secrets beyond that point. §8.01(b)(i), §8.03.

It is unclear how fiduciary duties and the contractual duty of loyalty differ in reach although, as we will see, they differ radically in remedies. Some courts take the view that a fiduciary relationship "establishes a distinct and separate obligation than the duty of loyalty" owing to "the 'peculiar' trust between the employee-agent and his employer-principal." *Rash v. J.Y. Intermediate, Ltd.*, 498 F.3d 1201, 1211 (10th Cir. 2007). From this perspective, fiduciaries are held to a higher standard than ordinary employees and could in theory be found in breach for conduct that would be permissible if perpetrated by a nonfiduciary employee. *See, e.g., id.* (noting that, under Texas law a fiduciary must show that she acted with the utmost good faith and most scrupulous honesty toward the principal, including placing the principal's interests before her own). Under this approach, the contours of the duty of loyalty will vary based on the employee's position, the relative status of the employee, and the vulnerability of the employer. Courts are likely to look harder at alleged breaches by high-level employees, including corporate executives, employees with long-term or exclusive relationships with customers, employees possessing highly specialized or unique skills or knowledge, and employees who have been entrusted with confidential information upon which their employer's business depends.

3. *Fiduciary Duties and Private Ordering.* Although the Restatement states that fiduciary duties cannot be disclaimed or modified, §8.01 cmt. a, this is incorrect, at least in the sense that the parties can agree to actions that, absent contrary agreement, would violate a fiduciary duty. For example, a corporate officer may not appropriate a corporate opportunity, but the parties are free to define some ventures as not corporate opportunities. *See, e.g.*, Del. Code Ann. tit. 8, §122(17) (2018) (authorizing corporations to renounce "any interest or expectancy of the corporation in, or in being offered an opportunity to participate in, specified business opportunities"). Further, the types of employees and executives who are most likely to be held liable as fiduciaries are also those likely to be able to bargain for concessions from their companies, including the right to moonlight and separation agreements authorizing the taking of certain accounts, customers, and opportunities. In addition, an employee can pursue a business opportunity otherwise "owned" by his or her employer by fully disclosing the opportunity and receiving advance permission to pursue it from the employer. *Cameco v. Gedicke*, 724 A.2d 783, 521-22 (N.J. 1999) (explaining that various considerations influence the determination of whether the duty of loyalty is breached, including contractual provisions, employer consent, "the status of the employee," and the "the nature of the employee's second source of income and its effect on the employer"); *see also* ALI PRINCIPLES OF CORPORATE GOVERNANCE §5.05

(1994) (addressing the appropriation of corporate opportunities by directors and senior executives).

4. *Solicitation.* A recurring issue in duty of loyalty cases is whether the departing employee solicited co-workers or clients before departure. In *Scanwell*, the competitor company hired most of Scanwell's employees and acquired many of its customers upon taking over its lease. Under the privilege to make preparations articulated in the case, what is an employee permitted to say to potential customers and employees prior to an anticipated departure?

The Colorado Supreme Court wrestled with this issue in *Jet Courier v. Mulei*, 771 P.2d 486 (Colo. 1989). Mulei was the head of the Denver office of an Ohio-based courier service when he decided to establish a competitive business. While still employed by Jet, Mulei met with several of Jet's Denver customers, told them he would be leaving, that he could "give them the same service," and that he "would be in a position, sometime later, to reduce cost." He also met with several of Jet's Denver employees and offered the Denver office staff better working conditions, insurance, and part ownership of his new endeavor if they joined him. The court held that "an employee may advise current customers of his employer that he will be leaving. However, any pretermination solicitation of those customers for a new competing business violates an employee's duty of loyalty." With respect to co-worker solicitation, the court established a multifactored test for determining whether the employee breached the duty of loyalty: "A court should consider the nature of the employment relationship, the impact or potential impact of the employee's actions on the employer's operations, and the extent of any benefits promised or inducements made to co-workers to obtain their services for the new competing enterprise. No single factor is dispositive[.]" *Id.* at 497.

How easy is it to draw a line between "advising" and "soliciting"? What if the departing employee asks co-workers about their job satisfaction and desire to stay with their current employer but doesn't actually ask them to defect? *See Kopka, Landau & Pinkus v. Hansen*, 874 N.E.2d 1065 (Ind. Ct. App. 2007) (no breach of duty of loyalty where law firm associate talked to other associates about their salary requirements and willingness to quit but made no offers of employment). The Restatement would bar "recruit[ing]" co-workers to leave "en masse" when that would "materially damage" the employer. §8.04 cmt. c. But it would simultaneously permit a "group of employees" to agree among themselves to leave for a new business or a competitor so long as there are not so many departures as to leave the present employer's business "immediately crippled." Cmt. d. This creates serious counseling difficulties for an attorney advising a group considering moving on.

5. *Tortious Interference with Contract.* In addition to breach of the duty of loyalty, solicitation cases sometimes give rise to intentional interference with contract claims against the new employer. *See* Chapter 5. However, a former employer may establish interference only in situations where the solicited individual was under a contract of which the new employer. *See Acclaim Sys. v. Infosys, Ltd.*, 679 F. App'x 207, 211-12 (3rd Cir. 2017) (intentional interference with contract relations requires proof that the defendant had specific knowledge of the contractual relationship, and such knowledge was lacking when all four workers were asked whether they were subject to a noncompete and each denied it); *See also Merritt Hawkins & Assocs., LLC v. Gresham*, 861 F.3d 143, 151-52 (5th Cir. 2017) (to recover exemplary damages for tortious interference, plaintiff must show malice by clear and convincing evidence, which requires a specific intent to cause substantial harm to plaintiff). Thus, solicitation of an at-will worker generally does not give rise to an interference claim. On the other hand, a tortious interference claim can arise if the departing employee or the competitor solicits a worker employed under a contract containing restrictive covenants or a fixed term of employment or a customer with an existing or prospective service or supply contract. *See, e.g., Volt Services v. Adecco Employment Services*, 35 P.3d 329, 337 (Or. App. 2001). The tort also lies if independently wrongful means are used. *Lewis-Gale Med. Ctr., LLC v. Alldredge*, 710 S.E.2d 716 (Va. 2011) (no showing of "improper methods," such as fraud or defamation). *See also W. Plains, L.L.C. v. Retzlaff Grain Co.*, 870 F.3d 774, 783 (8th Cir. 2017) (a jury could find unjust interference when defendant knowingly recruited, and seized plaintiff's workforce, infrastructure, and customer relationships; while it might have been permissible to recruit employees individually, its arranging for a group resignation which would decimate the company was not permissible); *Western Blue Print Co., LLC v. Roberts*, 367 S.W.3d 7 (Mo. 2012) (defendants were guilty of tortious interference by, inter alia, inducing other employees to leave their jobs with the plaintiff in a staggered fashion that impeded its ability to function effectively).

6. *Employer Remedies for the Conduct of "Faithless Servants."* What is the appropriate remedy in a case involving breach of loyalty? It is typically too late to enjoin the employee's competitive conduct. In cases where an employee usurps clients or a corporate opportunity, the employee may be required to pay for the losses sustained by the employer or to turn over profits gleaned from the competitive behavior. However, the losses or profits sought must be attributable to the disloyal behavior. *See Cameco v. Gedicke*, 724 A.2d 783, 521-22 (N.J. 1999).

Another possible remedy goes under the quaint name of the "faithless servant doctrine," which, where applicable, permits forfeiture (sometimes called disgorgement) of compensation paid during the period of breach. In addition to paying any damages due to the employer and being liable for any profits attributable to the disloyalty, the employee is obligated to return any salary or other compensation he received from the employer during his period of disloyalty. *See, e.g., Design Strategies, Inc. v. Davis*, 469 F.3d 284 (2nd Cir. 2006) (requiring former sales manager to pay damages equivalent to salary for periods corresponding to time during which he promoted competitor company). This approach has sometimes been used in situations where the breach of loyalty stems not from competitive behavior but from serious misconduct of the employee. *Astra USA, Inc. v. Bildman*, 914 N.E.2d 36 (Mass. 2009), for instance, involved a CEO who engaged in a pattern of sexual harassment, retaliation, and cover-up, as well as a variety of financial misdeeds. Applying New York's faithless servant doctrine, the court held that the employee must "forfeit all of his salary and bonuses from Astra for the period of disloyalty" even if the faithless servant "otherwise performed valuable services for his principal." Perhaps most surprisingly, and unlike other situations where a party materially breaches a contract, the wrongdoer was not permitted to recover in restitution for the reasonable value of the other services he rendered during the period of his faithlessness. Does this strike you as an unusually harsh remedy? Although the defendant in *Astra* was a former CEO, the court suggested in dicta that the disgorgement remedy could apply to lower-level employees as well. *Id.* at 49. *See also Morgan Stanley v. Skowron*, 989 F. Supp. 2d 356 (S.D.N.Y. 2013) (insider trading in violation of firm's code of conduct, which also imposes an affirmative duty to report misconduct, constitutes faithlessness sufficient to allow former employer to recover $31 million of compensation paid to employee during the period of his faithlessness). *But see Rash v. J.Y. Intermediate, Ltd.*, 498 F.3d 1201 (10th Cir. 2007) (forfeiture applicable only to " 'clear and serious' violations of fiduciary duty" considering such factors as the gravity, timing, and willfulness of the breach, the harm caused by the breach, and the adequacy of other remedies); *see also* RESTATEMENT OF EMPLOYMENT LAW §9.09(b); *see generally* Charles A. Sullivan, *Mastering the Faithless Servant?: Reconciling Employment Law, Contract Law, and Fiduciary Duty*, 2011 WIS. L. REV. 777.

7. *Liability of the New Employer.* As a practical matter, even if a court awards damages to the aggrieved employer, the company may face hurdles trying to recover the judgment. For this reason, employers commonly sue not only the breaching employee but also the new employer, often for tortious interference with contract. But Chan was not under contract with Scanwell, and the claims against her were based entirely on tort law. In such instances, the former employer can argue that the new employer "aided and abetted" or "conspired with" the employee to breach the duty of loyalty. In *Scanwell*, the lower court held Dimerco liable along with Chan under this theory. While Dimerco and Chan were clearly working together to spin off Scanwell's business, in other cases the competitor's role is less obvious, creating questions as to whether the new employer had the requisite knowledge or intent to justify liability. *Compare Design Strategies*, 469 F.3d at 303-04 (defendant IT Web not liable to former employer; although it knew about its co-defendant's employment, he had told it that plaintiff was not interested in expanding into the business area in question) *with Security Title Agency, Inc. v. Pope*, 200 P.3d 977 (Ariz. App. 2008) (defendant liable for aiding and abetting defecting branch manager who brought 66 employees to new employer where, inter alia, it participated in recruiting sessions, prepared written comparison of two companies' job benefits and agreed to indemnify the manager in any suit by plaintiff). Aiding and abetting liability generally requires knowledge that the conduct encouraged will constitute a breach of loyalty. *See Security Title* 200 P.3d at 987. If you represent a company recruiting an employee from a competitor or undertaking a business venture with an individual employed elsewhere, would you recommend that the client ask about the employee's duties to their current employer? What are the pros and cons of remaining ignorant? What are the ethical implications of this course of action?

8. *Whistleblowing.* It should be apparent that a broad duty of loyalty regarding confidential information is in considerable tension with the public policy tort and the federal and state statutes we explored in Chapter 4. Put simply, a duty of confidentiality would seem often to prevent an employee from doing exactly what those laws encourage. The solution of the Restatement of Employment Law is straightforward in theory, if perhaps not so easy to apply in practice: The duty of loyalty "must be interpreted in a manner consistent with the employee's rights and responsibilities" under those and other laws providing a right to "cooperate with regulatory authorities." §8.01(c); *see also* §8.02 cmt. a ("Information regarding an employer's illegal activities is not a 'trade secret' . . . nor is such information protectable by means of restrictive covenant. . . ."); *see generally* Peter S. Menell, *Tailoring a Public Policy Exception to Trade Secret Protection*, 105 CAL. L. REV. 1 (2017). That has not prevented some employers from trying to contract to limit employee rights in this sphere. *See* Jennifer M. Pacella, *Silencing Whistleblowers by Contract*, 55 AM. BUS. L. J. 261 (2018) (recommending extending SEC's Rule 21F-17, prohibiting contracts restricting employee rights to become whistleblowers, to also protect employee who provide otherwise-confidential documents to the Commission).

Recently, the use of nondisclosure agreements in settlements of sexual harassment claims have been challenged as freeing serial harassers to continue their predatory behavior. As a result, several states have either passed law or introduced bills to limit such agreements. *E.g.*, 2017 Wash. SB 5966. There has been considerable debate as to the effect of such legislation. *See generally* Ian Ayres, *Targeting Repeat Offender NDAs*, 71 STAN. L. REV. ONLINE 76 (2018) (given both the potential value to both alleged victims and accused harassers of limiting disclosure and the risks that nondisclosure agreements resolving a harassment claim will enable serial harassment, such agreements should be subject to the requirement of a statement of the charges in an "information escrow" that would become available to the EEOC if future charges were filed).

9. *Post-Employment Contractual Restraints.* The most significant limitation on the duty of loyalty is that it applies only while the employment relationship exists. To extend protection beyond termination, the employer may obtain a contractual commitment from the employee. These may take several forms: a covenant not to compete, under which an employee promises not to engage in competition with the employer for a period of time following employment; a promise not to solicit the employer's clients or other employees (a nonsolicitation agreement); and a commitment not to disclose any confidential information learned during employment (a nondisclosure agreement). The enforceability of restrictive covenants generally and noncompetes in particular is the subject of the next section.

PROBLEM

8-1. Sam Miller was vice president of H&R Metals, a company that processed scrap metal. He was employed at will with no written contract. On behalf of H&R, Miller investigated the purchase of a high-tech "shredder" from Newell Manufacturing that would increase H&R's operations. Miller negotiated preliminary terms for the purchase; however, H&R's board of directors subsequently voted not to go through with the deal, considering the investment in new technology premature. Dissatisfied with the direction of the business, Miller met with the president of H&R and told him he was planning to leave the company unless H&R made him an equity partner in the business. The president refused. Subsequently, and while still employed by H&R, Miller secured a small business loan from a local bank and contracted with Newell to purchase the shredder himself. He also filed the necessary paperwork to incorporate "Miller's Metals," obtained the state and local permits needed to run a shredding operation, and engaged an advertising company to prepare brochures and other informational materials that he planned to distribute once his business became operational.

One week before tendering his resignation, Miller had lunch with H&R Metals' operations manager, Georgia Sidway. Miller told Sidway about his disagreement with the president and his plans to open a competitive venture. Sidway asked Miller if he was offering her a job. Miller responded, "Well, at the moment I'm still on company time. But there are options out there. Why don't we have lunch again next week." The following week, Miller quit H&R, and Miller's Metals became operational. Due to his extensive advance planning, the business was able to secure its first contract and begin processing metal within a week. Miller met again with Georgia Sidway and offered her a job at a salary that he knew was far above what she had been paid at H&R. Together, Miller and Sidway met with several scrap metal suppliers who had previously provided metal to H&R. One of these suppliers, Packwell Parts, held a one-year contract to supply its scrap output to H&R on a monthly basis. As a result of the meetings, Packwell and three other suppliers decided to shift their business to Miller's Metals.

Suppose H&R learns of Miller's activities and files suit. What causes of action would you expect the former employer to pursue? What defenses would you raise if you were defending Miller? Who is likely to succeed? Regardless of your answer, is there anything you would have told Miller to do differently to avoid this lawsuit? *See generally Metzner v. Maryland Metals*, 382 A.2d 564 (Md. App. 1978).

B. POST-EMPLOYMENT RESTRAINTS ON COMPETITION

Contracts purporting to restrict post-employment competition are ubiquitous. *See* Norman D. Bishara, Kenneth J. Martin, and Randall S. Thomas, *An Empirical Analysis of Noncompetition Clauses and Other Restrictive Post-Employment Covenants*, 68 VAND. L. REV. 1 (2015) (A random sample drawn from S&P 1500 companies showed that 80 percent had noncompetes, usually from 1 to 2 years and often with a broad geographic scope; 76 percent had nonsolicitation agreements and 87 percent had nondisclosure agreements; the study noted a trend of more such clauses over time). Such contracts also expand on the protection offered by trade secret law, discussed later in the chapter. Although, unlike the duty of loyalty, trade secret protection continues after the employment relationship ends, it generally proscribes only the use and disclosure of protected information, not competition per se.

Contractual protection—covenants not to compete, nonsolicitation clauses, and nondisclosure clauses—provide employers a more reliable route to protecting their interests following an employee's departure. And they are easy to obtain from most employees, being required as part of normal onboarding procedures, along with acknowledgements of at-will status and agreements to arbitrate disputes. Some employers are even using clickwraps to obtain employee consent to such agreements. *See Newell Rubbermaid, Inc. v. Storm*, 2014 Del. Ch. LEXIS 45, 23-25 (Del. Ch. Mar. 27, 2014) (upholding a TRO against plaintiff for violation of confidentiality and nonsolicitation agreement made by "clickwrap"). Nevertheless, as we will see, the enforceability of such covenants in individual cases is far from certain.

The most controversial of these clauses—because it is the most restrictive—is the noncompetition agreement, under which an employee agrees not to work in a competitive endeavor for a designated period of time, typically also within a designated geographical area. Depending on how broadly they are drafted, these agreements can have the effect of keeping an individual out of the work force (or tied to his or her current employer); they have therefore been subject to significant judicial scrutiny

and scholarly debate. As we will see, some common ground exists among many jurisdictions on how to approach noncompete enforcement. However, there is significant
variation in results because of the fact-specific nature of most courts' approach, and
there are also outlier jurisdictions such as California, which prohibits enforcement
of employee noncompete agreements in that economically important state. The first
part of this section provides an overview of the competing doctrinal approaches and
policy issues at stake in enforcing contractual restraints on competition. The next
parts explore how those jurisdictions that enforce noncompetes negotiate these tensions in three commonly occurring factual scenarios: disputes over skills and training,
disputes over trade secrets and information, and disputes over customers and clients.

1. Approaches to Noncompete Enforcement

Cal. Bus. & Prof. Code §§16600 et seq. (2018)

§16600. Void Contracts

[E]very contract by which anyone is restrained from engaging in a lawful
profession, trade, or business of any kind is to that extent void.

Restatement (Second) of Contracts

§188 Ancillary Restraints on Competition

(1) A promise to refrain from competition . . . is unreasonably in restraint
of trade if

(a) the restraint is greater than is needed to protect the promisee's
legitimate interest, or

(b) the promisee's need is outweighed by the hardship to the promisor
and the likely injury to the public.

≡≡≡ *Outsource International, Inc. v. Barton*
≡≡≡ *192 F.3d 662 (7th Cir. 1999)*

[Defendant Barton was a staffing consultant for Plaintiff Outsource's predecessor company. He signed a noncompete, nonsolicitation, and confidentiality agreement upon
hire. Six years later, Outsource acquired Barton's employer, and Barton resigned and
opened his own temporary staffing company within the geographic area proscribed by
his employment agreement. The Seventh Circuit affirmed the district court's finding
that Outsource had presented a prima facie case for a preliminary injunction against
Barton under Illinois law.]

POSNER, Chief Judge, dissenting.

I regret my inability to agree with the court's disposition of the case, because it
is the right disposition from the standpoint of substantive justice. Mr. Barton is an
adult of sound mind who made an unequivocal promise, for which he was doubtless
adequately compensated, not to compete with his employer within 25 miles for a year
after he ceased being employed. He quit of his own volition—quit in fact to set up

in competition with his employer. And all the customers whom he obtained for his new company, before the preliminary injunction which the court affirms today put him temporarily out of business, were customers of his former employer. So he broke his contract. But Illinois law, to which we must of course bow in this diversity suit, is hostile to covenants not to compete found in employment contracts. An Illinois court would not enforce this covenant.

There is no longer any good reason for such hostility, though it is nothing either new or limited to Illinois. The English common law called such covenants "restraints of trade" and refused to enforce them unless they were adjudged "reasonable" in time and geographical scope. *Mitchel v. Reynolds*, 24 Eng. Rep. 347 (K.B. 1711). The original rationale had nothing to do with restraint of trade in its modern, antitrust sense. It was paternalism in a culture of poverty, restricted employment, and an exiguous social safety net. The fear behind it was that workers would be tricked into agreeing to covenants that would, if enforced, propel them into destitution. This fear, though it continues to be cited, has no basis in current American conditions.

Later, however, the focus of concern shifted to whether a covenant not to compete might have anticompetitive consequences, since the covenant would eliminate the covenantor as a potential competitor of the covenantee within the area covered by, and during the term of, the covenant. This concern never had much basis, especially when the covenant was found in an employment contract. It would be unlikely for the vitality of competition to depend on the ability of a former employee to compete with his former employer. So unlikely that it would make little sense to place a cloud of suspicion over such covenants, rather than considering competitive effects on a case by case basis.

At the same time that the concerns behind judicial hostility to covenants not to compete have waned, recognition of their social value has grown. The clearest case for such a covenant is where the employee's work gives him access to the employer's trade secrets. The employer could include in the employment contract a clause forbidding the employee to take any of the employer's trade secrets with him when he left the employment, as in fact the employer did in this case. Such clauses are difficult to enforce, however, as it is often difficult to determine whether the former employee is using his former employer's trade secrets or using either ideas of his own invention or ideas that are in the public domain. A covenant not to compete is much easier to enforce, and to the extent enforced prevents the employee, during the time and within the geographical scope of the covenant, from using his former employer's trade secrets.

A related function of such a covenant is to protect the employer's investment in the employee's "human capital," or earning capacity. The employer may give the employee training that the employee could use to compete against the employer. If covenants not to compete are forbidden, the employer will pay a lower wage, in effect charging the employee for the training. There is no reason why the law should prefer this method of protecting the employer's investment to a covenant not to compete.

I can see no reason in today's America for judicial hostility to covenants not to compete. It is possible to imagine situations in which the device might be abused, but the doctrines of fraud, duress, and unconscionability are available to deal with such situations. A covenant's reasonableness in terms of duration and geographical scope is merely a consideration bearing on such defenses. . . . Had Barton signed a covenant in which he agreed that if he ever left the employ of Outsource he would never again work in the business of providing temporary industrial labor anywhere in the world, there would be at least a suspicion that he had been forced or tricked into signing the covenant and therefore that it should not be enforced. There is no suggestion of that here, and so if I were writing on a clean slate I would agree wholeheartedly with the district court's granting a preliminary injunction against Barton's violating the covenant.

But the Illinois courts approach covenants not to compete in a different way, not radically different perhaps but different enough to require a reversal in this case. Their view is that a covenant not to compete that is contained in an employment contract is enforceable in only two circumstances—either where the covenant protects a "near permanent" relationship between the former employer and his customers, or where it protects "confidential information" (that is, trade secrets) of the former employer. . . .

The Illinois courts appear to place the burden of proving that the covenant meets one of the two criteria of validity on the employer. In effect Illinois requires the employer to prove that the covenant not to compete serves a social purpose. Such a requirement is inconsistent with the idea of freedom of contract, which animates contract law and a corollary of which is that courts do not limit the enforcement of contracts to those the social point of which the court can see. They enforce a contract unless there is some reason to think it imposes heavy costs on third parties, offends the moral code, fails to comply with formal requirements (such as those imposed on some contracts by the statute of frauds), or doesn't embody an actual deal between competent consenting adults.

Still, we must take the Illinois law as we find it, and apply it as best we can to the facts of the case. . . . There is no question that he violated the covenant not to compete in his employment contract, which barred him for one year after his employment ended from competing with Outsource in the Chicago area. But there is no evidence that he stole any of Outsource's trade secrets. Outsource's customer list [was not secret.] The wages that Outsource pays its workers are not secret either. Barton did not take the list of workers on Outsource's roster, but obtained workers for his customers in the same way that Outsource does, by radio and newspaper advertisements. . . .

[With respect to customers, the] only users of temp labor who testified at the preliminary injunction hearing agreed that such users have no sense of loyalty to particular suppliers. Both witnesses used multiple agencies. It was feasible for Barton to use standard selling techniques, rather than any techniques that he had learned from Outsource or information that he took with him when he left Outsource, to get customers for his new business. . . .

[A]s far as this record shows, all he used in signing up customers for his new venture were the standard sales techniques used in this business.

Since the irreparable harm to Barton from the grant of a preliminary injunction to Outsource exceeds the irreparable harm that Outsource would experience from the denial of the injunction (as a start-up, Barton would find it difficult to prove damages from being frozen out of business for a year as a result of the enforcement of the covenant), Outsource must prove not just that it has a better case than Barton but that it has a much better case. It has a worse case. . . .

NOTES

1. *A Spectrum of Approaches.* The three excerpts—from the California state code, the Restatement (Second) of Contracts, and Judge Posner's dissenting decision in *Outsource v. Barton*—above offer a range of approaches to enforcing noncompetes signed by employees. Judge Posner's opinion offers a pure freedom of contract perspective: Noncompetes are contracts and should be enforced like any other legal agreement. However, Posner acknowledges that this is not the law in Illinois. In fact, it is not the law in any jurisdiction, owing in part to the countervailing policy concerns Posner raises (albeit to dismiss them!).

At the opposite extreme is California, which categorically prohibits noncompete agreements between employers and employees. California has repeatedly reiterated this position. *See, e.g., Edwards v. Arthur Andersen*, 189 P.3d 285 (Cal. 2008) (employer's refusal to release former employee from noncompete agreement except on his waiver of claims against the company, resulting in employee not being hired by prospective employer, constituted an "independently wrongful act" supporting employee's claim for tortious interference with prospective economic advantage); *Silguero v. Cretguard, Inc.*, 113 Cal. Rptr. 3d 653 (Cal. App. 2010) (finding employee stated claim for wrongful termination in violation of public policy where new employer fired her upon learning of her noncompete with former employer because of an "understanding" between the two despite acknowledging the agreement was unenforceable under California law). *See also Golden v. Cal. Emergency Physicians Med. Grp.*, 896 F.3d 1018, 1019 (9th Cir. 2018) (although a settlement agreement barring a physician from working for his former employer did not violate § 16600 since it reached only one employer, a provision that limited his ability to work for third parties, even those with service contracts with the employer, was invalid given its broad scope). North Dakota, has a similarly restrictive statute. N.D. Cent. Code §9-08-06 (2013); *see also* Colo. Rev. Stat. 8-2-113(2) (barring such covenants subject to certain exceptions).

Most jurisdictions (like Illinois) follow some version of the Restatement approach, which enforces "reasonable" noncompetes necessary to protect employers' "legitimate interests," although the "near permanent" standard seems peculiar to that state. However, since *Outsource*, Illinois has made the test less hostile to noncompetes. *See Reliable Fire Equip. Co. v. Arredondo*, 965 N.E.2d 393, 403 (Ill. 2011) (relegating "near permanence" to merely one factor in the analysis of legitimate business interests).

> But this tripartite division of approaches to covenants not to compete might suggest a coherence that does not exist. Even within single jurisdiction, it is very difficult to predict the outcome of potential litigation over noncompetition clauses.

Daniel P. O'Gorman, *Contract Theory and Some Realism About Employee Covenant Not to Compete Cases*, 65 SMU L. Rev. 145, 147-48 (2012). Whether such uncertainty on balance benefits employers, employees, or both is unclear.

In the last several years, there has been renewed interest in regulating noncompetes. In 2018, Massachusetts passed a sweeping reform of noncompetition laws with the aim of dramatically reducing employer leverage. While not as hostile to such agreements as California, the new rules collectively greatly restrict employer leeway. The law, 2018 Mass. ALS 228, 2018 Mass. Ch. 228, 2017 Mass. HB 4732, is most notable for its requirement of "garden leave" for employees required to sit out. Such individuals are entitled to 50 percent of their base salary during the restricted period, although the statute provides that an agreement not so providing may be valid so long as the employee received "mutually-agreed upon consideration." The statute also includes provisions barring noncompetes for more than a year for anyone and entirely for lower wage workers and those laid off or terminated without cause. But it does not apply to other restrictions, such as nondisclosure and nonsolicitation agreements, so it is probable that employers will enhance those protections. Other recent state enactments include a California law protecting its employees from contractual choice-of-law clauses that would deprive them of the benefits of that state's ban on employment noncompetes. CAL. LAB. CODE § 925 (2018), and Illinois barring noncompetes for "low-wage" employees, 820 ILCS 90/1 *et seq. See* https://www.jacksonlewis.com/publication/massachusetts-legislature-close-deal-non-compete-law.

2. *Of Paternalism and Employee Bargaining Power.* Posner describes judicial disfavor of noncompetes as rooted in a fear of employee abuse that "has no basis in current American conditions." Do you agree? Certainly, employees today are more mobile and have more flexibility than in the eighteenth century, when noncompete law developed. Does that mean they are more autonomous? More able to refuse a noncompete agreement? *See* Charles A. Sullivan, *The Puzzling Persistence of Unenforceable Contract Terms*, 70 OHIO ST. L.J. 1127 (2009) (exploring why employers rationally choose to use noncompetition clauses that are too broad to be enforced as written); Rachel Arnow-Richman, *Cubewrap Contracts and Worker Mobility: The Dilution of Employee Bargaining Power via Standard Form Noncompetes*, 2006 MICH. ST. L. REV. 963 (asserting that employers frequently present noncompetes to workers in the form of standardized agreements to be signed as routine paperwork after hire when their ability to refuse employment on such terms is highly constrained); Katherine V.W. Stone, *The New Psychological Contract*, 48 UCLA L. REV. 519 (2001) (providing examples of employers' use of noncompete agreements with lower-level employees, including manicurists and deliverymen); *see also* J.J. Prescott, Norman D. Bishara & Evan Starr, *Understanding Noncompetition Agreements: The 2014 Noncompete Survey Project*, 2016 MICH. ST. L. REV. 369, 370 (reporting that state law has little influence on the use of noncompetition agreements in employee contracts).

In assessing the enforceability of noncompetes, courts often seem more willing to find in favor of an employer if the departing employee participated in drafting the agreement or demonstrated bargaining ability in some other capacity. *See, e.g., Campbell Soup Co. v. Desatnik*, 58 F. Supp. 2d 477, 479-81 (D.N.J. 1999); *Delli-Gatti v. Mansfield*, 477 S.E.2d 134 (Ga. Ct. App. 1996). Should the current rules of reasonableness be replaced by a heightened examination of employee volition? Some commentators have suggested that such an approach could be useful. *See, e.g.*, Rachel Arnow-Richman, *Bargaining for Loyalty in the Information Age*, 80 OR. L. REV. 1163, 1235-36 (2001).

3. *What Can You Get for Giving Up Your Right to Compete?* In contrast to this view, some scholars, consistent with Judge Posner's analysis, believe that judicial refusal to enforce noncompetes deprives employees of the opportunity to freely negotiate the sale of their skills and human capital. *See* Stewart E. Sterk, *Restraints on the Alienation of Human Capital*, 79 VA. L. REV. 383 (1993). From this perspective, employees who sign noncompetes should realize some additional benefits—higher wages, better employment conditions, or enhanced opportunities for training and promotion—in compensation for their concession. However, empirical data suggest otherwise. Studies show that employees who sign noncompetes have lower executive compensation, are less likely to invest in human capital, and are more likely to take "occupational detours" that amount to a step back in their careers. *See* Orly Lobel,

TALENT WANTS TO BE FREE (2013). *See also* Evan Starr, *Are Noncompetes Holding Down Wages,* available at SSRN: https://ssrn.com/abstract=3223659 or http://dx.doi.org/10.2139/ssrn.3223659 ("The quasi-experimental evidence . . . is consistent: worker mobility and wages are both reduced in state states that enforce noncompetes. In contrast, two studies of actual noncompetes, neither of which claims to separate causation from correlation, find that noncompetes themselves are associated with higher wages.").

4. *The Complex Economics of Noncompete Agreements.* Whether individual workers are better or worse off is a different question from whether society as a whole benefits or suffers from noncompete enforcement. On this score, are you surprised to discover that Judge Posner, a pillar of the law and economics school, would advocate for the enforcement of agreements that interfere with interfirm competition? Noncompete agreements pit two core law and economics principles against one another: freedom of contract for the individual parties to the agreement and freedom of competition generally. Judge Posner expresses what has been the dominant economic view of these agreements—that their anticompetitive effects are minimal and they should be enforced like other contracts. *See* Michael J. Trebilcock, THE COMMON LAW OF RESTRAINTS OF TRADE (1986); Stewart E. Sterk, *Restraints on the Alienation of Human Capital,* 79 VA. L. REV. 383 406-7 (1993).

Not everyone agrees. Professor Ronald Gilson has argued that California statutory law prohibiting noncompetes in employment contributed to the vast development of the high-tech industry in Silicon Valley during the late twentieth century by enabling healthy information "spillovers" between firms. He described Silicon Valley industrial organization as "remarkably porous to outside influence," with high employee mobility between firms and cross-cutting personal relationships, which institutionalized knowledge spillovers. In this setting:

> [A] postemployment covenant not to compete prevents knowledge spillover of an employer's proprietary knowledge . . . by blocking the mechanism by which the spillover occurs: employees leaving to take up employment with a competitor or to form a competing start-up. . . . Given the speed of innovation and the corresponding telescoping of product life cycles, knowledge more than a year or two old likely no longer has significant competitive value. The hiatus imposed by a covenant not to compete thus assures that . . . [t]he value of proprietary tacit knowledge embedded in the employee's human capital . . . will have dissipated over the covenant's term. Nothing of value is left to spill over to a new employer or start-up venture. . . .

Ronald J. Gilson, *The Legal Infrastructure of High Technology Industrial Districts: Silicon Valley, Route 128, and Covenants Not to Compete,* 74 N.Y.U. L. REV. 575, 589-603 (1999); *see also* Orly Lobel, *The New Cognitive Property: Human Capital Law and the Reach of Intellectual Property,* 93 TEX. L. REV. 789, 853 (2015) ("Restrictions on the flow of knowledge [through noncompetes and other devices] contaminate market flows and diminish both the incentives to move efficiently in the market and the incentives to innovate."); Yifat Aran, Note, *Beyond Covenants Not to Compete: Equilibrium in High-Tech Startup Labor Markets,* 70 STAN. L. REV. 1235,1238-40 (2018) (it is not merely California's prohibition of employee noncompetes but also the industry's tendency to provide workers with stock options that "explains Silicon Valley's efficiency in matching talent with ventures"; the latter allow employee retention for successful start-ups while pushing them away if the company stumbles); Charles A. Sullivan, *Revisiting the "Neglected Stepchild": Antitrust Treatment of Postemployment Restraints of Trade,* 1977 U. ILL. L. F. 621, 647-50.

Yet another perspective suggests that noncompetes may be self-defeating in terms of employer interests by dampening employees' incentives to improve their skills. On Amir & Orly Lobel, *Driving Performance: A Growth Theory of Noncompete Law*, 16 STAN. TECH. L. REV. 833 (2013) (reporting an experimental study showing that postemployment restrictions "may discourage employees from investing in their own human capital and work performance").

As you read the following materials, keep in mind these different views of the costs and benefits of noncompetes, both to individuals and to society.

2. Disputes over Skills and Training

Rem Metals Corporation v. Logan
565 P. 2d 1080 (Or. 1977)

TONGUE, Justice.

This is a suit in equity to enforce "noncompetition" provisions of two employment agreements between plaintiff and defendant, who had been employed by plaintiff as a welder of precision titanium castings. Defendant appeals from a decree enjoining him from engaging in such work for a period of six months in Oregon for Precision Castparts Corporation, a competitor of plaintiff. We reverse.

The primary question presented for decision in this case, according to plaintiff Rem, is whether, as an employer, it had a sufficient "protectable interest" in the skills and knowledge of defendant as a skilled craftsman engaged as a repair welder of precision titanium castings, so as to justify enforcement of such a "noncompetition" agreement as a "reasonable restraint" upon defendant.

The titanium castings on which defendant Logan worked as a repair welder were produced by his employer, the plaintiff, under contract with Pratt & Whitney Aircraft Division for use as bearing housings for jet aircraft engines under exceedingly strict specifications. Only three companies are engaged in the production of such castings for Pratt & Whitney. These include plaintiff, Precision Castparts (its principal competitor) and Misco of Michigan (a smaller company).

In the process of the production of such castings any defects are repaired by welding performed by skilled welders who are "certified" by Pratt & Whitney inspectors as being sufficiently skilled to be entrusted with this important work. There was also some evidence that titanium is a "rare" or "reactive" metal and is difficult to weld.

Defendant was one of two or three "certified" welders employed by plaintiff and was plaintiff's best welder, with a proficiency rating of 98.3 per cent. Other welders rated below 95 per cent. There was testimony, however, that three other welders had been able to become sufficiently qualified so as to be "certified" for Pratt & Whitney work after 20 hours of training and that during 1966 seven of plaintiff's welders (including defendant) were so "certified."

Defendant Logan had been previously employed by Wah Chang Corporation, where he learned to weld electrodes of titanium. He was employed by plaintiff in 1969 and subsequently signed two employment contracts, as did nearly all Rem employees, including provisions to the effect that for a period of one year after termination he would not engage in any business in competition with Rem within the United States, "whether as principal, agent, employer, consultant or otherwise."

In 1972 defendant was transferred to the welding department. He testified that he became "certified" in "less than two weeks," and that no one gave him "any instruction before he took the certification test" for the welding of titanium.

Plaintiff offered testimony describing its training program for welders. When asked whether Rem had any "trade secrets in the welding department that are not generally known in the industry," that witness answered that "Rem was able to do a better job," to ship ahead of its schedules, and with fewer "rejects" from Pratt & Whitney than its competitors, so that "there is something we must be doing that our competitors are not doing." Rem's president testified that defendant received job training at Rem and "extensive written procedures prepared by Rem" which enabled him to weld titanium castings. He also testified, however, that it was nevertheless not surprising that defendant Logan was able to become "certified" within "a matter of a few days," as testified by Logan. Rem's supervisor of welding testified that:

> I don't think it's a matter of disclosing inasmuch as it is its instructional nature. If a welder's in the tank doing the work, we're qualifying it and giving what instructions we are capable of.

There was also testimony by another former Rem titanium welder, since employed by Precision Castparts, that he observed no differences in the welding procedures and techniques at Rem and at PCP except that Rem uses a "vacuum tank," while PCP uses a "plastic bubble," both of which are standard techniques.

On September 18, 1976, defendant Logan, after being refused a wage increase of 50 cents per hour by Rem, went to work at that increased rate for Precision Castparts. Plaintiff offered evidence that, as a result, it was unable for a period of two weeks to ship castings worth approximately $25,000 to Pratt & Whitney and that it then had difficulty in maintaining its shipping schedules of such titanium castings because it did not have welders who were "able to complete the weld repair cycle in a satisfactory manner." It appears, however, that Rem was then able to train two welders who "shortly thereafter were able to pass the qualification test of Pratt & Whitney." Plaintiff's witnesses also testified to their concern over Rem's continued ability to compete with Precision Castparts, its principal competitor, which by then had 14 or 15 titanium welders, including defendant Logan.

[On the subject of the enforcement of noncompetition provisions in employment contracts, the general rule is as follows:]

> Three things are essential to the validity of a contract in restraint of trade: (1) it must be partial or restricted in its operation in respect either to time or place; (2) it must be on some good consideration; and (3) it must be reasonable, that is, it should afford only a fair protection to the interests of the party in whose favor it is made, and must not be so large in its operation as to interfere with the interests of the public.

Eldridge v. Johnson, 245 P.2d 239, 250 (Or. 1952). As also stated in *North Pacific Lbr. v. Moore*, 551 P.2d 431, 434 (1976):

> To be entitled to the protection which a noncompetition covenant purports to provide, the employer must show that he has a legitimate interest entitled to protection.

At the outset, it is important to bear in mind that this is not a case involving an employee whose regular duties involved frequent dealings with customers of his employer and who had access to "customer lists" or other similar confidential information relating to customers. . . .

In our judgment, this case falls within the rule as stated in Blake, *Employee Agreements Not to Compete*, 73 Harv. L. Rev. 625, 652 (1960), as follows:

> . . . It has been uniformly held that general knowledge, skill, or facility acquired through training or experience while working for an employer appertain exclusively to the employee. The fact that they were acquired or developed during the employment does not, by itself, give the employee a sufficient interest to support a restraining covenant, even though the on-the-job training has been extensive and costly. In the absence, of special circumstances the risk of future competition form the employee falls upon the employer and cannot be shifted, even though the possible damages is greatly increased by experience gained in the course of the employment.

. . . We recognize, however, as does Blake, that on any given set of facts it may be difficult to "draw a line" between "training in the general skills and knowledge of the trade, and training which imparts information pertaining especially to the employer's business" and that this is the "central problem" in such cases. In other words, as stated by Blake:

> Its objective is not to prevent the competitive use of the unique personal qualities of the employee—either during or after the employment but to prevent competitive use, for a time, of information or relationships which pertain peculiarly to the employer and which the employee acquired in the course of the employment. . . .

In such a case, however, the burden of proof is upon the employer to establish the existence of "trade secrets," "information or relationships which pertain peculiarly to the employer," or other "special circumstances" sufficient to justify the enforcement of such a restrictive covenant.

Based upon our examination of this record, which we review de novo, and under the facts and circumstances of this case, we hold that this employer failed to sustain that burden of proof. Although defendant received training and experience while employed by plaintiff which developed his skill as a repair welder of titanium castings, plaintiff did not, in our judgment, establish by sufficient and credible evidence "special circumstances" of such a nature as to entitle Rem to demand the enforcement upon this defendant by injunction of this "noncompetition" clause as a "reasonable restraint."

NOTES

1. *The Threshold Issue. Rem Metals* introduces a critical threshold question in assessing the enforceability of noncompete agreements: Does the employer have an underlying interest justifying protection? This inquiry is unique to the law of restrictive covenants in employment. In theory, it protects workers by limiting the situations in which they can be contractually constrained. One justification is simple fairness, but is Logan in need of judicial protection? Who is the more vulnerable party in *Rem Metals*, the employer or employee?

In answering that question, consider the following. First, it appears uncontradicted that Rem Metals lost $25,000 in the two weeks following Logan's departure before it was able to train replacements. But that damage flowed from Logan's departure, not from his competition, and he was an at-will worker, so there was no breach of contract. The employer would have suffered the same loss had Logan retired suddenly. Second, Logan was obviously an exceptionally good worker with a skill that is in demand. Maybe he was in a better position than most employees to protect himself in negotiating the terms of his employment, although his inability to secure a raise suggests otherwise. Finally, what would have happened had the employer prevailed? Would Logan have found equally lucrative employment opportunities if he were precluded from competing with Rem Metals for one year? Do your answers explain the court's application of the "protectable interest" requirement?

2. *Protecting General Training: A Law and Economics View. Rem Metals* articulates the majority rule that an employer may not enforce a noncompete to protect employer investments in general knowledge and training. Maybe the justification for the rule is not fairness per se but rather property-like notions.

Professor Gary Becker's well-known human capital theory distinguishes between specific training that is useful only to one employer and general training that is useful to many. He contends that employers have an incentive to invest in specific training of employees because it benefits their business and cannot be usurped by competitors. On the other hand, employers are unlikely to invest in general training, meaning the worker must either pay for outside schooling or, in the case of on-the-job training, accepting lower wages during the training period. This theory supports the general rule in *Rem Metals*: Since the employee pays for the training herself, the employer should not be permitted to use a noncompete to prevent his sale of that human capital to a competitor. *See* Gary S. Becker, Human Capital: A Theoretical and Empirical Analysis 19-37 (2d ed. 1975); Edmund W. Kitch, *The Law and Economics of Rights in Valuable Information*, 9 J. Legal Stud. 683, 684 (1980) (summarizing Becker's theories).

Several commentators disagree that employees pay for their own general training. Professors Rubin and Shedd note that some forms of general training are too costly for an employee to finance out of her wages, as where an employer imparts to an employee a trade secret worth millions to competitors. In that situation, the employer would require a noncompetition agreement to prevent the employee from defecting to another firm willing to pay her a premium for her valuable knowledge. Of course, trade secrets are theoretically protectable without a noncompete, but, as Judge Posner suggested, misappropriation of trade secrets is sometimes hard to prove and a valid covenant not to compete solves that problem. Were such noncompetes unenforceable, firms would have less incentive to invest in acquiring this type of highly valuable information or sharing it with its workforce. *See* Paul H. Rubin & Peter Shedd, *Human Capital and Covenants Not to Compete*, 10 J. Legal Stud. 93, 96-7 (1981).

Still, Professors Rubin and Shedd acknowledge that employers may over-enforce noncompete agreements, and therefore ultimately conclude that noncompetes should not be enforceable to protect general training unless the training includes trade secrets or confidential information. *Id*. at 109-10. This is the approach that most courts take. *See, e.g., Ag Spectrum Co. v. Elder*, 865 F.3d 1088, 1092-93 (8th Cir. 2017) (finding a noncompetition agreement unenforceable when, inter alia, there was no showing that plaintiff provided training and information to the defendant); *Tom James Co. v. Mendrop*, 819 S.W.2d 251, 253 (Tex. App. 1991) (measuring methods and tools used in custom tailored men's clothing business were not specific enough to justify protection). *But see* Fla. Stat. Ann. §542.335(1)(b)(5) (recognizing "extraordinary or specialized training" as a legitimate business interest justifying a noncompete). As we will see, employers sometimes try to circumvent this by requiring employees to sign training repayment agreements, an approach that has been sanctioned by at least some jurisdictions. *See, e.g.*, COLO. REV. STAT. 8-2-113(2) (2018) (recognizing exception to prohibition on noncompetes to allow enforcement of an agreement "providing for recovery of the expense of educating and training" against an employee who has worked less than two years). The Restatement of Employment Law takes this approach, stating that recoupment of training investments justifies repayment promises but not a noncompetition agreement. §8.07, cmt. f.

3. *Training and Customer Goodwill.* In holding against the employer, *Rem Metals* distinguishes situations in which the employee has frequent dealings with customers. In some circumstances, employers' asserted interests in training elide with a more particularized interest in preserving client contacts or customer goodwill. This might occur, for instance, where the employee is a salesperson who had no prior experience in the employer's industry and the on-the-job experience and "training" she receives allows her to develop relationships with customers that she may use to her competitive advantage upon departure. *See Roberson v. C.P. Allen Construction Co.*, 50 So. 3d 471, 476 (Ala. App. 2010). We will talk about the viability of noncompetes and other techniques designed to protect this distinct interest beginning at page 528. For now, it is important to be aware that, even if the type of training provided to an employee does not support a noncompete, there may be other justifications for enforcement.

4. *Noncompetes as Alternatives to Fixed-Term Contracts.* If an employer's principal concern is worker retention—and in the case of an interest in employee skills and training, it often is—why doesn't the employer simply obtain a fixed-term employment contract? Indeed, if the employer forgoes such a contract, perhaps because it does not want to make an equivalent commitment to retaining the employee for a fixed term, why should it be permitted to use a noncompete to achieve the same result? One possible answer is that, because fixed-term contracts cannot be specifically enforced against employees, they do not adequately address employers' concerns about retention. Employers may also be unable to predict the precise length of employment needed to protect their interests, and noncompetes provide greater flexibility. On the other hand, does it trouble you that noncompetes give employers the discretion to seek enforcement based on their unilateral assessment of the circumstance at the time of departure? In part because of such concerns, some commentators have suggested that certain noncompetes should be enforced only if the employer promised the employee some degree of job security in exchange for the covenant. *See* Rachel Arnow-Richman, *Noncompetes, Human Capital, and Contract Formation: What Employment Law Can Learn from Family Law*, 10 TEX. WESLEYAN L. REV. 155 (2003).

5. *The Departure Dispute as Morality Play.* Another way of understanding the result in *Rem Metals* is to consider general concepts of fairness. It is hard to feel sorry for an employer who refuses its star welder a $0.50 pay increase. Similarly, it is not surprising to see courts enforcing noncompetes against employees who affirmatively take or destroy documents or otherwise attempt to sabotage the employer's business upon departure. In this way, disputes about competition often turn on assessments of fairness and loyalty. *See* Alan Hyde, WORKING IN SILICON VALLEY: ECONOMIC AND LEGAL ANALYSIS OF A HIGH-VELOCITY LABOR MARKET 37 (2003). As you read the cases in this chapter, pay attention to how courts' assessment of fault and loyalty correlate with its decisions in favor of or against enforcement of restraints against competition.

   6. *The Costs of Litigation.* No matter who is right, disputes over competition can be costly, and that burden weighs more heavily on employees, who are usually less able to bear the expense of defending themselves against a company. Logan's new employer financed the litigation, and the new employer is often a co-defendant in litigation over employee competition. Indeed, in the case of a coveted employee, the new employer may well contemplate and plan for the possibility of future litigation in its recruiting and hiring process. *See, e.g., Saks Fifth Ave. v. James, Ltd.*, 630 S.E.2d 304, 307 (Va. 2006) (new employer obtained employees' noncompetes during interview process, referred them to its attorneys, and agreed in writing to defend employees in the event of legal challenge by former employer); *see* also Kevin J. Delaney & Robert A. Guth, *Ruling Lets Lee Go to Work at Google*, Wall St. J., Sept. 14, 2005, B2 (recounting a high-profile dispute between Google and Microsoft over Google's hiring of former Microsoft vice president).

   7. *Legitimate Interests.* If general training is not a basis for enforcing a noncompete, what is? What might have worked for Rem Metals in terms of a protectable interest justifying an injunction? Would it have made a difference, for instance, if the certification Rem Metals provided took three months and cost $3,000 to administer? What if Logan had told Rem Metals' contractors that he was leaving Rem Metals, and the contractors decided to bring their future business to Logan's new employer? *See White v. Mederi Caretenders Visiting Servs., LLC*, 226 So. 3d 774 (Fla. 2017) (home health service referrals may be a protected legitimate business interests under Florida statute such that former employees may be prohibited from contacting the employer's sources such as doctors and hospitals).We will explore the two most commonly recognized "legitimate interests" of employers in the next sections—employer confidential information and employer customer relations—but note that other legitimate interests have been recognized. Thus, the Restatement of Employment Law also recognizes noncompetes to protect the employer's investment in the employee's reputation in the market or the purchase of an employee-owned business. §8.07(b)(3), (4).

3.   Disputes over Information

CTI, Inc. v. Software Artisans, Inc.
3 F.3d 730 (4th Cir.), vacated, 1993 U.S. App. Lexis 28601 (1993)

Williams, Circuit Judge.

   [Comprehensive Technologies International, Inc., "CTI," brought this action against several former employees and Software Artisans, Inc., "SA," asserting trade secret misappropriation and breach of contract in connection with the defendants' development of a computer program called "Transend." The district court entered judgment for the defendants. In 1988, the founder and CEO of CTI, Celestino Beltran, established a Software Product Group, headed by defendant Dean Hawkes, to expand the company in the area of electronic data interchange ("EDI"). EDI is the computer-to-computer transmission of business transactions in proprietary or standard formats. Hawkes was given responsibility for developing software that would enable clients to process and transmit data through EDI technology. Defendant Filippides was hired to market the software, and the other defendant employees wrote the code.]

Each of the Defendant employees except Hawkes signed CTI's standard Confidentiality and Proprietary Information Agreement. Under the Agreement, each employee agreed not to disclose or use, directly or indirectly, during his employment and for three years thereafter any confidential, proprietary, or software-related information belonging to CTI. The Agreement specifically identified the Claims Express and EDI Link projects as confidential. [Hawkes signed] an Employment Agreement that contained similar but more restrictive provisions. In addition to promising confidentiality, Hawkes agreed that during the term of his employment he would not compete with CTI, solicit CTI's customers, or employ CTI's current or former employees.

The Software Products Group undertook to develop two software packages for personal computers. The first, Claims Express, is an electronic medical billing system. Claims Express transmits information that conforms to two specific insurance claims forms [and] has been successfully marketed. CTI's second software package, EDI Link, is not specific to the health care industry. It is designed to permit users to create generic forms, enter data on the forms electronically, test that data for errors, and store both the forms and the data on a computer. Although CTI expended substantial effort on EDI Link, at the time of trial the program had not been completed and had never been sold or marketed. Trial testimony indicated that between 35 and 85 percent of the program had been completed.

In February 1991, all of the Defendant employees left CTI. . . .

In April 1991, the Defendants incorporated Software Artisans, Inc., located in Fairfax, Virginia. By July 1991, SA had developed and begun to market its own program called Transend. According to its User's Manual, Transend creates a "paperless office environment" by enabling its users to process business forms on a computer. Transend is similar to Claims Express and EDI Link in that it is designed to prepare forms for transmission by EDI. Transend permits the user to input data, check the data for errors, and prepare the data for transmission by EDI.

. . . III

Trade Secrets

The district court . . . found that CTI did not prove that the Defendants misappropriated a trade secret. Under Virginia law a "trade secret" is information, including but not limited to, a formula, pattern, compilation, program, device, method, technique, or process, that:

1. Derives independent economic value, actual or potential, from not being generally known to, and not being readily ascertainable by proper means by, other persons who can obtain economic value from its disclosure or use, and

2. Is the subject of efforts that are reasonable under the circumstances to maintain its secrecy.

Va. Code Ann. §59.1-336. For purposes relevant to this case, "misappropriation" means the "use of a trade secret of another without express or implied consent by a person who . . . [a]t the time of . . . use, knew or had reason to know that his knowledge of the trade secret was . . . [a]cquired under circumstances giving rise to a duty to maintain its secrecy or limit its use." *Id.*

In denying CTI's claim for trade secret misappropriation, the district court found that CTI did not possess any trade secrets and that, even if CTI did possess trade secrets, the Defendants had not misappropriated them. The court found no evidence that CTI's purported trade secrets—the organization of Claims Express and EDI Link, the database access techniques of the two programs, and the unique identifiers of the two programs—derived independent economic value from not being generally known or were not readily ascertainable by proper means. Consequently, the court concluded that CTI's purported trade secrets failed to satisfy all of the elements necessary to prove a trade secret. The district court also concluded that the Defendants did not "copy" any trade secrets, implying that Defendants did not "use" or otherwise misappropriate them.

CTI argues that in granting judgment for Defendants on its trade secrets claim, the district court misapplied the law. . . .

CTI reads the district court's opinion as ruling as a matter of law that the organization of its database, its database access techniques, and its unique identifiers could not constitute trade secrets because each of their composite elements was in the public domain. CTI argues vociferously (and correctly) that although a trade secret cannot subsist in information in the public domain, it can subsist in a combination of such information, as long as the combination is itself secret. *See Integrated Cash Management v. Digital Transactions*, 920 F.2d 174 (2d Cir. 1990). According to CTI, each of its alleged trade secrets is just such a combination of publicly available information.

[However, CTI misreads the district court's opinion, which simply found that] CTI failed to present any evidence that its database organization, its access techniques, and its identifiers were not themselves publicly available. The court specifically found that the arrangement and interaction of the functions of Claims Express and EDI Link were "common to all computer programs of this type." Information that is generally known cannot qualify as a trade secret. . . .

Even if CTI had demonstrated that these items constituted trade secrets, CTI has not convinced us that the district court clearly erred in finding that the Defendants did not misappropriate any of CTI's alleged trade secrets. CTI points to the short development time and the complete lack of design documentation for Transend as strong circumstantial evidence of misappropriation. Although this evidence does raise some suspicions, Defendants provided a colorable explanation for the absence of design documentation. First, Defendant's expert . . . testified that it was not atypical for small software companies to neglect to prepare extensive design documentation. Second, [Defendant] Sterba testified that he and the others disliked the amount of paperwork involved in documenting their designs, that they preferred to use a "whiteboard" for their design work, and that they placed much of the information that would ordinarily appear in design documentation in the code itself. In light of this testimony, CTI's circumstantial evidence is not enough to convince us that the district court clearly erred in finding that the Defendants did not copy (or "use") any of CTI's alleged trade secret information. . . .

IV

Covenant Not to Compete

CTI next argues that the district court should have enforced Dean Hawkes's covenant not to compete. In his Termination Agreement, Hawkes agreed that, for a period of twelve months following his departure from CTI, he would not engage directly or indirectly in any business within the United States (financially as an investor or lender or as an employee, director, officer, partner, independent contractor, consultant or owner or in any other capacity calling for the rendition of personal services or acts of management, operation or control) which is in competition with the business of CTI. For purposes of this Agreement, the "business of CTI" shall be defined as the design, development, marketing, and sales of CLAIMS EXPRESS and EDI LINK type PC-based software with the same functionality and methodology. . . .

Virginia has established a three-part test for assessing the reasonableness of restrictive employment covenants. Under the test, the court must ask the following questions:

1. Is the restraint, from the standpoint of the employer, reasonable in the sense that it is no greater than is necessary to protect the employer in some legitimate business interest?
2. From the standpoint of the employee, is the restraint reasonable in the sense that it is not unduly harsh and oppressive in curtailing his legitimate efforts to earn a livelihood?
3. Is the restraint reasonable from the standpoint of a sound public policy?

If a covenant not to compete meets each of these standards of reasonableness, it must be enforced. As a general rule, however, the Virginia courts do not look favorably upon covenants not to compete, and will strictly construe them against the employer. The employer bears the burden of demonstrating that the restraint is reasonable.

The district court refused to enforce the covenant not to compete because it concluded that the covenant was broader than necessary to protect CTI's legitimate business interests. First, the court held that the scope of the employment restrictions was too broad because the restrictions precluded Hawkes from working for a competitor in any capacity, even as a janitor. The court implied that CTI did not have a legitimate interest in preventing Hawkes from working for a competitor in a menial capacity. Second, the district court concluded that the geographic scope of the agreement was broader than necessary to protect CTI's interests. The court found that CTI had marketed Claims Express only in Virginia, Nebraska, and perhaps one other state, and therefore CTI did not have a legitimate interest in restricting Hawkes's employment throughout the United States.

Although the district court believed that the covenant was categorically overbroad because it precluded Hawkes from working for a competitor of CTI in any capacity, the Virginia Supreme Court has enforced similarly broad restrictions. . . .

Moreover, as Vice President of CTI's Software Products Group, Hawkes necessarily came in contact with confidential information concerning both CTI's products and its customers. Hawkes's access to such confidential information makes the covenant not to compete more reasonable. As the Virginia Supreme Court has noted,

[t]he fact that the employment is of such a character as to inform the employee of business methods and trade secrets which, if brought to the knowledge of a competitor, would prejudice the interests of the employer, tends to give an element of reasonableness to a contract that the employee will not engage in a similar business for a limited time after the termination of his employment, and is always regarded as a strong reason for upholding the contract.

Stoneman [*v. Wilson*], 192 S.E. [816, 819 (Va. 1938)]. Similarly, in *Roanoke Engineering* [*v. Rosenbaum*, 290 S.E. 2d 882, 885 (Va. 1982)], an employee had access to confidential financial records, lists of customers and suppliers, and detailed knowledge of overhead factors, pricing policies, and bidding techniques. The Virginia Supreme Court held that this information enabled the employee to become a "formidable competitor" of his former employer, and concluded that a restriction barring the employee from working for competitors in any capacity was no greater than necessary to protect the employer's legitimate business interests.

Hawkes poses a similar danger to CTI's business. As the individual primarily responsible for the design, development, marketing and sale of CTI's software, Hawkes became intimately familiar with every aspect of CTI's operation, and necessarily acquired information that he could use to compete with CTI in the marketplace. When an employee has access to confidential and trade secret information crucial to the success of the employer's business, the employer has a strong interest in enforcing a covenant not to compete because other legal remedies often prove inadequate. It will often be difficult, if not impossible, to prove that a competing employee has misappropriated trade secret information belonging to his former employer. On the facts of this case, we conclude that the scope of the employment restrictions is no broader than necessary to protect CTI's legitimate business interests.

As a second ground for invalidating the covenant not to compete, the district court concluded that the geographic scope of the employment restrictions—"within the United States"—was greater than necessary to protect CTI's business. The district court merely noted that CTI had marketed Claims Express in only three states and therefore did not have a national market for its product.

The district court clearly erred in concluding that CTI did not have a national market for Claims Express. CTI licensed Claims Express in at least ten states. . . . CTI also identified for the district court specific customer prospects in [nineteen states] and the District of Columbia. CTI presented Claims Express and EDI Link (albeit in preliminary form) at national EDIA trade shows in both 1989 and 1990. Finally, CTI presented evidence that it faced direct [and potential] competition from companies located [throughout the country]. Given the breadth of the market for Claims Express, we cannot see how anything less than a nationwide prohibition could conceivably protect CTI's business interests. . . .

Having determined that the covenant not to compete is reasonable from CTI's point of view, we must next determine whether the covenant is reasonable from Hawkes's point of view, i.e., whether the curtailment on Hawkes's ability to earn a living is unduly harsh or oppressive. Although the agreement applies throughout the United States, it restricts Hawkes from engaging in only an extremely narrow category of business. Hawkes may not render personal services to, or perform acts of management, operation, or control for, any business in competition with "the business of CTI," which the agreement defines as "the design, development, marketing and sales of CLAIMS EXPRESS™ and EDI LINK™ type PC-based software with the same functionality and methodology." The agreement therefore permits Hawkes to design, develop, market and sell any software of a type different from Claims Express or EDI Link, any software of the same type having a different functionality or methodology, or any software of the same type having the same functionality and methodology that is not designed to run on personal computers. Hawkes is also free to compete with any other branch of CTI's business. Because Hawkes retains broad employability under the agreement, the agreement is not unduly harsh or oppressive.

In light of the foregoing, we conclude that the covenant not to compete is no greater than necessary to protect CTI's business and is not unduly harsh or oppressive. . . .

NOTES

1. *Trade Secret Defined.* Although the parties' settlement resulted in the vacation of this opinion, the court's discussion throws considerable light on various aspects of trade secret law. CTI's primary cause of action against its former employees was misappropriation of a trade secret. Virginia, like a majority of states, has adopted the Uniform Trade Secrets Act ("UTSA"), which lists two requirements for a trade secret: The item in question must derive independent economic value from not being generally known and it must be subject to the employer's reasonable efforts to maintain its secrecy. *See* UTSA, 14 U.L.A. 437 (1990); *see also* the Defend Trade Secrets Law of 2016, 18 U.S.C. § 1839(3) (2018); RESTATEMENT OF EMPLOYMENT LAW §8.02. Older trade secret cases often involved disputes over particular manufacturing processes or the "secret sauce" for a particular product. The recipe for Coca-Cola is often cited as the paradigmatic trade secret. Today, however, many employers seek trade secret protection for more general information, either technical information (as is the case in *CTI*) or confidential business information (financial documentation, marketing strategies, etc.). This poses new challenges in identifying what constitutes a trade secret. Although CTI may have made efforts to keep its project under wraps, according to the court the actual components of CTI's programs and their structure followed techniques and configurations that were in common use.

2. *Independently Valuable Information.* Another question that arises in analyzing trade secrets in information is whether that information—even if not generally known—has independent economic value. Professor Arnow-Richman interprets it to mean that information sought to be protected must be useable to competitors outside of the employer's project or business environment, which often is not the case with secret information that is highly technical and company-specific. Rachel Arnow-Richman, *Bargaining for Loyalty in the Information Age: A Reconsideration of the Role of Substantive Fairness in Enforcing Employee Noncompetes*, 80 OR. L. REV. 1163, 1190 (2001); *see also* Catherine Fisk, *Working Knowledge: Trade Secrets, Restrictive Covenants in Employment, and the Rise of Corporate Intellectual Property*, 1800-1920, 52 HASTINGS L. J. 441, 503-04 (2001). Was this part of the problem in *CTI*? In other words, was the employer trying to protect the work its employees were doing rather than a particular programming technique? If so, is that a good reason for denying CTI trade secret protection, or should the definition of a trade secret be understood to include such interests? The Restatement explicitly rejects protection of information "acquired by employees through their general experience, knowledge, and skills during the ordinary course of employment." §8.02cb)(3).

3. *Evidence of Misappropriation.* To succeed on its trade secret claim, CTI had to show not only that its software products were trade secrets but also that those secrets had been misappropriated. The UTSA offers an expansive definition of misappropriation. The portion most relevant in the competitive employment context defines the concept as

> disclosure or use of a trade secret of another without express or implied consent by a person who . . . at the time of disclosure or use knew or had reason to know that his knowledge of the trade secret was . . . acquired under circumstances giving rise to a duty to maintain its secrecy or limit its use.

14 U.L.A. 437; *see also* RESTATEMENT §8.03 (disclosure or use of a trade secret breaches the duty of loyalty).

As *CTI* illustrates, it can be difficult to prove misappropriation of trade secrets. However, the increasing sophistication of computer forensics has made it easier to track the downloading, copying, and e-mailing of files, allowing companies to demonstrate that particular documents were taken by departing employees. *See, e.g., Bimbo Bakeries USA Inc. v. Botticella*, 613 F.3d 102 (3d Cir. 2010) (employer's computer expert identified pattern of accessing multiple documents consistent with copying in the week leading up to former employee's departure and established that portable hard drives had been attached to the computer). But where alleged secrets are intangible and do not exist in written form, or where the employee resorts to less technical means of "copying," the employer must rely on circumstantial evidence of misappropriation. *See, e.g., San Jose Construction, Inc. v. S.B.C.C., Inc.*, 67 Cal. Rptr. 3d 54 (Cal. App. 2007) (similarities between project proposals submitted by plaintiff's former construction manager and those he submitted for same projects while in plaintiff's employ created issue of fact on misappropriation, notwithstanding his return of all project files); *Sunbelt Rentals, Inc. v. Head & Engquist Equip.*, 620 S.E.2d 222, 229 (N.C. Ct. App. 2005) (treating as evidence of misappropriation defendant's new company's speedy evolution from having no customers to converting several of plaintiff's customers and making extraordinarily high profit in first year of operation following mass defection of plaintiff's employees). If you were representing the employer, what other evidence of misappropriation would you look for and how would you go about obtaining it? If you were counseling an employee about to engage in competition with a former employer, what precautions would you recommend taking to help avoid or potentially defend against a misappropriation claim?

4. *The Role of Contract in Protecting Information.* To avoid the challenges facing employers in pursuing trade secret misappropriation claims, employers often seek contractual protection for information through a nondisclosure or noncompete clause. *See* Ronald J. Gilson, *The Legal Infrastructure of High Technology Industrial Districts: Silicon Valley, Route 128, and Covenants Not to Compete*, 74 N.Y.U. L. REV. 575 (1999); Gillian Lester, *Restrictive Covenants, Employee Training, and the Limits of Transaction-Cost Analysis*, 76 INDIANA L. J. 49, 53 (2001). This is illustrated by the unsuccessful tort claim and successful contract claim in *CTI.*

A criticism of employers' use of noncompetes is that it circumvents the threshold requirements of trade secret law, showing of a legitimate interest to justify enforcement. What is CTI's "legitimate" interest in enforcing a noncompete against Hawkes if there are no trade secrets to protect? Consider Professor Katherine Stone's perspective:

The long-standing view has been that to be enforceable, a covenant not to compete must protect an employer's legitimate interest in a trade secret or confidential information. This view creates a paradox, however, because if a court requires a trade secret or confidential information in order to enforce a covenant, the existence of the covenant becomes, at least theoretically, irrelevant. Disclosure of trade secrets and confidential information can be restrained in the absence of such a covenant.

If the law of noncompete covenants merely restates or incorporates the law of trade secrets and confidential relationships, then there is little independent role for the covenant.

Katherine V. W. Stone, *The New Psychological Contract*, 48 UCLA L. REV. 519, 583-84 (2001). Professor Stone attempts to explain this paradox, noting the possibility that a covenant makes it easier for an employer to obtain injunctive relief before the secret is disclosed.

In contrast to trade secret law, misappropriation is *not* a prerequisite to noncompete enforcement in most jurisdictions. *See Certainteed Corp. v. Williams*, 481 F.3d 528 (7th Cir. 2007) (noting that a noncompete protects a former employer "when the executive's use of trade secrets would be hard to detect"). But noncompete law does require a threshold showing of the employer's interest in the information to be protected. As Stone puts it: "In theory, the standard of proof for finding a trade secret in the two cases should be no different, unless the court is sub rosa imposing a different test for finding a trade secret where there is a contractual obligation." She goes on:

> . . . A case in point is [*CTI*]. While the court did not find that the knowledge the employee possessed was a trade secret, it justified its decision on the ground that the employee had access to confidential information concerning both the products and customers of the former employer, so that "it will often be difficult . . . to prove that a competing employee has misappropriated trade secret information belonging to his former employer." This rationale suggests that the court acted to protect the trade secret, not to enforce the parties' agreement, but the existence of the covenant enabled it to sidestep the difficult trade secret issue.

Id. at 585. Do you see why a court might be more inclined to find for an employer on the basis of a noncompete than on a trade secret claim? Do you understand Professor Stone's concern about this practice?

Consider that a contractual expansion of employer rights beyond that conferred by trade secret law has implications not only for the worker but for society. One criticism of the use of noncompetes in this manner is that it upsets the balance struck by the background intellectual property regime, which is intentionally limited so as to preserve public access to information while still incentivizing creation. *See* Viva R. Moffat, *The Wrong Tool for the Job: The IP Problem with Non-Competition Agreements*, 52 WILL. & MARY L. REV. 873 (2010).

5. *Narrower Restraints as Alternatives.* Requiring employees to sign nondisclosure agreements may be necessary to show the employer made reasonable efforts to maintain secrecy, one of the elements for trade secret protection, but do nondisclosure agreements (NDAs) pose similar problems to noncompetes? Admittedly, their narrower scope reduces the concern, although we'll encounter the "inevitable disclosure" doctrine later in this chapter. *See* p. 496. But employers often combine a noncompete with an NDA as a kind of belt-and-suspender strategy: Even if a court ultimately refuses to enforce the noncompete, it might enforce the nondisclosure promise.

Some courts apply the same rule of reasonableness to lesser restraints like nondisclosure and nonsolicitation clauses. But such clauses are more likely to be found reasonable if only because they are more tailored to the interest to be protected and less onerous. A nondisclosure clause, for example, may prevent an employee from using certain knowledge but not bar her from working for a competitor. And a nonsolicitation clause might allow the former employee to work for a competitor as long as she did not contact, or perhaps deal with, former customers. Nevertheless, such clauses can still pose a serious obstacle to an employee mobility. *See Manitowoc Co. v. Lanning*, 906 N.W.2d 139 (Wis. 2018) (finding a nonsolicitation agreement barring "poaching" of the employer's workers to be unenforceable even though less burdensome than a noncompete); *AssuredPartners, Inc. v. Schmitt*, 44 N.E.3d 463 (Ill. App. Ct. 2015) (nonsolicitation provision unenforceable because it prevented the former employee from soliciting business from not only from plaintiff's existing customers but also from potential customers). *But see Orthofix, Inc. v. Hunter*, 630 F. App'x 566, 573 (6th Cir. 2015) (nondisclosure agreements are enforceable even without geographic and durational limits so long as the agreement does not prohibit employees from using general knowledge, skill, and experience acquired in their former employment; if it does so, it is more properly viewed as a noncompete). As a result, even applying the same rule regarding validity to these lesser restraints may lead to a different assessment of the balance of hardships.

★ **6.** *Reasonableness.* Even if an employer is using a noncompete agreement to protect a legitimate interest, the agreement is not enforceable unless it is "reasonable." *CTI* discusses two factors that courts consider in assessing whether a noncompete is reasonable—its geographic reach and the scope of competition prohibited. (A third factor, duration of the restraint, is taken up in the next case.) Note the relationship between the two factors the court considers. The court permits a very broad geographic reach (the whole country) in part because the definition of competition is extremely narrow (only companies developing PC software with the same functionality and methodology). In past decades, courts frequently struck down noncompetes precluding nationwide competition as categorically overbroad, reflecting the view (and probably the reality in that era) that few businesses could be meaningfully competitive beyond the borders of their state or geographic region. In today's world, however, such geographic provisions are both more common and more commonly enforced, particularly if the scope of prohibited competition is narrowly drawn. Illustration 7 of the Restatement's §8.06 approves a "worldwide" ban on competition when reasonably tailored to protect the employer's interest. Indeed, courts have occasionally enforced worldwide restrictions on narrow forms of competitive behavior on behalf of companies operating in an international market. *See, e.g., Superior Consulting Co. v. Walling*, 851 F. Supp. 839, 847 (E.D. Mich. 1994); *Farr Assocs., Inc. v. Baksin*, 530 S.E.2d 878, 882 (N.C. Ct. App. 2000).

Note on Injunctive Relief and the Mechanics of Enforcement

If negotiations fail and the employer decides to sue a departing employee, it will typically seek preliminary injunctive relief from the court. That is, the employer will obtain an immediate, abbreviated hearing at which it will argue that the court should enjoin the employee from disclosing a trade secret and/or breaching his or her noncompete agreement, pending a full trial.

Although the tests vary somewhat among circuits, to obtain a preliminary injunction, an employer must show that there is a danger of irreparable harm, that it is likely to succeed on the merits at trial, that a balance of the equities favors issuing the injunction, and that an injunction will not violate the public interest. *See, e.g., SI Handling Systems, Inc. v. Heisley* 753 F.2d 1244, 1254 (3d Cir. 1985). During the preliminary injunction stage, the parties typically have a compressed discovery schedule and will often mount a full-blown minitrial at the hearing. Speed is important not only because harm may transpire during any delay but also because some courts refuse to issue a preliminary injunction if a decision is not reached before the noncompetition period expires. *See EMC Corp. v. Arturi*, 655 F.3d 75, 76 (1st Cir. 2011). Other courts, however, will recognize "equitable extensions" to account for delays in the legal system. *Guy Carpenter & Co. v. Provenzale*, 334 F.3d 459, 464 (5th Cir. 2003). In any event, so much effort is put into obtaining or defeating a temporary order because the preliminary injunction proceeding is often the only step that matters in this kind of litigation. By the time the case goes to trial on the merits, months may have passed. From the employer's perspective, any damage to its interests will have already been done. Although an employer who succeeds at trial after losing at the preliminary injunction stage may obtain damages, monetary injury in such cases is often hard to quantify, and damage awards can be difficult to collect from an individual employee.

For the employee, the issuance of a preliminary injunction means that he may be unemployed or underemployed, at least until trial. Even if he ultimately succeeds on the merits, he may not be able to recoup wages lost during the preliminary injunction period, and often the competitive employment opportunity that he sought to pursue will have disappeared. *See, e.g., FLIR Syst. v. Parrish*, 95 Cal. Rptr. 3d 307 (Cal. App. 2009). For some high-level employees, a competitor may be willing to wait for the employee to "sit out" the period of his noncompetition agreement. But for many ordinary employees, a preliminary injunction means lost career time, lost income, and lots of legal bills.

If an employer is successful in obtaining injunctive relief, what will the court order say? Where the employer successfully alleges breach of a noncompete, the court will enjoin the employee from competing. The scope of the injunction will reflect the terms of the contract, subject to any modifications the court may fashion to ensure that its effects are not unduly burdensome to the employee. In the case of a trade secret claim, the scope of the injunction is less clear. Trade secret law does not prohibit competition per se; rather, it prohibits misuse of certain information. Therefore, a preliminary injunction in a trade secret case might simply enjoin the employee from using or disclosing that information.

What if the former employer alleges the employee's new job is so closely related to his or her former position that the employee will inevitably use the employer's trade secrets? In *PepsiCo v. Redmond*, 54 F.3d 1262 (7th Cir. 1995), Pepsi sought to enjoin the former General Manager of its California Business Unit from taking a comparable position with rival drink manufacturer Quaker. It argued that Redmond had extensive knowledge of the company's annual operating plan, its pricing architecture, and its marketing and distribution strategies for the upcoming year. Redmond had signed a confidentiality agreement with Pepsi, but not a noncompete. Pepsi nonetheless sought an injunction against competition. The court granted it, finding that "unless Redmond possessed an uncanny ability to compartmentalize information, he would necessarily be making decisions about [Quaker's]

Gatorade and Snapple by relying on his knowledge of [Pepsi's] trade secrets." *Id.* at 1269. The court explained:

> Admittedly, PepsiCo has not brought a traditional trade secret case, in which a former employee has knowledge of a special manufacturing process or customer list and can give a competitor an unfair advantage by transferring the technology or customers to that competitor. PepsiCo has not contended that Quaker has stolen the [Pepsi] All Sport formula or its list of distributors. Rather PepsiCo has asserted that Redmond cannot help but rely on PCNA trade secrets as he helps plot Gatorade and Snapple's new course, and that these secrets will enable Quaker to achieve a substantial advantage by knowing exactly how PCNA will price, distribute, and market its sports drinks and new age drinks and being able to respond strategically. . . .
>
> The defendants' arguments [that Quaker has not and does not intend to use Pepsi's confidential information, much of which would be useless to it anyway] fall somewhat short of the mark. . . . In other words, PepsiCo finds itself in the position of a coach, one of whose players has left, playbook in hand, to join the opposing team before the big game. Quaker and Redmond's protestations that their distribution systems and plans are entirely different from PCNA's are thus not really responsive.

Id. at 1269-70. Is *PepsiCo* consistent with what *CTI* teaches about the elements of a trade secret claim? Is it consistent with the distinction *Rem Metals* draws between protectable information and an employee's skills and experience? Note that both parties in *PepsiCo* agreed that Redmond had not taken any documents upon departure, nor was he likely to use directly any of the information he remembered. Consider Professor Alan Hyde's opinion of the case:

> PepsiCo never identified any specific piece of information that Redmond had and Quaker wanted. PepsiCo did not show that Redmond knew the recipe for All Sport, or new flavors being worked on secretly, or which athletes had been approached for endorsements, or anything of that sort.
>
> What *did* Redmond know? He was far from the key figure in All Sport. He was one of many regional general managers. He had access, said PepsiCo, to its "Strategic Plan" and "Annual Operating Plan" covering "financial goals, marketing plans, promotional event calendars, growth expectations, and operational changes." He knew which markets Pepsi would focus on, and some aspects of a new delivery system. In other words, he knew what any manager knows.
>
> The *PepsiCo* decision is unusually proplaintiff, [and therefore] not typical. It inhabits a world in which all managers on distribution lists for "strategic plans" and "annual operating plans" serve for life, and may have their departures to work in the area they know enjoined at the option of their employer. It seems not to relate at all to today's world of corporate downsizing and managerial layoffs. It does not rest on any economic analysis of the efficiency advantages of letting Redmond go as against letting PepsiCo enjoin him, even though the Court of Appeals for the Seventh Circuit is famous for its law and economic approach. Nor does it reinforce employment-at-will, to which, in other cases, that court has paid homage. Employees with other options, such as competent managers, may choose not to accept employment at will if, following involuntary termination, they will be unable to work in their area of expertise.

Alan Hyde, WORKING IN SILICON VALLEY: ECONOMIC AND LEGAL ANALYSIS OF A HIGH-VELOCITY LABOR MARKET 34-35 (2003). The inevitable disclosure doctrine has not fared well in the courts, *e.g.*, *Holton v. Physician Oncology Servs., LP*, 742 S.E.2d 702 (Ga. 2013) (no stand-alone inevitable disclosure doctrine in Georgia), although some continue to rely on it. *See Bimbo v. Botticella*, 613 F.3d 102, 118 (3d Cir. 2010) (the defendant was properly enjoined from competing when he posed a "substantial threat" of trade secret disclosure of the "nooks and crannies" texture of Thomas's English Muffins, in large part because of "suspicious conduct during his final weeks of employment."). Professor Hyde's views substantially influenced the Restatement of Employment Law, which provides that no injunction should issue absent "actual use or disclosure" or "a high likelihood, based on the employee's statements or conduct" that the employee will violate the restriction. §8.05, cmt. B. The Defend Trade Secrets Law of 2016 also rejects the inevitable disclosure doctrine. 18 U.S.C. § 1836 (3)(a). It seems likely, therefore, that future suits will focus on whether there was actual use, or some reason to suspect an intent to use, confidential information. However, if courts are less likely to enjoin prophylactically disclosure of trade secrets, and if proof of actual disclosure is often difficult to establish, employers will have even more incentive to rely on noncompetition clauses to achieve their goals. To the extent that occurs, a lesser restraint will be replaced by a greater one.

Still, this does not mean that noncompetition terms moored to the former employer's interest in protecting disclosure of trade secrets are easily enforced. On the contrary, such clauses might fail for a host of reasons. Consider the court's refusal to enter an injunction based on a noncompetition agreement in *EarthWeb, Inc. v. Schlack*, 71 F. Supp. 2d 299 (S.D.N.Y. 1999). The court first rejected the EarthWeb's inevitable disclosure of trade secrets claim against its former employee (Schlack) who had left to take a job with an Internet startup (ITworld.com). The court then refused to enforce the noncompetition agreement Schlack had signed, concluding that ITworld was not a directly competitive business with Earthlink and that, in any event, the one-year restriction was too long "given the dynamic nature of this industry." *Id.* at 313. Even aside from these concerns, the court was not convinced an injunction was justified to protect the claimed secrets, including the claim that Schlack was intimately familiar with the "strategic thinking" behind the company's websites and its overall business plan). Such thinking might be revealed when the websites went public. *Id.* at 315.

As the final nail in the coffin, the court found that "enforcement of this provision would work a significant hardship on Schlack. When measured against the IT industry in the Internet environment, a one-year hiatus from the workforce is several generations, if not an eternity." *Id.* at 316.

Even if, unlike in *EarthWeb*, a noncompetition agreement premised on trade secrets protection is enforceable by injunction, remedies beyond such equitable relief can be problematic. Consider the next case.

≡
≡ *Fishkin v. Susquehanna Partners, G.P.*
≡ *340 F. App'x 110 (3d Cir. 2009)*

Van Antwerpen, Circuit Judge.

This appeal stems from a dispute between Appellant Susquehanna International Group, LLP ("SIG"), a securities trading firm, and two of its former employees, Cal Fishkin and Igor Chernomzav, who left SIG and formed a competing securities trading joint venture, TABFG, LLC ("TABFG"), in partnership with NT Prop Trading, LLC ("NT Prop"). . . .

I . . .

In the spring of 1999, Cal Fishkin and Igor Chernomzav began working for SIG as securities traders, and each executed an employment contract containing restrictive covenants. One such covenant, the "Non-Competition" clause, provided in part that,

> [f]or a period of nine (9) months following the later of the termination of [Employee's] employment or the third anniversary following Employee's entry into the training course, Employee shall not trade in any products in which he or she was trading for [SIG] at any time during the three (3) month period prior to the termination of Employee's employment.

The noncompetition clause also barred Fishkin and Chernomzav from disclosing confidential information about SIG's business and restricted them from associating with anyone employed at SIG during the nine months prior to their termination for a period of five years. The employment agreement provided SIG with alternative remedies in the event of a breach: (a) liquidated damages of $700,000 or $800,000, depending on when the breach occurred; or (b) injunctive relief and other remedies to which it was entitled at law.

In August 1999, SIG assigned Francis Wisniewski to trade Dow Futures, which are futures contracts in the Dow Jones Industrial Average ("DJIA"),[1] in the trading pit at the Chicago Board of Trade. Following about a month of unsuccessful trading, Wisniewski developed a formula for calculating the expected values of Dow Futures based on his observation that successful traders of Dow Futures monitored trading data for the S&P 500 Index. Because all of the individual stocks in the DJIA are also included in the S&P 500 Index, Dow Futures and S&P Futures tend to move in the same direction, with S&P Futures typically adjusting to market movements slightly before such adjustments are reflected in the price of Dow Futures. Accordingly, SIG's Dow Fair Value formula reflected the relationship between S&P Futures and Dow Futures. After developing this formula, Wisniewski created a spreadsheet to make the formula's calculations more quickly. After two months of trading Dow Futures, SIG reassigned Wisniewski. He saved the spreadsheet containing the Dow Fair Value formula.

In August 2001, SIG reassigned Wisniewski to the Dow Futures pit and, shortly thereafter, assigned Fishkin to trade Dow Futures (and engage in related hedging transactions) with Wisniewski. They used the Dow Fair Value formula that Wisniewski previously developed and traded the product until March 2003; for the year 2002, Wisniewski and Fishkin earned SIG net trading profits of approximately $30 million.

Fishkin grew dissatisfied with his compensation and, in June 2002, sought to negotiate a new employment contract with SIG. SIG did not immediately respond to his request. Later that year, Fishkin was approached by a non-SIG trader representing a group that later became NT Prop about whether he would be interested in forming

---

1. A "future" is a derivative, which is a security that derives its value from an underlying security or asset. Specifically, a future is a contract to buy or sell a particular commodity at a specific price at a set time in the future. The futures at issue in this litigation were contracts to buy or sell stocks in the DJIA or Standard & Poor's ("S&P") 500 Index—Dow Futures and S&P Futures, respectively—at a set price on a set date.

a new company to trade Dow Futures. Fishkin indicated that he would be interested in participating in the new trading group as of March 2003, when his contract with SIG expired. Between December 2002 and April 2003, Fishkin met with NT Prop representatives several times to discuss a trading venture; at one such meeting, NT Prop representatives asked Fishkin about SIG's profitability in trading Dow Futures. Fishkin told them that confidentiality provisions precluded him from revealing such information, but, when asked if he made more than $5 million at SIG, Fishkin replied by saying "you'll be pleased." In February 2003, Fishkin stopped trading for SIG and officially left the company in March 2003 (along with Chernomzav) to start a competing business, TABFG, LLC. On March 31, 2003, articles of incorporation were filed for TABFG. In late April 2003, TABFG and NT Prop entered into a joint venture to trade securities and financial products on the Chicago Board of Trade (as well as other exchanges). TABFG began trading on April 25, 2003; it traded for four and one-half months until September 16, 2003, when it was enjoined from doing so by the District Court.

[Fishkin, Chernomzav, and Wisniewski filed suit, seeking to have the noncompetition agreements in their employment contracts with SIG declared unenforceable. SIG counterclaimed, seeking an injunction preventing Fishkin and Chernomzav from trading as well as damages for breach of contract, misappropriation of trade secrets, conversion, tortious interference with contract, and civil conspiracy. SIG was granted a preliminary injunction to enforce Fishkin's and Chernomzav's noncompetition agreements by restraining them and TABFG from trading in violation of the former employees' promises; that injunction was ultimately made permanent. This appeal does not consider that ruling.]

III.

A. *Damages for Contractual Breach*

SIG appeals the District Court's ruling that, because SIG could not establish its lost profits resulting from Fishkin's and Chernomzav's breach of their employment contracts, it was entitled only to nominal damages on its breach of contract claim. SIG argues that the District Court erred in denying its motion for summary judgment and in barring it from recovering restitution damages measured by the net trading profits made by TABFG during the four and one-half months of 2003 during which it actively traded at the Chicago Board of Trade.

Pennsylvania law recognizes three possible remedies for a breach of contract: expectation damages, reliance damages, and restitution damages. *Ferrer v. Trustees of Univ. of Pa.,* 825 A.2d 591, 609 (2002); *see also ATACS Corp. v. Trans World Commc'ns, Inc.,* 155 F.3d 659, 669 (3d Cir. 1998); *Trosky v. Civil Serv. Commc'n,* 652 A.2d 813, 817 (1995); RESTATEMENT (SECOND) OF CONTRACTS §344 (ALI 1981). Although the preferred remedy for a contractual breach is the award of expectation damages, "measured by 'the losses caused and gains prevented by defendant's breach,'" *ATACS Corp.,* a party may also sue for reliance or restitution damages in limited instances. "This is especially so where an injured party is entitled to recover for breach of contract, but recovery based on traditional notions of expectation damages is clouded because of the uncertainty in measuring the loss in value to the aggrieved contracting party." *Id.*

Before the District Court, SIG conceded that it could not calculate its lost profits resulting from the breach, thereby rendering inappropriate the preferred remedy of expectation damages. Nevertheless, SIG argued that it was entitled to restitution damages, which require a breaching party to "disgorge the benefit he has received by returning it to the party that conferred it." *Trosky* (quoting RESTATEMENT (SECOND) OF CONTRACTS §344). In particular, SIG asserts that it conferred benefits on Fishkin and Chernomzav, in the form of training and opportunities to learn the market and develop goodwill with other traders, and that the proper measure of restitution for those benefits would require the breaching parties to "disgorge" their net trading profits.

The District Court concluded that this Court's decision in *American Air Filter* barred SIG's claim for disgorgement of TABFG and NT Prop's profits. In that case, American Air Filter sued its former employee, McNichol, and his new employer for breach of a noncompetition agreement. . . . On appeal, American Air Filter sought to establish damages via (1) an accounting of profits made by McNichol's new employer, (2) McNichol's commissions earned with his new employer, and (3) its own decrease in profit in the territory served by the former employee after it left the company. This Court rejected American Air Filter's attempt to measure its damages by the profits of the breaching party's new employer, observing that "[t]he basic failing of the plaintiff's theory is that the defendant's profits are not necessarily equivalent to the plaintiff's losses. . . . To compel defendant to disgorge these profits could give plaintiff a windfall and penalize the defendant, neither of which serves the purpose of contract damages." *Id.* ("[A] defendant's profits are not the measure of a contract plaintiff's losses. . . .")

[*ATACS* recognized] the possible remedy of restitution damages as measured by "'the fair value of [the subcontractor's contribution]'" [which] corresponds to RESTATEMENT (SECOND) OF CONTRACTS §344's characterization of a party's restitutionary interest as the "interest in having restored . . . any benefit that [it] has conferred on the other party." *See Trosky* (discussing §344). Although SIG asserts that the benefits it conferred on Fishkin and Chernomzav "reasonably equate [] to the $3.5 million in profit they generated for themselves and their co-venturers," it has failed to demonstrate that the value of the benefit it conferred in the form of training and opportunities corresponds to the breaching parties' net trading profits. As the District Court noted, "the 'basic failing' of SIG's theory is that the counterclaim defendant's profits are not necessarily equivalent to SIG's losses, whether those losses are viewed as SIG's lost profits or SIG's restitution interest in the benefit of its training." Because SIG did not prove that the value of the benefit conferred equated to net trading profits earned by the breaching parties, the District Court's rejection of SIG's claim for restitution damages was proper.

We acknowledge that, in the securities trading industry, harm occasioned by the breach of a noncompetition covenant can be uniquely difficult to calculate. Nevertheless, securities trading firms are not without a means to protect themselves against this difficulty; they can include liquidated damages clauses in their employment agreements that provide for the disgorgement of profits by the breaching party. *See, e.g., Worldwide Auditing Servs., Inc. v. Richter*, 587 A.2d 772, 777–78 (1991) (holding that a liquidated damages provision that provided for disgorgement of profit attributable to breaching party's violation of contractual covenant was enforceable). The parties' contract did include a liquidated damages provision—drafted by SIG—that did not provide for disgorgement. Instead, the provision gave SIG the choice to (a) accept liquidated damages of $700,000 or $800,000, or (b) pursue an injunction and other available, legal remedies. SIG chose the latter.

Accordingly, we will affirm the District Court's denial of SIG's claim for restitution damages.

B. Trade Secret Misappropriation

SIG also appeals the District Court's [Order] denying trade secret protection for the knowledge that SIG's Dow Futures trading methodology was profitable.[11] In particular, SIG asserts that, during Fishkin's discussions with NT Prop representatives between December 2002 and April 2003, Fishkin was asked about the profitability of SIG's Dow Futures trading. Although Fishkin told NT Prop that confidentiality provisions precluded him from revealing profitability information, when asked whether he made more than $5 million trading for SIG, Fishkin responded by saying "[y]ou'll be pleased." SIG contends that Fishkin's disclosure contained an implied assertion that its Dow Futures trading method was profitable to some degree greater than $5 million and that the disclosure of the extent of SIG's profitability motivated NT Prop's representatives to form a joint venture with TABFG to trade Dow Futures with Fishkin and Chernomzav.

To prevail on a claim for trade secret protection in Pennsylvania,[12] the party seeking protection must demonstrate:

> (1) that the information constitutes a trade secret; (2) that it was of value to the employer and important in the conduct of his business; (3) that by reason of discovery or ownership the employer had the right to the use and enjoyment of the secret; and (4) that the secret was communicated to the defendant while employed in a position of trust and confidence under such circumstances as to make it inequitable and unjust for him to disclose it to others, or to make use of it himself, to the prejudice of his employer.

Doeblers' Pa. Hybrids, Inc. v. Doebler, 442 F.3d 812, 829 (3d Cir. 2006).

As the District Court noted, "[t]he threshold inquiry in a trade secret misappropriation claim under Pennsylvania law is whether the information is a trade secret." Pennsylvania courts have adopted the definition of a trade secret as set forth in RESTATEMENT OF TORTS §757 cmt. b. *See Doebler.* This provision states that "[a] trade secret may consist of any formula, pattern, device or compilation of information which is used in one's business, and which gives him an opportunity to obtain an

---

11. The District Court also concluded that SIG's Dow Fair Value concept, formula, and spreadsheet did not warrant trade secret protection because, although SIG took steps to keep its method secret and the method was valuable for SIG, the Dow Fair Value trading approach was known and used by other traders, SIG did not invest a tremendous amount of time or money to develop the method, and other traders could duplicate SIG's approach fairly easily. On appeal, SIG abandons its claim that the trading strategy itself merited trade secret protection.

12. . . . Although Pennsylvania adopted the Uniform Trade Secrets Act, 12 Pa. Cons. Stat. Ann. §5301 *et seq.,* effective April 19, 2004, the Act does not apply to misappropriation occurring before its effective date. Because the conduct at issue occurred before April 19, 2004, the Uniform Trade Secrets Act does not apply; instead, Pennsylvania's common law governing trade secrets applies.

advantage over competitors who do not know or use it." Information is not entitled to trade secret protection if it is generally known, or easily derived from available information, in the relevant business community.

This Court has enumerated several factors to consider when determining whether information constitutes a trade secret deserving of protection:

> (1) the extent to which the information is known outside of the owner's business; (2) the extent to which it is known by employees and others involved in the owner's business; (3) the extent of measures taken by the owner to guard the secrecy of the information; (4) the value of the information to the owner and to his competitors; (5) the amount of effort or money expended by the owner in developing the information; and (6) the ease or difficulty with which the information could be properly acquired or duplicated by others.

Doebler; accord RESTATEMENT OF TORTS §757 cmt. b.

In some circumstances, courts have applied Pennsylvania law to permit trade secret protection of information concerning a company's profitability, such as that company's specific profit margins. *SI Handling Sys., Inc.*[*v. Heisley*, 753 F.2d 1244, 1260 (3d Cir. 1985)] (concluding that "range of data relating to materials, labor, overhead, and profit margin, among other things" qualified for trade secret protection to extent it was not "readily obtainable by anyone in the industry"); *see also Den–Tal–Ez, Inc. v. Siemens Capital Corp.*, 566 A.2d 1214, 1230 (1989) ("[I]nformation like . . . inventory data and projections, details unit costs and product-by-product profit margin data is protectable as trade secrets.").

Despite the recognition that some profitability information may warrant trade secret protection, the District Court properly rejected SIG's misappropriation claim. The information for which SIG sought protection was not its specific profit margins or its precise profitability; it was the fact of its profitability coupled with a limited suggestion of the extent of its profitability. In particular, Fishkin's statement that NT Prop representatives would be "pleased" with the profitability of SIG's Dow Futures trading method implied that SIG was profitable to some extent greater than $5 million.

As the District Court noted, the fact that Fishkin and Wisniewski were making money for SIG was already known to other traders. Under the circumstances, Fishkin's statement, while implying a certain threshold of profitability, did not sufficiently convey the extent of SIG's profitability to merit trade secret protection. Indeed, at the same time that Fishkin stated NT Prop would be pleased, he also declined to provide actual profitability information. A suggestion about the extent of a company's profitability, without more, is of limited value to the competitor and could easily be interpreted as mere puffery. Thus, Fishkin's statement is akin to the knowledge of the "hotness" of a product, which the Pennsylvania Supreme Court has rejected as a basis for trade secret protection. *See Van Products Co.* [*v. Gen. Welding & Fabricating Co.*, 213 A.2d 769 (Pa. 1965) (denying trade secret protection to a drying machine manufacturer when its former employee joined a competitor and disclosed fact that deliquescent desiccant air dryers were "hot product[s]"). Just as the Pennsylvania Supreme Court held that the "hotness" of a particular product was ascertainable to industry competitors in *Van Products,* other industry participants could observe and determine that SIG's trading in Dow Futures was profitable. . . .

NOTES

1. *Enforcing the Noncompete.* The *Fishkin* case illustrates a number of complications at the intersection of noncompetition and trade secret law. First, SIG did "win" in the sense that it enforced its noncompete clause, with the apparent legitimate interest supporting that clause being preservation of confidential information. That may have caused real pain to the defendants, but it didn't put a dime in the plaintiffs' pocket.

With respect to its damages remedy, SIG failed to get any meaningful recovery for breach of the noncompete because, according to the court, it could not establish its damages resulting from the defendants' breach on any of the three bases that contracts law usually provides. This should not be so mysterious: The harm suffered by SIG did not flow from the defendants not working for SIG (since they did not have a contractual commitment to do so, their leaving was no violation). Instead, the expectation interest would be measured by the harm flowing from business lost to a competitor, and there was apparently no proof of that. *Cf. Southwest Stainless, LP v. Sappington,* 582 F.3d 1176 (10th Cir. 2009) (upholding damage award for lost profits employer suffered as a result of ex-employees' breach of noncompetition clause as measured by the loss of orders from two customers). As the court suggests, there are other measures of contract recovery (reliance and restitution), but neither did SIG any good: The court simply refused to equate what the defendants earned after their employment with the training it provided while they were employed—which seems consistent with *Rem Metals.* What SIG wanted—and failed to get—on its contract theory was the profits the defendants made by competing. This is standard contract analysis, although we have seen that where disloyalty by a current employee occurs, *see* Note 6 on page 472, such profits may be disgorged. In an omitted footnote 9, the court noted that SIG had also sought restitution of the costs of its training program, which the district court had held inappropriate under Pennsylvania law.

2. *Liquidated Damages.* Difficulties of proof of damages are a classic reason for parties to include liquidated damages clauses in their noncompetition agreements. And, in fact, SIG had done just that—and pretty hefty ones. We will discuss the standards for valid liquidated damages clauses at the end of this chapter, but the important point for present purposes is that SIG forfeited its right to obtain up to $800,000 when it sought compensatory damages. Do you think the company (or its attorneys) should have been surer of their theory and their facts before they made that decision? Of course, hindsight is always 20/20, and maybe there were problems with the enforceability of the liquidated damages provision.

3. *Another Arrow.* But SIG had another arrow in its quiver—a claim for misappropriation of trade secrets. As the court's citation to the Restatement of Torts suggests, such a claim was traditionally viewed as a tort (in part because it reached those who "discovered the secret by improper means," §757(a)) although it had a contractual aspect (when "disclosure or use constitutes a breach of confidence," §757(b), with the entrusting typically arising by virtue of an employment relationship). While in a few states, trade secret law continues to be a common law creature, most jurisdictions, as happened in Pennsylvania, have now adopted the Uniform Trade Secrets Act. As you might guess, the remedy for misappropriation of a trade secret is more attractive than the remedy for a mere breach of contract. While the UTSA provides for both injunctive relief and damages measured by "the actual loss caused by misappropriation," it also permits recovery of "the unjust enrichment caused by misappropriation that is not taken into account in computing actual loss." §3. This was exactly the measure SIG sought—and failed to get—for the contract breach. Admittedly, "disgorgement" is a remedy fiduciary law provides for a "faithless servant," *see* page 472, but most, if not all, of the defendant's profits were earned after they ceased employment for the plaintiff—which meant they did not breach any duty of loyalty.

4. *Qualifying as a Trade Secret.* Both the Restatement of Torts, §757, cmt. b, and Pennsylvania's six-factor test try to define "trade secret," but a more rigorous formulation is found in the Uniform Trade Secrets Act:

> Information, including a formula, drawing, pattern, compilation including a customer list, program, device, method, technique or process that:
>> (1) Derives independent economic value, actual or potential, from not being generally known to, and not being readily ascertainable by proper means by, other persons who can obtain economic value from its disclosure or use.
>> (2) Is the subject of efforts that are reasonable under the circumstances to maintain its secrecy.

UTSA §1; *See generally* ROGER MILGRIM AND ERIC E. BENSEN ON TRADE SECRETS (2013).

5. *Back to* SIG. The district court ruled against plaintiff as to the "Dow Fair Value concept, formula, and spreadsheet," because the approach was "known and used by other traders." More plausibly protected was the employer's profitability, but the problem for SIG was that Fishkin's disclosure "while implying a certain threshold of profitability, did not sufficiently convey the extent of SIG's profitability to merit trade secret protection."

6. *Intersection of Noncompetition Law with Trade Secret Law.* As Professor Stone has suggested, *see* page 494, there is an interesting intersection of trade secret law and the law governing noncompetition agreements. From the employer's perspective, trade secret law is clearly superior in the remedies available, but, as *SIG* makes clear, that is true only when the employer can prove misappropriation of a trade secret. The decline of the inevitable disclosure doctrine has made it much less likely that trade secret law can bar an employer's competition where such proof is lacking.

A noncompete has the advantage of being prophylactic—it will prevent use of confidential information by barring the former employee from competing with her ex-employer. But a noncompete requires a legitimate employer interest, and one such interest is protecting trade secrets. Thus, an employer may have to be prepared to establish the existence of trade secrets to support an agreement not to compete. In *SIG* itself, information as to plaintiff's profitability would probably have sufficed to support the noncompete—and the district court did enjoin the defendants—even though the court did not find an actual misappropriation.

But might a noncompetition clause be justified where no trade secret is concerned? The Restatement of Employment Law says yes: An employer has a legitimate interest in protecting "trade secrets . . . and other protectable confidential information that does not meet the definition of a trade secret." §8.07(b)(1). The Restatement is singularly unhelpful in explaining what non-trade secret confidential information might be, and the justification for this broader approach—the employee "was put on

Competition, Employee Loyalty, and the Allocation

notice of which information the employer considered confidential and proprietary"—seems dubious. The Restatement does caution that it does not include public domain information or "information that would be considered part of the general experience, knowledge, and skills that employee acquires" through her employment. Cmt. b. In any event, the Restatement is correct that some courts would enforce a noncompete or a nondisclosure agreement in the absence of a trade secret. *E.g., Bernier v. Merrill Air Eng'rs*, 770 A.2d 97, 103 (Me. 2001) ("The confidential knowledge or information protected by a restrictive covenant need not be limited to information that is protected as a trade secret by the UTSA."); *Lamorte Burns & Co. v. Walters*, 770 A.2d 1158, 1166 (N.J. 2001) ("information need not rise to the level of a trade secret to be protected").

7. *"Negative Knowledge."* In some cases, the plaintiff seeks to protect what has been called "negative knowledge." In *EarthWeb*, discussed above, for example, EarthWeb sought to protect the former employee's knowledge of the trial-and-error process EarthWeb had undertaken in implementing its products. The court discounted this information. Is it not valuable? Or is there simply no way to protect it in a way that does not unfairly disadvantage the employee? Courts take different approaches to this issue, with some reaching results contrary to *EarthWeb*. *See, e.g., Metallurgical Indus. Inc. v. Fourtek, Inc.*, 790 F.2d 1195, 1203 (5th Cir. 1986) (finding no distinction between "positive" and "negative" knowledge because "knowing what not to do often leads to knowing what to do"); *On-line Technologies, Inc. v. Perkin-Elmer Corp.*, 253 F. Supp. 2d 313, 323 (D. Conn. 2003) (finding "negative knowledge" to be a recognized form of "using" a trade secret proscribed under state law). The Restatement recognizes information that has "negative or 'dead end' value." §8.02 cmt. b & Ill. 3.

8. *Reasonable Duration of a Noncompete in an Information Economy. EarthWeb* is also interesting because the court found a one-year duration in Schlack's contract to be unreasonably long. The same duration received implicit approval in *CTI*. Why? Is the difference due to the nature of the information being protected? The nature of the subsequent employment? The industry in question? Or is it just a difference in perspective between two courts deciding cases six years apart? In the last decade, courts have generally been stricter in deciding what constitutes a reasonable duration, recognizing that in many dynamic industries, knowledge does not remain secret or valuable for very long. *See, e.g., Estee Lauder Cos., Inc. v. Batra*, 430 F. Supp. 2d. 158 (S.D.N.Y. 2006) (reducing 12-month restraint with international scope to 5 months in recognition of limited long-term utility of marketing information). On the other hand, some courts are willing to enforce noncompetes of as much as three years or more, particularly where the industry in question is more stable or different interests, such as long-term client relationships, are at stake.

9. *Competition Defined.* The reach of any noncompetition agreement depends on the definition of "competition," which is why it is best drafting practice to define the term. But there are landmines in the process. Using a very general definition of competition can sometimes help employers avoid a court finding that the at-issue activity is not competition, but it also creates the risk of overbreadth. If an agreement does not set out a clear definition of competition, the court must reach its own conclusion based on the facts submitted about the nature of the two businesses. *See, e.g., Victoria's Secret Stores, Inc. v. May Dept. Stores Co.*, 157 S.W.3d 256, 261 (Mo. App. 2004) (finding that specialty lingerie store and department store that carried lingerie were not in "material competition" under terms of the noncompete).

PROBLEM

8-2.   Julie Hanaco was a biomedical engineer. While in graduate school, she worked for a university-sponsored hospital outreach program as a technical liaison for wheelchair-bound patients. Her job consisted of assessing and translating the medical needs of patients into technical requirements for the production of customized wheelchairs. After graduating, she was hired by Invocare Corp. as a product manager in its sales and marketing department with responsibility for research and development of motorized wheelchairs. Upon hire, she signed a contract prohibiting her "for a period of three years from termination of employment with Invocare, from rendering services as an officer, director, partner or employee, or otherwise providing assistance to, any competitor in the production of custom wheelchairs or other custom medical equipment."

Hanaco worked for Invocare for three years, during which time she was a key employee in the research, testing, and production of Invocare's "Mark V" motorized wheelchair. Although she was not primarily responsible for marketing, she was copied on documents containing the marketing strategy for the Mark V and related financial documentation. One month prior to the public debut of the Mark V, Hanaco left Invocare and opened her own biomedical engineering consulting company. She was immediately approached by Suncare, an Invocare competitor in the end stages of a two-year development process for a new prototype chair. Suncare wants to hire Hanaco as a technical liaison to conduct field trials with potential users of its new chair.

How would you advise Hanaco? Can she take the position with Suncare? If she declines, is she still at risk of liability by running her consulting company? Would it make a difference to know that the typical lead time for developing and producing a new prototype wheelchair is two years? Or that once a new chair debuts, it is common in the industry for competitors to "reverse engineer" the product to discern its technical components?

Note on Employee Creative Works and Inventions

The preceding cases dealt with disputes over information—the employers alleged that the workers had a competitive advantage as a result of the knowledge they obtained or the confidences they received during the course of their employment. In some instances, however, particularly in creative or technically innovative fields, a dispute will arise over ownership of a particular invention that the employee wishes to use subsequent to employment, either herself or on behalf of a competitor. Questions of ownership are typically avoided by private ordering: Worker and firm agree in advance how to allocate such rights. When such an agreement does not exist, however, intellectual property law, including copyright and patent protection, dictates the result. We have seen one example of a dispute between workers and firms over ownership of work product in *Natkin v. Winfrey* in Chapter 1, reproduced at page 36. In that case the plaintiffs were photographers, hired to shoot photos at the *Oprah Winfrey Show*, who claimed the show had violated their copyright rights by using their photos in publicity material. This note provides a brief overview of the legal framework governing claims to such property interests.

A. Employee-Authored Creative Works

The Copyright Act of 1976 provides that copyright protection subsists "in original works of authorship fixed in any tangible medium of expression, now known or later developed, from which they can be perceived, reproduced, or otherwise communicated." 17 U.S.C. §102. Works of authorship include literary works, artistic works, motion pictures, sound recordings, and other works including some forms of software code. The statute gives copyright owners the exclusive right to reproduce the copyrighted work; to prepare derivative works; to distribute, license, and sell the work; and, in certain circumstances, to display and perform the work. *See id.* Subject to various qualifications, a copyright owner has the sole prerogative to exercise these rights and to exclude others from doing so during the term of the copyright, which is the life of the author plus 70 years. *See* 17 U.S.C. §302.

Copyright ownership "vests initially in the author or authors of the work." 17 U.S.C. §201(a). Generally, the "author" is the party who actually creates the copyrightable work, but the statute provides an important exception for "works made for hire." *See id.* at §201(b). If the work is for hire, "the employer or other person for whom the work was prepared is considered the author" and owns the copyright, unless there is a written agreement to the contrary. *Id.* A work is for hire if it was "prepared by an employee within the scope of his or her employment" or, in some circumstances, specially ordered or commissioned by written agreement. *See* 17 U.S.C. §101.

Thus, the operative inquiry in most copyright disputes between firm and worker is whether the worker created the work as an employee acting within the scope of employment, rather than as an independent contractor. As *Natkin* indicated, the Supreme Court set forth a nonexhaustive, 13-factor test for determining employment status for such purposes in *Community for Creative Non-Violence v. Reid*, 490 U.S. 730 (1989). The *Reid* inquiry has resulted in significant litigation, and the contours of the employment relationship therefore may be important in the many areas of the economy in which creative activity is important to business operations, including the creative arts, publishing, advertising, music, media, technology, and communications sectors.

Of course, as the statutory scheme clearly contemplates, the difficulties in distinguishing employees from independent contractors usually may be avoided by contract. The "work for hire" rule is merely the default. The underlying relationship does not matter if the parties have agreed in writing to share one or more rights to the work or allocate all rights to one party. This works both ways: An "employee" can contract to retain her copyright, or an independent contractor can contract to assign it. Again, *Natkin* provides a good example: The dispute between the photographers and the production company over employment status could have been avoided if the parties had negotiated a commission or licensing agreement clearly allocating rights regarding the photographs.

The book you are reading was written by law professors as part of their scholarly duties, and with the support of their law schools. Neither of the law schools involved has a specific policy dealing with copyrights. Do Professors Glynn, Sullivan, and Arnow-Richman own the copyright, or do Seton Hall and Denver have a claim? Who else might have an ownership interest? Look at the copyright page to determine one party's (admittedly not disinterested) views on the matter. How do you think this entity (who is neither the employee nor the employer) obtained copyright ownership?

B. Employee Inventions

Under the existing patent regime, *see* 35 U.S.C. §101 *et seq.*, whoever invents or discovers any new, useful, and nonobvious "process, machine, manufacture, or composition of matter, or any new and useful improvement thereof" may obtain a patent for such invention or discovery, subject to various conditions. When such an invention is made, the inventor often has a choice between trade secret protection and patent protection (although not every trade secret satisfies the requirements for patentability). The basic trade-off is between the time-limited but exclusive rights given by patent law and the theoretically perpetual (but less absolute) protection provided by trade secret law. As we have seen, a trade secret essentially evaporates once it becomes generally known.

In contrast, the patent holder has the right to exclude others from making, using, or selling the patented invention or discovery during the term of the patent, generally 20 years from the date of filing. *See* 35 U.S.C. §271. Federal law provides that patent rights may be assigned only in writing, *see* 35 U.S.C. §261, but the enforceability of assignments in the employment context is usually governed by state law. *See, e.g., University Patents, Inc. v. Kligman*, 762 F. Supp. 1212, 1219 (E.D. Pa. 1991); *see also United States v. Dubilier Condenser Corp.*, 289 U.S. 178 (1933).

If a person invents or discovers something patentable during employment, he or she is the presumptive owner of the invention and of the resulting patent. RESTATEMENT OF EMPLOYMENT LAW §8.09(a). The operative default rule in the patent context is therefore opposite that in copyright. As with the copyright regime, however, patent law recognizes the primacy of private ordering through agreements allocating rights between worker and firm. *See Dubilier Condenser Corp.*, 289 U.S. at 187-88. Further, it shifts the default principle in one important way: Even absent an employee's outright assignment of the patent, the employer will own the patent if it hired the employee to invent or discover its subject. *See id.* at 187 ("One employed to make an invention, who succeeds, during his term of service, in accomplishing that task, is bound to assign to his employer any patent obtained."). *See* RESTATEMENT §8.09(b). When the employment contract expressly so provides, the right of assignment and the default rule coincide. *See id.* In the absence of an express agreement, however, the employer may demonstrate from the circumstances of employment an implied agreement by the employee to invent on behalf of the employer. *See id.* at 187-88. Such an agreement may be inferred from employer instructions and employee duties, among other things, although courts sometimes express reluctance to recognize such implied terms. *See, e.g., id.* at 188; *Standard Parts Co. v. Peck*, 264 U.S. 52, 58-59 (1923); *see also Scott Sys., Inc. v. Scott*, 996 P.2d 775, 778 (Colo. Ct. App. 2000) ("If an employee's job duties include the responsibility for inventing or for solving a particular problem that requires invention, any invention created by that employee during the performance of those responsibilities belongs to the employer . . . and the courts will find an implied contract obligation to assign any rights to the employer.").

Obviously then, firms that foresee substantial, innovative activity have a strong incentive to include job descriptions and assignment clauses in employment agreements that clarify ownership rights and the employee's inventive duties. Workers seeking to retain the fruits of their activity have a countervailing incentive to bargain for ownership or co-ownership rights for their inventions or to include language limiting the scope of their duties to the employer. State law often places some restrictions on employee assignments of rights to inventions; for example, some state statutes preclude assignments of inventions unrelated to the employer's business, developed entirely on the employees' own time, or for which no employer equipment or resources were used. For example, California Labor Code §2870 (2018) bars employers from enforcing agreements for the assignment of employee inventions when the invention was one that "the employee developed entirely on his or her own time without using the employer's equipment, supplies, facilities, or trade secret information," with exceptions that are vague enough to frequently generate fact disputes. *See Mattel v. MGA*, 616 F.3d 904 (9th Cir 2010). *See generally* ORLY LOBEL, YOU DON'T OWN ME: HOW MATTEL V. MGA ENTERTAINMENT EXPOSED BARBIE'S DARK SIDE (2018). *See also*; MINN. STAT. ANN. §181.78 (2018); N.C. GEN. STAT. §66-57.1 (2018). Nevertheless, employee assignment clauses are standard among firms engaged in research and development, and such assignments are typically enforced if reasonably tied to the nature of the employee's position.

Some employers seek even more protection by including so-called "holdover" or "trailer" clauses in their employment agreements. These clauses commonly require an employee to assign to the employer patent rights for inventions created within a defined period after termination of the employment relationship if the invention is related to or conceived as a result of the employee's work for the employer. In determining whether such clauses are enforceable, courts may engage in a "reasonableness" or "balancing" inquiry akin to those applied to restrictive covenants; that is, they assess the extent to which holdover provisions may protect legitimate employer interests, prevent a former employee from seeking other employment, and adversely affect the public interest. *See, e.g., Ingersoll-Rand Co. v. Ciavatta*, 542 A.2d 879, 888 (N.J. 1988).

Even if an employee retains ownership of a patent created during the course of employment, the employer may be entitled to a limited equitable use known as a "shop right." A shop right grants—or compels the employee to grant—the employer a non-exclusive right to practice or use the employee-owned invention when the employee conceived of and perfected the invention during the hours of employment, working with the employer's materials, tools, and other resources. *See Dubilier Condenser Corp.*, 289 U.S. at 187-88; *Francklyn v. Guilford Packing Co.*, 695 F.2d 1158, 1161 (9th Cir. 1983); RESTATEMENT OF EMPLOYMENT LAW §8.10.

For further discussion of employee creative works and inventions, and the application of copyright and patent law within the workplace, *see* Dan L. Burk, *Intellectual Property and the Firm*, 71 U. CHI. L. REV. 3 (2004); Catherine L. Fisk, *Authors at Work: The Origins of the Work-for-Hire Doctrine*, 15 YALE J. L. & HUMAN. 1 (2003); Robert P. Merges, *The Law and Economics of Employee Inventions*, 13 HARV. J. L. & TECH. 1 (1999).

4.   Disputes over Customers and Co-workers

═══ *Hopper v. All Pet Animal Clinic, Inc.*
═══ 861 P.2d 531 (Wyo. 1993)

TAYLOR, Justice.

[This appeal tests the enforceability of a covenant not to compete in an employment contract. The district court found that the covenant was reasonable and enjoined
a veterinarian from practicing small animal medicine for three years within a five-mile
radius. She appealed.]

We hold that the covenant's three-year duration imposed an unreasonable
restraint of trade permitting only partial enforcement of a portion of that term of the
covenant. . . .

II.   Facts

Following her graduation from Colorado State University, Dr. Glenna Hopper
(Dr. Hopper) began working part-time as a veterinarian at the All Pet Animal Clinic,
Inc. (All Pet) in July of 1988. All Pet specialized in the care of small animals; mostly
domesticated dogs and cats, and those exotic animals maintained as household pets.
Dr. Hopper practiced under the guidance and direction of the President of All Pet,
Dr. Robert Bruce Johnson (Dr. Johnson).

Dr. Johnson, on behalf of All Pet, offered Dr. Hopper full-time employment
in February of 1989. The oral offer included a specified salary and potential for
bonus earnings as well as other terms of employment. According to Dr. Johnson,
he conditioned the offer on Dr. Hopper's acceptance of a covenant not to compete,
the specific details of which were not discussed at the time. Dr. Hopper commenced
full-time employment with All Pet under the oral agreement in March of 1989 and
relocated to Laramie, discontinuing her commute from her former residence in
Colorado.

A written Employment Agreement incorporating the terms of the oral agreement was finally executed by the parties on December 11, 1989. Ancillary to the
provisions for employment, the agreement detailed the terms of a covenant not to
compete:

> 12. This agreement may be terminated by either party upon 30 days' notice to the
> other party. Upon termination, Dr. Hopper agrees that she will not practice small animal
> medicine for a period of three years from the date of termination within 5 miles of the
> corporate limits of the City of Laramie, Wyoming. Dr. Hopper agrees that the duration
> and geographic scope of that limitation is reasonable.

The agreement was antedated to be effective to March 3, 1989.

[The parties subsequently agreed to an Addendum in 1990 which raised Hopper's
salary, eliminated the bonus, and added a newly acquired corporate entity, Alpine
Animal Hospital, Inc. (Alpine), Laramie, to share Hopper's services. The modified
agreement reaffirmed the covenant not to compete.]

One year later, reacting to a rumor that Dr. Hopper was investigating the purchase of a veterinary practice in Laramie, Dr. Johnson asked his attorney to prepare a letter which was presented to Dr. Hopper. The letter, dated June 17, 1991, stated:

> I have learned that you are considering leaving us to take over the small animal part of Dr. Meeboer's practice in Laramie.
>
> When we negotiated the terms of your employment, we agreed that you could leave upon 30 days' notice, but that you would not practice small animal medicine within five miles of Laramie for a three-year period. We do not have any non-competition agreement for large-animal medicine, which therefore does not enter into the picture.
>
> I am willing to release you from the non-competition agreement in return for a cash buy-out. I have worked back from the proportion of the income of All-Pet and Alpine which you contribute and have decided that a reasonable figure would be $40,000.00, to compensate the practice for the loss of business which will happen if you practice small-animal medicine elsewhere in Laramie.
>
> If you are willing to approach the problem in the way I suggest, please let me know and I will have the appropriate paperwork taken care of.
>
> Sincerely,
> |Signed|
> R. Bruce Johnson,
> D.V.M.

Dr. Hopper responded to the letter by denying that she was going to purchase Dr. Meeboer's practice. Dr. Hopper told Dr. Johnson that the Employment Agreement was not worth the paper it was written on and that she could do anything she wanted to do. Dr. Johnson terminated Dr. Hopper's employment and informed her to consider the 30-day notice as having been given. . . .

[Dr. Hopper subsequently purchased a small and large animal practice within the city of Laramie. The practice grew from 368 clients at the time of purchase to approximately 950 at the time of trial, including 187 clients who were also clients of All Pet or Alpine. Small animal work contributed around 52 percent of Dr. Hopper's gross income in the practice.]

IV. Discussion. . . .

Two principles, the freedom to contract and the freedom to work, conflict when courts test the enforceability of covenants not to compete. There is general recognition that while an employer may seek protection from improper and unfair competition of a former employee, the employer is not entitled to protection against ordinary competition. . . .

A valid and enforceable covenant not to compete requires a showing that the covenant is: (1) in writing; (2) part of a contract of employment; (3) based on reasonable consideration; (4) reasonable in durational and geographical limitations; and (5) not against public policy. *A.E.P. Industries, Inc. v. McClure*, 302 S.E.2d 754, 760 (N. C. 1983). Wyo. Stat. §1-23-105 (1988). The reasonableness of a covenant not to compete is assessed based upon the facts of the particular case and a review of all of the circumstances. . . .

Wyoming has previously recognized that the legitimate interests of the employer, covenantee, which may be protected from competition include: (a) the employer's trade secrets which have been communicated to the employee during the course of employment; (b) confidential information communicated by the employer to the employee, but not involving trade secrets, such as information on a unique business method; and (c) special influence by the employee obtained during the course of employment over the employer's customers.

The enforceability of a covenant not to compete using the rule of reason analysis depends upon a determination, as a matter of law, that the promise not to compete is ancillary to the existence of an otherwise valid transaction or relationship. . . .

[While the oral promise of employment did not specify a geographic radius or time restriction, the written agreement did, and the covenant not to compete in it can be considered ancillary to Dr. Hopper's employment] *as long as it is supported by consideration* and meets other requirements for enforceability. . . .

Wyoming has never determined whether a promise not to compete made during the employment relationship is supported merely by the consideration of continued employment or must be supported by separate contemporaneous consideration. This court's decision in *Ridley* [*v. Krout*, 180 P.2d 124 (Wyo. 1947)] offers useful insight. An employment relationship with a mechanic was formed prior to the execution of the written contract containing the employee's ancillary promise not to compete. *Ridley*. While we did not specifically address the sufficiency of the consideration, the written contract with the mechanic contained separate consideration. In addition to the promise to continue employment for a term of ten years, the employer agreed, as consideration for the promise not to compete, to teach the mechanic new skills as a locksmith and in business operation.

Authorities from other jurisdictions are not in agreement on whether continued employment provides sufficient consideration or whether separate consideration is required to create an ancillary covenant not to compete made during the existence of the relationship. *See* Howard A. Specter & Matthew W. Finkin, Individual Employment Law and Litigation §8.02 (1989) (collecting cases). We believe strong public policy favors separate consideration.

> The better view, even in the at-will relationship, is to require additional consideration to support a restrictive covenant entered into during the term of the employment. This view recognizes the increasing criticism of the at-will relationship, the usually unequal bargaining power of the parties, and the reality that the employee rarely "bargains for" continued employment in exchange for a potentially onerous restraint on the ability to earn a living.

Id., §8.02 at 450. The separate consideration necessary to support an ancillary promise not to compete made after creation of the employment relationship would include promotion, pay raise, special training, employment benefits or other advantages for the employee.

The written Employment Agreement Dr. Hopper signed contains no evidence of separate consideration, such as a pay raise or other benefit, in exchange for the covenant not to compete. Standing alone, the covenant not to compete contained in the Employment Agreement failed due to lack of separate consideration. However, on June 1, 1990, the parties executed the Addendum to Agreement. In that agreement, Dr. Hopper accepted a pay raise of $550.00 per month. This agreement restates, by incorporation, the terms of the covenant not to compete. We hold that the Addendum to Agreement, with its pay raise, represented sufficient separate consideration supporting the reaffirmation of the covenant not to compete. Therefore, the district court's findings that the covenant was ancillary to an employment contract and that consideration was received in exchange for the covenant are not clearly erroneous. . . .

Employers are entitled to protect their business from the detrimental impact of competition by employees who, but for their employment, would not have had the ability to gain a special influence over clients or customers. . . .

The special interests of All Pet and Alpine identified by the district court as findings of fact are not clearly erroneous. Dr. Hopper moved to Laramie upon completion of her degree prior to any significant professional contact with the community. Her introduction to All Pet's and Alpine's clients, client files, pricing policies, and practice development techniques provided information which exceeded the skills she brought to her employment. While she was a licensed and trained veterinarian when she accepted employment, the additional exposure to clients and knowledge of clinic operations her employers shared with her had a monetary value for which the employers are entitled to reasonable protection. . . .

Enforcement of the practice restrictions Dr. Hopper accepted as part of her covenant not to compete does not create an unreasonable restraint of trade. While the specific terms of the covenant failed to define the practice of small animal medicine, the parties' trade usage provided a conforming standard of domesticated dogs and cats along with exotic animals maintained as household pets. As a veterinarian licensed to practice in Wyoming, Dr. Hopper was therefore permitted to earn a living in her chosen profession without relocating by practicing large animal medicine, a significant area of practice in this state. The restriction on the type of activity contained in the covenant was sufficiently limited to avoid undue hardship to Dr. Hopper while protecting the special interests of All Pet and Alpine.

In addition, as a professional, Dr. Hopper certainly realized the implications of agreeing to the terms of the covenant. While she may have doubted either her employers' desires to enforce the terms or the legality of the covenant, her actions in establishing a small animal practice violated the promise she made. In equity, she comes before the court with unclean hands. If Dr. Hopper sought to challenge the enforceability of the covenant, her proper remedy was to seek a declaratory judgment.

The public will not suffer injury from enforcement of the covenant. . . . While Dr. Hopper provided competent care to All Pet's and Alpine's clients, her services there were neither unique nor uncommon. Furthermore, the services which Dr. Hopper provided in her new practice to small animal clients were available at several other veterinary clinics within Laramie. Evidence did not challenge the public's ability to receive complete and satisfactory service from these other sources. Dr. Hopper's short-term unavailability resulting from enforcement of a reasonable restraint against unfair competition is unlikely, as a matter of law, to produce injury to the public. . . .

The geographical limit contained in the covenant not to compete restricts Dr. Hopper from practicing within a five-mile radius of the corporate limits of Laramie. As a matter of law, this limit is reasonable in this circumstance. The evidence presented at trial indicated that the clients of All Pet and Alpine were located throughout the county. Despite Wyoming's rural character, the five-mile restriction effectively limited unfair competition without presenting an undue hardship. Dr. Hopper could, for example, have opened a practice at other locations within the county.

A durational limitation should be reasonably related to the legitimate interest which the employer is seeking to protect.

In determining whether a restraint extends for a longer period of time than necessary to protect the employer, the court must determine how much time is needed for the risk of injury to be reasonably moderated. When the restraint is for the purpose of protecting customer relationships, its duration is reasonable only if it is no longer than necessary for the employer to put a new [individual] on the job and for the new employee to have a reasonable opportunity to demonstrate his [or her] effectiveness to the customers. If a restraint on this ground is justifiable at all, it seems that a period of several months would usually be reasonable. If the selling or servicing relationship is relatively complex, a longer period may be called for. Courts seldom criticize restraints of six months or a year on the grounds of duration as such, and even longer restraints are often enforced.

Blake, 73 Harv. L. Rev. at 677.

[Expert testimony at trial indicated that 70 percent of veterinary clients visit a clinic more than once per year. The remaining 30 percent of the clients use the clinic at least one time per year. In addition,] Dr. Johnson estimated that at All Pet and Alpine, the average client seeks veterinarian services one and one-half times a year. . . . Dr. Johnson admitted that influence over a client disappears in an unspecified "short period of time," but expressed a view that three years was "safe." He also agreed that the number of clients possibly transferring from All Pet or Alpine to Dr. Hopper would be greatest in the first year and diminish in the second year.

We are unable to find a reasonable relationship between the three-year durational requirement and the protection of All Pet's and Alpine's special interests. . . . Based on figures of client visits, a replacement veterinarian at All Pet and Alpine would be able to effectively demonstrate his or her own professionalism to virtually all of the clinics' clients within a one year durational limit. . . .

Under the formulation of the rule of reason inquiry, [in] the first Restatement of Contracts, the unreasonableness of any non-divisible term of a covenant not to compete made the entire covenant unenforceable. . . .

The conceptual difficulty of the position taken in the former Restatement of Contracts, *supra*, §518 leads to strong criticism by noted authors and the rejection of this so-called "blue pencil rule" by many courts. In very many cases the courts have held the whole contract to be illegal and void where the restraint imposed was in excess of what was reasonable and the terms to the agreement indicated no line of division that could be marked with a "blue pencil." In the best considered modern cases, however, the court has decreed enforcement as against the defendant whose breach has occurred within an area in which restriction would clearly be reasonable, even though the terms of the agreement imposed a larger and unreasonable restraint. Thus, the seller of a purely local business who promised not to open a competing store anywhere in America has been prevented by an injunction from running such a store with the same block as the one that he sold.

We believe the ability to narrow the term of a covenant not to compete and enforce a reasonable restraint permits public policy to be served in the most effective manner. Businesses function through the efforts of dedicated employees who provide the services and build the products desired by customers. Both the employer and the employee invest in success by expressing a commitment to one another in the form of a reasonable covenant not to compete. For the employer, this commitment may mean providing the employee with access to trade secrets, customer contacts or special training. These assets of the business are entitled to protection. For the employee, who covenants as part of a bargained for exchange, the covenant provides notice of the limits both parties have accepted in their relationship. The employee benefits during his tenure with the employer by his or her greater importance to the organization as a result of the exposure to the trade secrets, customer contacts or special training. When the employer-employee relationship terminates, a reasonable covenant not to compete then avoids unfair competition by the employee against the former employer and the specter, which no court would enforce, of specific performance of the employment agreement. When the parties agree to terms of a covenant, one of which is too broad, the court is permitted to enforce a narrower term which effectuates these public policy goals without arbitrarily invalidating the entire agreement between the parties and creating an uncertain business environment. In those instances where a truly unreasonable covenant operates as a restraint of trade, it will not be enforced.

. . . We, therefore, affirm the district court's conclusions of law that the type of activity and geographic limitations contained in the covenant not to compete were reasonable and enforceable as a matter of law. Because we hold that the covenant's three-year durational term imposed a partially unreasonable restraint of trade, we remand for a modification of the judgment to enjoin Dr. Hopper from unfair competition for a duration of one year from the date of termination.

NOTES

1. *Consideration.* *All Pet* begins with a treatment of contract formalities. Generally, an offer of employment is treated as the requisite consideration for the employee's covenant not to compete. However, where the employee signs an agreement after employment commences, courts take different approaches. Some, probably most, hold that continued employment is sufficient consideration for the noncompete agreement where the worker is employed at will and could otherwise be terminated. *See, e.g., Summits 7, Inc. v. Kelly*, 886 A.2d 365, 372-73 (Vt. 2005); *Lake Land Emp. Group of Akron, LLC v. Columber*, 804 N.E.2d 27, 31-32 (Ohio 2004). Others, like *All Pet*, require further consideration to support the post-hire agreement. *See, e.g., McKasson v. Johnson*, 315 P.3d 1138 (Wash. App. 2013) (continued employment not sufficient consideration); *Fifield v. Premier Dealer Servs., Inc.*, 993 N.E.2d 938, 943-44 (Ill. App. Ct. 2013) ("Illinois courts have repeatedly held that there must be at least two years or more of continued employment to constitute adequate consideration," even if the employee resigns instead of being terminated.). *See generally* Tracy L. Staidl, *The Enforceability of Noncompetition Agreements When Employment Is At-Will: Reformulating the Analysis*, 2 EMPLOYEE RTS. & EMP. POL'Y J. 95 (1998). Do you recognize this concept of "separate" consideration from courts' treatment of employer modifications of contractually binding handbooks? *See* Chapter 3.

In this case, Dr. Hopper received a pay raise upon re-executing her employment contract, which included the noncompete. How meaningful is that raise if her employment is at will and she can be fired at any time? What other types of consideration might support a post-hire noncompete? What if Dr. Johnson offered Hopper an All Pet Animal Clinic T-shirt? Would the noncompete be enforceable?

2. *Involuntarily Terminated Employees.* A related question is whether noncompetes are enforceable if the at-will employee is terminated involuntarily. Although Dr. Hopper may have been planning to leave, she was fired by Dr. Johnson. Some courts have concluded that an employer that terminates its employee forfeits the right to enforce that employee's noncompete agreement. *See, e.g., Wrigg v. Junkermier, Clark, Campanella, Stevens, P.C.*, 265 P.3d 646, 653 (2011) ("[A]n employer normally lacks a legitimate business interest in a covenant when it chooses to end the employment relationship. Maintenance of the employment relationship represents an employer's best method to prevent competition from an employee."). Other courts disregard the manner of termination, focusing solely on the reasonableness of the restraint. *See, e.g., James Roberson & Penhall Co. v. C.P. Allen Const. Co., Inc.*, 50 So. 3d 471 (Ala. App. 2010); *Twenty Four Collection v. Keller*, 389 So. 2d 1062 (Fla. Dist. Ct. App. 1980). Yet a third approach relies on principles of good faith and fair dealing. In an omitted part of the decision, *All Pet* considered the good faith of Dr. Johnson's actions. Noting that the agreement permitted termination at will, subject to a notice requirement, the court stated:

> Without more, the terms present the potential for an unreasonable restraint of trade. For example, if an employer hired an employee at will, obtained a covenant not to compete, and then terminated the employee, without cause, to arbitrarily restrict competition, we believe such conduct would constitute bad faith. Simple justice requires that a termination by the employer of an at will employee be in good faith if a covenant not to compete is to be enforced.
>
> Under the present facts, we cannot say that the termination of Dr. Hopper occurred in bad faith. Trial testimony presented evidence of increasing tension prior to termination in the professional relationship between Dr. Johnson and Dr. Hopper. This tension, however, did not appear to result in the termination. The notice of termination was given after Dr. Hopper was confronted about her negotiations to purchase a competitive practice and after Dr. Hopper had termed the employment contract worthless.

Hopper, 861 P.2d. at 541-42; *see also Rao v. Rao*, 718 F.2d 219, 223 (7th Cir. 1983) (concluding that implied contractual covenant of good faith and fair dealing precludes employer enforcement of noncompete following unjustified termination of employee). The Restatement of Employment Law would make restrictive covenants generally unenforceable where the employer materially breaches the governing contract, §8.06 cmt. G, or, failing that, for employees terminated without cause or who quit "for cause attributable to the employer." §8.06 cmt. f.

3. *Negotiating a Buy-Out.* Prior to termination, the employer in *All Pet* offered to release Hopper from the noncompete agreement for $40,000. Private resolution of noncompete disputes, like other legal disputes, is common, and a "buy out" is one way to settle. Dr. Hopper's decision to reject her employer's offer was apparently based, at least in part, on her belief that the agreement was "not worth the paper it was written on." Maybe she should have consulted an attorney in advance. Or maybe she did: given the vagueness of the governing principles, what would you have advised her? Do you see how uncertainty about the law would have influenced any negotiations?

4. *The Public Interest. All Pet* explicitly takes account of the effects of the employer's restraint on the public. As traditionally articulated, the controlling test requires the court to weigh the interest of the employer against "hardship to the promisor and the likely injury to the public." RESTATEMENT (SECOND) OF CONTRACTS §188. However, in most cases, courts do not treat societal interest as a separate factor to be considered in the analysis; rather, the assumption is that a covenant that is reasonable in relation to a protectable interest is unlikely to be harmful to the public. Those instances where courts give societal interest distinct attention tend to involve highly specialized employees providing essential services. *See, e.g., Columbus Med. Serv. LLC v. Thomas*, 308 S.W.3d 368 (Tenn. Ct. App. 2009) (noncompete agreement between physical therapists and staffing company that placed therapists in residential facility for disabled was not enforceable when doing so would interrupt continuity of care for vulnerable patient population); *Cmty. Hosp. Grp., Inc. v. More*, 869 A.2d 884 (N.J. 2005) (while not finding restrictions on medical practice per se unreasonable, such restraints should be limited to avoid harm to patients). Other jurisdictions address public concerns by statutorily prohibiting noncompetes in certain fields, most notably medicine. *See, e.g.*, Mass. Gen. Law Ann. 112 §12X (2018) (declaring void any restriction on a physician's right to practice in an employment or professional agreement); 6 Del. C. §2707 (2018) (same). The Model Rules of Professional Conduct similarly prohibit noncompetes between lawyers. *See* MRPC 5.6. Is the protection of public choice a more important concern for lawyers than doctors? Or is the Model Rule simply an example of lawyers protecting themselves? *See generally* Kevin D. Horvitz, Note, *An Unreasonable Ban on Reasonable Competition: The Legal Profession's Protectionist Stance Against Noncompete Agreements Binding In-House Counsel*, 65 Duke L.J. 1007 (2016).

5. *Reasonableness Assessments from the Employee's Perspective.* While "fairness" rarely plays an independent role in contracts analysis, *cf. Williams v. Walker-Thomas*, 350 F.2d 445 (D.C. Cir. 1965) (unconscionability), some formulations of the test for reasonableness of a noncompetition agreement speak of the restraint not being too great a hardship on the employee. *E.g.*, Restatement of Contracts §188(1)(b). It is, however, a rare case where this consideration is more than a makeweight in the reasonableness inquiry.

6. *Reasonableness from the Employer's Perspective.* Most courts require the employer to demonstrate the reasonableness of its noncompete. *See, e.g., Omniplex World Services Corp. v. U.S. Investigations Services, Inc.*, 618 S.E.2d 340, 342 (Va. 2005). Regardless of the burden of proof, whether a restraint is reasonable with respect to each of the relevant considerations—duration, geography, and definition of competition—depends on an assessment of the particular interest the employer seeks to protect, in this case All Pet's customers. This is why the *All Pet* parties sought expert testimony about patient relationships in the veterinary industry. The analysis is undertaken in relation to the nature and extent of the work the former employee performed since that ensures that the noncompete does not restrain the employee other than in relying on information or contacts he gained on the job. Thus, in the case of an employer's legitimate interest in customers, a restraint that prohibits the employee from competing only in the region where he had customer contact is more likely to be found reasonable than one based broadly, albeit accurately, on the geographic scope of the employer's business. *See, e.g., Home Paramount Pest Control Cos. v. Shaffer*, 718 S.E.2d 762 (Va. 2011) (noncompete provision in contract with employee of pest-control company was unenforceable since it barred the employee from working in the pest control industry in any capacity or even being a passive stockholder of a publicly traded company in that business); *King v. Head Start Family Hair Salons*, 886 So. 2d 769 (Ala. 2004) (finding noncompete prohibiting hairdresser from working within two miles of any of employer's salons overbroad and modifying geographic scope to a two-mile radius of the location where employee worked). If customer relationships are the interest being protected, is it arguable that a noncompete is always overbroad to the extent it bars the former employee from dealing with others in the geographic area? *See* Restatement of Employment Law §8.07, cmt. c ("Because a covenant prohibiting former employees from soliciting customers with whom they dealt while employed will ordinarily fully protect this legitimate interest, a broader restriction barring all competition by former employees ordinarily is not enforceable.").

7. *Successorship.* What happens when a company having noncompetes with its employees merges with another company? Might the scope of the noncompete suddenly change radically because the employer is now operating in more markets? Reversing field after an initial decision to the contrary, the Supreme Court of Ohio held that an LLC could step into the shoes of the original contracting company in order to enforce noncompetition agreements. *Acordia of Ohio, L.L.C. v. Fishel*, 978 N.E.2d 823 (2012). However, it simultaneously suggested that employees could raise the question "whether the numerous mergers in this case created additional obligations or duties so that the agreements should not be enforced on their original terms." *Id.* at 826.

8. *Judicial Responses to Overbroad Agreements.* As *All Pet* illustrates, jurisdictions vary in their response to noncompetes that satisfy the protectable interest requirement but are overbroad in scope. As the First Circuit explains:

> Courts presented with restrictive covenants containing unenforceable provisions have taken three approaches: (1) the "all or nothing" approach, which would void the restrictive covenant entirely if any part is unenforceable, (2) the "blue pencil" approach, which enables the court to enforce the reasonable terms provided the covenant remains grammatically coherent once its unreasonable provisions are excised, and (3) the "partial enforcement" approach, which reforms and enforces the restrictive covenant to the extent it is reasonable, unless the "circumstances indicate bad faith or deliberate overreaching" on the part of the employer.

Ferrofluidics Corp. v. Advanced Vacuum Components, 968 F.2d 1463 (1st Cir. 1992). Which approach does *All Pet* adopt? Is that the right rule? *Team Environmental Services v. Addison*, 2 F.3d 124, 127 (5th Cir. 1993), expressed concern over the *in terrorem* effects of overbroad agreements:

> An employee barred from plying his trade within 200 miles of his home would be far more hesitant to leave his job than if the proscription affected a substantially smaller area. This increased hesitancy obviously impacts the bargaining relationship with the current employer. Were courts to reform and enforce agreements like those at bar, employers would be free routinely to present employees with grossly overbroad covenants not to compete. While the employer presumptively would know that the agreement would be enforced only to the limit of the law, the employee likely would not.

Id. at 127. Scholars have raised similar concerns. *See, e.g.*, Charles A. Sullivan, *The Puzzling Persistence of Unenforceable Contract Terms*, 70 OHIO ST. L.J. 1127 (2009); Rachel Arnow-Richman, *Cubewrap Contracts and Worker Mobility: The Dilution of Employee Bargaining Power Via Standard Form Noncompetes*, 2006 MICH. ST. L. REV. 963.

On the other hand, refusal to enforce any form of restraint in the face of an overbroad agreement penalizes those employers who draft their agreements in good faith, denying even their legitimate rights. As one court put it, "The man who wildly claims that he owns all the cherry trees in the country cannot be denied protection of the orchard in his backyard." *Sidco Paper Co. v. Aaron*, 351 A.2d 250 (Pa. 1976). The Restatement of Employment Law would allow deletion or modification of overbroad covenants if "the employer lacked a reasonable and good-faith basis for believing the covenant was enforceable," and "gross overbreadth alone" permits such finding. §8.08; *see AssuredPartners, Inc. v. Schmitt*, 44 N.E.3d 463 (Ill. App. Ct. 2015) (modification of overbroad covenants was inappropriate when the court was "not dealing with one minor deficiency, but with several deficiencies" that render the clause unreasonable). Noncompetition agreements tend to be off-the-shelf documents applicable to all employees or at least to all employees at certain levels, which has led to some truly bizarre situations. Neil Irwin, *When the Guy Making Your Sandwich Has a Noncompete Clause*, http://www.nytimes.com/2014/10/15/upshot/when-the-guy-making-your-sandwich-has-a-noncompete-clause.html?_r=0&abt=0002&abg=1. Would that necessarily mean that a firm does not have a reasonable, good faith basis for enforcing any noncompete even for high-level employees?

However, overbroad agreements can be discouraged in ways other than by refusing to blue pencil them. In *Sentinel Integrity Solutions, Inc. v. Mistras Grp., Inc.*, 414 S.W.3d 911 (Tex. App. 2013), the court, applying a provision of the Texas Business and Commerce Code, upheld an award of $750,000 in attorneys' fees to a defendant who successfully defended a suit for alleged breach of a noncompetition agreement. And, in a man-bites-dog case, *Guinn v. Applied Composites Eng'y, Inc.*, 994 N.E.2d 1256 (Ind. Ct. App. 2013), a court held that a former employee stated a claim of intentional interference with contract against his prior employer based on its threat of an interference suit against the plaintiff's new employer, which caused his discharge; the basis of the threat was alleged to be an overbroad and unenforceable noncompetition agreement.

PROBLEMS

8-3. Reexamine the noncompete agreement in Problem 8-2 in light of *All Pet*'s treatment of reasonableness. Assuming Julie Hanaco's former employer has a legitimate interest in protecting the technical and marketing information related to its new wheelchair, is its restraint reasonable? In what respects—duration, geographic scope, and definition of competition—might Hanaco argue it is overbroad? If she were to prevail on such an argument, how would a court respond under each of the three approaches to overbroad agreements discussed above? How would you recommend the employer redraft its agreement to ensure that it is enforceable as written in the maximum number of jurisdictions?

8-4. KFN is a national executive search firm that helps Fortune 500 companies recruit and hire key employees. KFN employs a large number of recruiters whose job it is to pair "prospects" and "talent," that is, to identify job opportunities at top companies and find suitably experienced job seekers to fill them. Recruiters spend significant time cultivating relationships with top personnel at the "prospect" companies, learning about the operations of the company and getting to know its work culture and hiring patterns in order to maintain that company's business. Recruiters also spend time researching "talent," which includes getting to know candidates who have registered with KFN as well as cold-calling employed executives to see if they might be interested in a job change. Frequently, recruiters develop an area of specialty, such as placing executives with expertise in technology or servicing companies seeking talent with experience in emerging markets. All of the information that KFN gleans about both its prospects and talent is kept in an extensive database that includes general information about the company or individual, a history of the services KFN has provided to the company or individual, and the recruiters' ideas and impressions about how to best market the individual or assist the company.

Up until now, KFN has never required its recruiters to sign any written agreement upon hire, largely because it feared such an agreement would impede its ability to hire experienced recruiters who bring prior contacts with them to the firm. However, it is revisiting the issue due to recent publicity about large-scale employee defections and data stealing in the job placement industry. Suppose KFN retains you. Would you advise the firm to use a contract containing restrictive covenants? What other practices and precautions would you recommend? If KFN asks you to draft a form contract for use with new recruiters, what would it look like?

C. INNOVATIONS IN NONCOMPETITION LITIGATION AND PRIVATE ORDERING

As the previous materials suggest, the laws surrounding competitive behavior of employees offer little certainty, even where the parties have planned for possible post-employment competition through contract. However conscientiously an employer may have drafted a noncompete agreement, it is often unclear whether a court will deem its underlying interests protectable and the terms of the restraint reasonable at the time enforcement is sought. How do parties (and lawyers) manage this type of uncertainty? For employers, better drafting and new types of contractual instruments are being developed to address (or circumvent) judicial hostility to standard noncompetes. Employees, on the other hand, may have limited ability to influence this process. Unless they are exceptionally skilled or highly sought after, employees will often have to accept the terms provided by employers. However, employees may be able to get a leg up in avoiding enforcement of such agreements by seeking to channel disputes into employee-friendly fora, resulting in some cases in a "race to the courthouse." This in turn has led employers to adopt second-order risk management techniques, such as the inclusion of choice-of-law and choice-of-forum clauses in their agreements. The variety of emerging strategies, in both the litigation and drafting contexts, are discussed in this section.

1. The Race to the Courthouse

Advanced Bionics Corp. v. Medtronic, Inc., 59 P. 3d 231 (Cal. 2002), sounds more like a Civil Procedure exam than a real case, but it illustrates the maneuvering that can occur in a federal system with states having radically different approaches to the enforceability of noncompetition clauses. The interjurisdictional tug-o-war commenced when Mark Stultz, a former employee of Medtronic, and his new California-based employer, Advanced Bionics, brought a suit in California state court. They sought a declaration that the noncompete Stultz signed with Medtronic, which included a choice-of-Minnesota-law clause but no choice-of-forum provision, was invalid under California law barring postemployment restraints. After delaying the California action by improperly removing it to federal court, Medtronic filed an action in Minnesota seeking to enforce the noncompete. In that action, it obtained first a TRO and then a preliminary injunction enjoining Advanced Bionics from hiring Stultz and barring both parties from seeking relief in another court. Back in California, once their case had been remanded back to state court, Stultz and Advanced Bionics obtained a TRO against Medtronic barring prosecution of the suit it had brought in Minnesota. Got it? Dueling injunctions prevented the parties from litigating in another court. On appeal, the California Supreme Court rejected the lower court's use of the TRO. Although the majority acknowledged California's strong interest in protecting employees from noncompetes, it concluded that California's commitment to the norms of judicial restraint and comity rendered the antisuit TRO improper. This was true despite the possibility that the foreign court would enter a judgment first, which, under full faith and credit, would then require enforcement by the California court. And it was true despite California's "strong interest in protecting its employees from noncompetition agreements," which might well lead to refusing to enforce the clause in that state. *Id.* at 237.

This result is in stark contrast to the approach of the Minnesota courts, which exhibited little restraint and no deference to the first-filed California action. Their actions could be viewed as an aggressive effort to ensure extraterritorial application of Minnesota's employer-friendly law, and the California Supreme Court's response opened the possibility of employers avoiding that state's pro-competition policy by careful drafting and strategic litigation.

Note that there is no "natural" forum in a dispute like this. Minnesota was where the contracting parties were located at all relevant times—both at the time of contract formation and during the course of the employment relationship. On the other hand, California is the jurisdiction where the alleged breach occurred, and ultimately the effects of any judgment will be felt there. The clash is between competing visions of good public policy, that of most states (here, Minnesota), which permit such clauses, and California, which does not. If California law trumps, Minnesota is unable to protect its employers—Medtronics—from "unfair" competition; if Minnesota law prevails, a California business—Advanced Bionics—will be cut off from highly valued workers, and thus disadvantaged in the interstate marketplace in which it seeks to compete.

In any event, the California court held that "the Minnesota action does not divest California of jurisdiction, and Advanced Bionics remains free to litigate the California action unless and until Medtronic demonstrates to the Los Angeles County Superior Court that any Minnesota judgment is binding on the parties." *Id.* at 238. That means that, in cases such as these, the competition is less a race to the courthouse (since both actions can proceed) as much as a race to judgment, since the first final judgment entered will preclude the competing suit. Or maybe not. While the full faith and credit clause requires a court to respect a *judgment* entered by a sister state, state courts are rarely required to enforce *injunctions* entered by sister states. *See Baker by Thomas v. GMC*, 522 U.S. 222 (1998). *See generally* Polly J. Price, *Full Faith and Credit and the Equity Conflict*, 84 VA. L. REV. 747 (1998). This might mean that a Minnesota injunction against Stultz and Advanced Bionics might not be enforced in California, suggesting that, as long as Stultz doesn't visit Minnesota again, the Minnesota judgment will be a nullity. Or maybe if Advanced Bionics did business in Minnesota, it might somehow be held to account? Note that the Minnesota court could issue a money judgment that California would be compelled to enforce, but, as we saw in *SIG*, proving damages in cases such as this, not to mention getting them from an employee, is notoriously difficult. And the Minnesota judgment would be preclusive in California, so Stultz and Advanced Bionics could not recover against Medtronic.

Just to complicate things even more, the California legislature has weighed in. A 2016 California law voids provisions in employment contracts that require an employee to litigate outside of the state or deprive the employee of the substantive protections of California law. The statute applies to a worker "who primarily resides or works" in that state, but there is an exception for employees represented by legal counsel who negotiate on their behalf. CALIF. LAB. Code §925 (2018). At the least, the statute might streamline a declaratory judgment action in that state, allowing the California court decision to become final while competing litigation in other states wrestles with noncompetition issues there.

If there is no way for Medtronic to win the war, even if it prevails in some important battles, perhaps it should rethink the way it manages the risk of employee competition by a geographically mobile worker. It might, for example, consider utilizing other risk management techniques, such as including arbitration clauses in its employment contracts. Such clauses will be addressed in detail in Chapter 13. Nevertheless, the utility of an arbitration provision might be limited since an arbitrator may not be able to provide the relief Medtronic is seeking, and, even if it could, Medtronic might face obstacles in attempting to enforce the arbitral ruling.

Would the problem of dueling courts have been avoided if Medtronic had used a choice-of-forum clause instead of or in addition to its choice-of-law provision? Using both is probably the more common strategy, since a state court is more likely to enforce a choice of law clause requiring its state's law to apply than would another state. Such a clause could have specified that claims could be pursued only in Minnesota. You might have run into choice-of-forum clauses in Civil Procedure in *Carnival Cruise Lines v. Shute*, 499 U.S. 585 (1991), which upheld a Florida forum clause for a cruise line despite the difficulties litigating in that forum caused the plaintiffs, who were citizens of Washington. But the enforceability of choice-of-forum clauses, like choice-of-law clauses, is a matter of state contract law. Stultz and Advanced Bionics still could have sued in California arguing that, under the circumstances, this clause also was invalid because, like the choice-of-law clause, it represented an attempt to frustrate California public policy. Two recent cases suggest that public policy can invalidate both choice-of-forum and choice-of-law clauses. *See Verdugo v. Alliantgroup, L.P.*, 187 Cal. Rptr. 613 (Cal. App. 2015) (a forum-selection clause violated public policy when the employer could not establish that the chosen forum would not diminish an employee's substantive unwaivable rights under California law because it did not stipulate to the application of California law there); *Brown & Brown, Inc. v. Johnson*, 34 N.E.3d 357 (N.Y. 2015) (a choice-of-law clause was unenforceable as it related to a non-solicitation provision because it violated New York public policy). *But see St. Jude Med. S.C., Inc. v. Biosense Webster, Inc.*, 818 F.3d 785 (8th Cir. 2016) (Minnesota choice-of-law provision in an employment agreement being performed in California was valid because the parties acted in good faith and without the intent to evade the law); *see generally* Timothy P. Glynn, *Interjurisdictional Competition in Enforcing Noncompetition Agreements: Regulatory Risk Management and the Race to the Bottom,* 65 WASH. & LEE L. REV. 1381 (2008).

2. Innovations in Contract Drafting

Heder v. City of Two Rivers
295 F.3d 777 (7th Cir. 2002)

EASTERBROOK, Cir. J.

After the City of Two Rivers decided that all of its firefighters must be certified as paramedics, the City and the firefighters' union agreed [to compensate the firefighters at half of their regular hourly rate for time spent in paramedic training]. The deal between the City and the union included a 3% increase in the wages of firefighters who held certifications, plus an undertaking that any firefighter leaving the City's employ within the next three years would reimburse the City for the cost of the training, which would give each firefighter a portable credential. Two and a half years after beginning his training, Heder quit. Two Rivers withheld all of Heder's pay from his last two pay periods. Heder filed suit under the [Fair Labor Standards Act ("FLSA")], and the City counterclaimed for the remainder of the money that it believes Heder owes under its memorandum of agreement with the union.

[The court first addressed Heder's FLSA claim. The City] concedes that Heder was entitled to compensation that the FLSA specifies as a statutory floor below which no contract may go. That means, in particular, that Heder was entitled to at least the statutory minimum wage for his final two pay periods (leaving the City to collect any residue as an ordinary creditor) and that Heder is entitled to time and a half for any overtime hours for which the FLSA requires that premium. But the parties do not agree on what this means in practice, because the firefighters do not work an ordinary 40-hour week. [Based on the way the City calculated work time, the City was required to pay time and a half for all hours over 204 per 27-day period, even if some of those hours were devoted to training.]

Next we must decide whether the City has a good claim for reimbursement of at least some outlays.

Heder depicts a repayment obligation as a covenant not to compete that is invalid under WIS. STAT. §103.465. The district judge adopted this characterization; we do not, because in Wisconsin (as in other states) a covenant not to compete must be linked to competition. An agreement to repay Two Rivers if a firefighter goes to work for a rival fire department would be treated as a covenant not to compete. But the agreement between Two Rivers and the firefighters' union does not restrict Heder's ability to compete against the City after leaving its employ. The obligation is unconditional: a firefighter departing before three years have expired must repay training costs even if he goes back to school, changes occupation, or retires. Competition has nothing to do with the matter.

According to Heder, Wisconsin would act as if this were a covenant not to compete, on the ground that repayment induces "involuntary servitude" that is more onerous than the agreements explicitly regulated under §103.465. Yet this is not what the Supreme Court of Wisconsin said in [*Union Central Life Insurance Co. v. Balistrieri*, 120 N.W.2d 126 (1963)]): there it limited application of §103.465 to agreements that condition repayment on going to work for the ex-employer's rival. True enough, as the district judge emphasized, Two Rivers' repayment obligation shares with genuine restrictive covenants the feature that it makes changing jobs costly. But that is not enough to throw a contract out the window. Employers offer their workers many incentives to stay, so that they can reap the benefit of training and other productivity enhancers that depend on employees' tenure with the firm. Pay that increases with longevity is one common device; an employee who leaves must start elsewhere at the bottom rung. Firm-specific training (the value of which is lost if the employee changes jobs) likewise penalizes departures. . . . Seniority systems that link duration of service to better assignments, protection against layoffs, and so on, have a similar effect; to quit is to give up accumulated seniority. Private employers give employees profit-sharing plans and stock options that vest later (if the person remains employed) and bonuses that accrue after extra years have been served. Defined-benefit pension systems usually are back-loaded, so that the last years of work before retirement add more to the monthly pension benefit than do earlier years. . . . The common formula that starts with multiplying the final salary by the number of years served produces this effect automatically because salaries tend to rise with inflation and years of service. Yet no one believes that this powerful financial incentive to stick with one's employer until retirement is unlawful, even though it is much larger than the amount Heder must repay Two Rivers for paramedic training. The parties do not cite, and we could not find, any Wisconsin decision that characterizes the kind of incentives mentioned above as restrictive covenants regulated by Wis. Stat. §103.465. Instead, Wisconsin applies Wis. Stat. §103.465 only to the extent that a consequence is linked on working for a competitor. . . .

Nor can we see any reason why Wisconsin would want to extend its precedents to block reimbursement agreements such as the one Two Rivers made with its union. Employees received considerable benefits as a result: paramedic training that will be useful for years to come, a 3% increase in compensation starting in 1998 (rising to 3.5% in 1999) for those who are certified paramedics, and extra compensation (at overtime rates) for the training time. Residents of Two Rivers received the benefit of a fire department more likely to save lives. Cities fearing that employees would take their new skills elsewhere would be less likely to provide these benefits. Or they might use other ways to acquire a workforce with better skills. They could, for example, require the employees to undergo and underwrite their own training, with none of the time compensated. This is what law firms do when they limit hiring to persons who already have law degrees, what school systems do when hiring only teachers who hold state certificates. The employer must pay indirectly, through a higher salary, but no court would dream of calling this system (under which employees finance their own training) "involuntary servitude." If an employer may require employees to pay up front, why can't the employer bear the expense but require reimbursement if an early departure deprives the employer of the benefit of its bargain? A middle ground also would be feasible (and lawful): The employer could require the worker to pay for his own training but lend the worker the money and forgive repayment if he sticks around. . . . A worker who left before the loan had been forgiven would have to come up with the funds from his own sources, just as Heder must do. If that system is lawful, as it is, then the economically equivalent system that Two Rivers adopted must be lawful. The cost of training equates to the loan, repayment of which is forgiven after three years.

The district judge objected to the cliff in the repayment system: instead of a slow reduction (equivalent to amortization of a loan), the collective bargaining agreement calls for full repayment before three years and none after. The judge inferred from this that the useful life of paramedic training is three years; as Heder quit with only 1/6 of this time remaining his union could not legally bind him to repay more than 1/6 of these expenses. The inference is unsound: One could as easily infer from the fact that the 3% wage boost is perpetual that paramedic training lasts indefinitely. We know from the record that Heder spent 582 hours undergoing the initial round of training and eight hours to re-certify two years later. This implies that paramedic skills have a useful life that can be extended indefinitely with small recurring investment—and it also implies that the three-year period is generous to workers. Two Rivers could have made the period much longer (say, 10 years). Then even if the debt had been amortized, as the district judge preferred, many workers (all who stayed longer than 3 years but quit or retired before 10) would have been worse off. The actual structure cannot be set aside as onerous—even if Wisconsin had a rule, which it does not, that no onerous term in a collective bargaining agreement is enforceable. The day Heder quit, his paramedic skills were effectively as valuable as the day he received his certification. We do not think that the Supreme Court of Wisconsin is apt to require employers and employees to amortize training costs with precision, to factor in the time value of money (the agreement does not require Heder to pay interest, though it might have done so), or to craft an individual schedule based on the number of years each employee is expected to remain able to work. The collective bargaining agreement is valid under state law, so Heder must repay the full cost of his books and tuition, which came to about $1,400.

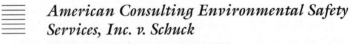

American Consulting Environmental Safety Services, Inc. v. Schuck

888 N.E.2d 874 (Ind. Ct. App. 2008)

FRIEDLANDER, J.

. . . American Consulting is an Indiana corporation that provides safety compliance services and materials to customers located within a 200-mile radius of South Bend, Indiana. To carry out its purpose, American Consulting evaluates the safety and accident prevention policies of businesses and offers programs and courses to bring them into compliance with regulatory agencies' requirements. On January 14, 2005, Schuck was hired by American Consulting as a safety instructor. Schuck signed an employment agreement setting forth the terms and conditions of her employment. Although Schuck had received training in occupational safety and health prior to coming to work for American Consulting, American Consulting required that Schuck undergo additional training. Specifically, Section 12 of the employment agreement provided [that the company would provide training to the employee at a cost of $3,000.00, which cost would be borne by the company if the employee remained working for 12 months. If, however, the Employee shall voluntarily terminate the employment or if the Employee is terminated by the Employer for good cause, the Employee shall reimburse the Company for the cost of training in accordance with a schedule that required the employee to repay progressively smaller amounts as she worked longer, but $3,000 if her employment was terminated in less than 3 months.]

Schuck's training by American Consulting consisted of spending one day watching videos and taking several short quizzes. The videos were part of a video library American Consulting had accumulated over the course of several years. Additional training included Schuck shadowing another American Consulting employee during visits to existing customers. In total, Schuck completed twelve and one-half days of "shadow training." During the training period, Schuck was paid $9.00 per hour and was not paid overtime.

In June 2005, Schuck informed American Consulting that she had been experiencing medical problems and had found out that she was pregnant. After five months of productive employment, Schuck felt it necessary, due to her pregnancy, to resign from her position. . . .

[American Consulting sued Schuck seeking repayment of $1,500.00 under Section 12 of her employment contract. T]he trial court made the following findings pertinent to our review:

> 13. In considering the facts of this case, the only credible evidence submitted as to the actual loss of the plaintiff is the wages paid to defendant during her training. Defendant testified that her hourly wage was $9.00 per hour and that she had one day of training by watching video tapes [and 12 days of shadow training by following an experienced employee] while that employee was actually earning money for the plaintiff while training employees of customer corporations. Assuming 13 days at 8 hours per day at $9.00 per hour equals $72.00 per day times 13 days equals $936.00. However, the plaintiff's schedule as found in Paragraph 12, provided that because the defendant had already worked six [sic] months at the time of her pregnancy-related request to leave employment, only one-half of that sum would be due, under the intent of the parties. The maximum damages that plaintiff could recover under the actual evidence would be $468.00, assuming that this provision is enforceable. Four Hundred Sixty-Eight Dollars ($468.00) is approximately thirty-one (31%) percent of the amount claimed by the plaintiff.
>
> 15. The lack of reasonableness of the stipulation for repayment of training costs under the circumstances of this case weighs in favor of finding that this is a penalty clause and is unenforceable.

. . . The term "liquidated damages" applies to a specific sum of money that has been expressly stipulated by the parties to a contract as to the amount of damages to be recovered by either party in the event of a breach of the contract by the other. Liquidated damages provisions are useful and generally enforceable in situations where actual damages would be uncertain or difficult to ascertain. To be enforceable, the sum stipulated as liquidated damages must "fairly be allowed as compensation for the breach." Where the stipulated sum is grossly disproportionate to the loss that may result from a breach of contract, we should treat the sum as a penalty rather than as liquidated damages.

As our Supreme Court has noted with regard to the history of litigation of liquidated damage clauses, in cases where actual damages could be readily ascertained and the amount stipulated exceeded the actual damages, then the contract provision has been treated as a "penalty" and only actual damages awarded. "The distinction between a penalty provision and a liquidated damages provision is that a penalty is imposed to secure performance of the contract, and liquidated damages are to be paid in lieu of performance."

In determining whether a stipulated sum payable on a breach of contract constitutes liquidated damages or a penalty, we will consider the facts, the intention of the parties, and the reasonableness of the stipulation under the circumstances of the case. Where there is uncertainty as to the meaning of a liquidated damages provision, classification as a penalty is favored. . . .

Here, Schuck's training consisted of watching videos accumulated over the years by American Consulting. These videos were also used to train other employees. Schuck also shadowed an American Consulting employee for twelve days. American Consulting did not send Schuck for specialized off-site training, seminars, or the like, or bring in specialists to provide on-site training. American Consulting failed to explain how the training it did provide amounted to its stated cost of $3,000.00. American Consulting also failed to demonstrate a reasonable relationship between the reimbursement amounts listed in the Section 12 schedule and the amount of actual damages incurred by the termination of employment.

To be sure, the primary damages American Consulting suffered (if indeed any damages at all) would have been the wage paid to Schuck during her training. This is precisely what the trial court used to compute American Consulting's damages. The trial court calculated Schuck's wage for thirteen days of training at a rate of $9.00 per hour for an eight-hour day and concluded that, at most, American Consulting's loss was $468.00, or thirty-one percent of American Consulting's claimed amount. American Consulting's claimed damages of $1,500.00 is not commensurate with or reasonably related to its actual damages. Furthermore, upon reading the contract, the purpose of Section 12 appears to be to secure performance of the contract for at least a twelve-month period, an earmark of a penalty provision. Based on the foregoing, we can only conclude that Section 12 amounts to an unenforceable penalty.

NOTES

1. *Training Repayment Agreements as an Alternative to Noncompetes.* In what ways might training repayment agreements better serve employers' interests than noncompetes? In theory, such agreements circumvent the problem of courts' general disfavor of noncompetes and the particular reluctance to recognize training as a protectable interest. As *Heder* illustrates, at least some courts have taken that view. *See also USS-Posco Indus. v. Case*, 197 Cal. Rptr. 3d 791, 801 (Cal. App. 2016) (repaying training costs did not run afoul of California's stringent rule against noncompetes), as have some state legislatures. *See* Colo. Rev. Stat. 8-2-113(2) (2018) (permitting enforcement of repayment agreements against employees who serve less than two years). There is also some reason to think that repayment agreements may be more efficient and less likely to overreach than noncompete agreements given that such agreements are tailored to a particular interest and usually apply only if the employee departs within a designated time period. *See* Gillian Lester, *Restrictive Covenants, Employee Training, and the Limits of Transaction-Cost Analysis*, 76 Ind. L. J. 49, 75-76 (2001).

However, training repayment agreements are hardly a panacea for employers or employees. Where the repayment obligation is tied to post-employment competition, courts are likely to view the agreement as a noncompete and evaluate its reasonableness under comparable standards. *See, e.g., Brunner v. Hand Indus.*, 603 N.E.2d 157 (Ind. Ct. App. 1992) (holding unenforceable agreement obligating former employee to repay costs of training if he joined competitor because employer had no protectable interest in general training and payments were unreasonable). In addition, as

Heder and *American Consulting* indicate, repayment agreements that do not hinge on noncompetition can still run afoul of other laws and doctrines such as restrictions on liquidated damage clauses and state and federal wage payment laws. *See also Sands Appliance Serv. v. Wilson*, 615 N.W.2d 241 (Mich. 2000) (finding training repayment arrangement violated state anti-kickback law prohibiting employer from requiring any form of compensation in exchange for job). From the employee's perspective, training repayment agreements might in some instances prove more onerous than noncompetes. Whereas an employee can comply with a noncompete by refraining from competition, a training repayment agreement requires that she have the funds to pay back the company. If the amount is high, it is easy to see how such an agreement can result in a total, if temporary, restraint on mobility.

2. *Liquidated Damages Analysis.* The two cases you read take very different analytical approaches to repayment agreements. *American Consulting* finds the repayment agreement to be an unenforceable penalty without regard to the law of restrictive covenants. *Heder*, on the other hand, concerns itself with whether the agreement is a noncompete, and upon concluding that it is not, enforces the repayment provision without regard to liquidated damages issues.

Although both liquidated damages provisions and restrictive covenants are matters of contract, the law treats the two types of clauses very differently. A liquidated damages provision that is part of a valid contract is presumptively enforceable, and the party seeking to avoid payment (the employee in repayment cases) bears the burden of overcoming that presumption by showing that the liquidated amount is disproportionate to probable or actual loss. *Cf. Sisters of Charity Health Sys. v. Farrago*, 21 A.3d 110 (Me. 2011) (a practice's patient base and goodwill were protectable business interests, which justified a liquidated damages clause that was a reasonable approximation of the damages that the employer would incur if a doctor left the practice to compete within a 25-mile radius). In contrast, we have seen that in most states, noncompetes are presumed void unless reasonable in relation to the employer's legitimate interests; it is the party seeking enforcement (the employer) who bears the burden of proof.

Why do the employees in *Heder* and *American Consulting* pursue such different legal theories? Is there any reason why the firefighters in *Heder* could not have availed themselves of the penalty argument that persuaded the court in *American Consulting*? Would a liquidated damages analysis lead to a different outcome in *Heder*? Or are competing results in the cases better explained by factual differences? If so, which facts?

Another question is whether a liquidated damages analysis is apt in either case. A typical liquidated damages provision is one that provides for a certain remedy in the event of a party's breach. For instance, an employer might include a repayment clause in a fixed-term contract under which an employee was bound to remain with the company for a set period, a technique you encountered in studying written contracts of high-level employees in Chapter 3. However, neither Heder nor Schuck had any contractual obligation to remain with their employers. *See Dresser-Rand Co. v. Bolick*, 14-12-00192-CV, 2013 WL 3770950 (Tex. App. July 18, 2013) (a repayment obligation for relocation expenses if an employee resigned within a year was not a liquidated damages provision when the defendant, as an at-will employee, had no obligation to work for the year and therefore did not breach to begin with).

Another situation in which employers might seek liquidated damages provisions is in settling claims. You will see an example of this in Chapter 13.

3. *"Garden Leave" Clauses.* Another way in which employers try to circumvent judicial disfavor of noncompetes is by adding clauses to their agreements promising to continue an employee's salary for the duration of the restraint. Offering pay—sometime referred to as "garden leave"—is a standard feature of many noncompete contracts in the United Kingdom, especially in the financial services sector. *See generally* Charles A. Sullivan, *Tending the Garden: Restricting Competition via "Garden Leave,"* 36 Berkeley J. Empl. & Lab. L. 293 (2016). Under such agreements, the employer essentially pays the worker to temporarily "sit out." In the UK, such workers typically remain formally employed; in the U.S., where such clauses are less often used, the worker is usually formally terminated. A variation on this idea is to give the employee a choice between not competing and receiving some form of compensation or competing and sacrificing that benefit. *See, e.g., Lucente v. IBM,* 310 F.3d 243, 248 (2d Cir. 2002).

Such clauses do not necessarily eliminate all of the harsh effects of noncompetes on employees—in fast-paced industries, skills can atrophy quickly, and an employee kept from the field may lose touch with cutting-edge developments and critical client contacts. Employers interested in hiring the defecting employee may not be willing to wait out the period of restraint, and the employee might miss out on key opportunities. Compensating the employee makes the restraint significantly less onerous, however, which could make some courts more willing to enforce the agreement, especially in satisfying the "balance of hardships" requirement for preliminary injunctions. *See, e.g., Nike v. McCarthy,* 379 F.3d 576, 587 (9th Cir. 2004) (finding Nike's obligation to pay employee full salary during restricted period a factor mitigating potential harm to the employee and supporting issuance of preliminary injunction). "Pay to sit out" clauses might increase the employer's chances of prevailing in other ways as well. Such clauses could support the employer's contention that it has a significant legitimate interest underlying the restraint. After all, it is unlikely that an employer would be willing to pay an employee *not* to work absent a significant economic reason to do so. *See* Cynthia L. Estlund, *Between Rights and Contract: Arbitration Agreements and Non-Compete Covenants as a Hybrid Form of Employment Law,* 155 U. Pa. L. Rev. 379, 425 (2006) (suggesting that mandatory garden leave could encourage employer self-policing in determining whether to seek noncompete enforcement). And, in California, at least if the worker remains formally employed, garden leave may be a way around the statutory prohibition on *post*employment restraints. Finally, given the relative recent use of such clauses, it is not surprising to find that serious interpretive questions have arisen. *See Reed v. Getco, LLC,* 65 N.E.3 904 (Ill. App. 2016) (no duty to mitigate by seeking other employment in light of language in the contract expressly providing that the employee would not compete for six months after his departure in return for the specified payment; employer had no unilateral power to reduce the defined period).

4. *No-Hire Agreements.* Still another option for employers is to bypass the employee altogether in favor of contracting directly with customers or competitors. Consulting and placement companies have long required clients to sign "no hire" agreements under which the client agrees that for a period of time it will not hire any employee leased to it by the consulting or placement company. *See, e.g., Blase Indus. v. Anorad Corp.,* 442 F.3d 235 (5th Cir. 2006). In some industries, competitors are adopting a similar technique, entering into mutual "no switching" agreements under which they agree not to "poach" one another's employees. These are more troubling than noncompetes because they can choke off competition between employers. They can, therefore, raise serious antitrust concerns, as indicated by litigation involving no-poaching agreements by some of the biggest technology firms in Silicon Valley. The Department of Justice entered a consent decree with the defendants, and a class action was subsequently brought on behalf of the engineers whose compensation was presumably suppressed by the agreement, leading to a large settlement. Government antitrust enforcement on this front also is ramped up. Department of Justice Antitrust Division/Federal Trade Commission, *Antitrust Guidance for Human Resource Professionals*, https://www.justice.gov/atr/file/903511/download. *See* Rochella T. Davis, *Talent Can't Be Allocated: A Labor Economics Justification for No-Poaching Agreement Criminality in Antitrust Regulation*, 12 Brook. J. Corp. Fin. & Com. L. 279-310 (2018).

5. *The Future of Private Ordering.* The legal significance of emerging contractual forms, like those described above, is as yet unknown. Both employers and companies must wait to see how courts and legislatures respond once such agreements start facing more consistent legal challenges. What is certain is that whatever way the law evolves in the area of employee competition, firms are likely to seek out newer and more creative ways of using private ordering to structure their relationships to maximum advantage.

Note on the Computer Fraud and Abuse Act

Although not limited to the scenario of competition by former employees, the Computer Fraud and Abuse Act ("CFAA"), 18 U.S.C. §1030 (2018), has played an increasingly important role in such situations and is worth noting in its own right. The CFAA was enacted in 1986 with the primary purpose of combating computer "hacking," but it reaches not only access to computers "without authorization" (the paradigmatic anonymous hacker), but also actions "exceeding authorized access," which obviously includes employees taking confidential information with them when they depart or sabotaging their former employer's systems. *See United States v. Steele*, 595 F. App'x 208 (4th Cir. 2014) (an ex-employee who continued to access his former employer's e-mail server for nine months after resigning to join a competitor violated the "without authorization" provision of CFAA). The CFAA creates criminal liability, but its use in the employment context is increasingly on the civil side with employers seeking compensatory damages or injunctive relief under the statute's authorization of suit by "[a]ny person who suffers damage or loss by reason of a violation." A typical civil case is an employer's suit against a former employee claiming misappropriation or destruction of its data.

A critical issue for CFAA litigation is whether an employee who violates the employer's restrictions on the use of information stored on a computer—for example, through an appropriate use policy—"exceeds authorized access." Some courts have been reluctant to read the statute this broadly, *e.g., WEC Carolina Energy Solutions LLC v. Miller*, 687 F.3d 199, 206 (4th Cir. 2012) ("[W]e adopt a narrow reading of the terms 'without authorization' and 'exceeds authorized access' and hold that they apply only when an individual accesses a computer without permission or obtains or alters information on a computer beyond that which he is authorized to access."); *United States v. Valle*, 807 F.3d 508, 511-12 (2d Cir. 2015) (2-1) (applying the rule of lenity to interpret "exceeds authorized access" to reach only accessing information without authorization for any purpose); *United States v. Nosal*, 676 F.3d 854,

863 (9th Cir. 2012) (en banc) ("we hold that the phrase 'exceeds authorized access' in the CFAA does not extend to violations of use restrictions. If Congress wants to incorporate misappropriation liability into the CFAA, it must speak more clearly."), but others have been more expansive. *E.g., Int'l Airport Centers, L.L.C. v. Citrin,* 440 F.3d 418 (7th Cir. 2006) (claim stated when an employee used a secure-erasure program to delete files on a laptop he had been assigned). Notice, of course, that a CFAA claim does not require a noncompetition clause nor does it require a finding that the information obtained is a trade secret or otherwise confidential. Rather, the gravamen of the claim is that the information was destroyed or taken without the necessary authority to do so. *See Brown Jordan Int'l, Inc. v. Carmicle,* 846 F.3d 1167 (11th Cir. 2017) (former employee's use of generic passwords to access other's accounts as well as his use of an app to remotely lock a laptop owned by the company violated the CFAA; it was unreasonable of him to use a generic password solely on a suspicion of dishonesty concerning the content of communications between others); *see generally,* Danielle J. Reid, Note, *Combating the Enemy Within: Regulating Employee Misappropriation of Business Information,* 71 VAND. L. REV. 1033 (2018).

PROBLEM

8-5.   Revisit the cases in this chapter in light of the developments in company contracting practices described above. Are there any cases in which it might have been prudent for the employer to use a "pay to sit out" clause, a training repayment agreement, or a "no-switching" contract? Are there other contract forms or clauses that you can think of that might have been appropriate? Choose one case and try your hand at drafting the alternative agreement.

Part Six

STATUTORY PROTECTIONS FOR EMPLOYEES

9
Antidiscrimination

A. THE POLICY BASES FOR ANTIDISCRIMINATION LAW

Federal laws bar discrimination by employers on a number of grounds: race, sex, religion, national origin, age, and disability. In addition, many state laws extend the list of prohibited grounds to marital status, political affiliation, and, increasingly, sexual orientation. While employers "discriminate" all the time in the sense that they differentiate between employees for all sorts of reasons, some bases of differentiation—race, sex, religion, national origin, age, disability—are impermissible, while others are perfectly legal. Still other bases, such as sexual orientation, are highly contested. The choice to prohibit discrimination emerges from two considerations. Most obviously, discrimination on the basis of certain characteristics, especially race and sex, is viewed as unfair since such characteristics are immutable and, therefore, beyond an individual's control. Because discrimination inflicts harm on victims for reasons they cannot control, it is also often viewed as immoral. This rationale, however, does not explain the prohibition against discrimination on the basis of religion, but discrimination on that basis or on the basis of other characteristics over which individuals exercise some degree of choice, such as political affiliation and marital status, is often viewed as wrongful because of deep-rooted concerns about human autonomy and the inalienability of fundamental rights. From this perspective, then, discrimination is wrongful because it damages the dignity of its victims.

Second, there is a socioeconomic agenda to antidiscrimination laws. This emerges most explicitly with respect to the Age Discrimination in Employment Act ("ADEA"), 29 U.S.C. §§621 et seq. (2018), and the Americans with Disabilities Act ("ADA"), 42 U.S.C.A. §§12101 et seq. (2018), where Congress stressed the waste of human resources caused by discrimination. Such action results not only in individual harm but also in the loss to society of the contributions of older workers and workers with disabilities whose abilities are not fully utilized. Although subordinate to dignity values, a concern for the potentially devastating economic consequences of discrimination was also prominent in the enactment of Title VII.

From this perspective, antidiscrimination statutes are united by two simple premises: First, the groups to be protected by the statute are disadvantaged economically; second, employers' discriminatory conduct causes, or at least contributes to, that disadvantage. Approached this way, the statutes seek to end discrimination in order to improve the economic condition of members of protected groups by allowing them to compete freely for jobs on the basis of their qualifications. Improving the economic condition of such groups can also redound to the benefit of society more generally.

Although equal employment opportunity has received almost unanimous support among all racial groups as an abstract principle, the antidiscrimination laws have often proved controversial in their application. The basic prohibition against express intentional racial discrimination is generally accepted, but a number of specific issues, including affirmative action, pregnancy discrimination, sexual harassment, disparate impact, and discrimination on the basis of sexual orientation, have generated intense national debate.

To begin, not everyone agrees that discrimination should be legally prohibited. Some even question the basic prohibition against express intentional discrimination on account of race. From the beginning, some defended both the wisdom and morality of discrimination or at least questioned the morality of legislating nondiscrimination. While few still subscribe to such views, it has been argued more recently that discrimination may be rational and efficient. Still another view is that, even if discrimination is wrongful, antidiscrimination laws are unnecessary either because market forces will eliminate discrimination without government interference or because discrimination is no longer a significant social problem. An employer that discriminates, after all, must pay a price: Artificially contracting the supply of available labor tends to raise the price of the labor purchased. If many employers discriminate, the price (wages) of their workforce will climb. Competitors will be free to exploit the pool of excluded black (or female) workers at lower wages, thus gaining a competitive advantage. As more employers seek lower-cost black workers, their value will rise. Thus, the market will correct discrimination, without the need for legal intervention. *See* John J. Donohue III, *Advocacy Versus Analysis in Assessing Employment Discrimination Law*, 44 STAN. L. REV. 1583, 1591 (1992) (recounting such opposition to Title VII's enactment); Richard A. Epstein, FORBIDDEN GROUNDS: THE CASE AGAINST EMPLOYMENT DISCRIMINATION LAWS (1992) (adding to the economic argument a strong libertarian critique of government intervention to eliminate discrimination).

Despite these theoretic objections, a variety of statistical studies suggest the continued existence of discrimination in a number of settings, ranging from sports to retail. In sports, for example, studies of basketball fouls seem to document race bias by referees. *See* Joseph Price & Justin Wolfers, *Racial Discrimination Among NBA Referees*, 125 Q. J. ECON. 1859 (2010) ("[M]ore personal fouls are called against players when they are officiated by an opposite-race refereeing crew than when officiated by an own-race crew. [W]e find appreciable differences in whether predominantly black teams are more likely to win or lose, based on the racial composition of the refereeing crew."). *See also* Ian Ayres, *Fair Driving: Gender and Race Discrimination in Retail Car Negotiations*, 104 HARV. L. REV. 817, 819 (1991). More relevant to our focus, Laura Giuliana, David I. Levine, & Jonathon Leonard, *Manager Race and the Race of New Hires*, 27 J. LAB. ECON. 589 (Oct. 2009), used data from a large retailer with frequent employee turnover to conclude that nonblack managers hire more whites and fewer blacks than do African American managers; in areas with large Hispanic populations, Hispanic managers hire more Hispanics and fewer whites than white managers.

This kind of statistical analysis of the persistence of discrimination in the workplace is confirmed by a number of field experiments. For example, Marianne Bertrand & Sendhil Mullainathan, *Are Emily and Greg More Employable than Lakisha and Jamal? A Field Experiment on Labor Market Discrimination*, 94 AM. ECON. REV. 991 (2004), report that, when identical fictitious resumes were sent to employers in Boston and Chicago, those receiving more favorable treatment were those containing non–African American sounding names. More recently, a study showed that legal memoranda supposedly written by black attorneys were rated much lower than the same work product supposedly written by white attorneys. Nextions, *Written in Black and White: Exploring Confirmation Bias in Racialized Perceptions of Writing Skills*, http://www.nextions.com/wp-content/files_mf/13972237592014040114WritteninBlackandWhiteYPS.pdf.

With respect to sex, Claudia Goldin & Cecilia Rouse, *Orchestrating Impartiality: The Impact of "Blind" Auditions on Female Musicians*, 90 AM. ECON. REV. 715 (2000), report that auditions held with the performer behind a screen substantially increased the likelihood that a female candidate would advance out of the preliminary round in an orchestra's selection process. And concerning age, Michael Winerip, *Three Men, Three Ages. Which Do You Like?*, N.Y. TIMES July 27, 2013, at B-1, reported a study in which three versions of the same person at three different ages were treated differently by a test group; the "assertive" version of the character was viewed more negatively than the younger versions when saying the same thing. *See generally* Nilanjana Dasgupta, *Implicit Ingroup Favoritism, Outgroup Favoritism, and Their Behavioral Manifestations*, 17 SOC. JUST. RES. 143 (2004).

Such findings are consistent with older studies showing that, when pairs of black and white "auditors" applied for jobs, the white applicant was able to advance farther through the hiring process than an equally qualified black counterpart in one of five audits. "In other words, the white was able to either submit an application, receive a formal interview, or the white was offered a job when the black was not. Overall, in one out of eight or 15 percent of the audits, the white was offered a job although his equally qualified black partner was not." Margery Austin Turner, Michael Fix, & Raymond J. Struyk, OPPORTUNITIES DENIED, OPPORTUNITIES DIMINISHED: DISCRIMINATION IN HIRING 31-32 (1991).

In an attempt to explain the discrepancy between economic theory and the reality on the ground, Gary Becker in THE ECONOMICS OF DISCRIMINATION (2d ed. 1971), posited that employers have a "taste for discrimination," for which they are willing to pay. Professor David A. Strauss, in *The Law and Economics of Racial Discrimination in Employment: The Case for Numerical Standards*, 79 GEO. L. J. 1619 (1991), notes that the "taste" may be that of the employer itself or of someone whose preferences the employer has to consider—other employees or customers. A version of this argument appeared in Professor Epstein's book FORBIDDEN GROUNDS, in which he claimed that homogeneity in a workplace could be conducive to productivity: where "individual tastes are grouped by race, by sex, by age, by national origin—and to some extent they are—then there is a necessary conflict between the commands of any antidiscrimination law and the smooth operation of the firm." *Id.* at 66-67; *see also* Devon Carbado & Mitu Galati, *The Law and Economics of Critical Race Theory: Crossroads, Directions, and a New Critical Race Theory*, 112 YALE L. J. 1757, 1762 (2003) (while disagreeing with Professor Epstein's normative view, agreeing that "employers have incentives to screen prospective employees for homogeneity); Scott A. Moss, *Women Choosing Diverse Workplaces: A Rational Preference with Disturbing Implications for Both Occupational Segregation and Economic Analysis of Law*, 27 HARV. WOMEN'S L. J. 1 (2004) (women rationally use the level of diversity as a proxy for discrimination and therefore tend to prefer workplaces with more women).

A related argument that seeks to explain (but not justify) the persistence of discrimination is that some protected characteristics are correlated with ability or other desirable characteristics. For instance, men are statistically more likely than women to have longer job tenure and not terminate or cut back employment after becoming a parent. This theory is sometimes called "statistical discrimination." Strauss, *supra*, at 1622. The logic of statistical discrimination does not require that racial or gender differences be inherent—any correlation with productivity could be the result of factors such as past societal discrimination. Further, "statistical discrimination" does not necessarily mean that the employer acts only on the basis of scientifically ascertained differences. Indeed, such discrimination will be more or less "rational" depending on the relationship between the stereotype used and statistical reality.

Is statistical discrimination objectionable even if it is accurate in group terms? Rational or not, relying on generalizations (perhaps better called stereotypes) excludes entire groups without any assessment of individual abilities. This is particularly problematic if the generalization is itself rooted in prior discrimination. Even if perceived productivity differences are real across groups, should employers be free to rely on them? Where does fairness to individuals fit into the equation? And wouldn't allowing such employment practices perpetuate the phenomenon by blunting incentives for acquiring human capital by members of such groups?

B. INDIVIDUAL DISPARATE TREATMENT DISCRIMINATION

1. Introduction

To address the pervasive problem of employment discrimination, Congress enacted a series of statutes dealing with various aspects of the phenomenon. These laws include Title VII of the Civil Rights Act of 1964; the Civil War Reconstruction statutes, especially 42 U.S.C. §1981; the Age Discrimination in Employment Act of 1967 ("ADEA"); and the Americans with Disabilities Act of 1990 ("ADA"), although the latter requires a separate discussion. See page 685. The avenues of relief under the statutes differ from each other in important ways, but all are concerned with discrimination in employment. The concept of "discrimination," however, has been developed in ways that are not always intuitively obvious. Indeed, "discrimination" is a term of art that embraces several different definitions, each with its own distinctive theory and methods of proof.

All of the statutes adopt a unitary definition of "disparate treatment" discrimination. The term originated in cases decided under Title VII and has been applied essentially unchanged in other antidiscrimination statutes. Disparate treatment, however, has developed in two distinct ways. Individual disparate treatment is the focus of this section, while systemic disparate treatment is taken up in section C. Individual disparate treatment is the theory most often asserted in court filings.

Title VII, 42 U.S.C. §§2000e to 2000e-17 (2018), which embraces almost all employers of 15 or more employees, proscribes discrimination in employment on the basis of race, color, religion, sex, or national origin. Section 703(a), 42 U.S.C. §2000e-2(a)(1), states the basic standard: It is an "unlawful employment practice" for an employer "to fail or refuse to hire or to discharge any individual, or otherwise to discriminate against any individual with respect to his compensation, terms, conditions, or privileges of employment, because of such individual's race, color, religion, sex, or national origin. . . ." The ADEA, 29 U.S.C. §§631-34 (2018), applies to employers with 20 or more workers. It tracks Title VII's language but ends each clause with "because of such individual's age." §623(a). The ADEA, however, defines "age" to include only those at least 40 years of age. §631(a).

Finally, in its present form, 42 U.S.C. §1981 (2018), guarantees "all persons within the jurisdiction of the United States . . . the same right in every State and Territory to make and enforce contracts . . . as is enjoyed by white citizens. . . ." Section 1981 originated in the Civil War Reconstruction era as one of several statutes intended to protect former slaves. While its success in promoting racial equality was limited for a century, doubts about whether it barred private discrimination ended in 1975 with *Johnson v. Railway Express Agency, Inc.*, 421 U.S. 454, 459-60 (1975), in which the Supreme Court wrote: "§1981 affords a federal remedy against discrimination in private employment on the basis of race."

Slack v. Havens
7 FEP 885 (S.D. Cal. 1973), aff'd as modified, 522 F.2d 1091 (9th Cir. 1975)

THOMPSON, J.

This action is brought by the plaintiffs, four black women, who allege they were discriminatorily discharged, due to their race, in violation of the Civil Rights Act of 1964, specifically 42 U.S.C. §2000e-2(a)(1). . . .

4. On January 31, 1968, plaintiffs Berrel Matthews, Emily Hampton, and Isabell Slack were working in the bonding and coating department of defendant Industries' plant, engaged in preparing and assembling certain tubing components for defendant's product. A white co-worker, Sharon Murphy, was also assigned to the bonding and coating department on that day and was performing the same general work as the three plaintiffs mentioned above. The fourth plaintiff, Kathleen Hale, was working in another department on January 31st.

Near the end of the working day, plaintiffs Matthews, Hampton, and Slack were called together by their immediate supervisor, Ray Pohasky, and informed that the following morning, upon reporting to work, they would suspend regular production and engage in a general cleanup of the bonding and coating department. The cleanup was to consist of washing walls and windows whose sills were approximately 12 to 15 feet above the floor, cleaning light fixtures, and scraping the floor which was caked with deposits of hardened resin. Plaintiffs Matthews, Hampton, and Slack protested the assigned work, arguing that it was not within their job description, which included only light cleanup in their immediate work areas, and that it was too hard and dangerous. Mr. Pohasky agreed that it was hard work and said that he would check to see if they had to do it.

5. On the following work day, February 1, 1968, plaintiffs Matthews, Hampton, and Slack reported to the bonding and coating department along with Sharon Murphy, their white co-worker. However, Mr. Pohasky excused Sharon Murphy to another department for the day, calling in plaintiff Kathleen Hale from the winding department where she had been on loan from the bonding and coating department for about a week. Mr. Pohasky then repeated his announcement that the heavy cleaning would have to be done. The four plaintiffs joined in protest against the heavy cleanup work. They pointed out that they had not been hired to do janitorial type work, and one of the plaintiffs inquired as to why Sharon Murphy had been excused from the cleanup detail even though she had very little seniority among the ladies in the bonding and coating department. In reply, they were told by Mr. Pohasky that they would do the work, "or else." There was uncontradicted testimony that at some-time during their conversation Pohasky injected the statement that "Colored people should stay in their places," or words to that effect. Some further discussion took place between plaintiffs and Pohasky and then with Gary Helming, plaintiffs' general supervisor, but eventually each of the plaintiffs was taken to the office of Mr. Helming where she was given her final paycheck and fired. Plaintiff Matthews testified without contradiction that on the way to Mr. Helming's office Mr. Pohasky made the comment that "Colored folks are hired to clean because they clean better."

6. The general cleanup work was later performed by newly-hired male employees. Sharon Murphy was never asked to participate in this cleanup before or after the plaintiffs' termination.

7. The day following the plaintiffs' firing a conference was held between plaintiffs and defendant Glenn G. Havens, together with Mr. Helming, Mr. Pohasky and other company officials, but the dispute was not resolved as to the work plaintiffs were expected to do. Apparently, the plaintiffs were offered reinstatement if they would now agree to do the same cleanup work. They refused. . . .

8. Having concluded that defendant Industries is an "employer" under Title VII of the Civil Rights Act for the purposes of this action, we must next consider whether plaintiffs' termination amounted to unlawful discrimination against them because of their race. Defendants deny that the facts support such a conclusion, contending that plaintiffs' case amounts to nothing more than a dispute as to their job classification.

Admittedly, the majority of the discussion between plaintiffs and Industries' management on January 31 and February 1, 1968 centered around the nature of the duties which plaintiffs were ordered to perform. Plaintiffs pointed out that they had not been hired with the understanding that they would be expected to perform more than light cleanup work immediately adjacent to their work stations. They were met with an ultimatum that they do the work—or else. Additionally, no explanation was offered as to why Sharon Murphy, a white co-worker, had been transferred out of the bonding and coating department the morning that the heavy cleaning was to begin there, while plaintiff Hale was called back from the winding department, where she had been working, to the bonding and coating area, specifically for participation in the general cleanup. It is not disputed that Sharon Murphy had less seniority than all of the plaintiffs except plaintiff Hale (having been hired 8 days prior to plaintiff Hale) and no evidence of a bona fide business reason was ever educed by defendants as to why Sharon Murphy was excused from assisting the plaintiffs in the proposed cleaning project.

The only evidence that did surface at the trial regarding the motives for the decisions of the management of defendant Industries consisted of certain statements by supervisor Pohasky, who commented to plaintiff Matthews that "colored folks were hired to clean because they clean better," and "colored folks should stay in their place," or words to that effect. Defendants attempt to disown these statements with the argument that Pohasky's state of mind and arguably discriminatory conduct was immaterial and not causative of the plaintiffs' discharge.

But defendants cannot be allowed to divorce Mr. Pohasky's conduct from that of Industries so easily. First of all, 42 U.S.C. §2000e(b) expressly includes "any agent" of an employer within the definition of "employer." Secondly, there was a definite causal relation between Pohasky's apparently discriminatory conduct and the firings. Had Pohasky not discriminated against the plaintiffs by demanding they perform work he would not require of a white female employee, they would not have been faced with the unreasonable choice of having to choose between obeying his discriminatory work order and the loss of their employment. Finally, by backing up Pohasky's ultimatum the top-level management of Industries ratified his discriminatory conduct and must be held liable for the consequences thereof. . . .

From all the evidence before it, this Court is compelled to find that defendant Industries, through its managers and supervisor, Mr. Pohasky, meant to require the plaintiffs to perform the admittedly heavy and possibly dangerous work of cleaning the bonding and coating department, when they would not require the same work from plaintiffs' white fellow employee. Furthermore, it meant to enforce that decision by firing the plaintiffs when they refused to perform that work. The consequence of the above was racial discrimination whatever the motivation of the management of defendant Industries may have been. Therefore, the totality of Industries' conduct amounted, in the Court's opinion, to an unlawful employment practice prohibited by the Civil Rights Act, specifically, 42 U.S.C. §2000e-2(a)(1).

NOTES

1. *Inroad into at Will.* As we have repeatedly seen, the traditional common law rule of employment contracts is that any contract not for a definite time is terminable at will by either party—for any reason or for no reason, for good reason or for bad reason. *Slack v. Havens* clearly changes this. How would you state the rule now?

2. *Proving Discrimination.* Would there be sufficient evidence of discrimination in the case without the statements of Pohasky—that "colored folks are hired to clean because they clean better"—to support a finding that the cleaning assignment was made to plaintiffs because they were African Americans? What other evidence supports the conclusion of race discrimination? Is there any evidence that the assignment was *not* made because of plaintiffs' race? Suppose you represented the defendant in *Slack*. What defenses might you consider when faced with this fact situation? What information would you look for with respect to Sharon Murphy?

3. *The Meaning of "Race."* While "race" seems an intuitive concept (and probably did to Pohasky), "race" as a legal concept is more complicated. In *Saint Francis College v. Al-Khazraji*, 481 U.S. 604 (1987), the Court considered a suit by a U.S. citizen who had been born in Iraq and claimed that he was denied tenure at the college based on his Arab ancestry. The district court rejected his §1981 claim because Arabs are generally considered Caucasians. The Supreme Court disagreed. While today we tend to think in terms of broader racial groups, many biologists and anthropologists criticize racial classifications as arbitrary and of

little use in understanding the variability of human beings. *See, e.g.*, Erik Lillquist & Charles A. Sullivan, *The Law and Genetics of Racial Profiling in Medicine*, 39 HARV. C.R.-C.L. L. REV. 391 (2004). Current scientific thinking on race, however, was ultimately irrelevant to the *Al-Khazraji* Court. Even if Arabs are now considered Caucasians, that was not the understanding in the nineteenth century when §1981 was enacted. At that time, "race" was used to include distinct tribes and ethnic groups: "The 1863 version of the New American Cyclopaedia divided the Arabs into a number of subsidiary races; represented the Hebrews as of the Semitic race, and identified numerous other groups as constituting races, including Swedes, Norwegians, Germans, Greeks, Finns, Italians (referring to mixture of different races), Spanish, Mongolians, Russians, and the like." *See also Shaare Tefila Congregation v. Cobb*, 481 U.S. 615, 617 (1987) (holding that a §1982 suit by a synagogue for defacement of its walls with anti-Semitic slogans was permissible because, when §1982 was adopted, "Jews and Arabs were among the people then considered to be distinct races and hence within the protection of the statute"). As a result, some "race" discrimination suits under §1981 are probably better characterized as "national origin" suits under Title VII.

4. *Admissions of Discriminatory Intent.* Pohasky's statements suffice to show his intent to discriminate because they constitute admissions of the state of mind that motivated him to assign the plaintiffs to this job. Where such statements can be proven, they are very powerful indications of discriminatory intent on various grounds:

a. In a race discrimination case, a police officer testified that the chief of police "loudly stated in my presence that he would not allow 'Spics and Niggers' to run his department within very close earshot of me." *Perez v. N.J. Transit Corp.*, 341 F. App'x 757, 761 (3d Cir. 2009).

b. In a sex discrimination case, plaintiff's supervisor "referred to women buyers as 'PMS,' 'menstrual,' and 'dragon lady.' He also stated that most women probably just wanted to stay home." *Passantino v. Johnson & Johnson Consumer Prods.*, 212 F.3d 493 (9th Cir. 2000).

c. In a religious discrimination case, a letter demoting plaintiff because he was a member of a church whose creed was white supremacy (and therefore the employees he supervised would not have confidence in his objectivity) constituted direct evidence of discriminatory intent on the basis of religion. *Peterson v. Wilmur Communications, Inc.*, 205 F. Supp. 2d 1014 (E.D. Wis. 2002).

d. In ADEA age discrimination cases, referring to an older worker as an "old short blond girl" while also stating that "older people didn't work as fast or were as productive as younger people," and commenting about the need for "fresh blood, younger employees." *Thomas v. Heartland Emp't Servs. LLC*, 797 F.3d 527, 530 (8th Cir. 2015)

e. In a national origin hostile work environment case, referring to a Mexican-American employee as "'Wetback,' 'Spic,' and 'Mexican Mother F_____.'" *Miller v. Kenworth of Dothan Inc.*, 277 F.3d 1269, 1273-74 (11th Cir. 2002).

In our society, such statements, at least until recently, seemed increasingly rare (whether or not the underlying belief systems have changed), but they continue to exist, as the national furor over the racist statements of Roseanne Barr indicates.

See John Koblin, *After Racist Tweet, Roseanne Barr's Show Is Canceled by ABC*, N.Y. TIMES, May 29, 2018, at A-1.

5. *Animus or Intent?* In these examples, the statement indicates the employer's animus or hostility to the group in question. But Pohasky apparently assigned plaintiffs to the cleaning work in question because he believed them to be better cleaners. Is this pejorative? If so, is it pejorative because it suggests that blacks can do only menial jobs like cleaning? Perhaps it does not matter. While discrimination may be motivated by hate, fear, or revulsion, the statutes do not require such negative impulses. If Pohasky chose the plaintiffs because he thought they were better workers than whites, at cleaning as well as everything else, he would still have been discriminating within the meaning of the statute. He would be intending to assign jobs by race.

6. *Conscious and Unconscious Stereotyping.* Mr. Pohasky was, presumably, aware of the beliefs he had about African Americans. If they were "stereotypes," he thought of them as true generalizations. Many stereotypes are like this—we employ them deliberately because they conform to our view of reality (whether or not that view is correct). But, as we have suggested earlier, there is a different view of how stereotypes operate in today's society. Professor Linda Hamilton Krieger, in *The Content of Our Categories: A Cognitive Bias Approach to Discrimination and Equal Employment Opportunity*, 47 STAN. L. REV. 1161 (1995), broke ground for a different view of intent to discriminate, one that has come to dominate the academic literature under rubrics such as "cognitive bias," "unreflective discrimination," "subtle bias," and "unconscious" (or "subconscious") "discrimination." As the diversity of labels indicates, the precise phenomena at issue are often contested, but Professor Krieger offers an excellent place to start. Using the insights provided by cognitive psychology, she concludes that stereotyping by race and gender is far more insidious than is often recognized because it is often an "unintended consequence" of the necessity for humans to categorize their sensory perceptions in order to make any sense of the world:

> [The] central premise of social cognition theory [is] that cognitive structures and processes involved in categorization and information processing can in and of themselves result in stereotyping and other forms of biased intergroup judgment previously attributed to motivational processes. The social cognition approach to discrimination comprises three claims relevant to our present inquiry. The first is that stereotyping . . . is nothing special. It is simply a form of categorization [of our sensory perceptions], similar in structure and function to the categorization of natural objects. According to this view, stereotypes, like other categorical structures, are cognitive mechanisms that all people, not just "prejudiced" ones, use to simplify the task of perceiving, processing, and retaining information about people in memory. They are central, and indeed essential to normal cognitive functioning.
>
> The second claim posited in social cognition theory is that, once in place, stereotypes bias intergroup judgment and decisionmaking. . . . [T]hey function as implicit theories, biasing in predictable ways the perception, interpretation, encoding, retention, and recall of information about other people. These biases are cognitive rather than motivational. They operate absent intent to favor or disfavor members of a particular social group. And, perhaps most significant for present purposes, they bias a decisionmaker's judgment long before the "moment of decision" [when the employment decision in question is made], as a decisionmaker attends to relevant data and interprets, encodes, stores, and retrieves it from memory. These biases "sneak up on" the decisionmaker, distorting bit by bit the data upon which his decision is eventually based.

The third claim follows from the second. Stereotypes, when they function as implicit prototypes or schemas [by which we evaluate each other], operate beyond the reach of decisionmaker self-awareness. Empirical evidence indicates that people's access to their own cognitive processes is in fact poor. Accordingly, cognitive bias may well be both unintentional and unconscious.

Id. at 1187-88; *see also* Tristin K. Green, in *Discrimination in Workplace Dynamics: Toward a Structural Account of Disparate Treatment Theory*, 38 HARV. C.R.-C.L. L. REV. 91, 128 (2003); Tristin K. Green, *Targeting Workplace Context: Title VII as a Tool for Institutional Reform*, 72 FORDHAM L. REV. 659 (2003).

When stereotyping is unintentional and unconscious, should acting based on stereotypes constitute individual disparate treatment discrimination? It is treating people differently based on their race or gender, but is that what antidiscrimination law proscribes? Or does intentional discrimination require a conscious intent to discriminate? For example, Professor Amy Wax argues in *Discrimination as Accident*, 74 IND. L.J. 1129 (1999), that, when discrimination is not conscious, employer efforts to reduce it will likely be unavailing. She therefore opposes liability for this variety of discrimination. *See also* Patrick Shin, *Liability for Unconscious Discrimination? A Thought Experiment in the Theory of Employment Discrimination Law*, 62 HASTINGS L. J, 67 (2010). But even Professor Wax agrees that, from a pure causation perspective, Title VII could be read to bar unconscious discrimination if it could be established as resulting in an adverse employment action. Amy L. Wax, *The Discriminating Mind: Define It, Prove It*, 40 CONN. L. REV. 979, 894 (2008). And others argue against limiting the antidiscrimination statutes to conscious actions. *See* Michael Selmi, *Discrimination as Accident: Old Whine, New Bottle*, 74 IND. L. J. 1234 (1999); Melissa Hart, *Subjective Decisionmaking and Unconscious Discrimination*, 56 ALA. L. REV. 741, 790-91 (2005). What do you think? Should disparate treatment discrimination require a conscious intent to discriminate, or is it enough to find that the plaintiff's protected class status caused the decision to occur? If a supervisor honestly believed he was acting for a nondiscriminatory reason, even if his unconscious biases in fact influenced his decision, should liability be imposed? If so, how would a plaintiff prove that, despite the supervisor's "honest belief," racial bias caused the decision?

7. *Are the Bad Old Days Still Around?* While most employment discrimination scholars agree that some variation of the cognitive bias theory explains an increasing percentage of cases in which women and minorities are disadvantaged relative to white males, others have warned against too quickly concluding that "old fashioned" discrimination is not a continuing and serious problem. *See* Michael L. Selmi, *Sex Discrimination in the Nineties, Seventies Style: Case Studies in the Preservation of Male Norms*, 9 EMPLOYEE RTS. & EMP. POL'Y J. 1 (2005) ("[T]here remains a significant amount of discrimination in the workplace that is not properly labeled as subtle but which involves the active and conscious exclusion of women from the workplace."). *See also* Ralph Richard Banks & Richard Thompson Ford, *(How) Does Unconscious Bias Matter?: Law, Politics, and Racial Inequality*, 58 EMORY L. J. 1053, 1059 (2009) ("While we do not doubt the existence of unconscious bias, we do doubt that contemporary racial bias accounts for all, or even most, of the racial injustice that bedevils our society."). Certainly, the continued litigation, challenging explicit sexual and racial harassment, suggests that not all discriminatory biases operate below the level of consciousness.

Another example of bias in labor markets is recent litigation challenging online recruiting. Athough digital job advertisements do not express a preference for particular groups on their face, segmenting of target populations enables them to be directed at particular demographics. Noam Scheiber, *Facebook Accused of Allowing Bias Against Women in Job Ads*, NY Times, Sept. 18, 2018, B1. Although this is clearly contrary to the thrust of the antidiscrimination laws, it is not so clear that it is unlawful either for the employer or the service provider. *See* Paulette T. Kim, *Discrimination in Online Employment Recruiting*, 63 St. Louis U. L. Rev. (forthcoming 2019).

8. *Intent, Motive, and the Prohibited Trait.* To this point, we have spoken of discriminatory "intent," which is often the way the Supreme Court has framed the individual disparate treatment theory. But the Court also often spoke of discriminatory "motive." As we will see in more detail, there is a distinction between the two concepts, although the Court often continues to speak of them as interchangeable. The distinction can be seen in *Hazen Paper Co. v. Biggins*, 507 U.S. 604 (1993), where a jury found violations under both the ADEA and ERISA when the 62-year-old plaintiff was fired as he approached a critical vesting date for his pension. The Supreme Court overturned the verdict, focusing on what has since come to be known as the "mixed motives" question: What should the law do when the employer acts because of two separate motives? While Hazen Paper obviously intended to fire the plaintiff, it might have been motivated to do so by his age, his pension status, a work-related reason, or all three. *Biggins* held that, when there were two or more potential motives, "a disparate treatment claim cannot succeed unless the employee's protected trait actually played a role in that process and had a determinative influence on the outcome." 507 U.S. at 610. This principle continues to operate under the Age Discrimination Act, *see Gross v. FBL Fin. Servs.*, 557 U.S. 167 (2009) (age must be the "but for" cause of adverse employment action), and for Title VII retaliation cases, *University of Texas Sw. Med. Ctr. v. Nassar*, 133 S. Ct. 2517 (2013), but we will see that it has been altered under Title VII for "status" discrimination. *See* page 580.

Biggins also focused more closely on the meaning of discriminatory motive. The Court held that firing someone to avoid his pension vesting, while a violation of ERISA, was not per se age discrimination.

> It is the very essence of age discrimination for an older employee to be fired because the employer believes that productivity and competence decline with old age. . . . Congress' promulgation of the ADEA was prompted by its concern that older workers were being deprived of employment on the basis of inaccurate and stigmatizing stereotypes.
>
> Although age discrimination rarely was based on the sort of animus motivating some other forms of discrimination, it was based in large part on stereotypes unsupported by objective fact. . . . Moreover, the available empirical evidence demonstrated that arbitrary age lines were in fact generally unfounded and that, as an overall matter, the performance of older workers was at least as good as that of younger workers. . . .
>
> When the employer's decision is wholly motivated by factors other than age, the problem of inaccurate and stigmatizing stereotypes disappears. This is true even if the motivating factor is correlated with age, as pension status typically is. Pension plans typically provide that an employee's accrued benefits will become nonforfeitable, or "vested," once the employee completes a certain number of years of service with the employer. On average, an older employee has had more years in the work force than a younger employee, and thus may well have accumulated more years of service with a particular employer. Yet an employee's age is analytically distinct from his years of service.

An employee who is younger than 40, and therefore outside the class of older workers as defined by the ADEA, may have worked for a particular employer his entire career, while an older worker may have been newly hired. Because age and years of service are analytically distinct, an employer can take account of one while ignoring the other, and thus it is incorrect to say that a decision based on years of service is necessarily "age-based."

Id. at 610-11 (citation omitted). The Court did recognize that it would violate the ADEA were the employer to use "[p]ension status [as] a proxy for age, not in the sense that the ADEA makes the two factors equivalent, but in the sense that the employer may suppose a correlation between the two factors and act accordingly." *Id.* at 613 (citation omitted).

But does this approach make sense? Suppose an employer discriminated against workers because they had gray hair. That's pretty highly—but not perfectly—correlated with age. How about wrinkles, which are even more highly (but still not perfectly) correlated with age? And there are many traits that are correlated with, but scarcely essential to, sex and race. We will see that the disparate impact theory protects against an employer's use of irrational but highly correlated factors, but isn't there something odd about saying that discrimination against gray-haired, wrinkled people isn't disparate treatment age discrimination?

9. *Employer Reaction to the Protected Trait. Biggins* focuses our attention on the employer's subjective reaction to the "protected class." In the case itself, of course, that class was older workers. While the Court viewed an employer's belief that "productivity and competence decline with old age" to be "the very essence of age discrimination," surely that cannot be the only impermissible kind of discriminatory intent within the statute: What if the jury found that Biggins was fired because the Hazens thought customers would not like working with older people? Older people are also often seen as "stuck in their ways," resistant to new ideas. If Hazen Paper viewed Biggins as not being sufficiently innovative, might that also indicate age stereotyping?

But *Biggins* can be generalized to other protected classes, most notably race, sex, national origin, or religion under Title VII. For liability to attach, the employer must have some aversion to the class in question. In *Slack*, that aversion was proven in part by Pohasky's remarks. While *Biggins* was remanded for further proceedings, this kind of "direct" evidence was lacking. Without such evidence, could Biggins prevail? How likely is it that the Hazens incorrectly believed Biggins's competence declined? Aren't employers more likely to act on "inaccurate and stigmatizing stereotypes" regarding competence in refusing to hire older workers than in firing them? The Hazens had the opportunity to watch plaintiff perform for almost a decade. If they fired him because they believed his competence was diminishing, how could that be the result of a stereotype? Or does Professor Krieger's article help explain this? To prevail, would Biggins have had to show (a) that they incorrectly evaluated his competence and (b) that they attributed his perceived loss of competence to his age? What if they correctly believed Biggins's performance was declining but also attributed it to his age?

10. *Looking Forward.* Neither *Slack* nor *Biggins* focuses on burdens of proof, but it has become clear that, under the disparate treatment theory, the plaintiff has the burden of establishing discriminatory intent. This raises two distinct problems. *Slack* primarily involved "direct" evidence of intent: Pohasky's statements indicating why he acted as he did. In contrast, *Biggins* primarily involved "circumstantial," or inferential, methods of proof. The next section considers the structure of an inferential case of individual disparate treatment.

2.   Proving Discrimination: The Traditional Framework

a.   *The Plaintiff's Prima Facie Case*

McDonnell Douglas Corp. v. Green
411 U.S. 792 (1973)

Justice POWELL delivered the opinion of the Court.

. . . Petitioner, McDonnell Douglas Corp., is an aerospace and aircraft manufacturer headquartered in St. Louis, Missouri, where it employs over 30,000 people. Respondent, a black citizen of St. Louis, worked for petitioner as a mechanic and laboratory technician from 1956 until August 28, 1964, when he was laid off in the course of a general reduction in petitioner's work force.

Respondent, a long-time activist in the civil rights movement, protested vigorously that his discharge and the general hiring practices of petitioner were racially motivated. As part of this protest, respondent and other members of the Congress on Racial Equality illegally stalled their cars on the main roads leading to petitioner's plant for the purpose of blocking access to it at the time of the morning shift change. The District Judge described the plan for, and respondent's participation in, the "stall-in" as follows:

[F]ive teams, each consisting of four cars would "tie up" five main access roads into McDonnell at the time of the morning rush hour. The drivers of the cars were instructed to line up next to each other completely blocking the intersections or roads. The drivers were also instructed to stop their cars, turn off the engines, pull the emergency brake, raise all windows, lock the doors, and remain in their cars until the police arrived. The plan was to have the cars remain in position for one hour.

Acting under the "stall in" plan, plaintiff [respondent in the present action] drove his car onto Brown Road, a McDonnell access road, at approximately 7:00 a.m., at the start of the morning rush hour. Plaintiff was aware of the traffic problem that would result. He stopped his car with the intent to block traffic. The police arrived shortly and requested plaintiff to move his car. He refused to move his car voluntarily. Plaintiff's car was towed away by the police, and he was arrested for obstructing traffic. Plaintiff pleaded guilty to the charge of obstructing traffic and was fined.

[O]n July 25, 1965, petitioner publicly advertised for qualified mechanics, respondent's trade, and respondent promptly applied for re-employment. Petitioner turned down respondent, basing its rejection on respondent's participation in the "stall-in." . . .

II

The critical issue before us concerns the order and allocation of proof in a private, non-class action challenging employment discrimination. The language of Title VII makes plain the purpose of Congress to assure equality of employment opportunities and to eliminate those discriminatory practices and devices which have fostered racially stratified job environments to the disadvantage of minority citizens. *Griggs v. Duke Power Co.*, 401 U.S. 424, 429 (1971) [reproduced at page 617]. As noted in *Griggs*, "Congress did not intend by Title VII, however, to guarantee a job to every person regardless of qualifications. In short, the Act does not command that any person be hired simply because he was formerly the subject of discrimination, or because he is a member of a minority group. Discriminatory preference for any group, minority or majority, is precisely and only what Congress has proscribed. What is required by Congress is the removal of artificial, arbitrary, and unnecessary barriers to employment when the barriers operate invidiously to discriminate on the basis of racial or other impermissible classification."

There are societal as well as personal interests on both sides of this equation. The broad, overriding interest, shared by employer, employee, and consumer, is efficient and trustworthy workmanship assured through fair and racially neutral employment and personnel decisions. In the implementation of such decisions, it is abundantly clear that Title VII tolerates no racial discrimination, subtle or otherwise. In this case, respondent, the complainant below, charges that he was denied employment "because of his involvement in civil rights activities" and "because of his race and color." Petitioner denied discrimination of any kind, asserting that its failure to re-employ respondent was based upon and justified by his participation in the unlawful conduct against it. Thus, the issue at the trial on remand is framed by those opposing factual contentions. . . .

The complainant in a Title VII trial must carry the initial burden under the statute of establishing a prima facie case of racial discrimination. This may be done by showing (i) that he belongs to a racial minority; (ii) that he applied and was qualified for a job for which the employer was seeking applicants; (iii) that, despite his qualifications, he was rejected; and (iv) that, after his rejection, the position remained open and the employer continued to seek applicants from persons of complainant's qualifications.[13] In the instant case, we agree with the Court of Appeals that respondent proved a prima facie case. Petitioner sought mechanics, respondent's trade, and continued to do so after respondent's rejection. Petitioner, moreover, does not dispute respondent's qualifications[14] and acknowledges that his past work performance in petitioner's employ was "satisfactory."

The burden then must shift to the employer to articulate some legitimate, nondiscriminatory reason for the employee's rejection. We need not attempt in the instant case to detail every matter which fairly could be recognized as a reasonable basis for a refusal to hire. Here petitioner has assigned respondent's participation in unlawful conduct against it as the cause for his rejection. We think that this suffices to discharge petitioner's burden of proof at this stage and to meet respondent's prima facie case of discrimination.

. . . Respondent admittedly had taken part in a carefully planned "stall-in," designed to tie up access to and egress from petitioner's plant at a peak traffic hour.[16]

---

13. The facts necessarily will vary in Title VII cases, and the specification above of the prima facie proof required from respondent is not necessarily applicable in every respect to differing factual situations.

14. We note that the issue of what may properly be used to test qualifications for employment is not present in this case. Where employees have instituted employment tests and qualifications with an exclusionary effect on minority applicants, such requirements must be "shown to bear a demonstrable relationship to successful performance of the jobs" for which they were used, *Griggs v. Duke Power Co.*

16. The trial judge noted that no personal injury or property damage resulted from the "stall-in" due "solely to the fact that law enforcement officials had obtained notice in advance of plaintiff's . . . demonstration and were at the scene to remove plaintiff's car from the highway."

Nothing in Title VII compels an employer to absolve and rehire one who has engaged in such deliberate, unlawful activity against it.[17] . . .

Petitioner's reason for rejection thus suffices to meet the prima facie case, but the inquiry must not end here. While Title VII does not, without more, compel rehiring of respondent, neither does it permit petitioner to use respondent's conduct as a pretext for the sort of discrimination prohibited by §703(a)(1). On remand, respondent must, as the Court of Appeals recognized, be afforded a fair opportunity to show that petitioner's stated reason for respondent's rejection was in fact pretext. Especially relevant to such a showing would be evidence that white employees involved in acts against petitioner of comparable seriousness to the "stall-in" were nevertheless retained or rehired. Petitioner may justifiably refuse to rehire one who was engaged in unlawful, disruptive acts against it, but only if this criterion is applied alike to members of all races.

Other evidence that may be relevant to any showing of pretext includes facts as to the petitioner's treatment of respondent during his prior term of employment; petitioner's reaction, if any, to respondent's legitimate civil rights activities; and petitioner's general policy and practice with respect to minority employment. On the latter point, statistics as to petitioner's employment policy and practice may be helpful to a determination of whether petitioner's refusal to rehire respondent in this case conformed to a general pattern of discrimination against blacks. *Jones v. Lee Way Motor Freight, Inc.*, 431 F.2d 245 (C.A. 10 1970); Blumrosen, *Strangers in Paradise:* Griggs v. Duke Power Co., *and the Concept of Employment Discrimination*, 71 MICH. L. REV. 59, 91-94 (1972).[19] In short, on the retrial respondent must be given a full and fair opportunity to demonstrate by competent evidence that the presumptively valid reasons for his rejection were in fact a coverup for a racially discriminatory decision.

NOTES

1. *Rationale for the Proof Structure. McDonnell Douglas* established the structure for litigating cases of individual disparate treatment based on what has been considered "circumstantial evidence" of discrimination, so much so that the case name has become a kind of mantra for analyzing the vast majority of employment discrimination cases. The first step, the prima facie case, was framed in terms of the four elements. It is obvious, however, that these elements do not fit every fact situation. Indeed, if you think about it, you will see that they describe very few cases: Most employment settings are competitive, which means that an employer hires B instead of A rather than leaving the job vacant. The employer's failure to rehire Green while still seeking other applicants was truly remarkable. More important than the four "elements" was the

---

17. The unlawful activity in this case was directed specifically against petitioner. We need not consider or decide here whether, or under what circumstances, unlawful activity not directed against the particular employer may be a legitimate justification for refusing to hire.

19. The District Court may, for example, determine after reasonable discovery that "the [racial] composition of defendant's labor force is itself reflective of restrictive or exclusionary practices." *See* Blumrosen, *supra*, at 92. We caution that such general determinations, while helpful, may not be in and of themselves controlling as to an individualized hiring decision, particularly in the presence of an otherwise justifiable reason for refusing to rehire. *See generally* Blumrosen, *supra*, n.19, at 93.

rationale for the prima facie case, which the Court described in *Teamsters v. United States*, 431 U.S. 324, 358 n.44 (1977):

> The *McDonnell Douglas* case involved an individual complainant seeking to prove one instance of unlawful discrimination. An employer's isolated decision to reject an applicant who belongs to a racial minority does not show that the rejection was racially based. Although the *McDonnell Douglas* formula does not require direct proof of discrimination, it does demand that the alleged discriminate demonstrate at least that his rejection did not result from the two most common legitimate reasons on which an employer might rely to reject a job applicant: an absolute or relative lack of qualifications or the absence of a vacancy in the job sought. Elimination of these reasons for the refusal to hire is sufficient, absent other explanation, to create an inference that the decision was a discriminatory one.

2. *Generalizing* McDonnell Douglas *to Different Contexts. McDonnell Douglas* is focused on the failure-to-rehire context. Suppose, however, that Green had never worked for the defendant. If you represented him, how would you prove the "qualification" aspect of element (ii)? What if Green had no prior experience in the industry and the employer required experience? Would Green not have a prima facie case? Similarly, what if the job Green sought had not remained open because the employer hired a white worker over Green? This would bar application of the fourth prong as *McDonnell Douglas* formulated it. How could Green then make out a prima facie case? By proving that the white was *less* qualified?

a. In the far more common situation where a plaintiff loses out to a competitor, the Supreme Court has not required plaintiff to prove that she was as well qualified as that competitor in order to make out a prima facie case. In *Patterson v. McLean Credit Union*, 491 U.S. 164, 186-87 (1989), a §1981 suit in which a black bank employee had been repeatedly passed over for promotions that were given to whites, the Court applied the *McDonnell Douglas* proof structure: "The burden [of establishing a prima facie case] is not onerous. Here, petitioner need only prove by a preponderance of the evidence that she applied for and was qualified for an available position, that she was rejected, and that after she was rejected respondent either continued to seek applicants for the position, or, as is alleged here, filled the position with a white employee." (citations omitted). Thus, to carry her initial burden, plaintiff need only show that she met the minimum qualifications for the job. Of course, if the defendant asserts the successful competitor's superior qualifications as its nondiscriminatory reason, plaintiff will have to challenge that claim at the pretext stage in order to prevail.

b. What are the elements of a prima facie case in a *discharge* case? Most discrimination cases involve discharges, and the lower courts have had to formulate the elements for this context. Indeed, two alternative formulations of *McDonnell Douglas* have emerged—one for individual discharges and the other for discharges in the course of reductions in force. In individual discharge cases, those involving a single employee, courts have tended to require him to show that he was doing "apparently satisfactory" work in order to carry his prima facie case burden. *E.g., Diaz v. Eagle Produce, Ltd.*, 521 F.3d 1201, 1207-8 (9th Cir. 2008); *Rivera v. City & County of Denver*, 365 F.3d 912, 920 (10th Cir. 2004). An alternative approach would allow the plaintiff to show that he was replaced by a person outside the protected class—say, a younger person in the ADEA context. *Wooler v. Citizens Bank*, 274 F. App'x 177, 179-80 (3d Cir. 2008).

c. In contrast, in reductions in force, that is, situations where a number of employees are terminated simultaneously, the "legitimate, nondiscriminatory reason"—the need to reduce expenses—is apparent on its face. Because *positions* are being eliminated, the power of proof that the plaintiff is doing an apparently satisfactory job diminishes. Courts have, therefore, tended to require a plaintiff to produce other evidence, such as identifying younger workers who were retained when she was discharged. *Lewis v. City of Detroit*, 702 F. App'x 274, 280-81 (6th Cir. 2017) ("If the termination arises as part of a work force reduction, this Court has further modified the fourth element to require the plaintiff to prove "additional direct, circumstantial, or statistical evidence tending to indicate that the employer singled out the plaintiff for discharge for impermissible reasons.").

d. Suppose a plaintiff is fired but replaced by a member of the same protected class? Most federal courts of appeals have held that, in an individual termination case, the plaintiff need not prove as part of the prima facie case that she was replaced by someone outside the relevant class. *E.g., Stella v. Mineta*, 284 F.3d 135, 146 (D.C. Cir. 2002). Why? However, even if this is correct for the prima facie case, the same-class replacement may make it extraordinarily difficult to prove pretext when defendant asserts a nondiscriminatory reason for its action. *See generally* Michael J. Zimmer, *A Chain of Inferences Proving Discrimination*, 79 U. Colo. L. Rev. 1243, 1279-80 (2008).

e. Given variations such as these, courts are increasingly likely to describe the plaintiff's burden tautologically: a plaintiff must first make out a *prima facie* case that: "(1) she was within the protected class; (2) she was qualified for the position; (3) she was subject to an adverse employment action; and (4) the adverse action occurred under circumstances giving rise to an inference of discrimination." *Tillery v. N.Y. State Office of Alcoholism & Substance Abuse Servs.*, No. 17-2366-cv, 2018 U.S. App. LEXIS 17139, at *3 (2d Cir. June 25, 2018). The fourth prong is not very helpful, is it?

3. *Consequences of the Prima Facie Case.* In *Texas Department of Community Affairs v. Burdine*, 450 U.S. 248 (1981), the Court described the consequences of proving a prima facie case:

> Establishment of the prima facie case in effect creates a presumption that the employer unlawfully discriminated against the employee. If the trier of fact believes the plaintiff's evidence, and if the employer is silent in the face of the presumption, the court must enter judgment for the plaintiff because no issue of fact remains in the case.

In accompanying footnote 7, *Burdine* said the use of the term "prima facie case" in *McDonnell Douglas* denoted "the establishment of a legally mandatory, rebuttable presumption"; it did *not* describe "the plaintiff's burden of producing enough evidence to permit the trier of fact to infer the fact at issue." That means that a plaintiff's proof of a prima facie case is not necessarily sufficient to create a jury question, but that plaintiff will nevertheless win if defendant fails to rebut the prima facie case and then fails to carry its burden of production. But defendant need not do much. *Burdine* made clear, however, that defendant had only a burden of production. If it introduces into evidence any nondiscriminatory reason, plaintiff then has the burden of persuasion as to pretext:

> The burden that shifts to the defendant, therefore, is to rebut the presumption of discrimination by producing evidence that the plaintiff was rejected, or someone else was preferred, for a legitimate, nondiscriminatory reason. The defendant need not persuade the court that it was actually motivated by the proffered reasons. It is sufficient if the defendant's evidence raises a genuine issue of fact as to whether it discriminated against the plaintiff. To accomplish this, the defendant must clearly set forth, through the introduction of admissible evidence, the reasons for the plaintiff's rejection. The explanation provided must be legally sufficient to justify a judgment for the defendant. If the defendant carries this burden of production, the presumption raised by the prima facie case is rebutted, and the factual inquiry proceeds to a new level of specificity. . . .
>
> The plaintiff retains the burden of persuasion. She now must have the opportunity to demonstrate that the proffered reason was not the true reason for the employment decision. This burden now merges with the ultimate burden of persuading the court that she has been the victim of intentional discrimination. She may succeed in this either directly by persuading the court that a discriminatory reason more likely motivated the employer or indirectly by showing that the employer's proffered explanation is unworthy of credence.

450 U.S. at 256. We will see that later cases went further to impose another requirement on the plaintiff: She must prove that the supposed legitimate nondiscriminatory reason was not only a pretext in the sense that it was untrue but that it was *a pretext for discrimination*, that is, that it hid a true discriminatory motive.

4. *The Role of Comparators.* "Disparate" treatment, as the phrase suggests, requires ultimately proving that the plaintiff was treated differently than a person of a different race or sex was (or would have been) treated. Thus, many disparate treatment cases turn on whether the plaintiff can identify "comparators" who are similarly situated to her except for her race, sex, and so forth, but were treated differently. The comparator may enter the analysis at the prima facie case stage or, more commonly, to show pretext by establishing that the defendant did not apply its supposed nondiscriminatory reason in, for example, a color- or sex-blind manner. *See generally* Charles A. Sullivan, *The Phoenix from the Ash: Proving Discrimination by Comparators*, 59 ALA. L. REV. 191 (2009). *But see* Suzanne B. Goldberg, *Discrimination by Comparison*, 120 YALE L.J. 728, 750 (2011).

The significance of comparators turns on how much similarity courts will require before dissimilar treatment will give rise to an inference of discrimination. *Ash v. Tyson Foods, Inc.*, 546 U.S. 454 (2006), rejected an extreme approach to comparative qualifications. The Eleventh Circuit had overturned a jury verdict for plaintiff, stating—apparently in all seriousness—that a plaintiff can use her asserted superior qualifications relative to a comparator to prove discrimination only when "the disparity in qualifications is so apparent as virtually to jump off the page and slap you in the face." *Id.* at 456-57. In reversing, the Supreme Court stressed that its prior decisions established that "qualifications evidence may suffice, at least in some circumstances, to show pretext," *id.* at 457 (quoting *Patterson v. McLean Credit Union*, 491 U.S. 164, 187-88 (1989)), and that plaintiff's proof that the employer "misjudged the qualifications" of the applicants "may be probative of whether the employer's reasons are pretexts for discrimination[,]" *id.* (quoting *Texas Dep't of Community Affairs v. Burdine*, 450 U.S. 248, 259 (1981)).

Perhaps not surprisingly, the Court then wrote that "[t]he visual image of words jumping off the page to slap you (presumably a court) in the face is unhelpful and imprecise as an elaboration of the standard for inferring pretext from superior qualifications." 456 U.S. at 457. While "slap in the face" was too restrictive, the Court did not endorse a particular alternative but did note other possible tests, and subsequent lower courts have tended to require plaintiff to show "that the disparities between the successful applicant's and her own qualifications were 'of such weight and significance that no reasonable person, in the exercise of impartial judgment, could have chosen the candidate selected over the plaintiff.'" *Brooks v. County Comm'n*, 446 F.3d 1160, 1163 (11th Cir. 2006) (citation omitted).

Ash dealt only with comparative *qualifications*, but comparisons can be drawn in other contexts, such as disparate discipline cases—that is, those in which plaintiff claims that, although he may have been guilty of misconduct, members of a different race or sex committed similar infractions with lesser discipline. In many circuits, the courts require a very close correspondence between the plaintiff and her putative comparator(s) before such proof is given much weight. *Gates v. Caterpillar, Inc.*, 513 F.3d 680 (7th Cir. 2008) (plaintiff, who was discharged for improper telephone and Internet use, was not similarly situated to three male employees who also misused employer's electronic equipment where they had a different supervisor, their conduct was limited to misuse of computers and did not involve telephone use, and they did not continue to engage in misconduct after being initially disciplined). *But see Jackson v. Fedex Corporate Servs.*, 518 F.3d 388, 397 (6th Cir. 2008) ("The district court's narrow definition of similarly situated effectively removed Jackson from the protective reach of the anti-discrimination laws. [Its] finding that Jackson had no comparables from the six other employees in the PowerPad project deprived Jackson of any remedy to which he may be entitled under the law.").

5. *Legitimate Nondiscriminatory Reason.* Defendant may rebut a prima facie case by "articulat[ing] some legitimate, nondiscriminatory reason" for its action. *McDonnell Douglas* established that disloyalty is such a reason. Suppose the court finds that Green was not rehired because he was a vegetarian. Is this a "legitimate, nondiscriminatory reason"? *Biggins* held that a firing to avoid a pension vesting, which would have been an ERISA violation, did not violate the ADEA; it was, therefore, "legitimate" under the latter statute. While the courts continue to speak of the employer's burden of producing a "legitimate nondiscriminatory reason," it seems clear that any reason is "legitimate" if it is "nondiscriminatory." This should not be so surprising in an at-will world.

6. *Retaliation. McDonnell Douglas* was framed as a discrimination case, that is, whether plaintiff was denied reemployment because of his race. You probably noticed that it might have been framed as what we would today call a public-policy case— he was not reemployed because of his civil rights activities. The law we studied in Chapter 4 on the public policy tort was largely nonexistent when *McDonnell Douglas* was handed down, but Title VII has its own ban on retaliation. Percy Green had raised this issue, but the Supreme Court did not address it. Retaliation under the antidiscrimination statutes is considered beginning at page 671.

Note on "Adverse Employment Actions"

Refusals to hire (as in *McDonnell Douglas*) and discharges (as in *Slack* and *Biggins*) are obviously sufficient to justify relief if wrongfully motivated. But not all differences in treatment because of race, sex, religion, or age have been viewed as actionable. Some courts, often relying on the notion that the antidiscrimination statutes reach only "terms and conditions" of employment, hold that minor harms do not give rise to a claim. They require "material adverse effects" for a suit to go forward, but often differ on what is material. *Compare Alexander v. Casino Queen, Inc.*, 739 F.3d 972, 980 (7th Cir. 2014) (floor assignments on the basis of race could constitute an adverse employment action because reduced tip income could have a significant financial impact), *with Kidd v. Mando Am. Corp.*, 731 F.3d 1196, 1204 (11th Cir. 2013) ("Kidd's demotion claim—grounded on a loss of supervisory responsibility of the accounts payable department, not a loss of salary or benefits—does not rise to" the level of an adverse employment actions); *see also Kuhn v. Washtenaw County*, 709 F.3d 612 (6th Cir. 2013) (investigation of a complaint of employee wrongdoing was not an adverse employment action when there was no disciplinary action, demotion, or change in job responsibilities).

Some courts seem far more receptive to holding actions with no direct economic consequences to be actionable. *E.g., Ortiz-Diaz v. United States HUD*, 867 F.3d 70, 71 (D.C. Cir. 2016) (otherwise lateral transfer away from a biased supervisor actionable given the potential adverse effects on plaintiff's career advancement); *Deleon v. Kalamazoo County Rd. Comm'n*, 739 F.3d 914, 919-920 (6th Cir. 2014) (adverse employment action could be found when a lateral transfer resulted in daily exposure to toxic and hazardous fumes).

Professor Rebecca Hanner White, in *De Minimis Discrimination*, 47 EMORY L. J. 1121, 1148, 1151 (1998), criticized the more restrictive decisions, arguing that the term "adverse employment action" is not found in the statutory language. The statute's bar on discrimination in connection with hiring, firing, or the "compensation, terms, conditions, or privileges" of employment "is better read as making clear that an employer who discriminates against an employee in a non-job-related context would not run afoul of Title VII, rather than as sheltering employment discrimination that does not significantly disadvantage an employee." *Id.; see also* Tristin K. Green, *Discrimination in Workplace Dynamics: Toward a Structural Account of Disparate Treatment Theory*, 38 HARV. C.R.-C.L. L. REV. 93, 102 (2003). *Cf.* Sandra Sperino, in *Justice Kennedy's Big New Idea*, 96 B.U.L. REV. 1789, 1791-92 (2017) (arguing that Title VII's adverse employment action requirement has been case into doubt by a recent Supreme Court's Fair Housing Act decision).

Note on "Reverse" Discrimination

In *McDonald v. Santa Fe Trail Transportation Co.*, 427 U.S. 273 (1976), the Court held that both Title VII and §1981 barred discrimination against whites. The plaintiffs, both white, were discharged for their involvement in misappropriating company property while an African American involved in the same incident was retained. The district court ruled that neither Title VII nor §1981 protected white plaintiffs from racial discrimination. The Supreme Court disagreed, holding that Title VII and §1981 protections are available to plaintiffs of all races. Since *Santa Fe*, whites have been protected against race discrimination under both Title VII and §1981. It is equally clear that men are protected against sex discrimination in employment under Title VII. Thus, all employees are protected, but they are protected only from discrimination on the prohibited ground. Indeed, this reality makes clear that the pervasive use of the term "protected classes" under those statutes is problematic. *See generally*

Jessica A. Clarke, *Protected Class Gatekeeping*, 92 N.Y.U.L. Rev. 101 (2017); *see also* Naomi Schoenbaum, *The Case for Symmetry in Antidiscrimination Law*, 2017 WIS. L. REV. 69; Bradley A. Areheart, *The Symmetry Principle*, 58 B.C.L. Rev. 1085 (2017). *Cf.* David Simson, *Fool Me Once, Shame on You; Fool Me Twice, Shame on You Again: How Disparate Treatment Doctrine Perpetuates Racial Hierarchy*, 59 HOUS. L. REV. (forthcoming 2019) (challenging the prevailing view that Title VII is a largely symmetrical).

In short, the employer need not have a good reason to discharge as long as its reason is not a prohibited one (e.g., race, sex, or age). While this is the law, employers are well advised to have defensible reasons for firing their workers. In that sense, the enactment of antidiscrimination statutes tends toward a just-cause rule since all workers—African Americans, Caucasians, women, men, older workers, individuals with disabilities, etc.—are free to challenge adverse decisions as discriminatory. While most such challenges will fail, the costs of litigation can themselves be considerable, and defensible employment decisions conduce to good employee morale. *See* Ann C. McGinley, *Rethinking Civil Rights and Employment at Will*, 57 OHIO ST. L.J. 1443 (1996).

Although *Santa Fe* makes clear that "reverse" discrimination is cognizable under both Title VII and §1981, the question of the validity of an affirmative action plan, reserved in footnote 8 in *Santa Fe*, was later resolved in favor of the voluntary use of racial and gender preferences. *Johnson v. Transportation Agency of Santa Clara County*, 480 U.S. 616 (1987) (approving affirmative action plan benefiting women); *United Steelworkers v. Weber*, 440 U.S. 969 (1979) (approving affirmative action plan benefiting African Americans). We will discuss these cases at page 611. And, while not explicitly an "affirmative action" case, *Ricci v. DeStefano*, 457 U.S. 457 (2009), reproduced at page 630, may suggest a new approach to the question. After you have read that decision, you will be finally in a position to assess the current status of affirmative action under Title VII.

Putting the affirmative action question aside, how does, say, a white plaintiff prove racial discrimination? *Santa Fe* did not explain how a white or male plaintiff makes out a prima facie case, and the lower courts seem unclear. In that case, did the plaintiffs make out a prima facie case by showing that they were whites who were fired, while a black was not, although he engaged in the same conduct? Clearly, an African American plaintiff would make out a prima facie case by proving that similarly situated white workers were favored. Does that mean that whites can also?

In some cases, there will be "direct evidence," *see Deets v. Massman Constr. Co.*, 811 F.3d 978 (7th Cir. 2016) (white construction worker told when laid off that the employer's "minority numbers" were too low), but absent that a number of circuits have adopted some version of a "background circumstances" test—that is, to establish a prima facie case, a "reverse" discrimination, plaintiff must establish "background circumstances" that support an inference that the defendant employer is "that unusual employer who discriminates against the majority." *Parker v. Baltimore & Ohio R.R. Co.*, 652 F.2d 1012, 1017 (D.C. Cir. 1981). While the notion has been criticized as "irremediably vague and ill-defined," *Iadimarco v. Runyon*, 190 F.3d 151, 161 (3d Cir. 1999), it continues to be applied to require something more for a white plaintiff than would be required were the plaintiff a member of a minority group. *Stockwell v. City of Harvey*, 597 F.3d 895, 901 (7th Cir. 2010). *See generally* Charles A. Sullivan, *Circling Back to the Obvious: The Convergence of Traditional and Reverse Discrimination in Title VII Proof*, 46 WM. & MARY L. REV. 1031 (2004).

b. Defendant's Rebuttal and Plaintiff's Proof of Pretext

[Handwritten margin note: Δ argues non-discriminatory reason EASY!!]

Assuming that the plaintiff establishes her prima facie case, the next step is for the defendant to put into evidence its nondiscriminatory reason. Given that this is merely a burden of production, employers almost always satisfy it. The *McDonnell Douglas* analysis then proceeds to the third and final step, in which the plaintiff attempts to prove that that reason is a pretext for discrimination. The courts have been rigorous in resisting efforts to collapse the employer's rebuttal case with the plaintiff's prima facie case. For example, *Ruiz v. County of Rockland*, 609 F.3d 486, 493 (2d Cir. 2010), held that, when plaintiff's performance evaluations showed satisfactory work, defendant's claim of his serious misconduct does not bar plaintiff from making out a prima facie case: "[T]he step at which the court considers such evidence is important" because "no amount of evidence permits a plaintiff to overcome a failure to make out a prima facie case." *But see Zayas v. Rockford Mem. Hosp.*, 740 F.3d 1154, 1158 (7th Cir. 2014) (prior satisfactory performance evaluations did not establish that plaintiff was meeting the employer's legitimate job expectations at the time she was fired, given more recent disciplinary actions").

As a practical matter, the vast majority of individual disparate treatment cases are resolved at the pretext stage, typically on a motion for summary judgment when the court finds that the plaintiff has not adduced sufficient evidence for a jury to determine the defendant's nondiscriminatory reason is pretextual. This is true despite the Supreme Court's permissive approach to proving pretext. In *Patterson v. McLean Credit Union*, 491 U.S. 164 (1989), plaintiff brought a §1981 suit challenging the defendant's repeated failures to promote her. On appeal, she questioned the district court's instructions to the jury that, in order to prevail, she had to show that she was better qualified than her successful white competitor. The Supreme Court agreed, finding this to be error. Applying the *McDonnell Douglas/Burdine* proof structure to claims of racial discrimination under §1981, the Court agreed that plaintiff "retains the final burden of persuading the jury of intentional discrimination" by proving that a defendant's legitimate nondiscriminatory reason was a pretext. However,

> [t]he evidence which petitioner can present in an attempt to establish that respondent's stated reasons are pretextual may take a variety of forms. Indeed, she might seek to demonstrate that respondent's claim to have promoted a better qualified applicant was pretextual by showing that she was in fact better qualified than the person chosen for the position. The District Court erred, however, in instructing the jury that in order to succeed petitioner was required to make such a showing. There are certainly other ways in which petitioner could seek to prove that respondent's reasons were pretextual. Thus, for example, petitioner could seek to persuade the jury that respondent had not offered the true reason for its promotion decision by presenting evidence of respondent's past treatment of petitioner, including the instances of the racial harassment which she alleges and respondent's failure to train her for an accounting position. While we do not intend to say this evidence necessarily would be sufficient to carry the day, it cannot be denied that it is one of the various ways in which petitioner might seek to prove intentional discrimination on the part of respondent. She may not be forced to pursue any particular means of demonstrating that respondent's stated reasons are pretextual.

Id. at 188. Earlier in this chapter, we saw that when plaintiff is passed over in favor of another, she need not prove her qualifications were equal or superior to those of the successful competitor to make out a prima facie case; it is enough to show that she has the minimum qualifications for the position. This is clearly the logic of *Patterson:* Plaintiff may establish her prima facie case without showing she is equal or superior to the whites promoted. However, the defendant will typically claim that it promoted the better-qualified persons, who happened to be white. Simply putting into evidence its view that the successful applicant was superior to plaintiff in some respects will suffice to carry the defendant's burden of production. Plaintiff must then prove pretext and, while *Patterson* holds that she may do this in a variety of different ways, the most obvious path is for plaintiff to show that her qualifications were equal or superior to those of the successful competitor. *See generally* Anne Lawton, *The Meritocracy Myth and the Illusion of Equal Employment Opportunity*, 85 MINN. L. REV. 587, 645 (2000). That, of course, brings us back to the whole question of comparators. *See* Note 4, page 552.

But even this inquiry reveals the complexity of the concept of "pretext." Suppose the plaintiff shows that the defendant's reason is objectively false—for example, the plaintiff proves she has a college degree, while the defendant claims it did not promote her because she did not have a degree. This would seem to prove pretext, but maybe not: Although the reason is not objectively true, the employer may have believed it to be true and acted on it, rather than on the basis of the employee's protected class. This "honest belief" rule has doomed many claims. *See, e.g., Loyd v. Saint Joseph Mercy Oakland,* 766 F.3d 580, 596 (6th Cir. 2014) (if an employer has an honest belief in the basis for the adverse employment action, and that belief arose from reasonable reliance on the particularized facts before the employer when it made the decision, the asserted reason will not be deemed pretextual, even if it was erroneous." *Johnson v. AT&T Corp.,* 422 F.3d 756, 762 (8th Cir. 2005) ("[T]he proper inquiry is not whether AT&T was factually correct in determining that Johnson had made the bomb threats. Rather, the proper inquiry is whether AT&T honestly believed that Johnson had made the bomb threats."); *cf. Loyd v. Saint Joseph Mercy Oakland,* 766 F.3d 580, 596 (6th Cir. 2014) (if an employer has an honest belief in the basis for the adverse employment action, "and that belief arose from reasonable reliance on the particularized facts before the employer when it made the decision," an erroneous decision will not be deemed pretextual). In such cases, the employer's asserted reason is not a "pretext" although it is factually incorrect. Of course, perhaps proof that the employer was objectively wrong is a reason for thinking that something more objectionable than an honest mistake explains the decision.

Alternatively, the defendant's reason might be true but fail to explain the decision. For example, if the employer claims the employee was discharged for tardiness, the female plaintiff might admit that she was frequently late, but claim that men who were also late were not fired. Again, we're discussing comparators: By proving that males were treated more favorably in regard to the asserted reason, the plaintiff undercuts the defendant's explanation. *See Ekokotu v. Fed. Express Corp.,* 408 F. App'x 331 (11th Cir. 2011) (if the plaintiff cannot show the asserted reason is false, she must establish that it was not applied to similarly situated individuals). To add a final layer of complication, a showing that others were guilty of the same act or omission as plaintiff does not necessarily prove that the adverse action taken against plaintiff was a pretext. Most obviously, the employer might have been unaware of the violations by others. *Mechnig v. Sears, Roebuck & Co.,* 864 F.2d 1359 (7th Cir. 1988).

Patterson allows plaintiff to challenge defendant's claimed reason indirectly, "by presenting evidence of respondent's past treatment of petitioner, including the instances of the racial harassment which she alleges and respondent's failure to train her for an accounting position." The partial dissent of Justices Brennan and Stevens argued that the jury instruction below was "much too restrictive," and argued for a broad approach that would include focusing on broader policies and practices, including past treatment of the plaintiff, such as failure to train her. *Id.* at 217. How is this proof relevant to the ultimate issue of whether the plaintiff was discriminated against?

1. Proving that the employer promoted whites without the asserted qualifications tends to show that the qualifications are unnecessary, even in the employer's own view.
2. Showing the employer's "general policy and practice with respect to minority employment" suggests that, if the employer generally discriminates, it is more likely it discriminated as to the particular plaintiff.
3. While harassment itself, if sufficiently severe, violates Title VII, *see* Section D, perhaps a company that condones racial harassment is more likely to be discriminatory in promotions.
4. Defendant's failure to train plaintiff, and its general past treatment of her may be probative of discrimination—unless the reason for adverse treatment was peculiar to plaintiff and unrelated to her race.

Will plaintiff at least get to the jury if she adduces evidence sufficient to raise a material issue of fact on one of these claims? *See Ridout v. JBS USA, LLC,* 716 F.3d 1079, 1084 (8th Cir. 2013) ("A strong showing that the plaintiff was meeting his employer's reasonable expectations at the time of termination may create a fact issue as to pretext when the employer claims that the employee was terminated for poor or declining performance."); *Hudson v. United Sys. of Ark.,* 709 F.3d 700 (8th Cir. 2013) (upholding jury verdict when there was evidence that defendant's supposed nondiscriminatory reason for plaintiff's discharge—her failure to call him on his cell phone when sick—was pretextual when plaintiff denied ever being informed of it and other executives testified that they never heard of this policy; in addition, there was evidence that the manager frequently belittled women, including plaintiff, whom he ordered "sit down, little girl").

Suppose defendant puts into evidence more than one nondiscriminatory reason. Some lower courts have required the plaintiff to adduce proof of the pretextual nature of *all* the reasons, *see e.g., Kautz v. Met-Pro Corp.,* 412 F.3d 463 (3d Cir. 2005). Other courts believe that proof that any reason is pretextual will usually permit the jury to infer that the pretext conceals a discriminatory motive. *See generally* Lawrence D. Rosenthal, *Motions for Summary Judgment When Employers Offer Multiple Justifications for Adverse Employment Actions: Why the Exceptions Should Swallow the Rule,* 2002 UTAH L. REV. 335, 335-36 (2002). Of course, sometimes an employer's multiple reasons will conflict, or change over time, thus providing another basis to infer pretext. *See, e.g., Hitchcock v. Angel Corps, Inc.,* 718 F.3d 733 (7th Cir. 2013) (at least four potentially different explanations for plaintiff's discharge were inconsistent or otherwise suspect); *Jones v. Nat'l Am. Univ.,* 608 F.3d 1039 (8th Cir. 2010) (a change in the employer's reasons from those offered the EEOC and those adduced at trial were evidence of pretext).

Employers have also attempted to buttress their nondiscriminatory reason with what is sometimes called the "same actor defense." Courts have often declined to infer a discriminatory intent when the person who hired an older worker also discharged him within a relatively short period of time. The rationale is that, had the employer held stereotypical views, he would not have hired the plaintiff in the first place. *Brown v. CSC Logic, Inc.* 82 F.3d 651 (5th Cir. 1996); *Proud v. Stone*, 945 F.2d 796 (4th Cir. 1991). A number of courts apply this inference, but the conditions are restrictive: Not only must the same supervisor must make both decisions, but the decisions must also be in tension with one another. For example, a person who hires an older worker or a woman for one position might be expected not to discriminate in discharging that person but could easily hold stereotypic views about the limitations of such persons with respect to higher-level jobs. Further, the time between the hiring and firing decisions may make a substantial difference as to the strength of the inference. *See Potter v. Synerlink Corp.*, 562 F. App'x 665 (10th Cir. 2014) (inference did not apply where the decisionmaker hired the plaintiff three and a half years before he fired her). The strength of the inference will also vary depending on the circumstances. *See EEOC v. Boeing Co.*, 577 F.3d 1044, 1052 (9th Cir. 2009). *See generally* Victor D. Quintanilla & Cheryl R. Kaiser, *The Same-Actor Inference of Nondiscrimination: Moral Credentialing and the Psychological and Legal Licensing of Bias*, 104 CAL. L. REV. 1 (2016); Natasha T. Martin, *Immunity for Hire: How the Same-Actor Doctrine Sustains Discrimination in the Contemporary Workplace*, 40 CONN. L. REV. 1117 (2008).

Patterson was not the Supreme Court's last encounter with the question of pretext. *St. Mary's Honor Center v. Hicks*, 509 U.S. 502 (1993), involved a race discrimination claim. At the bench trial, the plaintiff established a prima facie case under *Burdine*, thus triggering the *McDonnell Douglas* presumption. Defendant, in turn, produced two alternative explanations to rebut the presumption, but both were rejected by the judge. Since he credited neither explanation, one might have thought that the judge would have necessarily found them to be "pretexts" for discrimination. However, that was not his conclusion. Rather, the trial judge believed that the action was taken on the basis of personal animosity by the supervisor toward the plaintiff, something the supervisor had denied on the stand. The court therefore determined that the plaintiff had not met his burden of persuasion that the adverse actions were based on race. The Court of Appeals reversed, reasoning that, since the judge disbelieved the proffered explanations, the defendants were in "no better position than if they had remained silent."

The Supreme Court disagreed. The *McDonnell Douglas* presumption shift did not shift the plaintiff's ultimate burden of persuasion. To this point, the opinion was consistent with *Burdine*. But the majority went further. Looking to statements in prior opinions that the plaintiff always carries the burden of persuading the trier of fact that the defendant intentionally discriminated against him, the majority held that mere disbelief of the defendant's asserted reason was not enough to find for plaintiff. Rather, the trier of fact had to also find that the rejected reasons were not just a pretext for some hidden motivation but were a pretext for discrimination.

After *Hicks*, a prima facie case creates a mandatory presumption in favor of the plaintiff, but one that disappears as soon as the defendant carries its burden of production. But what is the effect of the proof that established the prima face case? In the wake of *Hicks*, some courts held that plaintiff had to produce *additional* evidence of discrimination, that is, evidence beyond the prima facie case and any proof of pretext (the so-called "pretext plus" rule). The alternative reading, the "pretext only" view, was that the trier of fact's disbelief of the purported nondiscriminatory reason permitted, although it did not require, a finding of discrimination. The Court resolved this dispute in the next case, opting for the pretext-only rule in an opinion which also casts light on the current approach to analyzing individual disparate treatment cases.

≡
≡ *Reeves v. Sanderson Plumbing Products, Inc.*
≡ *530 U.S. 133 (2000)*

Justice O'CONNOR delivered the opinion of the Court.

This case concerns the kind and amount of evidence necessary to sustain a jury's verdict that an employer unlawfully discriminated on the basis of age. Specifically, we must resolve whether a defendant is entitled to judgment as a matter of law when the plaintiff's case consists exclusively of a prima facie case of discrimination and sufficient evidence for the trier of fact to disbelieve the defendant's legitimate, nondiscriminatory explanation for its action. . . .

I

In October 1995, petitioner Roger Reeves was 57 years old and had spent 40 years in the employ of respondent, Sanderson Plumbing Products, Inc., a manufacturer of toilet seats and covers. Petitioner worked in a department known as the "Hinge Room," where he supervised the "regular line." Joe Oswalt, in his mid-thirties, supervised the Hinge Room's "special line," and Russell Caldwell, the manager of the Hinge Room and age 45, supervised both petitioner and Oswalt. Petitioner's responsibilities included recording the attendance and hours of those under his supervision, and reviewing a weekly report that listed the hours worked by each employee.

In the summer of 1995, Caldwell informed Powe Chesnut, the director of manufacturing and the husband of company president Sandra Sanderson, that "production was down" in the Hinge Room because employees were often absent and were "coming in late and leaving early." Because the monthly attendance reports did not indicate a problem, Chesnut ordered an audit of the Hinge Room's timesheets for July, August, and September of that year. According to Chesnut's testimony, that investigation revealed "numerous timekeeping errors and misrepresentations on the part of Caldwell, Reeves, and Oswalt." Following the audit, Chesnut, along with Dana Jester, vice president of human resources, and Tom Whitaker, vice president of operations, recommended to company president Sanderson that petitioner and Caldwell be fired. In October 1995, Sanderson followed the recommendation and discharged both petitioner and Caldwell.

At trial, respondent contended that it had fired petitioner due to his failure to maintain accurate attendance records, while petitioner attempted to demonstrate that respondent's explanation was pretext for age discrimination. Petitioner introduced evidence that he had accurately recorded the attendance and hours of the employees under his supervision, and that Chesnut, whom Oswalt described as wielding "absolute power" within the company, had demonstrated age-based animus in his dealings with petitioner.

[The jury returned a verdict in favor of petitioner of $35,000 in compensatory damages, which the judge doubled as liquidated damages pursuant to the jury's finding that the employer's age discrimination was "willful." The judge also awarded plaintiff $28,490.80 in front pay for two years' lost income. The Fifth Circuit reversed], holding that petitioner had not introduced sufficient evidence to sustain the jury's finding of unlawful discrimination. After noting respondent's proffered justification for petitioner's discharge, the court acknowledged that petitioner "very well may" have offered sufficient evidence for "a reasonable jury [to] have found that [respondent's] explanation for its employment decision was pretextual." The court explained, however, that this was "not dispositive" of the ultimate issue—namely, "whether Reeves presented sufficient evidence that his age motivated [respondent's] employment decision." Addressing this question, the court weighed petitioner's additional evidence of discrimination against other circumstances surrounding his discharge. Specifically, the court noted that Chesnut's age-based comments "were not made in the direct context of Reeves's termination"; there was no allegation that the two other individuals who had recommended that petitioner be fired (Jester and Whitaker) were motivated by age; two of the decision makers involved in petitioner's discharge (Jester and Sanderson) were over the age of 50; all three of the Hinge Room supervisors were accused of inaccurate record keeping; and several of respondent's management positions were filled by persons over age 50 when petitioner was fired. On this basis, the court concluded that petitioner had not introduced sufficient evidence for a rational jury to conclude that he had been discharged because of his age. . . .

II . . .

When a plaintiff alleges disparate treatment, "liability depends on whether the protected trait (under the ADEA, age) actually motivated the employer's decision." *Hazen Paper Co. v. Biggins.* That is, the plaintiff's age must have "actually played a role in [the employer's decision making] process and had a determinative influence on the outcome." [The lower courts "have employed some variant of the framework articulated in *McDonnell Douglas* to analyze ADEA claims that are based principally on circumstantial evidence," and the Court assumed, arguendo, that the *McDonnell Douglas* framework is fully applicable" under the ADEA as well as Title VII.]

[Under this framework, petitioner established a prima facie case and respondent rebutted it.] Although intermediate evidentiary burdens shift back and forth under this framework, "the ultimate burden of persuading the trier of fact that the defendant intentionally discriminated against the plaintiff remains at all times with the plaintiff." And in attempting to satisfy this burden, the plaintiff—once the employer produces sufficient evidence to support a nondiscriminatory explanation for its decision—must be afforded the "opportunity to prove by a preponderance of the evidence that the legitimate reasons offered by the defendant were not its true reasons, but were a pretext for discrimination." That is, the plaintiff may attempt to establish that he was the victim of intentional discrimination "by showing that the employer's proffered explanation is unworthy of credence." Moreover, although the presumption of discrimination "drops out of the picture" once the defendant meets its burden of production, the trier of fact may still consider the evidence establishing the plaintiff's prima facie case "and inferences properly drawn therefrom . . . on the issue of whether the defendant's explanation is pretextual."

In this case, the evidence supporting respondent's explanation for petitioner's discharge consisted primarily of testimony by Chesnut and Sanderson and documentation of petitioner's alleged "shoddy record keeping." Chesnut testified that a 1993 audit of Hinge Room operations revealed "a very lax assembly line" where employees were not adhering to general work rules. As a result of that audit, petitioner was placed on 90 days' probation for unsatisfactory performance. In 1995, Chesnut ordered another investigation of the Hinge Room, which, according to his testimony, revealed that petitioner was not correctly recording the absences and hours of employees. Respondent introduced summaries of that investigation documenting several attendance violations by 12 employees under petitioner's supervision, and noting that each should have been disciplined in some manner. Chesnut testified that this failure to discipline absent and late employees is "extremely important when you are dealing with a union" because uneven enforcement across departments would keep the company "in grievance and arbitration cases, which are costly, all the time." He and Sanderson also stated that petitioner's errors, by failing to adjust for hours not worked, cost the company overpaid wages. Sanderson testified that she accepted the recommendation to discharge petitioner because he had "intentionally falsified company pay records."

Petitioner, however, made a substantial showing that respondent's explanation was false. First, petitioner offered evidence that he had properly maintained the attendance records. Most of the timekeeping errors cited by respondent involved employees who were not marked late but who were recorded as having arrived at the plant at 7 A.M. for the 7 A.M. shift. Respondent contended that employees arriving at 7 A.M. could not have been at their workstations by 7 A.M., and therefore must have been late. But both petitioner and Oswalt testified that the company's automated timeclock often failed to scan employees' timecards, so that the timesheets would not record any time of arrival. On these occasions, petitioner and Oswalt would visually check the workstations and record whether the employees were present at the start of the shift. They stated that if an employee arrived promptly but the timesheet contained no time of arrival, they would reconcile the two by marking "7 A.M." as the employee's arrival time, even if the employee actually arrived at the plant earlier. On cross-examination, Chesnut acknowledged that the timeclock sometimes malfunctioned, and that if "people were there at their work stations" at the start of the shift, the supervisor "would write in seven o'clock." Petitioner also testified that when employees arrived before or stayed after their shifts, he would assign them additional work so they would not be overpaid.

Petitioner similarly cast doubt on whether he was responsible for any failure to discipline late and absent employees. Petitioner testified that his job only included reviewing the daily and weekly attendance reports, and that disciplinary write-ups were based on the monthly reports, which were reviewed by Caldwell. Sanderson admitted that Caldwell, and not petitioner, was responsible for citing employees for violations of the company's attendance policy. Further, Chesnut conceded that there had never been a union grievance or employee complaint arising from petitioner's record keeping, and that the company had never calculated the amount of overpayments allegedly attributable to petitioner's errors. Petitioner also testified that, on the day he was fired, Chesnut said that his discharge was due to his failure to report as absent one employee, Gina Mae Coley, on two days in September 1995. But petitioner explained that he had spent those days in the hospital, and that Caldwell was therefore responsible for any overpayment of Coley. Finally, petitioner stated that on previous occasions that employees were paid for hours they had not worked, the company had simply adjusted those employees' next paychecks to correct the errors.

Based on this evidence, the Court of Appeals concluded that petitioner "very well may be correct" that "a reasonable jury could have found that [respondent's] explanation for its employment decision was pretextual." Nonetheless, the court held that this showing, standing alone, was insufficient to sustain the jury's finding of liability: "We must, as an essential final step, determine whether Reeves presented sufficient evidence that his age motivated [respondent's] employment decision." And in making this determination, the Court of Appeals ignored the evidence supporting petitioner's prima facie case and challenging respondent's explanation for its decision. The court confined its review of evidence favoring petitioner to that evidence showing that Chesnut had directed derogatory, age-based comments at petitioner, and that Chesnut had singled out petitioner for harsher treatment than younger employees. It is therefore apparent that the court believed that only this additional evidence of discrimination was relevant to whether the jury's verdict should stand. That is, the Court of Appeals proceeded from the assumption that a prima facie case of discrimination, combined with sufficient evidence for the trier of fact to disbelieve the defendant's legitimate, nondiscriminatory reason for its decision, is insufficient as a matter of law to sustain a jury's finding of intentional discrimination.

In so reasoning, the Court of Appeals misconceived the evidentiary burden borne by plaintiffs who attempt to prove intentional discrimination through indirect evidence. This much is evident from our decision in *St. Mary's Honor Center.* There we held that the factfinder's rejection of the employer's legitimate, nondiscriminatory reason for its action does not compel judgment for the plaintiff. The ultimate question is whether the employer intentionally discriminated, and proof that "the employer's proffered reason is unpersuasive, or even obviously contrived, does not necessarily establish that the plaintiff's proffered reason . . . is correct." In other words, "it is not enough . . . to disbelieve the employer; the factfinder must believe the plaintiff's explanation of intentional discrimination."

In reaching this conclusion, however, we reasoned that it is permissible for the trier of fact to infer the ultimate fact of discrimination from the falsity of the employer's explanation. Specifically, we stated:

> The factfinder's disbelief of the reasons put forward by the defendant (particularly if disbelief is accompanied by a suspicion of mendacity) may, together with the elements of the prima facie case, suffice to show intentional discrimination. Thus, rejection of the defendant's proffered reasons will permit the trier of fact to infer the ultimate fact of intentional discrimination.

Proof that the defendant's explanation is unworthy of credence is simply one form of circumstantial evidence that is probative of intentional discrimination, and it may be quite persuasive. [*St. Mary's Honor Center.*] ("Proving the employer's reason false becomes part of (and often considerably assists) the greater enterprise of proving that the real reason was intentional discrimination.") In appropriate circumstances, the trier of fact can reasonably infer from the falsity of the explanation that the employer is dissembling to cover up a discriminatory purpose. Such an inference is consistent with the general principle of evidence law that the factfinder is entitled to consider a party's dishonesty about a material fact as "affirmative evidence of guilt." *Wright v. West,* 505 U.S. 277 (1992); 2 J. WIGMORE, EVIDENCE §278(2), p. 133 (J. Chadbourn rev. ed. 1979). Moreover, once the employer's justification has been eliminated, discrimination may well be the most likely alternative explanation, especially since the employer is in the best position to put forth the actual reason for its decision. *Cf. Furnco Constr. Corp. v. Waters,* 438 U.S. 567, 577 (1978) ("When all legitimate reasons for rejecting an applicant have been eliminated as possible reasons for the employer's actions, it is more likely than not the employer, who we generally assume acts with some reason, based his decision on an impermissible consideration"). Thus, a plaintiff's prima facie case, combined with sufficient evidence to find that the employer's asserted justification is false, may permit the trier of fact to conclude that the employer unlawfully discriminated.

This is not to say that such a showing by the plaintiff will always be adequate to sustain a jury's finding of liability. Certainly there will be instances where, although the plaintiff has established a prima facie case and set forth sufficient evidence to reject the defendant's explanation, no rational factfinder could conclude that the action was discriminatory. For instance, an employer would be entitled to judgment as a matter of law if the record conclusively revealed some other, nondiscriminatory reason for the employer's decision, or if the plaintiff created only a weak issue of fact as to whether the employer's reason was untrue and there was abundant and uncontroverted independent evidence that no discrimination had occurred. *See Fisher v. Vassar College*, 114 F.3d 1332, 1338 (2d Cir. 1997) ("If the circumstances show that the defendant gave the false explanation to conceal something other than discrimination, the inference of discrimination will be weak or nonexistent"). To hold otherwise would be effectively to insulate an entire category of employment discrimination cases from review under Rule 50, and we have reiterated that trial courts should not "treat discrimination differently from other ultimate questions of fact." *St. Mary's Honor Center.*

Whether judgment as a matter of law is appropriate in any particular case will depend on a number of factors. Those include the strength of the plaintiff's prima facie case, the probative value of the proof that the employer's explanation is false, and any other evidence that supports the employer's case and that properly may be considered on a motion for judgment as a matter of law. For purposes of this case, we need not—and could not—resolve all of the circumstances in which such factors would entitle an employer to judgment as a matter of law. It suffices to say that, because a prima facie case and sufficient evidence to reject the employer's explanation may permit a finding of liability, the Court of Appeals erred in proceeding from the premise that a plaintiff must always introduce additional, independent evidence of discrimination.

III . . .

A

[The Court went on to decide whether the employer was nevertheless entitled to judgment as a matter of law under Rule 50, holding no. In entertaining a motion for judgment as a matter of law, the court should review all of the evidence in the record.] In doing so, however, the court must draw all reasonable inferences in favor of the nonmoving party, and it may not make credibility determinations or weigh the evidence. *Lytle v. Household Mfg., Inc.*, 494 U.S. 545, 554-55 (1990). "Credibility determinations, the weighing of the evidence, and the drawing of legitimate inferences from the facts are jury functions, not those of a judge." *Anderson v. Liberty Lobby*, 477 U.S. 242 (1986). Thus, although the court should review the record as a whole, it must disregard all evidence favorable to the moving party that the jury is not required to believe. *See* Wright & Miller 299. That is, the court should give credence to the evidence favoring the nonmovant as well as that "evidence supporting the moving party that is uncontradicted and unimpeached, at least to the extent that that evidence comes from disinterested witnesses."

B

Applying this standard here, it is apparent that respondent was not entitled to judgment as a matter of law. In this case, in addition to establishing a prima facie case of discrimination and creating a jury issue as to the falsity of the employer's explanation, petitioner introduced additional evidence that Chesnut was motivated by age-based animus and was principally responsible for petitioner's firing. Petitioner testified that Chesnut had told him that he "was so old [he] must have come over on the Mayflower" and, on one occasion when petitioner was having difficulty starting a machine, that he "was too damn old to do [his] job." According to petitioner, Chesnut would regularly "cuss at me and shake his finger in my face." Oswalt, roughly 24 years younger than petitioner, corroborated that there was an "obvious difference" in how Chesnut treated them. He stated that, although he and Chesnut "had [their] differences," "it was nothing compared to the way [Chesnut] treated Roger." Oswalt explained that Chesnut "tolerated quite a bit" from him even though he "defied" Chesnut "quite often," but that Chesnut treated petitioner "in a manner, as you would . . . treat . . . a child when . . . you're angry with [him]." Petitioner also demonstrated that, according to company records, he and Oswalt had nearly identical rates of productivity in 1993. Yet respondent conducted an efficiency study of only the regular line, supervised by petitioner, and placed only petitioner on probation. Chesnut conducted that efficiency study and, after having testified to the contrary on direct examination, acknowledged on cross-examination that he had recommended that petitioner be placed on probation following the study.

Further, petitioner introduced evidence that Chesnut was the actual decision-maker behind his firing. Chesnut was married to Sanderson, who made the formal decision to discharge petitioner. Although Sanderson testified that she fired petitioner because he had "intentionally falsified company pay records," respondent only introduced evidence concerning the inaccuracy of the records, not their falsification. A 1994 letter authored by Chesnut indicated that he berated other company directors, who were supposedly his co-equals, about how to do their jobs. Moreover, Oswalt testified that all of respondent's employees feared Chesnut, and that Chesnut had exercised "absolute power" within the company for "as long as [he] can remember."

In holding that the record contained insufficient evidence to sustain the jury's verdict, the Court of Appeals misapplied the standard of review dictated by Rule 50. Again, the court disregarded critical evidence favorable to petitioner—namely, the evidence supporting petitioner's prima facie case and undermining respondent's nondiscriminatory explanation. The court also failed to draw all reasonable inferences in favor of petitioner. For instance, while acknowledging "the potentially damning nature" of Chesnut's age-related comments, the court discounted them on the ground that they "were not made in the direct context of Reeves's termination." And the court discredited petitioner's evidence that Chesnut was the actual decisionmaker by giving weight to the fact that there was "no evidence to suggest that any of the other decision makers were motivated by age." Moreover, the other evidence on which the court relied—that Caldwell and Oswalt were also cited for poor record keeping, and that respondent employed many managers over age 50—although relevant, is certainly not dispositive. In concluding that these circumstances so overwhelmed the evidence favoring petitioner that no rational trier of fact could have found that petitioner was fired because of his age, the Court of Appeals impermissibly substituted its judgment concerning the weight of the evidence for the jury's.

The ultimate question in every employment discrimination case involving a claim of disparate treatment is whether the plaintiff was the victim of intentional discrimination. Given the evidence in the record supporting petitioner, we see no reason to subject the parties to an additional round of litigation before the Court of Appeals rather than to resolve the matter here. The District Court plainly informed the jury that petitioner was required to show "by a preponderance of the evidence that his age was a determining and motivating factor in the decision of [respondent] to terminate him." The court instructed the jury that, to show that respondent's explanation was a pretext for discrimination, petitioner had to demonstrate "1, that the stated reasons were not the real reasons for [petitioner's] discharge; and 2, that age discrimination was the real reason for [petitioner's] discharge." Given that petitioner established a prima facie case of discrimination, introduced enough evidence for the jury to reject respondent's explanation, and produced additional evidence of age-based animus, there was sufficient evidence for the jury to find that respondent had intentionally discriminated. The District Court was therefore correct to submit the case to the jury, and the Court of Appeals erred in overturning its verdict.

Justice GINSBURG, concurring. . . .

I write separately to note that it may be incumbent on the Court, in an appropriate case, to define more precisely the circumstances in which plaintiffs will be required to submit evidence beyond these two categories in order to survive a motion for judgment as a matter of law. I anticipate that such circumstances will be uncommon. As the Court notes, it is a principle of evidence law that the jury is entitled to treat a party's dishonesty about a material fact as evidence of culpability. Under this commonsense principle, evidence suggesting that a defendant accused of illegal discrimination has chosen to give a false explanation for its actions gives rise to a rational inference that the defendant could be masking its actual, illegal motivation. Whether the defendant was in fact motivated by discrimination is of course for the finder of fact to decide; that is the lesson of *St. Mary's Honor Center v. Hicks.* But the inference remains—unless it is conclusively demonstrated, by evidence the district court is required to credit on a motion for judgment as a matter of law, that discrimination could not have been the defendant's true motivation. If such conclusive demonstrations are (as I suspect) atypical, it follows that the ultimate question of liability ordinarily should not be taken from the jury once the plaintiff has introduced [evidence supporting a prima facie case and evidence supporting a finding of pretext.] Because the Court's opinion leaves room for such further elaboration in an appropriate case, I join it in full.

NOTES

1. *Beyond Pretext Plus.* Professor Michael Zimmer, *Slicing & Dicing of Individual Disparate Treatment Law,* 61 LA. L. REV. 577 (2001), views *Reeves* as broader than merely rejecting the lower court's "pretext-plus" rule. Not only does the evidence supporting plaintiff's prima facie case remain relevant once defendant puts in evidence its nondiscriminatory, *id.* at 587-88, but *Reeves* also made clear that all the evidence in the record needs to be reviewed in deciding motions for summary judgment or judgment as a matter of law: "Slicing and dicing away plaintiff's evidence to leave only evidence supporting defendant's case is inconsistent with the true nature of the *McDonnell Douglas* method of analyzing individual disparate treatment cases." *Id.* at 591-92.

2. *"Unreasonable" Decision Versus Business Judgment.* Courts have often recognized that the more unusual and idiosyncratic a decision is—in terms of the way business is normally conducted—the more appropriate it is to infer discrimination. This principle is in obvious tension with what has sometimes been called the "business judgment" rule, which is that courts should not second-guess business decisions. One illustration of the conflict is *White v. Baxter Healthcare Corp.*, 533 F.3d 381, 393 (6th Cir. 2008), in which the majority reaffirmed that "the plaintiff may also demonstrate pretext by offering evidence which challenges the reasonableness of the employer's decision 'to the extent that such an inquiry sheds light on whether the employer's proffered reason for the employment action was its actual motivation'" (citation omitted). It went on:

> [O]ur Circuit has never adopted a "business-judgment rule" which requires us to defer to the employer's "reasonable business judgment" in Title VII cases. Indeed, in most Title VII cases the very issue in dispute is whether the employer's adverse employment decision resulted from an objectively unreasonable business judgment, i.e., a judgment that was based upon an impermissible consideration such as the adversely-affected employee's race, gender, religion, or national origin. In determining whether the plaintiff has produced enough evidence to cast doubt upon the employer's explanation for its decision, we cannot . . . unquestionably accept the employer's own self-serving claim that the decision resulted from an exercise of "reasonable business judgment." Nor can we decide "as a matter of law" that "an employer's proffered justification is reasonable." The question of whether the employer's judgment was reasonable or was instead motivated by improper considerations is for the jury to consider. . . .

Id. at 394 n.6; *see also DeJesus v. WP Co. LLC*, 841 F.3d 527 (D.C. Cir. 2016) (a jury could find a supervisor's interpretation of plaintiff's actions as insubordination "was so unreasonable that it could not be honestly held"). Nevertheless, scholars suggest that, even when a business reason seems implausible, courts are too willing to look to other factors—whether personal animosity or cronyism—to explain such decisions. *See* Ann C. McGinley, *The Emerging Cronyism Defense and Affirmative Action: A Critical Perspective on the Distinction Between Color-Blind and Race-Conscious Decision Making Under Title VII*, 39 Ariz. L. Rev. 1003 (1997); Chad Derum & Karen Engle, *The Rise of the Personal Animosity Presumption in Title VII and the Return to "No Cause" Employment*, 81 Tex. L. Rev. 1177, 1182 (2003).

3. *"Me, Too" Proof of Pretext.* In *Sprint/United Management Co. v. Mendelsohn*, 552 U.S. 379 (2007), a reduction-in-force case, plaintiff wanted to call as witnesses five other older workers who claimed that they, too, were discriminated against because of their age in the downsizing. The Supreme Court found "such evidence [to be] neither *per se* admissible nor *per se* inadmissible." *Id.* at 381. Emphasizing the broad discretion accorded trail courts' evidentiary rulings—reviewable under a deferential abuse of discretion standard—the trial court should make the admissibility determination: "With respect to evidentiary questions in general [including "relevance" under federal Rule of Evidence 401] and Rule 403 [as to "prejudice"] in particular, a district court virtually always is in the better position to assess the admissibility of the evidence in the context of the case before it." *Id.* at 387. Discrimination cases are well suited to this general approach since a relevance decision "is fact based and depends on many factors, including how closely related the evidence is to the plaintiff's circumstances and theory of the case," while determining if evidence "is prejudicial also requires a fact-intensive, context-specific inquiry." *Id.* at 388. One scholar has argued that the focus on "insular individualism" of supervisors and managers is inconsistent with how workplaces operate in practice, with any particular decision being influenced by a web of other decisions and practices, sometimes influencing individual actors in ways they do not themselves understand. Tristin Green, *Insular Individualism: Employment Discrimination Law After* Ledbetter v. Goodyear, 43 HARV. C.R-C.L. L. REV. 353 (2008).

After *Mendelsohn* the determination in every case will be contextual, taking into account the requirements of FED. R. EVID. 401 and 403. As to Rule 401, Sprint claimed that any discrimination by other supervisors was simply irrelevant to the question at issue: Did plaintiff's supervisor pick her for discharge because of her age? If the intent of a single individual is the touchstone, isn't that right? What about the possibility that a supervisor would feel freer to discriminate if others were so acting?

As for prejudice under Rule 403, "[a]lthough relevant, evidence may be excluded if its probative value is substantially outweighed by the danger of unfair prejudice, confusion of the issues, or misleading the jury, or by considerations of undue delay, waste of time, or needless presentation of cumulative evidence." Thus, a low level of relevance may not be sufficient to justify admission of evidence if it is likely to prejudice the jury. *See Mattenson v. Baxter Healthcare Corp.*, 438 F.3d 763, 770-71 (7th Cir. 2006) (in a division of 7,000 employees with hundreds of executives, the fact that some may dislike old workers and even fire old workers because of their age is weak evidence that a particular older employee was fired because of his age; absent proof of a pervasive culture of prejudice, such evidence may be excluded under Rule 403, although it not reversible error to admit it). Isn't there a real danger that a jury would punish Sprint for being a "bad employer" if all this evidence were admitted, even if the decision as to Mendelsohn herself was not discriminatory?

3. Proving Discrimination: Mixed-Motive Analysis

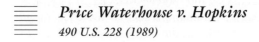

Price Waterhouse v. Hopkins
490 U.S. 228 (1989)

Justice BRENNAN announced the judgment of the Court and delivered an opinion, in which Justice MARSHALL, Justice BLACKMUN, and Justice STEVENS join. . . .

. . . At Price Waterhouse, a nationwide professional accounting partnership, a senior manager becomes a candidate for partnership when the partners in her local office submit her name as a candidate. All of the other partners in the firm are then invited to submit written comments on each candidate—either on a "long" or a "short" form, depending on the partner's degree of exposure to the candidate. Not every partner in the firm submits comments on every candidate. After reviewing the comments and interviewing the partners who submitted them, the firm's Admissions Committee makes a recommendation to the Policy Board. This recommendation will be either that the firm accept the candidate for partnership, put her application on "hold," or deny her the promotion outright. The Policy Board then decides whether to submit the candidate's name to the entire partnership for a vote, to "hold" her candidacy, or to reject her. The recommendation of the Admissions Committee, and the decision of the Policy Board, are not controlled by fixed guidelines: a certain number of positive comments from partners will not guarantee a candidate's admission to the partnership, nor will a specific quantity of negative comments necessarily defeat her application. Price Waterhouse places no limit on the number of persons whom it will admit to the partnership in any given year.

Ann Hopkins had worked at Price Waterhouse's Office of Government Services in Washington, D.C., for five years when the partners in that office proposed her as a candidate for partnership. Of the 662 partners at the firm at that time, 7 were women. Of the 88 persons proposed for partnership that year, only 1—Hopkins—was a woman. Forty-seven of these candidates were admitted to the partnership, 21 were rejected, and 20—including Hopkins—were "held" for reconsideration the following year. Thirteen of the 32 partners who had submitted comments on Hopkins supported her bid for partnership. Three partners recommended that her candidacy be placed on hold, eight stated that they did not have an informed opinion about her, and eight recommended that she be denied partnership.

In a jointly prepared statement supporting her candidacy, the partners in Hopkins' office showcased her successful 2-year effort to secure a $25 million contract with the Department of State, labeling it "an outstanding performance" and one that Hopkins carried out "virtually at the partner level." Despite Price Waterhouse's attempt at trial to minimize her contribution to this project, Judge Gesell specifically found that Hopkins had "played a key role in Price Waterhouse's successful effort to win a multimillion-dollar contract with the Department of State." Indeed, he went on, "[n]one of the other partnership candidates at Price Waterhouse that year had a comparable record in terms of successfully securing major contracts for the partnership."

The partners in Hopkins' office praised her character as well as her accomplishments, describing her in their joint statement as "an outstanding professional" who had a "deft touch," a "strong character, independence and integrity." Clients appear to have agreed with these assessments. At trial, one official from the State Department described her as "extremely competent, intelligent," "strong and forthright, very productive, energetic and creative." Another high-ranking official praised Hopkins' decisiveness, broadmindedness, and "intellectual clarity"; she was, in his words, "a stimulating conversationalist." Evaluations such as these led Judge Gesell to conclude that Hopkins "had no difficulty dealing with clients and her clients appear to have been very pleased with her work" and that she "was generally viewed as a highly competent project leader who worked long hours, pushed vigorously to meet deadlines and demanded much from the multidisciplinary staffs with which she worked."

On too many occasions, however, Hopkins' aggressiveness apparently spilled over into abrasiveness. Staff members seem to have borne the brunt of Hopkins' brusqueness. Long before her bid for partnership, partners evaluating her work had counseled her to improve her relations with staff members. Although later evaluations indicate an improvement, Hopkins' perceived shortcomings in this important area eventually doomed her bid for partnership. Virtually all of the partners' negative remarks about Hopkins—even those of partners supporting her—had to do with her "interpersonal skills." Both "[s]upporters and opponents of her candidacy," stressed Judge Gesell, "indicated that she was sometimes overly aggressive, unduly harsh, difficult to work with and impatient with staff."

There were clear signs, though, that some of the partners reacted negatively to Hopkins' personality because she was a woman. One partner described her as "macho"; another suggested that she "overcompensated for being a woman"; a third advised her to take "a course at charm school." Several partners criticized her use of profanity; in response, one partner suggested that those partners objected to her swearing only "because it[']s a lady using foul language." Another supporter explained that Hopkins "ha[d] matured from a tough-talking somewhat masculine hard-nosed mgr to an authoritative, formidable, but much more appealing lady ptr candidate." But it was the man who, as Judge Gesell found, bore responsibility for explaining to Hopkins the reasons for the Policy Board's decision to place her candidacy on hold who delivered the coup de grace: in order to improve her chances for partnership, Thomas Beyer advised, Hopkins should "walk more femininely, talk more femininely, dress more femininely, wear make-up, have her hair styled, and wear jewelry."

Dr. Susan Fiske, a social psychologist and Associate Professor of Psychology at Carnegie-Mellon University, testified at trial that the partnership selection process at Price Waterhouse was likely influenced by sex stereotyping. Her testimony focused not only on the overtly sex-based comments of partners but also on gender-neutral remarks, made by partners who knew Hopkins only slightly, that were intensely critical of her. One partner, for example, baldly stated that Hopkins was "universally disliked" by staff, and another described her as "consistently annoying and irritating"; yet these were people who had had very little contact with Hopkins. According to Fiske, Hopkins' uniqueness (as the only woman in the pool of candidates) and the subjectivity of the evaluations made it likely that sharply critical remarks such as these were the product of sex stereotyping—although Fiske admitted that she could not say with certainty whether any particular comment was the result of stereotyping. Fiske based her opinion on a review of the submitted comments, explaining that it was commonly accepted practice for social psychologists to reach this kind of conclusion without having met any of the people involved in the decisionmaking process.

In previous years, other female candidates for partnership also had been evaluated in sex-based terms. As a general matter, Judge Gesell concluded, "[c]andidates were viewed favorably if partners believed they maintained their femin[in]ity while becoming effective professional managers"; in this environment, "[t]o be identified as a 'women's lib[b]er' was regarded as [a] negative comment." In fact, the judge found that in previous years "[o]ne partner repeatedly commented that he could not consider any woman seriously as a partnership candidate and believed that women were not even capable of functioning as senior managers—yet the firm took no action to discourage his comments and recorded his vote in the overall summary of the evaluations."

Judge Gesell found that Price Waterhouse legitimately emphasized interpersonal skills in its partnership decisions, and also found that the firm had not fabricated its complaints about Hopkins' interpersonal skills as a pretext for discrimination. Moreover, he concluded, the firm did not give decisive emphasis to such traits only because Hopkins was a woman; although there were male candidates who lacked these skills but who were admitted to partnership, the judge found that these candidates possessed other, positive traits that Hopkins lacked.

The judge went on to decide, however, that some of the partners' remarks about Hopkins stemmed from an impermissibly cabined view of the proper behavior of women, and that Price Waterhouse had done nothing to disavow reliance on such comments. He held that Price Waterhouse had unlawfully discriminated against Hopkins on the basis of sex by consciously giving credence and effect to partners' comments that resulted from sex stereotyping. Noting that Price Waterhouse could avoid equitable relief by proving by clear and convincing evidence that it would have placed Hopkins' candidacy on hold even absent this discrimination, the judge decided that the firm had not carried this heavy burden. . . .

II . . .

In passing Title VII, Congress made the simple but momentous announcement that sex, race, religion, and national origin are not relevant to the selection, evaluation, or compensation of employees. Yet, the statute does not purport to limit the other qualities and characteristics that employers may take into account in making employment decisions. The converse, therefore, of "for cause" legislation, Title VII eliminates certain bases for distinguishing among employees while otherwise preserving employers' freedom of choice. This balance between employee rights and employer prerogatives turns out to be decisive in the case before us.

Congress' intent to forbid employers to take gender into account in making employment decisions appears on the face of the statute. In now-familiar language, the statute forbids an employer to "[discriminate] *because of* such individual's . . . sex." (emphasis added). We take these words to mean that gender must be irrelevant to employment decisions. To construe the words "because of" as colloquial shorthand for "but-for causation," as does Price Waterhouse, is to misunderstand them.

But-for causation is a hypothetical construct. In determining whether a particular factor was a but-for cause of a given event, we begin by assuming that that factor was present at the time of the event, and then ask whether, even if that factor had been absent, the event nevertheless would have transpired in the same way. The present, active tense of the operative verbs of §703(a)(1) ("to fail or refuse"), in contrast, turns our attention to the actual moment of the event in question, the adverse employment decision. The critical inquiry, the one commanded by the words of §703(a)(1), is whether gender was a factor in the employment decision *at the moment it was made*. Moreover, since we know that the words "because of" do not mean "solely because of,"[8] we also know that Title VII meant to condemn even those decisions based on a mixture of legitimate and illegitimate considerations. When, therefore, an employer considers both gender and legitimate factors at the time of making a decision, that decision was "because of" sex and the other, legitimate considerations—even if we may say later, in the context of litigation, that the decision would have been the same if gender had not been taken into account.

---

8. Congress specifically rejected an amendment that would have placed the word "solely" in front of the words "because of." 110 Cong. Rec. 2728, 13837 (1964).

To attribute this meaning to the words "because of" does not, as the dissent asserts, divest them of causal significance. A simple example illustrates the point. Suppose two physical forces act upon and move an object, and suppose that either force acting alone would have moved the object. As the dissent would have it, neither physical force was a "cause" of the motion unless we can show that but-for one or both of them, the object would not have moved; to use the dissent's terminology, both forces were simply "in the air" unless we can identify at least one of them as a but-for cause of the object's movement. Events that are causally overdetermined, in other words, may not have any "cause" at all. This cannot be so.

[Congress did not intend to require a plaintiff "to identify the precise causal role played by legitimate and illegitimate motivations"; it meant only to require her "to prove that the employer relied upon sex-based considerations" in its decision.]

To say that an employer may not take gender into account is not, however, the end of the matter, for that describes only one aspect of Title VII. The other important aspect of the statute is its preservation of an employer's remaining freedom of choice. We conclude that the preservation of this freedom means that an employer shall not be liable if it can prove that, even if it had not taken gender into account, it would have come to the same decision regarding a particular person. The statute's maintenance of employer prerogatives is evident from the statute itself and from its history, both in Congress and in this Court. . . .

The central point is this: while an employer may not take gender into account in making an employment decision . . ., it is free to decide against a woman for other reasons. We think these principles require that, once a plaintiff in a Title VII case shows that gender played a motivating part in an employment decision, the defendant may avoid a finding of liability only by proving that it would have made the same decision even if it had not allowed gender to play such a role. This balance of burdens is the direct result of Title VII's balance of rights.

Our holding casts no shadow on *Burdine*, in which we decided that, even after a plaintiff has made out a prima facie case of discrimination under Title VII, the burden of persuasion does not shift to the employer to show that its stated legitimate reason for the employment decision was the true reason. We stress, first, that neither court below shifted the burden of persuasion to Price Waterhouse on this question, and in fact, the District Court found that Hopkins had not shown that the firm's stated reason for its decision was pretextual. Moreover, since we hold that the plaintiff retains the burden of persuasion on the issue whether gender played a part in the employment decision, the situation before us is not the one of "shifting burdens" that we addressed in *Burdine*. Instead, the employer's burden is most appropriately deemed an affirmative defense: the plaintiff must persuade the factfinder on one point, and then the employer, if it wishes to prevail, must persuade it on another. *See NLRB v. Transportation Management Corp.*, 462 U.S. 393 (1983).[12]. . .

---

12. [Contrary to the dissent, it is] perfectly consistent to say both that gender was a factor in a particular decision when it was made and that, when the situation is viewed hypothetically and after the fact, the same decision would have been made even in the absence of discrimination. . . . [W]here liability is imposed because an employer is unable to prove that it would have made the same decision even if it had not discriminated, this is not an imposition of liability "where sex made no difference to the outcome." In our adversary system, where a party has the burden of proving a particular assertion and where that party is unable to meet its burden, we assume that that assertion is inaccurate. Thus, where an employer is unable to prove its claim that it would have made the same decision in the absence of discrimination, we are entitled to conclude that gender did make a difference to the outcome.

C

In saying that gender played a motivating part in an employment decision, we mean that, if we asked the employer at the moment of the decision what its reasons were and if we received a truthful response, one of those reasons would be that the applicant or employee was a woman. In the specific context of sex stereotyping, an employer who acts on the basis of a belief that a woman cannot be aggressive, or that she must not be, has acted on the basis of gender.

. . . As to the existence of sex stereotyping in this case, we are not inclined to quarrel with the District Court's conclusion that a number of the partners' comments showed sex stereotyping at work. As for the legal relevance of sex stereotyping, we are beyond the day when an employer could evaluate employees by assuming or insisting that they matched the stereotype associated with their group. . . . An employer who objects to aggressiveness in women but whose positions require this trait places women in an intolerable and impermissible Catch-22: out of a job if they behave aggressively and out of a job if they don't. Title VII lifts women out of this bind.

Remarks at work that are based on sex stereotypes do not inevitably prove that gender played a part in a particular employment decision. The plaintiff must show that the employer actually relied on her gender in making its decision. In making this showing, stereotyped remarks can certainly be evidence that gender played a part. In any event, the stereotyping in this case did not simply consist of stray remarks. On the contrary, Hopkins proved that Price Waterhouse invited partners to submit comments; that some of the comments stemmed from sex stereotypes; that an important part of the Policy Board's decision on Hopkins was an assessment of the submitted comments; and that Price Waterhouse in no way disclaimed reliance on the sex-linked evaluations. This is not, as Price Waterhouse suggests, "discrimination in the air"; rather, it is, as Hopkins puts it, "discrimination brought to ground and visited upon" an employee. By focusing on Hopkins' specific proof, however, we do not suggest a limitation on the possible ways of proving that stereotyping played a motivating role in an employment decision, and we refrain from deciding here which specific facts, "standing alone," would or would not establish a plaintiff's case, since such a decision is unnecessary in this case. *But see* [O'Connor, J., at page 604, concurring in the judgment].

As to the employer's proof, in most cases, the employer should be able to present some objective evidence as to its probable decision in the absence of an impermissible motive.[15] Moreover, proving "that the same decision would have been justified . . . is not the same as proving that the same decision would have been made." An employer may not, in other words, prevail in a mixed-motives case by offering a legitimate and sufficient reason for its decision if that reason did not motivate it at the time of the decision. Finally, an employer may not meet its burden in such a case by merely showing that at the time of the decision it was motivated only in part by a legitimate reason. The very premise of a mixed-motives case is that a legitimate reason was present, and indeed, in this case, Price Waterhouse already has made this showing

[handwritten margin note: Employer must assert affirmative defense]

---

15. Justice White's suggestion that the employer's own testimony as to the probable decision in the absence of discrimination is due special credence where the court has, contrary to the employer's testimony, found that an illegitimate factor played a part in the decision, is baffling.

574 ≡≡≡≡ 9. Antidiscrimination

by convincing Judge Gesell that Hopkins' interpersonal problems were a legitimate concern. The employer instead must show that its legitimate reason, standing alone, would have induced it to make the same decision.

III

The courts below held that an employer who has allowed a discriminatory impulse to play a motivating part in an employment decision must prove by clear and convincing evidence that it would have made the same decision in the absence of discrimination. We are persuaded that the better rule is that the employer must make this showing by a preponderance of the evidence. . . .

IV

[Price Waterhouse challenged as clearly erroneous the district court's findings both that stereotyping occurred and that it played any part in the decision to place Hopkins' candidacy on hold. The plurality disagreed.]

In finding that some of the partners' comments reflected sex stereotyping, the District Court relied in part on Dr. Fiske's expert testimony. Without directly impugning Dr. Fiske's credentials or qualifications, Price Waterhouse insinuates that a social psychologist is unable to identify sex stereotyping in evaluations without investigating whether those evaluations have a basis in reality. This argument comes too late. At trial, counsel for Price Waterhouse twice assured the court that he did not question Dr. Fiske's expertise and failed to challenge the legitimacy of her discipline. Without contradiction from Price Waterhouse, Fiske testified that she discerned sex stereotyping in the partners' evaluations of Hopkins and she further explained that it was part of her business to identify stereotyping in written documents. We are not inclined to accept petitioner's belated and unsubstantiated characterization of Dr. Fiske's testimony as "gossamer evidence" based only on "intuitive hunches" and of her detection of sex stereotyping as "intuitively divined." Nor are we disposed to adopt the dissent's dismissive attitude toward Dr. Fiske's field of study and toward her own professional integrity.

Indeed, we are tempted to say that Dr. Fiske's expert testimony was merely icing on Hopkins' cake. It takes no special training to discern sex stereotyping in a description of an aggressive female employee as requiring "a course at charm school." Nor, turning to Thomas Beyer's memorable advice to Hopkins, does it require expertise in psychology to know that, if an employee's flawed "interpersonal skills" can be corrected by a soft-hued suit or a new shade of lipstick, perhaps it is the employee's sex and not her interpersonal skills that has drawn the criticism.

Price Waterhouse also charges that Hopkins produced no evidence that sex stereotyping played a role in the decision to place her candidacy on hold. As we have stressed, however, Hopkins showed that the partnership solicited evaluations from all of the firm's partners; that it generally relied very heavily on such evaluations in making its decision; that some of the partners' comments were the product of stereotyping; and that the firm in no way disclaimed reliance on those particular comments, either in Hopkins' case or in the past. Certainly a plausible—and, one might say, inevitable—conclusion to draw from this set of circumstances is that the Policy Board in making its decision did in fact take into account all of the partners' comments, including the comments that were motivated by stereotypical notions about women's proper deportment. . . .

V

We hold that when a plaintiff in a Title VII case proves that her gender played a motivating part in an employment decision, the defendant may avoid a finding of liability only by proving by a preponderance of the evidence that it would have made the same decision even if it had not taken the plaintiff's gender into account. . . .

Justice O'CONNOR, concurring in the judgment.

I agree with the plurality that on the facts presented in this case, the burden of persuasion should shift to the employer to demonstrate by a preponderance of the evidence that it would have reached the same decision concerning Ann Hopkins' candidacy absent consideration of her gender. I further agree that this burden shift is properly part of the liability phase of the litigation. I thus concur in the judgment of the Court. My disagreement stems from the plurality's conclusions concerning the substantive requirement of causation under the statute and its broad statements regarding the applicability of the allocation of the burden of proof applied in this case. . . .

I

. . . The legislative history of Title VII bears out what its plain language suggests: a substantive violation of the statute only occurs when consideration of an illegitimate criterion is the "but-for" cause of an adverse employment action. The legislative history makes it clear that Congress was attempting to eradicate discriminatory actions in the employment setting, not mere discriminatory thoughts. Critics of the bill that became Title VII labeled it a "thought control bill," and argued that it created a "punishable crime that does not require an illegal external act as a basis for judgment." Senator Case . . . responded:

> The man must do or fail to do something in regard to employment. There must be some specific external act, more than a mental act. Only if he does the act because of the grounds stated in the bill would there be any legal consequences.

Thus, I disagree with the plurality's dictum that the words "because of" do not mean "but-for" causation; manifestly they do. We should not, and need not, deviate from that policy today. . . .

The evidence of congressional intent as to which party should bear the burden of proof on the issue of causation is considerably less clear. . . . [In the area of tort liability,] the law has long recognized that in certain "civil cases" leaving the burden of persuasion on the plaintiff to prove "but-for" causation would be both unfair and destructive of the deterrent purposes embodied in the concept of duty of care. Thus, in multiple causation cases, where a breach of duty has been established, the common law of torts has long shifted the burden of proof to multiple defendants to prove that their negligent actions were not the "but-for" cause of the plaintiff's injury.

See, e.g., Summers v. Tice, 199 P.2d 1 (Cal. 1948). The same rule has been applied where the effect of a defendant's tortious conduct combines with a force of unknown or innocent origin to produce the harm to the plaintiff. *See Kingston v. Chicago & N.W.R. Co.*, 211 N.W. 913, 915 (Wis. 1927). . . . *See also* 2 J. Wigmore, Select Cases on the Law of Torts, §153, p. 865 (1912). . . .

[At times, however, the but-for] "test demands the impossible. It challenges the imagination of the trier to probe into a purely fanciful and unknowable state of affairs. He is invited to make an estimate concerning facts that concededly never existed. The very uncertainty as to what might have happened opens the door wide for conjecture. But when conjecture is demanded it can be given a direction that is consistent with the policy considerations that underlie the controversy."

. . . There is no doubt that Congress considered reliance on gender or race in making employment decisions an evil in itself. . . . Reliance on such factors is exactly what the threat of Title VII liability was meant to deter. While the main concern of the statute was with employment opportunity, Congress was certainly not blind to the stigmatic harm which comes from being evaluated by a process which treats one as an inferior by reason of one's race or sex. . . . At the same time, Congress clearly conditioned legal liability on a determination that the consideration of an illegitimate factor caused a tangible employment injury of some kind.

Where an individual disparate treatment plaintiff has shown by a preponderance of the evidence that an illegitimate criterion was a substantial factor in an adverse employment decision, the deterrent purpose of the statute has clearly been triggered. More importantly, as an evidentiary matter, a reasonable factfinder could conclude that absent further explanation, the employer's discriminatory motivation "caused" the employment decision. The employer has not yet been shown to be a violator, but neither is it entitled to the same presumption of good faith concerning its employment decisions which is accorded employers facing only circumstantial evidence of discrimination. Both the policies behind the statute, and the evidentiary principles developed in the analogous area of causation in the law of torts, suggest that at this point the employer may be required to convince the factfinder that, despite the smoke, there is no fire. . . .

[The plurality, however, goes too far by holding that the burden shifts when "a decisional process is 'tainted' by awareness of sex or race in any way."] In my view, in order to justify shifting the burden on the issue of causation to the defendant, a disparate treatment plaintiff must show by direct evidence that an illegitimate criterion was a substantial factor in the decision. . . .

NOTES

1. *The Holding of* Price Waterhouse. Understanding the significance of *Price Waterhouse* is complicated by the lack of a majority opinion for the Court. There was a four-judge plurality opinion written by Justice Brennan with separate concurrences by Justices O'Connor and White. In such circumstances, the holding of the Court is said to be the narrowest point on which five justices concurring in the judgment agree. *See Marks v. United States*, 430 U.S. 188 (1977). Although Justice White had also concurred, the narrowest holding was generally accepted by the lower courts to be found in the opinion of Justice O'Connor.

To put it simply, the trial judge had found that Price Waterhouse had relied on Hopkins's gender in putting her application for partnership on "hold," but it also found that legitimate objections to plaintiff's interpersonal skills were a factor in the decision. The plurality held that in a situation where a defendant's motives were mixed—that is, where legitimate and illegitimate considerations were both present—a plaintiff need only prove by a preponderance of the evidence that her gender or other protected characteristic was "a motivating factor" for the challenged decision. Upon that showing, the burden of persuasion shifted to the defendant to avoid liability by proving as an affirmative defense that it would have made the same decision absent the discrimination.

If Justice O'Connor's concurrence controlled, it narrowed the plurality's rule in two ways: First, she raised the bar by requiring the plaintiff to show that the impermissible factor, such as plaintiff's sex, was a "substantial," not just a "motivating," factor. And, second, to trigger the *Price Waterhouse* shift in the burdens, she required plaintiff to introduce "direct" evidence of discrimination. Finding this concurrence to be the narrowest holding, the lower courts generally applied *Price Waterhouse* only when the plaintiff had sufficient direct evidence to determine that discrimination was a "substantial" factor. If the trier of fact so found, plaintiff would prevail unless defendant carried the burden of persuasion that it would have made the same decision even if the prohibited trait was not a substantial factor.

2. *Direct Evidence.* What is "direct" evidence anyway? If the term means anything, it refers to evidence that, if believed, would establish a fact at issue without the need to draw any inferences. In disparate treatment cases, the fact at issue is whether the employer relied on a prohibited characteristic in making its decision. An evidence purist would say that there can't be direct evidence of anyone's state of mind because intent is internal and beyond observation. *See generally* Charles A. Sullivan, *Accounting for* Price Waterhouse: *Proving Disparate Treatment Under Title VII*, 56 Brook. L. Rev. 1107 (1991). But as used by Justice O'Connor, "direct evidence" would seem to require a statement by the decision maker that showed he was motivated by illegitimate considerations with respect to the at-issue decision.

Analytically, this raises at least two questions. First, what did the decision maker actually say? The decision maker may, of course, testify as to his reasons. But testimony of out-of-court statements can be admissible even if the party allegedly making the statement now denies that he did so. *EEOC v. Warfield-Rohr Casket Co.*, 364 F.3d 160, 163-64 (4th Cir. 2004) ("[T]here is no requirement that an employee's testimony be corroborated in order to apply the mixed-motive framework."). Second, does the comment reflect illegitimate considerations? Obviously some comments are explicitly racist or sexist, but less explicit comments may also suffice. *Ash v. Tyson Foods, Inc.*, 546 U.S. 454 (2006), held that a manager's use of "boy" to refer to an African American man could reveal discriminatory intent: "The speaker's meaning may depend on various factors including context, inflection, tone of voice, local custom, and historical usage. Insofar as the Court of Appeals held that modifiers or qualifications are necessary in all instances to render the disputed term probative of bias, the court's decision is erroneous." *Id.* at 456; *see also McGinest v. GTE Serv. Corp.*, 360 F.3d 1103, 1116-17 (9th Cir. 2004) (the use of "code words" for race, like "drug dealer," can indicate discrimination). *But see Putman v. Unity Health Sys.*, 348 F.3d 732 (8th Cir. 2003) (comments about plaintiff not being "humble enough" and being "too prideful" not clearly linked to race). *See generally* Leora F. Eisenstadt, *The N-Word at Work: Contextualizing Language in the Workplace*, 33 Berkeley J. Emp. & Lab. L. 299, 303 (2012).

3. *Lower Court Confusion About "Direct" Evidence.* The circuits evolved a range of definitions of "direct evidence." Some courts read *Price Waterhouse* as applying only in cases involving "direct evidence," in the classic evidentiary sense of the term, that is, that the evidence proves the fact at issue without need to draw any inferences. A startling example is *Shorter v. ICG Holdings, Inc.*, 188 F.3d 1204 (10th Cir. 1999), which held that defendant's manager referring to plaintiff as an "incompetent nigger" within a day or two of having fired her was not direct evidence of discriminatory intent. The statement was merely a matter of personal opinion.

As we will see in the next principal case, however, "direct" evidence is no longer a meaningful category under Title VII, since the Supreme Court has held that the Civil Rights Act of 1991 overturned any requirement of direct evidence for what we have termed mixed-motive cases. And the Court's decision in *Gross v. FBL Fin. Servs.*, 557 U.S. 167 (2009), rejecting any "mixed-motive" burden-shifting under the ADEA altogether, rendered the concept of "direct" evidence inapplicable under that statute as a legal category. *See also Univ. of Texas Sw. Med. Ctr. v. Nassar*, 570 U.S. 338 (2013) ("motivating factor" causation not applicable to Title VII retaliation suits brought under §704(a); thus, there is no burden shifting in such cases even if there is "direct evidence"). However, the "directness" of the evidence at issue, that is, how closely it was linked to the decision in question and how probative it is of discriminatory motivation, can be expected to continue to influence courts in deciding more "gestalt" questions—such as whether a reasonable jury could find discrimination on the available evidence.

• **4.** *Causation.* Perhaps the most significant aspect of *Price Waterhouse* was the Court's conclusion that an employer could be liable even if the discriminatory intent *did not actually cause* an employment action. All that was necessary is that such intent be a "motivating factor." Even Justice O'Connor would impose liability without proof of causation where discriminatory intent was a "substantial factor." But this description of causation may be somewhat deceptive—for all these justices, if the employer established it would have made the same decision in any event, the employer is not liable. Thus, the plaintiff need not show but-for causation to win a judgment, but plaintiff will lose if the defendant shows no such causation. In that sense, *Price Waterhouse* can still be said to be consistent with *Biggins'* requirement that discrimination be a "determinative influence." After *Price Waterhouse*, the question was not so much causation as who proves causation.

• **5.** *No Harm, No Foul?* This requirement of causation, however, did not last long. Ironically, the one point on which all nine justices agreed in *Price Waterhouse*—that the discriminatory intent had to cause harm before Title VII liability attached—was legislatively rejected by the Civil Rights Act of 1991, which added a new §703(m), 42 U.S.C. §2000e-2(m). That section provides that "an unlawful employment practice is established when the complaining party demonstrates that race, color, religion, sex, or national origin was a motivating factor for any employment practice, even though other factors also motivated the practice." Thus, the "motivating factor" test of the *Price Waterhouse* plurality is accepted, as is the corollary of "mixed-motive" violations. Perhaps even more significant, the amendment also modifies *Price Waterhouse* by establishing that the plaintiff's proof of an illegitimate "motivating factor" does not merely shift the burden of proving no causation to the defendant, but actually establishes a violation, without regard to what the defendant can prove on rebuttal. "But-for" or "determinative factor" causation has been replaced by "motivating factor" causation. Precisely how strong a factor must be in order to count as motivating is unclear. *See* Martin J. Katz, *The Fundamental Incoherence of Title VII: Making Sense of Causation in Disparate Treatment Law*, 94 Geo. L.J. 489 (2006) (describing the concept as "minimal causation"). As we will see, both *Gross* and *Nassar* are predicated on the notion that "status discrimination" under Title VII is subject to a lesser causal standard than but-for.

Nevertheless, the 1991 statute offers an opportunity for defendants to limit plaintiff's remedies even if a violation has been established. Section 706(g), 42 U.S.C. §2000e-5(g), now provides that, in §703(m) cases, if a respondent can "demonstrate" that it "would have taken the same action in the absence of the impermissible motivating factor," plaintiff's remedies are limited. Thus, a court

> (i) may grant declaratory relief, injunctive relief (except as provided in clause (ii)), and attorney's fees and costs demonstrated to be directly attributable only to the pursuit of a claim under section 703(m); and (ii) shall not award damages or issue an order requiring any admission, reinstatement, hiring, promotion, or payment. . . .

In such a situation, then, the plaintiff is essentially limited to a declaration of defendant's liability plus attorney's fees. She is not entitled to any monetary damages. While this scheme continues to govern discrimination cases under Title VII, the Supreme Court rejected such analysis for the ADEA in *Gross v. FBL Fin. Servs.*, 557 U.S. 167 (2009), where plaintiff's burden is to prove that age was a determinative factor in all cases. Further, *University of Texas Southwestern Medical Center v. Nassar*, 133 S. Ct. 2517 (2013), held that "motivating factor" causation is not applicable to Title VII retaliation suits brought under §704(a) since §703(m) was limited to "status" discrimination claims under §703; thus, there is no burden shifting even if there is "direct evidence." Requiring but-for causation can make an enormous difference in the outcome of case even when there are statements admitting bias. *E.g.*, *Arthur v. Pet Dairy*, 593 F. App'x 211, 221 (4th Cir. 2015); *Johnson v. Securitas Sec. Servs. USA, Inc.*, 769 F.3d 605, 614 (8th Cir. 2014). *Gross* and *Nassar* also suggest that but-for causation is likely to be the plaintiff's burden under statutes that do not explicitly require otherwise, such as the ADA, *e.g.*, *Lewis v. Humboldt Acquisition Corp.*, 681 F.3d 312 (6th Cir. 2012) (en banc) (ADA suit requires determinative factor proof); *Serwatka v. Rockwell Automation, Inc.*, 591 F.3d 957 (7th Cir. 2010) (same), even though some have argued that the ADA's incorporation by reference of VII procedures and remedies requires a different result under that statute. *See* Catherine T. Struve, *Shifting Burdens: Discrimination Law Through the Lens of Jury Instruction*, 51 B.C. L. Rev. 279 (2010).

• **6.** *No Blacks Need Apply.* Suppose an employer places a sign outside its personnel office, saying, "No blacks need apply." Is that a violation of §703? Surprisingly, the plurality opinion in *Price Waterhouse* suggests that the answer is "not necessarily" because the sign might not be a causative factor in any particular decision. What is the law now that §703(m) and (g) have been added? Wouldn't a plaintiff still need to prove that race was a motivating factor in denying her a job in order to establish a violation?

• **7.** *Expert Testimony on Stereotyping and Cognitive Bias.* Can expert testimony be used to prove that ambiguous comments reflect bias? What were the various views in *Price Waterhouse* about Dr. Susan Fiske? In his dissent, Justice Kennedy wrote that "Fiske purported to discern stereotyping in comments that were gender neutral— e.g., 'overbearing and abrasive'—without any knowledge of the comments' basis in reality and without having met the speaker or subject." Is this criticism valid? May not certain statements be susceptible of varying meanings, with expert testimony helping the factfinder in deciding whether the statements are likely to reflect stereotyping? *See generally* Tristin K. Green, *"It's Not You, It's Me": Assessing an Emerging Relationship Between Law and Social Science*, 46 CONN. L. REV. 287 (2013); Melissa Hart & Paul M. Secunda, *A Matter of Context: Social Framework Evidence in Employment Discrimination Class Actions*, 78 FORDHAM L. REV. 37 (2009); David L. Faigman, Nilanjana Dasgupta, & Cecilia L. Ridgeway, *A Matter of Fit: The Law of Discrimination and the Science of Implicit Bias*, 59 HASTINGS L. J. 1389, 1426-27 (2008). More recently, there have been doubts expressed about the implicit bias narrative. Michael Selmi, *The Paradox of Implicit Bias and a Plea for a New Narrative*, 50 ARIZ. ST. L.J. 193 (2018); Samuel R. Bagenstos, *Implicit Bias's Failure*, BERKELEY J. EMPL. & LABOR L. (forthcoming 2018).

* * *

The plurality in *Price Waterhouse* noted that at "some point in the proceedings . . . the District Court must decide whether a particular case involves mixed motives." 490 U.S. at 247 n.12. At what point in the trial does this decision take place? How would you prepare jury instructions on *McDonnell Douglas/Burdine* and *Price Waterhouse*? If the instructions accurately stated the law, would jurors be likely to understand them? The next case might help.

≡ ### *Desert Palace, Inc. v. Costa*
≡ *539 U.S. 90 (2003)*

Justice THOMAS delivered the opinion of the Court.

The question before us in this case is whether a plaintiff must present direct evidence of discrimination in order to obtain a mixed-motive instruction under Title VII of the Civil Rights Act of 1964, as amended by the Civil Rights Act of 1991. We hold that direct evidence is not required.

I

A

Since 1964, Title VII has made it an "unlawful employment practice for an employer . . . to discriminate against any individual . . ., *because of* such individual's race, color, religion, sex, or national origin." (Emphasis added.) In *Price Waterhouse v. Hopkins*, the Court considered whether an employment decision is made "because of" sex in a "mixed-motive" case, *i.e.*, where both legitimate and illegitimate reasons motivated the decision. The Court concluded that, under §2000e-2(a)(1), an employer could "avoid a finding of liability . . . by proving that it would have made the same decision even if it had not allowed gender to play such a role." The Court was divided, however, over the predicate question of when the burden of proof may be shifted to an employer to prove the affirmative defense.

Justice Brennan, writing for a plurality of four Justices, would have held that "when a plaintiff . . . proves that her gender played a *motivating* part in an employment decision, the defendant may avoid a finding of liability only by proving by a preponderance of the evidence that it would have made the same decision even if it had not taken the plaintiff's gender into account." The plurality did not, however, "suggest a limitation on the possible ways of proving that [gender] stereotyping played a motivating role in an employment decision."

Justice White and Justice O'Connor both concurred in the judgment. Justice White would have held that the case was governed by *Mt. Healthy City Bd. of Ed. v. Doyle*, 429 U.S. 274 (1977), and would have shifted the burden to the employer only when a plaintiff "showed that the unlawful motive was a *substantial* factor in the adverse employment action." Justice O'Connor, like Justice White, would have required the plaintiff to show that an illegitimate consideration was a "substantial factor" in the employment decision. But, under Justice O'Connor's view, "the burden on the issue of causation" would shift to the employer only where "a disparate treatment plaintiff [could] show by *direct evidence* that an illegitimate criterion was a substantial factor in the decision."

Two years after *Price Waterhouse*, Congress passed the 1991 Act "in large part [as] a response to a series of decisions of this Court interpreting the Civil Rights Acts of 1866 and 1964." *Landgraf v. USI Film Products*, 511 U.S. 244 (1994). In particular, §107 of the 1991 Act, which is at issue in this case, "responded" to *Price Waterhouse* by "setting forth standards applicable in 'mixed motive' cases" in two new statutory provisions.[1] [The Court quoted §2000e-2(m).] The second [§ 706(g)(2)(B)] provides that, with respect to "'a claim in which an individual proves a violation under section 2000e-2(m),'" the employer has a limited affirmative defense that does not absolve it of liability, but restricts the remedies available to a plaintiff. The available remedies include only declaratory relief, certain types of injunctive relief, and attorney's fees and costs. In order to avail itself of the affirmative defense, the employer must "demonstrate that [it] would have taken the same action in the absence of the impermissible motivating factor."

Since the passage of the 1991 Act, the Courts of Appeals have divided over whether plaintiff must prove by direct evidence that an impermissible consideration was a "motivating factor" in an adverse employment action. Relying primarily on Justice O'Connor's concurrence in Price Waterhouse, a number of courts have held that direct evidence is required to establish liability under §2000e-2(m). In the decision below, however, the Ninth Circuit concluded otherwise.

B

Petitioner Desert Palace, Inc., dba Caesar's Palace Hotel & Casino of Las Vegas, Nevada, employed respondent Catharina Costa as a warehouse worker and heavy equipment operator. Respondent was the only woman in this job and in her local Teamsters bargaining unit.

Respondent experienced a number of problems with management and her co-workers that led to an escalating series of disciplinary sanctions, including informal rebukes, a denial of privileges, and suspension. Petitioner finally terminated respondent after she was involved in a physical altercation in a warehouse elevator with fellow

---

1. This case does not require us to decide when, if ever, §107 applies outside of the mixed-motive context.

Teamsters member Herbert Gerber. Petitioner disciplined both employees because the facts surrounding the incident were in dispute, but Gerber, who had a clean disciplinary record, received only a 5-day suspension.

. . . At trial, respondent presented evidence that (1) she was singled out for "intense 'stalking'" by one of her supervisors, (2) she received harsher discipline than men for the same conduct, (3) she was treated less favorably than men in the assignment of overtime, and (4) supervisors repeatedly "stacked" her disciplinary record and "frequently used or tolerated" sex-based slurs against her.

Based on this evidence, the District Court denied petitioner's motion for judgment as a matter of law, and submitted the case to the jury with instructions, two of which are relevant here. First, without objection from petitioner, the District Court instructed the jury that "the plaintiff has the burden of proving . . . by a preponderance of the evidence" that she "suffered adverse work conditions" and that her sex "was a motivating factor in any such work conditions imposed upon her."

Second, the District Court gave the jury the following mixed-motive instruction:

> You have heard evidence that the defendant's treatment of the plaintiff was motivated by the plaintiff's sex and also by other lawful reasons. If you find that the plaintiff's sex was a motivating factor in the defendant's treatment of the plaintiff, the plaintiff is entitled to your verdict, even if you find that the defendant's conduct was also motivated by a lawful reason.
>
> However, if you find that the defendant's treatment of the plaintiff was motivated by both gender and lawful reasons, you must decide whether the plaintiff is entitled to damages. The plaintiff is entitled to damages unless the defendant proves by a preponderance of the evidence that the defendant would have treated plaintiff similarly even if the plaintiff's gender had played no role in the employment decision.

Petitioner unsuccessfully objected to this instruction, claiming that respondent had failed to adduce "direct evidence" that sex was a motivating factor in her dismissal or in any of the other adverse employment actions taken against her. The jury rendered a verdict for respondent, awarding backpay, compensatory damages, and punitive damages. The District Court denied petitioner's renewed motion for judgment as a matter of law. . . .

II

This case provides us with the first opportunity to consider the effects of the 1991 Act on jury instructions in mixed-motive cases. Specifically, we must decide whether a plaintiff must present direct evidence of discrimination in order to obtain a mixed-motive instruction under 42 U.S.C. §2000e-2(m). Petitioner's argument on this point proceeds in three steps: (1) Justice O'Connor's opinion is the holding of *Price Waterhouse*; (2) Justice O'Connor's *Price Waterhouse* opinion requires direct evidence of discrimination before a mixed-motive instruction can be given; and (3) the 1991 Act does nothing to abrogate that holding. Like the Court of Appeals, we see no need to address which of the opinions in *Price Waterhouse* is controlling: the third step of petitioner's argument is flawed, primarily because it is inconsistent with the text of §2000e-2(m).

Our precedents make clear that the starting point for our analysis is the statutory text. And where, as here, the words of the statute are unambiguous, the "judicial inquiry is complete." Section 2000e-2(m) unambiguously states that a plaintiff need only "demonstrate" that an employer used a forbidden consideration with respect to "any employment practice." On its face, the statute does not mention, much less require, that a plaintiff make a heightened showing through direct evidence. Indeed, petitioner concedes as much.

Moreover, Congress explicitly defined the term "demonstrates" in the 1991 Act, leaving little doubt that no special evidentiary showing is required. Title VII defines the term "'demonstrates'" as to "meet the burdens of production and persuasion." §2000e(m). If Congress intended the term "'demonstrates'" to require that the "burdens of production and persuasion" be met by direct evidence or some other heightened showing, it could have made that intent clear by including language to that effect in §2000e(m). Its failure to do so is significant, for Congress has been unequivocal when imposing heightened proof requirements in other circumstances, including in other provisions of Title 42 . . . 42 U.S.C. §5851(b)(3)(D) (providing that "relief may not be ordered" against an employer in retaliation cases involving whistleblowers under the Atomic Energy Act where the employer is able to "*demonstrate by clear and convincing evidence* that it would have taken the same unfavorable personnel action in the absence of such behavior") (emphasis added); *cf. Price Waterhouse* ("Only rarely have we required clear and convincing proof where the action defended against seeks only conventional relief.").

In addition, Title VII's silence with respect to the type of evidence required in mixed-motive cases also suggests that we should not depart from the "conventional rule of civil litigation [that] generally applies in Title VII cases." That rule requires a plaintiff to prove his case "by a preponderance of the evidence," using "direct or circumstantial evidence," *Postal Service Bd. of Governors v. Aikens*, 460 U.S. 711, 714, n.3 (1983). We have often acknowledged the utility of circumstantial evidence in discrimination cases. For instance, in *Reeves v. Sanderson Plumbing Products, Inc.* we recognized that evidence that a defendant's explanation for an employment practice is "unworthy of credence" is "one form of *circumstantial evidence* that is probative of intentional discrimination." (emphasis added). The reason for treating circumstantial and direct evidence alike is both clear and deep-rooted: "Circumstantial evidence is not only sufficient, but may also be more certain, satisfying and persuasive than direct evidence." *Rogers v. Missouri Pacific R. Co.*, 352 U.S. 500, 508, n.17 (1957). . . .

For the reasons stated above, we agree with the Court of Appeals that no heightened showing is required under §2000e-2(m).

In order to obtain an instruction under §2000e-2(m), a plaintiff need only present sufficient evidence for a reasonable jury to conclude, by a preponderance of the evidence, that "race, color, religion, sex, or national origin was a motivating factor for any employment practice." Because direct evidence of discrimination is not required in mixed-motive cases, the Court of Appeals correctly concluded that the District Court did not abuse its discretion in giving a mixed-motive instruction to the jury. Accordingly, the judgment of the Court of Appeals is affirmed. . . .

[Justice O'CONNOR, concurred, agreeing that the evidentiary rule she urged in Price Waterhouse had been superseded by the Civil Rights Act of 1991.]

NOTES

1. *What Was the Fuss About?* If you were a newcomer to discrimination law and had not been steeped in the intricacies of *McDonnell Douglas* and *Price Waterhouse*

proof structures, you might wonder what all the fuss was about in *Desert Palace* and why the Court was so focused on questions of proof more than 40 years after Title VII was enacted. After all, what is so remarkable about a case holding that "[i]n order to obtain an instruction under §2000e-2(m), a plaintiff need only present sufficient evidence for a reasonable jury to conclude, by a preponderance of the evidence, that 'race, color, religion, sex, or national origin was a motivating factor for any employment practice.'"? This seems simple to the point of banality.

However, having struggled with the prior cases, you should understand *Desert Palace's* potential significance. Congress had modified *Price Waterhouse* in 1991 by adopting Justice Brennan's "motivating factor" articulation of plaintiff's burden and, indeed, expanded on the plurality's holding by providing that plaintiff's proof of a motivating factor was sufficient for liability. While, as under *Price Waterhouse*, defendant could still carry its same decision burden, the 1991 amendments narrowed that defense to reducing plaintiff's remedies.

Congress, however, did not explicitly address Justice O'Connor's "direct" evidence threshold for applying this method of analysis, and the lower courts generally continued to require some version of "direct evidence" in order to trigger *Price Waterhouse* burden-shifting. In this light, the significance of *Desert Palace* is to eliminate the direct evidence barrier to burden-shifting and avoid the complicated inquiry into whether evidence is sufficiently "direct." If a plaintiff can prove, by any kind of evidence, that a particular factor motivated the at-issue decision, the plaintiff prevails—although the defendant may limit the plaintiff's remedies if it establishes it would have made the same decision anyway.

2. *Have O'Connor's Worst Fears Been Realized?* In *Price Waterhouse*, Justice O'Connor expressed concern about not imposing liability on the employer, or even shifting a burden of persuasion, because of inconclusive indications of discrimination:

> Thus, stray remarks in the workplace . . . cannot justify requiring the employer to prove that its hiring or promotion decisions were based on legitimate criteria. Nor can statements by nondecisionmakers, or statements by decisionmakers unrelated to the decisional process itself suffice to satisfy the plaintiff's burden in this regard. In addition, in my view testimony such as Dr. Fiske's in this case, standing alone, would not justify shifting the burden of persuasion to the employer. Race and gender always "play a role" in an employment decision in the benign sense that these are human characteristics of which decisionmakers are aware and may comment on in a perfectly neutral and nondiscriminatory fashion. For example, in the context of this case, a mere reference to "a lady candidate" might show that gender "played a role" in the decision, but by no means could support a rational factfinder's inference that the decision was made "because of" sex. What is required is what Ann Hopkins showed here: direct evidence that decisionmakers placed substantial negative reliance on an illegitimate criterion in reaching their decision.

After *Desert Palace*, can "stray remarks" create a jury question on motivating factor? *See generally* Michael J. Zimmer, *A Chain of Inferences Proving Discrimination*, 79 U. COLO. L. REV. 4 (2008) ("Direct, direct-lite, or circumstantial evidence" (or any combination) can be used to prove individual disparate treatment discrimination; discriminatory motivation can be shown by unequal treatment, defendant's admissions that it discriminated, actions based on stereotypes, and the *McDonnell Douglas* approach); *see also* Kerri Lynn Stone, *Shortcuts in Employment Discrimination Law*, 56 ST. LOUIS U. L.J. 111 (2011).

3. *Does* Desert Palace *End* McDonnell Douglas? While *Desert Palace* eliminates direct evidence as a precondition to what used to be called a *Price Waterhouse* case, is it even more radical? Does it eliminate the whole *McDonnell Douglas* proof structure? *Desert Palace* can be read narrowly. For example, footnote 1 indicates that the Court was not deciding the impact of this decision "outside of the mixed-motive context." But prior to *Desert Palace*, one boundary between *Price Waterhouse* and *McDonnell Douglas* was "direct" evidence. With direct evidence gone, have the two proof structures been collapsed into one?

After *Price Waterhouse*, the distinction between the *Price Waterhouse* and *McDonnell Douglas* cases had been framed in two ways. First, *Price Waterhouse* governed "direct evidence" cases, while *McDonnell Douglas* applied to "circumstantial evidence" proof. Second, *Price Waterhouse* involved "mixed motives," while *McDonnell Douglas* involved a single motive. If circumstantial evidence can be used to prove liability using §703(m)'s "motivating factor" standard of liability, such cases can no longer be viewed as a "direct" evidence proof structure in contrast to *McDonnell Douglas's* "circumstantial" or "indirect" evidence structure.

What about "single motive" vs. "mixed motives"? Finding a "single motive" based on the process of elimination is the core of *McDonnell Douglas*—plaintiff proves that the most obvious nondiscriminatory reasons do not apply to her case, thereby establishing a prima facie case; defendant introduces evidence of a nondiscriminatory reason in rebuttal; plaintiff then introduces evidence that defendant's reason is not the true reason in order to establish that such a reason is a pretext for discrimination. This process leads to the factfinder thinking about the case as an either/or proposition: either the defendant's reason explains the decision or the plaintiff's claim of discrimination explains it. That makes the method seem to be about "single motives." However, *Price Waterhouse* also noted that Congress did not establish a sole cause standard under Title VII, and even under the most restrictive schemes, the plaintiff need only establish but-for or determinative factor causation, not that no other motive was involved. Thus, under *Gross* or *Nassar*, the plaintiff wins even if the factfinder finds that another reason is involved, as long as discrimination is the but-for reason. Is that possible in a traditional *McDonnell Douglas* case? Has describing *McDonnell Douglas* as involving a "single motive" always been metaphorical?

St. Mary's Honor Center v. Hicks may shed some light here. As you will recall, in *Hicks*, the trial had determined that personal animosity, not discrimination, explained the adverse decision, even though the individual defendant denied such animosity. Thus, the court found a fact claimed by neither party. The narrow holding of *Hicks* is that disbelief of the supposed nondiscriminatory reason was not necessarily sufficient: The trier had to find not merely that the defendant's reason was pretextual but that it was a pretext for discrimination. But the broader holding of the case is that the trier of fact can make any determination justified by the record before it. This would seem to point toward letting the jury reach the motivating factor question even in a pure *McDonnell Douglas* setting if the factfinder so determined from the record. A jury could find that both impermissible and permissible reasons motivated a decision, even though the parties each claim only one motivation—plaintiff's claim of discrimination and defendant's claim of a nondiscriminatory reason. Thus, after *Desert Palace*, a jury could disbelieve both plaintiff's claim that discrimination entirely explained the challenged decision and defendant's claim that nondiscrimination entirely explained it.

586 9. *Antidiscrimination*

But even if that's true, such that a jury would be free to find mixed motive liability in a case litigated under the *McDonnell Douglas* structure, *McDonnell Douglas* may still survive *Desert Palace* for other reasons. When faced with a motion for summary judgment, can't plaintiffs still rely on the process of elimination of nondiscriminatory reasons that then supports the drawing of an inference that the reason for defendant's action was discrimination? If so, *McDonnell Douglas* appears to live, at least at that procedural level. Can plaintiff use this process of elimination argument before the jury?

After *Desert Palace*, the Seventh Circuit restructured its analysis in terms of the "indirect" and "direct methods of proof." The indirect method is *McDonnell Douglas*. The direct method is either "direct evidence," of discriminatory motivation, such as admissions by the employer, or a " 'convincing mosaic' of circumstantial evidence" that would justify that inference without the employer's admission. *Coleman v. Donahoe*, 667 F.3d 835, 860, (7th Cir. 2012) (citations and internal quotations omitted). Although numerous cases, both in the Seventh Circuit and elsewhere, deployed that language, a recent Seventh Circuit panel rejected the view that that "convincing mosaic" was a legal test. *Ortiz v. Werner Enters., Inc.*, 834 F.3d 760, 765 (7th Cir. 2016), held that the real question is "simply whether the evidence would permit a reasonable factfinder to conclude that the plaintiff's [protected class] caused the discharge or other adverse employment action." Further, "[e]vidence must be considered as a whole, rather than asking whether any particular piece of evidence proves the case by itself-or whether just the 'direct' evidence does so, or the 'indirect' evidence. Evidence is evidence. Relevant evidence must be considered and irrelevant evidence disregarded, but no evidence should be treated differently from other evidence because it can be labeled 'direct' or 'indirect.' "

4. *Splitting the Baby. Desert Palace* seems to favor plaintiffs because it lowers the requirements for access to the lower "motivating factor" causal standard. But is there a downside for them? While §703(m) provides the "motivating factor" standard for liability, it is subject to §706(g)(2)(B)'s same decision defense. On the one hand, a jury finding that defendant discriminated may be unlikely to believe defendant's proof that it would have made the same decision even if it had not discriminated; on the other, a jury may be tempted to "split the baby," that is, accept both the plaintiff's proof that discrimination was a motivating factor *and* the defendant's proof that it would have made the same decision regardless. That would substantially limit the remedies plaintiff would get. Some have cautioned about the professional responsibility tensions this situation creates—the prospect of attorneys' fees for the plaintiff's lawyer and no recovery at all for the plaintiff. *Coe v. N. Pipe Prods., Inc.*, 589 F. Supp. 2d 1055, 1098 (N.D. Iowa 2008).

5. *Lower Courts and Commentators.* Will the lower courts continue to maintain the single-versus-mixed-motive distinction after *Desert Palace*? So far, they have been reluctant to inter so long-standing and influential a doctrine as the *McDonnell Douglas* framework, although they have not persuasively justified its survival. One recent decision, *Quigg v. Thomas County School District*, 814 F.3d 1227, (11th Cir. 2016), summarized the problem and the different approaches among the circuits. It began by noting that the *McDonnell Douglas* "framework is fatally inconsistent with the mixed-motive theory of discrimination because the framework is predicated on proof of a single, 'true reason' for an adverse action." . . . Thus, if an employee cannot rebut her employer's proffered reasons for an adverse action but offers evidence demonstrating that the employer also relied on a forbidden consideration, she will not meet her burden. Yet, this is the exact type of employee that the mixed-motive theory of discrimination is designed to protect." *Id.* at 1237-38.

Quigg relied heavily on *White v. Baxter Healthcare Corp.*, 533 F.3d 381 (6th Cir. 2008), but found support for rejecting the application of *McDonnell Douglas* to a mixed motive case in four other circuits to consider the issue," citing, *e.g.*, *Holcomb v. Iona Coll.*, 521 F.3d 130 (2d Cir. 2008); *Makky v. Chertoff*, 541 F.3d 205, 214 (3d Cir. 2008). Four more circuits allow plaintiffs employees to survive a motion for summary judgment either through *McDonnell Douglas* or "by simply showing a genuine issue of material fact exists as to whether an illegal reason was a motivating factor in an adverse action." *E.g.*, *McGinest v. GTE Serv. Corp.*, 360 F.3d 1103 (9th Cir. 2004); *Fogg v. Gonzales*, 492 F.3d 447, 451 (D.C. Cir. 2007). Indeed, "the Eighth Circuit is alone in holding that, post-*Desert Palace*, the *McDonnell Douglas* approach must be applied in the present context." *See Griffith v. City of Des Moines*, 387 F.3d 733 (8th Cir. 2004).

As for the appropriate rule, *Quigg* adopted the framework put forth by the Sixth Circuit in *White*, which had held that

> to survive a defendant's motion for summary judgment, a Title VII plaintiff asserting a mixed-motive claim need only produce evidence sufficient to convince a jury that: (1) the defendant took an adverse employment action against the plaintiff; and (2) "race, color, religion, sex, or national origin was a *motivating factor*" for the defendant's adverse employment action. 42 U.S.C. §2000e-2(m) (emphasis added). This burden of producing some evidence in support of a mixed-motive claim is not onerous and should preclude sending the case to the jury only where the record is devoid of evidence that could reasonably be construed to support the plaintiff's claim. [It] is irrelevant, for purposes of a summary judgment determination, whether the plaintiff has presented direct or circumstantial evidence in support of the mixed-motive claim, *see Desert Palace*.

533 F.3d at 400 (citations omitted). Nevertheless, both *Quigg*, 814 F.3d at 1238 n.7 and *White*, 533 F.3d at 400 n.10, viewed this approach as inapplicable to single-motive cases.

This is contrary to the commentators, who, at the time, generally read *Desert Palace* as destroying *McDonnell Douglas*, in effect if not in theory. *E.g.*, Michael J. Zimmer, *The New Discrimination Law:* Price Waterhouse *Is Dead, Whither* McDonnell Douglas?, 53 EMORY L. J. 1887 (2004); Kenneth R. Davis, Price-*Fixing: Refining the* Price Waterhouse *Standard and Individual Disparate Treatment Law*, 31 FLA. ST. U. L. REV. 859, 861 (2004); William R. Corbett, McDonnell Douglas, *1973-2003: May You Rest in Peace?*, 6 U. PA. J. LAB. & EMP. L. 199, 212-13 (2003); Henry L. Chambers, Jr., *The Effect of Eliminating Distinctions Among Title VII Disparate Treatment Cases*, 57 SMU L. REV. 83, 102-3 (2004).

Even if the commentators are correct and *McDonnell Douglas* is doctrinally no longer required, the case law applying it will continue to have utility. And it certainly is true that *McDonnell Douglas* continues to be cited in decision after decision. Even if a court *need* no longer pursue the three-step ritual, it will still have to decide whether evidence of a motivating discriminatory reason is sufficient for a jury to find for plaintiff. This includes assessing whatever evidence the plaintiff adduces to exclude the nondiscriminatory reasons—whether those would have been the "most common" legitimate reasons that in the past were negated as part of plaintiff's prima facie case or the more specific reason articulated in defendant's case. While plaintiff will not need to exclude all potential nondiscriminatory reasons, she may have to cast sufficient doubt on innocent reasons to allow the jury to find in her favor by a preponderance of the evidence that an impermissible reason was a motivating factor. Some would say that this is *McDonnell Douglas* in substance if not form.

In practice, then, we might expect to see courts continue to use the *McDonnell Douglas/Reeves* structure as a way of implementing the more gestalt "sufficient evidence" approach of *Desert Palace*. But a court that wished to save itself time in granting summary judgment to defendant might summarize the evidence and conclude that it was not sufficient for a reasonable jury to find intent to discriminate motivating the challenged decision. Nevertheless, such a court would be well advised to find "sufficient evidence" in a case such as *Reeves*, where the Supreme Court has held that proof of a prima facie case plus proof of pretext will generally be sufficient at least to allow the trier of fact to decide that discrimination occurred.

Note on Discrimination in Complex Organizations

While disparate treatment is often discussed in terms of the intent of the "employer," employers typically are corporations or other business organizations, and employment decisions in such entities pose complications for discrimination law. Recall Pohasky (in *Slack*). He was biased, but he was not the actual decision maker in the challenged terminations—that was Gary Helming, "plaintiff's general supervisor." We do not know whether Helming was biased, or even aware of Pohasky's bias. What's the law to do about this situation, that is, where the ultimate decision maker is unbiased but is influenced by a biased subordinate? Often described as cat's paw or subordinate bias liability, the question is increasingly important.

The Supreme Court first addressed this "cat's paw"* question in *Staub v. Proctor Hospital*, 562 U.S. 411 (2011). That case arose under the Uniformed Services Employment and Reemployment Rights Act of 1994, but it is likely to have its primary effect under Title VII since it has a structure similar to Title VII's 703(m) in that an employer violates USERRA when uniformed service membership is "a motivating factor in the employer's action, unless the employer can prove that the action would have been taken in the absence of such membership." *Id*. at 416-17.

Plaintiff Staub, a member of the United States Army Reserve, claimed to have been fired because of the actions of his immediate supervisor and her supervisor. He presented strong evidence that the two were hostile to Staub's military obligations. A series of disagreements over his performance, which plaintiff claimed were pretextual, culminated in his discharge. The decision to fire Staub was made by Linda Buck, Proctor's vice president of human resources but based on information provided by the two supervisors. Before the discharge, however, Buck reviewed Staub's personnel file; after the discharge, she reviewed the matter again when Staub challenged his

---

* The term "cat's paw" was introduced into the discrimination lexicon by Judge Posner in *Shager v. Upjohn Co.*, 913 F.2d 398, 405 (7th Cir, 1990). He derived it from an Aesop fable, put into verse by La Fontaine in 1679. In the fable, a monkey induces a cat to pull roasting chestnuts from the fire. The cat does so, burning its paws, while the monkey makes off with the chestnuts. How accurately the fable maps onto the employment situation is less clear, other than that the decision maker is in some sense duped.

firing through Proctor's grievance process. At trial, Staub did not claim that Buck had any hostility to his military service but rather that the two supervisors did, and that their actions influenced Buck's ultimate employment decision. A jury found that Staub's "military status was a motivating factor in [the] decision to discharge him." *Id*. at 415.

In a very complicated opinion (on which *see* Charles A. Sullivan, *Tortifying Employment Discrimination*, 62 B.U. L. Rev. 1431 (2012), which distinguished between "intent" (in the sense of desire to cause a particular outcome) and "motive" (in the sense of bias)), the Court concluded with a relatively straightforward rule:

> We therefore hold that if a supervisor performs an act motivated by antimilitary animus that is *intended* by the supervisor to cause an adverse employment action, and if that act is a proximate cause of the ultimate employment action, then the employer is liable. . . .

Id. at 422.

Since both intent and motive must exist, the absence of the requisite intent is fatal even if bias is present. Thus, "an unfavorable entry on the plaintiff's personnel record was caused to be put there, with discriminatory animus" will not establish the tort if there was no intent to cause Staub's dismissal. *Id*. at 417-18; *see also Cherry v. Siemens Healthcare Diagnostics, Inc.*, 829 F.3d 974 (8th Cir. 2016) (no cat's paw liability when the supervisor, even if racially motivated in his negative performance evaluation, did not know of the planned reduction in force and therefore could not have intended the resultant adverse employment action). "Intent" in this context "denotes that the actor desires to cause consequences of his act, or that he believes that the consequences are substantially certain to result from it." Under traditional tort law, "'intent' . . . denote[s] that the actor desires to cause consequences of his act, or that he believes that the consequences are substantially certain to result from it." 562 U.S. at 422 n.3.

Further, if motive and intent reside in a lower level individual, the plaintiff must still show that that individual's conduct caused the resulting adverse action. Exactly what the notion of "proximate" cause adds to the analysis in this context is unclear, *see* Charles A. Sullivan, *Tortifying Employment*, 92 B.U. L. Rev. 1431 (2012); Sandra F. Sperino, *Discrimination Statutes, the Common Law, and Proximate Cause*, 2013 U. Ill. L. Rev. 1 (2013); Sandra F. Sperino, *Statutory Proximate Cause*, 88 Notre Dame L. Rev. 1199 (2013), but the Court stressed that "[w]e do not think that the ultimate decisionmaker's exercise of judgment automatically renders the link to the supervisor's bias 'remote' or 'purely contingent.' The decisionmaker's exercise of judgment is *also* a proximate cause of the employment decision, but it is common for injuries to have multiple proximate causes." *Id*. at 419-20.

The Court rejected a hard-and-fast rule that, even if the decision maker's mere exercise of independent judgment did not break the causal link, her "independent investigation (and rejection) of the employee's allegations of discriminatory animus ought to do so." *Id*. at 420. That is because "the supervisor's biased report may remain a causal factor if the independent investigation takes it into account without determining that the adverse action was, apart from the supervisor's recommendation, entirely justified." *Id*. at 421. However, subsequent courts have frequently found the causal chain broken by what is described as independent investigations. *See Sami v. Detroit Med. Ctr.*, 591 F. App'x 419, 426-27 (6th Cir. 2014); *Lobato v. N.M. Env't Dep't*, 733 F.3d 1283, 1296 (10th Cir. 2013).

In a footnote, the Court confined its opinion to situations where a supervisor's actions would be imputed to the employer under traditional agency principles. *Id.* at 422 n.4. Further, it did not pass on "whether the employer would be liable if a co-worker, rather than a supervisor, committed a discriminatory act that influenced the ultimate employment decision." *Id.* That footnote also noted that "Staub took advantage of Proctor's grievance process, and we express no view as to whether Proctor would have an affirmative defense if he did not." *Id.*

Thus, *Staub* resolves many cat's paw questions, and the lower courts have applied its analysis in a number of cases. However, the decision leaves important issues unresolved including the meaning of proximate cause in the discrimination context, the extent to which subordinate bias liability may flow from the actions of co-workers, *see Smyth-Riding v. Scis. & Eng'g Servs., LLC*, 699 F. App'x 146, 156 (4th Cir. 2017) ("To extend cat's paw liability to influence by co-workers 'would constitute an expansion of the theory to a context in which its application has not been recognized'"), and whether a grievance or other alert to the possibility of discrimination might be required of the plaintiff to trigger such liability. Whatever the answer to those questions, it is clear that the plaintiff must be able to at least establish but-for causation between the actions of the biased individual and those of the final decisionmaker. *See EEOC v. DynMcdermott Petroleum Operations Co.*, 537 F. App'x 437 (5th Cir. 2013) (fact that one manager was the cat's paw of another could be inferred from the former's influence or leverage over the latter given his power over discipline and compensation); *Sharp v. Aker Plant Servs. Grp., Inc.*, 726 F.3d 789, 797 (6th Cir. 2013) (although a manager was not the ultimate decision maker, those who were relied solely on his forced rankings and recommendation of who could be fired without disrupting current projects, and there was no process to scrub any bias).

However, what questions it left unanswered, the impact of *Staub* may have been drastically limited by a subsequent decision. Recall that *Staub* addressed the influence of "supervisors" on ultimate decision makers, and only two years after *Staub* was decided, the Court handed down *Vance v. Ball State University*, 570 U.S. 421, 424 (2013), which held that "an employee is a 'supervisor' for purposes of vicarious liability under Title VII if he or she is empowered by the employer to take tangible employment actions against the victim. . . ." The Court rejected the lower court cases taking "the more open-ended approach advocated by the EEOC's Enforcement Guidance, which ties supervisor status to the ability to exercise significant direction over another's daily work." *Id.* at 431.

If the *Vance* approach applies to the *Staub* scenario, the *Staub* holding will shrink in significance. To appreciate this, consider that it is not so clear that the two "supervisors" whose intent and motive were proximate causes of Staub's discharge by Buck, would qualify as supervisors under *Vance*. They certainly did not have the power to discharge Staub, which is why Buck was involved in the first place, although it's possible that they had power to take other "tangible employment actions" against him.

Perhaps "supervisor" means two different things in the two contexts. Or maybe the Court will resolve the question it explicitly avoided and decide that "subordinate bias liability" can follow from the actions of "co-workers." Or maybe the "delegation" concept will turn nonsupervisors (in a formal sense) into supervisors (in a practical sense), a possibility suggested by Alito's concurrence in *Staub*. 562 U.S. at 425 ("Where the officer with formal decisionmaking authority merely rubberstamps the recommendation of others, the employer, I would hold, has actually delegated the decisionmaking responsibility to those whose recommendation is rubberstamped.

I would reach a similar conclusion where the officer with the formal decisionmaking authority is put on notice that adverse information about an employee may be based on antimilitary animus but does not undertake an independent investigation of the matter."). The lower courts have grappled with these questions. *E.g., Shazor v. Prof'l Transit Mgmt.*, 744 F.3d 948 (6th Cir. 2014). See page 900 (dealing with liability for harassment).

* * *

Note on Age Discrimination Variations on the Individual Disparate Treatment Theme

To some extent, the law developed under Title VII, §1981, and the ADEA is similar. For example, in describing the core violation, *Hazen Paper Co v. Biggins*, 507 U.S. 604 (1993), drew heavily on Title VII precedents establishing the disparate treatment theory. After quoting from the *Teamsters v. United States*, 431 U.S. 324, 335 n.15 (1977), description of disparate treatment, the Court went on to state that "[t]he disparate treatment theory is of course available under the ADEA, as the language of that statute makes clear." *Id.* at 609. Implementing this perception, the Supreme Court has assumed the *McDonnell Douglas* framework applies to age discrimination claims, although it has inexplicably refused to so hold. *Reeves v. Sanderson Plumbing Prods., Inc.*, 530 U.S. 133, 142 (2000).

Although the Court has not explicitly revisited the *McDonnell Douglas* framework's applicability to cases under the ADEA, it has driven a wedge between the analysis of Title VII claims and ADEA claims in terms of causation. In *Gross v. FBL Financial Services*, 557 U.S. 167 (2009), the Supreme Court not only rejected the application of Title VII's motivating factor analysis under §703(m) to cases under the ADEA, but also refused to apply *Price Waterhouse* analysis to ADEA cases, reaffirming that a plaintiff claiming age discrimination must prove that discrimination was a determinative factor in a challenged decision.

The majority adopted a three-step rationale. First, it held that the amendment of Title VII in the 1991 to add the "motivating factor" standard of liability in §703(m) did not apply to the ADEA. Thus, *Desert Palace* is limited to Title VII cases. Given *Smith v. City of Jackson*, 544 U.S. 228 (2005), which focused on differences between the ADEA's language and Title VII's as a result of the 1991 amendment to Title VII, this step was not surprising. The second step, however, was startling, which was to also hold that the burden-shifting approach established by the Court for Title VII in *Price Waterhouse* did not apply. Given the Court's stress on statutory language in *City of Jackson*, and the fact that *Price Waterhouse* interpreted identical language in the pre-1991 version of Title VII and the ADEA, the Court's analysis is inexplicable. The third step in rejecting applying *Price Waterhouse* to the ADEA was even more bizarre: *Gross* appeared to overrule *Price Waterhouse* even though it had just found it inapplicable to the ADEA, and, as to Title VII, it had already been superseded by the 1991 amendments to Title VII. If there is a point to this, it might be to foreclose the application of *Price Waterhouse* to other statutes, such as §1981. Indeed, the court recently applied but-for causation to Title VII retaliation cases, reasoning that §703(m)'s motivating factor analysis did not explicitly reach those claims, which are governed by a different statutory provision, §704(a). *University of Texas Sw. Med. Ctr. v. Nassar*, 133 S. Ct. 2517 (2013). *See generally* Catherine T. Struve, *Shifting Burdens: Discrimination Law*

Through the Lens of Jury Instruction, 51 B.C. L. REV. 279 (2010); Martin J. Katz, Gross *Disunity*, 114 PENN ST. L. REV. 857 (2010); Michael C. Harper, *The Causation Standard in Federal Employment Law: Gross v. FBL Financial Services, Inc., and the Unfulfilled Promise of the Civil Rights Act of 1991*, 58 BUFFALO L. REV. 69 (2010). The lower courts have generally applied *Gross* broadly to reach all statutes that lack language like §703(m). *E.g.*, *Lewis v. Humboldt Acquisition Corp.*, 681 F.3d 312 (6th Cir. 2012) (ADA suit requires determinative factor proof); *Serwatka v. Rockwell Automation, Inc.*, 591 F.3d 957 (7th Cir. 2010) (same); *Palmquist v. Shinseki*, 689 F.3d 66, 73-74 (1st Cir. 2012) (same for Rehabilitation Act); and the *Nassar* opinion is likely to reinforce that trend.

However, the circuit courts have so far read *Gross* not to affect the application of *McDonnell Douglas* analysis in ADEA cases. *E.g.*, *Sims v. MVM, Inc.*, 704 F.3d 1327, 1333 (11th Cir. 2013) ("Our continued application of the *McDonnell Douglas* framework in ADEA cases is also consistent with all of our sister circuits that have addressed the issue."). They have also continued to look to something like "direct evidence"— not as a burden-shifting device but rather as a reason to find that age was a determinative factor. *Wilson v. Cox*, 753 F.3d 244, 247 (D.C. Cir. 2015) (decision maker's statement that older worked "came here to retire" were sufficient to require a trial).

While *Gross* creates a formal split between the analyses of cases under both statutes, the ADEA also differs in other respects from Title VII. For example, *Biggins* itself noted that "age discrimination rarely was based on the sort of animus motivating some other forms of discrimination," although the Court recognized that "it was based in large part on stereotypes unsupported by objective fact." *Id.* at 610-11. Some commentators have agreed that age discrimination is different but warn that it may actually be worse because of "opportunistic" conduct by employers. In GOVERNING THE WORKPLACE: THE FUTURE OF LABOR AND EMPLOYMENT LAW 64-65 (1988), Professor Paul Weiler argued that workers tend to be paid less than they are worth when first hired and more than they are worth in the later stages of their careers. Compensation tends to be linked to seniority in the firm, and workers with greater seniority receive more than their increased productivity would justify. This structure tends to keep employees loyal to the firm throughout their working lives but also creates a potential for "opportunistic" employer behavior, that is, taking advantage of the situation by replacing senior employees with younger, lower-paid workers. Older discharged workers rarely will be able to command the same compensation from another employer because their skills tend to be firm-specific. By narrowly defining what it means to discriminate on account of age, *Biggins* freed employers to make productivity-based judgments and perhaps resurrected the problem of opportunistic behavior. When you study disparate impact discrimination, *see* page 617, consider whether the ADEA version of that theory offers a better way to challenge this phenomenon than disparate treatment.

Another dramatic difference between Title VII and the ADEA flows from the fact that, given the limitation of the ADEA to those 40 and older, age discrimination against individuals below the cutoff is legal. Further, the Supreme Court has held that, even within the protected class of those over 40, it is permissible to discriminate against younger workers in favor of older workers (although not vice versa). *General Dynamics Land Systems, Inc. v. Cline*, 540 U.S. 581, 586 (2004) (while the ADEA's language could be read as flatly barring all "age" discrimination, "Congress's interpretive clues speak almost unanimously to an understanding of discrimination as directed against workers who are older than the ones getting treated better.").

Still another difference between the ADEA and Title VII arises because, unlike race and sex, which tend to be viewed as discrete points, age is a continuum. Inferring age discrimination from differences in treatment, therefore, is more or less plausible depending on the size of the age disparity at issue. In *O'Connor v. Consolidated Coin Caterers Corp.*, 517 U.S. 308, 311-12 (1996), the lower court had found that a 56-year-old plaintiff had not made out a prima facie case of age discrimination under *McDonnell Douglas/Burdine* because he was replaced by a worker over age 40 and thus in the same protected group as plaintiff. The Supreme Court rejected this approach. The bar on discrimination "because of age," means that it is irrelevant "that one person in the protected class has lost out to another person in the protected class . . .so long as he has lost out because of his age. Or to put the point more concretely, there can be no greater inference of age discrimination (as opposed to '40 or over' discrimination) when a 40-year-old is replaced by a 39-year-old than when a 56-year-old is replaced by a 40-year-old." *Id.* *O'Connor* held that an inference of age discrimination "cannot be drawn from the replacement of one worker with another worker insignificantly younger. Because the ADEA prohibits discrimination on the basis of age and not class membership, the fact that a replacement is substantially younger than the plaintiff is a far more reliable indicator of age discrimination than is the fact that the plaintiff was replaced by someone outside the protected class." 517 U.S. at 313. How large an age discrepancy is necessary to infer age discrimination from a comparison? *See Emmett v. Kwik Lok Corp.*, 528 F. App'x 257, 260 n.2 (3d Cir. 2013) ("five-year difference between Emmett and the average age of the three individuals who took over his job duties—is very thin"); *Ramlet v. E.F. Johnson Co.*, 507 F.3d 1149 (8th Cir. 2007) (one year's and five years' age difference between plaintiff and comparators insufficient to establish a prima facie case). Obviously, this is highly contextual, depending on what other evidence is available.

Note on Pleading

In 2002, the Supreme Court reversed a Second Circuit decision that had required plaintiff to plead at least a *McDonnell Douglas* claim in order to survive a Rule 12(b)(6) motion to dismiss for failure to state a claim. *Swierkiewicz v. Sorema, N.A.*, 534 U.S. 506 (2002). The plaintiff had alleged that he had been first demoted and ultimately fired by his employer because of his national origin and age in violation of Title VII of the Civil Rights Act of 1964 and the ADEA. He did plead his age (49) and national origin (Hungarian) and the younger age (32) and different national origin (French) of the favored co-worker. He also alleged that he had 25 years' more experience than the co-worker. For the Second Circuit that was not enough—he had to at least plead a prima facie case under the *McDonnell Douglas* proof structure.

In a unanimous opinion written by Justice Thomas, the Supreme Court reversed, reaffirming the traditional view of notice pleading under the Federal Rules of Civil Procedure. Put simply, the plaintiff's complaint gave the defendant employer adequate notice of both the act being challenged—plaintiff's discharge—and of the legal bases upon which he was suing—national origin discrimination in violation of Title VII and age discrimination in violation of the ADEA. Since the employer knew what adverse actions were being charged, who the supposed favored employee was, and what statutory requirements were allegedly violated, it had all the information that notice pleading requires. As for the failure to plead a prima facie case under *McDonnell Douglas*, the Court noted that *McDonnell Douglas* provides "an evidentiary standard, not a pleading requirement"; therefore, "under a notice pleading system, it is not appropriate to require a plaintiff to plead facts establishing a prima facie case." 534 U.S. at 511. Whatever hurdles employment discrimination plaintiffs had to face in their quest for vindication, pleading problems appeared to be a thing of the past. For example, in *Bennett v. Schmidt*, 153 F.3d 516, 518 (7th Cir. 1998), the Seventh Circuit wrote "[b]ecause racial discrimination in employment is 'a claim upon which relief can be granted,' this complaint could not be dismissed under Rule 12(b)(6). 'I was turned down for a job because of my race' is all a complaint has to say."

This certainty, however, has been severely shaken by two remarkable cases, *Bell Atlantic Corp. v. Twombly*, 550 U.S. 544 (2007), and *Ashcroft v. Iqbal*, 556 U.S 662 (2009), where the Court adopted a "plausibility pleading" standard for Rule 12(b)(6) motions, a standard whose operational meaning remains unclear but that many believe has radically changed pleading requirements under the Federal Rules.

The *Iqbal* opinion essentially sets out an analytic structure that suggest that a court analyze a complaint under "[t]wo working principles." 556 U.S at 678. Drawing on *Twombly*, *Iqbal* requires a court deciding a Rule 12(b)(6) motion to identify the "factual" allegations as distinct from legal conclusions in a complaint. "Facts" plead must be taken as true, but allegations that do not state "facts" need not be credited: "[T]he tenet that a court must accept as true all of the allegations contained in a complaint is inapplicable to legal conclusions. Threadbare recitals of the elements of a cause of action, supported by mere conclusory statements, do not suffice." *Id*. Obviously, what counts as a "fact" as opposed to a legal conclusion is key to understanding this first prong of *Iqbal*. For purposes of this course, one critical question is whether a complaint alleging "discrimination" pleads a fact or a conclusion.

Once the facts alleged are identified, the second *Iqbal* step is to determine whether, accepting such allegations as true, the "complaint that states a plausible claim for relief." Quoting heavily from *Twombly*, the Court explained:

> To survive a motion to dismiss, a complaint must contain sufficient factual matter, accepted as true, to "state a claim to relief that is plausible on its face." A claim has facial plausibility when the plaintiff pleads factual content that allows the court to draw the reasonable inference that the defendant is liable for the misconduct alleged. The plausibility standard is not akin to a "probability requirement," but it asks for more than a sheer possibility that a defendant has acted unlawfully. Where a complaint pleads facts that are "merely consistent with" a defendant's liability, it "stops short of the line between possibility and plausibility of 'entitlement to relief.'"

Id. This is "a context-specific task that requires the reviewing court to draw on its judicial experience and common sense." *Id*. at 679. If a plaintiff's allegations of "discrimination" are only conclusions, the court must look to the rest of the complaint for "facts" that show that the claim of discrimination is plausible."

The $64 question is whether *Swierkiewicz* survives the new regime. *Twombly* cited it with apparent approval, but *Iqbal* did not cite it at all. Some commentators argue that *Swierkiewicz* remains good law, and therefore that plausible pleading, properly understood, will have relatively little effect on employment discrimination claims. *E.g.*, Joseph A. Seiner, *After* Iqbal, 45 WAKE FOREST L. REV. 179, 194 (2010); Joseph A. Seiner, *Pleading Disability*, 51 B.C. L. REV. 95 (2010); Joseph A. Seiner, *The Trouble with* Twombly: *A Proposed Pleading Standard for Employment Discrimination Cases*,

2009 U. Ill. L. Rev. 1011. This view is supported by numerous cases that continue to apply *Swierkiewicz.* Others are more skeptical. *E.g.,* Suzette M. Malveaux, *Front Loading and Heavy Lifting: How Pre-Dismissal Discovery Can Address the Detrimental Effect of* Iqbal *on Civil Rights Cases,* 14 Lewis & Clark L. Rev. 65, 82 (2010); Suja A. Thomas, *The New Summary Judgment Motion: The Motion to Dismiss Under* Iqbal *and* Twombly, 14 Lewis & Clark L. Rev. 15 (2010). This view is supported by the lower court authority viewing *Swierkiewicz* as overruled at least in part. *See McCleary-Evans v. Md. DOT,* 780 F.3d 582, 587-88 (4th Cir. 2015) (*Swierkiewicz's* more lenient pleading standard has been superseded, and plaintiff's averments of discrimination were mere conclusions when she failed to allege a prima facie case or other basis for inferring more than the possibility of discrimination); *Fowler v. UPMC Shadyside,* 578 F.3d 203, 211 (3d Cir. 2009) ("We have to conclude, therefore, that because *Conley* has been specifically repudiated by both *Twombly* and *Iqbal,* so too has *Swierkiewicz,* at least insofar as it concerns pleading requirements and relies on *Conley.*"). And one commentator, looking at the worst-case scenario, offers suggestions for effectively pleading claims under the new pleading standard. Charles A. Sullivan, *Plausibly Pleading Employment Discrimination,* 52 Wm. & Mary L. Rev. 1613, 1622 (2011); *see also* Michael J. Zimmer, *Title VII's Last Hurrah: Can Discrimination Be Plausibly Pled?,* 2014 U. Chi. Legal F. 19. A partial reconciliation of competing perspective is *Littlejohn v. City of New York,* 795 F.3d 297, 310 (2d Cir. 2015), which agreed that *Iqbal* applied to Title VII complaints but found it

> does not affect the benefit to plaintiffs pronounced in the *McDonnell Douglas* quartet. To the same extent that the *McDonnell Douglas* temporary presumption reduces the facts a plaintiff would need to *show* to defeat a motion for summary judgment prior to the defendant's furnishing of a non-discriminatory motivation, that presumption also reduces the facts needed to be *pleaded* under *Iqbal.* . . . The facts alleged must give plausible support to the reduced requirements that arise under *McDonnell Douglas* in the initial phase of a Title VII litigation. The facts required by *Iqbal* to be alleged in the complaint need not give plausible support to the ultimate question of whether the adverse employment action was attributable to discrimination. They need only give plausible support to a minimal inference of discriminatory motivation.").

Of course, this would suggest that plaintiff must at least plead a prima facie case, which is a retreat from *Swierkiewicz.*

PROBLEM

9-1. In response to a help-wanted ad, Jane Armstrong, a 38-year-old woman, applies for a job as a cab driver at the Hacker Cab Company. She has a valid driver's license and has driven extensively, but not for pay, for 20 years. She is a vegetarian and a Capricorn. After a brief interview, at which all these facts emerge, she is rejected by "Tip" O'Neill, Hacker's president. Armstrong comes to you for legal counsel. You do some investigation. The first call you make is to O'Neill, who admits that the job is still open, but explains that he rejected Armstrong because "Capricorns make lousy drivers; besides she's too old to adjust to the rigors of cab driving, especially since she doesn't eat meat." When asked whether Armstrong's gender played a part in the decision, O'Neill replied, "Hell no. Some of my best friends are women. I don't care if my brother marries one. Har, har." A "windshield survey" of the Hacker Cab Company at shift-changing times reveals an almost total absence of women drivers. It is common knowledge that there is a heavy turnover in the cab-driving business.

How would you analyze this case based on *Price Waterhouse, McDonnell Douglas,* and *Desert Palace*?

C. SYSTEMIC DISCRIMINATION

We have seen that individual challenges to adverse employment decisions require the courts to focus on how a particular plaintiff has been treated by a defendant. But employment policies that sweep more broadly can also be challenged—for example, an employer's policy to hire only men, to fire older workers, or to separate employees by race, gender, or age. Challenges might also be mounted against employer practices that are not consciously designed to exclude, but that have the effect of disproportionately disadvantaging employees with protected characteristics. Such policies and practices raise systemic issues that may be addressed through one of the two concepts of systemic discrimination presently governing Title VII actions: systemic disparate treatment and disparate impact.

1. Systemic Disparate Treatment

Systemic disparate treatment can be proven in two ways. First, the plaintiff may simply demonstrate that the employer has an announced, formal policy of discrimination. Second, the plaintiff who fails to prove a formal policy may nevertheless establish that the defendant's employment decisions reveal a "pattern or practice" of disparate treatment. In both cases, motive is critical, but it is obvious from the facial discrimination in a formal policy and inferable from the impact of the practices.

a. *Formal Policies of Discrimination*

Historically, formal systems excluding women and minority group members or segregating them into inferior jobs were common. While there were rarely "white only" signs outside workplaces in the same way such signs were posted near public restrooms and drinking fountains in the South, many employers, particularly in the South, formally segregated jobs by race, with blacks typically consigned to lower-paying, less-attractive jobs. For example, Duke Power in North Carolina limited African Americans to the "Labor Department," the lowest-level jobs in the company. *See Griggs v. Duke Power Co.*, 401 U.S. 424 (1971). Most employers also segregated many jobs by gender, again with lower-level jobs assigned to female workers. Before the 1964 Civil Rights Act, it was standard practice for newspaper classified employment advertisements to be separately listed under "help wanted male" and "help wanted female."

With the passage of Title VII in 1964, most formal discriminatory policies of race or sex discrimination ended. Similarly, prior to the passage of the ADEA, employers typically imposed mandatory retirement at age 65. Since the ADEA now generally bars age discrimination for those over 40, most such formal discriminatory policies have disappeared.

Nevertheless, not all formal policies were rescinded without court intervention. An example is *Trans World Airlines, Inc. v. Thurston*, 469 U.S. 111 (1985), in which the defendant airline permitted pilots disqualified from serving in that capacity for reasons other than age to transfer automatically to the position of flight engineer but barred those who were required by a federal regulation to stop flying as pilots at age 60 from doing so. The Court had no trouble finding the policy facially discriminatory. "Since [the policy] allows captains who become disqualified for any reason other than age to 'bump' less senior flight engineers, [the] transfer policy is discriminatory on its face." *Id.* at 121. Because the policy drew an age line, it necessarily reflected an intent to discriminate on that basis. *But see Ky. Ret. Sys. v. EEOC*, 554 U.S. 125 (2008) (permitting a retirement plain to explicitly take age into account when there was no reason to believe it systematically disadvantaged older workers).

Today, most employers understand the requirements of the antidiscrimination laws and would not normally adopt a facially discriminatory plan unless the employer believed that the plan did not violate the statute, either because it was not technically discrimination or because it believed the policy to be permissible under a statutory exception. The first possibility is not as far-fetched as one might think. Sex distinctions in employer dress and grooming codes generally have been held not to constitute illegal sex discrimination under Title VII when they treat male and female employees separately but equally. *See* page 667. We will also encounter racial and gender preferences that are sometimes permissible under Title VII as part of valid affirmative action plans. *See* page 619. As for exceptions to the statute, police and fire departments continue to have age restrictions because of an exception written into the ADEA. And with respect to gender, age, and national origin, the bona fide occupational qualification ("BFOQ") defense permits classification on these bases in limited circumstances where the protected characteristic is strongly enough related to success on the job. In *Thurston*, the court rejected the airline's attempt to use this defense because many pilots over age 60 continued to work as flight engineers for TWA, thus undercutting the claim that being younger than 60 was a BFOQ.

b. Systemic Practices

Trans World Airlines v. Thurston involved a formal policy that facially treated older workers differently. There was no need, therefore, to search further for intent to discriminate. But the systemic disparate treatment theory goes beyond formal policies to reach pervasive practices rooted in intentional discrimination. Thus, the second type of systemic disparate treatment arises where no formal, announced policy of using race or gender can be established, but the plaintiff nevertheless shows a pattern of decisions explainable by the operation of bias in employment decisions.

In short, the plaintiff can establish a prima facie case of such treatment by show-ing that the employer's personnel practices reveal discrimination by decisionmakers. Whether described as a covert "policy" or simply the cumulative result of biased individual decisions, the result is the same. Such a showing is usually by statistical evidence of a gross and long-lasting disparity between, say, the racial or gender com-position of the employer's workforce and the composition that would be expected, given the labor market from which the defendant picks its workers. The statistical evidence can be buttressed by anecdotal evidence supporting the inference that the employer had a policy of discriminating. For example, in *Teamsters v. United States*, 431 U.S. 324 (1977), the plaintiff showed that almost no black or Hispanic workers had been assigned to the "line driver" job despite their availability in the lower-status "city driver" jobs and in the general population from which the employer selected its employees. Buttressing this "inexorable zero" in minority representation in the line driver jobs was testimony by workers that supervisors had told them that the com-pany was not ready for black and Hispanic line drivers. The Court undertook a similar analysis in *Hazelwood School District v. United States*, 433 U.S. 299 (1977), although there the question was whether a school district could be shown to have discriminated in hiring when the representation of minority teachers was compared to the racial composition of the relevant labor market for teachers.

Where plaintiff's case is based primarily on statistical evidence, as in *Teamsters*, determining whether there is disparate treatment often leads to a battle between the parties' statistical experts. The defendant may challenge the plaintiff's prima facie case by introducing evidence showing that plaintiff's statistical data or techniques are flawed. For instance, a common tactic is to challenge the labor pool on which the expectancy for female or minority work force representation was based.

Alternatively, the employer may admit the disparity but offer an explanation for the statistics that negates its intent to discriminate. Perhaps the most famous exam-ple of this defense is *EEOC v. Sears, Roebuck & Co.*, 839 F.2d 302 (7th Cir. 1988). Women constituted some 60 percent of the applicants for full-time sales jobs at Sears (both commissioned and noncommissioned) but only 27 percent of the newly hired commissioned salespeople. Median hourly wages were about twice as high for com-missioned as for noncommissioned salespeople. The EEOC argued that, given the desirability of the commissioned jobs, this disparity could be explained only by an inference of intentional discrimination by Sears and that, even though the Commission had the burden of proving such intent, the statistics were a sufficient basis to carry that burden.

The employer, however, successfully blunted the EEOC's statistical showing by convincing the trial court that the large disparity between men and women in com-mission sales jobs was explained by women generally lacking interest in those jobs, in part because of the competitive nature of the work. To be more precise, the dis-trict court found that the EEOC had not sustained its burden because, in light of the lack of interest argument, it had not established that the disparity resulted from Sears' discrimination. Ironically, Sears based its defense on a school of feminist think-ing that stresses the differences between men and women, reasoning that the diver-gent life experiences of men and women lead them to develop different perspectives and attitudes. Thus, Sears argued it was the women's lack of interest in commission sales jobs, not the employer's discrimination, that resulted in underrepresentation of women in those jobs. While *Sears* illustrates the upsides and downsides of even apparently strong statistical showings, it may be equally indicative of a major failure of trial strategy by the EEOC, which produced not a single female employee or applicant to testify as to having been denied a commissioned position. *See also EEOC v. Consolidated Service Systems*, 989 F.2d 233 (7th Cir. 1993) (a finding a statistically significant overrepresentation of Koreans in the employer's workforce resulted from word-of-mouth recruiting, not intent to prefer Koreans).

Sears was a major setback for the systemic disparate treatment, but perhaps a worse setback for the theory was *Dukes v. Wal-Mart Stores, Inc.*, 564 U.S. 338 (2011), where the Supreme Court reversed the Ninth Circuit certification of a class action on behalf of a class of over a million current and former employees. Although that opinion focused on whether the "commonality" requirement for a class action was met (an inquiry that is not necessary when the EEOC sues, as in *Sears*), the opinion did not bode well for the robustness of systemic disparate treatment as a theory of liability. The plaintiffs relied largely on expert evidence, which included statistical evidence of the lower relative success of female workers as compared with men within Wal-Mart (as in *Sears*) as well as statistical evidence showing that female success at Wal-Mart was lower than at other big box retailers. Finally, the plaintiffs introduced "social framework" expert testimony that sought to link the statistics to company policies permitting the operation of bias in promotion and compensation decisions by delegating largely standardless and unreviewed decisions to lower-level managers.

The majority opinion, written by Justice Scalia, recognized that if the plaintiffs could establish that Wal-Mart operated under a *general policy* of discrimination that manifested itself in the pay and promotion practices of the company, then certification of the class would be justified. However, the Court found such proof lacking. Wal-Mart had no formal policy of discrimination; indeed, the majority emphasized that its policies emphasized equal opportunity. To avoid this problem, the plaintiffs relied heavily on "social framework" testimony from a Dr. Bielby that Wal-Mart's "strong corporate culture" makes it "vulnerable" to "gender bias." Even accepting this testimony, however, the expert could not go on to "determine with any specificity how regularly stereotypes play a meaningful role in employment decisions at Wal-Mart," which for the majority did "nothing to advance respondents' case. '[W]hether 0.5 percent or 95 percent of the employment decisions at Wal-Mart might be determined by stereotyped thinking' is the essential question on which respondents' theory of commonality depends. If Bielby admittedly has no answer to that question, we can safely disregard what he has to say. It is worlds away from 'significant proof' that Wal-Mart 'operated under a general policy of discrimination.'" *Id.* at 354-55.

In fact, Wal-Mart's according discretion to local managers seemed, to the majority, to be the diametric opposite of a uniform employment discrimination practice: In a company the size of Wal-Mart, it is "quite unbelievable" that all managers would exercise their discretion in a common, much less commonly discriminatory way without a common direction. *Id.* at 356. Even if the plaintiffs had established a pattern of gender-linked pay and promotion discrepancies in all of Wal-Mart's 3,400 stores, the Court continued, commonality would still not exist because there could be different explanations for the discrepancies in different stores and regions. Finally, although (unlike the EEOC in *Sears*), the plaintiffs had also submitted 120 declarations of female workers regarding discrimination they suffered, the Court deemed this anecdotal evidence too weak to raise an inference that all the stores' personnel decisions were discriminatory given the small number of declarations compared to the large size of the class.

Since the *Wal-Mart* decision was formally about commonality for class action purposes, it does not necessarily suggest a dilution of the systemic disparate treatment theory, which can be asserted either in a government enforcement action (as in *Teamsters* or *Hazelwood*) or in a private class action. While *Wal-Mart* makes it much harder to have a class action certified, it does not necessarily affect EEOC "pattern or practice" suits, such as *Sears*. Nevertheless, the opinion may portend greater problems for that theory in the future. *See* Noah D. Zatz, Tristin K. Green, Melissa Hart, Richard Ford, *Working Group on the Future of Systemic Disparate Treatment Law*, 32 BERKELEY J. EMP. & LAB. L. 387 *et seq.* (2011).

To the extent the theory remains robust, the establishment of a prima facie of systemic disparate treatment has been held to result in a *Price Waterhouse*-like shifting of the burden of persuasion. That is, when systemic disparate treatment toward the class is proven, and an individual plaintiff is shown to be a member of that class, discrimination as to the individual is established—subject to the defendant carrying a burden of proof that the individual was not harmed by the pattern of discrimination. *See Teamsters; Franks v. Bowman Transp. Co.*, 424 U.S. 747, 772 (U.S. 1976) ("petitioners here have carried their burden of demonstrating the existence of a discriminatory hiring pattern and practice by the respondents and, therefore, the burden will be upon respondents to prove that individuals who reapply were not in fact victims of previous hiring discrimination."). However, this burden shifting is available only in an EEOC suit or class action, not to an individual plaintiff. *E.g., Daniels v. UPS*, 701 F.3d 620 (10th Cir. 2012); *Chin v. Port Auth. of N.Y. & N.J.*, 685 F.3d 135, 147 (2d Cir. 2012).

c. Bona Fide Occupational Qualifications

Section 703(e) of Title VII provides:

> Notwithstanding any other provision of this title . . . it shall not be an unlawful employment practice for an employer to hire and employ employees . . . on the basis of religion, sex, or national origin in those certain instances where religion, sex, or national origin is a bona fide occupational qualification reasonably necessary to the normal operation of that particular business or enterprise.

The ADEA also provides a BFOQ defense that uses language identical to Title VII. The defense, under both statutes has been read very narrowly, and the Title VII provision does not by its terms allow race discrimination to be a BFOQ. *See Chaney v. Plainfield Healthcare Ctr.*, 612 F.3d 908 (7th Cir. 2010) (holding that honoring a patient's request for white caregivers was not a justification for discrimination in job assignments, even if the employer had a good faith belief that it was required by state law to honor such requests). *See also Ferrill v. The Parker Group, Inc.*, 168 F.3d 468 (11th Cir. 1999) (rejecting, in a §1981 case, a BFOQ for racially segregating telemarketers aimed at getting out the vote for an election, with blacks calling blacks and whites calling whites).

The Supreme Court's first meaningful treatment of the BFOQ defense was in *Dothard v. Rawlinson*, 433 U.S. 321 (1977), in which the Court upheld a rule requiring prison guards in "contact" positions to be the same gender as the inmates they guarded. The majority stressed that Alabama's penitentiaries had been held unconstitutional because of their dangerous and inhumane conditions. Further, the 20 percent of sex offenders were scattered throughout the dormitories. While characterizing the BFOQ defense as "an extremely narrow exception to the general prohibition of discrimination on the basis of sex," the Court recognized that in an "environment of violence and disorganization, it would be an over-simplification to characterize [the rule against women] as an exercise in 'romantic paternalism.'" *Id.* at 334-35. Title VII normally allows individual women to decide whether jobs are too dangerous for them, but the Alabama prisons conditions made it likely that women could not perform the essence of the correctional counselor's job—to maintain security:

> A woman's relative ability to maintain order in a male, maximum-security, unclassified penitentiary of the type Alabama now runs could be directly reduced by her womanhood. There is a basis in fact for expecting that sex offenders who have criminally assaulted women in the past would be moved to do so again if access to women were established within the prison. There would also be a real risk that other inmates, deprived of a normal heterosexual environment, would assault women guards because they were women.

Id. at 336. Thus, an employee's "very womanhood" could undermine her ability to do the job. The dissent by Justice Marshall protested this analysis as justifying discrimination by the barbaric state of the prisons. Those conditions violate the Constitution and, therefore, cannot constitute "the normal operation of that particular business or enterprise" required by the BFOQ defense. Further, the notion that the employee's "very womanhood" makes assaults more likely

> regrettably perpetuates one of the most insidious of the old myths about women—that women, wittingly or not, are seductive sexual objects. The effect of the decision, made I am sure with the best of intentions, is to punish women because their very presence might provoke sexual assaults. It is women who are made to pay the price in lost job opportunities for the threat of depraved conduct by prison inmates. Once again, "[t]he pedestal upon which women have been placed has . . ., upon closer inspection, been revealed as a cage." It is particularly ironic that the cage is erected here in response to feared misbehavior by imprisoned criminals.

Id. at 345 (Marshall, J., dissenting).

The Supreme Court's next encounter with the BFOQ defense was in a suit under the ADEA. *Western Air Lines v. Criswell*, 472 U.S. 400 (1985), involved whether an airline could limit flight engineer positions to pilots no older than 60 under the BFOQ exception to the ADEA. Flight engineers monitored side-facing instrument panels in commercial aircraft of that era such as the Boeing 727. A Federal Aviation Administration ("FAA") regulation barred those over age 60 from the other two pilot jobs—captain and first officer—but did not set any standard for flight engineers.

Defendant's evidence focused on the possibility that flight engineers would suffer a heart attack, the risks of which generally increase with age. Plaintiff's evidence established that physiological deterioration was individualized and could be ascertained through physical examinations that the FAA required for all flight engineers. Further, other airlines allowed flight engineers over age 60 to continue to fly without any apparent safety problems.

The Court upheld a jury instruction that included a "two-part inquiry [, which] properly identifies the relevant considerations for resolving a BFOQ defense to an age-based qualification purportedly justified by considerations of safety." *Id.* at 416. That test was whether it was (1) highly impractical to make individualized determinations as to ability to perform the job safely; and (2) some persons over the defined age possess "traits of a physiological, psychological or other nature which preclude safe and efficient job performance that cannot be ascertained by means other than knowing their age." *Id.*

The Court later elaborated on this test and applied it in the sex discrimination context in *International Union, UAW v. Johnson Controls, Inc.*, 499 U.S. 187 (1991), which involved a "fetal protection policy" that broadly excluded women from jobs that exposed them to lead. Lower courts had reached conflicting results in deciding whether such policies even distinguished workers on the basis of sex, as opposed to a neutral characteristic, such as fetal safety. However, the Supreme Court had no difficulty with that question: "The bias in Johnson Controls' policy is obvious. Fertile men, but not fertile women, are given a choice as to whether they wish to risk their reproductive health for a particular job." *Id.* at 197. Further, "the absence of a malevolent motive does not convert a facially discriminatory policy into a neutral policy with a discriminatory effect." *Id.* at 199. While a discriminatory policy can nevertheless be justified as a bona fide occupational qualification, Johnson Controls' policy did not meet the strict requirements of this exception:

> The wording of the BFOQ defense contains several terms of restriction that indicate that the exception reaches only special situations. The statute thus limits the situations in which discrimination is permissible to "certain instances" where sex discrimination is "reasonably necessary" to the "normal operation" of the "particular" business. Each one of these terms—certain, normal, particular—prevents the use of general subjective standards and favors an objective, verifiable requirement. But the most telling term is "occupational"; this indicates that these objective, verifiable requirements must concern job-related skills and aptitudes.

Id. at 201. The majority rejected the argument that "occupational" merely meant "related to a job," holding, rather, that the term related to "qualifications that affect an employee's ability to do the job." *Id.* Since susceptibility of a fetus to lead poisoning was entirely unconnected to whether its mother could make batteries, this approach effectively foreclosed the BFOQ defense.

The Court recognized that the safety of third parties had been important in cases such as *Criswell* but drew a distinction, observing that in those cases

> safety concerns were not independent of the individual's ability to perform the assigned tasks, but rather involved the possibility that, because of age-connected debility, a flight engineer might not properly assist the pilot, and might thereby cause a safety emergency. Furthermore, although we considered the safety of third parties in *Dothard* and *Criswell*, those third parties were indispensable to the particular business at issue. In *Dothard*, the third parties were the inmates; in *Criswell*, the third parties were the passengers on the plane. We stressed that in order to qualify as a BFOQ, a job qualification must relate to the "essence," or to the "central mission of the employer's business."

Id. at 202-3. While the health of future children was a deep social concern, the BFOQ did not render it essential to battery making.

The *Johnson Controls* reasoning was reinforced by the Pregnancy Discrimination Act, which had amended Title VII in 1978 to declare that pregnancy discrimination was sex discrimination. The Court described the PDA as "contain[ing] a BFOQ standard of its own: Unless pregnant employees differ from others 'in their ability or inability to work,' they must be 'treated the same' as other employees 'for all employment-related purposes.'" *Id.* at 204. This meant that "women as capable of doing their jobs as their male counterparts may not be forced to choose between having a child and having a job." *Id.*

While the Court was not persuaded that tort liability to fetuses was a real danger, it did note that "[w]e, of course, are not presented with, nor do we decide, a case in which costs would be so prohibitive as to threaten the survival of the employer's business. We merely reiterate our prior holdings that the incremental cost of hiring women cannot justify discriminating against them." Finally, the majority specifically noted that its decision did not suggest that sex could not constitute a BFOQ when privacy interests are implicated.

In the wake of *Johnson Controls*, most BFOQ claims have arisen in the institutional context, most often prisons, as in the next principal case, but also in hospitals, *Slivka v. Camden-Clark Mem'l Hosp.*, 594 S.E.2d 616 (W. Va. 2004), and psychiatric facilities, *Healey v. Southwood Psychiatric Hospital*, 78 F.3d 128 (3d Cir. 1996). Can you guess why?

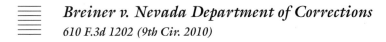

Breiner v. Nevada Department of Corrections
610 F.3d 1202 (9th Cir. 2010)

BERZON, Circuit Judge:

The Nevada Department of Corrections (NDOC) hires only female correctional lieutenants at a women's prison. The district court granted summary judgment upholding NDOC's discriminatory employment policy, concluding that the policy imposed only a "de minimis" restriction on male prison employees' promotional opportunities and, alternatively, that the policy falls within Title VII's exception permitting sex discrimination in jobs for which sex is a bona fide occupational qualification, 42 U.S.C. §2000e-2(e)(1). We reverse as to both holdings.

Factual & Procedural Background

[While being operated by a private company, Corrections Corporation of America (CCA), problems at the Southern Nevada Women's Correctional Facility (SNWCF) prompted an investigation by the NDOC's inspector general. The inspector general concluded] that SNWCF had become "an uninhibited sexual environment." He noted "frequent instances of inappropriate staff/inmate interaction," "flirtatious activities between staff and inmates," and "widespread knowledge" of "long-term inmate/inmate sexual relationships." In exchange for sex, prison staff "routinely introduce[d] . . . contraband into the institution, including alcohol, narcotics, cosmetics, [and] jewelry." The inmates' sexual behavior—which they freely admitted was designed to "compromise staff and enhance inmate privileges"—was, in the Inspector General's view, "predictable." The Inspector General attributed the guards' misconduct to "a lack of effective supervisory management oversight and control. . . . There is no evidence that supervisors or managers recognize this risky behavior or do anything to stop it." To address this "leadership void," the Inspector

General recommended that "line supervisors undergo leadership training" and that "subordinate staff undergo re-training with emphasis on inmate con games and ethical behavior."

In the wake of the Inspector General's report, which ignited "very high profile" media coverage, CCA announced that it was terminating its contract to operate SNWCF. NDOC resumed control of the facility and, according to Crawford, faced intense political pressure to "mitigate the number of newspaper articles" and to "assure the State of Nevada that we would not be embarrassed like this again." To achieve this goal, Crawford decided to restaff the facility so that seventy percent of the front-line staff at SNWCF would be women.

Crawford also decided to hire only women in SNWCF's three correctional Lieutenant positions. The correctional lieutenants are shift supervisors and are the senior employees on duty seventy-five percent of the time. Correctional lieutenants report to wardens or deputy wardens and are responsible for supervising the prison's day-to-day operations, including directing the work of subordinate staff, inspecting the facility and reporting infractions, and monitoring inmates' activities and movement through the facility. There is one correctional lieutenant assigned to SWNCF per shift. Although the correctional lieutenant posting specified that "only female applicants will be accepted for these positions," several males applied for the positions, which were eventually filled by three women.

[Three male Nevada correctional officers brought suit although they had not applied for the lieutenant positions. They challenged only the gender limitation with respect to that position; the "seventy-percent-female restriction on front line guards" was, therefore, not at issue in this litigation.]

A. The "De Minimis" Theory

NDOC asserts that the three SNWCF positions were the only correctional lieutenant promotions in the NDOC system as a whole restricted to women applicants and that twenty-nine out of thirty-seven correctional lieutenant positions filled over a four-year period went to men. Relying on these statistics, NDOC maintains that the concededly discriminatory policy of excluding men from the SNWCF correctional lieutenant positions had only a "de minimis" impact on the plaintiffs and so did not violate Title VII with regard to them. This conclusion reflects a fundamental misunderstanding of the basic precepts of Title VII and is not supported by our case law.

[The court stressed the desirability of the positions at issue and noted "[t]hat another opportunity may later arise for which the applicant is eligible does not negate the injury of being denied an earlier position on the basis of one's sex, with the resulting loss of pay for a period and delayed eligibility for another promotion." Further, positions are not fungible, and some may be more desirable for individuals than others, for example, because of location. Cases like *Robino v. Iranon*, 145 F.3d 1109 (9th Cir. 1998), were inapposite. That decision approved assigning only female guards to certain posts to protect female inmate privacy, but involved only assignments within the prison, not positions.] *Robino*'s premise, then, was necessarily that a minor impact on job assignments was too minimal to be actionable. This very limited concept has no application to NDOC's policy. An employer's "fail[ure] or refus[al] to hire" on the basis of sex is, without limitation, actionable under Title VII. 42 U.S.C. §2000e-2(a)(1). NDOC's refusal to hire men in the correctional lieutenant positions therefore violates Title VII unless NDOC can demonstrate that gender is a BFOQ for the positions. NDOC cannot meet that burden, as we now explain.

B.   Gender as a Bona Fide Occupational Qualification . . .

NDOC has not explicitly articulated the "job qualification" for correctional lieutenants for which it claims sex is a legitimate proxy. We are left to try to adduce what that "qualification" might be from the declarations by NDOC officials on which the defendants rely in their briefs as justification for the facially discriminatory policy. . . .

From this panoply of explanations, it appears that NDOC administrators sought to "reduce the number of male correctional employees being compromised by female inmates," and that they believed the gender restriction on shift supervisors would accomplish this because (1) male correctional lieutenants are likely to condone sexual abuse by their male subordinates; (2) male correctional lieutenants are themselves likely to sexually abuse female inmates; and (3) female correctional lieutenants possess an "instinct" that renders them less susceptible to manipulation by inmates and therefore better equipped to fill the correctional lieutenant role.[5]

The first theory fails because NDOC has not shown that "all or nearly all" men would tolerate sexual abuse by male guards, or that it is "impossible or highly impractical" to assess applicants individually for this qualification. As to the second theory, there is no "basis in fact," *Dothard*, for believing that individuals in the correctional lieutenant role are particularly likely to sexually abuse inmates. The third theory—and, to a significant degree, the first two—relies on the kind of unproven and invidious stereotype that Congress sought to eliminate from employment decisions when it enacted Title VII.

[The court reviewed *Dothard*, concluding that its finding of a BFOQ] was premised on a level of violence among inmates atypical even among maximum security facilities. *See Gunther v. Iowa State Men's Reformatory*, 612 F.2d 1079, 1085 (8th Cir. 1980).

Appellate courts, including this court, have followed *Dothard* in requiring prison administrators to identify a concrete, logical basis for concluding that gender restrictions are "reasonably necessary." In *Everson v. Michigan Department of Corrections*, 391 F.3d 737 (6th Cir. 2004), the Sixth Circuit upheld a gender restriction imposed by the Michigan Department of Corrections (MDOC) to eradicate "rampant sexual abuse of female prisoners." MDOC had "pledged . . . to minimize access to secluded areas and one-on-one contact between male staff and female inmates" pursuant to settlement of two lawsuits, one brought by the United States Department of Justice, alleging that the failure to protect female inmates from ongoing sexual abuse violated their constitutional rights. To effectuate the settlement agreements, MDOC

---

5. NDOC also suggests that privacy and rehabilitation were among the "factors . . . considered important" in implementing the gender restriction. Neither in its briefs nor at oral argument, however, was NDOC able to direct the court to any evidence that Crawford or other administrators actually considered privacy or rehabilitation in developing the policy. This void is not surprising, as it is the guards who have direct daily contact with the inmates, not the correctional lieutenants. As noted, NDOC, in a separate policy not here challenged, restricts the number of front-line guards in female prisons. As there is no evidence in this record to indicate that concern about privacy or rehabilitation was a basis for the decision to preclude men from serving in the supervisory positions, we do not consider those rationales in our BFOQ analysis.

employed only female guards in the housing units of women's prisons. MDOC data showed that most allegations of sexual abuse, and all of the sustained allegations, involved male employees, and that sexual abuse occurred most frequently in the housing units. This data, the court held, "established that the exclusion of male [guards] will decrease the likelihood of sexual abuse."

In *Henry v. Milwaukee County*, 539 F.3d 573 (7th Cir. 2008), a juvenile detention center decided to staff each housing "pod" with at least one guard of the same sex as the juveniles housed on that pod, to achieve a "direct role model/mentoring form of supervision." During the day, one of the two guards on each male "pod" could be female, but the sole night shift slot on each pod had to be staffed by a man. The Seventh Circuit accepted the administrator's "professional judgment" that same-gender mentoring was "necessary to achieve the [facility's] mission of rehabilitation." Yet, the court found no factual support for the administrator's conclusion that the program's effectiveness required same-sex staff at all times, including on the night shift, when the juvenile inmates were sleeping.

In *Robino*, we held that even had the gender-based restriction on assignments been actionable under Title VII, it fell within the BFOQ exception. The prison, based on "a study conducted by a specially appointed task force in compliance with an EEOC settlement agreement," designated as female only those posts that "require[d] the [guard] on duty to observe the inmates in the showers and toilet areas . . . or provide[d] unsupervised access to the inmates." Because "a person's interest in not being viewed unclothed by members of the opposite sex survives incarceration," we held that protecting inmate privacy and preventing sexual misconduct warranted the restriction.

These cases illustrate that, even in the unique context of prison employment, administrators seeking to justify a BFOQ must show "a high correlation between sex and ability to perform job functions." *Johnson Controls*. Moreover, the particular staffing restriction at issue must match those "job functions" with a high degree of specificity to be found reasonably necessary. *See id.*; *Robino*. In *Henry*, for example, the application of the gender restriction on the night shift would not address privacy concerns, as "the vast majority of the time that the juveniles were unclothed occurred during [ ] daytime shifts" when women were permitted to staff the pods, and was not justified by the mentoring objective because "the opportunity . . . to interact with the juveniles on the [night] shift [wa]s very minimal."

Applying this "high correlation" requirement, NDOC's first rationale for restricting the supervisory correctional lieutenant positions to women cannot suffice. Crawford's testimony suggests that because the supervisors employed by CCA were male and had failed to prevent sexual abuse, NDOC was entitled to conclude that men as a class were incapable of adequately supervising front line staff in female prisons. While we must defer to the reasoned judgment of prison administrators, *see Robino*, CCA's acknowledged leadership failure falls far short of providing "a factual basis for believing that all or substantially all [men] would be unable to safely and effectively perform the duties of the job," or that it would be "impossible or highly impracticable to determine job fitness"—here, the ability to enforce workplace rules prohibiting sexual misconduct—"on an individualized basis." *Williams v. Hughes Helicopters, Inc.*, 806 F.2d 1387, 1391 (9th Cir. 1986) [ADEA]. The fundamental switch in operational responsibility to NDOC, moreover, made any inference from the experience under CCA's extremely poor management all the weaker.

NDOC's second rationale fares no better. There is no evidence indicating that any correctional lieutenant at SNWCF had sexual relationships with an inmate. In contrast, in *Everson*, copious data about the actual incidence of sexual abuse in Michigan's women's prisons supported the conclusion that the gender restriction on guards in the housing units would be effective. In *Robino*, prison administrators used "a study by a specially appointed task force" and "an extensive inventory of post duties" to limit the gender restriction to those posts that "provide[d] unsupervised access to the inmates." NDOC, however, offers neither data nor logical inferences about the opportunities for abuse inherent in the correctional lieutenant position to support the restriction.

In fact, the one substantiated case of sexual abuse Crawford mentioned was the front-line guard who impregnated an inmate, yet NDOC continues to employ men in thirty percent of these positions. *See Everson*. When asked why the complete prohibition on the hiring of men was limited to correctional lieutenants, Crawford stated, "We did not want to go globally on this. We wanted to be specifically, what can we do to bring this thing under control . . .? And it was the recommendation that we just look at . . . not the line level, but the supervisor level." This explanation falls short of the "reasoned decision-making process, based on available information and experience," *Robino*, that can support a BFOQ.

Even if there were a factual basis to believe that any correctional lieutenant sexually abused any inmate, there is no basis to presume that sexual abuse, by correctional lieutenants or by guards with their supervisors' tacit permission, would continue after the state resumed control over the prison. CCA's lax oversight provided male correctional lieutenants "the opportunity not to take action against male correctional subordinates that sexually abused female inmates." That opportunity cannot be presumed to exist after the wholesale change of SNWCF's leadership, designed precisely to cure wholesale management defects going well beyond the sexual abuse issue.

To hold otherwise would be to absolve NDOC from their fundamental responsibility to supervise their staff, from wardens to front-line guards. In *Dothard*, the inmates' violent behavior, which prison administrators could not directly control, rendered the gender restriction reasonably necessary. Neither *Dothard* nor any of the cases on which NDOC relies support finding a BFOQ based on the bald assertion that it would be "impossible . . . to ensure that any given male correctional lieutenant will take action to prevent and stop sexual misconduct." Where, as here, the problem is *employee* behavior, prison administrators have multiple resources, including background checks, prompt investigation of suspected misconduct, and severe discipline for infractions, to ensure compliance with institutional rules.

NDOC has not demonstrated that these alternative approaches—including the Inspector General's suggestion of enhanced training for both supervisors and front-line guards—are not viable. . . .

Disturbingly, in suggesting that all men are inherently apt to sexually abuse, or condone sexual abuse of, female inmates, NDOC relies on entirely specious gender stereotypes that have no place in a workplace governed by Title VII. NDOC's third theory, that women are "maternal," "patient," and understand other women, fails for the same reason. To credit NDOC's unsupported generalization that women "have an instinct and an innate ability to discern . . . what's real and what isn't" and so are immune to manipulation by female inmates would violate "the Congressional purpose to eliminate subjective assumptions and traditional stereotyped conceptions regarding the . . . ability of women to do particular work." *Rosenfeld v. S. Pac. Co.*, 444 F.2d 1219, 1225 (9th Cir. 1971). "The harmful effects of occupational cliches," *Gerdom v. Continental Airlines*, 692 F.2d 602, 607 (9th Cir. 1982), are felt no less strongly when invoked as a basis for one gender's unique suitability for a particular job than when relied on to exclude members of that sex from employment. Simply put, "we are beyond the day when an employer could . . . insist[ ] that [employees] matched the stereotype associated with their group." *Price Waterhouse v. Hopkins.* . . .

In sum, NDOC has not met its burden of showing "a basis in fact," *Dothard*, for concluding that all male correctional lieutenants would tolerate sexual abuse by their subordinates; that all men in the correctional lieutenant role would themselves sexually abuse inmates; or that women, by virtue of their gender, can better understand the behavior of female inmates. Nor has it refuted the viability of alternatives that would achieve that goal without impeding male employees' promotional opportunities. . . .

NOTES

1. *Adverse Employment Action?* The court's rejection of the de minimis argument might suggest that any sex discrimination is impermissible unless justified by a BFOQ. But a closer reading suggests that this is not true. As we saw on page 553, a "de minimis" exception seems alive and well under Title VII, although it is framed in terms of whether the at-issue decision constitutes an "adverse employment action." For many courts, a "lateral transfer," that is, one that does not result in loss of pay or a demotion, is not actionable. In jurisdictions with stringent definitions of adverse employment action, an employer may be able to assign individuals by sex, age, or even race without having to establish a BFOQ. *See Tipler v. Douglas County*, 482 F.3d 1023, 1025 (8th Cir. 2007 (BFOQ "analysis is unnecessary if (1) the policy requiring female-only supervision of female inmates is reasonable, and (2) such a policy imposes only a 'minimal restriction' on the employee"). *But see Piercy v. Maketa*, 480 F.3d 1192 (10th Cir. 2007) (facial discrimination might be actionable when it was not clear that assignments were purely lateral). *Cf. EEOC v. AutoZone, Inc.*, 860 F.3d 564 (7th Cir. 2017) (even if a black employee was transferred to keep a store's staff "predominantly Hispanic," plaintiff had no cause of action where the transfer did not reduce his pay or responsibilities). *See generally* Rebecca Hanner White, *De Minimis Discrimination*, 47 EMORY L. J. 1121, 1148, 1172-73 (1998) (arguing that, where discrimination has been found, "the 'de minimis' nature of the discrimination should not serve as a basis for dismissing the claim. That the discrimination may be viewed as 'trivial' or 'de minimis' goes merely to remedies and not to liability.").

2. *Avoiding Sexual Harassment and Exploitation.* Although it could be described in "privacy" terms, *Breiner* is about more than privacy in the sense of an interest in not being seen unclothed by members of the opposite sex. The scandal that gave rise to the policy at issue indicates the serious problems that can arise in custodial settings, which may explain why employers in such settings often resort to such policies. And, while the court struck down the sex-limitation for lieutenants, it made clear that the policy as to the sex of the front-line guards themselves was not at issue. In purely numerical terms, the number of positions reserved for female guards undoubtedly dwarfed the three supervisory slots at issue in the case. If a male guard sued the prison, would he win? It's safe to assume that avoiding harassment and exploitation of female inmates is an appropriate goal, but is a gender line reasonably necessary to achieve it? *See generally* Kim Shayo Buchanan, *Beyond Modesty: Privacy in Prison and the Risk of Sexual Abuse*, 88 MARQ. L. REV. 751 (2005) ("[W]hen women prisoners are sexually exploited by guards, they are victims of sexual aggression; feminists do them no favor by pretending that they are not.").

Since *Breiner*, the Ninth Circuit has decided two prison cases, approving gender-specific staffing issues in one and suggesting a problem in the other. *Compare Teamsters Local Union No. 117 v. Wash. Dep't of Corr.*, 789 F.3d 979 (9th Cir. 2015) (a plan designating 110 female-only correctional position to patrol housing units, prison grounds, and work sites was valid under the BFOQ exception since it reflected an individualized, well-researched response to problems in women's prisons of sexual abuse and misconduct by prison guards, breaches of inmate privacy, and security gaps) *with Ambat v. City & Cnty. of S.F.*, 757 F.3d 1017 (9th Cir. 2014) (triable issue as to whether an employer's policy of prohibiting male deputies from supervising female jail inmates was a BFOQ because of questions about its factual basis and justification").

3. *Rehabilitation.* The court finds that neither rehabilitation nor privacy concerns were proffered as justifications for the sex limitation. In some cases, however, courts have found rehabilitation to be a legitimate basis for a BFOQ. In *Healey v. Southwood Psychiatric Hospital*, 78 F.3d 128, 132-33 (3d Cir. 1996), plaintiff challenged a gender-based assignment of childcare specialists at a hospital for emotionally disturbed children and adolescents, some of whom had been sexually abused. The court upheld summary judgment for the employer:

> The "essence" of Southwood's business is to treat emotionally disturbed and sexually abused adolescents and children. Southwood has presented expert testimony that staffing both males and females on all shifts is necessary to provide therapeutic care. "Role modeling," including parental role modeling, is an important element of the staff's job, and a male is better able to serve as a male role model than a female and vice versa. A balanced staff is also necessary because children who have been sexually abused will disclose their problems more easily to a member of a certain sex, depending on their sex and the sex of the abuser. If members of both sexes are not on a shift, Southwood's inability to provide basic therapeutic care would hinder the "normal operation" of its "particular business." Therefore, it is reasonably necessary to the normal operation of Southwood to have at least one member of each sex available to the patients at all times.

See also Torres v. Wisconsin Dep't of Health & Social Services, 859 F.2d 1523 (7th Cir. 1988) (rehabilitation in a prison context).

4. *Privacy.* The *Breiner* court cites *Rubino* for the proposition that an individual's interest in not being seen unclothed by a member of the opposite sex survives incarceration. A number of cases have concurred, but they have often stressed, as in *Robino* itself, that measures short of denying individuals jobs because of their sex can suffice. *E.g., Henry v. Milwaukee County*, 539 F.3d 573 (7th Cir. 2008). What about the privacy of patients and clients? The *Johnson Controls* majority denied that its opinion would do away with privacy protections, 99 U.S. 187, 206 n.4.

5. *Deference.* Many BFOQ cases turn on the level of deference courts accord the professional judgment of employers. Particularly in the prison context, the cases tend to at least claim to be deferring to some extent. In *Breiner* itself, the prison officials' cavalier rationale for their own rule probably was largely responsible for the opinion's evident disdain. But the Ninth Circuit stated that some deference was due. How much? *See also Henry*, 539 F.3d 580-81 (administrators "are entitled to substantial deference" but the discretion accorded is not unlimited).

6. *Essence of the Business.* Although not at issue in *Breiner*, some BFOQ cases have turned not on whether one gender was better than another in some respect but rather whether such superiority went to the "'essence' of the business." This test originated in *Diaz v. Pan American Airways, Inc.*, 442 F.2d 385 (5th Cir. 1971), holding that sex was not a BFOQ for the job of flight attendant—despite the asserted superiority of women in being sexually attractive to male passengers and comforting to female passengers—because those characteristics are peripheral to the airline's essential concern with safe transportation. *Johnson Controls* confirms the importance of "essence" analysis in applying the BFOQ. However, the fact that a policy furthers an essential function is not sufficient to establish a BFOQ: "Title VII's standard is not satisfied simply because a policy promotes an essential function of an institution. Although sex-based assignments might be helpful in pursuing [the goals of rehabilitation, security, and privacy], in order to satisfy the anti-discrimination strictures of Title VII, [the employer] must show that the contested sex classifications are "'reasonably necessary.'" *Henry*, 539 F.3d 581. In *Henry*, the court held that "Although reducing the number of opposite-sex staff on the pods may *help* to promote security, efficient risk management and privacy, Milwaukee County has failed to establish that its policy was *reasonably necessary* for these goals." *Id.* at 581.

7. *Customer Preference.* Whatever the correct view of privacy, it would support relatively narrow inroads into Title VII's proscriptions. It does, however, tend to merge into a larger question: When, if ever, is "customer preference" a basis for a BFOQ? So framed, the courts have not been sympathetic. For example, the Ninth Circuit rejected a BFOQ claim in *Fernandez v. Wynn Oil Co.*, 653 F.2d 1273 (9th Cir. 1981), where the defendant argued that the plaintiff could not be made vice president of international operations because Latin American clients would react negatively to a woman in such a position. Although finding the defense not factually supported, the Ninth Circuit also held it inadequate as a matter of law because customer preference cannot justify gender discrimination. *Id. See also EEOC v. HI 40 Corp.*, 953 F. Supp. 301 (W.D. Mo. 1996) (being female was not a BFOQ for counselors at weight-loss centers, despite the centers' mostly female customers' preference for female counselors). There is, however, rising concern that discriminatory customer preferences are influencing employment decisions in less visible ways. *See generally* Dallan F. Flake, *When Should Employers Be Liable for Factoring Biased Customer Feedback into Employment Decisions?*, 102 MINN. L. REV. 2169 (2018).

8. *Sex Appeal as a BFOQ.* Is selling sex appeal a BFOQ? *Frank v. United Airlines*, 216 F.3d 845 (9th Cir. 2000), struck down the airlines' maximum weight requirements for women, which were stricter than those for men. Women were required to weigh 14 to 25 pounds less than male colleagues of the same height and age. There was no showing that "having disproportionately thinner female than male flight attendants bears a relation to flight attendants' ability to greet passengers, push carts, move luggage, and, perhaps most importantly, provide physical assistance in emergencies." *Id.* at 855. Why would United adopt such a policy? Is it to satisfy customer preference for conventional views of attractiveness? *See also Wilson v. Southwest Airlines Co.*, 517 F. Supp. 292 (N.D. Tex. 1981) (being female was not a BFOQ for defendant who marketed itself as "love airline," using the female allure and sex appeal of its employees).

A more recent example is Hooters, a chain of restaurants that hires only women, who are clad in provocative outfits, to serve food to customers. In an investigation by the EEOC in the mid-1990s, the company defended its practice by arguing that "[a] lot of places serve good burgers. The Hooters' Girls, with their charm and All-American sex appeal, are what our customers come for." *Restaurant Chain to Resist Hiring Men*, N.Y. Times, Nov. 16, 1995, at A20, col. 5. The EEOC dropped its investigation against Hooters after the company's massive public relations campaign. A private action was then settled, under terms that allowed Hooters to continue to hire only women as waitpersons. The men who were discriminated against by this company policy did, however, receive monetary compensation. *Hooters to Pay $3.75 Million in Sex Suit*, USA Today, Oct. 1, 1997, at 1A; *see also* Richard Morgan, *The Inevitable Rise of the Gay Hooters*, NY Times, June 21, 2018, MB-1. ("Avoiding high style and serving lots of fried bar snacks, a gay sports-bar franchise looks to expand. The half-naked bartenders are part of the plan."). *See generally* Kimberly A. Yuracko, *Private Nurses and Playboy Bunnies: Explaining Permissible Sex Discrimination*, 92 Cal. L. Rev. 147, 191 (2004) (differentiating approaches taken by courts to cases raising issues of patient privacy versus sexual titillation). Similar issues arise in the visual arts regarding race. *See* Michael Paulson, *"Hamilton" Producers Will Change Job Posting, But Not Commitment to Diverse Casting*, NY Times, Mar. 30, 2016, C2. *See also* Russell Robinson, *Casting and Caste-ing: Reconciling Artistic Freedom and Antidiscrimination Norms*, 95 Cal. L. Rev. 1, 5 (2007) ("[W]hen it comes to casting, an entire industry effectively disregards Title VII.").

d. Voluntary Affirmative Action

As we have seen, Title VII and §1981 bar race discrimination, not merely discrimination against African Americans and other racial minorities. Title VII also bars sex discrimination, not merely discrimination against women. Accordingly, discrimination against whites and males is as impermissible as discrimination against minorities and women, although we have also seen that "reverse" discrimination may be harder to prove. One kind of reverse discrimination that is subject to somewhat different rules are racial and gender preferences pursuant to a valid affirmative action plan.

The Supreme Court first encountered this problem in *United Steelworkers of America v. Weber*, 443 U.S. 193 (1979), where a five-to-two majority upheld an employer's use of a voluntary affirmative action plan benefiting unskilled black workers. Kaiser Aluminum had negotiated with the union representing its workers to create a training program for incumbent, unskilled workers to fill skilled job categories. Until this plan was adopted, craft positions were filled by people with craft experience, typically learned in craft unions that had historically excluded blacks from membership. In order to address the resultant lack of trained minorities, the plan reserved for black employees 50 percent of the openings in these newly created in-plant training programs until the percentage of skilled black craft workers approximated the percentage of blacks in the local labor force. While the plan provided as many training openings for whites as for blacks, African Americans with less seniority than whites were admitted to it because there were far fewer of them available.

After holding that Title VII's prohibition against racial discrimination does not condemn all private, voluntary, race-conscious affirmative action plans, the Court upheld the plan and rejected the plaintiffs' discrimination claim.

> We need not today define in detail the line of demarcation between permissible and impermissible affirmative action plans. It suffices to hold that the challenged Kaiser-USWA affirmative action plan falls on the permissible side of the line. The purposes of the plan mirror those of the statute. Both were designed to break down old patterns of racial segregation and hierarchy. Both were structured to "open unemployment opportunities for Negroes in occupations which have been traditionally closed to them."
>
> At the same time, the plan does not unnecessarily trammel the interests of the white employees. The plan does not require the discharge of white workers and their replacement with new black hirees. . . . Nor does the plan create an absolute bar to the advancement of white employees; half of those trained in the program will be white. Moreover, the plan is a temporary measure; it is not intended to maintain racial balance, but simply to eliminate a manifest racial imbalance.

Id. at 208.

The Court reaffirmed *Weber* in *Johnson v. Transportation Agency, Santa Clara County, California*, 480 U.S. 616 (1987), and extended its application to affirmative action on behalf of women. The employer had promoted Diane Joyce to the position of road dispatcher, making her the first woman included among the 238 skilled craft worker jobs. A male, who had scored two points higher on an interview, sued, claiming reverse discrimination. Although Diane Joyce was qualified for the job, the district court found that the woman's sex was the determining factor in her selection.

When the case reached the Supreme Court, it used the opportunity to broadly approve affirmative action plans. As to the litigation structure of such cases, the Court held that, when a defendant claims it has acted in accordance with an affirmative action plan, the plaintiff has the burden of persuasion in establishing the invalidity of that affirmative action plan. Interestingly, the Court used the *McDonnell Douglas* inferential method of proof even though the decision maker admitted that sex was a factor in the selection decision. But the employer's explanation that it had relied upon its affirmative action plan was viewed by the Court as a "legitimate, nondiscriminatory reason," leaving it up to the male plaintiff to prove the plan invalid. Thus, in a reverse discrimination case, the plaintiff bears the burden of persuasion to prove discrimination, either because the challenged action was not taken pursuant to an affirmative action plan, *see* page 554, or because it was taken pursuant to an invalid plan. As to the substantive standard, *Weber* and *Johnson* focus on two aspects, that the plan address a "manifest imbalance" and that it "not unduly trammel" other workers' prospects.

i. Manifest Imbalance

The plan's use of race or sex must be aimed at remedying a "manifest imbalance in a traditionally segregated job category." Such an imbalance brings the affirmative action plan into alignment with the purposes of Title VII, which include breaking down historic patterns of discrimination. Justice Blackmun's concurrence in *Weber* demonstrated how broad this first factor is: "[T]he Court considers a job category to be 'traditionally segregated' when there has been a societal history of purposeful exclusion of blacks from the job category, resulting in a persistent disparity between the proportion of blacks in the labor force and the proportion of blacks among those who hold jobs within the category." *Weber*, 443 U.S. at 212.

This approach is cast in terms of statistical disparity alone, without regard to the underlying cause of the disparity. *Weber* made clear that an employer may adopt an affirmative action plan in the absence of any prior discrimination on its own part; remedying the effects of societal discrimination will suffice. *See id.* at 214. As for determining whether a manifest imbalance in a traditionally segregated job category exists, the *Johnson* Court observed that the proper comparison is between the percentage of minorities or women in the job category in the employer's work force and the percentage of those workers in the *relevant labor pool.* 480 U.S. at 632. A comparison with general population figures is appropriate only when the job involves no skills or skills easily acquired by the general population. *Id.* For skilled jobs, the appropriate comparison is to the skilled labor pool. *See Hazelwood Sch. Dist. v. United States*, 433 U.S. 299 (1977). Because *Johnson* involved skilled trade positions, the Court viewed the appropriate comparison to be that between the percentage of skilled workers in the employer's work force (zero) and the percentage of women in the relevant labor market having the requisite skills. *Johnson*, 480 U.S. at 632. Once the proper comparison is established, it is still necessary to determine whether the imbalance is great enough to justify the affirmative action remedy. *See Shea v. Kerry*, 796 F.3d 42 (D.C. Cir. 2015) (the employer adduced proof that its plan addressed manifest imbalances in senior-level Foreign Service Officer positions resulting from past discrimination).

An important, and as yet unresolved, issue is whether a voluntary affirmative action plan must be "remedial"—in the sense of aimed at remedying a manifest imbalance—to be lawful under Title VII. The affirmative action plans in both *Weber* and *Johnson* were designed to ameliorate a traditionally segregated job category, and the Court's decisions in those cases addressed when such a remedial interest would support an affirmative action plan. But when no such manifest imbalance exists, may a voluntary affirmative action plan yet be permissible? *Taxman v. Board of Education of Township of Piscataway*, 91 F.3d 1547 (3d Cir. 1996) (en banc), involved a claim by a white school teacher who had been laid off while an equally qualified black teacher was retained. The Third Circuit rejected the school district's use of race under its affirmative action plan to choose between two equally qualified teachers when one needed to be laid off. Since there was no underrepresentation of blacks in the Piscataway school system, the board did not assert a remedial purpose for the plan but instead relied upon a diversity rationale, reasoning that students would benefit from a racially diverse teaching staff. The Third Circuit, however, held that a nonremedial interest would not support an affirmative action plan under Title VII. In the wake of the Supreme Court's decision approving nonremedial affirmative action under the Equal Protection Clause in the context of higher education in *Grutter v. Bollinger*, 539 U.S. 306 (2003), the lower courts might be more open to such justifications in the context of Title VII, but *Parents Involved in Community Schools v. Seattle School Dist. No. 1*, 551 U.S. 701 (2007), cuts the other way. *See generally* Kingsley R. Browne, *Title VII and Diversity*, 14 NEV. L.J. 806 (2014).

ii. Not Unduly Trammel

The second prong for determining the legitimacy of an affirmative action plan under *Weber* and *Johnson* is that the plan must not "unduly trammel" the interests of majority group members. A common criticism of affirmative action by its opponents is that such programs disadvantage majority workers. In *Weber*, the Court suggested that a plan might be invalid if it (1) deprives white employees of their jobs; (2) was an absolute bar to their advancement; or (3) was not temporary since its goal was to maintain, not attain racial balance. The plan in *Weber* did not contravene any of these considerations. *Weber*, 443 U.S. at 209.

Most affirmative action plans focus on hiring and promotion, making them more easily defensible under the second prong of the *Weber/Johnson* standard. *Weber* itself involved a training program to which no one had automatic entitlement. Similarly, in *Johnson*, the male plaintiff had no entitlement to the position but was one of several qualified applicants for the job. Moreover, the plan did not block plaintiff from being promoted in the future, and he in fact received a promotion when another opening arose. *Johnson*, 480 U.S. at 639, n.15. The Court emphasized that no rigid quotas had been set; instead, sex was only one factor out of several considered by the employer in deciding whom to promote. An affirmative action plan used to determine layoffs, as opposed to hiring or promotion, would likely find more difficulty satisfying this prong.

Again, the *Taxman* case provides a useful comparison. Using race as a tiebreaker to decide which teacher to lay off when seniority and qualifications were equal was viewed by the Third Circuit as unduly trammeling the interests of Taxman, who lost her job and was unemployed for some time. In *Weber* and *Johnson*, no one lost a job or any position to which they were otherwise entitled. Even if the Court were to approve adoption of voluntary affirmative action plans for nonremedial purposes, upholding the application of such plans in a layoff context seems unlikely.

Although the Supreme Court has not decided a Title VII affirmative action case since *Johnson*, *Ricci v. DeStefano*, 457 U.S. 457 (2009), reproduced at page 630, may have cast doubt on *Weber* and *Johnson*. *Ricci* arose from a promotion test administered by the fire department in New Haven, Connecticut, which yielded racially skewed results. The rate of white candidates who passed the test was significantly higher than the rate of minority candidates. When the city decided not to certify the test results because of potential disparate impact liability, white firefighters sued the city. In a sharply divided opinion, the Supreme Court determined that the city's actions amounted to intentional disparate treatment of the white firefighters and granted them summary judgment. The fact that the racial disparity in the test results created a prima facie case for disparate impact was not a defense to the disparate treatment claim unless the employer had a "strong basis in evidence" to believe that it would be liable for disparate impact discrimination. *Id.* at 563. In order to meet this requirement, an employer had to demonstrate a strong basis to believe that the test was not a business necessity or job-related or, if it were, that practices with less discriminatory impact on minorities were available. *Id.* at 587.

The meaning of *Ricci* for affirmative action is unclear. On the one hand, the majority never cited either *Johnson* or *Weber*, perhaps suggesting that there are simply two lines of authority governing two different situations. This is bulwarked by the fact that the city did not articulate the usual justifications for affirmative action but rather simply argued that its refusal to certify results was justified by its fear of disparate impact liability. On the other hand, *Ricci* takes a more stringent approach to practices designed to help minorities, which may portend a much more stringent approach to affirmative action under Title VII.

The Second Circuit has opted for the two different lines of authority reading of the law. In *United States v. Brennan*, 650 F.3d 65, 72 (2d Cir. 2011), it held that

Johnson and *Weber* do not apply to all race- or gender-conscious employer actions. In light of *Ricci*, the "manifest imbalance" and "no unnecessary trammeling" analysis of those cases extends, at most, to circumstances in which an employer has undertaken a race- or gender-conscious affirmative action plan designed to benefit all members of a racial or gender class in a forward-looking manner only. Where, as here, the employer instead provides individualized race- or gender-conscious benefits as a remedy for previous disparate impact, the employer must satisfy the requirements of *Ricci*, not *Johnson* and *Weber*, in order to avoid disparate-treatment liability.

See also Shea v. Kerry, 796 F.3d 42, 54 (D.C. Cir. 2015) (finding *Weber/Johnson* to control a challenge to an affirmative action plan, despite *Ricci*, because those opinions "are directly applicable to this case" and the Supreme Court has cautioned against the lower courts finding its decisions overruled by implication).

Note on Voluntary Affirmative Action Plans of Public Employers

A public employer's affirmative action plan may be lawful under Title VII but still fall afoul of the Equal Protection Clause when a constitutional claim is brought. As you learned in Constitutional Law, all racial classifications by the state, local, or federal government are to be measured by strict scrutiny. Under this test, "such classifications are constitutional only if they are narrowly tailored measures that further compelling governmental interests." *Adarand Constr. v. Pena*, 515 U.S. 200 (1995); *Richmond v. J.A. Croson*, 488 U.S. 469 (1989). According to the Supreme Court, providing a remedy for the victims of proven discrimination is a sufficiently important governmental interest to withstand constitutional attack but remedying the effects of societal discrimination is not. *Wygant v. Jackson Bd. of Educ.*, 476 U.S. 262 (1986). Thus, one way to withstand a reverse equal protection claim is for an employer to have convincing evidence of its own prior discrimination before embarking on an affirmative action program.

Are there other compelling governmental interests justifying racial preferences? The Court addressed race-conscious decision making in the public sector in five-to-four decisions in four higher education cases. The first two, *Grutter v. Bollinger*, 539 U.S. 306 (2003), and *Gratz v. Bollinger*, 539 U.S. 244 (2003), involved challenges by white students denied admission to the University of Michigan. In both cases, the Supreme Court upheld diversity, at least for an educational institution, as a compelling governmental interest. And Justice O'Connor, speaking for the Court in *Grutter*, implied that diversity may be a compelling governmental interest in areas beyond higher education by citing favorably the amici briefs of large corporations and the brief of military leaders arguing in favor of racially diverse workforces.

The Court disagreed, however, about whether the programs at issue were sufficiently tailored to achieving that diversity interest. In *Grutter*, the Court upheld the law school admissions program as narrowly tailored to the diversity objective; however, in *Gratz*, dealing with undergraduate admissions, the Court struck down that program as not being tailored enough. The essential difference between the two programs was that the law school assessed the complete admissions file of each individual applicant, including membership in underrepresented minority groups, while the undergraduate program mechanically gave applicants who were members of underrepresented minority groups certain points. *See also Parents Involved in Community Schools v. Seattle School Dist. No. 1*, 551 U.S. 701 (2007) (striking down the use of race to achieve greater diversity in elementary and secondary schools).

The Court revisited diversity in college admissions in a pair of decisions, both involving the same University of Texas affirmative action plan. The first, *Fisher v. University of Texas at Austin,* 570 U.S. 297 (2013) ("*Fisher I*"), reversed the Fifth Circuit's approval of the university's admissions plan, but it did not disturb *Grutter*'s core premise that diversity could be a sufficiently compelling state interest to survive strict scrutiny. Rather, the majority believed that the Fifth Circuit had been too deferential to the university's tailoring of its plan to the diversity interest claimed. According to the Court, "[n]arrow tailoring also requires that the reviewing court verify that it is 'necessary' for a university to use race to achieve the educational benefits of diversity," which requires "a careful judicial inquiry into whether a university could achieve sufficient diversity without using racial classifications." *Id.* at 312.

Although that set what some believed was an impossibly high standard for the plan, on remand, the Fifth Circuit again upheld the admissions program, and this time the Supreme Court, somewhat surprisingly, affirmed. *Fisher v. Univ. of Tex.,* 136 S. Ct. 2198 (2016). *Fisher II,* rejected plaintiff's challenge to the concreteness of the compelling interest being pursued because, first, UT may not set a goal of minority enrollment that is "reduced to pure numbers," *id.* at 2210, and, second, the University had sufficiently identified the educational values it sought to realize. *Id.* at 2211. The Court also found that UT had justified its need for explicit consideration of race despite progress in that regard as a result of state's Ten Percent Plan. *Id.* at 2212. The Court was dismissive with respect to the viability of other possible strategies to achieve this objective. Although *Fisher II* was historic in preserving *Grutter*'s approval of diversity rationales for race consciousness, it is a very limited decision given the peculiarities of the facts involved. Indeed, the majority described the UT process at issue as "sui generis." *Id.* at 2209.

And regardless of the status of race consciousness admissions in institutions of higher education, *Fisher II,* like *Fisher I,* provided only the most tentative guidance on the limits of affirmative action in the employment context. Prior to *Fisher* but after the Michigan cases, the Seventh Circuit considered the "diversity" question in that setting. At issue was a challenge to the Chicago police department's practice of racially "standardizing" test scores to increase the number of African Americans and Hispanics promoted within the force. In rejecting a suit by white officers, the court held that "there is an even more compelling need for diversity in a large metropolitan police force charged with protecting a racially and ethnically divided major American city like Chicago. Under the *Grutter* standards, we hold, the City of Chicago has set out a compelling operational need for a diverse police department." *Petit v. Chicago,* 352 F.3d 1111, 1117-18 (7th Cir. 2003).

Despite *Petit,* the constitutionality of affirmative action in the employment context is uncertain. Two circuits, including the Seventh which decided *Petit,* have sustained challenges to race-conscious diversity programs on the basis of the Equal Protection Clause. *Alexander v. City of Milwaukee,* 474 F.3d 437, 446 (7th Cir. 2007) (*Petit* "never approved such a loose and indeed effectively standardless approach" as the one at issue); *Lomack v. City of Newark,* 463 F.3d 303, 310 (3d Cir. 2006) (unlike *Petit,* "the City does not argue that diversity within individual fire companies is in any other way necessary, or even beneficial, to the Fire Department's mission of fighting fires, *i.e.,* that the Department has an operational need for diverse fire companies").

Adarand, Grutter/Gratz, Parents Involved, and the two *Fishers* are all constitutional, not statutory, decisions, but public employers' affirmative action plans must fall within both constitutional and statutory limits. That the Court found diversity to be a compelling state interest in the context of university admissions in *Grutter* does not necessarily mean it will be viewed as a compelling state interest in the employment setting, were a constitutional challenge brought. *See generally* Deborah C. Malamud, *The Strange Persistence of Affirmative Action Under Title VII*, 118 W. VA. L. REV. 1, 23 (2015).

2. Systemic Disparate Impact Discrimination

While disparate treatment discrimination is the purposeful exclusion of minorities or women from jobs, disparate impact discrimination exists when employment policies, regardless of intent, adversely affect one group more than another and cannot be justified. This section briefly outlines the structure of disparate impact analysis, the policies subject to disparate impact analysis, and defenses to a disparate impact case.

As we will see, the disparate impact theory clearly applies under Title VII of the Civil Rights Act of 1964 and under the ADA. It also operates under the ADEA, although in a very diluted form. *See Meacham v. Knolls Atomic Power Lab.*, 554 U.S. 84 (2008); *Smith v. City of Jackson*, 544 U.S. 228 (2005). *See* page 645. The Supreme Court has held that disparate impact is *not* available under 42 U.S.C. §1981 (2018); *see Gen. Bldg. Contractors Ass'n v. Pennsylvania*, 458 U.S. 5 (2002), or under 42 U.S.C. §1983 (2018) in suits enforcing the equal protection clause of the United States Constitution; *see, e.g., Personnel Admin. of Mass. v. Feeney*, 442 U.S. 256, 272 (1979).

Even under Title VII, where disparate impact originated as a theory of liability, recent developments have altered the landscape. The theory originated in 1971 in *Griggs v. Duke Power Co.*, 401 U.S. 424 (1971), and was elaborated on in a number of Supreme Court decisions until 1989. In that year, *Wards Cove Packing Co. v. Atonio*, 490 U.S. 642 (1989), radically reconceptualized the law. Congress, in turn, revived disparate impact analysis as the centerpiece (and most controversial part) of the Civil Rights Act of 1991. Most recently, the Supreme Court decided *Ricci v. DeStefano*, 457 U.S. 457 (2009), which at least limited the disparate impact theory and which some believe signals its end.

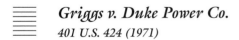

Griggs v. Duke Power Co.
401 U.S. 424 (1971)

Chief Justice BURGER delivered the opinion of the Court.

[Prior to the effective date of Title VII, Duke Power explicitly discriminated on the basis of race. "Negroes were employed only in the Labor Department where the highest paying jobs paid less than the lowest paying jobs in the other four 'operating' departments in which only whites were employed." With the enactment of Title VII, the Company abandoned its prior policy and allowed blacks to be hired into, or transfer to, any other department. However, Duke Power applied to these workers a high school diploma requirement that had applied for a decade to white workers seeking operating jobs. Further, on the effective date of Title VII, Duke Power for the first time required satisfactory scores on two professionally prepared tests for initial employment (although for current employees only the high school diploma was required for transfer). Shortly thereafter, Duke Power permitted incumbent employees who lacked a high school education to transfer by passing the two tests, the Wonderlic Personnel Test, which purports to measure general intelligence, and the Bennett Mechanical Comprehension Test. The district court found neither test directed or intended to measure the ability to learn to perform a particular job or category of jobs. The requisite scores used for both initial hiring and transfer approximated the national median for high school graduates. The test standards would thus screen out approximately half of all high school graduates.

[Both the district court and the Fourth Circuit found that, despite the prior policy of overt racial discrimination, there was no showing of a racial purpose or invidious intent in the adoption of the high school diploma or test requirements and that these standards had been applied fairly to whites and Negroes alike.]

The objective of Congress in the enactment of Title VII is plain from the language of the statute. It was to achieve equality of employment opportunities and remove barriers that have operated in the past to favor an identifiable group of white employees over other employees. Under the Act, practices, procedures, or tests neutral on their face, and even neutral in terms of intent, cannot be maintained if they operate to "freeze" the status quo of prior discriminatory employment practices.

The Court of Appeals' [judges] agreed that, on the record in the present case, "whites register far better on the Company's alternative requirements" than Negroes.[6]

This consequence would appear to be directly traceable to race. Basic intelligence must have the means of articulation to manifest itself fairly in a testing process. Because they are Negroes, petitioners have long received inferior education in segregated schools and this Court expressly recognized these differences in *Gaston County v. United States,* 395 U.S. 285 (1969). There, because of the inferior education received by Negroes in North Carolina, this Court barred the institution of a literacy test for voter registration on the ground that the test would abridge the right to vote indirectly on account of race. Congress did not intend by Title VII, however, to guarantee a job to every person regardless of qualifications. In short, the Act does not command that any person be hired simply because he was formerly the subject of discrimination, or because he is a member of a minority group. Discriminatory preference for any group, minority or majority, is precisely and only what Congress has proscribed. What is required by Congress is the removal of artificial, arbitrary, and unnecessary barriers to employment when the barriers operate invidiously to discriminate on the basis of a racial or other impermissible classification.

Congress has now provided that tests or criteria for employment or promotion may not provide equality of opportunity merely in the sense of the fabled offer of milk to the stork and the fox. On the contrary, Congress has now required that the posture and condition of the job-seeker be taken into account. It has—to resort again to the fable—provided that the vessel in which the milk is proffered be one all seekers

---

6. In North Carolina, 1960 census statistics show that, while 34% of white males had completed high school, only 12% of Negro males had done so. U.S. Bureau of the Census, U.S. Census of Population: 1960, Vol. 1, Characteristics of the Population, pt. 35, Table 47.

Similarly, with respect to standardized tests, the EEOC in one case found that use of a battery of tests, including the Wonderlic and Bennett tests used by the Company in the instant case, resulted in 58% of whites passing the tests as compared with only 6% of the blacks. Decision of EEOC, CCH Empl. Prac. Guide, ¶17,304.53 (Dec. 2, 1966). *See also* Decision of EEOC 70-552, CCH Empl. Prac. Guide, ¶6139 (Feb. 19, 1970).

can use. The Act proscribes not only overt discrimination but also practices that are fair in form, but discriminatory in operation. The touchstone is business necessity. If an employment practice which operates to exclude Negroes cannot be shown to be related to job performance, the practice is prohibited.

On the record before us, neither the high school completion requirement nor the general intelligence test is shown to bear a demonstrable relationship to successful performance of the jobs for which it was used. Both were adopted, as the Court of Appeals noted, without meaningful study of their relationship to job-performance ability. Rather, a vice president of the Company testified, the requirements were instituted on the Company's judgment that they generally would improve the overall quality of the work force.

The evidence, however, shows that employees who have not completed high school or taken the tests have continued to perform satisfactorily and make progress in departments for which the high school and test criteria are now used. The promotion record of present employees who would not be able to meet the new criteria thus suggests the possibility that the requirements may not be needed even for the limited purpose of preserving the avowed policy of advancement within the Company. In the context of this case, it is unnecessary to reach the question whether testing requirements that take into account capability for the next succeeding position or related future promotion might be utilized upon a showing that such long-range requirements fulfill a genuine business need. In the present case the Company has made no such showing.

The Court of Appeals held that the Company had adopted the diploma and test requirements without any "intention to discriminate against Negro employees." We do not suggest that either the District Court or the Court of Appeals erred in examining the employer's intent; but good intent or absence of discriminatory intent does not redeem employment procedures or testing mechanisms that operate as "built-in headwinds" for minority groups and are unrelated to measuring job capability.

The Company's lack of discriminatory intent is suggested by special efforts to help the undereducated employees through Company financing of two-thirds the cost of tuition for high school training. But Congress directed the thrust of the Act to the *consequences* of employment practices, not simply the motivation. More than that, Congress has placed on the employer the burden of showing that any given requirement must have a manifest relationship to the employment in question.

The facts of this case demonstrate the inadequacy of broad and general testing devices as well as the infirmity of using diplomas or degrees as fixed measures of capability. History is filled with examples of men and women who rendered highly effective performance without the conventional badges of accomplishment in terms of certificates, diplomas, or degrees. Diplomas and tests are useful servants, but Congress has mandated the common sense proposition that they are not to become masters of reality.

[The Court also rejected the defendant's argument that §703(h) justified the test requirements. That provision authorizes the use of "any professionally developed ability test" that is not "designed, intended or used to discriminate because of race." Looking to EEOC guidelines and the legislative history of the statute, "the conclusion is inescapable that the EEOC's construction of §703(h) to require that employment tests be job related comports with congressional intent."]

Nothing in the Act precludes the use of testing or measuring procedures; obviously they are useful. What Congress has forbidden is giving these devices and mechanisms controlling force unless they are demonstrably a reasonable measure of job performance. Congress has not commanded that the less qualified be preferred over the better qualified simply because of minority origins. Far from disparaging job qualifications as such, Congress has made such qualifications the controlling factor, so that race, religion, nationality, and sex become irrelevant. What Congress has commanded is that any tests used must measure the person for the job and not the person in the abstract. . . .

NOTES

1. *Disparate Impact History in a Nutshell.* The disparate impact theory was refined by the Court in a number of decisions from 1971 until 1989, at which point the Supreme Court decided *Wards Cove Packing Co. v. Atonio*, 490 U.S. 642 (1989), which most observers viewed as essentially gutting the theory. *Wards Cove* generated a national controversy about the disparate impact theory that was ultimately resolved by the enactment of the Civil Rights Act of 1991, whose centerpiece was a debate over "quotas," *Wards Cove*, and the appropriate structure of the disparate impact theory. During the debates, proponents argued that a strong impact theory was needed to open up job opportunities to minorities and women. Opponents vociferously claimed that disparate impact would result in quotas by encouraging employers to hire minorities and women, without regard to qualifications, merely to avoid potential liability.

In any event, since 1991 disparate impact has largely been framed in terms of the meaning of the amendments made by the Civil Rights Act. As we will see, however, those amendments refer back to prior law, so that some of the history of disparate impact must be revisited to determine what the present statute prohibits and permits. And the Supreme Court's 2009 decision in *Ricci v. DeStefano* once again cast doubt on the viability of the theory.

2. *Rationales for Disparate Impact.* Why should a showing of adverse impact alone, without intent to discriminate, be sufficient to establish illegal discrimination? Is it because defendants may be acting with intent to discriminate, but proof of such intent is not available to plaintiff? Duke Power imposed the challenged rules just as Title VII became effective. Was the Supreme Court merely trying to get around the lower court's finding of no intent to discriminate? "It might be possible to defend the [disparate impact theory] by framing it as simply an evidentiary tool used to identify genuine, intentional discrimination—to 'smoke out,' as it were, disparate treatment. But arguably the disparate-impact provisions sweep too broadly to be fairly characterized in such a fashion—since they fail to provide an affirmative defense for good-faith (i.e., nonracially motivated) conduct, or perhaps even for good faith plus hiring standards that are entirely reasonable." *Ricci v. DeStefano*, 557 U.S. 557, 595 (2009) (Scalia, J., concurring) (citations omitted).

Or perhaps the North Carolina school system was responsible. *Griggs* dealt with an educational prerequisite and test results that probably correlate highly with increased level and quality of education. These requirements were imposed in a state that segregated African Americans in underfunded and inferior school systems. Is it this de jure discrimination in education that caused blacks in North Carolina to be disproportionately affected by Duke Power's rule? If so, why should the employer be responsible? Ramona L. Paetzold & Steven L. Willborn, in *Deconstructing Disparate Impact: A View of the Model Through New Lenses*, 74 N.C. L. Rev. 325, 353-54

(1995), argue that the cause of impact is irrelevant to the disparate impact theory since "[t]he law treats the employer's criterion as the cause of a disparity, even though it may be only one of a wide array of factors necessary to produce the disparity."

Another rationale for employer liability in such cases is grounded in efficiency. Professor Paulette Caldwell believes that Title VII was designed to increase productive efficiency by allowing individuals to achieve their full economic potential. *See* Paulette Caldwell, *Reaffirming the Disproportionate Effects Standard of Liability in Title VII Litigation*, 46 U. Pitt. L. Rev. 555 (1985). Her point is that, in the long run, efficiency will be improved if the pool of potential workers is widened by adding persons whose full potential would never be developed if denied entry-level positions. Is this what Chief Justice Burger meant when he wrote in *Griggs* that "[h]istory is filled with examples of men and women who rendered highly effective performance without the conventional badges of accomplishment in terms of certificates, diplomas, and degrees?" If so, does it have much to do with "discrimination"?

At first blush, whatever the underlying justifications, disparate impact seems in tension with the basic premise of antidiscrimination legislation: Because members of protected groups are indistinguishable from similarly situated members of the majority, they ought not be treated differently in the workplace. While group differences may exist, disparate treatment ignores those differences and focuses instead on members of the protected group who are similarly situated to other individuals. In contrast, impact analysis not only acknowledges, but also focuses on, differences between groups. Individuals will be entitled to a remedy precisely because they are members of a group that is different.

The impact approach, however, does not abandon the equality principle. The business necessity defense permits the employer to rely on differences between employees when those differences are relevant to the job. Employers are prohibited from considering only differences that are not related to job performance. Thus, for purposes of qualifying for work, the underlying premise remains true: *Protected group members should be treated equally when their work qualifications are the same.*

Disparate impact liability effectively creates a duty for employers to identify and eliminate employment practices that unnecessarily operate as "built-in headwinds" for protected groups that have not yet achieved economic parity with white males. Viewed in this light, disparate impact can be considered a form of liability for negligence—an employer who does not intend to discriminate may nonetheless be liable for failing to exercise its duty of care toward protected group members. *See* David Benjamin Oppenheimer, *Negligent Discrimination*, 141 U. Pa. L. Rev. 899 (1993); *cf.* Stephanie Bornstein, *Reckless Discrimination*, 105 Calif. L. Rev. 1055 (2017).

3. *Proving Impact.* The Court's use of statistics in *Griggs* is unsophisticated— even naive—compared with later refinements. The impact statistics on high school diplomas and tests were not linked in any direct way to the defendant's practices. Nevertheless, *Griggs* is a landmark case because it validates a statistical approach to discrimination litigation. Further, the decision establishes another critical point: When data that relates directly to the practices of the defendant itself is not available, a plaintiff may make out a prima facie case with more general statistics, leaving the defendant to show the inapplicability of those statistics to its practices.

In contrast, in *Wards Cove Packing Co. v. Atonio*, 490 U.S. 642 (1989), the Supreme Court undertook a much more sophisticated view of statistical proof. At issue in that case was a remote, seasonal salmon-canning facility with two main classes of workers—cannery jobs (almost all Native Alaskan and Filipino) and noncannery jobs (almost all white). The comparison between the racial breakdown of those working in cannery jobs and those in unskilled noncannery jobs was more dramatic than the comparative pass rates in *Griggs*, and the plaintiffs in *Wards Cove* sought to prove the discriminatory impact of a number of neutral hiring practices, including "nepotism, a rehire preference, a lack of objective hiring criteria, separate hiring channels, [and] a practice of not promoting from within." *Id.* at 647. Consider how the plaintiffs could establish disparate impact based on the employer's use of the practices in hiring. If the unskilled noncannery workforce is predominantly white, nepotism and rehire preferences are likely to yield predominantly white hiring. But to what group should the workforce numbers be compared to determine whether the results are disparate?

Wards Cove held that the "proper comparison [is] between the racial composition of [the at-issue jobs] and the racial composition of the qualified . . . population in the relevant labor market." The concept of the relevant labor market is borrowed from systemic disparate treatment law. Is the relevant labor market concept as used in disparate treatment cases appropriate for disparate impact analysis? Consider two systemic disparate treatment cases discussed in the previous section. In *Teamsters v. United States* (*see* page 598), the relevant labor market was the general population, while in *Hazelwood*, it was persons certified to teach in the relevant geographic area. In *Teamsters*, there was no reason to believe that the subset of those interested in and otherwise qualified for truck-driving jobs varied much from the general population. That was obviously not true in *Hazelwood*, which involved school teachers. In both cases, however, the issue was whether the statistics supported an inference of discriminatory intent. The Court was seeking to identify the pool from which the employer drew its employees so it could compare that pool with the group selected in order to determine whether the difference between the two was significant enough to suggest intentional discrimination.

The question in a disparate impact case is not whether the statistics allow an inference of discriminatory intent but whether the employer's neutral employment practice has a disparate impact on a statutorily protected group. For purposes of this inquiry, what is the "relevant labor market"? Is it the applicant pool, the labor pool from which the employer recruited, the labor pool in the geographic area surrounding the workplace, or the general population—and, if the last, the general population where? Each of these options creates potential problems. The applicant pool is perhaps the most relevant comparison group because it is directly affected by the employer's practices. The applicant pool, however, might be distorted by the employer's choice of recruitment sources, or posted qualifications, or reputation for discrimination. Similarly, the employer's choice of labor pool may not be appropriate because that pool may be distorted by the employer's practices. The geographic area "around" the workplace may not be appropriate because the job in question may require a broader search. Is the best choice the labor pool from which a reasonable nondiscriminatory employer would draw its employees? But a reasonable employer who had no intent to discriminate might select a local and homogenous labor pool just because it is convenient. Should that pool be compared with the most diverse pool of qualified applicants available in order to determine whether there is a disparate impact? Does impact analysis impose on employers a duty to seek out the most diverse labor pool?

4. *Who Can Use the Disparate Impact Theory?* The cases invoking disparate impact have almost all involved minorities or women. Can whites or males invoke the theory? *See* Charles A. Sullivan, *The World Turned Upside Down?: Disparate Impact*

Claims by White Males, 98 Nw. U. L. Rev. 1505 (2004) (concluding that, while as a matter of pure statutory interpretation, Title VII is better read not to permit such suits, it should be construed to permit them because of equal protection concerns).

5. *Current Applications of the Impact Theory.* The most successful challenges under disparate impact have undoubtedly been to tests, often traditional pen-and-paper (or computer-administered examinations) but also often to physical fitness tests. *See* page 627. Disparate impact analysis, however, can be aimed at a wide variety of practices, including objective criteria such as height and weight requirements, and subjective ones such as unstructured interviews. Three current issues concern the possible disparate impact of policies against hiring those who are currently unemployed, *see* Jennifer Jolly-Ryan, *Have a Job to Get a Job: Disparate Treatment and Disparate Impact of the "Currently Employed" Requirement*, 18 Mich. J. Race & L. 189 (2012); those with low credit scores (probably highly correlated with unemployment), *see* Lea Shepard, *Toward a Stronger Financial History Antidiscrimination Norm*, 53 B.C. L. Rev. 1695 (2012); and those with arrest and conviction records, *see* Johnathan J. Smith, *Banning the Box but Keeping the Discrimination?: Disparate Impact and Employers' Overreliance on Criminal Background Checks*, 49 Harv. C.R.-C.L. L. Rev. 197 (2014); Terence G. Connor & Kevin J. White, *The Consideration of Arrest and Conviction Records in Employment Decisions: A Critique of the EEOC Guidance*, 43 Seton Hall L. Rev. 971 (2013). Some states and cities have addressed some of these questions without framing the issue as racial discrimination. For example, "ban the box" legislation limits the timing of inquiries about criminal history. Michael Pinard, *Criminal Records, Race and Redemption*, 16 N.Y.U. J. Legis. & Pub. Pol'y 963, 985-86 (2013)

A fourth potential application of disparate impact has yet to be reflected in case-law or in governmental regulation, but it looms increasingly large: workplace analytics, including the use of artificial intelligence, as a means of selecting employees. *See generally* Charles A. Sullivan, *Employing AI*, 63 Vill. L. Rev. 395 (2018). Although efforts in this direction are still in early stages, the technique of using big data to identify candidates likely to be successful in one or more measures of job performance threatens both to result in substantial disparate impact and challenges traditional notions of business necessity. Solon Barocas and Andrew Selbst, *Big Data's Disparate Impact*, 104 Calif. L. Rev. 671, 677 (2016), write that data mining seeks to discover statistically significant correlations between the "target variables" (the sought-after characteristics of better workers) and the traits of potential workers to the extent they can be found in the data. And, assuming that the target variable is itself job related, the algorithm will identify traits that correlate with that variable—even though there may be no causal explanation available for why that might be true. Thus, these commentators conclude that traditional validation techniques are likely to be satisfied: "Data mining will likely only be used if it is actually predictive of something, so the business necessity defense solely comes down to whether the trait sought is important enough to job performance to justify its use in any context." *Id.* at 709. *See also* Pauline Kim, *Data-Driven Discrimination at Work*, 58 Wm. & Mary L. Rev. 857, 860 (2017).

a. Plaintiff's Proof of a Prima Facie Case

Section 703(k)(1)(A)(i) states the general rule for a disparate impact case: Plaintiff carries the burden of persuasion that the employer "uses a particular employment practice that causes disparate impact on the basis of race, color, religion, sex, or national origin." This embraces two questions that arose before the 1991 Amendments: (1) Is every employment-related action of an employer a qualifying "employment practice"? (2) How does a plaintiff establish that a disparate impact resulted from a "particular" practice as opposed to a congeries of causes?

Both points can be illustrated by *Connecticut v. Teal*, 457 U.S. 440 (1982), which involved a two-part selection process: a written test and a more subjective assessment of the candidates who passed the written test. The employer attempted to avoid disparate impact analysis of its written test on the ground that the "bottom line"—the end product of the employer's total selection procedure—did not have a disparate racial impact, even though the test considered by itself had such an impact. The Supreme Court rejected that approach, focusing on the right of individual black applicants to be free from barriers in the employment process that impact blacks as a group. While blacks were not disproportionately screened out of jobs in *Teal*, they were disproportionately screened out of the opportunity to compete for those jobs by the test. The 1991 Civil Rights Act, by requiring the plaintiff to prove "a particular employment practice that causes disparate impact," essentially codifies *Teal*.

Teal, however (like *Griggs*), involved a challenge to an objective, pass/fail requirement. The plaintiffs in *Griggs* challenged the employer's requirements for a high school diploma and a passing score on two standardized tests. The *Teal* plaintiffs also challenged a test. Thus, the practices being challenged in both cases were objective requirements, and the impact of each could be readily measured. What would have happened if the test in *Teal* did not have a disparate impact but plaintiffs had been able to show that the subjective portion of the selection process resulted in the disproportionate exclusion of African Americans? Can subjective components comprise "a particular employment practice" under the amended statute? The answer seems clearly yes. In *Watson v. Fort Worth Bank & Trust*, 487 U.S. 977 (1988), the Court unanimously held that subjective employment practices could also be attacked under the disparate impact theory. *Id*. at 989. Watson's employer relied upon supervisors' subjective assessments of employees in deciding who would receive promotions. Rejecting the employer's argument that subjective practices did not lend themselves to disparate impact analysis, the Court determined that its "decisions in *Griggs* and succeeding cases could largely be nullified if disparate impact analysis were applied only to standardized selection practices." *Id*. at 990. The Court was persuaded that "disparate impact analysis is in principle no less applicable to subjective employment criteria than to objective or standardized tests. In either case, a facially neutral practice, adopted without discriminatory intent, may have effects that are indistinguishable from intentionally discriminatory practices." *Id*. Accordingly, the Court held that disparate impact claims may be brought to attack either objective or subjective practices. In light of *Watson*, §703(k) will undoubtedly be read to include subjective practices that have an impact.

This suggests that the disparate impact theory will sweep very broadly, but there are some statutory and judicially crafted exceptions. Thus, §703(k)(3) exempts employer rules prohibiting the employment of an individual who currently, knowingly, and illegally uses or possesses a controlled substance. Additional limitations may be created by the courts. An example of a "volitional exception" is *Garcia v. Spun Steak Co.*, 998 F.2d 1480 (9th Cir. 1993), where the employer required its bilingual employees to speak only English while on the job. Although the impact of the rule fell more harshly on employees of Hispanic origin, the Ninth Circuit found the rule immune from impact attack: Bilingual employees could comply with the rule and thus could avoid discipline simply by obeying. The court, moreover, found that employees have no affirmative right to speak their language of choice or otherwise to express their cultural heritage at work. *See also Lanning v. SEPTA*, 308 F.3d 286, 293 (3d Cir. 2002) (suggesting that the ability of women to improve their performance on a physical fitness test by training for it was relevant to assessing the test's validity). *But see Maldonado v. Altus*, 433 F.3d 1294, 1304-5 (10th Cir. 2006) (holding that English-only rules can create or contribute to a hostile work environment under disparate treatment and disparate impact theories).

Another judge-made exception may be employer passivity: At least one circuit has held that, for a disparate impact claim, the practice being challenged must be affirmatively adopted by the employer. In *EEOC v. Chicago Miniature Lamp Works*, 947 F.2d 292, 305 (7th Cir. 1991), the employer relied upon a word-of-mouth recruiting method for hiring new employees. Although the EEOC contended this resulted in a disparate impact on blacks, the court refused to permit an impact claim to proceed, reasoning it was the employees' actions of referring their friends and relatives, not any employer policy, that had caused the impact. "Passive reliance" on employee action is not an employer policy for purposes of disparate impact analysis, said the court.

While these kinds of limitations on disparate impact may be significant, the most difficult problem for plaintiffs is likely to be identifying the "particular" employment practice that causes an impact. We have seen that in *Connecticut v. Teal*, the Supreme Court rejected the "bottom line" defense to disparate impact claims, reasoning that if a particular component of a selection process had a disparate impact, that component could be challenged even if the overall result of the selection process produced no impact. *Teal*, 457 U.S. 440. In *Wards Cove v. Atonio*, the Court confronted the flip side of *Teal*, and held that plaintiffs could *not* mount a disparate impact challenge to the bottom line results of the employer's hiring practices: "[A] Title VII plaintiff does not make out a case of disparate impact simply by showing that, 'at the bottom line' there is racial *imbalance* in the work force. As a general matter, a plaintiff must demonstrate that it is the application of a specific or particular employment practice that has created the disparate impact under attack." *Wards Cove*, 490 U.S. at 657; *see generally* Charles A. Sullivan, *Disparate Impact: Looking Past the* Desert Palace *Mirage*, 47 Wm. & Mary L. Rev. 911, 960-64 (2005).

In the 1991 Civil Rights Act, Congress essentially codified this aspect of *Wards Cove*. Section 703(k)(1)(A) provides that an unlawful employment practice based on disparate impact is established only if "(i) a complaining party demonstrates that a respondent uses a particular employment practice that causes a disparate impact. . . ." Importantly, however, the statute provides an exception: Plaintiffs may attack the bottom line if they can show that the individual components of the whole process are not capable of separation for analysis. §703(k)(1)(B)(i).

Thus, if more than one employment practice is involved in a selection process (as in *Teal*), plaintiff must identify the component or components that are causing the disparate impact and must prove the impact of each. This is not a dramatic change in the law. *Griggs*, after all, involved a challenge to both standardized testing and to the high school diploma requirement. Evidence of the impact of each was presented to and relied upon by the Court. Discovery of employer records and testimony may produce evidence to support a showing of impact. If the plaintiff cannot prove the impact of each separate practice of the overall selection process, she will have to prove the components are not capable of separation for analysis. Presumably, such a plaintiff will have to show that she has taken all reasonable steps to establish the impact of the separate practices. *Compare Chin v. Port Auth. of N.Y. & N.J.*, 685 F.3d 135, 154-155 (2d Cir. 2012) (while a promotion process involved three steps, the recommendations in the first two steps could not be separated from the third for statistical analysis since both played an indeterminate role), *with Davis v. Cintas Corp.*, 717 F.3d 476 (6th Cir. 2013) (plaintiff neither identified a "particular employment practice" by including several distinct subjective elements of a multi-interview hiring system nor showed that the "many steps were so intertwined that they were not capable of separation for analysis").

Yet another question is how much disparity must the plaintiff show to establish disparate impact? In *Griggs*, for example, the disparate pass rates on the tests of whites and blacks were substantial. Even with respect to high school diplomas, the white graduation rate was three times that of the blacks. Might some practices have a real impact, but one that is not large enough to satisfy the statute? The answer is unclear. The EEOC uses a "four-fifths rule" as evidence of impact—that is, it regards "a selection rate for any race, sex, or ethnic group which is less than four-fifths (4/5) (or eighty percent) of the rate for the group with the highest rate" as sufficient and "a greater than four-fifths rate" as generally insufficient. The Supreme Court has neither adopted nor rejected the four-fifths rule, *see Connecticut v. Teal*, 457 U.S. 440, 453 n.12 (1982) (stressing that the rule was designed to allocate government enforcement resources, not to define liability). It has been cited by a number of courts, even when recognized only as a rule of thumb. *See EEOC v. Joint Apprenticeship Committee*, 186 F.3d 110 (2d Cir. 1998); *Bullington v. United Air Lines, Inc.*, 86 F.3d 1301 (10th Cir. 1999). *But see Bew v. City of Chicago*, 252 F.3d 891 (7th Cir. 2001) (upholding a finding of a prima facie case of disparate impact even though 98.24 percent of blacks and 99.96 percent of whites had passed a test because there was a statistical correlation between race and test failure).

Once the plaintiff has made such a showing, the statute further provides that:

> If the respondent demonstrates that a specific employment practice does not cause the disparate impact, the respondent shall not be required to demonstrate that such practice is required by business necessity.

Section 703(k)(B)(ii); 42 U.S.C. §2000e-2(k)(B)(ii). The new Act does not further define this "no cause" defense.

PROBLEM

9-2. The Naperville police department chief wants to replace the traditional police revolver used as standard equipment with the much more powerful Smith & Wesson Model 59 semi-automatic. The Model 59 is very powerful and is quite large, with a wide hand grip. National data show that over 50 percent of all women and about 10 percent of all men would be unable to handle the gun because of the size of the hand grip. Assume the police chief asks you if there would be any legal problem with the department adopting the Model 59. What additional facts would you like to know before you render an opinion? Is this an "employment practice" to begin with? Even if not, is hiring only those who can use the weapon such a practice or does this push the disparate impact theory too far? Could you recommend that the department take any steps before requiring that the Model 59 be used by all department officers that might help insulate the department from disparate impact liability?

---

b. Defendant's Rebuttal

There are several rebuttal possibilities available to the employer to respond to a prima facie case of disparate impact discrimination. The most obvious is simply for employers to try to undermine the plaintiff's showing of a prima facie case by introducing evidence that the data on which plaintiff relied were flawed. The second is for the employer to attempt to carry the burden of persuasion that the practice at issue is within the statutory business necessity/job-related defense. *Griggs* provides one example of a failed effort: The fact that the employer had legitimate, and even plausible, justifications for its policies was not sufficient absent some kind of empirical demonstration that its policies conduced to greater productivity. Other Supreme Court cases have taken a hard line toward what suffices where testing is concerned. *See Albemarle Paper Co. v. Moody*, 422 U.S. 405 (1975); *but see Washington v. Davis*, 426 U.S. 229 (1976). We will encounter a taste of the complications of testing validation and, indeed, of business necessity in *Ricci*, but a brief recounting of one case suggests some of the complications.

Lanning v. Southeastern Pennsylvania Transportation Authority, 181 F.3d 478 (3d Cir. 1999) (*Lanning I*), involved a physical fitness test instituted by SEPTA to upgrade the quality of its transit police force. Designed by an expert exercise physiologist with extensive experience in creating physical fitness tests for law enforcement agencies, the test required applicants to complete a 1.5 mile run within 12 minutes. This would require an aerobic capacity of 42.5 mL/kg/min, the aerobic capacity the expert determined would be necessary to perform the job of SEPTA transit officer. Implementation of the test had a strongly disparate impact on women: Between 6 and 12 percent of women applicants passed it as compared to 55 to 60 percent of male applicants. While SEPTA rigorously applied the test to new applicants, it did not impose similar requirements on incumbents, merely offering incentives for current officers to meet such aerobic levels. Most did, but many did not, and SEPTA never attempted to measure the performance of those who failed to keep fit. Indeed, some "unfit" incumbent officers were promoted and also given special recognition, commendations, and satisfactory performance evaluations.

Turning to the meaning of business necessity, *Lanning I* interpreted the 1991 Amendments as endorsing the business necessity standard enunciated in *Griggs* (and not *Wards Cove*'s watering down of that standard). It concluded:

> Taken together, *Griggs*, *Albemarle* and *Dothard* teach that in order to show the business necessity of a discriminatory cutoff score an employer must demonstrate that its cutoff measures the minimum qualifications necessary for successful performance of the job in question. Furthermore, because the Act instructs us to interpret its business necessity language in conformance with *Griggs* and its pre-*Wards Cove* progeny, we must conclude that the Act's business necessity language incorporates this standard.

Lanning I, 181 F.3d at 489. Thus, what you learned about business necessity from reading *Griggs* seems largely applicable.

But if the *Lanning I* approach to the proper standard is simply a return to *Griggs*, the application of that standard generated greater difficulties. The aerobic test at issue was "job related" in the sense that everyone who passed it will be fit, at least aerobically, for the job. It might not be "job related" if that term means that those who fail the test are not fit to be police officers. The majority in *Lanning I* believed that the aerobic test must measure only the *minimum* qualifications necessary for the job. What is wrong with the "more is better" approach? Is it that more may be *better* for business but not *necessary*? Since SEPTA did not require aerobic fitness of current employees, although it did encourage such fitness, how could the specified aerobic level be "necessary"?

Lanning I, thus, took a very stringent approach to business necessity and seemed to presage a victory for plaintiffs. However, the court remanded, and on remand the district court found that the test satisfied the Third Circuit's requirements. In *Lanning II*, 308 F.3d 286 (3d Cir. 2002), the court of appeals affirmed:

> SEPTA argued that the run test measures the "minimum qualifications necessary" because the relevant studies indicate that individuals who fail the test will be much less likely to successfully execute critical policing tasks. For example, the District Court credited a study that evaluated the correlation between a successful run time and performance on 12 job standards. The study found that individuals who passed the run test had a success rate on the job standards ranging from 70% to 90%. The success rate of the individuals who failed the run test ranged from 5% to 20%. The District Court found that such a low rate of success was unacceptable for employees who are regularly called upon to protect the public. In so doing, the District Court implicitly defined "minimum qualifications necessary" as meaning "likely to be able to do the job."
>
> Plaintiffs argued, however, that within the group that failed the run test, significant numbers of individuals would still be able to perform at least certain critical job tasks. They argued that as long as some of those failing the run test can do the job, the standard cannot be classified as a "minimum." In essence, plaintiffs proposed that the phrase "minimum qualifications necessary" means "some chance of being able to do the job." Under this logic, even if those failing the test had a 1% chance of successfully completing critical job tasks, the test would be too stringent.
>
> We are not saying, as our distinguished brother in dissent suggests we are saying, that "more is better." While, of course, a higher aerobic capacity will translate into better field performance—at least as to many job tasks which entail physical capability—to set an unnecessarily high cutoff score would contravene *Griggs*. It would clearly be unreasonable to require SEPTA applicants to score so highly on the run test that their predicted rate of success be 100%. It is perfectly reasonable, however, to demand a chance of success that is better than 5% to 20%. . . .
>
> [W]e reject without more the argument that applicants—male and female—should not be tested until they have graduated from the police academy, perhaps two and one-half years after they first applied to SEPTA; indeed, the dissent recognizes but relegates to a footnote the increase in SEPTA's costs and the uncertainty in planning and recruitment this would occasion. [And] all incumbents—male and female—are now required to take a physical fitness test every six months, another step toward improving the workforce. In this connection, it bears mention that SEPTA is unable to discipline incumbents who do not pass the test only because of the patrol officers' union's challenge, sustained by an arbitrator. With the union's blessing, however, SEPTA offers financial incentives to those officers who do pass.
>
> One final note. While it is undisputed that SEPTA's 1.5 mile run test has a disparate impact on women, it is also undisputed that, in addition to those women who

could pass the test without training, nearly all the women who trained were able to pass after only a moderate amount of training. It is not, we think, unreasonable to expect that women—and men—who wish to become SEPTA transit officers, and are committed to dealing with issues of public safety on a day-to-day basis, would take this necessary step.

Lanning II, 308 F.3d at 291-93. Are you convinced that it is a "business necessity" to require only recruits to be fit? Is the last paragraph the real basis for the result, that the impact could easily have been avoided by the female candidates? If so, how does that fit into the statutory analysis?

PROBLEM

9-3.   Kaplan offers undergraduate and graduate degrees to students across the country. Some of its students obtain financial aid through programs operated by the Department of Education; consequently, some employees have access to those students' financial information. The Department has regulations that circumscribe the manner in which Kaplan can access and use students' information. Violations of those regulations can bring severe penalties.

About a decade ago, Kaplan discovered that some of its financial-aid officers had stolen payments that belonged to students and that some executives had engaged in self-dealing, by hiring relatives as vendors. In response, Kaplan implemented a number of measures, one of which was to run credit checks on applicants for senior-executive positions, accounting, and other positions with access to company financials or cash, and positions with access to student financial-aid information. The credit checks are performed by a third-party vendor, which reports, among other things, whether the applicant has ever filed for bankruptcy, is delinquent on child-support payments, has any garnishments on earnings, or has outstanding civil judgments exceeding $2,000. If an applicant's credit history includes any of the enumerated items, the vendor flags the applicant's file for "review." At that point, Kaplan reviews the file and makes an ad hoc decision as to whether to move forward with the application. The credit-check process is racially blind: The vendor does not report the applicant's race with her other information.

The EEOC has launched an investigation of whether Kaplan's use of credit checks screens out more African-American applicants than white applicants, creating a disparate impact in violation of Title VII. Assume that such an impact can be proved and that it is substantial. If you were representing Kaplan, how would you establish the business necessity of this practice? Are you assisted by the fact that the EEOC itself uses this kind of credit check for 84 of the agency's 97 positions, noting that "overdue just debts increase temptation to commit illegal or unethical acts as a means of gaining funds to meet financial obligations"?

These facts drawn from *EEOC v. Kaplan Higher Educ. Corp.*, 748 F.3d 749 (6th Cir. 2014), although the court there never reached the business necessity question.

c. Alternative Employment Practices

The Civil Rights Act of 1991 permits a plaintiff to prevail by showing a particular employment practice with a disparate impact if the employer fails to establish job relation and business necessity. But a disparate impact violation also exists when, despite the employer's successful proof of job relation and business necessity, the plaintiff shows that there exists an alternative employment practice "and the [employer] refuses to adopt such alternative employment practice." §703(k)(1)(A).

Proving an "alternative employment practice" is not easy, however, and there is little case law holding an employer liable under this alternative path. Most cases find a failure of plaintiff's proof in this regard. *See IBEW v. Miss. Power & Light Co*, 442 F.3d 313 (5th Cir. 2006); *Allen v. City of Chicago*, 351 F.3d 306 (7th Cir. 2003). One of the few exceptions is *Jones v. City of Boston*, 845 F.3d 28 (1st Cir. 2016), where plaintiffs had established the disparate impact on African Americans of a police department's tests on hair to determine the presence of illegal drugs. While the employer established the business necessity of drug testing police officers, plaintiffs established a triable case of an alternative employment practice: A reasonable factfinder could conclude that the police department did not adopt an available alternative—adding urinalysis confirmation—that would have met the department's legitimate needs with less disparate impact. *Id.* at 31.

Among unanswered questions is whether the alternative practice need be non-discriminatory or merely less discriminatory in effect. A second question is whether this path to liability exists when the alternative devices are effective, but not *equally* effective, or when they are costlier. In *Jones*, the court noted that urinalysis would have required additional supervision by, and cost for, the department, but it did not consider those costs sufficient to make the alternative unreasonable given that it did exactly that with other officers. Further, under the statute, a successful alternative selection practice claim also requires that the employer "refuse" to adopt the alternative practice. "Refuse" seems to mean more than mere failure to use the alternative practice, and *Jones* looked to the fact that plaintiffs provided the department with an expert's statement proposing this alternative as the basis for finding "refusal."

d. Another Defense

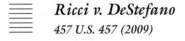

Ricci v. DeStefano
457 U.S. 457 (2009)

Justice KENNEDY delivered the opinion of the Court.

. . . In 2003, 118 New Haven firefighters took examinations to qualify for promotion to the rank of lieutenant or captain. Promotion examinations in New Haven (or City) were infrequent, so the stakes were high. The results would determine which firefighters would be considered for promotions during the next two years, and the order in which they would be considered. Many firefighters studied for months, at considerable personal and financial cost.

When the examination results showed that white candidates had outperformed minority candidates, the mayor and other local politicians opened a public debate that turned rancorous. Some firefighters argued the tests should be discarded because the results showed the tests to be discriminatory. They threatened a discrimination lawsuit if the City made promotions based on the tests. Other firefighters said the exams were neutral and fair. And they, in turn, threatened a discrimination lawsuit if the City, relying on the statistical racial disparity, ignored the test results and denied promotions to the candidates who had performed well. In the end the City took the side of those who protested the test results. It threw out the examinations.

Certain white and Hispanic firefighters who likely would have been promoted based on their good test performance sued the City and some of its officials. . . .

We conclude that race-based action like the City's in this case is impermissible under Title VII unless the employer can demonstrate a strong basis in evidence that, had it not taken the action, it would have been liable under the disparate-impact statute. The respondents, we further determine, cannot meet that threshold standard. As a result, the City's action in discarding the tests was a violation of Title VII. In light of our ruling under the statutes, we need not reach the question whether respondents' actions may have violated the Equal Protection Clause.

I . . .

A . . .

[The City's promotion process was governed by its charter, which included a civil service merit system as determined by job-related tests, as well as by a collective bargaining agreement with the firefighters' union and state and federal law. The charter imposed a "rule of three"—whoever was promoted had to be among the top three scorers. The CBA with the union required that, for promotion eligibility, a written examination would account for 60% and an oral examination 40% of each applicant's total score.

[The City hired Industrial/Organizational Solutions, Inc. (IOS) to develop and administer the examinations, at a cost of $100,000. IOS specializes in designing entry-level and promotional examinations for fire and police departments. It began its work by performing job analyses to identify the tasks, knowledge, skills, and abilities essential for the lieutenant and captain positions. This entailed interviews of incumbents and ride-alongs with on-duty officers. It also involved writing job-analysis questionnaires for incumbent battalion chiefs, captains, and lieutenants. "At every stage of the job analyses, IOS, by deliberate choice, oversampled minority firefighters to ensure that the results—which IOS would use to develop the examinations—would not unintentionally favor white candidates."

[IOS then developed the written and oral examinations to measure the candidates' job-related knowledge using training manuals and procedures approved by the New Haven fire chief and assistant fire chief. The written test for each position was multiple-choice, with each test having 100 questions written below a 10th-grade reading level. Candidates were then provided a 3-month study period and a list that identified the source material for the questions. The oral examinations concentrated on job skills and abilities, using hypothetical situations to test incident-command skills, firefighting tactics, interpersonal skills, leadership, and management ability, among other things. Candidates would be presented with these hypotheticals and asked to respond before a panel of three assessors. The assessors were battalion chiefs, assistant chiefs, and chiefs from departments of similar sizes to New Haven's throughout the country, and 66 percent were minorities, with each three-member assessment panels containing two minority members.]

B

[Although the City's contract with IOS contemplated "a technical report" by IOS after the examinations, City officials, including its counsel, Thomas Ude, met in early 2004 with IOS Vice President Chad Legel, who had led the IOS team that developed and administered the tests. They] expressed concern that the tests had discriminated against minority candidates. Legel defended the examinations' validity, stating that any numerical disparity between white and minority candidates was likely due to various external factors and was in line with results of the Department's previous promotional examinations.

Several days after the meeting, Ude sent a letter to the CSB [New Haven Civil Service Board] purporting to outline its duties with respect to the examination results. Ude stated that under federal law, "a statistical demonstration of disparate impact," standing alone, "constitutes a sufficiently serious claim of racial discrimination to serve as a predicate for employer-initiated, voluntar[y] remedies-even . . . race-conscious remedies."

[There ensured great controversy as the CSB considered certifying the results over the course of several meetings. Submissions were made detailing the racially disparate impact of the scores, although not the names of the candidates. Although unaware whether they had passed or failed, some firefighter-candidates spoke in favor of certifying the test results and argued that they had put great effort into studying the materials. Others spoke against certifying the test results, challenging the questions' relevance to firefighting practices in New Haven. Legel defended IOS's record and approach, but Christopher Hornick, an industrial/organizational psychologist from Texas who operates a consulting business competing with IOS, stressed that the scores indicated a "relatively high adverse impact." He also said that "the collective-bargaining agreement's requirement of using written and oral examinations with a 60/40 composite score might account for the statistical disparity." And Hornick argued for "assessment centers," where "candidates face real-world situations and respond just as they would in the field, allow[ing] candidates 'to demonstrate how they would address a particular problem as opposed to just verbally saying it or identifying the correct option on a written test.'"

[Other input to the CSB included (1) statements by a Homeland Security fire program specialist who viewed the questions as job-relevant, and (2) statements by a Boston College professor specializing in "race and culture as they influence performance on tests," who had not reviewed the tests themselves but viewed the racial impact as consistent with results across the country. The City's counsel argued against the tests, claiming that they "had one of the most severe adverse impacts that he had seen" and that "there are much better alternatives to identifying [firefighting] skills." He offered his "opinion that promotions . . . as a result of these tests would not be consistent with federal law." The mayor's representative took a similar tack. Ultimately, the CSB voted 2 to 2 on the use of the test results, which meant that the results would not be certified.]

II . . .

A . . .

[The Court seemed to suggest that disparate impact was somehow a subordinate theory of liability, writing that "[a]s enacted in 1964, Title VII's principal nondiscrimination provision held employers liable only for disparate treatment. That section retains its original wording today." But it recognized that "in *Griggs v. Duke Power Co.* interpreted the Act to prohibit, in some cases, employers' facially neutral practices that, in fact, are 'discriminatory in operation,'" and that the Civil Rights Act of 1991 "included a provision codifying the prohibition on disparate-impact discrimination."]

B

Petitioners allege that when the CSB refused to certify the captain and lieutenant exam results based on the race of the successful candidates, it discriminated against them in violation of Title VII's disparate-treatment provision. The City counters that its decision was permissible because the tests "appear[ed] to violate Title VII's disparate-impact provisions."

Our analysis begins with this premise: The City's actions would violate the disparate-treatment prohibition of Title VII absent some valid defense. All the evidence demonstrates that the City chose not to certify the examination results because of the statistical disparity based on race—*i.e.*, how minority candidates had performed when compared to white candidates. As the District Court put it, the City rejected the test results because "too many whites and not enough minorities would be promoted were the lists to be certified." Without some other justification, this express, race-based decisionmaking violates Title VII's command that employers cannot take adverse employment actions because of an individual's race.

The District Court did not adhere to this principle, however. It held that respondents' "motivation to avoid making promotions based on a test with a racially disparate impact . . . does not, as a matter of law, constitute discriminatory intent." And the Government makes a similar argument in this Court. It contends that the "structure of Title VII belies any claim that an employer's intent to comply with Title VII's disparate-impact provisions constitutes prohibited discrimination on the basis of race." But both of those statements turn upon the City's objective—avoiding disparate-impact liability—while ignoring the City's conduct in the name of reaching that objective. Whatever the City's ultimate aim—however well intentioned or benevolent it might have seemed—the City made its employment decision because of race. The City rejected the test results solely because the higher scoring candidates were white. The question is not whether that conduct was discriminatory but whether the City had a lawful justification for its race-based action.

We consider, therefore, whether the purpose to avoid disparate-impact liability excuses what otherwise would be prohibited disparate-treatment discrimination. Courts often confront cases in which statutes and principles point in different directions. Our task is to provide guidance to employers and courts for situations when these two prohibitions could be in conflict absent a rule to reconcile them. In providing this guidance our decision must be consistent with the important purpose of

Title VII—that the workplace be an environment free of discrimination, where race is not a barrier to opportunity.

With these principles in mind, we turn to the parties' proposed means of reconciling the statutory provisions. . . . Petitioners would have us hold that, under Title VII, avoiding unintentional discrimination cannot justify intentional discrimination. That assertion, however, ignores the fact that, by codifying the disparate-impact provision in 1991, Congress has expressly prohibited both types of discrimination. We must interpret the statute to give effect to both provisions where possible. We cannot accept petitioners' broad and inflexible formulation.

Petitioners next suggest that an employer in fact must be in violation of the disparate-impact provision before it can use compliance as a defense in a disparate-treatment suit. Again, this is overly simplistic and too restrictive of Title VII's purpose. The rule petitioners offer would run counter to what we have recognized as Congress's intent that "voluntary compliance" be "the preferred means of achieving the objectives of Title VII." *Firefighters v. Cleveland*, 478 U. S. 501, 515 (1986). Forbidding employers to act unless they know, with certainty, that a practice violates the disparate-impact provision would bring compliance efforts to a near standstill. Even in the limited situations when this restricted standard could be met, employers likely would hesitate before taking voluntary action for fear of later being proven wrong in the course of litigation and then held to account for disparate treatment.

At the opposite end of the spectrum, respondents and the Government assert that an employer's good-faith belief that its actions are necessary to comply with Title VII's disparate-impact provision should be enough to justify race-conscious conduct. But the original, foundational prohibition of Title VII bars employers from taking adverse action "because of . . . race." §2000e-2(a)(1). And when Congress codified the disparate-impact provision in 1991, it made no exception to disparate-treatment liability for actions taken in a good-faith effort to comply with the new, disparate-impact provision in subsection (k). Allowing employers to violate the disparate-treatment prohibition based on a mere good-faith fear of disparate-impact liability would encourage race-based action at the slightest hint of disparate impact. A minimal standard could cause employers to discard the results of lawful and beneficial promotional examinations even where there is little if any evidence of disparate-impact discrimination. That would amount to a *de facto* quota system, in which a "focus on statistics . . . could put undue pressure on employers to adopt inappropriate prophylactic measures." *Watson*. Even worse, an employer could discard test results (or other employment practices) with the intent of obtaining the employer's preferred racial balance. That operational principle could not be justified, for Title VII is express in disclaiming any interpretation of its requirements as calling for outright racial balancing. §2000e-2(j). The purpose of Title VII "is to promote hiring on the basis of job qualifications, rather than on the basis of race or color." *Griggs*.

In searching for a standard that strikes a more appropriate balance, we note that this Court has considered cases similar to this one, albeit in the context of the Equal Protection Clause of the Fourteenth Amendment. The Court has held that certain government actions to remedy past racial discrimination—actions that are themselves based on race—are constitutional only where there is a "'strong basis in evidence'" that the remedial actions were necessary. *Richmond v. J. A. Croson Co.*, 488 U.S. 469, 500 (1989). This suit does not call on us to consider whether the statutory constraints under Title VII must be parallel in all respects to those under the Constitution. That does not mean the constitutional authorities are irrelevant, however. Our cases discussing constitutional principles can provide helpful guidance in this statutory context. . . .

The same interests [as operated in *Wygant* and *Croson*] are at work in the interplay between the disparate-treatment and disparate-impact provisions of Title VII. Congress has imposed liability on employers for unintentional discrimination in order to rid the workplace of "practices that are fair in form, but discriminatory in operation." *Griggs.* But it has also prohibited employers from taking adverse employment actions "because of" race. Applying the strong-basis-in-evidence standard to Title VII gives effect to both the disparate-treatment and disparate-impact provisions, allowing violations of one in the name of compliance with the other only in certain, narrow circumstances. The standard leaves ample room for employers' voluntary compliance efforts, which are essential to the statutory scheme and to Congress's efforts to eradicate workplace discrimination. And the standard appropriately constrains employers' discretion in making race-based decisions: It limits that discretion to cases in which there is a strong basis in evidence of disparate-impact liability, but it is not so restrictive that it allows employers to act only when there is a provable, actual violation.

Resolving the statutory conflict in this way allows the disparate-impact prohibition to work in a manner that is consistent with other provisions of Title VII, including the prohibition on adjusting employment-related test scores on the basis of race. *See* §2000e-2(*l*). Examinations like those administered by the City create legitimate expectations on the part of those who took the tests. As is the case with any promotion exam, some of the firefighters here invested substantial time, money, and personal commitment in preparing for the tests. Employment tests can be an important part of a neutral selection system that safeguards against the very racial animosities Title VII was intended to prevent. Here, however, the firefighters saw their efforts invalidated by the City in sole reliance upon race-based statistics.

If an employer cannot rescore a test based on the candidates' race, §2000e-2(*l*), then it follows *a fortiori* that it may not take the greater step of discarding the test altogether to achieve a more desirable racial distribution of promotion-eligible candidates—absent a strong basis in evidence that the test was deficient and that discarding the results is necessary to avoid violating the disparate-impact provision. Restricting an employer's ability to discard test results (and thereby discriminate against qualified candidates on the basis of their race) also is in keeping with Title VII's express protection of bona fide promotional examinations. *See* §2000e-2(h) ("[N]or shall it be an unlawful employment practice for an employer to give and to act upon the results of any professionally developed ability test provided that such test, its administration or action upon the results is not designed, intended or used to discriminate because of race"); *cf. AT&T Corp. v. Hulteen*, 556 U.S. 701 (2009).

For the foregoing reasons, we adopt the strong-basis-in-evidence standard as a matter of statutory construction to resolve any conflict between the disparate-treatment and disparate-impact provisions of Title VII.

Our statutory holding does not address the constitutionality of the measures taken here in purported compliance with Title VII. We also do not hold that meeting the strong-basis-in-evidence standard would satisfy the Equal Protection Clause in a future case. As we explain below, because respondents have not met their burden under Title VII, we need not decide whether a legitimate fear of disparate impact is ever sufficient to justify discriminatory treatment under the Constitution.

Nor do we question an employer's affirmative efforts to ensure that all groups have a fair opportunity to apply for promotions and to participate in the process by which promotions will be made. But once that process has been established and employers have made clear their selection criteria, they may not then invalidate the test results, thus upsetting an employee's legitimate expectation not to be judged on the basis of race. Doing so, absent a strong basis in evidence of an impermissible disparate impact, amounts to the sort of racial preference that Congress has disclaimed, §2000e-2(j), and is antithetical to the notion of a workplace where individuals are guaranteed equal opportunity regardless of race.

Title VII does not prohibit an employer from considering, before administering a test or practice, how to design that test or practice in order to provide a fair opportunity for all individuals, regardless of their race. And when, during the test-design stage, an employer invites comments to ensure the test is fair, that process can provide a common ground for open discussions toward that end. We hold only that, under Title VII, before an employer can engage in intentional discrimination for the asserted purpose of avoiding or remedying an unintentional disparate impact, the employer must have a strong basis in evidence to believe it will be subject to disparate-impact liability if it fails to take the race-conscious, discriminatory action.

C

The City argues that, even under the strong-basis-in-evidence standard, its decision to discard the examination results was permissible under Title VII. That is incorrect. Even if respondents were motivated as a subjective matter by a desire to avoid committing disparate-impact discrimination, the record makes clear there is no support for the conclusion that respondents had an objective, strong basis in evidence to find the tests inadequate, with some consequent disparate-impact liability in violation of Title VII.

On this basis, we conclude that petitioners have met their obligation to demonstrate that there is "no genuine issue as to any material fact" and that they are "entitled to judgment as a matter of law." Fed. Rule Civ. Proc. 56(c). . . .

[The majority agreed with the City that the adverse racial impact here was significant, which required it "to take a hard look at the examinations to determine whether certifying the results would have had an impermissible disparate impact." But] a prima facie case of disparate-impact liability—essentially, a threshold showing of a significant statistical disparity, *Connecticut v. Teal*, and nothing more—is far from a strong basis in evidence that the City would have been liable under Title VII had it certified the results. That is because the City could be liable for disparate-impact discrimination only if the examinations were not job related and consistent with business necessity, or if there existed an equally valid, less-discriminatory alternative that served the City's needs but that the City refused to adopt. We conclude there is no strong basis in evidence to establish that the test was deficient in either of these respects. . . .

1

There is no genuine dispute that the examinations were job-related and consistent with business necessity. The City's assertions to the contrary are "blatantly contradicted by the record" [including the statements of Chad Legel and city officials outlining the detailed steps taken to develop and administer the examinations. The only outside witness who reviewed the examinations in any detail was the only one with any fire-fighting experience, and he stated that the "questions were relevant for both exams."].

2

Respondents also lacked a strong basis in evidence of an equally valid, less-discriminatory testing alternative that the City, by certifying the examination results, would necessarily have refused to adopt. Respondents raise three arguments to the contrary, but each argument fails. First, respondents refer to testimony before the CSB that a different composite-score calculation—weighting the written and oral examination scores 30/70—would have allowed the City to consider two black candidates for then-open lieutenant positions and one black candidate for then-open captain positions. (The City used a 60/40 weighting as required by its contract with the New Haven firefighters' union.) But respondents have produced no evidence to show that the 60/40 weighting was indeed arbitrary. In fact, because that formula was the result of a union-negotiated collective-bargaining agreement, we presume the parties negotiated that weighting for a rational reason. Nor does the record contain any evidence that the 30/70 weighting would be an equally valid way to determine whether candidates possess the proper mix of job knowledge and situational skills to earn promotions. Changing the weighting formula, moreover, could well have violated Title VII's prohibition of altering test scores on the basis of race. *See* §2000e-2(*l*). On this record, there is no basis to conclude that a 30/70 weighting was an equally valid alternative the City could have adopted.

Second, respondents argue that the City could have adopted a different interpretation of the "rule of three" [such as "banding," which is "rounding scores to the nearest whole number and considering all candidates with the same whole-number score as being of one rank." However, had] the City reviewed the exam results and then adopted banding to make the minority test scores appear higher, it would have violated Title VII's prohibition of adjusting test results on the basis of race. §2000e-2(*l*); *see also Chicago Firefighters Local 2 v. Chicago*, 249 F. 3d 649, 656 (CA7 2001) (Posner, J.) ("We have no doubt that if banding were adopted in order to make lower black scores seem higher, it would indeed be . . . forbidden"). As a matter of law, banding was not an alternative available to the City when it was considering whether to certify the examination results.

Third, and finally, respondents refer to statements by Hornick in his telephone interview with the CSB regarding alternatives to the written examinations. Hornick stated his "belie[f]" that an "assessment center process," which would have evaluated candidates' behavior in typical job tasks, "would have demonstrated less adverse impact." But Hornick's brief mention of alternative testing methods, standing alone, does not raise a genuine issue of material fact that assessment centers were available to the City at the time of the examinations and that they would have produced less adverse impact. . . .

3

On the record before us, there is no genuine dispute that the City lacked a strong basis in evidence to believe it would face disparate-impact liability if it certified the examination results. In other words, there is no evidence—let alone the required strong basis in evidence—that the tests were flawed because they were not job-related or because other, equally valid and less discriminatory tests were available to the City. Fear of litigation alone cannot justify an employer's reliance on race to the detriment of individuals who passed the examinations and qualified for promotions. The City's discarding the test results was impermissible under Title VII, and summary judgment is appropriate for petitioners on their disparate-treatment claim.

* * *

The record in this litigation documents a process that, at the outset, had the potential to produce a testing procedure that was true to the promise of Title VII: No individual should face workplace discrimination based on race. Respondents thought about promotion qualifications and relevant experience in neutral ways. They were careful to ensure broad racial participation in the design of the test itself and its administration. As we have discussed at length, the process was open and fair.

The problem, of course, is that after the tests were completed, the raw racial results became the predominant rationale for the City's refusal to certify the results. The injury arises in part from the high, and justified, expectations of the candidates who had participated in the testing process on the terms the City had established for the promotional process. Many of the candidates had studied for months, at considerable personal and financial expense, and thus the injury caused by the City's reliance on raw racial statistics at the end of the process was all the more severe. Confronted with arguments both for and against certifying the test results—and threats of a lawsuit either way—the City was required to make a difficult inquiry. But its hearings produced no strong evidence of a disparate-impact violation, and the City was not entitled to disregard the tests based solely on the racial disparity in the results.

Our holding today clarifies how Title VII applies to resolve competing expectations under the disparate-treatment and disparate-impact provisions. If, after it certifies the test results, the City faces a disparate-impact suit, then in light of our holding today it should be clear that the City would avoid disparate-impact liability based on the strong basis in evidence that, had it not certified the results, it would have been subject to disparate-treatment liability. . . .

Justice SCALIA, concurring.

I join the Court's opinion in full, but write separately to observe that its resolution of this dispute merely postpones the evil day on which the Court will have to confront the question: Whether, or to what extent, are the disparate-impact provisions of Title VII of the Civil Rights Act of 1964 consistent with the Constitution's guarantee of equal protection? The question is not an easy one. *See generally* Primus, *Equal Protection and Disparate Impact: Round Three*, 117 HARV. L. REV. 493 (2003).

The difficulty is this: Whether or not Title VII's disparate-treatment provisions forbid "remedial" race-based actions when a disparate-impact violation would *not* otherwise result—the question resolved by the Court today—it is clear that Title VII not only permits but affirmatively *requires* such actions when a disparate-impact violation *would* otherwise result. But if the Federal Government is prohibited from discriminating on the basis of race, *Bolling v. Sharpe*, 347 U. S. 497, 500 (1954), then surely it is also prohibited from enacting laws mandating that third parties—*e.g.*, employers, whether private, State, or municipal—discriminate on the basis of race. As the facts of these cases illustrate, Title VII's disparate-impact provisions place a racial thumb on the scales, often requiring employers to evaluate the racial outcomes of their policies, and to make decisions based on (because of) those racial outcomes. That type of racial decisionmaking is, as the Court explains, discriminatory. . . .

The Court's resolution of these cases makes it unnecessary to resolve these matters today. But the war between disparate impact and equal protection will be waged sooner or later, and it behooves us to begin thinking about how—and on what terms—to make peace between them.

Justice ALITO, with whom Justice SCALIA and Justice THOMAS join, concurring.

[The concurrence "join[ed] the Court's opinion in full" but wrote separately to correct important omissions in Justice GINSBURG's dissent. The major thrust of the concurrence was that, even were the Court to accept the dissent's "good cause" standard, resolving the case required a trial as to whether the avoidance of disparate impact liability was a pretext because there was a genuine issue of material fact, even under that lower standard, whether "the City's real reason was illegitimate, namely, the desire to placate a politically important racial constituency."]

Justice GINSBURG, with whom Justice STEVENS, Justice SOUTER, and Justice BREYER join, dissenting.

[The dissent started with the observation that, when Title VII was applied to public employment in 1972 "municipal fire departments across the country, including New Haven's, pervasively discriminated against minorities." She noted that in the early 1970's, "African-Americans and Hispanics composed 30 percent of New Haven's population, but only 3.6 percent of the City's 502 firefighters. The racial disparity in the officer ranks was even more pronounced: '[O]f the 107 officers in the Department only one was black, and he held the lowest rank above private.'" While some progress had been made, "[b]y order of this Court, New Haven, a city in which African-Americans and Hispanics account for nearly 60 percent of the population, must today be served— as it was in the days of undisguised discrimination—by a fire department in which members of racial and ethnic minorities are rarely seen in command positions." . . .]

Neither Congress' enactments nor this Court's Title VII precedents (including the now-discredited decision in *Wards Cove*) offer even a hint of "conflict" between an employer's obligations under the statute's disparate-treatment and disparate-impact provisions. Standing on an equal footing, these twin pillars of Title VII advance the same objectives: ending workplace discrimination and promoting genuinely equal opportunity.

Yet the Court today sets at odds the statute's core directives. When an employer changes an employment practice in an effort to comply with Title VII's disparate-impact provision, the Court reasons, it acts "because of race"—something Title VII's disparate-treatment provision generally forbids. This characterization of an employer's compliance-directed action shows little attention to Congress' design or to the *Griggs* line of cases Congress recognized as pathmarking . . . [Because a court is bound to read the provisions of any statute as harmonious] Title VII's disparate-treatment and disparate-impact proscriptions must be read as complementary.

In codifying the *Griggs* and *Albemarle* instructions, Congress declared unambiguously that selection criteria operating to the disadvantage of minority group members can be retained only if justified by business necessity. In keeping with Congress' design, employers who reject such criteria due to reasonable doubts about their reliability can hardly be held to have engaged in discrimination "because of" race. A reasonable endeavor to comply with the law and to ensure that qualified candidates of all races have a fair opportunity to compete is simply not what Congress meant to interdict. I would therefore hold that an employer who jettisons a selection device when its disproportionate racial impact becomes apparent does not violate Title VII's disparate-treatment bar automatically or at all, subject to this key condition: The employer must have good cause to believe the device would not withstand examination for business necessity. *Cf. Faragher v. Boca Raton*, 524 U. S. 775, 806 (1998) (observing that it accords with "clear statutory policy" for employers "to prevent violations" and "make reasonable efforts to discharge their duty" under Title VII). . . .

This litigation does not involve affirmative action. But if the voluntary affirmative action at issue in *Johnson* [*v. Transportation Agency, Santa Clara Cty.*] does not discriminate within the meaning of Title VII, neither does an employer's reasonable effort to comply with Title VII's disparate-impact provision by refraining from action of doubtful consistency with business necessity. . . .

NOTES

1. *Putting It All Together or Tearing It All Apart?* If you want an opportunity to think about big concepts spread across this entire chapter, *Ricci* has it all: systemic disparate treatment, disparate impact, testing, and affirmative action from a statutory or constitutional perspective. What more could a professor (or student) ask for? The other perspective on *Ricci*, however, is that it tears apart quite a lot of what you've learned to this point. Indeed, there are those who think that it is the end of disparate impact liability. That may be an overstatement, but *Ricci* is at least a sea change that will reverberate in a variety of ways.

2. *The Holding.* The majority was clear: Defendants' decision to scrub the test because its use would have meant no promotions for African Americans and only two for Hispanics, who together made up over half of the test takers, was intentional disparate treatment discrimination against the white test takers who would have been promoted had the test been certified. That the test results amounted to a prima facie case of disparate impact discrimination was not a defense to a disparate treatment case unless the employer also had a strong basis in evidence to believe that it would be liable for disparate impact discrimination, which means that it would have no business necessity/job relation defense and that there is no viable alternative employment practice.

What exactly is a "strong basis"? *United States v. Brennan*, 650 F.3d 65, 109-10 (2d Cir. 2011), tried to explain:

> [W]e hold that, under *Ricci*, a "strong basis in evidence" of non-job-relatedness or of a less discriminatory alternative requires more than speculation, more than a few scattered statements in the record, and more than a mere fear of litigation, but less than the preponderance of the evidence that would be necessary for actual liability. This is what it means when courts say that the employer must have an objectively reasonable fear of disparate-impact liability.

See generally Herman N. Johnson, Jr., *The Evolving Strong-Basis-In-Evidence Standard*, 32 BERKELEY J. EMP. & LAB. L. 347 (2011).

3. *Relation to Affirmative Action.* Only Justice Ginsburg in dissent puts *Ricci* in context with the Court's Title VII affirmative action decisions. Recall that under

Weber/Johnson, see page 611, a prima facie case of disparate treatment is not required in order to justify an affirmative action plan; all that is necessary is a manifest imbalance in a traditionally segregated job category and no unnecessary trammeling of majority rights. In *Ricci*, however, even an uncontested prima facie case of disparate impact (a clear manifest imbalance in terms of the test itself) is not enough to permit the employer to take steps to reduce or eliminate the impact.

The parallels between affirmative action analysis under Title VII and *Ricci's* approach to the intersection of disparate treatment and disparate impact are obvious. In both, race may influence an employer's decision, but only under certain circumstances. For a valid affirmative action plan, there must be a manifest imbalance, and majority interests must not be unduly trammeled. In the case of tests with a disparate impact, the test may be thrown out precisely because of that impact, but only under a strong basis in evidence test. So both doctrines allow disparate treatment under more-or-less tight constraints.

Prior to *Ricci*, some wondered if the Roberts Court would overrule *Weber/Johnson's* approval of voluntary affirmative action. Does *Ricci* suggest that the answer is no because it allows some systemic disparate treatment? On the other hand, *Ricci* was not an affirmative action case, at least as that term is normally used. No one was preferred over anyone else, although white firefighters lost promotions they would otherwise have gotten. Since the majority condemned actions taken for racial reasons absent a strong basis in evidence for disparate impact liability, *Ricci* can be viewed as harsher than the affirmative action cases. And the "strong basis in evidence test" seems to require more in the way of proof than "manifest imbalance" does in the affirmative action context.

In *United States v. Brennan*, 650 F.3d 65 (2d Cir. 2011), the Second Circuit distinguished between the *Weber/Johnson* affirmative action analysis and *Ricci's* "strong basis in evidence" defense: The threshold determination is now "whether the race- and sex-conscious action constitutes an affirmative action plan at all." *Id.* at 97. In its view,

> when an employer, acting ex ante, although in the light of past discrimination, establishes hiring or promotion procedures designed to promote equal opportunity and eradicate future discrimination, that may constitute an affirmative action plan. But where an employer, already having established its procedures in a certain way—such as through a seniority system—throws out the results of those procedures ex post because of the racial or gender composition of those results, that constitutes an individualized grant of employment benefits which must be individually justified, and not affirmative action.

Id. at 99-100. Where only ex post benefits are at issue, therefore, "the employer may not invoke the 'affirmative action' defense of *Johnson* and *Weber.*" *Id.* at 104; *see also Shea v. Kerry*, 796 F.3d 42, 54 (D.C. Cir. 2015) (finding *Weber/Johnson* to control a challenge to an affirmative action plan, despite *Ricci*, because those opinion "are directly applicable to this case" and the Supreme Court has cautioned against the lower courts finding its decisions overruled by implication).

4. *Does Knowledge Equal Intentional Discrimination?* The majority finds intent to discriminate against whites because the City acted to avoid disparate impact liability to blacks (absent the "strong evidence" defense). But does the fact that the City acted because it knew of a "statistical disparity based on race" necessarily lead to the conclusion that it rejected the test "solely because the higher scoring candidates were white"? Is there a difference between intending not to disadvantage African American and Hispanic candidates and intending to discriminate against the white candidates? Did New Haven invalidate the test in order to deprive whites of promotions? Or was that merely a foreseeable consequence? Or does it matter? *See generally* Michael J. Zimmer, *Ricci's Color-Blind Standard in a Race Conscious Society: A Case of Unintended Consequences?*, 2010 BYU L. Rev. 1257 (2010); Cheryl I. Harris & Kimberly West-Faulcon, *Reading* Ricci: *White(ning) Discrimination, Race-ing Test Fairness*, 58 UCLA L. Rev. 73 (2010); Kerri Stone, *The Unexpected Appearance of Transferred Intent in Title VII*, 55 Loy. L. Rev. 752 (2010); Nancy L. Zisk, *Failing the Test: How* Ricci v. DeStefano *Failed to Clarify Disparate Impact and Disparate Treatment Law*, 34 Hamline L. Rev. 27, 28-29 (2011); Helen Norton, *The Supreme Court's Post-Racial Turn Towards a Zero-Sum Understanding of Equality*, 52 Wm. & Mary L. Rev. 197 (2010); Charles A. Sullivan, Ricci v. DeStefano: *End of the Line or Just Another Turn on the Disparate Impact Road?*, 104 Nw. U. L. Rev. 411 (2010).

5. *A Hierarchy of Theories?* The majority thinks that disparate treatment is the main evil that Congress proscribed; disparate impact is a late addition to the statute and must be tailored to minimize any conflict with the disparate treatment bar. Justice Ginsburg takes an opposite view—*Griggs* made clear that disparate impact was implicit in Title VII from the beginning. This difference influences the approach of each side: Disparate treatment can be sacrificed to disparate impact, for the majority, only if the "strong basis in evidence" test is met, thus ensuring that disparate treatment is generally avoided. (You might also wonder why it matters to the majority that disparate impact was added only in the 1991 Civil Rights Act. Doesn't the application of the theory, no matter when, require trying to reconcile both in a nongrudging manner?)

But let's probe Justice Ginsburg's view a bit more. She sees no conflict between disparate treatment and disparate impact claims. Disparate treatment prohibits intentional discrimination but, even if the employer's practices were not intentionally discriminatory, there is a duty to not use practices with a disparate impact unless the practices were justified as job-related and consistent with business necessity. By enacting both theories, Congress thus intended to allow race consciousness to avoid an unjustified racial impact. To put it another way, such race consciousness could not be the kind of disparate treatment Title VII meant to proscribe. For the dissent, the *Ricci* Court's invalid equation of consciousness of race with intent to discriminate creates the tension that it then resolves with its new hierarchy of theories.

6. *What's the Disagreement on the Standard?* The various opinions disagree about a lot, especially the application of the appropriate standard to the facts of the case. But Supreme Court decisions are usually more about law than facts, and, on the law, is there much difference between the majority and the Ginsburg dissent? The majority articulates the "strong basis in evidence" standard. Justice Ginsburg found no violation if the employer has "good cause to believe the device would not withstand examination for business necessity." So the difference is "strong basis" versus "good cause." A tempest in a teapot?

At one point, Justice Ginsburg argues against the majority's standard because "[i]t is hard to see how these requirements differ from demanding that an employer establish 'a provable, actual violation' *against itself*." (emphasis in original). In the affirmative action cases, some justices sought to avoid requiring an employer, in defending an affirmative action plan favoring minorities, having to adduce proof that would make it liable to minorities. This would, obviously, discourage the adoption of such plans. But how does this argument apply here? By definition, if there is such a "strong basis," the employer can scrub the test. There will then be no disparate impact liability because the test is never used, and there will be no disparate treatment liability because of the strong basis for disparate impact liability.

7. *Isn't There Strong Basis for Disparate Impact Liability?* The Court wrote "a prima facie case of disparate-impact liability—essentially a threshold showing of a significant statistical disparity and nothing more—is far from a strong basis in evidence that the City would have been liable under Title VII had it certified the results." Can that be true in light of §703(k), which shifts the burden of persuasion to the defendant upon the showing of disparate impact? In other words, if black firefighters were to mount a disparate impact attack, they would win upon showing the fact of impact—unless the employer carried its burden of showing business necessity/job relation defense. *Ricci*, however, requires the employer seeking to avoid disparate impact liability in the first place to show that it has no business necessity, or at least show that it has a strong basis in evidence that it has no business necessity. *Wards Cove* shifted the burden of proving no business necessity to black plaintiffs. Is *Ricci* a very convoluted way of doing the same thing, with the employer acting as a kind of proxy for potential black plaintiffs?

8. *Was the Test Job-Related/Business Necessity as a Matter of Law?* Given (a) the majority's strong basis in evidence test, (b) its acknowledgment of the existence of a prima facie case, and (c) its grant of summary judgment to the white firefighters, it must follow that the test was valid as a matter of law. While we haven't explored test validation in detail, is it so clear that the test was valid? The mere fact that effort is put into test design isn't necessarily enough to validate it under governing principles. Indeed, the *Ricci* majority does not address the jurisprudence associated with the test exception in original §703(h). Why?

9. *Alternative Employment Practices.* The Court agrees that even a valid test can't be used if there's an alternative employment practice that achieves the same purposes with lesser racial impact. The record before the CSB showed alternatives that were less discriminatory—simply altering the ratio of written to oral scores (as did Bridgeport, a city just down the interstate from New Haven), using "assessment centers," or altering the "rule of three" to a banding approach—all were alternatives that may have had less impact and that may have equally served the employer's needs. So why not remand on this question?

10. *Suppose Minority Test Takers Claim Disparate Impact?* Pursuant to *Ricci* decision, the City certified the test results, and a black plaintiff brought suit challenging the promotions in the *Ricci* case. He wasn't a party to the *Ricci* litigation, which means that under normal principles of res judicata, he wasn't technically bound by the result, *Martin v. Wilks*, 490 U.S. 755 (1989), although admittedly a provision added to Title VII by the 1991 CRA, 42 U.S.C. §2000e-2(n) (2006), might foreclose his suit. Charles A. Sullivan, Ricci v. DeStefano: *End of the Line or Just Another Turn on the Disparate Impact Road?*, 104 Nw. U. L. Rev. 411, 424-25 (2010). But, civil procedure principles aside, Justice Kennedy concluded the opinion for the Court with a statement about a subsequent disparate impact suit:

> If, after it certifies the test results, the City faces a disparate-impact suit, then in light of our holding today it should be clear that the City would avoid disparate-impact liability based on the strong basis in evidence that, had it not certified the results, it would have been subject to disparate-treatment liability.

Relying heavily on this sentence, the district court dismissed the suit, but the Second Circuit reversed:

> [W]e cannot reconcile all of the indications from the Supreme Court in *Ricci*. After a careful review of that decision and relevant nonparty preclusion and Title VII case law, we conclude that Briscoe's claim is neither precluded nor properly dismissed. *Ricci* did not substantially change Title VII disparate-impact litigation or preclusion principles in the single sentence of dicta targeted at the parties in this action.

Briscoe v. City of New Haven, 654 F.3d 200, 209 (2d Cir. 2011).

11. *The End of Disparate Impact?* Is the disparate impact theory of liability gone? In other words, while the *Ricci* majority *allows* an employer to take race into account when it has the requisite strong basis in fact, does Kennedy's sentence suggest that the employer can *choose* never to apply disparate impact because doing so will always be disparate treatment? Under this view, avoidance of disparate treatment is always a complete defense to disparate impact. Or does the sentence make sense only when the employer does not (as New Haven didn't) have a strong basis to believe that it was subject to disparate impact liability? Under this view, an employer *must* avoid a practice with a disparate impact, even if it results in disparate treatment, so long as it has the requisite strong basis in evidence. But hold it—that can't be right. Before *Ricci*, an employer could prevail in a suit by black firefighters only by proving that it had a business necessity for its practice, not by showing that it had a strong basis in evidence that it had a business necessity. *See generally* Joseph Seiner & Benjamin Gutman, *Does* Ricci *Herald a New Disparate Impact?* 90 BU. L. REV. 2181 (2010) (arguing that the sentence suggests the creation of yet another affirmative defense to disparate impact discrimination).

12. *Or Maybe It Matters When? Ricci* focuses on New Haven's decision whether to certify the test. At that point, the CSB had to favor either those who were successful or those who were not, with obvious racial consequences. As Kennedy wrote, "[t]he problem, of course, is that *after the tests were completed*, the raw racial results became the predominant rationale for the City's refusal to certify the results." (emphasis added). He went on to stress that "[t]he injury arises in part from the high, and justified, expectations of the candidates who had participated in the testing process on the terms the City had established for the promotional process." Elsewhere, he spoke of "competing expectations."

But the majority recognized that, in deciding whether or what to test, and before the competing expectations crystallized, potential racial effects can be taken into account:

> Title VII does not prohibit an employer from considering, before administering a test or practice, how to design that test or practice in order to provide a fair opportunity for all individuals, regardless of their race. And when, during the test-design stage, an employer invites comments to ensure the test is fair, that process can provide a common ground for open discussions toward that end.

This strongly suggests that an employer need not be color-blind in its approach to test design.

13. *New Light on Disparate Impact.* In *Texas Department of Housing and Community Affairs v. Inclusive Communities Project, Inc.*, 135 S. Ct. 2507 (2015), the Supreme Court found the disparate impact theory applicable under the Fair

Housing Act. While not directly addressing Title VII, the majority opinion looked to employment discrimination law for its interpretation of the FHA. Citing *Griggs* and the plurality in *Smith v. City of Jackson*, 544 U.S. 228 (2005), an ADEA case approving the disparate impact theory under that statute, see page note on impact analysis under the ADEA, the Court wrote that the

> antidiscrimination laws must be construed to encompass disparate-impact claims when their text refers to the consequences of actions and not just to the mindset of actors, and where that interpretation is consistent with statutory purpose. These cases also teach that disparate-impact liability must be limited so employers and other regulated entities are able to make the practical business choices and profit-related decisions that sustain a vibrant and dynamic free-enterprise system. And before rejecting a business justification—or, in the case of a governmental entity, an analogous public interest—a court must determine that a plaintiff has shown that there is "an available alternative . . . practice that has less disparate impact and serves the [entity's] legitimate needs."

Inclusive Communities Project, 135 S. Ct. at 2518. The Court also acknowledged that disparate impact liability under the FHA "also plays a role in uncovering discriminatory intent: It permits plaintiffs to counteract unconscious prejudices and disguised animus that escape easy classification as disparate treatment. In this way disparate-impact liability may prevent segregated housing patterns that might otherwise result from covert and illicit stereotyping." *Id*. at 2511-12.

While approving FHA disparate impact liability generally, the majority cautioned that the theory "has always been properly limited in key respects that avoid the serious constitutional questions that might arise under the FHA," for instance, if such liability were imposed based solely on a showing of a statistical disparity. It stressed the role of the business necessity defense in Title VII as restraining too broad an application of the principle. "To be sure, the Title VII framework may not transfer exactly to the fair-housing context, but the comparison suffices for present purposes." *Id*. at 2523. Similarly, the Court stressed that a "disparate-impact claim that relies on a statistical disparity must fail if the plaintiff cannot point to a defendant's policy or policies causing that disparity. A robust causality requirement ensures that '[r]acial imbalance . . . does not, without more, establish a prima facie case of disparate impact' and thus protects defendants from being held liable for racial disparities they did not create" (quoting *Wards Cove*). *Id*.

Justice Alito's dissent, joined by the Chief Justice and Justices Scalia and Thomas, rejected disparate impact liability largely by reading "because of" in the FHA to mean the reason a person acts. Justice Thomas separately dissented in a truly remarkable opinion that was a frontal assault on *Griggs*, which he viewed as illegitimate and therefore not to be extended further than stare decisis might require. *See generally* Samuel R. Bagenstos, *Disparate Impact and the Role of Classification and Motivation in Equal Protection Law after* Inclusive Communities, 101 Cornell L. Rev. 1115 (2016).

Note on Impact Analysis Under the ADEA

In *Smith v. City of Jackson*, 544 U.S. 228 (2005), the Supreme Court held that disparate impact is available under ADEA but in a considerably diluted form. *City of Jackson* involved a challenge by older police officers to raises that disparately favored younger workers. The Court reasoned that the ADEA should be interpreted identically to Title VII to the extent that both statutes were identical. Two textual differences between the ADEA and Title VII, however, combined to lead the Court to conclude that the scope of the disparate-impact theory is narrower under the ADEA. The first textual difference is ADEA §4(f)(1), 29 U.S.C. §623(f)(1), which lacks any Title VII analog. That section expressly permits differentiations "based on reasonable factors other than age." This indicated to the Court that Congress thought that factors correlated with age, albeit not age-based themselves, sometimes have relevance in employment decisions. *See* Judith J. Johnson, *Rehabilitate the Age Discrimination in Employment Act: Resuscitate the "Reasonable Factors Other Than Age" Defense and the Disparate Impact Theory*, 55 HASTINGS L. J. 1399 (2004).

Further developing the significance of the reasonable factor other than age ("RFOA") language, *Meacham v. Knolls Atomic Power Lab.*, 554 U.S. 84 (2008), held that the RFOA was an affirmative defense as to which the defendant bore the burden of persuasion. Further, *Meacham* ruled that the RFOA defense superseded the normal business necessity/job relation defense for disparate impact claims under Title VII: "[W] are now satisfied that the business necessity test should have no place in ADEA disparate-impact cases." *Id*. at 97. Rather, the only question is whether a non-age factor that produces an age impact is "reasonable," although what that means and how it might differ from normal business necessity/job relation analysis is not clear.

The second difference is the Civil Rights Act of 1991, which amended Title VII but not the ADEA with respect to refining disparate impact. In short, the 1991 CRA was widely seen as restoring disparate impact law to its state under *Griggs v. Duke Packing*, following the Court's more limiting decision in *Wards Cove Packing Co. v. Atonio*. Since that amendment did not apply to the ADEA, the Court concluded that the *Wards Cove* version of disparate impact applies in age discrimination cases.

Applying this standard to the case, the *City of Jackson* majority found that the plaintiffs had not sufficiently identified the challenged practice with the supposed impact to satisfy *Wards Cove. See also Allen v. Highlands Hosp. Corp.*, 545 F.3d 387, 404 (6th Cir. 2008) (while the plaintiffs alleged to reduce labor cost, including those for employees with greater seniority, they "have not established that this corporate desire evolved into an identifiable practice that disproportionately harms workers who are at least 40 years old"). *City of Jackson* also stated that, in any event, the City's decision to grant raises based on seniority and positions was reasonable given the City's goal of raising employees' salaries to match those in surrounding communities.

D. SEXUAL AND OTHER DISCRIMINATORY HARASSMENT

In this section, we consider employees' rights to a workplace in which they are free from sexual and other discriminatory harassment. Under Title VII, the ADEA, and the ADA, employees have a cause of action for harassment when the harassment is on the basis of membership in a protected group. Harassment poses different challenges than the theories of discrimination discussed previously in this chapter. For example, some conduct that would be described as harassment if it occurred in the workplace is unobjectionable in other contexts. Further, sexual harassment, like other kinds of discriminatory harassment, typically does not result in any adverse economic impact on the victim, even if the emotional distress is severe. The decision to find a violation of the discrimination laws under such circumstances is in sharp contrast to efforts in other antidiscrimination contexts to require an "adverse employment action." In addition, discriminatory harassment typically occurs in violation of, rather than in compliance with, company policy, and harassers typically are satisfying their own personal interests, rather than seeking to further their employer's interests. This attribute of discriminatory harassment raises a new issue: What is the employer's liability for harassment by supervisors and co-workers in violation of company policy? Finally, because controlling workplace harassment by disciplining harassing employees may relieve an employer of liability, discriminatory harassment raises questions about the rights of alleged perpetrators.

Although the lower federal courts were originally dismissive of sexual harassment as a theory of liability under Title VII, the Supreme Court decision in *Meritor Savings Bank v. Vinson*, 477 U.S. 57 (1986), signaled a sea change. The facts in *Meritor* were extreme. Sidney Taylor, a vice president of Meritor and manager of one of its branch offices, hired Michelle Vinson and became her supervisor. Vinson started as a trainee but ultimately was promoted to assistant branch manager. While her advancement at the bank was based on merit, she alleged that she had been constantly harassed by Taylor during her four years of employment. According to Vinson's testimony, Taylor "invited her out to dinner and, during the course of the meal, suggested that they go to a motel to have sexual relations. At first she refused, but out of what she described as fear of losing her job she eventually agreed. . . . Taylor thereafter made repeated demands upon her for sexual favors, usually at the branch, both during and after business hours; she estimated that over the next several years she had intercourse with him some 40 or 50 times. In addition, Taylor fondled her in front of other employees, followed her into the women's restroom when she went there alone, exposed himself to her, and even forcibly raped her on several occasions." *Meritor*, 477 U.S. at 60.

The Supreme Court declared that: "Without question, when a supervisor sexually harasses a subordinate because of the subordinate's sex, that supervisor 'discriminate[s]' on the basis of sex." *Id*. at 64. As importantly, the Court rejected the argument that harassment was limited to economic losses. Looking in large part to EEOC Guidelines on Sexual Harassment, 29 C.F.R. §1604.11, the Court held that "a plaintiff may establish a violation of Title VII by proving that discrimination based on sex has created a hostile or abusive work environment." *Meritor*, 477 U.S. at 66. It did caution, however, that "not all workplace conduct that may be described as 'harassment' affects a 'term, condition, or privilege' of employment within the meaning of Title VII. For sexual harassment to be actionable, it must be sufficiently severe or pervasive 'to alter the conditions of [the victim's] employment and create an abusive working environment.'" *Id*. at 67. The Court also made clear that "the fact that sex-related conduct was 'voluntary,' in the sense that the complainant was not forced to participate against her will, is not a defense to a sexual harassment suit brought under Title VII. The gravamen of any sexual harassment claim is that the alleged sexual advances were 'unwelcome.'" *Id*. at 68.

Meritor established what was essentially a new cause of action under Title VII, one that is in many ways very different than the kind of discrimination we have studied to this point. However, it left a myriad of questions to be answered. Two of the most important were when the offensive conduct was "because of sex" and what conduct is sufficiently "severe or pervasive" to be actionable.

Oncale v. Sundowner Offshore Services, Inc.
523 U.S. 75 (1998)

Justice SCALIA delivered the opinion of the Court.

This case presents the question whether workplace harassment can violate Title VII's prohibition against "discrimination . . . because of . . . sex," when the harasser and the harassed employee are of the same sex.

I

The District Court having granted summary judgment for respondent, we must assume the facts to be as alleged by petitioner Joseph Oncale. The precise details are irrelevant to the legal point we must decide, and in the interest of both brevity and dignity we shall describe them only generally. In late October 1991, Oncale was working for respondent Sundowner Offshore Services on a Chevron U.S.A., Inc. oil platform in the Gulf of Mexico. He was employed as a roustabout on an eight-man crew which included respondents John Lyons, Danny Pippen, and Brandon Johnson. Lyons, the crane operator, and Pippen, the driller, had supervisory authority. On several occasions, Oncale was forcibly subjected to sex-related, humiliating actions against him by Lyons, Pippen, and Johnson in the presence of the rest of the crew. Pippen and Lyons also physically assaulted Oncale in a sexual manner, and Lyons threatened him with rape.

Oncale's complaints to supervisory personnel produced no remedial action; in fact, the company's Safety Compliance Clerk, Valent Hohen, told Oncale that Lyons and Pippen "picked [on] him all the time too," and called him a name suggesting homosexuality. Oncale eventually quit—asking that his pink slip reflect that he "voluntarily left due to sexual harassment and verbal abuse." When asked at his deposition why he left Sundowner, Oncale stated "I felt that if I didn't leave my job, that I would be raped or forced to have sex."

[The district court held that "Mr. Oncale, a male, has no cause of action under Title VII for harassment by male co-workers." The Fifth Circuit affirmed.]

II . . .

Title VII's prohibition of discrimination "because of . . . sex" protects men as well as women, *Newport News* [*Shipbuilding & Dry Dock Co. v. EEOC*, 462 U.S. 669, 678 (1983)], and in the related context of racial discrimination in the workplace we have rejected any conclusive presumption that an employer will not discriminate against members of his own race. "Because of the many facets of human motivation, it would be unwise to presume as a matter of law that human beings of one definable group will not discriminate against other members of that group." *Castaneda v. Partida*, 430 U.S. 482 (1977). In *Johnson v. Transportation Agency*, Santa Clara County, 480 U.S. 616 (1987), a male employee claimed that his employer discriminated against him because of his sex when it preferred a female employee for promotion. Although we ultimately rejected the claim on other grounds, we did not consider it significant that the supervisor who made that decision was also a man. If our precedents leave any doubt on the question, we hold today that nothing in Title VII necessarily bars a claim of discrimination "because of . . . sex" merely because the plaintiff and the defendant (or the person charged with acting on behalf of the defendant) are of the same sex.

Courts have had little trouble with that principle in cases like *Johnson*, where an employee claims to have been passed over for a job or promotion. But when the issue arises in the context of a "hostile environment" sexual harassment claim, the state and federal courts have taken a bewildering variety of stances. Some, like the Fifth Circuit in this case, have held that same-sex sexual harassment claims are never cognizable under Title VII. Other decisions say that such claims are actionable only if the plaintiff can prove that the harasser is homosexual (and thus presumably motivated by sexual desire). Still others suggest that workplace harassment that is sexual in content is always actionable, regardless of the harasser's sex, sexual orientation, or motivations.

We see no justification in the statutory language or our precedents for a categorical rule excluding same-sex harassment claims from the coverage of Title VII. As some courts have observed, male-on-male sexual harassment in the workplace was assuredly not the principal evil Congress was concerned with when it enacted Title VII. But statutory prohibitions often go beyond the principal evil to cover reasonably comparable evils, and it is ultimately the provisions of our laws rather than the principal concerns of our legislators by which we are governed. Title VII prohibits "discrimination . . . because of . . . sex" in the "terms" or "conditions" of employment. Our holding that this includes sexual harassment must extend to sexual harassment of any kind that meets the statutory requirements.

Respondents and their amici contend that recognizing liability for same-sex harassment will transform Title VII into a general civility code for the American workplace. But that risk is no greater for same-sex than for opposite-sex harassment, and is adequately met by careful attention to the requirements of the statute. Title VII does not prohibit all verbal or physical harassment in the workplace; it is directed only at "discrimination . . . because of . . . sex." We have never held that workplace harassment, even harassment between men and women, is automatically discrimination because of sex merely because the words used have sexual content or connotations. "The critical issue, Title VII's text indicates, is whether members of one sex are exposed to disadvantageous terms or conditions of employment to which members of the other sex are not exposed." *Harris* [*v. Forklift Systems, Inc.*, 510 U.S. 17 (1993)].

Courts and juries have found the inference of discrimination easy to draw in most male-female sexual harassment situations, because the challenged conduct typically involves explicit or implicit proposals of sexual activity; it is reasonable to assume those proposals would not have been made to someone of the same sex. The same chain of inference would be available to a plaintiff alleging same-sex harassment, if there were credible evidence that the harasser was homosexual. But harassing conduct need not be motivated by sexual desire to support an inference of discrimination on the basis of sex. A trier of fact might reasonably find such discrimination, for example, if a female victim is harassed in such sex-specific and derogatory terms by another woman as to make it clear that the harasser is motivated by general hostility to the presence of women in the workplace. A same-sex harassment plaintiff may also, of course, offer direct comparative evidence about how the alleged harasser treated members of both sexes in a mixed-sex workplace. Whatever evidentiary route the plaintiff chooses to follow, he or she must always prove that the conduct at issue was not merely tinged with offensive sexual connotations, but actually constituted "discrimination . . . because of . . . sex."

And there is another requirement that prevents Title VII from expanding into a general civility code: As we emphasized in *Meritor* and *Harris*, the statute does not reach genuine but innocuous differences in the ways men and women routinely interact with members of the same sex and of the opposite sex. The prohibition of harassment on the basis of sex requires neither asexuality nor androgyny in the workplace; it forbids only behavior so objectively offensive as to alter the "conditions" of the victim's employment. "Conduct that is not severe or pervasive enough to create an objectively hostile or abusive work environment—an environment that a reasonable person would find hostile or abusive—is beyond Title VII's purview." *Harris*. We have always regarded that requirement as crucial, and as sufficient to ensure that courts and juries do not mistake ordinary socializing in the workplace—such as male-on-male horseplay or intersexual flirtation—for discriminatory "conditions of employment."

We have emphasized, moreover, that the objective severity of harassment should be judged from the perspective of a reasonable person in the plaintiff's position, considering "all the circumstances." *Harris*. In same-sex (as in all) harassment cases, that inquiry requires careful consideration of the social context in which particular behavior occurs and is experienced by its target. A professional football player's working environment is not severely or pervasively abusive, for example, if the coach smacks him on the buttocks as he heads onto the field—even if the same behavior would reasonably be experienced as abusive by the coach's secretary (male or female) back at the office. The real social impact of workplace behavior often depends on a constellation of surrounding circumstances, expectations, and relationships which are not fully captured by a simple recitation of the words used or the physical acts performed. Common sense, and an appropriate sensitivity to social context, will enable courts and juries to distinguish between simple teasing or roughhousing among members of the same sex, and conduct which a reasonable person in the plaintiff's position would find severely hostile or abusive. . . .

NOTES

• 1. *Sex-as-Conduct versus Gender. Oncale* makes clear that, regardless of the sex of the harasser and victim, the central issue for purposes of establishing liability under Title VII is whether the terms and conditions of the victim's employment were altered because of "sex." This term has generated some confusion because "sex" is sometimes used to refer to sexual conduct and sometimes to refer to biological sex. Although *Oncale* establishes that same-sex harassment is actionable under Title VII, the question remains: When is harassment because of or on the basis of sex? The Court confirms prior opinions that the gender of the target must cause the harassment. Thus, an inference of sex-based discrimination was often drawn by the lower courts based on sexual advances made by a heterosexual toward a victim of the opposite sex. Consistent with this logic, the Court indicates that sexual advances by a homosexual toward an individual of the same sex also may give rise to the inference that such action is "because of sex." *See* Rebecca Hanner White, *There's Nothing Special About Sex: The Supreme Court Mainstreams Sexual Harassment*, 7 WM. & MARY BILL RTS. J. 725, 734 (1999) ("The fact that harassment is sexual in nature may (and often will) be powerful evidence that the victim is suffering harassment because of her sex. The defendant may, however, avoid liability if the fact finder is convinced that the victim was not a target of harassment because of her sex, whether or not the harassment was sexual in nature."); Steven Willborn, *Taking Discrimination Seriously:* Oncale *and the Fate of Exceptionalism in Sexual Harassment Law*, 7 WM. & MARY BILL RTS. J. 677 (1999). In contrast, David S. Schwartz, *When Is Sex Because of Sex? The Causation Problem in Sexual Harassment Law*, 150 U. PA. L. REV. 1697 (2002), argues for a "sex per se" rule that would go beyond a presumption and find sexual conduct sufficient to satisfy the "because of sex" requirement.

Another approach finds harassment to be sexual when it is predicated on a plaintiff's failure to conform to gender norms. The paradigm for gender-nonconformity discrimination is an "effeminate" male or a "butch" woman. *See, e.g., EEOC v. Boh Bros. Constr. Co., LLC,* 731 F.3d 444, 456 (5th Cir. 2013) (en banc) (*Price Waterhouse's* treatment of sex stereotyping reaches sexual harassment claim; "[t]hus, the EEOC may rely on evidence that Wolfe viewed Woods as insufficiently masculine to prove its Title VII claim."); *Smith v. Salem*, 378 F.3d 566, 572 (6th Cir. 2004) (transsexual stated a Title VII claim by alleging that he was a victim of discrimination because his conduct and mannerisms "did not conform with his employers' and co-workers' sex stereotypes of how a man should look and behave").

This theory comes very close to finding discrimination on the basis of sexual orientation to be actionable. Although courts often go to great lengths to distinguish between sex discrimination and sexual orientation discrimination, *e.g., Vickers v. Fairfield Med. Ctr.*, 453 F.3d 757, 759 (6th Cir. 2006), a number of commentators argue that such discrimination is properly viewed as sex discrimination within the meaning of Title VII. *See* Luke A. Boso, *Real Men*, 37 HAWAII L. REV. 107, 108 (2015); Brian Soucek, *Perceived Homosexuals: Looking Gay Enough for Title VII*, 63 AM. U. L. REV. 715 (2014); Katherine M. Franke, *What's Wrong with Sexual Harassment?*, 49 STAN. L. REV. 691, 732 (1997); Zachary A. Kramer, *The Ultimate Gender Stereotype: Equalizing Gender-Conforming and Gender-Nonconforming Homosexuals Under Title VII*, 2004 U. ILL. L. REV. 465, 465 (2004); Camille Hébert, *Sexual Harassment as Discrimination "Because of . . . Sex": Have We Come Full Circle?* 27 OHIO N.U. L. REV. 439 (2001).

• **2.** *Gender Harassment. Oncale's* notion that sexual harassment is only a subset of sex discrimination is underscored by cases in which women complain not of unwelcome sexual advances but of environments that are hostile to women in other ways. For example, recall *Desert Palace*, reproduced at page 580. This was a discriminatory discharge case, not a contaminated work environment case, and thus, the Supreme Court apparently did not find it necessary to include most of the lurid facts. But consider the facts as recounted in the Ninth Circuit's opinion from the hostile environment perspective:

> Costa also presented evidence that she was penalized for her failure to conform to sexual stereotypes. Although her fellow Teamsters frequently lost their tempers, swore at fellow employees, and sometimes had physical altercations, it was Costa, identified in one report as "the lady Teamster," who was called a "bitch," and told "you got more balls than the guys." Even at trial, and despite testimony that she "got along with most people" and had "few arguments," Caesars' managers continued to characterize her as "strong willed," "opinionated," and "confrontational," leading counsel to call her "bossy" in closing argument. Supervisor Karen Hallett, who later signed Costa's termination order, expressly declared her intent to "get rid of that bitch," referring to Costa.
>
> Supervisors frequently used or tolerated verbal slurs that were sex-based or tinged with sexual overtones. Most memorably, one co-worker called her a "fucking cunt."

When she wrote a letter to management expressing her concern with this epithet, which stood out from the ordinary rough-and-tumble banter, she received a three-day suspension in response. Although the other employee admitted using the epithet, Costa was faulted for "engaging in verbal confrontation with co-worker in the warehouse resulting in use of profane and vulgar language by other employee."

Costa v. Desert Palace, 299 F.3d 838, 845-46 (9th Cir. 2002) (en banc).

Her co-workers didn't desire to have sex with Costa—they wanted to drive her out of the workplace. One inference is that they did so because she was a woman—the only woman in that position. Thus, the courts have found that harassing conduct of a non-sexual nature can constitute sexual harassment. *See, e.g., Pucino v. Verizon Communs., Inc.*, 618 F.3d 112 (2d Cir. 2010) (proof that a female employee was subject to disparately harsh working conditions compared to men could establish a violation, especially when coupled with proof of her supervisor's constant use of "bitch"); *EEOC v. Fairbrook Medical Clinic, P.A*, 609 F.3d 320, 327 (4th Cir. 2010) ("Although Kessel made offensive remarks in front of both male and female audiences, his use of 'sex-specific and derogatory terms' indicates that he intended to demean women."). *But see Smith v. Hy-Vee, Inc.*, 622 F.3d 904, 908 (8th Cir. 2010) (despite evidence that harasser touched plaintiff and made sexual references, there was no sufficient basis to infer that she was motivated by sexual desire because she subjected both men and women to the same behavior); *Love v. Motiva Enters. LLC*, 349 F. App'x 900, 903 (5th Cir. 2009) (although harassment was framed in sexual terms, there was no reason to believe that the harasser was either making implicit proposals for sexual activity or was lesbian given her "rude and obnoxious persona, which was directed at all co-workers generally").

Vicki Schultz, in *Reconceptualizing Sexual Harassment*, 107 YALE L. J. 1683, 1686-87, 1689 (1998), argues against the "sexual desire-dominance paradigm" for sexual harassment because that paradigm "has served to exclude from legal understanding many of the most common and debilitating forms of harassment faced by women (and many men) at work each day." One of Schultz's solutions is for courts to employ a rebuttable presumption of illegal harassment when the harassment is directed at women who work in traditionally segregated job categories. *See also* Rebecca Hanner White, *There's Nothing Special About Sex: The Supreme Court Mainstreams Sexual Harassment*, 7 WM. & MARY BILL RTS. J. 725, 735-6 (1999) ("[Schultz's] approach makes sense intuitively, and is consistent with *Oncale*, provided that courts keep in mind that only an inference of sex-discrimination is created, not a conclusive method of proof. After all, a woman in a male-dominated workplace may be harassed because she is a woman, or she may be harassed because she is a jerk."). Given that Costa was the only woman in her workplace, how would the trier of fact decide the abuse aimed at her was because she was a woman doing "men's work" or because she was "a jerk"?

• **3.** *Sex, Not Sexual Orientation*. If Oncale's employer can establish that his co-workers harassed him because he is a homosexual, can he nonetheless establish an actionable claim under Title VII? After years of uniform circuit court holdings that discrimination on the basis of sexual orientation is not generally actionable under Title VII, three circuits have recently reached the opposite conclusion on various grounds. *See* page 669. The law in the remaining circuits thus currently requires courts to distinguish between actions on the basis of sexual orientation (legal) and those on the basis of sex, including gender nonconformity (illegal). Does this make any sense? *See* Zachary A. Kramer, *Heterosexuality and Title VII*, 103 NW. U. L. REV. 205, 208-9 (2009) ("For lesbian and gay employees, sexual orientation is a burden because courts are primed to reject otherwise actionable discrimination claims on the theory that such claims are an attempt to bootstrap protection for sexual orientation into Title VII."). L. Camille Hébert, *Transforming Transsexual and Transgender Rights*, 15 WM. & MARY J. WOMEN & L. 535 (2009) (the term "sex" should be defined more broadly than courts have seen fit to do with respect to sexual minorities, to extend protection not only on biological status but gender-linked traits, including gender identity).

• **4.** *The Equal-Opportunity Harasser.* Suppose a supervisor harasses both men and women. The "equal opportunity harasser" appears often in the literature and sometimes in the cases. In the heterosexual context, female plaintiffs have encountered the sometimes successful defense that the harasser directs his offensive conduct and remarks against both men and women and therefore does not violate Title VII. *See Reine v. Honeywell Int'l Inc.*, 362 F. App'x 395 (5th Cir. 2010) (both men and women were treated badly and only a few of the harassing comments related to sex). *But see Beckford v. Dep't of Corr.*, 605 F.3d 951, 960 (11th Cir. 2010) (although harassment of both sexes occurred, female workers "presented evidence that the inmates called them cunts, whores, bitches, and sluts, and we have ruled that these gender-specific and highly offensive epithets evidence sex-based harassment under Title VII"); *Venezia v. Gottlieb Mem'l Hosp., Inc.*, 421 F.3d 468, 473 (7th Cir. 2005) (harassment of both husband and wife by different individuals did not necessarily mean that there was no sex discrimination). *See generally* Martin J. Katz, *Reconsidering Attraction in Sexual Harassment*, 79 IND. L.J. 101, 125-39 (2004); Ronald Turner, *Title VII and the Inequality-Enhancing Effects of the Bisexual and Equal Opportunity Harasser Defenses*, 7 U. PA. J. LAB. & EMP. L. 341, 342, 345 (2005).

5. *Disparate Impact Theory.* If a court concludes that harassment was not because of sex in the intent sense but nevertheless had a greater effect on women than on men, perhaps because it occurred in a sex-segregated workplace, the disparate impact theory suggests a possible way to attack the mistreatment. *See* Camille Hébert, *The Disparate Impact of Sexual Harassment: Does Motive Matter?*, 53 KAN. L. REV. 341 (2004) (arguing that disparate impact should be applicable to sexual harassment cases because women as a group are disproportionately disadvantaged by sexually harassing conduct in the workplace); Kelly Cahill Timmons, *Sexual Harassment and Disparate Impact: Should Non-Targeted Workplace Sexual Conduct be Actionable Under Title VII?*, 81 NEB. L. REV. 1152, 1155 (2003) (concluding "that non-targeted sexual conduct in the workplace should be actionable only if the conduct's disproportionate impact on women is great").

EEOC v. Sunbelt Rentals, Inc.
521 F.3d 306 (4th Cir. 2008)

WILKINSON, Circuit Judge:

This case arises from a Title VII action brought by the United States Equal Employment Opportunity Commission on behalf of Clinton Ingram, a Muslim American, against Sunbelt Rentals, Inc. The EEOC alleges that Ingram, while working at Sunbelt, was subjected to a religiously hostile work environment in violation of Title VII. The district court granted summary judgment for Sunbelt and dismissed the claim.

Title VII extends the promise that no one should be subject to a discriminatorily hostile work environment. In the wake of September 11th, some Muslim Americans, completely innocent of any wrongdoing, became targets of gross misapprehensions

654 ===== 9. Antidiscrimination

and overbroad assumptions about their religious beliefs. But the event that shook the foundations of our buildings did not shake the premise of our founding—that here, in America, there is no heretical faith. Because the evidence, if proven, indicates that Ingram suffered severe and pervasive religious harassment in violation of Title VII, we reverse the district court's grant of summary judgment and remand with directions that this case proceed to trial.

I.

A.

Sunbelt is a company that rents and sells construction equipment. In October 2001, a month after the September 11th attacks, it hired Ingram to work at its Gaithersburg, Maryland store. After initially working as a truck driver, Ingram was later promoted to the position of rental manager, a position he held until his termination in February 2003. As a rental manager, Ingram primarily worked at a rental counter located inside the store's showroom and was responsible for assisting customers with equipment rentals.

Ingram worked in close quarters with several other Sunbelt employees. In addition to Ingram, there were three other rental managers at the Gaithersburg location: David Gray, John "Hank" Parater, and Barry Fortna. Gray and Parater had work stations on either side of Ingram at the office's rental counter, and Fortna, the "lead rental manager," worked at a desk behind the counter.

In addition to his fellow rental managers, Ingram frequently interacted with Mike Warner, the store's shop foreman, and Steve Riddlemoser, the overall manager of the Gaithersburg office. When Riddlemoser was not in the office, Warner served as the "acting manager." If both Riddlemoser and Warner were absent, then Fortna was left in charge. The regional manager for the Gaithersburg location was Eddie Dempster.

Prior to joining Sunbelt, Ingram, who is an African American, converted to Islam while serving in the United States Army. It is undisputed that Sunbelt, as well as Ingram's coworkers, knew Ingram was a Muslim. In fact, Sunbelt permitted Ingram to use a private, upstairs room for short prayer sessions that were required by Ingram's faith. In addition, Sunbelt allowed Ingram to attend a weekly congregational prayer session that took place from 1:00-1:45 p.m. on Friday afternoons. Ingram also observed tenets of his faith at the workplace by keeping a beard and wearing a kufi, a traditional headgear worn by Muslim men. Notably, Ingram was the only Muslim employee at the Gaithersburg office.

During his time at Sunbelt, Ingram claims he was subjected to a hostile work environment on the basis of his religion. According to Ingram, the abusive environment was marked by a steady stream of demeaning comments and degrading actions directed against him by his coworkers—conduct that went unaddressed and unpunished by Sunbelt supervisors.

For instance, coworkers used religiously-charged epithets and often called Ingram names such as "Taliban" and "towel head." In addition, fellow employees frequently made fun of Ingram's appearance, challenged his allegiance to the United States, suggested he was a terrorist, and made comments associating all Muslims with senseless violence. Sometimes Ingram's supervisors personally participated in the harassment.

Sunbelt responds, in turn, that Ingram also used profane and derogatory language in the workplace.

Additionally, Ingram was the victim of several religiously charged incidents. For instance, on one occasion, Gray held a metal detector to Ingram's head and, after the detector did not go off, called Ingram a "fake ass Muslim want-to-be turbine wearing ass." In a separate incident, Gray showed Ingram a stapler and said that "if anyone upsets you pretend this stapler is a model airplane [and] just toss it in the air, just repeatedly catch it, [and] don't say anything." Ingram understood this to be a reference to the September 11 attacks and another attempt by Gray to equate Ingram with terrorists. Finally, a cartoon was posted in the store's dispatch area depicting persons "dressed in Islamic or Muslim attire" as suicide bombers. [In the cartoon, an instructor with a bomb strapped to his body tells the others: "okay, pay attention" because "I'm only showing you . . . how this works once."] Taking offense, Ingram complained about the cartoon to the dispatcher and eventually tore it down.

In addition to these explicitly religious incidents, Ingram suffered from other forms of harassment. For example, his timecard, which was used to punch time in and out, was frequently hidden, especially on Fridays when he went to congregational prayer. Likewise, coworkers constantly unplugged his computer equipment and, on one occasion, defaced his business card by writing "dumb ass" over his name.

After nearly every incident of harassment, Ingram verbally complained to Riddlemoser, and sometimes Dempster and Warner. [These complaints did not resolve the matter and ultimately Ingram complained to Sunbelt's Human Resources Department. This, too, failed to stop the harassment.]

B.

[The district court granted summary judgment to Sunbelt, finding the harassment not sufficiently severe or pervasive to establish a prima facie case of a hostile work environment. The district court stated] "[t]here's a lot of coarse behavior that goes on in the workplace," and Sunbelt was "a little more rough and ready than, let us say, the Century Club of New York of which fine ladies are members." Second, the court stated that several of the incidents that Ingram complained about, such as the hiding of his timecard, lacked a direct "nexus with religion." Third, the court explained that if the explicitly religious incidents involving his coworkers were sufficiently severe or pervasive, Ingram would have included them in his written complaint to Human Resources. Because he did not, the district court presumed they must not have been sufficiently severe or pervasive. . . .

II . . .

In order to prove that Ingram suffered from a "discriminatorily hostile or abusive work environment," *Harris v. Forklift Systems, Inc.*, 510 U.S. 17 (1993), the EEOC must demonstrate that the harassment was (1) unwelcome, (2) because of religion, (3) sufficiently severe or pervasive to alter the conditions of employment and create an abusive atmosphere, and (4) imputable to the employer.

[The court had no difficulty finding the conduct "unwelcome," given Ingram's response to his co-workers and his complaints to management. Nor did it have any difficulty with the religious nature of the comments, given that, for example, "Taliban" or "towel head" would not have been applied to a non-Muslim employee, and the co-workers "teased [him] about his appearance, particularly his kufi and beard."]

C.

The main area of contention here is whether the harassment alleged by Ingram was "sufficiently severe or pervasive to alter the conditions of [his] employment and create an abusive working environment." *Harris* (quoting *Meritor*). Viewed on summary judgment, the evidence establishes that Ingram persistently suffered from religious harassment of the most demeaning, degrading, and damaging sort. The district court erred when it held the EEOC had failed to satisfy this requirement.

1.

The "severe or pervasive" element of a hostile work environment claim "has both subjective and objective components." *Ocheltree v. Scollon Prods., Inc.*, 335 F.3d 325, 333 (4th Cir. 2003) (en banc) (citing *Harris*). First, the plaintiff must show that he "subjectively perceive[d] the environment to be abusive." *Harris*. Next, the plaintiff must demonstrate that the conduct was such that "a reasonable person in the plaintiff's position" would have found the environment objectively hostile or abusive. *Oncale v. Sundowner Offshore Servs., Inc.*. Because Sunbelt does not, and could not, challenge the EEOC's contention that the harassment seemed severe and pervasive to Ingram personally, we focus our attention on the element's objective component.

This objective inquiry "is not, and by its nature cannot be, a mathematically precise test." *Harris*. Rather, when determining whether the harassing conduct was objectively "severe or pervasive," we must look "at all the circumstances," including "the frequency of the discriminatory conduct; its severity; whether it is physically threatening or humiliating, or a mere offensive utterance; and whether it unreasonably interferes with an employee's work performance." *Id.*; *Ocheltree*. "[N]o single factor is" dispositive, *Harris*, as "[t]he real social impact of workplace behavior often depends on a constellation of surrounding circumstances, expectations, and relationships which are not fully captured by a simple recitation of the words used or the physical acts performed," *Oncale*.

While this standard surely prohibits an employment atmosphere that is "permeated with discriminatory intimidation, ridicule, and insult," *Harris*, it is equally clear that Title VII does not establish a "general civility code for the American workplace," *Oncale*. This is because, in order to be actionable, the harassing "conduct must be [so] extreme [as] to amount to a change in the terms and conditions of employment." *Faragher v. City of Boca Raton*, 524 U.S. 775, 788 (1998). Indeed, as the Court observed, "simple teasing, offhand comments, and isolated incidents (unless extremely serious) will not amount to discriminatory changes in the terms and conditions of employment." *Id.*; *see also Clark County Sch. Dist. v. Breeden*, 532 U.S. 268, 270-71 (2001).

Our circuit has likewise recognized that plaintiffs must clear a high bar in order to satisfy the severe or pervasive test. Workplaces are not always harmonious locales, and even incidents that would objectively give rise to bruised or wounded feelings will not on that account satisfy the severe or pervasive standard. Some rolling with the punches is a fact of workplace life. Thus, complaints premised on nothing more than "rude treatment by [coworkers]," *Baqir v. Principi*, 434 F.3d 733, 747 (4th Cir. 2006), "callous behavior by [one's] superiors," *Bass v. E.I. DuPont de Nemours & Co.*, 324 F.3d 761, 765 (4th Cir. 2003), or "a routine difference of opinion and personality conflict with [one's] supervisor," *Hawkins v. PepsiCo, Inc.*, 203 F.3d 274, 276 (4th Cir. 2000), are not actionable under Title VII.

The task then on summary judgment is to identify situations that a reasonable jury might find to be so out of the ordinary as to meet the severe or pervasive criterion. That is, instances where the environment was pervaded with discriminatory conduct "aimed to humiliate, ridicule, or intimidate," thereby creating an abusive atmosphere. *Jennings v. Univ. of North Carolina*, 482 F.3d 686, 695 (4th Cir. 2007) (en banc) (citing *Meritor*). With these principles in mind, we examine whether a reasonable person in Ingram's position would have found the environment to be sufficiently severe or hostile.

2.

The evidence indicates that Ingram suffered religious harassment that was "persistent, demeaning, unrelenting, and widespread." *Harris v. L & L Wings, Inc.*, 132 F.3d 978, 984 (4th Cir. 1997). It is impossible as an initial matter to ignore the context in which the harassment took place. In the time immediately following September 11th, religious tensions ran higher in much of the country, and Muslims were sometimes viewed through the prism of 9/11, rather than as the individuals they were. Sunbelt's Gaithersburg office was no exception. After the terrorist attacks took place, there was lots of talk amongst Sunbelt employees, especially by Gray, about how the "Muslim religion is bad." Likewise, after it was publicized that the D.C. snipers were Muslim, anti-Islam sentiment rose in the Sunbelt workplace. Ingram, the lone Muslim employee, was left to bear the verbal brunt of anti-Islamic sentiment.

Specifically, Ingram was subject to repeated comments that disparaged both him and his faith. Several coworkers, including one with supervisory authority, referred to Ingram in harshly derogatory terms. Mike Warner, the store's shop foreman, called Ingram "Taliban" "over and over again," as well as "towel head." Likewise, Sal Rindone, a Sunbelt mechanic, told Ingram that he thought Ingram was a member of the Taliban. This same coworker also challenged Ingram's allegiance to the United States, asking Ingram "are you on our side or are you on the Taliban's side," and telling him that if "you don't like America or where we stand, you can just leave." Ingram, a veteran of the United States Army, responded that he was not a member of the Taliban but rather "an American and a Muslim."

In addition, Ingram was persistently harassed about his appearance, particularly his kufi and beard. For example, Warner, when making fun of Ingram's appearance, "would make it known that" he thought Ingram actually "look[ed] like a Taliban." On at least one occasion, Gray called Ingram a "fake Muslim" because of his beard. As Gray later admitted, such "comments were made often." According to Ingram, the harassment by Gray was "an ongoing thing, daily."

Ingram was also harassed about his short, Sunbelt-sanctioned prayer sessions. Gray told Ingram "several times" that he had a "problem" with Ingram leaving his desk to pray. In addition, Ingram's timecard was often hidden on Fridays, the day he went to congregational prayer. Even more severe was a comment made by Warner to another coworker, which was later related to Ingram. Warner said that if he ever caught Ingram praying upstairs, that would be "the end of him."

In addition to the abusive comments made to and about Ingram personally, several coworkers made hostile remarks about Islam generally. For instance, rental manager Hank Parater told Ingram that the United States should go to Saudi Arabia and "kill them all," referring to Muslims in the Arab world. Parater also said that he wanted to be a Muslim so he could have eight wives. After it was announced on a television in the store's showroom that the D.C. snipers had been apprehended, another coworker stared at Ingram and shouted, "I should have known they were Muslims." Gray admitted that the treatment of Ingram likely stemmed from "the events of September 11th and the sniper attacks in our area."

Ingram was also the object of anti-Muslim crudities that associated Ingram, and the Muslim faith, with violence and terrorism. [The court repeated the metal detector, staple, and cartoon incidents. While focusing primarily on Ingram's "personal experience," the court also noted the affidavits of two Sunbelt customers who were Muslims, one of whom attested that Sunbelt employees called him a litany of derogatory names, including "Bin Laden," "Hezbullah," "Ayatollah," "Kadaffi," "Saddam Hussein," "terrorist," and "sun nigger."]

Ingram also was forced to endure harassment lacking a direct religious nexus. Coworkers frequently hid Ingram's timecard, unplugged his computer equipment, and defaced his business card with terms such as "dumb ass." Although similar pranks were played on other Sunbelt employees, there is evidence suggesting that Ingram suffered such harassment more often than others and more likely because of his religion. For instance, Ingram's timecard was hidden most frequently on Fridays, the day he went to congregational prayer. On the Friday before Ingram filed the written complaint, his timecard was hidden on at least five separate occasions. In light of the extensive, explicitly religious harassment by the same coworkers, a reasonable jury could infer that other harassing incidents were also motivated by a disdain for Ingram's faith.

Sunbelt makes much of the fact that those who participated in the harassment were merely Ingram's coworkers, and not anyone with supervisory authority over him. However, the evidence presented creates at least a triable issue in that regard. Warner, the store's shop foreman and a primary harasser of Ingram's, served as the acting manager whenever Riddlemoser was absent. At the very least, he was viewed as a "higher up" within the office. Similarly, Fortna, the lead rental manager, supervised Ingram's work and even signed the "supervisor" line on Ingram's disciplinary forms. As a result, a jury could infer that the harassment by Warner and Fortna had a greater impact given their supervisory status. *See Faragher*.

Likewise, Sunbelt insists the harassment could not have been sufficiently severe because, *inter alia*, it was never "physically threatening." While the presence of "physical threats undeniably strengthens a hostile work environment claim," we have not held that such evidence is required. *White v. BFI Waste Servs.*, 375 F.3d 288, 298 n.6 (4th Cir. 2004). Names can hurt as much as sticks and stones, and the Supreme Court has never indicated that the humiliation so frequently attached to hostile environments need be accompanied by physical threat or force.

While the district court suggested that the harassment might be discounted because the environment was inherently coarse, Title VII contains no such "crude environment" exception, and to read one into it might vitiate statutory safeguards for those who need them most. Of course, if Sunbelt's environment was somehow so universally crude that the treatment of Ingram was nothing out of the ordinary, the jury would be entitled to take that into account. However, the evidence here suggests that the jury could also take the opposite view—that the harassment of Ingram was unique.

Any of the above incidents, viewed in isolation, would not have been enough to have transformed the workplace into a hostile or abusive one. No employer can lightly be held liable for single or scattered incidents. We cannot ignore, however, the habitual use of epithets here or view the conduct without an eye for its cumulative effect. Our precedent has made this point repeatedly. *See Amirmokri v. Baltimore Gas & Elec. Co.*, 60 F.3d 1126, 1131 (4th Cir. 1995) (finding the alleged harassment was sufficiently severe or pervasive because an Iranian plaintiff was called "names like 'the local terrorist,' a 'camel jockey' and 'the Emir of Waldorf'" on an almost daily basis).

Companies cannot, of course, be charged with cleansing their workplace of all offensive remarks. Such a task would be well-nigh impossible, and would encourage companies to adopt authoritarian traits. But we cannot regard as "merely offensive," and thus "beyond Title VII's purview," *Harris*, constant and repetitive abuse founded upon misperceptions that all Muslims possess hostile designs against the United States, that all Muslims support jihad, that all Muslims were sympathetic to the 9/11 attack, and that all Muslims are proponents of radical Islam.

If Americans were forced to practice their faith under the conditions to which Ingram was subject, the Free Exercise Clause and the embodiment of its values in the Title VII protections against workplace religious prejudice would ring quite hollow. Title VII makes plain that religious freedom in America entails more than the right to attend one's own synagogue, mosque, or church. Free religious exercise would mean little if restricted to places of worship or days of observance, only to disappear the next morning at work. In this regard, Title VII helps ensure the special nature of American unity, one not premised on homogeneity but upon the common allegiance to and customary practice of our constitutional ideals of mutual respect.

D.

[The court finally turned to the basis of the employer's liability for the actions of its workers and managers, finding that the standards for such liability were met.]

NOTES

1. *Other Bases of Discriminatory Harassment.* As *Sunbelt* illustrates, harassment claims under the antidiscrimination statutes have not been limited to sexual harassment. While sexual harassment predominates among the hostile environment cases under Title VII, the first case to recognize hostile environment as a basis for liability under Title VII, *Rogers v. EEOC*, 454 F.2d 234 (5th Cir. 1971), concerned an employer who "created an offensive work environment for employees by giving discriminatory service to its Hispanic clientele." Sexual harassment cases such as *Meritor* revived litigation over work environments contaminated by racial, national origin, or age discrimination. *See Cooler v. Layne Christensen Co.*, 710 F. App'x 842 (11th Cir. 2017) (use of "nigger" on one occasion is not sufficient to establish a hostile work environment claim but two uses, together with references to plaintiff as "boy" and "you people," sufficed); *Castleberry v. STI Grp.*, 863 F.3d 259, 262 (3d Cir. 2017) (use of a single racial slur in front of plaintiffs and their non-African-American coworkers, when accompanied by threats of termination, which ultimately occurred, was sufficient severe); *Rivera v. Rochester Genesee Reg'l Transp. Auth.*, 702 F.3d 685

(2d Cir. 2012) (Puerto Rican and African American plaintiffs established triable cases of national origin and racial harassment by each testifying to several instances where epithets like "spic," "Taco Bell," and "nigger" were used; there was also evidence about extensive bullying and physical harassment which could be found by a jury to be connected to the slurs).

Sunbelt was itself a religious harassment case under Title VII, but there have also been successful claims under the ADA, *see Arrieta-Colon v. Wal-Mart P.R., Inc.*, 434 F.3d 75 (1st Cir. 2006) (upholding jury verdict of disability discrimination for plaintiff who was harassed because his penile implants left him in a constant state of semi-erection), and presumably age-based harassment would also be actionable.

2. Harris. The *Sunbelt* court repeatedly refers to *Harris v. Forklift Systems, Inc.*, 510 U.S. 17 (1993), where a unanimous Court, building on *Meritor*, established the standards for "severe or pervasive." Although the district court had recognized the severity of the harassment, it had dismissed because the comments were not "so severe as to be expected to seriously affect [Harris's] psychological well-being." Quoting *Meritor*, the Court wrote:

> When the workplace is permeated with "discriminatory intimidation, ridicule, and insult," that is "sufficiently severe or pervasive to alter the conditions of the victim's employment and create an abusive working environment," Title VII is violated.
>
> This standard, which we reaffirm today, takes a middle path between making actionable any conduct that is merely offensive and requiring the conduct to cause a tangible psychological injury. As we pointed out in *Meritor*, "mere utterance of an . . . epithet which engenders offensive feelings in an employee," does not sufficiently affect the conditions of employment to implicate Title VII. Conduct that is not severe or pervasive enough to create an objectively hostile or abusive work environment—an environment that a reasonable person would find hostile or abusive—is beyond Title VII's purview. Likewise, if the victim does not subjectively perceive the environment to be abusive, the conduct has not actually altered the conditions of the victim's employment, and there is no Title VII violation.
>
> But Title VII comes into play before the harassing conduct leads to a nervous breakdown. A discriminatorily abusive work environment, even one that does not seriously affect employees' psychological well-being, can and often will detract from employees' job performance, discourage employees from remaining on the job, or keep them from advancing in their careers. Moreover, even without regard to these tangible effects, the very fact that the discriminatory conduct was so severe or pervasive that it created a work environment abusive to employees because of their race, gender, religion, or national origin offends Title VII's broad rule of workplace equality. The appalling conduct alleged in *Meritor*, and the reference in that case to environments " 'so heavily polluted with discrimination as to destroy completely the emotional and psychological stability of minority group workers,' " quoting *Rogers v. EEOC*, merely present some especially egregious examples of harassment. They do not mark the boundary of what is actionable.

530 U.S. at 21-22. Thus, while Title VII certainly "bars conduct that would seriously affect a reasonable person's psychological well-being, . . . the statute is not limited to such conduct. So long as the environment would reasonably be perceived, and is perceived, as hostile or abusive, there is no need for it also to be psychologically injurious." *Id.* at 22.

The *Harris* Court stressed that "[t]his is not, and by its nature cannot be, a mathematically precise test," *id.* Rather, it requires "looking at all the circumstances. These may include the frequency of the discriminatory conduct; its severity; whether it is physically threatening or humiliating, or a mere offensive utterance; and whether it unreasonably interferes with an employee's work performance." *Id*. The employee's "psychological well-being" is relevant, but by no means the only factor. The harasser's role in the employer's hierarchy may also be important. Susan Grover & Kimberley Piro, *Consider the Source: When the Harasser Is the Boss*, 79 FORDHAM L. REV. 499 (2010).

• **3.** *Applying* Harris. As *Sunbelt* well illustrates, *Harris* provides little in the way of answers even if it sets the governing analytic structure. The divergent views of the same conduct by the district court and the Fourth Circuit illustrate how indeterminate the "severe or pervasive" concepts are even after *Harris*. You might find a parallel in the tort of intentional infliction of emotional distress in Chapter 5, but courts in discriminatory harassment cases have tended to find claims stated far more often than under the common law. Is that because it's somehow more harmful to make an employee's life miserable for reasons related to her protected status?

In any event, many courts have applied the *Harris* standard, and the results are anything but consistent. *Compare Desardouin v. City of Rochester*, 708 F.3d 102 (2d Cir. 2013) (comments made on a weekly basis over several months, though not threatening, were more than merely offensive; for a male supervisor to repeatedly say to a female subordinate that her husband was "not taking care of [her] in bed" could readily be found to be a solicitation for sexual relations coupled with a claim of sexual prowess); *with Stevens v. Saint Elizabeth Med. Ctr., Inc.*, 533 F. App'x 634 (6th Cir. 2013) (conduct not such that a reasonable person would find objectively hostile when multiple text messages were neither offensive nor vulgar, and most were innocuous; the texts that inappropriately expressed continued affection and physical interactions in the office including kissing may have been unwanted or unsolicited but did not result "in a working environment permeated with discriminatory intimidation or ridicule, nor was it physically threatening such that it would have unreasonably interfered" with plaintiff's work performance).

• **4.** *A Few Comments Not Enough?* Courts have sometimes resisted finding actionable harassment based only on a few offensive comments. In *Clark County School District v. Breeden*, reproduced at page 671, the Supreme Court held that no reasonable person could believe that telling a single joke with a sexual innuendo constituted actionable harassment. *See also Sprague v. Thorn Americas, Inc.*, 129 F.3d 1355 (10th Cir. 1997) (sporadic comments over 16-month period, including joking request that plaintiff undo her top button, staring down her dress and joking about it, and referring to a jewelry item as "kinky," did not create a hostile environment). Might #MeToo change the way courts look at such conduct? As in *Sunbelt*, courts have been more open to finding a hostile environment based on verbal harassment when the comments are alleged to be "commonplace," "ongoing," and "continuing" over a long period of time. *E.g., Mosby-Grant v. City of Hagerstown*, 630 F.3d 326 (4th Cir. 2010) (finding a triable claim when police academy recruit produced evidence that she was targeted because of her sex, consistently made to feel like an outsider by her classmates and some instructors, sexist comments were frequently made to her or in her presence, and she was consistently subjected to taunting); *Vera v. McHugh*, 622 F.3d 17, 28 (1st Cir. 2010) (male supervisor's staring at plaintiff in a sexual way, repeatedly standing too close to her, and once calling her "babe," could support a reasonable jury finding of sexual harassment; although some lack of privacy and personal space was inherent in the situation, "Rodriguez went out of his way to violate Vera's privacy and the integrity of her personal space"). And sometimes a claim can be stated with neither touching nor comments. *See Billings v. Town of Grafton*, 515 F.3d 39 (1st Cir. 2008) (even absent touching, sexual advances, or overtly sexual comments, a manager's repeatedly staring at his subordinate's breasts could constitute actionable harassment).

• **5.** *Blue Collar Versus White Collar.* In discussing the requirement that conduct be severe or pervasive to be actionable, the *Oncale* court states, "in same-sex (as in all) harassment cases, that inquiry requires careful consideration of the social context in which particular behavior occurs and is experienced by its target." One possible meaning of this is that actions that may be severe in one context are mild in another. We saw a variation on this in *Sunbelt* where the employer argued that the religion-based comments were somehow less objectionable because of the general atmosphere of workers riding each other. In *Williams v. General Motors*, 187 F.3d 553 (6th Cir. 1999), the court held that the standard for establishing sexual harassment does not vary with the work environment. The same standard applies, therefore, whether the complaint is asserted in a coarse blue-collar environment or in a more refined professional environment. Is this holding consistent with *Oncale*?

• **6.** *Is "Unwelcome" Still a Requirement? Harris* framed the core question for harassment cases as whether "the environment would reasonably be perceived, and is perceived, as hostile or abusive." This formulation conspicuously omitted any reference to whether particular conduct had to be "unwelcome" in order to be actionable, a requirement that *Meritor* had explicitly imposed. As a result, many believe that *Harris* modified *sub silentio* that part of *Meritor*: If conduct is subjectively experienced by the subject as hostile or abusive, it can scarcely be "welcomed" by the subject. *See, e.g., Carr v. Allison Gas Turbine Div., Gen. Motors Corp.*, 32 F.3d 1007, 1008 (7th Cir. 1994) (" 'Welcome sexual harassment' is an oxymoron"). Such a view of *Harris* also avoided one of the few aspects of *Meritor* that feminists found objectionable: the Court's statement that evidence of "a complainant's sexually provocative speech or dress" is "obviously relevant" to deciding "whether he or she found particular sexual advances unwelcome." The Court did recognize the possibility that such evidence would be unduly prejudicial as compared to its probative value but stressed that "there is no per se rule against its admissibility." *Meritor*, 477 U.S. at 69. Assessing a plaintiff's sexual history or her personal style in order to resolve a case, whether it be a criminal prosecution for rape or a civil suit for sexual harassment, is profoundly disturbing and has resulted in amendments to the Rules of Evidence to restrict such inquiries. *See* Jane H. Aiken, *Protecting Plaintiffs' Sexual Pasts: Coping with Preconceptions Through Discretion*, 51 EMORY L. J. 559 (2002) (exploring the civil application of Rule 412).

But is unwelcomeness truly gone? Not according to the *Sunbelt* court, although it had no trouble in finding the religious comments to be unwelcome to Ingram. Some argue that this aspect of *Meritor* is alive and well, together with *Meritor*'s authorization of an inquiry into plaintiff's "dress and personal fantasies." Under this view, welcomeness is not a question of the victim's subjective reaction but, rather, what a reasonable person in the shoes of the alleged harasser would believe she wanted, welcomed, or would otherwise find unobjectionable. Even under such a view, some courts have been resolute in sharply restricting inquiries into the plaintiff's life. An extreme example is *Burns v. McGregor Electronic Industries*, 989 F.2d 959 (8th Cir. 1993), where the Eighth Circuit twice had to reverse the district court, which clearly disapproved of plaintiff's lifestyle. The Eighth Circuit held that a woman's *off-work* dress and activities were irrelevant to whether she welcomed advances at work. Similarly, the fact that she might welcome advances from some individuals does not mean that any man was free to make them:

> The plaintiff's choice to pose for a nude magazine outside work hours is not material to the issue of whether plaintiff found her employer's work-related conduct offensive. This is not a case where Burns posed in provocative and suggestive ways at work. Her private life, regardless how reprehensible the trier of fact might find it to be, did not provide lawful acquiescence to unwanted sexual advances at her work place by her employer. To hold otherwise would be contrary to Title VII's goal of ridding the work place of any kind of unwelcome sexual harassment. . . .

Burns, 989 F.2d at 963. The trial court made explicit findings that the conduct was not invited or solicited despite plaintiff posing naked for a nationally distributed magazine. The court believed, however, that because of her outside conduct, including her "interest in having her nude pictures appear in a magazine containing much lewd and crude sexually explicit material," the uninvited sexual advances of her employer were not "in and of [themselves] offensive to her." *Id.* The trial court also explained that Burns "would not have been offended if someone she was attracted to did or said the same thing," but the appeals court rejected this approach: "This rationale would allow a complete stranger to pursue sexual behavior at work that a female worker would accept from her husband or boyfriend. This standard would allow a male employee to kiss or fondle a female worker at the workplace." *Id.* at 963.

But notice that even *Burns*, which essentially excludes off-work conduct, did not reject the welcomeness inquiry explicitly. Had plaintiff "posed in provocative and suggestive ways at work," it presumably would have admitted that evidence, although it may run afoul of Rule 412. While *Burns* was decided before *Harris*, post-*Harris* cases, like *Sunbelt*, continue to ask whether conduct was invited or welcomed. *E.g., EEOC v. Prospect Airport Servs.*, 621 F.3d 991, 997-98 (9th Cir. 2010) ("welcomeness is inherently subjective" but "unwelcomeness has to be communicated"). Such cases put a burden on plaintiff to rebuff sexual advances or otherwise object to sexualized conduct before the harasser can be held responsible and therefore seem to provide harassers a one-time get-out-of-jail-free card until the target communicates her distaste.

. **7.** *When Is Severe or Pervasive Harassment OK?* Can harassment ever be justified? Establishments such as Hooters restaurants hire females as waitresses, dress them in outfits designed to be provocative, and advertise not just the food but also the sexually attractive personnel. If a Hooters waitress complains of sexual harassment by customers, can the employer justify it, perhaps as a BFOQ? The only decided case to raise this issue starkly is *Lyle v. Warner Brothers Television Productions*, 132 P.3d 211, 225-26 (Cal. 2006), where a writer for the "Friends" sitcom failed to recover under the state's fair employment law for the sexually oriented atmosphere in the studio:

> There is no dispute *Friends* was a situation comedy that featured young sexually active adults and sexual humor geared primarily toward adults. Aired episodes of the show often used sexual and anatomical language, innuendo, wordplay, and physical gestures to create humor concerning sex, including oral sex, anal sex, heterosexual sex, gay sex, "talking dirty" during sex, premature ejaculation, pornography, pedophiles, and "threesomes." The circumstance that this was a creative workplace focused on generating scripts for an adult-oriented comedy show featuring sexual themes is significant in assessing the existence of triable issues of facts regarding whether the writers' sexual antics and coarse sexual talk were aimed at plaintiff or at women in general, whether plaintiff and other women were singled out to see and hear what happened, and whether the conduct was otherwise motivated by plaintiff's gender.

Concluding that the record showed that the sexual discussions, including of the writers' own personal sexual experiences were "nondirected" conduct, the court found there was no harassment because of sex.

8. *Nontargeted Harassment.* As *Lyle* suggests, there has been some question as to whether harassment must be targeted at women in order to be actionable. *See Ocheltree v. Scollon Prods.*, 335 F.3d 325, 327 (4th Cir. 2003) (en banc). But the cases have generally not found the absence of targeting to be fatal to a claim. *See Hoyle v. Freightliner, LLC*, 650 F.3d 321 (4th Cir. 2011) (given the number of incidents and consistent describing of women in a sexually subservient and demeaning light, a reasonable jury could find an abusive work environment); *Gallagher v. C.H. Robinson Worldwide, Inc.*, 567 F.3d 263, 274 (6th Cir. 2009) ("Whether the offensive conduct was intentionally directed specifically at Gallagher or not, the fact remains that she had no means of escaping her co-workers' loud insulting language and degrading conversations; she was unavoidably exposed to it.").

Further, when harassment is targeted at the plaintiff, harassment of other women may be relevant to establishing that the conduct is actionable. After recognizing that its precedents permitted the factfinder to "consider similar acts of harassment of which a plaintiff becomes aware during the course of his or her employment, even if the harassing acts were directed at others or occurred outside of the plaintiff's presence," *Hawkins v. Anheuser-Busch, Inc.*, 517 F.3d 321, 336 (6th Cir. 2008), went on:

> [T]he appropriate weight to be given a prior act will be directly proportional to the act's proximity in time to the harassment at issue in the plaintiff's case. The further back in time the prior act occurred, in other words, the weaker the inference that the act bears a relationship to the current working environment. On the other hand, more weight should be given to acts committed by a serial harasser if the plaintiff knows that the same individual committed offending acts in the past. This is because a serial harasser left free to harass again leaves the impression that acts of harassment are tolerated at the workplace and supports a plaintiff's claim that the workplace is both objectively and subjectively hostile.

Id. at 336-37. *See also Ziskie v. Mineta*, 547 F.3d 220 (4th Cir. 2008) (affidavits of plaintiff's female c-workers could lend credence to plaintiff's mistreatment claims, show the harassment was pervasive, or support a finding that she was treated poorly by coworkers because of her sex, and not some other reason).

9. *Harassment in Splitsville.* The recurring problem of consensual relationships gone bad has troubled harassment law. Even if welcomeness is, generally speaking, not a viable defense separate and apart from the *Harris* requirements, there is one situation where it might arise—where a consensual relationship ends. Although firing one's former lover seems analytically indistinguishable from discharging a person who will not have sex with the harasser in the first place, some courts have been more ambivalent about this scenario. *Compare Pipkins v. Temple Terrace*, 267 F.3d 1197, 1201 (11th Cir. 2001) (stating that, construing plaintiff's allegations in the light most favorable to her, "she merely portrays any action by Klein to have been taken because of his disappointment in their failed relationship. Again, such a motivation is not 'because of . . . sex.'") *with Green v. Adm'rs of the Tulane Educ. Fund*, 284 F.3d 642, 657 (5th Cir. 2002) ("[I]t was only after the relationship ended that Richardson began to harass her. This fact alone supports a jury's inference that he harassed her because she refused to continue to have a casual sexual relationship with him. As such, we conclude that there was sufficient evidence to support the jury's finding of sexual harassment."). *See also Forrest v. Brinker Int'l Payroll Co., LP*, 511 F.3d 225, 229 (1st Cir. 2007) ("reasoning that the harassment could not have been motivated by the victim's sex because it was instead motivated by a romantic relationship gone sour establishes a false dichotomy. Presumably the prior relationship would never have occurred if the victim were not a member of the sex preferred by the harasser, and thus the victim's sex is inextricably linked to the harasser's decision to harass.").

Believe it or not, some management attorneys recommend a "love contract" for couples entering consensual relationships. Sharon Rabin-Margalioth, *Love at Work*, 13 DUKE J. GENDER L. & POL'Y 237, 253 n.98 (2006), writes that a typical love contract will be written something like this:

> We hereby notify the Company that we wish to enter into a voluntary and mutual consensual social relationship. In entering into this relationship, we both understand and agree that we are both free to end the social relationship at any time. Should the social relationship end, we both agree that we shall not allow the breakup to negatively impact the performance of our duties. Prior to signing this Consensual Relationship Contract, we received and reviewed the Company Sexual Harassment Policy, a copy of which is attached hereto. By signing below, we acknowledge that the social relationship between us does not violate the Company's Sexual Harassment Policy, and that entering into the social relationship has not been made a condition or term of employment.

See also Vicki Schultz, *The Sanitized Workplace*, 112 YALE L.J. 2061, 2126-28 (2003). Do you think this would exonerate an employer of liability? Might it create other problems even if it did?

10. *Harassment Meets the First Amendment.* Hostile environment sexual harassment liability frequently is based on sexually offensive, obscene, or denigrating speech. Some harassment cases, however, have involved speech that is not sexually explicit and more clearly political in nature. An individual is free to get on a soap box and argue that women belong in the kitchen, not the workplace. Can that same individual bring his soapbox into the workplace and argue the same thing there? *See Lipsett v. University of Puerto Rico*, 864 F.2d 881, 903-4 (1st Cir. 1988) (female resident stated a Title VII claim by alleging that she was subjected to comments that women should not be surgeons). Is harassment law limited by the First Amendment? *See* David Bernstein, YOU CAN'T SAY THAT!: THE GROWING THREAT TO CIVIL LIBERTIES FROM ANTIDISCRIMINATION LAWS (2003); Helen L. Norton, *You Can't Ask (or Say) That: The First Amendment Implications of Civil Rights Restrictions on Decisionmaker Speech*, 11 WM. & MARY BILL RTS. J. 727, 729, 777 (2003); Eugene Volokh, *What Speech Does "Hostile Work Environment" Harassment Law Restrict?*, 85 GEO. L.J. 627 (1997); Kingsley R. Browne, *Zero Tolerance for the First Amendment: Title VII's Regulation of Employee Speech*, 27 OHIO N.U. L. REV. 563 (2001); Charles R. Calleros, *Title VII and the First Amendment: Content-Neutral Regulation, Disparate Impact, and the "Reasonable Person,"* 58 OHIO ST. L.J. 1217 (1997); Cynthia L. Estlund, *Freedom of Expression in the Workplace and the Problem of Discriminatory Harassment*, 75 TEX. L. REV. 687 (1997).

Despite the outpouring of scholarship on the subject, few cases have raised First Amendment problems with such suits, and the Supreme Court has, in dicta in

R.A.V. v. City of St. Paul, Minnesota, 505 U.S. 377 (1992), suggested that there is no free speech concern:

> [S]ince words can in some circumstances violate laws directed not against speech but against conduct (a law against treason, for example, is violated by telling the enemy the nation's defense secrets), a particular content-based subcategory of a proscribable class of speech can be swept up incidentally within the reach of a statute directed at conduct rather than speech. Thus, for example, sexually derogatory "fighting words," among other words, may produce a violation of Title VII's general prohibition against sexual discrimination in employment practices, 42 U.S.C. §2000e-2; 29 C.F.R. §1604.11 (1991). *See also* 18 U.S.C. §242; 42 U.S.C. §§1981, 1982. Where the government does not target conduct on the basis of its expressive content, acts are not shielded from regulation merely because they express a discriminatory idea or philosophy.

R.A.V., 505 U.S. at 389. Since *R.A.V.*, the Court decided *Harris* in which the sexually harassing behavior was primarily evidenced by offensive remarks. Although the constitutionality of imposing liability on the employer for those remarks was raised in briefs submitted in that case, the Court did not address the issue in its opinion. Does the dictum in *R.A.V.* explain why Hardy's statements in *Harris* are not protected?

11. *Constructive Discharge.* In many harassment cases, the plaintiff, unable to resolve the matter internally, quits. That was true, for example, in *Harris.* Assuming the sexual harassment was actionable, and the employer liable, can such a plaintiff recover for lost future earnings, or is she limited to the emotional distress caused by the harassment during the time she was employed? The question is one of "constructive discharge," that is, situations in which an employee's formal quitting is viewed as equivalent to being fired. The Supreme Court has held that the fact that harassment may be sufficiently severe or pervasive to contaminate the work environment but not necessarily sufficient to establish a constructive discharge. *Pennsylvania State Police v. Suders*, 542 U.S. 129 (2004), held that "A hostile-environment constructive discharge claim entails something more: A plaintiff who advances such a compound claim must show working conditions so intolerable that a reasonable person would have felt compelled to resign." Had Ingram quit, would he have been constructively discharged?

In *Green v. Brennan*, 136 S. Ct. 1769 (2016), the Supreme Court resolved a question regarding the timeliness of constructive discharge claims, with the majority holding that plaintiffs had to meet filing requirements as measured from the moment they gave notice of their resignation, not as measured from the employer's acts creating the intolerable conditions that led to that resignation. Beyond expanding the time to bring suit, *Green* also seems to reject the rule in some circuits that the employer had to intend to force the employee to quit in order for a resignation to count as a constructive discharge. See *EEOC v. Consol Energy, Inc.*, 860 F.3d 131 (4th Cir. 2017).

12. *Employer Liability.* Conduct by a supervisor, coworker, or even customer may be harassment without making the employer liable for such conduct. In *Sunbelt* itself, the court, having found a triable claim of harassment, still had to go on to decide whether the employer was liable for such conduct. Because they are part and parcel of more general employer efforts to comply with the law and reduce legal exposure, issues of employer liability are treated in Chapter 13 on risk management.

Note on Grooming and Dress Codes ♠

Perhaps the most blatant remaining form of gender discrimination in employment is employer dress and grooming codes, which frequently have disparate standards for males and females. How can such standards survive Title VII's prohibition of gender discrimination? In *Willingham v. Macon Telegraph Publ'g Co.*, 507 F.2d 1084, 1091-92 (5th Cir. 1975) (en banc), the Fifth Circuit denied a man's challenge to an employer's rule prohibiting male (but not female) employees from having hair longer than shoulder length:

> Equal employment *opportunity* may be secured only when employers are barred from discriminating against employees on the basis of immutable characteristics, such as race and national origin. Similarly, an employer cannot have one hiring policy for men and another for women *if* the distinction is based on some fundamental right. But a hiring policy that distinguishes on some other ground, such as grooming codes or length of hair, is related more closely to the employer's choice of how to run his business than to equality of employment opportunity. . . . [A] line must be drawn between distinctions grounded on such fundamental rights as the right to have children or to marry and those interfering with the manner in which an employer exercises his judgment as to the way to operate a business. Hair length is not immutable and in the situation of employer vis à vis employee enjoys no constitutional protection. If the employee objects to the grooming code he has the right to reject it by looking elsewhere for employment, or alternatively he may choose to subordinate his preference by accepting the code along with the job. . . .
>
> We adopt the view, therefore, that distinctions in employment practices between men and women on the basis of something other than immutable or protected characteristics do not inhibit employment *opportunity* in violation of Sec. 703(a). Congress sought only to give all persons equal access to the job market, not to limit an employer's right to exercise his informed judgment as to how best to run his shop.
>
> We are in accord also with the alternative ground. . . . "From all that appears, equal job opportunities are available to both sexes. It does not appear that defendant fails to impose grooming standards for female employees; thus in this respect each sex is treated equally."

Willingham has received general acceptance: gender-specific differences in dress and grooming codes do not per se violate Title VII. *See, e.g., Harper v. Blockbuster Entm't Corp.*, 139 F.3d 1385 (11th Cir. 1998); *Tavora v. New York Mercantile Exch.*, 101 F.3d 907 (2d Cir. 1997).

No one seems to doubt that permitting female, but not male, employees to have shoulder-length hair is sex discrimination in an analytic sense. As the Court said in another context, "[s]uch a practice does not pass the simple test of whether the evidence shows 'treatment of a person in a manner which but for that person's sex would be different.'" *City of L.A. Dep't of Water & Power v. Manhart*, 435 U.S. 702, 711 (1978). What, then, is the justification for permitting it? Does *Willingham* establish a de minimis test under which trivial sex distinctions do not warrant federal court intervention? That would explain the court's distinction between cases involving hair length and cases involving "fundamental rights." Remember, also, that some courts have required different treatment to have material adverse effects in order to constitute discrimination. Maybe hair length requirements are not material. Or is *Willingham* an example of a "volition" exception to Title VII: Employer requirements that can easily be met by an employee are not within the statutory proscription?

Declining protection because the different treatment is trivial is consistent with the courts' treatment of sexual harassment that is not sufficiently serious or pervasive to create a hostile environment. But even a minor incident of sexual harassment becomes actionable as a quid pro quo case when job benefits are contingent on acceptance of the discriminatory remarks or conduct. What if an employee is threatened with the loss of his job on the ground that his hair is too long? How can this be viewed as trivial?

Many commentators look on grooming cases as sui generis, that is, that they shouldn't be read to have much meaning beyond the context in which they arise, perhaps because the issues they address are perceived by many to be insignificant. But don't these cases reflect stereotypes so ingrained that they are not even recognized as such? *See* Karl E. Klare, *Power/Dressing: Regulation of Employee Appearance*, 26 NEW ENG. L. REV. 1395 (1992). Why is it that an employer can legally prohibit males from wearing dresses or eye shadow? Is it because there is something wrong with males assuming "female" roles? Is a man wrong to assume such roles in turn because females are inferior and a man demeans himself by aping them? Is it merely coincidence that society looks more favorably on women who appropriate "male" attire (e.g., the pants suit) than the other way around? Or perhaps the courts are simply applying what they perceive as legislative intent: Whatever Congress *said*, it did not *mean* to bar this kind of employer rule. Isn't it clear that the 1964 Congress did not intend Title VII to require a unisex dress code?

Several decisions have found Title VII violated when the employer's dress code did not treat women equally. In *Carroll v. Talman Federal Savings & Loan Ass'n*, 604 F.2d 1028 (7th Cir. 1979), the court considered a dress code allowing males to wear "customary business attire" but requiring women to wear uniforms. Although disclaiming any intent to pass on the reasonableness of general employer dress regulations, the court distinguished the case before it: "While there is nothing offensive about uniforms per se, when some employees are uniformed and others not there is a natural tendency to assume that the uniformed women have a lesser professional status than their male colleagues attired in normal business clothes." *Id*. at 1033; *see also Frank v. United Air Lines*, 216 F.3d 845 (9th Cir. 2000) (an airline's differential weight standards for flight attendants were facially discriminatory because they imposed unequal burdens on men and women in how they were calculated). Expectations that there would be a shift in the law in this area were, however, dashed by *Jespersen v. Harrah's Operating Co.*, 444 F.3d 1104 (9th Cir. 2006)(7-4), which rejected a claim that sex-differentiated grooming policies were illegal because they placed an unequal burden on women due to the time and expense entailed in applying make-up.

The issue of appearance restrictions, whether framed as a discrimination issue or as a matter of personal autonomy has generated considerable attention in the law reviews. The *Duke Journal of Gender & Law* devoted an entire symposium issue to it in 2007, in volume 14. Similar challenges have been made to grooming rules that affect African Americans without great success. *EEOC v. Catastrophe Mgmt. Sols.*, 852 F.3d 1018 (11th Cir. 2016) (holding an employer's rule against "excessive hairstyles" interpreted to bar dreadlocks was not actionable race discrimination). *See generally* D. Wendy Greene, *Splitting Hairs: The Eleventh Circuit's Take on Workplace Bans Against Black Women's Natural Hair in* EEOC v. Catastrophe Management Solutions, 71 U. MIAMI L. REV. 987 (2017); Angela Onwuachi-Willig, *Another Hair Piece: Exploring New Strands of Analysis Under Title VII*, 98 GEO. L. J. 1079 (2010).

Allowance of sex-based differences has not always been limited to the grooming code scenario. In *Bauer v. Lynch*, 812 F.3d 340 (4th Cir. 2016), the court upholding gender-normed physical fitness tests for FBI trainees by rejecting the simple *Manhart* test of whether "the evidence shows treatment of a person in a manner which but for that person's sex would be different" in favor of asking whether the test imposes a greater burden on one sex than the other. Can you explain this decision?

PROBLEM

9-4. You work as an employment lawyer. A young woman has come to see you seeking advice. She tells you that she works at a nearby mid-sized law firm. She is a relatively young associate, and this is her first job after her clerkship. She tells you she made a "big mistake" by getting "involved" with a partner at the firm. While she does not work in his practice group, she is sometimes assigned out to work with that group, which is how she got to know him. From her point of view, the relationship "didn't work out" and "wasn't that big a deal." However, she is beginning to be concerned that it's a much bigger deal for him.

She broke up with him two weeks ago, sending him an e-mail from her G-mail account, telling him the usual stuff. He responded with a series of three e-mails ranging from confused to hurt to angry. His last e-mail stated, "You'll be sorry about this. We had a very good thing going." He has not since communicated with her directly, but he snubs her when they meet in the halls, and she has heard from a senior associate that "Joe's badmouthing you with the partners big-time."

Your client will not be considered for partner for several years, but her annual review was last week, and she received a 7 (out of a scale of 10). In last year's annual review, she was rated an 8.5. The reviewing partner, who is in charge of her group, told her, "Don't worry about it, I'm sure you'll bounce back and there's no impact on salary or bonus." But she did not find her explanations for the slippage very satisfactory.

How would you advise her?

Note on Sexual Orientation Discrimination ⚓

Sexual orientation is not listed as a protected characteristic under Title VII, and discrimination on the basis of sexual orientation per se was long uniformly held not actionable under federal law. *See, e.g., DeSantis v. Pac. Telephone & Telegraph Co.* 608 F.2d 327 (9th Cir. 1979). In 2017, however, in a dramatic break from prior precedents, the en banc Seventh Circuit decided *Hively v. Ivy Tech Cmty. Coll. of Ind.*, 853 F.3d 339 (7th Cir. 2017), holding that discrimination on the basis of sexual orientation is a form of sex discrimination prohibited by Title VII. Going beyond the cases that had recognized a gender nonconformity theory that allowed some gays to sue for discrimination against them, the majority held that sexual orientation discrimination per se equated with sexual discrimination on either of two theories. First, looking to "switch the categories" analysis, it noted that the lesbian plaintiff would not have been discharged had she been a male whose preferences were for women as sexual partners. Secondly, looking to interracial association cases (those that found a violation when whites were terminated for their associations with blacks), it found that discrimination on the basis of the sex of those whom one marries or with whom one has romantic relationships was discrimination on the basis of sex. The Seventh Circuit was soon joined by the Second. *Zarda v. Altitude Express, Inc.*, 883 F.3d 100 (2d Cir. 2018); *see also Franchina v. City of Providence*, 881 F.3d 32 (1st Cir. 2018) (finding discrimination against a lesbian actionable under the sex-plus theory, that is, that sex plus another factor, in this case sexual orientation, caused the adverse action); *cf. EEOC v. R.G. & G.R. Harris Funeral Homes*, 884 F.3d 560, 571, 575 (6th Cir. 2018) ("Discrimination on the basis of transgender and transitioning status is necessarily discrimination on the basis of sex, and thus the EEOC should have had the opportunity to prove that the Funeral Home violated Title VII by firing Stephens because she is transgender and transitioning from male to female"; "it is analytically impossible to fire an employee based on that employee's status as a transgender person without being motivated, at least in part, by the employee's sex."). *See generally* William N. Eskridge, Jr., *Title VII's Statutory History and the Sex Discrimination Argument for LGBT Workplace Protections,*127 YALE L. J. 322 (2016); Brian Soucek, Hively's *Self-Induced Blindness*, 127 YALE L. J. F. 115 (2017); Brian Soucek, *Queering Sexual Harassment Law*, 128 YALE L. J. F. 67 (2018).

Most other circuits have not held sex orientation discrimination to equate to sex discrimination, but they do permit attack on such bias when the adverse actions can be linked to gender stereotyping: a so-called gender nonconformity claim. Similar arguments can be made with respect to transgender or transsexual individuals. Early cases rejected such a theory. *See, e.g., DeSantis* (finding that male could be legally fired for being effeminate, even if he was not gay). The authority of such decisions was radically undercut by *Price Waterhouse v. Hopkins* (reproduced at page 568), however, which held it impermissible to discriminate against a woman because she is too masculine. It would seem that discrimination against a male for "effeminacy" or other failures to conform to male stereotypes would also be impermissible, and the circuits courts have generally so held. In *Nichols v. Azteca Restaurant Enterprises, Inc.*, 256 F.3d 864 (9th Cir. 2001), the court found plaintiff had stated a claim under Title VII when he alleged he was discriminated against for acting "too feminine." It said *Price Waterhouse* prohibits discrimination based on sex stereotyping and thus, to the extent *DeSantis* conflicts with *Price Waterhouse*, it is no longer good law. *See also Prowel v. Wise Bus. Forms, Inc.*, 579 F.3d 285 (3d Cir. 2009) (although the plaintiff might have been subjected to harassment because of his sexual orientation per se, there was enough basis to suspect that the harassment was because of his failure to conform to gender stereotypes to warrant a trial).

The absence of a federal statute prohibiting discrimination on the basis of sexual orientation has led to a number of other legal theories attacking such conduct. In public employment, sexual orientation discrimination has been challenged on the basis of the right of privacy, due process, free speech, and equal protection. Until recently, these constitutional attacks had very limited success, but developments such as *Lawrence v. Texas*, 539 U.S. 558 (2003) (striking down Texas same-sex sodomy law), and *Romer v. Evans*, 517 U.S. 620 (1996) (striking down Colorado law as discriminating against gays), augur more success for such claims, as does the Supreme Court's invalidation of the Defense of Marriage Act in *United States v. Windsor*, 570 U.S. 744 (2013).

Further, challenges based on state constitutions have also been successful; *see Gay Law Students Ass'n v. Pacific Telephone & Telegraph Co.*, 595 P.2d 592 (Cal. 1979) (holding that gays could sue a public utility for employment discrimination under the equal protection clause of the California Constitution). In addition, a number of states have enacted their own civil rights legislation expressly covering sexual orientation. Such statutes typically protect against discrimination on the basis of sexual orientation, normally defined as including heterosexuality, bisexuality, and homosexuality. For a comprehensive listing, *see* http://www.lambdalegal.org. While versions of an Employment Nondiscrimination Act ("ENDA") have been perennially introduced in Congress, it has yet to pass.

The Supreme Court's decision in *Obergefell v. Hodges*, 135 S. Ct. 2584 (2015), striking down state bans on same-sex marriage, seems likely to have strong reverberations across many legal areas, including employment. *See generally* Matthew W. Green, Jr., *Same-Sex Sex and Immutable Traits: Why* Obergefell v. Hodges *Clears a Path to Protecting Gay and Lesbian Employees from Workplace Discrimination Under Title VII*, 20 J. Gen. Race & Just. 1 (2017); Keith Cunningham-Parmeter, *Marriage Equality, Workplace Inequality: The Next Gay Rights Battle*, 67 Fla. L. Rev. 1099 (2015); Stephen F. Befort & Michael J. Vargas, *Same-Sex Marriage and Title VII*, 56 Santa Clara L. Rev. 207 (2016).

E. RETALIATION

In addition to prohibiting discrimination on the grounds of race, sex, religion, national origin, and age, Title VII, §1981, and the ADEA create a remedy for certain retaliatory conduct. Retaliation is also prohibited by the ADA in somewhat different terms.

Section 704(a) of Title VII, 42 U.S.C. §2000e-3(a), provides:

> It shall be an unlawful employment practice for an employer to discriminate against any of his employees or applicants for employment . . . because he has opposed any practice made an unlawful employment practice by this title, or because he has made a charge, testified, assisted, or participated in any manner in an investigation, proceeding, or hearing under this title.

The ADEA prohibits retaliation in substantially identical language. 29 U.S.C. §623(d). Even though §1981 does not expressly prohibit retaliation, it has been held to do so through its prohibition of discrimination on account of race. *CBOCS West, Inc. v. Humphries*, 553 U.S. 442 (2008); *see also Jackson v. Birmingham Bd. of Educ.*, 544 U.S. 167 (2005) (retaliation for opposing sex discrimination was sex discrimination within the meaning of Title IX).

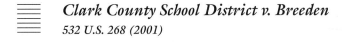

Clark County School District v. Breeden
532 U.S. 268 (2001)

Per Curiam.

[Plaintiff sued her employer, the Clark County School District, alleging that the District had taken two separate adverse employment actions against her in response to two different protected activities in which she had engaged.]

On October 21, 1994, [Ms. Breeden's] male supervisor met with [her] and another male employee to review the psychological evaluation reports of four job applicants. The report for one of the applicants disclosed that the applicant had once commented to a co-worker, "I hear making love to you is like making love to the Grand Canyon." At the meeting [Ms. Breeden's] supervisor read the comment aloud, looked at [her] and stated, "I don't know what that means." The other employee then said, "Well, I'll tell you later," and both men chuckled. [Ms. Breeden] later complained about the comment to the offending employee, to Assistant Superintendent George Ann Rice, the employee's supervisor, and to another assistant superintendent of petitioner. Her first claim of retaliation asserts that she was punished for these complaints.

The Court of Appeals for the Ninth Circuit has applied §2000e-3(a) to protect employee "opposition" not just to practices that are actually "made . . . unlawful" by Title VII, but also to practices that the employee could reasonably believe were unlawful. We have no occasion to rule on the propriety of this interpretation, because even assuming it is correct, no one could reasonably believe that the incident recounted above violated Title VII.

Title VII forbids actions taken on the basis of sex that "discriminate against any individual with respect to his compensation, terms, conditions, or privileges of employment." 42 U.S.C. §2000e-2(a)(1). Just three Terms ago, we reiterated, what was plain from our previous decisions, that sexual harassment is actionable under Title VII only if it is "so 'severe or pervasive' as to 'alter the conditions of [the victim's] employment and create an abusive working environment.'" (Only harassing conduct that is "severe or pervasive" can produce a "constructive alteration in the terms or conditions of employment"); *Faragher v. Boca Raton*, 524 U.S. 775 (1998), quoting *Meritor; Oncale v. Sundowner Offshore Services, Inc.*, [reproduced at page 648] (Title VII "forbids only behavior so objectively offensive as to alter the 'conditions' of the victim's employment"). Workplace conduct is not measured in isolation; instead, "whether an environment is sufficiently hostile or abusive" must be judged "by 'looking at all the circumstances,' including the 'frequency of the discriminatory conduct; its severity; whether it is physically threatening or humiliating, or a mere offensive utterance; and whether it unreasonably interferes with an employee's work performance.'" *Faragher v. Boca Raton* (quoting *Harris*). Hence, "[a] recurring point in [our] opinions is that simple teasing, offhand comments, and isolated incidents (unless extremely serious) will not amount to discriminatory changes in the 'terms and conditions of employment.'" *Faragher v. Boca Raton*.

No reasonable person could have believed that the single incident recounted above violated Title VII's standard. The ordinary terms and conditions of [Ms. Breeden's] job required her to review the sexually explicit statement in the course of screening job applicants. Her co-workers who participated in the hiring process were subject to the same requirement, and indeed, in the District Court [she] "conceded that it did not bother or upset her" to read the statement in the file. Her supervisor's comment, made at a meeting to review the application, that he did not know what the statement meant; her co-worker's responding comment; and the chuckling of both are at worst an "isolated incident" that cannot remotely be considered "extremely serious," as our cases require, *Faragher v. Boca Raton*. The holding of the Court of Appeals to the contrary must be reversed.

Besides claiming that she was punished for complaining to [the School District's] personnel about the alleged sexual harassment, [Ms. Breeden] also claimed that she was punished for filing charges against petitioner with the Nevada Equal Rights Commission and the Equal Employment Opportunity Commission (EEOC) and for filing the present suit. [She] filed her lawsuit on April 1, 1997; on April 10, 1997, [her] supervisor, Assistant Superintendent Rice, "mentioned to Allin Chandler, Executive Director of plaintiff's union, that she was contemplating transferring plaintiff to the position of Director of Professional Development Education"; and this transfer was "carried through" in May. In order to show, as her defense against summary judgment required, the existence of a causal connection between her protected activities and the transfer, [Ms. Breeden] "relied wholly on the temporal proximity of the filing of her complaint on April 1, 1997 and Rice's statement to plaintiff's union representative on April 10, 1997 that she was considering transferring plaintiff to the [new] position." The District Court, however, found that [Ms. Breeden] did not serve [the School District] with the summons and complaint until April 11, 1997, one day after Rice had made the statement, and Rice filed an affidavit stating that she did not become aware of the lawsuit until after April 11, a claim that [Ms. Breeden] did not challenge. Hence, the court concluded, [she] "had not shown that any causal connection exists between her protected activities and the adverse employment decision."

The Court of Appeals reversed, relying on two facts: The EEOC had issued a right-to-sue letter to [Ms. Breeden] three months before Rice announced she was contemplating the transfer, and the actual transfer occurred one month after Rice learned of [her] suit. The latter fact is immaterial in light of the fact that [the School District] concededly was contemplating the transfer before it learned of the suit. Employers need not suspend previously planned transfers upon discovering that a Title VII suit has been filed, and their proceeding along lines previously contemplated, though not yet definitively determined, is no evidence whatever of causality.

As for the right-to-sue letter: [Ms. Breeden] did not rely on that letter in the District Court and did not mention it in her opening brief on appeal. Her demonstration of causality all along had rested upon the connection between the transfer and the filing of her lawsuit—to which connection the letter was irrelevant. When, however, [the School District] answering brief in the Court of Appeals demonstrated conclusively the lack of causation between the filing of [Ms. Breeden's] lawsuit and Rice's decision, [she] mentioned the letter for the first time in her reply brief. The Ninth Circuit's opinion . . . suggests that the letter provided [the School District] with its first notice of [her] charge before the EEOC, and hence allowed the inference that the transfer proposal made three months later was [its] reaction to the charge. This will not do.

First, there is no indication that Rice even knew about the right-to-sue letter when she proposed transferring respondent. And second, if one presumes she knew about it, one must also presume that she (or her predecessor) knew *almost two years earlier* about the protected action (filing of the EEOC complaint) that the letter supposedly disclosed. . . . The cases that accept mere temporal proximity between an employer's knowledge of protected activity and an adverse employment action as sufficient evidence of causality to establish a prima facie case uniformly hold that the temporal proximity must be "very close," *Neal v. Ferguson Constr. Co.*, 237 F.3d 1248, 1253 (CA10 2001). *See, e.g., Richmond v. Oneok, Inc.*, 120 F.3d 205, 209 (CA10 1997) (3-month period insufficient); *Hughes v. Derwinski*, 967 F.2d 1168, 1174-1175 (CA7 1992) (4-month period insufficient). Action taken (as here) 20 months later suggests, by itself, no causality at all. . . .

NOTES

‣ **1.** *Public Policy Tort.* Recall the public policy discussion in Chapter 4. Retaliation under the antidiscrimination statutes is simply a version of the rule that an employee cannot be discharged in violation of public policy. As will be explained in these Notes, however, the doctrine has developed under the antidiscrimination laws in more elaborate but not always intuitive ways.

⸜ **2.** *Prima Facie Case of Retaliation.* A standard formulation of the prima facie case for retaliation is found in *Kwan v. Andalex Grp., LLC,* 737 F.3d 834, 844 (2d Cir. 2013), which requires the plaintiff to show "(1) 'participation in a protected activity'; (2) the defendant's knowledge of the protected activity; (3) 'an adverse employment action'; and (4) 'a causal connection between the protected activity and the adverse employment action.'" If plaintiff is able to establish such a case, the burden of production shifts to the employer to put into evidence a nonretaliatory reason for its action. At that point, the plaintiff may still prevail by proving that reason is a pretext for retaliation. *Jute v. Hamilton Sundstrand Corp.,* 420 F.3d 166, 179 (2d Cir. 2005).

At issue in *Breeden* were the first and third prongs. Proving causation is often the most difficult hurdle for plaintiffs, since temporal proximity is typically not enough, even for a prima facie case, unless the protected conduct and the adverse action are very close in time. *Tyler v. Univ. of Ark. Bd. of Trs.,* 628 F.3d 980, 986-87 (8th Cir. 2011) ("Generally, 'more than a temporal connection is required to present a genuine factual issue on retaliation,' and only in cases where the temporary proximity is very close can the plaintiff rest on it exclusively."). (Citations omitted.) Even assuming such proximity establishes a prima facie case, it may do little to prove that the defendant's nonretaliatory reason is a pretext. *El Sayed v. Hilton Hotels Corp.,* 627 F.3d 931, 933 (2d Cir. 2010). *See* Note 5, page 675.

3. *Opposition and Participation.* Shirley Breeden presented two distinct claims of protected conduct. One was for opposition conduct (her internal complaints), and the other was for participation conduct (her filing of charges to the state agency and the EEOC). Many courts and commentators perceive a sharp distinction between the protections of the "opposition" clause and the "participation" clause. While a plaintiff invoking the opposition clause must demonstrate a reasonable, good faith belief that the conduct complained of is unlawful, the participation clause may protect conduct without regard to its basis. One of the first "participation" cases, *Pettway v. American Cast Iron Pipe Co.,* 411 F.2d 998 (5th Cir. 1969), set the tone for these decisions by finding actionable retaliation when a worker was fired for filing an allegedly false and malicious charge with the EEOC—namely, that the employer had bought off an EEOC investigator. The court wrote: The purpose of §704(a) "is to protect the employee who utilizes the tools provided by Congress to protect his rights. The Act will be frustrated if the employer may unilaterally determine the truth or falsity of charges and take independent action." *Id.* at 1004-05; *see also Glover v. S. Carolina Law Enf.,* 170 F.3d 411 (4th Cir. 1999) (unreasonable deposition testimony protected by participation clause). *But see Benes v. A.B. Data, Ltd.,* 724 F.3d 752, 753 (7th Cir. 2013) (even participation in EEOC-sponsored mediation is not protected if the employee would have been fired for such conduct had it occurred in another context), discussed by Charles A. Sullivan, *Taking Civility Too Far* in http://lawprofessors.typepad.com/laborprof_blog/2013/08/taking-civility-too-far.html.

After the *Breeden* Court disposed of the plaintiff's "opposition clause" claim by deciding that no reasonable person could believe that she had been sexually harassed, it went on to consider the causation issue on her "participation" clause claim. It would have had no need to do so if filing of an "unreasonable" charge was unprotected. *Breeden* thus implicitly confirms the lower courts that have held that the participation clause prohibits retaliation, even where the underlying discrimination claim lacks a reasonable basis. Would even a charge filed in bad faith be protected? *See* Lawrence D. Rosenthal, *Reading Too Much into What the Court Doesn't Write: How Some Federal Courts Have Limited Title VII's Participation Clause's Protections After* Clark County School District v. Breeden, 83 WASH. L. REV. 345 (2008) (arguing that some courts are incorrectly applying the reasonable belief standard to participation clause claims).

4. *Reasonable Belief.* While the reasonableness of a plaintiff's belief in the illegality of the challenged conduct may be irrelevant for participation, it can be critical for a successful opposition claim. *Breeden* assumed, but did not decide, that the opposition clause's protections attach if the challenged practice is not in fact unlawful. In other words, a reasonable, good faith belief that the employer has acted unlawfully may or may not suffice under the opposition clause. While the statutory language supports limiting the statute's protections only to opposition to conduct that is in fact unlawful, would such an interpretation be consistent with the policy objectives of §704? *See Robinson v. Shell Oil*, 519 U.S. 337 (1997) (the policy of §704 furthered by including former employees within the protections of the statute).

Assuming a reasonable, good faith belief is necessary, problems arise as to when an employee's perceptions are reasonable. *Compare Kelly v. Howard I. Shapiro & Assocs. Consulting Eng'rs, P.C.*, 716 F.3d 10 (2d Cir. 2013) ("paramour preferences" not actionable under Title VII so plaintiff's complaints about "sexual favoritism" did not suggest that she was being discriminated against because of her sex), *with Battaglia v. United Parcel Service, Inc.*, 70 A.3d 602 (N.J. 2013) (plaintiff protected under state law for opposing continued use in management meetings of grossly sexist language even though no particular woman heard the remarks and therefore there was no actionable harassment). *See* Terry Smith, *Everyday Indignities: Race, Retaliation, and the Promise of Title VII*, 34 COLUM. HUM. RTS. L. REV. 529 (2003); Deborah L. Brake & Joanna L. Grossman, *The Failure of Title VII as a Rights Claiming System*, 86 N.C. L. REV. 859 (2008); Lawrence D. Rosenthal, *To Report or Not to Report: The Case for Eliminating the Objectively Reasonable Requirement for Opposition Activities Under Title VII's Anti-Retaliation Provision*, 39 ARIZ. ST. L.J. 1127 (2007).

5. *Temporal Proximity.* Assuming protected conduct, the plaintiff must still show an adverse action and a causal link between the protected conduct and the adverse action. Does *Breeden* mean that the plaintiff always loses on summary judgment where the only evidence of causation is that the adverse employment action occurred three months or more after the decision maker learned of the protected activity? Is it possible to assess the role of temporal proximity without looking at the other facts in the case? *See Twigg v. Hawker Beechcraft Corp.*, 659 F.3d 987, 1001-02, (10th Cir. 2011) ("[E]vidence of temporal proximity has minimal probative value where intervening events provide a legitimate basis for the employer's action."); *Pinkerton v. Colorado Dept. of Transp.*, 563 F.3d 1052 (10th Cir. 2009) (termination within a few days of the complaint plaintiff filed with employer, together with evidence that employer's reasons for firing plaintiff may not have been credible, held sufficient); *see also Fuhr v. Hazel Park Sch. Dist.*, 710 F.3d 668, 676 (6th Cir. 2013) ("while temporal proximity alone cannot establish a causal connection, a lack of temporal proximity alone can be fatal to an attempt to establish a causal connection").

6. *Balancing Opposition and Employer Interests.* Opposition conduct may be less protected than participation conduct in another way. Where participation is concerned, the courts have not been sympathetic to countervailing employer interests. For example, courts have found employers guilty of unlawful retaliation when they treat differently an employee who files a discrimination charge, even if the employer's action seems justified from a business perspective. *See, e.g., Watford v. Jefferson Cty. Pub. Sch.*, 870 F.3d 448, 454 (6th Cir. 2017) (a collective bargaining agreement that required a grievance to be "held in abeyance" once an EEOC charge was filed constituted retaliation since reasonable employees would be dissuaded from filing a charge). *But see Richardson v. Comm'n on Human Rights & Opportunities*, 532 F.3d 114 (2d Cir. 2008) (election-of-remedies provision in a collective bargaining agreement, which provided that employee alleging discrimination may not arbitrate a dispute as a grievance if she filed a charge, did not violate Title VII). That the employer is invoking a neutral rule that would have been applied to employees engaging in other forms of litigation does not mean those rules may be applied to persons who have engaged in participation activities under employment discrimination statutes. In a sense, §704's participation clause entitles plaintiffs to special treatment.

But what about the opposition clause? Can the form the employee's opposition takes remove her from the protections of the Act? As should be obvious from *McDonnell Douglas Corp. v. Green*, reproduced at page 547, the answer is yes. Recall that Green had engaged in a "stall in" to protest alleged discrimination by the company, and the company had asserted his participation in those activities as the explanation for why Green was not rehired. Although *McDonnell Douglas* did not directly rule on §704(a), which was not before the Court, it wrote, in language broad enough to embrace §704(a): "Nothing in Title VII compels an employer to absolve and rehire one who has engaged in such deliberate, unlawful activity against it." *McDonnell Douglas*, 411 U.S. at 803. How far does *McDonnell Douglas* go in allowing an employer to discriminate because of the nature or form of an employee's "opposition"? Is it merely a "law and order" decision in that it permits retaliation where the opposition violates criminal statutes, or can it be read more broadly?

Rather than establishing a "disloyalty" bright line, the lower courts seem to be balancing employer and employee interests. *See, e.g, Hatmaker v. Mem'l Med. Ctr.*, 619 F.3d 741 (7th Cir. 2010) (holding that participation in an internal investigation is opposition, not participation, but, in any event, such conduct "doesn't insulate an employee from being discharged for conduct that, if it occurred outside an investigation, would warrant termination"); *Argyropoulos v. City of Alton*, 539 F.3d 724 (7th Cir. 2008) (employee who secretly recorded meeting with supervisors not protected). If so, what goes on the scales? *See Cruz v. Coach Stores, Inc.*, 202 F.3d 560 (2d Cir. 2000) (slapping co-worker in response to sexual harassment not a protected activity, certainly when other options were available to plaintiff); *Douglas v. DynMcDermott Petro. Oper. Co.*, 144 F.3d 364 (5th Cir. 1998) (unethical disclosure by attorney justified discharge even if that conduct was in opposition to discrimination). What if the employee is a high-level affirmative action official? *Johnson v. Univ. of Cincinnati*, 215 F.3d 561 (6th Cir. 2000) (Title VII protects VP for Human Resources advocating on behalf of women and minorities). Is the validity of the allegation or the employer's reaction a factor? What about the extent of any resulting disruption? *See Robbins v. Jefferson Cty. Sch. Dist.*, 186 F.3d 1253 (10th Cir. 1999). Could even substantial disruption be outweighed by employer provocation? Should the court consider whether the plaintiff was more disruptive than necessary or whether the plaintiff had ulterior motivations?

7. *Distinguishing Opposition from Participation.* Because the opposition and participation clauses offer different degrees of protection, it is important to distinguish between the two. In *Crawford v. Metro Gov't of Nashville & Davidson Counties*, 555 U.S. 271 (2008), the Supreme Court held that an employee's involvement in an employer's internal investigation into possible harassment was protected under the opposition clause because opposition "goes beyond 'active, consistent,' behavior in ordinary discourse," as when people are said to "oppose" capital punishment even if they don't take public positions. Thus, "a person can 'oppose' by responding to someone else's question just as surely as by provoking the discussion, and nothing in the statute requires a freakish rule protecting an employee who reports discrimination on her own initiative but not one who reports the same discrimination in the same words when her boss asks a question." 555 U.S. at 277-78 (citation omitted); *see also Sayger v. Riceland Foods, Inc.*, 735 F.3d 1025, 1032 (8th Cir. 2013) (employees who respond to internal efforts to address discrimination also protected).

The *Crawford* Court did not reach the question of whether it was also protected under the participation clause. The result was to assure a minimum level of protection but leave open whether the employee reasonably believed that the conduct she reported was harassment. Suppose she didn't. For example, suppose she just answered her employer's question without even thinking about whether the conduct was illegal. If that's not opposition, might it still be "participation," or does the statute require at least a formal charge or suit by somebody? *See generally* Deborah L. Brake, *Retaliation in an EEO World*, 89 IND. L.J. 115 (2014) (by deciding *Crawford* under the opposition clause the Court left witnesses still subject to the requirement that their answers reflect a reasonable belief in illegality). Professor Brake's fears have been borne out. *See EEOC v. Rite Way Serv.*, 819 F.3d 235 (5th Cir. 2016) (even a plaintiff who is merely acting as a third-party witness to questions about possible discrimination must have a reasonable belief in the conduct's illegality to be protected from retaliation). If not, is *Crawford's* protection nearly as broad as it might first appear?

8. *Third-party Retaliation*: The Supreme Court held that Title VII bars third-party retaliation, that is, situations where the individual alleging retaliation did not personally engage in any protected activity but suffers an adverse employment action because of another person's protected conduct. In *Thompson v. North Am. Stainless, LP*, 562 U.S. 170 (2011), the plaintiff was terminated after his fiancée, a co-worker, filed a sex discrimination claim with the EEOC. It was undisputed that the fiancée's filing was protected participation, and the Court had little trouble holding that retaliation against a third party—the plaintiff—was unlawful retaliation since a reasonable worker—the fiancée—might well be deterred from engaging in such conduct if she had known the consequences. We'll discuss that standard in the next principal case.

The Court viewed the more difficult question as being whether the plaintiff—as opposed to his fiancée—had standing to sue for the retaliation, but it ultimately so held. The Court rejected as "absurd" a standard that would allow anyone to sue when injured by a violation: "For example, a shareholder would be able to sue a company for firing a valuable employee for racially discriminatory reasons, so long as he could show that the value of his stock decreased as a consequence." *Id.* at 176-77. It also rejected the defendant's argument that only the person participating in the protected conduct could file suit, choosing instead to look to the "zone of interests" test from administrative law and holding that Title VII "incorporates this test, enabling suit by any plaintiff with an interest 'arguably [sought] to be protected by the statutes.'" *Id.* at 177-78. Under this test, the plaintiff had standing to challenge his discharge: He was an employee and "not an accidental victim of the retaliation—collateral damage, so to speak, of the employer's unlawful act. To the contrary, injuring him was the employer's intended means of harming Regalado. Hurting him was the unlawful act by which the employer punished her." *Id.* at 178.

9. *Expanding Protection Against Retaliation. Crawford* and *North American Stainless* both expanded protection against retaliation. But they are not the only cases that have done so. In other recent decisions, the Court has held that the antidiscrimination provisions of 42 U.S.C. §1981, *CBOS West, Inc. v Humphries*, 553 U.S. 442 (2008), and the federal employee sections of Title VII, *Gomez-Perez v. Potter*, 553 U.S. 474 (2008), implicitly bar retaliation. However, the plaintiffs' winning streak came to an abrupt end in *University of Texas Southwestern Med. Center v. Nassar*, 570 U.S. 338 (2013), where, as we have seen at page 579, the Court required but-for causation to prove a retaliation claim rather than the motivating factor standard applicable to "status discrimination." In its opinion, the majority offered a policy justification that suggests a majority of the Justices may be having second thoughts about the retaliation provisions:

> In addition, lessening the causation standard could also contribute to the filing of frivolous claims, which would siphon resources from efforts by employer, administrative agencies, and courts to combat workplace harassment. Consider in this regard the case of an employee who knows that he or she is about to be fired for poor performance, given a lower pay grade, or even just transferred to a different assignment or location. To forestall that lawful action, he or she might be tempted to make an unfounded charge of racial, sexual, or religious discrimination; then, when the unrelated employment action comes, the employee could allege that it is retaliation. . . . Even if the employer could escape judgment after trial, the lessened causation standard would make it far more difficult to dismiss dubious claims at the summary judgment stage. It would be inconsistent with the structure and operation of Title VII to so raise the costs, both financial and reputational, on an employer whose actions were not in fact the result of any discriminatory or retaliatory intent. Yet there would be a significant risk of that consequence if respondent's position were adopted here.

Id. at 358-59. What do you think of that argument? Even before *Nassar*, some commentators have argued for greater reliance on state antiretaliation provisions to correct holes in federal protection. Alex B. Long, *Viva State Employment Law! State Law Retaliation Claims in a Post-*Crawford/Burlington Northern *World*, 77 TENN. L. REV. 253, 257 (2010); Sandra F. Sperino, *Revitalizing State Employment Discrimination Law*, 20 GEO. MASON L. REV. 545 (2013).

Nevertheless, plaintiffs can have success despite the heightened causation requirement. *See Baines v. Walgreen Co.*, 863 F.3d 656, 663-64 (7th Cir. 2017) (sufficient evidence of retaliatory intent in refusing to rehire an employee given evidence of unusual intervention from a district manager, a showing that plaintiff's application and interview scores were mysteriously missing, and the fact that the employer hired someone with less experience); *Donathan v. Oakley Grain, Inc.*, 861 F.3d 735 (8th Cir. 2017) (plaintiff had a triable issue of retaliation when she was terminated within eight days of complaining of sex discrimination despite a strong work history when the position had not been previously subject to seasonal layoffs and a less qualified replacement was soon hired).

Burlington Northern & Santa Fe Ry. Co. v. White
548 U.S. 53 (2006)

BREYER, J.

Title VII of the Civil Rights Act of 1964 forbids employment discrimination against "any individual" based on that individual's "race, color, religion, sex, or national origin." A separate section of the Act—its anti-retaliation provision—forbids an employer from "discriminating against" an employee or job applicant because that individual "opposed any practice" made unlawful by Title VII or "made a charge, testified, assisted, or participated in" a Title VII proceeding or investigation. . . .

We conclude that the anti-retaliation provision does not confine the actions and harms it forbids to those that are related to employment or occur at the workplace. We also conclude that the provision covers those (and only those) employer actions that would have been materially adverse to a reasonable employee or job applicant. In the present context that means that the employer's actions must be harmful to the point that they could well dissuade a reasonable worker from making or supporting a charge of discrimination.

[Shortly after Sheila White, the only woman working in her department at the Railroad's Tennessee yard, complained of harassment by her supervisor, she was reassigned from her position operating a forklift to a track laborer job, a more physically demanding and dirtier job. The pay and benefits, however, were the same. After White filed a charge of discrimination with the EEOC, she was suspended without pay for 37 days, a suspension that would have become a termination had she not filed a grievance. The company contended White had been suspended because she was insubordinate. White did grieve her suspension, and the hearing officer found she had not been insubordinate and ordered her reinstated with backpay. White filed suit, alleging that the change in her job responsibilities and her suspension constituted actionable retaliation under Title VII. A jury agreed with White. The Sixth Circuit, en banc, affirmed the judgment in White's favor.]

II

Title VII's anti-retaliation provision forbids employer actions that "discriminate against" an employee (or job applicant) because he has "opposed" a practice that Title VII forbids or has "made a charge, testified, assisted, or participated in" a Title VII "investigation, proceeding, or hearing.". . . .

A

[The Court rejected the argument that Title VII's antiretaliation provision should be read *in pari materia* with the anti-discrimination provision to require a link between the challenged retaliatory action and the terms, conditions, or status of employment.] We cannot agree. The language of the substantive provision differs from that of the anti-retaliation provision in important ways. [Section 703(a) speaks in terms of discrimination in various aspects of employment or employment opportunities. In contrast, § 704(a) declares it unlawful to discriminate against an employee or applicant for engaging in protected conduct.]

[The words in § 703(a)] —"hire," "discharge," "compensation, terms, conditions, or privileges of employment," "employment opportunities," and "status as an employee"—explicitly limit the scope of that provision to actions that affect employment or alter the conditions of the workplace. No such limiting words appear in the anti-retaliation provision. Given these linguistic differences, the question here is not whether identical or similar words should be read *in pari materia* to mean the same thing. Rather, the question is whether Congress intended its different words to make a legal difference. We normally presume that, where words differ as they differ here, " 'Congress acts intentionally and purposely in the disparate inclusion or exclusion.' " *Russello v. United States*, 464 U.S. 16, 23 (1983).

There is strong reason to believe that Congress intended the differences that its language suggests, for the two provisions differ not only in language but in purpose as well. The anti-discrimination provision seeks a workplace where individuals are not discriminated against because of their racial, ethnic, religious, or gender-based status. *See McDonnell Douglas Corp. v. Green*, [reproduced at page 547]. The anti-retaliation provision seeks to secure that primary objective by preventing an employer from interfering (through retaliation) with an employee's efforts to secure or advance enforcement of the Act's basic guarantees. The substantive provision seeks to prevent injury to individuals based on who they are, *i.e.*, their status. The anti-retaliation provision seeks to prevent harm to individuals based on what they do, *i.e.*, their conduct.

To secure the first objective, Congress did not need to prohibit anything other than employment-related discrimination. The substantive provision's basic objective of "equality of employment opportunities" and the elimination of practices that tend to bring about "stratified job environments," would be achieved were all employment-related discrimination miraculously eliminated.

But one cannot secure the second objective by focusing only upon employer actions and harm that concern employment and the workplace. Were all such actions and harms eliminated, the anti-retaliation provision's objective would *not* be achieved. An employer can effectively retaliate against an employee by taking actions not directly related to his employment or by causing him harm *outside* the workplace. *See, e.g., Rochon v. Gonzales*, 438 F.3d [1211, 1213 (CADC 2006)] (FBI retaliation against employee "took the form of the FBI's refusal, contrary to policy, to investigate death threats a federal prisoner made against [the agent] and his wife"); *Berry v. Stevinson Chevrolet*, 74 F.3d 980, 984, 986 (CA10 1996) (finding actionable retaliation where employer filed false criminal charges against former employee who complained about discrimination). A provision limited to employment-related actions would not deter the many forms that effective retaliation can take. Hence, such a limited construction would fail to fully achieve the anti-retaliation provision's "primary purpose," namely, "maintaining unfettered access to statutory remedial mechanisms." *Robinson v. Shell Oil Co.*, 519 U.S. 337 (1997).

Thus, purpose reinforces what language already indicates, namely, that the anti-retaliation provision, unlike the substantive provision, is not limited to discriminatory actions that affect the terms and conditions of employment. . . .

For these reasons, we conclude that Title VII's substantive provision and its anti-retaliation provision are not coterminous. The scope of the anti-retaliation provision extends beyond workplace-related or employment-related retaliatory acts and harm. We therefore reject the standards applied in the Courts of Appeals that have treated the anti-retaliation provision as forbidding the same conduct prohibited by the anti-discrimination provision and that have limited actionable retaliation to so-called "ultimate employment decisions."

B

The anti-retaliation provision protects an individual not from all retaliation, but from retaliation that produces an injury or harm. As we have explained, the Courts of Appeals have used differing language to describe the level of seriousness to which this harm must rise before it becomes actionable retaliation. We agree with the formulation set forth by the Seventh and the District of Columbia Circuits. In our view, a plaintiff must show that a reasonable employee would have found the challenged action materially adverse, "which in this context means it well might have 'dissuaded a reasonable worker from making or supporting a charge of discrimination.'" *Rochon.* We speak of *material* adversity because we believe it is important to separate significant from trivial harms. Title VII, we have said, does not set forth "a general civility code for the American workplace." *Oncale v. Sundowner Offshore Services, Inc.,* [reproduced at page 648]; *see Faragher* (judicial standards for sexual harassment must "filter out complaints attacking 'the ordinary tribulations of the workplace, such as the sporadic use of abusive language, gender-related jokes, and occasional teasing'"). An employee's decision to report discriminatory behavior cannot immunize that employee from those petty slights or minor annoyances that often take place at work and that all employees experience. *See* 1 B. LINDEMANN & P. GROSSMAN, EMPLOYMENT DISCRIMINATION LAW 669 (3d ed. 1996) (noting that "courts have held that personality conflicts at work that generate antipathy" and "'snubbing' by supervisors and co-workers" are not actionable under §704(a)). The anti-retaliation provision seeks to prevent employer interference with "unfettered access" to Title VII's remedial mechanisms. *Robinson.* It does so by prohibiting employer actions that are likely "to deter victims of discrimination from complaining to the EEOC," the courts, and their employers. *Ibid.* And normally petty slights, minor annoyances, and simple lack of good manners will not create such deterrence. *See* 2 EEOC 1998 MANUAL §8, p. 8-13.

We refer to reactions of a *reasonable* employee because we believe that the provision's standard for judging harm must be objective. An objective standard is judicially administrable. It avoids the uncertainties and unfair discrepancies that can plague a judicial effort to determine a plaintiff's unusual subjective feelings. We have emphasized the need for objective standards in other Title VII contexts, and those same concerns animate our decision here. *See, e.g., Pennsylvania State Police v. Suders,* 542 U.S. 129 (2004) (constructive discharge doctrine); *Harris v. Forklift Systems, Inc.* (hostile work environment doctrine).

We phrase the standard in general terms because the significance of any given act of retaliation will often depend upon the particular circumstances. Context matters. "The real social impact of workplace behavior often depends on a constellation of surrounding circumstances, expectations, and relationships which are not fully captured by a simple recitation of the words used or the physical acts performed." A schedule change in an employee's work schedule may make little difference to many workers, but may matter enormously to a young mother with school age children. *Cf., e.g., Washington* [*v. Ill. Dep't of Revenue,* 420 F.3d 658 (CA7 2005)] (finding flex-time schedule critical to employee with disabled child). A supervisor's refusal to invite an employee to lunch is normally trivial, a nonactionable petty slight. But to retaliate by excluding an employee from a weekly training lunch that contributes significantly to the employee's professional advancement might well deter a reasonable employee from complaining about discrimination. *See* 2 EEOC 1998 MANUAL §8, p. 8-14.

Hence, a legal standard that speaks in general terms rather than specific prohibited acts is preferable, for an "act that would be immaterial in some situations is material in others." *Washington.*

Finally, we note that contrary to the claim of the concurrence, this standard does *not* require a reviewing court or jury to consider "the nature of the discrimination that led to the filing of the charge." Rather, the standard is tied to the challenged retaliatory act, not the underlying conduct that forms the basis of the Title VII complaint. By focusing on the materiality of the challenged action and the perspective of a reasonable person in the plaintiff's position, we believe this standard will screen out trivial conduct while effectively capturing those acts that are likely to dissuade employees from complaining or assisting in complaints about discrimination.

III

Applying this standard to the facts of this case, we believe that there was a sufficient evidentiary basis to support the jury's verdict on White's retaliation claim. [The trial court's instructions required the . . . jury to determine whether respondent "suffered a materially adverse change in the terms or conditions of her employment." While today's decision makes clear that the jury was not required to find a relation to the terms and conditions of employment], insofar as the jury also found that the actions were "materially adverse," its findings are adequately supported.

First, Burlington argues that a reassignment of duties cannot constitute retaliatory discrimination where, as here, both the former and present duties fall within the same job description. We do not see why that is so. Almost every job category involves some responsibilities and duties that are less desirable than others. Common sense suggests that one good way to discourage an employee such as White from bringing discrimination charges would be to insist that she spend more time performing the more arduous duties and less time performing those that are easier or more agreeable. That is presumably why the EEOC has consistently found "retaliatory work assignments" to be a classic and "widely recognized" example of "forbidden retaliation." 2 EEOC 1991 MANUAL §614.7, pp. 614-31 to 614-32. . . .

To be sure, reassignment of job duties is not automatically actionable. Whether a particular reassignment is materially adverse depends upon the circumstances of the particular case, and "should be judged from the perspective of a reasonable person in the plaintiff's position, considering 'all the circumstances.' " *Oncale.* But here, the jury had before it considerable evidence that the track labor duties were "by all accounts more arduous and dirtier"; that the "forklift operator position required more qualifications, which is an indication of prestige"; and that "the forklift operator position was objectively considered a better job and the male employees resented White for occupying it." Based on this record, a jury could reasonably conclude that the reassignment of responsibilities would have been materially adverse to a reasonable employee.

Second, Burlington argues that the 37-day suspension without pay lacked statutory significance because Burlington ultimately reinstated White with backpay. . . . White did receive backpay. But White and her family had to live for 37 days without income. They did not know during that time whether or when White could return to work. Many reasonable employees would find a month without a paycheck to be a serious hardship. And White described to the jury the physical and emotional hardship that 37 days of having "no income, no money" in fact caused. ("That was the worst Christmas I had out of my life. No income, no money, and that made all of us feel bad. . . . I got very depressed.") Indeed, she obtained medical treatment for her emotional distress. A reasonable employee facing the choice between retaining her job (and paycheck) and filing a discrimination complaint might well choose the former. That is to say, an indefinite suspension without pay could well act as a deterrent, even if the suspended employee eventually received backpay. . . . Thus, the jury's conclusion that the 37-day suspension without pay was materially adverse was a reasonable one. . . .

[Justice Alito's concurring opinion omitted.]

NOTES

1. *Retaliation Outside the Workplace.* Prior to *Burlington*, the Court had held that former employees were protected from retaliation in terms of unfavorable references. *Robinson v. Shell Oil Co.*, 519 U.S. 337 (1997). In some sense, of course, that case involved retaliation outside the workplace. *Burlington* confirms that, holding that, while §703 reaches only actions that affect employment, §704 is *not* limited to discriminatory acts that affect the terms and conditions of employment.

Occasionally a question has arisen as to whether an employer violates the retaliation provisions of the antidiscrimination statutes by bringing suit against the employee in retaliation for protected conduct. For example, would it be permissible for an employer to bring defamation charges against an employee who has alleged discrimination? The Supreme Court addressed a similar issue under the National Labor Relations Act. *BE&K Construction Co. v. NLRB*, 536 U.S. 516 (2002), held, in light of First Amendment concerns, that the NLRA did not prohibit reasonably based but unsuccessful lawsuits filed with a retaliatory purpose. A baseless suit would lack this justification and, after *Burlington*, would seem actionable.

2. *Adverse Employment Actions Under §703?* Given that the actions White complained of clearly affected her employment, why do you think the Court felt it necessary to decide whether §704 applied to actions that did not affect the terms and conditions of employment? Perhaps the Court reached out to resolve this question because it did not believe the actions, even though arising from the workplace, would have stated a claim under §703? Obviously, this would have important implications for the concept of "adverse employment action" we discussed at page 553. In his concurring opinion in *Burlington*, Justice Alito disagreed with the majority's analysis, believing that the scope of §§703 and 704 are the same and both reach only materially adverse employment actions. But he found the actions White challenged to be materially adverse within the meaning of either section. As applied to §703, this would be a more pro-plaintiff position in discrimination cases than many predicted of Justice Alito. *See generally* Lisa Durham Taylor, *Parsing Supreme Court Dicta and the Example of Non-Workplace Harms*, 57 Drake L. Rev. 75 (2008); Lisa Durham Taylor, *Adding Subjective Fuel to the Vague-Standard Fire: A Proposal for Congressional Intervention After* Burlington Northern & Santa Fe Railway Co. v. White, 9 U. Pa. J. Lab. & Emp. L. 533 (2007); Ernest F. Lidge III, *What Types of Employer Actions Are Cognizable Under Title VII?: The Ramifications of* Burlington Northern & Santa Fe Railroad Co. v. White, 59 Rutgers L. Rev. 497, 535 (2007).

3. *Third-Party Retaliation and Material Adversity.* The *North American Stainless* Court thought it "obvious that a reasonable worker might be dissuaded from engaging in protected activity if she knew that her fiancé would be fired." 562 U.S. 170, but recognized that line-drawing problems would arise in deciding when the *Burlington Northern* standard would be satisfied when the retaliatory action was aimed at a third party: "We must also decline to identify a fixed class of relationships for which third-party reprisals are unlawful. We expect that firing a close family member will almost always meet the *Burlington* standard, and inflicting a milder reprisal on a mere acquaintance will almost never do so, but beyond that we are reluctant to generalize." *Id.* at 175. The Court did, however, stress that the inquiry was to be "objective." *Id.* But, after *Burlington*, isn't the question whether the retaliatory action is viewed as likely to deter a reasonable employee from engaging in protected conduct? That would suggest that subjectivity enters the picture where the *employer's* motives are concerned. Isn't the correct test whether the actual employer (not a reasonable one) believed that acting against X would deter/punish protected conduct by Y, or at least by a reasonable employee in Y's position? For an excellent pre-*Thompson* discussion of the entire question of third-party retaliation, *see* Alex. B. Long, *The Troublemaker's Friend: Retaliation Against Third Parties and the Right of Association in the Workplace*, 59 FLA. L. REV. 931 (2007).

The *North American Stainless* Court's stress about context is playing out in the lower courts, which reflect a wide range of results as to when the *Burlington Northern* standard is satisfied. *E.g., Rodríguez-Vives v. P.R. Firefighters Corps of P.R.*, 743 F.3d 278 (1st Cir. 2014) (the cumulative effect of a series of petty acts of retaliation, such as refusal to allow plaintiff to join other firefighters to travel on fire vehicles to lunch and being assigned to cook and clean, might dissuade a reasonable employee from opposing discrimination); *Colon v. Tracey*, 717 F.3d 43 (1st Cir. 2013) (summary judgment affirmed for employer when plaintiff claimed that she was demoted by being reassigned from human resources "generalist" to human resources "business partner," with no effect on her salary or job title, and the change was only temporary).

4. *Threats Just Fine?* The Seventh and First Circuits seem to take the position that an unfulfilled threat by itself cannot violate the antiretaliation provisions of the federal statutes or, at least, cannot support a claim for constructive discharge. *Chapin v. Fort-Rohr Motors, Inc.*, 621 F.3d 673 (7th Cir. 2010) (no constructive discharge in retaliation setting when employee quit work in response to threat to discharge him if he did not withdraw EEOC charge); *Goodman v. NSA, Inc.*, 621 F.3d 651, 656 (7th Cir. 2010) (unfulfilled threats to transfer plaintiff to positions she could not work were not actionable); *see also Ahern v. Shinseki*, 629 F.3d 49, 56 (1st Cir. 2010) (proposing a change in schedule does not itself, constitute a materially adverse action until brought to fruition). Can't threats satisfy the *Burlington* standard? How about a threat of physical violence? *See Brandon v. Sage Corp.*, 808 F.3d 266, 271 (5th Cir. 2015) (while "a realistic, drastic pay cut threat" might deter opposition, a mere threat of such action by someone outside plaintiff's chain of command made to "a reasonable high-placed person" familiar with the organization would not have deterred that person from protected activity). More generally, Professor Sandra F. Sperino, in *Retaliation and the Reasonable Person*, 67 FLA. L. REV. 2031 (2016), challenges lower courts' application of the *Burlington Northern* standard both on theoretical grounds and in view of an empirical study revealing that subjects viewed various employer responses as more likely to discourage reporting than do many court decisions.

F. DISABILITY DISCRIMINATION

Protecting individuals with disabilities from discrimination in employment poses difficult problems. Legally, disability discrimination poses the threshold question of who is protected, that is, who is a "disabled" individual. Further, disabilities are sometimes relevant to an individual's ability to work. While many disabilities don't affect the performance of many jobs at all, some disabilities deprive people of the physical and/or mental prerequisites to perform essential job functions of particular positions. Prohibiting "discrimination" against such individuals would unduly interfere with employers' ability to select a qualified workforce. Other disabled individuals may be qualified to work but only if the employer accommodates their disability in some way. Such individuals, unlike most other statutorily protected groups, require some form of different treatment to enjoy equal access to employment opportunities. Merely guaranteeing equal treatment for similarly situated individuals in those situations does not adequately respond to the problem of promoting employment of the disabled.

The ADA seeks to deal with these problems in two separate ways. First, while generally barring disability discrimination, the statute broadens the defenses available to employers as compared with other antidiscrimination statutes. Employers are permitted to engage in disparate treatment on the basis of disability if the disabled employee is unable to perform the essential functions of the job. In addition, employers are free to use qualification standards that screen out disabled individuals if those qualifications are job-related and consistent with business necessity.

Counterbalancing this, disabled individuals have rights beyond those guaranteed to other groups protected by antidiscrimination legislation. The centerpiece of disability discrimination law is the employer's affirmative duty to provide reasonable accommodation to ensure that individuals with disabilities secure equal employment opportunities and benefits. The focus of the duty to accommodate is on equal employment opportunity, not merely equal treatment.

As a result, employers are legally obligated to treat covered employees equally or differently depending on the circumstances—employers must treat individuals with disabilities equally to nondisabled persons if they are qualified and their disabilities do not require accommodation; employers are permitted to treat such individuals differently, that is, to discriminate against them, if their disabilities cannot be accommodated; and employers are required to treat such individuals differently, and better than other workers, if reasonable accommodations are necessary to ensure equal employment opportunity and benefits. Further, since accommodation providing equal opportunity for individuals with disabilities can be costly for employers, the ADA includes an "undue hardship" defense, which makes cost, usually irrelevant under the disparate treatment provisions of other antidiscrimination statutes, an express statutory defense to discrimination based on the duty to accommodate.

The focus of this section will be Title I of the ADA, which deals with employment, although other parts of the statute deal with important issues beyond employment. The ADA and associated regulations borrow extensively from the Rehabilitation Act of 1973, 29 U.S.C. §§701-95 (2014), which was a narrower federal statute covering only federal contractors and federal employers. The Rehabilitation Act continues to operate in its original sphere, and its precedents influence ADA decisions, and the ADA regulations and Interpretive Guidance of the (EEOC) borrow from regulations under the earlier act.

The ADA was passed in 1990, but the first decade and a half of its life proved profoundly disappointing to disability advocates. The amorphous definition of disability permitted the courts to narrowly circumscribe the statute's reach. While we will examine the details of this development, the net result was that most cases under Title I of the ADA were dismissed because the plaintiffs were either not disabled within the meaning of the statute (as construed by the courts) or too disabled to perform the essential functions of the jobs they sought. The result of increasing dissatisfaction with a number of Supreme Court decisions was the Americans with Disabilities Act Amendment Act of 2008, Pub. L. 110-325, signed into law in on September 2008 and effective January 1, 2009. *See generally* Michelle A. Travis, *Impairment as Protected Status: A New Universality for Disability Rights,* 46 GA. L. REV. 937 (2012); Stacy A. Hickox, *The Underwhelming Impact of the Americans with Disabilities Act Amendments Act,* 40 U. BALT. L. REV. 419, 422-23 (2011); Alex B. Long, *Introducing the New and Improved Americans with Disabilities Act: Assessing the ADA Amendments Act of 2008,* 103 NW. U. L. REV. COLLOQUY 217 (2008); *see also* Jeffrey Douglas Jones, *Enfeebling the ADA: The ADA Amendments Act of 2008,* 62 OKLA. L. REV. 667, 669 (2010).

1. The Meaning of "Disability"

In contrast to other statutes prohibiting discrimination in employment, establishing membership in the ADA's protected classification often requires extensive legal and factual analysis. Generally speaking, to claim protection under the ADA, a plaintiff must be "a qualified individual with a disability"; that is, the plaintiff must be an individual with a disability who can perform essential job functions with or without reasonable accommodation. 42 U.S.C. § 12102(1) provides three definitions of "disability":

A. a physical or mental impairment that substantially limits one or more of the major life activities of . . . [an] individual;
B. a record of such an impairment; or
C. being regarded as having such an impairment.

This definition requires three inquiries. First, whether the individual has an impairment. The first part of the definition deals with an individual who has an actual impairment. It contains three elements, each of which is further defined in the EEOC's ADA regulations. Section 1630.2(h) of the regulations defines physical or mental *impairment* as:

1. Any physiological disorder or condition, cosmetic disfigurement, or anatomical loss affecting one or more of the following body systems: neurological, musculoskeletal, special sense organs, respiratory (including speech organs), cardiovascular, reproductive, digestive, genitor-urinary, hemic and lymphatic, skin, and endocrine; or
2. Any mental or psychological disorder, such as mental retardation, organic brain syndrome, emotional or mental illness, and specific learning disabilities.

The second inquiry is whether a "major life activity" is limited by the impairment. Originally, the definition of such activities was left to the EEOC's regulations, but the ADAAA added a statutory definition that both incorporated the EEOC's approach and broadened it. For purposes of determining whether an individual has an actual disability,

> (A) major life activities include, but are not limited to, caring for oneself, performing manual tasks, seeing, hearing, eating, sleeping, walking, standing, lifting, bending, speaking, breathing, learning, reading, concentrating, thinking, communicating, and working.
>
> (B) . . . a major life activity also includes the operation of a major bodily function, including but not limited to, functions of the immune system, normal cell growth, digestive, bowel, bladder, neurological, brain, respiratory, circulatory, endocrine, and reproductive functions.

42 U.S.C. §12102(2).

The third inquiry is whether the limitation is "substantial." As you might guess, this was a major point of debate both under the original ADA and in framing the Americans with Disabilities Act Amendments Act ("ADAAA"), and, as we will see, Congress's solution was less than elegant.

ADA coverage, however, does not depend on establishing an actual, present disability. As noted, §12102(B) also reaches individuals with a "record" of an impairment, and paragraph (C) protects those that the employer "regards" as having an impairment. Once you have a better sense of what constitutes an actual disability, we will explore the "record" and "regarded as" prongs of the statutory prohibition.

a. Actual Disability

The Supreme Court first considered the meaning of disability in *School Board of Nassau County v. Arline*, 480 U.S. 273 (1987). *Arline* was a Rehabilitation Act case construing the definition of what was then called a "handicapped individual," which is identical to the ADA's definition of individual with a disability. The school board fired Arline, an elementary school teacher, because it believed her active tuberculosis posed a threat to the health of others. When she sued, the board contended that a person with a contagious disease was not protected by the Rehabilitation Act if the adverse employment action was based on the employee's contagiousness and not on the condition itself. The Supreme Court disagreed. In finding Arline to be a handicapped individual, the Court refused to allow the school to disassociate the contagious effects of the teacher's impairment from the impairment itself. As the Court stated, "Arline's contagiousness and her physical impairment each resulted from the same underlying condition, tuberculosis. It would be unfair to allow an employer to seize upon the distinction between the effects of a disease on others and the effects of a disease on a patient and use that distinction to justify discriminatory intent." *Id.* at 282.

In light of *Arline*'s holding, is a person who tests positively for HIV, the virus that causes AIDS, an "individual with a disability"? Given that a contagious disease can be a "disability," a person who has developed AIDS is undoubtedly an "individual with a disability" under both the Rehabilitation Act and the ADA. That is, active AIDS clearly qualifies as a physical impairment and also substantially limits major life activities. But *Arline* left open the question whether an asymptomatic person can be considered "handicapped" solely on the basis of contagiousness.

In *Bragdon v. Abbott*, 524 U.S. 624 (1998), the plaintiff, infected with HIV, sued her dentist when he required her cavity to be filled in a hospital instead of in his office. She sued under Title II of the statute, which prohibits discrimination in public accommodations; however, the definition of discrimination under Title II is the same as that under Title I, thus rendering *Bragdon* relevant to employment. Applying the three-step analysis we have sketched, the Court first asked whether the condition at issue was a "physical impairment." *id.* at 632, and, given its effects on the immune system, found that HIV is a "physical impairment" from the moment of infection, regardless of the presence of symptoms. *Id.* Second, the Court asked whether the impairment affected a major life activity. *Id.* at 637. The plaintiff in this case relied successfully on the major life activities of reproduction and child bearing, but the Court noted that HIV affects many other major life activities. *Id.* at 638-39. Third, the Court examined whether the impairment's effect on reproduction was "substantial," *id.* at 639, concluding that HIV substantially limits the plaintiff's ability to bear children because of the risk of transmitting the disease. *Id.* The Court elaborated that, "the Act addresses substantial limitations on major life activities, not utter inabilities." *Id.* at 641. Accordingly, *Bragdon* upheld the plaintiff's claim under the ADA since HIV infection is a physical impairment that substantially limits the major life activity of reproduction. *Id.*

In a passage that has influenced numerous later cases, the Court stressed that "whether respondent has a disability covered by the ADA is an individualized inquiry." *Id.* at 657. Thus, what is a disability for one person may not be disabling for another. That meant the Court did not rule on whether HIV infection is a per se disability under the ADA, irrespective of its limiting effects on the activities of the particular plaintiff. *Id.* at 642.

Bragdon was not only the first case decided by the Court but it was also the high point of jurisprudence under the original ADA in terms of broadly reading the statute's coverage. Every other Court decision under Title I restricted the reach of the statute. One of the most significant retrenchments was *Toyota Motor Mfg., Kentucky, Inc. v. Williams*, 534 U.S. 184 (2002). Plaintiff there was employed on a Toyota assembly line, where she worked with pneumatic tools. Ms. Williams developed carpal tunnel syndrome and related impairments that restricted her ability to perform manual tasks at her job. Toyota initially modified her job duties to accommodate her condition but ultimately refused to provide her the accommodation she sought; it then discharged her after her condition had worsened to the extent that she could not work at all.

The central issue before the Court was what major life activities counted. Williams claimed that the activity at stake was performing manual tasks, and the Court held that "to be substantially limited in performing manual tasks, an individual must have an impairment that prevents or severely restricts the individual from doing activities that are of central importance to most people's daily lives." 534 U.S. at 187. Thus, the opinion simultaneously broadened what counted as a major life activity and broadened what was necessary to be substantially limited. Do you see how that double play dramatically narrowed the ADA's reach? The narrower an activity may be defined and still count as major, the more likely it is that a plaintiff can prove she is substantially limited. For example, suppose a person is unable to walk long distances. If "walking" is a major life activity, the individual would be limited but perhaps not substantially limited; on the other hand, walking long distances is less likely to be viewed as a major life activity, but the person is more likely to be considered substantially limited.

In justifying its decision, the Court wrote that "substantially limited and major life activities" both "need to be interpreted strictly to create a demanding standard for qualifying as disabled" to implement Congress's goals in passing the ADA. 534 U.S. at 197. Congress didn't agree, and it expressed that disagreement in a variety of ways in the ADAAA. Thus, it commanded that "[t]he definition of disability in this Act shall be construed in favor of broad coverage of individuals under this Act, to the maximum extent permitted by the terms of this Act," §12102(4)(A), in the process explicitly rejecting the *Williams* strict interpretation language. More specifically, as we have seen, the new statute defined major life activities very broadly.

As for "substantially limited," the ADAAA was more circuitous although very clear in its thrust. Thus, the amendments do not directly define the term. However, the ADAAA states that *Toyota* "has created an inappropriately high level of limitation necessary to necessary to obtain coverage under the ADA." Congress then went on to disapprove the then-effective EEOC regulations by expressing its "expectation" that the EEOC would revise its regulations. The ADAAA simultaneously answered a question the Supreme Court had raised by explicitly providing authority to the EEOC to issue regulations defining disability, and the agency has in fact issued regulations, 29 C.F.R. Pt. 1630 (2018).*

Finally, Congress commanded that "[t]he term 'substantially limits' shall be interpreted consistently with the findings and purposes" of the ADAAA. §12102(4)(B).

Note on Impairments

The threshold requirement for a disability is an impairment, and with the ADAAA's broadening of "major life activities" and its watering down of "substantially limited," that threshold question is more often resolved in favor of the plaintiffs. *See generally* Stephen F. Befort, *An Empirical Analysis of Case Outcomes Under the ADA Amendments Act*, 70 Wash & Lee L. Rev. 2027 (2013); Nicole B. Porter, *The New ADA Backlash*, 82 Tenn. L. Rev. 1 (2014). Foreseeing some problems, the ADAAA explicitly provided that "[a]n impairment that is episodic or in remission is a disability if it would substantially limit a major life activity when active." §12102(4)(D). Does that mean, for instance, that multiple sclerosis is an impairment, even though, in its early stages, it can be relatively asymptomatic? The EEOC's proposed regulations list multiple sclerosis as an example of "Impairments that Will Consistently Meet the Definition of Disability." §1630.2(j).

---

* The extent to which courts should defer to EEOC regulations was more than a little confused before the ADAAA, and some uncertainty remains. Title I of the originally ADA conferred substantive rule-making authority on the EEOC, 42 U.S.C.A. §12116, which would seem to require the courts to accord substantial deference under *Chevron U.S.A., Inc. v. Nat. Resources Defense Council, Inc.*, 467 U.S. 837 (1984), and its progeny. However, two problems arose. First, the EEOC carried out that mandate by issuing both regulations and an "Interpretive Guidance," and there has been question as to whether the Guidance is due the same deference as the regulations. Rebecca Hanner White, *Deference and Disability Discrimination*, 9 Mich. L. Rev. 532 (2000).

Secondly, *Sutton v. United Air Lines, Inc.*, refused to defer to the EEOC because the agency at that time had authority to interpret only Title I, and the interpretation at issue involved the prefatory umbrella provisions of the statute. This question has been resolved by the ADAAA, which expressly gives the EEOC (and other agencies charged with administering other Titles of the ADA) the authority to issue regulations relating to the definition of disability. 42 U.S.C.A. §12205a. And deference to EEOC regulations now seems mandated by *Chevron U.S.A., Inc. v. Echazabal*, 536 U.S. 73 (2002) (deferring to EEOC interpretation of the "direct threat" defense even though it was broader than the statutory language).

Despite this broad approach, the Act and its regulations specifically exclude certain conditions from the definition of impairment. ADA Sections 508 and 511 expressly exclude certain sex-related practices or conditions, such as homosexuality, bisexuality, transvestism, pedophilia, transexualism, and exhibitionism. Also excluded are compulsive gambling, kleptomania, pyromania, and disorders resulting from the current illegal use of psychoactive drugs. Further, the EEOC's Interpretive Guidance, 29 C.F.R. Part 1630 Appendix, provides that the term "physical or mental impairment" does not include physical characteristics, such as weight, height, and eye color, that are in the "normal range" and are not the result of a physiological disorder. §1630.2(h); *see Fischer v. Minneapolis Pub. Sch.*, 792 F.3d 985, 989 (8th Cir. 2015) (an employer's belief that plaintiff could not perform "the physical labor of a medium strength worker" was not the same as that he suffered a physical impairment). The Interpretive Guidance also excludes common personality traits, illiteracy, economic disadvantages, and advanced age, although physical and mental impairments associated with aging may be covered. *See* 29 C.F.R. pt. 1630, app. §1630.2(h), (j).

Although pregnancy shares many of the characteristics of a disability as defined by the ADA, the EEOC Interpretive Guidance states that pregnancy per se is not a disability covered by the statute because pregnancy is not an impairment. *See* 29 C.F.R. pt. 1630, app. §1630.2(h); *see generally* Melissa Cole, *Beyond Sex Discrimination: Why Employers Discriminate Against Women with Disabilities When Their Employee Health Plans Exclude Contraceptives from Prescription Coverage*, 43 Ariz. L. Rev. 501, 521 (2001) (while most women's pregnancies do not constitute disabilities, some face grave health risks and "the very potential of pregnancy constitutes a disability, a substantial limitation on the major life activity of reproduction"). However, as suggested in the next paragraph, the regulations do view temporary impairments as potentially being actual disabilities, and pregnancy often entails impairments such as lifting limitations. *See also Young v. UPS, Inc.*, 135 U.S. 1338 (2015), reproduced at page 753 (referring to the EEOC's ADA regulations as also potentially imposing a duty to accommodate pregnancy).

Interestingly, the proposed regulations are similar to the earlier regulations in suggesting that temporary conditions can be impairments, although it views them as unlikely to be disabilities: "Temporary, non-chronic impairments of short duration with little or no residual effects (such as the common cold, seasonal or common influenza, a sprained joint, minor and non-chronic gastrointestinal disorders, or a broken bone that is expected to heal completely) usually will not substantially limit a major life activity." §1630.2(j). Is any physical characteristic outside what is considered the normal range an "impairment"? Consider unusual strength or high intelligence. Are these impairments (because they are out of the normal range), but not disabilities (because they do not substantially impair life activities)? Or are they not impairments at all because they are out of the normal range on the "positive," rather than the "negative," side? Is being left-handed an impairment?

What about individuals with genetic propensities but no actual disease at the moment? It seems unlikely that such individuals are currently actually disabled within the ADA, in part because such an individual will not ordinarily be substantially limited in a major life activity—although like *Bragdon*, some such conditions may limit reproduction for fear of passing on the condition to offspring. But most genetic propensities will likely not be viewed as impairments because they are not certain to eventuate. A few diseases, like Huntington's, are inevitable for those with the allele, although they may not manifest the symptoms until late in life. Most "genetic diseases," however, simply make individuals more susceptible to the condition (although sometimes increasing the risk factor enormously). Is someone with the Huntington's allele but no symptoms impaired? If so, does this impairment substantially limit any major life activity? Even if the answer is yes, what about those genetic diseases whose appearance is not inevitable? *See generally* John V. Jacobi, *Genetic Discrimination in a Time of False Hopes*, 30 FLA. ST. U.L. REV. 363 (2003).

The Genetic Information Non-Discrimination Act of 2008 ("GINA"), 22 Stat. 881, codified at 42 U.S.C.A. §2000ff (2018), provides a separate source of protection against certain kinds of genetic discrimination. GINA prohibits discrimination by employers and health insurers based on genetic information. The EEOC is charged with enforcement of the employment provisions of the act and has promulgated final regulations to carry out Title II, the employment chapter. 29 C.F.R. Pt. 1635 (2018). In a nutshell, Title II of GINA prohibits the use of genetic information in employment, prohibits the intentional acquisition of genetic information about applicants and employees, and imposes strict confidentiality requirements. It applies to employers, public and private, with 15 or more employees. The EEOC's regulations regard the protections of GINA as absolute when it comes to an employer's *use* of genetic information; any use is strictly prohibited. Moreover, acquisition of genetic information by employers is restricted. *See generally* Jessica Roberts, *Preempting Discrimination: Lessons from the Genetic Information Nondiscrimination Act*, 63 VAND. L. REV. 439 (2010).

A final question about impairments relates to physical conditions caused at least in part by voluntary conduct. The First Circuit considered whether such conditions constitute impairments in *Cook v. Rhode Island Dept. of Mental Health*, 10 F.3d 17 (1st Cir. 1993). Bonnie Cook was morbidly obese, meaning that she weighed more than 100 pounds over her optimal weight. In response to her claim of discrimination under the Rehabilitation Act, the defendant argued that " 'mutable' conditions are not the sort of impairments" covered by the Act because Cook could "simply lose weight and rid herself of any concomitant disability." *Id.* at 23. Although the court questioned whether "immutability is a prerequisite to the existence" of an "impairment," it found evidence in the record to support a finding that the dysfunctional metabolism underlying morbid obesity is permanent. The defendant also argued that morbid obesity cannot be an impairment because it is "caused, or at least exacerbated, by voluntary conduct." The court rejected that limitation, noting that "the Act indisputably applies to numerous conditions that may be caused or exacerbated by voluntary conduct, such as alcoholism, AIDS, diabetes, cancer resulting from cigarette smoking, [and] heart disease." *Id.* at 24. *See generally* Jane Byeff Korn, *Fat*, 77 B.U. L. REV. 25 (1997). Does the ADAAA's command to broadly construe the definition of disability resolve this? *See* Jane Byeff Korn, *Too Fat*, 17 VA. J. SOC. POL'Y & L. 209, 211 (2010) the ADAAA "will probably not protect people who are obese absent a significant change in our thinking about obesity").

Bearing out Professor Korn's prediction is *Morris v. BNSF Ry. Co.*, 817 F.3d 1104, 1112-13 (8th Cir. 2016). It held, first, as to actual disability, "for obesity, even morbid obesity, to be considered a physical impairment, it must result from an underlying physiological disorder or condition," a pre-existing standard not altered by the ADAAA, "which did not affect the definition of physical impairment." Second, as for regarded as liability, plaintiff could prevail only by showing that his employer "perceived his obesity to be a condition that met the definition of 'physical impairment.'

The ADA does not prohibit discrimination based on a perception that a physical characteristic—as opposed to a physical impairment—may eventually lead to a physical impairment as defined under the Act. Instead, the plain language of the ADA prohibits actions based on an existing impairment or the perception of an existing impairment." *Id*. at 1113.

≡ ## *Summers v. Altarum Inst., Corp.,*
≡ ### *740 F.3d 325 (4th Cir. 2014)*

DIANA GRIBBON MOTZ, Circuit Judge:

Pursuant to recent amendments to the Americans with Disabilities Act, a sufficiently severe temporary impairment may constitute a disability. Because the district court held to the contrary, we reverse and remand.

I.

A.

Carl Summers appeals the dismissal of his complaint for failure to state a claim on which relief can be granted. Accordingly, we recount the facts as alleged by Summers.

[In July 2011, Summers began work as a senior analyst for the Altarum Institute, a government contractor with an office in Alexandria, Virginia. His job required him to travel to the Maryland offices of Altarum's client, the Defense Centers of Excellence for Psychological Health and Traumatic Brain Injury ("DCoE").] On October 17, 2011, Summers fell and injured himself while exiting a commuter train on his way to DCoE. With a heavy bag slung over his shoulder, he lost his footing and struck both knees against the train platform. Paramedics took Summers to the hospital, where doctors determined that he had sustained serious injuries to both legs. Summers fractured his left leg and tore the meniscus tendon in his left knee. He also fractured his right ankle and ruptured the quadriceps-patellar tendon in his right leg. Repairing the left-leg fracture required surgery to fit a metal plate, screws, and bone into his tibia. Treating Summers's ruptured right quadriceps required another surgery to drill a hole in the patella and refasten his tendons to the knee.

Doctors forbade Summers from putting any weight on his left leg for six weeks and estimated that he would not be able to walk normally for seven months at the earliest. Without surgery, bed rest, pain medication, and physical therapy, Summers alleges that he would "likely" not have been able to walk for more than a year after the accident.

While hospitalized, Summers contacted an Altarum human-resources representative about obtaining short-term disability benefits and working from home as he recovered [which DCoE permitted for "extra hours"]. The Altarum representative agreed to discuss "accommodations that would allow Summers to return to work," but suggested that Summers "take short-term disability and focus on getting well again." Summers sent emails to his supervisors at Altarum and DCoE seeking advice about how to return to work; he suggested "a plan in which he would take short-term disability for a few weeks, then start working remotely part-time, and then increase his hours gradually until he was full-time again."

Altarum's insurance provider granted Summers short-term disability benefits. But Altarum never followed up on Summers's request to discuss how he might successfully return to work. The company did not suggest any alternative reasonable accommodation or engage in any interactive process with Summers. Nor did Altarum tell Summers that there was "any problem with his plan for a graduated return to work." Instead, on November 30, Altarum simply informed Summers "that Altarum was terminating [him] effective December 1, 2011, in order to place another analyst in his role at DCoE."

B.

[Summers sued, alleging, inter alia, that Altarum discriminated against him by wrongfully discharging him on account of his disability. The lower court dismissed his termination claim because Summers had failed to allege that he was disabled. The court reasoned that a "temporary condition, even up to a year" isn't within the ADA, and it] suggested that Summers was not disabled because he could have worked with the assistance of a wheelchair. . . .

II . . .

A. . . . .

Summers alleges that he was disabled under the ADA's actual-disability prong. Specifically, he asserts that his impairment "substantially limit[ed]" his ability to walk—which the ADA recognizes as one of the "major life activities" whose substantial limitation qualifies as a disability. *Id.* §12102(2)(A). Accordingly, if Summers's impairment substantially limited his ability to walk, he suffered a "disability" for purposes of the ADA.

B.

In September 2008, Congress broadened the definition of "disability" by enacting the ADA Amendments Act of 2008 ("ADAAA" or "amended Act"). In response to a series of Supreme Court decisions that Congress believed improperly restricted the scope of the ADA, it passed legislation with the stated purpose of "reinstating a broad scope of protection to be available under the ADA." §2(b)(1). Particularly relevant to this case, Congress sought to override *Toyota Motor Manufacturing, Kentucky, Inc. v. Williams*, 534 U.S. 184, 199 (2002), in which the Supreme Court had adopted a strict construction of the term "disability" and suggested that a temporary impairment could not qualify as a disability under the Act. Congress believed that *Toyota* set an "inappropriately high level of limitation necessary to obtain coverage under the ADA." §2(b)(5).

Abrogating *Toyota*, the amended Act provides that the definition of disability "shall be construed in favor of broad coverage of individuals under this chapter, to the maximum extent permitted by [its] terms." 42 U.S.C. §12102(4)(A). Further, Congress instructed that the term "substantially limits" be interpreted consistently with the liberalized purposes of the ADAAA. §12102(4)(B).[1] And Congress directed the [EEOC] to revise its regulations defining the term "substantially limits" to render them consistent with the broadened scope of the statute. §2(b)(6).

After notice and comment, the EEOC promulgated regulations clarifying that "[t]he term 'substantially limits' shall be construed broadly in favor of expansive coverage" and that the term is "not meant to be a demanding standard." 29 C.F.R. §1630.2(j)(1)(i) (2013). The EEOC regulations also expressly provide that "effects of an impairment *lasting or expected to last fewer than six months* can be substantially limiting" for purposes of proving an actual disability. §1630.2(j)(1)(ix) (emphasis added).

According to the appendix to the EEOC regulations, the "duration of an impairment is one factor that is relevant in determining whether the impairment substantially limits a major life activity." §1630.2(j)(1)(ix)(app.). Although "[i]mpairments that last only for a short period of time are typically not covered," they may be covered "if sufficiently severe." *Id.* The EEOC appendix illustrates these principles: "[I]f an individual has a back impairment that results in a 20-pound lifting restriction that lasts for several months, he is substantially limited in the major life activity of lifting, and therefore covered under the first prong of the definition of disability." *Id.*

III.

In dismissing Summers's wrongful-discharge claim, the district court held that, even though Summers had "suffered a very serious injury," this injury did not constitute a disability because it was temporary and expected to heal within a year. That holding represented an entirely reasonable interpretation of *Toyota* and its progeny. But in 2008, Congress expressly abrogated *Toyota* by amending the ADA. We are the first appellate court to apply the amendment's expanded definition of "disability." Fortunately, the absence of appellate precedent presents no difficulty in this case: Summers has unquestionably alleged a "disability" under the ADAAA sufficiently plausible to survive a Rule 12(b)(6) motion.

A.

Summers alleges that his accident left him unable to walk for seven months and that without surgery, pain medication, and physical therapy, he "likely" would have been unable to walk for far longer.[3] The text and purpose of the ADAAA and its implementing regulations make clear that such an impairment can constitute a disability.

In the amended Act, after concluding that courts had construed the term "disability" too narrowly, Congress stated that it intended to liberalize the ADA "in favor

---

1. The ADAAA provides, with respect to the "regarded-as" prong, that a plaintiff will not be disabled if his impairment is "transitory and minor," i.e., of "an actual or expected duration of 6 months or less." *Id.* §12102(3)(B). It contains no similar durational requirement for the "actual-disability" prong.

3. In enacting the ADAAA, Congress clarified that courts must disregard so-called "mitigating measures" when determining whether an impairment constitutes a disability. The new statute and regulations require courts to evaluate a plaintiff's impairment as it would manifest without treatments such as medication, mobility devices, and physical therapy. 42 U.S.C. §12102(4)(E)(i); 29 C.F.R. §1630.2(j)(5). . . . Because Summers's impairment could constitute a disability with or without surgery, we need not address whether his surgeries constituted mitigating measures.

of broad coverage." 42 U.S.C. §12102(4)(A). Congress also mandated that the ADA, as amended, be interpreted as broadly as its text permits. *Id.* Furthermore, the EEOC, pursuant to its delegated authority to construe "disability" more generously, adopted new regulations providing that an impairment lasting less than six months can constitute a disability. 29 C.F.R. §1630.2(j)(1)(ix). Although short-term impairments qualify as disabilities only if they are "sufficiently severe," *id.* §1630.2(j)(1)(ix)(app.), it seems clear that the serious impairment alleged by Summers is severe enough to qualify. If, as the EEOC has concluded, a person who cannot lift more than twenty pounds for "several months" is sufficiently impaired to be disabled within the meaning of the amended Act, *id.*, then surely a person whose broken legs and injured tendons render him completely immobile for more than seven months is also disabled.

In holding that Summers's temporary injury could not constitute a disability as a matter of law, the district court erred not only in relying on pre-ADAAA cases but also in misapplying the ADA disability analysis. The court reasoned that, because Summers could have worked with a wheelchair, he must not have been disabled. This inverts the appropriate inquiry. A court must first establish whether a plaintiff is disabled by determining whether he suffers from a substantially limiting impairment. Only then may a court ask whether the plaintiff is capable of working with or without an accommodation. *See* 42 U.S.C. §12102(4)(E)(i)(III) (the determination whether an impairment is substantially limiting "shall be made without regard to the ameliorative effects of . . .reasonable accommodations"). If the fact that a person could work with the help of a wheelchair meant he was not disabled under the Act, the ADA would be eviscerated.

B.

Despite the sweeping language of the amended Act and the clear regulations adopted by the EEOC, Altarum maintains that a temporary impairment cannot constitute a disability. In doing so, Altarum principally relies on pre-ADAAA cases that, as we have explained, the amended Act abrogated. Additionally, Altarum briefly advances two other arguments why Summers's leg injuries did not "substantially limit" his ability to walk.

1.

First, Altarum contends that the EEOC regulations defining a disability to include short-term impairments do not warrant deference under *Chevron, U.S.A., Inc. v. Natural Resources Defense Council, Inc.*, 467 U.S. 837 (1984). Altarum argues that Congress's intent "not to extend ADA coverage to those with temporary impairments expected to fully heal is evident," because such a "dramatic expansion of the ADA would have been accompanied by some pertinent statement of Congressional intent."

When a litigant challenges an agency's interpretation of a statute, we apply the familiar two-step *Chevron* analysis. First, we evaluate whether Congress has "directly spoken" to the precise question at issue. If traditional rules of statutory construction render the intent of Congress clear, "that is the end of the matter." *Chevron.* If the statute is "silent or ambiguous" with respect to the question at issue, we proceed to the second step—determining whether the agency's interpretation of the statute is reasonable. *Id.* An agency's reasonable interpretation will control, even if better interpretations are possible. *Id.*

Although Altarum contends that Congress's intent to withhold ADA coverage from temporarily impaired employees is "evident," no such intent seems evident to us. To be sure, the amended Act does preserve, without alteration, the requirement that an impairment be "substantial" to qualify as a disability. But Congress enacted the ADAAA to correct what it perceived as the Supreme Court's overly restrictive definition of this very term. And Congress expressly directed courts to construe the amended statute as broadly as possible. Moreover, while the ADAAA imposes a six-month requirement with respect to "regarded-as" disabilities, it imposes no such durational requirement for "actual" disabilities, thus suggesting that no such requirement was intended. *See Hamdan v. Rumsfeld*, 548 U.S. 557, 578 (2006) ("[A] negative inference may be drawn from the exclusion of language from one statutory provision that is included in other provisions of the same statute."). For these reasons, we must reject Altarum's contention that the amended Act clearly evinces Congress's intent to withhold ADA coverage for temporary impairments. At best, the statute is ambiguous with respect to whether temporary impairments may now qualify as disabilities.

Accordingly, we turn to step two of the *Chevron* analysis—determining whether the EEOC's interpretation is reasonable. We conclude that it is. The EEOC's decision to define disability to include severe temporary impairments entirely accords with the purpose of the amended Act. The stated goal of the ADAAA is to expand the scope of protection available under the Act as broadly as the text permits. The EEOC's interpretation—that the ADAAA may encompass temporary disabilities—advances this goal. Moreover, extending coverage to temporarily impaired employees produces consequences less "dramatic" than Altarum seems to envision. Prohibiting employers from discriminating against temporarily disabled employees will burden employers only as long as the disability endures. Temporary disabilities require only temporary accommodations.

2.

Alternatively, Altarum argues that, even deferring to the EEOC regulations, Summers's impairment does not qualify as a disability. Altarum maintains that the EEOC regulations do not apply to Summers's impairment because those regulations do not cover "temporary impairments due to injuries" even if they do cover "impairments due to permanent or long-term conditions that have only a short-term impact."

But, in fact, the EEOC regulations provide no basis for distinguishing between temporary impairments caused by injuries, on one hand, and temporary impairments caused by permanent conditions, on the other. The regulations state only that the "effects of an impairment lasting or expected to last fewer than six months can be substantially limiting"—they say nothing about the cause of the impairment. 29 C.F.R. §1630.2(j)(1)(ix).

Nor do the regulations suggest that an "injury" cannot be an "impairment." Rather, the EEOC defines an impairment broadly to include "[a]ny physiological disorder or condition, cosmetic disfigurement, or anatomical loss affecting one or more body systems," including the "musculoskeletal" system. *Id.* §1630.2(h)(1). This expansive definition surely includes broken bones and torn tendons. And the EEOC elsewhere uses the terms "injury" and "impairment" interchangeably. *See id.* §1630.2(j)(5) n.3 (app.); *id.* §1630.15(f) (app.).

In sum, nothing about the ADAAA or its regulations suggests a distinction between impairments caused by temporary injuries and impairments caused by permanent conditions. Because Summers alleges a severe injury that prevented him from walking for at least seven months, he has stated a claim that this impairment "substantially limited" his ability to walk.

IV.

Under the ADAAA and its implementing regulations, an impairment is not categorically excluded from being a disability simply because it is temporary. The impairment alleged by Summers falls comfortably within the amended Act's expanded definition of disability. . . .

NOTES

1. *The Analysis.* Mr. Summers won this round, but he will not necessarily win his claim. We now know that he is actually disabled, but we do not know whether he is "qualified": If his disability keeps him from performing the essential functions of his job (with or without reasonable accommodation), he will lose. As we will see, coming to work as usual might (or might not) be an essential function, and his limitation in that regard might (or might not) be reasonably accommodated (say, by some telecommuting). But once Summers established his actual disability and qualifications, Altarum (1) cannot discriminate against him on that basis, and (2) has to reasonably accommodate that disability—short of undue hardship.

Had the temporary nature of his condition meant he wasn't actually disabled, Summers might have claimed that Altarum "regarded" him as disabled. If the employer fired him because of his physical limitations, that might seem like a slam dunk. Proof of "regarded as" status would mean that Summers was (1) protected from discrimination but (2) not entitled to an accommodation. In this scenario, he need not be allowed to telecommute. But wait: Temporary conditions—those expected to last less than six months—are excluded from "regarded as" protection. So protection under this prong is not as obvious as it seems. If the impairment is neither an actual disability nor a "regarded as" disability, Altarum is free to fire Summers because of his injury.

2. *Temporary and Episodic Disabilities.* The *Summers* case is all about what "substantially limits" means, but it focuses on only one aspect of that inquiry: whether a temporary impairment is by definition not substantially limiting. The court holds no, at least when the impairment is "sufficiently severe." This may seem like a no-brainer, at least in scenarios like the one confronted in the case—a serious injury coupled with long-term recovery. But the *Summers* opinion thinks the district court got it right under the original ADA—it was only the ADAAA that changed the analysis. This may give you some idea of why Congress reacted so strongly to judicial construction of the original statute.

But do you think the Fourth Circuit was correct under the amended law? Doesn't the statute allow employers to discriminate against short-term impairments under the "regarded as" prong? Isn't it odd that Congress seems to allow the very kind of discrimination under one prong that would be barred under another prong? Indeed, it's even odder since, as we've seen, an employer need not accommodate "regarded as" disabilities, only actual disabilities (and, according to the EEOC, "record of" disabilities). In short, the standard for coverage seems lower under the more demanding prong of the statute.

Maybe this is where the EEOC regulations and the "*Chevron* two-step" come in. Even assuming this result would be odd as a matter of statutory interpretation, the statute is at worse "ambiguous" because it leaves a "gap" by failing to expressly address the status of temporary impairments for the "actually disabled" prong. That's the first step of the *Chevron* analysis, and satisfaction of it essentially authorizes the EEOC to fill that gap. Since the Commission's regulations clearly include temporary actual disabilities so long as they are sufficiently severe, we move to the second step, which asks whether the agency's interpretation is a reasonable (not necessarily preferable) one. Since the court isn't prepared to say the agency interpretation is unreasonable, the regulation stands.

Related to the notion of a temporary disability is the question of episodic ones—flare-ups of an underlying condition that are themselves temporary in nature even though the condition causing them is not. Unlike Summers, whose condition was expected to heal within a year, those who have the underlying impairment may expect such episodic manifestations to arise periodically in the future. But with respect to this question, there is no need to look to the regulations since the ADAAA speaks clearly, explicitly providing that "[a]n impairment that is episodic or in remission is a disability if it would substantially limit a major life activity when active." §12102(4)(D). *See Gogos v. AMS Mech. Sys., Inc.*, 737 F.3d 1170, 1173 (7th Cir. 2013) (an episode of a blood-pressure spike and vision loss may be covered disabilities when both problems may be "episodic" manifestations of a longstanding blood-pressure condition).

3. *Major Life Activity.* There is no need to look to major life activities for the "regarded as" prong: It is enough that the employer discriminates on the basis of a nontemporary impairment. But to be protected from discrimination under the "actual disability" prong (and thus to be also entitled to reasonable accommodation), an employee must not only have an impairment, but that impairment must substantially limit a major life activity.

Consider the ADAAA's effect on major life activities. This can be complicated. Recall that, in *Bragdon*, where the question was whether HIV affected a major life activity, the Court focused on the activity of reproduction since the plaintiff was a female who claimed to be substantially limited in her ability to bear a child because of the risk of passing on the disease to it. Where a male with HIV is concerned, however, there is no danger in fathering a child with HIV. Under the original ADA, such a plaintiff might have had to claim that his condition substantially limited him in having sex because of the aversion of potential sexual partners or his unwillingness to put them at risk. But the ADAAA short circuits the whole question—major life activities now "include the operation of a major bodily function," and specifically lists the immune system. And there is not much doubt that a plaintiff with HIV is substantially limited in terms of the functioning of his immune system.

Note on Major Life Activities

The ADAAA's inclusion of a definition of major life activities significantly reduces the need to interpret that term. But it might be useful to survey some of the pre-ADAAA decisions to appreciate the confusion. Some of these decisions remain good law; many do not. For example, *Pack v. Kmart Corp.*, 166 F.3d 1300 (10th Cir. 1999), held that sleep is a major life activity, but concentration is not. The ADAAA lists both. *Head v. Glacier Northwest, Inc.*, 413 F.3d 1053, 1058 (9th Cir. 2005), viewed thinking, reading, interacting with others, and sleeping as major life activities. The ADAAA embraces all of these except "interacting with others," and it does include "communicating," which might or might not be the same thing. *Reeves v. Johnson Controls World Servs., Inc.*, 140 F.3d 144 (2d Cir. 1998), wrote that "everyday mobility" is not a major life activity where agoraphobia restricted plaintiff's ability to travel. The ADAAA doesn't list "everyday mobility" as a major life activity, but its list is not exhaustive.

Arline, Bragdon, and Williams all had physical disabilities, but as some of the cases we've just surveyed indicate, the ADA encompasses mental and emotional disabilities as well as physical ones. According to Ann Hubbard:

> There can be no doubt that Congress intended major life activities to reach beyond what makes life merely possible to what makes it enjoyable and meaningful. An activity's importance must be assessed in light of the full array of aspirations and opportunities our modern society offers. These include the everyday activities that allow an individual to participate in every aspect of our modern society: civic, social, educational, economic, vocational, professional, political, commercial, recreational and cultural. Activities in all of these public spheres, as well as in personal and family life, must therefore be included in the category of "major."

The Major Life Activity of Belonging, 39 WAKE FOREST L. REV. 217, 224-25 (2004); *see also* Ann Hubbard, *Meaningful Lives and Major Life Activities*, 55 ALA. L. REV. 997 (2004); Ann Hubbard, *The Major Life Activity of Caring*, 8 IOWA J. GENDER, RACE & JUST. 327 (2004); Ann Hubbard, *The Myth of Independence and the Major Life Activity of Caring*, 8 J. GENDER RACE & JUST. 327 (2004).

Prior to the ADAAA, there was also considerable confusion about whether working could be considered a major life activity. Both *Sutton v. United Airlines, Inc.* 527 U.S. 471 (1999), and *Toyota* explicitly reserved this question. The ADAAA, however, explicitly includes "working" in its list of major life activities. Nevertheless, *Sutton* looked to the then-existing EEOC regulations, which provided plaintiffs are substantially limited in working only if they establish that they are excluded from "either a class of jobs or a broad range of jobs" as compared to persons with "comparable training, skills and abilities." *Id*. at 491 (quoting the applicable regulation). "The inability to perform a single, particular job does not constitute a substantial limitation in the major life activity of working." *Id*. The current regulations omit that language, but do not replace it with any meaningful definition. *See Ferrari v. Ford Motor Co.*, 826 F.3d 885, 893-94 (6th Cir. 2016) (Ford barred Ferrari only from a single, particular job and thus did not regard his opioid use as a substantial limitation on the major life activity of working).

Note on Substantially Limited

Once a major life activity is defined, the remaining question is whether the impairment substantially limits plaintiff's participation in it. The primary question before the *Toyota* court was whether Williams' impairment substantially limited her major life activity of performing manual tasks. The Court answered that question by stating that only if the impairment "prevents or severely restricts the individual from doing activities that are of central importance to most people's daily lives" will it be considered substantially limiting. Moreover, the Court required that the impairment's impact must also be permanent or long term. 534 U.S. at 198.

The ADAAA explicitly disapproved of *Toyota's* approach as setting "an inappropriately high level of limitation," and for good measure it also disapproved of the extant EEOC regulations as "expressing too high a standard." 42 U.S.C.A. §12101. Responding to this concern, §1630.2(j)(1)(i) of the new EEOC's regulations now provides a number of "rules of construction," designed to expand statutory protection. The most sweeping sets the stage for the others: "The term 'substantially limits' shall be construed broadly in favor of expansive coverage, to the maximum extent permitted by the terms of the ADA. [It] is not meant to be a demanding standard." Subsequent rules provide more detail but cut in favor of broad reach. Thus, an impairment is a disability within the meaning of this section if it " 'substantially limits' the ability of an individual to perform a major life activity as compared to most people in the general population," §1630.2(j)(1)(iii), but it "need not prevent, or significantly or severely restrict, the individual from performing a major life activity in order to be considered a disability." *Id.* Further, "[i]n determining whether an individual has a disability, the focus is on how a major life activity is substantially limited, not on what an individual can do in spite of an impairment." §1630.2(j)(1)(iv).

In short, if, as in *Summers*, the courts give deference to the EEOC regulations, much of the prior case law will be abrogated, and limitations will have to be much less "substantial" than before to meet the ADA's threshold.

Note on Mitigating Measures

One of the targets of the ADAAA was *Sutton v. United Airlines, Inc.* 527 U.S. 471 (1999), a case that held that individuals who used mitigating or ameliorative measures to deal with their impairment should be assessed in their mitigated state. While *Sutton* itself involved pilots rejected by an airline because they needed glasses for 20/20 vision, the opinion and two companion cases—*Murphy v. UPS*, 527 U.S. 516 (1999) (plaintiff's high blood pressure should be considered in his medicated state to assess substantial limitation), and *Albertson's, Inc. v. Kirkingburg*, 527 U.S. 555 (1999) (plaintiff's subconscious adjustments to his monocular vision should be considered in assessing substantial limitation)—threatened to radically cut back on the protected class. Indeed, Justice Stevens's dissent in *Sutton* argued that the majority's approach would permit an employer to discriminate against a veteran who lost a leg if his prosthesis was effective. 527 U.S. 497-98.

The ADAAA explicitly disapproved of *Sutton* and provides that "the determination of whether an impairment substantially limits a major life activity shall be made *without regard* to the ameliorative effects of mitigating measures," listing a number of mitigating measures such as medication, prosthetics, hearing aids, etc. However, the amended statute goes on to provide that "the ameliorative effects of the mitigating measures of ordinary eyeglasses or contact lenses shall be considered in determining whether an impairment substantially limits a major life activity." Accordingly, while Congress amended the statute in direct response to the result in *Sutton*, it essentially agreed that the *Sutton* plaintiffs were not to be considered persons with *actual* disabilities within the meaning of the ADA.

In the wake of the ADAAA, there remains a problem regarding those who do not use measures when they are available. Such individuals will be disabled (a matter that divided the courts prior to the ADAAA), but the failure to mitigate may sometimes make them unqualified. As we will see, a disabled person is otherwise qualified if she can perform the essential functions of the position with or without reasonable accommodation. The obvious question that will arise is the extent to which an employer must accommodate an individual who does not use mitigating measures to enable her to do the job at issue. *See generally* Jeannette Cox, *"Corrective" Surgery and the Americans with Disabilities Act*, 46 SAN DIEGO L. REV. 113 (2009). Finally, the use of a mitigating measure might itself create a disability where none previously existed. *Sulima v. Tobyhanna Army Depot*, 602 F.3d 177, 187 (3d Cir. 2010), held that the side effects from medical treatment may themselves constitute an impairment under the ADA even if the condition treated is not itself disabling; however, since " 'disability' connotes an involuntary condition," a plaintiff seeking protection on this theory must show both that the treatment was required in the "prudent judgment" of the medical profession and that there was not an equally efficacious alternative without similarly disabling side effects.

PROBLEMS

9-5.   Sarah Smith is an assembly-line worker who is diabetic and dependent on insulin injections to maintain her glucose level. She must inject up to four times a day to maintain ideal glucose levels. If her glucose level drops too low, she will become hypoglycemic and go into a coma. If her glucose level is too high, it will cause long-term physical deterioration of numerous body systems. Since eating increases glucose levels, Sarah needs to inject one half hour before eating larger meals. Her doctor has recommended that she eat smaller and more frequent meals to help modulate variations in her glucose levels. Outside of work, Sarah leads an active life and exercises regularly. She must be careful to time her injections depending on her exercise and eating patterns. Exercise reduces glucose levels on a short-term basis and can upset the balance of insulin and glucose in the body, possibly resulting in a hypoglycemic reaction. Because Sarah is careful about her eating, exercise, and treatment regimen, her diabetes is reasonably well controlled. She does not yet exhibit any physical damage related to excess glucose levels. She carries small amounts of sugar with her to minimize the incidence of hypoglycemic reactions. Assembly-line workers operate on a very rigid schedule. Sarah wants to seek accommodations from her employer to make it easier for her to maintain her glucose levels while at work. Was Sarah an individual with a disability under the original ADA? What about under the ADA as amended?

9-6.   Alpha-1 antitrypsin ("AAT") is a serum protein that protects the lungs from proteolytic enzymes. Approximately 80 percent of individuals who inherit an AAT deficiency from both parents develop chronic obstructive pulmonary disease ("COPD"). Individuals who inherit the deficiency from only one parent have an increased risk of developing COPD (one in ten), especially if they smoke or work in dusty environments. Tuan Lee, who inherited AAT deficiency from both of his parents, does not yet suffer from any symptoms of COPD. Is Tuan impaired? If so, is he substantially limited with respect to a major life activity and, therefore, protected under the ADA as amended?

b. Record of Such an Impairment

Section 3(2) of the ADA defines disability to include having a record of an impairment that substantially limits a major life activity. A variety of "records" contain such information, including employment records, medical records, and education records. However, "[t]he impairment indicated in the record must be an impairment that would substantially limit one or more of the individual's major life activities." 29 C.F.R. pt. 1630, app. §1630.2(k). *See Colwell v. Suffolk County Police Dept.*, 158 F.3d 635, 645 (2d Cir. 1998) (hospitalization for cerebral hemorrhage was too vague and too short to be record of impairment); *Sherrod v. American Airlines, Inc.*, 132 F.3d 1112, 1120-21 (5th Cir. 1998) (hospitalization for back surgery was not a record of an impairment that would substantially limit a major life activity). *See generally* Alex B. Long, *(Whatever Happened to) The ADA's "Record of" Prong(?)*, 81 WASH. L. REV. 669 (2006).

PROBLEM

9-7. Reconsider Problems 9-5 and 9-6. Could you make a "record of impairment" argument on behalf of Sarah or Tuan?

c. Regarded as Having Such an Impairment

We saw earlier that individuals are protected by the ADA even if they are not actually impaired or if they are "regarded" by their employers as being impaired. *Sutton* read this provision narrowly, but the ADAAA changes this radically; § 12102(3)(A) now provides that an individual is regarded as having an impairment "if the individual establishes that he or she has been subjected to an action prohibited under this Act because of an actual or perceived physical or mental impairment whether or not the impairment limits or is perceived to limit a major life activity."

In other words, to be liable, the employer must still discriminate on the basis of an impairment, but there is no requirement that the employer believe the impairment to be substantially limiting. Under the original statute, for example, *Brown v. Lester E. Cox Medical Center*, 286 F.3d 1040 (8th Cir. 2002), upheld a jury verdict for the plaintiff on her "regarded as" claim only when evidence showed that the employer regarded the plaintiff's multiple sclerosis as substantially limiting her ability to think because it believed her condition made her unfit for further employment in any capacity at the medical center. Under the ADAAA's approach, proving that the employer discriminated against the plaintiff because of her MS would suffice with no further inquiry (assuming the plaintiff to be otherwise qualified). Think about discrimination based on obesity. If that's an impairment, the inquiry is at an end under the "regarded as" prong.

"Regarded as" discrimination may be more common than might first appear. Professor Michelle Travis, in *Perceived Disabilities, Social Cognition, and "Innocent Mistakes,"* 55 VAND. L. REV. 481 (2002), contends that "at least some perceived disabilities are likely to result not from consciously held, group-based prejudices or generalizations, but from nonmotivational cognitive processing errors," *id.* at 491, that is, errors that do not derive from conscious prejudices or even conscious group-based decision making. Of course, as we saw in *Summers*, the sweep of this prong is limited by the statutory provision that it "shall not apply to impairments that are transitory and minor. A transitory impairment is an impairment with an actual or expected duration of 6 months or less." Nevertheless, the "regarded as" prong now provides the broadest statutory protection. *But see EEOC v. BNSF Ry. Co.*, 853 F.3d 1150, 1159 (10th Cir. 2017) (plaintiff was neither regarded as nor actually disabled when a hand injury prevented him from complying with a three-point-contact rule while climbing and gripping tools with both hands; neither limitation prevented him from working in a broad class of job and both are "jobs-centered tasks, which do not amount to major life activities").

Counterbalancing this dramatic expansion, however, the ADAAA effectively created a two-tiered structure for disability claims. For actual (and presumably "record of") disabilities, the statute continues both to forbid discrimination and to mandate accommodation. But for "regarded as" claims, the ADAAA bars discrimination only; it does not mandate accommodation. *See generally* Stephen F. Befort, *Let's Try This Again: The ADA Amendments Act of 2008 Attempts to Reinvigorate the "Regarded As" Prong of the Statutory Definition of Disability*, 2010 UTAH L. REV. 993. *But see* Jeannette Cox, *Reasonable Accommodations and the ADA Amendments' Overlooked Potential*, 24 GEO. MASON L. REV. 147 (2016) (arguing that, ADA provisions, such as requiring a business necessity for job qualifications standards, provide accommodation-like protection for the regarded-as disabled).

How would this apply to the *Sutton* plaintiffs? They presumably have no actual disability under the ADA, originally or as amended, since their corrective lenses may be taken into account in determining whether their visual impairments substantially limit one or more major life activities. But, corrected or not, they do have myopia, an impairment. And their prospective employer denied them employment because of their myopia. They thus would be considered individuals with a disability under the "regarded as" prong under the amended statute, although the "qualification standard" defense might avoid liability for United.

2. The Meaning of "Qualified Individual with a Disability"

Establishing the existence of a disability is necessary but not sufficient to bring an individual within Title I's protections since that statute prohibits discrimination only against "a *qualified* individual with a disability because of the disability of such individual." 42 U.S.C. §12112(a) (2014) (emphasis added). In turn, Title I in §12111(8) defines a "qualified individual with a disability" as:

> an individual with a disability who, with or without reasonable accommodation, can perform the essential functions of the employment position that such individual holds or desires. For the purposes of this title, consideration shall be given to the employer's judgment as to what functions of a job are essential, and if an employer has prepared a written description before advertising or interviewing applicants for the job, this description shall be considered evidence of the essential functions of the job.

This definition protects disabled individuals who can perform the essential tasks of their jobs and thus prevents employers from denying employment because a disability precludes the performance of nonessential or relatively unimportant aspects of the job. On the other hand, denying employment to someone who cannot perform the essential functions of the job—with or without reasonable accommodation—is perfectly legal. *See Majors v. GE Elec. Co.*, 714 F.3d 527 (7th Cir. 2013) (because plaintiff was permanently unable to lift more than twenty pounds, she could not perform an essential function of the auditor position without accommodation and having another worker lift heavy objects for her was "not a reasonable accommodation"); *Olsen v. Capital Region Med. Ctr.*, 713 F.3d 1149, 1154 (8th Cir. 2013) (plaintiff's frequent epileptic seizures prevented her from being qualified for her position since an essential function of mammography technician was insuring patient safety, and she was unable to "adequately perform that function during the indefinite periods in which she was incapacitated"). Accordingly, to determine whether an individual is qualified, it is necessary to distinguish the essential functions of the job from those that are not, an inquiry which tends to entail the question of whether a reasonable accommodation is available.

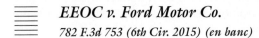

EEOC v. Ford Motor Co.
782 F.3d 753 (6th Cir. 2015) (en banc)

McKEAGUE, Circuit Judge.

The Americans with Disabilities Act (ADA) requires employers to reasonably accommodate their disabled employees; it does not endow all disabled persons with a job—or job schedule—of their choosing. Jane Harris, a Ford Motor Company employee with irritable bowel syndrome, sought a job schedule of her choosing: to work from home on an as-needed basis, up to four days per week. Ford denied her request, deeming regular and predictable on-site attendance essential to Harris's highly interactive job. Ford's papers and practices—and Harris's three past telecommuting failures—backed up its business judgment.

Nevertheless, the federal Equal Employment Opportunity Commission (EEOC) sued Ford under the ADA. It alleged that Ford failed to reasonably accommodate Harris by denying her telecommuting request and retaliated against her for bringing the issue to the EEOC's attention. The district court granted summary judgment to Ford on both claims. We affirm.

I.

The Ford Motor Company employs about 224,000 employees worldwide. True to its founder's vision, Ford uses its employees in assembly lines to perform independent yet interconnected tasks. Resale buyers of steel come early on the lines—before any assembling begins. They purchase raw steel from steel suppliers and then, as their name suggests, resell the steel to parts manufacturers known as "stampers." The stampers then supply the steel parts to the vehicle assemblers, who put together the vehicles.

As an intermediary between steel and parts suppliers, the resale buyer's job is highly interactive. Some of the interactions occur by email and telephone. But many require good, old-fashioned interpersonal skills. During core business hours, for example, resale buyers meet with suppliers at their sites and with Ford employees and stampers at Ford's site—meetings that Ford says are most effectively performed face to face. And Ford's practice aligns with its preaching: It requires resale buyers to work in the same building as stampers so they can meet on a moment's notice. This high level of interactivity and teamwork is why, in Ford's judgment, "a resale buyer's regular and predictable attendance in the workplace" is "essential to being a fully functioning member of the resale team."

A former Ford resale buyer with irritable bowel syndrome takes center stage in this case: Jane Harris. [The court spent considerable time detailing Harris's limitations as an employee, both her poor performance and high absenteeism, and stressed that when she missed work, her teammates had to pick up the slack, including by taking on the functions that Harris could not perform at home." It did acknowledge that her "irritable bowel syndrome of course contributed to the situation. It gave her uncontrollable diarrhea and fecal incontinence," occasionally preventing her from making the one-hour drive to work without an accident. "The vicious cycle continued, as her symptoms increased her stress, and the increased stress worsened her symptoms—making her less likely to come to work."

[Ford tried to help, for example, including allowing Harris to "telecommute on an ad hoc basis" in an "Alternative Work Schedule." But despite the *ad hoc* telecommuting and flexible schedules, problems persisted. Harris nevertheless sought permission to "to work up to four days per week from home." Ford denied permission. "Ford's practice and policy limited telecommuting for resale buyers. In practice, Ford's buyers telecommuted, at most, on *one* set day per week," which "aligned with its policy, which makes clear that those jobs that require 'face-to-face contact'—and those individuals who were not 'strong performer' and who had poor time-management skills—were among those not 'appropriate for telecommuting.'" Ford ultimately decided Harris requested accommodation as unreasonable although it did meet with Harris to explore it and offered to accommodate her in other ways, such as moving her closer to the restroom or looking for jobs better suited for telecommuting. Harris turned down each alternative accommodation and filed a charge with the EEOC. Ultimately, the "rest of Harris's time at Ford did not go well," and she was terminated.

[The EEOC sued claiming inter alia, failure to reasonably accommodate Harris's disability, but the district court granted summary judgment in favor of Ford. A divided panel of the Sixth Circuit reversed, and the court took the case en banc.]

II.

Many disabled individuals require accommodations to perform their jobs. The ADA addresses this reality by requiring companies like Ford to make "reasonable accommodations to the known . . . limitations of an otherwise qualified individual with a disability" where such an accommodation does not cause the employer "undue hardship." 42 U.S.C. § 12112(b)(5). To comply with the ADA, then, Ford must "reasonabl[y] accommodat[e]" Harris (undisputedly a disabled individual for purposes of this appeal) if she is "*qualified*." §§ 12112(a), (b)(5) (emphasis added); *see Smith v. Ameritech*, 129 F.3d 857, 866 (6th Cir. 1997).

To be "qualified" under the ADA, Harris must be able to "perform the essential functions of [a resale buyer]" "with or without reasonable accommodation." 42 U.S.C. § 12111(8). A "reasonable accommodation" may include "job restructuring [and] part-time or modified work schedules." *Id.* at § 12111(9)(B). But it does *not* include removing an "essential function[]" from the position, for that is *per se* unreasonable. *Brickers v. Cleveland Bd. of Educ.*, 145 F.3d 846, 850 (6th Cir. 1998); *see Sch. Bd. of Nassau Cnty. v. Arline*, 480 U.S. 273, 287 n.17 (1987). The district court held that Harris was *not* qualified because her excessive absences prevented her from performing the essential functions of a resale buyer. We agree.

A

Is regular and predictable on-site job attendance an essential function (and a prerequisite to perform other essential functions) of Harris's resale-buyer job? We hold that it is.

1

We do not write on a clean slate. Much ink has been spilled establishing a general rule that, with few exceptions, "an employee who does not come to work cannot perform any of his job functions, essential or otherwise." *EEOC v. Yellow Freight Sys., Inc.*, 253 F.3d 943, 948 (7th Cir. 2001) (en banc). We will save the reader a skim by omitting a long string cite of opinions that agree, but they do. *E.g., Samper v. Providence St. Vincent Med. Ctr.*, 675 F.3d 1233, 1237-38 (9th Cir. 2012) (collecting cases); *Mason v. Avaya Commc'ns, Inc.*, 357 F.3d 1114, 1122-24 (10th Cir. 2004) (same). Our Circuit has not bucked the trend. And for good reason: "most jobs require the kind of teamwork, personal interaction, and supervision that simply cannot be had in a home office situation." *Rauen v. U.S. Tobacco Mfg. L.P.*, 319 F.3d 891, 896 (7th Cir. 2003).

That general rule—that regularly attending work on-site is essential to most jobs, especially the interactive ones—aligns with the text of the ADA. Essential functions generally are those that the employer's "judgment" and "written [job] description" prior to litigation deem essential. *See* 42 U.S.C. § 12111(8). And in most jobs, especially those involving teamwork and a high level of interaction, the employer will require regular and predictable on-site attendance from all employees (as evidenced by its words, policies, and practices).

The same goes for the EEOC's regulations. They define essential functions as those that are "fundamental" (as opposed to "marginal"), 29 C.F.R. § 1630.2(n)(1), so that a job is "fundamentally alter[ed]" if an essential function is removed. 29 C.F.R. § Pt. 1630(n), App. at 394. To guide the essential-function inquiry, the regulations speak in factors—seven of them. The first two restate the statutory considerations. 29 C.F.R. § 1630.2(n)(3)(i)-(ii). The remaining five add other considerations. 29 C.F.R. § 1630.2(n)(3)(iii)-(vii). In many jobs, especially the interactive ones, all seven point toward finding regular and predictable on-site attendance essential. Take the amount of time performing that function, for example, § 1630.2(n)(3)(iii): Most of one's *work* time is spent *at work*, and many interactive functions simply cannot be performed off site. Or take the consequences of failing to show up for work, § 1630.2(n)(3)(iv): They can be severe. Ditto for the terms of the collective bargaining agreement, § 1630.2(n)(3)(v): They certainly won't typically exempt regular attendance. Other employees' work practices are no different, § 1630.2(n)(3)(vi)-(vii): Other employees usually attend work at the worksite. And so on, such that most jobs would be *fundamentally altered* if regular and predictable on-site attendance is removed.

The EEOC's informal guidance on the matter cuts in the same direction. An employer may refuse a telecommuting request when, among other things, the job requires "face-to-face interaction and coordination of work with other employees," "in-person interaction with outside colleagues, clients, or customers," and "immediate access to documents or other information located only in the workplace." EEOC Fact Sheet, *Work At Home/Telework as a Reasonable Accommodation* (Oct. 27, 2005), http://www.eeoc.gov/facts/telework.html. That is because, as the EEOC elsewhere explains, "the inquiry into essential functions is not intended to second guess an employer's business judgment with regard to production standards." 29 C.F.R. § Pt. 1630(n), App. at 395. Nor is it meant "to require employers to lower such standards." *Id.* But that's what would happen in many jobs if regular, in-person attendance was not required.

A sometimes-forgotten guide likewise supports the general rule: common sense. *Waggoner v. Olin Corp.*, 169 F.3d 481, 482-84 (7th Cir. 1999). Non-lawyers would readily understand that regular on-site attendance is required for interactive jobs. Perhaps they would view it as "the basic, most fundamental" "activity" of their job. Webster's Third New International Dictionary 777, 920 (1986) (defining "essential" and "function"). But equipped with a 1400-or-so page record, standards of review, burdens of proof, and a seven-factor balancing test, the answer may seem more difficult. Better to follow the commonsense notion that non-judges (and, to be fair to judges, our sister circuits) hold: Regular, in-person attendance is an essential function—and a prerequisite to essential functions—of most jobs, especially the interactive ones. That's the same rule that case law from around the country, the statute's language, its regulations, and the EEOC's guidance all point toward. And it's the controlling one here.

2

That rule has straightforward application here: Regular and predictable on-site attendance was essential for Harris's position, and Harris's repeated absences made her unable to perform the essential functions of a resale buyer. The required teamwork, meetings with suppliers and stampers, and on-site "availability to participate in . . . face-to-face interactions," all necessitate a resale buyer's regular and predictable attendance. For years Ford has required resale buyers to work in the same building as stampers, further evidencing its judgment that on-site attendance is essential. And the practice has been consistent with the policy: all other resale buyers regularly and predictably attend work on site. Indeed, even those who telecommute do so only one set day per week and agree in advance to come into work if needed. Sealing the deal are Harris's experiences and admissions. Her excessive absences caused her to make mistakes and caused strife in those around her. And she agreed that four of her ten primary duties could not be performed from home. On this record, the EEOC cannot show that regularly attending work was merely incidental to Harris's job; it was *essential* to her job.

It follows that Harris's up-to-four-days telecommuting proposal—which removed that essential function of her job—was unreasonable. *Brickers; Mason*. The *employee* bears the burden of proposing an accommodation that will permit her to effectively perform the essential functions of her job. *Jakubowski v. Christ Hosp., Inc.*, 627 F.3d 195, 202 (6th Cir. 2010). Harris proposed only one accommodation—one that would exempt her regular and predictable attendance from her resale-buyer job. In failure-to-accommodate claims where the employee requests an "accommodation that *exempts* her from an essential function," "the essential functions and reasonable accommodation analyses [] run together." *Samper*. One conclusion (the function is essential) leads to the other (the accommodation is not reasonable). That's this case. Harris's proposed accommodation was unreasonable.

Nor could Harris perform the essential functions of her job with Ford's past reasonable accommodations. . . .

B

The EEOC sees it differently. It argues that three sources—(1) Harris's own testimony, (2) other resale buyers' telecommuting practices, and (3) technology—create a genuine dispute of fact as to whether regular on-site attendance is essential. But none does.

[The court would not permit an employee's "unsupported testimony" to create a *genuine* "dispute of fact," as to the essential functions of the positions and, in any event, "Harris's testimony does not add much." As for other employees' telecommuting schedules, that evidence may be relevant in theory but not on this record: "Harris's coworkers worked from home on materially *different* schedules: on one set day per week—no more, and sometimes less. The most any employee was even *authorized* to work from home was two days per week." Further, looking to any telecommunication for any employee as a basis for accommodation everyone would mean that "once an employer allows *one* person the ability to telecommute on a *limited* basis, it must allow *all* people with a disability the right to telecommute on an *unpredictable* basis up to 80% of the week (or else face trial). That's 180-degrees backward. It encourages—indeed, requires—employers to *shut down* predictable and limited telecommuting as an accommodation for *any* employee."]

(3) *Technology*. Despite its commonsense charm, the EEOC's appeal to technology ultimately fails to create a genuine fact issue. It is "self-evident," the EEOC declares without citation to the record or any case law, that "technology has advanced" enough for employees to perform "at least some essential job functions" at home. In the abstract, no doubt, this is precisely right. *E.g., Vande Zande v. Wis. Dep't of Admin.*, 44 F.3d 538, 544 (7th Cir. 1995) (recognizing as much). But technology changing *in the abstract* is not technology changing *on this record*. Our review of a district court's summary-judgment ruling is confined to the record. And no record evidence—*none*—shows that a great technological shift has made this highly interactive

job one that can be effectively performed at home. The proper case to credit advances in technology is one where the record *evinces* that advancement. There is no such evidence here.

In fact, the evidence here shows the opposite: technology has *not* changed so as to make regular in-person attendance marginal for this job. . . .

One more point, for clarification. None of this is to say that whatever the employer says is essential necessarily becomes essential. . . . Our ruling does not, in other words, require blind deference to the employer's stated judgment. But it *does* require granting summary judgment where an employer's judgment as to essential job functions—evidenced by the employer's words, policies, and practices and taking into account all relevant factors—is "job-related, uniformly-enforced, and consistent with business necessity." *Tate v. Farmland Indus., Inc.*, 268 F.3d 989, 993 (10th Cir. 2001). That aptly describes Ford's judgment regarding regular and predictable on-site attendance for resale buyers. The district court accordingly properly granted summary judgment.

C

Our conclusion that Harris was unqualified for her position makes it unnecessary to consider whether Ford showed bad faith in the discussions to work out a reasonable accommodation while Harris was still employed. Even if Ford did not put sufficient effort into the "interactive process" of finding an accommodation, 29 C.F.R. § 1630.2(o)(3), "that failure is actionable only if it prevents identification of an appropriate accommodation *for a qualified individual*." *Basden v. Prof'l Transp., Inc.*, 714 F.3d 1034, 1039 (7th Cir. 2013) (emphasis added) . . .

[The majority also upheld the district court's grant of summary judgment on the EEOC's retaliation claim.]

KAREN NELSON MOORE, Circuit Judge, dissenting. . .

I dissent because the majority refuses to engage in the fact-intensive, case-by-case determination required by the EEOC regulations and repeatedly refuses to take the facts in the light most favorable to Harris, as summary judgment requires. When we apply both standards properly, the EEOC has presented sufficient evidence to dispute whether Harris is a qualified individual, either because physical presence is not an essential function of her job or because telework is a reasonable accommodation for her. There is also a genuine dispute about whether Ford retaliated against Harris for filing a charge with the EEOC.

I.   Analysis

A.   *Harris's request to telework*

. . . The key point is that Harris proposed to be out of the office *up to* four days each week, not four days per week, every week. The relevant questions in this case are therefore whether physical presence every day of the week is an essential function of Harris's job, and whether telework some days each week is a reasonable accommodation.

B. The EEOC created a genuine dispute of material fact whether physical presence at the work-site is an essential function of Harris's job.

I agree that we should consider Ford's judgment that physical presence in the office is an essential function of Harris's job. However, Ford gave *only one reason* for why physical presence is an essential function—that the resale buyer position requires a great deal of face-to-face teamwork. Ford did not and could not argue that Harris needed to be in the office to use key equipment or to provide services to outside clients, for example. What exactly is the teamwork that Ford claims must be performed face-to-face? Based on the limited record of this case, it appears to be two things: (1) spur-of-the-moment meetings to address unexpected problems in the supply chain, and (2) scheduled meetings.

In contrast, the EEOC presented two pieces of evidence that directly contradict Ford's claim that the teamwork functions of Harris's job required her to be physically present in the office. First, Harris attested in her declaration that she actually performed 95% of her job on the phone or through email, *even when in the office*. Second, Ford allowed other resale buyers to telework. This suggests that, to perform effectively, resale buyers do not need to be prepared to handle unexpected problems in the supply chain through face-to-face interactions every day of the week.

A reasonable jury might ultimately agree with Ford, or it might agree with Harris. The point is that there is a genuine dispute of material fact that *only* a jury should resolve. . . .

3. Ford's own judgment

Ford's own judgment that physical presence in the office is an essential function of Harris's job certainly is entitled to consideration, but that judgment is not dispositive. In defining "[q]ualified individual," the ADA states only that "*consideration* shall be given to the employer's judgment as to what functions of a job are essential." 42 U.S.C. § 12111(8) (emphasis added). Noticeably absent is the word "deference." The EEOC regulations interpreting this section similarly include the employer's judgment *as just one of seven factors* courts should consider. 29 C.F.R. § 1630.2(n)(3). Yes, the EEOC regulations provide that "inquiry into the essential functions is not intended to second guess an employer's business judgment with regard to production standards," but they also state that "whether a particular function is essential 'is a factual determination that must be made on a case by case basis [based upon] *all* relevant evidence.'" *Deane v. Pocono Med. Ctr.*, 142 F.3d 138, 148 (3d Cir. 1998) (quoting 29 C.F.R. § 1630, app. § 1630.2(n)) (alterations in original). Other circuits also treat the employer's judgment as just one factor to consider in assessing whether a particular function is essential. *See, e.g., Rohan v. Networks Presentations LLC*, 375 F.3d 266, 279 n.22 (4th Cir. 2004); *Gillen v. Fallon Ambulance Serv., Inc.*, 283 F.3d 11, 25 (1st Cir. 2002); *Cripe v. City of San Jose*, 261 F.3d 877, 887 (9th Cir. 2001).

The majority's test for when an employer's judgment that a function is essential can be overcome—if it is not "job-related, uniformly-enforced, [or] consistent with business necessity"—is thus not compelled by the ADA or the EEOC regulations. And in fact, the majority's test is in direct tension with the regulations' insistence that the inquiry is a fact-intensive, case-by-case determination.

Moreover, the majority's insistence that the "general rule" is that physical attendance at the worksite is an essential function of most jobs does not advance the analysis in this case. . . . When courts have addressed the issue, the record had, in fact, established that the employee had to be physically present to access equipment or materials located only in the office, or to provide direct services to clients or customers. *See, e.g., Samper v. Providence St. Vincent Med. Ctr.*, 675 F.3d 1233, 1238-39 (9th Cir. 2012) (neo-natal nurse who provided direct patient care).

Here, in contrast, the sole reason given by Ford for why Harris needs to be physically present in the workplace is that the resale buyer position requires a high degree of face-to-face teamwork. Ford does not claim that necessary physical equipment or files can be accessed only on-site, or that Harris must interact with outside clients at Ford's work-site.

Nor do cases noting teamwork as one reason for finding physical presence an essential job function resolve this case. Of the cases cited by Ford, all but two involved jobs that otherwise obviously require physical attendance—materials located only in the office or direct client interaction. The courts therefore did not need to consider squarely whether teamwork might be effectively accomplished remotely because other aspects of the employees' jobs clearly required them to be physically present at work. *See, e.g., Samper* (neo-natal nurse who provided direct patient care); *Hypes* (loan review analyst who used confidential documents that could not leave the office). And in one of the two remaining cases, the employee did not actually contest that her teamwork responsibilities could be performed only on-site; rather, she argued that another employee could take up the in-person teamwork duties of her job. *Mason v. Avaya Comm'ns, Inc.*, 357 F.3d 1114, 1120-21 (10th Cir. 2004).

Therefore, only the Seventh Circuit's decision in *Vande Zande v. Wisconsin Department of Administration*, 44 F.3d 538 (7th Cir. 1995), arguably presents a set of facts similar to the present case. In *Vande Zande*, the plaintiff had a job that did not require her to use materials present only in the workplace or to interact directly with clients on-site. The *Vande Zande* court specifically stated that its conclusion that "team work under supervision generally cannot be performed at home" would "no doubt change as communications technology advances." Technology has undoubtedly advanced since 1995 in facilitating teamwork through fast and effective electronic communication such that it should no longer be assumed that teamwork must be done in-person.

Thus, neither the general case law on physical presence at the work-site nor prior case law on teamwork resolves this case. Ford gave only one reason for why Harris's physical presence at the worksite is an essential function of her job—that the resale buyer position requires a great deal of face-to-face teamwork. The EEOC presented two pieces of evidence that directly contradict this claim. Summary judgment is therefore not appropriate.

Finally, the majority's claim that failure to grant summary judgment to Ford would turn telework into a "weapon" completely overstates the reach of this case and itself sets a problematic precedent for other failure-to-accommodate cases. First, providing telework is not just a good deed; sometimes it is legally required under the ADA. Second, in any given case, employees seeking telework as a reasonable accommodation partly on the basis that other employees are permitted to telework would need to show that those other employees have similar job duties to their own. They cannot point to just any employee. Here, Harris pointed to telework agreements of other resale buyers. More fundamentally, in assessing whether a function is essential, the EEOC regulations expressly invite courts to consider the experience of other employees "in similar jobs." 29 C.F.R. § 1630.2(n)(3)(vii). Indeed, the majority's test for whether a function is essential also requires assessing how the employer treats other employees. Thus, this kind of comparison is inevitable in order to evaluate properly many reasonable-accommodation claims. The majority would privilege Ford's overstated perverse-incentives argument at the expense of properly and carefully assessing reasonable-accommodation claims as the ADA and the EEOC regulations require. Finally, I doubt that Ford and other employers would actually limit telework so drastically based on the slight risk that in certain reasonable-accommodation cases, the telework agreements of employees with similar job duties might be relevant. The majority ignores the myriad other reasons why employers might choose to provide telework to their employees, such as incentivizing individuals to come work for them or reducing the size of the physical workplace.

C. The EEOC created a genuine dispute of material fact whether telework is a reasonable accommodation for Harris.

Alternatively, there is a genuine dispute of material fact whether Harris was qualified with the reasonable accommodation of telework. Many of Ford's arguments that telework would not be a reasonable accommodation for Harris confuse flex-time arrangements—when an employee might work after regular business hours or on the weekends—with telework during core business hours only—when Ford's offices are open. Harris's request can be construed as a request to telework during core business hours only. If Harris teleworked during core business hours only, Ford's concerns that she could not access pricing information from other Ford employees or be available to interact with team members would not arise. . . .

[The dissent also argued that Ford's efforts to accommodate did not satisfy its obligations to pursue an interactive process.]

NOTES

1. *A Bleeding Edge Decision.* The overturned panel decision was a dramatic departure from most of the circuit court authority on the issue of whether physical presence was an essential function of most jobs in the modern workplace. The panel majority was, therefore, breaking new ground—although it stressed that its result was largely just a reflection of shifting practices in the workplace, often as a result of technological changes that meant that work no longer had to be rooted to a physical environment. The Sixth Circuit voted to take the case en banc, and restored the status quo ante in a decision that is very hostile to accommodations that excuse disabled workers from normal attendance requirements. Nevertheless, the analytical structure for ADA accommodation means that each case is to be decided individually, which means that absenteeism or telecommuting may be more viable in some settings than others, and a subsequent decision by the Sixth Circuit indicates precisely that *Hostettler v. Coll.*

of Wooster, 895 F.3d 844, 857 (6th Cir. 2018) ("full-time presence at work is not an essential function of a job simply because an employer says that it is. If it were otherwise, employers could refuse *any* accommodation that left an employee at work for fewer than 40 hours per week. That could mean denying leave for doctor's appointments, dialysis, therapy, or anything else that requires time away from work.").

2. *Essential Functions*. What makes a job function "essential"? The EEOC's regulations define the term to mean the "fundamental job duties," as opposed to the "marginal functions" of the job. Factors to consider in making that distinction are whether the position exists to perform the function, the number of employees available to perform it, and/or whether the function is highly specialized, thus requiring special expertise. In addition to the employer's job description, other evidence to consider includes, although it is not limited to, the employer's judgment, the amount of time spent performing the function, the work experience of people previously or currently in the job or similar jobs, and the terms of any collective bargaining agreement. *See* 29 C.F.R. §1630.2(n). Further, the fact that a function is performed rarely does not mean it is nonessential. *Hennagir v. Utah Dep't of Corr.*, 587 F.3d 1255 (10th Cir. 2009) (prison health care worker unable to complete emergency response training was not qualified to perform an essential job function no matter how rarely emergencies might arise).

Numerous cases find a disability to disqualify individuals from particular jobs. *See EEOC v. Picture People, Inc.*, 684 F.3d 981 (10th Cir. 2012) (employee, who was congenitally and profoundly deaf but communicated by writing notes, gesturing, pointing, and miming was not qualified to do the essential functions of a photo studio job—with or without accommodation—in interacting with customers and selling photo packages); *Shannon v. New York City Transit Auth.*, 332 F.3d 95 (2d Cir. 2003) (color-blind bus driver unable to perform essential functions of the job, which included recognizing traffic signals). *See generally* Michelle A. Travis, *Disqualifying Universality Under the Americans with Disabilities Act Amendments Act*, 2015 MICH. ST. L. REV. 1689.

3. *Showing Up*. It's sometimes said that the biggest factor in success is "showing up." *Ford* concurs, holding whether "showing up" was an essential function of at least this resale buyer job. Some would say that being present is often a way of doing a task, not the task itself. *See generally* Michelle A. Travis, *Recapturing the Transformative Potential of Employment Discrimination Law*, 62 WASH. & LEE L. REV. 3 (2005). But, as the majority makes clear, *Ford* is in the mainstream and the dissent is the outlier. Although short-term leaves with a fixed endpoint may be a reasonable accommodation for some disabilities, *cf. Murphy v. Samson Res. Co.*, 525 F. App'x 703 (10th Cir. 2013) ("a leave of absence is not a reasonable accommodation where, as here, an employee continues to seek leave and it is uncertain if or when she will be able to return to work"), most courts have drawn the line at requiring employers to accommodate employees by permitting them to work remotely or use flex-time to a greater extent than other workers. These issues are played out well in *Ford*'s majority and dissent. Who has the better of the argument?

By the way, note that the ADAAA does not bear directly on this issue since it did not amend the statute with respect to "qualified" or "reasonable accommodation." Of course, one could argue that the broad purpose of the ADAAA was to make the ADA more effective, which could support the dissent. Or one could argue that Congress was presumably aware of the numerous cases holding that showing up was an essential function and chose not to alter that interpretation.

4. *Mixing Concepts.* A court approaching the qualifications questions often is confronted with two questions: Can the plaintiff perform the job without accommodation, and, if not, can he perform it with accommodation? Because accommodation can bear on the qualified question, the two concepts are often inextricably intertwined. Nevertheless, this reality can create confusion—as *Ford* illustrates. If attendance is not an essential function, Harris might be qualified to do her job without any accommodation. Second, even if plaintiff were unable to do her job if Ford treated her as it treated other employees (limited telecommuting), she might be able to perform the work if Ford were to allow her to telecommute more often, that is to say, she would be qualified after a reasonable accommodation was provided. Dividing the world this way is pretty artificial, isn't it, at least in this case? After all, the only way plaintiff could do her job remotely is if she were to telecommute. Or is the point Professor Travis's: Presence is a *way* of performing, not the *task* that is being performed?

5. *Job Descriptions & Business Judgment.* The outcome in *Ford* may be explained less by a neutral evaluation of the facts than by the level of deference the respective opinions accord the employer's views of what's essential to perform the job. The ADA itself suggests some deference: §12111(8) states that "consideration shall be given to the employer's judgment as to what functions of a job are essential" and that written job descriptions prepared prior to advertising or interviewing applicants "shall be considered evidence of the essential functions of the job." But such documentation is only "evidence." Doesn't that term suggest that the court can look behind what the employer says is essential?

To some extent this is certainly true. What is important is not necessarily what the employer claims to be an essential function but rather whether the employer treats a function as essential. *See Carmona v. Sw. Airlines Co.*, 604 F.3d 848 (5th Cir. 2010) (although unable to work regularly, plaintiff could perform the essential functions of his job as a flight attendant when he did work, and the employer's lenient policy regarding attendance allowed the jury to find that that was sufficient). On the other hand, there is little doubt that many courts seem to bend over backwards to defer to the employer's claims about essential job functions. *See generally* Michelle A. Travis, *Disqualifying Universality Under the Americans with Disabilities Act Amendments Act*, 2015 MICH. ST. L. REV. 1689. Who gets the deference question right in *Ford*?

6. *Who Proves What?* A plaintiff is not protected by the ADA unless she can perform the essential functions of the job. That would suggest that she has to establish what the essential functions are and her ability to perform them. Note, however, that the *Ford* majority put the burden on the employee to prove that attendance was essential, and other courts agree. *E.g., Supinski v. UPS*, 413 F. App'x 536, 540 (3d Cir. 2011); *Rehrs v. Iams Co.*, 486 F.3d 353, 356 (8th Cir. 2007).

With respect to reasonable accommodation, the plaintiff has the burden of showing that some accommodation is reasonable, while the defendant has the burden of establishing that a reasonable accommodation is an undue hardship. This may seem odd, and indeed it is: How can something both be reasonable and unduly burdensome? The Supreme Court's explanation is, essentially, that plaintiff's burden is "only [to] show that an 'accommodation' seems reasonable on its face, i.e., ordinarily or in the run of cases," at which point the employer "then must show special (typically case-specific) circumstances that demonstrate undue hardship in the particular circumstances." *US Airways, Inc. v. Barnett*, 535 U.S. 391, 401-02 (2002). *Contra* Hawkins v. *Schwan's Home Serv.*, 778 F.3d 877, 879 (10th Cir. 2015) (while the employer may have a burden of production on essential functions, plaintiff failed to carry his burden of persuasion that driving a truck was not essential, even though he had performed his work for more than two years without driving a truck).

7. *Quality and Quantity of Work as Essential.* Suppose an individual can perform all the essential job tasks but cannot meet the speed or quality standards set by the employer. The Interpretive Guidance provides:

> [T]he inquiry into essential functions is not intended to second guess an employer's business judgment with regard to production standards, whether qualitative or quantitative, nor to require employers to lower such standards. . . . If an employer requires its typists to be able to accurately type 75 words per minute, it will not be called upon to explain why an inaccurate work product, or a typing speed of 65 words per minute, would not be adequate. . . . However, if an employer does require accurate 75 word per minute typing . . ., it will have to show that it actually imposes such requirements on its employees in fact, and not simply on paper.

29 C.F.R. pt. 1630, app. §1630.2(n); *see Milton v. Scrivner, Inc.*, 53 F.3d 1118 (10th Cir. 1995) (pace set by employer's new production standard constituted an essential function of grocery selector job). What arguments would you make on essential functions on behalf of a dyslexic lawyer who produces a good work product but is denied partnership on the basis of (relatively) low productivity? Is she a qualified individual with a disability? Note that the statute prohibits discriminatory qualification standards unless job-related for the position in question and consistent with business necessity and the duty of reasonable accommodation. *See* 42 U.S.C. §12112(b)(6) (2014). Is the Interpretive Guidance consistent with this statutory provision?

8. *Associational Discrimination.* Even if an employee is not herself disabled under any of the three prongs, she may still not be discriminated against because of her relationship with a person who is disabled. 42 U.S.C. §12112(b)(4) bars discrimination against "a qualified individual because of the known disability of an individual with whom the qualified individual is known to have a relationship or association." In this scenario, the protected person must be qualified, but the disabled person need not be.

For example, in *Dewitt v. Proctor Hosp.*, 517 F.3d 944 (7th Cir. 2008), a claim of discrimination on account of the plaintiff's association with her disabled husband was allowed to proceed where there was evidence that her discharge was an effort to avoid the high costs of her husband's cancer treatment; her supervisor's comments about "creative" cost-cutting and her suggestion that less expensive hospice care be considered, coupled with plaintiff's discharge shortly after review of medical claims, allowed inference that employer was concerned that husband might require treatment indefinitely. *See also Trujillo v. PacifiCorp*, 524 F.3d 1149 (10th Cir. 2008) (married employees raised factual issue as to whether the alleged reason for their discharges was a pretext for avoiding the high costs of their son's medical expenses). In *Dewitt*, Judge Posner concurred, suggesting, however, that, if the employer would have discriminated against anyone who ran up such high medical bills, there would have been no discrimination on the basis of disability. What do you think of that argument?

3.   The Duty of Reasonable Accommodation

We have seen that a qualified individual with a disability is one who can perform the essential functions of the job she holds or desires—with or without reasonable accommodation. The concept of reasonable accommodation distinguishes the ADA from other antidiscrimination statutes. Under the ADA, it is not enough for an employer to treat its disabled employees the same—no better and no worse—than it treats its nondisabled employees. In appropriate circumstances, the employer must take affirmative steps that will allow disabled employees to perform their jobs—it must provide a "reasonable accommodation" where that will not result in "undue hardship." Failing to provide reasonable accommodations constitutes one form of discrimination under the statute.

While we have necessarily met the duty to reasonably accommodate as part of the "qualified" inquiry, we defer further consideration of it until Chapter 10, which discusses that question together with the Family and Medical Leave Act, the other major statute requiring employers to accommodate certain personal needs of their employees.

But it is important to remember that sometimes what might be viewed as a failure to accommodate could instead be analyzed as garden-variety discrimination. Thus, some courts have stressed that there is no ADA duty of accommodation (as opposed to the prohibition of discrimination) when the employer has a policy of excusing workers from all or some of their duties when they are temporarily incapacitated. In such cases, failure to treat a disabled worker equally is impermissible. *See Duello v. Buchanan County Bd. of Supervisors*, 628 F.3d 968, 974 (8th Cir. 2010) (employee failed to adduce evidence that the employer regularly excused workers from operating heavy machinery when they were temporarily unable to do so).

4. Discriminatory Qualification Standards

The ADA prohibits the use of discriminatory standards or selection criteria in hiring and classifying employees. Section 102(b) provides that "discriminate" includes

> 3. utilizing standards, criteria, or methods of administration . . . that have the effect of discrimination on the basis of disability, . . .
> 6. using qualification standards, employment tests, or other selection criteria that screen out or tend to screen out an individual with a disability or a class of individuals with disabilities unless the standard, test or other selection criteria, as used by the covered entity, is shown to be job-related for the position in question and is consistent with business necessity. . . .

Employers have at least three possible defenses to an allegation of discrimination under this definition. First, the language of the prohibition on discriminatory standards and selection criteria is reminiscent of disparate impact under Title VII; not surprisingly, ADA regulations indicate that both paragraphs are subject to a job-relatedness and business necessity defense similar to that permitted in disparate impact cases. *See* 29 C.F.R. §§1630.7, 1630.10. Section 103(a), however, which sets forth defenses, provides that the use of criteria with a disparate impact on the basis of disability must also be consistent with the employer's duty to provide reasonable accommodation. *See* 29 C.F.R. §1630.15(b)(1), (c). Second, standards or selection criterion may also be defended on the basis that they are permitted or required by another federal statute or regulation. *See* 29 C.F.R. §1630.15(e). Third, ADA §103(b) provides that "[t]he term 'qualification standards' may include a requirement that an individual shall not pose a direct threat to the health or safety of other individuals in the workplace."

In short, qualification standards that are either facially discriminatory or that have a disparate impact on disabled individuals can violate the ADA, but all discriminatory qualification standards may be defended as job-related and consistent with business necessity, permitted or required by another federal statute or regulation, or necessary to prevent a direct threat to health and safety.

Most challenges to qualification standards do not raise significant factual issues about whether the challenged standard or criteria actually screens out disabled individuals. Challenged standards frequently are facially discriminatory, such as vision requirements for drivers. Even standards or criteria that do not expressly implicate a disabling impairment are generally challenged on the ground that a disabled individual cannot meet the standard because of his or her disability. Thus, the fact that the standard or criteria screens out an individual with a disability is obvious. The primary issue in these cases, therefore, is whether the discriminatory standard or criteria can be defended.

This section first examines the direct threat defense. Second, it considers the job-relatedness and business necessity defense as applied to qualification standards that screen out disabled individuals, including those promulgated by the federal government. Finally, it addresses the disparate impact theory in disability discrimination cases.

a. Direct Threat

ADA §103(b) provides that "[t]he term 'qualification standards' may include a requirement that an individual shall not pose a direct threat to the health or safety of other individuals in the workplace." Direct threat is defined by §101(3) as a "significant risk to the health or safety of others" that cannot be eliminated by a reasonable accommodation. The EEOC requires the "direct threat" determination to be based on a reasonable medical judgment that considers such factors as the duration of the risk, the nature and severity of the potential harm, the likelihood of the potential harm, and the imminence of the potential harm. *See* 29 C.F.R. §1630.2(r). Direct threat is simultaneously relevant to whether the individual with a disability is "qualified" to perform essential functions, whether the employer is justified in basing an employment decision on the individual's disability, and whether the employer has a duty to accommodate the individual's disability. It seems likely that the employer has the burden of proof on this issue. *EEOC v. Wal-Mart Stores, Inc.*, 477 F.3d 561 (8th Cir. 2007); *contra LaChance v. Duffy's Draft House, Inc.*, 146 F.3d 832, 835 (11th Cir. 1998) (plaintiff must prove absence of direct threat).

The ADA's "direct threat" provision is derived from the Supreme Court's decision in *School Board of Nassau County v. Arline*, 480 U.S. 273 (1987), which was decided under §504 of the Rehabilitation Act. The Court held that an individual with tuberculosis was not otherwise qualified to be an elementary school teacher if she posed a significant risk of transmitting the disease to others and if that risk could not be eliminated through reasonable accommodation. In *Bragdon v. Abbott*, 524 U.S. 624 (1998), the defendant, a dentist, asserted that whether a risk is significant is to be assessed from the point of view of the person denying the service.

The Court, however, stated that such assessments are to be made on the basis of medical or other objective evidence available at the time that the allegedly discriminatory action occurred. A good-faith belief that a significant risk exists is not enough, nor would any special deference be afforded a defendant who is himself a medical professional.

The EEOC's regulation interpreting "direct threat" defines the term to include "a significant risk of substantial harm to the health or safety *of the individual or others* that cannot be eliminated or reduced by reasonable accommodation." 29 C.F.R. §1630.2(r). (Emphasis added.) The validity of that regulation was at issue in *Chevron U.S.A. Inc. v. Echazabal*, 536 U.S. 73 (2002). Echazabal suffered from hepatitis C, which caused severe liver damage. Chevron had refused to hire him because the position in question involved exposure to toxins in Chevron's refinery that posed elevated risk of harm to his damaged liver. The trial court granted summary judgment for Chevron based on the EEOC's regulation, but the Ninth Circuit invalidated that regulation. Since the ADA specifically provided for a "threat to others" defense, but was silent on the issue of "threat to self," the Ninth Circuit reasoned that Congress intended to exclude "threat to self." The Supreme Court disagreed, since the text of the statute suggests that an employer's qualification standards "may include," but not be limited to, harm to others. Second, the Court held that there is no evidence that Congress made a deliberate choice to omit "threat to self" from the affirmative defense's scope.

While *Echazabal* involved one direct-threat issue, others often arise in the workplace. Thus, courts assessing the risk of hiring HIV-infected individuals have reached different results depending on the nature of the work involved. *Compare Chalk v. United States Dist. Court*, 840 F.2d 701 (9th Cir. 1988) (teacher with AIDS did not pose a "significant risk" in the workplace and his condition could be monitored to ensure that any secondary infections he contracted also would not pose a significant risk), *with Waddell v. Valley Forge Dental Assocs.*, 276 F.3d 1275 (11th Cir. 2001) (HIV-positive dental hygienist posed a direct threat to the health and safety of others).

The direct-threat defense is often raised in the context of employees with mental disabilities. In *The ADA, The Workplace, and the Myth of the "Dangerous Mentally Ill,"* 34 U.C. DAVIS L. REV. 849, 850-51 (2001), Professor Ann Hubbard notes that public fears concerning persons with mental disabilities are strikingly disproportionate to the risk of violence actually posed and cautioned that a direct-threat defense may not be based on erroneous risk assessments. *See also* Jane Byeff Korn, *Crazy (Mental Illness Under the ADA)*, 36 U. MICH. J.L. REFORM 585 (2003); Ann Hubbard, *Understanding and Implementing the ADA's Direct Threat Defense*, 95 NW. U. L. REV. 1279 (2001).

Another issue that arises in connection with a direct-threat situation is whether the risk can be reasonably accommodated. For instance, can an accommodation that would reduce health or safety risks be unreasonable because of the burden it would place on co-workers? Suppose co-workers could protect themselves against an individual's contagious disease by being vaccinated, wearing face masks and plastic gloves, or avoiding close contact with the person with a disability? *See Treadwell v. Alexander*, 707 F.2d 473 (11th Cir. 1983) (a proposed accommodation that would result in substantially increased workloads for co-workers was unreasonable); *cf.* 29 C.F.R. pt. 1630, app. §1630.15(d) (describing accommodations that are an undue hardship).

b. Job-related and Consistent with Business Necessity

If a qualification standard excludes disabled individuals, it may still be permissible when it is "job-related and consistent with business necessity." In *Albertsons, Inc. v. Kirkingburg*, 527 U.S. 555 (1999), the employer fired the plaintiff from his job as a commercial truck driver because he failed to meet federal vision standards. Kirkingburg sued his employer under the ADA when it failed to rehire him after he attained a waiver from the Department of Transportation ("DOT") that would have licensed him despite his condition. Kirkingburg contended that the ADA forbids an employer from requiring as a job qualification that an employee meet a federal standard when that employee obtained a waiver of the applicable standard. The Supreme Court held that "it was error to read the regulations establishing the waiver program as modifying the content of the basic visual acuity standard in a way that disentitled an employer like Albertsons to insist on it." *Id.* at 571. The Court added that the waiver program was an "experiment" without "empirical evidence," and it would not require an employer to participate. Justice Thomas concurred in the judgment on the grounds that Kirkingburg was not a "qualified individual with a disability" since he did not meet the minimum visual acuity level required by the government.

Kirkingburg thus holds that employers hiring drivers covered by DOT's regulations may adopt blanket rules excluding drivers who do not meet DOT's physical requirements. In other words, individualized assessments are not required in this context, and the employer need not present evidence of the job-relatedness or business necessity of the qualification. *Cf.* 29 C.F.R. §1630.15(e) (1998) (providing that compliance with another federal law or regulation is a defense to liability under the ADA).

Bates v. UPS, 511 F.3d 974 (9th Cir. 2007) (en banc), approached the questions of justification more generally. It first rejected a BFOQ analysis (which the court had previously adopted). Instead:

> To show "job-relatedness," an employer must demonstrate that the qualification standard fairly and accurately measures the individual's actual ability to perform the essential functions of the job. When every person excluded by the qualification standard is a member of a protected class—that is, disabled persons—an employer must demonstrate a predictive or significant correlation between the qualification and performance of the job's essential functions.
>
> To show that the disputed qualification standard is "consistent with business necessity," the employer must show that it "substantially promote[s]" the business's needs. "The 'business necessity' standard is quite high, and is not to be confused with mere expediency." For a safety-based qualification standard, "[i]n evaluating whether the risks addressed by . . . [the] qualification standard constitute a business necessity, the court should take into account the magnitude of possible harm as well as the probability of occurrence."
>
> Finally, to show that "performance cannot be accomplished by reasonable accommodation," the employer must demonstrate either that no reasonable accommodation currently available would cure the performance deficiency or that such reasonable accommodation poses an "undue hardship" on the employer.

Id. at 996 (citations and footnotes omitted). The court then turned to the qualification standard allocation of burdens of proof, which it viewed as parallel to those for the direct-threat defense. It explained:

> Because UPS has linked hearing with safe driving, UPS bears the burden to prove that nexus as part of its defense to use of the hearing qualification standard. The employees,

however, bear the ultimate burden to show that they are qualified to perform the essential function of safely driving a package car. . . .

By requiring UPS to justify the hearing test under the business necessity defense, but also requiring plaintiffs to show that they can perform the essential functions of the job, we are not saying, nor does the ADA require, that employers must hire employees who cannot safely perform the job, particularly where safety itself is an essential function. Nor are we saying that an employer can never impose a safety standard that exceeds minimum requirements imposed by law. However, when an employer asserts a blanket safety-based qualification standard—beyond the essential job function—that is not mandated by law and that qualification standard screens out or tends to screen out an individual with a disability, the employer—not the employee—bears the burden of showing that the higher qualification standard is job-related and consistent with business necessity, and that performance cannot be achieved through reasonable accommodation.

Id. at 992. *See also Atkins v. Salazar*, 677 F.3d 667 (5th Cir. 2011) (upholding as business necessity certain physical requirements for park rangers).

c. Disparate Impact

Disparate impact discrimination is applicable under the ADA. For example, in *Raytheon Company v. Hernandez*, 540 U.S. 44 (2003), plaintiff was forced to resign from defendant's employ after testing positive for cocaine. Two years later, he reapplied for employment, but his application was denied. The company contended it had a policy of refusing to rehire anyone who had been terminated for violation of workplace conduct rules. The Supreme Court ruled the Ninth Circuit had mistakenly treated this as a disparate treatment claim when it was at most a disparate impact analysis. To the extent that a neutral policy (no rehiring of discharged workers) resulted in not rehiring addicts, it was not because of intentional discrimination against the disabled but because a neutral rule disproportionately affected them. While the Court recognized that disparate impact is viable under the ADA, its opinion left unexamined whether the defendant's "no rehire" policy would run afoul of the statute under disparate impact analysis because the plaintiff had not properly pled the disparate impact claim. *See* Elizabeth Roseman, Comment, *A Phoenix from the Ashes? Heightened Pleading Requirements in Disparate Impact Cases*, 36 SETON HALL L. REV. 1043 (2006). It also did not reach the question of whether the ADA requires an employer to bend neutral rehiring policies as a form of reasonable accommodation of a disabled worker. *See generally* Christine Neylon O'Brien, *Facially Neutral No-Rehire Rules and the Americans with Disabilities Act*, 22 HOFSTRA LAB. & EMP. L.J. 114 (2004).

Framing reasonable accommodation claims as disparate impact claims can in some cases raise difficult policy issues. Consider, for example, the request of a covered individual for extra sick leave to deal with medical problems. Restricting sick leave would not directly exclude the person from work, but it might make it more difficult for her to schedule doctor's appointments, or more expensive because she must take unpaid personal days to see the doctor. As a consequence, this type of policy could result in fewer disabled persons being employed. This policy would "impact" individuals with disabilities because their needs differ from those of other individuals. Should disparate impact liability apply to claims like this?

The closest the Court has come to answering this is *Alexander v. Choate*, 469 U.S. 287 (1985), decided under the Rehabilitation Act. There, the Court rejected the claim that the Tennessee Medicaid Program's 14-day limitation on inpatient coverage would have an unlawful disparate impact on the disabled. How might *Choate* affect a claim by an individual with a disability for more sick leave than other individuals receive? Under the ADA, can such an employee attack a sick leave policy that restricts paid leave to 14 days on the ground that the policy has a disparate impact on employees with disabilities? The EEOC suggests that such a claim is not viable, but that an employee affected by such a policy may be entitled to leave as a reasonable accommodation:

> It should be noted, however, that some uniformly applied employment policies or practices, such as leave policies, are not subject to challenge under the adverse impact theory. "No-leave" policies (e.g., no leave during the first six months of employment) are likewise not subject to challenge under the adverse impact theory. However, an employer, in spite of its "no-leave" policy, may, in appropriate circumstances, have to consider the provision of leave to an employee with a disability as a reasonable accommodation, unless the provision of leave would impose an undue hardship.

29 C.F.R. pt. 1630, app. §1630.15(c). Does this mean that the policy is legal but that accommodation is always required unless it is an undue hardship? Is there much difference between that view and declaring the policy illegal vis-à-vis the disabled except where undue hardship exists, which would then make the policy a business necessity?

Note on a Rock and a Hard Place

When a disabled worker is discharged, she often needs to seek disability benefits, typically Social Security disability. Eligibility for such benefits is generally contingent on inability to work. This creates a tension between the disabled worker's claim that she is sufficiently disabled to be eligible for those benefits and her possible ADA challenge to the discharge, which requires that she be a "qualified individual." In *Cleveland v. Policy Management Systems Corporation*, 526 U.S. 795 (1999), the plaintiff lost her job after suffering a stroke. She then filed a Social Security Disability Insurance ("SSDI") claim since she was "unable to work" because of her "condition." *Id.* at 798. After receiving those benefits, the plaintiff filed an ADA claim against her employer for failing to provide her with "reasonable accommodations" so that she could have continued to perform her essential job functions. *Id.* Although the lower courts had held that a plaintiff cannot maintain two inconsistent positions for the purposes of SSDI and the ADA, the Supreme Court determined that a plaintiff's claim of total disability under the SSDI does not necessarily bar the plaintiff from filing an ADA claim for failure to make reasonable accommodations. *Id.* at 803. The Court stated that a plaintiff can be "unable to work" for purposes of the SSDI, and still may have been able to work if the employer had made "reasonable accommodations." *Id.* The Court noted that factual or legal inconsistencies must be explained by the plaintiff for the claim to survive summary judgment. *Id.* at 806.

After *Cleveland*, courts no longer presume that a claim for disability benefits is necessarily inconsistent with an ADA claim but instead closely examine the factual statements made in the benefits proceedings. *See, e.g., Smith v. Clark Cnty. Sch. Dist.,* 727 F.3d 950 (9th Cir. 2013) *Kiely v. Heartland Rehabilitation Services Inc.,* 359 F.3d 386 (6th Cir. 2004). Suppose an employer requires employees who seek employer-provided disability benefits to sign a statement asserting, "I cannot perform the essential functions of any job with or without reasonable accommodation." Will signing such a statement bar a subsequent ADA claim?

If you were advising a discharged employee who you believe has a viable claim for disability discrimination, would you advise him to seek disability benefits? What factors would go into your advice?

G. PROCEDURES AND REMEDIES

Title VII creates an amalgam of methods—administrative and judicial—for enforcement of its substantive proscriptions, which both the ADA and ADEA follow with a few variations. The basic Title VII procedures for enforcement of the substantive rights it creates are found in 42 U.S.C. §2000e-5 (2014) and are very complicated, especially for unrepresented individuals. Many of the complications arise from two distinct periods of limitation, which together mean that it is relatively easy for a plaintiff to get to court after it's too late. *See generally* Charles A. Sullivan & Lauren Walter, Employment Discrimination Law & Practice (2008), ch. 12.

Title VII time limitations were forced onto the national stage by *Ledbetter v. Goodyear Tire & Rubber Co.,* 550 U.S. 618 (2007), which held that Title VII's charge filing period begins to run when the employee is notified of an adverse employment decision. In the case itself, the plaintiff, who had won a jury verdict, had learned about her raise (but not the raises of her male co-workers) years before she filed her charge. *Ledbetter*'s rejection of her claim struck a nerve both on the Court and in Congress. Justice Ginsburg read a strong dissent from the bench in which she called on Congress to override the majority, and Congress responded with the Lilly Ledbetter Fair Pay Act of 2009 ("FPA"), Pub. L. No. 111-2, §3, 123 Stat. 5, 5-6 (2009). The FPA, however, while both retroactive and applicable to other antidiscrimination laws, is limited to expanding the governing limitations period only for "a discriminatory compensation decision or other practice," thus leaving other acts of discrimination still subject to very complex and very rigorous limitations periods. *See generally* Charles A. Sullivan *Raising the Dead?: The Lilly Ledbetter Fair Pay Act,* 84 Tul. L. Rev. 499 (2010) (examining the statutory scheme and arguing for a "causation-only" interpretation of the FPA).

Most suits under the antidiscrimination laws are individual disparate treatment claims brought by private persons. But the EEOC may also sue (recall *Ford*), and, as we saw in connection with the two systemic theories, class actions are often invoked to prosecute systemic claims. In such settings, the complications of discrimination law are magnified by the complications of class action law. All of this came to a head before the Supreme Court in *Wal-Mart Stores, Inc. v. Dukes,* 564 U.S. 338 (2011), which both tightened the "commonality" requirements for class actions under Federal Rule of Civil Procedure 23(a) and required most such suits to be certified under Rule 23(b)(3), which requires notice to class members and an opportunity for them to opt out of the class. There is little doubt that this has been a major blow to private enforcement, although class actions continue to be certified. *See generally* Joseph A. Seiner, *Weathering Wal-Mart*, 89 Notre Dame L. Rev. 1343 (2014). Title VII, §1981, the ADEA, and Title I of the ADA have similar, but distinct, remedial schemes. *See generally* Sullivan & Walter, ch. 13. As a result, the availability of, and limitations on, different forms of relief vary from statute to statute. Generally speaking, however, the statutes offer a successful plaintiff the possibility of instatement or reinstatement (with appropriate seniority) as well as back pay and attorneys' fees. In appropriate cases, front pay (the same as back pay but measured from the time of judgment to the time the plaintiff resumes her rightful position) is also available. *See Pollard v. E. I. du Pont de Nemours & Co.*, 532 U.S. 843 (2001). However, back pay awards under all the statutes are to be reduced by amounts that were earned and could have been earned with reasonable diligence through alternative employment.

Title VII, the ADA, and §1981 also offer compensatory and punitive damages, although both are capped under Title VII and the ADA. *See Pollard v. E. I. du Pont de Nemours & Co.*, 532 U.S. 843 (2001); Rebecca Hollander-Blumoff & Matthew T. Bodie, *The Effects of Jury Ignorance About Damage Caps: The Case of the 1991 Civil Rights Act*, 90 Iowa L. Rev. 1365 (2005). But neither is available under the ADEA, which instead offers potential double recovery under the term "liquidated damages." Where available, compensatory damages include emotional injury.

Punitive damages may be awarded only upon a showing of "malice" or "reckless indifference" by an employer. *Kolstad v. American Dental Ass'n*, 527 U.S. 526 (1999). *See generally* Joseph Seiner, *The Failure of Punitive Damages in Employment Discrimination Cases: A Call for Change*, 50 Wm. & Mary L. Rev. 735 (2008); Stacy A. Hickox, *In Reduction of Punitive Damages for Employment Discrimination: Are Courts Ignoring Our Juries?*, 54 Mercer L. Rev. 1081, 1121 (2003).

A final remedial issue is whether the person who committed the discriminatory act has personal liability or whether liability is limited to the employer. *Miller v. Maxwell's Int'l, Inc.*, 991 F.2d 583 (9th Cir. 1993), held that neither Title VII nor the ADEA imposes personal liability. The court reasoned that these statutes are addressed to "employers," and even though this term is defined to include "agents" of the employer, this inclusion was intended to incorporate the doctrine of respondeat superior. Moreover, because both statutes exempt small employers from coverage, the court thought it "inconceivable" that Congress would have intended to impose liability on individual employees. Other appellate decisions have agreed that supervisory employees do not have personal liability to the discriminatee under Title VII, ADA Title I, and the ADEA. But employees do have personal liability to the discriminatee under §1981 and may be reachable under state law analogs to the federal discrimination laws. *See generally* Rebecca Hanner White, *Vicarious and Personal Liability for Employment Discrimination*, 30 Ga. L. Rev. 509 (1996).

10

Accommodating Workers' Lives

This chapter addresses the obligations that arise when employees require some accommodation in order to meet the demands of the workplace. Of course, many familiar employment practices can be viewed as accommodating the needs of some classes of workers while also meeting the needs of employers. For example, part-time work may allow some workers—for instance, parents of young children, and mothers in particular—more flexibility while enabling employers to tailor labor costs more closely to demand. "Seasonal" work also allows matching the needs of employees who cannot work all year (e.g., students) to fill employer needs during peak demand. "Temporary" work (a word that reflects actual expectations rather than legal status given the ubiquity of the at-will rule) also allows a better matching of employer needs and employee availability than the more traditional full-time, full-year job. Finally, working from home, which has grown substantially with the advent of technology, reduces employer overhead and may maximize worker convenience especially for workers who are unable to commute to the traditional workplace due to physical problems or family commitments. Literally millions of individuals work in each of these statuses. *See generally* Katherine V.W. Stone, *Legal Protections for Atypical Employees: Employment Law for Workers Without Workplaces and Employees Without Employers*, 27 Berkeley J. Emp. & Lab. L. 251, 255-56 (2006).

However, such employment structures are not without their problems. In Chapter 1, for example, we saw that "temp" help has morphed in some areas from its traditional form—rather than providing truly short-term workers, the agency provides "leased" workers on a long-term basis. In such structures neither the employee nor the workplace at which she labors views the arrangement as temporary. Rather, the relationship is recast to shift costs and risks from the firm at which the contingent workers labor to the "employer" who leases them to that firm. And part-time employment has been criticized as frequently a device used to reduce labor costs not only by paying workers (usually female) lower rates than full-time workers but also by denying them fringe benefits such as health insurance. Similarly, seasonal work, while a useful mechanism for matching the needs of employers and employees in many sectors of the economy, also generates huge social problems as "migrant workers" crisscross the country as employment opportunities open and close. Finally, working from home has strong positives and strong negatives since telecommuting uses both very high-value employees and very low-value workers, such as telemarketers.

Beyond such structures, and the focus of this chapter, is the question of the extent to which the law does, or should, require employers to "accommodate" the differing needs of individuals who aspire to be as "normal" or "regular" as their circumstances permit. The two primary examples are workers with family caretaking responsibilities, in particular pregnant women and mothers, and disabled individuals, who may be able to perform effectively if the employer accommodates their disabilities. *See generally* Nicole Buonocore Porter, *Accommodating Everyone*, 47 SETON HALL L. REV. 85 (2016) (arguing for universal accommodations but with a less demanding undue hardship exception for less compelling reasons); Nicole Buonocore Porter, *Mutual Marginalization: Individuals with Disabilities and Workers with Caregiving Responsibilities*, 6 FLA. L. REV. 1099 (2014). While a pregnant worker will usually be physically incapacitated for a relatively short time, the intermittent disruption caused by several pregnancies and the continuing demands of childcare create difficulties for many women far beyond any period of physical incapacity. Some difficulties may be traced to employer perceptions about the "commitment" of mothers or the "distractions" children represent for mothers, but many women face significant challenges in managing their professional and personal lives beyond those addressed by the antidiscrimination mandates. Put simply, treating mothers equally with fathers will often not result in equality of outcomes.

As for the disabled, the courts originally gave a narrow construction to the definition of "disability" under the original Americans with Disabilities Act ("ADA"), meaning that the duty of accommodation imposed by that Act reached relatively few individuals. With the 2008 passage of the Americans with Disabilities Amendments Act ("ADAAA"), the protected class of those with "actual" disabilities was greatly expanded, even though the new statute also made clear that there was no need to accommodate those who were merely "regarded as" disabled rather than actually disabled. *See* Chapter 9. The result is a renewed focus on accommodating individuals who have difficulty meeting the normal demands of a workplace but who could provide effective work if they were accommodated.

Similarly, feminists argue that Title VII's prohibition of pregnancy discrimination has had limited success because problems for women's success are posed less by the demands of pregnancy and the first few months of infant care than by the continuing demands on women's time and attention of raising a family and, increasingly, taking care of elderly parents. *See also* Peggie R. Smith, *Elder Care, Gender, and Work: The Work-Family Issue of the 21st Century*, 25 BERKELEY J. EMP. & LAB. L. 351 (2004). While some men face similar challenges in reconciling the demands of home and the workplace, such responsibilities still fall disproportionately on women.

The law's response to this problem has been very limited but nevertheless highly controversial. The Family and Medical Leave Act ("FMLA") ensures 12 weeks of *unpaid* leave a year for a variety of purposes related to child-rearing and care for ill family members. The FMLA, however, covers larger employers only, applies to only relatively unusual life events (i.e., it does not permit leave for many garden-variety demands on worker time), and, in the end, provides only for unpaid leave, thus exacting a high price from the workers it protects.

Underlying this entire problem is the question of whether the traditional structure of most workplaces, which relies on permanent "full-time face-time" workers is necessary to productivity. *See* Michelle Travis, *Recapturing the Transformative*

Potential of Employment Discrimination Law, 62 WASH. & LEE L. REV. 3, 6 (2005). The business world's resistance to the FMLA, and the courts' narrow construction of both Title VII's prohibition of pregnancy discrimination and the ADA's definition of disability are predicated to a large extent on the perception that the traditional model of employment is not only natural but also necessary for American businesses to continue to be competitive in a global economy.

This chapter attempts to grapple with the questions of accommodating various needs relating to workers' lives. While the focus will be on current legal regimes, the student should keep in mind two points. First, for their own business reasons, firms may well take a more accommodationist stance than the law requires. For that reason, the law may prove ultimately to be far less important than economics; Michelle A. Travis, *What a Difference a Day Makes, or Does It? Work/Family Balance and the Four-Day Work Week*, 42 CONN. L. REV. 1223 (2010). Second, whatever the current state of the law, concern is increasing that it is not proactive enough in dealing with the legitimate life-cycle needs of the current workforce. Legal change has begun, and more may well be in the offing.

Section A deals with how the antidiscrimination laws bear on workers needing certain types of accommodations, briefly discussing the Title VII duty of reasonable accommodation of religion and then focusing on the more robust ADA duty of reasonable accommodation of disability. This sets the stage for section B, which considers the extent to which the general prohibition of sex discrimination under Title VII and the Pregnancy Discrimination Act may assist mothers in the workplace. It then turns to the FMLA, which protects both men and women whose health problems or family issues collide with the demands of the workplace.

A. ACCOMMODATION UNDER THE AMERICANS WITH DISABILITIES ACT

Title VII imposes very limited obligations on employers to address the needs of employees seeking accommodations. As we will see, the statute bars discrimination on the basis of pregnancy, but it merely requires equal treatment of pregnant workers—there is no requirement that pregnancy or childbirth, much less child-rearing, be accommodated.

One provision of Title VII does mandate that employers "reasonably accommodate" the religious practices and beliefs of their employees, but this command has been read so narrowly as to pose few demands on employers. Section 701(j) provides:

> The term "religion" includes all aspects of religious observance and practice, as well as belief, unless an employer demonstrates that he is unable to reasonably accommodate to an employee's or prospective employee's religious observance or practice without undue hardship on the conduct of the employer's business.

See also EEOC v. Abercrombie & Fitch Stores, Inc., 135 S. Ct. 2028 (2015) (failure to hire an individual because the employer suspected she might need a religious accommodation would violate Title VII). However, despite the apparent sweep of this provision, the Supreme Court has interpreted it to minimize its demands. Thus, *Trans World Airlines, Inc. v. Hardison*, 432 U.S. 63 (1977), upheld the discharge of an employee whose religion forbade him to work on his Sabbath. It rejected a variety of possible accommodations, including alterations in the seniority system established by a collective agreement. As for accommodations that would have left the seniority system intact, they, too, were not required since each involved some cost to the employer, and "[t]o require TWA to bear more than a de minimis cost in order to give Hardison Saturdays off is an undue hardship." *Id.* at 84. While the employee was free to seek shift-swaps from co-workers, honoring such voluntary swaps may often satisfy the employer's duty. *See also Ansonia Bd. of Educ. v. Philbrook*, 479 U.S. 60, 68 (1986) (employer's duty satisfied when it provides a reasonable accommodation even if not the worker's preferred accommodation). *See also Walker v. Indian River Transp. Co.*, No. 17-10501, 2018 U.S. App. LEXIS 20878, at *13-17 (11th Cir. July 27, 2018) (employer offered plaintiff a reasonable accommodation when it offered him a truck route that did not require Sunday work and thus eliminated the conflict between work requirements and religious practices, even though the new route paid less than the earlier one).

The ADA, although using basically the same language as Title VII's religion clause, nevertheless imposes a more robust duty of accommodation. Thus, it declares as discriminatory

> not making reasonable accommodations to the known physical or mental limitations of an otherwise qualified individual with a disability who is an applicant or employee, unless such covered entity can demonstrate that the accommodation would impose an undue hardship on the operation of the business of such covered entity. . . .

§12112(b)(5)(A). The duty is a species of strict liability since there need be no inquiry into employer intent. *See Punt v. Kelly Servs.*, 862 F.3d 1040, 1048 (10th Cir. 2017) (failure to provide a reasonable accommodation "establishes the required nexus between the disability and the alleged discrimination without the need to delve into the employer's subjective motivations." While the ADA is treated in more detail in Chapter 9, our present concern is not with the protected class (qualified individuals with disabilities) but with the employer's duty of accommodation. Under the current statute, qualified persons with "actual" disabilities must be accommodated; those who are only "regarded as" disabled may not be discriminated against on the basis of their impairment but need not be accommodated

The ADA's complicated structure makes reasonable accommodation relevant both to establishing and to defending against a failure to accommodate claim. As we saw in Chapter 9, a person with a statutory "disability" is protected only if he or she is a "qualified individual," which is in turn defined as "an individual with a disability who, with or without reasonable accommodation, can perform the essential functions of the employment position that such individual holds or desires." §12111(8). If a disabled individual can perform essential functions only with reasonable accommodation, the employer has a duty to provide those accommodations—short of an "undue hardship." While an employer need not accommodate the nonessential duties of a position other than excusing the employee from performing them, *Hoffman v. Caterpillar, Inc.*, 256 F.3d 568 (7th Cir. 2001), the ADA also requires employers to make existing facilities readily accessible to individuals with disabilities. *See Feist v. Louisiana, Dep't of Justice, Office of the Atty. Gen.*, 730 F.3d 450 (5th Cir. 2013) (a parking spot may be a reasonable accommodation for mobility-impaired worker). But if the disabled individual cannot perform the job without accommodations that are not reasonable or that impose an undue hardship, she or he is not a "qualified individual," and therefore disparate treatment on the basis of disability is permitted and accommodating the disability is not required.

What, then, is a "reasonable accommodation"? The statute provides that such accommodations include the following:

> (A) making existing facilities used by employees readily accessible to and usable by individuals with disabilities; and
> (B) job restructuring, part-time or modified work schedules, reassignment to a vacant position, acquisition or modification of equipment or devices, appropriate adjustment or modifications of examinations, training materials or policies, the provision of qualified readers or interpreters, and other similar accommodations for individuals with disabilities.

How far does "job restructuring" or "reassignment to a vacant position" go?

U.S. Airways, Inc. v. Barnett
535 U.S. 391 (2002)

Justice BREYER delivered the opinion of the Court.

The Americans with Disabilities Act of 1990 prohibits an employer from discriminating against an "individual with a disability" who, with "reasonable accommodation," can perform the essential functions of the job. This case, arising in the context of summary judgment, asks us how the Act resolves a potential conflict between: (1) the interests of a disabled worker who seeks assignment to a particular position as a "reasonable accommodation," and (2) the interests of other workers with superior rights to bid for the job under an employer's seniority system. In such a case, does the accommodation demand trump the seniority system?

In our view, the seniority system will prevail in the run of cases. As we interpret the statute, to show that a requested accommodation conflicts with the rules of a seniority system is ordinarily to show that the accommodation is not "reasonable." Hence such a showing will entitle an employer/defendant to summary judgment on the question—unless there is more. The plaintiff remains free to present evidence of special circumstances that make "reasonable" a seniority rule exception in the particular case. And such a showing will defeat the employer's demand for summary judgment.

I

In 1990, Robert Barnett, the plaintiff and respondent here, injured his back while working in a cargo-handling position at petitioner U.S. Airways, Inc. He invoked seniority rights and transferred to a less physically demanding mailroom position. Under U.S. Airways' seniority system, that position, like others, periodically became open to seniority-based employee bidding. In 1992, Barnett learned that at least two employees senior to him intended to bid for the mailroom job. He asked U.S. Airways to accommodate his disability-imposed limitations by making an exception that would allow him to remain in the mailroom. After permitting Barnett to continue his mailroom work for five months while it considered the matter, U.S. Airways eventually decided not to make an exception. And Barnett lost his job.

Barnett then brought this ADA suit claiming, among other things, that he was an "individual with a disability" capable of performing the essential functions of the mailroom job, that the mailroom job amounted to a "reasonable accommodation" of his disability, and that U.S. Airways, in refusing to assign him the job, unlawfully discriminated against him.

[The District Court granted summary judgment to U.S. Airways, stressing the decades-old use of a seniority system by USAir and that such seniority policies were common in the airline industry. In this context, "USAir employees were justified in relying upon the policy. As such, any significant alteration of that policy would result in undue hardship to both the company and its nondisabled employees." The Ninth Circuit reversed en banc, finding that a seniority system was merely a factor in a fact-intensive undue hardship analysis.]

II

In answering the question presented, we must consider the following statutory provisions. First, the ADA says that an employer may not "discriminate against a qualified individual with a disability." 42 U.S.C. §12112(a). Second, the ADA says that a "qualified" individual includes "an individual with a disability who, *with* or without *reasonable accommodation*, can perform the essential functions of" the relevant "employment position." §12111(8) (emphasis added). Third, the ADA says that "discrimination" includes an employer's "*not making reasonable accommodations* to the known physical or mental limitations of an otherwise qualified . . . employee, *unless* [the employer] can demonstrate that the accommodation would impose an *undue hardship* on the operation of [its] business." §12112(b)(5)(A) (emphasis added). Fourth, the ADA says that the term "'reasonable accommodation' may include . . . reassignment to a vacant position." §12111(9)(B).

The parties interpret this statutory language as applied to seniority systems in radically different ways. In US Airways' view, the fact that an accommodation would violate the rules of a seniority system always shows that the accommodation is not a "reasonable" one. In Barnett's polar opposite view, a seniority system violation never shows that an accommodation sought is not a "reasonable" one. Barnett concedes that a violation of seniority rules might help to show that the accommodation will work "undue" employer "hardship," but that is a matter for an employer to demonstrate case by case. . . .

A

U.S. Airways' claim that a seniority system virtually always trumps a conflicting accommodation demand rests primarily upon its view of how the Act treats workplace "preferences." Insofar as a requested accommodation violates a disability-neutral workplace rule, such as a seniority rule, it grants the employee with a disability treatment that other workers could not receive. Yet the Act, U.S. Airways says, seeks only "equal" treatment for those with disabilities. *See, e.g.*, 42 U.S.C. §12101(a)(9). It does not, it contends, require an employer to grant preferential treatment. *Cf.* H. R. Rep. No. 101-485, pt. 2, p. 66 (1990); S. Rep. No. 101-116, pp. 26-27 (1989) (employer has no "obligation to prefer *applicants* with disabilities over other *applicants*" (emphasis added)). Hence it does not require the employer to grant a request that, in violating a disability-neutral rule, would provide a preference. . . .

While linguistically logical, this argument fails to recognize what the Act specifies, namely, that preferences will sometimes prove necessary to achieve the Act's basic equal opportunity goal. The Act requires preferences in the form of "reasonable accommodations" that are needed for those with disabilities to obtain the same workplace opportunities than those without disabilities automatically enjoy. By definition any special "accommodation" requires the employer to treat an employee with a disability differently, i.e., preferentially. And the fact that the difference in treatment violates an employer's disability-neutral rule cannot by itself place the accommodation beyond the Act's potential reach.

Were that not so, the "reasonable accommodation" provision could not accomplish its intended objective. Neutral office assignment rules would automatically prevent the accommodation of an employee whose disability-imposed limitations require him to work on the ground floor. Neutral "break-from-work" rules would automatically prevent the accommodation of an individual who needs additional breaks from work, perhaps to permit medical visits. Neutral furniture budget rules would automatically prevent the accommodation of an individual who needs a different kind of chair or desk. Many employers will have neutral rules governing the kinds of actions most needed to reasonably accommodate a worker with a disability. *See* 42 U.S.C. §12111(9)(b) (setting forth examples such as "job restructuring," "part-time or modified work schedules," "acquisition or modification of equipment or devices," "and other similar accommodations"). Yet Congress, while providing such examples, said nothing suggesting that the presence of such neutral rules would create an automatic exemption. . . .

In sum, the nature of the "reasonable accommodation" requirement, the statutory examples, and the Act's silence about the exempting effect of neutral rules together convince us that the Act does not create any such automatic exemption. The simple fact that an accommodation would provide a "preference"—in the sense that it would permit the worker with a disability to violate a rule that others must obey—cannot, in and of itself, automatically show that the accommodation is not "reasonable." As a result, we reject the position taken by U.S. Airways and Justice Scalia to the contrary. . . .

B

Barnett argues that the statutory words "reasonable accommodation" mean only "effective accommodation," authorizing a court to consider the requested accommodation's ability to meet an individual's disability-related needs, and nothing more. On this view, a seniority rule violation, having nothing to do with the accommodation's effectiveness, has nothing to do with its "reasonableness." It might, at most, help to prove an "undue hardship on the operation of the business." . . . Barnett adds that any other view would make the words "reasonable accommodation" and "undue hardship" virtual mirror images—creating redundancy in the statute. And he says that any such other view would create a practical burden of proof dilemma.

The practical burden of proof dilemma arises, Barnett argues, because the statute imposes the burden of demonstrating an "undue hardship" upon the employer, while the burden of proving "reasonable accommodation" remains with the plaintiff, here the employee. This allocation seems sensible in that an employer can more frequently and easily prove the presence of business hardship than an employee can prove its absence. But suppose that an employee must counter a claim of "seniority rule violation" in order to prove that an "accommodation" request is "reasonable." Would that not force the employee to prove what is in effect an absence, i.e., an absence of hardship, despite the statute's insistence that the employer "demonstrate" hardship's presence?

These arguments do not persuade us that Barnett's legal interpretation of "reasonable" is correct. For one thing, in ordinary English the word "reasonable" does not mean "effective." It is the word "accommodation," not the word "reasonable," that conveys the need for effectiveness. An ineffective "modification" or "adjustment" will not accommodate a disabled individual's limitations. Nor does an ordinary English meaning of the term "reasonable accommodation" make of it a simple, redundant mirror image of the term "undue hardship." The statute refers to an "undue hardship on the operation of the business." 42 U.S.C. §12112(b)(5)(A). Yet a demand for an effective accommodation could prove unreasonable because of its impact, not on business operations, but on fellow employees—say because it will lead to dismissals, relocations, or modification of employee benefits to which an employer, looking at the matter from the perspective of the business itself, may be relatively indifferent.

Neither does the statute's primary purpose require Barnett's special reading. The statute seeks to diminish or to eliminate the stereotypical thought processes, the thoughtless actions, and the hostile reactions that far too often bar those with disabilities from participating fully in the Nation's life, including the workplace. *See* generally §§12101(a) and (b). These objectives demand unprejudiced thought and reasonable responsive reaction on the part of employers and fellow workers alike. They will sometimes require affirmative conduct to promote entry of disabled people into the workforce. They do not, however, demand action beyond the realm of the reasonable. . . .

Finally, an ordinary language interpretation of the word "reasonable" does not create the "burden of proof" dilemma to which Barnett points. Many of the lower courts, while rejecting both U.S. Airways' and Barnett's more absolute views, have reconciled the phrases "reasonable accommodation" and "undue hardship" in a practical way.

They have held that a plaintiff/employee (to defeat a defendant/employer's motion for summary judgment) need only show that an "accommodation" seems reasonable on its face, i.e., ordinarily or in the run of cases. *See, e.g., Reed v. Lepage Bakeries, Inc.*, 244 F.3d 254, 259 (CA1 2001) (plaintiff meets burden on reasonableness by showing that, "at least on the face of things," the accommodation will be feasible for the employer).

Once the plaintiff has made this showing, the defendant/employer then must show special (typically case-specific) circumstances that demonstrate undue hardship in the particular circumstances. *See Reed* ("'undue hardship inquiry focuses on the hardships imposed . . . in the context of the particular [employer's] operations'").

Not every court has used the same language, but their results are functionally similar. In our opinion, that practical view of the statute, applied consistently with ordinary summary judgment principles, *see* Fed. Rule Civ. Proc. 56, avoids Barnett's burden of proof dilemma, while reconciling the two statutory phrases ("reasonable accommodation" and "undue hardship").

III

The question in the present case focuses on the relationship between seniority systems and the plaintiff's need to show that an "accommodation" seems reasonable on its face, i.e., ordinarily or in the run of cases. We must assume that the plaintiff, an employee, is an "individual with a disability." He has requested assignment to a mailroom position as a "reasonable accommodation." We also assume that normally such a request would be reasonable within the meaning of the statute, were it not for one circumstance, namely, that the assignment would violate the rules of a seniority system. *See* §12111(9) ("reasonable accommodation" may include "reassignment to a vacant position"). Does that circumstance mean that the proposed accommodation is not a "reasonable" one?

In our view, the answer to this question ordinarily is "yes." The statute does not require proof on a case-by-case basis that a seniority system should prevail. That is because it would not be reasonable in the run of cases that the assignment in question trump the rules of a seniority system. To the contrary, it will ordinarily be unreasonable for the assignment to prevail.

A

Several factors support our conclusion that a proposed accommodation will not be reasonable in the run of cases. Analogous case law supports this conclusion, for it has recognized the importance of seniority to employee-management relations. [The Court cited its Title VII *Hardison* opinion and numerous lower court decisions under the Rehabilitation Act and the ADA holding that seniority systems found in collective bargaining agreements trump requested accommodations. The Court then noted that the advantages and disadvantages resulting from upending seniority systems did not belong to collectively bargained systems alone.]

For one thing, the typical seniority system provides important employee benefits by creating, and fulfilling, employee expectations of fair, uniform treatment. These benefits include "job security and an opportunity for steady and predictable advancement based on objective standards." They include "an element of due process," limiting "unfairness in personnel decisions." And they consequently encourage employees to invest in the employing company, accepting "less than their value to the firm early in their careers" in return for greater benefits in later years.

Most important for present purposes, to require the typical employer to show more than the existence of a seniority system might well undermine the employees' expectations of consistent, uniform treatment—expectations upon which the seniority system's benefits depend. That is because such a rule would substitute a complex case-specific "accommodation" decision made by management for the more uniform, impersonal operation of seniority rules. Such management decision making, with its inevitable discretionary elements, would involve a matter of the greatest importance to employees, namely, layoffs; it would take place outside, as well as inside, the confines of a court case; and it might well take place fairly often. *Cf.* ADA, 42 U.S.C. §12101(a)(1) (estimating that some 43 million Americans suffer from physical or mental disabilities). We can find nothing in the statute that suggests Congress intended to undermine seniority systems in this way. And we consequently conclude that the employer's showing of violation of the rules of a seniority system is by itself ordinarily sufficient.

B

The plaintiff (here the employee) nonetheless remains free to show that special circumstances warrant a finding that, despite the presence of a seniority system (which the ADA may not trump in the run of cases), the requested "accommodation" is "reasonable" on the particular facts. That is because special circumstances might alter the important expectations described above. The plaintiff might show, for example, that the employer, having retained the right to change the seniority system unilaterally, exercises that right fairly frequently, reducing employee expectations that the system will be followed—to the point where one more departure, needed to accommodate an individual with a disability, will not likely make a difference. The plaintiff might show that the system already contains exceptions such that, in the circumstances, one further exception is unlikely to matter. We do not mean these examples to exhaust the kinds of showings that a plaintiff might make. But we do mean to say that the plaintiff must bear the burden of showing special circumstances that make an exception from the seniority system reasonable in the particular case. And to do so, the plaintiff must explain why, in the particular case, an exception to the employer's seniority policy can constitute a "reasonable accommodation" even though in the ordinary case it cannot.

IV

[We conclude that "ordinarily" the ADA does not require] an employer to assign a disabled employee to a particular position even though another employee is entitled to that position under the employer's "established seniority system." . . . Hence, a showing that the assignment would violate the rules of a seniority system warrants summary judgment for the employer—unless there is more. The plaintiff must present evidence of that "more," namely, special circumstances surrounding the particular case that demonstrate the assignment is nonetheless reasonable. . . .

Justice SCALIA, with whom Justice THOMAS joins, dissenting. . . .

I

The Court begins its analysis by describing the ADA as declaring that an employer may not "discriminate against a qualified individual with a disability." In fact the Act says more: an employer may not "discriminate against a qualified individual with a disability *because of the disability* of such individual." 42 U.S.C. §12112(a) (emphasis added). It further provides that discrimination includes "not making reasonable accommodations *to the known physical or mental limitations* of an otherwise qualified individual with a disability." §12112(b)(5)(A) (emphasis added).

Read together, these provisions order employers to modify or remove (within reason) policies and practices that burden a disabled person "because of [his] disability." In other words, the ADA eliminates workplace barriers only if a disability prevents an employee from overcoming them—those barriers that would not be barriers but for the employee's disability. These include, for example, work stations that cannot accept the employee's wheelchair, or an assembly-line practice that requires long periods of standing. But they do not include rules and practices that bear no more heavily upon the disabled employee than upon others—even though an exemption from such a rule or practice might in a sense "make up for" the employee's disability. It is not a required accommodation, for example, to pay a disabled employee more than others at his grade level—even if that increment is earmarked for massage or physical therapy that would enable the employee to work with as little physical discomfort as his co-workers. That would be "accommodating" the disabled employee, but it would not be "making . . . accommodation to the known physical or mental limitations" of the employee, §12112(b)(5)(A), because it would not eliminate any workplace practice that constitutes an obstacle because of his disability.

So also with exemption from a seniority system, which burdens the disabled and nondisabled alike. In particular cases, seniority rules may have a harsher effect upon the disabled employee than upon his co-workers. If the disabled employee is physically capable of performing only one task in the workplace, seniority rules may be, for him, the difference between employment and unemployment. But that does not make the seniority system a disability-related obstacle, any more than harsher impact upon the more needy disabled employee renders the salary system a disability-related obstacle. When one departs from this understanding, the ADA's accommodation provision becomes a standardless grab bag—leaving it to the courts to decide which workplace preferences (higher salary, longer vacations, reassignment to positions to which others are entitled) can be deemed "reasonable" to "make up for" the particular employee's disability. . . .

[These dissenters would have affirmed summary judgment for the defendant without providing the plaintiffs an opportunity to show that creating an exception to the seniority system was reasonable in the circumstances.]

[Justice SOUTER, with whom Justice GINSBURG joined, dissented.]

NOTES

1. *Collectively Bargained Versus Unilaterally Created Seniority Systems.* The *Barnett* decision is reminiscent of the Supreme Court's refusal in *Hardison* to read Title VII's duty of religious accommodation to require modifications in the employer's seniority system. However, in at least two ways, *Barnett* is more dramatic. First, the ADA lacks Title VII's language privileging seniority systems. *See* 42 U.S.C. §2000e-2(h) ("[I]t shall not be an unlawful employment practice for an employer to apply . . . different terms, conditions, or privileges of employment pursuant to a bona fide seniority . . . system"). Second, unlike TWA, the employer in *Barnett* was not caught between a rock and a hard place by virtue of a contractually enforceable collective bargaining agreement. Was the Supreme Court correct in its assumption that such a system generally confers the same advantages on workers as do those that result from collective bargaining? In an omitted concurrence, Justice O'Connor argued that a system could grant such advantages if it were legally enforceable; thus, she would have preferred to limit the presumption in favor of seniority systems to those the employer was contractually obligated to follow. She joined the Court's opinion, however, observing that the majority's rule and her preferred one will generally reach the same result. *See generally* Seth D. Harris, *Re-thinking the Economics of Discrimination:* U.S. Airways v. Barnett, *the ADA, and the Application of Internal Labor Market Theory*, 89 Iowa L. Rev. 123, 126 (2003) ("Justice Breyer's *Barnett* opinion can be best explained with reference to the view that an employer's seniority system can play an important role in shaping and protecting the employer's sunk investments/delayed dividends contract with its employees.").

2. *Accommodation as Preference.* The *Barnett* Court expressly acknowledged that the ADA will sometimes require that the disabled worker receive a preference. The notion that the ADA requires employers to favor disabled individuals in at least some circumstances, and therefore to incur greater costs for such persons than for their nondisabled co-workers, has generated considerable debate about the normative and economic justifications for this mandate. In short, why has Congress defined unlawful "discrimination" to include failing to accommodate?

The Equal Employment Opportunity Commission's ("EEOC") Interpretive Guidance describes reasonable accommodation in terms of according individuals with a disability "equal employment opportunity," which means "an opportunity to attain the same level of performance, or to enjoy the same level of benefits and privileges of employment as are available to the average similarly situated employee without a disability." 29 C.F.R. pt. 1630, app. §1630.9. As you will see, this is the same argument made for pregnant women: Formal equality, in the sense of treating such individuals the same as other workers, will not allow them to participate equally in the workplace given the special demands placed on them by their family responsibilities. Is the argument stronger for the disabled? Why?

Failure to accommodate is discrimination by definition under the ADA, but there is an obvious difference between discrimination per se and a failure to accommodate. This has led to a lively literature on whether the duty to accommodate is consistent with the antidiscrimination commands of other statutes we have studied. Some of this literature views the disparate impact theory under Title VII as providing a rough analog to the ADA's duty to accommodate and therefore finds little difference between accommodation and antidiscrimination. *See, e.g.*, Mary Crossley, *Reasonable Accommodation as Part and Parcel of the Antidiscrimination Project*, 35 Rutgers L.J. 861 (2004); Michael Ashley Stein, *Same Struggle, Different Difference: ADA Accommodations as Antidiscrimination*, 153 U. Pa. L. Rev. 579 (2004); J. H. Verkerke, *Disaggregating Antidiscrimination and Accommodation*, 44 Wm. & Mary L. Rev. 1385 (2003); Stewart J. Schwab & Steven L. Willborn, *Reasonable Accommodation of Workplace Disabilities*, 44 Wm. & Mary L. Rev. 1197 (2003); Samuel R. Bagenstos, *"Rational Discrimination," Accommodation, and the Politics of (Disability) Civil Rights*, 89 Va. L. Rev. 825 (2003).

3. *Accommodation Beyond Seniority Systems.* Although *Barnett* was decided in the context of a dispute over a seniority system, the issue raised by the case is much broader. Roughly speaking, accommodations can impose costs on the employer, fellow workers, both, or neither. *Barnett* expanded the notion of unreasonableness beyond the effect on business operations to the impact on co-employees. The Court held

that, where a seniority system exists, such costs "ordinarily" need not be imposed. But suppose there's no seniority system?

When, if ever, will a disabled employee's request for reassignment to a vacant position entitle him to the job over other equally qualified (or better qualified) applicants? Recall that the Court "assumed" that plaintiff's request for reassignment to a vacant position would "normally . . . be reasonable within the meaning of the statute" but for the seniority system, which specified that seniority-based bidding would fill such vacancies. The lower courts had sharply disagreed on their answer to this question. *Compare Huber v. Wal-Mart Stores, Inc.*, 486 F.3d 480, 483 (8th Cir. 2007), *cert. dismissed*, 552 U.S. 1136 (2008) ("[T]he ADA is not an affirmative action statute and does not require an employer to reassign a qualified disabled employee to a vacant position when such a reassignment would violate a legitimate nondiscriminatory policy of the employer to hire the most qualified candidate."), *with Smith v. Midland Brake, Inc.*, 180 F.3d 1154, 1164-65 (10th Cir. 1999) (en banc). *Huber* has since been somewhat undercut by the Seventh Circuit's overruling of a decision on which *Huber* had relied. *EEOC v. United Airlines, Inc.*, 693 F.3d 760 (7th Cir. 2012), found that the *Barnett* majority's analysis required a different result. Nevertheless, the next circuit to address the question sided with *Huber*. *United States EEOC v. St. Joseph's Hosp., Inc.*, 842 F.3d 1333, 1347 (11th Cir. 2016) (ADA does not require preferential noncompetitive reassignment); *see generally* Stacy M. Hickox, *Transfer as an Accommodation: Standards from Discrimination Cases and Theory*, 62 Ark. L. Rev. 195 (2009); Nicole B. Porter, *Reasonable Burdens: Resolving the Conflict Between Disabled Employees and Their Coworkers*, 34 Fla. St. U. L. Rev. 313 (2007); Alex B. Long, *The ADA's Reasonable Accommodation Requirement and "Innocent Third Parties,"* 68 Mo. L. Rev. 863 (2003); Cheryl L. Anderson, *"Neutral" Employer Policies and the ADA: The Implications of* U.S. Airways Inc. v. Barnett *Beyond Seniority Systems*, 51 Drake L. Rev. 1 (2002). But surely the question of whether an accommodation is reasonable (or an undue hardship) can't turn solely on whether it involves costs. Or can it? We'll explore the cost question below. Reconsider this question after you read the next case.

Whatever the parameters of reasonable accommodation when an employer has a "vacant" position, any such obligation depends on the position in fact being available, since, whatever the reassignment obligations of an employer might be to a disabled employee, they do not require a promotion, *Brown v. Milwaukee Bd. of Sch. Dirs.*, 855 F.3d 818 (7th Cir. 2017), nor creating a new job, *Toronka v. Cont'l Airlines, Inc.*, 411 F. App'x 719, 726 (5th Cir. 2011). Further, the courts have tended to view positions as not vacant for the purposes of the accommodation if any other worker might have a claim on them. *E.g., Duvall v. Georgia-Pacific Consumer Prods., L.P.*, 607 F.3d 1255, 1262 (10th Cir. 2010) (a position is vacant for accommodation purposes only "if it if it would be available for a similarly-situated non-disabled employee").

4. *Knowing About the Need for Accommodation.* The employer's duty of accommodation is normally triggered by an employee's request. "In general . . . it is the responsibility of the individual with a disability to inform the employer that an accommodation is needed." 29 C.F.R. pt. 1630, app. §1630.9. As we will see, the regulations then envision an "interactive process" in which possible accommodations are considered. But the accommodation duty is in tension with the notion that an employer normally should not inquire into the existence of a disability. Obviously, when the employee raises her disability in a request for accommodation, the employer can ask for further information as part of the "interactive process," which we will explore shortly. But is it ever appropriate for the employer to raise the accommodation question on its own initiative? The regulations provide that "[i]f an employee with a known disability is having difficulty performing his or her job, an employer may inquire whether the employee is in need of a reasonable accommodation." 29 C.F.R. pt. 1630, app. §1630.9. Suppose you represent an employer who suspects that an employee's deteriorating job performance is related to a disability. Do you advise your client to inquire about it? Wouldn't that elevate the risk of a disability discrimination claim if an adverse employment action was later taken against the individual? On the other hand, isn't there some risk in not initiating a conversation?

* * *

Although the ADA is now a quarter century old, there were relatively few cases developing the duty of reasonable accommodation because, as explored in Chapter 9, the courts so often found plaintiffs were either not disabled to begin with or were so disabled as to be unqualified to do the essential functions of the job. The 2008 passage of the ADAAA by liberalizing the definition of disability has brought reasonable accommodation back to center stage.

In that endeavor, two aspects of the ADA duty intersect. One is procedural, the "interactive process" that the governing regulations require when an accommodation is requested. The second is substantive: What makes an accommodation "reasonable"? And when is hardship on the employer "undue"? This latter question is complicated by the fact that, although one could view hardship as merely one factor in the question of whether an accommodation was reasonable, *Barnett* divides them into two separate inquiries, with the burden of persuasion varying depending on what inquiry is the focus of concern. Thus, the *Barnett* Court endorsed the lower courts that placed the burden of proving an accommodation is reasonable on its face, "i.e., ordinarily or in the run of cases," with the employer then able to rebut by showing "special (typically case-specific) circumstances that demonstrate undue hardship in the particular circumstances."

≡≡ *Lowe v. Independent School District No. 1 of Logan County,*
≡≡ *Oklahoma*
   363 F. App'x 548 (10th Cir. 2010)

[Plaintiff Terianne Lowe filed suit against her former employer, Independent School District No. 1 of Logan County, Oklahoma, for failure to reasonably accommodate her post-polio condition in violation of the ADA. The district court granted summary judgment in favor of the District, but the Tenth Circuit reversed.]

Ms. Lowe had polio as a child and, as a result, has worn leg braces for most of her life and has had several knee replacements. She has been advised by her physician that she will have to be in a wheelchair at some point and that walking and standing for long periods will accelerate the deterioration of her leg muscles.

[Ms. Lowe was certified to teach a variety of science courses for grades seven through twelve and had experience as a classroom teacher, but for many years she had been working under an "extra duty" contract as a high school counselor; that was a sedentary position that required no accommodation for her disability.]

In the fall of 2005, as a result of complaints from parents and staff about Ms. Lowe's performance as a counselor at Guthrie High School, Terry Simpson, the District Superintendent, determined that Ms. Lowe's extra-duty contract as a counselor would not be renewed for the 2006–07 school year and that Ms. Lowe would, instead, be reassigned as a classroom teacher. Ms. Lowe was informed of this decision in March 2006 by Jan Chadwick, the principal of Guthrie High School. Ms. Lowe understood that her base salary as a teacher would not be affected by the reassignment but that she would lose the approximately $5,700.00 in additional income she earned under the extra-duty contract as a counselor.

In May 2006, the temporary teaching contract of Mary Rhinehart expired and was not renewed by the District. Ms. Rhinehart had taught physical science at the high school in one of the smallest and most crowded classrooms that, as then configured, would not accommodate a walker or a wheelchair in the aisles between the lab tables. The physical science class, and all other science classes at the high school, were laboratory classes. The physical science class was the only opening for a science teacher at the high school for the 2006–07 school year.

Ms. Lowe, for reasons explained below, eventually came to understand that she would be reassigned to teach physical science in Ms. Rhinehart's small, crowded classroom. In order to plan for that contingency, Ms. Lowe met with Lori Allen, head of the Guthrie High School science department, to share with Ms. Allen her concerns about the reassignment in light of her disability. Ms. Allen did not question the need for such a meeting because she had learned from a school board member that Ms. Rhinehart was not retained in order to open up a teaching slot for Ms. Lowe in Ms. Rhinehart's former classroom. Together, Ms. Lowe and Ms. Allen compiled a list of accommodations they believed necessary in order for Ms. Lowe to teach physical science in the laboratory science classroom formerly used by Ms. Rhinehart. Before the end of the 2005–06 school year, Ms. Lowe presented the list of accommodations and a letter from her physician to principal Chadwick, her immediate supervisor, to Don Bowman, the District's human resources director, and to Superintendent Simpson. Shortly thereafter, Ms. Chadwick was told by Don Bowman that no accommodation would be made and that Ms. Lowe should be assigned to a non-laboratory science class.[2] Ms. Chadwick passed this information along to Ms. Lowe.

By August 2006, Ms. Lowe had heard nothing from the District regarding her request for accommodation, other than the message from Mr. Bowman, relayed by Ms. Chadwick, that no accommodation would be made. Two weeks before school was to begin, Mary Pratz, an advocacy specialist and representative with the Oklahoma Education Association, set up a meeting attended by Superintendent Simpson, Ms. Lowe, Michelle Redus, president of the Guthrie Association of Classroom Teachers, and herself. The purpose of the meeting was to discuss the accommodations Ms. Lowe believed she would need in order to teach physical science in Ms. Rhinehart's former classroom. It is clear that, at the time of the August meeting, Ms. Lowe believed that such would be her assignment come the start of the new school year.

As we will discuss below, there is significant disagreement among those present at the August meeting as to what actually was said. One thing is clear: Ms. Lowe was dissatisfied with the result of the meeting and submitted her resignation two days later. . . .

---

2. Apparently at this point, Mr. Bowman, like Superintendent Simpson, did not know that all high-school science classes were laboratory classes.

III.   Discussion . . .

In order "[t]o establish her claim under the ADA, [Ms. Lowe] must show: (1) she is a disabled person within the meaning of the ADA; (2) she is able to perform the essential job functions with or without reasonable accommodation; and (3) [defendant] discriminated against her because of her disability." *Albert v. Smith's Food & Drug Ctrs., Inc.*, 356 F.3d 1242, 1249 (10th Cir. 2004).

There is no dispute as to the first two requirements. The issue is whether the District discriminated against Ms. Lowe because of her disability. "The ADA defines the term 'discriminate' to include 'not making *reasonable accommodations* to the known physical or mental limitations of an otherwise qualified individual with a disability who is an applicant or employee, unless such covered entity can demonstrate that the accommodation would impose an undue hardship on the operation of the business of such covered entity. . . .' "

[In *Smith v. Midland Brake, Inc.*, 180 F.3d 1154 (10th Cir. 1999) (en banc)] "[w]e noted that the employer and employee must engage in an interactive process to determine what [accommodation] would be appropriate." "The obligation to engage in an interactive process is inherent in the statutory obligation to offer a reasonable accommodation to an otherwise qualified disabled employee."

Once the District was in receipt of Ms. Lowe's list of possible accommodations and the letter from her doctor regarding the reassignment, it was required to proceed "in a reasonably interactive manner" with Ms. Lowe to determine what reasonable accommodation might be made to the physical-science-teaching job in order for her to perform it successfully. *Id.* "The interactive process is typically an essential component of the process by which a reasonable accommodation can be determined," and "includes good-faith communications between the employer and employee." *Id.* "Neither party may create or destroy liability by causing a breakdown of the interactive process." *Albert.* A question of fact as to whether an employer has failed to interact in good faith and thus failed to reasonably accommodate will preclude summary judgment for the employer.

Defendant argues that "the interactive process is merely a means to achieve a reasonable accommodation rather than an independent substantive requirement." While that is true, *see Rehling v. City of Chicago*, 207 F.3d 1009, 1015-16 (7th Cir. 2000) (recognizing that the interactive process the ADA contemplates is not an end in itself), a plaintiff can prevail if she can "show that the result of the inadequate interactive process was the failure of the [employer] to fulfill its role in determining what specific actions must be taken . . . in order to provide the qualified individual a reasonable accommodation." In other words, a plaintiff must show "that the employer's failure to engage in an interactive process resulted in a failure to identify an appropriate accommodation for the qualified individual."

The first step in analyzing Ms. Lowe's failure-to-accommodate claim is to determine whether her ultimate resignation was, as the district court concluded, based merely on her speculation as to where she would be reassigned. Contrary to the district court, we think that, given the information available to Ms. Lowe, she could have reasonably concluded that she would be assigned to teach a physical science class in a small and crowded classroom.

Given all the evidence available to Ms. Lowe, much of it coming from defendant's agents, we think the district court erred in concluding that Ms. Lowe's view of the situation was based merely on her personal speculation. The fact that, even after the August meeting, Superintendent Simpson never informed Ms. Lowe that she would not have to teach in Ms. Rhinehart's classroom justified Ms. Lowe in her belief that she would not be able to resume duties as a classroom science teacher at Guthrie High School. Further, the District's late-advanced theory that it could have placed Ms. Lowe in a junior high science class was never conveyed to her.

We turn now to the facts relative to the interactive process. Early on, as mentioned above, Ms. Lowe learned from Principal Chadwick that no accommodation would be made. Ms. Chadwick had been told this by the District's human resources director, Don Bowman, shortly after the District received the letter from Ms. Lowe's doctor outlining necessary accommodations. After this indirect contact by Mr. Bowman, the District failed for at least four months to respond directly to Ms. Lowe's suggestions for accommodation and only did so when prodded to act by Mary Pratz, an official from the Oklahoma Education Association.

When a meeting was finally convened at Ms. Pratz's behest, even Superintendent Simpson admitted that he did not prepare for it, had not reviewed Ms. Lowe's list of suggested accommodations, and did not know coming into the meeting that all science classes at the high school were lab classes. There is no dispute that Ms. Redus stated that the master schedule for the upcoming year at the high school indicated that Ms. Lowe would be teaching physical science, although there is also evidence that master schedules are sometimes changed at the last minute.

The pivotal issue is whether Ms. Lowe was told, at any time, that she would either be accommodated to teach the physical science class or that she would not have to teach a lab science class at all. The evidence on this point is contradictory [and thus raises a genuine issue of material fact. Most of those present thought that Lowe was told no accommodation would be made although Superintendent Simpson testified, "I believe I indicated that there was a possibility she would not be in a lab science."]

In addition to concluding that Ms. Lowe's failure-to-accommodate claim was too speculative, the district court held that "[b]ecause plaintiff resigned before classes started, she cannot show that the defendant failed to accommodate her disability." We think this is wrong for two reasons.

First, Ms. Lowe's resignation did not preclude her failure-to-accommodate claim. In *Albert v. Smith's Food & Drug Ctrs., Inc.*, the plaintiff's severe asthma prevented her from continuing her job as a cashier. She applied unsuccessfully for other jobs with the defendant and worked for three weeks in customer service. The defendant then told her there were no more hours for her in customer service, but she could have her old cashier job back if her physician would approve. When he would not, the plaintiff stopped working and filed for unemployment. The fact that plaintiff had stopped working for the defendant did not preclude her from pursuing her failure-to-accommodate claim. Indeed, this court held that because the material facts about the interactive process were in dispute, it was error to grant summary judgment to the defendant.

To the extent the District implies that, had Ms. Lowe not resigned, it would have continued to work with her toward a reasonable accommodation, we note that the existence of a dispute concerning the status of the interactive process raises a genuine issue of material fact as to whether the District failed in its duty to reasonably accommodate Ms. Lowe.

Second, Ms. Lowe has raised a genuine issue of material fact on her constructive discharge claim. "Constructive discharge occurs when an employer unlawfully creates working conditions so intolerable that a reasonable person in the employee's position would feel forced to resign." *Strickland v. United Parcel Serv., Inc.*, 555 F.3d 1224, 1228 (10th Cir. 2009) (quotation omitted). "The standard is objective: the employer's subjective intent and the employee's subjective views on the situation are irrelevant. Whether a constructive discharge occurred is a question of fact." We conclude that a genuine issue of material fact exists as to whether a reasonable person, faced with a teaching assignment that will require much standing and moving about, and knowing that such activity will hasten her muscular degeneration and the need for a wheelchair, would have no other choice but to resign. *See Sanchez v. Denver Pub. Schs.*, 164 F.3d 527, 534 (10th Cir. 1998) (holding that the conditions of the job must be objectively intolerable and that the plaintiff must show that she had no other choice but to quit). . . .

IV. Conclusion

The evidence produced by Ms. Lowe raises a genuine issue of material fact as to whether, by failing to engage in the interactive process in good faith, the District failed to identify an appropriate accommodation and thus violated the ADA. It also raises a genuine issue of material fact as to whether a reasonable person, under the circumstances, would have felt compelled to resign. . . .

O'BRIEN, J., concurring.

[Although joining in the Order and Judgment, the concurrence stressed that Lowe was not happy to hear that she would be reassigned from her counselor position to that of a classroom teacher because she preferred being a counselor and did not want to return to the classroom. In April she applied for a position with Guthrie Job Corps, citing the reason for wanting to leave her position with the school district as "retirement." She was offered full-time employment by the Job Corps, which she accepted on June 12, 2006. While Lowe's assumptions about where and what she would teach may have been reasonable, she also knew that teachers were often reassigned at the last minute before school started. Further, Simpson may have simply wanted to keep his options open.]

On August 4, two days after the meeting and without requesting a definitive answer from Simpson as to what he would do in response to her concerns, Lowe sent her resignation letter, saying only, "Consider this my resignation. I am retiring." The letter gave no notice she was resigning due to the School District's failure to make reasonable accommodations, nor did she condition her resignation on such a failure. An employer is not liable for failing to assure an employee reasonable accommodations will be made. The statute imposes liability for "*not making* reasonable accommodations to the known physical or mental limitations of an otherwise qualified individual with a disability who is an applicant or employee. . . ." 42 U.S.C. §12112(b)(5)(A) (emphasis added). Lowe's resignation may have short-circuited the process by not giving the School District an adequate time to respond. We cannot know whether a reasonable accommodation would or would not have been forthcoming. . . .

The School District argues, correctly, I think, that the interactive process is merely a method of facilitating statutory goals. It is a recommendation, not a statutory requirement. . . . While it may be an essential component to understand the employee's needs, "a plaintiff cannot base a reasonable accommodation claim solely on the allegation that the employer failed to engage in an interactive process." *Rehling v. City of Chicago*, 207 F.3d 1009, 1016 (7th Cir. 2000) ("[T]he interactive process is a means and not an end in itself."). Clearly an employer could, with impunity, ignore the interactive process so long as it reasonably accommodated employee needs.

This case comes down to whether the School District would have accommodated Lowe's needs by reassignment to a non-laboratory classroom (as it could have done) had she not resigned in a huff.[7] Since the record does not supply an answer to that question with reasonable certainty this case must be tried.

NOTES

1. *Not Getting to the Merits.* Are you surprised that the court never determined whether the proposed accommodations were reasonable/not an undue hardship? Or did it? *Lowe* does say that the mere failure to pursue the interactive process is not a violation of the ADA. In this regard, the Tenth Circuit agrees with most other circuits that have been unwilling to impose liability on an employer solely for failure to engage in the interactive process. There must also be a showing that a reasonable accommodation could have been found had the process been pursued. *See Basden v. Prof'l Transp., Inc.*, 714 F.3d 1034, 1039 (7th Cir. 2013). However, failure to engage in the process may be unwise. *See Snapp v. United Transp. Union*, 889 F.3d 1088, 1100 (9th Cir. 2018) (while it remains appropriate to shift the burden of proof to the employer as to the availability of a reasonable accommodation when the employer fails to satisfy its interactive process duty because of inadequate information about potential accommodations, such shifting is not appropriate at trial where the plaintiff must shoulder a burden of persuasion on the issue). *See also EEOC v. Dolgencorp, LLC*, 899 F.3d 428, 434 (6th Cir. 2018) (uphold a jury verdict for failure to accommodate when the diabetic plaintiff was fired for violating a no-drink policy after the employer refused to allow her to keep fruit juice nearby to deal with low blood sugar; although alternative accommodations, such as glucose pills, may have been sufficient accommodation, such possibilities were irrelevant give the employer's failure to engage in the interactive process). In this light, did the *Lowe* court necessarily find at least a genuine issue of material fact that plaintiff could have been reasonably accommodated without undue hardship? Or just that it could not obtain summary judgment on that ground?

2. *A Two-Way Street?* By definition, an "interactive process" involves both sides working together toward an accommodation. The *Lowe* concurrence suggests that plaintiff might have failed to do her part, which implies a downside to the interactive process requirement for employees: An employee who fails to participate in discussions about accommodation may forfeit protection against failure-to-accommodate discrimination. *E.g., Goos v. Shell Oil Co.*, 451 F. App'x 700 (9th Cir. 2011) (employee's

---

7. The School District's behavior is not a model for interactive engagement. However, the interactive process creates a duty on both parties to act in good faith. *Smith v. Midland Brake, Inc.* Lowe's good faith in the process is equally as questionable as the School District's. It was no secret Lowe resented her removal from the counseling position and did not want to return to the classroom. Lowe testified "[t]here were some places that they could have put me and that were discussed with Mary Pratz and with Lori Allen [head of high school science department] and with Michelle Redus. There were places that they could have put me." But Lowe never presented these alternatives to Simpson. Lowe also testified there were some science classrooms at the high school where she could teach which would only require the lowering of the blackboard. The record does not indicate Lowe suggested she be assigned to these classrooms. Under these circumstances, it seems rather arbitrary to mention only the School District's shortcomings in the process.

failure to accommodate claim dismissed when she failed to engage in the interactive process in good faith). In *Reed v. Lepage Bakeries, Inc.*, 244 F.3d 254 (1st Cir. 2001), the court ruled that Lepage had no obligation to accommodate Reed's disability because Reed had failed to provide Lepage with the information necessary to create a suitable means to accommodate her bipolar disorder. Is that the point of the concurrence—especially footnote 7—that at trial, plaintiff may have somehow waived her rights by not participating in the process? But the majority says, "[n]either party may create or destroy liability by causing a breakdown of the interactive process." If the employer's failure to interact is not a violation of the ADA unless there was a reasonable accommodation possible, perhaps the employee's failure is not a bar to suit if such participation would have been futile?

3. *The Effect of Plaintiff's Resignation.* The *Lowe* court had to dispose of three threshold issues to get to the merits. The first was whether plaintiff's resignation was based on mere speculation or rather her reasonable belief that she would not be accommodated. The second was whether, even if her belief were reasonable, her resignation somehow mooted her failure to accommodate claim. And the third issue was whether the failure to accommodate resulted in a constructive discharge. Plaintiff survived all three challenges. But suppose Ms. Lowe had consulted you after the August meeting. Would you have advised her to return to working, at least until it was clear that she would be assigned to the small classroom? The denial of an accommodation will frequently make it difficult, but not impossible, for a disabled employee to continue to work, which means that some hard choices may have to be made. Given the demanding standard for constructive discharge, it is certainly possible that an employee who quits when she is not accommodated will have forfeited any ADA claim.

4. *What Accommodations?* In ADA accommodation cases, the devil is often in the details. Ms. Lowe's treating doctor wrote that his patient "has a functional limitation which requires sedentary work only. She is unable to repetitively climb stairs; is unable to kneel, squat, or crawl." Appendix. Given those limitations, these were Ms. Lowe's proposed "Laboratory Safety Modifications for Physical Disabilities":

> Classroom will need to be modified so teacher can be accessible to each table. (Wider aisles to allow wheel chair/walker access)
> - Lab stations will need to be lowered.
> - Chalkboards/whiteboards will need to be lowered so are accessible from a sitting position.
> - Overhead cart and screen will need to be modified to accommodate a sitting position.
> - Eyewash station will need to be added that is accessible.
> - Fume hood will need to be added that is accessible.
> - Safety Shower will need to be added that is accessible.
> - Fire extinguisher and fire blanket need to be lowered.
> - Chemical and flammable storage will need to be modified so it is accessible.
> - General lab equipment storage will need to be modified so it is accessible.
> - Teacher aide will be needed to gather lab equipment, transport chemicals, and monitor safety issues during labs.

5. *Costs of Accommodation.* These classroom changes are significant direct costs, and there is also the possibility of indirect costs—such as potential lost student space. Of course, maybe some changes could have been eliminated had there been an interactive process. And plaintiffs are not entitled to their preferred accommodations: As long as the employer offers an accommodation that reasonably meets their needs, the statutory duty is satisfied. *Bunn v. Khoury Enters.*, 753 F.3d 676 (7th Cir. 2014) (once an employer provided a reasonable accommodation, it had discharged its obligations under the law, whether or not it engaged in the interactive process to explore other possible accommodations); *Hill v. Walker*, 737 F.3d 1209, 1217 (8th Cir. 2013) (Arkansas Department of Family Services not required to remove plaintiff family service worker from one particularly stressful case to accommodate her depression and anxiety when she rejected its proposed accommodation of having a supervisor attend visits with her). Could Ms. Lowe safely teach in the lab without all of the proposed changes?

Suppose Bowman and Sampson called you for advice before the meeting, and suppose that they told you that their physical plant staff had estimated the costs of the accommodation at $10,000. Is this reasonable? An undue hardship? The language of the statute suggests that real costs may have to be incurred in order to accommodate. Thus, §101(9) provides that qualified readers or interpreters may be a reasonable accommodation. Further, the Interpretive Guidance suggests that reasonable accommodations include providing personal assistants such as a page turner for an employee with no hands or a travel attendant for an employee who is blind. 29 C.F.R. pt. 1630, app. §1630.2(o). *See generally* Mark C. Weber, *Unreasonable Accommodation and Due Hardship*, 62 FLA. L. REV. 1119 (2010) ("The duty to accommodate is a substantial obligation, one that may be expensive to satisfy, and one that is not subject to a cost-benefits balance, but rather a cost-resources balance; it is also subject to increase over time.").

The cases have not yet gone so far. *Vande Zande v. Wis. Dep't of Admin.*, 44 F.3d 538 (7th Cir. 1995), is the seminal reasonable accommodation case, and it involved a paraplegic plaintiff, who was employed by the state for three years. To enable her to perform her job duties, the State Department "made numerous accommodations" but refused her request for an at-home computer when pressure ulcers prevented her from going to work. Despite this refusal, the plaintiff was able to complete all but 16.5 hours of work during her eight-week home confinement. The remaining time was covered by her paid sick leave reserves. She filed suit under the ADA alleging that her employer failed to reasonably accommodate her disability.

The Seventh Circuit, in an opinion written by Judge Posner, held that "[t]he employee must show that the accommodation is reasonable in the sense both of efficacious and proportionate to costs," 44 F.3d at 543, the approach later approved by *Barnett*. The court elaborated that an employer is not required to accommodate a disability by allowing the disabled worker to work, unsupervised, from home, since productivity would inevitably be reduced. *Id*. at 544-45. Accordingly, the employer's action was deemed reasonable as a matter of law. *Id*. at 545. The court also rejected the plaintiff's claim that the State Department was required to lower the communal kitchen sink by two inches so that she could use it instead of the bathroom sink. *Id*. at 546. "The duty of reasonable accommodation is satisfied when the employer does what is necessary to enable the disabled worker to work in *reasonable comfort*." *Id*. (emphasis added).

If we assume that Lowe could show that her proposals were "efficacious," can she also show that the hypothetical $10,000 is proportionate? Professor Sunstein critiques Posner's opinion for not providing any real content to the concept of "proportionate." Cass R. Sunstein, *Cost-Benefit Analysis Without Analyzing Costs or*

Benefits: Reasonable Accommodation, Balancing, and Stigmatic Harms, 74 U. CHI. L. REV. 1895, 1904-05 (2007). With respect to Posner's statement that employees can't be accommodated by working from home because of concerns about supervision, he writes:

> Talk about casual empiricism! If the question is whether the costs of the accommodation are disproportionate to the benefits, we might want to make some kind of serious inquiry into both costs and benefits. What is the evidence that if workers telecommute, "their productivity will inevitably be greatly reduced"? In assessing benefits, do we ask how much disabled people are willing to pay to telecommute? Or do we ask how much they would have to be paid to be denied the right to telecommute? More particularly, what is the evidence that Vande Zande's own productivity was reduced? Did her productivity fall during the eight-week period in which she worked at home? What, in fact, is the nature of her job, such that "team work under supervisors" is required? It would seem important to ask and answer that question to assess her request to telecommute. But Judge Posner does not inquire.

Indeed, Sunstein suggests that *Vande Zande's* analysis boils down to nothing more than a judge's intuitions. Given the risk of a judge's reaction being negative, would you err on the side of granting the accommodation if you were advising the school district in *Lowe? See also Reyazuddin v. Montgomery Cnty.*, 789 F.3d 407, 418 (4th Cir. 2015) (finding it error to "reduce a multi-factor analysis to a single factor—cost"; cost is important but must be viewed in relation to other factors, such as whether other similar facilities accommodated those kinds of disabilities).

Finally, to the extent that costs have to be "proportionate" to benefits, some scholars have argued that benefits for nondisabled workers ought to be taken into account. *See* Michelle A. Travis, *Lashing Back at the ADA Backlash: How the Americans with Disabilities Act Benefits Americans Without Disabilities*, 76 TENN. L. REV. 311 (2009); Elizabeth F. Emens, *Integrating Accommodation*, 156 U. PA. L. REV. 839 (2008). That doesn't seem applicable in *Lowe*, but suppose installation of a ramp or elevator benefits not only the disabled worker but also other workers and improves their productivity?

6. *Looking at Undue Hardship.* Suppose that, as the district's counsel, you conclude that the accommodation Lowe seeks may well be reasonable. *Barnett* nevertheless allows an employer to prevail if such an accommodation would be an undue hardship, a question that is analyzed separately. Section 101(10) of the ADA provides that "undue hardship" means "an action requiring significant difficulty or expense, when considered in light of" the following factors:

   (i) the nature and cost of the accommodation needed under this Act;

   (ii) the overall financial resources of the facility or facilities involved in the provision of the reasonable accommodation; the number of persons employed at such facility; the effect on expenses and resources, or the impact otherwise of such accommodation upon the operation of the facility;

   (iii) the overall financial resources of the covered entity; the overall size of the business of a covered entity with respect to the number of its employees; the number, type, and location of its facilities; and

   (iv) the type of operation or operations of the covered entity, including the composition, structure, and functions of the workforce of such entity; the geographic separateness, administrative, or fiscal relationship of the facility or facilities in question to the covered entity.

42 U.S.C. §12111(10).

In *Borkowski v. Valley Cent. Sch. Dist.*, 63 F.3d 131 (2d Cir. 1995), the court discussed these criteria, concluding that the issue of "undue hardship" is one of degree: "[E]ven this list of factors says little about how great a hardship an employer must bear before the hardship becomes undue." The court held that employers are not required to show that they would be driven to the brink of insolvency. It relied on ADA legislative history rejecting a provision that would have defined an undue hardship as one that threatened the continued existence of the employer. *Id.* at 139. "Where the employer is a government entity, Congress could not have intended the only limit on the employer's duty to make reasonable accommodation to be the full extent of the tax base on which the government entity could draw." *Id.; see generally* Steven B. Epstein, *In Search of a Bright Line: Determining When an Employer's Financial Hardship Becomes "Undue" Under the Americans with Disabilities Act*, 48 VAND. L. REV. 391 (1995); *see also Vande Zande*, 44 F.3d at 543 (an accommodation is an undue hardship when it is unduly costly "in relation to the benefits of the accommodation to the disabled worker as well as to the employer's resources"). Do you understand how undue hardship might help the district in *Lowe?*

7. *Putting the Two Terms Together.* As a practical matter, one would expect that a plaintiff would typically be able to prove that a proposed accommodation was efficacious. The more serious question is likely to be whether its costs are proportionate to its benefits (although you should note that employees have incentives to propose less costly accommodations whose costs are, therefore, more likely to be proportionate). Costs, then, will tend to be the determinative factor as to the reasonableness of an accommodation. And they will, at least in extreme cases, be relevant to the undue hardship question. Despite the different burdens, aren't these the same question? Judge Posner's grand synthesis in *Vande Zande* was as follows:

> [C]osts enter at two points in the analysis of claims to an accommodation to a disability. The employee must show that the accommodation is reasonable in the sense both of efficacious and of proportional to costs. Even if this prima facie showing is made, the employer has an opportunity to prove that upon more careful consideration the costs are excessive in relation either to the benefits of the accommodation or to the employer's financial survival or health. . . . One interpretation of "undue hardship" is that it permits an employer to escape liability if he can carry the burden of proving that a disability accommodation reasonable for a normal employer would break him.

And *Barnett* seems to endorse this approach of looking to costs twice.

8. *Back to* Lowe. Now that you know what reasonable accommodation and undue hardship mean as a matter of law, was there a reasonable accommodation available in *Lowe?* It might have been costly to modify the classroom in question, especially if the result was space for fewer students. But why could the school not just assign Lowe to another, less cramped classroom? It might require bumping another teacher into Ms. Rhinehart's cramped space, but is that a problem? Does your answer depend on whether there's a seniority system in place regarding classrooms? And what about assigning Lowe to junior high classes?

9. *Full-time Face-time.* As *Vande Zande* suggests, a frequent question is whether an employer need accommodate by allowing an employee to work at home. Most circuits, in agreement with Posner, have found regularly and timely attendance at

work to be an essential job function for most positions, thus foreclosing any need to accommodate individuals whose disabilities prevent them from working more or less normal schedules. If such individuals are unable to come to work regularly, they are not "otherwise qualified." If they are able to come to work but request an accommodation, that accommodation will not be reasonable if it deviates substantially from regular and timely attendance. *See, e.g., Basden v. Prof'l Transp., Inc.*, 714 F.3d 1034 (7th Cir. 2013). Employers, therefore, generally are not required to accommodate disabled individuals by allowing numerous absences or by granting leaves of absence of indefinite duration. *See, e.g., Murphy v. Samson Res. Co.*, 525 F. App'x 703 (10th Cir. 2013); *Wilson v. Dollar Gen. Corp.*, 717 F.3d 337 (4th Cir. 2013). However, despite the "full-time face-time" norm, a short-term leave of absence often will be viewed as a reasonable accommodation, *Robert v. Bd. of County Comm'rs of Brown County*, 691 F.3d 1211, 1218 (10th Cir. 2012) (a leave may be reasonable when the employee provides an estimated date of return and some assurance that she will be able to perform her essential duties in the "near future"), particularly when the employer's own policies provide for paid or unpaid leave as great as that requested by the disabled employee. *See, e.g., Nunes v. Wal-Mart Stores, Inc.*, 164 F.3d 1243 (9th Cir. 1999) (jury question on reasonableness when plaintiff was terminated before leave period under employer's policy expired); *see generally* Stacy A. Hickox & Joseph M. Guzman, *Leave as an Accommodation: When Is Enough, Enough?* 62 CLEV. ST. L. REV. 437 (2014); Stephen F. Befort, *The Most Difficult Reasonable Accommodation Issues: Reassignment and Leave of Absence*, 37 WAKE FOREST L. REV. 439 (2002). Do you think that the continued judicial skepticism about the reasonableness of working from home is justified in light of changes in American work patterns and the increased availability of technology enabling individuals to work remotely?

10. *"Voluntary" Accommodations.* Wisconsin provided Vande Zande with a number of accommodations. For example, it had bathrooms modified, had a step ramped, and bought adjustable furniture for plaintiff. *Vande Zande*, 44 F.3d at 544. These may or may not have been required in light of the court's opinion. The ADA Interpretive Guidance indicates that an employer is permitted to provide accommodations beyond those required. *See* 29 C.F.R. pt. 1630, app. §1630.9 ("nothing in this part [relating to reasonable accommodation] prohibits employers or other covered entities from providing accommodations beyond those required by this part"). If an employer provides a noncompulsory accommodation, can the employer withdraw the accommodation or refuse to extend it to other similarly situated disabled individuals? This might seem like a rhetorical question since providing the accommodation would seem to establish both that it is reasonable and not an undue hardship. But the courts generally say yes. *Boyle v. City of Pell City*, 866 F.3d 1280 (11th Cir. 2017); *Credeur v. Louisiana*, 860 F.3d 785 (5th Cir. 2017). The explanation is probably less logic than a desire not to disincentivize employers from responding generously. *See generally* Nicole Buonocore Porter, *Withdrawn Accommodations*, 63 DRAKE L. REV. 885 (2015).

We will see, however, that the fact that an employer provides nonmandated accommodations to a disabled male employee may have implications for its duty to provide accommodations to pregnant women under the nondiscrimination commands of Title VII.

11. *Norms Trumping Law.* Many employers, often counseled by attorneys, have taken the initiative in developing protocols for engaging proactively with disabled employees about their need for accommodation. Such internal procedures often apply whenever an individual suffers a physical or mental limitation, whether or not that condition constitutes a recognized disability. This means that other workers may reap a benefit from the reasonable-accommodation requirement and that, in at least some instances, voluntary accommodations are achieved without the need for a protracted legal dispute. This reality has been described as "a quiet revolution that gets little coverage in the case reporter system. All over the United States, disabled employees and human resources managers are joining together to invent mutually acceptable workplace solutions in the form of reasonable accommodations." Stephen Befort, *Accommodation at Work: Lessons from the Americans with Disabilities Act and Possibilities for Alleviating the American Worker Time Crunch*, 13 CORNELL J. L. & PUB. POL'Y 615, 628 (2004); *see also* Rachel Arnow-Richman, *Public Law and Private Process: Toward an Incentivized Organizational Justice Model of Equal Employment Quality for Caregivers*, 2007 UTAH L. REV. 25 (2007).

PROBLEMS

10-1. Sam is hearing impaired. He has applied and been turned down for a secretarial job that included answering phones. He comes to you for advice, informing you that he told the interviewer that he could perform all aspects of the job, except for answering the phone, without any accommodation. With respect to answering the phone, he proposed two alternatives at the interview: (1) eliminating the phone responsibilities or (2) providing a telecommunications device (TDD) that would allow him to answer the phone. The interviewer rejected Sam because neither alternative was "feasible."

In advising Sam, first focus on whether he is qualified for this job. What arguments can he make? What arguments can the employer make? If you conclude that Sam is qualified, which, if either, of the two alternatives is reasonable and not an undue hardship? What further information would you need to answer this question?

10-2. About five years ago, Jan developed a violent, and potentially fatal, food allergy to paprika. She is so sensitive that aromas from coworkers' food can trigger an attack, and an attack can, unless treated immediately, kill her. To avoid exposure, Jan uses a service dog named Penny, who has been trained at a cost of $10,000 to Jan to sniff paprika and warn Jan of its presence. Jan takes Penny everywhere, including to work. There was never a problem until recently, when a coworker claimed that he was allergic to Penny and asked that she be removed from the workplace. You are advising the employer. What advice do you give? *See* Steven Greenhouse, *When Treating One Worker's Allergy Sets Off Another's*, N.Y. TIMES, May 11, 2010, Section A-10. *See generally* Jeannette Cox, *Disability Stigma and Intraclass Discrimination*, 62 FLA. L. REV. 429, 432-33 (2010); Kelly Cahill Timmons, *Accommodating Misconduct Under the American with Disabilities Act*, 57 FLA. L. REV. 187 (2005).

B.   ANTIDISCRIMINATION, ACCOMMODATION, AND THE PROBLEM OF WORK-FAMILY BALANCE

In addition to needs that arise as a result of disability, many employees have family responsibilities that impact their ability to work. Perhaps the most common problem is the conflict faced by many workers, particularly women, in attempting to balance the demands of work and the responsibilities of caring for young children. But workers face a variety of life demands that can have such effects, ranging from obligations to aging parents to family emergencies and sudden illnesses to personal needs relating to their own health and well-being.

The legal obligations of employers in responding to such life needs are modest. Unlike disability, there is no general duty to accommodate workers' family and personal responsibilities. However, because most workers can expect to face such demands at some point in their lives, the limited rights that they have in such situations are profoundly important. For the same reason, employers can expect to face difficult questions about whether and when to accommodate the life needs of its workforce, both as a legal compliance problem and as a business strategy. This section considers two laws that apply to workers facing a subset of life events that can affect work: Title VII, as amended by the Pregnancy Discrimination Act, which prohibits discrimination on the basis of pregnancy; and the FMLA, which provides up to 12 weeks of unpaid leave to workers who need such leave for the birth or care of a new child or for their own illness or that of a family member. It goes on to consider perspectives on whether the law can and should be expanded in this area to require greater accommodation of workers' lives in light of the diversified needs of the modern workforce.

1.   Pregnancy Under Title VII: The Limits of Formal Equality

In one of its first decisions under Title VII, the Supreme Court determined that discrimination against women on account of parentage, a quality they share with males, was illegal. In *Phillips v. Martin Marietta Corp.*, 400 U.S. 542 (1971), the employer barred the employment of women who were parents of preschool-age children while similarly situated men were hired. The Supreme Court held such conduct illegal. While *Phillips* did recognize that such discrimination might be permissible if the employer could prove that not having preschool children was within the narrow "bona fide occupational qualification" ("BFOQ") exception for sex discrimination, *see* Chapter 9, the case has come to stand for the bedrock proposition that individuals must be treated as such and cannot be stereotyped as members of the sex or race to which they belong. Even if it were true, as Martin Marietta claimed, that, as a group, mothers of small children had worse attendance records than fathers, Title VII would render it illegal to treat individual mothers adversely on the basis of their gender.

Phillips was an easy case—it prohibited discrimination on account of a woman's status as a parent, a condition mothers shared with fathers. But the question of whether employers could treat women differently on account of pregnancy—a female physical condition that has no analog for males—proved more difficult for the Court. The Supreme Court's initial encounter with this problem was in *General Electric Co. v. Gilbert*, 429 U.S. 125 (1976), which held that discrimination on account of pregnancy was not per se sex discrimination within the meaning of Title VII. The case involved a fringe benefit plan for employees who could not work as a result of disabilities, but it excluded pregnancy-related disabilities. The Court rejected the plaintiff's claims, relying on its prior decision in *Geduldig v. Aiello*, 417 U.S. 484 (1974), which had upheld a similar state disability insurance plan against an equal protection challenge. In deciding *Gilbert*, the Court held that a pregnancy classification is not per se disparate treatment because of sex:

> The lack of identity between the excluded disability and gender as such under this insurance program becomes clear upon the most cursory analysis. The program divides potential recipients into two groups—pregnant women and nonpregnant persons. While the first group is exclusively female, the second includes members of both sexes.

429 U.S. at 135 (quoting *Geduldig*, 417 U.S. at 496-97 n.20). Thus, under *Gilbert* employers not only had no duty to accommodate pregnancy or motherhood but could also freely discriminate against "pregnant people."

In 1978, Congress responded by enacting the Pregnancy Discrimination Act ("PDA"), which added §701(k) to Title VII. That section begins: "The terms 'because of sex' or 'on the basis of sex' include, but are not limited to, because of or on the basis of pregnancy, childbirth or related medical conditions. . . ." This sentence overruled *Gilbert* and promised more restrictions on how employers could treat women, at least during their pregnancies. It appears to proscribe all explicit pregnancy classifications that cannot be justified under the BFOQ defense, *see* Chapter 9, which allows sex discrimination only in highly exceptional circumstances.

While some hoped that that the PDA would not only proscribe discrimination but also trigger a broader duty to accommodate pregnancy, those hopes have for years been frustrated. After defining "sex" to include pregnancy and related conditions, the PDA goes on to impose the following standard for the treatment of pregnant women by employers: "Women affected by pregnancy, childbirth, or related medical conditions shall be treated the same for all employment-related purposes, including receipt of benefits under fringe benefit programs, as other persons not so affected but similar in their ability or inability to work." The circuit courts generally cut back on the breadth of the proscription of pregnancy discrimination in the first clause of §701(k) by viewing this second clause as limiting the first. Under this reading, the key is whether a woman "affected by pregnancy" is "treated the same" as a similarly situated man would be, that is, a man facing similar physical restrictions and limitations due to a different medical condition. If so, there is no violation of the statute even if pregnancy actually disadvantages a woman. *See generally* Joanna L. Grossman, *Pregnancy, Work, and the Promise of Equal Citizenship*, 98 Geo. L.J. 567, 570 (2010); Kimberly A. Yuracko, *Trait Discrimination as Sex Discrimination: An Argument Against Neutrality*, 83 Tex. L. Rev. 167 (2004).

An early case so holding was *Marafino v. St. Louis County Circuit Court*, 707 F.2d 1005 (8th Cir. 1983), which found that the failure to hire the plaintiff as a law clerk for a state judge because she was pregnant did not violate §701(k). The court reasoned that the employer would not have hired anyone requiring a leave of absence shortly after beginning a short-term position. Thus, the employer did not discriminate against pregnant women but rather against persons (including but not limited to pregnant women) who would have to take a leave in the foreseeable future.

Another example is Judge Posner's opinion in *Troupe v. May Department Stores Co.*, 20 F.3d 734 (7th Cir. 1994), which found no violation in a department store's discharge of a saleswoman. Plaintiff's morning sickness "of unusual severity" during her first trimester resulted in recurring lateness, despite warnings from the employer. She was fired the day before her maternity leave was due to begin. Although there was some evidence of the employer's suspicion that she would not return to work after her half-pay leave, Posner's opinion stressed "[t]he great, the undeniable fact is the plaintiff's tardiness." *Id.* at 737. While no moral blame attached to her inability to work a normal schedule, nothing in the PDA "requires an employer to treat an employee afflicted by morning sickness better than the employer would treat an employee who was equally tardy for some other health reason. . . . If an employee who (like Troupe) does not have an employment contract cannot work because of illness, nothing in Title VII requires the employer to keep the employee on the payroll." *Id.* There did not seem to be another employee with whom Troupe could be compared, but that did not phase Judge Posner:

> We must imagine a hypothetical Mr. Troupe, who is as tardy as Ms. Troupe was, also because of health problems, and who is about to take a protracted sick leave growing out of those problems at an expense to Lord & Taylor equal to that of Ms. Troupe's maternity leave. If Lord & Taylor would have fired our hypothetical Mr. Troupe, this implies that it fired Ms. Troupe not because she was pregnant but because she cost the company more than she was worth to it.

Id. at 738. Having conjured up the hypothetical Mr. Troupe, Posner then apparently required plaintiff to prove that he did not exist, rather than requiring Lord & Taylor to prove he did. "Troupe would be halfway home if she could find one nonpregnant employee of Lord & Taylor who had not been fired when about to begin a leave similar in length to hers. She either did not look, or did not find. Given the absence of other evidence, her failure to present any comparison evidence doomed her case." *Id.* at 739.

Scholars have argued that Kimberly Troupe fell victim to sex stereotyping because Lord & Taylor would probably not have concluded that a similarly situated employee, about to take disability leave, would fail to return to work after the leave. *See* Ann C. McGinley & Jeffrey W. Stempel, *Condescending Contradictions: Richard Posner's Pragmatism and Pregnancy Discrimination*, 46 FLA. L. REV. 193, 221 (1994). Permitting the defendant to act on the assumption that Troupe would not return to work after her baby was born validates exactly the type of stereotype about women, especially pregnant women, that the PDA was intended to overcome. *Id.* In that sense, the hypothetical Mr. Troupe will never be similarly situated to Ms. Troupe.

In short, like *Marafino, Troupe* interprets the PDA to prohibit only conduct that treats pregnant women differently than "similarly situated" nonpregnant people. Despite a slight liberalization of the law even in the Seventh Circuit, *see Maldonado v. U.S. Bank*, 186 F.3d 759, 767 (7th Cir. 1999) (employer discharge of bank teller because of her projected absence due to childbirth not permissible unless the employer "has a good faith basis, supported by sufficiently strong evidence, that the normal inconveniences of an employee's pregnancy will require special treatment."); Joanna L. Grossman, *Pregnancy, Work, and the Promise of Equal Citizenship*, 98 GEO. L. J. 567, 607 (2010) ("*Maldonado* stands for the right of pregnant workers not to be *presumed* incapable."), it remained true until recently that Title VII not only permitted pregnancy to be a basis for discharge in some cases but also imposed no duty of accommodation of pregnancy.

This conclusion was both cast into doubt and reaffirmed in the Supreme Court's latest encounter with the PDA, an opinion that does not require employers who provide no accommodations for anyone to accommodate pregnancy but simultaneously expands the notion of intent to discriminate in a way that will require employers to more frequently accommodate pregnant women when they accommodate other workers than was true under the *Marafino/Troupe* regime.

Young v. UPS
135 S. Ct. 1338 (2015)

Justice BREYER delivered the opinion of the Court.

The Pregnancy Discrimination Act makes clear that Title VII's prohibition against sex discrimination applies to discrimination based on pregnancy. It also says that employers must treat "women affected by pregnancy . . . the same for all employment-related purposes . . . as other persons not so affected but similar in their ability or inability to work." 42 U.S.C. §2000e(k). We must decide how this latter provision applies in the context of an employer's policy that accommodates many, but not all, workers with nonpregnancy-related disabilities.

In our view, the Act requires courts to consider the extent to which an employer's policy treats pregnant workers less favorably than it treats nonpregnant workers similar in their ability or inability to work. And here—as in all cases in which an individual plaintiff seeks to show disparate treatment through indirect evidence— it requires courts to consider any legitimate, nondiscriminatory, nonpretextual justification for these differences in treatment. See *McDonnell Douglas Corp.* v. *Green* [reproduced at page 547]. Ultimately the court must determine whether the nature of the employer's policy and the way in which it burdens pregnant women shows that the employer has engaged in intentional discrimination. The Court of Appeals here affirmed a grant of summary judgment in favor of the employer. Given our view of the law, we must vacate that court's judgment.

I

A

We begin with a summary of the facts. The petitioner, Peggy Young, worked as a part-time driver for the respondent, United Parcel Service (UPS). Her responsibilities included pickup and delivery of packages that had arrived by air carrier the previous night. In 2006, after suffering several miscarriages, she became pregnant. Her doctor told her that she should not lift more than 20 pounds during the first 20 weeks of her pregnancy or more than 10 pounds thereafter.

UPS required drivers like Young to be able to lift parcels weighing up to 70 pounds (and up to 150 pounds with assistance). UPS told Young she could not work while under a lifting restriction. Young consequently stayed home without pay during most of the time she was pregnant and eventually lost her employee medical coverage.

Young subsequently brought this federal lawsuit. We focus here on her claim that UPS acted unlawfully in refusing to accommodate her pregnancy-related lifting restriction. Young said that her co-workers were willing to help her with heavy packages. She also said that UPS accommodated other drivers who were "similar in their . . . inability to work." She accordingly concluded that UPS must accommodate her as well.

UPS responded that the "other persons" whom it had accommodated were (1) drivers who had become disabled on the job, (2) those who had lost their Department of Transportation (DOT) certifications, and (3) those who suffered from a disability covered by the Americans with Disabilities Act of 1990. UPS said that, since Young did not fall within any of those categories, it had not discriminated against Young on the basis of pregnancy but had treated her just as it treated all "other" relevant "persons."

B

Title VII of the Civil Rights Act of 1964 forbids a covered employer to "discriminate against any individual with respect to . . . terms, conditions, or privileges of employment, because of such individual's . . . sex." In 1978, Congress enacted the Pregnancy Discrimination Act, which added new language to Title VII's definitions subsection. The first clause of the 1978 Act specifies that Title VII's "ter[m] 'because of sex' . . . include[s] . . . because of or on the basis of pregnancy, childbirth, or related medical conditions." § 2000e(k). The second clause says that

> women affected by pregnancy, childbirth, or related medical conditions shall be treated the same for all employment-related purposes . . . as other persons not so affected but similar in their ability or inability to work. . . .

This case requires us to consider the application of the second clause to a "disparate-treatment" claim—a claim that an employer intentionally treated a complainant less favorably than employees with the "complainant's qualifications" but outside the complainant's protected class. *McDonnell Douglas.* We have said that "[l]iability in a disparate-treatment case depends on whether the protected trait actually motivated the employer's decision." *Raytheon Co.* v. *Hernandez,* 540 U.S. 44, 52 (2003). We have also made clear that a plaintiff can prove disparate treatment either (1) by direct evidence that a workplace policy, practice, or decision relies expressly on a protected characteristic, or (2) by using the burden-shifting framework set forth in *McDonnell Douglas.* See *Trans World Airlines, Inc.* v. *Thurston,* 469 U.S. 111 (1985).

[The majority described the *McDonnell Douglas* litigation structure and then noted that employment discrimination law also recognized disparate-impact claim, but Young had not alleged disparate impact nor a "pattern-or-practice" claim.

[In responding to UPS's motion for summary judgment, Young pointed to a number of facts. In addition to those stated above, they included:]

7. UPS, in a collective-bargaining agreement, had promised to provide temporary alternative work assignments to employees "unable to perform their normal work assignments due to an *on-the-job* injury." (Emphasis added.)

8. The collective-bargaining agreement also provided that UPS would "make a good faith effort to comply . . . with requests for a reasonable accommodation because of a permanent disability" under the ADA.

9. The agreement further stated that UPS would give "inside" jobs to drivers who had lost their DOT certifications because of a failed medical exam, a lost driver's license, or involvement in a motor vehicle accident.

10. When Young later asked UPS' Capital Division Manager to accommodate her disability, he replied that, while she was pregnant, she was "too much of a liability" and could "not come back" until she " 'was no longer pregnant.' " . . .

As direct evidence of intentional discrimination, Young relied, in significant part, on the statement of the Capital Division Manager (10 above). As evidence that she had made out a prima facie case under *McDonnell Douglas*, Young relied, in significant part, on evidence showing that UPS would accommodate workers injured on the job (7), those suffering from ADA disabilities (8), and those who had lost their DOT certifications (9). That evidence, she said, showed that UPS had a light-duty-for-injury policy with respect to numerous "other persons," but not with respect to pregnant workers.

Young introduced further evidence indicating that UPS had accommodated several individuals when they suffered disabilities that created work restrictions similar to hers. UPS contests the correctness of some of these facts and the relevance of others. But because we are at the summary judgment stage, and because there is a genuine dispute as to these facts, we view this evidence in the light most favorable to Young, the nonmoving party:

13. Several employees received accommodations while suffering various similar or more serious disabilities incurred on the job [a 10-pound lifting limitation, foot injury, and an arm injury].

14. Several employees received accommodations following injury, where the record is unclear as to whether the injury was incurred on or off the job [recurring knee injury, ankle injury, knee injury, stroke, and leg injury].

15. Several employees received "inside" jobs after losing their DOT certifications [for a DUI conviction, high blood pressure, and sleep apnea diagnosis].

16. Some employees were accommodated despite the fact that their disabilities had been incurred off the job.

17. According to a deposition of a UPS shop steward who had worked for UPS for roughly a decade, "the only light duty requested [due to physical] restrictions that became an issue" at UPS "were with women who were pregnant."

[The District Court granted UPS' motion for summary judgment and the Fourth Circuit affirmed.]

D

We note that statutory changes made after the time of Young's pregnancy may limit the future significance of our interpretation of the Act. In 2008, Congress expanded the definition of "disability" under the ADA to make clear that "physical or mental impairment[s] that substantially limi[t]" an individual's ability to lift, stand, or bend are ADA-covered disabilities. ADA Amendments Act of 2008, 42 U.S.C. §§ 12102(1)-(2). As interpreted by the EEOC, the new statutory definition requires employers to accommodate employees whose temporary lifting restrictions originate off the job. See 29 CFR pt. 1630, App., § 1630.2(j)(1)(ix). We express no view on these statutory and regulatory changes.

II

The parties disagree about the interpretation of the Pregnancy Discrimination Act's second clause. As we have said, the Act's first clause specifies that discrimination "'because of sex'" includes discrimination "because of . . . pregnancy." But the meaning of the second clause is less clear; it adds: "[W]omen affected by pregnancy, childbirth, or related medical conditions shall be treated the same for all employment-related purposes . . . as *other persons* not so affected but *similar in their ability or inability to work.*" 42 U.S.C. § 2000e(k) (emphasis added). Does this clause mean that courts must compare workers *only* in respect to the work limitations that they suffer? Does it mean that courts must ignore all other similarities or differences between pregnant and nonpregnant workers? Or does it mean that courts, when deciding who the relevant "other persons" are, may consider other similarities and differences as well? If so, which ones?

The differences between these possible interpretations come to the fore when a court, as here, must consider a workplace policy that distinguishes between pregnant and nonpregnant workers in light of characteristics not related to pregnancy. Young poses the problem directly in her reply brief when she says that the Act requires giving "the same accommodations to an employee with a pregnancy-related work limitation as it would give *that employee* if her work limitation stemmed from a different cause but had a similar effect on her inability to work." Suppose the employer would not give "*that* [*pregnant*] *employee*" the "same accommodations" as another employee, but the employer's reason for the difference in treatment is that the pregnant worker falls within a facially neutral category (for example, individuals with off-the-job injuries). What is a court then to do?

The parties propose very different answers to this question. Young and the United States believe that the second clause of the Pregnancy Discrimination Act "requires an employer to provide the same accommodations to workplace disabilities caused by pregnancy that it provides to workplace disabilities that have other causes but have a similar effect on the ability to work." In other words, Young contends that the second clause means that whenever "an employer accommodates only a subset of workers with disabling conditions," a court should find a Title VII violation if "pregnant workers who are similar in the ability to work" do not "receive the same [accommodation] even if still other non-pregnant workers do not receive accommodations."

UPS takes an almost polar opposite view. It contends that the second clause does no more than define sex discrimination to include pregnancy discrimination. Under this view, courts would compare the accommodations an employer provides to pregnant women with the accommodations it provides to others *within* a facially neutral category (such as those with off-the-job injuries) to determine whether the employer has violated Title VII. . . .

A

We cannot accept either of these interpretations. . . .

The problem with Young's approach is that it proves too much. It seems to say that the statute grants pregnant workers a "most-favored-nation" status. As long as an employer provides one or two workers with an accommodation—say, those with particularly hazardous jobs, or those whose workplace presence is particularly needed, or those who have worked at the company for many years, or those who are over the age of 55—then it must provide similar accommodations to *all* pregnant workers (with comparable physical limitations), irrespective of the nature of their jobs, the employer's need to keep them working, their ages, or any other criteria.

Lower courts have concluded that this could not have been Congress' intent in passing the Pregnancy Discrimination Act. And Young partially agrees, for she writes that "the statute does not require employers to give" to "pregnant workers all of the benefits and privileges it extends to other" similarly disabled "employees when those benefits and privileges are . . . based on the employee's tenure or position within the company" [such as seniority, full-time work, and different job classifications].

Young's last-mentioned concession works well with respect to seniority, for Title VII itself contains a seniority defense, see 42 U.S.C. § 2000e-2(h). Hence, seniority is not part of the problem. But otherwise the most-favored-nation problem remains, and Young's concession does not solve it. How, for example, should a court treat special benefits attached to injuries arising out of, say, extra-hazardous duty? If Congress intended to allow differences in treatment arising out of special duties, special service, or special needs, why would it not also have wanted courts to take account of differences arising out of special "causes"—for example, benefits for those who drive (and are injured) in extrahazardous conditions?

We agree with UPS to this extent: We doubt that Congress intended to grant pregnant workers an unconditional most-favored-nation status. The language of the statute does not require that unqualified reading. The second clause, when referring to nonpregnant persons with similar disabilities, uses the open-ended term "other persons." It does not say that the employer must treat pregnant employees the "same" as "*any* other persons" (who are similar in their ability or inability to work), nor does it otherwise specify *which* other persons Congress had in mind.

Moreover, disparate-treatment law normally permits an employer to implement policies that are not intended to harm members of a protected class, even if their implementation sometimes harms those members, as long as the employer has a legitimate, nondiscriminatory, nonpretextual reason for doing so. See, *e.g., Raytheon; McDonnell Douglas.* There is no reason to believe Congress intended its language in the Pregnancy Discrimination Act to embody a significant deviation from this approach. Indeed, the relevant House Report specifies that the Act "reflect[s] no new legislative mandate." H. R. Rep. No. 95-948, pp. 3-4 (1978) (hereinafter H. R. Rep.). And the Senate Report states that the Act was designed to "reestablis[h] the law as it was understood prior to" this Court's decision in *General Electric Co.* v. *Gilbert.* S. Rep. No. 95-331, p. 8 (1978) (hereinafter S. Rep.).

B

[The Court traced the somewhat inconsistent history of EEOC pronouncements. After certiorari had been granted in *Young*, the EEOC promulgated a guideline barring employers from looking to the source of an employee's limitations in any policy regarding accommodations. The majority refused to defer to this guidance in part because it seemed tailored to the present case, in part because its position was inconsistent with those the Government has long advocated, and in part because the position was insufficiently rationalized.]

C

We find it similarly difficult to accept the opposite interpretation of the Act's second clause. UPS says that the second clause simply defines sex discrimination to include pregnancy discrimination. But that cannot be so.

The first clause accomplishes that objective when it expressly amends Title VII's definitional provision to make clear that Title VII's words "because of sex" and "on the basis of sex" "include, but are not limited to, because of or on the basis of pregnancy, childbirth, or related medical conditions." 42 U.S.C. § 2000e(k). We have long held that " 'a statute ought, upon the whole, to be so construed that, if it can be prevented, no clause' " is rendered " 'superfluous, void, or insignificant.' " *TRW Inc.* v. *Andrews*, 534 U.S. 19, 31 (2001). But that is what UPS' interpretation of the second clause would do.

The dissent, basically accepting UPS' interpretation, says that the second clause is not "superfluous" because it adds "clarity." It makes "plain," the dissent adds, that unlawful discrimination "includes disfavoring pregnant women relative to other workers of similar inability to work." Perhaps we fail to understand. *McDonnell Douglas* itself makes clear that courts normally consider how a plaintiff was treated relative to other "persons of [the plaintiff's] qualifications" (which here include disabilities). If the second clause of the Act did not exist, we would still say that an employer who disfavored pregnant women relative to other workers of similar ability or inability to work had engaged in pregnancy discrimination. In a word, there is no need for the "clarification" that the dissent suggests the second sentence provides.

Moreover, the interpretation espoused by UPS and the dissent would fail to carry out an important congressional objective. [The PDA was designed to overturn both the holding and the reasoning of *Gilbert*, which had upheld a plan denying pregnancy-related health benefits.] In short, the *Gilbert* majority reasoned in part just as the dissent reasons here. The employer did "not distinguish between pregnant women and others of similar ability or inability *because of pregnancy*." It distinguished between them on a neutral ground—*i.e.*, it accommodated only sicknesses and accidents, and pregnancy was neither of those.

Simply including pregnancy among Title VII's protected traits (*i.e.*, accepting UPS' interpretation) would not overturn *Gilbert* in full—in particular, it would not respond to *Gilbert*'s determination that an employer can treat pregnancy less favorably than diseases or disabilities resulting in a similar inability to work. . . .

III

The statute lends itself to an interpretation other than those that the parties advocate and that the dissent sets forth. Our interpretation minimizes the problems we have discussed, responds directly to *Gilbert*, and is consistent with longstanding interpretations of Title VII.

In our view, an individual pregnant worker who seeks to show disparate treatment through indirect evidence may do so through application of the *McDonnell Douglas* framework. That framework requires a plaintiff to make out a prima facie case of discrimination. But it is "not intended to be an inflexible rule." *Furnco Constr. Corp.* v. *Waters*, 438 U.S. 567, 575 (1978). Rather, an individual plaintiff may establish a prima facie case by "showing actions taken by the employer from which one can infer, if such actions remain unexplained, that it is more likely than not that such actions were based on a discriminatory criterion illegal under" Title VII. *Id.* The burden of making this showing is "not onerous." In particular, making this showing is not as burdensome as succeeding on "an ultimate finding of fact as to" a discriminatory employment action. *Furnco.* Neither does it require the plaintiff to show that those whom the employer favored and those whom the employer disfavored were similar in all but the protected ways. See *McDonnell Douglas* (burden met where plaintiff showed that employer hired other "qualified" individuals outside the protected class); *Furnco* (same). Thus, a plaintiff alleging that the denial of an accommodation constituted disparate treatment under the Pregnancy Discrimination Act's second clause may make out a prima facie case by showing, as in *McDonnell Douglas*, that she belongs to the protected class, that she sought accommodation, that the employer did not accommodate her, and that the employer did accommodate others "similar in their ability or inability to work."

The employer may then seek to justify its refusal to accommodate the plaintiff by relying on "legitimate, nondiscriminatory" reasons for denying her accommodation. But, consistent with the Act's basic objective, that reason normally cannot consist simply of a claim that it is more expensive or less convenient to add pregnant women to the category of those ("similar in their ability or inability to work") whom the employer accommodates. After all, the employer in *Gilbert* could in all likelihood have made just such a claim.

If the employer offers an apparently "legitimate, non-discriminatory" reason for its actions, the plaintiff may in turn show that the employer's proffered reasons are in fact pretextual. We believe that the plaintiff may reach a jury on this issue by providing sufficient evidence that the employer's policies impose a significant burden on pregnant workers, and that the employer's "legitimate, nondiscriminatory" reasons are not sufficiently strong to justify the burden, but rather—when considered along with the burden imposed—give rise to an inference of intentional discrimination.

The plaintiff can create a genuine issue of material fact as to whether a significant burden exists by providing evidence that the employer accommodates a large percentage of nonpregnant workers while failing to accommodate a large percentage of pregnant workers. Here, for example, if the facts are as Young says they are, she can show that UPS accommodates most nonpregnant employees with lifting limitations while categorically failing to accommodate pregnant employees with lifting limitations. Young might also add that the fact that UPS has multiple policies that accommodate nonpregnant employees with lifting restrictions suggests that its reasons for failing to accommodate pregnant employees with lifting restrictions are not sufficiently strong—to the point that a jury could find that its reasons for failing to accommodate pregnant employees give rise to an inference of intentional discrimination.

This approach, though limited to the Pregnancy Discrimination Act context, is consistent with our longstanding rule that a plaintiff can use circumstantial proof to rebut an employer's apparently legitimate, nondiscriminatory reasons for treating individuals within a protected class differently than those outside the protected class . . . . In particular, it is hardly anomalous (as the dissent makes it out to be) that a plaintiff may rebut an employer's proffered justifications by showing how a policy operates in practice. In *McDonnell Douglas* itself, we noted that an employer's "general policy and practice with respect to minority employment"—including "statistics as to" that policy and practice—could be evidence of pretext. Moreover, the continued focus on whether the plaintiff has introduced sufficient evidence to give rise to an inference of *intentional* discrimination avoids confusing the disparate-treatment and disparate-impact doctrines.

Our interpretation of the Act is also, unlike the dissent's, consistent with Congress' intent to overrule *Gilbert*'s reasoning and result. The dissent says that "[i]f a pregnant woman is denied an accommodation under a policy that does not discriminate against pregnancy, she *has* been 'treated the same' as everyone else." This logic would have found no problem with the employer plan in *Gilbert*, which "denied an accommodation" to pregnant women on the same basis as it denied accommodations to other employees—*i.e.*, it accommodated only sicknesses and accidents, and pregnancy was neither of those. In arguing to the contrary, the dissent's discussion of *Gilbert* relies exclusively on the opinions of the dissenting Justices in that case. But Congress' intent in passing the Act was to overrule the *Gilbert majority* opinion, which viewed the employer's disability plan as denying coverage to pregnant employees on a neutral basis.

IV

[Under this interpretation, there was adequate evidence to deny the defendant summary judgment.] Viewing the record in the light most favorable to Young, there is a genuine dispute as to whether UPS provided more favorable treatment to at least some employees whose situation cannot reasonably be distinguished from Young's. In other words, Young created a genuine dispute of material fact as to the fourth prong of the *McDonnell Douglas* analysis.

Young also introduced evidence that UPS had three separate accommodation policies (on-the-job, ADA, DOT). Taken together, Young argued, these policies significantly burdened pregnant women. See (shop steward's testimony that "the only light duty requested [due to physical] restrictions that became an issue" at UPS "were with women who were pregnant"). The Fourth Circuit did not consider the combined effects of these policies, nor did it consider the strength of UPS's justifications for each when combined. That is, why, when the employer accommodated so many, could it not accommodate pregnant women as well?

We do not determine whether Young created a genuine issue of material fact as to whether UPS's reasons for having treated Young less favorably than it treated these other nonpregnant employees were pretextual. We leave a final determination of that question for the Fourth Circuit to make on remand, in light of the interpretation of the Pregnancy Discrimination Act that we have set out above. . . .

Justice ALITO, concurring in the judgment.

[Violation of the PDA's first clause requires an employer's intent to discriminate because of or on the basis of pregnancy. Under this clause, it does not matter whether the employer's ground for the unfavorable treatment is reasonable; all that matters is the employer's actual intent. But the second clause raises more difficult questions of interpretation. "[T]his clause does not merely explain but instead adds to the language that precedes it," a reading consistent with the statutory text's use of the word "and." Further, the "second clause makes no reference to intent, which is the linchpin of liability under the first clause," and "the second clause is an affirmative command (an employer 'shall' provide equal treatment), while the first clause is negative (it prohibits discrimination)." Finally, "if the second clause does not set out an additional restriction on employer conduct, it would appear to be largely, if not entirely, superfluous."]

This leads to the second question: In determining whether pregnant employees have been given the equal treatment that this provision demands, with whom must the pregnant employees be compared? I interpret the second clause to mean that pregnant employees must be compared with employees performing the same or very similar jobs. [An employer need not treat workers whose positions do not entail heavy lifting the same as those who do.]

This conclusion leads to a third, even more difficult question: When comparing pregnant employees to nonpregnant employees in similar jobs, which characteristics of the pregnant and nonpregnant employees must be taken into account? [The concurrence agreed with the majority in rejecting the "most favored employee" interpretation but recognized the resulting conundrum: pregnant workers were treated the same as some "other persons" while differently than other "other persons." . . .] An interpretation that leads to such a problem cannot be correct.

I therefore turn to the other possible interpretation of the phrase "similar in their ability or inability to work," namely, that "similar in the ability or inability to work" means "similar *in relation* to the ability or inability to work." Under this interpretation, pregnant and non-pregnant employees are not similar in relation to the ability or inability to work if they are unable to work for different reasons. And this means that these two groups of employees are not similar in the relevant sense if the employer has a neutral business reason for treating them differently. I agree with the Court that a sufficient reason "normally cannot consist simply of a claim that it is more expensive or less convenient to add pregnant women to the category of those . . . whom the employer accommodates."[5] Otherwise, however, I do not think that the second clause of the PDA authorizes courts to evaluate the justification for a truly neutral rule. . . .

III.

[Justice Alito agreed with the majority that the record was "sufficient (albeit barely)" to survive summary judgment under the first clause and also agreed that summary judgment should be denied under the second clause. Under the UPS policy, drivers physically unable to perform the usual tasks of the position fell into three groups.]

First, some drivers were reassigned to less physically demanding positions. Included in this group were (a) those who were unable to work as drivers due to an injury incurred on the job, (b) those drivers who were unable to work as drivers due to a disability as defined by the Americans With Disabilities Act of 1990 (ADA), and (c) those drivers who, as the result of a medical condition or injury, lost the Department of Transportation (DOT) certification needed to work in that capacity.

The second group of drivers consisted of those who were not pregnant and were denied transfer to a light-duty job. Drivers who were injured off the job fell into this category. The third group was made up of pregnant drivers like petitioner.

---

5. If cost alone could justify unequal treatment of pregnant employees, the plan at issue in *General Electric Co.* v. *Gilbert* would be lawful. But this Court has repeatedly said that the PDA rejected " 'both the holding and the reasoning' " in *Gilbert.*

It is obvious that respondent had a neutral reason for providing an accommodation when that was required by the ADA. Respondent also had neutral grounds for providing special accommodations for employees who were injured on the job [since otherwise they would have been eligible for workers' compensation benefits.]

The accommodations that are provided to drivers who lost their DOT certifications, however, are another matter. A driver may lose DOT certification for a variety of reasons, including medical conditions or injuries incurred off the job that impair the driver's ability to operate a motor vehicle. Such drivers may then be transferred to jobs that do not require physical tasks incompatible with their illness or injury. It does not appear that respondent has provided any plausible justification for treating these drivers more favorably than drivers who were pregnant.

The Court of Appeals provided two grounds for distinguishing petitioner's situation from that of the drivers who had lost their DOT certifications, but neither is adequate. First, the Court of Appeals noted that "no legal obstacle [stood] between [petitioner] and her work." But the legal obstacle faced by drivers who have lost DOT certification only explains why those drivers could not continue to perform all the tasks required by their ordinary jobs; it does not explain why respondent went further and *provided such drivers with a work accommodation. . . .*

[The Fourth Circuit's second distinction was that loss of DOT certification did not mean that the driver was unable to perform a range of demanding physical tasks, but the concurrence thought it "doubtful that this is true in all instances," which means that at least sometimes such drivers were] assigned to jobs that did not require them to perform tasks that they were incapable of performing due to the medical condition that caused the loss of DOT certification. Respondent has not explained why pregnant drivers could not have been given similar consideration. . . .

Justice SCALIA, with whom Justice KENNEDY and Justice THOMAS join, dissenting. . . .

I . . .

[Plaintiff did not establish liability under either the disparate treatment or disparate impact theories, which forced Young and the Court to turn to § 2000e(k). But the] most natural way to understand the same-treatment clause is that an employer may not distinguish between pregnant women and others of similar ability or inability *because of pregnancy.* Here, that means pregnant women are entitled to accommodations *on the same terms* as other workers with disabling conditions. If a pregnant woman is denied an accommodation under a policy that does not discriminate against pregnancy, she *has* been "treated the same" as everyone else. UPS's accommodation for drivers who lose their certifications illustrates the point. A pregnant woman who loses her certification gets the benefit, just like any other worker who loses his. And a pregnant woman who keeps her certification does not get the benefit, again just like any other worker who keeps his. That certainly sounds like treating pregnant women and others the same.

There is, however, another way to understand "treated the same," at least looking at that phrase on its own. One could read it to mean that an employer may not distinguish *at all* between pregnant women and others of similar ability. Here, that would mean pregnant women are entitled, not to accommodations on the same terms as others, but to *the same accommodations* as others, no matter the differences (other than pregnancy) between them. UPS's accommodation for decertified drivers illustrates this usage too. There is a sense in which a pregnant woman denied an accommodation (because she kept her certification) has *not* been treated the same as an injured man granted an accommodation (because he lost his certification). He got the accommodation and she did not.

Of these two readings, only the first makes sense in the context of Title VII. The point of Title VII's bans on discrimination is to prohibit employers from treating one worker differently from another *because of a protected trait*. It is not to prohibit employers from treating workers differently for reasons that have nothing to do with protected traits. . . .

Prohibiting employers from making *any* distinctions between pregnant workers and others of similar ability would elevate pregnant workers to most favored employees. If Boeing offered chauffeurs to injured directors, it would have to offer chauffeurs to pregnant mechanics. And if Disney paid pensions to workers who can no longer work because of old age, it would have to pay pensions to workers who can no longer work because of childbirth. It is implausible that Title VII, which elsewhere creates guarantees of *equal* treatment, here alone creates a guarantee of *favored* treatment. . . .

II

The Court agrees that the same-treatment clause is not a most-favored-employee law, but at the same time refuses to adopt the reading I propose—which is the only other reading the clause could conceivably bear. The Court's reasons for resisting this reading fail to persuade.

The Court starts by arguing that the same-treatment clause must do more than ban distinctions on the basis of pregnancy, lest it add nothing to the part of the Act defining pregnancy discrimination as sex discrimination. Even so read, however, the same-treatment clause *does* add something: clarity. . . .

This clarifying function easily overcomes any charge that the reading I propose makes the same-treatment clause "'superfluous, void, or insignificant.'" Perhaps, as the Court suggests, even without the same-treatment clause the best reading of the Act would prohibit disfavoring pregnant women relative to disabled workers. But laws often make explicit what might already have been implicit, "for greater caution" and in order "to leave nothing to construction." . . .

That brings me to the Court's remaining argument: the claim that the reading I have set forth would not suffice to overturn our decision in *Gilbert*. Wrong. *Gilbert* upheld an otherwise comprehensive disability-benefits plan that singled pregnancy out for disfavor. The most natural reading of the Act overturns that decision, because it prohibits singling pregnancy out for disfavor.

The Court goes astray here because it mistakenly assumes that the *Gilbert* plan excluded pregnancy on "a neutral ground"—covering sicknesses and accidents but nothing else. In reality, the plan in *Gilbert* was not neutral toward pregnancy. [The dissent in *Young* cited the dissenters in *Gilbert* to this effect.]

III

Dissatisfied with the only two readings that the words of the same-treatment clause could possibly bear, the Court decides that the clause means something in-between. It takes only a couple of waves of the Supreme Wand to produce the desired result. Poof!: The same-treatment clause means that a neutral reason for refusing to accommodate a pregnant woman is pretextual if "the employer's policies impose a significant burden on pregnant workers." Poof!: This is so only when the employer's reasons "are not sufficiently strong to justify the burden."

How we got here from the same-treatment clause is anyone's guess. There is no way to read "shall be treated the same"—or indeed anything else in the clause—to mean that courts must balance the significance of the burden on pregnant workers against the strength of the employer's justifications for the policy. That is presumably why the Court does not even *try* to connect the interpretation it adopts with the text it purports to interpret. The Court has forgotten that statutory purpose and the presumption against superfluity are tools for choosing among competing reasonable readings of a law, not authorizations for making up new readings that the law cannot reasonably bear.

The fun does not stop there. Having ignored the terms of the same-treatment clause, the Court proceeds to bungle the dichotomy between claims of disparate treatment and claims of disparate impact. Normally, liability for disparate treatment arises when an employment policy has a "discriminatory motive," while liability for disparate impact arises when the effects of an employment policy "fall more harshly on one group than another and cannot be justified by business necessity." *Teamsters.* In the topsy-turvy world created by today's decision, however, a pregnant woman can establish disparate *treatment* by showing that the *effects* of her employer's policy fall more harshly on pregnant women than on others (the policies "impose a significant burden on pregnant workers," and are inadequately justified (the "reasons are not sufficiently strong to justify the burden"). The change in labels may be small, but the change in results assuredly is not. Disparate-treatment and disparate-impact claims come with different standards of liability, different defenses, and different remedies. §§ 1981a, 2000e-2(k). For example, plaintiffs in disparate-treatment cases can get compensatory and punitive damages as well as equitable relief, but plaintiffs in disparate impact cases can get equitable relief only. See §§ 1981a, 2000e-5(g). A sound reading of the same-treatment clause would preserve the distinctions so carefully made elsewhere in the Act; the Court's reading makes a muddle of them.

But (believe it or not) it gets worse. In order to make sense of its conflation of disparate impact with disparate treatment, the Court claims that its new test is somehow "limited to the Pregnancy Discrimination Act context," yet at the same time "consistent with" the traditional use of circumstantial evidence to show intent to discriminate in Title VII cases. A court in a Title VII case, true enough, may consider a policy's effects and even its justifications—along with "'all of the [other] surrounding facts and circumstances'"—when trying to ferret out a policy's motive. *Hazelwood School Dist.* v. *United States,* 433 U.S. 299 (1977). The Court cannot possibly think, however, that its newfangled balancing test reflects this conventional inquiry. It has, after all, just marched up and down the hill telling us that the same-treatment clause is not (no-no!) "'superfluous, void, or insignificant.'" If the clause merely instructed courts to consider a policy's effects and justifications the way it considers other circumstantial evidence of motive, it *would* be superfluous. So the Court's balancing test must mean something else. Even if the effects and justifications of policies are not enough to show intent to discriminate under ordinary Title VII principles, they could (Poof!) still show intent to discriminate for purposes of the pregnancy same-treatment clause. Deliciously incoherent.

And all of this to what end? The difference between a routine circumstantial-evidence inquiry into motive and today's grotesque effects-and-justifications inquiry into motive, it would seem, is that today's approach requires judges to concentrate on effects and justifications to the exclusion of other considerations. But Title VII *already* has a framework that allows judges to home in on a policy's effects and justifications—disparate impact. Under that framework, it is *already* unlawful for an employer to use a practice that has a disparate impact on the basis of a protected trait, unless (among other things) the employer can show that the practice "is job related . . . and consistent with business necessity." §2000e-2(k)(1)(A)(i). The Court does not explain why we need (never mind how the Act could possibly be read to contain) today's ersatz disparate-impact test, under which the disparate-impact element gives way to the significant-burden criterion and the business-necessity defense gives way to the sufficiently-strong-justification standard. Today's decision can thus serve only one purpose: allowing claims that belong under Title VII's disparate-impact provisions to be brought under its disparate-treatment provisions instead.

IV

[The dissent also took issue with Justice Alito's concurrence for allowing an employer to] deny a pregnant woman a benefit granted to workers who perform similar tasks only on the basis of a "neutral business ground." This requirement of a "business ground" shadows the Court's requirement of a "sufficiently strong" justification, and, like it, has no footing in the terms of the same-treatment clause. . . . His] need to engage in this text-free broadening in order to make the concurrence's interpretation work is as good a sign as any that its interpretation is wrong from the start. . . .

Justice KENNEDY, dissenting.

[Although joining Justice Scalia's dissent, this separate dissent noted "little doubt that women who are in the work force—by choice, by financial necessity, or both—confront a serious disadvantage after becoming pregnant." This reality is partially addressed by the PDA and the parental leave provisions of the FMLA, and perhaps by the ADA Amendments Act of 2008, as interpreted by implementing regulations that "may require accommodations for many pregnant employees, even though pregnancy itself is not expressly classified as a disability. Additionally, many States have enacted laws providing certain accommodations for pregnant employees. These Acts honor and safeguard the important contributions women make to both the workplace and the American family."]

NOTES

1. *How Big a Change?* The critical statutory language reads: "[W]omen affected by pregnancy, childbirth, or related medical condition shall be treated the same for all employment-related purposes as other persons not so affected but similar in their ability or inability to work." All the justices rejected the "most-favored nation" reading of this second clause of the PDA, and the majority does so because this reading essentially writes intent to discriminate out of the statute for pregnancy accommodation disparate treatment cases. But at the same time, the majority purports to apply *McDonnell Douglas,* which is all about intent, to the question of pregnancy accommodations. Even more confusingly, it makes clear that its analysis applies only to the pregnancy question. In short, the Court seems to be reformulating what it means to intend to discriminate, but only for cases of pregnancy accommodation. *See generally* Joanna L. Grossman, *Expanding the Core: Pregnancy Discrimination Law as It Approaches Full Term,* 52 IDAHO L. REV. 825 (2016).

2. *The Test.* The critical sentence seems to be: "[T]he plaintiff may reach a jury on this issue by providing sufficient evidence that the employer's policies impose a significant burden on pregnant workers, and that the employer's 'legitimate, nondiscriminatory' reasons are not sufficiently strong to justify the burden, but rather—when considered along with the burden imposed—give rise to an inference of intentional discrimination." So the factfinder still has to find intent, but that issue gets to the jury when there's evidence of "a significant burden" and evidence that the employer's reasons are not "sufficiently strong."

Up to this point, you've learned that intent to discriminate requires, well, intent. The strength or weakness of the employer's reasons is irrelevant so long as the factfinder determines that a prohibited characteristic did not play a role in the decision. Of course, very weak reasons might allow a jury to infer intent since the jury might not credit that an employer in fact acted for what seemed a silly or irrational reason. Does *Young* change this? If it doesn't, why did the majority limit its rule to pregnancy? If it does, what does intent mean in the pregnancy setting?

Professor Deborah Brake, *The Shifting Sands of Employment Discrimination: From Unjustified Impact to Disparate Treatment in Pregnancy and Pay,* 105 GEO. L. J. 559, 584-85 (2017), finds *Young* remarkable. First, the demand for sufficiently strong reasons "rips the seams out of the traditional understanding of what separates impact from treatment claims. Time and again, the Court has reiterated that proof that a practice has a disparate impact does not establish proof of intent to discriminate." Secondly, the plaintiff now need not prove pretext in its original meaning, "that the employer's reason was not its genuine motivation for acting. Rather, the plaintiff need show only that it was not a 'strong' enough reason 'to justify the burden' on pregnant women." *See also* Michael C. Harper, *Confusion on the Court: Distinguishing Disparate Treatment from Disparate Impact in* Young v. UPS *and* EEOC v. Abercrombie & Fitch, Inc., 96 B.U.L. REV. 543 (2016); William Corbett, *Young v. United Parcel Service, Inc.: McDonnell Douglas to the Rescue?,* 92 WASH. U. L. REV. 1683 (2015).

3. *Significant Burden and Sufficiently Strong.* The Court provided some guidance on the two key concepts for its new test. A plaintiff can get to the jury on a significant burden "by providing evidence that the employer accommodates a large percentage of nonpregnant workers while failing to accommodate a large percentage of pregnant workers." As applied to the case before the Court, a showing would suffice that "UPS accommodates most nonpregnant employees with lifting limitations while categorically failing to accommodate pregnant employees with lifting limitations." The second half of the statement is certainly true, but did Young show that UPS accommodated "most nonpregnant employees with lifting limitations"? If so, is that because having a lifting limitation is an ADA-defined disability?

As for the strength of the employer's reasons, the majority noted, and Justice Alito agreed, that "consistent with the Act's basic objective, that reason normally cannot consist simply of a claim that it is more expensive or less convenient to add pregnant women to the category of those ('similar in their ability or inability to work') whom the employer accommodates." As for Young herself, she could argue that UPS's multiple policies accommodating nonpregnant employees with lifting restrictions suggest that its reasons for failing to accommodate pregnant employees "are not sufficiently strong—to the point that a jury could find that its reasons for failing to accommodate pregnant employees give rise to an inference of intentional discrimination."

Professor Deborah Widiss predicts that most pregnancy accommodation cases will be influenced by ADA-mandated accommodations since a prima facie case can be established by looking to any group of favored workers and a pretext finding is possible even for workers favored by statutory mandate because the employer will have to explain why it did not extend such accommodations to pregnant workers. *The Interaction of the Pregnancy Discrimination Act with the Americans with Disabilities Act after* Young v. UPS, 50 U.C. DAVIS L. REV. 1423 (2017). But remember Justice Alito's concurrence. He would find compliance with the ADA and accommodations for those injured on the job to be sufficiently strong. Only the DOT disqualification apparently suffices. Do you think the majority would agree if forced to confront the issue?

In a post-*Young* decision, *Legg v. Ulster Cnty.*, 820 F.3d 67 (2d Cir. 2016), the court overturned defendant's post-trial judgment as a matter of law. Plaintiff had established a prima facie case by showing that she was denied light duty accommodation for her pregnancy when workers injured on the job were accommodated. While the employer's duty under state law to continue to pay worker injured on the job was a neutral reason, a reasonable jury could find it to be pretextual when no one testified that that was the reason for the denial and the evidence showed that a large number of other workers were accommodated when one woman was not. In addition, a reasonable jury could find "the defendants' reasons were not 'sufficiently strong,' when considered alongside the burden imposed, to justify the denial of accommodation to pregnant employees," when there was only one such worker and the cost of the accommodation could have been found to be a factor in the decision, contrary to *Young's* teaching. *Id.* at 77.

4. *Merging Disparate Treatment and Disparate Impact.* Looking to the strength of the employer's reasons (rather than merely their honesty) is a radical shift in approach to disparate treatment. Indeed, Justice Scalia's dissent accused the majority of importing disparate impact analysis into a disparate treatment framework. Is that a fair observation? Although factfinders could always draw an inference of intent to discriminate from the use of a practice with a disparate impact, that was rare in the lower courts when sophisticated statistical evidence was not available. If Scalia is right, is that a bad thing? By the way, the disparate impact theory had had almost no traction in the pregnancy context before *Young*. Joanna L. Grossman, in *Pregnancy, Work, and the Promise of Equal Citizenship*, 98 GEO. L.J. 567, 616 (2010) ("The reality is that plaintiffs almost never prevail on such claims in the pregnancy context."). *See also* L. Camille Hebert, *Disparate Impact and Pregnancy: Title VII's Other Accommodation Requirement*, 24 AM. U.J. GENDER SOC. POL'Y & L. 107 (2015); *see also* Michelle A. Travis, *Recapturing the Transformative Potential of Employment Discrimination Law*, 62 WASH. & LEE L. REV. 3 (2005).

5. *Stepping Back from the Doctrine.* Whatever the doctrinal implications of *Young,* the significance of the case for at least larger employers is clear: Failing to accommodate pregnant workers when other workers are so accommodated is risky under Title VII. Second, as the majority noted, and Justice Kennedy stressed, the ADA may impose its own requirements of accommodation of some pregnancy restrictions, such as heavy lifting for at least some jobs. When the possible application of the Americans with Disabilities Act to pregnancy as a temporary disability is factored in, that risk becomes much greater. *See generally* Deborah A. Widiss, Gilbert *Redux: The Interaction of the Pregnancy Discrimination Act and the Amended Americans with Disabilities Act,* 46 U.C. Davis 961 (2013). Finally, state laws are increasingly requiring accommodation of pregnancy. *See* National Women's Law Center, https://nwlc. org/resources/pregnancy-accommodations-states/. *But see* Bradley A. Areheart, *Accommodating Pregnancy,* 67 Ala. L. Rev. 1125 (2016) (favoring parental or even universalist accommodation rather than accommodating through the ADA or targeted statutes dealing with pregnancy). The bottom line is that at least larger employers whose operations occur in such states will feel the need to revise their policies in a more pregnancy-friendly way.

6. *Related Conditions.* Pregnancy, as such, is not the only condition affected by the PDA. Because of the "related medical conditions" language of the statute, *Young* may require re-examination of employer breastfeeding rules. *See Hicks v. City of Tuscaloosa,* 870 F.3d 1253, 1260 (11th Cir. 2017) (discrimination on account of breastfeeding is prohibited by the PDA; although employers "do not have to provide *special* accommodations to breastfeeding workers," plaintiff claimed only that she be treated the same as other employees with temporary injuries who were given "alternative duty"); *see also* 29 U.S.C. §207(r) (2018) (requiring employers provide lactation support for their workers).

Given the prior approach of the lower courts, however, it is not clear whether *Young* will have an impact on other gender-related issues. For example, questions have arisen about the extent to which employers can exclude fertility treatments and birth control from coverage, which could be viewed as pertaining to pregnancy-related conditions. *See In re Union Pac. R.R. Emp't Practices Litig.,* 479 F.3d 936, 938 (8th Cir. 2007) (the PDA did not require an employer to cover contraception for women when it did not do so for men); *Saks v. Franklin Covey Co.,* 316 F.3d 337 (2d Cir. 2003) (rejecting a claim that denial of fertility treatments violated Title VII). *But see Hall v. Nalco Co.,* 534 F.3d 644 (7th Cir. 2008) (finding denial of in vitro fertilization to be sex discrimination against women); *see generally* Stephen F. Befort & Elizabeth C. Borer, *Equitable Prescription Drug Coverage: Preventing Sex Discrimination in Employer-Provided Health Plans,* 70 La. L. Rev. 205 (2009).

7. *Child-care Discrimination?* Although discrimination against those with child-care responsibilities is not per se illegal under the statute, *Piantanida v. Wyman Ctr., Inc.,* 116 F.3d 340 (8th Cir. 1997), we've seen that one of the first Title VII cases involved an explicit employer policy excluding women with school-age children. *Phillips v. Martin Marietta Corp.,* 400 U.S. 542 (1971). Title VII's basic prohibition of sex discrimination, then, especially coupled with the PDA, may provide relief even in more individualized cases when an employer treats mothers worse than other workers. An example is *Walsh v. National Computer Systems,* 332 F.3d 1150 (8th Cir. 2003), where plaintiff was treated much more harshly than her coworkers during her pregnancy and upon her return from maternity leave. A jury found Walsh had been subjected to a hostile work environment and had been constructively discharged based on pregnancy or sex discrimination. The appeals court upheld the verdict, rejecting the employer's argument that the only discrimination proven was against parents or on the basis of childcare duties, which is not prohibited by Title VII. Rather, the evidence supported the plaintiff's claim that "she was discriminated against not because she was a new parent, but because she is a woman who had been pregnant, had taken a maternity leave, and might become pregnant again." *Id.* at 1160. Admittedly, Walsh's case was far stronger than many because of the numerous statements of her supervisor explicitly referring to her past or potential future pregnancy. But even absent such statements, it will often be possible to prove disparate treatment of mothers. *See* Joan C. Williams & Stephanie Bornstein *The Evolution of "FReD": Family Responsibilities Discrimination and Developments in the Law of Stereotyping and Implicit Bias*, 59 HASTINGS L. J. 1311 (2008); Joan C. Williams & Nancy Segal, *Beyond the Maternal Wall: Relief for Family Caregivers Who Are Discriminated Against on the Job*, 26 HARV. WOMEN'S L. J. 77 (2003).

8. *The Employer's Perspective.* In light of all this, think about the accommodation problem from the employer's planning perspective. The risk of liability tied to the differential treatment of workers needing accommodations requires that employers be conscientious in deciding how to respond to workers' requests for deviations from regular work practices. If you were an employer, what type of policy would you institute? Would you (1) accommodate everyone; (2) accommodate no one; (3) trust your supervisors to make "appropriate" accommodation decisions; or (4) locate the decisions within HR to ensure consistency? With respect to the last two options, wouldn't your decision depend on the kind of work involved? The cost of the requested accommodations? The value of the particular employee to your team or the business as a whole? The anticipated duration of the accommodation? The need for managerial consistency?

As you approach this question, don't forget the possibility that some accommodations may actually be in the employer's interests. For example, "flex-time" is increasingly offered by larger employers and innovations like the four-day work week have received positive reviews. Symposium, *Redefining Work: Implications of the Four-Day Work Week*, 42 CONN. L. REV. 1031 *et seq.* (2010). *But see* Robert C. Bird, *The Promise and Peril of Flexible Working Time*, 118 W. VA. L. REV. 327 (2015) (survey finding most employers do not have such policies).

And as you formulate policies for the employer, you might have to consider whether some accommodations of some workers might themselves generate legal problems. Within some limits, employers are permitted to accommodate pregnant workers. *California Federal Savings & Loan Ass'n v. Guerra*, 479 U.S. 272 (1987), held that employers could provide some preferential treatment to pregnant workers without violating Title VII's prohibition of sex discrimination. In that case, the Court found no conflict between Title VII's prohibition of sex discrimination and a California statute which, in effect, created a right to unpaid maternity leave by granting women a right to return to comparable employment after delivery. The PDA was "a floor beneath which pregnancy disability benefits may not drop—not a ceiling above which they may not rise." *Id.* at 280. But there are limits to such preferences. *Schafer v. Bd. of Pub. Educ. of the Sch. Dist. of Pittsburgh, Pa.*, 903 F.2d 243 (3d Cir. 1990), struck down a policy giving women one year's maternity leave while denying comparable paternity leave for men. Since the leave far exceeded the normal period of disability related to child-*bearing*, it was really child-*rearing* leave. According to the court, *Guerra* did not justify preferring mothers over fathers for this purpose since either parent could care for the child. *Id. Cf. Johnson v. Univ. of Iowa*, 431 F.3d 325 (8th Cir. 2005) (allowing biological mothers, but not fathers, to use accrued paid sick leave for absences after birth of a child is not gender discrimination because additional paid leave is provided to women for pregnancy-related disability, not child-rearing purposes). *See generally* Keith Cunningham-Parmeter, *Men at Work, Fathers at Home: Uncovering the Masculine Face of Caregiver Discrimination*, 24 COLUM. J. GENDER & L. 253 (2013).

Because the protection provided by Title VII is limited, commentators have suggested a variety of responses beyond proposals for reinterpreting existing statutes. The closest the nation has come to developing law requiring work-family accommodations is the FMLA, which is treated next.

2. The Family and Medical Leave Act

Partly in response to some of the limits of discrimination law discussed in the previous section, Congress enacted the Family and Medical Leave Act ("FMLA") of 1993, which, together with its state analogs, is the major thrust of accommodation law for those who do not count as "disabled."

The FMLA is administered by the Department of Labor, which has elaborate regulations implementing the statute. 29 C.F.R. §825 (2014). The FMLA differs from the PDA in several ways. The statute goes beyond issues of gender discrimination and the challenges posed by pregnancy in an attempt to target the problem of work-family balance more broadly. It seeks to do this by extending rights to workers both for family care and for self-care. Thus, leave is required not only in connection with the birth of a child and to deal with serious family illnesses (family care) but also to deal with the worker's own serious illness (self-care). It protects workers in gender-neutral terms, providing the same rights to men and women workers with family responsibilities.

At the same time, the FMLA raises many of the same issues associated with existing discrimination law, including concerns about the limits of equality and the problem of preferential treatment. In addition, it has been subject to significant criticism, both by employers, who believe it improperly intrudes on managerial prerogative, and by advocates and feminists, who find it insufficient in addressing workers' needs, particularly those of mothers.

29 U.S.C. §2612. Leave Requirement

(a) In general.

(1) *Entitlement to leave.* Subject to section 103, an eligible employee shall be entitled to a total of 12 workweeks of leave during any 12-month period for one or more of the following:

(A) Because of the birth of a son or daughter of the employee and in order to care for such son or daughter.

(B) Because of the placement of a son or daughter with the employee for adoption or foster care.

(C) In order to care for the spouse, or a son, daughter, or parent, of the employee, if such spouse, son, daughter, or parent has a serious health condition.

(D) Because of a serious health condition that makes the employee unable to perform the functions of the position of such employee.

(E) Because of any qualifying exigency (as the Secretary shall, by regulation, determine) arising out of the fact that the spouse, or a son, daughter, or parent of the employee is on covered active duty (or has been notified of an impending call or order to covered active duty) in the Armed Forces . . . .

(c) *Unpaid leave permitted.* Except as provided in subsection (d) [pertaining to the ability of the employer require or employee to elect to substitute existing paid leave for FMLA leave], leave granted under subsection (a) may consist of unpaid leave. . . .

29 U.S.C. §2614. Employment and Benefits Protection

(a) Restoration to position

Except as provided in subsection (b) of this section, any eligible employee who takes leave under section 2612 of this title for the intended purpose of the leave shall be entitled, on return from such leave—

(A) to be restored by the employer to the position of employment held by the employee when the leave commenced; or

(B) to be restored to an equivalent position with equivalent employment benefits, pay, and other terms and conditions of employment.

(2) Loss of benefits

The taking of leave under section 2612 of this title shall not result in the loss of any employment benefit accrued prior to the date on which the leave commenced.

(3) Limitations

Nothing in this section shall be construed to entitle any restored employee to—

(A) the accrual of any seniority or employment benefits during any period of leave; or

(B) any right, benefit, or position of employment other than any right, benefit, or position to which the employee would have been entitled had the employee not taken the leave.

NOTES

1. *FMLA Coverage.* The FMLA has far more limited coverage than most of the other statutory schemes we treat in this book. For example, Title VII and the ADA reach all employers with 15 or more employees. By contrast, the FMLA applies only to employers with 50 or more employees. Further, unlike the antidiscrimination statutes, not all employees of covered employers are protected. Part-time employees, first-year employees, and even employees who work for small offices of larger employers are not entitled to leave under the FMLA. This is because the statute requires "eligible" employees to have worked for the employer for at least 12 months, §2611(2)(A)(1), and for at least 1,250 hours during the year preceding the start of the leave, §2611(2)(A)(ii), and to be employed at a worksite where the employer employs at least 50 employees within a 75-mile radius. §2611(2)(B)(ii). *See Staunch v. Cont'l Airlines, Inc.*, 511 F.3d 625 (6th Cir. 2008) (flight attendant not entitled to FMLA leave when she had worked fewer than 1,250 hours).

2. *FMLA Benefits.* The statute's basic command is *unpaid* leave, which is defined as reinstating the employee to the same or an equivalent job when the leave ends. Elsewhere, the statute permits the employee to elect, or the employer to require, the use of any paid leave the employee may have accrued under the employer's other policies (vacation, paid sick time, etc.) during FMLA leave. *See* 29 U.S.C. §2612(d)(2). As a practical matter, most employers insist on this, in part for administrative convenience and in part to ensure that employees do not take 12 weeks of FMLA leave and existing paid leave consecutively, resulting in a longer absence from work. The other principal advantage conferred by the FMLA is the requirement that employers maintain preexisting benefits, including health insurance, while the employee is on FMLA leave. However, the employee is obligated to continue paying his or her portion of the premiums, which can be onerous during a time in which the employee is not receiving a salary.

The fact that FMLA leave is unpaid is the key limitation and source of criticism of the statute. Only a relatively privileged class of workers is likely to be able to take full advantage of its benefits. A number of commentators have called for the provision of paid family/medical leave, funded by either the employer or government sources. *See, e.g.*, Gillian Lester, *A Defense of Paid Family Leave*, 28 HARV. J.L. & GENDER 1 (2005); Michael Selmi, *Family Leave and the Gender Wage Gap*, 78 N.C. L. REV. 707, 770-73 (2000). There have also been initiatives to require paid leave at the state level. Currently only a handful of states have implemented such a program, in all cases funded through a temporary disability insurance program. *See* Paid Family Leave Resources, Nat'l Conf. St. Legislatures, http://www.ncsl.org/research/labor-and-employment/ paid-family-leave-resources.aspx.

3. *Limitations on FMLA Rights.* Despite the FMLA's general authorization of leave, the statute does have some limitations. For example, the statute expressly provides that seniority need not accrue during any statutory-mandated leave. §2614(a)(3). Further, §2614(b) creates an exception to the reinstatement right for "highly compensated employees" (the top ten percent of all employees in a designated geographic area), but only if reinstatement would cause "substantial and grievous economic injury." 29 C.F.R. §825.218; *see Kephart v. Cherokee County, N.C.*, 229 F.3d 1142 (4th Cir. 2002). Third, the statute itself limits the family members for whose care leave may be taken, although the courts have not been grudging in interpreting this provision. *Gienapp v. Harbor Crest*, 756 F.3d 527, 531 (7th Cir. 2014) ("Employees are entitled to leave to provide 'care' for their children," regardless of whether they are the "primary" caregiver); *Ballard v. Chi. Park Dist.*, 741 F.3d 838, 839 (7th Cir. 2014) (the FMLA requires leave to physically care for a terminally ill parent's medical, hygienic, or nutritional needs even if the care was not part of ongoing treatment of the condition).

Finally, an employee who takes leave for her own health condition may be asked to provide a doctor's certification of her ability to resume work. §2614(a)(4). *See Wallace v. FedEx Corp.*, 764 F.3d 571 (6th Cir. 2014) (upholding 29 C.F.R. §825.305(a) which allows an employer to require a medical-certification form within 15 days but also requires that employer to advise the employee of the consequences of failure to provide such a certification). There is some flexibility about leave, *see Hansen v. Fincantieri Marine Group, LLC*, 763 F.3d 832 (7th Cir. 2014) (employer may not deny intermittent FMLA leave merely because requests exceed the estimated length in his medical certification form), but an employee who exhausts her permitted leave and is still unable to work is not entitled to keep her job. *Hatchett v. Philander Smith Coll.*, 251 F.3d 670, 677 (8th Cir. 2001).

4. *Resistance and Reaction to Enactment of the FMLA.* The relatively narrow coverage of the FMLA and its limited unpaid benefit reflect strong resistance to the statute on the part of corporate America. The first President Bush vetoed two earlier versions of the statute, but the bill gained momentum when it was framed as addressing a "family" issue rather than a feminist one. Opponents of the FMLA argued that it started down the slippery slope of government-mandated policies, reducing corporate control over employee benefit programs. Employers worried about the effectiveness of temporary replacements and/or morale problems resulting from redistribution of work to cover FMLA leaves. Small business owners, in particular, complained of administrative costs, especially the statute's record-keeping and notice provisions.

5. *Impact of the FMLA.* In the more than two decades since the FMLA has been in effect, millions of employees have taken advantage of the rights it provides. Corporate America has seemed to adjust to its demands without substantial evidence of either the disruption of operations or the effects on morale of employees asked to pick up the slack when a coworker takes leave. Thus, the high costs that corporations believed would come from compliance with the FMLA have apparently not materialized. Indeed, there is reason to think that the statute has resulted in some benefits to employers in improved staff retention, morale, and productivity. *See* Jane Waldfogel, *Family-Friendly Policies for Families with Young Children*, 5 EMP. RTS. & EMP. POL'Y J. 273, 290-91 (2001). Of course, this success is perhaps attributable to the very limited protections afforded by the FMLA. A more aggressive statute, such as one requiring paid leave, might generate a very different response.

6. *FMLA Irony.* There has been no constitutional challenge to the statute as far as it reaches private employment, but the Supreme Court has considered a claim that the FMLA could not constitutionally apply to the states because of the Eleventh Amendment. In *Nevada Department of Human Resources v. Hibbs*, 538 U.S. 721 (2003), the Court rejected that argument in an opinion replete with irony. The plaintiff in that case, William Hibbs, worked for the Department's Welfare Division. He sought, and was granted, leave under the FMLA to care for his ailing wife, who was recovering from a car accident, but he and the Department disagreed about the amount of leave. He was terminated when he failed to report to work when the Department required him to do so. He sued, and the Department interposed a claim of Eleventh Amendment immunity.

While the Eleventh Amendment generally bars private suits against the state without their consent, *Board of Trustees of Univ. of Ala. v. Garrett*, 531 U.S. 356 (2001) (barring ADA suits); *Kimel v. Fla. Bd. of Regents*, 528 U.S. 62 (2000) (barring ADEA suits), Congress may "abrogate such immunity in federal court if it makes its intention to abrogate unmistakably clear in the language of the statute and acts pursuant to a valid exercise of its power under §5 of the Fourteenth Amendment." 538 U.S. at 726. Title VII has been interpreted to validly abrogate such immunity. *Fitzpatrick v. Bitzer*, 427 U.S. 445 (1976). Since there was no doubt that Congress had intended to abrogate states' immunity, *Hibbs* turned on whether Congress acted within its §5 power in either attacking equal protection violations or enacting "prophylactic legislation that proscribes facially constitutional conduct, in order to prevent and deter unconstitutional conduct." *Id.* at 721-22. The Court held yes.

In enacting the FMLA, Congress looked to evidence that states continued to rely on invalid gender stereotypes in the employment context, specifically in the administration of leave benefits. That evidence, however, was not of continued discrimination against women but rather of discrimination against male workers. For example, one survey stated that 37 percent of surveyed private-sector employees were covered by maternity leave policies, while only 18 percent were covered by paternity leave policies. *Id.* at 730. Further, there was also evidence of "differential leave policies [for men and women that] were not attributable to any differential physical needs of men and women, but rather to the pervasive sex-role stereotype that caring for family members is women's work." *Id.* at 731. Finally, "even where state laws and policies were not facially discriminatory, they were applied in discriminatory ways." *Id.* at 732. The Court concluded that "the States' record of unconstitutional participation in, and fostering of, gender-based discrimination in the administration of leave benefits is weighty enough to justify the enactment of prophylactic §5 legislation." *Id.* at 735. The importance of the gender basis of the FMLA is underscored by *Coleman v. Court of Appeals*, 566 U.S. 30 (2012), a case dealing with the "self-care" provisions of the FMLA. There, the Court found an insufficient basis for concluding that states had discriminated on the basis of sex in this regard, thus rendering that aspect of the statute unenforceable against state employees by private suit for damages. The irony of *Hibbs* was that, although the gender-neutral statute was largely designed to address the work-life concerns of women, it was upheld because of evidence of Congress's concern about discrimination against men.

In *Family Leave and the Gender Wage Gap*, 78 N.C. L. Rev. 707, 708 (2000), Professor Michael Selmi argues that not only are employers' attitudes toward men as caregivers part of the problem, but male attitudes themselves also must change if women are to play a more central role in the workplace: "[I]ncreasing workplace equality will require persuading men to behave more like women, rather than trying to induce women to behave more like men. Achieving this objective would create a new workplace norm where all employees would be expected to have and spend time with their children, and employers would adapt to that reality." Accordingly, he would create greater incentives for men to take leave for the birth or adoption of a child. Does this go too far in urging that men be pressured or incentivized into taking leave? Is he too optimistic about the ability of the law to assist societal change? Along these lines, Keith Cunningham-Parmeter, *(Un)Equal Protection: Why Gender Equality Depends on Discrimination*, 109 NW. U. L. Rev. 1 (2015), advocates paid leave bonuses only for fathers in order to shift societal expectations.

7. *Has It Worked?* While passage of the FMLA is often viewed as a major, if very limited, advance in requiring employers to become more "family friendly" in gender-neutral terms, many commentators remain sharply critical of the inadequate response of the law to the obstacles faced by pregnant women and working mothers. The FMLA's principal contribution is that it supplements Title VII's prohibition of pregnancy discrimination by requiring accommodation of at least some of the more exigent demands of pregnancy and motherhood. Today, Ms. Troupe could take FMLA leave rather than lose her job. The statute guarantees employees who could otherwise be legally discharged under Title VII the right to return to their jobs after taking time off to give birth or care for their children. But even viewed together, the FMLA and Title VII provide a very limited accommodation regime for mothers. Normal childcare responsibilities are not addressed by the FMLA, and even caring for an ill child is not protected if a "serious health condition" is not in play. What

constitutes a "serious health condition" is sometimes complicated, but most routine aliments that keep children home from school, such as colds and earaches, are not FMLA leave–eligible.

As a result, there have been calls for expanded accommodation of what one commentator calls the "caregiver conundrum," defined as the obstacles generated by "a set of norms in the workplace that were shaped by and for men." Nicole Buonocore Porter, *Synergistic Solutions: An Integrated Approach to Solving the Caregiver Conundrum for "Real" Workers*, 39 STETSON L. REV. 777, 781 (2010). As she sees it,

> The caregiver conundrum affects caregivers in three primary ways. First, many (perhaps most) caregivers need and want more workplace flexibility to meet the demands of their families, yet most workplaces do not provide the flexibility needed. Second, caregivers who choose to work reduced hours or part-time in order to spend more time taking care of their families do so at the significant cost of marginalizing their careers and being underpaid for their efforts. Third, parents and other caregivers in the lower-income brackets might need flexibility or reduced hours to meet their caregiving obligations but are financially unable to take time off for caregiving needs. These caregivers may also have difficulty meeting their workplace requirements because of inadequate or unreliable daycare.

Id. She offers as one solution a "Part-Time Parity Act," which would mandate pay and benefits proportional to those of full-time workers. *Id.* at 828-33. Other proposals would require FMLA leave for more quotidian childrearing, mandated accommodation in the form of required workplace flexibility, and accommodation tailored to individual caregiving needs similar to that granted religion and disability under other laws. *See also* Debbie N. Kaminer, *The Work-Family Conflict: Developing a Model of Parental Accommodation in the Workplace*, 54 AM. U. L. REV. 305 (2004); Laura T. Kessler, *The Attachment Gap: Employment Discrimination Law, Women's Cultural Caregiving, and the Limits of Economic and Liberal Legal Theory*, 34 U. MICH. J. L. REFORM 371, 386-87 (2001); Peggie R. Smith, *Accommodating Routine Parental Obligations in an Era of Work-Family Conflict: Lessons from Religious Accommodations*, 2001 WIS. L. REV. 1443 (2001). *Cf.* Rachel Arnow-Richman, *Incenting Flexibility: The Relationship Between Public Law and Voluntary Action in Enhancing Work-Life Balance*, 42 CONN. L. REV. 1081, 1099 (2010) (arguing that reasons such as "lack of information, cognitive biases, transaction costs, and other impediments" lead to suboptimal decisions with respect to leave: "In the context of workplace accommodations, this may mean that employers are under-serving caregivers (and in some instances themselves) by failing to make cost-neutral and even mutually advantageous accommodations.").

Might further measures also, at some point, create their own problems? Does privileging pregnancy, childbirth, and the early months of childrearing reinforce the notion that women's primary role is childrearing? Would extending such rights in a gender-neutral fashion solve that problem if, as Professor Selmi argues, women will be the primary ones to invoke such benefits? And, to the extent that benefits used primarily by women are costly for employers, would imposing such requirements lead employers to avoid hiring women in the first place? While such conduct would violate Title VII, it might frequently be impossible to detect.

In part as a result of such concerns, some commentators have urged moving the focus away from enabling caregiving to making work more accessible to people of all backgrounds and family situations, for instance by reducing the work week and eliminating mandatory overtime. *See, e.g.*, Marion Crain, *"Where Have All the Cowboys Gone?": Marriage and Breadwinning in Postindustrial Society*, 60 Ohio St. L. J. 1877 (1999); Vicki Schultz, *Life's Work*, 100 Colum. L. Rev. 1881 (2000). Might such proposals be more likely to garner public and political support? Are they likely to be as helpful to women with caregiving responsibilities? The Great Recession led some employers, largely in terms of saving money, to institute different work arrangements, most notably, the 4/40 workweek (four days of ten hours each). But there is reason to doubt that such changes will contribute substantially to better work-family balance, especially for women. Michelle A. Travis, *What a Difference a Day Makes, or Does It? Work/Family Balance and the Four-Day Work Week*, 42 Conn. L. Rev. 1223 (2010).

8. *Substantive Benefits and Redistributive Concerns.* The FMLA contains an affirmative directive—eligible employees must receive a specific substantive benefit—making it more of an accommodation statute like the ADA than a nondiscrimination statute like Title VII. Any kind of accommodation requirement raises redistribution concerns, particularly where the laws in question impose the costs of redistribution not on society generally but on the employers who are required to accommodate the workers in question. *See* Samuel R. Bagenstos, *The Future of Disability Law*, 114 Yale L. J. 1 (2004) (arguing that, because the ADA may serve as an open-ended tool of redistribution to people with disabilities, courts have limited its reach, resulting in the law's failure to undo deep-rooted structural barriers to employment for people with disabilities).

Professor Arnow-Richman argues that the history of the ADA, and in particular courts' narrow interpretation of its accommodation mandate, bode poorly for the future of work-family accommodation. This is particularly true, she suggests, in what she describes as the contemporary "Me, Inc." economy:

> The desirability of employer-supported accommodation rests on two assumptions: (i) basic features of the contemporary workplace represent choices about work structure that can and should be changed; and (ii) it is reasonable to expect employers to absorb the costs associated with making those changes or with providing necessary benefits to employee caregivers.
>
> These assumptions are . . . especially problematic when examined against the history of government intervention in the workplace and the nature of modern employment relationships. [V]oluntarily-provided employer benefits . . . have been the dominant mode of addressing employee lifecycle needs for the majority of the twentieth century. Such an allocation of rights and responsibilities at work was enabled by a particular "social contract" of employment, one in which employers and employees anticipated a long-term symbiotic relationship often governed by a collective bargaining agreement. In contrast, today's work relationships are defined by a "Me, Inc." work culture—an employment environment in which workers are increasingly independent, short-term employment relationships predominate, collective action is all but absent, and employer reliance on contingent labor has dramatically expanded. In an economy where employees' futures depend not on their current employer but on the value of their human capital within the external labor market, the incentives for voluntary accommodation of employees' lifecycle needs are generally absent.

See Rachel Arnow-Richman, *Accommodation Subverted: The Future of Work/Family Initiatives in a "Me, Inc." World*, 12 Tex. J. Women & L. 345, 373-88 (2003). She concludes that responding to the problem of inadequate accommodation of caregiving through government mandates "shows inadequate consideration for contemporary expectations about the way people work," and therefore imposing "extensive employer-funded accommodation in this context may overreach and spawn backlash." *Id.* at 374. Are you convinced by these concerns, or is Arnow-Richman's account overly pessimistic? Rather than caving to the "Me, Inc." work culture, should the law make wider efforts to dismantle what might appear to some observers as a race to the bottom?

9. *Hurting the People We Are Trying to Help?* Separate from concerns about fairness for employers are concerns about the impact of accommodation mandates on the group intended to benefit from them. Some scholars have raised questions about the consequences of statutes such as the FMLA and ADA. Christine Jolls, *Accommodation Mandates*, 53 STAN. L. REV. 223, 225, 291 (2000), writes that newer accommodation mandates, such as the ADA and FMLA are directed to "discrete, identifiable groups of workers, such as the disabled" to accommodate their "unique needs." For the FMLA, she warns that, because of significant occupational segregation, such an accommodation mandate will tend "to lower the relative wages of disadvantaged workers and to increase or decrease their relative employment levels depending on whether the value of the mandated accommodation exceeds or falls short of its cost." She predicts that, because the cost of unpaid leave is hard to monetize, a mandate that imposes such costs "may be more likely to be reflected in reductions in the relative employment levels of disadvantaged workers and less likely to be reflected in reductions in their relative wages." *Id; see also* John J. Donohue III, *Understanding the Reasons for and Impact of Legislatively Mandated Benefits for Selected Workers*, 53 STAN. L. REV. 897 (2001); *cf.* Cass R. Sunstein, *Human Behavior and the Law of Work*, 87 VA. L. REV. 205, 206-8 (2001) (supporting mandates as a default rule but allowing them to be waived). If Professor Jolls is correct, more accommodation would mean less employment for women (mothers) but more accommodating employment for those who obtain jobs. Is that a worthwhile trade-off? Who should decide?

10. *A Procedural Approach?* Is there a middle road that can expand caregiver rights while avoiding the pitfalls of accommodation mandates? Professor Arnow-Richman proposes that employers should have a duty to discuss caregiving accommodations with their employees, somewhat along the lines of the ADA's interactive process. Unlike the ADA, however, there would be no substantive duty to accommodate. "A procedural requirement imposed on the employer upon the conclusion of FMLA leave recognizes, for instance, that an employee who gives birth or adopts a new child cannot be expected to seamlessly return to full-time work upon the conclusion of the child's third month." Rachel Arnow-Richman, *Public Law and Private Process: Toward an Incentivized Organizational Justice Model of Equal Employment Quality for Caregivers*, 2007 UTAH L. REV. 25, 57. This approach would also have the advantage of shifting "the blunt effect of a one-size-fits-all mandated benefit" to a more flexible response by the employer and employee. *Id.* Framing the new right as procedural only with no substantive component "is critical to the political viability of the proposal both in terms of congressional adoption and the reliability of judicial enforcement." To what extent do procedural protections assist employees in the absence of mandates? In other words, does an employer have any incentive to accommodate an employee if the law does not so require? If not, do the litigation incentives proposed by Professor Arnow-Richman help? Might they impose additional risks?

Goelzer v. Sheboygan County, Wisconsin
604 F.3d 987 (7th Cir. 2010)

WILLIAMS, Circuit Judge.

After two decades of employment with her county government, Dorothy Goelzer was fired from her job. Her supervisor informed her of the termination decision two weeks before she was scheduled to begin two months of leave under the Family and Medical Leave Act (FMLA). This leave did not mark the first time Goelzer was away from work on FMLA leave, as Goelzer had taken a significant amount of authorized FMLA leave during the four preceding years to deal with her own health issues and those of her mother and husband. After she lost her job, Goelzer brought this suit and alleged that her employer had interfered with her right to reinstatement under the FMLA and had retaliated against her for taking FMLA leave. The defendants contend that her supervisor simply decided to hire another person with a larger skill set. [The district court granted summary judgment against plaintiff, but the Seventh Circuit reversed.]

I. Background

[Sheboygan County hired Dorothy Goelzer in 1986 as Clerk Typist in its office of the Register of Deeds. By 1999, she was the administrative assistant to Adam Payne, the Board's Administrative Coordinator. Payne consistently gave Goelzer good performance reviews and merit increases. In some of his evaluations, he praised her for rarely being absent.]

Goelzer began to have significant health issues in 2002. She had eye surgery in July and took approximately a month of FMLA leave during her surgery and recovery. She also had multiple doctors' appointments in the months before and after her surgery. All in all, she used 312.50 hours of sick leave in 2002, the equivalent of nearly eight forty-hour weeks. Payne wrote in Goelzer's 2002 performance evaluation that, "[t]hough Dorothy has had an excellent record in the past, (36 hours of sick leave in 2001), she utilized 312 hours or 39 days of sick leave in 2002."

Goelzer continued to have health problems in 2003. She . . . took time off on thirty-two different days during 2003 for her health issues and used a total of 176.50 hours of leave. Payne commented on Goelzer's use of sick leave again in that year's performance evaluation, stating: "Dorothy utilized 176.50 hours or 22 days of sick leave in 2003." He gave her an overall rating of 3.36, with a 3.5 in the attendance category. He did not award her a merit pay increase. [When Goelzer disagreed with Payne about no merit increase, Payne responded with a February 5, 2004, memorandum that again referred to her leave: "In fact, the past two years, use of sick leave and vacation combined, you were out of the office 113 days. As the only support person in the office, this has presented challenges in the functionality and duties associated with the office."]

Goelzer used 94 hours of sick leave in 2004. She received a merit increase of 1.5% after her 2004 evaluation. The next year, Goelzer's health was stable, but her mother's health was not. Goelzer took FMLA leave on nine days in 2004 for appointments related to her mother or husband, and her 2005 FMLA applications included requests for intermittent leave to care for her mother. Goelzer received a 1.25% merit increase after 2005. Goelzer stated in an affidavit that when she asked why she did not receive a higher merit pay increase, Payne responded that she had missed a lot of time at work due to appointments with her mother.

Goelzer learned in 2006 that she would need foot surgery that year. On May 10, 2006, Goelzer submitted an FMLA leave request for time away from work from September 22, 2006 to November 20, 2006 for her foot surgery and recovery. At Payne's request, Goelzer provided a medical certification for the foot surgery to Human Resources Director Michael Collard on June 1, 2006. Collard wrote directly to Goelzer's doctor five days later and asked whether Goelzer could return to light duty office work before November 19, 2006, and if so, when. Goelzer's doctor responded that she would be totally disabled and unable to work during that time period. The County eventually approved Goelzer's FMLA leave request on August 8.

On August 15, 2006, the Sheboygan County Board passed an ordinance that converted the position of County Administrative Coordinator to that of County Administrator. The Board also appointed Payne to serve as County Administrator. With this change, Payne now had the power under Wisconsin Statute §59.18(3) to discharge Goelzer on his own, a power he did not previously have. Within the next ten days, Payne told Collard that he wanted to meet to discuss options for terminating Goelzer's employment. In preparation for the August 25, 2006 meeting, Collard prepared notes related to options, with a list that included "term outright, just need to change," "eliminate position," "Change T/O—reshuffle—create new position not qualified for," "Raise expectations & evaluate," and "Retaliation for FMLA?".

On September 8, 2006, two weeks before Goelzer was to commence FMLA leave for her foot surgery, Payne discharged Goelzer with an effective date of November 30, 2006. (Payne placed Goelzer on paid leave until November 30, 2006 so that she would receive the FMLA leave that had been previously approved.) At the time, Goelzer had used 67 hours of leave in 2006 and was scheduled to take an additional 328 hours related to her foot surgery. . . .

Payne did not immediately replace Goelzer. Instead, he first utilized an unpaid college intern. On January 16, 2007, the County Board enacted an ordinance that eliminated Goelzer's former position and replaced it with the position of "Assistant to the Administrator." It also increased the pay grade for the role from Grade 6 to Grade 8. Payne hired Kay Lorenz as the Assistant to the Administrator on March 19, 2007. . . .

II.   Analysis . . .

The FMLA allows an eligible employee with a serious health condition that renders the employee unable to perform her position to take twelve workweeks of leave during each twelve-month period. 29 U.S.C. §2612(a)(1)(D). An employee may also utilize this leave to care for certain immediate relatives, including a parent or spouse, with a serious health condition. *Id.* §2612(a)(1)(C). Under the FMLA, an employee on leave is entitled to the right to be restored to the same or an equivalent position that she had before she took qualifying leave. *Id.* §2614(a)(1)-(2). An employer may not "interfere with, restrain, or deny the exercise of or the attempt to exercise" any FMLA rights. *Id.* §2615(a)(1).

In addition, the FMLA affords protection to employees who are retaliated against because they exercise rights protected by the Act. *Lewis v. Sch. Dist. #70*, 523 F.3d 730, 741 (7th Cir. 2008). Pursuant to 29 U.S.C. §2615(a)(2), it is "unlawful for any employer to discharge or in any other manner discriminate against any individual for opposing any practice made unlawful by this subchapter." The Act also makes it unlawful to "discharge" or "discriminate" against a person for taking part in proceedings or inquiries under the FMLA. 29 U.S.C. §2615(b). We have construed these provisions as stating a cause of action for retaliation.

[The court determined that Goelzer's complaint alleged both interference and retaliation. One paragraph cited 29 U.S.C. §2614(a)(1), the FMLA provision barring interference, while a different passage used the language of §2615(a)(2), prohibiting retaliation.]

A. FMLA Interference

We first address Goelzer's interference argument. The plaintiff carries the burden of proving an FMLA interference claim. *Darst v. Interstate Brands Corp.*, 512 F.3d 903, 908 (7th Cir. 2008). To establish such a claim, an employee must show that: (1) she was eligible for the FMLA's protections; (2) her employer was covered by the FMLA; (3) she was entitled to take leave under the FMLA; (4) she provided sufficient notice of her intent to take leave; and (5) her employer denied her FMLA benefits to which she was entitled. *Burnett v. LFW, Inc.*, 472 F.3d 471, 477 (7th Cir. 2006). There is no dispute regarding the first four requirements; it is clear that the FMLA allowed Goelzer to take the leave that she did. The only issue is whether the defendants fired her to prevent her from exercising her right to reinstatement to her position. *See Simpson v. Office of the Chief Judge of the Circuit Court of Will County*, 559 F.3d 706, 712 (7th Cir. 2009) ("Firing an employee to prevent her from exercising her right to return to her prior position can certainly interfere with that employee's FMLA rights.").

An employee's right to reinstatement is not absolute. The FMLA allows an employer to refuse to restore an employee to the "former position when restoration would confer a 'right, benefit, or position of employment' that the employee would not have been entitled to if the employee had never left the workplace." *Kohls v. Beverly Enters. Wis., Inc.*, 259 F.3d 799, 805 (7th Cir. 2001) (citing 29 U.S.C. §2614(a)(3)(B)); *see also* 29 C.F.R. §825.216(a) ("An employee has no greater right to reinstatement or to other benefits and conditions of employment than if the employee has been continuously employed during the FMLA leave period."). In other words, an employee is not entitled to return to her former position if she would have been fired regardless of whether she took the leave.

The question at this stage of the proceedings, then, is whether a jury could find that the defendants did not reinstate Goelzer because she exercised her right to take FMLA leave. Payne and the County maintain that the answer is "no," as their position is that Goelzer's employment would have been terminated regardless of whether she took FMLA leave. They maintain that after Payne received a promotion to County Administrator, he simply exercised his new authority to replace Goelzer on his own with a person of his choosing. They stress that before his promotion, Payne would have needed the approval of the County through its Executive Committee before he could terminate Goelzer's employment. With the promotion to County Administrator, however, Payne could now make the termination decision on his own. And three weeks after he assumed his new role, Payne notified Goelzer she was losing her job, a decision he says had nothing to do with Goelzer's use of FMLA leave.

Michael Collard, the County's Human Resources Director, supports Payne's account. Collard asserts that Payne had expressed frustration for some time that Goelzer was not performing the tasks Payne had envisioned for her, and Collard also says that Payne had expressed a desire for an assistant with a greater skill set. In addition, although Payne did not immediately replace Goelzer and instead first utilized a college intern, Payne maintains that in the longer term he wanted the position to be enhanced to allow him to assign more sophisticated tasks beyond those that he says Goelzer could handle.

The defendants' account provides one possible explanation for the termination decision, and a jury might well choose to believe it. But there is another possibility as well. Goelzer contends that she lost her job because Payne and the County were not happy that she had exercised her right to take FMLA leave. . . . Even though the leave was authorized, we conclude that the evidence Goelzer introduced in response to the defendants' motion for summary judgment could lead a jury to find that she was denied reinstatement not because Payne simply wanted a different assistant, but because she had exercised her right to take leave under the FMLA.

A jury might be swayed by comments Payne made that could suggest frustration with Goelzer's use of FMLA leave. In her 2002 performance evaluation, for instance, Payne explicitly contrasted Goelzer's use of FMLA leave with her past "excellent" attendance, saying, "[t]hough Dorothy has had an excellent attendance record in the past, (36 hours of sick leave in 2001), she utilized 312 hours or 39 days of sick leave in 2002." Payne gave her a 3.5 rating in the "attendance" category in 2002. He noted her use of sick leave in the following year's performance evaluation as well, stating "Dorothy utilized 176 hours of 22 days of sick leave in 2003," and he gave her an overall rating of 3.36 that year but did not award a merit increase. Notably too, when Goelzer asked Payne in 2006 why she did not receive a higher merit increase based on her 2005 performance, she says that Payne responded that she had missed too much time from work to attend to appointments with her mother.

A jury might also look to the memorandum Payne wrote in 2004 in response to Goelzer's view that she should have received a merit increase, where he said in part: "you were out of the office having eye surgery in 2002 and 2003. In fact, the past two years, use of sick leave and vacation combined, you were out of the office 113 days. As the only support person in the office, this has presented challenges in the functionality and duties associated with the office." A jury might view this memorandum as evidence that Goelzer lost her job because she exercised her right to take FMLA leave, as it might Payne's comments in an evaluation he wrote in January 2006: "On occasion, I have been concerned with office and phone coverage. Dorothy had numerous appointments the past year and needs to be more cognitive of the time she is away from her desk or corresponding with others on non-related work activities." The defendants do not dispute that the FMLA protected Goelzer's attendance at these appointments, and a jury could look to those comments as indication that Payne was not pleased Goelzer had been absent for many FMLA-covered appointments, even though she was permitted to take them by the Act and an employer is not to interfere with that right.

Moreover, although Payne now maintains he had concerns about Goelzer's skill set and performance, he consistently gave her favorable performance reviews. He says now that her satisfactory performance ratings reflect his "lowered expectations" of her abilities, but the performance ratings themselves do not speak of lowered expectations, and a jury would not be compelled to credit this explanation. In fact, just over seven months before Payne told Goelzer she was being terminated, he had conducted Goelzer's annual performance review and concluded that her performance met or exceeded expectations in all areas.

A factfinder might also consider that, if Payne had serious problems with Goelzer's performance, he could have asked the County Board to terminate Goelzer's employment before he received the promotion, yet he did not do so. In addition, although Payne asserts that he wanted an assistant with a larger skill set, there are no documents evidencing a plan to restructure the assistant position before Goelzer's termination. And, of course, Payne told Goelzer that she was losing her job two weeks before she was scheduled to take two months of FMLA leave. In short, we are left with two competing accounts, either of which a jury could believe. So summary judgment is not appropriate, and we reverse its grant.

B. FMLA Retaliation

Goelzer also contends her FMLA retaliation theory should proceed to trial. The FMLA provides that it is unlawful for an employer "to discharge or in any manner discriminate against" any employee for opposing any practice the FMLA makes unlawful. 29 U.S.C. §2615(a)(2). The difference between a retaliation and interference theory is that the first "requires proof of discriminatory or retaliatory intent while [an interference theory] requires only proof that the employer denied the employee his or her entitlements under the Act." *Kauffman [v. Fed. Express Corp.*, 426 F.3d 880, 884 (7th Cir. 2005)]. To succeed on a retaliation claim, the plaintiff does not need to prove that "retaliation was the *only* reason for her termination; she may establish an FMLA retaliation claim by 'showing that the protected conduct was a substantial or motivating factor in the employer's decision'" *Lewis*.

A plaintiff may proceed under the direct or indirect methods of proof when attempting to establish an FMLA retaliation claim. *Burnett*. Under the direct method, the only method Goelzer employs, a plaintiff must present evidence that her employer took a materially adverse action against her because of her protected activity. If the plaintiff's evidence is contradicted, the case must proceed to trial unless the employer presents unrebutted evidence that it would have taken the adverse action against the plaintiff even if it did not have a retaliatory motive. That is, the plaintiff survives summary judgment by "'creating a triable issue of whether the adverse employment action of which she complains had a discriminatory motivation.'" *Lewis*.

Payne and the County maintain that a jury could not conclude that they intentionally discriminated against Goelzer for using FMLA leave. In addition to the evidence to which she pointed in support of her interference claim, Goelzer also directs our attention to Human Resources Director Collard's inquiry to Goelzer's physician that asked "[w]hether Ms. Goelzer would be physically able to work light duty in an office environment prior to November 19, 2006, and if so, when would be an appropriate time that we would expect her to return." [This inquiry likely violated the regulations which, at the time, prohibited an employer contacting an employee's physician without his permission. 29 C.F.R. §825.307. As since amended, the regulation allows an employer to "contact the health care provider for purposes of clarification and authentication of the medical certification . . . after the employer has given the employee an opportunity to cure any deficiencies. . . ." While the FMLA does not appear to provide a right to relief unless a violation of this regulation results in interference with the employee's rights under the statute, plaintiff] asserts that Collard's inquiry to her doctor supports her claim that the defendants had retaliated against her for using her FMLA leave.

Even if Collard's inquiry is put to the side, there is enough evidence in the record for a jury to find that the defendants fired Goelzer because she had utilized FMLA leave and not because Payne wanted to hire a new person with more skills. For example, Goelzer had received positive performance reviews, and none suggest on their face that they were the result of any "lowered expectations" from Payne. Payne denies that he made any oral derogatory comments regarding Goelzer's FMLA use, but that is for the jury to decide, and in any event the jury might view his written comments on Goelzer's performance evaluations regarding her use of FMLA leave as evidence that her use of FMLA leave motivated the termination decision. Payne also communicated the termination decision after he knew Goelzer planned to be out for two months on FMLA leave, and she had utilized a significant amount of FMLA leave in the years preceding the decision. Although the defendants disclaim any causal connection between Goelzer's requests for and use of FMLA leave and her firing, we conclude that a jury could find otherwise. As is the case with her interference theory, then, summary judgment is not appropriate on her retaliation action, and we reverse its grant in the defendants' favor. . . .

NOTES

1. *Qualifying Conditions.* There was no dispute in *Goelzer* that plaintiff's various leaves were both authentic and qualifying. That is, the defendant did not challenge either the genuineness of plaintiff's reasons for seeking leave or that these reasons satisfied the FMLA's requirements. The genuineness of employee claims is obviously often a difficult question for human resource departments, and the problem is made more difficult by the FMLA's limitations on contacting the plaintiff's doctor. Do you see why an employer might be satisfied with a doctor's note, and not wish to inquire further?

2. *Serious Health Conditions.* As for whether a particular set of circumstances qualifies for FMLA leave, that is often a complicated question. Perhaps the most difficult issue arises with respect to whether the plaintiff (or a family member) has a "serious health condition." As you might expect, "serious health condition" is a term of art under the statute, and one that is extensively addressed by Department of Labor regulations. To appreciate some of the complexities, consider *Russell v. N. Broward Hosp.*, 346 F.3d 1335 (11th Cir. 2003). There, the defendant did not deny that Russell was out for medical reasons, but it argued that her absences were nonetheless not protected leave under the FMLA. Although Russell was badly injured (she fell at work and was diagnosed with a fractured right elbow and a sprained ankle and related problems), the court found that her injury did not constitute a "serious health condition" under the FMLA. That was because the statute defines a "serious health condition" as "an illness, injury, impairment, or physical or mental condition that involves—(A) inpatient care in a hospital, hospice, or residential medical care facility; or (B) continuing treatment by a health care provider." *Id.* §2611(11). Russell was not admitted to a hospital, so eligibility turned on whether she had undergone continuing treatment. While the statute itself does not define that term, the Department of Labor provided a detailed definition:

> (2) *Continuing Treatment* by a health care provider. A serious health condition involving continuing treatment by a health care provider includes any one or more of the following:
>
> > (i) A period of incapacity (i.e., inability to work, attend school or perform other regular daily activities due to the serious health condition, treatment therefor, or recovery therefrom) of more than three consecutive calendar days, and any subsequent treatment or period of incapacity relating to the same condition, that also involves:
> >
> > > (A) Treatment two or more times by a health care provider, by a nurse or physician's assistant under direct supervision of a health care provider, or by a provider of health care services (e.g., physical therapist) under orders of, or on referral by, a health care provider; or
> > >
> > > (B) Treatment by a health care provider on at least one occasion which results in a regimen of continuing treatment under the supervision of the health care provider. . . .

29 C.F.R. §825.113(a)(2)(i). Because Ms. Russell was not incapacitated for "more than three consecutive days," she was not entitled to FMLA leave. Although she was partially incapacitated for a number of days over a ten-day period, she was not fully incapacitated for the requisite time. While the regulations also provide for other varieties of "continuing treatment," such as incapacity due to pregnancy or prenatal care or due to a chronic serious health condition such as asthma, diabetes, or epilepsy, §825.113, none of these alternatives was applicable to plaintiff's situation. *See generally* Leslie A. Barry, Note, *Determining the Proper Standard of Proof for Incapacity Under the Family and Medical Leave Act*, 97 Iowa L. Rev. 931 (2012).

3. *Denial of Merit Raises.* Plaintiff in the principal case seemed to challenge only her dismissal. What if she had challenged the denial of a merit raise? Payne's own statements would seem to establish that her leave was a factor in denying a raise. That would mean that she should win on such a claim, regardless of the reason for her ultimate termination. Or is there something odd about having to factor in as much as 12 weeks of absenteeism in making merit determinations?

4. *Interference.* Do you understand the difference between the "interference" and "retaliation" claims at issue in *Goelzer*? Section 2615(a)(1) of the Act sets out the interference claim, providing:

> Exercise of rights. It shall be unlawful for any employer to interfere with, restrain, or deny the exercise of or the attempt to exercise, any right provided under this subchapter.

The paradigm cases under this provision are an employer's denial of a leave in the first place or its refusal to reinstate the employee to a comparable position when the leave is over. These disputes, then, typically boil down to whether the employee is leave-eligible. However, the interference claim is not limited to such situations. *Gordon v. United States Capitol Police*, 778 F.3d 158, 165 (D.C. Cir. 2015), held that "an employer action with a reasonable tendency to 'interfere with, restrain, or deny' the 'exercise of or attempt to exercise' an FMLA right may give rise to a valid interference claim under § 2615(a)(1) even where the action fails to actually prevent such exercise or attempt." Thus, suit was validly predicated on expressed hostility to plaintiff's FMLA leave and actions taken to punish her before she took that leave.

The statute, however, expressly provides that a restored employee is *not* entitled to "any right, benefit, or position of employment other than any right, benefit, or position to which the employee would have been entitled had the employee not taken the leave." 29 U.S.C. 2614(a)(3)(B). Thus, an employer may deny reinstatement to an employee on FMLA leave if that employee would have been terminated or her job eliminated had she continued working. *See* 29 C.F.R. 825.216; *Batacan v. Reliant Pharms., Inc.*, 228 F. App'x 702, 704 (9th Cir. 2007) (since an employee on leave has no greater right to reinstatement than if she had been continuously employed, "an employee taking FMLA leave may be terminated pursuant to a legitimate reduction in force").

These provisions raise the question of who has the burden of persuasion on an interference claim. As *Goelzer* frames it, "an employee must show that: (1) she was eligible for the FMLA's protections; (2) her employer was covered by the FMLA; (3) she was entitled to take leave under the FMLA; (4) she provided sufficient notice of her intent to take leave; and (5) her employer denied her FMLA benefits to which she was entitled." That last prong, according to *Goelzer*, includes negating any employer claim that the worker would have been terminated in any event. But *Goelzer* quotes the Department of Labor regulations that appear to place a burden on the employer in this situation: "An employer must be able to show that an employee would not otherwise have been employed at the time reinstatement is requested in order to deny restoration to employment." 29 C.F.R. §825.216(a)(1). Other circuits have required the employer "to prove the reason for termination was unrelated to FMLA." *Phillips v. Matthews*, 547 F.3d 905, 911 (8th Cir. 2008); *accord Smith v. Diffee Ford-Lincoln-Mercury, Inc.*, 298 F.3d 955, 963 (10th Cir. 2002) ("[T]he regulation validly shifts to the employer the burden of proving that an employee, laid off during FMLA leave, would have been dismissed regardless of the employee's request for, or taking of, FMLA leave."); *see generally* Rachel Arnow-Richman, *Accommodation Subverted: The Future of Work/Family Initiatives in a "Me, Inc." World*, 12 Tex. J. Women & L. 345, 371 (2003); Martin H. Malin, *Interference with the Right to Leave Under the Family and Medical Leave Act*, 7 Emp. Rts. & Emp. Pol'y J. 329 (2003).

5. *Retaliation.* Section 2615(a)(2) provides that it is unlawful for an employer "to discharge or in any other manner discriminate against any individual for opposing any practice made unlawful by this subchapter." The paradigm case for this is the employer who grants leave and reinstates the employee but then later discharges her for taking such leave. The circuits have agreed that lesser adverse actions will also support an FMLA retaliation claim, adopting the Title VII approach of *Burlington Northern & Santa Fe Railway v. White*, 548 U.S. 53 (2006), *see* page 679, which looks to whether the action taken would deter a reasonable employee from exercising his statutory rights. *See Crawford v. JP Morgan Chase & Co.*, 531 F. App'x 622, 627 (6th Cir. 2013) ("We join our sister circuits in concluding that *Burlington* applies to retaliation claims under the FMLA.").

Unlike an interference claim, a plaintiff making a retaliation claim must demonstrate not only a right to leave but also that the employer had a discriminatory reason for denying reinstatement or taking other adverse action. *See, e.g., Capps v. Mondelez Global, LLC*, 847 F.3d 144 (3d Cir. 2017) (a retaliation claim requires proof of employer intent to retaliate, and a finding that the adverse employment action taken because of the employer's "honest belief" that the plaintiff was misusing FMLA leave precludes finding such an intent). The courts generally apply Title VII proof structures to determine whether the requisite intent exists. *See, e.g., Brungart v. BellSouth*

Telecomms., Inc. 231 F.3d 791, 798 (11th Cir. 2000). And some circuits have carried over the "honest belief" rule from Title VII cases to the FMLA. *See* page 557. In other words, a retaliation claim will fail even though the employee suffered an adverse employment action for seeking or using FMLA leave if the employer honestly believed the employee was abusing such leave. *E.g., Tillman v. Ohio Bell Tel. Co.*, 545 F. App'x 340, (6th Cir. 2013); *Medley v. Polk Co.*, 260 F.3d 1202, (10th Cir. 2001).

You may have noticed that the *Goelzer* court applied the "motivating factor analysis" to the causation issue regarding plaintiff's retaliation claim. The origins of this rule under the FMLA precede the Supreme Court's interpretation of the ADEA, *Gross v. FBL Fin. Servs., Inc.*, 557 U.S. 167 (2009), and, more pointedly, the retaliation protection of Title VII, *Univ. of Tex. Sw. Med. Ctr. v. Nassar*, 570 U.S. 338 (2013), both of which require plaintiff to prove "determinative factor" or but-for causation. *See* pages 579. *Goelzer's* application of "contributing factor" in an FMLA case, accordingly, is suspect.

6. *Role of the Regulations.* Given the vagueness of the statute and the (comparative) specificity of the regulations, a frequent question under the FMLA will be the meaning and validity of the Department of Labor's regulations. *See Downey v. Strain*, 510 F.3d 534 (5th Cir. 2007) (upholding regulations requiring employers to provide workers with individual notice that leave would be viewed as FMLA leave). The FMLA delegated to the Secretary of Labor the authority to "prescribe such regulations as are necessary to carry out" the FMLA's general requirements for leave. 29 U.S.C. §2654. Under familiar principles of administrative law, that means substantial deference to the agency's interpretation of the statute.

We have encountered the "*Chevron* question" of the validity of administrative agency regulations in the context of the ADA in Chapter 9 where we saw that the pattern of deference was pretty checkered; indeed, the ADAAA was passed in part to reinforce EEOC authority. *See Summers v. Altarum Inst., Corp.*, reproduced at page 692. Neither has the Department of Labor gotten a free pass from the Court. *Ragsdale v. Wolverine World Wide, Inc.*, 535 U.S. 81 (2002), rejected a Department of Labor regulation providing that leave may not count against an employee's FMLA entitlement unless the employer promptly notified the employee that the leave has been designated as FMLA leave. The Court viewed the regulation as inconsistent with the statutory requirement of only 12 weeks of leave a year. Importantly, Ragsdale could not show that she had been prejudiced or harmed by the employer's failure to give notice. The Court did not decide what would happen in a case when an employee could show harm flowing from the employer's failure to provide notice.

7. *Intermittent Leave.* Notice that in *Goelzer* the plaintiff often took "intermittent leave," typically for doctors' appointments. While leave is frequently thought of in extended terms, FMLA leave may be taken intermittently in blocks as small as an hour at a time (and, as discussed in the next note, without prior notice if the need for leave is unforeseeable). Obviously, some triggers for FMLA leave do not raise the question of intermittent leave (for example, illness for three days), while others often will (continuing treatment by a health care provider). Intermittent leave is required only when it is medically necessary, *Haggard v. Levi Strauss & Co.*, 8 F. App'x 599 (8th Cir. 2001) (physician's note for employee working half-days did not trigger right to intermittent leave because it did not state the medical necessity for the leave), which distinguishes it from other kinds of leave under the statute.

Because of the scheduling difficulties and potential disruption of such leave (and, perhaps because there is less of a pay "hit" for employees availing themselves of intermittent leave), some employers assert that this one is of the most onerous requirements of the FMLA. *See* Eric Paltell, *Intermittent Leave Under the Family and Medical Leave Act of 1993: Job Security for the Chronically Absent Employee?*, 10 Lab. Law. 1 (1994). Do you think such concerns are legitimate or are they likely overstated? Do the facts in *Goelzer* influence your opinion?

Responding to these kinds of concerns, the statute and its regulations allow an employer to transfer an employee who seeks intermittent leave from a job where attendance is vital to an equivalent position where the employee's periodic absences will be less burdensome. 29 U.S.C. §2612(b)(2); 29 C.F.R. §825.204; *see Spangler v. Fed. Home Loan Bank of Des Moines*, 278 F.3d 847, 853 (8th Cir. 2002); *see also Carmona v. Sw. Airlines Co.*, 604 F.3d 848, 860 n.3 (5th Cir. 2010) ("[W]hile the FMLA can excuse an employee from his employer's ordinary attendance requirements, it does not do so where the employee requests the right to take intermittent leave without notice indefinitely. The FMLA also does not prevent the employee from being transferred to a different job with equivalent pay and benefits where his periodic absences will do less damage to the business."). *See generally* S. Elizabeth Wilborn Malloy, *The Interaction of the ADA, the FMLA, and Workers' Compensation: Why Can't We Be Friends?*, 41 Brandeis L.J. 821, 837 (2003).

8. *Employee Notice Requirements.* Another compliance issue that frequently arises in FMLA litigation concerns the law's notice requirements. The statute provides that, when the need for leave is foreseeable, an employee must generally give her employer no less than 30 days' advance notice, although there is some flexibility built into the regulations when it is not possible to do so. *See* 29 U.S.C. §2612(e)(1) & (2)(B); 29 C.F.R. §825.302. Goelzer apparently met these requirements, but not all employees are so careful. *See Righi v. SMC Corp. of Am.*, 632 F.3d 404 (7th Cir. 2011) (plaintiff's nine-day absence during a period that included six work days required notice; his vague reference to needing "the next couple days" could not be considered adequate notice of a request for FMLA leave of that more substantial duration). *Cf. Gienapp v. Harbor Crest*, 756 F.3d 527, 531 (7th Cir. 2014) (when an employee took qualified leave to care for her daughter who was suffering from cancer, the length of that leave was unforeseeable; employees are not required to tell the employer how much leave they need when they do not yet know themselves); *see also Hansler v. Lehigh Valley Hosp. Network*, 798 F.3d 149 (3d Cir. 2015) (the employer may have a duty to inquire further when an employee's certification is "ambiguous or non-responsive"; in such cases, the employer must identify deficiencies and provide an opportunity for cure before taking an adverse action).

While the statute does not address notice requirements when leave is unforeseeable, the regulations provide that notice be given to the employer "as soon as practicable," and that should generally be "within the time prescribed by the employer's usual and customary notice requirements applicable to such leave." 29 C.F.R. §825.303(a). The regulations go on to detail to whom notice may be given, by whom notice may be given, and how it may be provided. 29 C.F.R. §825.303(b). "The employee need not expressly assert rights under the FMLA or even mention the FMLA, but need only state that leave is needed. The employer will be expected to obtain any additional required information through informal means." *Id. See Clinkscale v. St. Therese of New Hope*, 701 F.3d 825 (8th Cir. 2012) (an employee's exhibiting signs of severe distress and anxiety, causing her to be instructed to go home followed by a doctor's note the next day, created a jury question as to whether she had provided the requisite notice of a potentially FMLA-qualifying condition).

This can create some compliance challenges for the employer who must determine when it is appropriate to seek such additional information. While the employer will want to know if the leave is FMLA-eligible, most routine illnesses and common injuries do not trigger statutory protection. The employer may wish to balance its desire for certainty against administrative convenience issues as well as the potential awkwardness (and other liability risks) that may result from probing into an employee's personal situation. Recall from *Goelzer* that the regulations do not give the employer a blank check in following up with a health care provider.

The notice provisions can also create pitfalls for employees. Although the regulations are very generous to employees, particularly with respect to unforeseen needs, employees will not be entitled to FMLA leave unless they provide their employer information "sufficient to reasonably apprise it of the employee's request to take time off for a serious health condition." The point is that, even if the employee has what constitutes a qualifying condition, the employee has a further obligation to adequately inform the employer. *Compare Carter v. Ford Motor Co.*, 121 F.3d 1146 (8th Cir. 1997) (notice insufficient when Carter informed Ford that he was sick and did not know when he could return to work but did not offer further information regarding his condition); *Collins v. NTN-Bower Corp.*, 272 F.3d 1006 (7th Cir. 2001) (telling employer that employee was "sick" not sufficient); *with Spangler v. Fed. Home Loan Bank*, 278 F.3d 847 (8th Cir. 2002) (requesting time off for "depression again" is possibly a valid request when employer knew employee suffered from depression).

9. *Perfect Attendance Programs.* The effect of the FMLA on incentive programs to reward attendance generated considerable controversy. A plain language reading of the statute would seem to make individuals on FMLA-leave eligible, but such incentive programs arguably substantially improve productivity. The amended regulations make clear that such programs are permissible, even when they exclude participation by those taking FMLA leave. 29 C.F.R. §215(c)(2).

10. *The FMLA and the ADA.* The ADA and the FMLA overlap to some extent. Individuals who are covered by both statutes have more than one option for dealing with an impairment that necessitates frequent absences. Even if leave would not be a reasonable accommodation given their employer's needs, leave without pay under the FMLA is a statutory right as long as the employer is provided with adequate notice. In addition, employees with attendance problems that are health related, but who are not disabled within the meaning of the ADA, will still be entitled to leave without pay if their health problem is a "serious health condition" under the FMLA. The overlap between the ADA and FMLA can create tricky compliance issues for the employer, as well. For example, while an employee with a serious health condition may max out her FMLA entitlement after 12 weeks, if the employee's condition qualifies as a disability and she requests additional leave, the employer must consider whether granting it would be a reasonable accommodation.

11. *Individual Liability.* Unlike the antidiscrimination statutes but similar to the Fair Labor Standards Act (FLSA), the FMLA has been held to provide for individual liability for individuals acting for the employer, at least where private employers are concerned and perhaps for public employers as well. *See* 29 C.F.R. §825.104(d); *Haybarger v. Lawrence Cnty. Adult Prob. & Parole*, 667 F.3d 408 (3d Cir. 2012). For example, Goelzer sued Adam Payne personally. *See generally* Sandra F. Sperino, *Under Construction: Questioning Whether Statutory Construction Principles Justify Individual Liability Under the Family and Medical Leave Act*, 71 Mo. L. Rev. 71 (2006); Sandra F. Sperino, *Chaos Theory: The Unintended Consequences of Expanding*

Individual Liability Under the Family and Medical Leave Act, 9 EMP. RTS. & EMP. POL'Y J. 175 (2005). Given what you know about the two statutes, does it make sense to hold individuals liable for FMLA and minimum wage violations and leave violations but not gender discrimination?

12. *Counseling the Employer.* Prior to her health problems, Goelzer was frequently praised by Payne for her good attendance. In hindsight, was that a mistake? It certainly helped plaintiff establish that her later attendance problems were likely to be viewed as very problematic by him. Or was the problem not the earlier praise but Payne's repeated references to her absences after she began using her leave? And what about "the problem employee," the one who frequently misses work for questionable reasons? In *Russell*, the plaintiff had had attendance problems well before the accident that led to her discharge. It's possible, even probable, that the hospital believed she was malingering, or at least making a mountain out of a molehill. Of course, the hospital might be right or wrong in this belief, but, in an at-will world, it would be free to discharge such workers without fear of liability. Does the FMLA unduly restrict employers' ability to deal with such problems? *See* Sara Schlaefer Muoz, *A Good Idea, But . . .: Some Businesses Complain That the Family and Medical Leave Act Should Be More Aptly Named the Slackers Protection Act*, WALL ST. J., Jan. 24, 2005. To what extent do problems like this suggest attorney involvement in what seem like normal human resources processes?

* * *

While a casebook tends to focus on cases, employers tend to view statutes like the FMLA as requiring systemic changes in employment policies. Thus, almost all covered employers have overhauled their leave policies in response to the passage of the statute. Attorneys representing employers will, therefore, frequently be involved in the task of drafting such policies and occasionally in the task of interpreting them when particularly problematic situations arise. One skill of the employer's lawyer, when wearing her drafting hat, is to create policies that are both legal and administrable by the Human Resources Department. The next problem asks you to do just that.

PROBLEMS

10-3. You are U.S. counsel for Ocyllis, Inc., a Canadian firm that has just acquired an American corporation. The Canadian general counsel, your boss, has asked you to review the possible application of several of Ocyllis's personnel policies for possible application and/or modification in the United States. The first such policy is reproduced below:

1. *Intent.* This policy is designed to facilitate reasonably flexible arrangements at the time of birth or adoption of children. The policy will enable both parents to combine a productive career with family responsibilities with minimal impact on the corporation.
2. *Eligibility.* Full-time and part-time employees, who have at least 13 weeks' continuous employment at the Corporation prior to the birth or adoption of a child are eligible for pregnancy, paternity, and/or parental leave. To be eligible for financial benefits from the Corporation, employees must have 26 weeks of continuous service prior to birth or adoption.

3. *Pregnancy Leave.* Pregnancy leave is available only to natural mothers. An eligible employee is entitled to paid pregnancy leave for up to 19 weeks at 85 percent of full pay. In exceptional circumstances, a pregnancy leave may be extended beyond the 19-week period, at the discretion of the Ocyllis Board of Directors. An employee is normally expected to give four weeks' notice of the date of return to work, should this be different from the previously agreed date.

4. *Paternity Leave.* Paternity leave is available only to natural fathers. An eligible employee is entitled to two weeks' leave with full salary, pay, and benefits. Leave must be taken within the first 26 weeks after the birth of the child.

5. *Parental Leave.* Parental leave is available to all parents, natural and adoptive. An eligible employee is entitled to unpaid leave for up to 35 weeks. For natural mothers and fathers, parental leave is in addition to pregnancy or paternity leave. For natural mothers, parental leave commences when pregnancy leave ends. For natural fathers and adoptive parents, parental leave must begin no later than 52 weeks after the birth of the child or the date the adopted child first comes into the custody, care, and control of the employee.

6. *Benefits During Leave.* Employees who take advantage of these provisions will incur no loss in salary level and will be entitled to pension, health disability, and other benefits provided the employee contributes the necessary amount of the cost of benefits. Vacation and sick leave shall continue to accrue during leave.

Advise Ocyllis to what extent U.S. law requires changes in this policy. Note also where the policy may be more generous than U.S. law requires and advise Ocyllis on whether extending those provisions to its American operations is desirable.

10-4. You have now learned some of the basic nuts and bolts of FMLA coverage and enforcement and have had the opportunity to try your hand at implementing the law through a workplace policy. In light of this knowledge, imagine that you are a legislative aide to a U.S. senator who has a strong interest in work/family issues and has publicly committed to introducing legislation to redress some of the perceived shortcomings of current law. She has asked you to do preliminary research and advise her about possible approaches. What would you recommend? Would you amend existing legislation like the FMLA or the PDA? Or might you propose new legislation? Who would your proposal protect and what would it require? Would it apply to all businesses and all workers, and, if not, how would you limit it? To the extent your proposal would generate costs, how should they be allocated among employers, workers, and/or taxpayers? Are there ways of framing your proposal that might be responsive to potential political and social resistance?

11

Employee Compensation

A. AN OVERVIEW OF WAGE AND FRINGE BENEFITS REGULATION

This chapter provides an introduction to direct regulation of employee compensation, which includes wages, in-kind wage substitutes, and—although not covered here—"fringe benefits." This contrasts with some of the mandates discussed in the previous chapters that can protect compensation, but less directly. *See generally* Nantiya Ryan & Nancy Reichman, *Hours Equity Is the New Pay Equity*, 59 Vill. L. Rev. 35 (2014) (discussing the various statutory frameworks for wage and hour equity in the workplace). For example, because worker pay and benefits are "terms and conditions of employment," the discriminatory behavior we studied in Chapter 9 that adversely affects these conditions is prohibited. In addition, in Chapter 10 we learned that the Family and Medical Leave Act mandates that employers maintain health benefits for employees during periods of leave covered by the statute, and the Pregnancy Discrimination Act requires employers to treat pregnancy-related leave the same as other types of short-term disability-based leave. Moreover, there are other employer-funded benefits or protections, such as mandated workers' compensation for work-related injuries and unemployment insurance.

Despite these limitations and the laws treated below, most compensation received by most workers is the result of private ordering. The vast majority of workers in the United States earn in excess of the wages mandated by the Fair Labor Standards Act ("FLSA"), 29 U.S.C.A. §201-19 (2018), and analog state laws. These wages, therefore, are a result of individual employee-employer negotiation, collective bargaining, or, more generally, labor market forces, rather than regulation. In addition, as discussed in Chapter 1, to the extent that workers and firms may structure their relationships to avoid "employment," most of the protections discussed in this chapter do not apply at all. And, as addressed below, many employees are exempt from the FLSA's wage requirements. Similarly, the law leaves the decision to provide fringe benefits largely to employers' discretion. Employers may do so unilaterally, by individual contract, or as a result of collective negotiations with representatives of the workers. Not only do the federal and state governments directly provide to all citizens only minimal retirement, disability, and health benefits, the law historically has not mandated that employers provide such benefits, beyond their contributions to unemployment insurance and workers' compensation. Even with regard to health and retirement benefits specifically, it is only an employer's decision to do so that triggers the mandates of the Employee Retirement Income Security Act ("ERISA"), 29 U.S.C. §1001-1461 (2018). However, as part of the health care reform package Congress passed in 2010, *see generally* Patient Protection and Affordable Care Act, Pub. L. No. 111-148, 124 Stat. 119 (2010), as modified by the Health Care and Education Reconciliation Act of 2010 (Pub. L. 111-152, 124 Stat. 1029 (2010)) (hereinafter the Affordable Care Act or "ACA") (codified principally in various sections of 26, 29, and 42 U.S.C.), a large employer faces tax penalties if it does not offer health care coverage or offers coverage that is not "affordable," *see* 26 U.S.C.A. §4980H (2018).

This chapter focuses on wage and hour protections and, in particular, the scope and limitations of the FLSA. Along the way, it will also touch on state wage and hour mandates. The chapter does *not* address fringe benefits regulation. The topic of pension and health benefits regulation under ERISA, the Internal Revenue Code, and employer provisions of the 2010 health care reform package is not covered because these benefits and related law are sufficiently complicated that they cannot be given justice here, even in an introductory manner. Nevertheless, we strongly urge students interested in practicing labor and employment law in general or employee benefits in particular, to take an Employee Benefits course, which most law schools offer as a stand-alone elective.

B. WAGE PROTECTIONS

Wage protections for workers have a mixed history in the United States. Long before federal labor statutes favoring collective bargaining, *see* National Labor Relations Act, codified as amended at 29 U.S.C. §151-69 (2018), there were attempts to regulate abuses by employers. Some of the earliest efforts were state laws restricting child labor. Although a number of jurisdictions also passed statutes controlling the hours of employment of adults, the most far-reaching were frequently struck down by the Supreme Court in the substantive due process period when the Supreme Court interpreted the Fourteenth Amendment to prohibit states from "interfering" with employment contracts. *See, e.g., Lochner v. New York*, 198 U.S. 45 (1905). One major exception to Supreme Court hostility to such regulation was with respect to women. The famous Brandeis Brief provided the Supreme Court in *Muller v. Oregon*, 208 U.S. 412 (1908), with a basis for upholding legislation "protecting" women by limiting their hours of employment, while similar statutes applied to men were being struck down.

With the demise of substantive due process, statutes directly regulating hours worked and wages paid became the norm in the United States. At the federal level, the FLSA is the primary mechanism for dealing with perceived employer abuses. However, a number of other federal, state, and local laws also directly regulate worker pay.

Of course, government control of wage levels has always had its critics. Some claim that establishing a minimum wage above market rates harms social welfare and has adverse effects on the working poor, including artificially reducing the demand for labor. David Neumark & William Wascher, *Minimum Wages and Low-Wage Workers: How Well Does Reality Match the Rhetoric?* 92 MINN. L. REV. 1296 (2008); *see also* John Foley, *Questioning the Merits of Federal Minimum Wage Legislation*, 5 GEO. J. L. & PUB. POL'Y 679 (2007) (arguing that the minimum wage increases unemployment, leads to higher inflation, and produces other detrimental effects on the poor). Others support the minimum wage on traditional and not-so-traditional grounds. *See, e.g.*, Bruce E. Kaufman, *Institutional Economics and the Minimum Wage: Broadening the Theoretical and Policy Debate*, 63 IND. & LAB. REL. REV. 427 (2010) (offering justifications for the minimum wage including addressing unequal bargaining power, promoting economic stability and long-term economic efficiency, and reducing labor market externalities); Noah D. Zatz, *The Minimum Wage as a Civil Rights Protection: An Alternative to the Antipoverty Arguments?*, 1 U. CHI. LEGAL F. 1 (2009) (arguing that the minimum wage is justified not only as a poverty reduction tool, but also as a civil rights protection). Although the debate continues, most recent studies—often made possible by state-to-state differences in minimum wage floors—support the view that (at least modest) increases to the minimum wage have few adverse effects on employment rates, and recent surveys of economists tend to support the view that the overall benefits of modest increases outweigh the costs. *See, e.g.*, Dale Belman & Paul Wolfson, *15 Years of Research on U.S. Employment and the Minimum Wage* (December 10, 2016), Tuck School of Business Working Paper No. 2705499. available at SSRN: https://ssrn.com/abstract=2705499 or http://dx.doi.org/10.2139/ssrn.2705499 (summarizing the research); John Schmitt, *Why Does the Minimum Wage Have No Discernible Effect on Employment?*, Center for Economic and Policy Research (February 2013), available at http://cepr.net/publications/reports/why-does-the-minimum-wage-have-no-discernible-effect-on-employment (same); Chicago Booth, *Minimum Wage*, IGM Forum (Feb. 13, 2013), available at http://www.igmchicago.org/igm-economic-experts-panel/poll-results?SurveyID=SV_br0IEq5a9E77NMV (showing economists' survey responses).

The issue of the government's role in regulating wages is debated cyclically in Congress when efforts are made to increase the FLSA minimum wage, and, as explored in Chapter 1, discussions of wage regulation and wages generally are tied to other hot-button issues, including immigration. Perhaps unsurprisingly, although the basic protections afforded by the FLSA have persisted, the opponents of government regulation of wages have gained the upper hand at times, at least at the national level. For example, as discussed below, some believe that the practical effect of Department of Labor ("DOL") regulations promulgated in 2004 was to exempt more workers from the FLSA's overtime protections. In addition, the last time Congress enacted legislation increasing the minimum wage was in 2007. The floor reached its high in 2009 at $7.25 an hour. *See* 29 U.S.C.A. §206(a)(1)(C) (2018). This increase also had an impact on state law, which may provide protection for workers excluded from coverage under the FLSA. For example, the federal increase boosted minimum wage levels in those jurisdictions that tie their wage requirements to federal law. As discussed below, a majority of states and some municipalities have enacted a wage floor above the federal level. In addition, states often enact other kinds of wage protections or requirements, including wage payment laws that provide for civil and criminal liability for failure to pay promised wages.

1. The FLSA

The original purposes of the FLSA were to prevent certain historic employer abuses of labor—including child labor—and to ensure that every covered employee received at least a basic minimum wage and a premium for work exceeding the standard number of hours per week. The statute's overtime provisions were also designed to create incentives to spread employment over a greater number of workers. Thus, the FLSA requires covered employers to pay covered employees a minimum wage (again, currently $7.25 for most covered workers); it also requires employers to pay workers an overtime premium at one half their "regular rate of pay" for hours worked in excess of 40 hours per week. *See* 29 U.S.C. §206(a)-(b), 207(a)(1) (2018). However, the FLSA's overtime provisions do not limit the number of hours an employee may be required to work and thus the statute does not protect from discharge workers who refuse to work overtime.

The FLSA also contains the Equal Pay Act, a very limited ban on sex discrimination in pay, *see id.* at §206(d), and provisions designed to curtail oppressive child labor and protect children's safety and educational opportunities, particularly for children under 16 years of age, *see id.* at §212(c). Finally, it establishes wage-related record-keeping requirements for employers. *See id.* at §211. Most of the planning, litigation, and public policy issues, however, relate to the minimum wage and overtime requirements.

With some exceptions, the substantive requirements of the FLSA are straightforward; in other words, when they are applicable, the FLSA's wage and hour requirements are fairly simple to apply. They are also mandatory and, hence, for the most part, cannot be waived via contract. Thus, private ordering plays a relatively small role where the FLSA operates. Of course, this raises an interesting, overarching policy question: Should the requirements of the FLSA be mandatory, or should employees and employers be allowed to waive these requirements, at least in some circumstances?

Nevertheless, given the current statutory and regulatory framework, FLSA litigation usually focuses on the statute's coverage—that is, issues surrounding who constitutes an "employee," who constitutes a covered employer, and who is otherwise exempt from the FLSA's protections or mandates. A few application issues have led to significant litigation, including determining what constitutes hours "worked" and calculating "rate of pay" for purposes of overtime.

a. Scope of Coverage

i. Employee and Employer

Because the FLSA broadly governs "employees" engaged in interstate commerce, the first step in determining whether the act applies at all is to determine whether a worker is an "employee" rather than another kind of worker—in most circumstances, an independent contractor. This definition of "employee" was addressed at length in Chapter 1, and its application in the FLSA context in particular was addressed in *Ansoumana v. Gristede's Operating Corp.*, reproduced at page 51.

Ansoumana also discussed aspects of who qualifies as an "employer" for FLSA purposes. Recall that there may be more than one "employer": A separate entity may be liable under the FLSA as a "joint employer." Moreover, supervisory personnel with direct control over employees may qualify as "employers" and, hence, may be individually liable for violations along with the firm or entity they control. Such personal liability for statutory violations is not unique but is quite rare. As *Ansoumana* indicated, extending liability to individual officers or controlling persons ensures that responsible parties have strong incentives to comply with the statute's mandates.

The *Ansoumana* decision, however, did not address the FLSA's "commerce" and "enterprise" coverage provisions. Any *employee* "engaged in commerce or in the production of goods for commerce" is covered by the Act, whether or not the employer is an enterprise engaged in commerce as statutorily defined. 29 U.S.C. §206(a), 207(a) (1) (2018); *see Brennan v. Arnheim & Neely, Inc.*, 410 U.S. 512, 516-17 (1973). To be engaged in commerce, individual employees must be "performing work involving or related to the movement of persons or things (whether tangibles or intangibles, and including information and intelligence)" between states. 29 C.F.R. §779.103. In addition, an employee is engaged in commerce when regularly engaging in interstate communication (such as using the mails or telephone) or when regularly traveling across state lines while working. Substantial, rather than sporadic or de minimis, interstate activities are required. Whether an employee's interstate activities are sufficiently substantial is a fact-intensive inquiry. *See, e.g., Locke v. St. Augustine's Episcopal Church*, 690 F. Supp. 2d 77 (E.D.N.Y. 2010) (holding that a church janitor was not an employee engaged in commerce under the FLSA, nor was his employer an enterprise engaged in commerce); *Bowrin v. Catholic Guardian Society*, 417 F. Supp. 2d 449 (S.D.N.Y. 2006) (finding that employees of a charitable organization were not engaged in commerce in most tasks they performed, but some tasks involving interstate travel were covered activities).

On the other hand, even an employee who is not individually engaged in such commerce will be covered if he or she is "employed in an enterprise engaged in commerce or in the production of goods for commerce." 29 U.S.C. §206(a), 207(a) (1). The most difficult and litigated aspect of this requirement is what constitutes an "enterprise." Indeed, the scope of the employing enterprise is important for several other reasons. First, the FLSA has a minimum dollar volume limitation; it currently does not apply to employing enterprises whose annual gross volume of sales is less than $500,000. 29 U.S.C. §203(s)(1)(A)(ii). In addition, whether several operations or entities constitute a single enterprise may be dispositive of whether the statute's overtime mandates have been satisfied; for example, if an employee works for two separate entities that constitute a single enterprise, the sum of the hours the employee works for both entities during a week will determine whether the employee is entitled to an overtime premium. Finally, if liability under the FLSA is established, recovery may depend on the scope of the enterprise when one part of an entity within it is insolvent.

The FLSA defines "enterprise" as follows:

> "Enterprise" means the related activities performed (either through unified operation or common control) by any person or persons for a common business purpose, and includes all such activities whether performed in one or more establishments or by one or more corporate or other organizational units including departments of an establishment operated through leasing arrangements, but shall not include the related activities performed for such enterprise by an independent contractor.

29 U.S.C. §203(r). Certain relationships or arrangements are exempted from enterprise treatment, including exclusive-dealership arrangements and franchises. *See id.* In *Brennan v. Arnheim & Neely, Inc.*, 410 U.S. 512, 518 (1973), the Supreme Court stated that the three main elements of this statutory definition are "related activities, unified operation or common control, and common business purpose." *See also* 29 C.F.R. §779.202 ("[T]he enterprise includes all such related activities which are performed through 'unified operation' or 'common control' . . . even if they are performed by more than one person, or in more than one establishment, or by more than one corporate or other organizational unit."). Obviously, these elements overlap, and various pieces of evidence may be relevant to more than one. "Activities are 'related' when they are the same or similar." *Arnheim & Neely, Inc.*, 410 U.S. at 518; *see also Chao v. A-One Med. Servs., Inc.*, 346 F.3d 908 (9th Cir. 2003) (holding two companies to be one enterprise because both provided home health care services even though they serviced different types of patients under different levels of care with differing eligibility requirements); *Pierce v. Coleman Trucking, Inc.*, 2005 WL 2338822 (N.D. Ohio Sept. 23, 2005) (finding related activities when two companies engaged in identical asbestos removal activities and differed only in their union relationships).

According to DOL regulations, "common control"

> includes the power to direct, restrict, regulate, govern, or administer the performance of the activities. "Common" control includes the sharing of control and it is not limited to sole control or complete control by one person or corporation. "Common" control therefore exists where the performance of the described activities are [sic] controlled by one person or by a number of persons, corporations, or other organizational units acting together.

29 C.F.R. §779.221; *see also Arnheim & Neely, Inc.*, 410 U.S. at 518 (finding that operations controlled through a fully integrated central office constituted a unified operation subject to common control). Common ownership is one factor in determining common control, but it is not dispositive. *See, e.g., Dole v. Odd Fellows Home Endowment Bd.*, 912 F.2d 689 (4th Cir. 1990).

Another regulation broadly defines common business purpose:

> Generally, the term "common business purpose" will encompass activities whether performed by one person or by more than one person, or corporation, or other business organization, which are directed to the same business objective or to similar objectives in which the group has an interest. The scope of the term "enterprise" encompasses a single business entity as well as a unified business system which performs related activities for a common business purpose.

29 C.F.R. §779.213. This definition is consistent with the Supreme Court's treatment in *Arnheim & Neely, Inc.*, 410 U.S. at 518, finding a real-estate management company's operations at a number of different, separately owned buildings had a common business purpose because the "activities at the several locations are tied together by the common business purpose of managing commercial properties for profit."

Finally, in 1974, Congress extended the definition of "employer" under the FLSA to include virtually all public employers. *See* Pub. L. 93-259, §6, 88 Stat. 58-62 (1974); 29 U.S.C. §203(d) (2014). The Supreme Court ultimately found this extension to be a proper exercise of Congress's Commerce Clause power and not inconsistent with the strictures of the Tenth Amendment. *See Garcia v. San Antonio*

Metro. Transit Auth., 469 U.S. 528 (1985). However, the combined effect of two subsequent Supreme Court decisions, *Seminole Tribe v. Florida*, 517 U.S. 44 (1996), and *Alden v. Maine*, 527 U.S. 706 (1999), renders states immune from *private* suits for damages under the FLSA. The Department of Labor may still enforce the FLSA against the states, but municipalities and other political subdivisions do not enjoy such sovereign immunity, and are, thus, frequently the target of private FLSA suits, *see, e.g., Acton v. City of Columbia*, 436 F.3d 969 (8th Cir. 2006).

ii.   Exemptions

Even if a worker is a covered employee employed by one or more covered employers, the employee may nevertheless be exempt from the FLSA's protections. The FLSA and implementing DOL regulations contain a significant number of exemptions excluding certain categories of employees from the minimum wage requirements, the overtime provisions, or both. Many of the exemptions apply to employees in specific industries or subsectors of specific industries, or those holding jobs in certain, defined job categories. For example, some workers under 20 years of age may receive wages as low as $4.25 for the first 90 days of employment. In addition, various categories of transportation and agricultural workers are exempt from the FLSA's overtime requirements, and the statute contains separate overtime requirements for firefighters and law enforcement officials. Some seasonal employees are exempt from both the minimum wage and overtime requirements as well. Moreover, domestic workers traditionally have been excluded as well under the exemption for "companion services." However, a DOL rule adopted under the Obama Administration, extended wage and hour protections to home health care workers employed through an agency or other third-party provider. *See* 29 C.F.R. §552.

Public employees are subject to a number of unique provisions. Most notably, section 7(o) of the statute, 29 U.S.C. §207(o), allows public employers to compensate employees who work overtime with compensatory time—that is, one and one-half hours off for every hour worked in excess of 40 hours per week—instead of overtime pay. A frequently debated policy question is whether that same option should be available to private sector employees. Currently, "comp time" in lieu of overtime is not permitted even if both parties would prefer it.

When you encounter FLSA in practice, the first place to begin is to ascertain whether the situation you are confronting falls within one of the many exceptions to the general coverage provisions we have sketched. This chapter does not attempt to cover all of the various exemptions in the statute, *see, e.g.*, 29 U.S.C. §213, but it does convey the flavor of the analysis while treating some of the more important exemptions in terms of numbers of workers excluded from the FLSA's protections.

Note on the "White Collar" Exemptions

The best-known FLSA exemptions tend to be labeled generically as the "white-collar" exemptions. Section 13(a)(1) of the FLSA completely exempts "any employee employed in a bona fide executive, administrative, or professional capacity." *See* 29 U.S.C. §213(a)(1). In subsequent amendments to the FLSA, Congress also added a special exemption for certain "computer employees" and "highly compensated" employees. *See* 29 U.S.C. §213(a)(17).

The original aim of the white-collar exemptions was to exclude from coverage those workers not engaged directly in production but rather involved in management, administration, and the learned or creative professions. The §13(a)(1) exemptions were "premised on the belief that the workers exempted typically earned salaries well above the minimum wage, and they were presumed to enjoy other compensatory privileges such as above average fringe benefits and better opportunities for advancement, setting them apart from the nonexempt workers entitled to overtime pay." *See* 69 Fed. Reg. 22,122, 22, 123-24 (April 23, 2004). In addition, Congress believed that the work such employees performed was "difficult to standardize to any time frame and could not be easily spread to other workers after 40 hours in a week, making compliance with the overtime provisions difficult and generally precluding the potential job expansion intended by the FLSA's time-and-a-half overtime premium." *Id.* at 22, 123. Such distinctions may be less meaningful today, as the American economy shifts from manufacturing to the provision of services, technology and communications, and creative professions. Views differ on whether this is a reason to expand or contract the exemptions.

DOL regulations govern the exemptions. *See* 20 C.F.R. §541. These regulations—which were first promulgated in the 1940s and remained largely unchanged until 2004—contained requirements that had to be satisfied in order for an employee to be treated as exempt. To qualify, an employee's compensation had to exceed a defined salary floor and had to be in the form of a set "salary," rather than an hourly wage subject to reductions based on the quality or quantity of work performed. In addition, an employee qualified for such exempt status only if his or her "primary duties" were "administrative," "professional," or "executive" in nature. Each of these duty classifications, in addition to the term "primary duty," was defined, although inexactly and, hence, was subject to widespread litigation.

In 2004, the DOL altered portions of the white-collar exemption regime. *See* Defining and Delimiting the Exemptions for Executive, Administrative, Professional, Outside Sales and Computer Employees, 29 C.F.R. §541. These changes generated great controversy in the mainstream media and in political circles because of their anticipated net effect; according to many commentators, they would significantly increase the number of workers exempt from the FLSA's protections wage and overtime protections.

The ultimate effect of the revised regulations is complex. In one way, the 2004 rules benefited employees: They raised the qualifying salary level for these exemptions to $455 a week or $23,660 per year, meaning more workers are nonexempt based on their wages alone, irrespective of their responsibilities. On the other hand, other provisions clearly exempted more employees. For example, the rules exempted from coverage an employee "who leads a team of other employees assigned to complete major projects for the employer," without regard to whether the employee has direct supervisory authority over other team members. *See* 29 C.F.R. §541.203(c). In addition, more workers with only *some* executive duties were exempted because the new "primary duty" test does not limit the amount of nonexempt work an employee can perform and still be considered an "executive." *See id.* Finally, the new regulations contain an additional exemption for employees earning more than $100,000 a year ("highly compensated employees"), without regard to primary duties; such an employee must perform only a single exempt task "customarily and regularly" in order to be exempt. *See* 29 C.F.R. §541.601. Since the $100,000 trigger is not inflation-indexed, more and more employees will reach this status over time.

In 2016, the DOL updated its regulations to, among other things, increase substantially the number of workers eligible for overtime benefits by increasing the wage floor for the white- collar exemptions. The Department summarized the change as follows:

> In the Final Rule, the Department updated the salary level above which certain "white collar" workers may be exempt from overtime pay requirements to equal the 40th percentile of earnings of full-time salaried workers from the lowest wage Census Region. This change raises the salary level from its previous amount of $455 per week (the equivalent of $23,660 per year) to a new level of $913 per week (the equivalent of $47,476 per year). Salaried white-collar employees paid below the updated salary level are generally entitled to overtime pay, while employees paid at or above the salary level may be exempt from overtime pay if they primarily perform certain duties. The Final Rule also raises the compensation level for highly compensated employees subject to a more minimal duties test from its previous amount of $100,000 to $134,004 annually.

See Guidance for Private Employers on Changes to the White Collar Exemption in the Overtime Final Rule, Wage and Hour Division, United States Department of Labor (May 18, 2016), https://www.dol.gov/whd/overtime/final2016/general-guidance.pdf. This means that the initial floor of $47,476 a year was to be increased every three years to reflect the earnings at the fortieth percentile of full-time salaried workers in the country's lowest-wage Census Region. *See also* Noam Scheiber, *White House Increases Overtime Eligibility by Millions*, N.Y. TIMES (May 17, 2016), http://www.nytimes.com/2016/05/18/business/white-house-increases-overtime-eligibility-by-millions.html?_r=1. Similarly, the threshold for the "highly compensated employee" exemption would be increased to $134,404 a year and updated every three years to reflect the earnings of the 90th percentile. *See Defining and Delimiting the Exemptions for Executive, Administrative, Professional, Outside Sales and Computer Employees*, 81 Fed. Reg. 32391 (May 23, 2016) (to be codified at 29 C.F.R. pt. 541).

Ten days before the new rule was to become effective, the District Court for the Eastern District of Texas issued a nationwide preliminary injunction preventing the new rule from going into effect. *Nevada v. United States DOL*, 218 F. Supp. 3d 520 (E.D. Tex. 2016), finding that, in enacting the new wage floors the DOL exceeded its authority under the statute. In August 2017, the court made the injunction permanent. It clarified, however, that while the new rule's significant increase in the wage floor is invalid, the 2004 minimum salary level is not. *See* 275 F. Supp. 3d 795 (E.D. Tex. 2017). The government appealed, but following the election of President Trump and the appointment of Secretary of Labor Alexander Acosta, it indicated that the DOL intends to revise the rule. Still, it asked the court to affirm that the DOL has the power to use salary levels to determine overtime eligibility. At the time this book went to press, the case is still pending. The DOL has stated that it is unlikely to enact a new rule until 2020. The new rule is likely to contain a salary threshold increase, but one far lower than the initial rule's level. *See* Chris Opfer, *Trump Administration Weighs New Overtime Pay Requirements*. BLOOMBERG LAW NEWS. Sept. 24, 2018.

The bottom line is that, for now, the 2004 rules remain in effect. A primary purpose of these rules was to reduce the uncertainty the prior regulations produced and the litigation that resulted. *See* 69 Fed. Reg. 22,122 (Apr. 23, 2004). Various aspects of the exemptions do provide greater clarity. For instance, "salary" and the effect of reductions in pay for various purposes are now defined more clearly. *See* 29 C.F.R. §541.602. Similarly, some exemptions are now better defined, including the computer employee, outside salesperson, and education exemptions. And added provisions set out categorical exclusions from the exemptions, including those for emergency response personnel, "blue collar" and other workers engaged only in manual or repetitive labor, *see* 29 C.F.R. §541.3(a), (b), and nurse practitioners, *see* 29 C.F.R. 541.301(e)(2). Moreover, these regulations provide a single primary duty test, abandoning the prior approach, which contained two different tests—the "long" and "short" tests—based on salary level. *See id.* at §541.700.

Nevertheless, much in the 2004 regulations parrots or parallels the prior regulations. For example, the purposes of the exemptions remain the same, and the basic distinction between production and administrative work continues to be paramount. Moreover, the definitions and terms that govern applicability of the exceptions are generally quite similar to those under the prior regime.

Also, determining whether an employee is exempt as an executive, administrator, or professional remains a highly fact-sensitive inquiry. And how the general rules governing these exemptions and the somewhat altered "primary duty test" may apply in particular situations continues to pose planning difficulties. Indeed, whether an employee who was nonexempt before is now exempt as an executive, administrator, or professional may not be clear. Few courts have applied the new regulations, and developing a guiding body of case law will take years. Employers and employees, therefore, will need to rely not only on the new regulations and the examples they provide in assessing exempt/nonexempt status but also on older case law, at least where the operative standards have not changed significantly.

The best way to appreciate the challenges facing employers, employees, and courts is to see how the white-collar exemptions are applied in relatively close cases. Thus, as a starting point, read the following case involving employees classified as "assistant managers" by their employers.

≡≡≡ *Costello v. Home Depot USA, Inc.*
928 F. Supp. 2d 473 (D. Conn. 2013)

JANET C. HALL, District Judge.

Introduction

[Plaintiff James Costello brought this action against defendant Home Depot U.S.A., Inc. (Home Depot), alleging that he was not paid for overtime work in violation of the Fair Labor Standards Act (the "FLSA"), 29 U.S.C. §207. Home Depot simultaneously filed this motion for summary judgment as to Costello arguing that there was no violation of the FLSA because he was properly categorized as an exempt executive employee in accordance with the FLSA's rules governing overtime payments. The motion was denied.]

III. Factual Background

[In 2004, two separate federal actions were filed alleging that Home Depot violated the FLSA with regard to merchandising assistant store managers ("MASMs"). The district court originally allowed the cases to proceed as a "collective" action (similar to a class action) but later reversed that decision. Separate multiple-plaintiff actions followed, including the present action. At this point, one of the remaining plaintiffs was James Costello.]

Home Depot operates large, warehouse-style retail stores that sell home improvement products and services. Home Depot stores are staffed by one Store Manager and up to seven Assistant Store Managers, a group that includes MASMs. MASMs are the second-highest-ranking employees in Home Depot stores, subordinate only to the Store Manager. The stores are divided into up to eleven core merchandising departments: Lumber, Building Materials, Flooring, Paint, Hardware, Plumbing, Electrical, Garden, Kitchen & Bath, Millwork, and Decor.

MASMs and Specialty ASMs [SASMs] oversee from one to eleven merchandising departments. Merchandising departments are staffed by sales associates and one department supervisor. MASMs supervise the department supervisors and associates assigned to their departments. Costello . . . dispute[s] whether all of the departments [he was] assigned to also had an assigned department supervisor, and [he] maintain[s] that the department supervisors are primarily responsible for supervision of associates in that department. The MASM job description states that, among other responsibilities, MASMs are responsible for "[m]aintaining department profitability," "provid[ing] leadership to Associates," and "[s]etting store objectives and ensuring [that] they are met." . . .

Costello was hired as a sales associate by Home Depot in March 1997. On July 29, 2002, Costello was promoted to the MASM position. Before his promotion, Costello went through a retail management assessment and training program. The parties dispute exactly what the training entailed or whether Costello received continuous training as an MASM, but agree the training included review of a Home Depot manual that covered various parts of store operations.

Costello began working as an MASM in Westerly, Rhode Island, in July 2002, and was transferred as an MASM to a store in Waterford, Connecticut, in September 2003, where he remained, with the exception of a temporary reassignment to a store in Lisbon, Connecticut, until his employment ended on January 1, 2006. At the Westerly store, Costello was assigned to the Lumber, Millwork, Building Materials, Hardware, Pro Desk, and Tool Rental Center departments, and for a short time, the Front Desk. The Pro Desk, Hardware, and Rental Center departments each had department supervisors, and there was a fourth department supervisor who managed the Lumber, Building Materials, and Millwork departments. These four department supervisors reported to Costello. When Costello was assigned to the Front Desk, an additional supervisor reported to him. A disputed number of other employees, including associates, also worked in the store.

[At the Waterford and Lisbon stores, Costello was likewise assigned to a number of departments, and the department supervisors reported to him.]

Costello resigned from Home Depot on either December 29, 2005, or January 1, 2006, and this resignation occurred around the time allegations by female employees were made against him. Home Depot claims that an investigation was performed relating to the complaints and that Costello was found to have violated the company's Code of Conduct and his employment was terminated.

The MASM job description states that the major tasks and responsibilities of the position include, "[r]ecruiting, interviewing applicants and making recommendations to the Store Manager about hiring for open positions." When assigned to the Westerly store, Costello assisted in preparing the store for its grand opening and was involved in hiring staff. Costello conducted 200 or 300 interviews and asked candidates about their product knowledge, departmental preferences, and previous experience. He made recommendations to the store manager or human resources manager about who should be hired based on his interviews, and at least some of these candidates were hired. Costello was then part of a group that was involved in deciding where the new employees would be placed and what salary they would be offered. Costello claims that the final hiring decisions were made by the store manager or human resources manager. Following the opening of the Westerly store, Costello conducted a few additional interviews and recommended that two employees be transferred in to the store from different Home Depot stores. Costello claims that he was not involved in the hiring process at the Waterford store.

Costello taught forklift training classes and, when he had a department supervisor who was training to be an ASM, he would involve him or her in performance review meetings with sales associates to observe how the process worked. The parties dispute whether Costello was responsible for ensuring that associates completed electronic training courses. Costello recommended that associates receive certain types of training for their development.

The MASM job description also states that the major tasks and responsibilities of MASMs includes, "[s]cheduling Associates' work and training time." As the stores where Costello worked, either the human resources manager or a store scheduler initially prepared the store schedule. Costello then had the opportunity to review the schedules, but the parties dispute whether Costello reviewed the schedules to ensure that the departments were adequately staffed. Costello would sometimes suggest changes to the store schedule when he determined there were not enough associates scheduled.

When Costello received a call that an employee would not be at work, Costello would attempt to get coverage for those positions for the departments he was responsible for, and would notify the department supervisors for the other affected departments. Costello did not need the store manager's approval to perform this task. Costello could approve or disapprove employee requests for the scheduling of vacation time, and requests for vacation time were first approved by department supervisors. Costello had the authority to sign off on edits to employee time records, but Costello asserts that this function was the principal responsibility of the operations manager.

Costello held meetings with department supervisors to communicate action items and set a timeline as to when the actions would get done. He also prepared task lists that needed to be done in a certain timeframe. When his store manager suggested areas for improvement, Costello developed plans to implement any necessary changes, and followed up to ensure the tasks he had assigned had been completed. The parties dispute how much of Costello's time was taken up with these activities.

The MASM job description also states that the major tasks and responsibilities of MASMs includes, "[c]oaching, training and developing Associates by providing both informal (e.g., on-floor coaching) and formal (e.g., written evaluation) job performance-based feedback." Costello was responsible for preparing performance evaluations for the hourly associates every six months, one for purposes of determining annual raises, and one interim review to track performance issues. Costello kept a file on each employee to track each employee's progress and updated these files on a monthly basis. Costello personally prepared performance reviews for department supervisors, but the parties dispute whether Costello delegated responsibility for the review process for sales associates. Costello met with department supervisors and sales associates to discuss the performance evaluations, and, at Waterford, the store managers would attend monetary reviews for department supervisors.

In the performance evaluations Costello completed, Costello was involved with the recommendation of leadership and potential codes for sales associates, which could impact pay raises. Costello estimates that his recommendations were accepted 90 percent of the time. Costello participated in meetings regarding annual raises of both sales associates and department supervisors and, made recommendations about the raises his employees should receive. Costello estimates those recommendations were followed 99 percent of the time. In addition to the semi-annual performance reviews, Costello could monitor and recognize associates' performance throughout the year. Costello was able to give merit badges to employees, the accumulation of which could lead to a $100 reward. Costello also recommended employees for various store awards.

Costello mentored employees to help them advance professionally and would discuss efficiency and profitability improvements with department supervisors. At the Westerly store, Costello would sometimes discuss with the store manager which associates were ready for a promotion; some of the individuals Costello identified were in fact promoted. At least one employee so identified was offered promotion but declined the offer.

The stores where Costello worked employed associates known as inventory management associates who put together initial merchandise orders and, in at least one performance evaluation, Costello was encouraged to have weekly meetings with those associates and department supervisors to ensure that departments were fully stocked. The parties dispute whether Costello was responsible for reviewing the orders. The parties dispute the degree to which Costello could determine what products to place along certain aisles and other parts of the store.

The MASM job description also states that the major tasks and responsibilities of MASMs includes, "[m]aintaining department profitability through report analysis, identifying trends, defining problems and developing appropriate responses in three or more departments." As part of his job as an MASM, Costello reviewed the Whole Store Report, which contained information related to profitability, "shrink," and labor hours, to see how his departments were doing. At meetings, Costello mentioned various actions he was taking to try to increase sales, including recommending increasing staff in critical time periods like weekends and holidays. Costello was responsible for ensuring the "shrink plan" was prepared and reviewing the shrink plan on a weekly basis. When shrink audits revealed that his departments were not performing well, Costello met with the department head and/or store manager to take corrective action.

Costello had the authority to discipline associates if he observed them acting contrary to Home Depot policies and procedures, including writing up the employee and determining corrective action. Costello disputes that the disciplinary action entailed involved more than filling out a form. Costello had the authority to send employees home if he determined they were behaving improperly, including if any employee disrespected a customer, was involved in a safety violation, brought weapons into the store, or was under the influence of alcohol or drugs. Costello exercised this authority when one of his employees climbed into a dumpster shoot. Costello stopped the employee, had him climb out of the shoot, punch out, and go home. Costello reported the incident to his store manager, and the employee was terminated. Costello attended the termination session.

Costello was responsible for coaching employees and memorializing verbal conversations about performance issues. Costello asserts this responsibility was shared by department supervisors. Consultation with human resources or the store manager was only required if the problem involved a safety or hazardous waste issue.

The MASM job description also states that the major tasks and responsibilities of MASMs includes, "[e]nsuring Safety of Customers and Associates." If there was a safety violation in the store when Costello was present, Costello was responsible for addressing it, and he would respond depending on the nature of the problem. Costello asserts this responsibility was shared with department supervisors. Costello walked his departments and inspected overhead material to make sure the items were properly situated, wrapped, and labeled. If there was a problem with the overhead items, Costello would find associates to fix the issue. Costello asserts that, if no associates were available, he was required by the store manager to fix the issue himself.

When Costello opened the store, he was responsible for walking the entire store to ensure there were no safety hazards; if he observed any safety issues, he would address it with the assistant manager for that department and have it corrected before the store was opened to the public. Costello ensured that anything outside the store was secured when he closed the store. The parties dispute whether Costello did this upon opening the store. Costello had the code for the store's alarms and was frequently called into work when the alarm went off. When called in to deal with the alarm, he had to shut off the alarm, deal with the police, walk the store, and reset the alarm.

Costello was responsible for helping to ensure customers were satisfied. Costello reviewed customer complaints, and had to devise a resolution within a day of receiving the complaint, which could include marking down the product, replacing the product, or calling the customer. Costello also reviewed secret shopper reports once a month to monitor the job performance of the sales associates. Costello addressed employee grievances, such as problems with other employees. In such a situation, Costello could coordinate the transfer of the employee to another department. Costello asserts such an action required approval of the store manager.

In the Westerly store, Costello sometimes served as the Manager on Duty ("MOD") for three to four hours for shifts when he either opened or closed the store. The parties dispute how often this occurred, and whether being MOD meant Costello was the only manager in the store at the time. . . .

Costello's starting salary as an MASM was $44,000 per year. In April 2003, this amount was increased to $45,800 per year. In April 2004, this amount was increased to $46,900 per year. In April 2005, this amount was increased to $50,000 per year. Costello understood that his salary was to cover all hours worked, and that he might have to work more than 55 hours per week.

In addition to his base salary, Costello was eligible for a bonus of up to 25 percent of his annual salary based on store sales and stock options based on his performance and the store's performance. Costello received a bonus for 2004 totaling $3,381.49. He received more than 1,300 stock options between 2003 and 2005.

Hourly associates were not eligible to receive stock options or bonuses. From 2004 to 2005, the midrange hourly rates for sales associates and department supervisors in the market where Costello worked were $12.64 and $16.97, respectively. Costello asserts that this pay was supplemented by overtime pay, and that top pay for sales associates reached $17.57 per hour and for department supervisors reached $22.23 per hour.

Costello was held accountable for the profitability of his departments and making his sales plans, and he was evaluated in part on department sales performance. . . . Costello spent up to three hours each week attending management meetings where he discussed sales plans, loss prevention, markdowns, new store programs, and shrink. Costello asserts that department supervisors also attended those meetings. Costello spent up to two hours each week walking the store by himself or with either his store manager or district manager. Costello spent an hour each week reviewing reports. Costello stated that keeping track of employees' performance issues was a "continuous operation."

Costello asserts that he spent the majority of his time on, and the majority of his duties concerned, customer service and manual labor. Costello also asserts that department supervisors were considered part of the management team and that they could serve as MOD. Costello asserts that department supervisors are directly responsible for supervising and counseling sales associates. Costello asserts that he did not make policy decisions for the stores in which he worked. . . .

IV.   Discussion

The sole issue before the court is whether summary judgment is appropriate as to whether Costello [was] misclassified as exempt from the overtime requirements of the FLSA. Home Depot argues no issue of material fact exists as to this point and that [he was] properly classified as exempt under the "executive employee" provision of the FLSA.

. . . [The FLSA's] overtime pay requirement does not apply to "any employee employed in a bona fide executive, administrative, or professional capacity." 29 U.S.C. §213(a)(1). . . .

"Since this exemption provides an affirmative defense to overtime claims, the employer has the burden of proving that a plaintiff is an exempt 'bona fide executive' by a preponderance of the evidence." *Scott v. SSP America, Inc.*, No. 09–CV–4339 (RRM) (VVP), 2011 WL 1204406, *6 (E.D.N.Y. Mar. 29, 2011). "Exemptions to the FLSA are 'narrowly construed against the employers seeking to assert them.'" *Bilyou* [v. *Dutchess Beer Distribs., Inc.*, 300 F.3d 217, 222 (2d Cir. 2002)] (quoting *Arnold v. Ben Kanowsky, Inc.*, 361 U.S. 388, 392 (1960)). "The determination of whether an employee is exempt from the overtime requirements of the FLSA is a 'highly fact intensive inquiry that must be made on a case-by-case basis in light of the totality of the circumstances.'" *Scott*. . . .

Under the "bona fide executive" exemption, as of 2004, federal regulations exempt an employee:

(1)   Compensated on a salary basis at a rate of not less than $455 per week. . .;

(2)   Whose primary duty is management of the enterprise in which the employee is employed or of a customarily recognized department or subdivision thereof;

(3) Who customarily and regularly directs the work of two or more other employees; and

(4) Who has the authority to hire or fire other employees or whose suggestions and recommendations as to the hiring, firing, advancement, promotion or any other change of status of other employees are given particular weight.

29 C.F.R. §541.100(a).

A. *Costello*

The court first turns to Costello. The court will consider the four factors governing application of the executive exemption.

1. First Factor

As to the first factor, concerning the rate of compensation, Costello does not dispute that this factor is satisfied as to him.

2. Third Factor

As to the third factor, concerning whether Costello customarily and regularly directed the work of two or more other employees, Costello does not appear to contest this fact. . . . Accordingly, the court deems this third factor satisfied for the purposes of this Motion for Summary Judgment.

3. Fourth Factor

The fourth factor concerns whether Costello had the authority to hire or fire other employees or whether his suggestions and recommendations as to the hiring, firing, advancement, promotion, or any other change of status of other employees were given particular weight. The regulations state:

> To determine whether an employee's suggestions and recommendations are given "particular weight," factors to be considered include, but are not limited to, whether it is part of the employee's job duties to make such suggestions and recommendations; the frequency with which such suggestions and recommendations are made or requested; and the frequency with which the employee's suggestions and recommendations are relied upon. Generally, an executive's suggestions and recommendations must pertain to employees whom the executive customarily and regularly directs. It does not include an occasional suggestion with regard to the change in status of a co-worker. An employee's suggestions and recommendations may still be deemed to have "particular weight" even if a higher level manager's recommendation has more importance and even if the employee does not have authority to make the ultimate decision as to the employee's change in status.

29 C.F.R. §541.105. Home Depot argues that the frequency of Costello's input into the interviewing process (over 200 interviews at the Westerly store), his input into the promotion and salary raise process for subordinates, and the relatively high frequency with which his suggestions were followed suggest that this factor is satisfied. Costello contends (briefly, and in a footnote) that because he did not have the ultimate authority to make these decisions (something Home Depot does not dispute), a material issue of fact remains as to whether his recommendations were given particular weight. The court notes that the regulations state that the frequency with which an employee's suggestions and recommendations are sought and relied upon are among the factors courts should consider when evaluating this factor. Here, Costello testified that 90 percent of his recommendations, which were relatively large in number, were ultimately agreed with. The court, however, notes the absence of affidavit testimony demonstrating that these recommendations actually had an impact on those receiving them. While such evidence is not absolutely necessary in order to grant a summary judgment motion, its absence fails to resolve the issue of material fact raised by Costello's testimony that his opinions were not accorded particular weight by his supervisors. Drawing all inferences in favor of Costello, as the court must on Home Depot's Motion for Summary Judgment, Home Depot has not established an absence of a material issue of fact as to this factor.

4.   Second Factor

The court now turns to the second factor, concerning whether Costello's primary duty was management of the enterprise. As with the bulk of cases involving the executive exemption, it is this factor that is most hotly contested between the parties.

Federal regulations provide further instructions with respect to the definitions of both "management" and "primary duty." Before 2004, the regulations provided a list of duties that were generally understood to be managerial, including:

> Interviewing, selecting, and training of employees; setting and adjusting their rates of pay and hours of work; directing their work; maintaining their production or sales records for use in supervision or control; appraising their productivity and efficiency for the purpose of recommending promotions or other changes in their status; handling their complaints and grievances and disciplining them when necessary; planning the work; determining the techniques to be used; apportioning the work among the workers; determining the type of materials, supplies, machinery or tools to be used or merchandise to be bought, stocked and sold; controlling the flow and distribution of materials or merchandise and supplies; providing for the safety of the men and the property.

29 C.F.R. §541.102(b) (2003). The 2004 regulations added three additional duties to this list, including "providing for the . . . security of the employees or the property; planning and controlling the budget; and monitoring or implementing legal compliance measures."

"'Primary duty' is defined by the regulations as 'the principal, main, major or most important duty that the employee performs.' To determine whether plaintiffs' performance of these exempt activities constitutes their 'primary duty,' a court must consider 'the character of an employee's job as a whole.'" *Mullins v. New York,* 653

F.3d 104, 106 (2d Cir. 2011) (quoting 29 C.F.R. §541.700(a)). The pre–2004 explanation of primary duty included four factors a court should consider, in addition to "[t]he amount of time spent in the performance of the managerial duties," including:

> the relative importance of the managerial duties as compared with other types of duties, the frequency with which the employee exercises discretionary powers, his relative freedom from supervision, and the relationship between his salary and the wages paid other employees for the kind of nonexempt work performed by the supervisor.

29 C.F.R. §541.103 (2003). The current [regulation] no longer mention "the frequency with which the employee exercises discretionary powers." *See* 29 C.F.R. §541.700. However, courts understand this factor to be incorporated into an analysis of an employee's "relative freedom from supervision." *See, e.g., Morgan v. Family Dollar Stores*, 551 F.3d 1233, 1270 n. 57 (11th Cir. 2008). Additionally, the regulations outlining the meaning of "primary duty" explain:

> Assistant managers in a retail establishment who perform exempt executive work such as supervising and directing the work of other employees, ordering merchandise, managing the budget and authorizing payment of bills may have management as their primary duty even if the assistant managers spend more than 50 percent of the time performing nonexempt work such as running the cash register. However, if such assistant managers are closely supervised and earn little more than the nonexempt employees, the assistant managers generally would not satisfy the primary duty requirement.

29 C.F.R. §541.700(c).

a. Relative Importance of Exempt Duties

The court turns first to the question of the relative importance of the managerial duties that Costello undertook.

Home Depot argues that Costello frequently performed managerial tasks as set out in 29 C.F.R. §541.102, and that those tasks were Costello's principal value to the company. Home Depot argues:

> [Costello] (1) interviewed between 200 and 300 candidates and helped select candidates for hire; (2) trained employees; (3) adjusted employee schedules; (4) provided input concerning employees' rate of pay; (5) reviewed and analyzed various reports relevant to the management of his departments; (6) appraised productivity and efficiency and recommended several individuals for promotion; (7) handled both employee and customer complaints; (8) disciplined employees; (9) planned, assigned, and monitored work; (10) reviewed and approved product orders; (11) ensured the safety of the store; and (12) enforced Home Depot policy.

Home Depot further contends that these duties constituted Costello's principal value to Home Depot, which it claims is evident from the inherent import of the tasks performed (such as the periods during which Costello served as Manager on Duty), the rigor of the process of promotion and training that prepared Costello for his MASM duties, company performance evaluations that concentrated criticism on Costello's more managerial duties, and Costello's compensation arrangement, which involved the receipt of bonuses and stock options that were based on store sales.

Costello disputes this characterization, and argues:

> [T]he ultimate success or failure of the store did not hinge on Plaintiff performing his management duties, but the store would have failed if Plaintiff did not complete his non-managerial work. Indeed, it is clear from the testimony and other evidence on record that Plaintiff and other MASMs were expected to . . . make sure the store was clean, that it was in stock and customers were served no matter how many hours it took them to accomplish all of those tasks.

Unlike some of the other cases to consider the relative importance of an employee's more managerial duties, here the court does not have any direct testimony from Home Depot officials as to how the company viewed the importance of the various tasks assigned to and carried out by Costello. Instead, the court is left to attempt to divine such conclusions, in part, from what can only be described as a somewhat intuitive assessment of what duties are critical to a large-scale retail operation. The Second Circuit, however, clearly contemplates courts making such assessments. In *Donovan v. Burger King Corp.,* the court observed:

> [T]he record fully supports Judge Sifton's finding that the principal responsibilities of Assistant Managers, in the sense of being most important or critical to the success of the restaurant, are managerial. Many of the employees themselves so testified and it is clear that the restaurants could not operate successfully unless the managerial functions of Assistant Managers, such as determining amounts of food to be prepared, running cash checks, scheduling employees, keeping track of inventory, and assigning employees to particular jobs, were performed. For that reason, as well as the fact that much of the oversight of the operation can be carried out simultaneously with the performance of non-exempt work, we believe the principal or most important work of these employees is managerial.

Donovan v. Burger King Corp., 675 F.2d 516, 521 (2d Cir. 1982).

It is undisputed that Costello performed at least some of the tasks that track those outlined in *Donovan,* although the frequency with which Costello performed those tasks, and whether he was the only person performing them, is a matter of contention. Also unclear is how other employees regarded the importance of what Costello was doing. As stated above, unlike in *Donovan,* the defendants here provide no corroborating testimony or evidence as to whether Costello's ostensibly managerial tasks were "critical to the success" of the store. In *Clougher v. Home Depot,* the court considered a similar claim by an MASM in a Home Depot store. In that case, the employee conceded to performing some managerial tasks, but claimed, similarly to Costello, to performing those tasks infrequently, and only in a supporting role to his other, more important non-exempt work. The court found this dispute sufficient to preclude summary judgment because of outstanding factual issues. *See Clougher v. Home Depot,* 696 F. Supp. 2d 285, 291-92 (E.D.N.Y. 2010). . . . Other courts have not found similar ambiguities sufficient to demonstrate a material issue of fact. . . .

Here, Costello certainly conducted a large number of interviews with potential hires over the course of his employment and had at least some input into the hiring process (although he did not make the ultimate determinations), participated in some training of lower-level employees, reviewed staffing schedules initially compiled by other employees (although Costello insists, and his deposition testimony seems to confirm, that Costello did not review those schedules for the purposes of ensuring adequate staffing), participated in worker performance evaluation, dealt with safety issues, and dealt with customer complaints. However, it also appears that many of these duties were sometimes shared by other employees, or, in the case of inventory orders, were sometimes carried out without any managerial supervision at all. The evidence in the record does not definitely answer these questions.

Perhaps the most potentially critical job function Costello performed related to his occasional duties as MOD, in which he would open or close the store, and was sometimes the only salaried manager in the store. Although sometimes accompanied by other managers, Costello would, during at least some of those periods, make sure the store had cashiers, open the vault, ensure department staffing, and run daily reports. Although a store manager held ultimate responsibility, Home Depot's argument that Costello's functions as MOD were indeed critical for store success are significantly more persuasive than its contentions regarding his other responsibilities. However, the amount of time actually spent on this activity is hotly disputed. . . . Here, given the absence of corroborating testimony from Home Depot officials or other employees regarding the importance of Costello's various tasks, divergent accounts of the amount of time actually spent on managerial tasks (including performance of MOD functions), the degree to which those functions were replicated by lower-level employees, Costello's testimony that he was informed by supervisors that customer service was his primary job function, and his somewhat uncertain degree of influence in hiring decisions, a material issue of fact remains as to the relative importance of Costello's managerial functions.

b. Time Spent Performing Non-Exempt Work

The court will also consider the amount of time Costello spent performing non-exempt work as part of its inquiry into whether managerial tasks constituted Costello's primary duty. The federal regulations state:

> The amount of time spent performing exempt work can be a useful guide in determining whether exempt work is the primary duty of an employee. This, employees who spend more than 50 percent of their time performing exempt work will generally satisfy the primary duty requirement. Time alone, however, is not the sole test, and nothing in this section requires that exempt employees spend more than 50 percent of their time performing exempt work. Employees who do not spend more than 50 percent of their time performing exempt duties may nonetheless meet the primary duty requirement if the other factors support such a conclusion.

29 C.F.R. §541.700(b). Analysis of this section here is not particularly illuminating as Home Depot does not appear to argue that Costello crossed the 50 percent threshold in the performance of exempt managerial work. As is obvious from the regulation however, this fact is not dispositive one way or the other, as "Employees who do not spend more than 50 percent of their time performing exempt duties may nonetheless meet the primary duty requirement if other factors support such a conclusion." Costello maintains that of a workweek that varied between 60 and 80 hours, around ten hours could be spent doing traditionally managerial tasks. Additionally (or possibly overlappingly), Costello engaged in MOD-related activities (either alone or with other managers) between nine and 40 hours per week.

In short, it is unclear which way this evidence cuts, or what the actual scope of Costello's duties, in terms of time spent, was. A variation between less than ten percent to nearly 50 percent of time spent, at least partially, doing managerial tasks is indeed a significant one for the purposes of this analysis. While perhaps less favorable to Costello's position than the issue of relative importance, the factual disputes here still create a material issue of fact as to Costello's primary duty that precludes determination as a matter of law. The court further notes that neither side has introduced evidence as to whether Costello was capable, given the tasks at hand, of simultaneously performing managerial and non-managerial tasks, something that courts which have found that employees were properly exempt have relied on when considering a situation in which the majority of an employee's time is spent on non-exempt tasks. . . . Given the fact-intensive nature of this inquiry, the court refrains from assuming the ease of such multitasking in the specific context of the Home Depot stores in which Costello worked. As such, a material issue of fact remains as to this factor which precludes determination as a matter of law.

c. Freedom from Direct Supervision. . .

Home Depot argues that Costello frequently exercised discretion, with a minimum of oversight, as a MASM. This discretion was primarily demonstrated through Costello's role in preparing performance reviews (a task Costello claims was often delegated to non-salaried employees), recommending annual raises and additional training, decisions related to dealing with employees who called out of work, dealing with customer complaints, and other such activities.

Further, Home Depot argues that, not only was Costello, when he was MOD, sometimes the only salaried manager in the store, even when the store manager was present Costello engaged in a great deal of discretionary activity as MASM as to the departments he was assigned to:

> [It] was Costello who: (1) ensured his departments were properly staffed; (2) planned the work to be done in each department; (3) delegated work to his subordinates and followed up to make sure it was done in a timely and correct manner; (4) ensured his subordinates were trained, both for their current position and so they would be ready to advance to the next level; (5) ensured proper merchandise was ordered; (6) inspected his departments for safety violations; (7) resolved employee and customer complaints; (8) made recommendations regarding annual raises for his employees; (9) counseled associates on disciplinary issues; (10) recognized his subordinates for exceptional performance; and (11) devised strategies to improved department sales.

Costello asserts that, while he performed many of these tasks, in many instances—particularly related to hiring, firing, and scheduling decisions—ultimate decision-making power and discretion lay elsewhere. Further he contends that he did so infrequently, and that when he did, he was in large part constrained by corporate policies. The existence of corporate policies does not, categorically, limit such discretion. Further, Costello does not actually explain how, and in what sense, his discretionary powers were limited by specific corporate policies. More substantively, while Costello was always subject in the corporate chain of command to the store manager, he was also often accompanied by other managers while MOD, and while some tasks, such as ordering supplies and scheduling, were carried out in large part by others, it seems clear that Costello had a relatively free hand within his areas of influence. Taken together, these facts lay out a scope of activity that lends itself to a conclusion that Costello was relatively free from direct supervision. While this is not dispositive of the Motion for Summary Judgment, this factor appears to weigh in favor of Home Depot.

d. Salary

The court next considers how Costello's salary compares to wages paid nonexempt workers for performing similar tasks. Costello earned between $44,000 and $50,000 during the course of his employment, during which he was expected to work at least 55 hours per week, and sometimes worked between 60 and 80 hours per week. Additionally, Costello could receive performance bonuses and stock options, and received a bonus in 2004 for $3,381.49 and 1,300 stock options between 2003 and 2005. It is unclear what the total value of those stock options are, or when Costello received them.

The parties do not provide a breakdown of how many weeks per year Costello was expected to work. Assuming a 55 hour work week and a 52 week per year work schedule, Costello earned between $15.38 per hour ($846.15 per week) and $17.42 per hour ($961.54 per week). From 2004 to 2005, the mid-range hourly rate for sales associates was $12.64 per hour and for department supervisors was $16.97. . . .

The court does recognize that bonuses and stock options were unavailable to lower-level employees, something that suggests greater importance and a more central role for Costello. However, the dollar amounts in question, particularly when factoring in unresolved factual questions of which hourly rates it should compare and the availability of overtime for lower-level employees, do not appear to yield a significant disparity in compensation that suggest as a matter of law that Costello's primary duty was management. As such, it is not clear in which party's favor this factor weighs.

Taking all these factors together, it is clear that material issues of fact exist as to Costello's primary duty at Home Depot, precluding summary judgment. Accordingly, Home Depot's Motion for Summary Judgment as to Costello is denied.

NOTES

1. *Initial Impressions.* Costello had the title of manager, had some supervisory duties, and had some authority to exercise judgment in his work. Stepping back from legal doctrine, wouldn't you consider Costello to be "white collar"? Indeed, one of the lingering problems with these exemptions is that both employees and employers often fail to understand their scope. For example, many employees who view themselves as white collar—perhaps in part because they receive a "salary" rather than "hourly wages"—may simply assume that they are exempt and thus not demand overtime pay. Such employees may instinctively prefer the exempt designation insofar as they associate that categorization with professional status, and they may well view it as a proxy for the importance of their jobs and their value to the company. Employers, too, may be mistaken about the law or share similar perceptions about the relationship between exempt status and employee value. Consider as well that the FLSA places significant record-keeping responsibilities on employers with respect to the hours and compensation levels of nonexempt workers. This can create administrative burdens for the employer and negatively affect morale among employees who must keep track of and regularly report all of their work time.

2. *Certainty and the "Old" and "New" Regulations.* As discussed above, a major criticism of the "old" regulations governing the exemptions for executive, administrative, and professional employees was how little guidance they provided. In *Costello*, the court applies the 2004 rules on the executive exemption but makes some reference to the pre-2004 rules, as well as draws some comparisons. Do you see much distinction between them in terms of certainty of outcomes or ease of application? Also, several of the precedents on which *Costello* relies applied the pre-2004 rules, further suggesting that the 2004 changes may not have altered the analysis significantly. Considering the purpose of the executive exemption inquiry—determining whether the workers at issue really do exercise significant authority—could it be any less fact-intensive? What might be the downside of bright-line rules that seek to categorize workers *ex ante*?

In March 2014, President Obama directed the Secretary of Labor to reconsider the 2004 rules, contending that the existing white-collar exemptions do not adequately protect worker wages and hours. *See* Executive Office of the President, *Memorandum for the Secretary of Labor*, Doc. No. 2014-06138, 79 Fed. Reg. 15209 (March 18, 2014). The fate of the resulting rule, and the Trump Administration's plans for a new regulation, are is discussed above at page 799.

3. *Right Result?* Do you think the *Costello* court reached the right result? Are the distinctions the court draws between Costello and those that are exempt under the executive exemption meaningful? Are you satisfied with the tests the court articulated for making these determinations?

4. *"Managers."* *Costello* is far from the only case in which employees identified as "managers" by their employers have successfully claimed that they are nonexempt. Indeed, Costello's claim was but one of 39 originally brought together by Home Depot assistant managers. Although the court severed the claims, each, including Costello's, could proceed separately. *See Costello v. Home Depot U.S.A., Inc.*, 888 F. Supp. 2d 258 (D. Conn. 2012). And similar claims have been brought against Home Depot by assistant managers working elsewhere the country. Indeed, in recent years, misclassification of store and single-facility managers has been a particularly fertile area for litigation and large settlements. *See, e.g.*, http://www.lawyersandsettlements.com/settlements/employment-settlements/ (listing hundreds of large settlements in employment-related cases on an updated basis, including claims brought by store and facility managers in the retail sector).

While much of this litigation has addressed assistant managers, other cases have involved the highest-ranking employees at their respective facilities. For example, in *McKinney v. United Store-All Centers LLC*, 656 F. Supp. 2d 114 (D.D.C. 2009), the court denied the employer's motion for summary judgment on the issue of whether employees hired as "primary managers" of its self-storage facilities—which leased storage units and rental trucks to customers—were exempt from the FLSA's overtime mandates under the administrative and executive employee exemptions. After engaging in a detailed analysis akin to that in *Costello*, the court concluded that, despite their rank at the firm's local facilities, there were genuine issues of material fact as to whether these employees' primary duties were executive (exercising significant authority) or administrative (exercising significant discretion) in nature.

5. *Administrative Employees.* Determining whether a worker is covered by the exemption for administrative employees, like the executive employee exemption, is often a highly fact-intensive inquiry. The current (2004) DOL regulations provide that an "employee employed in a bona fide administrative capacity" means any employee:

> (1) Compensated on a salary or fee basis at a rate of not less than $455 per week . . . exclusive of board, lodging or other facilities;
> (2) Whose primary duty is the performance of office or non-manual work directly related to the management or general business operations of the employer or the employer's customers; and
> (3) Whose primary duty includes the exercise of discretion and independent judgment with respect to matters of significance.

29 C.F.R. §541.200. As the regulations recognize, this exemption overlaps with the one for executive employees. *See* 29 C.F.R. §541.201. The key distinction is that administrative employees need not manage or supervise others—they need simply exercise discretion and independent judgment on important business matters. The exercise of discretion and independent judgment encompasses "the comparison and the evaluation of possible courses of conduct, and acting or making a decision after the various possibilities have been considered." 29 C.F.R. §541.202. The employee must have the "authority to make an independent choice, free from immediate direction or supervision," although one can exercise discretion and independent judgment even if his or her decisions or recommendations are reviewed at a higher level. The regulations list a number of factors to consider in determining whether an employee exercises discretion and independent judgment. *See id.*

"Matters of significance" refers to the level of importance or consequence of the work performed. Areas in which work might qualify for the exemption include "tax; finance; accounting; budgeting; auditing; insurance; quality control; purchasing; procurement; advertising; marketing; research; safety and health; personnel management; human resources; employee benefits; labor relations; public relations, government relations; computer network, internet and database administration; legal and regulatory compliance; and similar activities." *See* 29 C.F.R. §541.201. A number of specific examples of qualifying work are set forth in Note 9 below.

6. *Professional Employees.* Another exemption is for "professional employees," but the framework for determining which employees are exempt as "professionals" parallels, in many cases, the tests for determining executive or administrative employee status. The current regulations provide that an "employee employed in a bona fide professional capacity" under the FLSA means an employee:

> (1) Compensated on a salary or fee basis at a rate of not less than $455 per week . . . exclusive of board, lodging, or other facilities; and
> (2) Whose primary duty is the performance of work:
> (i) Requiring knowledge of an advanced type in a field of science or learning customarily acquired by a prolonged course of specialized intellectual instruction; or
> (ii) Requiring invention, imagination, originality or talent in a recognized field of artistic or creative endeavor

29 C.F.R. §541.300. Note, however, that certain categories of licensed professionals are exempt regardless of their salary. *See, e.g.,* 29 C.F.R. §541.304 (exempting employees who have "a valid license or certificate permitting the practice of law or medicine or any of their branches and is actually engaged in the practice thereof" as

well as residents and interns pursuing such a profession). Yet courts tend to construe these categories narrowly. *See, e.g., Lola v. Skadden, Arps, Slate, Meagher & Flom LLP,* 620 F. App'x 37 (2d Cir. 2015) (holding that a contract attorney who performed document review did not engage in the "practice of law" because the attorney used predetermined criteria to sort documents and exercised no legal judgment whatsoever); *Belt v. Emcee, Inc.* 444 F.3d 403 (5th Cir. 2006) (holding that nurse practitioners and physician assistants fell outside of the "practice of medicine" exception to the salary-basis test for determining professional exemption from overtime-pay requirements).

7. *The Outside Sales Exemption.* The FLSA and underlying regulations also provide an exemption for an "outside salesman," for whom the minimum salary requirements applicable to the previously discussed exemptions do not apply. *See* 29 U.S.C.A. §213(a)(1); 29 C.F.R. §541.500. The regulation defines outside salesman as any employee:

(1) Whose primary duty is:
  (i) making sales within the meaning of section 3(k) of the Act, or
  (ii) obtaining orders or contracts for services or for the use of facilities for which a consideration will be paid by the client or customer; and
(2) Who is customarily and regularly engaged away from the employer's place or places of business in performing such primary duty.

29 C.F.R. §541.500(a).

This exemption, too, has been the subject of a fair amount of litigation. Indeed, in a recent decision of great significance to the pharmaceutical industry, the Supreme Court broadly construed the exemption, holding that pharmaceutical sales representatives whose primary duty was to obtain nonbinding commitments from physicians to prescribe their employer's prescription drugs in appropriate cases qualified as "outside salesmen" exempt from FLSA's minimum wage and maximum hours requirements. This rejected the Department of Labor's view (of its own regulation) that a "sale" required more than such a nonbinding commitment. *See Christopher v. SmithKline Beecham Corp.,* 567 U.S. 142 (2012).

Note that some states impose stricter standards under their wage and hour statutes for quantifying the "outside" element of this exemption. Those states look to the actual time spend engaged in outside vs. inside sales work to determine exempt salespeople. For example, California uses a "primarily engaged" standard that requires sales directors to spend half their time working away from the community, and Colorado requires a bona fide salesperson to spend at least 80 percent of his or her work activities on outside sales. *See DLSE—Glossary,* State of California, Department of Industrial Relations (2016), http://www.dir.ca.gov/dlse/Glossary.asp? Button1=O#outside%20salesperson; *Colorado Minimum Wage Order Number 32,* Department of Labor and Employment, Division of Labor, https://www.sos.state.co.us/CCR/GenerateRulePdf.do?ruleVersionId=6534&fileName=7%20CCR%201103-1.

8. *The Auto Dealer "Salesman" Exemption.* The exempt status of "service advisors" at automobile dealerships—that is, whether they fall within the statutory exemption for "salesman," *see* 29 U.S.C. § 213(b)(10)(A)—has been another frequently contested issue. In 1970, the DOL issued a regulation defining "salesman" to mean "an employee who is employed for the purpose of and is primarily engaged in making sales or obtaining orders or contracts for sale of the vehicles . . . which the establishment is primarily engaged in selling." 29 CFR § 779.372(c)(1) (1971). The regulation excluded service advisors, who sell repair and maintenance services but not vehicles, from the exemption. In 1978, the DOL issued an opinion letter departing from its previous position and stating that service advisors could be exempt under the statute. In 2011, however, the Department issued a final rule that followed the original 1970 regulation and interpreted the statutory term "salesman" to mean only an employee who sells vehicles. *See* 76 Fed. Reg. 18859.

In *Encino Motors, LLC v. Navarro*, 136 S. Ct. 2117 (2016), the Supreme Court found that this 2011 regulation was not entitled to *Chevron* deference because the DOL had failed to give a reasoned explanation for its decision to abandon its practice of treating service advisors as exempt under section 213(b)(10)(A). It therefore held that Section 213(b)(10)(A) must be construed without placing controlling weight on this regulation. On remand, however, the Ninth Circuit held that service advisors do not fall within the exemption because, under the most natural reading of the statute, Congress did not intend to exempt such advisors, and, even if the text were ambiguous, the legislative history confirms that Congress intended to exempt only those selling and servicing cars. *See Navarro v. Encino Motorcars, LLC*, 845 F.3d 925 (9th Cir. 2017).

9. *Guidance and Planning Implications.* Employment counsel are frequently called upon to make *ex ante* assessments of whether employees are exempt. Now that you are familiar with the tests for determining whether an employee is exempt under the executive and administrative exemptions, how comfortable would you be in making such assessments? Do the standards articulated facilitate category-wide treatment, or, as an attorney, would you feel it necessary to evaluate each person in each job? Further, to the extent that jobs often vary in reality from the corresponding job description, might you find it useful to visit each location to discuss the work with supervisors or even employees? Can you anticipate some problems in doing that?

There are some additional sources of guidance available beyond judicial decisions applying the regulations. Individual employers can seek feedback from the DOL on the exempt status of their employees. Upon such request, the DOL will issue a nonbinding opinion letter regarding the employees' status based on the facts the employer provided. In addition, the regulations themselves provide some particularized examples of workers who are or are not exempt. Consider, for instance, some of the examples provided in the regulations on the administrative exemption:

(a) Insurance claims adjusters generally meet the duties requirements for the administrative exemption, whether they work for an insurance company or other type of company, if their duties include activities such as interviewing insured's, witnesses and physicians; inspecting property damage; reviewing factual information to prepare damage estimates; evaluating and making recommendations regarding coverage of claims; determining liability and total value of a claim; negotiating settlements; and making recommendations regarding litigation. . . .

(c) An employee who leads a team of other employees assigned to complete major projects for the employer (such as purchasing, selling or closing all or part of the business, negotiating a real estate transaction or a collective bargaining agreement, or designing and implementing productivity improvements) generally meets the duties requirements for the administrative exemption, even if the employee does not have direct supervisory responsibility over the other employees on the team.

(d) An executive assistant or administrative assistant to a business owner or senior executive of a large business generally meets the duties requirements for the administrative exemption if such employee, without specific instructions or prescribed procedures, has been delegated authority regarding matters of significance.

(e) Human resources managers who formulate, interpret or implement employment policies and management consultants who study the operations of a business and propose changes in organization generally meet the duties requirements for the administrative exemption. However, personnel clerks who "screen" applicants to obtain data regarding their minimum qualifications and fitness for employment generally do not meet the duties requirements for the administrative exemption. . . .

(g) Ordinary inspection work generally does not meet the duties requirements for the administrative exemption. Inspectors normally perform specialized work along standardized lines involving well-established techniques and procedures which may have been catalogued and described in manuals or other sources. Such inspectors rely on techniques and skills acquired by special training or experience. They have some leeway in the performance of their work but only within closely prescribed limits.

29 C.F.R. §541.203.

Although employers' counsel ought to scrutinize carefully such examples, the guidance they provide may still be of limited assistance since they focus on relatively few of the thousands of positions in the American workplace. Moreover, as *Costello* and the qualifying language in each of the foregoing examples suggest, individual variations in the nature and scope of employees' duties can be dispositive even within an individual job category established by an employer.

10. *Overtime Pay.* Given the higher social standing of white-collar workers, why would plaintiffs such as Costello want to *not* be exempt? While it may be too obvious to stress, they are not concerned with whether they were paid $7.25 an hour—undoubtedly, they receive more than that. These are not "minimum wage" cases at all, but illustrate that the FLSA can play an important role for higher-status employees who work overtime. Home Depot may have violated the law, but it may not have done so "willfully." Can you understand how easy it might be for an employer dealing with "white collar" or even "professional" workers not to focus on problems such as those raised in these cases?

11. *Remedies and Enforcement.* Uncertainty is not the only reason that white-collar exemptions are frequently litigated: The amount of money potentially at stake provides an obvious incentive for these claims. This is particularly true for those cases brought as "collective" actions, a form of representative action (similar to a class action) expressly provided for in the FLSA, *see* 29 U.S.C. §216(b), in which large numbers of employees may join together to seek relief. *Costello* is fairly typical: The litigation was pursued at least initially as a collective action involving many employees who were not paid overtime over long periods. In these kinds of cases, if the employer turns out to be wrong, liability for unpaid overtime compensation alone may climb into the millions of dollars. Indeed, if you do a little math in your head (time and a half for any hours over 40 during a week for a year or beyond), you will see how the damages for even one of these assistant managers will run deep into the tens of thousands of dollars. Then multiply that by the number of such assistant managers in the region who were originally joined the action. THEN multiply by the number of assistant managers who might be bringing similar actions around the country.

Costello also illustrates that employers may be subject to "liquidated damages"—an additional amount equal to the amount of unpaid wages—for violations of the

FLSA's overtime and minimum wage mandates. *See* 29 U.S.C. §216(b). The court may, however, in its discretion award lesser or no liquidated damages if it finds that the employer's actions giving rise to FLSA liability were in good faith and that the employer had reasonable grounds for believing that his act or omission was not a violation. *See* 29 U.S.C. §260; 29 C.F.R. §790.22. Moreover, prevailing FLSA plaintiffs are also awarded their reasonable attorneys' fees. *See* 29 U.S.C. §216(b). Finally, any person who willfully violates the provisions of the FLSA may be subject to criminal fines and imprisonment. *See* 29 U.S.C. §216(a).

As discussed in the notes following the *Ansoumana* case in Chapter 1, page 51, there have been a number of successful and high-profile minimum-wage suits. However, as also mentioned, enforcement of wage and hour laws at the low end of the labor market is difficult and rare. *See id.* For this reason, wage and hour violations—sometimes referred to as "wage theft"—are widespread. *See, e.g.,* Brishen Rogers, *Toward Third-Party Liability for Wage Theft*, 11 BERKELEY J. EMPL. & LAB. L. 1, 10 n.33 (2010) (citing numerous recent studies showing that violations are common); *see also* ANNETTE BERNHARDT ET AL., THE GLOVES-OFF ECONOMY: WORKPLACE STANDARDS AT THE BOTTOM OF THE LABOR MARKET 7-8 (2008) (same). Indeed, while enforcement activities have been on the rise in recent years, so too are underlying violations across the low-wage workforce. *See, e.g.,* Steven Greenhouse, *More Workers Are Claiming "Wage Theft,"* N.Y. TIMES, Sept. 1, 2014, at A1; Marianne Levine, *Behind the Minimum Wage Fight, a Sweeping Failure To Enforce the Law,* Feb. 18, 2018, https://www.politico.com/story/2018/02/18/minimum-wage-not-enforced-investigation-409644.

Chapter 1 discusses a number of phenomena that contribute to this underenforcement problem, including "employer" coverage questions, insolvency of fly-by-night labor contractors, and the socioeconomic vulnerability and immigrant status of workers. Insufficient remedies to incentivize private attorneys to bring these claims are another reason, since, in contrast to claims for overtime by higher-wage workers, the potential damages for lost wage claims for low-wage workers often are not substantial. Furthermore, due to a chronic lack of resources, the DOL and state agencies traditionally have been unable to fill the enforcement gap. Technology, including electronic payroll systems, also can facilitate wage theft and exacerbate enforcement problems. For example, by using software that rounds down increments of time worked or automatically subtracts break deductions whether or not a break is actually taken, employers can reduce at paid time in ways that are difficult to detect. *See, e.g.,* Elizabeth Tippett, *How Employers Profit from Digital Wage Theft Under the FLSA,* 66 AMERICAN B.L. JOUR. 55 (2018); *see also* Charlotte Alexander & Elizabeth Chika Tippett, *The Hacking of Employment Law,* 82 Mo L. REV. 973 (2017).

Still another factor is the array of procedural hurdles workers must overcome to obtain relief under the FLSA, including the statute's collective action mechanism for consolidating claims, 29 U.S.C. §216(b), which, unlike ordinary class actions, require workers to opt into the suit. *See* Craig Becker & Paul Strauss, *Representing Low-Wage Workers in the Absence of a Class: The Peculiar Case of Section 16 of the Fair Labor Standards Act and the Underenforcement of Minimum Labor Standards,* 92 MINN. L. REV. 1317 (2006); Nantiya Ruan, *Facilitating Wage Theft: How Courts Use Procedural Rules to Undermine Substantive Rights of Low-Wage Workers,* 63 VAND. L. REV. 727 (2010); Scott A. Moss & Nantiya Ruan, *The Second-Class Class Action: How Courts Thwart Wage Rights by Misapplying Class Action Rules,* 61 AM. U. L. REV. 523 (2012); *see also Genesis Healthcare Corp. v. Symczyk,* 569 U.S. 66

(2013) (holding that a collective action brought by single employee on behalf of herself and all similarly situated employees for employer's alleged violation of the FLSA became moot as result of offer of judgment by employer in an amount sufficient to make her whole). And, as discussed in detail in Chapter 13, collective enforcement of wage and hour laws also has been made more difficult by the Supreme Court's recent Federal Arbitration Act decisions. *See* Chapter 13, page 943; *Epic Systems Corp. v. Lewis,* 138 S. Ct. 1612 (2018).

In response to these concerns and developments, several states have amended existing wage statutes to expand the remedies by which workers can address "wage theft." These remedies include the public posting of violations by the State in workplaces, increased fines for violations, liquidated damage clauses, and reinstatement of workers who are fired because they bring wage theft claims against their employer. *See e.g.,* N.Y. LAB. LAW § 195 (2018); D.C. CODE § 32-1302 (2018). For a discussion of potential tax liability for wage theft and suggestions for improving enforcement, *see* Sachin S. Pandya, *Tax Liability for Wage Theft,* 3 COLUM. J. TAX L. 113 (2012).

12. *Erring on the Side of Safety?* Unlike mistakenly classifying an employee as exempt, mistakenly classifying an employee as nonexempt is unlikely to harm the employee. Since erroneously treating the employee as exempt poses great risks to the employer in terms of unpaid overtime plus interest, liquidated damages, and paying its own attorneys' fees and litigation costs and those of the plaintiff, it would seem that employers might choose to err on the side of classifying workers as nonexempt. But employers might discount the risks of liability by the (un)likelihood that the employee or the DOL will actually bring suit and prevail. Depending on the employer's view of the risks, it may be willing to accept the risk of downstream liability to avoid paying overtime in the near term. And erring on the side of nonexempt status has its own obvious problem: the risk of substantial overtime payments. However, an employer who chooses this path could also limit such costs by avoiding overtime and hiring additional workers. Can you appreciate how complex a legal and business decision it is to decide whether positions are exempt or not? Realize too that over the course of time, even correct decisions may have to be reconsidered in light of changing workplace practices.

13. *Private Ordering Again.* We started our discussion of the FLSA by saying that there is relatively little role for private ordering. That's certainly true with respect to the substantive provisions—the workers could not prospectively waive their rights to overtime compensation in order to, say, get more overtime hours. But the exemptions analyzed in these cases can be viewed as opening a door to private ordering. An employer's structuring a job in certain ways will bring the employee within or without the exemption. Of course, there are real, if not legal, constraints on this type of planning. Hiring subordinates might result in exemption for the supervisor, but it also results in two more workers protected by the FLSA.

PROBLEM

11-1. Suppose you are an attorney at a large law firm. You have been asked by the firm's managing partner to give her advice on whether various "paralegals" are exempt employees. You are confident that the vast majority of paralegals are not exempt as "learned professionals," given that the new regulations explicitly provide that only paralegals possessing specialized degrees in other professional fields and applying that knowledge are exempt as such professionals. *See* 29 C.F.R. §541.301(e)(7). But might some paralegals be administrative employees?

You know that most paralegals in your firm—like the bulk of paralegals elsewhere—simply assist attorneys in completing various tasks, including drafting and filing legal documents and forms, preparing for trial, reviewing documents, communicating with clients, organizing documents and materials, performing basic compilations, and engaging in basic legal research. As to whether paralegals whose primary duties fit this description are exempt under the administrative exemption, your research reveals a recent Department of Labor Opinion Letter—providing a nonbinding legal opinion based on the facts provided by the employer—that offers a fairly definitive "no," indicating that such employees do not exercise the level of judgment and discretion necessary to satisfy the exemption's requirements:

> It continues to be our opinion that the duties of paralegal employees do not involve the exercise of discretion and independent judgment of the type required by section 541.200(a)(3) of the final regulations, thus an analysis of whether their work is related to management or general business operations is not necessary. The outline of the duties of the paralegal employees you provide describes the use of skills rather than discretion and independent judgment. The paralegals typically are drafting particular documents to assist attorneys on a particular case or matter. The paralegals are not themselves formulating or implementing management policies, utilizing authority to waive or deviate from established policies, providing expert advice, or planning business objectives in accordance with the dictates of 29 C.F.R. §541.202(b). Thus, . . . the paralegal employees appear to fit more appropriately into that category of employees who apply particular skills and knowledge in preparing assignments. Employees who apply such skills and knowledge generally are not exercising independent judgment, even if they have some leeway in reaching a conclusion. In addition, most jurisdictions have strict prohibitions against the unauthorized practice of law by laypersons. Under the American Bar Association's Code of Professional Responsibility, a delegation of legal tasks to a lay person is proper only if the lawyer maintains a direct relationship with the client, supervises the delegated work, and has complete professional responsibility for the work produced. The implication of such strictures is that the paralegal employees you describe would not have the amount of authority to exercise independent judgments with regard to legal matters necessary to bring them within the administrative exemption.

Wage and Hour Division, U.S. Department of Labor, Opinion Letter FLSA 2005-54, 2005 WL 3638473 (December 16, 2005).

Despite the Opinion Letter, you know that paralegal duties vary enormously in your firm, and there is no formal job description for any of them. Indeed, some of the more experienced and successful paralegals in your firm have responsibilities requiring a significant amount of judgment. Accordingly, you inquire further and learn some pertinent information with regard to four such paralegals. In addition to performing the basic duties described above:

- Adrianne works in the Family Law group and is largely responsible for initial client screening and intake decisions;

- Boris, who has worked in the firm's Corporate Group for 15 years, has authority to update and edit the department's library of standard forms;
- Carlos is the person primarily responsible for pretrial document management in several multimillion-dollar cases for the Commercial Litigation group; and
- Devon, who works in your firm's human resources department, exercises fairly broad de facto authority to make various types of regulatory compliance decisions.

Under any of these circumstances, would the paralegal be exempt as an administrative employee? Do the examples from the regulations discussed in Note 8 above help? Does the Department's Opinion letter determine the outcome for any of them, or does its discussion of the discretion and independent judgment factor suggest rather that the outcome is far from clear? What other information, if any, might be helpful in making your assessment?

---

b. FLSA Application Problems

When an employee is entitled to the FLSA's minimum wage protections, overtime protections, or both, application of the requirements is often straightforward. Nevertheless, a few application issues have produced litigation. One set of these issues involves the calculation of hours or compensable time, and another involves rate-of-pay determinations.

i. Compensable Time

In applying the FLSA's minimum wage and overtime mandates, one must determine the number of hours an employee has worked. The original statute contained no definition of "work," "compensable time," or any other term addressing what counts as work or working hours. In a series of early cases, the Supreme Court held that the statute's definition of "employ"—"to suffer or permit to work"—means that employers must pay employees for productive activities they control or require and are for the employer's primary benefit. *See Tennessee Coal, Iron, & R.R. Co. v. Muscoda Local No. 123*, 321 U.S. 590 (1944); *Armour & Co. v. Wantock*, 323 U.S. 126 (1944); *Skidmore v. Swift & Co.*, 323 U.S. 134 (1944). The Court also held, however, that time spent in "incidental" activities is also compensable. *See Skidmore, supra*. This lack of clarity led Congress to pass the Portal-to-Portal Act of 1947, *see* 29 U.S.C. §254 (2018), which explicitly *excludes* from compensable time (1) travel to and from work and the work site prior to or after the workday or principal work activities and (2) activities that are "preliminary to or postliminary to said principal activity or activities," unless such travel or activities are included as compensable time pursuant to custom or contract.

What constitutes "preliminary or postliminary" activities, however, has been the subject of a fair amount of litigation. In general, an employee's activities preparing for work or after ending work, such as putting on or taking off work clothes, are noncompensable. However, where such activities are "an integral and indispensable part of the principal activities," they remain compensable. *Mitchell v. King Packing Co.*, 350 U.S. 260, 262-63 (1956). Thus, while donning work clothes is normally noncompensable, putting on and taking off uniforms at work pursuant to employer requirements or industry custom, or for safety reasons, is compensable. *See, e.g., IBP, Inc. v. Alvarez*, 546 U.S. 21 (2005) (finding that where putting on and taking off required work gear and uniforms are integral and indispensable activities, time spent moving to and from changing areas to work areas constitutes compensable time as does time waiting to doff gear). *But see Sandifer v. U.S. Steel Corp.*, 134 S. Ct. 870 (2014) (finding that donning and doffing of clothes and safety gear is subject to collective bargaining and hence not compensable pursuant to section 203(o) of the FLSA, when the safety gear was relatively de minimis compared to the clothing). It is also worth noting that preparing necessary tools or equipment is also compensable. *Mitchell*, 350 U.S. at 262-63 (finding knife-sharpening in a meat-packing plant is integral and indispensable to employee's principal activity of butchering); *see also* 29 C.F.R. §790.8(c) (protective clothing for workers in a chemical plant).

Nevertheless, interpretation and application issues with regard to preliminary and postliminary activities continue to arise. For example, in *Integrity Staffing Sols., Inc. v. Busk*, 135 S. Ct. 513 (2014), the Supreme Court finally resolved the much disputed question of whether time employees spend waiting for and undergoing security screenings before leaving work constitutes compensable activity, concluding that it does not.

Various other questions with regard to compensable time are addressed by detailed Department of Labor regulations. These include rules that distinguish compensable break times, sleep time, lunch and other meal times, and other "down" times from nonproductive portions of the day that are not compensable. In recent years, lawsuits over uncompensated break, meal, and other time have received significant attention. *See, e.g.*, Wage and Hour Lawsuits against Wal-Mart Settled for over $350 Million, December 30, 2008, *available at* http://www.aboutlawsuits.com/wage-and-hour-lawsuits-against-wal-mart-settled-2211/ (discussing Wal-Mart's agreement to pay between $352 million and $640 million to settle 63 wage and hour lawsuits filed in 42 states). The federal courts have developed two tests to determine whether meal time is compensable under the FLSA. One focuses on whether the employee was relieved from all duties during the meal break; the other, which is now the majority view, inquires whether the employer or employee received the "predominant benefit" of the meal break. *See, e.g., Babcock v. Butler County*, 806 F.3d 153 (3d Cir. 2015) (discussing both tests and adopting the predominant benefit approach, which it describes as the clear majority view).

The status of "on-call" time is another area in which there is much controversy and litigation. This issue has produced many disputes in certain job categories—for example, emergency response personnel, automated equipment and information systems maintenance personnel, and nonexempt medical workers. This is unsurprising considering the number of hours at issue and, hence, the enormous economic stakes for both employees and employers.

Pabst v. Oklahoma Gas & Electric Co.
228 F.3d 1128 (10th Cir. 2000)

LUCERO, Circuit Judge.

[W]e conclude that plaintiffs' on-call duties requiring them to continually monitor automated alarms by pager and computer were compensable under the FLSA. In so holding, we reject the argument that on-call monitoring time is not compensable unless contemporaneously reported to the employer as overtime. Further, we uphold the district court's determination that the employer's FLSA violation was not willful, and affirm both the award of prejudgment interest and the denial of liquidated damages. . . .

I

Plaintiffs are Electronic Technicians in Oklahoma Gas & Electric's ("OG&E") Facility Operations Department. Plaintiffs Pabst and Gilley were Electronic Technician I's ("Tech 1s") and plaintiff Barton was an Electronic Technician II ("Tech 2"). The three plaintiffs, along with two other employees, monitored automated heat, fire, and security systems in several OG&E buildings. Prior to an August 1994 reduction in force, these duties required twelve on-site employees working three eight-hour shifts.

Plaintiffs were on call to monitor OG&E building alarms weekdays from 4:30 p.m. to 7:30 a.m. and twenty-four hours a day on weekends. During these hours, alarms went to computers at Pabst's and Gilley's homes, as well as to pagers for all plaintiffs. After October 1994, Barton began to receive alarms at home via laptop computer. Plaintiffs were required to respond to the alarms initially within ten minutes, then, after October 1996, within fifteen minutes. Failure to respond within the time limit was grounds for discipline. Each plaintiff was assigned, and required always to carry, an alpha-numeric pager. These pagers were only 70% reliable. The short response time, coupled with unreliable pagers, forced plaintiffs to remain at or near their homes while on call.

The district court found that plaintiffs received an average of three to five alarms per night, not including pages for security issues. Although not all alarms required plaintiffs to report to the office—it appears many could be fixed by remote computer— the district court found it took an average of forty-five minutes to respond to each alarm. Neither party disputes those findings on appeal.

[The district court also found that the employer did not utilize a rotational on-call schedule. A rotation "would not have been feasible because of the frequency of alarms and plaintiffs' differing areas of expertise."]

According to plaintiffs, their supervisor instructed them to report only on-call time spent responding to an alarm. OG&E paid plaintiffs for at least one hour for each alarm to which they responded, and two hours if they had to return to OG&E facilities. Plaintiffs apparently reported some, but not all, of the alarms they answered, but did not claim as overtime the remainder of their time spent on call.

Considerable testimony was presented regarding the extent to which monitoring interfered with plaintiffs' personal activities. Most significantly, an average of three to five alarms per night, each requiring on average forty-five minutes of work, severely disrupted plaintiffs' sleep habits; indeed, they testified to rarely experiencing more than five hours of uninterrupted sleep per night. In addition, even during waking hours, plaintiffs were unable to pursue many personal activities while on call because of the need to come into their homes to check their computers every fifteen minutes.

The district court found plaintiffs' on-call time compensable under the FLSA and awarded them compensation for fifteen hours per weekday and twenty-four hours per Saturday and Sunday, less any hours already paid for responding to alarms. . . .

II. . .

"Employ" is defined as including "to suffer or permit to work." §203(g). The pertinent question, and one with which courts have struggled, is whether on-call time is "work" for purposes of the statute. The FLSA does not explicitly address the issue of on-call time.[1] Courts, however, have developed a jurisprudence of on-call time, based on the Supreme Court cases of *Armour & Co. v. Wantock*, 323 U.S. 126 (1944), and *Skidmore v. Swift & Co.*, 323 U.S. 134 (1944). Those cases determine the relevant inquiry to be whether an employee is "engaged to wait" or "waiting to be engaged," *Skidmore*, or, alternatively, whether on-call time is spent predominantly for the benefit of the employer or the employee, *see Armour*. Necessarily, the inquiry is highly individualized and fact-based, and "requires consideration of the agreement between the parties, the nature and extent of the restrictions, the relationship between the services rendered and the on-call time, and all surrounding circumstances," *Boehm v. Kansas City Power & Light Co.*, 868 F.2d 1182, 1185 (10th Cir. 1989) (citing *Skidmore*). We also focus on the degree to which the burden on the employee interferes with his or her personal pursuits. *See Armitage v. City of Emporia*, 982 F.2d 430, 432 (10th Cir. 1992). Several facts are relevant in assessing that burden: number of calls, required response time, and ability to engage in personal pursuits while on call. *See id.; Renfro v. City of Emporia*, 948 F.2d 1529, 1537-38 (10th Cir. 1991).

A

OG&E argues that it did not know plaintiffs were working the entire time they were on call and thus did not "suffer or permit" them to work. 29 U.S.C. §203(g). Its theory goes as follows: Plaintiffs were responsible for reporting their own overtime;[2]

---

1. Although regulations promulgated by the Department of Labor address that issue, they are unhelpful to our analysis because they fail to anticipate a scenario, like that in the present case, in which an on-call employee is able to perform his or her duties from a location away from the employer's premises. *See* 29 C.F.R. §785.17 (stating that an "on call" employee is working if "required to remain on call on the employer's premises or so close thereto that he cannot use the time effectively for his own purposes"). More helpful are those regulations applicable to fire protection and law enforcement employees. *See* 29 C.F.R. §553.221(d) (stating that time spent on call is compensable if "the conditions placed on the employee's activities are so restrictive that the employee cannot use the time effectively for personal pursuits").

2. Plaintiffs worked a forty-hour week in addition to their time on call. Thus, to the extent on-call time was working time, it was compensable at the overtime rate. *See* 29 U.S.C. §207.

B. *Wage Protections* === 825

because they reported only time spent responding to calls (and apparently not even all of that), rather than *all* of their on-call time, OG&E lacked knowledge that they were working and therefore did not suffer or permit them to work. This argument misinterprets the nature of the on-call time inquiry and borders on the disingenuous.

As a factual matter, OG&E's purported lack of actual knowledge is dubious. Plaintiffs cite record testimony detailing a reprimand Pabst received for attempting to report the entire time spent monitoring systems as overtime. . . . More significantly, OG&E's policy informed plaintiffs they would be compensated only for on-call time spent responding to an alarm. The only logical inference was that they would not be compensated for time spent monitoring their computers and pagers, unless they took some specific action responding to an alarm. To claim, then, that OG&E did not know plaintiffs were working because they did not report every hour of their evenings and weekends as overtime is misleading. While OG&E arguably may have lacked knowledge of the legal proposition that the FLSA required compensating plaintiffs for their on-call time under the system at issue, OG&E certainly knew that plaintiffs were performing the duties they had been assigned.

OG&E relies heavily on *Davis v. Food Lion*, 792 F.2d 1274, 1276 (4th Cir. 1986), for its knowledge theory. In *Davis*, the court found that "Food Lion has an established policy which prohibits employees from working unrecorded, so-called 'off-the-clock,' hours." Davis argued that Food Lion's "Effective Scheduling" system required him to work such off-the-clock hours in order to perform his required duties and avoid reprimand. The Fourth Circuit held the FLSA "required Davis to prove Food Lion's actual or constructive knowledge of his overtime work," and found no clear error in the district court's "factual finding that Food Lion has no actual or constructive knowledge of Davis's off-the-clock work."

Davis is not applicable to the case before us. First, there is no evidence of anything like an explicit prohibition on plaintiffs' performing after-hours monitoring duties; on the contrary, such was the very essence of their responsibilities. Moreover, *Davis* was not, as plaintiffs correctly note, an on-call time case. In the on-call context, an employer who creates an on-call system obviously has constructive, if not actual, knowledge of employees' on-call duties. An employer must evaluate whether those duties are compensable under the FLSA, and if the employer concludes they are not, the employees do not bear the burden of submitting overtime requests for hours that fall outside the definition of what the employer classifies as compensable. Plaintiffs reported (apparently with some omissions) the hours to which they were entitled under OG&E's policy. That they did not report the entirety of their remaining on-call hours does not preclude the obvious conclusion that OG&E had knowledge of their on-call status.

[OG&E argued that its rotating on-call schedule meant that it had neither actual nor constructive knowledge of the full extent of plaintiffs' on-call hours. The argument was that OG&E believed only one plaintiff to be on call during a given week, and thus it did not know of the other two. But the district court noted that there was strong evidence against any such rotational schedule and that even OG&E conceded that there were weeks when two employees recorded time despite the supposed rotation. There was no clear error in the district court's findings.]

B

Whether a particular set of facts constitutes compensable "work" under the FLSA is a legal question we review de novo. *See Berry v. County of Sonoma*, 30 F.3d 1174, 1180 (9th Cir. 1994). In *Renfro*, we granted FLSA compensation to firefighters for their on-call time. *Renfro*'s facts include the following:

> the firefighter must be able to report to the stationhouse within twenty minutes of being paged or be subject to discipline; that the on-call periods are 24-hours in length; and primarily that the calls are frequent—a firefighter may receive as many as 13 calls during an on-call period, with a stated average frequency of 3-5 calls per on-call period.

OG&E emphasizes that all but one published Tenth Circuit case addressing on-call time have found it non-compensable. Counting published cases, however, is meaningless in resolving a fact-intensive question such as the compensability of on-call time. Rather, the proper question is which case is most analogous. . . . In sum, this case is far more analogous to *Renfro* than to the more numerous precedents cited by OG&E.

Although OG&E complains bitterly against having to compensate plaintiffs for working twenty-four hours a day, seven days a week, the cost to an employer of an "always on call" arrangement does not mean that such a system is not cognizable under the FLSA, so long as the on-call time qualifies as work under the relevant FLSA precedents. While one circuit has held that always being on call, while extremely burdensome, does not in and of itself make the on-call time compensable for FLSA purposes, *see Bright v. Houston Northwest Med. Ctr. Survivor, Inc.*, 934 F.2d 671, 678-79 (5th Cir. 1991) (en banc), another circuit found that requiring employees to monitor and respond all day, every day is a factor weighing in favor of compensability, *see Cross v. Arkansas Forestry Comm'n*, 938 F.2d 912, 916-17 (8th Cir. 1991) (holding that on-call time is compensable under the FLSA because employees were required to continuously monitor transmissions and respond within thirty minutes, and because they were subject to on-call status twenty-four hours per day for every day of a work period). We agree with both *Bright* and *Cross*. Although always being on call is not dispositive, such an added burden is relevant in assessing the extent to which all-the-time on-call duty deprives employees of the ability to engage in personal activities.

The only significant difference between the burden on the plaintiffs in *Renfro* and the burden on Pabst, Gilley, and Barton is that plaintiffs here often did not have to report to the employer's workplace in order to respond to calls. This lighter burden, however, is offset by the fact that plaintiffs, unlike the firefighters in *Renfro*, were not on call for "six shifts of twenty-four hours each in a 19-day cycle," but rather during *all* of their off-premises time. The frequency of calls here actually is greater than in *Renfro* because plaintiffs' calls during weekdays occurred during a fifteen hour, rather than a twenty-four hour, period. Additionally, in *Renfro*, we found on-call time compensable despite the fact that the firefighters "had participated in sports activities, socialized with friends and relatives, attended business meetings, gone shopping, gone out to eat, babysitted, and performed maintenance or other activities around their home." *Renfro* controls the application of the FLSA to the facts before us, and leads us to hold that the district court was correct in finding plaintiffs' on-call time compensable.

III

We next consider OG&E's claims that the award of overtime compensation should be reduced by subtracting out several time periods.

We reject, as a matter of law, OG&E's argument that time spent in personal pursuits should be subtracted. The relevant inquiry in on-call cases is not whether plaintiffs' duties prevented them from engaging in any and all personal activities during on-call time; rather it is "whether 'the time is spent predominantly for the employer's benefit or the employee's.'" *Boehm* (quoting *Armour*). This is a yes-no inquiry—whose benefit predominated? OG&E cites no authority for the proposition that a court must determine whose benefit predominated during each on-call hour. *Cf. Renfro* (holding firefighters' on-call time compensable even though they engaged in some personal pursuits during that time). OG&E's other arguments for reductions in the damages award, which pertain to individual plaintiffs, are factual issues subject to clear error review.

OG&E argues that Barton should not have been awarded overtime compensation from October 1994 through October 1, 1996 because during that time he was monitoring alarms only by pager and not by computer. OG&E primarily focuses on the comparatively small amount of remote overtime Barton charged during that period, as compared to Gilley and Pabst. However, we are persuaded the district court did not clearly err in determining that Barton, like Gilley and Pabst, received between three and five pages per night during this period, despite the comparatively smaller amount of overtime Barton recorded. . . .

[The court affirmed the district court's denial of liquidated damages, finding that the court did not abuse its discretion in concluding that OG&E's actions were reasonable and in good faith, despite its mistaken belief that the on-call time was noncompensable.]

NOTES

1. *A Costly Mistake.* Although this case was brought by only three employees, and the court ultimately rejected their bid for liquidated damages, OG&E's liability was still significant, given that these employees consistently worked a 24/7 schedule. Had OG&E known that the FLSA required overtime compensation for this time, how might it have structured its on-call regime to limit the amount it would have to pay out to its technicians? It might have instituted a real rotation system. Might it have been cheaper to hire a fourth tech for a night shift than to pay overtime? Might knowledge of potential liability also have influenced how OG&E ran its operations— for example, what equipment it uses, what times of day this equipment should be running, how many resources it puts into daytime maintenance? The possibility of more reliable pagers jumps off the page.

2. *Disparate Outcomes and Planning Implications.* The *Pabst* court recognizes the differing views of the various circuit courts on when on-call time is compensable. Indeed, these differences are even more profound when one digs a little deeper. For example, *Bright v. Houston Northwest Medical Center Survivor, Inc.*, 934 F.2d 671 (5th Cir. 1991) (en banc), did not simply hold, as *Pabst* suggests, that always being on-call "does not in and of itself make the on-call time compensable for FLSA purposes." Rather, the *Bright* court held as a matter of law that a biomedical equipment repair technician on-call around the clock was not entitled to compensation for on-call periods except those in which he actually worked because (1) he was not required to remain at or very near the hospital where he worked, (2) he was free to be at his home or at any place he chose without advising his employer, and (3) he was "subject only to the restrictions that he be reachable by beeper, not be intoxicated, and be able to arrive at the hospital in 'approximately' twenty minutes." *Id*. at 676; *see also Adair v. Charter Cty. of Wayne*, 452 F.3d 482 (6th Cir. 2006) (finding officers employed by county airport were not entitled to overtime pay for off-duty time during which they were required to carry pagers and remain relatively near to work because they could engage in regular activities); *Beck v. Okla. Gas & Elec. Co.*, 2017 U.S. Dist. LEXIS 30089, *1 (W.D. Okla. March 3, 2017) (granting defendant's motion for summary judgment against five employees seeking pay for on-call time because it found that the restrictions of being on-call were not burdensome, services provided during a regular shift were not related to those while on-call, and the employees were called less frequently than in *Pabst* and had the ability to engage in personal activities).

In light of these differing approaches and outcomes, the issue of on-call time provides a nice example of the planning difficulties for employers with operations in more than one part of the country. Should such an employer treat similarly situated employees differently based on local circuit law?

3. *From Pagers to PDAs.* Pabst involved a pager, technology that is so last-millennium. In an era of smart phones, employees are increasingly expected to respond during what are, in theory, nonworking hours. Even when such responses are not required, employees often do answer e-mails or calls off hours. This is an area of considerable liability risk for employers. The Seventh Circuit's decision in *Allen v. Chicago*, 865 F.3d 936 (7th Cir. 2017), drives home this point in the context of a dispute over whether Chicago needed to compensate police officers for off-duty work (checking communications, etc.) on cellphones. The court declared that an employer must "pay for all work [managers] know about, even if they did not ask for the work, even if they did not want the work done, and even if they had a rule against doing the work." *Id*. at 938. Ultimately, the employees lost in the case because they had not requested payment at the time and the City did not have actual or constructive knowledge of the uncompensated off-duty work. *Id*. at 942-43. Nevertheless, by articulating a "knew or should have known" standard, the court made clear that, to avoid potential liability for such otherwise compensable off-duty work, employers must carefully instruct employees on work expectations when they are off-duty, have a system for reporting off-duty or overtime work that does not deter such reporting, and ensure there is not an unspoken or unwritten expectation among managers that employees respond or otherwise engage in work when they are off-duty. Also, as we saw in Chapter 6, employers typically have the legal freedom and technological ability to track employee use of employer equipment 24/7. *See generally* Sean L. McLaughlin, Comment, *Controlling Smart-Phone Abuse: The Fair Labor Standards Act's Definition of "Work" in Non-exempt Employee Claims for Overtime*, 58 U. Kan. L. Rev. 737 (2010). If you were an employer's attorney, would you consider instructing employees not to use company e-mail, phone, or other electronic devices during nonwork hours? That seems extreme, but the risks of liability might be pretty high. The alternative of monitoring such use and reacting on a more individual basis also seems problematic.

4. *Line Drawing.* Compensation for on-call time provides yet another example of the difficulty of drawing lines under the FLSA and the corresponding costs and risks for employers and employees trying to determine *ex ante* what the terms of their relationship will be. Congress may be institutionally incapable of drawing finer distinctions to avoid such problems. But, why doesn't the DOL attempt to make things clearer? In answering this question, consider the potential costs and risks of clarity. For example, are unforeseen loopholes and other unintended consequences more likely? Also, does greater specificity increase the need for more frequent regulatory amendments?

5. *Computer Personnel.* One obvious growth area in the "on-call" context in recent years involves information technology and computer personnel. Given that virtually all public and private employers use such technology, and many, if not most, need their systems to operate 24 hours a day, employees are needed who can respond when there are software, hardware, and other problems. However, these employees pose an additional wrinkle to the "on-call" question. As mentioned above, some computer personnel are exempt under the special exemption for computer employees. *See* 29 U.S.C.A. §213(a)(17). The new governing regulation, which closely tracks the statutory language, provides as follows:

29 C.F.R. §541.400 General Rule for Computer Employees. . . .

(b) The section 13(a)(1) exemption applies to any computer employee compensated on a salary or fee basis at a rate of not less than $455 per week . . ., exclusive of board, lodging or other facilities, and the section 13(a)(17) exemption applies to any computer employee compensated on an hourly basis at a rate not less than $27.63 an hour. In addition, under either section 13(a)(1) or section 13(a)(17) of the Act, the exemptions apply only to computer employees whose primary duty consists of:

(1) The application of systems analysis techniques and procedures, including consulting with users, to determine hardware, software or system functional specifications;

(2) The design, development, documentation, analysis, creation, testing or modification of computer systems or programs, including prototypes, based on and related to user or system design specifications;

(3) The design, documentation, testing, creation or modification of computer programs related to machine operating systems; or

(4) A combination of the aforementioned duties, the performance of which requires the same level of skills.

The exemption does not include employees primarily engaged in the manufacture or repair of computer hardware and related equipment or those who merely use computers in their work. *See* 29 C.F.R. §541.401.

In light of this exemption, think about the various kinds of computer or information employees with whom you have worked at school or while employed. Are any or all of your school's or your employer's IT employees exempt? Recall, of course, that some may already be exempt under the administrative or executive exemptions. Is this easy to determine or would you require more detail regarding duties to make an assessment? *Cf.* Wage and Hour Division, U.S. Department of Labor, Opinion Letter FLSA FLSA2006-42, 2006 WL 3406603 (October 26, 2006) (opining that an IT Support Specialist position in which the employee is primarily responsible for "installing, configuring, testing, and troubleshooting computer applications, networks, and hardware" does not involve the exercise of sufficient discretion to qualify for the administrative exemption and does not involve the "application of systems analysis techniques and procedures, including consulting with users, to determine hardware, software or system functional specifications" necessary to qualify for the computer employee exemption).

Among computer employees, how many are "on-call," at least some of the time? What about the *Pabst* plaintiffs? The employer never argued that these employees were exempt, only that their on-call time was not compensable. Do you see why?

In terms of policy, does it make sense to exempt these computer employees from the FLSA's strictures, including the overtime provisions that might mandate premium compensation for when they are on-call (assuming such time would otherwise satisfy the test articulated in *Pabst*)? In other words, are these computer employees more like learned and creative professionals or more like the technicians in *Pabst*? In answering this question consider not only what such computer employees do, but also their relative ability to protect themselves in the market. Is your answer today different than it might have been in 2000, at the height of the Internet and technology boom?

6. *New Frontiers in On-Call Work: "Just-In-Time" Employment.* Another emergent issue in this context is so-called just-in-time scheduling, in which employers in the service sector use software to track customer demand and then adjust workers' schedules as needed. This is highly efficient from the employer perspective since an employer can maintain a fairly exacting labor-hours-to-demand ratio. However, this technique leaves employees with little certainty about their schedule or the number of hours they will work and results in fluctuating hours that disrupt family responsibilities and preclude employees from working elsewhere. Currently, such idle time is not compensable under the FLSA. Moreover, although some states have sought to regulate work scheduling, scholars argue these protections are also inadequate. *See* Charlotte Alexander, Anna Haley-Lock, & Nantiya Ruan, *Stabilizing Low-Wage Work: Legal Remedies for Unpredictable Work Hours and Income Instability*, 50 Harv. CR-CL L. Rev. 1 (2015); *see also* Steven Greenhouse, *Part-Time Schedules, Full-Time Headaches*, N.Y. Times, July 18, 2014 at B1 (discussing the phenomenon and fledgling efforts at regulation at the state and local level).

PROBLEM

11-2. *Oops, I Did It [Violated the FLSA?] Again. . . .* This item appeared in Yahoo! News on March 30, 2006:

Former Spears Bodyguards Sue for Overtime

Three men hired to guard pop star Britney Spears have filed a lawsuit claiming they worked long hours and were not paid overtime.

The lawsuit, filed Tuesday in Superior Court, names three companies—Britney Brands Inc., Britney Touring Inc. and Team Tours Inc.—as responsible for not properly compensating former bodyguards Lonnie Jones, Randy Jones and Silas Dukes.

Together, the three men are seeking damages exceeding $25,000 for unpaid wages and benefits, their attorney Daniel Emilio said Wednesday. Messages left at the office of Spears' publicist Leslie Sloane Zelnick were not immediately returned.

Randy Jones and Dukes worked 12- to 16-hour shifts and were required to be on call 24 hours a day during trips with Spears, according to the lawsuit. Lonnie Jones worked 12-hour shifts, the suit said.

The trio claimed they were only paid a "straight salary," missed meals and didn't receive overtime pay.

Hired in 2004, the men claim they were laid off on Nov. 30, 2005 without receiving a final paycheck.

http://news.yahoo.com/s/ap/20060330/ap_on_en_mu/people_spears.

Suppose you were contacted by Ms. Spears' legal team and asked to assist in determining the risk of liability under the FLSA and preparing a possible defense. They send you the complaint, which, under California's liberal pleading regime, provides little detail in addition to what is set forth above. Their two questions for you are (1) whether these bodyguards might be exempt under the white-collar exemptions and (2) if not, whether their "on-call" time might constitute compensable hours. As to the first question, what additional information would you need to make this determination? Given what you know at this point, how likely is it that these bodyguards are exempt? As to the second question, what information would you need to determine whether the on-call time is compensable? Again, given what you know at this point, how likely is it that this time is compensable? Additionally, based on the facts provided so far, is there a possible further line of defense here? Hint: Take a look back at *Ansoumana. But see Schultz v. Capital Intern. Security, Inc.*, 460 F.3d 595 (4th Cir. 2006) (holding workers hired to provide security for Saudi prince were "employees" covered by FLSA because, among other things, prince and security company exercised nearly complete control over their jobs, they were paid a set rate per shift, some worked for the prince for several years, and he preferred workers who would stay over the long term).

Finally, switch gears and consider the plaintiffs' perspective. Although the complaint appears not to have done so at this point, could and should the plaintiffs have named Ms. Spears as a defendant in her personal capacity? After all, she's "not that innocent." Wouldn't that up the settlement value of the case?

---

ii. Calculating "Regular Rate of Pay"

As we have seen, the FLSA's overtime provisions require employers to pay covered workers "time and a half," that is, one and one-half times their "regular rate of pay" for hours in excess of 40 hours in any given week. *See* 29 U.S.C. §207 (2018). What constitutes an employee's "regular rate of pay" is a fairly easy calculation when an employee receives only hourly wages or receives a salary and has a work week with standard hours. Thus, for example, an employee who receives a weekly salary of $1,000 for 40 hours of work has a regular rate of pay of $25 per hour. If the employee works 50 hours in a given week, the employer will have to pay the employee $1,375 for that week—$1,000 weekly salary for the first 40 hours plus $375 for the additional 10 hours ($25 multiplied by the 10 additional hours multiplied by the one-and-one-half overtime premium rate).

If the employee's salary compensates for fewer than 40 hours a week, then the employee is entitled to his or her regular rate for additional hours up to 40 hours, and the premium rate thereafter. Thus, for example, an employee who receives a weekly salary of $750 for 30 hours of work a week has a regular rate of $25 dollars per hour. If the employee works 50 hours in a given week, the employer will have to pay the employee $1,375 for that week—$750 weekly salary for 30 hours, plus $250 for 10 additional hours ($25 multiplied by 10), plus $375 for the remaining 10 hours ($25 multiplied by the 10 additional hours plus one-half that amount, representing the overtime premium).

The regular rate of pay calculation becomes more difficult, however, when the employee receives a salary for hours that are contemplated to fluctuate week-to-week or receives forms of compensation in addition to his or her hourly wage or salary. In this situation, a DOL regulation allows the employer to use a fluctuating workweek computation method to determine the regular rate and overtime pay. *See* 29 C.F.R. §778.114. This method still guarantees an overtime premium for each overtime hour worked, but, by allowing a recomputation of the regular rate each week based on the total hours worked, it in effect allows the employer to pay less of a premium per hour the more hours the employee works in any given week.

This calculation method, however, is available only when (1) there is "a clear mutual understanding of the parties" that the salary is compensation for "the hours worked each workweek, whatever their number, rather than for working 40 hours or some other fixed weekly work period"; (2) the salary is sufficient to ensure a rate not less than the applicable minimum wage rate for every hour worked in any week (regardless of the number of hours worked); and (3) the employee actually receives the extra compensation, in addition to the base salary, for all overtime hours worked at a rate not less than one-half the employee's regular rate of pay. Thus, this is one context in which private ordering can alter an employee's rights under the FLSA, although the statute limits the potential impact of such ordering and its requirements provide baseline protections against employer abuse.

In terms of determining the employee's regular rate of pay when the employee receives compensation in addition to a regular wage or salary, the FLSA provides that this rate shall include "all remuneration for employment paid to, or on behalf of, the employee," unless the type of additional compensation falls within one of eight exclusions, such as Christmas or birthday gifts, vacation pay, bonuses, and fringe benefits. *See* 29 U.S.C. §207(e). Determining the meaning of "remuneration for employment" and interpreting and applying the exclusions have proven difficult in some circumstances. *See, e.g., Flores v. City of San Gabriel*, 824 F.3d 890 (9th Cir. 2016) (holding that the city's cash-in-lieu of benefits payments are not properly excluded from the calculation of the regular rate of pay under either § 207(e)(2) or (e)(4)).

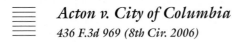

Acton v. City of Columbia
436 F.3d 969 (8th Cir. 2006)

Lay, Circuit Judge.

Chris N. Acton and ninety-nine current and former firefighters (the "firefighters") employed by the City of Columbia, Missouri (the "City") brought suit against the City for failing to include a series of payments in the firefighters' regular rate of pay, in violation of 29 U.S.C. §207(e) (the Fair Labor Standards Act or "FLSA").

[The district court granted the firefighters' summary judgment] motion in part, ruling that sick leave buy-back monies should be included in the firefighters' regular rate of pay. However, the district court also denied the firefighters' motion in part, ruling that monies received under the City's meal allowance program were excluded from the regular rate. Finally, the district court found no evidence that the City willfully violated the FLSA. . . .

IV. Sick Leave Buy-Back

Under the City's sick leave buy-back program, firefighters who work twenty-four hour work shifts during the course of one year accumulate ten days of sick leave. Firefighters who fail to use their sick leave are entitled to "sell back" any of the ten unused sick days to the City in exchange for a lump sum payment equal to 75% their regular hourly pay, provided the firefighter has amassed at least six months sick leave. The firefighters contend that all monies received from the sale of sick leave should be included in their regular rate of pay. The regular rate of pay calculation is critical because it provides the base point from which the firefighters' overtime compensation is calculated.

A. *The Fair Labor Standards Act*

Section 207(e) of the FLSA provides, in relevant part, that "all remuneration for employment paid to, or on behalf of, the employee" must be included in the employee's regular rate of pay, provided such remuneration is not prohibited by one of eight statutory exclusions listed under §207(e)(1)-(8). 29 U.S.C. §207(e). There is a statutory presumption "that remuneration in any form is included in the regular rate calculation. The burden is on the employer to establish that the remuneration in question falls under an exception." *Madison v. Res. for Human Dev. Inc.*, 233 F.3d 175, 187 (3d Cir. 2000).

Before beginning our analysis, we must clarify a preliminary matter of statutory construction under the FLSA that has been a point of confusion between the parties. First, the City argues sick leave buy-back monies do not constitute remuneration for employment. Next, the City contends sick leave buy-back monies are also excluded under §207(e)(2) because they "are not made as compensation for [the employee's] hours of employment." *Id.* However, the language "not made as compensation for [the employee's] hours of employment" posited in §207(e)(2) is but a mere re-articulation of the "remuneration for employment" requirement set forth in the preambulary language of §207(e). Section 207(e)(2), properly understood, operates not as a separate basis for exclusion, but instead clarifies the types of payments that do not constitute remuneration for employment for purposes of §207. Therefore, we treat the City's "remuneration for employment" and §207(e)(2) arguments under the same mode of analysis. Finally, because both provisions modify one other, we must necessarily consider the express requirements of §207(e)(2) and the federal regulations interpreting it when determining if sick leave buy-back monies constitute remuneration for employment.

1. Remuneration for Employment

Regulation 29 C.F.R. §778.223 provides the touchstone for our inquiry because it addresses the scope of §207(e)(2). Specifically, regulation §778.223 addresses whether monies paid to employees for remaining on call are excluded from the regular rate under §207(e)(2). The regulation concludes that monies paid to employees to remain on call, while not related to "any specific hours of work," are nevertheless awarded as "compensation for performing a duty involved in the employee's job"— namely, the employee's willingness and commitment to work unscheduled hours if requested. *See* 29 C.F.R. §778.223. The plain language of the regulation makes clear that all monies paid as compensation for either a general or specific work-related duty should be included in the regular rate. The critical question before this court is whether sick leave buy-back monies compensate the firefighters for some specific or general duty of employment.

In order to qualify for sick leave buy-back payments, firefighters must come to work regularly for a period of several years in order to amass the requisite six month sick leave reserve. Then, the firefighters must also accrue additional sick leave in the present year in order to be eligible for buy-back. Thus, the primary effect of the buy-back program is to encourage firefighters to come to work regularly over a significant period of their employment tenure. We recognize consistent workplace attendance to be a general duty of employment and, therefore, rule that sick leave buy-back monies constitute remuneration for employment.[10]

The City sets forth three primary arguments to support its conclusion that sick leave buy-back payments are not remuneration for employment. First, the City argues its buy-back program was intended to promote two objectives unrelated to employee compensation. On the one hand, the sick leave buy-back program was intended to provide firefighters with a form of short-term disability insurance because the City does not have a disability policy covering employee illness or disability lasting six months or less. The sick leave buy-back program, with its six-month accrued sick leave requirement, was devised as a mechanism for employees to self-insure against personal illness or disability. Alternatively, the City argues its sick leave buy-back program discourages employees from treating sick leave as another form of vacation or personal leave because the program creates a money incentive for employees to accrue, but not use, their sick leave.

These arguments are not compelling. Even if the sick leave buy-back program was intended to provide employees with a form of short-term disability insurance and to discourage misuse of sick leave, one plain effect of the program is to reward regular workplace attendance through a non-discretionary, year-end, lump sum payment. The City's proffered justifications do not change the undisputed fact that the firefighters are plainly rewarded for regularly showing up for work over a period of years.

Second, the City also cites 29 C.F.R. §825.125, a Department of Labor opinion letter, and a decision from a federal district court in the Northern District of Illinois

---

10. We also note that sick leave buy-back monies do not resemble any of the payments expressly excluded under §207(e)(2). *See* 29 C.F.R. §778.224(a) (noting that payments excluded from the regular rate under §207(e)(2) must "be 'similar' in character to the payments specifically described" in (e)(2)). Sick leave buy-back monies, in contrast to §207(e)(2) payments, are awarded to employees for coming to work consistently, not for work that was never performed.

to support its claim that bonuses awarded for perfect attendance do not require performance by the employee, but rather contemplate the absence of occurrences. 29 C.F.R. §825.215 ("Bonuses for perfect attendance and safety do not require performance by the employee but rather contemplate the absence of occurrences."); Opinion Letter from Maria Echaveste, Administrator, U.S. Department of Labor (Mar. 21, 1994) ("Bonuses premised on 'perfect attendance' or 'perfect safety' are rewards not for work or production, but for compliance with rules."); *Dierlam v. Wesley Jessen Corp.*, 222 F. Supp. 2d 1052, 1057 (N.D. Ill. 2002) (noting that a bonus that does not require its recipient to meet production goals or quality standards "simply contemplates the non-occurrence of an event—[the recipient's] absence from work").

However, none of these three authorities address the applicability of §207. Instead, each confronts the issue of whether an employee is entitled to a bonus for good attendance upon returning to work under the Family Medical Leave Act. The City's attempt to cite language taken out of context from authorities interpreting another federal statute in no way binds us in this case. To the extent the City uses these authorities to argue that consistent workplace attendance does not "require performance by the employee," we flatly disagree. We believe consistent workplace attendance *does* require performance. In the modern workplace, regular and prompt workplace attendance is a valued commodity, one for which the City appropriately rewards its employees.

Finally, the City cites the Sixth Circuit's decision in *Featsent v. City of Youngstown*, 70 F.3d 900 (6th Cir. 1995), to support its argument that sick leave buy-back monies do not constitute remuneration for employment. In *Featsent*, the Sixth Circuit ruled that monies paid to employees who did not submit medical claims and failed to use accrued sick leave were excluded from the regular rate of pay under §207(e)(2) because such payments are "unrelated to the [employee's] compensation for services and hours of service."

We decline to follow the Sixth Circuit's decision in *Featsent*. The *Featsent* court failed to articulate any basis for its reasoning. The court did not distinguish regulation §778.223 in reaching its conclusion, nor did it recognize and explain how payments awarded to an employee for not using accrued sick leave, which necessarily requires employees to work more days than they are required, is not tantamount to payment for services rendered. Because we are unpersuaded by the Sixth Circuit's analysis, we reject its conclusion.

2. Statutory Exceptions. . . .

Section 207(e)(5) provides:

[E]xtra compensation provided by a premium rate paid for certain hours worked by the employee in any day or workweek because such hours are hours worked in excess of eight in a day or in excess of the maximum workweek applicable to such employee under subsection (a) or in excess of the employee's normal working hours or regular working hours, as the case may be[.]

The dissent argues sick leave monies should be excluded under §207(e)(5) because they constitute premium payments for specific hours worked. This analysis fails for several reasons. First, sick leave monies are not paid for specific hours worked. Instead, these payments compensate employees for a record of consistent attendance over the course of several years, not simply for working days during a given year they are otherwise entitled to take off.

Second, in order for payments to be excluded under §207(e)(5), they must be "paid for certain hours worked by the employee in any day or workweek because such hours are hours worked in excess of eight in a day or in excess of the maximum [required in a] workweek." *Id*. Even assuming, as the dissent does, that sick leave buy-back payments are paid in sole recognition for the specific days a firefighter chooses to work instead of calling in sick, there is still no basis to exclude such payments under §207(e)(5). Section 207(e)(5), by its own terms, limits its applicability to payments made for certain hours worked in excess of the employee's normal daily or weekly schedule. Under the dissent's approach, buy-back payments are, at best, premium payments for working normally scheduled hours.

Finally, §207(e)(5) plainly excludes only "premium" payments—that is, payments no less than one and one-third the employee's regular rate. *See* 29 C.F.R. §778.308(b). The dissent creatively "compounds" sick leave buy-back payments, which are awarded at the sub-premium rate of 75% the firefighters' hourly wage, with the firefighters' base hourly wage. This ignores the fact that the premium payments themselves must be at least one and one-third the employee's hourly rate. *See id*. Be this as it may, the dissent's approach, taken to its logical conclusion, yields unsettling results. Under the dissent's theory, all extra monies paid to employees for specific hours worked may be "compounded" with the employee's regular hourly rate and excluded under §207(e)(5), in contravention of the express requirements of 29 C.F.R. §778.207(b). *See* 29 C.F.R. §778.207(b) (stating that non-overtime premiums for specific hours worked, such as nightshift differentials and hazard pay, must be included in the regular rate). Therefore, we rule that §207(e)(5) does not exclude sick leave buy-back payments from the regular rate of pay. . . .

LOKEN, Chief Judge, dissenting. . . .

Sick leave buy-back payments admittedly do not fit comfortably within the exclusion in 29 U.S.C. §207(e)(2) for "payments made for occasional periods when no work is performed." But the court is wrong to suggest that such payments "are not related to specific duties or hours worked." In my view, sick leave buy-back payments are functionally equivalent to premium overtime pay that is expressly excluded from an employee's regular rate. Like overtime, and unlike true attendance bonuses, these payments relate to specific hours *worked*—the days that the employee chose to work rather than to use paid sick leave.

As the Supreme Court said in the FLSA's formative years, "[t]o permit overtime premium to enter into the computation of the regular rate would be to allow overtime premium on overtime premium—a pyramiding that Congress could not have intended." *Bay Ridge Operating Co. v. Aaron*, 334 U.S. 446, 464 (1948). This principle was codified in 1949. *See* 29 U.S.C. §207(e)(5)-(e)(7). If sick leave buy-back payments fit awkwardly under §207(e)(2) because they relate to hours worked, rather than to hours not worked, these payments are squarely within the purview of the three exclusions found in subsections (e)(5)-(e)(7) that apply to "extra compensation provided by a premium rate paid for certain hours worked."[14]

---

14. Unlike the exclusion in §207(e)(2) for payments for hours not worked, compensation excluded from the employee's regular rate under subsections (e)(5)-(e)(7) "shall be creditable toward overtime compensation payable pursuant to this section." §207(h). . . .

Section 207(e)(5) excludes "extra compensation provided by a premium rate paid for certain hours worked . . . because such hours are hours worked . . . in excess of the employee's . . . regular working hours." A firefighter who works one or more paid sick leave days has worked in excess of his "regular working hours." If otherwise eligible under the City's program, he may sell unused sick leave to bring his total pay for sick leave hours worked up to 175% of his regular rate. The related exclusion in §207(e)(6) applies to "extra compensation provided by a premium rate paid for work by the employee on . . . regular days of rest" if the premium rate is not less than one and one-half times the regular rate. These exclusions were intended to prevent the pyramiding of "overtime on overtime." They have been applied to a variety of overtime compensation programs.

In response, the court asserts that sick leave buy-back payments are not compensation at a premium rate. This ignores economic reality. The City agreed to pay the plaintiff firefighters for ten days of sick leave each year. If sick leave is used, the City must pay another employee to do the work, presumably at a rate at least equal to the regular rate of the firefighter on sick leave. If the firefighter instead works, leaving his sick leave unused, the City through the buy-back program pays, on top of the regular rate already paid, a premium equal to 75% of the firefighter's regular rate. Thus, for those days worked, the firefighter is paid 175% of his regular rate. This premium is greater than and functionally no different than the premium the FLSA requires employers to pay for overtime work—not less than one and one-half times (150%) the employee's regular rate. *See* 29 U.S.C. §207(a). And like overtime, extra compensation paid for unused sick leave is offset by the employer not incurring the expense of hiring additional workers or paying other employees to fill in.

It may make little difference whether the City's sick leave buy-back payments are excluded from a firefighter's regular rate under §207(e)(2) because they are "similar to payments made when no work is performed due to illness," *Featsent*, or under §207(e)(5) or (6) as overtime compensation paid at a premium rate. But the contrary decision of the district court and this court to include those payments in the regular rate both distorts FLSA principles and discourages use of a creative overtime payment device that benefits both employers and employees. I respectfully dissent from this decision.

NOTES

1. *Remuneration and Exclusions.* The majority engaged in a two-step inquiry. First, it had to decide whether the sick leave buy-back payments are "remuneration." That seems pretty clear, doesn't it? Why the fuss? Second, the court had to determine whether the payments, although remuneration, fell within one of the exclusions in the statute. The majority's explanation makes sense, doesn't it? But so does the dissent's! They come at the question using different paradigms. Who has the better approach? Why?

2. *Seeing the Forest.* Although the interpretation of the language of the statute and underlying regulations dominates the discussion, what are the real stakes in this case? In other words, now that the firefighters have prevailed, what effect will it have on their compensation? Who, in the buy-back program circumstance, may be benefiting under the surface? If you were the employer's counsel, would you recommend

eliminating this or adjusting the employees' base rate of pay? Think about whether, going forward, this result is likely to be good, bad, or neutral for employees and employers.

3. *Planning Problems Continued.* Far more important than the particulars of the analysis in this case are the broader lessons for employment law counselors and human resources personnel. This case and the others in this chapter suggest that there are a number of traps for the unwary, and that each compensation decision must be analyzed from a number of perspectives to ensure the FLSA is not violated. Given the complexity and how costly mistakes may be, personnel and compensation decisions with potential FLSA implications ought to be undertaken with great care. And a new wrinkle has been added to the analysis by the rise of timekeeping software, *see* Elizabeth Tippett, Charlotte Alexander, & Zev Eigen, *When Timekeeping Software Undermines Compliance*, 19 YALE J. L. & TECH 1, 3 (2017), which provides employers the ability to "deprive employees of earned pay by editing down their hours worked, setting up automatic default rules that shave time, and disguising edits to employees' time records."

2. Other Wage Protections

At the federal level, the FLSA is the primary mechanism for dealing with perceived wage and hour abuses. However, federal law provides a number of other more narrowly drawn protections in certain contexts. For example, prevailing wage laws require various firms contracting with the federal government to compensate their workers at the prevailing minimum wage for like workers in the local labor market. *See, e.g.*, 40 U.S.C. §§3141-44, 3146, 3147 (Davis-Bacon Act); 41 U.S.C. §§35-43, 43a, 43b, 44, 45 (Walsh-Healey Act). Moreover, as mentioned previously, the Equal Pay Act mandates that male and female employees doing equal work in a workplace receive the same pay, absent some justification unrelated to sex.

But, as mentioned previously, there are also state and local wage and hour protections. This is because, unlike the NLRA or ERISA, the FLSA does not preempt the field; that is, its protections are not exclusive. Thus, state and local governments may provide for wage and hour protections that exceed those in the FLSA. For example, many states have enacted their own prevailing wage laws for government contractors. Most states also have wage payment laws (including so-called "theft of service" statutes) that provide for civil and criminal liability for failure to pay promised wages. Indeed, to ensure wages are paid, New York and Wisconsin have taken the extraordinary step of imposing pro rata liability on certain shareholders for unpaid wages when the corporation does not meet its wage obligations. *See* N.Y. BUS. CORP. §630; WIS. STAT. §180.0622. States also impose what might be deemed "procedural" wage and hour protections; for instance, a California statute requires that commission agreements with certain sales representatives be in writing, and that the writing contain various information, including how the commission is computed. The statute also requires documentation of how payment is calculated when an employee's commissions are paid. *See* CAL. CIV. CODE §§1738.10-.16

(2018); *Baker v. American Horticulture Supply, Inc.* 111 Cal. Rptr.3d 695 (Cal. Ct. App. 2010) (discussing the statute).

In addition, many states have their own minimum wage and overtime protections, which may increase the wage floor, further regulate hours or documentation, and/or extend protections to employees exempted by the FLSA (e.g., agricultural workers, seasonal workers, uncovered domestic workers, and workers employed by uncovered employers). Unsurprisingly, these laws vary greatly. *See, e.g.*, U.S. Department of Labor, Wage and Hour Division, *Minimum Wage Laws in the States*, July 1, 2018, *available at* https://www.dol.gov/whd/minwage/america.htm (listing state minimum wage and overtime protections) [hereinafter DOL WHD]; Economic Policy Institute, *Minimum Wage Tracker*, *available at* https://www.epi.org/minimum-wage-tracker/?gclid=Cj0KCQjw9NbdBRCwARIsAPLsnFa8AW9t1ervIjUcadXimYbA6uH2-mgppWlqMPeUs6wRT1dTLzBHd3oaAtJHEALw_wcB#/min_wage/Washington%20D.C. [hereinafter EPI] According to the DOL, as of July 1, 2018, five states have no minimum wage and two states (Georgia and Wyoming) have minimum wage requirements that are lower than the federal minimum. *See* DOL WHD, *supra*. Of course, the FLSA minimum wage governs most workers in these jurisdictions, and, thus, lower minimum wage standards will provide the floor only for those not within the FLSA. Fourteen states track the federal mandate, although their coverage may be broader. The remaining states and the District of Columbia have higher minimum wage requirements. *See id.*

At the time this book went to press, the District of Columbia's minimum wage of $13.25 an hour is higher than any state's, and this floor will increase to $15.00 in 2020. California and Massachusetts, however, have enacted stepped minimum wage increases that will reach $15.00 an hour in 2023. *See* EPI, *supra*. New York State's minimum wage for the New York City metropolitan area will reach the $15.00 level in 2021. *See id.* Numerous states also index their minimum wage levels, so these will increase over time as well. *See id.* In July 2018, the District also passed a ballot measure that will eliminate its lower, "tipped" minimum wage. Seven states pay both tipped and untipped workers the same minimum wage. Paul Schwartzman & Fenit Nirappil, *D.C. Voters Approve Initiative to Raise Minimum Wage for Tipped Workers to $15*, WASHINGTON POST, June 19, 2018, *available at* https://www.washingtonpost.com/local/dc-politics/district-voters-head-to-the-polls/2018/06/18/e945273e-730e-11e8-b4b7-308400242c2e_story.html?utm_term=.73c7bd2b53f7. These significantly higher wage floors and their periodic increases indicate that, although minimum wage increases happen only sporadically at the federal level, proponents continue to enjoy success in particular regions of the country.

Several states also have their own overtime regulations. California, for example, requires that firms pay workers double-time (twice the regular rate) for hours worked in excess of 12 hours per day or 48 hours per week. *See id.* It is worth noting that such a double-overtime regime could have profound effects on litigation awards and, hence, employer incentives and planning. Consider, for example, how the bodyguards' potential recovery in the Spears case—*see* Problem 11-2—might differ under the California statute.

When possible under state law, municipalities also may regulate wages of employees within their borders. For example, Seattle was first city to enact a $15.00 per hour minimum, to be effective in 2021. San Francisco followed, but its $15.00 floor became effective in 2018. Chicago and other cities around the country have enacted minimums well above their state mandates. *See e.g.*, EPI, *supra*; Greg Persio, *The Top Five Cities with the Highest Minimum Wage*, INVESTOPEDIA, available at https://www. investopedia.com/articles/investing/080515/top-5-us-cities-highest-minimum-wage.asp. Another recent effort in this direction is the movement to have cities enact "living wage" laws governing municipal contractors. *See generally* Scott L. Cummings & Steven A. Boutcher, *Mobilizing Local Government Law for Low-Wage Workers*, 1 CHI. LEGAL F. 187, 195 (2009) (discussing the broad reach of the Los Angeles Living Wage Ordinance, which imposes wage obligations above the federal and state minimums on employers that receive financial benefits from the municipality); Clayton P. Gillette, *Local Redistribution, Living Wage Ordinances, and Judicial Intervention*, 101 Nw. U. L. REV. 1057 (2007) (discussing the growing number of local living wage ordinances and legal challenges to them).

12

Worker Safety and Health

From industrial accidents to occupational diseases, safety and health problems are pervasive in the workplace. The causes range from debatable dangers to evident perils, and emanate from physical surroundings, machinery, vehicles, chemicals, and, of course, other humans. Some risks are inherent in certain occupations (at least given present technology), but others can be reduced or even eliminated. For a host of reasons, the American workplace, as a whole, has gotten safer. For example, while the number and rate of workplace fatalities ticked up in 2016, the long-term trend is one of marked decline. Indeed, both figures are lower than in 2006 and have declined substantially since 1992. U.S. DEPARTMENT OF LABOR, BUREAU OF LABOR STATISTICS (hereinafter "DOL, BLS"), CENSUS OF FATAL OCCUPATIONAL INJURIES CHARTS – CURRENT AND REVISED DATA (2106), *available at* http://www.bls.gov/iif/oshcfoi1.htm#charts (with charts containing fatal injury statistics from 1992 to 2016). Similarly, the rate of occupational injury and illness cases in private industry has steadily declined, from 5.0 per 100 full-time equivalent workers in 2003 to 2.9 in 2016. DOL, BLS, 2016 SURVEY OF OCCUPATIONAL INJURIES & ILLNESSES CHARTS PACKAGE (Nov. 9, 2017), *available at* https://www.bls.gov/iif/osch0060.pdf.

Nevertheless, many industries and sectors—for example, construction, agriculture, trucking, mining, and commercial fishing—remain relatively dangerous. And general improvements in safety do not assure that any particular worker or workplace will be injury-free: In 2016, despite a decline from prior years, 2.9 million workers suffered some kind of job-related injury or illness. DOL, BLS, ECONOMIC NEWS RELEASE, Employer-Reported Workplace Injury and Illnesses, 2016, *available at* https://www.bls.gov/news.release/osh.nr0.htm. In addition, some incidents produce many injuries or deaths. In 2010, for example, the explosion of BP's Deepwater Horizon platform in the Gulf of Mexico killed 11 workers and injured 17, and the disaster at Massey Energy's Upper Big Branch Mine in West Virginia resulted in the deaths of 29 miners. Reports also may significantly understate the incidence of workplace injury, disease, and death. *See, e.g.*, Kathleen M. Fagan & Michael J. Hodgson, *Under-Recording of Work-Related Injuries and Illnesses: An OSHA Priority*, J. OF

SAFETY RESEARCH (2016), *available at* https://www.osha.gov/ooc/underrecording_ fagan_hodgson.pdf (stating that the substantial undercounting of workplace injuries and illnesses is well documented and discussing recent studies).

The problems of worker safety and health can be addressed in various ways. One is through private ordering. Health and safety issues are a frequent subject of collective bargaining agreements, and most such agreements, in addition to providing for health insurance, deal with at least some workplace safety issues, including safety standards and leave policies for injuries and illnesses. But collective bargaining is an imperfect means of improving worker safety and health, not only because such bargaining does not guarantee employer concessions or significant improvements, but also because the vast majority of workers are nonunionized. In theory, employees could bargain for health and safety protections individually, but, with the exception of health and disability insurance, terms addressing these issues directly are rarely part of individual employment agreements, even where such agreements exist.

The statutory and other mandates discussed throughout this casebook address aspects of the problem in a variety of ways, albeit neither directly nor comprehensively. For example, as discussed in Chapter 4, whistleblower statutes and the public policy tort protect employees who have reported suspected safety hazards, refused to engage in dangerous activities, or otherwise assisted government officials in addressing safety concerns. We also saw in Chapter 7 that the National Labor Relations Act ensures even nonunionized workers the right to engage in "concerted activity" for a variety of ends, one of which is workplace health and safety. *See NLRB v. Washington Aluminum Co.*, 370 U.S. 9 (1962) (holding that a group of workers leaving their employment because of extreme cold was protected activity). Moreover, as covered in Chapters 9 and 10, fostering workplace safety and health plays an important role under the Americans with Disabilities Act, as either a by-product of the employer's obligation to reasonably accommodate disabled workers or, conversely, as a reason for refusing to provide certain accommodations. Likewise, other antidiscrimination provisions and the Family and Medical Leave Act implicate safety and health in various ways, including health- or injury-related leave policies and real or perceived gender-related health or safety risks, as addressed in a number of bona fide occupational qualification cases. Finally, as considered in Chapter 11, the Fair Labor Standards Act's ("FLSA") child labor provisions are premised on protecting the health and safety of this particularly vulnerable group.

Despite the pervasiveness of concerns over the safety and health of workers, the law has developed only two major regimes that deal directly and primarily with the question. One is state workers' compensation systems; the other is the federal Occupational Safety and Health Act ("OSHA"), 29 U.S.C. §§651 *et seq.* (2018). Much like pension law, workers' compensation has become its own discipline: Most law schools offer a separate course on it and many attorneys practice primarily or exclusively in this area. Nevertheless, because it is important that you have at least some acquaintance with workers' compensation and OSHA, both regimes are addressed briefly below.

The two systems have proven to be both important and, unsurprisingly, controversial. As mentioned in Chapter 5, in the early twentieth century, the workers' compensation system replaced the common-law tort of negligence with an administrative regime of strict liability for work-related injuries and diseases. This system provides more certain recovery for employees for physical injuries in accidents arising out of their employment, but subject to a trade-off: Workers' compensation restricts the amount of recovery and preempts others claims through workers' compensation exclusivity. There is some question as to whether the costs of this system create adequate incentives for employers to reduce safety hazards. *See, e.g.*, Alison Morantz, et al., *Economic Incentives in Workers' Compensation: A Holistic, International Perspective*, 69 RUTGERS L. REV. 1015 (2017) (discussing why employer incentives are in decline). Limitations on employer liability might reduce incentives to eliminate workplace hazards below the point a tort system would set and perhaps below what is acceptable from a societal perspective. *See generally* Emily A. Spieler, *(Re)Assessing the Grand Bargain: Compensation for Work Injuries in the United States, 1900-2017*, 69 RUTGERS L. REV. 891, 1011 (2017) (arguing that the scope of exclusivity should be re-examined to ensure adequate incentives for employers to reduce workplace hazards). Despite exclusivity, costs for employers under workers' compensation rose in the last quarter of the twentieth century, contributing to recurrent talk of a compensation crisis. *See generally* Martha T. McCluskey, *Insurer Moral Hazard in the Workers' Compensation Crisis: Reforming Cost Inflation, Not Rate Suppression*, 5 EMP. RTS. & EMPLOY. POL'Y J. 55 (2001); *see also* Spieler, *supra*, at 931-32. Since then, however, many states have imposed limitations on benefits and made other changes that have significantly reduced both the costs of workers' compensation for employers and benefits for workers. *See* Spieler, *supra*, at 936-48 (discussing the many statutory changes states have enacted since 1990, which have caused a downward spiral in workers' compensation benefits).

The other major legal regime addressing workplace safety is OSHA, which was enacted by Congress in 1970 and remains the most direct attack on the problem. Together with state counterparts and a few other federal safety regimes covering specific industries (such as the Mine Safety and Health Administration), OSHA seeks to prevent (instead of merely compensate) workplace injuries. *See generally* Mark Rothstein, OCCUPATIONAL SAFETY AND HEALTH LAW (2018 ed.). However, while the workplace has grown somewhat safer, it is not clear that OSHA gets much of the credit. Over time, many have questioned whether that regime, which consists largely of a regulatory scheme enforced by periodic agency inspection of worksites, rather than lawsuits brought by affected workers, is an effective means of ensuring safety and compliance. *See generally* Charlotte Alexander, *Transmitting the Costs of Unsafe Work*, 54 AM. BUS. L.J. 463 (2017) (discussing scholarly criticisms of OSHA's regulatory regime, the shortcomings of its oversight structure, and studies showing the barriers workers face in taking advantage of OSHA's purported protections). And there has been a wave of highly critical assessments of OSHA's performance in recent years. *See generally id.; see also* Jason R. Bent, *An Incentive-Based Approach to Regulating Workplace Chemicals*, 73 OHIO ST. L.J. 1389 (2012); CTR. FOR PUB. INTEGRITY, BROKEN GOVERNMENT: AN EXAMINATION OF EXECUTIVE BRANCH FAILURES SINCE 2000 10-11 (2008); Susan Bisom-Rapp, *What We Learn in Troubled Times: Deregulation and Safe Work in the New Economy*, 55 WAYNE L. REV. 1097, 1231-39 (2009); Lynn Rhinehart, *Workers at Risk: The Unfulfilled Promise of the Occupational Safety and Health Act*, 111 W. VA. L. REV. 117, 121-23 (2008); *see also* David C. Vladeck, *The Failed Promise of Workplace Health Regulation*, 111 W. VA. L. REV. 15 (2008) (discussing coal mine disasters and the failure of federal workplace health and safety regimes to protect workers).

This chapter offers a brief overview of workers' compensation regimes and OSHA. It is not designed to be comprehensive. Rather, its aim is to introduce the history and structure of these two regimes; key elements, limitations, and litigated issues;

and current controversies. The coverage of OSHA in particular is truncated, due in large part to the fact that a deeper dive would require detailed study of the regulations and the particulars with regard to individual regulations and enforcement actions.

A. WORKERS' COMPENSATION

1. The History of Workers' Compensation

In the late nineteenth and early twentieth centuries, workers often could not recover compensation for workplace injuries because of the "unholy trinity" of common law defenses: the fellow servant rule (which provided that the employer was not vicariously liable for worker injuries caused by negligent co-workers), assumption of risk, and contributory negligence. As courts gradually began removing these barriers, employers' fears of liability for workplace injuries grew. On the other side of the debate, those interested in protecting employees were concerned about the pace and completeness of common law change. These competing perspectives ultimately led to the "grand bargain," the universal adoption of workers' compensation schemes. In summarizing the origins of workers' compensation, Price Fishback and Shawn Kantor write:

> The American movement for compensation legislation began in 1898, when the New York Social Reform Club presented the New York legislature with a compensation bill emulating the 1897 British law. The bill was killed in committee and deemed "too radical to pass" by the bill's legislative sponsor. As the economic and political environment changed over the next decade, the legislation obtained increasing support in response to an increase in employment in dangerous industries, an increased public awareness of workplace accident problems, and employers' worries about an increasingly unfavorable liability climate.
>
> Public awareness of workplace accidents during the period increased as shifts in employment across industries led to an increase in the share of workers in more dangerous jobs in manufacturing and mining and as the reporting of accident risk increased sharply. . . . [T]here was increased public awareness of workplace accidents because state labor departments, with their increasing budgets, improved their reporting of workplace injuries; therefore, the reported level of accident risk was rising. Reformers used these statistics to publicize the dangers and consequent financial hardships associated with workplace accidents.
>
> The greater attention paid to accident risk added to the consternation of employers because it occurred within an increasingly unfavorable liability climate. . . . [T]he number of states with employers' liability laws that restricted one or more of the employers' [common law tort] defenses for nonrailroad accidents rose from 7 in 1900 to 25 by 1913. The courts also modified the common-law defenses, which further exacerbated employers' uncertainty about the negligence liability system. Greater uncertainty about the law led employers and injured workers to accept the relatively high costs of litigation and test the bounds of the law more often, which in turn led to an increase in court cases at every level. In fact, the increased uncertainty was associated with a more than three-fold rise in the number of state supreme court cases related to nonrailroad workplace accident litigation from 154 in 1900 to 490 in 1911. [Expanded liability combined with legal uncertainty] contributed to an increase in the liability insurance premiums that employers paid. . . .

Employers' worsening accident liability status in the early 1900s encouraged employer-supported lobbying groups to explore the possibility of a switch to a no-fault compensation system. Between 1908 and 1910 the National Civic Federation, which was composed of leaders from major corporations and conservative unions, devoted substantial time in their meetings to developing and promoting a workers' compensation bill. Meanwhile, the National Association of Manufacturers in 1910 called on its members to provide voluntary accident insurance, but then in 1911 the National Association of Manufacturers fully endorsed workers' compensation as a solution to the accident compensation problem. After forming in 1907 the American Association of Labor Legislation became one of the leading advocates for workers' compensation. The federal government, which often preceded most employers in offering relatively generous workplace benefits, established workers' compensation for federal workers in 1908 as a result of Theodore Roosevelt's strong support.

Employers' shift in interest toward workers' compensation coincided with changing sentiments among organized labor, whose ranks expanded from 868,000 in 1900 to 2.14 million in 1910, growing nearly three times faster than the labor force. The attitudes of major labor organizations went through a substantial change as they gained more experience with the results of employers' liability laws. Around the turn of the century, the American Federation of Labor believed that better accident compensation could be achieved by stripping employers of their three [tort] defenses. Organized labor's reluctance to embrace workers' compensation was part of a more general opposition to government regulation of the workplace on the theory that business interests controlled politics, and, thus, better benefits for workers could be achieved only through the voluntary organization of workers. But organized labor harshly criticized the fact that large numbers of injured workers were left uncompensated by the negligence system and that a large percentage of the insurance premiums that employers paid for liability never reached injured workers. In 1909, therefore, the American Federation of Labor switched its position and passed four resolutions supporting workers' compensation legislation, and the organization, at the federal level and through its state affiliates, became a vocal proponent of no-fault accident compensation.

The support from major employers' groups and organized labor led to the widespread adoption of workers' compensation. . . . In the second decade of the century . . . 43 states adopted workers' compensation. By 1930 all the states except Arkansas, Florida, Mississippi, and South Carolina had enacted the legislation. As Harry Weiss noted, "No other kind of labor legislation gained such general acceptance in so brief a period in this country."

The Adoption of Workers' Compensation in the United States, 1900-30, 41 J. L. & ECON. 305, 315-19 (1998); *see also* Lex K. Larson, LARSON'S WORKERS' COMPENSATION LAW §§2.07-.08 (Matthew Bender and Co., Inc., Rev. Ed. 2018); *see generally* Spieler, *supra*, at 859-955. Fishback and Kantor go on to explain that the basic trade-offs between employer and employee interests:

Instead of being imposed by one interest group at the expense of other groups, workers' compensation was enacted because a broad-based coalition of divergent interests saw gains from reforming the negligence liability system. Employers anticipated a reduction in labor friction, a reduction in the uncertainty of their accident and court costs, and a reduction in the gap between what they paid for insurance and what injured workers received. In addition, they were able to pass at least some of the additional costs of workers' compensation benefits on to their workers in the form of lower real wages. Workers, on average, anticipated higher post-accident benefits from the new legislation. Even if they "bought" the better benefits through lower wages, they anticipated better "insurance" coverage against workplace accident risk. Further, insurers believed that the shift to workers' compensation would reduce problems with adverse selection, and thus they could expand their coverage of workplace accidents.

In her detailed critique of the state of workers' compensation regimes today, however, Professor Emily Spieler discusses why, after a quarter century of states' cutting benefits and limiting coverage while retaining (and sometimes expanding) exclusivity, this "grand bargain" now often favors the interests of employers over that of workers:

> The bargain is a "*quid pro quo* in which the sacrifices and gains of employees and employers are to some extent put in balance." . . . Today, many injured workers never receive compensation—but they are nevertheless foreclosed from bringing tort actions. Those who successfully pursue compensation claims often receive too little, given the design of the benefits and the long-term consequences of injuries. The system is not, and has never been, "adequate," in the sense articulated by the National Commission. The current political environment means that attacks on benefit adequacy will continue in many states. At the same time, the protection of employers from tort litigation has remained largely intact.

Spieler, *supra*, at 1005-06 (footnotes and citations omitted).

2. The Basic Structure of Workers' Compensation Statutes

Today, all states have workers' compensation regimes. Since their enactment in the early part of the last century, the basic structure of these statutes has remained the same. Because workers' compensation is a creature of state law, there are important variations; however, these regimes contain the same core components:

> 1. Insurance. A WC [workers' compensation] statute requires employers to secure and provide insurance for their employees against the losses suffered by reason of workplace injuries. Such insurance must come either from approved carriers or from the employer's own resources for self-insurance, as certified by a state agency.
> 2. Entitlement. Unlike the tort system, in which recovery against the employer (and its liability insurer) depends upon proof of both the employer's fault (and also the absence of worker fault), the injured employee may draw upon WC insurance if the injury was in any way caused by the job—i.e., if it "arose out of and in the course of employment."
> 3. Benefits. While a WC regime expands the basis of employer responsibility to encompass all job-related injuries, it reduces correspondingly the extent of the employer's legal responsibility for any particular injury. Rather than award full tort compensation for all economic and noneconomic losses suffered by each victim, the typical WC benefit scheme reimburses the victim [for medical costs and some portion of net wages lost due to temporary and permanent disabilities].
> 4. Administration. Primary responsibility for administering a WC scheme is conferred upon an administrative tribunal: the expectation is that this process will give workers quicker, easier, and less expensive access to the above benefit structure. Ideally, such ready access is also facilitated by substituting "cause" for "fault" as the precondition for recovery, and by replacing at-large damages tailored to each victim with the schedule formula designed for the average worker.

5. Exclusivity. The tacit assumption of the no-fault model is that victims as a group are better protected, ex ante, by such a guarantee of more limited redress for crucial financial losses from workplace injuries, even granting that in particular cases, viewed ex post, the individual worker who can establish fault would likely be able to collect more substantial tort compensation for all the economic and noneconomic consequences of the injury. Having made such an assumption and required the employer to provide and pay for this preferred WC system, the legislature then grants employers the *quid pro quo* of statutory immunity from any liability for these workplace injuries under the background tort system. . . .

Paul C. Weiler, *Workers' Compensation and Product Liability: The Interaction of a Tort and Non-Tort Regime*, 50 OHIO ST. L.J. 825, 826-30 (1989). While the core elements persist despite local variations, these laws have not been static over time; for example, benefits were liberalized in the 1970s, and, as a result of rising insurance costs many states retrenched in the late 1990s, enacting reforms limiting workers' compensation benefits and recoveries. *See generally* Spieler, *supra*, at 936-48.

Assuming a worker's injury is a compensable one to begin with, a topic that is addressed in the next section, workers' compensation laws provide benefits for physical injuries and illnesses—that is, medical benefits and wage-loss benefits for disabling conditions—and limited death benefits. Although medical expenses are normally completely covered, lost wages are subject to a statutory cap. Critically, workers' compensation also excludes pain and suffering damages and some emotional distress damages. Most states finance such benefits by requiring employers to self-insure (and satisfy the state that they are solvent enough to do so), purchase private workers' compensation insurance, or participate in a state-provided insurance plan.

The standard benefits—which again, vary in size and applicability by state—generally include:

- *Medical Expenses.* Workers' compensation regimes usually require complete coverage of all medical expenses reasonably required to cure or relieve the effects of workplace injuries and covered occupational diseases. These ordinarily include not only direct medical services, but also necessary incidental services such as transportation and medical equipment.
- *Temporary Disability Benefits.* All states' regimes provide for temporary disability benefits for a period of recovery after a worker has been injured. These benefits, which cover both total and partial disabilities, normally run from the time of the injury plus a waiting period (three to seven days) until the conclusion of the healing period. The healing period ends when the worker is able to return to work or has reached maximum medical improvement and must seek permanent disability benefits. Temporary benefits tend to be calculated based on a percentage (normally two-thirds, but sometimes only half) of the employee's lost wages, which in turn is based on the worker's average weekly wage for a preceding period—often 3, 6, or 12 months. However, such benefits are capped at a particular level per week, and the cap varies by jurisdiction.
- *Permanent Disability Benefits.* Permanent disabilities normally are broken into two categories: unscheduled and scheduled.
  - *Scheduled disabilities* refers to permanent disabilities listed in a statutorily adopted schedule of possible injuries to designated parts of the body. These

are compensated according to predetermined statutory amounts for the loss of particular body parts—that is, the actual loss of the limb or part or, in many cases, the loss of the use of that limb or part. The statute mandates a fixed rate that is paid for a specific number of weeks. These scheduled benefits are supposed to reflect roughly the standard amount of earning capacity lost from the injury.

- *Unscheduled disabilities* refer to those injuries not listed in the existing schedule. They are compensated based on the loss of earning capacity, normally determined after fact-finding by a vocational expert and capped at a statutory maximum. The amount awarded may be calculated based on a variety of factors, including prior average earnings, the loss of physical functions to the injured body part, the education and employment history of the worker, and the worker's ability to continue employment. If the worker can return to work, only functional impairment will be taken into account, and there is a cap (varying by state) on the amount that can be received. Although the method differs by state, a standard calculation provides the worker with her average salary for the time period she was completely incapacitated up to a maximum amount, and, thereafter, a percentage of the maximum amount allowed tied to the percentage of earning capacity lost (i.e., if the worker lost 40 percent of earning capacity, she would receive 40 percent of the maximum benefits). Given the calculation method, unscheduled benefits are specific to the worker and the injury suffered. States have allowed separate recovery for scheduled and unscheduled injuries if the employee can demonstrate that the loss of earning capacity is separate for the two injuries.

- *Vocational Rehabilitation Services.* Vocational services are aimed at getting the injured worker back to work in some capacity.

- *Death Benefits.* All states provide death benefits for spouses and dependents of employees who suffer fatal work-related injuries, although the benefits vary widely in both amount and duration. These benefits tend to be based on a percentage of the employee's average weekly wage, tied to the number of dependents, capped at a statutory maximum amount, and limited to a specified statutory period. Many states also provide limited benefits for funeral expenses. Some states have separate statutory provisions that increase the amount of death benefits for the dependents of certain types of workers, including police officers, firefighters, and paramedics.

Obviously, disputes may arise over what medical expenses are necessary and reasonable, whether and to what the extent an employee is disabled, the average weekly wages the employee earned prior to injury or death, who is a "dependent," and a host of other issues. Given their standardized structure, however, the amount of benefits owed in a particular case is far more predictable and certain than tort damages, facilitating efficient resolution of many potential disputes.

3. Coverage and Compensable Injuries

Given the structure of workers' compensation regimes, and in particular the fact that workers' compensation is no-fault and its benefits structure standardized, disputes that do arise as a result of workplace injuries and illnesses typically involve coverage and compensability—that is, whether the worker, employer, and particular injury fall within the scope of the regime. Such issues are addressed in Chapter 1, pages 5-50.

When worker and firm are found to be employee and employer, participation in the state's workers' compensation scheme is mandatory for the employer in all states except Texas. Oklahoma passed legislation similar to the Texas approach but the Oklahoma Supreme Court struck down the employer opt-out provisions on state constitutional grounds; *see Vasquez v. Dillard's, Inc.*, 381 P.3d 768 (Okla. 2016). Elsewhere, very small employers are sometimes exempted, and many states exempt or limit coverage for certain agriculture and domestic workers. Nevertheless, the vast majority of employees are covered.

Where these threshold issues of employment and statutory coverage are satisfied, the next issue is whether the injury or illness is compensable. Compensable injuries are accidental injuries that occur in the course of employment and arise out of employment. The concept of "accident," the notion of "course of employment," and the requirement that an injury "arise out" of employment have each raised questions as to the reach of workers' compensation coverage. Further, some workplace illnesses, including occupational diseases, are subject to separate statutory treatment since they may not be accidental in the sense that they were not sudden or unexpected. This section considers each of these concepts.

a. Injuries Sustained "in the Course of" Employment

In most cases, determining whether a worker sustains an injury in the course of employment or outside of employment is easy. However, sometimes this issue is far from clear-cut because the worker's conduct or actions are outside of or inconsistent with the worker's job duties and are not for the benefit of the employer. Most cases falling into this gray area involve situations in which worker injuries occurred while the worker was traveling to or from work, on a "frolic or detour," engaging in "horseplay" or unauthorized conduct at work, participating in extracurricular activities somehow related to work, or acting in pursuit of personal interest. As you read, keep in mind that, while the "in the course of" employment inquiry is similar to the one courts use to determine whether an employer is liable for an employee's tort under the doctrine of respondeat superior (something you may have studied in your torts class and this book touched on in Chapter 1), the law governing this issue in the workers' compensation context is somewhat different, embodying its own set of considerations.

Kindel v. Ferco Rental, Inc.
899 P.2d 1058 (Kan. 1995)

LOCKETT, Judge.

A worker was killed on his return trip home from work. The worker's surviving spouse and minor children claimed death benefits. The Administrative Law Judge (ALJ) denied their claim, finding that the worker had abandoned his employment and therefore the accident did not arise out of and in the course of his employment. On review, the Workers Compensation Board (the Board) reversed the ALJ, finding that the worker's death arose out of and in the course of his employment. The employer appealed . . . .

Donald L. Kindel was employed by Ferco Rental, Inc. (Ferco). On October 11, 1991, Kindel was transported in a company pickup truck from his home in Salina, Kansas, to a construction job site in Sabetha, Kansas. James Graham, Kindel's supervisor, was the driver of the truck. The company truck had been checked out to Graham to transport Kindel and other employees to and from the job site.

On the way to Sabetha, Graham and Kindel passed a former employee of Ferco. Kindel held up a note inviting the former co-worker to join them at the Outer Limits, a "striptease" bar adjacent to Interstate 70 on the west side of Topeka. At approximately 3:30 p.m., after completing the day's work at the job site in Sabetha, Graham and Kindel proceeded back toward Salina. On the way, the two men stopped at the Outer Limits for approximately four hours, where they became inebriated.

Graham suffers from amnesia and cannot recall any of the events occurring after they stopped at the Outer Limits. Graham testified, however, that it was Kindel's idea to stop at the Outer Limits; that Kindel made the arrangements to meet the former co-worker at the Outer Limits after work that day; and that if Kindel would have wanted to proceed straight home, Graham would have done so.

At approximately 8:50 p.m., the Kansas Highway Patrol received a call of a motor vehicle accident on Interstate 70. . . . When Trooper McCool arrived at the accident scene, he observed the Ferco truck overturned and lying in the south ditch of the westbound lane near an entrance to a rest area. Graham, who was driving, and Kindel had been partially ejected out of the truck's windshield. Kindel was deceased. Subsequent tests determined that Graham and Kindel had blood alcohol levels of .225 and .26, respectively.

Prior to the accident, Graham and Kindel were aware that Ferco had a policy that, except to obtain food or fuel, company vehicles were to be used only to go directly from the shop to the job site. Company vehicles were not to be used for personal pleasure or business. Ferco had a comprehensive drug and alcohol policy in place at the time of the accident which, among other things, prohibited workers from using the company equipment while under the influence of alcohol. Employees were not authorized to use a company vehicle to stop at a bar to consume alcohol. Kindel signed off on this policy on December 8, 1990. The employer asserted that when the employees stopped at the bar, authorization to use the company vehicle ceased and any further use of the company vehicle was not part of their employment.

At the time of the accident on October 11, 1991, Graham possessed a valid Kansas driver's license. Ferco was aware of Graham's propensity for drinking and driving. Graham had been charged with DUI some six days prior to this incident and had a previous conviction for which he had had his driver's license suspended. Graham understood that he was prohibited from drinking while using company equipment. Graham testified that the reason for stopping at the Outer Limits was to pursue pleasure and to have a good time. He said it was his understanding that when he pulled up at the Outer Limits, his work was over for the day.

Kindel's surviving spouse and minor children filed a workers compensation claim, seeking death benefits pursuant to K.S.A.1991 Supp. 44-510b. The ALJ found "that the deviation was so substantial and there is not a causal connection between the deviation and the purpose of employment, nor a causal nexus between the resulting accident and death as to say that the claimant had ever returned to the scope of his employment. . . . The subsequent death, therefore, did not arise out of and in the course of his employment."

The ALJ made no findings as to whether Kindel's death resulted substantially from his intoxication. The claimants appealed.

After reviewing the record, the Board reached the opposite conclusion, finding that Kindel's death arose out of and in the course of his employment. The Board acknowledged case law from other jurisdictions supporting the ALJ's decision, but found case law supporting a finding of compensability to be more persuasive. The Board first noted that Kindel's trip to and from Sabetha, absent the detour, would have been considered a part of his employment. The Board stated that even if it assumed that the deviation from employment increased the risk of injury, the injury and resulting death resulted from the combined personal and work-related risks. The Board concluded that, under Kansas law, the increased risk attributable to the deviation did not, by itself, bar recovery. . . .

[The Board went on to conclude that "this case is not materially different from any other where a claimant deviates from his employment but has returned at the time of the accident. The Appeals Board therefore finds that claimant's death arose out of and in the course of his employment."]

The Board reversed the decision of the ALJ and remanded the case for a determination of the appropriate benefits. The employer appealed. . . .

Arising out of and in the Course of Employment

Although K.S.A.1991 Supp. 44-508(f), a codification of the longstanding "going and coming" rule, provides that injuries occurring while traveling to and from employment are generally not compensable, there is an exception which applies when travel upon the public roadways is an integral or necessary part of the employment. *See Blair v. Shaw*, 233 P.2d 731 (Kan. 1951); *Messenger v. Sage Drilling Co.*, 680 P.2d 556 (Kan. App. 1984). Because Kindel and other Ferco employees were expected to live out of town during the work weeks, and transportation to and from the remote site was in a company vehicle driven by a supervisor, this case falls within the exception to the general rule.

In any employment to which workers compensation laws apply, an employer is liable to pay compensation to an employee where the employee incurs personal injury by accident arising out of and in the course of employment. Whether an accident arises out of and in the course of the worker's employment depends upon the facts peculiar to the particular case.

The two phrases arising "out of" and "in the course of" employment, as used in our Workers Compensation Act, K.S.A. 44-501 *et seq.*, have separate and distinct meanings; they are conjunctive, and each condition must exist before compensation is allowable. The phrase "out of" employment points to the cause or origin of the accident and requires some causal connection between the accidental injury and the employment. An injury arises "out of" employment when there is apparent to the rational mind, upon consideration of all the circumstances, a causal connection between the conditions under which the work is required to be performed and the resulting injury. Thus, an injury arises "out of" employment if it arises out of the nature, conditions, obligations, and incidents of the employment.

The phrase "in the course of" employment relates to the time, place, and circumstances under which the accident occurred and means the injury happened while the worker was at work in the employer's service.

Both the ALJ and the Board acknowledge the separate considerations inherent in the determination whether the death arose "out of" and "in the course of" employment. The ALJ concluded that the length of time Kindel spent at the Outer Limits and his substantial consumption of alcohol removed his subsequent activity from arising "in the course of" his employment, notwithstanding the fact he was on his homeward route at the time of the accident. The Board, on the other hand, determined that Kindel's injury and death resulted from combined risks attributable to his personal deviation *and* his employment, and held that the increased risk factor attributable to the deviation should not bar recovery. The point of disagreement between the ALJ and Board is whether the deviation was so substantial as to permanently remove the worker from the course of his employment, even though he later continued his homeward route. The parties cite various cases for support of their respective positions.

Two Kansas cases address a somewhat similar situation and determined whether the worker had abandoned his employer's business. They are *Angleton v. Starkan, Inc.*, 828 P.2d 933 (Kan. 1992), and *Woodring v. United Sash & Door Co.*, 103 P.2d 837 (Kan. 1940). . . . Angleton, who was employed as a truck driver for Starkan, was hauling a load of cattle when a pair of hijackers began following him in another truck. By conversation over the citizens band radio, one of the hijackers persuaded Angleton to pull off the highway to smoke marijuana. Angleton stopped his truck and got into the hijackers' truck. While Angleton was smoking a marijuana cigarette, one of the hijackers shot and killed him. . . .

The *Angleton* court first determined that absent the alleged marijuana episode, the accident occurred in the course of Angleton's employment. The court noted that at the time of his death, Angleton was en route to deliver his load of cattle to a feedlot on the route designated by his employer and that at the time Angleton pulled off the highway, he was driving his load in fulfillment of his employment obligations. The court further observed that Angleton was killed because he was responsible for the Starkan truck and cattle and his employment for Starkan transporting valuable cargo exposed him to an increased risk of injury of being robbed while on the highway.

The *Angleton* court then examined whether the alleged use of marijuana changed the district court's conclusion that the accident resulting in Angleton's death arose out of and in the course of his employment. The district court had noted that the only testimony that Angleton pulled off the highway to smoke marijuana was the testimony by one of the hijackers and found that testimony to be inherently unreliable. . . . The *Angleton* court determined that the record supported the district court's finding that the hijacker's testimony was unreliable and held that the testimony was not sufficient or reliable to support a finding that the worker's conduct constituted a deviation from his employment. The court found that Angleton's death arose in the course of and out of his employment.

In *Woodring* . . ., the claimant was a traveling salesman who lived in Salina. Woodring was sent by his employer to meet a client in Enterprise, Kansas, to further the employer's business. Prior to arriving at Enterprise, the claimant went to Minneapolis, Kansas, and picked up three friends who made the journey to Enterprise with him. When the worker arrived at Enterprise, he discovered the man he was supposed to meet was in Abilene. The claimant made no further attempts to contact the client, and instead proceeded to a local drinking establishment with his friends for "an hour or so" where he imbibed intoxicating liquor. Thereafter, while driving recklessly on his return journey to Salina, claimant was injured when his car overturned. . . .

The *Woodring* court then observed that where a business errand is the purpose of a worker's journey, the social incident of taking a few guests along for the pleasure of their company would not affect the worker's right to compensation for an injury sustained in the performance of that errand. The *Woodring* court noted that an intruding question was whether a worker, engaged in the employer's service, could be permitted to recover compensation for an injury sustained while operating an automobile on the public highway under the influence of intoxicating liquor in violation of a Kansas statute which made such an act a criminal offense punishable by fine or imprisonment or both. It found that because the district court had determined the business errand was finished or abandoned and that the worker had set about the pursuit of his own pleasure or indulgence, there was no theory of law or of justice which would impose on the employer the obligation to pay compensation for any injury sustained by the worker under such circumstances.

The claimants rely heavily on *Angleton* . . . for support of a finding of compensability in this case. The claimants seek to distinguish *Woodring*, noting that Kindel was a passenger being driven home by his supervisor in a company vehicle and that the supervisor was required to return his employer's vehicle. The employer fails to address the *Angleton* precedent, but contends that the rationale of *Woodring* should be applied to this case. It is important to note that in *Angleton* and *Woodring* there were allegations that the worker was violating the law. Here, although Kindel was intoxicated, the fact he drank was not a violation of the law nor was he violating a law, at the time he was killed.

In support of their arguments, both parties cite numerous cases from outside of Kansas. The most favorable case for the employer is *Calloway v. Workmen's Comp.*, 268 S.E.2d 132 (W. Va. 1980). In *Calloway*, the West Virginia Supreme Court found the claimant salesman's activity of drinking and tavern-hopping from midafternoon until 11 p.m. amounted to an abandonment of any business purpose such that the injuries he received in an accident shortly thereafter while being transported home were not compensable. The *Calloway* court acknowledged that workers compensation laws generally recognize that an employee is entitled to compensation for an injury received while travelling on behalf of his employer's business.

The court noted that where an employee deviates from the employer's business, the employee may be denied compensation if the injury occurs during the deviation and that once the employee ceases the deviation and returns to the employer's business, a subsequent injury is ordinarily compensable. The court then observed:

> In the case of a major deviation from the business purpose, most courts will bar compensation recovery on the theory that the deviation is so substantial that the employee must be deemed to have abandoned any business purpose and consequently cannot recover for injuries received, even though he has ceased the deviation and is returning to the business route or purpose. [Citations omitted.]
>
> . . . A deviation generally consists of a personal or nonbusiness-related activity. The longer the deviation exists in time or the greater it varies from the normal business route or in purpose from the normal business objectives, the more likely that it will be characterized as major.

The *Calloway* court then reviewed a number of cases in which various courts have characterized an employee's deviations to be sufficiently major to deny compensation. The *Calloway* court concluded:

> In the present case, there is no dispute that the claimant was initially traveling on behalf of his employer in an attempt to solicit new business in the Logan County area. However, even under the facts liberally construed in his behalf, he had completed any company business in the midafternoon when he and his fellow employee began to frequent taverns. The continuation of this activity until 11:00 p.m. was a major deviation, not only in time but also in its nature. It can only be viewed as an abandonment of any business purpose.

The most favorable case for the claimants is *Rainear v. C.J. Rainear & Co.*, 307 A.2d 72 (N.J. 1973). In *Rainear*, the New Jersey Supreme Court held that where an automobile accident had occurred while the decedent was on his way home from work along a proper and permissible route, decedent's 10-hour stop at a restaurant and bar to eat and drink did not amount to such a departure from the decedent's reasonable sphere of employment as to bar a compensation award. In that case, the decedent's travel expenses were being paid by his employer. There was nothing in the record to confirm that drinking caused the accident. The *Rainear* court reviewed a number of cases awarding compensation to employees injured following a deviation. The court stated:

> There is nothing in the compensation law which fixes an arbitrary limit to the number of hours of deviation which may be terminated with travel coverage resumed. Thus if the decedent ate dinner at [the restaurant and bar] en route home and stayed there simply watching television for hours before continuing on his intended travel home, there clearly would be no rational basis for failing to apply the broad remedial principles embraced in [other New Jersey workers compensation cases]. While the fact that he also did some drinking there may have influenced the Appellate Division's negative result, the drinking really has no legal bearing here since there was no proof that the accident or death resulted from intoxication.

A deviation from the employer's work generally consists of a personal or nonbusiness-related activity. The longer the deviation exists in time or the greater it varies from the normal business route or in purpose from the normal business objectives, the more likely that the deviation will be characterized as major. In the case of a major deviation from the business purpose, most courts will bar compensation recovery on the theory that the deviation is so substantial that the employee must be deemed to have abandoned any business purpose and consequently cannot recover for injuries received, even though he or she has ceased the deviation and is returning to the business route or purpose.

Is there substantial evidence to support the Board's finding of compensability, *i.e.*, that Kindel's death arose in the course of his employment? The employer provided transportation. Kindel was a passenger and not the driver. He was being transported home after completion of his duties. Despite approximately four hours at the Outer Limits, the distance of the deviation was less than one quarter of a mile. Kindel was killed after resuming the route home. Under the facts, even though the worker was intoxicated, as a passenger in his employer's vehicle, he was not committing a violation of Kansas law. Kindel was killed while engaging in an activity contemplated by his employer while traveling on a public interstate highway. The fact he had been drinking has no legal bearing on the present compensation determination since there was no proof that the accident or Kindel's death resulted from Kindel's intoxication.

The workers compensation statutes are to be liberally construed to effect legislative intent and award compensation where it is reasonably possible to do so. We note that the workers compensation law does not fix an arbitrary limit on the number of hours of deviation, which may be terminated with travel coverage resumed. Whether there was a deviation, and if that deviation had terminated, is a question of fact to be determined by the administrative law judge or the Workers Compensation Board. Under our standard of review, we find that the Board did not act unreasonably, arbitrarily, or capriciously and there is substantial evidence to support the Board's conclusion that the fatal injury occurred in the course of Kindel's employment.

Did Death Result Substantially from Intoxication?

[Kansas has a statutory provision disallowing compensation when the employee's injury "results . . . substantially from the employee's intoxication." But the fact that Kindel was merely a passenger in the vehicle prevented a finding that his "intoxication was a substantially causative factor in bringing about his death." In the course of so deciding, the court found inapplicable a Kansas common law negligence rule that required a passenger "to exercise that care which a reasonably careful person would use for his or her own protection under the existing circumstances," because "[c]ommon-law defenses to tort theories of negligence do not apply to workers compensation claims."]

Clodgo v. Rentavision, Inc.
701 A.2d 1044 (Vt. 1997)

GIBSON, Justice.

Defendant Rentavision, Inc. appeals a decision of the Commissioner of the Vermont Department of Labor and Industry awarding workers' compensation benefits to claimant Brian Clodgo. Rentavision argues the Commissioner erred in awarding compensation for an injury sustained while claimant and another employee were engaged in horseplay. We reverse.

On July 22, 1995, claimant was working as manager of Rentavision's store in Brattleboro. During a lull between customers, claimant began firing staples with a staple gun at a co-worker, who was sitting on a couch watching television. The co-worker first protested, but then, after claimant had fired twenty or thirty staples at him, fired three staples back at claimant. As claimant ducked, the third staple hit him in the eye. Claimant eventually reported the injury and filed a claim for workers' compensation benefits. Rentavision contested the award, arguing that claimant was engaged in noncompensable horseplay at the time of the injury. Following a hearing in March 1996, the Commissioner awarded permanent partial disability and vocational rehabilitation benefits, medical expenses, and attorney's fees and costs. This appeal followed. . . .

Compensable injuries under Vermont's Workers' Compensation Act are those received "by accident arising out of and in the course of . . . employment." 21 V.S.A. §618. Although only work-related injuries are compensable, we recognize that "even [employees] of maturer years [will] indulge in a moment's diversion from work to joke with or play a prank upon a fellow [employee]." *Leonbruno v. Champlain Silk Mills,* 128 N.E. 711, 711 (N.Y. 1920). For such a horseplay-related injury to be compensated, however, claimant must show that it both (1) arose out of the employment, and (2) occurred in the course of the employment. A nonparticipant injured by the horseplay of others will nearly always be able to meet this test, *see* 2 A. Larson & L. Larson, WORKERS' COMPENSATION LAW §23.61, at 5-199 (1997), while a participant may or may not recover. *See* 2 Larson & Larson, *supra,* §23.20, at 5-182 to 5-183.

. . . Whether a horseplay participant is entitled to recover usually hinges on whether the injury occurred in the course of employment, which, in turn, depends on the extent of the employee's deviation from work duties. . . .

The question certified for review is whether claimant's horseplay bars him from recovery for the resulting injury under Vermont's Workers' Compensation Act. Rentavision contends the Commissioner misapplied the law in concluding that claimant's horseplay-related injury was compensable. We agree. An injury arises out of employment if it would not have occurred but for the fact that the conditions and obligations of the employment placed claimant in the position where he or she was injured. Thus, claimant must show that "but for" the employment and his position at work, the injury would not have happened.

Although the accident here would not have happened but for claimant's participation in the horseplay and therefore was not exclusively linked to his employment, it also was not a purely personal risk that would have occurred regardless of his location and activity on that day. He was injured during work hours with a staple gun provided for use on the job, and thus the findings support a causal connection between claimant's work conditions and the injury adequate to conclude that the accident arose out of his employment.

Nonetheless, claimant must also show that the injury occurred in the course of the employment. An accident occurs in the course of employment when it was within the period of time the employee was on duty at a place where the employee was reasonably expected to be *while fulfilling the duties of the employment contract.* Thus, while some horseplay among employees during work hours can be expected and is not an automatic bar to compensation, the key inquiry is whether the employee deviated too far from his or her duties.

The Commissioner must therefore consider (1) the extent and seriousness of the deviation; (2) the completeness of the deviation (i.e., whether the activity was commingled with performance of a work duty or was a complete abandonment of duty); (3) the extent to which the activity had become an accepted part of the employment; and (4) the extent to which the nature of the employment may be expected to include some horseplay. The Commissioner found that although shooting staples was common among employees, such activity was not considered acceptable behavior by Rentavision. She made no finding concerning whether Rentavision knew that staple-shooting occurred at work, but did find that claimant made material misrepresentations of fact designed to avoid an inference of horseplay or inappropriate behavior in order that he might obtain workers' compensation benefits. Claimant makes no showing that shooting staples at fellow employees was an accepted part of claimant's employment or furthered Rentavision's interests.

The facts show that the accident was unrelated to any legitimate use of the staplers at the time, indicating there was no commingling of the horseplay with work duties. The Commissioner focused on the slack time inherent in claimant's job, but this factor alone is not dispositive. Although some horseplay was reasonably to be expected during idle periods between customers, the obvious dangerousness of shooting staples at fellow employees and the absence of connection between duties as a salesperson and the horseplay events indicates the accident occurred during a substantial deviation from work duties. Therefore, we reverse the Commissioner's award.

Reversed.

MORSE, Justice, dissenting.

I respectfully dissent. The Court reverses a decision of the Commissioner of the Vermont Department of Labor and Industry awarding workers' compensation benefits for an injury sustained while claimant was engaged in "horseplay" with another employee. The basic criteria of analysis utilized by the Commissioner are not disputed by the Court. Rather, the Court disagrees with the Commissioner's application of the law to the facts, holding that the horseplay constituted a substantial deviation from the course of employment and therefore was not compensable.

Under settled standards of review, the Court has stepped out of its proper role. The Court is not to second-guess the Commissioner's conclusions. . . .

With respect to the extent and seriousness of the deviation, as well as its completeness, the Commissioner found that claimant and his fellow employee had completed virtually all the work that needed to be done in the absence of customers and that business was very slow that day. When the injury occurred, claimant and his fellow employee were in a period of enforced idleness while they waited for customers. They were not actively pursuing any specific tasks and were passing the time as required by their jobs. As Larson points out, when there is a lull in work, there are no duties to abandon. During such periods, the deviation can be more substantial than at other times when an employee may be actively pursuing a task directly related to employment. *Id.* §23.65, at 5-219, 5-226 to 5-227. The Commissioner could thus reasonably conclude that the horseplay in this case did not constitute an abandonment of duties or even a serious deviation from the demands of work at that time of day.

Regarding the extent to which such horseplay had become an accepted activity, the Commissioner found that it had been a commonplace occurrence at the store. Although the executive assistant to defendant's president testified that claimant's horseplay was not considered acceptable behavior, he acknowledged that an employee would not be fired for engaging in such activity. The Commissioner thus reasonably concluded that the horseplay as engaged in by claimant, while not condoned by the employer, was a tacit part of employment.

Finally, the Commissioner could reasonably conclude that work in a retail establishment might be expected to include such horseplay. The Commissioner characterized the claimant and his fellow employee as "suffering through a very slow day in a retail establishment," having quoted Larson as noting that "idleness breeds mischief, so that if idleness is a fixture of the employment, its handmaiden mischief is also." (Quoting 2 Larson & Larson, *supra*, §23.65, at 5-219.) Retail work necessitates passing time if there are no customers demanding attention. . . . The Commissioner's determination that the nature of the business lent itself to the horseplay in question was fairly and reasonably supported by the facts.

In sum, the Commissioner applied the proper legal standard to the facts, and the evidence fairly and reasonably supports the Commissioner's conclusion, a conclusion that, I might add, is a reasonable one given the policy of the law to help alleviate the consequences of injury in the workplace. . . .

NOTES

1. *A Sufficient Connection with Employment?* Ultimately, the "in the course of" and "arises out of" requirements seek to ensure that the injury was sufficiently connected with work or the workplace to justify shifting the risk of loss to the employer and the workers' compensation system. Based on your reading of *Kindel* and *Clodgo*, what is the legal standard for determining if an injury occurs "in the course of" employment? Why do the courts reach opposite conclusions on whether the injuries in question satisfied this standard? One could strongly argue that the horseplay at issue in *Clodgo* was not as significant a deviation from the workers' duties as conduct at issue in *Kindel*, which involved spending several hours at an off-site location. How can the cases be reconciled, if at all?

As discussed above, there is an ongoing debate about the efficiency and efficacy of workers' compensation—a system that costs billions of dollars a year. If cost containment is a legitimate concern, why should the employer be responsible for injuries sustained outside the workplace and outside an employee's specified work duties and tasks? Why might such broad coverage be socially beneficial (i.e., worth the costs)? Even if you conclude that the employer's responsibility ought to extend beyond the scope of workplace duties in some circumstances, can the result in *Kindel* be justified?

2. *The Journey to and from Work.* Under the "going and coming rule," an injury occurring during a worker's journey to and from work—before and after work, or during the lunch break—is not compensable, unless it occurs on the work premises or in the employer's vehicle. *See* Larson, *supra*, at §§13.01, 15.01. However, there are a number of exceptions to this principle. Most importantly, travel to and from work is compensable if the journey itself is a substantial part of the worker's service or if, based on the employer's needs or requests, the journey is made with a special degree of inconvenience or urgency. Thus, for example, where travel to different locations is part of the job, the employee travels on a "special errand" for the employer, or the employee must travel to remote sites, such travel is often considered in the course of employment. *See id.* at §§13.01, 14.01-.07. Of increasing importance in the era of telecommuting, travel between home and work may be in the course of employment if home is a regular "second office." Why did the court find that the commute from work at issue in *Kindel* was in the course of employment?

3. *Worker Intoxication and Misconduct.* Injuries resulting from or relating to the use or abuse of alcohol or drugs are common subjects of controversy in the workers' compensation context. As we saw in *Kindel*, many states now limit recovery for injuries sustained as a result of intoxication, although the extent to which alcohol must have "caused" the injuries varies by statute and is a frequently litigated issue. *See, e.g., Cyr v. McDermott's, Inc.* 996 A.2d 709 (Vt. 2010) (although the worker was intoxicated when he ingested chemicals from a soda bottle that had been given to him while at work, an issue remained whether the intoxication caused his resulting injuries); *see generally* Larson, *supra*, at §§36.01-.03. Why were Kindel's wife and children still able to recover benefits despite the intoxication provision in the Kansas statute? Were Graham's injuries compensable?

Some states also provide a statutory defense for "willful misconduct." Although this kind of defense could be interpreted broadly, courts generally have limited its application to deliberate or intentional violations of regulations designed to prevent serious injury or intentional and knowing violations of statutes designed to prevent the type of injury that occurred. *See* Larson, *supra*, at §§34.01-.03, 37.03. Thus, mere horseplay like that at issue in *Clogdo* would not constitute willful misconduct, although, as that case makes clear, such conduct may still fall outside the course of employment. Does the narrow reading of willful misconduct make sense in light of what you know about the purpose of the workers' compensation system and the "trade-offs" that it embodies?

Finally, note that the *Kindel* court rejects the employer's attempt to use common-law tort defenses, including the defense that a passenger is obliged to take reasonable care to ensure his or her own safety under the circumstances. Here again we see the trade-off underlying workers' compensation: Just as injured employees cannot bring common-law tort claims, employers cannot escape workers' compensation liability by presenting common-law defenses.

4. *Work-related Recreational or "Extracurricular" Activities.* A recurrent issue involving the connection between the injury and employment is whether recreational and social activities—for example, sports, exercising, games, social gatherings—are within the course of employment. As a general matter, they are—if they occur on the employers' premises during normal work breaks or otherwise incident to employment. In addition, such activities are within the course of employment when required by the employer or when the employer derives some direct benefit from the activity beyond mere enhancement of employee health or morale. *See generally* Larson, *supra*, at §§22.01-.05. The more tenuous the nexus between the activity and the workplace, work terms and hours, and direct employer sponsorship or support, the less likely it is that it will be found to be "in the course of" employment. *See id.* at §22.04; *compare Bender v. Dakota Resorts Mgmt., Inc.*, 700 N.W.2d 739 (S.D. 2005) (finding compensable injury sustained by employee of ski resort injured while skiing at the resort during his break); *E.C. Styberg Engineering Co., Inc. v. Lab. and Indus. Rev. Comm'n*, 692 N.W.2d 322 (Wis. Ct. App. 2004) (same for softball injury sustained during paid break) *with Montgomery County v. Smith*, 799 A.2d 406 (Md. Ct. App. 2002) (denying workers' compensation benefits to a worker injured while playing basketball after his workday in gym at detention center where he worked where employer did not require or sponsor activity). Courts remain deeply split over whether injuries occurring during employer-sponsored parties, picnics, and other events are within the course of employment, although distinctions sometimes hinge on the degree of employer pressure to attend or participate. *See* Larson, *supra*, at §22.04; *see, e.g., Young v. Taylor-White, LLC*, 181 S.W.3d 324 (Tenn. 2005) (rejecting claim for benefits where injury occurred in a voluntary "three-legged race" at an employer-sponsored picnic); *State v. Dalton*, 878 A.2d 451 (Del. 2005) (awarding benefits where worker was hurt in charity softball game where evidence suggested that participation by police officers was expected). Some states have statutorily barred benefits for injuries sustained during recreational activities absent employer compulsion to participate. *See* Larson, *supra*, at §22.02.

5. *"Personal Comfort" Doctrine.* Another issue that arises often in "in the course of" employment cases is the extent to which injuries that occur during employee deviations from work tasks to seek "personal comfort"—for example, eating, using the restroom, washing, resting, getting warm, and so forth—are compensable. The so-called "personal comfort" doctrine provides that such deviations are in the course of employment unless the departure is sufficiently great that it constitutes an intent to abandon the job temporarily or unless the method chosen is unusual or unreasonable, such that it cannot be considered incidental to employment. *See generally* Larson, *supra*, at §§21.01-.08. Although the inquiry is fact-specific, injuries are usually compensable in run-of-the-mill cases involving breaks for personal comfort at work during work hours. *See id.* Greater deviations, however, often are not compensable. *See, e.g., Galaida v. Autozone, Inc.*, 882 So.2d 1111 (Fla. Ct. App. 2004) (finding that, although an authorized cigarette break might qualify under the doctrine, a gunshot wound an employee received during such a break was not compensable because the employee's conduct—dropping a firearm while reaching for a cigarette—and resulting injury were not a foreseeable consequence of the break). Indeed, the doctrine applies only to injuries occurring on work premises or other areas where workers are authorized to be during work hours.

b. "Arises out of" Employment

Odyssey/Americare of Oklahoma v. Worden
948 P.2d 309 (Okla. 1997)

HODGES, Justice.

Odyssey/Americare of Oklahoma (Employer) and its insurer seek vacation of a Court of Civil Appeals opinion in this matter which sustained an order of the Workers' Compensation Court awarding benefits to Cheryl Worden (Claimant). The trial tribunal found that Claimant's injury arose out of her employment. This Court finds that there was not competent evidence to support that determination.

Claimant was a field nurse for Employer. She lived approximately twenty miles away from Employer's office. She went to Employer's office about once a week. Otherwise, she worked out of her home scheduling appointments with patients and traveling to visit them. At trial, the parties submitted a stipulation that Claimant was Employer's employee covered under the Workers' Compensation Act. Claimant testified that as she was walking to her car to go to a patient appointment, she slipped on wet grass in her yard and fell injuring her foot and ankle. The grass was wet from rain. But for the patient appointment, she would not have left the house.

The trial tribunal originally denied the claim, finding that her injury did not arise out of and in the course of her employment. According to the court, "the claimant's injuries were as a result of a risk which was purely personal to the claimant and not as a result of a hazardous risk associated with the claimant's employment." . . .

Oklahoma law requires that an employer pay compensation only for "accidental personal injury sustained by the employee arising out of and in the course of his employment, without regard to fault. . . ." OKLA. STAT. tit. 85, §11 (1991). The term "in the course of employment" relates to the time, place, or circumstances under which the injury is sustained. The term "arise out of employment" contemplates the causal connection between the injury and the risks incident to employment. The two requirements are distinct and are not synonymous. *Id.* Only the "arise out of" requirement is at issue in this matter. The parties agree that Claimant was in the course of her employment at the time of injury.

There are three categories of injury-causing risk an employee may encounter while in the course of employment: risks solely connected with employment, which are compensable; personal risks, which are not compensable; and neutral risks, such as weather risks, which are neither distinctly connected with employment nor purely personal. *See* 1 LARSON'S WORKERS' COMPENSATION LAW §7.30 (1997). Whether a neutral risk that causes an injury is employment-related or personal is a question of fact to be decided in each case.

Nationwide, there have been five lines of interpretation of the "arising out of" requirement. 1 LARSON *supra* at §6. The "peculiar risk" doctrine required the claimant "to show that the source of the harm was in its nature peculiar to his occupation." *Id.* at §6.20. At one time the peculiar risk doctrine was the dominant test in American Workers' Compensation jurisprudence but it was gradually replaced by the "increased risk" doctrine.

The "increased risk" test "differs from the peculiar-risk test in that the distinctiveness of the employment risk can be contributed by the increased *quantity* of a risk that is *qualitatively* not peculiar to the employment." *Id.* The rule is often stated as a determination of whether the claimant's employment exposed the worker to more risk than that to which the general public was exposed.

An easier test for a claimant to meet is that of "actual risk." "Under this doctrine, a substantial number of courts are saying, in effect, 'We do not care whether the risk was also common to the public, if in fact it was a risk of *this* employment.'" *Id.* at §6.40.

A number of courts now apply the "positional risk" doctrine. It states that "[a]n injury arises out of employment if it would not have occurred *but for* the fact that the conditions on the employment placed claimant in the position where he was injured." *Id.* at §6.50.

A rarely used line of interpretation is that of "proximate cause." This test demands "that the harms be foreseeable as a hazard of this kind of employment, and that the chain of causation be not broken by any independent intervening cause, such as an act of God." *Id.* at §6.60. This line of authority is "encountered occasionally in opinions and old texts." *Id.*

Prior to the 1986 amendments to Oklahoma's Workers' Compensation Act, Oklahoma cases relied primarily on the increased risk doctrine to determine whether a risk arose out of a worker's employment. However, the peculiar risk and positional risk tests had also been applied. But in 1986, the Oklahoma Legislature amended section 3(7) of title 85 to require that "only injuries having as their source a risk not purely personal but one that is reasonably connected with the conditions of employment shall be deemed to arise out of employment." The Legislature also repealed the provision which required an employer to produce "substantial evidence" to overcome a presumption that an injury was compensable under the Workers' Compensation Act. *See* OKLA. STAT. tit. 85, §27 (1981) (repealed). The presumption and its corresponding burdens of production and persuasion were abolished.

These statutory changes to the analysis of the "arise out of" requirement were explained in *Am. Mgmt. Sys., Inc. v. Burns*, 903 P.2d 288 (Okla. 1995). In *Burns,* a worker visiting Oklahoma City on a business trip for his employer was murdered in his hotel room by an unknown assailant with unknown motive. This Court explained that a claimant now has the burden of establishing the causal connection between injury and employment. "To establish injury or death as attributable to an employment-related risk, the operative force of a hazard, other than that which affects the public in general, must be identified." This Court specifically held that the positional risk test is now "unavailable for proving an injury's causal nexus to employment." Burn[s'] widow failed to establish that her husband's death arose out of his employment rather than from the ever-present risk of crime faced by the general public.

Despite the holding in *Burns*, the Court of Civil Appeals in this matter held that "because the risk responsible was clearly presented by the requirements of her employment, it does not matter whether the risk of injury to her was no greater than the risk to the general public." Thus, it applied essentially the positional risk test rejected in the 1986 amendments to the Workers' Compensation Act as explained in *Burns*.

The Court of Civil Appeals read two post-*Burns* cases as controlling this controversy, *Darco Transp. v. Dulen*, 922 P.2d [591 (Okla. 1996)] and *Stroud Mun. Hosp. v. Mooney*, 933 P.2d 872 (Okla. 1996). It noted that in each case compensation was allowed for traffic collision injuries even though the employee was exposed to the same street risk faced by the general motoring public. That is true, but for reasons that are not present in the instant claim.

In *Darco*, a cross-country truck driver was injured when the tractor-trailer rig he was driving was struck by a train at a crossing where the warning equipment had malfunctioned. The test this Court applied was the same increased risk test that had been applied in *Burns*. However, the accident risk the truck driver encountered in *Darco* arose out of his employment "because the perils of this servant's travel for his master [were] co-extensive with the risks of employment." *Darco*. Thus, for that truck driver the risk of traffic accident arose from the very nature of his employment.

The Court of Civil Appeals also read *Stroud Mun. Hosp. v. Mooney*, as modifying the rule in *Burns*. *Mooney* involved an exception to the "general rule that an injury sustained while going to or from an employer's premises is not one arising out of and in the course of employment." There, the special mission exception applied because the employee was instructed to return immediately from his lunch break at home to the emergency room of his employer's hospital in order for him to perform emergency blood work. The employee was injured in an automobile accident while he was attempting to comply with his employer's instruction. . . .

In this matter, there are no facts to indicate that Claimant was on a special mission outside regular working hours for her employer. In fact, the record demonstrated that she was within her regular working hours performing her usual tasks. *Mooney*'s special mission exception was not asserted by Claimant nor does it apply to these facts.

Neither *Darco* nor *Mooney* abrogate or modify the increased risk test required by the Workers' Compensation Act and described in *Burns*. . . .

This case is controlled by the increased risk test for the arising out of element of coverage provided in the Workers' Compensation Act. . . . The question is whether Claimant's employment subjected her to a risk that exceeded the ordinary hazards to which the general public is exposed. It did not.

Claimant encountered the neutral risk of wet and therefore slippery grass due to rain. Her employment exposed her to no more risk of injury from wet grass than that encountered by any member of the general public. No evidence was presented linking the risk to her employment. Although Claimant was undeniably in the course of her employment at the time of her injury, the injury did not arise from her employment. The trial tribunal's initial order denying coverage was correct. The order allowing compensation was error.

City of Brighton v. Rodriguez
318 P.3d 496 (Colo. 2013)

Chief Justice RICE delivered the Opinion of the Court.

We granted certiorari to consider whether an "unexplained" fall—i.e., a fall with a truly unknown cause or mechanism—satisfies the "arising out of" employment requirement of Colorado's Workers' Compensation Act, section 8-41-301(1)(c), C.R.S. (2013), and is thus compensable as a work-related injury. . . .

Respondent Helen Rodriguez injured herself after falling down a flight of stairs at work. While we agree with the court of appeals' holding that Rodriguez's unexplained fall was compensable, we disagree with its reasoning. The court of appeals erred when it endorsed Rodriguez's view that her injuries arose out of employment because "uncertainty about the cause of an injury cannot properly bar a workers' compensation claim if every one of the potential causes satisfie[d] the conditions of recovery." . . . We hold that an unexplained fall necessarily stems from a "neutral" risk, *i.e.*, a risk that is attributable neither to the employment itself nor to the employee him- or herself. Under our longstanding "but-for" test, such an unexplained fall "arises out of" employment if the fall would not have occurred but for the fact that the conditions and obligations of employment placed the employee in the position where he or she was injured. Rodriguez's unexplained fall arose out of employment under this test. . . .

I. Facts and Procedural History

Rodriguez worked as a special events coordinator for the City of Brighton. On January 8, 2009, Rodriguez was walking to her office, which was located in the basement of the Brighton City Hall building ("City Hall"). She paused at the top of a flight of concrete stairs running along the outside of City Hall to greet two of her co-workers, Scott Miller and Dennis Williams, who were standing toward the bottom of the stairs. After a brief chat with Miller and Williams, she began to walk down the stairs, which were dry and unobstructed. All of a sudden, she tumbled forward. Rodriguez hit her head, lost consciousness, and did not remember precisely how she fell—for example, she did not know whether she tripped, slipped, lost her balance, or something else entirely. Prior to falling, Rodriguez was not experiencing a headache, neck pain, dizziness, or vision problems.

After her fall, Rodriguez was taken by ambulance to a nearby emergency room. She underwent Computed Tomography ("CT") and Magnetic Resonance Angiogram ("MRA") scans, which revealed four unruptured aneurysms on the right side of her brain. A few weeks later, she underwent surgery for these aneurysms.

As a result of her fall, Rodriguez experienced head, neck, and back injuries. . . . [The City argued] that the injuries resulting from Rodriguez's fall were not compensable because they did not "arise out of" her employment. Specifically, the City argued that either (1) her fall was caused by her brain aneurysms, or (2) her fall was "unexplained." A hearing on this matter was held before Administrative Law Judge Ted A. Krumreich ("the ALJ") in December of 2010.

Miller and Williams, the only witnesses to Rodriguez's fall, testified at this hearing. Both were located toward the bottom of the stairs when they paused to chat with Rodriguez. Neither knew why Rodriguez fell as she did. For example, neither saw her trip, slip, or lose her balance. Both testified that the stairs appeared to be dry and unobstructed. Specifically, Miller stated that Rodriguez took two to four steps, and then "all of a sudden just went forward." Williams testified that he observed Rodriguez descend a few steps prior to pitching forward, and that it appeared as if someone "just literally yanked a rug out from underneath her." Miller and Williams also testified that Rodriguez had been speaking and acting normally immediately prior to her fall.

At the hearing, the ALJ also heard testimony from Dr. Jeffrey Wunder, who had performed an independent medical examination of Rodriguez at the City's request. Dr. Wunder opined that the "most likely" cause of Rodriguez's fall was a fainting or dizziness episode caused by Rodriguez's brain aneurysms, although he could not state this conclusion with a "reasonable degree of medical probability." The ALJ also reviewed two opposing reports from Dr. Lynn Parry and Dr. Alexander Feldman. Both Dr. Parry and Dr. Feldman opined that Rodriguez's brain aneurysms were not the cause of her fall, as the aneurysms were asymptomatic prior to the fall.

In his Order, the ALJ specifically discredited Dr. Wunder's testimony and credited the testimony of the two other doctors. The ALJ found that Rodriguez's fall was not precipitated by her brain aneurysms, nor was it caused by her tripping or missing a step or by any dangerous condition on the stairs. The ALJ noted that the witnesses to the fall were unable to state precisely why it occurred and that Rodriguez herself could not remember. Thus, he concluded that Rodriguez's fall was "unexplained." As a result, he concluded that her injuries were noncompensable, because in failing to describe her fall's precise causal mechanism, Rodriguez also failed to show that her injury "arose out of" her employment as required by section 8-41-301(1)(c) . . .

[The Industrial Claims Appeals Office affirmed the ALJ's decision, and Rodriguez appealed. The court of appeals set aside the ICAO's order on procedural grounds, in the process endorsing Rodriguez's argument that uncertainty about the cause of an injury alone cannot bar a workers' compensation claim.]

III. Analysis

First, we review the well-established analytical categories that we have used to evaluate the three types of risks that cause injuries to employees in the workplace. We hold that an "unexplained" fall—*i.e.*, a fall with a truly unknown cause or mechanism—falls into the "neutral risk" category. Consistent with our longstanding precedent regarding neutral risks, we also hold that the "but-for" test applies to determine whether unexplained falls "arise out of" employment. Next, we apply this test to the facts of Rodriguez's case and hold that her injury "arose out of" employment under section 8-41-301(1)(c) and is accordingly compensable under the Act. . . .

A. *Rodriguez's Unexplained Fall Arose Out of Employment and Was Compensable Under the "But-For" Test*

To recover benefits under the Act, an employee's injury must both occur "in the course of" employment and "aris[e] out of" employment. §8-41-301(1)(c).

The employee must meet this standard by a preponderance of the evidence. §8-43-201(1). The parties in this case agree that Rodriguez's injury occurred "in the course of" her employment; thus, our analysis focuses on determining whether her unexplained fall "arose out of" her employment.

The term "arising out of" refers to the origin or cause of an employee's injury. *Horodyskyj v. Karanian,* 32 P.3d 470, 475 (Colo. 2001). Specifically, the term calls for examination of the causal connection or nexus between the conditions and obligations of employment and the employee's injury. *Id.* An injury "arises out of" employment when it has its "origin in" an employee's work-related functions and is "sufficiently related to" those functions so as to be considered part of employment. *Id.* It is not essential, however, that an employee be engaged in an obligatory job function or in an activity resulting in a specific benefit to the employer at the time of the injury. *City of Boulder v. Streeb,* 706 P.2d 786, 791 (Colo. 1985). . . .

Here, the City concedes that the activity causing Rodriguez's injury—walking down the stairs to her basement office—was sufficiently work-related to be considered part of Rodriguez's employment. It argues, however, that Rodriguez necessarily could not provide a sufficient causal connection between her work activities and her injuries because she could not provide evidence regarding the precise *mechanism* for her fall down the stairs (e.g., tripping, slipping, or losing her balance). We disagree.

All risks that cause injury to employees can be placed within three well-established, overarching categories: (1) *employment risks,* which are directly tied to the work itself; (2) *personal risks,* which are inherently personal or private to the employee him- or herself; and (3) *neutral risks,* which are neither employment related nor personal. 1 ARTHUR LARSON & LEX K. LARSON, LARSON'S WORKERS' COMPENSATION LAW §§4.01-4.03, at 4-1 to 3 (2013) (hereinafter LARSON); *see also Horodyskyj,* 32 P.3d at 475-77 (dividing assaults by co-employees into these three categories for the purpose of determining whether an assault "arose out of" employment).

The first category, employment risks, encompasses risks inherent to the work environment itself. Employment risks include, for example, a gas explosion at work that burns an employee's body, *Rio Grande Motor Way v. De Merschman,* 68 P.2d 446, 447 (Colo. 1937), or the breakdown of an industrial machine that partially amputated an employee's finger, *Leffler v. ICAO,* 252 P.3d 50, 50 (Colo. App. 2010). The causal connection between such prototypical industrial risks and employment is intuitive and obvious, and the resulting injuries are universally considered to "arise out of" employment under the Act. *See id.; see also* LARSON, §4.01, at 4-2. Rodriguez's injury does not fit into this first risk category because the stairs were dry and free of obstructions, and the ALJ specifically found that nothing about the condition of the stairs contributed to Rodriguez's fall. *See In re Margeson,* 27 A.3d 663, 667 (N.H. 2011) ("Typically, a slip and fall is only attributable to an employment-related risk if it results from tripping on a defect or falling on an uneven or slippery surface on an employer's premises.").

In contrast, the second category contains risks that are entirely personal or private to the employee him- or herself. *See Horodyskyj,* 32 P.3d at 475-77; LARSON, §4.02, at 4-2. These risks include, for example, an employee's preexisting idiopathic illness or medical condition that is completely unrelated to his or her employment, such as fainting spells, heart disease, or epilepsy. *See, e.g., Irwin v. Indus. Comm'n,* 695 P.2d 763, 765-66 (Colo. App.1985) (holding that an employee who had a medical history of blacking out and who did so at work did not suffer an injury "arising out of" employment); *Gates Rubber Co. v. Indus. Comm'n,* 705 P.2d 6, 7 (Colo. App. 1985) (holding same, regarding an employee who had an epileptic seizure and struck his head on a level, nonslippery concrete floor). Such "personal risks" also include an assault at work arising solely from an employee's private, and not professional, life. *See, e.g., Velasquez v. Indus. Comm'n,* 581 P.2d 748, 749 (Colo. App. 1978) (holding that employees who were shot by a co-worker at work did not suffer injuries "arising out of" employment because the assailant had purely personal, and not employment-related, motivations for the attack). . . .

These types of *purely* idiopathic or personal injuries are generally not compensable under the Act, unless an exception applies. *See Velasquez,* 581 P.2d at 749; *see also Irwin,* 695 P.2d at 765. Here, however, the ALJ specifically found that Rodriguez's fall was not attributable to her preexisting brain aneurysms and that there was no other evidence to indicate that her fall was caused by an idiopathic condition. We are bound by that factual finding. *See Metro Moving & Storage Co. v. Gussert,* 914 P.2d 411, 415 (Colo. App. 1995) (stating that a reviewing court should defer to the ALJ's resolution of conflicts in the evidence, including the medical evidence). Thus, Rodriguez's fall was not caused by a personal risk.

The third category includes injuries caused by so-called "neutral risks." *Horodyskyj,* 32 P.3d at 477. Such risks are considered neutral because they are not associated with either the employment itself nor with the employee him- or herself. *Id.* For example, a neutral risk was implicated when: (1) an employee was killed by car thieves on the way back from an employment errand, *Indus. Comm'n of Colo. v. Hunter,* 214 P. 393, 394 (Colo. 1923); (2) a farm hand was killed by a lightning strike while tending to his employer's horses, *Aetna Life Ins. Co. v. Indus. Comm'n,* 254 P. 995, 995 (Colo. 1927); (3) an employee was murdered by a random, insane man while on the job, *London Guarantee & Accident Co. v. McCoy,* 45 P.2d 900, 901-02 (Colo. 1935); and (4) an employee was injured after a co-employee accidentally discharged a hunting rifle in the employer's parking lot, *Kitchens v. Dep't of Labor & Emp't,* 486 P.2d 474, 475-77 (Colo. App. 1971).

We hold that an unexplained fall necessarily constitutes a neutral risk. It is clear that Rodriguez's fall was not the result of an occupational hazard or a personal risk. Because the precise mechanism of her unexplained fall was neither occupational nor personal, by definition, such a fall is fundamentally similar to other neutral risks—like car thieves, lightning, murderous lunatics, and stray bullets—because none of these risks has a connection with the employee's work or with the employee him- or herself. *See* LARSON, §7.04[1][c], at 7-31 ("[W]here the neutral-risk concept has been accepted for other purposes, a lot of confusion, circumlocutions, and fictions could be avoided in the unexplained-fall cases by merely accepting the proposition that what is unexplained is neutral.").

Importantly, however, injuries stemming from neutral risks, whether such risks be an employer's dry and unobstructed stairs or stray bullets, "arise out of" employment because they would not have occurred *but for* employment. That is, the employment causally contributed to the injury because it obligated the employee to engage in employment-related functions, errands, or duties at the time of injury. *See Horodyskyj,* 32 P.3d at 477 ("[A]n injury is compensable under the Act as long as it is triggered by a neutral source that is not specifically targeted at a particular employee and would have occurred to any person who happened to be in the position of the injured employee at the time and place in question."); *Circle K Store No. 1131 v. Indus. Comm'n,* 796 P.2d 893, 898 (Ariz. 1990) ("In a pure unexplained-fall case, there is no way in which an award can be justified as a matter of causation theory except by a recognition that . . . but-for reasoning satisfie[s] the 'arising [out of]' requirement" (internal quotation marks omitted)).

For over eighty years, this Court has consistently applied the "but-for" test (otherwise known as the "positional-risk" test) to injuries caused by neutral risks. *See Aetna*, 254 P. at 995 (holding that a lightning accident "arose out of" employment because the "employment required [the employee] to be in a position where the lightning struck him). . . . We reaffirm *Aetna*'s holding that injuries from neutral risks "arise out of" employment. We therefore hold that the "but-for" test applies to unexplained falls because an unexplained fall stems from a neutral risk. The "but-for" test provides that an injury from a neutral risk "arises out of" employment "if it would not have occurred *but for* the fact that the conditions and obligations of the employment placed [the] claimant in the position where he [or she] was injured." *Horodyskyj*, 32 P.3d at 477 (emphasis added) (quoting LARSON, §3.05, at 3-5 to -6).

By applying the "but-for" test to unexplained falls, we reverse the court of appeals to the extent it held that an unexplained fall is compensable when "every one of the potential causes [of the fall] satisfies the conditions of recovery." Such a holding misses the mark because it introduces a kind of speculative fiction about all of the possible causes of a fall; such speculation is unhelpful when the evidence indicates that the cause of a fall is unknown. *See* LARSON, §7.04[1][c], at 7-31. This fiction is also entirely avoidable if a fall is properly categorized as arising from *either* an employment-related risk or a personal/idiopathic risk or a neutral risk. If a fall is the result of an employment-related risk, it very likely "arose out of" employment; if it is the result of a preexisting, idiopathic condition, it did not (unless an exception applies). If the cause of a fall is truly unknown, however, and the fall thus stems from a neutral risk, the "but-for" test is applied to determine whether the fall "arose out of" employment. Specifically, the resulting injury "arises out of" employment if it would not have occurred *but for* the fact that the conditions and obligations of the employment placed the employee in the position where he or she was injured.

Moreover, some form of the "but-for" test appears to be the approach taken by the majority of states that have addressed unexplained falls. *See* LARSON, 7.04[1][a], at 7-24 ("In appraising the extent to which courts are willing to accept this general but-for theory . . . it is significant to note that most courts confronted with the unexplained-fall problem have seen fit to award compensation."). We are simply more persuaded by this approach than other possible alternatives.

Significantly, the "but-for" test does not relieve the employee of the burden of proving causation, nor does it suggest that all injuries that occur at work are compensated under workers' compensation law. Rather, it acknowledges that an employee meets his or her burden to prove that an injury "arose out of" employment when the employee proves that an injury (1) had its "origin in" his or her work-related functions and is "sufficiently related to" those functions so as to be considered part of employment, and (2) arose from a neutral risk, whether that neutral risk is an unexplained fall down an employer's staircase or "an arrow out of nowhere." *See* LARSON, §7.04[1][b], at 7-28.

Demanding more precision about the exact mechanism of a fall is inconsistent with the spirit of a statute that is designed to compensate workers for workplace accidents regardless of fault. Such an approach would also be antithetical to the clear remedial purposes of the Act. . . .

Additionally, a more demanding causation approach with regard to unexplained falls is inconsistent with our longstanding precedent regarding the compensability of injuries caused by neutral risks. For over eighty years, we have awarded benefits in cases involving neutral risks, which—by definition—are not connected to the employment itself. *See, e.g., Hunter,* 214 P. at 394 (murder by car thieves); *Aetna,* 254 P. at 995 (lightning strike); *McCoy,* 45 P.2d at 901–02 (murder by random insane man); *Kitchens,* 29 486 P.2d at 475–77 (co-employee accidentally shooting another co-employee with hunting rifle). Indeed, employees must only demonstrate that there were specific connections to employment in cases *not* involving neutral risks. For example, if an employee has epilepsy and is injured after having a seizure at work, the employee must show that he or she was exposed to an additional "special hazard" of employment. *See, e.g., Ramsdell v. Horn,* 781 P.2d 150, 152 (Colo. App. 1989) (holding that a carpenter's injuries from a fall were compensable because even though he fell as a result of an epileptic seizure, he did so while located on a twenty-five-foot-high scaffold, a "special hazard" of employment).

The City relies on *Finn v. Industrial Commission,* 437 P.2d 542 (Colo.1968), for the proposition that an unexplained fall can never "arise out of" employment. Specifically, the City points to the following language:

> We do not agree that a presumption exists that an employee found injured on his employer's premises is presumably injured from something arising out of his work, *i.e.,* that the doctrine of [r]es ipsa loquitur or some variation of it applies here. On the contrary, the burden of proof in these cases is on the claimant who must show a direct causal relationship between his employment and his injury

Id. at 544. A close examination of *Finn*'s facts reveals, however, that this Court upheld the denial of benefits in that case because the employee's injury was idiopathic. . . .

Thus, while *Finn*'s rationale is not a model of clarity, its central holding—that an injury due to a "mysterious innerbody malfunction" does not "arise out of" employment merely because that injury occurs at work—is entirely consistent with this Court's precedent regarding the non-compensability of idiopathic injuries. . . . We clarify here, however, that our statement in *Finn* that an employee must show a "direct causal relationship between his employment and his injury," applies only to cases involving idiopathic—and thus not unexplained—falls.

In sum, it is clear that Rodriguez's fall "arose out of" her employment. The ALJ specifically found that her fall was not caused by an employment-related risk (e.g., slippery, obstructed, or otherwise dangerous stairs), nor by a personal, idiopathic risk (e.g., her aneurysms). Rather, the cause was unknown, and thus her fall was unexplained. We hold that such an unexplained fall is necessarily caused by a neutral risk. Because Rodriguez's fall would not have occurred but for the fact that the conditions and obligations of her employment—namely, walking to her office during her work day—placed her on the stairs where she fell, her injury "arose out of" employment and is compensable. . . .

Justice EID, dissenting.

To the majority, an unexplained injury that occurs at work is equivalent to being attacked by car thieves, struck by lightning, or hit by a stray bullet. I disagree. The cause of such "neutral risks" in those cases is perfectly clear—that is, the car thieves, the lightning bolt, or the stray bullets. Such injuries are covered by workers compensation because work put the claimant in the position to be injured by the causal force—that is, the thief, bolt, or bullet. Here, by contrast, the ALJ determined that the cause of Rodriguez's injury was unexplained, and therefore found the injury (correctly in my view) non-compensable. To put it differently, Rodriguez failed to prove that her injury "arose out of" her employment. By deeming such unexplained injuries compensable, the majority significantly expands the scope of workers' compensation coverage in Colorado. Because such decisions are, in my view, better left to the legislature, I respectfully dissent. . . .

In this case, as the majority observes, the ALJ did eliminate some potential causes of Rodriguez's injuries, finding that neither the condition of the stairs nor her preexisting brain aneurysms caused the fall. But eliminating these two potential causes only shows two factors which did not cause the fall, and none that did. Without sufficient evidence to determine why Rodriguez fell, the ALJ ultimately concluded that the cause of the fall was "unexplained."

Because the cause of the fall was unexplained, Rodriguez could not, and did not, establish causation, and thus she did not carry her burden to show by a preponderance of the evidence that her injuries arose out of employment. In my view, we should simply affirm the ALJ's determination in all respects.

The majority nevertheless breathes new life into Rodriguez's claim by placing her unexplained fall on equal footing with "neutral risks" like car thieves, lightning bolts, or stray bullets. These risks are not merely neutral, however; they are also known. If an injury were to arise from any of these causes, the claimant could demonstrate to the ALJ not only how she was injured, but more importantly, that the injury "would not have occurred but for the fact that the conditions and obligations of employment placed the employee in the position" where she was exposed to the risk of being injured.

The majority's error, however, is to expand the concept of "neutral risks" to include injuries that occur at work *where the cause is not known*. Such an unexplained injury is not categorically "neutral," as the majority would have it. Rather, an unexplained injury defies categorization. It could have been caused by a neutral risk, but it could also be the result of an entirely personal risk of harm, or of an occupational hazard. In other words, "but for" the claimant's presence at work, the injury could have occurred anyway. Unlike an injury resulting from a known, neutral threat, an unexplained fall by definition does not establish causation, and therefore cannot satisfy the claimant's obligation to demonstrate that an injury arose out of employment.

Significantly, the majority does not question the ALJ's conclusion that the cause of Rodriguez's injury could not be determined, or offer a cause of its own. Yet somehow, the majority finds it "clear" that "Rodriguez's fall was not the result of an occupational hazard, nor a personal risk." In doing so, the majority extends the ALJ's ruling well beyond its purview. Far from ruling out all occupational hazards or personal risks as potential causes of the injury, the ALJ held only that the fall was not precipitated by Rodriguez's brain aneurysms, or by her tripping or missing a step or by any dangerous condition on the stairs. After eliminating these potential causes—and only these potential causes—the ALJ then concluded that the fall was "unexplained." Rather than extrapolating from this modest holding the broad conclusion that no occupational hazard or personal risk could have caused the injury, the majority should take the ALJ's determination for what it is: a testament to Rodriguez's failure to establish that her injuries arose out of her employment.

Compounding this error, the majority next implies that the ALJ required Rodriguez to prove the "precise mechanism" of her fall, and thus applied too strict of a causal test. That simply is not the case. The ALJ applied the well-established "preponderance of the evidence" standard. By finding that the cause of the fall was unexplained, however, the ALJ correctly determined that Rodriguez could not meet the burden of proof required to establishing the cause of her injury. Thus, the ALJ's determination was not the result of Rodriguez being required to bear an excessive burden. The burden which the ALJ placed upon Rodriguez was correct; she simply failed to carry that burden.

More significantly, the majority's position extends the ability to receive worker's compensation well beyond the scope prescribed by statute. The majority denies that its holding suggests "that all injuries that occur at work are compensated under workers' compensation law." But by placing unexplained injuries on equal ground with injuries with neutral (and known) causes, the majority makes it possible to receive compensation after merely demonstrating that an injury was sustained on the job. This has never been enough, at least until today, to establish entitlement to workers' compensation—a causal connection must be shown. Otherwise, it would have been unnecessary for the legislature to have included the "arising out of" requirement. *See Fetzer v. N.D. Workforce Safety and Ins.,* 815 N.W.2d 539,543–44 (N.D. 2012) (holding, in a case involving an unexplained fall, that the "but-for reasoning of the positional risk doctrine is inconsistent with our statute that requires claimants to prove a causal connection between their employment and injury"). Thus, by holding that unexplained injuries are compensable, the majority significantly expands the scope of workers' compensation coverage in Colorado. Because I believe this expansion is an issue best left to the legislature, I respectfully dissent from the majority's opinion.

NOTES

1. *Comparing the Cases and the "Arising Out of" Tests.* The "arising out of" employment test is concerned with the causal connection between employment and the injury. Work your way through the *Worden* and *Rodriguez* analyses. First, consider how similar the analyses are in terms of the focus of the inquiry and categorization of risks. What types of risks are universally compensable and what types clearly are not? Then turn to the differences in the tests the courts articulate for assessing the causal connection to employment with regard to neutral risks. Did these differences matter in these two cases? In other words, were the outcomes different because of the tests the courts articulated or because of distinguishable facts?

2. *The Five Approaches.* *Worden* lists the five traditional approaches to assessing a causal connection in cases involving neutral or mixed risks of injury. As the court indicates, the most stringent of the five, the proximate-cause test (requiring foreseeability and no intervening cause), is now rarely deployed. *See* LARSON, *supra*, at §§3.01, 3.06. The peculiar-risk doctrine, also fairly stringent, has largely been abandoned as well. *See id.* at §§3.01-.02. A sizable number of jurisdictions have adopted the most permissive of the approaches, the positional-risk test, including Colorado, as reaffirmed in *Rodriguez*. *See* LARSON, *supra*, at §§3.05, 8.04. However, in recent years, other jurisdictions, including North Dakota (in the *Fetzger* case cited in the dissent in *Rodriguez*), have eschewed the positional-risk test, opting instead for one of the stricter approaches. *See, e.g., Fetzer*, 815 N.W.2d at 543–44; *Dykhoff v. Xcel Energy*, 840 N.W.2d 821 (Minn. 2013) (holding employee injured from a slip and fall at work could not recover because the employer had not exposed her to a condition that placed her at an increased risk of injury beyond what she would experience in her nonwork life); *Mitchell v. Clark Cnty. Sch. Dist.,* 111 P.3d 1104, 1106 (Nev. 2005) (refusing to adopt the positional-risk test in the context of an unexplained injury at work).

Nevertheless, with the facts of *Worden* and *Rodriguez* as a backdrop, consider how the three principal approaches—actual risk, increased risk, and positional risk— might affect the outcome in close cases. In light of this, and the purposes of the workers' compensation regime, which of the three is the most appropriate? To test your understanding, what would have happened had Worden slipped on wet grass on arriving at a patient's home rather than on leaving her own home?

Now look back at *Kindel* and *Clodgo.* In both cases, the courts found that the employee's injuries arose out of employment. Why? Would it matter which of the three approaches the court had adopted?

3. *Proving Causation for Downstream Harm.* The *Rodriguez* court never reached the question of whether further "downstream" disabilities potentially traced to the original fall were causally connected to her employment and, hence, compensable. Obviously, an employee like Rodriguez will have won the battle but lost the war if on remand she is denied compensation for consequences such as worsening injuries caused by intervening medical malpractice. Fortunately for such injured workers, most of the time, when the primary injury has arisen from employment, all such consequences are also compensable, absent an intervening cause attributable to the worker's own conduct. *See* LARSON, *supra,* at §§10.01-.12. Why do you suppose workers' compensation regimes take this liberal approach? In other words, what is to be gained by making the employer—via greater insurance premiums—bear the risk for all such downstream consequences, including even tortious medical treatment? Do these social benefits justify "charging" the employer for the injurious consequences of others?

4. *Workplace Assaults.* Whether an assault in the course of employment—by a co-worker or other third-party—"arises out of" employment has been the subject of much litigation and legislation. Assaults normally arise out of employment if, at a minimum, the risk of an assault is increased by the nature of the job or the work setting or if it was precipitated by a work-related dispute (e.g., an assault upon a supervisor). This means that, generally, assaults by co-workers or other third parties that are motivated by personal or private reasons do not arise out of employment, unless employment facilitates an assault that would not otherwise be made—for example, where the dangerous nature of the job increases the risk of an assault or, at least sometimes, where work friction and proximity are a contributing factor. *See, e.g., Sanderson Farms, Inc. v. Jackson,* 911 So. 2d 985 (Miss. Ct. App. 2005) (holding that employee's injuries from assault by co-employee following argument over personal loan did not arise out of employment); *see generally* LARSON, *supra,* at §§8.01-.03. However, some courts have held that an assault in the workplace (or during work hours) by a co-worker or third party is enough to establish that it arose out of employment. *See id.* at §8.01. The "assault exception" to workers' compensation coverage is sometimes separately codified rather than simply a variation of the "arising out of" employment analysis. *See, e.g.,* MINN. STAT. §176.011, subd. 16 ("Personal injury does not include an injury caused by the act of a third person or fellow employee intended to injure the employee because of personal reasons, and not directed against the employee as an employee, or because of the employment.").

5. *In the Course of and Arising out of Employment.* Now that we have seen four cases addressing either the "in the course of" "arising out of" employment requirements, take a moment to consider what each element addresses. What type of connections with employment, specifically, is each requirement designed to test? For instance, why is it that, while the "arising out of" issue was hotly contested in both *Worden* and *Rodriguez*, the "in the course of" issue was not? Although these tests are distinct, keep in mind that, in many circumstances, the facts and analyses underlying the resolution of each are not so easily separated. For example, consider how a finding that an injury occurred in the course of employment is likely to affect the "arising out of" analysis under the positional risk doctrine. Similarly, in most jurisdictions, the "street-risk doctrine" provides that street- or highway-related injuries for employees—for example, delivery and sales people—whose duties increase their exposure to the hazards of "the street" arise out of employment. *See* LARSON, *supra*, at §§6.01-.05. Thus, if an employee is consistently on the road in the course of his or her employment, any injuries he or she might sustain during such travels are likely to also "arise out of" employment.

The leading treatise on workers' compensation suggests that there is interplay between the two inquiries: Where there is a weak "in the course of" connection, courts may require a stronger "arising out of" connection to support a finding of compensability, and vice versa. *See id*. at §29.01. Might this sliding scale or "balancing out" process account for the varying results in the four cases we have read in this section?

c. *"Accidental" or "By Accident"*

In addition to the requirements that an injury arise in the course of employment and out of employment to be compensable, most state statutes also require that it normally be "accidental" or "by accident." The touchstone for whether the injury is "accidental" is unexpectedness: "an unlooked for mishap or an untoward event which is not expected or designed." *See* LARSON, *supra*, at §42.02 (quoting the seminal English case of *Fenton v. Thorley & Co.*, [1903] A.C. 443). A further element of "accidental" recognized in many jurisdictions—although a highly criticized one—is that the injury must be traceable to a definite time, place, and occasion or cause, at least within reasonable limits. In other words, courts read "accident" or "by accident" to require that "an accident" be shown to have given rise to the injury. *See id*.

The main fault line running through the cases analyzing this element involves whether the notion of unexpectedness inherent in "accidental" requires an accidental cause or merely an accidental result. *Id*. at §§42.02, 43.01. The leading treatise provides the classic example of a situation in which the work-related cause is expected but the result is not: "A worker who, for years, has lifted hundred-pound sacks many times a day suffers a heart attack while lifting one in the usual way, and medical testimony confirms that the heavy lift did in fact cause the attack." *Id*. at §42.02. Whether unexpected injuries resulting from such "usual" exertion or exposure are compensable varies by jurisdiction and the nature and definiteness of the injury. The vast majority of courts have found that sudden mechanical or structural changes in the body, such as something breaking, rupturing, or herniating, are accidental—even where the exertion causing the change is usual. Similarly, courts almost always find usual exposure causing freezing or sunstroke to be accidental. A less sizable majority find "generalized conditions"—for example, heart attacks, back injuries, muscle strains, and other similar problems—resulting from usual exertion to be accidental. The other jurisdictions require the injured worker to demonstrate that some kind of unusual or abnormal exertion or exposure (including, for example, excessive strain or work, or sudden shocks or falls) caused the injury. *See generally id.* at §§43.01-03. Of course, determining what constitutes a sufficiently unusual or abnormal exertion often poses difficult issues.

It is worth noting that workplace assaults may be "accidental." A workplace assault or battery by a co-worker or third-party, although intentional on the part of the perpetrator, may be sudden and unexpected by the employee and unexpected and unintended by the employer. Obviously, if the assault or other injurious action is intended by or attributable to the employer, then the injury is not accidental, and the employee may sue the employer in tort. In addition, as we have seen, even if deemed accidental, a co-worker or third-party assault resulting from a personal or private motive may nevertheless be excluded from workers' compensation coverage because it does not arise out of employment or is otherwise subject to a statutory "assault exception."

Relatedly, as discussed at the end of Chapter 5, a frequent subject of litigation is whether sexual harassment and other forms of discrimination are covered under workers' compensation or excluded as intentional or quasi-intentional conduct. The question typically arises not when the plaintiff files a compensation claim but rather when a harassed worker sues in tort or under a state antidiscrimination statute because the remedies that are available under such regimes—in particular those addressing mental and emotional distress—are unavailable under workers' compensation. Normally, if there is no physical injury associated with such conduct, the victim will not be covered under the workers' compensation regime, and hence there will be no exclusivity. Where, however, the harassing or discriminatory behavior caused some type of physical injury—for example, a sexually-motivated assault or battery—the question is much closer, and, as discussed in Chapter 5, courts have not agreed on the answer. Of course, workers' compensation law does not preempt federal discrimination law, and thus, if the conduct rises to the level of actionable discrimination against the employer under Title VII or another federal antidiscrimination statute (*see* Chapter 9), the employee may bring such claims.

Another particularly troublesome category of "accident" cases involves diseases, including infectious diseases acquired through exposure at work, diseases aggravated by work exertion, diseases brought on or made worse by the work environment or temperature, and "occupational diseases" caused by exposure—sometimes over long periods—to harmful conditions tied to particular types of employment. There are circumstances in which diseases are clearly compensable, such as when the disease follows as a natural consequence of a work-related injury that is accidental or when it is a direct result of a particular workplace mishap, malfunction, or other unusual event. *See* LARSON, *supra*, at §42.03.

In many other contexts, however, the disease inquiry has proven difficult. One problem is the cause-result issue discussed above, and courts have been divided over whether routine exposure to conditions causing or aggravating diseases is compensable. Beyond this, some diseases, including occupational ones, are not unexpected at all—think of, for example, "black lung" disease, a condition not only expected but in fact anticipated when one works for extended periods in coal mines. Another concern involves indefiniteness, given the frequent difficulty of tracing diseases to particular occasions and causes or showing that they developed suddenly and unexpectedly. With diseases that are common in the general population, simply establishing a connection to work can be difficult. The employee may need to show that the disease was caused by work conditions rather than by routine or normal exposure to germs, toxins, or the actions of the worker herself. Consider, for instance, a worker whose job exposes him to toxins associated with lung cancer but who is also a smoker. Finally, the time element—that is, the delay in manifestation of the disease—also raises a host of potential proof and other problems, most notably in the occupational disease context.

All states have addressed aspects of these problems statutorily, and there are some federal regimes addressing particular diseases or industries. All state statutes include specific sections covering occupational diseases, and many are general in scope, covering all employment-related diseases. Others contain lists of covered conditions, but typically these statutes also include catchall provisions that extend to nonspecified diseases. Such statutes do *not* require evidence of unexpected or sudden triggering events. Rather, occupational disease coverage depends on whether there is a sufficiently recognizable link between the disease and the particular type of work at issue—work that at least increases the risk of such disease.

Note on Compensability of "Mental Injuries"

Whether work-related injuries that may be characterized as "mental," "stress-related," or "psychological" in nature are compensable under workers' compensation has produced an enormous amount of litigation and controversy. Early on, only "physical injuries" were contemplated under workers' compensation regimes, and thus, emotional distress and mental injuries were not compensable absent some corresponding physical injury or disorder. Over time, however, greater recognition has developed not only of the seriousness of various "mental injuries" but also of the need to compensate at least some such ailments. In addressing the physical-mental divide, courts and commentators have separated claims into four general categories: (1) physical stimuli causing physical injuries, (2) mental stimuli causing physical injuries (so-called "mental-physical"), (3) physical stimuli causing mental injuries ("physical-mental"), and (4) mental or nervous injuries caused by mental stimulus ("mental-mental"). *See generally* LARSON, *supra*, at §§56.01-.04.

Provided the injury is sufficiently connected to work and is accidental, category 1 claims have always been compensable. There is now general agreement that claims in categories 2 and 3 (mental-physical and physical-mental) are compensable as well, although states and courts may impose various proof requirements and limit recovery for mental injuries in a number of ways. A common example of a category 2 claim is a stress-induced heart attack; category 3 includes claims for psychological conditions that result from or are exacerbated by a physical injury.

Thus, currently, the controversy focuses largely on the final category—mental-mental claims. This group of workers' compensation claims raises the same types of concerns as emotional distress claims in tort, including floodgates issues, causation and diagnostic problems, and questions of proof. They also raise concerns about the cost of the workers' compensation system. Although most states now provide workers' compensation coverage for mental-mental claims, some do not. *See id.* at

§56.06. Of the states that accept such claims, some require no greater showing than that required for claims for physical injuries; others require a showing that a sudden stimulus caused the psychological or mental injury; and still others require a showing that the mental stress was unusual in the given context. *See id.* Some state legislatures have amended their statutes to limit such claims in various ways, including requiring a heightened level or particular type of stress or mental impairment, increasing the burden of proof, imposing specific diagnostic guidelines, altering causation standards, limiting the amount of benefits, or excluding benefits altogether. *See id.* Of course, compensability for such claims would benefit many employees, but those who prefer to sue in tort or some other state-law theory would be barred from doing so due to workers' compensation exclusivity.

Note on Exclusivity

Exclusivity is a core component of all workers' compensation regimes, and, as we have seen, the scope of the bar is frequently litigated in contexts in which tort or other remedies would otherwise be available and would be superior for the worker (e.g., offering greater damages for lost wages, damages for emotional and mental stress, and the potential for punitive damages). Whether workers' compensation provides the exclusive remedy normally depends on resolution of the various scope questions addressed above—that is, whether the worker is a covered "employee," whether the injury or illness arose in the course of and out of employment, whether the injury was accidental or the illness was an otherwise covered occupational disease, and whether the type of injury—for example, mental-mental—is compensable. In a few cases, however, courts have found that exclusivity extends beyond the scope of covered injuries, although these holdings are highly controversial. *See, e.g., Bias v. E. Associated Coal Corp.*, 640 S.E.2d 540 (W. Va. 2006) (holding that a common-law negligence claim for stress-related injuries employee sustained at work is preempted by workers' compensation exclusivity even though a statute precluding benefits for mental-mental injuries bars recovery under the state's workers' compensation regime).

As states have narrowed the scope of compensable conditions and reduced benefits under their workers' compensation regimes, exclusivity has come under scrutiny. *See, e.g., Tooey v. AK Steel Corp.*, 81 A.3d 851 (Pa. 2013) (rejecting exclusivity on statutory grounds of claims arising from contraction of work-related mesothelioma because a contrary conclusion would leave the employee "with *no remedy* against his or her employer, a consequence that clearly contravenes the Act's intended purpose of benefitting the injured worker"); Robert F. Williams, *Can State Constitutions Block the Workers' Compensation Race to the Bottom?*, 69 RUTGERS L. REV. 1081 (2017) (describing possible state constitutional challenges to exclusivity where benefits are dramatically reduced or unavailable to workers). After detailing the general decline in benefits and compensability across the country, Professor Spieler offers a similarly critical assessment:

> The scope of exclusivity needs to be reevaluated and measured against the adequacy of workers' compensation benefits for injured workers. Employers' duty to provide safe workplaces should not be obscured by the leveling attained through a social benefit system that allows for claims suppression and limited adjustment of insurance rates for

claims that are paid. Despite improvements in safety records overall, the incentives to establish and maintain safe workplaces are remarkably weak. If we take seriously the need for incentives to encourage continuous safety improvement in workplaces, then expansion of tort remedies in situations in which the employers allow the persistence of known hazards needs to be reevaluated.

Spieler, *supra*, at 1011-12.

Note, however, that even if workers' compensation is the exclusive remedy vis-à-vis the employer or employers (*see* Chapter 1), the worker may have a viable tort claim against third parties whose conduct contributed to the injury. Furthermore, in many contexts in which an employee is injured or becomes ill, counsel will pursue additional remedies against third-party tortfeasors with resources, including manufacturers of defective products used by the employee, landowners, and other firms whose actions may affect the safety of the employee or workplace. Co-employees, customers, or other individuals whose negligent or intentional conduct causes the harm also may be liable, but often such tortfeasors lack sufficiently deep pockets to be worth suing. Finally, a few courts have recognized that employers are in some cases effectively "third parties" and subject to tort suit under the "dual capacity" doctrine, which provides that an employee may recover in tort against an employer if the employer caused or aggravated the injury while acting in a non-employer capacity. For example, an employer may be subject to a tort suit for providing negligent medical care for the employee that aggravated the employee's condition or for manufacturing a defective product that harms the employee at work. *See generally* Robert L. Rubin, *Accommodating Tort Law: Alternative Remedies for Workplace Injuries*, 69 RUTGERS L. REV. 1119 (2017).

B. OSHA

Workers' compensation regimes are meant to create incentives for employers to improve workplace safety by mandating compensation for occupational injuries and diseases. In contrast, OSHA, the Occupational Safety and Health Act of 1970, 29 U.S.C. §§651-78 (2018), is designed to address safety directly by setting and enforcing standards to prevent workplace injuries and diseases. It does so through a top-down regulatory structure rather than through private enforcement or injury claims. OSHA is therefore an entirely different type of legal regime than workers' compensation. As a result, it produces a different kind of litigation—mostly addressing the setting of standards—and its own unique set of problems and controversies.

One rarely discussed issue is whether OSHA and workers' compensation should be viewed as interdependent rather than as entirely separate and distinct regimes. For example, might the social utility of the trade-off underlying workers' compensation depend to some extent on the quality of the OSHA regime? For a detailed treatment of the shortcomings under current law with regard to regulating workplace chemicals and a proposed reform designed to alter incentives under the workers' compensation regime and push chemical manufacturing employers to cooperate in developing new OSHA exposure limits, *see* Jason R. Bent, *An Incentive-Based Approach to Regulating Workplace Chemicals*, 73 OHIO ST. L.J. 1389 (2012).

1. A Glance at OSHA's History and Structure

Prior to adoption of OSHA, state legislation had long regulated some workplace health and safety matters, and federal legislation had addressed particular industries notorious for their history of safety problems, such as coal mining. Yet OSHA marked the first comprehensive national effort to deal with workplace safety. Sweeping in its coverage, it excludes only state and local government employers, employers covered by other safety regimes, and workplaces in states with approved safety plans. OSHA preempts state occupational safety laws unless the state adopts a plan approved by the Occupational Safety and Health Administration, in which case the state plan precludes federal activity. Nevertheless, more general state and local laws, such as those relating to fire safety, continue unaffected by OSHA, and workers' compensation regimes are expressly saved from preemption, despite their obvious relationship to workplace safety.

The statute created an elaborate administrative mechanism for its enforcement. The acronym OSHA is often used both to mean the Act itself and the agency within the Labor Department—the Occupational Safety and Health Administration— charged with implementing the statute. The administrative structure created by the statute is more complicated than those governing many other federal agencies, but the Secretary of Labor, acting through OSHA, is charged with promulgating and enforcing safety standards.

a. Safety Standards

Under §5(a) of the Act, 29 U.S.C. §654, safety standards come in two basic forms: the statute's "general duty clause," and the specific standards promulgated by OSHA. The general duty clause is a catchall provision requiring a safe workplace even in the absence of more specific standards. However, it is residual in that it governs a potential workplace hazard only if no specific promulgated standard addresses the hazard.

The general duty provision states that an employer "shall furnish to each of his employees employment and a place of employment which are free from recognized hazards that are causing or are likely to cause death or serious physical harm to his employees." To prove a violation of the clause, the Secretary of Labor must establish that the employer failed to keep the workplace free of a hazard to which employees were exposed, that the hazard was "recognized" based on standard knowledge in the industry, that the hazard was likely to cause death or serious physical harm, and that there are feasible methods or measures for addressing the hazard. An employer, therefore, may violate the clause even though no employee has yet been harmed. The various elements of a violation of this clause have been the subject of occasional controversy, as has its application to particular hazards arguably addressed by specific standards.

Most of the debate, however, has focused on OSHA's promulgation of specific standards. The Act requires that employers "comply with occupational safety and health standards" promulgated by OSHA. Three kinds of specific standards are con-templated under the Act: interim standards, new or permanent standards, and tem-porary standards. In deriving specific standards, OSHA is assisted by a research agency, the National Institute for Occupational Safety and Health ("NIOSH"), located in the Department of Health and Human Services. NIOSH has no power to adopt standards; it simply advises OSHA.

Temporary standards are, in essence, emergency standards that OSHA may adopt with minimal procedures if it finds that a particular substance or new hazard poses a grave danger to employees and that an emergency measure is necessary to protect employees from such danger. *See* 29 U.S.C. §655(c). Given the high bar, OSHA has rarely adopted such emergency standards.

OSHA was also authorized to adopt so-called interim standards, which were intended to be placeholders for more considered efforts. These provisions were largely based on federal standards existing prior to OSHA or "consensus" (lowest common denominator) standards of various standards-producing institutions. OSHA adopted thousands of such standards shortly after the statute was enacted, creating a storm of controversy, in part because they imposed an immediate and complex array of new safety requirements on many employers. Many of these provisions were later abolished by statute, but, over four decades later, "interim" standards continue to make up the bulk of specific standards under OSHA.

After the initial period in which interim standards were to be adopted, OSHA was authorized to promulgate new or permanent standards (which may be completely new or may modify or revoke interim standards). Enactment of such standards, however, is subject to more rigorous administrative procedures and greater substantive limits than apply to interim standards. The substantive limits in particular have been the subject of legal challenges to proposed standards and the basis for criticism of the OSHA workplace safety regime.

Part of the difficulty stems from the generality of the statutory delegation. For example, §6(b)(5) of the statute states that the Secretary, in dealing with toxic or harmful physical agents, "shall set the standard which most adequately assures, to the extent feasible, on the basis of the best available evidence, that no employee will suffer material impairment of health or functional capacity." It also states that that "other considerations shall be the latest available scientific data in the field, the feasibility of the standards, and the experience gained under this and other health and safety laws." Section 3(8) of the statute defines a health and safety standard as one that is "reasonably necessary and appropriate to safe or healthful employment."

Through judicial refinement, some clearer requirements now have emerged. For example, to promulgate any permanent standard, OSHA must demonstrate that the regulation will reduce or eliminate a "significant risk" to worker health or safety. *Indus. Union Dep't v. Am. Petroleum Inst.*, 448 U.S. 607, 641 (1980). This risk must be sufficiently quantified to enable OSHA to characterize it as significant. *See id.* at 656. In addition, OSHA must demonstrate that the risk to health or safety is "material," *AFL-CIO v. OSHA*, 965 F.2d 962, 973 (11th Cir. 1992), and that the proposed standard is feasible—that is, "capable of being done, executed, or effected" by the regulated industry, both technologically and economically. *Am. Textile Mfrs. Inst. v. Donovan* ("*ATMI*"), 452 U.S. 490, 508-09 (1981). However, OSHA usually need not engage in a cost-benefit analysis—a determination of whether the costs of compliance with the proposed standard are reasonable when compared to its benefits. *See ATMI*, 452 U.S. at 506-22.

The agency's determinations with regard to risk, materiality, and feasibility are conclusive if they are "supported by substantial evidence in the record considered as a whole," 29 U.S.C. §655(f), a standard that is not as deferential as "arbitrary and capricious" review but still falls far short of requiring scientific certainty or allowing de novo judicial inquiry. Nevertheless, these requirements do mandate that OSHA demonstrate that its standards are premised on available scientific evidence of probable benefits to worker health or safety—a significant hurdle in certain occupational disease and chemical exposure contexts.

Although not insurmountable, this need for substantial scientific support in a world of scientific uncertainty, combined with challenges by industry, other procedural hurdles, and resistance or delays within OSHA itself has resulted in few permanent standards actually being promulgated. *See generally* David Michaels & Celeste Monforton, *Scientific Evidence in the Regulatory System: Manufacturing Uncertainty and the Demise of the Formal Regulatory System*, 13 J. L. & POL'Y 17 (2005); *see also* Bent, *supra*, at 1420-26 (describing the full spectrum of causes for OSHA's failure to promulgate and enforce standards). For example, since its inception, OSHA has promulgated comprehensive standards for only about 30 chemical toxins, *see* Michaels & Monforton, *supra*, at 28, sometimes only after being compelled to do so following judicial challenges by labor or workplace safety advocates. Consider how all of these factors combined to delay promulgation of the standards at issue in the next case, which involves exposure to a particular toxin (hexavalent chromium) that clearly threatens worker health.

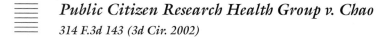

Public Citizen Research Health Group v. Chao
314 F.3d 143 (3d Cir. 2002)

BECKER, Chief Judge.

This opinion addresses a Petition by Public Citizen Health Research Group ("Public Citizen") to review the inaction of [OSHA], and to require OSHA to commence a rulemaking that would lower the permissible exposure limit for hexavalent chromium. It is not disputed that hexavalent chromium, which is widely used in various industries and which has been classified as a carcinogen, can have a deleterious effect on worker health. [NIOSH] has for several decades recommended that OSHA adopt a far more stringent permissible exposure limit ("PEL") for hexavalent chromium than the consensus [interim] standard it promulgated in 1971. In response to a 1993 petition for rulemaking, OSHA agreed that there was clear evidence that exposure to hexavalent chromium at the consensus level can result in excess risk of lung cancer and other chromium-related illnesses, and announced that it was initiating a rulemaking that it expected would conclude in 1995. However, nearly a decade after this announcement, nothing has happened, evincing a clear pattern of delay.

This matter was before us once before. . . . In that [1998] case, we declined Public Citizen's request to compel agency action. . . . At that time, OSHA represented that it intended to issue a proposed rule by September 1999, and we found such a deadline permissible in light of alleged competing policy priorities. . . . Yet, at the time of oral argument in this case, which was nine years after OSHA initially announced its intention to begin the rulemaking process, no rulemaking had yet been initiated, and it appeared that none would be in the foreseeable future. Indeed, at oral argument, OSHA's counsel admitted the possibility that OSHA might not promulgate a rule for another ten or twenty years, if at all.

We concluded that the delay had become unreasonable, and that while competing policy priorities might explain slow progress, they could not justify indefinite delay and recalcitrance in the face of an admittedly grave risk to public health. We therefore determined to grant the petition and to direct OSHA to proceed expeditiously with its hexavalent chromium rulemaking process. This opinion was drafted on an expedited basis . . . when we received OSHA's announcement that it had instituted the long-sought rulemaking process, stating that: "The health risks associated with occupational exposure to hexavalent chromium are serious and demand serious attention. . . . We are committed to developing a rule that ensures proper protection to safeguard workers who deal with hexavalent chromium."

This notice appears to have been prompted by the displeasure clearly evidenced by the panel during oral argument, especially the question posed to counsel whether they would be receptive to mediation regarding the timeframe for a judicially-ordered rulemaking. [In any event, the notice does not render the case moot because] the agency's action does not resolve an important facet of the case, namely Public Citizen's request that we order OSHA to issue a proposed rule within 90 days and supervise OSHA's progress.

Accordingly, we will publish the opinion that had been prepared to resolve the remedy issue, and will direct that Public Citizen and OSHA submit to a course of mediation for sixty days before The Honorable Walter K. Stapleton. If the parties cannot agree to a workable timetable during that period, the panel will issue and enforce a schedule of its own device. . . .

I. Facts and Procedural Posture

Hexavalent chromium is a compound found only rarely in nature but used widely in industry—for chrome plating, stainless steel welding, alloy production, and wood preservation. The dangers of exposure to it have long been recognized, and include ulceration of the stomach and skin, necrosis, perforation of the nasal septum, asthma, and dermatitis. More significantly, there is strong evidence that inhaled hexavalent chromium is carcinogenic. Since 1980, the Department of Health and Human Service's National Toxicology Program has designated various hexavalent chromium compounds as human carcinogens. The Environmental Protection Agency has been in accord since 1984. . . . Disturbingly, the primary evidence of hexavalent chromium's carcinogenicity comes not from animal studies, but from epidemiological studies of workers exposed to it; in short, as Public Citizen states, "the principal evidence is actual human body counts."

Soon after [OSHA] took effect in 1970, OSHA established a 100 $\mu g/m^3$ [a weight-to-volume ratio that can be converted to "parts per billion" by multiplying by the chemical weight of the compound] permissible exposure limit ("PEL") for inhalation exposure to hexavalent chromium. That level did not reflect OSHA's independent judgment about the appropriate standard, but rather constituted a "lowest common denominator" consensus standard to provide workers some measure of protection pending OSHA's consideration of the optimal long-term standard. The 1971 standard remains in effect. However, although today's foremost health concern regarding hexavalent chromium is its carcinogenicity, OSHA did not take that into account when promulgating the standard. . . .

Shortly after OSHA promulgated the consensus standard, NIOSH . . . urged OSHA to adopt a PEL of 1.9 µg/m³, a level 1/52 of the existing standard. At that time, NIOSH concluded that the evidence of the carcinogenicity of a few specified hexavalent chromium compounds was lacking, but that all other forms were carcinogenic. Subsequently, however, NIOSH concluded that all forms of hexavalent chromium should be considered carcinogenic, and it recommended that the 1.9 µg/m³ standard be applied to all such compounds.

In 1993, Public Citizen petitioned OSHA to issue an emergency temporary standard that would set a PEL of 0.5 µg/m³ as an 8-hour weighted average. The Occupational Safety and Health Act requires OSHA to issue an emergency temporary standard without the usual notice-and-comment procedures if it finds that such action is needed to protect employees against grave danger. 29 U.S.C. §655(c). OSHA denied the petition because it contended that "the extremely stringent judicial and statutory criteria for issuing" an emergency standard were not met. It did, however, acknowledge that its existing standard was inadequate. . . . It therefore announced that [it would begin rulemaking on the matter and anticipated notice would be published in March 1995].

This timetable was short-lived. Only a month after its response to Public Citizen's rulemaking petition, OSHA reported that the date for issuance of a proposed standard had slipped from March to May 1995, and by May 1995 the anticipated issuance date had been pushed back again to December 1995. Thus began a pattern of delay. . . .

Amidst this ongoing delay, OSHA commissioned a comprehensive risk assessment of hexavalent chromium. This assessment, which became known as the "Crump Report," concluded that exposure at the current PEL (100 µg/m³) over a 45-year working lifetime could be expected to result in between 88 and 342 excess cancer deaths per thousand workers. Moreover, the Crump Report concluded that significant numbers of excess cancer deaths could be expected even at much lower levels of exposure. . . .

OSHA's November 1996 semiannual regulatory agenda endorsed the Crump analysis, and OSHA explicitly acknowledged that "[t]here appears to be no dispute that the current PEL is too high" and "must be greatly reduced." Accordingly, OSHA stated that it was considering a new standard 10 to 100 times lower than the existing one. . . . Even at that level, it noted, there would be significant risk of excess cancer deaths.

Addressing these events in its present brief, OSHA contends that it was then concerned with methodological imperfections in the available data. For example, the Crump Report did not control for the effects of smoking or asbestos, factors obviously related to lung cancer incidence; if the studied populations of chromium-exposed workers smoked more than the general population, smoking could have accounted for some of the excess deaths. Industry groups therefore pressured OSHA to wait for the results of the then-forthcoming Johns Hopkins study, which, in the industry's view, was "expected to be the most accurate and complete database on chromium exposure and mortality available." OSHA also represents that budget cuts, government shutdowns, and new responsibilities under the Small Business Regulatory Enforcement Fairness Act of 1996 limited the resources available for hexavalent chromium rulemaking. In August 1997, OSHA explained to Public Citizen that work on the rule was continuing, but that these considerations had delayed progress and prevented it from expediting the rulemaking.

Public Citizen, discouraged by what it viewed as a pattern of inaction, urged OSHA in March 1997 to commit to a timetable for rulemaking. [OSHA did not so commit and, in 1997, Public Citizen sought review of OSHA's allegedly unreasonable delay before this Court.]

We declined Public Citizen's request to compel agency action, for we concluded that the facts did not yet "demonstrate that inaction is . . . unduly transgressive of the agency's own tentative deadlines." Key to our decision [were] our observation[s] that the Secretary of Labor has "quintessential discretion . . . to allocate OSHA's resources and set its priorities," [that the delays might be reasonable, and that the intervenors raised serious questions about the data underlying Public Citizen's calculations]. Given these scientific questions, OSHA's superior technical expertise, and its professed plan to issue a deadline for proposed rulemaking in September 1999, we concluded that OSHA's delay was not yet unreasonable.

Following our ruling, OSHA adhered to its September 1999 pledge in each of its regulatory agendas published through April 1999. But it in fact issued no proposed rule in September 1999, and in its November 1999 agenda it announced that its new target date was June 2001. . . .

Meanwhile, August 2000 saw the release of the long-awaited Johns Hopkins study on hexavalent chromium.[3] . . . [The Hopkins Study confirmed the elevated lung cancer risk from hexavalent chromium exposure observed in other studies.]

Although the Hopkins Study explicitly sought to address the shortcomings in previous empirical research, namely the lack of controls for smoking, asbestos, and other environmental factors, its release did not spur OSHA into action. The study was released in August 2000, but OSHA's November 2000 agenda pushed the date for a proposed rule back to September 2001. OSHA's second-most-recent agenda, issued December 3, 2001, reflected another, more radical departure from previous plans: for the first time since 1994, the hexavalent chromium rulemaking was denominated a "long-term action," and the timetable for action stated that the date for a proposed rule was "to be determined."

OSHA offers a number of explanations for the delay that has now become indefinite. It notes that "[t]he day the [Bush] Administration took office, it instructed the agencies that any new regulatory actions must be reviewed and approved by a department or agency head appointed after January 20, 2001." As it was not headed by a presidential appointee until August 3, 2001, OSHA contends that it could not begin to set its new regulatory priorities until that time. Even then, it asserts, two extraordinary unforeseen events—the attacks on the World Trade Center and Pentagon and the anthrax mailings—required it immediately to divert significant resources to safety efforts.

Even amidst these distractions, OSHA represents, it has continued to evaluate the need for a new hexavalent chromium rule. . . .

In OSHA's submission, the problem is that it "believes that the information now available is inconclusive on important issues, such as whether the epidemiological studies . . . apply to all Cr VI compounds and the utility of the data to establish a dose-response relationship." Although the Hopkins Study was a step forward, OSHA points out that its authors acknowledged certain limitations, particularly in

---

3. Public Citizen alleges that many of the Hopkins study's results, if not its actual data, had been available to OSHA since 1995.

estimating the cumulative exposure for the different individuals in the cohort. The study also did not resolve the dispute over whether all hexavalent chromium compounds present the same degree of risk. Because OSHA has decided that it would benefit from public input and expert criticism on these issues, it has published a request for information (RFI) in its August 2002 regulatory agenda. After the time for response, OSHA states, it will evaluate all of the information available and decide how to proceed.

Public Citizen brought the present petition for review alleging that "[d]eference to an agency's priorities and timetables only goes so far," and arguing that, "at some point, a court must tell an agency that enough is enough." The Administrative Procedure Act, 5 U.S.C. §706(1), creates a right of action by an aggrieved party to compel unreasonably delayed agency action. When the action sought is the promulgation of an occupational exposure standard under 29 U.S.C. §655, the federal courts of appeals have exclusive jurisdiction under 29 U.S.C. §655(f), which we have interpreted to provide "jurisdiction to conduct judicial review over the health and safety standards issued by the Secretary of Labor, as well as over claims in which the Secretary has not yet acted but where her delay is allegedly unreasonable." [*Oil, Chem. & Atomic Workers Union v. OSHA*, 145 F.3d 120, 122 (3d Cir. 1998).]

II. Discussion

. . . Our polestar is reasonableness, and while in 1997 we found reasonable OSHA's delay in the face of scientific uncertainty and competing regulatory priorities, we now find ourselves further from a new rule than we were then. We examine each of OSHA's justifications in turn.

A. Has OSHA's Delay Been Excessive?

In 1993, OSHA acknowledged that the existing hexavalent chromium standard is inadequate and "that there is clear evidence that exposure to Cr VI at the current PEL of 100 µg/m³ can result in an excess risk of lung cancer and other Cr VI-related illnesses." That was fully nine years ago, and its first target date for a proposed rule—March 1995—is now more than seven years past. OSHA has missed all ten of its self-imposed deadlines, including the September 1999 target it offered to this Court in *Oil Workers*. Far from drawing closer to a rulemaking, all evidence suggests that ground is being lost. OSHA's December 2001 regulatory agenda demoted the rulemaking from a "high priority" to a "long-term action" with a timetable "to be determined." In fact, at oral argument, OSHA's counsel admitted the possibility that another ten or even twenty years might pass before it issues a rule, if it ever does.

OSHA responds that Public Citizen's concerns about the missed deadlines and recent reclassification are misconceived. It explains that under the Regulatory Flexibility Act, 5 U.S.C. §602, agencies must publish regulatory agendas that include all rules the agency intends to propose or promulgate that are "likely to have a significant economic impact on a substantial number of small entities." A rule's inclusion in an agency's agenda does not, however, require the agency to consider or act on that item. *See* 5 U.S.C. §602(d). . . .

Regarding hexavalent chromium's recent downgrade to a "long-term project," OSHA clarifies that this is a reflection of whether the rulemaking will be completed in a short period of time and represents that the designation carries no implication about a rulemaking's relative importance to other matters OSHA is considering. The items listed as "high priority" in the December 2001 agenda, it says, were simply those on which OSHA intended to take action in fiscal 2002. It therefore contends that the priority downgrade was more a clarification than a change in the agency's priorities.

We find neither of these explanations satisfactory. We agree with OSHA insofar as its failure strictly to follow its published agenda is not actionable, but this defense misses the point: OSHA's persistent failure to meet deadlines is not the disease itself, but rather a symptom of its dilatory approach to the hexavalent chromium rulemaking process. Similarly, even if OSHA's decision to downgrade the project's priority truly represents a clarification rather than a change, it still gives clear evidence that at least another year will pass before OSHA takes even the first formal step toward promulgating a rule. . . .

Section 6(b) of the Occupational Safety and Health Act requires the Secretary of Labor to "set the standard which most adequately assures, to the extent feasible, on the basis of the best available evidence, that no employee will suffer material impairment of health or functional capacity even if such employee has regular exposure to the hazard dealt with by such standard for the period of his working life." 29 U.S.C. §655(b). The Supreme Court has found that this language compels action: "Both the language and structure of the Act, as well as its legislative history, indicate that it was intended to require the elimination, as far as feasible, of significant risks of harm." *Indus. Union Dep't, AFL-CIO v. Am. Petroleum Inst.*, 448 U.S. 607, 641 (1980). As such, the agency's priorities are judicially reviewable, and this Court and others have compelled OSHA to take action to address significant risks. . . .

We find extreme OSHA's nine-year (and counting) delay since announcing its intention to begin the rulemaking process, even relative to delays other courts have condemned in comparable cases. Indeed, in no reported case has a court reviewed a delay this long without compelling action. . . .

OSHA contends that [among the various reported cases, in only one] did a court compel the agency to issue a *proposed* rule; the others dealt with situations where the agency had issued a proposed rule but was allegedly dilatory in issuing a final regulation. It further notes that [that one case was later characterized as exceptional and the project at issue was conceded to be urgent].

While we acknowledge that . . . the other cases are in some ways distinguishable from this one, we nonetheless regard them as valuable precedent. . . . At all events, we think it "exceptionally rare" that an agency would for years classify an action as a "high priority," only to demote it to a "long term project" upon the release of a study that provides more convincing evidence of the danger than had previously existed.

We are satisfied that OSHA's delay in this case is objectively extreme, and we find its regression alarming in the face of its own 1996 statement that "there appears to be no dispute that the current PEL is too high." We therefore conclude that, absent a scientific or policy-based justification for its delay, we must compel it to act.

B. Does Scientific Uncertainty Justify OSHA's Delay?

In . . . the first installment of this case, Public Citizen relied upon the Crump Report's finding that between 88 and 342 out of every 1,000 workers exposed to hexavalent chromium will die from cancer attributable to that exposure. We recognized, however, that there were "serious questions about the validity of the data and assumptions underlying Petitioner's calculations." For example, . . . it was "wrong to assume that all workers in industries dealing with chromium in some way or another are exposed to 100 µg/m³ hexavalent chromium, every working day for 45 years." We likewise observed that some workers breathe through respirators that protect them from exposure to chromium, and that Public Citizen's calculations failed to distinguish between lead chromate and other hexavalent chromium compounds with potentially different carcinogenicities. Finally, and most importantly, we were troubled by the Crump Report's failure to control for smoking and asbestos inhalation, two factors likely related to lung cancer incidence.

Based on this imperfect science and our recognition that "OSHA . . . possesses enormous technical expertise we lack," we concluded that we were "not in a position to tell the Secretary how to do her job." OSHA offers several reasons for us to continue that deferential posture. First, OSHA allegedly "has not yet completed its evaluation of the Hopkins study." It points out that the study's authors acknowledged certain limitations of their data, particularly in estimating the cumulative exposure for different individuals in the cohort, and also that the study did not address the previous dispute over whether all hexavalent chromium compounds present the same degree of risk. OSHA summarizes that, "even assuming the Hopkins study is the most useful single study available, it does not answer all of the technically complex questions about carcinogenicity and other health effects that OSHA would need to resolve in developing a Cr VI rule."

Second, OSHA alleges that "Public Citizen virtually ignores the other critical components of a Cr VI rulemaking." One of OSHA's requirements is that a standard must be technologically feasible, and given that one governing hexavalent chromium would apply to numerous industries, the feasibility analysis is quite complex. While it admits that it has successfully addressed issues of comparable complexity in the past, it notes that "these efforts have not been successful where courts have found insufficient rigor in the agency's analysis of scientific and economic issues." See, e.g., Indus. Union Dep't; AFL-CIO v. OSHA, 965 F.2d 962 (11th Cir. 1992). The bottom line, OSHA states, is that "[t]he belief that a chemical may be carcinogenic does not lead easily to the appropriate PEL for that chemical," and forcing it to issue a rule prematurely will likely result in that rule being overturned in court.

We agree with OSHA that the evidence may be imperfect, that the feasibility inquiry is formidable, and that premature rulemaking is undesirable. But given the history chronicled above, we find these concerns insufficient to justify further delay in regulating hexavalent chromium. First, while it is true that the Hopkins study's authors recognized certain limitations of their data, the epidemiological data as of the mid-1990s were sufficient for EPA, ATSDR, NIOSH, the National Toxicology Program, and the International Agency for Research on Cancer to find hexavalent chromium carcinogenic; for OSHA to commence a rulemaking proceeding; and for OSHA's contractor to estimate that exposures at a fraction of the current PEL would result in significant excess cancer deaths.

Moreover, OSHA based its delay on its professed desire to consider that study because of its superior data and ability to control for smoking. It was released in August 2000, more than two years ago, but it has hardly facilitated the rulemaking process.[5] OSHA now offers it as a justification for further inaction, claiming that it has not completed its evaluation of the study's findings and that the study's conclusions "can be much better assessed when experts in the field have had the opportunity to review and criticize it."

We are unconvinced. Public Citizen points out that, as the study was published in a peer-reviewed journal, experts in the field have already had the opportunity to criticize it. Notably, in the two years since its publication, "no response or letter criticizing it has been published." Especially since many of the study's findings have been available since 1995, the time for examining it has passed; we also note that, if further professional criticism is absolutely necessary, the notice-and-comment process will provide an ample opportunity.

Nor do we find persuasive OSHA's broad assertion that the Hopkins study "does not answer *all* of the technically complex questions . . . that OSHA would need to resolve in developing a Cr VI rule." This is obviously true, but without more it is irrelevant, for the Occupational Safety and Health Act does not *require* scientific certainty in the rulemaking process. Indeed, read fairly, the Act virtually forbids delay in pursuit of certainty—it requires regulation "on the basis of the best *available* evidence," 29 U.S.C. §655(b)(5) (emphasis added), and courts have warned that "OSHA cannot let workers suffer while it awaits the Godot of scientific certainty." *United Steelworkers of Am. v. Marshall*, 647 F.2d 1189, 1266 (D.C. Cir. 1980).

OSHA points to one specific shortcoming of the Hopkins study—that it "did not address the previous dispute over whether all hexavalent chromium compounds present the same degree of risk." That is indeed a question it did not resolve, and this uncertainty is the principal topic of [the brief filed by the intervenor, an industry advocate], which argues that the lead chromate used in pigments is not as carcinogenic as other hexavalent chromium compounds. The Hopkins study casts no light on this issue because its test population did not work in the pigment industry, but even without better data than that which existed in *Oil Workers* in 1997, we find this uncertainty insufficient to delay rulemaking further. Even if the chromate in pigments is not carcinogenic, an argument that, tellingly, OSHA itself does not offer, requiring concrete findings on this distinction would effectively hold hostage the thousands of workers who are exposed to non-pigment hexavalent chromium. We will not sanction that result when [OSHA flagged this issue in the prior litigation four years ago].

Finally, while we are sympathetic to OSHA's claim that a thorough feasibility analysis is both highly important and quite difficult, we cannot allow an imperfect analysis to justify indefinite delay. OSHA first announced a rulemaking nine years ago, and by its own account it has been examining the issue through NIOSH for at least four years. OSHA does not explain why this particular feasibility determination requires an extreme length of time, and it does not offer even a projection of how much time it might ultimately require. In such a situation, our traditional agency deference begins to resemble judicial abdication, and we conclude that scientific uncertainties and technical complexities, while no doubt considerable, can no longer justify delay. Judges on this court are not paid to decide the easy cases, and neither is OSHA.

---

5. Indeed, the Hopkins study's results were first presented publicly in 1995.

Difficult challenges go with the territory, and courts and agencies regularly surmount them. The notice-and-comment process should itself provide a fertile forum for gathering information on feasibility.

C.   Do Competing Priorities Justify OSHA's Delay?

[OSHA argues that it exercised its discretion to concentrate its resources elsewhere. For example, in 1999 and 2000, OSHA "focused most of its rulemaking resources on issuing an ergonomics standard before the end of the former Administration's term." Because the Clinton Administration placed such great emphasis on quickly finalizing those standards, the process was remarkably compressed; OSHA issued a proposed rule on November 23, 1999, and a final rule less than a year later, on November 14, 2000, "a timetable that required tremendous agency resources."]

OSHA represents that the delays became worse when the Bush administration took office, [given the administration's directive not to approve new standards without approval of the new agency head, the delay in the appointment of an agency head, and the September 11 attacks and anthrax mailings].

We do not lightly discount these admittedly significant competing priorities . . . [but] we reach the ineluctable conclusion that hexavalent chromium has progressively fallen by the wayside. This is unacceptable. . . .

D.   What Is the Proper Remedy?

Public Citizen requests that we direct OSHA to issue a proposed rule within 90 days, and to submit a schedule for finalizing the rule within 12 months thereafter. Neither OSHA's brief nor its recent announcement contains a proposed timetable, but it insists that Public Citizen's proposed pace of rulemaking "is unrealistic in light of the procedural, consultative, and analytical duties that constrain OSHA rulemaking and the historical time frames required for OSHA to develop a toxic chemical standard." For example, the Regulatory Flexibility Act, 5 U.S.C. §§601-12, requires it to prepare a regulatory flexibility analysis if the rule will have a "significant economic impact upon a substantial number of small entities," a mandate this rulemaking is sure to trigger. Also, the Small Business Regulatory Enforcement Fairness Act, 5 U.S.C. §609(b), requires it to convene a review panel to address the rule's potential impacts on small entities. Finally, Executive Order 12866 requires that OSHA submit its proposal, including a detailed economic analysis, to the Office of Management and Budget, which is to review it within 90 days.

While we are certain that the time for action has arrived, we are cognizant of our lack of expertise in setting permissible exposure limits, and we recognize the damage that an ill-considered limit might cause. At oral argument, we presented the parties with a somewhat novel possibility: that they would submit to a course of mediation, conducted by a senior judge of this Court, in which they might work together toward a realistic timetable that we would then enforce. Both sides stated their willingness to engage in this process, and we think it the most promising way to develop a reasonable and workable schedule. We are, however, highly aware that this presents yet another opportunity for potentially indefinite bargaining and delay. We will therefore submit the matter to mediation for a period not to exceed sixty days, after which time, if the parties have not reached an accord, the panel will promulgate a schedule it deems appropriate. . . .

NOTES

1. *Even More Delays.* The Third Circuit's decision by no means ended the matter. When the parties could not agree, the Court adopted the mediator's recommendation and directed OSHA to publish a proposed rule no later than October 4, 2004, and to publish a final standard no later than January 18, 2006. The Court subsequently granted OSHA an extension to February 28, 2006. *See* National Metal Finishing Resource Center, *OSHA Hexavalent Chromium PEL Page, available at* http://www.nmfrc.org/compliance/pel2.cfm. OSHA published its final rule that day, *see* 71 Fed. Reg. 10099-10385 (Feb. 28, 2006), some 13 years after OSHA agreed that there was evidence that the level of exposure to hexavalent chromium allowed by the 1971 interim standard posed an excessive risk to worker health. The final standard provides for a PEL of 5.0 μg/m^3, as opposed to the 0.5 μg/m^3 for which Public Citizen had petitioned. Thereafter, both Public Citizen and industry representatives filed suit challenging the final standard. OSHA issued corrections to the rule on June 23, 2006, and an amendment on October 30, 2006, reflecting a settlement agreement with various parties. *See* 71 Fed. Reg. 36,008 (June 23, 2006); 71 Fed. Reg. 63,238 (Oct. 30, 2006). Nevertheless, litigation continued on both the standard and OSHA's decision to alter certain employee notification requirements. Ultimately, the Third Circuit upheld the promulgated rules, except for the change in the notification requirements, which it remanded back to OSHA for further consideration. *See Public Citizen Health Research Group v. U.S. Dept. of Labor*, 557 F.3d 165 (3d Cir. 2009). Yet further delays occurred in implementing inspection and compliance programs; for example, the National Emphasis Program targeting hexavalent chromium did not go into effect until February 2010. *See* OSHA, *National Emphasis Program—Hexavalent Chromium*, Directive No. CPL 02-02-076 (Feb. 23, 2010), *available at* http://www.osha.gov/OshDoc/Directive_pdf/CPL_02-02-076.pdf.

2. *A Rare, Hard-Fought Victory.* As the history of this case and the tone of the court's opinion suggests, federal courts are loath to order agencies, including OSHA, to promulgate rules. Indeed, courts view themselves as far better equipped to review and reject agency actions, although, even in that context, they must be deferential to the agency's determinations. And inaction by OSHA is common.

So why, ultimately, did the Third Circuit take such an exceptional step in this case and order OSHA to act? Do you think the court overstepped? Certainly, some question whether a court should ever interfere when an agency chooses not to regulate, absent a clear congressional directive to act. What reasons, if any, justify court interference with an agency's discretion to determine whether to engage in the rulemaking process?

3. *The Role of Scientific and Technological Uncertainty.* Assuming OSHA's concerns about scientific and technological uncertainty were not simply a *post hoc* justification for dragging its feet, this case demonstrates how uncertainty arguments from regulated industries have deterred OSHA from acting, particularly with regard to allegedly harmful chemicals and substances. Consider how the substantial evidence requirement, combined with scientific and technological uncertainty regarding health risks and feasibility, may affect OSHA's decision making. First, developing the science to determine risk and feasibility takes time and resources. Given the nature of the inquiry, OSHA itself may have good-faith doubts about the science even after accumulating greater knowledge. For example, it may question the causal connection between exposure and disease, the levels of exposure that pose a danger, whether all forms of the substance pose equal problems, and so forth. Beyond this, OSHA officials know what to expect downstream—if the agency forges ahead with the rule-making process where any doubt exists, industry groups will challenge the scientific and technological bases for the proposed standards during the notice and comment period. *See generally* Michaels & Monforton, *supra*. If these challenges fail, these groups can seek relief from Congress and, if that fails, they may bring suit challenging the final version of the rule.

That said, what is the alternative? Should the requirements for OSHA to promulgate specific standards be more lenient? Alternative approaches to rule making or judicial review might strike the balance in favor of greater regulation to the benefit of workers. For example, Congress could amend the statute to provide for more deferential "arbitrary and capricious" review or to streamline procedures by reducing opportunities for public comment and participation. On the other hand, given the substantial costs on regulated employers, might it be good policy to require OSHA both to engage in a full notice and comment process and to make the rigorous showing of significant risk and feasibility that the law currently requires?

4. *Other Factors Contributing to Agency Inaction.* Uncertainty clearly was not the only reason for OSHA's inaction on hexavalent chromium. The various other reasons—limited resources, unforeseen events, other priorities, new procedural hurdles, changing agency leadership, and ideological preferences—played critical roles. Won't at least one of these factors always be present as OSHA attempts to regulate workplace hazards? If so, is this simply a story of a lack of political will or, alternatively, "capture" of the agency or Congress by powerful interest groups? In other words, perhaps OSHA's approach to promulgating standards cannot be fixed. If it can be, how and by whom?

b. Enforcement

OSHA enforcement historically has been largely of the "command and control" variety. That is, OSHA inspectors issue citations for violations of specific standards or of the general duty clause. These citations may range from "de minimis," ones with no penalty, to "serious" and "willful" violations, whose penalties can range up to $70,000. For a failure to abate violations, a $7,000 penalty per day is possible. Citations are not initially enforced in court. Rather, if contested, they are adjudicated administratively by the Occupational Safety and Health Review Commission ("OSHRC"), composed of three commissioners appointed by the president. Only after the OSHRC decision can an employer seek review in the appropriate court of appeals. Criminal sanctions are also available, but only when an employer makes false statements to an inspector, intentionally interferes with an inspection, or has actual knowledge of a dangerous condition that leads to a fatality. OSHA also provides some ancillary protections, including antiretaliation and disclosure provisions.

OSHA engages in regular inspections and will also inspect employers in response to employee complaints. Generally, inspections are conducted without advance notice, but, absent OSHA obtaining a warrant, an employer can refuse to allow access to its establishment. OSHA need not demonstrate probable cause of a criminal violation to obtain an administrative search warrant, but it must have specific evidence of a violation or show satisfaction of reasonable standards for conducting the particular inspection. *See Marshall v. Barlow's, Inc.*, 436 U.S. 307 (1978). In many instances, however, employers waive the warrant requirement. Why do you think that is? *See generally* Note, *The Permissible Scope of OSHA Complaint Inspections*, 49 U. CHI. L. REV. 203 (1982).

Data from recent years provides some sense of the scope of OSHA's enforcement activity. In 2011, OSHA conducted 40,614 inspections and found 85,514 violations of OSHA's standards and regulations, of which about three quarters were "serious." In 2016, the agency conducted fewer inspections (31,948) and violations decreased substantially, to 58,702. The percentage of violations deemed serious was close to the same. *See* OSHA, 2016 Enforcement Summary, *available at* https://www.osha. gov/dep/2016_enforcement_summary.html. Note that these inspections are supplemented by those conducted by cooperating state agencies; in 2017, for example, the number of such inspections was 43,551. OSHA, COMMONLY USED STATISTICS (2017) [hereinafter "OSHA CUS"], *available at* https://www.osha.gov/oshstats/ commonstats.html. Although the number of inspections and cited violations have increased over historic lows in the mid-1990s, both total inspections and found violations are down dramatically from earlier years. *See* Public Citizen Health Research Group, *Report Detailing Occupational Safety and Health Administration Enforcement Actions from 1972 through 1998* (HRG Publication #1494), *available at* http://www. citizen.org/publications/release.cfm?ID=6693. Moreover, since OSHA was enacted in 1970, workplace deaths have fallen from 38 to 14 per day and occupational injury and illness rates have fallen from 10.9 incidents per 100 workers to 2.9. *See* OSHA CUS, *supra*.

Still, OSHA's resources and capacity remain severely limited. Indeed, despite the growth in the economy and the workforce, OSHA's budget declined from 2016 to 2018. *See id.* Along with those working with state partners, OSHA can muster only about 2,100 inspectors (fewer than in earlier years). To put this in perspective, because OSHA is responsible for the health and safety of 130 million workers (employed at more than 8 million worksites), this translates into about one inspector for every 59,000 workers. *See id.*

A very important aspect of OSHA's structure is what it does not permit: Unlike statutes such as Title VII and the FLSA, OSHA does not authorize private enforcement. As *Public Citizen* suggests, private parties may be able in extreme cases to compel OSHA to promulgate standards, but they cannot compel it to enforce those standards against particular violators. Occasionally, OSHA standards have been used to establish a standard of care in suits based on other theories, such as negligence. *See generally* Rothstein, *supra*, §§501, 502, and 513. Nevertheless, given the general absence of private enforcement, the significance of administrative enforcement (or the lack thereof) cannot be overstated.

2. OSHA's Troubled Past and Present, and Its Uncertain Future

The implementation and enforcement of OSHA have been much criticized from all sides. Employers have complained about the burdensomeness of the regulations, the "nitpickiness" of inspectors and excessiveness of citations, and the lack of recognition for good-faith efforts to comply. These types of criticisms and related advocacy efforts have had an impact, including the repeal of some of the interim regulations, the limited promulgation of new and permanent standards, successful challenges to certain OSHA initiatives, and reductions in OSHA's enforcement resources. In addition, as discussed in the *Public Citizen* case above, various changes in the law—including the Regulatory Flexibility Act and the Small Business Regulatory Enforcement Fairness Act—have imposed constraints on OSHA's ability to promulgate and enforce new standards.

On the other hand, labor and workplace safety advocates have long bemoaned OSHA's ineffectiveness in purging the workplace of preventable safety hazards, despite the overall decline in reported workplace fatalities, injuries, and violations. Many have expressed concern about the various substantive and procedural barriers to OSHA's promulgation of new specific regulations. But most critics have focused on enforcement, arguing that OSHA's efforts and the penalties resulting from violations are woefully inadequate. They argue, for example, that there are far too few inspections and resulting sanctions to create sufficient incentives for employers to comply with OSHA's mandates, particularly given the relatively weak penalties for most violations. *See, e.g.*, Charlotte Alexander, *Transmitting the Costs of Unsafe Work*, 54 AM. BUS. L.J. 463, 480-81 (2017); Susan Bisom Rapp, *What We Learn in Troubled Times: Deregulation and Safe Work in the New Economy*, 55 WAYNE L. REV. 1197, 1211, (2009) ("given its current level of resources, OSHA can conduct inspections of 'each workplace under its jurisdiction on average once every 133 years.'"). In addition, the effectiveness of OSHA's antiretaliation regime has been the subject of much criticism. *See, e.g.*, GAO, WHISTLEBLOWER PROTECTION: SUSTAINED MANAGEMENT ATTENTION NEEDED TO ADDRESS LONG-STANDING PROGRAM WEAKNESSES (August 2010), *available at* http://www.gao.gov/new.items/d10722.pdf; *see also* Jarod S. Gonzalez, *A Pot of Gold at the End of the Rainbow: An Economic Incentives-Based Approach to OSHA Whistleblowing*, 14 EMPL. RTS & EMPLOY. POL'Y J. 325 (2010) (discussing the weaknesses and limitations of OSHA's existing antiretaliation regime). In the eyes of these critics, the long-term trend toward reduced enforcement in the OSHA context and deregulation more generally have simply made things worse.

The vexing questions, then, are the extent to which the critiques of OSHA, from either side, are valid, and if so, whether realistic reforms might make the regime more effective. These questions, and the sharp differences of opinion on both the agency's role and how to conduct regulatory oversight have produced disparate approaches in recent administrations.

For example, partially in response to industry pressure, during the George W. Bush administration in particular, OSHA shifted its focus towards greater self-regulation—that is, allowing employers to avoid an ordinary inspection schedule if they demonstrate their ability to comply with health and safety standards and improve their safety records. All of these programs were voluntary. Industry groups were able to defeat the one compelled self-regulation program—the Cooperative Compliance

Program—that they viewed as imposing obligations that were too onerous. *See* Orly Lobel, *Interlocking Regulatory and Industrial Relations: The Governance of Workplace Safety*, 57 ADMIN. L. REV. 1071, 1124-28 (2005).

In her article discussing the trends at the time, Professor Lobel discussed how efforts to improve OSHA and, more generally, workplace safety and health, had shifted away from the traditional bilateral debate between more or less regulation. For example, she discussed recent OSHA reforms that focus on neither top-down enforcement nor further deregulation but rather on promoting safety and health compliance or "self-regulation" efforts within regulated firms. Examples of this "third way" include OSHA's longstanding but then recently expanded Voluntary Protection Program ("VPP") and its Safety and Health Achievement Recognition Program ("SHARP"), both of which were designed to reward firms with certain levels of safety achievement and self-regulatory structures. The reward included exemption from general, scheduled inspections. *Id.* at 1105-07 (footnotes and citations omitted).

Early studies showed these programs to be successful. *See id.* at 1108 (noting that a GAO study "found that participation in the programs has considerably reduced injury and illness rates, improved relationships with OSHA, improved productivity, and decreased worker compensation costs"). Looking ahead, Professor Lobel noted the potential of compliance-centered regimes, although cautioning that, to prevent such public/private cooperation from becoming merely deregulation in disguise, steps must be taken to ensure that OSHA will indeed return to direct enforcement where firms fail to comply or improve safety through self-governance and that workers—the stakeholders OSHA is supposed to protect—have a voice in the governance. *See id.* at 1112-15.

In a contemporaneous article, Professor Cynthia Estlund critiqued the new self-governance approach under OSHA. *See generally* Cynthia Estlund, *Rebuilding the Law of the Workplace in an Era of Self-Regulation*, 105 COLUM. L. REV. 319 (2005). Like Lobel, she discussed both the potential promise in self-regulation and the dangers of insufficient corresponding government oversight and the lack of worker involvement. Professor Estlund asserted that, for this kind of self-regulatory approach to be effective in achieving statutory goals, it must embody tripartite involvement of workers, employers, and government regulators. In addition, appropriate incentives must be sustained through ongoing monitoring by independent outsiders, the threat of sanctions and civil lawsuits for noncompliance with safety standards, and meaningful antiretaliation protection for whistleblowers. *See id.*

Unfortunately, agency leaders appear not to have heeded fully these kinds of suggestions and warnings. A 2009 GAO report found that, while VPP programs expanded significantly during the last years of the Bush administration, OSHA failed to develop adequate internal controls and mechanisms for assessing the programs' performance. The agency therefore was unable to ensure that only qualified worksites were allowed to participate in the program and that participants remained compliant with health and safety standards. The GAO also found significant rates of noncompliance among certain types of participating firms. *See generally* GAO, OSHA's VOLUNTARY PROTECTIONS PROGRAM: IMPROVED OVERSIGHT AND CONTROLS WOULD BETTER ENSURE PROGRAM QUALITY (May 2009), *available at* http://www.gao.gov/new.items/d09395.pdf.

In light of these findings and other enforcement priorities, the Obama Administration shifted resources away from voluntary compliance to other OSHA programs. *See* Steve Tuckey, *OSHA's Deeper Bite: The Obama Administration Injects New Power into the Occupational Safety Agency as Employers Find Themselves on the Defensive*, CBS Money Watch.com, April 1, 2010, *available at* http://find-articles.com/p/articles/mi_m0BJK/is_3_21/ai_n53519363/. Although it chose to scale back and tighten the VPP program rather than abandon it, the Obama administration's efforts, too, have come under scrutiny. *See* DOL OIG, Voluntary Protection Program: Controls Are Not Sufficient to Ensure Only Worksites with Exemplary Safety and Health Systems Remain in Program (December 16, 2013), *available at* http://www.oig.dol.gov/public/reports/oa/2014/02-14-201-10-105.pdf.

Moving beyond self-regulatory approaches, the Obama Administration turned its emphasis to greater agency and state enforcement efforts, including implementing a number of new regulatory initiatives, targeting enforcement in particular sectors, modestly increasing OSHA's budget, and hiring additional inspectors. *See, e.g.*, Laura Walter, *DOL 2011 Budget Request Includes OSHA Increase, Focus on Enforcement*, EHS Today, Feb. 1, 2010, *available at* http://ehstoday.com/standards/osha/dol-budget-request-osha-increase-focus-enforcement-2414/. As discussed above, these initiatives may have had some impact, as the number of violations dropped from 2011 to 2016 even as inspections declined. *See* 2016 Enforcement Summary, *supra*. Nevertheless, given OSHA's limited resources, few doubt that the agency never uncovers many violations.

The pendulum has swung again in the wake of the election of President Trump. His administration made clear early on that it intended to reduce what it perceives as regulatory burdens on businesses generally, and, accordingly, it moved quickly to reduce OSHA's rulemaking activities. *See, e.g.*, Stephen Lee & Marissa Horn, *Trump's OSHA Slashes Many Worker Safety Rulemaking Plans*, Bloomberg BNA (July 20, 2017), *available at* https://www.bna.com/trumps-osha-slashes-n73014462036/. OSHA inspections also slightly declined in 2017, and, again, the agency's budget shrunk modestly as well. *See* OSHA CUS, *supra*. While the administration's deregulatory emphasis and early changes have received substantial criticism from worker, health and safety, and environmental advocates, it remains to be seen what overall impact these changes will have on worker health and safety.

PROBLEM

12-1. Suppose you work for the Workplace Safety and Health Institute, a nonpartisan "think tank" devoted to developing and advocating innovative and efficient ways to improve workplace safety and reduce work-related injuries and diseases. Given what you have seen in this chapter, what kinds of legal reforms might you advocate? In thinking about solutions, consider all possibilities, including, *inter alia*, greater direct regulation and enforcement of the "command and control" variety (more regulations and inspections and greater sanctions); alternative regulatory arrangements that seek to promote "third way" self-regulation; greater protection against retaliation for whistleblowers or injured workers; reintroduction of tort liability for employer negligence; enhanced civil and criminal liability for responsible supervisors or officers; and employee empowerment, including greater protections for collective bargaining and bargaining units. At a general level, what are the costs and benefits of these various approaches? In light of the nature of the modern workplace, what are the practical impediments to implementation? Which methods might work in combination, and which would not?

Part Seven

RISK MANAGEMENT

13

Managing the Risks and Costs of Liability in Employment Disputes

To a considerable extent, this entire book has been about "risk management." Private ordering allows parties to structure their relationship as they see fit, creating certain legal obligations and limiting others. Chapters 1 through 3 dealt with the initial choice to create an employment relationship and on what terms. We saw that contracting parties can sometimes avoid "employment" altogether, a strategy often pursued by firms seeking to avoid the legal liabilities associated with that status. Even where an employment relationship exists, the ability to set terms contractually—coupled with the at-will presumption—often permits employers to limit their obligations to employees, for instance, by disclaiming contractual right to job security.

Such risk management is largely in the hands of employers. Most workers face a take-it-or-leave-it choice as to whether a particular job carries employment status and the terms of any relationship that may be offered. Chapter 3 dealt primarily with the rather exceptional, highly valued worker, who may be able to trade salary and other benefits for enhanced job security or other favorable employment terms. More often, however, freedom of contract merely affords workers an ability to take or reject what the employer offers; they must then work with the tools that the public law regime provides to "employees," assuming they can establish that status, to maximize their position.

This does not mean, however, that the employer has free rein in structuring work relationships. Any decision it makes involves trade-offs. We saw in Chapters 1, 5, and 12 that the employer that avoids tort liability to workers by structuring its relationships as "employment" thereby assumes tort liability to third parties for its workers' actions and subjects itself to the workers' compensation regime. It also undertakes a host of other statutory risks and duties to its employees, including the antidiscrimination laws and the Family and Medical Leave Act, treated in Chapters 9 and 10, and the wage laws discussed in Chapter 11.

Moreover, employers cannot always be confident that their election of a particular status or set of terms will actually determine their legal obligations. We saw in Chapter 1 that the test for employment status is multi-factored and dependent on circumstances beyond the intent of the parties. Similarly, although employers may designate a particular relationship at will, alterations in at-will status may occur due to the promises and assurances of supervisors, written employment manuals, or implicit company policies and practices. Thus, despite the availability of contract law, and regardless of the ultimate structure chosen, both employers and employees often find their legal relationship ambiguous.

Perhaps most importantly, there are significant limits on the extent to which the law permits private ordering in workplace relationships. For instance, we saw in Chapter 8 that employers can use noncompetition agreements and related contract mechanisms to safeguard their trade secret rights and to reduce the risk of employee defection in an at-will world. However, the enforceability of such agreements is constrained by public policy, and employers are often unable to predict whether such contracts will provide the protection they seek. In addition, employers have very limited ability to structure or restructure terms of employment mandated by statutory law. An employer may not, for instance, limit its liability under state workers' compensation law in exchange for larger payments, nor may it substitute time off for overtime pay under federal wage and hour law, even if both parties would prefer that arrangement. And, of course, employers have no—or very limited—ability to "waive" substantive obligations arising under constitutional, tort, and antidiscrimination laws discussed in Chapters 4, 5, 7, 9, and 10.

In sum, the patchwork of laws governing workplace relationships—a combination of contract law principles operating against a backdrop of tort rules and general and employment-specific statutes and regulations—presents serious challenges to the cost-conscious, compliance-oriented employer. Thus, an important question to think about as you complete your study of employment law is the interaction between firms and workers in what might be described as "second level" efforts at risk management. These techniques are "second" level because they attempt to reduce employers' risks entailed by the initial policy choice as to whether to offer employment at all and in what form. They include efforts to ensure compliance with the law, prevent disputes, and reduce the costs associated with legal disputes when they inevitably arise. Larger employers frequently consult with attorneys and human resource experts before implementing policies or making personnel decisions to avoid running afoul of the law or even appearing to do so for fear of drawing a costly (even if ultimately unsuccessful) lawsuit. Similarly, where an employee contests a decision, employers frequently seek cost-effective ways of dealing with the dispute short of litigation, such as private resolution or settlement.

This chapter explores several ways in which employers respond to the risk of litigation and legal liability and employee responses to such efforts. It begins in Section A with employer efforts to prevent and resolve disputes in-house, with particular emphasis on sexual harassment. As a result of two seminal Supreme Court decisions on vicarious liability for hostile work environment claims, employers have strong incentives to take precautions against harassment and respond aggressively if it occurs.

The chapter then turns in Section B to employer termination practices and the use of severance and release agreements to avoid possible litigation. Particularly in large layoff situations, employers typically promise post-termination pay, and perhaps other benefits, in exchange for the employee's promise not to sue the employer.

Section C then considers several mechanisms that employers have used to reduce risks in litigation. The first is the increasingly common practice of requiring employees to sign pre-dispute arbitration agreements. Under such agreements, parties do not waive or settle the merits of claims but rather agree that, should a dispute arise, they will resolve it through a private arbitration process rather than through traditional litigation. The second is the use of stipulated damages clauses to safeguard employer interests by ensuring a monetary remedy is available in the event that an employee breaches its obligations to the employer.

Section D turns to yet another kind of risk management—passing the risk to others. It addresses the use of insurance as a means of managing the costs of liability to employees. Finally, Section E very briefly considers bankruptcy, which might be viewed, at least in some contexts, as the ultimate risk-management technique of employers.

As you read, you will understand that the study of risk management begins with techniques employers implement, but, as in the rest of this book, the focus quickly shifts to the responses of employees and the policy choices implicated in deciding how far the law should permit private ordering in this setting. From the employer's perspective, consider whether these risk management tools are effective in achieving employer goals and, if not, how they might be made more effective. Equally important, consider the effects of such measures on employees' ability to vindicate their rights. Are there places where private ordering has gone too far?

A. PREVENTIVE MEASURES AND CORRECTIVE ACTION

1. Anticipating and Responding to Hostile Work Environment Harassment

The best way to avoid litigation expenses is to resolve disputes internally, and employers use a variety of methods to do this. A common technique is to develop internal procedures through which employees can raise concerns before they develop into a legal problem. For instance, many companies have written complaint procedures under which employees are directed to report their concerns to designated individuals and follow up with reports to successively higher levels of management if the employee remains dissatisfied. A less formal approach is to establish an "open door" policy that invites employees to speak to any manager, or particular management personnel, on an as-needed basis. Depending on the employer, these approaches may be adopted in tandem and may have a greater or lesser degree of formality and structure.

For example, a Publix Supermarket Policy provides:

> It is just a fact of life that occasionally there will be problems and misunderstandings among people. If something bothers you, or if you need clarification of a Publix policy or procedure, please talk to a manager about it. Always remember, as a Publix associate you can talk to anyone in management. Experience has shown, however, that many problems can best be worked out by the following steps:

1. Discuss your problem or raise your question directly with your immediate Supervisor/Manager/Department Head.
2. If the matter is not resolved or you still have a question or concern, go to the next highest level of management (for example, Store Manager, District Manager, Regional Director of Retail Operations, or a Vice-President).
3. Just remember—you can discuss your problem with anyone in management all the way to the top level. Also, your Divisional Human Resources Department is available to assist you with any matter at any time, and you may contact the Employee Assistance Department in Lakeland for confidential counseling.

Madray v. Publix Supermarkets, Inc., 208 F.3d 1290, 1295 (11th Cir. 2000).

Although such policies are common, they are not without some risk to employers. Employees have sometimes attempted to use open door policies as the basis of a contract claim when they are discharged. They might allege, for instance, that the employer failed to follow or participate in all steps of its process or that they were retaliated against for invoking the policy. While the Publix policy does not explicitly promise nonretaliation, some grievance policies purport to immunize employees who invoke company procedures. Thus, an occasional court has recognized a cause of action where the employee can show that she was retaliated against for pursuing open door avenues. *See, e.g., Vida v. El Paso Employees' Fed. Credit Union*, 885 S.W.2d 177 (Tex. App. 1994) (cause of action if employer retaliated against plaintiff for use of its grievance procedure when the employee manual explicitly assured that no retaliation would occur). Most courts have rejected such claims, however, in some cases because of language disclaiming the binding nature of the policy and in other instances because the policy did not constitute a sufficiently definite promise. *See, e.g., Haynes v. Level 3 Communs., LLC*, 167 F. App'x 712 (10th Cir. 2006) (employer's open-door policy too vague to constitute a contract or support a claim of promissory estoppel); *Stefano v. Micron Tech., Inc.*, 65 F. App'x 139 (9th Cir. 2003) (existence of open-door policy did not bring plaintiff within any exception to at-will employment).

As a result, there is relatively little legal downside in adopting such policies, and they have significant advantages. In addition to limiting costly litigation, they may result in more favorable outcomes for both employees and employers. While litigation often entails a permanent severing of the employment relationship, successful internal resolution can enable the aggrieved employee to continue working. If the attempted resolution is not successful and the dispute winds up in litigation (whether court or arbitration), the employer's internal response can be a critical aid in its defense.

This is most true with respect to employment discrimination. In the Title VII context, the Supreme Court decided two cases in 1998 dealing with a sexual hostile work environment created by a supervisor in which employer efforts to prevent and respond to harassment figured prominently. In *Burlington Industries, Inc. v. Ellerth*, 524 U.S. 742 (1998), the harassment took place while the supervisor and victim were away from the office on a business trip. In the other, *Faragher v. Boca Raton*, 524 U.S. 775 (1998), the victims were lifeguards who were harassed at a beach remote from the city employer. In both cases, the employees failed to complain about the harassment until after leaving their jobs. It was assumed for the purposes of the case that the conduct in question, if attributable to the employers, would have constituted actionable hostile environment harassment under Title VII, an issue you considered in Chapter 9. The employers essentially defended by arguing that they were not liable for the harassing conduct of the supervisors because the harassment did not result in any tangible employment action by the supervisor, such as a termination or demotion, and because the employees had not complained before leaving the company. Thus, the question before the Court was when an employer should be liable for harassing conduct, given lack of knowledge of the behavior by upper level management. This question is critical under Title VII since personal liability does not attach to an individual actor under the federal discrimination laws. *See* Rebecca Hanner White, *Vicarious and Personal Liability for Employment Discrimination*, 30 GA. L. REV. 509, 545-61 (1996). While some state antidiscrimination statutes provide for individual liability, *see, e.g., Elezovic v. Ford Motor Co.*, 697 N.W.2d 851, 861 (Mich. 2005), it can be difficult for plaintiffs to collect on those judgments. As a result, an employee typically has no recovery—despite having proven harassment in the workplace—if the employer is not liable for the actions of the harasser.

Drawing on agency principles, the *Ellerth* and *Faragher* opinions laid out the structure for employer liability for supervisory harassment. First, there is automatic employer liability when a "supervisor" subjects plaintiff to "a tangible employment action, such as discharge, demotion, or undesirable reassignment." *Faragher*, 524 U.S. at 808. In such cases, the employer's liability is absolute and not subject to any defense. Second, when such a supervisor subjects plaintiff to conduct that is *not* a tangible employment action, such as a contaminated work environment, the employer is liable but subject to an affirmative defense. The Court explained:

> When a supervisor makes a tangible employment decision, there is assurance the injury could not have been inflicted absent the [supervisor's] agency relation [with the employer]. A tangible employment action in most cases inflicts direct economic harm. As a general proposition, only a supervisor, or other person acting with the authority of the company, can cause this sort of injury. A co-worker can break a co-worker's arm as easily as a supervisor, and anyone who has regular contact with an employee can inflict psychological injuries by his or her offensive conduct. But one co-worker (absent some elaborate scheme) cannot dock another's pay, nor can one co-worker demote another. . . .
>
> Tangible employment actions are the means by which the supervisor brings the official power of the enterprise to bear on subordinates. A tangible employment decision requires an official act of the enterprise, a company act. . . . The supervisor often must obtain the imprimatur of the enterprise and use its internal processes.
>
> For these reasons, a tangible employment action taken by the supervisor becomes for Title VII purposes the act of the employer. Whatever the exact contours of the aided in the agency relation standard, its requirements will always be met when a supervisor takes a tangible employment action against a subordinate. . . .
>
> Whether the agency relation aids in commission of supervisor harassment which does not culminate in a tangible employment action is less obvious. . . . On the one hand, a supervisor's power and authority invests his or her harassing conduct with a particular threatening character, and in this sense, a supervisor always is aided by the agency relation. On the other hand, there are acts of harassment a supervisor might commit which might be the same acts a co-employee would commit, and there may be some circumstances where the supervisor's status makes little difference. . . .
>
> In order to accommodate the agency principles of vicarious liability for harm caused by misuse of supervisory authority, as well as Title VII's equally basic policies of encouraging forethought by employers and saving action by objecting employees, we adopt the following holding. . . . An employer is subject to vicarious liability to a

victimized employee for an actionable hostile environment created by a supervisor with immediate (or successively higher) authority over the employee. When no tangible employment action is taken, a defending employer may raise an affirmative defense to liability or damages. . . . The defense comprises two necessary elements: (a) that the employer exercised reasonable care to prevent and correct promptly any sexually harassing behavior, and (b) that the plaintiff employee unreasonably failed to take advantage of any preventive or corrective opportunities provided by the employer or to avoid harm otherwise. While proof that an employer had promulgated an antiharassment policy with complaint procedure is not necessary in every instance as a matter of law, the need for a stated policy suitable to the employment circumstances may appropriately be addressed in any case when litigating the first element of the defense. And while proof that an employee failed to fulfill the corresponding obligation of reasonable care to avoid harm is not limited to showing any unreasonable failure to use any complaint procedure provided by the employer, a demonstration of such failure will normally suffice to satisfy the employer's burden under the second element of the defense. No affirmative defense is available, however, when the supervisor's harassment culminates in a tangible employment action, such as discharge, demotion, or undesirable reassignment.

Ellerth, at 761-65.

Notice that the Court also alluded to a third scenario where employer liability for hostile work environment may be implicated: sexual harassment by a nonsupervisor, such as a co-worker (or even a customer). While *Ellerth* and *Faragher* did not address that situation directly, it is now clear that an employer is liable for nonsupervisory harassment only if it is negligent. *Vance v. Ball State University,* 570 U.S. 421, 427 (2013) ("[A]n employer is directly liable for an employee's unlawful harassment if the employer was negligent with respect to the offensive behavior."). Thus, co-worker hostile environment harassment will not result in liability unless the employer knew or should have known of the problem and did not reasonably address it. This is viewed as a form of direct liability for the employer's own negligence as opposed to vicarious liability for the conduct of the harasser. However, the employer's policies and practices are still relevant to this assessment, insofar as negligence may occur where the employer fails to have processes in place to discover and reasonably respond to harassing behavior. As a practical matter, then, the employer's mechanisms to prevent and correct harassment apply both in the supervisor harassment and co-worker harassment cases, although the burdens of proof are reversed in the two situations.

This structure obviously makes the question of whether the harasser is a "supervisor" critical for either automatic or presumptive liability, since harassment by a nonsupervisor subjects the employer to liability only if it is negligent. *Vance* defined the term very narrowly: "[A]n employer may be vicariously liable for an employee's unlawful harassment only when the employer has empowered that employee to take tangible employment actions against the victim, i.e., to effect a 'significant change in employment status, such as hiring, firing, failing to promote.'" *Id.* at 431. The dissent by Justice Ginsburg, joined by Justices Breyer, Kagan, and Sotomayor would have taken a more functional approach, including "employees who control the day-to-day schedules and assignments of others." *Id.* at 458.

The majority stressed the workability of such a definition in contrast to the "nebulous" definition of the EEOC and some lower courts since "supervisory status can usually be readily determined, generally by written documentation." *Id.* at 432. As for the suggestion that this approach leaves "employees unprotected against harassment by co-workers who possess the authority to inflict psychological injury by assigning unpleasant tasks or by altering the work environment in objectionable ways," the majority was unpersuaded: "[T]he victims will be able to prevail simply by showing that the employer was negligent in permitting this harassment to occur, and the jury should be instructed that the nature and degree of authority wielded by the harasser is an important factor to be considered in determining whether the employer was negligent." *Id.* at 445-46.

Despite the supposed clarity of the rule, there will be gray areas given the Court's indication that a person may be a supervisor even if he or she lacks hiring or firing authority but can effect "reassignment with significantly different responsibilities, or a decision causing a significant change in benefits." *Id.* at 431 (quoting *Ellerth*). Further, the *Vance* majority cautioned that:

> [E]ven if an employer concentrates all decisionmaking authority in a few individuals, it likely will not isolate itself from heightened liability under *Faragher* and *Ellerth*. If an employer does attempt to confine decisionmaking power to a small number of individuals, those individuals will have a limited ability to exercise independent discretion when making decisions and will likely rely on other workers who actually interact with the affected employee. Under those circumstances, the employer may be held to have effectively delegated the power to take tangible employment actions to the employees on whose recommendations it relies. *See Ellerth*.

Id. at 446-47. This obviously requires a focus on the realities of workplace decision making rather than the formalities and may implicate the cat's paw possibility we encountered in Chapter 9 at page 588.

In any event, post-*Vance*, most harassment cases will proceed as negligence claims, which means that the employee has the burden of proving the employer knew (or should have known) of the harassment and failed to respond reasonably. In most cases, then, there will be no strict liability and the burden of proof will shift from the employer having to establish an affirmative defense to the employee to establish both elements of her claim.

While allocating burdens might be very important in the litigation context, employers need to be more concerned with whether they are acting appropriately in preventing and correcting illegality. An employer who reacts reasonably to harassment in situations where no supervisor is involved will avoid direct liability, no matter how extreme the co-worker or customer harassment. And, absent a tangible employment action, an employer who takes appropriate steps to "prevent and correct" violations by supervisors will have satisfied the first prong of the affirmative defense and be halfway to avoiding vicarious liability.

Thus, *Ellerth* and *Faragher* understandably generated a cottage industry among lawyers and employment relation specialists about appropriate prevention and correction strategies. In the cases that follow, consider which employer actions are effective and which are not. Does the result in each case correspond to the effectiveness of the employer's response? In other words, does the existence of the affirmative defense encourage good employer practices, or does it encourage superficial efforts that simply make the employer look good in court, what has been dubbed "paper compliance" with the law? How could the employer have been more successful in avoiding and/or responding in each case?

≡ ## Nichols v. Tri-National Logistics, Inc.
≡ *809 F.3d 981 (8th Cir. 2016)*

MURPHY, Circuit Judge.

During 2011 and 2012 Rebecca Nichols drove a semi truck for Tri-National Logistics and RMR Driver Services (collectively "TNI"). During the period from May 25 until June 1, 2012 her fellow driver, James Paris, made unwelcome sexual advances. Then on a mandatory layover, he took away her truck keys and cell phone while continuing to proposition her. On May 25, 2012 Nichols reported his behavior to TNI and again up to June 1. After TNI terminated Nichols on June 25, 2012, citing her poor safety record, she brought this action charging TNI with discrimination on the basis of sex [and] termination in retaliation for her complaints. . . . The district court granted summary judgment to the defendants, and Nichols appeals. We reverse and remand.

I

[Although Rebecca Nichols had had a checkered record in working as a truck driver in 2011 and had been terminated for two incidents causing damage, she was rehired in October 2011 but informed that she could no longer drive alone and was responsible for finding her own driving partner. The first three partners all viewed her as an unsafe driver.] At that point Nichols began driving with James Paris. During their first trip Paris asked Nichols if she was interested in a romantic relationship. Nichols declined the offer but did not report it to TNI. She was scheduled to drive with Paris again from May 25 to 30. Their truck on that trip had a sleeping compartment in the back of the cab separated from the two driver seats by a curtain. According to her deposition testimony, Paris opened the cab's curtain and exposed himself while Nichols was driving. Upset, she told him to get dressed and "not to behave that way." According to Nichols, she immediately reported this incident to Melissa Foust in TNI's safety department.

Nichols testified that after this initial incident, Paris would often stand in the back of the cab while she was in the driver seat, lean over her in his underwear with his hands on the overhead compartment. Nichols testified that this happened on three or four occasions and that at least once his genitals were visible through a hole in his underwear. When asked at her deposition if he had ever done this more than once on the same day, Nichols replied "Not that I remember offhand." Nichols told Melissa Foust about similar conduct by Paris five times during their six-day trip. Nichols told Foust that she nevertheless did not want to change assignments before she could find another driving partner because she needed to work to pay her bills. Nichols also reported Paris' conduct to a TNI dispatcher, Bob Oliver, several days before May 30. According to her deposition, Oliver just told Nichols to try to "endure it" until the trip was complete, at which point he would help find her another partner.

After Nichols and Paris made their delivery in Laredo, Texas on May 30, they drove approximately three hours to his home in Pharr, Texas for a mandatory 34-hour rest period. Nichols testified that she went along with Paris to Pharr because she had been told another driver would not be available until after the rest period. Her request to take the truck to a place where she could stay overnight was denied because Paris had personal possessions in the cab. Nichols complained to the dispatcher, "Bob, I can't believe your telling me that. Didn't I just tell you maybe an hour ago that the man was trying to control me to no hilt and I couldn't get away from him?" Oliver responded "[t]ry to get along with him until you guys get back out on the road" and offered to pay half the cost of a motel room. Nichols decided to sleep in the truck instead on the night of May 30.

When Nichols asked Paris to take her to a motel on May 31, he asked her to sleep with him. He proposed that in return he would forgive an eight hundred dollar debt she owed him. Nichols testified that when she refused, Paris became "excessively mad," verbally degraded her, and twice forcibly took away her keys and cell phone. Eventually Paris did take Nichols to a motel where she spent the night, and on the next day he drove her back to Laredo where she got on the truck of another TNI driver, Chris Loya. Nichols then reported Paris' conduct in Pharr to TNI and said that it had caused her to feel abused, scared, and degraded.

[For the next few weeks Nichols drove with Loya who reported several safety violations by her. She was terminated on June 25, 2012.]

II. . .

The district court erred when analyzing Nichols' sexual harassment claim by not considering all that had occurred during the 34-hour rest period in Pharr. Under Title VII "offensive conduct does not necessarily have to transpire at the workplace in order for a juror reasonably to conclude that it created a hostile working environment." *Dowd v. United Steelworkers of Am., Local No. 286*, 253 F.3d 1093, 1102 (8th Cir. 2001). For example, in *Moring v. Arkansas Department of Corrections*, 243 F.3d 452 (8th Cir. 2001), a Title VII sexual harassment verdict was upheld on appeal where the offensive conduct had occurred in a hotel room after business hours. Nichols' time in Pharr was part of her work trip because she stopped there during a mandatory rest period, and Oliver told her he would only find her a driver after it was completed. The TNI truck was the only form of transport available to her at the time, and Oliver instructed Nichols she could not use it to drive to a motel.

The district court treated Nichols' decision to remain with the truck as her own choice, but the law does not require an employee to "quit or want to quit" when faced with a Hobson's choice. *See Davis v. U.S. Postal Serv.*, 142 F.3d 1334, 1341 (10th Cir. 1998). Such a requirement could force an employee to choose between her employment and her right to file a legal claim. The appropriate test is whether Nichols subjectively perceived her work environment as offensive.

The record contains genuine issues of material fact about all that happened on the trip and whether Nichols subjectively perceived Paris' actions as offensive. Nichols testified at her deposition that after he exposed himself, she was upset, told him not to behave that way, and complained immediately to TNI. Nichols also testified that she complained to Melissa Foust about Paris five times throughout the trip and reported to Oliver on June 1 that she felt abused, degraded, and scared. A psychiatrist who performed an independent medical examination testified that Nichols felt sexually harassed and suffered from depression and post-traumatic stress disorder due to Paris' aggressive conduct seeking sex. Although Nichols need not prove psychological injury, the psychiatrist's testimony bolsters her claim that she felt abused and harassed. *See Harris v. Forklift Sys., Inc.*, 510 U.S. 17, 22 (1993).

The district court erred in finding that Nichols did not report Paris' conduct to TNI until June 1. Nichols alleges that after Paris first exposed himself, she immediately reported it to Melissa Foust, a TNI safety department employee. . . . The test of whether a company is considered to have actual knowledge of harassing conduct is whether sufficient information comes "to the attention of someone who [had] the power to terminate the harassment." *Sandoval v. Am. Bldg. Maint. Indus., Inc.,* 578 F.3d 787, 802 (8th Cir. 2009).

When the evidence is viewed in the light most favorable to Nichols, her initial report to Foust about Paris must have been on Friday, May 25. It could not have been on Saturday, May 26 or Sunday, May 27 because Foust had not worked on the weekend. She could also not have initially reported during the last three days of the trip. When the evidence is viewed in the light most favorable to Nichols, there were four distinct days during which Paris leaned over her in his underwear. Foust's regular work hours were 8:00 AM to 5:00 PM, and the record reflects that on Friday, May 25 Nichols called TNI six times between 2:48 PM and 5:47 PM.

TNI argues that even if Nichols did report Paris' conduct prior to June 1, she has not shown that the company failed to take appropriate remedial action. The factors to consider when assessing the reasonableness of an employer's actions "include the amount of time that elapsed between the notice and remedial action, the options available to the employer, . . . and whether or not the measures ended the harassment." [*E.E.O.C. v.*] *CRST* [*Van Expedited, Inc.,* 679 F.3d 657, 692-93 (8th Cir. 2012)]. In *CRST,* we determined that the employer took appropriate remedial action by: "(1) removing the [harassed] woman from the truck as soon as practicable [within 24 hours], arranging overnight lodging at a motel and subsequent transportation to a CRST terminal at the company's expense; (2) requesting a written statement from the [victim]; (3) relieving the [victim] from future assignments with the alleged harasser; and (4) reprimanding the alleged harasser and barring him from team-driving with women indefinitely." We further noted that these "actions, not necessarily in combination, constitute the type of prompt and effective remedial action that our precedents prescribe."

Unlike the employer in *CRST,* TNI did not remove Paris from her truck within 24 hours, proceed to investigate the alleged misconduct, or reprimand Paris. Nichols notified TNI about his harassment on May 25, and seven days elapsed before TNI arranged for Chris Loya to pick her up in Laredo. TNI could have ordered Nichols to leave Paris' truck as soon as it learned about the problem and promptly help[ed] her find another driving partner, reprimanded Paris for his behavior, or arranged lodging for her in Laredo instead of permitting her to accompany him to Pharr on May 30. Instead, TNI allegedly took no action to remove her despite her consistent complaints of sexual harassment, but allowed her to go to Paris' apartment in Pharr, and stranded her there with no available alternate form of transportation.

The dissent suggests that TNI's response was reasonable in comparison to several other cases it cites, but none of these cases involved a workplace at all like the confined environment of an over the road truck cab in which Nichols was isolated for a multiday trip. . . . In contrast—in our case there are genuine issues of material fact in this record. These include whether TNI took appropriate remedial action in response to Nichols' personal plea to save her from further harassment. On this full record the district court erred by dismissing Nichols' sexual harassment claim. . . .

IV

[The Eighth Circuit affirmed the district court's grant of summary judgment to defendants on plaintiff's claim that she was fired in retaliation for reporting Paris' conduct to the company because of "sufficient evidence that TNI was concerned about Nichols' unsafe driving well before she complained about sexual harassment."].
SMITH, Circuit Judge, dissenting.

I respectfully dissent. After reviewing the record in the light most favorable to Nichols, I conclude that Nichols has not demonstrated that TNI acted negligently in addressing her complaints. When an employee alleges sexual harassment by a coworker, "[a]n employer must be allowed some time to gauge the credibility of the complainant." *Dhyne v. Meiners Thriftway, Inc.*, 184 F.3d 983, 988 (8th Cir. 1999). As a result, an employee often must "tolerate some delay" by an employer taking appropriate remedial action. *See id.*

Sexual harassment by a coworker is not a violation of Title VII unless an "employer knew or should have known of the harassment in question and failed to take proper remedial action." *Moylan v. Maries Cty.*, 792 F.2d 746, 750 (8th Cir. 1986). Consistent with the negligence standard used to evaluate an employer's response, we have refrained from requiring specific remedial measures. Instead, we have stated that "[f]actors in assessing the reasonableness of remedial measures *may include* the amount of time that elapsed between the notice and remedial action, the options available to the employer, . . . and whether or not the measures ended the harassment." *Carter v. Chrysler Corp.*, 173 F.3d 693, 702 (8th Cir.1999) (emphasis added). "Proper remedial action need be only 'reasonably calculated to stop the harassment'. . . ." *Engel v. Rapid City Sch. Dist.*, 506 F.3d 1118, 1125 (8th Cir. 2007) (quoting *Carter*).

[The dissent disagreed that the record showed that Nichols' first report was on Friday, May 25. When "the record is read to favorably harmonize Nichols's testimony, May 28 is the earliest Nichols could have called Foust to report Paris."]. As such, TNI's opportunity to take appropriate remedial action is significantly reduced. No specific time requirement exists for employers to respond to sexual harassment claims, but it must be reasonable under the circumstances. *Carter.* Applying existing circuit precedent, TNI took remedial action within a reasonable time of receiving notice from Nichols. In *Barrett v. Omaha National Bank*, we found an employer's response to an employee's sexual harassment complaint within four days to be prompt remedial action. 726 F.2d 424, 427 (8th Cir. 1984). Likewise, in *Green v. Franklin National Bank of Minneapolis*, we rejected an employee's claim that an employer failed to act promptly enough when it took remedial action nearly a month after learning of the harassment. 459 F.3d 903, 912 (8th Cir. 2006).

. . . The majority is correct that in *CRST* we determined that the employer took appropriate remedial action by removing the harassed employee from the truck within 24 hours; however, we did not set 24 hours as a minimum standard. An employer's response need not be ideal in every case but must be reasonable under the circumstances. *See, e.g., Green*; *Lapka v. Chertoff*, 517 F.3d 974, 987 (7th Cir. 2008).

Here, Paris's alleged harassment of Nichols ended not later than June 1. To be sure, no one should have to endure harassing conduct for any period, but employers can only be legally responsible for conduct of which they are made aware and fail to take timely, reasonable steps to correct. The time period between May 28 and June 1 is the very type of delay employees must unfortunately sometimes endure. . . .

This case also presents important contextual considerations in determining whether TNI acted negligently. [That the harassment occurred in a truck scheduled to be on the road limited the employer's options.] The majority is correct that TNI could have reprimanded Paris. However, TNI's decision not to reprimand Paris immediately does not constitute actionable conduct. In choosing not to reprimand Paris before determining fault, TNI did not delay unreasonably in taking remedial action. *See Dhyne* [*v. Meiners Thriftway, Inc.,* 184 F.3d 983, 988 (8th Cir. 1999)] (holding that an employer must be allowed some time to gauge the credibility of the complainant).

Contrary to the majority's characterization, I do not think TNI knew or should have known that Nichols needed to be saved. At most, TNI knew Paris was exposing himself to Nichols but that Nichols did not consider the conduct so intolerable that she required immediate removal from the truck. . . .

NOTES

1. *Knowledge.* Paris was certainly not Nichols' supervisor, which means that employer liability turned first on when the employer knew of should have known of the misconduct. Although it's possible for employers to have knowledge other than from reports by the victim, *see Duch v. Jakubek,* 588 F.3d 757 (2d Cir. 2009) (jury could conclude that supervisor had constructive knowledge of co-worker harassment where employee requested shift change, supervisor employer observed her "teary and red" when asked about the harasser, and supervisor knew harasser had engaged in past misconduct toward female employees), such reports will be the typical way in which an employer learns there is a problem. That means that the employer will usually not be liable for conduct that occurred before the report if it acts appropriately after receiving it. Given the documented tendency of women to attempt to deal with harassment in less confrontational ways, *see* Linda Hamilton Krieger, *Employer Liability for Sexual Harassment—Normative, Descriptive, and Doctrinal Interactions: A Reply to Professors Beiner and Bisom-Rapp,* 24 U. ARK. LITTLE ROCK L. REV. 169, 180-83 (2001), that also means that much harassment will go unaddressed.

And note also the division between the majority and dissent over the date of the report: the reasonableness of the response is in part dependent on how quickly the employer acts, which depends on when it learns of the misconduct. *See also Smith v. Rock-Tenn Servs.,* 813 F.3d 298 (6th Cir. 2016) (a reasonable jury could find that total inaction for ten days, where the employer had warned the harasser that further complaints would result in termination, was unreasonable).

2. *Prevention.* The *Nichols* opinions spend no time on TNI's efforts to prevent harassment, focusing entirely on correcting such conduct once it occurs. Where supervisor harassment triggers presumptive liability, that would be erroneous since the employer has the burden of proving reasonable preventive *and* corrective action. But it would probably be harmless in any event because, although a few cases question the effectiveness of employer policies, *see Williams v. Spartan Communications,* page 913, most employers' antiharassment policies and training have been found adequate. For co-worker negligence cases, then, liability will almost always turn on "correction," that is, how quickly and effectively the employer responded to a report, although whether it followed its own policies may be important.

3. *Correction.* The majority and the dissent part company on the appropriateness of the company's response to the reported harassment. Who do you agree with? Recall that the dispute is not about whether the response was appropriate but whether a reasonable jury could find it wasn't. *Nichols* was written before #MeToo. Might even Judge Smith view things differently today? Might society have a different view of how long a woman can be expected to put up with objectionable conduct pending company action?

As for response, TNI ultimately separated Nichols and Paris. That ended the harassment as far as Nichols was concerned. But are you surprised that the opinion does not report whether Paris was even disciplined or discharged? Aside from its effects on Nichols's suit, wouldn't it be an enormous risk for TNI to continue to employ him? And might not a discharge play well before a jury that must make the final determination as to the reasonableness of the employer's response?

More generally, a recurring factual question is whether the employer's response was adequate under the circumstances, and that turns in the first instance on an employer's verification of a report. *Nichols* never got to the question of whether the alleged harassment occurred, but a typical complaint will generate an investigation that may or may not be conclusive on the issue. *See Sutherland v. Wal-Mart Stores, Inc.*, 632 F.3d 990 (7th Cir. 2011) (finding affirmative defense established after an internal investigation that the plaintiff's claims could not be corroborated). If the employer acts against the alleged harasser, however, it risks penalizing an innocent employee, which can itself have legal consequences. One solution is just to separate the complainant and the alleged harasser. Might that be what TNI was doing?

4. *Unreasonable Failure to Report.* While Nichols assessed negligence liability, the second prong of the affirmative defense to presumptive employer liability for supervisory harassment focuses not on the employer's actions but on the victim's. We've seen that victims are typically hesitant to report, hoping they can "handle" it themselves and worried that a report might brand them as "troublemakers" and damage their careers. The law encourages such reluctance because hostile environment claims require severe or pervasive conduct, and victims are probably correct in thinking that a few minor incidents do not constitute illegal behavior. *See Clark County Sch. Dist. v. Breeden*, reproduced at page 671. *But see Boyer-Liberto v. Fontainebleau Corp.*, 786 F.3d 264 (4th Cir. 2015) (en banc) ("[R]ather than encourage the early reporting vital to achieving Title VII's goal of avoiding harm, [too strict a standard] deters harassment victims from speaking up by depriving them of their statutory entitlement to protection from retaliation."). But when does delay become so unreasonable as to satisfy that part of the affirmative defense? Courts have reached widely different results on this question. *Compare Mota v. Univ. of Tex. Houston Health Sci. Ctr.*, 261 F.3d 512 (5th Cir. 2001) (nine-month delay was reasonable) *with Pinkerton v. Colorado DOT*, 563 F.3d 1052 (10th Cir. 2009) (two-month delay was unreasonable); *Conatzer v. Medical Prof. Bldg. Serv.*, 95 F. App'x 276 (10th Cir. 2004) (17-day delay was unreasonable).

5. *Effective Remedial Action Not Enough in Supervisor Harassment Cases.* Because the two prongs of the affirmative defense in supervisor harassment cases are conjunctive, an employer is vicariously liable despite its taking reasonable preventive and corrective action when the victim promptly complains. *See, e.g., Chapman* *v. Carmike Cinemas*, 307 F. App'x 164 (10th Cir. 2009) (summary judgment for employer improper where plaintiff immediately reported sexual assault despite the fact that employer terminated perpetrator because employer cannot establish unreasonable failure to report). *But see McCurdy v. Ark. State Police*, 375 F.3d 762 (8th Cir. 2004). Some commentators argue that, for policy reasons, the affirmative defense should remain available to employers who respond effectively, whether or not the employee unreasonably delays reporting. *See* Zev J. Eigen, Nicholas Menillo & David Sherwyn, *When Rules Are Made to Be Broken*, 109 Nw. L. Rev. 109 (2014); David Sherwyn et al., *Don't Train Your Employees and Cancel Your "1-800" Harassment Hotline: An Empirical Examination and Correction of the Flaws in the Affirmative Defense to Sexual Harassment Charges*, 69 FORDHAM L. REV. 1265, 1280-84 (2000-01). On the other hand, is there a competing rationale for finding liability despite the employer's admirable response? *See* Joanna L. Grossman, *The First Bite Is Free: Employer Liability for Sexual Harassment*, 61 U. PITT. L. REV. 671, 711-15 (2000) (arguing that decisions focusing solely on employer corrective action impermissibly substitute a negligence standard for the Supreme Court's vicarious liability rule); Krieger, *supra*, at 169, 196-97 (suggesting that harassment is a reasonably foreseeable harm flowing from the operation of a business whose costs should be internalized).

6. *Victim Requests for Confidentiality.* What if the victim promptly reports but insists that the matter be kept confidential? Several courts have found in favor of employers in those situations, treating the victim's complaint as ineffective. *See, e.g., Hardage v. CBS Broad., Inc.*, 427 F.3d 1177, 1185-88 (9th Cir. 2005); *Olson v. Lowe's Home Ctrs. Inc.*, 130 F. App'x 380, 390 (11th Cir. 2005). There is also contrary authority, however. *Malik v. Carrier Corp.*, 202 F.3d 97, 105-06 (2d Cir. 2000) ("Prudent employers will compel harassing employees to cease all such conduct and will not, even at a victim's request, tolerate inappropriate conduct that may, if not halted immediately, create a hostile environment."). Suppose you are an employer formulating a policy regarding harassment. How should you direct your supervisors to handle a "confidential" complaint of harassment? Recall that, while the particular employee demanding confidentiality may thereby be precluded from suit, future employees who are harassed will be able to show the employer knew of the problem and failed to deal with it; in other words, as to potential victims, the employer will not be able to show reasonable steps to prevent the harassment.

7. *Report to Whom?* To trigger potential negligence liability, it is enough that the employer "knew or should have known" of the misconduct. To establish the affirmative defense to presumptive liability in supervisor harassment cases, an employer must show failure of the employee to "unreasonably take advantage of" corrective opportunities provided by the employer. In either case, a report to a particular person might or might not suffice. Some courts have even held that victims satisfy their reporting obligations in such situations when the offending supervisor is designated as a proper recipient for complaints under the policy. *See, e.g., Gorzynski v. JetBlue Airways Corp.*, 596 F.3d 93 (2d Cir. 2010). Others hold that employees who do not escalate their complaint up the chain of command or who bypass the offending manager by using other channels designated in the employer's harassment policy failed to satisfy their reporting obligations. *See, e.g., Madray v. Publix*, 208 F.3d 1290, 1301-02 (11th Cir. 2000) (finding unreasonable failure to report by employee harassed by store manager where policy required employee to report either

to store manager, district manager, or division manager, and employee reported only to assistant managers within her store).

These kinds of questions have led employers to seek to limit their risk designating only a few individuals to whom complaints can be made. *See* Anne Lawton, *Operating in an Empirical Vacuum: The* Ellerth *and* Faragher *Affirmative Defense*, 13 COLUM. J. GENDER & L. 197 (2005). In *Nichols*, suppose the employer's harassment policy had so provided. Would her reports to Faust and Oliver not have counted for negligence liability? The court says that the test for actual knowledge is "whether sufficient information comes 'to the attention of someone who [had] the power to terminate the harassment.'" That's unlikely to be true of either individual. But wouldn't a reasonable employer require reports such as this to be escalated quickly to someone who could deal with them?

Employers also seek to discourage complaints or at least place the employee in a bad light by requiring complaints to be made within a very short time of the harassment. *See Rennard v. Woodworker's Supply, Inc.*, 101 F. App'x 296, 300 (10th Cir. 2004) (plaintiff disciplined for failing to report sexual harassment within one week as required by employer policy); Anne Lawton, *The Bad Apple Theory in Sexual Harassment*, 13 GEO. MASON L. REV. 817, 850-55 (2005). On the other hand, does the first prong of the defense limit the extent to which employers can use such strategies successfully? In other words, can a policy that significantly limits the manner and time frame in which a victim is required to report harassment still satisfy the preventive action component of the defense?

8. *Tangible Employment Actions.* The *Ellerth/Faragher* defense applies only to hostile work environment claims. The Supreme Court made clear in both cases that, where the supervisor engages in a tangible employment action that adversely affects the victim, vicarious liability is automatic. And *Vance v. Ball State University* makes clear that whether a harasser is a supervisor turns on whether he or she is able to inflict a tangible employment action. As a result, plaintiffs often argue that the harassment they endured culminated in a more tangible adverse action. Courts disagree as to the definition of tangible employment act. Some hold that a tangible employment act means an "ultimate" employment decision, such as a discharge. *See, e.g., Lutkewitte v. Gonzales*, 436 F.3d 248, 252 (D.C. Cir. 2006). Others take the view that any act that substantially affects a term or condition of employment suffices. *See, e.g., Green v. Administrators of Tulane Educational Fund*, 284 F.3d 642, 654-55 (5th Cir. 2002) (finding that "demotion, together with the substantial diminishment of her job responsibilities, was sufficient to constitute a tangible employment action" despite absence of any economic loss). A parallel debate in the retaliation context was resolved by the Supreme Court, which rejected an "ultimate employment action" test. *See Burlington Northern & Santa Fe Ry. v. White*, 548 U.S. 53 (2006) (the anti-retaliation provision "covers those (and only those) employer actions that would have been materially adverse to a reasonable employee or job applicant."). Does this holding suggest a relaxed standard for tangible employment actions is appropriate in the sexual harassment context, or are these two different doctrines?

What is clear is that the act in question must be an official exercise of managerial judgment. In *Pennsylvania State Police v. Suders*, 542 U.S. 129 (2004), the Supreme Court addressed the question whether the *Ellerth/Faragher* defense was available to employers in situations where harassment culminated in a constructive discharge. The Third Circuit had held a constructive discharge, as the equivalent of a termination, constituted a tangible employment action, rendering the employer strictly liable for the victim's harassment. The Supreme Court reversed, explaining:

> Like the harassment considered in our pathmarking decisions [*Ellerth* and *Faragher*], harassment so intolerable as to cause a resignation may be effected through co-worker conduct, unofficial supervisory conduct, or official company acts. Unlike an actual termination, which is *always* effected through an official act of the company, a constructive discharge need not be. . . .
>
> To be sure, a constructive discharge is functionally the same as an actual termination in damages-enhancing respects. . . . But when an official act does not underlie the constructive discharge, the *Ellerth* and *Faragher* analysis, we here hold, calls for extension of the affirmative defense to the employer. As those leading decisions indicate, official directions and declarations are the acts most likely to be brought home to the employer, the measures over which the employer can exercise greatest control. Absent "an official act of the enterprise," as the last straw, the employer ordinarily would have no particular reason to suspect that a resignation is not the typical kind daily occurring in the work force. And as *Ellerth* and *Faragher* further point out, an official act reflected in company records—a demotion or a reduction in compensation, for example—shows "beyond question" that the supervisor has used his managerial or controlling position to the employee's disadvantage.

Id. at 147-48. Do you agree with the Court's analysis? Does its resolution of the constructive discharge question shed any light on how it might resolve the outstanding question whether a tangible employment action requires an "ultimate" employment decision?

9. *Liability to the Putative Harasser?* The structure of the affirmative defense clearly encourages employers to discipline, even discharge, harassers. That's why TNI's apparent failure to take such action against Paris was surprising. Since he was likely an at-will employee, contractual liability seems foreclosed, and the public policy tort is inapposite. In contrast, maybe there was a union involved. If so, the governing collective bargaining agreement would typically have constrained the employer's action, including limitations on the discipline that may be meted out: Even a person properly found to have been guilty of harassment can be disciplined only proportionate to the offense. *See Westvaco Corp. v. United Paperworkers Int'l Union*, 171 F.3d 971, 977 (4th Cir. 1999) ("the general public policy against sexual harassment is not sufficient to supplant labor arbitration of employee disciplinary sanctions"). Similarly, civil service laws and academic tenure protections might limit employer responses to harassment and other wrongful conduct by supervisors or co-workers in government and university settings.

What about privacy concerns and defamation? Suppose Paris was in fact innocent of any wrongful conduct but word of the charges against him went around the workplace? Might TNI be liable for defamation if its actions had caused the rumors? Revisit Chapter 5 for these issues. Finally, what about sex discrimination? Might an employer's response to a charge of harassment be viewed as a violation of Title VII? *See Sassaman v. Gamache*, 566 F.3d 307 (2d Cir. 2009) (discharge of male on the basis that men had a propensity to harass, subjecting employer to potential liability by female claiming harassment, was actionable). *See also Russell v. City of Kansas City*, 414 F.3d 863, 868 (8th Cir. 2005) (white female supervisor demoted for allegedly fostering racially harassing workplace may have been the victim of discrimination when black and white males were given only a "slap on the wrist").

Williams v. Spartan Communications
No. 99-1566, 2000 U.S. App. LEXIS 5776 (4th Cir. March 30, 2000)

MOTZ, C.J.

Veneal Williams sold advertising from 1989 to 1995 for Spartan Communications, Incorporated, which runs a television station in Spartanburg, South Carolina. Her immediate supervisor was Local Sales Manager Mitchell Maund, who was promoted to that position in 1992. Williams alleges that between 1992 and 1995 Maund sexually assaulted her three times during business trips that the two took together. The second assault assertedly occurred in Williams' van, while the two were watching an R-rated movie rented on Maund's instructions.

On May 24, 1995, Williams reported Maund's assaults to Spartan General Sales Manager Greg Rose and Spartan Personnel Manager Donna Groothedde. Maund was out of town that day, but Rose, Groothedde and Spartan Vice President and General Manager Jack West met with him the following day, May 25. At that time, Maund admitted to renting and watching the movie in Williams' van. That afternoon, Maund, Rose, Groothedde, and West met again; as a result of Maund's admitted rental of the movie, he resigned. Maund received five months' severance pay in return for releasing Spartan from liability for his dismissal. Due to the distress of continued sexual harassment, Williams left her job with Spartan and is now unemployed and in counseling.

[A magistrate judge granted summary judgment to Spartan. On appeal, the issue] is whether Spartan has established, as a matter of law, its entitlement to an affirmative defense to Williams' hostile environment claim. The Supreme Court has explained that "when no tangible employment action is taken, a defending employer may raise an affirmative defense" to a claim of "vicarious liability . . . for an actionable hostile environment created by a supervisor with immediate . . . authority over the employee." *Faragher v. Boca Raton*, 524 U.S. 775, 807 (1998); *Burlington Indus. v. Ellerth*, 524 U.S. 742, 765 (1998). To do so an employer must demonstrate by the "preponderance of the evidence" that (1) it "exercised reasonable care to prevent and correct promptly any sexually harassing behavior" and (2) "the plaintiff employee unreasonably failed to take advantage of any preventative [sic] or corrective opportunities provided by the employer or to avoid harm otherwise." The magistrate judge held that Spartan had satisfied both elements of the affirmative defense as a matter of law and so granted the company summary judgment.

We believe that this ruling was error. We need only discuss the first prong of the defense—whether Spartan has established, as a matter of law, that it "exercised reasonable care to prevent and correct promptly" the sexually harassing behavior.

The magistrate judge found that the following evidence demonstrated that Spartan had indisputably satisfied this prong: (1) Williams admitted that she knew of Spartan's anti-harassment policy, had attended a meeting at which it was discussed, and saw a posted notice of it, which identified persons to whom she could report improper conduct, and (2) Spartan forced Maund to resign as soon as it learned of Williams' allegations.

This rationale fails to recognize that while the existence of an antiharassment policy and prompt corrective action pursuant to it provides important evidence that an employer has acted to meet the first prong of the affirmative defense, such evidence does not compel this conclusion. Rather, any anti-harassment policy offered to satisfy the first prong of the *Faragher-Ellerth* defense must be "both reasonably designed and reasonably effectual." *Brown v. Perry*, 184 F.3d 388, 396 (4th Cir. 1999). Moreover, a prompt response to complaints of harassment made pursuant to a policy banning harassment does not necessarily establish the first prong of the affirmative defense.

The magistrate judge also entirely ignored substantial relevant evidence submitted by Williams that could lead a factfinder to conclude that Spartan's anti-harassment policy was not an effective preventive program. This evidence included: (1) Maund's deposition testimony that he received no training on sexual harassment and did not even recall any specific discussion of the anti-harassment policy; (2) senior Spartan management's toleration of and participation in lewd conversations and publication of sexually explicit jokes and cartoons in the workplace; (3) evidence that an employee's complaint to a Spartan manager about foul language and sexist jokes in the workplace produced no corrective action; (4) General Sales Manager Rose's comment that a secretary had been fired because "she didn't give him a blow job"; (5) Vice President and General Manager West's remark to male managers looking at female participants in a management training function, "Boys, I've stepped over better than that just to jack off"; (6) General Sales Manager West's comment after a sexual harassment training meeting, "does this mean we can't fuck the help any more"; (7) the close relationship between Maund (the alleged harasser) and West, Rose, and other senior managers at Spartan; and (8) the anti-harassment policy's failure, in contravention of EEOC guidelines, to assure those reporting harassment that they would not be subject to retaliation, particularly when the policy provided that "an employee who in bad faith falsely accuses another employee of harassment will be subject to disciplinary action up to and including termination." . . .

Here Spartan disseminated an anti-harassment policy which failed to provide that complainants would be free from retaliation, and yet warned that false reports of harassment would subject a complainant to disciplinary action, "including termination." Although these features do not, in themselves, render the policy ineffective, when considered in conjunction with the conduct of most senior Spartan management, a policy with such features could be found to be ineffective. The outrageous comments by Vice President and General Manager West ("does this mean we cannot fuck the help anymore") and General Sales Manager Rose (a secretary was terminated because "she didn't give him a blow job") suggest not only that a complaint made pursuant to this anti-harassment policy might fall on deaf ears, but also that such a complaint might cause the complainant's termination. Indeed, Williams produced evidence that a Spartan employee decided not to complain of harassment because of fear of being fired. The long and close personal relationships between those managers who made the denigrating comments, West and Rose, and the alleged harasser, Maund, were so well known that several of the witnesses described them as members of the "Augusta Boys Club." Given these relationships, a factfinder could conclude that a complaint about Maund would receive a particularly skeptical response from Spartan management.

We note that Spartan's policy states that "any employee who feels they are being subjected to any form of harassment in violation of this policy should bring their complaint to the attention" of one of four members of management: "[1] the[] immediate supervisor, [2] the General Manager, [3] the appointed liaison, or [4] the Manager of Corporate Human Resources." Providing an employee recourse to multiple members of management is commendable. But Williams produced evidence that could lead a factfinder to determine that the extra protection seemingly afforded by this provision was illusory in her case. This is so because one of the four suggested recipients of harassment complaints was the harasser himself, Maund; another was his good friend, Vice President and General Manager West (the source of the "does this mean we can't fuck the help any more" and the "I've stepped over better than that just to jack off" remarks); and the remaining two managers reported to West, the General Manager of the station and Vice President of the entire company. Thus, the conduct of Spartan's senior management could be found to have isolated Williams from effective channels of complaint. A factfinder could conclude that the language in the anti-harassment policy together with the conduct of Spartan's most senior management "discouraged complaining about a supervisor's harassing behavior." *Smith.*

This is not to say that Williams has demonstrated that Spartan cannot establish the first prong of *Faragher's* affirmative defense. A factfinder may well ultimately conclude that Spartan's anti-harassment policy and prompt corrective action do establish this prong. However, we believe that when Williams' evidence is considered in the light most favorable to her, Spartan has not established the first prong as a matter of law. For these reasons, we reverse the district court's grant of summary judgment to Spartan.

REVERSED.

WILKINSON, C.J., dissenting.

I agree with the district court that Spartan Communications has established both prongs of the affirmative defense under *Faragher* and *Ellerth.* I would therefore uphold the grant of summary judgment. . . .

As to the first prong of the defense, Spartan exercised reasonable care to prevent and correct the sexually harassing behavior that Williams reported. Spartan put in place a strong anti-harassment policy that states the "working environment should be free of intimidation and harassment." The policy defines and prohibits sexual harassment and encourages employees to come forward with complaints. A complaint may be reported to any one of at least four different people, including the department head, general manager, appointed EEO liaison, and the manager of corporate human resources. Williams admits that she was aware of this policy. She attended a meeting at which the policy was discussed by the corporate personnel director and saw a posted notice prohibiting sexual harassment and identifying various persons to whom she could report any improper conduct. Spartan also took swift action to correct the alleged harassment. When Williams finally reported Maund's inappropriate behavior, Spartan immediately conducted an investigation and asked Maund to resign only two days after receiving Williams' complaint.

Though the existence of an anti-harassment policy is not sufficient to satisfy the first part of the affirmative defense, the policy here is "both reasonably designed and reasonably effectual." *Brown v. Perry,* 184 F.3d 388, 396 (4th Cir. 1999). The majority attempts to discredit the effectiveness of the policy by referring to lewd statements by management and to the fact that Spartan's policy did not contain an explicit anti-retaliation provision. Yet the majority does not assert that the policy was ineffective when complaints were reported or that Spartan had retaliated against any employee who made a complaint. There is simply "no evidence that [the] employer adopted or administered an anti-harassment policy in bad faith or that the policy was otherwise defective or dysfunctional." There is only the evidence that Spartan immediately terminated Maund when it learned of his misconduct. Because it had an effective policy, Spartan has satisfied the first part of the affirmative defense.

The majority's litany of crude remarks attributed to management does not undermine Spartan's affirmative defense. It is a rare case when some remarks could not be dredged up or alleged in order to challenge management's reasonableness. The affirmative defense focuses not on remarks, however, but on the conduct of employers and employees in preventing and addressing sexual harassment complaints. A collection of off-hand remarks unrelated to the harassment simply does not preclude Spartan from establishing the first prong of the affirmative defense on summary judgment. Indeed, the remarks related by the majority were not directed toward Williams. She was not even present when most of them were made. While no one would approve of the comments, Title VII is not intended to allow courts to act as censors of workplace speech or impose a general workplace civility code.

As to the second prong of the defense, Williams failed to take advantage of the opportunities provided by Spartan to avoid the sexual harassment. "[A] demonstration of such failure will normally suffice to satisfy the employer's burden under the second element of the defense." *Faragher.* . . . Williams knew about Spartan's policy, knew whom to contact with grievances, and yet waited three years to report the harassment. During this time, plaintiff was allegedly assaulted twice more, once while watching an R-rated movie in her van with Maund and again while with Maund in her hotel room. *Faragher* and *Ellerth* encourage employees to report such conduct precisely to avoid continued harassment. Spartan has established that Williams unreasonably failed to take advantage of the company's preventive and corrective measures. Williams "should not recover damages that could have been avoided if she had done so." *Faragher.*

By denying summary judgment in a case where the affirmative defense has been clearly established, the majority simply indicates an aversion to the Supreme Court's mandate in *Faragher* and *Ellerth*. In doing so, the majority creates the worst of all possible worlds. Despite the existence of a reasonable and effective complaint procedure, the employee continues to be harassed for nearly three years because no misconduct was reported. The company in turn has no opportunity to rectify unacceptable behavior. Such an outcome is the antithesis of Title VII's primary objective, which is "not to provide redress but to avoid harm." *Faragher.* . . .

NOTES

1. *"Paper Compliance?" Williams* raises an important question—does a sexual harassment policy actually prevent harassment? More importantly, should the existence of such a policy absolve an employer of liability for harassment that occurs nevertheless? Many commentators have criticized the Supreme Court's decisions in *Ellerth* and *Faragher* for granting too much deference to employer policies and practices. *See, e.g.,* Elizabeth Tippett, *Harassment Trainings*, 39 BERKELEY J. EMP. & LAB. L. ___ (forthcoming 2018); Susan Bisom-Rapp, *An Ounce of Prevention Is a Poor Substitute for a Pound of Cure: Confronting the Developing Jurisprudence of Education and Prevention in Employment Discrimination Law*, 22 BERKELEY J. EMP. & LAB. L. 1 (2001); Susan D. Carle, *Acknowledging Informal Power Dynamics in the Workplace: A Proposal for Further Development of the Vicarious Liability Doctrine in Hostile Environment Sexual Harassment Cases*, 13 DUKE J. GENDER L. & POL'Y 85 (2006); Joanna L. Grossman, *The Culture of Compliance: The Final Triumph of Form Over Substance in Sexual Harassment Law*, 26 HARV. WOMEN'S L.J. 3 (2003); Anne Lawton, *Operating in*

an Empirical Vacuum: The Ellerth *and* Faragher *Affirmative Defense*, 13 COLUM. J. GENDER & L. 197 (2005). These commentators argue that the affirmative defense creates incentives for employers to go through the motions of being tough on harassment, establishing strongly worded policies and implementing training programs, but that such practices do not get at the root cause of harassing behavior. Professor Lawton suggests that those practices come at the expense of more aggressive efforts to equalize the workplace and to respond to acts of discrimination, *id.* at 233-35, and she concludes that courts' equating policies with prevention essentially shifts the burden of proof to the employee on the reasonableness of the employer's prevention efforts. *Id.* at 235; *see also* Vicki Schultz, *The Sanitized Workplace*, 112 YALE L.J. 2061, 2174-77 (2003) (suggesting that liability for hostile environment harassment should turn on the extent of sex segregation in the particular workplace rather than employer's aggressiveness in policing sexual conduct).

    Williams certainly demonstrates that it is possible for an employer to have a policy on the books and at the same time tolerate a work culture in which objectionable behavior endures. The question is whether courts will hold such employers accountable. *Williams* and other decisions find that an employer must do more than institute a policy or a training program to prevent and correct harassment. *See, e.g., Hawkins v. Anheuser-Busch, Inc.* 517 F.3d 321 (6th Cir. 2008) (concluding that "an employer's responsibility to prevent future harassment is heightened where it is dealing with a known serial harasser"). However, the *Williams* decision provoked a strong dissent, and other courts have adopted the dissenting judge's more deferential view of employer practices. *See, e.g., Barrett v. Applied Radiant Energy Corp.*, 240 F.3d 262 (4th Cir. 2001) ("Distribution of an anti-harassment policy provides 'compelling proof' that the company exercised reasonable care in preventing and promptly correcting sexual harassment.").

    2. *Conjunctive Elements.* The *Williams* court deals only with the first prong of the defense, and only with its first element—whether the employer engaged in preventive action. Since a reasonable jury could find that the employer failed to reasonably prevent harassment, the other aspects of the defense were irrelevant; if the jury so finds, the employer will be liable. Assume, however, that the court went on to complete the analysis. How would the employer fare? Prompt and effective *corrective* action was taken: Immediately after Williams reported Maund's behavior, he resigned. As for the second prong, the harassment perpetrated against Williams continued for three years before she reported it, which strongly suggests she was unreasonable in failing to report. Given these facts, the court's willingness to look beyond the employer's policy on harassment in assessing prevention was critical to the plaintiff's success.

    3. *Reasonable Failures to Report.* Alternatively, could Williams successfully argue that her significant delay in reporting Maund's harassing behavior was reasonable? Note the employer's sexual harassment policy did not offer assurances of nonretaliation, and, as the court makes clear, the past comments of senior managers could give an employee good reason to fear that her complaint of harassment would not be taken seriously. Courts often are reluctant to find a failure to report reasonable where the victim cites only general fear and embarrassment. *See, e.g., Matvia v. Bald Head Isle Mgmt.*, 259 F.3d 261, 270 (4th Cir. 2001) (finding that general fear of negative reactions from co-workers, which ultimately came to fruition, did not justify failure to report). Other courts, however, have found that a victim's failure to report promptly could be reasonable in similar circumstances, as where the employer's work culture discouraged reporting or the victim had a specific basis for fearing retaliation. *See, e.g., Reed v. MBNA Mktg. Sys.*, 333 F.3d 27, 36-37 (1st Cir. 2003) (finding 17-year-old victim's failure to report reasonable where harasser told her she would be fired for reporting); *Mota v. Univ. of Tex. Houston Health Sci. Ctr.*, 261 F.3d 512 (5th Cir. 2001) (finding untenured professor's delay in reporting harassment by prominent department head reasonable, especially given that the victim's immigration status could be jeopardized if he no longer worked as university employee).

4. *Supervisor versus Co-worker.* In *Williams,* the courts treated the harassment as being cause by a "supervisor." After *Vance v. Ball State University* that seems unlikely to be correct. That means that today Spartan would be liable only for negligence, and the failure of plaintiff to report the harassment for years almost certainly means that the employer did not know or have reason to know of it. Since Spartan fired the harasser within two days of learning of the conduct, it would almost certainly not be liable. Judge Wilkerson seems to have been unduly worried.

5. *Beyond Sexual Harassment.* Although the Supreme Court's decisions in *Ellerth* and *Faragher* involved sexual harassment in particular, most courts have applied the affirmative defense to hostile work environment claims based on other protected characteristics and arising under sources of law other than Title VII's prohibition on sex discrimination. Might the concept of employer prevention and corrective action have bearing on employer liability for other forms of discrimination as well? Proactive employer behavior can also limit the employee's damage award upon a successful showing of discrimination. *See Kolstad v. American Dental Ass'n*, 527 U.S. 526, 545 (1999) ("[I]n the punitive damages context, an employer may not be vicariously liable for the discriminatory employment decisions of managerial agents where these decisions are contrary to the employer's 'good-faith efforts to comply with Title VII.'").

6. *Treatment of the Harasser.* The *Williams* court noted that "as a result of Maund's admitted rental of the movie, he resigned. Maund received five months' severance pay in return for releasing Spartan from liability for his dismissal." The majority does not further explore this, and the dissent seems to think that the employer did as much as could be expected when it "fired" Maund. Why pay an admitted harasser severance? If you were the employer's counsel, would you have recommended paying him five months' salary? The President of the University of Southern California resigned, in part because of a termination payout to a gynecologist accused of sexually assaulting students. *USC President to Step Down Amid Sexual Misconduct Claims Against Gynecologist*, May 26, 2018, https://www.huffingtonpost.com/entry/cl-max-nikias-usc-step-down-president_us_5b09b119e4b0802d69cbca20.

PROBLEMS

13-1. Spectrum Stores, a regional convenience store chain, asks you to review its policy on sexual harassment. Spectrum owns approximately 25 stores and 2 warehouses across two states and employs over 300 employees. Approximately 20 of those employees, including its officers and human resources personnel, work in Spectrum's corporate headquarters. Orientation for all store personnel is conducted at the headquarters, and the following policy is distributed to all employees at that time:

Spectrum Stores does not and will not tolerate harassment of our employees, applicants or customers. The term "harassment" includes but is not limited to: slurs, jokes and other verbal, graphic or physical conduct relating to an individual's race, color, sex, sexual orientation, or religion. "Harassment" also includes sexual advances, requests for sexual favors, unwelcome touching and other verbal, graphic or physical conduct of a sexual nature.

VIOLATION OF THIS POLICY WILL SUBJECT THE EMPLOYEE TO DISCIPLINARY ACTION.

If you feel that you are being harassed in any way you should notify your immediate supervisor. If you believe that a supervisor or a member of management has acted inconsistently with this policy and you are not comfortable bringing a complaint regarding harassment to your immediate supervisor or if you believe that your complaint concerning a co-worker, a customer, or a vendor has not been handled to your satisfaction, please immediately contact either the Vice President of Human Resources or the Executive Vice President.

Please do not assume Spectrum is aware of your problem. Please bring your complaints and concerns to our attention so that we can resolve them.

Is there anything you would recommend adding to or changing in this policy? Are there any other practices or procedures you would recommend that Spectrum adopt? If you need further information to answer, what questions would you ask Spectrum's management before offering advice?

13-2. Terri Munroe was a shipping and receiving clerk in one of Spectrum Stores' warehouses and the only female employee at her worksite. Reed Gilbelt, a co-worker, frequently subjected Terri to sexual comments and lewd behavior. Among other things, he referred to her as "luscious" and "sweet cheeks," and on two occasions he suggested that Terri accompany him to the Red Roof Inn during a break. He frequently sent suggestive e-mails to her.

After enduring this behavior for six months, Terri reported Reed's conduct to her supervisor, Vincent Sing. Vincent laughed when he read the e-mails Terri showed him and told Terri that she should "resolve the problem on her own." Over the next three months, Vincent engaged in suggestive behavior as well. He told Terri that he "had a job for her under his desk," remarked that Terri should wear shorter shorts on one occasion when he saw her standing on high equipment, and invited Terri out with him on three occasions. Once when Terri asked to be permitted to clock out early due to illness, Vincent told her she could only leave if she came home with him. When Terri refused, Vincent forced her to work until the end of her regular shift.

Three months after first reporting Reed's behavior to Vincent, Terri reported the behavior of both employees to Diane O'Connor, Spectrum's Human Resources Vice President. Diane placed Terri on paid leave and launched an immediate investigation, during which she interviewed over a dozen employees during the course of two weeks. As a result of the investigation, Spectrum terminated Reed, and Vincent resigned. Diane informed Terri of this outcome, and Terri returned to work. She did not experience any further harassment upon her return; however, she resigned from employment one month later citing her distress at the behavior she had endured prior to the investigation and being "shunned" upon her return to work by some co-workers who were upset about the departures of Reed and Vincent.

Assume that Spectrum maintains the sexual harassment policy laid out in problem 13-1 above and that the company provides sexual harassment training to all its employees. Suppose you represent Terri. Enumerate all of the discrimination claims and theories of liability that you can pursue against Spectrum. If Terri's experience amounts to severe and pervasive hostile behavior based on sex, can she establish that Spectrum should be vicariously liable for Reed's conduct? What about for Vincent's conduct? Think about how you would go about establishing this element of her claim(s), anticipate what arguments Spectrum is likely to make, and explain how you would respond to them.

---

2. Employer Investigations of Workplace Misconduct

Internal investigations of sexual harassment complaints are now standard practice among sophisticated employers, and they are used not only in dealing with allegations of discrimination, but in ensuring compliance with regulatory and criminal laws and dealing with civil liability on many fronts. Some internal investigations receive a great deal of media attention, such as the after-the-fact inquiry into the Penn State scandal by former FBI Director Louis Freer, *The Paterno Legacy, Changed Forever*, NY TIMES, July 13, 2012, at B11, and the New Jersey governor's office's internal investigation that exonerated Governor Chris Christie of personal involvement in the "Bridgegate" scandal. Michael Barbaro, *Report Details Claims by Ally: Christie Knew of Bridge Lane Closings*, N.Y. TIMES, Mar. 27, 2014, at A-1. They may be conducted by line managers, compliance officers, corporate counsel, or, as in the Penn State and New Jersey cases, outside counsel.

A firm might wish to have an attorney, often an outside attorney, conduct its internal investigation for a number of reasons. Foremost is the fact that investigations do not normally trigger privilege protections when conducted by nonlawyers. *See* Kathryn W. Munson, Comment, *Why Don't You Do Right? Corporate Fiduciary Law and the Self-Critical Analysis Privilege*, 88 TUL. L. REV. 651 (2014). Another advantage is the perception of impartiality when an investigation is conducted by someone without a direct stake in the outcome. *See* Joanna L. Grossman, *The Culture of Compliance: The Final Triumph of Form over Substance in Sexual Harassment Law*, 26 HARV. WOMEN'S L. J. 3, 57-63 (2003) (discussing institutional and other biases in internal investigations). For the latter reason as well, the tendency is to have special counsel retained to investigate serious cases, especially when a higher-level official is the subject of a complaint. Using special counsel avoids disqualification that may result from the same law firm both conducting the investigation and litigating any suit that ensues if the investigating attorney becomes a necessary witness. *See* Jeffrey A. Van Detta, *Lawyers as Investigators: How* Ellerth *and* Faragher *Reveal a Crisis of Ethics and Professionalism Through Trial Counsel Disqualification and Waivers of Privilege in Workplace Harassment Cases*, 24 J. LEGAL PROF. 261 (1999/2000).

At the same time, investigations have generated difficult ethical questions for lawyers, who may be faced with conflicts of interest or even risk criminal liability should their work help hide client wrongdoing or obstruct investigations by outside authorities. *See* Peter J. Henning, *Targeting Legal Advice*, 54 AM. U. L. REV. 669, 694 (2005) (quoting the SEC's Director of Enforcement, Stephen Cutler, "One area of particular focus for us is the role of lawyers in internal investigations of their clients or companies. We are concerned that, in some instances, lawyers may have conducted investigations in such a manner as to help hide ongoing fraud, or may have taken actions to actively obstruct such investigations.").

a. *Representing the Employer in an Investigation*

From the employer's perspective, the purpose of an internal investigation is to ascertain the facts in order to determine the optimal course of action—while trying to avoid making matters worse. The resulting choices might include making no changes after finding no wrongdoing, improving procedures to avoid even the perception of future problems despite a finding of no wrongdoing, self-reporting violations to enforcement authorities or regulators, taking steps to remedy the situation by disciplining or discharging those responsible for illegal or unwise conduct, and making settlement offers to aggrieved persons. Of course, the employer's response will usually itself be constrained by various legal doctrines. For example, the antidiscrimination laws prohibit retaliation against those who participate in legal proceedings and even those who oppose discrimination. The Supreme Court reaffirmed this in *Crawford v. Metropolitan Gov't of Nashville & Davidson County*, 555 U.S. 271 (2009) (holding that an employee's response to questions during a harassment investigation constituted protected "opposition" conduct under Title VII's antiretaliation principle).

Whatever the ultimate action taken, the first step is to ascertain the facts. Practitioners have developed a number of strategies for maximizing the efficacy of fact seeking in these investigations while minimizing the risks the investigations themselves may create. For example, it is both common sense and standard practice to identify and safeguard electronic files and relevant documents since employees may well wish to hide or destroy them to protect themselves and/or the corporation. It is also important to have a set of protocols for conducting witness interviews. One set of commentators recommends two rounds of interviews, the first and more informal is "designed to stake out the field of inquiry," and the second round is more focused:

> The purposes of the preliminary round of interviews is to: (a) introduce the investigating attorney, explain what is happening, and secure the witness's cooperation and understanding of the need for confidentiality; (b) learn the witness's background and connection to the matter under investigation; (c) give each witness an idea of what is going to happen in the investigation; and (d) attempt to identify the universe of witnesses and pertinent documents.
>
> In the initial interview, every effort should be made to put the witness at ease and convey the notion that the investigating attorney views the witness as a collaborator in a joint effort to find out exactly what happened. The initial interview should be a conversation—*not* an examination. The less the investigating attorney professes to know about the client and the client's industry during the initial interview, the better. Ideally, the investigating attorney assumes the role of student and asks the witness to assume the role of teacher. . . . The witness will probably end up telling the investigator the witness's version of what happened without much additional prompting. If the witness is not

forthcoming, the investigating attorney will have to proceed to a second, more adversarial interview, as described below. . . .

[I]f there is some material disagreement between witnesses, or between witnesses and available documents, the investigating attorney will need to conduct a second round of interviews with those witnesses whose stories seem to conflict with those of other witnesses or with available documents. In contrast to the preliminary interview, the second interview should be more in the nature of an examination than a conversation. . . .

[T]he investigating attorney may want to employ a professional court reporter for this purpose. A verbatim transcript will remove any doubt as to what the witness actually said during the interview. An employee witness in fear of losing his or her job, or perhaps even of prosecution, may later deny having made crucial disclosures. . . . [A court reporter may also help convince the government that "the company has engaged in a serious and professional effort to discover and document the facts."]

However, creating a verbatim transcript of witness interviews is contrary to the conventional wisdom of many practitioners . . . to protect against disclosure of such materials in the event a decision is made to voluntarily disclose the results of an internal investigation to the government. Instead, investigating attorneys often prepare post-interview memoranda that include the attorney's mental impressions and opinions so the memoranda will be protected by the work product doctrine. . . . [P]reserving applicable privileges is vitally important in conducting witness interviews. However, the government is requesting waiver of privileged materials with increasing frequency as a condition for the disclosing entity to receive credit for full cooperation. Therefore, preservation of privileges is ultimately uncertain, and may be less important than ensuring the accuracy of the testimony of critical witnesses. . . .

Ames Davis & Jennifer L. Weaver, *A Litigator's Approach to Interviewing Witnesses in Internal Investigations,* 17 HEALTH LAWYER 8, 9 (2005).

This passage suggests a number of the problems with internal investigations, including the very controversial practice of the Department of Justice and other state and federal regulatory authorities to demand (they might say "request") waivers of attorney-client privilege and work product protection as a condition of settlement discussions. The Department of Justice has adopted varying positions over time, but its current stance is reflected in the "Yates Memorandum," "Individual Accountability for Corporate Wrongdoing," Memorandum from Sally Q. Yates, Deputy Attorney Gen., U.S. Dep't of Justice, to All Component Heads and United States Attorneys (Sept. 9, 2015), https://www.justice.gov/dag/file/769036/download. As its title suggests, the Memorandum seeks to hold individuals liable for violations and to that end suggests conditioning deferral of prosecution of the corporation on corporate internal investigations turning over responsible individuals. That will typically require waiver of the corporate attorney-client privilege. *See generally* Katrice Bridges Copeland, *The Yates Memo: Looking for "Individual Accountability" in All the Wrong Places,* 102 IOWA L. REV. 1897, 1925 (2017).

Despite that possibility at the end of the day, as Davis and Weaver suggest, the attorney investigator should make every effort to preserve the privilege. Other commentators recommend a series of steps to protect the privilege and work product protection, including:

- Early lawyer involvement
- Explicit corporate request for legal (as opposed to business) advice
- Documenting the confidentiality of communications
- Restricting the internal flow of information

- Obtaining information from highest possible sources
- Labeling documents judiciously to avoid diluting protection for sensitive material
- Interposing legal conclusions, mental impressions, and strategies in all notes
- Treating former employee contacts as confidential for work product protection
- Deciding whether to release the report to a governmental agency, underwriter's counsel, accountants, or the press in light of the effect on privileges
- Express legal conclusions, opinions, and recommendations in the report to the board of directors

Thomas R. Mulroy & Eric J. Munoz, *The Internal Corporate Investigation*, 1 DePaul Bus. & Comm. L. J. 49, 82-84 (2002).

While the careful attorney will do her best to ensure that the privilege applies, she will also be aware that the protections may well be waived should a prosecutor threaten criminal charges or a regulator threaten a civil enforcement action. Further, the corporation may choose to waive its privilege even if not pressed by a government agency. For example, while the EEOC does not demand privilege waivers as part of its investigations, an employer seeking to allay Commission doubts about the effectiveness of its sexual harassment or antidiscrimination policies might want to provide such reports.

One of the central problems of the internal investigation is the relationship of the investigator to the employee being questioned. That individual may not understand that the investigator is in no sense that person's attorney—especially if the investigation begins with a version of the informal "conversation" described by Davis and Weaver. The potential for misunderstanding the role of the attorney is especially great if (as is often the case) the attorney investigating the matter on behalf of the employer has previously worked with the individual being questioned in matters in which the interests of the employer and employee were aligned.

New Jersey saw this play out in a high-profile case, *Speeney v. Rutgers*, 369 F. App'x 357 (3d Cir. 2010), which started with sexual harassment complaints by several students against a Rutgers University professor. Rutgers retained what was then the firm of Carpenter, Bennett & Morrissey both to represent it in the university's internal de-tenuring proceeding against the harasser and to defend it against a suit by him. Ultimately, both proceedings were resolved without any findings but with the professor leaving Rutgers. The students were apparently unhappy with the settlement and/or with any compensation to be paid to them on their own claims.

They were also unhappy with the law firm. In its representation of Rutgers, the firm interviewed the students who later became key witnesses in the internal proceedings and, presumably, would have been key to Rutgers's defense of the professor's suit. When the students brought suit, they not only pursued claims against Rutgers for the harassment, but also sued Carpenter for malpractice, asserting that they were not mere witnesses but rather clients of the firm. And, for good measure, they sought to have the firm disqualified from representing Rutgers in their suit against it.

The Third Circuit's decision was scarcely definitive. Since the plaintiffs ultimately settled their claims against Rutgers, the disqualification motion was moot when the matter reached court. But there was still the plaintiffs' malpractice claim against "their" lawyers, the Carpenter firm. While the district court had found that there was no attorney-client relationship, the Third Circuit remanded for another determination in light of new evidence the plaintiffs claim to have had. *See also Morin v. Me. Educ. Ass'n*, 993 A.2d 1097 (Me. 2010) (trial court exceeded its discretion in disqualifying employer's law firm in employee's discrimination suit; while attorney may have misrepresented his role in investigation by calling it "independent" and saying he did not represent employer, plaintiff was unable to show actual prejudice from employer being represented by attorneys from the same firm).

As *Speeney* suggests, the safest course of action is for the investigating attorney to inform the employee explicitly that the investigator is not representing him, a so-called *Upjohn* warning,

> which explains to the interviewee that: a) interviewing counsel represents the company, and not the individual employee; b) because the interviewer is conducting the interview to gather information to provide legal advice to the company, the substance of the interview is protected by the attorney-client privilege; c) that privilege belongs to the company, not the interviewee; d) the interviewee must maintain the confidentiality of the information disclosed during the interview; and e) the company, in its sole discretion, may decide to waive that privilege at some future point.

William Athanas & Christopher Terrell, *Conducting an Internal Investigation: Recognizing and Resolving Key Issues from an Internal and External Perspective*, 75 ALA. LAW. 307, 310 (2014). Those who resist any standard warning agree that it dispels any possible confusion about the relationship of the investigator to the witness but stress the risk is that it will discourage frank disclosure by the employee. Do you think that Davis and Weaver would favor providing such a warning? Wouldn't the warning tend to raise witness defenses, especially in the first, putting-the-witness-at-ease stage they recommend? Which approach would you use?

b. The Employee as Witness or Target

In the typical internal investigation, the individuals interviewed will be current employees, although former employees and "outsiders" such as suppliers or independent contractors may sometimes be asked to provide information. With outsiders, the biggest problem for the investigator is obtaining cooperation when she has neither legal process nor a command-and-control relationship. With current employees, the attorney likely has the necessary leverage to obtain cooperation, simply because the employer can require the witness' participation. That leverage, however, creates its own risks, most notably the possibility that the employee participating under compulsion will not be truthful.

Some employees, of course, have incentives to cooperate or, at least, few disincentives. The person alleging sexual harassment, for example, will need to cooperate because of her responsibility to take advantage of her employer's mechanisms for correcting problems. True "innocent bystanders" in the firm may see no reason not to cooperate simply because they have little stake in the dispute and cooperation will clearly be expected as part of the job. But the person accused of wrongdoing or anyone who fears that he or she will be accused or blamed by the target, has more to worry about; and coworkers, subordinates, or supervisors of targets may be concerned about the consequences for them—whichever way the investigation proceeds.

Suppose an employee has been given an *Upjohn* warning and has concerns about either being (or becoming) a target or risking the ire of the target or of those close to him. Can he refuse to cooperate, or at least demand that an attorney be present? In the union setting, federal labor law often accords members the right to have a union representative present. *See* Michael D. Moberly & Andrea G. Lisenbee, *Honing Our* Kraft?: *Reconciling Variations in the Remedial Treatment of* Weingarten *Violations*, 21 Hofstra Lab. & Emp. L. J. 523 (2004). It is possible some such rights exist outside the union context, but the National Labor Relations Board has vacillated on this issue and currently does not recognize such a right. *See* Ann C. Hodges, *The Limits of Multiple Rights and Remedies: A Call for Revisiting the Law of the Workplace*, 22 Hofstra Lab. & Emp. L. J. 601 (2005); Christine Neylon O'Brien, *The NLRB Waffling on* Weingarten *Rights*, 37 Loy. U. Chi. L. J. 111 (2005). As a result, it is not uncommon for employers to prohibit witnesses from bringing their own representative to an investigation.

There is, of course, no legal compulsion for the employee to answer questions, and the employee could refuse to appear without her attorney. Further, at least in circumstances where criminal liability is possible (rare in sexual harassment investigation, but common in a wide range of other investigations such as investigations into embezzlement), the employee's statements—particularly untruthful or misleading ones—can be used against her in subsequent criminal proceedings. Thus, a refusal to cooperate is sometimes the employee's wisest course of conduct. *See Hopp & Flesch, LLC v. Backstreet*, 123 P.3d 1176 (Colo. 2005) (attorney did not commit malpractice by advising employee not to participate in internal investigation because her statements could be used in subsequent criminal proceedings).

On the other hand, employees who do not cooperate risk discipline or termination and likely have little legal recourse against their employer. Generally speaking, there is no exception to the at-will rule that would prevent an employer from discharging an employee who refuses to cooperate. *Merkel v. Scovill, Inc.*, 787 F.2d 174 (6th Cir. 1986); *Costello v. St. Francis Hosp.*, 258 F. Supp. 2d 144 (E.D.N.Y. 2003). Indeed, it might even be good cause sufficient to justify firing even where an employee has some preexisting right to job security.

Privacy claims are also likely unavailing since the employer's need to ascertain whether there was a violation of law or company policy will almost always trump any privacy concerns, provided the inquiry is not overly broad. These issues will be front and center in many sexual harassment investigations. Of course, limitations on how information is gathered during an investigation still apply, such as the general prohibition on polygraph tests and any constraints imposed by tort law. *See Vasarhelyi v. New School for Social Research*, 646 N.Y.S.2d 795 (App. Div. 1996) (upholding a claim for intentional infliction of emotional distress arising out of outside attorneys' investigation); *see generally* Chapters 5 and 6. Thus, an employer could be subject to claims of false imprisonment or intentional infliction of emotional distress in the case of egregious employer misconduct. *But see Jones v. Dep't of Pub. Safety & Corr.*, 923 S. 2d 699 (La. Ct. App. 2005) (upholding discharge based in part on refusal of corrections officer to take a polygraph examination as part of a sexual harassment investigation).

The one situation where an employee could have greater legal protection is in a public employment setting. While a demand for cooperation on threat of dismissal seems permissible in the private sector, authority is split as to whether a public entity's threat to discharge an employee who does not cooperate means any resulting statements were inadmissible as coerced self-incrimination. *See People v. Sapp*, 934 P.2d 1367, 1374 (Colo. 1997) (statement cannot be used against him). *But see Debnam v. North Carolina Dep't of Correction*, 432 S.E.2d 324 (N.C. 1993) (employer did not violate employee's right against self-incrimination by terminating him for refusing to answer possibly incriminating questions even though it did not affirmatively inform employee on use immunity).

c. Employee Right to Indemnification or a Defense?

Another issue is who will pay for the attorneys' fees of an employee who does seek the advice of counsel. Prosecutors sometimes frown on advances of legal fees and even indemnification of employees, Sarah Helene Duggin, *Internal Corporate Investigations: Legal Ethics, Professionalism and the Employee Interview*, 2003 COLUM. BUS. L. REV. 859, 914-15, and internal investigators therefore tend to avoid committing on this issue prior to the conclusion of the investigation. For employees who cannot afford their own counsel, corporate punting on reimbursement may be the equivalent of saying no.

> At any rate, problems can arise when the employer considers whether to provide for representation. First, assume the employer decides to do so, whether or not it feels obligated to take that step. Court Rule 1.8(f) controls cases in which an attorney "accept[s] compensation for representing a client from one other than the client," requiring informed consent and no interference with the attorney's independent judgment, and, as indicated by *In re State Grand Jury Investigation*, 983 A.2d 1097 (N.J. 2009), arranging for such representation can be problematic. In that case, the state sought to disqualify attorneys representing employees of a target firm because of how the firm had arranged for representation. While rejecting disqualification on the facts before it, the opinion recognized the potential for interference with the lawyer's professional judgment in representing his client, and established a number of principles, including prohibitions on communications between the payer and attorney and no termination of payments "without leave of court brought on prior written notice to the lawyer and the client." *Id.* at 495-97. Although *In re State Grand Jury Investigation* arose in the criminal context, Rule 1.8(f) presumably applies to all situations where an employer pays the litigation expenses of its workers. Thus, attorneys would be well advised to take the Court's six factors into account when entering into any such relationship.

Assuming the employer is not willing to pay for counsel, the question is whether it has an obligation to do so. Whether any employee who does retain counsel, either for the investigation itself or any subsequent proceedings against him, has a right to indemnification is a complicated question, and may depend on whether the employer is in the public or private sector. In the public sector, state statutes often set the ground rules. *See, e.g., Prado v. State*, 895 A.2d 1154 (N. J. 2006) (state statute required Attorney General to defend employees subject to some exceptions). In the private sector, many state corporate statutes require mandatory indemnification of expenses, including attorneys' fees, but they are usually limited to corporate "officers" acting in good faith in pursuit of the best interests of the employer. Some statutes, however, are broad enough to reach ordinary employees.805 ILCS 5/8.75(c). Other states reach similar results under common-law principles. The RESTATEMENT (THIRD) OF AGENCY (ALI 2006), for example, would impose on a principal a duty to indemnify the agent if there is an agreement to do so. §8.14(1); *see also Harris v. Howard Univ.*,

Inc., 28 F. Supp. 2d 1, 14 (D.D.C. 1998) (finding pursuant to university by-laws that employer was required to indemnify plaintiff vice president for acts committed in good faith but not for those attributable to gross negligence). But a formal agreement is not necessary. The Restatement goes on to provide that, unless otherwise agreed, the principal should reimburse the agent who "suffers a loss that fairly should be borne by the principal in light of their relationship." § 8.14(2)(b). Cmt. d is more specific: "a principal has a duty to indemnify the agent against [reasonable] expenses and other losses incurred by the agent in defending against actions brought by third parties if the agent acted with actual authority in taking the action challenged by the third party's suit." *Id.* The underlying notion is akin to unjust enrichment. That is, to the extent that an employee is sued for pursuing the interests of his employer, the costs of defense are ones that are expended on behalf of that employer, and the employer has been unjustly enriched to the extent the employee, not the employer, has incurred them.

However, the Restatement's requirement to repay the costs of a defense is subject to the limitation that it does not reach "losses that result from the agent's own negligence, illegal acts, or other wrongful conduct." Cmt. b; *see also* cmt. d ("A principal does not have a duty to indemnify an agent against . . . losses caused solely by wrongful acts committed by the agent."). Thus, it may be critical to indemnification that the employee prevails in defending himself on the underlying claim or at least settles before a determination of liability.

A further problem is whether the employer is required to *advance* attorneys' fees, as opposed to repaying such fees when they have been incurred. As a practical matter, an employer refusing to pay fees until the conclusion of the litigation will put enormous pressure on most employees, and, in complex cases, it may well result in the employee being unable to retain an attorney. Thus, where the employer and employee's interests align, it is in the employer's interest to advance fees, as in the New Jersey *Grand Jury* case, although there is little legal compulsion on employers to do so. The exception is where the obligation to indemnify stems from a contractual commitment or a provision of the company's by-laws, as is sometimes the case with officers and high-level employees. For a dramatic example of complicated litigation involving who counts as an "officer," see *Aleynikov v. Goldman Sachs Grp., Inc.*, 155 A.3d 370 (Del. 2017); *see also Homestore, Inc. v. Tafeen*, 888 A.2d 204, 211-14 (Del. 2005) (upholding advancement of litigation expenses to former officer required by corporate by-laws and rejecting argument that company need not advance litigation expenses because employee personally profited by alleged wrongdoing; *International Airport Ctrs., L.L.C. v. Citrin*, 455 F.3d 749 (7th Cir. 2006) (rejecting an employer's effort to enjoin an employee's action seeking advancement under Delaware law). Since in most cases advancement of fees is voluntary, employers may condition their commitment on an undertaking of the employee to repay the moneys advanced if he is ultimately determined to have committed wrongdoing.

Finally, it is doubtful that any of these principles apply when an employee seeks recovery of costs of the counsel in the course of an internal investigation. The indemnification issue is cast in terms of shifting the costs from the agent to the principal when a third party sues. While the rule might apply even in the absence of formal proceedings, such as a settlement for "nuisance value," the internal investigation pits the employee-witness against the employer, not against any third party. This is particularly true where the investigation is in response to a harassment complaint. In such instances, the employer conducts the investigation with hopes of taking corrective action that will enable it to avoid vicarious liability in a subsequent lawsuit by the complaining party.

Should the internal investigation result in the discharge of the employee, who is then sued by the third party whose complaint may have triggered the investigation, a statutory or common law right of indemnification may well apply but may be dependent upon the employee being exonerated in the course of the proceedings. Further, to the extent the former employer refuses to advance attorneys' fees and costs, the former employee will be in a very difficult situation—regardless of the theoretic right to indemnification.

The bottom line, of course, is that the employee who is interviewed during, or is even the target of, an internal investigation is often faced with a number of unpalatable alternatives. The employee can refuse to cooperate and risk discipline or dismissal; the employee can cooperate and risk discipline, dismissal, and even the use of statements she makes in later criminal proceedings against her. *See* Saul Elbeinmarch, *When Employees Confess, Sometimes Falsely*, N.Y. Times, Mar. 9, 2014, at BU1 (reporting an assessment of numerous suits by ex-employees of Autozone that suggest that internal investigations by investigators trained in the same high-pressure techniques as the police, can result in false confessions as employees see the alternative of discharge as more attractive than potential arrest by the police). The employee can insist on an attorney to help her decide on her course of action, and she will probably (but not certainly) have the request accommodated, but she may well be responsible for the attorneys' fees involved. Should the investigation result in her discharge, she will probably have no right against her former employee, except perhaps a right to indemnification should she prevail in any suit brought against her.

PROBLEMS

13-3. You have been consulted by an individual you know slightly from the local gym. He tells you that he is a midlevel manager at the local branch of Pal-Mart, a chain of superstores. He has had some recent disagreements with a female subordinate. Yesterday, he was told by a Human Resource specialist that he was being suspended with pay pending Pal-Mart's investigation of a complaint of sexual harassment. He was told to expect a call from an attorney with a large firm in the nearby city, who would be handling the investigation.

He has not been provided any further information, but he is sure that the complaint was made by his subordinate. He wants to know how to proceed. What further questions do you have for him?

13-4. You have been retained by Pal-Mart as special counsel to investigate the matter raised in Problem 13-3. You have a barebones complaint from the subordinate naming her supervisor and accusing him of "disgusting, inappropriate comments." Sketch out your strategy for investigating the matter.

B. CONDUCTING LAYOFFS AND OBTAINING RELEASE AGREEMENTS

One important risk management technique for employers is to obtain contractual releases of liability from terminated employees. It is generally understood that employees cannot *prospectively* waive substantive claims under any of the federal employment statutes; such legislation would be rendered wholly inoperative if employees could be required to waive or release rights as a condition of employment. *See Alexander v. Gardner-Denver Co.*, 415 U.S. 36, 51 (1974) ("[W]e think it clear that there can be no prospective waiver of an employee's rights under Title VII."). However, once a cause of action arises, the employee may release any claims he or she may have subject to certain conditions. Effective release agreements are typically obtained by providing terminated employees with severance pay contingent upon signing a waiver of rights.

Such "buy outs" often occur in cases of individual terminations, and they can be notorious when high-level executives leave major companies with "golden handshakes." *See In re the Walt Disney Co. Deriv. Litig.*, 906 A.2d 27 (Del. 2006) (rejecting breach of duty claims against board of directors for decisions to hire and shortly thereafter, fire the CEO with multimillion-dollar buy-out). However, much more modest packages are particularly common in the context of large-scale reductions in force ("RIFs"). RIFs pose many legal and practical challenges for employers. Companies must ensure they do not select employees for layoff based on an impermissible criterion, such as age. In addition, they must comply with certain statutory requirements, such as providing advance notice of layoffs. For example, the federal Workers Adjustment and Retraining Notification Act, 29 U.S.C. §2101 et seq. (2018) ("WARN"), requires covered employers engaging in "plant closings" or "mass layoffs" to usually provide 60 days' notice to affected workers. Perhaps most importantly, employers must be cognizant that the financial, social, and emotional effects of layoffs can be devastating to the affected employees and in the case of a closing, may have repercussions throughout the community where the company is located. Even smaller-scale layoffs may negatively affect the morale and productivity of those workers who remain employed. For all of these reasons, careful advance planning can be critical in maintaining a successful working environment post-layoff as well as avoiding liability to those who are "let go."

Williams v. Phillips Petroleum Co.
23 F.3d 930 (5th Cir. 1994)

WILLIAMS, J.

[In 1992, Phillips Petroleum Company, Phillips Gas Holding Company, Inc. ("PGHC"), and Phillips 66 Company, a division of Phillips Petroleum Company, reduced their work forces at their Houston Chemical Complex ("HCC") and laid off over 500 employees at their Bartlesville, Oklahoma, location. PGHC provided the Bartlesville workers 60 days' notice prior to the reduction in force. The defendants also laid off 27 workers at several locations in Houston to whom they did not provide notice. Six of the laid off Houston workers (the "original plaintiffs") brought suit alleging that defendants had violated WARN by failing to provide 60 days' notice. Subsequently, four of the workers laid off from the Bartlesville location (the "Bartlesville plaintiffs") sought to join the suit. All of the original and Bartlesville plaintiffs signed releases in connection with their terminations in exchange for what the employer described as enhanced layoff benefits. The district court refused to permit joinder of the Bartlesville plaintiffs and awarded summary judgment to the employer on the original plaintiffs' claims.]

III

A

The district court rendered summary judgment because no mass layoff occurred at the single sites of employment where the original plaintiffs worked. . . .

WARN requires covered employers to provide "affected employees" notice of a mass layoff. "Affected employees" include "employees who may reasonably be expected to experience an employment loss as a consequence of a proposed plant closing or mass layoff by their employer." 29 U.S.C. §2101(a)(5). A "mass layoff" is defined as any employment loss at a single site of employment that involves one-third of the employees at that site and at least fifty employees, or at least 500 employees. 29 U.S.C. §2101(a)(3); 20 C.F.R. §639.3(c). If a "mass layoff" occurs, the employer must provide written notice to each affected employee at least sixty days prior to the layoff and inform various state and local officials of the mass layoff. 29 U.S.C. §2102. An employer who violates WARN is liable for back pay, lost benefits, civil penalties, and attorneys' fees. 29 U.S.C. §2104.

The statute does not define a "single site of employment." The rules promulgated by the Secretary of Labor provide that "[n]on-contiguous sites in the same geographic area which do not share the same staff or operational purpose should not be considered a single site." 20 C.F.R. §639.3(i)(4). . . .

The Houston and Bartlesville layoffs cannot be aggregated to bootstrap the Houston plaintiffs over the WARN minimum required for a mass layoff. . . . It is not plausible, under any reasonable or good-faith reading of the regulations, that the Houston and Bartlesville plants—located in different states and hundreds of miles apart—could be considered a "single site" for purposes of WARN.

Employees were not rotated between the different sites, and the locations did not share staff and equipment. *See* 20 C.F.R. §639.3(i)(3). No other "unusual circumstances" have been alleged that would support classifying the two plants as a "single site." *See* 20 C.F.R. §639.3(i)(8); *Carpenters Dist. Counsel of New Orleans v. Dillard*, 15 F.3d 1275, 1290 (5th 1994). . . . The Bartlesville layoffs, accordingly, are irrelevant to the issue of whether the Houston employees were entitled to notice under WARN.

No mass layoff occurred at the single sites of employment where the original plaintiffs worked. Five of the plaintiffs worked at HCC's operations in three different locations in and around Houston. HCC laid off twenty-seven employees over a ten-month period. One of the named plaintiffs worked for PGHC in Houston; PGHC laid off eight employees who worked at that site. The layoffs at HCC and PGHC were not mass layoffs as defined by the Act, as the number of employees laid off did not meet the fifty-employee minimum. Thus, the Houston employees were not entitled to WARN notification. . . .

B

The district court also rendered summary judgment for Phillips because the plaintiffs had signed releases covering the allegations made in their complaint. . . .[2] Normally the release of federal claims is governed by federal law. *See, e.g., O'Hare v. Global Natural Resources, Inc.*, 898 F.2d 1015, 1017 (5th Cir. 1990) (ADEA); *Rogers v. General Elec. Co.*, 781 F.2d 452, 454 (5th Cir. 1986) (Title VII). Public policy favors voluntary settlement of claims and enforcement of releases, *Rogers*, but a release of an employment or employment discrimination claim is valid only if it is "knowing" and "voluntary," *Alexander v. Gardner-Denver Co.*, 415 U.S. 36, 52 n.15 (1974). Once a party establishes that his opponent signed a release that addresses the claims at issue, received adequate consideration, and breached the release, the opponent has the burden of demonstrating that the release was invalid because of fraud, duress, material mistake, or some other defense. We examine the totality of circumstances to determine whether the releasor has established an appropriate defense. *O'Hare.*

1.

Each original plaintiff signed a release shortly after his or her termination of employment. The releases stated that signing the release was a condition to participation in the company's enhanced supplemental layoff pay plan, advised the employee to consult an attorney, gave ample time to consider the release, and specifically covered all claims relating to the individual's employment or layoff. The Bartlesville plaintiffs signed similar releases.

The requirements of WARN pertain to an individual's employment and termination, issues addressed in the releases. Phillips provided enhanced benefits for those employees who signed the releases. These benefits were in addition to the basic severance plan benefits that the employees would have received regardless of whether they had signed the releases. The original plaintiffs are making claims on matters addressed in their release, and the Bartlesville plaintiffs attempted to join the lawsuit that involved claims on matters addressed in their release. Thus, all elements of a valid release are present.

Williams has provided no credible evidence that the releases were obtained by fraud or duress. There is no genuine issue of material fact that the releases were valid.

Williams contends that the releases were invalid because they did not mention WARN. This argument is meritless. There is no obligation under WARN or the common law for the defendants to mention WARN for the releases to be valid. The

---

2. Although this discussion is unnecessary to the issue of whether WARN was violated, given our holding in part III.A., *supra*, we include it as a further indication that this action is frivolous.

releases stated that they included all claims relating to the "time of my employment or to my layoff. . . ." WARN applies to layoffs and the releases addressed all claims related to the plaintiffs' layoffs; thus, the releases barred WARN claims.

Plaintiffs also argue that the waivers did not comply with the Older Workers Benefit Protection Act ("OWBPA"), 29 U.S.C. §626(f). Plaintiffs have asserted no age discrimination claim, and their proffered analogy between WARN and the ADEA does not survive scrutiny. The OWBPA places specific requirements on waivers of age discrimination claims in order for them to be considered knowing and voluntary. This statute is a change from the common law, and there is no similar obligation imposed on employers under WARN.

Williams contends that the waivers are invalid under a totality of the circumstances test. She claims that the combination of five factors makes the waivers invalid, but she identifies no precedent suggesting that these factors are dispositive. Williams carried the burden to demonstrate that there was a genuine issue of material fact on a defense to the validity of the releases. She was obligated to produce some evidence of fraud, duress, or other basis for holding the release invalid. She has not done so, thus summary judgment was appropriate.

Even if we accept Williams's statement of the totality of circumstances test, she cannot prevail. She identifies several elements to consider: (1) a plaintiff's education and business experience; (2) the role of each plaintiff and class member in deciding the terms of the release; (3) the clarity of the agreement and all related documents referred to in the releases; (4) whether each plaintiff and class member was represented by or consulted with an attorney; and (5) the amount of time each plaintiff and class member had possession of or access to the release before signing it.

Concerning the plaintiffs' education and business experience, there [is] no evidence suggesting that they could not read or understand the releases. The cases relied upon by the plaintiffs are distinguishable by whether the individual who signed the release understood the claims released. There is nothing in the record establishing a genuine issue of material fact that the plaintiffs did not know what they were doing.

Plaintiffs argue that none of them negotiated the terms of the releases. There is no evidence that plaintiffs were denied an opportunity to negotiate, nor that they were given a "take it or leave it" offer. The releases informed each employee that he should consult a lawyer and allowed a reasonable period, in most instances up to forty-five days, to consider the releases. The plaintiffs signed the releases and never asserted in their declarations that Phillips had precluded them from negotiating. There is no evidence sufficient to create a genuine issue of material fact.

The releases were clear, simple, and easily understood. The release precluded all claims related to the plaintiffs' "employment" or "layoff." This is not technical jargon, and it covers the plaintiffs' WARN claims. The plaintiffs do not indicate what provisions could have been incomprehensible to them, as they were written in plain English. There is also no evidence of duress that could have forced them to sign involuntarily.

The plaintiffs also claim that the releases should be invalidated because the defendants presented no evidence that each plaintiff and class member actually consulted with an attorney. The releases signed by the plaintiffs stated:

> You should thoroughly review and understand the effect of the release before signing it. To the extent that you have any claims covered by this release, you will be waiving

potentially valuable rights by signing. You are also advised to discuss this release with your lawyer.

Thus, defendants advised the plaintiffs to consult a lawyer. Plaintiffs suggest that Phillips should have offered to supply a lawyer, but they offer no authority imposing this duty. Even without signing the releases, plaintiffs were entitled to substantial layoff benefits that could have been used to finance a lawyer, either individually or jointly. It is not Phillips's fault that the plaintiffs chose not to consult a lawyer after being advised to do so. Plaintiffs do not contest the final element of the test, as they were given as much as forty-five days to consider the releases.

2.

Even if a release is tainted by misrepresentation or duress, it is ratified if the releasor retains the consideration after learning that the release is voidable. A person who signs a release, then sues his or her employer for matters covered under the release, is obligated to return the consideration. Offering to tender back the consideration after obtaining relief in the lawsuit would be insufficient to avoid a finding of ratification. *Grillet v. Sears, Roebuck & Co.*, 927 F.2d 217, 220-21 (5th Cir. 1991).

For signing the releases, the original plaintiffs as a group received $ 210,853.65 in consideration in an enhanced plan benefits and $56,632.38 in basic plan benefits. The original plaintiffs did not return the consideration to the defendants, even after making claims that the releases were voidable. Thus, the plaintiffs ratified the releases even if, *arguendo*, they were not knowingly and voluntarily signed. *Grillet.* . . .

NOTES

1. *A Tale of Several Regimes.* Understanding when a release agreement is effective depends on the applicable legal standard, which varies depending on the substantive claim being released. *Williams* deals with the standard for the validity of releases under WARN, a federal statute that does not deal explicitly with requirements for releasing claims. In upholding the plaintiffs' releases, the court applies a general "knowing and voluntary standard," which it drew from a Title VII case, *Alexander v. Gardner-Denver Co.*, 415 U.S. 36, 52, n.15 (1974). This test, elaborated in a variety of ways by the lower courts, applies to WARN, Title VII, the Americans with Disabilities Act, and the Family and Medical Leave Act.

In contrast, some statutes—most notably the ADEA—contain provisions directly governing release agreements or have been interpreted to impose special requirements. *Williams* alludes to, but declines to apply, the more demanding regime that exists under the Older Workers Benefit Protection Act, a 1991 amendment to the ADEA, which requires that a release be "knowing and voluntary" and that, "at a minimum," the employer comply with a variety of procedural requirements including:

(A) the waiver is part of an agreement between the individual and the employer that is written in a manner calculated to be understood by such individual, or by the average individual eligible to participate;

(B) the waiver specifically refers to rights or claims arising under this chapter;

(C) the individual does not waive rights or claims that may arise after the date the waiver is executed;

(D) the individual waives rights or claims only in exchange for consideration in addition to anything of value to which the individual already is entitled;

(E) the individual is advised in writing to consult with an attorney prior to executing the agreement;

(F) (i) the individual is given a period of at least 21 days within which to consider the agreement; or

(ii) if a waiver is requested in connection with an exit incentive or other employment termination program offered to a group or class of employees, the individual is given a period of at least 45 days within which to consider the agreement;

(G) the agreement provides that for a period of at least 7 days following the execution of such agreement, the individual may revoke the agreement, and the agreement shall not become effective or enforceable until the revocation period has expired. . . .

29 U.S.C. §626(f)(1). More specific disclosures are also required "if a waiver is requested in connection with an exit incentive or other employment termination program offered to a group or class of employees," *id*. at (H), and the statute has particular provisions governing settlement once an EEOC charge or suit has been filed. *Id*. at §626(f)(2). Even more protective of employees is the Fair Labor Standards Act, which generally deems waivers and settlement of claims unenforceable without Department of Labor supervision. *See* Evan Hudson-Plush, Note, *WARN's Place in the FLSA/Employment Discrimination Dichotomy: Why a Warning Cannot Be Waived*, 27 CARDOZO L. REV. 2929, 2945-48 (2006).

Finally, where the underlying claims involve only state law, a release is likely to be subjected to an even lower level of scrutiny than would be true under the general "knowing and voluntary" standard applied in *Williams* under WARN. Most likely, the validity of such releases would be determined as a matter of ordinary contract law, although state-to-state variations are possible.

2. *Comparing Standards: "Knowing and Voluntary" Versus Common Law.* Invalidating a release agreement under basic contract principles is quite difficult. The requisite consideration and assent are generally present and easy to establish: The employer provides severance or other benefits in exchange for the release, and both parties typically sign a written agreement. The only way for an employee to void the contract is to demonstrate a defense like fraud or duress. And, as the "tender back" discussion in *Williams* indicates, exercising a right to void a contract may require the return of the consideration received.

While a few federal courts treat the enforceability of releases as a matter of normal contract principles, the vast majority apply a "totality of the circumstances" test to all non-OWBPA federal statutory claims to determine whether a waiver is knowing and voluntary. That test looks to a number of factors, as one commentator explains:

To determine whether a person's consent is knowing and voluntary under the totality of the circumstances, courts apply a list of factors: the person's education and business experience, the person's role in determining the release's provisions, the release's clarity and specificity, the time the person had to review and consider the release, whether the person read the release and considered its terms before signing it, whether the person knew or should have known his or her rights upon executing the release, whether the person was represented by an attorney or had other independent advice, whether there was consideration for the release, and whether the person's consent was induced by improper conduct by the employer, including whether the employer encouraged or discouraged the person from consulting with an attorney. This list is not exhaustive, and the absence of any one factor is not dispositive. The factors are not to be treated as a checklist, and courts do not insist on rigid adherence to them.

Daniel P. O'Gorman, *A State of Disarray: The "Knowing and Voluntary" Standard for Releasing Claims Under Title VII of the Civil Rights Act of 1964*, 8 U. PA. J. LAB. & EMP. L. 73, 85-88 (2005). *See also* Daniel P. O'Gorman, *Show Me the Money: The Applicability of Contract Law's Ratification and Tender-Back Doctrines to Title VII Releases,* 84 TUL. L. REV. 675, 728 (2010); Craig Robert Senn, *Knowing and Voluntary Waivers of Federal Employment Claims: Replacing the Totality of Circumstances Test with a "Waiver Certainty" Test*, 58 FLA. L. REV. 305 (2006). Which standard does *Williams* apply? Contract? Totality of the circumstances? Something in between? Further, it's not always clear what law the court thinks it is applying—federal or state.

3. *Comparing Standards: "Knowing and Voluntary" versus OWBPA.* A large overlap obviously exists between the factors used in the knowing and voluntary standard and the requirements OWBPA prescribes, but OWBPA is harder-edged. For example, while one factor under the knowing and voluntary test is the time the employee had to consider the release, OWBPA requires a minimum of 21/45 days and also prescribes a week's "cooling off" period for revocation. Courts have tended to require strict compliance with OWBPA. *See Am. Airlines, Inc. v. Cardoza-Rodriguez*, 133 F.3d 111 (1st Cir. 1998) (invalidating release for failure to explicitly advise employees to consult an attorney).

From a positivist perspective, it is easy to explain why ADEA claims are subject to more stringent requirements than claims under most other federal statutes—Congress so provided. But what justifies OWBPA's imposition of these highly specialized criteria? In other words, what is so special about releases of age discrimination claims in general and releases of such claims following a RIF in particular? Should comparable requirements be placed on other types of waivers, such as those in *Williams*, or ordinary severance agreements? What about waivers of procedural rights, like the right to a jury trial or agreements to shorten applicable statutes of limitations? *See Rodriguez v. Raymours Furniture Co.*, 138 A.3d 528 (N.J. 2016) (invalidating an agreement imposed on applicants as a condition of hiring that shortened the statute of limitations under New Jersey's antidiscrimination law). We will revisit this last question when we look at pre-dispute arbitration agreements in the next section.

4. *Back to the Common Law.* Despite the development of specialized standards, the common law is not entirely irrelevant to assessing a release either under the knowing and voluntary standard or under OWBPA. For example, both incorporate the requirement of "consideration," and all releases are subject to contractual defenses. Note that *Williams* considers and rejects the applicability of the defenses of fraud and duress. *See Gilkerson v. Neb. Colocation Ctrs.*, LLC, 859 F.3d 1115, 1119-20 (8th Cir. 2017) (triable issue of duress when plaintiff was induced to sign an agreement forfeiting his contractual status in return for not being fired immediately). The presence of undue influence, *see Odorizzi v. Bloomfield School Dist.*, 54 Cal. Rptr. 533 (Ct. App. 1966), unconscionability, *see* discussion on page 956, or mistake could negate a release as well. These defenses may be relevant even in the ADEA context since OWBPA provides a floor, not a ceiling. But, as the *Williams* court stresses, the common law places the burden of persuasion on the party challenging the release. Once the employer shows offer and acceptance and consideration, the contract is established, albeit subject to the employee proving some invalidating factor. In contrast, under OWBPA, the burden is on the employer to demonstrate its compliance with the statutory requirements.

5. *What About Bargaining Power?* In *Williams*, the plaintiffs, unable to prove fraud or duress, urged that their releases should be void in light of their lack of sophistication, limited education, and inability to negotiate vis-à-vis the employer. Why do you think the Fifth Circuit rejects this line of argument? At one point, the court disparages the contention that the release agreement was a "take it or leave it offer," finding no evidence to support this claim. Is the court suggesting that the employees had more power to bargain than they realized? It seems unlikely that Phillips would have negotiated different terms with different employees, but that is not impossible. Is the court implicitly stating that the ability to dicker over terms is important to the validity of a contract? Or is the court simply unsympathetic to the plaintiffs given that they stood to gain $2 million in additional compensation and benefits under the release? Could an argument like the one advanced by the plaintiffs work in the OWBPA context, even if the technical requirements of the statute have been satisfied?

6. *The Two-Way Release.* While the main benefit for workers of signing a release is severance pay, there are sometimes other advantages, as where the release is reciprocal (waiving claims by the employer against the employee) or where it supersedes past agreements imposing duties on the employee. In *Avery Dennison Corp., v. Naimo*, 25 IER Cases 690 (N.D. Ill. 2006), a release including a merger clause was held to preclude the employer from enforcing a prior written employment agreement containing a noncompete. The employer in *Avery* most likely sought to merge the prior employment contract into the separation agreement in order to avoid any future employee claims to salary or benefits; in the process it failed to consider the prior contract's non-competition clause. *Avery* also offers a reminder to employees. Getting laid off is difficult enough without a noncompete hampering one's prospects of re-employment. The presentation of a termination agreement is a good time to try to secure other benefits besides severance, such as a release from such commitments.

7. *"Good" Releases Crowding out "Bad" Ones.* Although *Williams* holds that OWBPA does not control outside the ADEA, risk-averse employers are well advised to satisfy the more demanding standards of OWBPA whenever they seek releases. Most releases, therefore, are structured along OWBPA lines. As a practical matter, this allows the employer to develop a single standardized release agreement and set of procedures that human resources personnel can use in all cases, without having to make individual judgments about whether a particular termination might implicate the ADEA. In addition, abiding by OWBPA requirements provides enhanced certainty that the release will hold up if challenged since any release that satisfies OWBPA is almost certain to satisfy other tests. For employees, this means that those offered a release will have the opportunity to review, consider, and even revoke their agreement, effectively reaping the benefits of the OWBPA irrespective of whether they raise ADEA claims or are even protected by the statute. *See, e.g., Neely v. Good Samaritan Hosp.*, 345 F. App'x 39 (6th Cir. 2009) (release was properly revoked by race discrimination plaintiff notwithstanding fact that she never raised age discrimination claim).

8. *Ratification and Tendering Back. Williams* states that even if a release is subject to a valid contract defense, the employee will "ratify" the agreement if she retains the benefits of the agreement (the severance pay) despite learning the release is voidable. In short, a plaintiff who seeks to challenge a release must tender back the consideration received where only the knowing and voluntary standard governs. In contrast, ratification is not possible under OWBPA if the release is inadequate; there is therefore no need to tender back the consideration received in order to file an ADEA suit. *See Oubre v. Entergy Operations*, 522 U.S. 422, 427 (1998) (rejecting any requirement of ratification or requiring return of consideration: any such rule "would frustrate the statute's practical operation as well as its formal command" since discharged employees will often have spent the money received and therefore be unable to tender back).

9. *Waivers of Administrative Rights.* Although employees can release their rights to sue under the federal discrimination laws, including the ADEA where the OWBPA waiver requirements are met, employees may not release their rights to file administrative charges with the EEOC. *See* 29 U.S.C. §629(f)(4); *EEOC v. Cosmair, Inc.*, 821 F.2d 1085 (5th 1987) (finding such a waiver to be against public policy). Thus, an employer may not treat the filing of an administrative charge as a breach of the agreement. The effect of such a provision on the rest of the release, however, is unclear. *See Wastak v. Lehigh Valley Health Network*, 342 F.3d 281, 292 (3d Cir. 2003) (finding administrative rights waiver severable and employee's promise not to sue enforceable notwithstanding the invalid clause). Employers are increasingly dealing with this possibility by explicitly providing in their releases that signatories continue to have a right to file charges with relevant agencies.

10. *Will Uncle Sam Foot Part of the Bill?* From an employee's perspective, a question that often arises is whether a settlement can be structured to reduce the tax consequences, especially where large amounts are paid out in a given year. Other than stretching payouts over several years to avoid pushing the employee into a higher income bracket, the answer is usually no. Severance pay, like the wages it replaces, is taxable. Indeed, the Internal Revenue Code, 26 U.S.C §104(a)(2) (2018), generally excludes from gross income only "the amount of any damages received (whether by suit or agreement) on account of personal injuries or sickness." As a result, not only severance but most employment-related recoveries—backpay, front pay, recoveries for emotional harm, etc.—are taxable. In only a few instances, for example, physical assault or physical sexual harassment, may it be possible to characterize some or all of the settlement as "personal injury" and thus nontaxable income. Further, the employee's attorney should alert her client that, if proceeds of a settlement are taxable, the employer may legally withhold taxes on any payment made. *Rivera v. Baker West, Inc.*, 430 F.3d 1253 (9th Cir. 2005). Taxation issues also loomed large where attorney's fees are involved, which were long treated as taxable to the employee as income. Congress responded to this problem by amending 26 U.S.C. §62(a)(20) (2018) to allow deduction of fees and costs, whether received in litigation or settlement, free of restrictions that earlier applied.

PROBLEM

13-5. Harold Brown was a 59-year-old district sales manager for AMF Bowling Products Group. After 26 years of service, he was offered early retirement. Harold requested and was given the opportunity to take the offer to an attorney. After consultation, he accepted the offer by executing the following "Severance Agreement":

I. Resignation

I, HAROLD BROWN do voluntarily submit my resignation from AMF Bowling Products effective August 1.

II. Severance Payout

Based on 1.5 weeks of pay per completed year of service, severance pay will total $30,581. (37.5 weeks). . . .

III. Waiver

I, HAROLD BROWN, accept the severance entitlement outlined above and understand that this represents the entire severance entitlement and no other provisions are express or implied. I accept the terms and conditions of this entitlement and release AMF from any outstanding obligations or litigation in this matter.

Harold has come to believe that he was pushed to resign because of his age and would like to pursue litigation. How would you advise him on the question whether the above agreement precludes suit? Besides possible procedural defects under the OWBPA, do you see any contract-based arguments for challenging the agreement?

Note on Employer Obligations and Exceptions Under WARN

As *Williams* makes clear, an employer contemplating an RIF must take a number of specific procedural steps in planning and executing a layoff. While an effective release will cover a multitude of legal mistakes, employers must first attempt to comply with the governing statutory requirements. With respect to WARN, the first question is whether a proposed action requires notice. Determining whether WARN's notice provisions are triggered often turns on a number of technical questions. Generally speaking, WARN requires employers with 100 or more employees to provide 60 days' notice to affected employees in the event of a mass layoff or plant closing. As *Williams* demonstrates, whether an RIF constitutes a "mass layoff" at "a single site" may result in litigation. This can generate difficult problems of who counts as laid off. *Compare Collins v. Gee W. Seattle LLC,* 631 F.3d 1001 (9th Cir. 2011) (a business shutdown qualified under WARN even though fewer than 30 employees remained when the company closed; the 120 employees who had left after an announcement of a likely closing had not "voluntarily departed" within the meaning of the statute), *with Ellis v. DHL Express Inc. (USA),* 633 F.3d 522 (7th Cir. 2011) (employees who accepted a union-negotiated severance agreement were "voluntary departures" not to be counted towards WARN's triggering requirement). While Phillips Petroleum engaged in a "mass layoff" at its Oklahoma location, its layoffs in Houston did not meet the statutory minimum. *Cf. Davis v. Signal Int'l Texas GP, LLC,* 728 F.3d 482 (5th Cir. 2013) (two facilities constituted a "single site" of employment due to regular sharing of staff and similar organizational purposes).

Another common area of WARN litigation is the various exceptions to its notice requirement, two of which tend to recur often. First, in the case of a plant closing, an employer is excused from the 60-day requirement where providing notice would impede its ability to obtain capital or business that would enable the employer to avoid the closing. Second, in the case of both plant closings and layoffs, an employer is excused from the 60-day requirement where the closing or layoff is due to business circumstances that were not reasonably foreseeable; the employer, however, must still provide whatever notice is reasonable in the circumstances. A high-profile example of a layoff implicating the latter exception is *Roquet v. Arthur Andersen*, 398 F.3d 585 (7th Cir 2005) (2-1). Workers who lost their jobs following the Department of Justice's indictment of Arthur Andersen in connection with the 2001 collapse of Enron brought a WARN suit against the accounting firm for failing to provide advance notice. Arthur Andersen defended by arguing that the DOJ indictment and subsequent demise of the firm were not reasonably foreseeable. The plaintiffs countered that, once the DOJ began investigating Arthur Andersen in the wake of the Enron scandal, the firm should have known that it would lose business and need to massively reduce staff. In a divided decision, the Seventh Circuit found for the defendant:

> [T]he Department of Labor has provided some guidance regarding when the "unforeseen business circumstances" exception applies. . . . A business circumstance may be reasonably unforeseeable if it was caused by some sudden, dramatic, and unexpected action, or by conditions outside the employer's control. 20 C.F.R. §639.9(b)(1). When determining whether a mass layoff was caused by unforeseeable business circumstances, courts evaluate whether a similarly situated employer exercising reasonable judgment could have foreseen the circumstances that caused the layoff. *Id*. §639.9(b)(2). Thus, a company will not be liable if, when confronted with potentially devastating occurrences, it reacts the same way that other reasonable employers within its own market would react.
>
> The parties dispute whether Andersen established either element of the exception—causation and foreseeability. The district court concluded that the need for mass layoffs was caused by the public announcement of the indictment on March 14. We agree. Up until then, Andersen suffered no marked loss of business despite a spate of negative publicity. It is clear that economic hemorrhaging really did not begin until word of the indictment got out. . . .
>
> In determining whether a crippling business circumstance is foreseeable, we must bear in mind that "it is the 'probability of occurrence that makes a business circumstance "reasonably foreseeable,"' rather than the 'mere possibility of such a circumstance.'" The layoffs began on April 23, which means that Andersen was required to notify employees 60 days earlier, or February 22. [As of that date,] it was not a foregone conclusion that Andersen would be indicted as a company—in the past, the government typically went after culpable individuals, not companies as a whole. By all accounts, this was an unusual move by the DOJ. There is evidence in the record suggesting that Andersen could have reasonably foreseen the indictment by March 1—the date it was told by the DOJ that it was being indicted. But hope still remained that the dreaded act could be stalled if not avoided.

Id. at 588-89. The court also noted that requiring notice under such circumstances could lead fragile companies to lay off workers prematurely rather than fighting to stay afloat. *Id*. at 589-90. *See also Varela v. AE Liquidation, Inc. (In re AE Liquidation, Inc.)*, 866 F.3d 515, 518 (3d Cir. 2017) (the duty to warn was not triggered until a layoff became more likely than not, which did not occur until the day of the layoff given constant reassurances to the employer of sufficient funds to continue operations); *Pearce v. Faurecia Exhaust Sys., Inc.*, 29 F. App'x 454 (6th Cir. 2013) (when layoffs were caused by the bankruptcy of the employer's primary customer, defense of "unforeseeable business circumstances" applied). Arthur Andersen is not the only high-profile WARN case. *See* Sara Randazzo, *Dewey Settles Layoff Claims for $4.5 Million*, WSJ Law Blog, June 12, 2014, available at http://blogs. wsj.com/law/2014/06/12/dewey-settles-layoff-claims-for-4-5-million/ (reporting proposed settlement of claims against the former Dewey & LeBoeuf law firm stemming from its 2012 collapse).

Remedies under WARN are limited. The goal of the statute is not job protection as such; it seeks merely to provide employees with a window of time to plan for the disruption of a layoff, begin searching for new employment, and, if necessary, obtain new skills. Consequently, an employee can receive only the wages and benefits to which he or she would otherwise have been entitled for each day of the violation (up to 60 days). For the employer who might have to pay this amount to each worker in a mass layoff, the stakes are high. In addition, employers who violate WARN may, in some instances, be assessed a daily statutory penalty. 29 U.S.C. §2104.

Note on Managing the Risk of Systemic Discrimination Claims in Planning an RIF

One of the most significant concerns of employers conducting a reduction in force is the risk of liability under discrimination laws. Particularly in large-scale layoffs, systemic claims may potentially be brought by class action. For these reasons, employers are well advised to carefully review the criteria they use in selecting employees for layoff. The employer must ensure not only that its managers do not intentionally base layoff decisions on protected status, but also that neutral criteria do not disparately impact workers with protected status, or, if they do, that the disparity can be legitimately explained by other business considerations. One group of practitioners offers the following checklist:

II. Create and Document the Layoff Plan

A. Articulate and document economic and other business justifications for the layoff. If an employee files a wrongful layoff case, this documentation will lay the foundation for the employer's case. . . .

C. Articulate and document the basis for determining the number of positions the employer will cut in each work unit.

1. Determine the positions and skills within each work unit which the employer must retain to achieve its articulated business goals. This assessment should precede, and should not take into account, an assessment of the skills of the individual incumbents.

2. Establish criteria for determining which positions an employer will eliminate within a work unit to achieve articulated business goals.

D. Standardize the methodology and criteria for selecting individuals for layoff.

1. Use objective criteria to the extent possible. . . .

3. Define the method by which the employer will determine the relative ranking of employees for layoff purposes. [I]t is inadvisable to rely solely on past performance

evaluations because these are likely to be written in highly complementary terms and are not designed for comparing employees on the skills, knowledge and abilities required for post-RIF jobs. Rather, it is more sensible to prepare special assessment ratings in connection with layoff selection which assess relative skills, knowledge, abilities and other qualifications. . . .

5. Accurately document the legitimate business factors that justify the particular layoff decision, e.g., comparative seniority, experience, performance evaluations and elimination of tasks performed by incumbent. . . .

V.   Review the Tentative Layoff

A. Conduct an adverse impact analysis of the tentative layoff list by race, sex and appropriate age bands under the attorney-client privilege. . . .

C. Review the impending layoff in light of the following questions:

1. Are WARN Act notices necessary?

2. Will the layoff breach employment contracts (express contracts or promises implied from oral assurances, length of service, commendations or salary increases), the covenant of good faith and fair dealing, employee handbooks, labor contracts, layoff policies or past practices?

3. Will the layoff impact whistleblowers, complainers or persons about to vest in pension or retiree health benefits or violate other public policies?

4. Will the reduction in force affect workers on pregnancy leave, family leave or medical leave?

5. Is collective bargaining necessary?

Ethan Lipsig et al., *Planning and Implementing Reductions in Force*, C922 ALI-ABA 1165, 1231-36 (1994). As a practical matter, an employer that plans to obtain OWBPA releases will necessarily have to take some of these steps in order to provide the requisite disclosures to employees. In addition to its procedural requirements, OWBPA provides that where "an exit incentive or other employment termination program [is] offered to a group or class of employees," the employer must provide each employee with information about all employees eligible for the incentive or program, including their ages and job titles. The purpose of this provision is to give employees adequate information on which to determine whether it is in their interest to waive potential substantive claims. In effect, OWBPA thus ensures a kind of pre-suit discovery to would-be plaintiffs. Although employers may dislike the provision for this reason, compliance can be useful from a risk management perspective. As the excerpt suggests, culling this information may alert the employer in advance to possible liability risks raised by the statistical composition of its selected class of workers.

Employers who run into trouble in conducting a layoff tend to be those who fail to employ objective criteria, fail to apply such criteria consistently, or fail to document their layoff procedure. Consider the court's description of the RIF selection process in *Oberg v. Allied Van Lines, Inc.*, 1996 U.S. Dist. LEXIS 4717 (N.D. Ill. April 11, 1996):

Allied thereafter launched a selection procedure in connection with its reduction which was unclear, undocumented and ripe for problems, including claims for discrimination. No written guidelines for termination were prepared. No documents were prepared to explain why certain employees were terminated compared to others and it appears that in some instances employees' evaluations were ignored.

Naturally, different supervisors interpreted the criteria in different ways and applied them based upon the circumstances attendant to their own business units rather than in some rigid, mathematical manner. As Allied's senior management considered the changes, the names of individuals whose employment status would be affected by the changes were forwarded on to Allied's RIF committee. The committee consisted of Allied Human Resources and Legal Department personnel.

Among the evidence plaintiffs sought to rely on was the following statement from a report authored by executives of Allied's parent company to assist in the RIF:

> Despite the recent incidence of high turnover there are still many managers in the organization with very long service. No doubt this has encouraged the atmosphere of insular bureaucracy that still pervades part of the business.

Id. Do you see how the way the RIF was conducted could have encouraged, or at least enabled, age discrimination? As the lawyer for Allied, what would you have recommended the company do differently in planning major layoffs? Incidentally, the employer in *Oberg* had obtained releases from the terminated employees; however, they were found invalid for failure to comply with all of the OWBPA disclosure requirements. *See Oberg v. Allied Van Lines, Inc.*, 11 F.3d 679 (7th Cir. 1993).

PROBLEM

13-6. Union Mortgage & Lending ("UML"), located in Boston, has acquired Connecticut Family Credit ("CFC"), located in Hartford, and plans to consolidate operations in Boston. CFC employed three accountants, of which UML must select two for layoff. Herk is a 61-year-old white male with 12 years of seniority. He currently earns $75,000 per year. His performance evaluations are consistently good but not outstanding. Joeline is a 42-year-old white woman with six years of seniority. She currently earns $68,000 per year. Her performance evaluations are similar to Herk's. She has strong ties to her previous employer of eight years, a large Connecticut-based bank with whom CFC did significant business. Miguel is a 29-year-old Hispanic male who arrived at CFC eight months ago from a big New York accounting firm. He earns $62,000 per year. His paper credentials exceed those of Herk and Joeline, and he has excellent interpersonal skills. Miguel's performance has not yet been formally evaluated; however, the general manager at CFC believes he is a "rising star." UML consults you about which accountant to retain. How would you advise your client to go about this decision? What risks are associated with laying off each of these three employees? What additional information might you seek from CFC before deciding? Are there any special precautions UML should take once it makes its decision? Once you have made your selections, draft a separation letter for UML to send to the affected employees apprising them of the decision.

C. MANAGING UNFAVORABLE FORA AND ADVERSE LAW

The previous sections of this chapter explored methods employers may use to prevent employment disputes or at least resolve them internally. Inevitably, some disputes escalate to the point that an aggrieved worker wishes to pursue legal action. The traditional step in such situations is for the employee to file a complaint in court, provided he or she has taken the requisite administrative steps in the case of claims arising under federal discrimination law. Such suits can often be brought as class or collective actions, and, although the FEDERAL RULES OF CIVIL PROCEDURE have been interpreted to restrict the extent to which some claims may be pursued in this fashion (*see, e.g., Wal-Mart Stores, Inc. v. Dukes*, 564 U.S. 338 (2011) (finding insufficient "commonality" among members of a million-plus employee class action to permit certification of a Title VII suit)), such suits still pose the risk of substantial employer liability. One way that employers seek to reduce the risks associated with this possibility is to alter contractually the default principle that disputes are litigated in the court the plaintiff chooses, complete with that forum's choice-of-law principles. Perhaps the most common method of doing this is to require all workers, as a condition of initial or continued employment, to arbitrate any dispute that may arise during the course of the employment relationship. Increasingly, employers go further and try to structure the arbitration terms to minimize the amount of exposure if a policy or practice is challenged. Perhaps the most dramatic way they do this is to foreclose not only any class action in court by requiring arbitration but also by framing such agreements to bar class arbitration. The result is that such mandatory arbitration agreements force employees to pursue dispute resolution individually, a choice that will often make it financially impossible for any claim to be pursued in any forum.

The issues regarding the validity of arbitration agreements are taken up in the first subsection. In addition, where law is uncertain or harm is difficult to prove, employers sometimes attempt to contractually define the financial consequences of a dispute, often through the use of a stipulated damages clause. This is covered in subsection 2.

1. Pre-Dispute Arbitration Agreements

Arbitration is an alternative to traditional court litigation through which parties employ a third-party, nonjudicial decision maker to adjudicate their dispute in a private proceeding. From the perspective of the employer, the purpose of a pre-dispute arbitration agreement is to avoid protracted and expensive litigation and steer potential disputes to fora that the employer considers more cost-efficient, predictable, and, perhaps, friendlier to its interests. Because it is private, the arbitration process varies depending on the particular forum and rules the parties select. In many instances, parties opt for an established arbitration service, such as the American Arbitration Association, which has an extensive set of rules and procedures for resolving employment disputes and a cadre of trained arbitrators. *See AAA National Rules for the*

Resolution of Employment Disputes (2005), *available at* http://www.adr.org/sp.asp?id=22075. But parties might also choose a less formal venue or develop their own set of rules and procedures. For these reasons, arbitrations vary significantly in terms of the expertise and background of the arbitrators; whether lawyers or other advocates participate; the formality with which testimony is presented; and the degree of attention to evidentiary and other procedural rules.

In theory, opting for arbitration does not reduce the risk of being on the losing end of a dispute but merely reduces the costs of resolving it by substituting a cheaper and speedier alternative mechanism. Such features could make arbitration a more accessible, and hence more effective, form of dispute resolution for employees who lack the time, financial resources, and access to counsel necessary to pursue litigation in court. *See* Samuel Estreicher, *Saturns for Rickshaws: The Stakes in the Debate over Predispute Employment Arbitration Agreements*, 16 OHIO ST. J. ON DISP. RESOL. 559 (2001). Indeed, arbitration is the typical means of resolving disputes in the collective bargaining context, although there the continued presence of the union as a "repeat player" may bulwark employee prospects for success. In contrast, Cynthia Estlund, in *The Black Hole of Mandatory Arbitration*, 96 N.C. L. REV. 679 (2018), argues that Professor Estreicher's benign view of arbitration's value for workers in the employment setting is incorrect. After undertaking an empirical study, she concludes that "the great bulk of disputes that are subject to mandatory arbitration agreements . . . simply evaporate before they are even filed. . . . Mandatory arbitration is less an 'alternative dispute resolution' mechanism than it is a magician's disappearing trick." *Id.* at 682.

Arbitration is quicker and less costly, however, precisely because certain procedures and safeguards associated with court litigation are abandoned. Further, since employers generally select the particular forum and its procedures, it is possible that arbitration will favor employers in both substantive outcomes and extent of remedies. Even in an objectively neutral forum and outside the collective bargaining context, the "repeat player" effect may lead arbitrators to favor those who are most likely to want to use their services in the future—employers. *See* Cynthia Estlund, *Rebuilding the Law of the Workplace in an Era of Self-Regulation*, 105 COLUM. L. REV. 319, 397-98 (2005).

Such concerns are heightened by the common employer practice of requiring employees to sign contracts to arbitrate upon applying for or commencing a job and well before a dispute actually arises. In contrast to the decision to arbitrate an existing dispute, an employee faced with a pre-dispute arbitration agreement is less likely to either appreciate the importance of choice of forum or consult counsel. *See* Matthew T. Bodie, *Questions About the Efficiency of Employment Arbitration Agreements*, 39 GA. L. REV. 1, 41 (2004) (pre-dispute arbitration agreements "are more likely to be based on primitive guesswork, or less, on the part of the employee" compared to post-dispute agreements, and employers are likely to have significant informational advantages that they may use to the employees' disadvantage). Moreover, such agreements are generally boilerplate documents that individual employees are rarely in a position to refuse. If employees are not able to negotiate the terms or arbitration agreements, or even rationally weigh the trade-offs involved in agreeing to the employer's chosen forum and procedures, such agreements could effectively serve as waivers of substantive employment rights. *See* David S. Schwartz, *Mandatory Arbitration and Fairness*, 84 NOTRE DAME L. REV. 1247 (2009); Katherine V.W. Stone, *Mandatory Arbitration of Individual Employment Rights: The Yellow Dog Contract of the 1990s*, 73 DENV. U. L. REV. 1017 (1996).

Yet another set of objections to arbitration stems from the fact that, as a private dispute resolution mechanism, arbitration may not serve the wider goals of the law, particularly the antidiscrimination statutes, even if it achieves justice in individual cases. Chief among the concerns are the confidentiality of the process, which arguably inhibits public education about discrimination and limits the development of the law by removing a large source of potential precedent cases. *See* Geraldine Szott Moohr, *Arbitration and the Goals of Employment Discrimination Law*, 56 WASH. & LEE L. REV. 395, 426-39 (1999).

Debates about the relative merits and limitations of arbitration as an alternative dispute resolution mechanism underlie an evolving body of doctrine on the legal enforceability of pre-dispute employment arbitration agreements. The starting point for that analysis is the 1925 Federal Arbitration Act ("FAA"), which provides that a written arbitration clause in any "contract evidencing a transaction involving commerce . . . shall be valid, irrevocable, and enforceable, save upon such grounds as exist at law or in equity for the revocation of any contract." 9 U.S.C. §2 (2014). If a party who has signed an arbitration agreement files suit in court, the FAA commands the judge to stay the proceedings on motion of the opposing party; this remits the plaintiff only to the designated arbitral forum for relief. While there are several limitations on the statute's scope, the Supreme Court has applied it sweepingly. *Circuit City Stores, Inc. v. Adams*, 532 U.S. 105 (2001) (holding most employment contracts within the FAA).

For our purposes, the most important set of issues concerns the relationship between private arbitration and employee statutory rights. Employment arbitration agreements typically apply to any workplace dispute, but they are most frequently invoked by employers defending against federal statutory claims, such as discrimination claims. The employee's right to be free from discrimination includes the statutory right to have her claims heard in a court of law before a jury. One of the foundational questions of private ordering in employment law is whether an employer can change that by private contract.

The question of enforceability of an arbitration agreement in the individual employment setting of a statutory employment claim was first addressed by the Supreme Court in *Gilmer v. Interstate/Johnson Lane Corp.*, 500 U.S. 20 (1995), an age discrimination suit. The plaintiff had signed an arbitration agreement in order to register as a securities representative with the New York Stock Exchange; that agreement, although not entered into with his employer, required Gilmer to arbitrate any dispute arising with other registered members of the exchange, including his employer. The Supreme Court held the agreement enforceable. It found nothing in the text or underlying policy of the ADEA that precluded the submission of age discrimination claims to private arbitration. *See generally* Charles A. Sullivan, *The Story of* Gilmer v. Interstate/Johnson Lane Corp: *Gilmering Antidiscrimination Law*, EMPLOYMENT DISCRIMINATION STORIES (Friedman ed., 2006).

In subsequent cases, the Court held that an arbitration agreement would be binding even if entered into directly between an employer and employee despite some arguable limiting language in the FAA, *Circuit City v. Adams*, 532 U.S. 105 (2001), and that a union could waive an individual's statutory right to a judicial forum in a collective bargaining agreement. *14 Penn Plaza, LLC v. Pyett*, 556 U.S. 247 (2009).

See generally Alan Hyde, *Labor Arbitration of Discrimination Claims After* 14 Penn Plaza v. Pyett: *Letting Discrimination Defendants Decide Whether Plaintiffs May Sue Them*, 25 Ohio St. J. Disp. Resol. 975, 976 (2010); Margaret L. Moses, *The Pretext of Textualism: Disregarding Stare Decisis in* 14 Penn Plaza v. Pyett, 14 Lewis & Clark L. Rev. 825 (2010).

The Court has also held that the courts may not invalidate a contractual waiver of class arbitration even if the plaintiff's cost of individually arbitrating a federal statutory claim exceeds potential recovery, *Am. Express Co. v. Italian Colors Rest.*, 570 U.S. 228 (2013), and that the FAA preempts state law to the extent that it would treat arbitration agreements differently than other contracts. *See Doctor's Assocs. v. Casarotto*, 517 U.S. 681 (1996) (striking down state law prescribing special procedural requirements for arbitration agreements). *See, e.g.*, David S. Schwartz, *Correcting Federalism Mistakes in Statutory Interpretation: The Supreme Court and the Federal Arbitration Act*, 67 L. & Contemp. Probs. 5 (2004) (arguing that FAA preemption is inconsistent with congressional intent and contrary to Court's conservative majority's purported support for federalism).

Nevertheless, these decisions still left open the possibility that either "general" state law—such as unconscionability principles—or other federal protections might limit employers' ability to preclude class or collective claims, either in court or in the arbitral forum. The Supreme Court largely closed the door on such a possibility in the next principal case, and in the case after that rejected the argument that such arbitration agreements violate the federal labor laws.

≡≡≡ *AT&T Mobility LLC v. Concepcion*
≡≡≡ *563 U.S. 333 (2011)*

Justice Scalia delivered the opinion of the Court.

Section 2 of the Federal Arbitration Act (FAA) makes agreements to arbitrate "valid, irrevocable, and enforceable, save upon such grounds as exist at law or in equity for the revocation of any contract." 9 U.S.C. §2. We consider whether the FAA prohibits States from conditioning the enforceability of certain arbitration agreements on the availability of classwide arbitration procedures.

I

In February 2002, Vincent and Liza Concepcion entered into an agreement for the sale and servicing of cellular telephones with AT&T Mobility LCC (AT&T). The contract provided for arbitration of all disputes between the parties, but required that claims be brought in the parties' "individual capacity, and not as a plaintiff or class member in any purported class or representative proceeding." The agreement authorized AT&T to make unilateral amendments, which it did to the arbitration provision on several occasions. The version at issue in this case reflects revisions made in December 2006, which the parties agree are controlling.

The revised agreement provides that customers may initiate dispute proceedings by completing a one-page Notice of Dispute form available on AT&T's Web site. AT&T may then offer to settle the claim; if it does not, or if the dispute is not resolved within 30 days, the customer may invoke arbitration by filing a separate Demand for Arbitration, also available on AT&T's Web site. In the event the parties proceed to arbitration, the agreement specifies that AT&T must pay all costs for nonfrivolous claims; that arbitration must take place in the county in which the customer is billed; that, for claims of $10,000 or less, the customer may choose whether the arbitration proceeds in person, by telephone, or based only on submissions; that either party may bring a claim in small claims court in lieu of arbitration; and that the arbitrator may award any form of individual relief, including injunctions and presumably punitive damages. The agreement, moreover, denies AT&T any ability to seek reimbursement of its attorney's fees, and, in the event that a customer receives an arbitration award greater than AT&T's last written settlement offer, requires AT&T to pay a $7,500 minimum recovery and twice the amount of the claimant's attorney's fees.

The Concepcions purchased AT&T service, which was advertised as including the provision of free phones; they were not charged for the phones, but they were charged $30.22 in sales tax based on the phones' retail value. [They later filed a complaint against AT&T, which was later consolidated with a putative class action alleging false advertising and fraud by AT&T's charging sales tax on phones it advertised as free. AT&T moved to compel arbitration under the terms of its contract with the Concepcions, and they opposed the motion on the ground that the arbitration agreement was unconscionable because it disallowed classwide procedures. Relying on the California Supreme Court's decision in *Discover Bank* v. *Superior Court*, 113 P.3d 1100 (2005), the district court found that the arbitration provision was unconscionable because AT&T had not shown that bilateral arbitration adequately substituted for the deterrent effects of class actions. The Ninth Circuit affirmed.]

II

The FAA was enacted in 1925 in response to widespread judicial hostility to arbitration agreements. *See Hall Street Associates, LLC v. Mattel, Inc.*, 552 U.S. 576, 581 (2008). Section 2, the "primary substantive provision of the Act," *Moses H. Cone Memorial Hospital v. Mercury Constr. Corp.*, 460 U.S. 1, 24 (1983), provides, in relevant part, as follows:

> A written provision in any maritime transaction or a contract evidencing a transaction involving commerce to settle by arbitration a controversy thereafter arising out of such contract or transaction . . . shall be valid, irrevocable, and enforceable, save upon such grounds as exist at law or in equity for the revocation of any contract.

9 U.S.C. §2.

We have described this provision as reflecting both a "liberal federal policy favoring arbitration," *Moses H. Cone*, and the "fundamental principle that arbitration is a matter of contract," *Rent-A-Center, West, Inc. v. Jackson*, 561 U.S. 63, 67 (2010). In line with these principles, courts must place arbitration agreements on an equal footing with other contracts, *Buckeye Check Cashing, Inc. v. Cardegna*, 546 U.S. 440, 443 (2006), and enforce them according to their terms, *Volt Information Sciences, Inc. v. Board of Trustees of Leland Stanford Junior Univ.*, 489 U.S. 468, 478 (1989).

The final phrase of §2, however, permits arbitration agreements to be declared unenforceable "upon such grounds as exist at law or in equity for the revocation of any contract." This saving clause permits agreements to arbitrate to be invalidated by "generally applicable contract defenses, such as fraud, duress, or unconscionability," but not by defenses that apply only to arbitration or that derive their meaning from the fact that an agreement to arbitrate is at issue. *Doctor's Associates, Inc. v. Casarotto,* 517 U.S. 681, 687 (1996); *see also Perry v. Thomas,* 482 U.S. 483, 492-93, n.9 (1987). The question in this case is whether §2 preempts California's rule classifying most collective-arbitration waivers in consumer contracts as unconscionable. We refer to this rule as the *Discover Bank* rule.

Under California law, courts may refuse to enforce any contract found "to have been unconscionable at the time it was made," or may "limit the application of any unconscionable clause." Cal. Civ. Code Ann. §1670.5(a) (West 1985). A finding of unconscionability requires "a 'procedural' and a 'substantive' element, the former focusing on 'oppression' or 'surprise' due to unequal bargaining power, the latter on 'overly harsh' or 'one-sided' results." *Armendariz v. Foundation Health Psychcare Servs.,* 6 P.3d 669, 690 (2000); accord, *Discover Bank.*

In *Discover Bank*, the California Supreme Court applied this framework to class-action waivers in arbitration agreements and held as follows:

> [W]hen the waiver is found in a consumer contract of adhesion in a setting in which disputes between the contracting parties predictably involve small amounts of damages, and when it is alleged that the party with the superior bargaining power has carried out a scheme to deliberately cheat large numbers of consumers out of individually small sums of money, then . . . the waiver becomes in practice the exemption of the party 'from responsibility for [its] own fraud, or willful injury to the person or property of another.' Under these circumstances, such waivers are unconscionable under California law and should not be enforced.

California courts have frequently applied this rule to find arbitration agreements unconscionable.

III

A

The Concepcions argue that the *Discover Bank* rule, given its origins in California's unconscionability doctrine and California's policy against exculpation, is a ground that "exist[s] at law or in equity for the revocation of any contract" under FAA §2. Moreover, they argue that even if we construe the *Discover Bank* rule as a prohibition on collective-action waivers rather than simply an application of unconscionability, the rule would still be applicable to all dispute-resolution contracts, since California prohibits waivers of class litigation as well.

When state law prohibits outright the arbitration of a particular type of claim, the analysis is straightforward: The conflicting rule is displaced by the FAA. *Preston v. Ferrer,* 552 U.S. 346, 353 (2008). But the inquiry becomes more complex when a doctrine normally thought to be generally applicable, such as duress or, as relevant here, unconscionability, is alleged to have been applied in a fashion that disfavors arbitration. In *Perry v. Thomas,* for example, we noted that the FAA's preemptive effect might extend even to grounds traditionally thought to exist " 'at law or in equity for the revocation of any contract.' *Id.* (emphasis deleted). We said that a court may not "rely on the uniqueness of an agreement to arbitrate as a basis for a state-law holding that enforcement would be unconscionable, for this would enable the court to effect what . . . the state legislature cannot." *Id.*

An obvious illustration of this point would be a case finding unconscionable or unenforceable as against public policy consumer arbitration agreements that fail to provide for judicially monitored discovery. The rationalizations for such a holding are neither difficult to imagine nor different in kind from those articulated in *Discover Bank.* A court might reason that no consumer would knowingly waive his right to full discovery, as this would enable companies to hide their wrongdoing. Or the court might simply say that such agreements are exculpatory—restricting discovery would be of greater benefit to the company than the consumer, since the former is more likely to be sued than to sue. *See Discover Bank* (arguing that class waivers are similarly one-sided). And, the reasoning would continue, because such a rule applies the general principle of unconscionability or public-policy disapproval of exculpatory agreements, it is applicable to "any" contract and thus preserved by §2 of the FAA. In practice, of course, the rule would have a disproportionate impact on arbitration agreements; but it would presumably apply to contracts purporting to restrict discovery in litigation as well.

Other examples are easy to imagine. The same argument might apply to a rule classifying as unconscionable arbitration agreements that fail to abide by the Federal Rules of Evidence, or that disallow an ultimate disposition by a jury (perhaps termed "a panel of twelve lay arbitrators" to help avoid preemption). Such examples are not fanciful, since the judicial hostility towards arbitration that prompted the FAA had manifested itself in "a great variety" of "devices and formulas" declaring arbitration against public policy. *Robert Lawrence Co. v. Devonshire Fabrics, Inc.*, 271 F.2d 402, 406 (CA2 1959). And although these statistics are not definitive, it is worth noting that California's courts have been more likely to hold contracts to arbitrate unconscionable than other contracts. Broome, *An Unconscionable Applicable of the Unconscionability Doctrine: How the California Courts Are Circumventing the Federal Arbitration Act*, 3 HASTINGS BUS. L.J. 39, 54, 66 (2006); Randall, *Judicial Attitudes Toward Arbitration and the Resurgence of Unconscionability*, 52 BUFF. L. REV. 185, 186-87 (2004).

The Concepcions suggest that all this is just a parade of horribles, and no genuine worry. "Rules aimed at destroying arbitration" or "demanding procedures incompatible with arbitration," they concede, "would be preempted by the FAA because they cannot sensibly be reconciled with Section 2." The "grounds" available under §2's saving clause, they admit, "should not be construed to include a State's mere preference for procedures that are incompatible with arbitration and 'would wholly eviscerate arbitration agreements.'"

We largely agree. Although §2's saving clause preserves generally applicable contract defenses, nothing in it suggests an intent to preserve state-law rules that stand as an obstacle to the accomplishment of the FAA's objectives. As we have said, a federal statute's saving clause "'cannot in reason be construed as [allowing] a common law right, the continued existence of which would be absolutely inconsistent with the provisions of the act. In other words, the act cannot be held to destroy itself.'" *American Telephone & Telegraph Co. v. Central Office Telephone, Inc.*, 524 U.S. 214, 227-228 (1998).

We differ with the Concepcions only in the application of this analysis to the matter before us. We do not agree that rules requiring judicially monitored discovery or adherence to the Federal Rules of Evidence are "a far cry from this case." The overarching purpose of the FAA, evident in the text of §§2, 3, and 4, is to ensure the enforcement of arbitration agreements according to their terms so as to facilitate streamlined proceedings. Requiring the availability of classwide arbitration interferes with fundamental attributes of arbitration and thus creates a scheme inconsistent with the FAA.

B

The "principal purpose" of the FAA is to "ensur[e] that private arbitration agreements are enforced according to their terms." *Volt; see also Stolt-Nielsen S. A. v. AnimalFeeds Int'l Corp.*, 559 U.S. 662 (2010). This purpose is readily apparent from the FAA's text. Section 2 makes arbitration agreements "valid, irrevocable, and enforceable" as written (subject, of course, to the saving clause); §3 requires courts to stay litigation of arbitral claims pending arbitration of those claims "in accordance with the terms of the agreement"; and §4 requires courts to compel arbitration "in accordance with the terms of the agreement" upon the motion of either party to the agreement (assuming that the "making of the arbitration agreement or the failure . . . to perform the same" is not at issue). In light of these provisions, we have held that parties may agree to limit the issues subject to arbitration, *Mitsubishi Motors Corp. v. Soler Chrysler-Plymouth, Inc.*, 473 U.S. 614, 628 (1985), to arbitrate according to specific rules, *Volt*, and to limit *with whom* a party will arbitrate its disputes, *Stolt-Nielsen.*

The point of affording parties discretion in designing arbitration processes is to allow for efficient, streamlined procedures tailored to the type of dispute. It can be specified, for example, that the decision maker be a specialist in the relevant field, or that proceedings be kept confidential to protect trade secrets. And the informality of arbitral proceedings is itself desirable, reducing the cost and increasing the speed of dispute resolution. *14 Penn Plaza LLC v. Pyett*, 556 U.S. 247, 269 (2009); *Mitsubishi Motors Corp.*

The dissent quotes *Dean Witter Reynolds Inc. v. Byrd*, 470 U.S. 213, 219 (1985), as " 'reject[ing] the suggestion that the overriding goal of the Arbitration Act was to promote the expeditious resolution of claims.' " That is greatly misleading. After saying (accurately enough) that "the overriding goal of the Arbitration Act was [not] to promote the expeditious resolution of claims," but to "ensure judicial enforcement of privately made agreements to arbitrate," *Dean Witter* went on to explain: "This is not to say that Congress was blind to the potential benefit of the legislation for expedited resolution of disputes. Far from it. . . ." It then quotes a House Report saying that "the costliness and delays of litigation . . . can be largely eliminated by agreements for arbitration." (Quoting H. R. Rep. No. 96, 68th Cong., 1st Sess., 2 (1924)). The concluding paragraph of this part of its discussion begins as follows:

> We therefore are not persuaded by the argument that the conflict between two goals of the Arbitration Act—enforcement of private agreements and encouragement of efficient and speedy dispute resolution—must be resolved in favor of the latter in order to realize the intent of the drafters.

In the present case, of course, those "two goals" do not conflict—and it is the dissent's view that would frustrate *both* of them.

Contrary to the dissent's view, our cases place it beyond dispute that the FAA was designed to promote arbitration. They have repeatedly described the Act as "embod[ying] [a] national policy favoring arbitration," *Buckeye Check Cashing*, and "a liberal federal policy favoring arbitration agreements, notwithstanding any state substantive or procedural policies to the contrary," *Moses H. Cone; see also Hall Street Assocs.* Thus, in *Preston v. Ferrer*, holding preempted a state-law rule requiring exhaustion of administrative remedies before arbitration, we said: "A prime objective of an agreement to arbitrate is to achieve 'streamlined proceedings and expeditious results,'" which objective would be "frustrated" by requiring a dispute to be heard by an agency first. That rule, we said, would "at the least, hinder speedy resolution of the controversy."[5]

California's *Discover Bank* rule similarly interferes with arbitration. Although the rule does not *require* classwide arbitration, it allows any party to a consumer contract to demand it *ex post*. The rule is limited to adhesion contracts, *Discover Bank*, but the times in which consumer contracts were anything other than adhesive are long past. The rule also requires that damages be predictably small, and that the consumer allege a scheme to cheat consumers. *Discover Bank*. The former requirement, however, is toothless and malleable . . . and the latter has no limiting effect, as all that is required is an allegation. Consumers remain free to bring and resolve their disputes on a bilateral basis under *Discover Bank*, and some may well do so; but there is little incentive for lawyers to arbitrate on behalf of individuals when they may do so for a class and reap far higher fees in the process. And faced with inevitable class arbitration, companies would have less incentive to continue resolving potentially duplicative claims on an individual basis.

Although we have had little occasion to examine classwide arbitration, our decision in *Stolt-Nielsen* is instructive. In that case we held that an arbitration panel exceeded its power under §10(a)(4) of the FAA by imposing class procedures based on policy judgments rather than the arbitration agreement itself or some background principle of contract law that would affect its interpretation. We then held that the agreement at issue, which was silent on the question of class procedures, could not be interpreted to allow them because the "changes brought about by the shift from bilateral arbitration to class-action arbitration" are "fundamental." This is obvious as a structural matter: Classwide arbitration includes absent parties, necessitating additional and different procedures and involving higher stakes. Confidentiality becomes more difficult. And while it is theoretically possible to select an arbitrator with some expertise relevant to the class-certification question, arbitrators are not generally knowledgeable in the often-dominant procedural aspects of certification, such as the protection of absent parties. The conclusion follows

---

5. Relying upon nothing more indicative of congressional understanding than statements of witnesses in committee hearings and a press release of Secretary of Commerce Herbert Hoover, the dissent suggests that Congress "thought that arbitration would be used primarily where merchants sought to resolve disputes of fact . . . [and] possessed roughly equivalent bargaining power." Such a limitation appears nowhere in the text of the FAA and has been explicitly rejected by our cases. "Relationships between securities dealers and investors, for example, may involve unequal bargaining power, but we [have] nevertheless held . . . that agreements to arbitrate in that context are enforceable." [*Gilmer v. Interstate/Johnson Lane Corp.*]

that class arbitration, to the extent it is manufactured by *Discover Bank* rather than consensual, is inconsistent with the FAA.

First, the switch from bilateral to class arbitration sacrifices the principal advantage of arbitration—its informality—and makes the process slower, more costly, and more likely to generate procedural morass than final judgment. "In bilateral arbitration, parties forgo the procedural rigor and appellate review of the courts in order to realize the benefits of private dispute resolution: lower costs, greater efficiency and speed, and the ability to choose expert adjudicators to resolve specialized disputes." [*Stolt-Nielsen*]. But before an arbitrator may decide the merits of a claim in classwide procedures, he must first decide, for example, whether the class itself may be certified, whether the named parties are sufficiently representative and typical, and how discovery for the class should be conducted. [The majority cited data indicating that class consumer arbitration took far longer than individual arbitration.]

Second, class arbitration *requires* procedural formality. The AAA's rules governing class arbitrations mimic the Federal Rules of Civil Procedure for class litigation. Compare AAA, Supplementary Rules for Class Arbitrations (effective Oct. 8, 2003), online at http://www.adr.org/sp.asp?id=21936, with FED. RULE CIV. PROC. *23*. And while parties can alter those procedures by contract, an alternative is not obvious. If procedures are too informal, absent class members would not be bound by the arbitration. For a class-action money judgment to bind absentees in litigation, class representatives must at all times adequately represent absent class members, and absent members must be afforded notice, an opportunity to be heard, and a right to opt out of the class. *Phillips Petroleum Co. v. Shutts*, 472 U.S. 797, 811-12 (1985). At least this amount of process would presumably be required for absent parties to be bound by the results of arbitration.

We find it unlikely that in passing the FAA Congress meant to leave the disposition of these procedural requirements to an arbitrator. Indeed, class arbitration was not even envisioned by Congress when it passed the FAA in 1925; as the California Supreme Court admitted in *Discover Bank*, class arbitration is a "relatively recent development." And it is at the very least odd to think that an arbitrator would be entrusted with ensuring that third parties' due process rights are satisfied.

Third, class arbitration greatly increases risks to defendants. Informal procedures do of course have a cost: The absence of multilayered review makes it more likely that errors will go uncorrected. Defendants are willing to accept the costs of these errors in arbitration, since their impact is limited to the size of individual disputes, and presumably outweighed by savings from avoiding the courts. But when damages allegedly owed to tens of thousands of potential claimants are aggregated and decided at once, the risk of an error will often become unacceptable. Faced with even a small chance of a devastating loss, defendants will be pressured into settling questionable claims. Other courts have noted the risk of "in terrorem" settlements that class actions entail, see, *e.g.*, *Kohen v. Pac. Inv. Mgmt. Co. LLC & PIMCO Funds*, 571 F.3d 672, 677-78 (CA7 2009), and class arbitration would be no different.

Arbitration is poorly suited to the higher stakes of class litigation. In litigation, a defendant may appeal a certification decision on an interlocutory basis and, if unsuccessful, may appeal from a final judgment as well. Questions of law are reviewed *de novo* and questions of fact for clear error. In contrast, 9 U.S.C. §10 allows a court to vacate an arbitral award *only* where the award "was procured by corruption, fraud, or undue means"; "there was evident partiality or corruption in the arbitrators"; "the arbitrators were guilty of misconduct in refusing to postpone the hearing . . . or in refusing to hear evidence pertinent and material to the controversy[,] or of any other misbehavior by which the rights of any party have been prejudiced"; or if the "arbitrators exceeded their powers, or so imperfectly executed them that a mutual, final, and definite award . . . was not made." . . . And parties may not contractually expand the grounds or nature of judicial review. *Hall Street Assocs.* We find it hard to believe that defendants would bet the company with no effective means of review, and even harder to believe that Congress would have intended to allow state courts to force such a decision.

The Concepcions contend that because parties may and sometimes do agree to aggregation, class procedures are not necessarily incompatible with arbitration. But the same could be said about procedures that the Concepcions admit States may not superimpose on arbitration. . . .

The dissent claims that class proceedings are necessary to prosecute small-dollar claims that might otherwise slip through the legal system. But States cannot require a procedure that is inconsistent with the FAA, even if it is desirable for unrelated reasons. Moreover, the claim here was most unlikely to go unresolved. As noted earlier, the arbitration agreement provides that AT&T will pay claimants a minimum of $7,500 and twice their attorney's fees if they obtain an arbitration award greater than AT&T's last settlement offer. The District Court found this scheme sufficient to provide incentive for the individual prosecution of meritorious claims that are not immediately settled, and the Ninth Circuit admitted that aggrieved customers who filed claims would be "essentially guarantee[d]" to be made whole. Indeed, the District Court concluded that the Concepcions were *better off* under their arbitration agreement with AT&T than they would have been as participants in a class action, which "could take months, if not years, and which may merely yield an opportunity to submit a claim for recovery of a small percentage of a few dollars."

* * *

Because it "stands as an obstacle to the accomplishment and execution of the full purposes and objectives of Congress," *Hines v. Davidowitz*, 312 U.S. 52, 67 (1941), California's *Discover Bank* rule is preempted by the FAA. . . .

[Justice THOMAS concurred. Although he "reluctantly" joined the Court's opinion, he wrote separately to argue that "[a]s I would read it, the FAA requires that an agreement to arbitrate be enforced unless a party successfully challenges the formation of the arbitration agreement, such as by proving fraud or duress." That reading would require reversal because the *Discover Bank* rule "does not relate to defects in the making of an agreement."]

Justice BREYER, with whom Justice GINSBURG, Justice SOTOMAYOR, and Justice KAGAN join, dissenting.

The Federal Arbitration Act says that an arbitration agreement "shall be valid, irrevocable, and enforceable, *save upon such grounds as exist at law or in equity for the revocation of any contract.*" 9 U.S.C. §2 (emphasis added). California law sets forth certain circumstances in which "class action waivers" in *any* contract are unenforceable. In my view, this rule of state law is consistent with the federal Act's language and primary objective. It does not "stan[d] as an obstacle" to the Act's "accomplishment and execution." *Hines v. Davidowitz*, 312 U.S. 52, 67 (1941). And the Court is wrong to hold that the federal Act pre-empts the rule of state law.

I

[The dissent reviewed the *Discover Bank* rule, concluding that it does not establish a "blanket policy" against class action waivers in the consumer context, but rather that "it represents the 'application of a more general [unconscionability] principle,'" citing *Gentry v. Superior Ct.*, 165 P. 3d 556, 564 (2007).]

II

A

The *Discover Bank* rule is consistent with the federal Act's language. It "applies equally to class action litigation waivers in contracts without arbitration agreements as it does to class arbitration waivers in contracts with such agreements." Linguistically speaking, it falls directly within the scope of the Act's exception permitting courts to refuse to enforce arbitration agreements on grounds that exist "for the revocation of *any* contract." 9 U.S.C. §2 (emphasis added). The majority agrees.

B

The *Discover Bank* rule is also consistent with the basic "purpose behind" the Act. *Dean Witter Reynolds Inc. v. Byrd*, 470 U.S. 213, 219 (1985). We have described that purpose as one of "ensur[ing] judicial enforcement" of arbitration agreements; *see also Marine Transit Corp. v. Dreyfus*, 284 U.S. 263, 274, n.2 (1932) ("'The purpose of this bill is to make *valid and enforcible* agreements for arbitration'" (quoting H. R. Rep. No. 96, 68th Cong., 1st Sess., 1 (1924); emphasis added)); 65 Cong. Rec. 1931 (1924) ("It creates no new legislation, grants no new rights, except a remedy to enforce an agreement in commercial contracts and in admiralty contracts"). As is well known, prior to the federal Act, many courts expressed hostility to arbitration, for example by refusing to order specific performance of agreements to arbitrate. *See* S. Rep. No. 536, 68th Cong., 1st Sess., 2 (1924). The Act sought to eliminate that hostility by placing agreements to arbitrate "'*upon the same footing as other contracts.*'" *Scherk v. Alberto-Culver Co.*, 417 U.S. 506, 511(1974) (quoting H. R. Rep. No. 96, at 2; emphasis added).

Congress was fully aware that arbitration could provide procedural and cost advantages. The House Report emphasized the "appropriate[ness]" of making arbitration agreements enforceable "at this time when there is so much agitation against the costliness and delays of litigation." And this Court has acknowledged that parties may enter into arbitration agreements in order to expedite the resolution of disputes. *See Preston v. Ferrer*, 552 U.S. 346, 357 (2008) (discussing "prime objective of an agreement to arbitrate"). *See also Mitsubishi Motors Corp. v. Soler Chrysler-Plymouth, Inc.*, 473 U.S. 614, 628 (1985).

But we have also cautioned against thinking that Congress' primary objective was to guarantee these particular procedural advantages. Rather, that primary objective was to secure the "enforcement" of agreements to arbitrate. . . .

Thus, insofar as we seek to implement Congress' intent, we should think more than twice before invalidating a state law that does just what §2 requires, namely, puts agreements to arbitrate and agreements to litigate "upon the same footing."

III

The majority's contrary view (that *Discover Bank* stands as an "obstacle" to the accomplishment of the federal law's objective), rests primarily upon its claims that the *Discover Bank* rule increases the complexity of arbitration procedures, thereby discouraging parties from entering into arbitration agreements, and to that extent discriminating in practice against arbitration. These claims are not well founded.

For one thing, a state rule of law that would sometimes set aside as unconscionable a contract term that forbids class arbitration is not (as the majority claims) like a rule that would require "ultimate disposition by a jury" or "judicially monitored discovery" or use of "the Federal Rules of Evidence." Unlike the majority's examples, class arbitration is consistent with the use of arbitration. It is a form of arbitration that is well known in California and followed elsewhere. . . . And unlike the majority's examples, the *Discover Bank* rule imposes equivalent limitations on litigation; hence it cannot fairly be characterized as a targeted attack on arbitration.

[The dissent challenged the majority's view that that individual, rather than class, arbitration is a fundamental attribute of arbitration. When the FAA was passed, arbitration was not yet well developed and Congress "may well have thought that arbitration would be used primarily where merchants sought to resolve disputes of fact, not law, under the customs of their industries, where the parties possessed roughly equivalent bargaining power." This would suggest "if anything, that California's statute is consistent with, and indeed may help to further, the objectives that Congress had in mind."]

For another thing, the majority's argument that the *Discover Bank* rule will discourage arbitration rests critically upon the wrong comparison. The majority compares the complexity of class arbitration with that of bilateral arbitration. And it finds the former more complex. But, if incentives are at issue, the *relevant* comparison is not "arbitration with arbitration" but a comparison between class arbitration and judicial class actions. After all, in respect to the relevant set of contracts, the *Discover Bank* rule similarly and equally sets aside clauses that forbid class procedures—whether arbitration procedures or ordinary judicial procedures are at issue. . . .

The majority's related claim that the *Discover Bank* rule will discourage the use of arbitration because "[a]rbitration is poorly suited to . . . higher stakes" lacks empirical support. . . .

Further, even though contract defenses, *e.g.*, duress and unconscionability, slow down the dispute resolution process, federal arbitration law normally leaves such matters to the States. . . . The *Discover Bank* rule amounts to a variation on this theme. California is free to define unconscionability as it sees fit, and its common law is of no federal concern so long as the State does not adopt a special rule that disfavors arbitration.

Because California applies the same legal principles to address the unconscionability of class arbitration waivers as it does to address the unconscionability of any other contractual provision, the merits of class proceedings should not factor into our decision. If California had applied its law of duress to void an arbitration agreement, would it matter if the procedures in the coerced agreement were efficient?

Regardless, the majority highlights the disadvantages of class arbitrations, as it sees them. But class proceedings have countervailing advantages. In general agreements that forbid the consolidation of claims can lead small-dollar claimants to abandon their claims rather than to litigate. I suspect that it is true even here, for as the Court of Appeals recognized, AT&T can avoid the $7,500 payout (the payout that supposedly makes the Concepcions' arbitration worthwhile) simply by paying the claim's face value, such that "the maximum gain to a customer for the hassle of arbitrating a $30.22 dispute is still just $30.22."

What rational lawyer would have signed on to represent the Concepcions in litigation for the possibility of fees stemming from a $30.22 claim?

NOTES

1. *A Consumer-Friendly Arbitration Agreement?* The AT&T arbitration agreement at issue was very consumer friendly, perhaps in an effort to make it more judicially palatable. A cynic might say that it was drafted to ensure that no class action or class arbitration proceeding would ever hold the corporation liable for millions of dollars while giving the seller the ability to refund the $30.22 to the relatively few consumers who actually filed a claim. That seems to be the dissent's assessment. Regardless of whether that's a correct view of the seller's motives, the Court's holding does not seem to be limited to "reasonable" arbitration provisions and, indeed, the Court soon held that the fact that individual arbitration would cost a plaintiff more than could be recovered from it was not a basis for invalidating an agreement to arbitrate. *Am. Express Co. v. Italian Colors Rest.*, 570 U.S. 228 (2013).

2. *Unconscionability.* Although *Concepcion* arose in the consumer context, it is applicable to employment and, prior to the decision, there were a surprising number of decisions striking arbitration clauses in the employment area as unconscionable. Indeed, arbitration may have been the only area of American law where unconscionability doctrine seemed alive and well. *See generally* Jeffrey W. Stempel, *Arbitration, Unconscionability, and Equilibrium: The Return of Unconscionability Analysis as a Counterweight to Arbitration Formalism*, 19 OHIO ST. J. DISP. RESOL. 757, 766-67 (2004).

However, despite the Court's ruling in *Concepcion*, it did not hold that arbitration agreements could never be unconscionable. Thus, the prior case law may still be relevant to attacks on arbitration agreements, but obviously after *Concepcion* neither the fact that an agreement was entered into as a condition of employment nor the fact that the agreement bars class arbitration is enough for unconscionability. This is illustrated by subsequent developments in California. *See Iskanian v. CLS Transportation Los Angeles, LLC*, 327 P.3d 129 (Cal. 2014) (holding that *Concepcion* had overruled an earlier California Supreme Court decision, *Gentry v. Superior Court*, 165 P.3d 556, 568 (Cal. 2007), invalidating a class action waiver in a case alleging violation of FLSA overtime requirements).

In short, in order to find an agreement invalid on this ground, there must be proof of a more focused defect. *See, e.g., Hall v. Treasure Bay Virgin Isle. Corp.*, 371

F. App'x 311 (3d Cir. 2010) (arbitration agreement imposing 30-day statute of limitations and requiring nonprevailing party to pay costs was substantively unconscionable); *Murray v. United Food & Commercial Workers Intl. Union*, 289 F.3d 297, 302-04 (4th Cir. 2002) (arbitration agreement giving employer discretion in naming possible arbitrators and constraining arbitrators' ability to rule on authority of employer's president was unconscionable and unenforceable).

3. *"Not Arbitration" or "Waiving Substantive Rights"?* Would it be better to view cases such as *Hall* and *Murray* not as "unconscionability" decisions but rather as holding that the dispute resolution system was too one-sided to be considered arbitration (*Hall*) or as agreements purporting to waive nonwaivable rights (*Murray*)? After all, merely calling something an arbitration agreement doesn't make it one and adding remedial limitations to an agreement calling for arbitration doesn't convert those clauses into arbitration provisions.

However, the existence of unenforceable provisions does not necessarily invalidate a contract. Courts sometimes "sever" bad clauses, striking down only the objectionable provisions while still enforcing the agreement to arbitrate. *See, e.g., Morrison v. Circuit City Stores, Inc.*, 317 F.3d 646, 675 (6th Cir. 2003) (limitation on Title VII remedies unenforceable); *see also Ragone v. Atl. Video*, 595 F.3d 115 (2d Cir. 2010) (when employer agrees to waive potentially unconscionable provisions regarding a shortened statute of limitations and attorneys' fees, the court should enforce the arbitration agreement after severing such terms; the court cautioned that it might have reached a different result if the employer tried to enforce the objectionable clauses). Is this a good response to unconscionable arbitration agreements? Note that the practice is similar to the "blue pencil" approach some courts have applied in enforcing overbroad noncompete agreements, as discussed in Chapter 8, and it raises similar questions of encouraging employer overreaching. Some courts have responded to this concern by refusing to sever agreements that they view as such. *See, e.g., Parilla v. IAP Worldwide Services, VI, Inc.*, 368 F.3d 269, 289 (3d Cir. 2004) ("[A] multitude of unconscionable provisions in an agreement to arbitrate will preclude severance and enforcement of arbitration if they evidence a deliberate attempt by an employer to impose an arbitration scheme designed to discourage an employee's resort to arbitration or to produce results biased in the employer's favor."). What are the ethics of attorney participation in such drafting? *See* Martin H. Malin, *Ethical Concerns in Drafting Employment Arbitration Agreements After* Circuit City *and* Green Tree, 41 Brandeis L.J. 779 (2003).

4. *Understanding the Legal Significance of* Concepcion. A number of California decisions had struck down arbitration agreements as unconscionable, but *Discover Bank v. Superior Court*, 113 P.3d 1100 (Cal. 2005), was seminal. As the Supreme Court indicates, it found the arbitration provision unconscionable because it disallowed class-wide proceedings, and it was followed by *Gentry v. Superior Court*, 165 P.3d 556, 568 (Cal. 2007), which invalidated a class action waiver in a case alleging violation of FLSA overtime requirements. Thus, California put a major crimp in the use of arbitration agreements to foreclose class or collective dispute resolution.

It was common ground to the majority and dissent that state law could not discriminate against arbitration agreements, but California did not do so: It found waivers of the right to bring class actions in court to be equally objectionable to waiving the right to bring class arbitrations. What makes *Concepcion* groundbreaking from a legal standpoint was the majority's invalidation of a state rule that did not discriminate against arbitration because that law "stands as an obstacle to the accomplishment and execution of the full purposes and objectives of Congress." While the FAA's language—"save upon such grounds that exist at law or in equity for the revocation of any contract"—might seem to authorize nondiscriminatory state laws, the Court viewed the statute as not permitting state rules that stand as an obstacle to the accomplishment of the FAA's objectives.

Concepcion, then, turned on whether a rule invalidating a waiver of the right to proceed as a class would impede the FAA's overarching purpose—which was is to ensure the enforcement of arbitration agreements according to their terms in order to facilitate informal, streamlined proceedings. Thus, parties may agree to limit the issues subject to arbitration, to arbitrate according to specific rules, and to limit with whom they will arbitrate. Class arbitration, unless agreed to by the parties, violated that principle because it would necessarily sacrifice arbitration's informality and make the process slower and costlier. Further, because it increased the risks to employers, the *Discover Bank* rule would discourage them from entering into arbitration agreements in the first place. The dissent, of course, disagreed, leaning heavily on what it saw as the nondiscriminatory thrust of the language.

5. *Understanding the Practical Significance of Concepcion.* It is hard to overstate the significance of the Court's decision. Class actions have been a battleground between employers and employees for years, but *Concepcion* provides an avenue for employers to avoid any such risk. A valid arbitration agreement will necessarily preclude any class court suit and a clause barring class arbitration will necessarily force employees into vindicating their rights, if at all, individually.

Given *Concepcion*, among the few potential remaining barriers to contractual bars to class claims in employment cases are the protections afforded by the National Labor Relations Act. Although the NLRA is sometimes mistakenly viewed as solely concerned with unionization and collective bargaining, it is framed in broader terms and protects the rights of covered workers to bring unfair labor practices charges before the NLRB and to engage in concerted or collective action. Indeed, the "speech" implications of this protection are discussed in Chapter 7. The Supreme Court's most recent encounter with arbitration posed the question of the relationship between this statutory regime and the FAA.

In *D.R. Horton, Inc.*, 357 NLRB, No. 184 (2012), the National Labor Relations Board took up the issue of whether a mandatory arbitration clause that prohibited individual employees from consolidating claims with those of other employees violates the NLRA. The Board held that the arbitration policy violated Sections 7 and 8(a) for two reasons: first, by being drafted broadly enough to convey to a reasonable employee that she was giving up her right to file unfair labor practice charges with the Board; and, second, by infringing on employee rights to act concertedly for mutual aid and protection by barring employees from pursuing both class or group actions and class or group arbitration. The implications of the second reason are far broader than the first, since, in the employment area, it had the potential to undermine *Concepcion*'s validation of agreements barring class arbitration and adjudication. On appeal, the Fifth Circuit upheld the Board on the first ground, but it reversed on the second. *See D.R. Horton, Inc. v. NLRB,* 737 F.3d 344 (5th Cir. 2013). The Supreme Court took up this issue after other circuits reached a contrary result.

Epic Systems Corp. v. Lewis
138 S. Ct. 1612 (2018)

Justice GORSUCH delivered the opinion of the Court.

* * *

[These three consolidated cases involved employer policies that bar employees from bringing claims jointly or collectively against the employer by requiring each employee to resort exclusively to individual arbitration.]

II

We begin with the Arbitration Act and the question of its saving clause.

Congress adopted the Arbitration Act in 1925 in response to a perception that courts were unduly hostile to arbitration. No doubt there was much to that perception. Before 1925, English and American common law courts routinely refused to enforce agreements to arbitrate disputes. But in Congress's judgment arbitration had more to offer than courts recognized—not least the promise of quicker, more informal, and often cheaper resolutions for everyone involved. So Congress directed courts to abandon their hostility and instead treat arbitration agreements as "valid, irrevocable, and enforceable." 9 U.S.C. § 2. The Act, this Court has said, establishes "a liberal federal policy favoring arbitration agreements." *Moses H. Cone Memorial Hospital* v. *Mercury Constr. Corp.*, 460 U. S. 1, 24 (1983) (citing *Prima Paint Corp.* v. *Flood & Conklin Mfg. Co.*, 388 U.S. 395 (1967)).

Not only did Congress require courts to respect and enforce agreements to arbitrate; it also specifically directed them to respect and enforce the parties' chosen arbitration procedures. Indeed, we have often observed that the Arbitration Act requires courts "rigorously" to "enforce arbitration agreements according to their terms, including terms that specify *with whom* the parties choose to arbitrate their disputes and *the rules* under which that arbitration will be conducted." *American Express Co.* v. *Italian Colors Restaurant*, 570 U.S. 228, 233 (2013) (some emphasis added; citations, internal quotation marks, and brackets omitted).

On first blush, these emphatic directions would seem to resolve any argument under the Arbitration Act. The parties before us contracted for arbitration. They proceeded to specify the rules that would govern their arbitrations, indicating their intention to use individualized rather than class or collective action procedures. And this much the Arbitration Act seems to protect pretty absolutely. See *AT&T Mobility LLC* v. *Concepcion*; *Italian Colors*. You might wonder if the balance Congress struck in 1925 between arbitration and litigation should be revisited in light of more contemporary developments. You might even ask if the Act was good policy when enacted. But all the same you might find it difficult to see how to avoid the statute's application.

Still, the employees suggest the Arbitration Act's saving clause creates an exception for cases like theirs. By its terms, the saving clause allows courts to refuse to enforce arbitration agreements "upon such grounds as exist at law or in equity for the revocation of any contract." § 2. That provision applies here, the employees tell us, because the NLRA renders their particular class and collective action waivers illegal. In their view, illegality under the NLRA is a "ground" that "exists at law . . . for the revocation" of their arbitration agreements, at least to the extent those agreements prohibit class or collective action proceedings.

The problem with this line of argument is fundamental. Put to the side the question whether the saving clause was designed to save not only state law defenses but also defenses allegedly arising from federal statutes. Put to the side the question of what it takes to qualify as a ground for "revocation" of a contract. Put to the side for the moment, too, even the question whether the NLRA actually renders class and collective action waivers illegal. Assuming (but not granting) the employees could satisfactorily answer all those questions, the saving clause still can't save their cause.

It can't because the saving clause recognizes only defenses that apply to "any" contract. In this way the clause establishes a sort of "equal-treatment" rule for arbitration contracts. *Kindred Nursing Centers L. P. v. Clark*, 137 S. Ct. 1431 (2017). The clause "permits agreements to arbitrate to be invalidated by 'generally applicable contract defenses, such as fraud, duress, or unconscionability.'" *Concepcion*. At the same time, the clause offers no refuge for "defenses that apply only to arbitration or that derive their meaning from the fact that an agreement to arbitrate is at issue." *Ibid*. Under our precedent, this means the saving clause does not save defenses that target arbitration either by name or by more subtle methods, such as by "interfer[ing] with fundamental attributes of arbitration." *Id.*; *see Kindred Nursing, supra*.

This is where the employees' argument stumbles. They don't suggest that their arbitration agreements were extracted, say, by an act of fraud or duress or in some other unconscionable way that would render *any* contract unenforceable. Instead, they object to their agreements precisely because they require individualized arbitration proceedings instead of class or collective ones. And by attacking (only) the individualized nature of the arbitration proceedings, the employees' argument seeks to interfere with one of arbitration's fundamental attributes.

We know this much because of *Concepcion*. . . . [The] Court held, the defense failed to qualify for protection under the saving clause because it interfered with a fundamental attribute of arbitration all the same. It did so by effectively permitting any party in arbitration to demand classwide proceedings despite the traditionally individualized and informal nature of arbitration. This "fundamental" change to the traditional arbitration process, the Court said, would "sacrific[e] the principal advantage of arbitration—its informality—and mak[e] the process slower, more costly, and more likely to generate procedural morass than final judgment." In the Court's judgment, the virtues Congress originally saw in arbitration, its speed and simplicity and inexpensiveness, would be shorn away and arbitration would wind up looking like the litigation it was meant to displace.

Of course, *Concepcion* has its limits. The Court recognized that parties remain free to alter arbitration procedures to suit their tastes, and in recent years some parties have sometimes chosen to arbitrate on a classwide basis. But *Concepcion*'s essential insight remains: courts may not allow a contract defense to reshape traditional individualized arbitration by mandating classwide arbitration procedures without the parties' consent. Just as judicial antagonism toward arbitration before the Arbitration Act's enactment "manifested itself in a great variety of devices and formulas declaring arbitration against public policy," . . . . a rule seeking to declare individualized arbitration proceedings off limits is, the Court held, just such a device.

The employees' efforts to distinguish *Concepcion* fall short. They note that their putative NLRA defense would render an agreement "illegal" as a matter of federal statutory law rather than "unconscionable" as a matter of state common law. But we don't see how that distinction makes any difference in light of *Concepcion*'s rationale and rule. Illegality, like unconscionability, may be a traditional, generally applicable contract defense in many cases, including arbitration cases. But an argument that a contract is unenforceable *just because it requires bilateral arbitration* is a different creature. A defense of that kind, *Concepcion* tells us, is one that impermissibly disfavors arbitration whether it sounds in illegality or unconscionability. . . . At the end of our encounter with the Arbitration Act, then, it appears just as it did at the beginning: a congressional command requiring us to enforce, not override, the terms of the arbitration agreements before us.

III

But that's not the end of it. Even if the Arbitration Act normally requires us to enforce arbitration agreements like theirs, the employees reply that the NLRA overrides that guidance in these cases and commands us to hold their agreements unlawful yet.

This argument faces a stout uphill climb. When confronted with two Acts of Congress allegedly touching on the same topic, this Court is not at "liberty to pick and choose among congressional enactments" and must instead strive "'to give effect to both.'" *Morton* v. *Mancari*, 417 U.S. 535, 551 (1974). A party seeking to suggest that two statutes cannot be harmonized, and that one displaces the other, bears the heavy burden of showing "'a clearly expressed congressional intention'" that such a result should follow. *Vimar Seguros y Reaseguros, S.A.* v. *M/V Sky Reefer*, 515 U.S. 528, 533 (1995). The intention must be "'clear and manifest.'" *Morton*. And in approaching a claimed conflict, we come armed with the "stron[g] presum[ption]" that repeals by implication are "disfavored" and that "Congress will specifically address" preexisting law when it wishes to suspend its normal operations in a later statute. *United States* v. *Fausto*, 484 U. S. 439, 452, 453 (1988).

These rules exist for good reasons. Respect for Congress as drafter counsels against too easily finding irreconcilable conflicts in its work. More than that, respect for the separation of powers counsels restraint. Allowing judges to pick and choose between statutes risks transforming them from expounders of what the law *is* into policymakers choosing what the law *should be*. Our rules aiming for harmony over conflict in statutory interpretation grow from an appreciation that it's the job of Congress by legislation, not this Court by supposition, both to write the laws and to repeal them.

Seeking to demonstrate an irreconcilable statutory conflict even in light of these demanding standards, the employees point to Section 7 of the NLRA. That provision guarantees workers "the right to self-organization, to form, join, or assist labor organizations, to bargain collectively through representatives of their own choosing, and to engage in other concerted activities for the purpose of collective bargaining or other mutual aid or protection." 29 U.S.C. § 157. From this language, the employees ask us to infer a clear and manifest congressional command to displace the Arbitration Act and outlaw agreements like theirs.

But that much inference is more than this Court may make. Section 7 focuses on the right to organize unions and bargain collectively. It may permit unions to bargain to prohibit arbitration. Cf. *14 Penn Plaza LLC* v. *Pyett*, 556 U.S. 247, 256–260 (2009). But it does not express approval or disapproval of arbitration. It does not mention class or collective action procedures. It does not even hint at a wish to displace the Arbitration Act—let alone accomplish that much clearly and manifestly, as our precedents demand.

Neither should any of this come as a surprise. The notion that Section 7 confers a right to class or collective actions seems pretty unlikely when you recall that procedures like that were hardly known when the NLRA was adopted in 1935. Federal Rule of Civil Procedure 23 didn't create the modern class action until 1966; class arbitration didn't emerge until later still; and even the Fair Labor Standards Act's collective action provision postdated Section 7 by years. And while some forms of group litigation existed even in 1935, Section 7's failure to mention them only reinforces that the statute doesn't speak to such procedures.

A close look at the employees' best evidence of a potential conflict turns out to reveal no conflict at all. The employees direct our attention to the term "other concerted activities for the purpose of . . . other mutual aid or protection." This catchall term, they say, can be read to include class and collective legal actions. But the term appears at the end of a detailed list of activities speaking of "self-organization," "form[ing], join[ing], or assist[ing] labor organizations," and "bargain[ing] collectively." 29 U.S.C. § 157. And where, as here, a more general term follows more specific terms in a list, the general term is usually understood to "'embrace only objects similar in nature to those objects enumerated by the preceding specific words.'" *Circuit City Stores, Inc.* v. *Adams*, 532 U.S. 105, 115 (2001) (discussing *ejusdem generis* canon). All of which suggests that the term "other concerted activities" should, like the terms that precede it, serve to protect things employees "just do" for themselves in the course of exercising their right to free association in the workplace, rather than "the highly regulated, courtroom-bound 'activities' of class and joint litigation." *Alternative Entertainment*, [858 F. 3d 393, 414-15 (CA6 2017)] (Sutton, J., concurring in part and dissenting in part) (emphasis deleted). None of the preceding and more specific terms speaks to the procedures judges or arbitrators must apply in disputes that leave the workplace and enter the courtroom or arbitral forum, and there is no textually sound reason to suppose the final catchall term should bear such a radically different object than all its predecessors.

The NLRA's broader structure underscores the point. After speaking of various "concerted activities" in Section 7, Congress proceeded to establish a regulatory regime applicable to each of them. The NLRA provides rules for the recognition of exclusive bargaining representatives, 29 U.S.C. § 159, explains employees' and employers' obligation to bargain collectively, § 158(d), and conscribes certain labor organization practices, §§ 158(a)(3), (b). The NLRA also touches on other concerted activities closely related to organization and collective bargaining, such as picketing, § 158(b)(7), and strikes, § 163. It even sets rules for adjudicatory proceedings under the NLRA itself. §§ 160, 161. Many of these provisions were part of the original NLRA in 1935, while others were added later. But missing entirely from this careful regime is any hint about what rules should govern the adjudication of class or collective actions in court or arbitration. Without some comparably specific guidance, it's not at all obvious what procedures Section 7 might protect. Would opt-out class action procedures suffice? Or would opt-in procedures be necessary? What notice might be owed to absent class members? What standards would govern class certification? Should the same rules always apply or should they vary based on the nature of the suit? Nothing in the NLRA even whispers to us on any of these essential questions. And it is hard to fathom why Congress would take such care to regulate all the other matters mentioned in Section 7 yet remain mute about this matter alone—unless, of course, Section 7 doesn't speak to class and collective action procedures in the first place.

[Congress well knows how to mandate particular dispute resolution procedures if it so desires, including statutes barring predispute arbitration.]

In response, the employees . . . suggest that the NLRA doesn't discuss any particular class and collective action procedures because it merely confers a right to use *existing* procedures provided by statute or rule, "on the same terms as [they are] made available to everyone else." But of course the NLRA doesn't say even that much. And, besides, if the parties really take existing class and collective action rules as they find them, they surely take them subject to the limitations inherent in those rules—including the principle that parties may (as here) contract to depart from them in favor of individualized arbitration procedures of their own design.

Still another contextual clue yields the same message. The employees' underlying causes of action involve their wages and arise not under the NLRA but under an entirely different statute, the Fair Labor Standards Act. The FLSA allows employees to sue on behalf of "themselves and other employees similarly situated," 29 U.S.C. § 216(b), and it's precisely this sort of collective action the employees before us wish to pursue. Yet they do not offer the seemingly more natural suggestion that the FLSA overcomes the Arbitration Act to permit their class and collective actions. Why not? Presumably because this Court held decades ago that an identical collective action scheme (in fact, one borrowed from the FLSA) does *not* displace the Arbitration Act or prohibit individualized arbitration proceedings. *Gilmer* v. *Interstate/Johnson Lane Corp.*, 500 U.S. 20, 32 (1991) (discussing Age Discrimination in Employment Act). In fact, it turns out that "[e]very circuit to consider the question" has held that the FLSA allows agreements for individualized arbitration. *Alternative Entertainment* (opinion of Sutton, J.) (collecting cases). Faced with that obstacle, the employees are left to cast about elsewhere for help. And so they have cast in this direction, suggesting that one statute (the NLRA) steps in to dictate the procedures for claims under a different statute (the FLSA), and thereby overrides the commands of yet a third statute (the Arbitration Act). It's a sort of interpretive triple bank shot, and just stating the theory is enough to raise a judicial eyebrow.

Perhaps worse still, the employees' theory runs afoul of the usual rule that Congress "does not alter the fundamental details of a regulatory scheme in vague terms or ancillary provisions—it does not, one might say, hide elephants in mouse-holes." *Whitman* v. *American Trucking Assns., Inc.*, 531 U.S. 457, 468 (2001). Union organization and collective bargaining in the workplace are the bread and butter of the NLRA, while the particulars of dispute resolution procedures in Article III courts or arbitration proceedings are usually left to other statutes and rules—not least the Federal Rules of Civil Procedure, the Arbitration Act, and the FLSA. It's more than a little doubtful that Congress would have tucked into the mousehole of Section 7's catchall term an elephant that tramples the work done by these other laws; flattens the parties' contracted-for dispute resolution procedures; and seats the Board as supreme superintendent of claims arising under a statute it doesn't even administer.

Nor does it help to fold yet another statute into the mix. At points, the employees suggest that the Norris-LaGuardia Act, a precursor of the NLRA, also renders their arbitration agreements unenforceable. But the Norris-LaGuardia Act adds nothing here. It declares "[un]enforceable" contracts that conflict with its policy of protecting workers' "concerted activities for the purpose of collective bargaining or other mutual aid or protection." 29 U.S.C. §§ 102, 103. That is the same policy the NLRA advances and, as we've seen, it does not conflict with Congress's statutory directions favoring arbitration. . . .

What all these textual and contextual clues indicate, our precedents confirm. In many cases over many years, this Court has heard and rejected efforts to conjure conflicts between the Arbitration Act and other federal statutes. In fact, this Court has rejected *every* such effort to date (save one temporary exception since overruled), with statutes ranging from the Sherman and Clayton Acts to the Age Discrimination in Employment Act, the Credit Repair Organizations Act, the Securities Act of 1933, the Securities Exchange Act of 1934, and the Racketeer Influenced and Corrupt Organizations Act. Throughout, we have made clear that even a statute's express provision for collective legal actions does not necessarily mean that it precludes "'individual attempts at conciliation'" through arbitration. *Gilmer*. And we've stressed that the absence of any specific statutory discussion of arbitration or class actions is an important and telling clue that Congress has not displaced the Arbitration Act. Given so much precedent pointing so strongly in one direction, we do not see how we might faithfully turn the other way here. . . .

The employees rejoin that our precedential story is complicated by some of this Court's cases interpreting Section 7 itself. But, as it turns out, this Court's Section 7 cases have usually involved just what you would expect from the statute's plain language: efforts by employees related to organizing and collective bargaining in the workplace, not the treatment of class or collective actions in court or arbitration proceedings. See, *e.g.*, *NLRB* v. *Washington Aluminum Co.*, 370 U. S. 9 (1962) (walkout to protest workplace conditions); *NLRB* v. *Textile Workers*, 409 U. S. 213 (1972) (resignation from union and refusal to strike); *NLRB* v. *J. Weingarten, Inc.*, 420 U. S. 251 (1975) (request for union representation at disciplinary interview). Neither do the two cases the employees cite prove otherwise. In *Eastex, Inc.* v. *NLRB*, 437 U. S. 556, 558 (1978), we simply addressed the question whether a union's distribution of a newsletter in the workplace qualified as a protected concerted activity. We held it did, noting that it was "undisputed that the union undertook the distribution in order to boost its support and improve its bargaining position in upcoming contract negotiations," all part of the union's "'continuing organizational efforts.'" *Id.*, at 575, and n. 24. In *NLRB* v. *City Disposal Systems, Inc.*, 465 U. S. 822, 831-832 (1984), we held only that an employee's assertion of a right under a collective bargaining agreement was protected, reasoning that the collective bargaining "process—beginning with the organization of the union, continuing into the negotiation of a collective-bargaining agreement, and extending through the enforcement of the agreement—is a single, collective activity." Nothing in our cases indicates that the NLRA guarantees class and collective action procedures, let alone for claims arising under different statutes and despite the express (and entirely unmentioned) teachings of the Arbitration Act.

That leaves the employees to try to make something of our dicta. The employees point to a line in *Eastex* observing that "it has been held" by other courts and the Board "that the 'mutual aid or protection' clause protects employees from retaliation by their employers when they seek to improve working conditions through resort to administrative and judicial forums." . . . But even on its own terms, this dicta about the holdings of other bodies does not purport to discuss what *procedures* an employee might be entitled to in litigation or arbitration. Instead this passage at most suggests only that "resort to administrative and judicial forums" isn't "entirely unprotected." Indeed, the Court proceeded to explain that it did not intend to "address . . . the question of what may constitute 'concerted' activities in this [litigation] context." So even the employees' dicta, when viewed fairly and fully, doesn't suggest that individualized dispute resolution procedures might be insufficient and collective procedures might be mandatory. Neither should this come as a surprise given that not a single one of the lower court or Board decisions *Eastex* discussed went so far as to hold that Section 7 guarantees a right to class or collective action procedures. As we've seen, the Board did not purport to discover that right until 2012, and no federal appellate court accepted it until 2016.

* * *

[The Court then discussed deference to the Labor Board as a matter of administrative law under the *Chevron* doctrine and held no deference due.]

IV

The dissent sees things a little bit differently. In its view, today's decision ushers us back to the *Lochner* era when this Court regularly overrode legislative policy judgments. The dissent even suggests we have resurrected the long-dead "yellow dog" contract. But like most apocalyptic warnings, this one proves a false alarm. Our decision does nothing to override Congress's policy judgments. As the dissent recognizes, the legislative policy embodied in the NLRA is aimed at "safeguard[ing], first and foremost, workers' rights to join unions and to engage in collective bargaining." Those rights stand every bit as strong today as they did yesterday. And rather than revive "yellow dog" contracts against union organizing that the NLRA outlawed back in 1935, today's decision merely declines to read into the NLRA a novel right to class action procedures that the Board's own general counsel disclaimed as recently as 2010.

Instead of overriding Congress's policy judgments, today's decision seeks to honor them. This much the dissent surely knows. Shortly after invoking the specter of *Lochner*, it turns around and criticizes the Court for trying *too hard* to abide the Arbitration Act's "'liberal federal policy favoring arbitration agreements,'" *Howsam* v. *Dean Witter Reynolds, Inc.*, 537 U.S. 79, 83 (2002), saying we "'ski'" too far down the "'slippery slope'" of this Court's arbitration precedent. But the dissent's real complaint lies with the mountain of precedent itself. The dissent spends page after page relitigating our Arbitration Act precedents, rehashing arguments this Court has heard and rejected many times in many cases that no party has asked us to revisit.

When at last it reaches the question of applying our precedent, the dissent offers little, and understandably so. Our precedent clearly teaches that a contract defense "conditioning the enforceability of certain arbitration agreements on the availability of classwide arbitration procedures" is inconsistent with the Arbitration Act and its saving clause. *Concepcion*. And that, of course, is exactly what the employees' proffered defense seeks to do.

Nor is the dissent's reading of the NLRA any more available to us than its reading of the Arbitration Act. The dissent imposes a vast construction on Section

966 ══ 13. *Managing the Risks and Costs of Liability in Employment Disputes*

7's language. But a statute's meaning does not always "turn solely" on the broadest imaginable "definitions of its component words." *Yates* v. *United States*, 135 S. Ct. 1074 (2015) (plurality opinion). Linguistic and statutory context also matter. We have offered an extensive explanation why those clues support our reading today. By contrast, the dissent rests its interpretation on legislative history. But legislative history is not the law. . . . Besides, when it comes to the legislative history here, it seems Congress "did not discuss the right to file class or consolidated claims against employers." *D. R. Horton*. So the dissent seeks instead to divine messages from congressional commentary directed to different questions altogether—a project that threatens to "substitute [the Court] for the Congress."

. . . . .The dissent proceeds to argue that its expansive reading of the NLRA conflicts with and should prevail over the Arbitration Act. The NLRA leaves the Arbitration Act without force, the dissent says, because it provides the more "pinpointed" direction. Even taken on its own terms, though, this argument quickly faces trouble. The dissent says the NLRA is the more specific provision because it supposedly "speaks directly to group action by employees," while the Arbitration Act doesn't speak to such actions. But the question before us is whether courts must enforce particular arbitration agreements according to their terms. And it's the Arbitration Act that speaks directly to the enforceability of arbitration agreements, while the NLRA doesn't mention arbitration at all. So if forced to choose between the two, we might well say the Arbitration Act offers the more on-point instruction. . . .

Ultimately, the dissent retreats to policy arguments. It argues that we should read a class and collective action right into the NLRA to promote the enforcement of wage and hour laws. But it's altogether unclear why the dissent expects to find such a right in the NLRA rather than in statutes like the FLSA that actually regulate wages and hours. Or why we should read the NLRA as mandating the availability of class or collective actions when the FLSA expressly authorizes them yet allows parties to contract for bilateral arbitration instead. While the dissent is no doubt right that class actions can enhance enforcement by "spread[ing] the costs of litigation," it's also well known that they can unfairly "plac[e] pressure on the defendant to settle even unmeritorious claims," *Shady Grove Orthopedic Associates, P. A.* v. *Allstate Ins. Co.*, 559 U.S. 393, 445, n. 3 (2010) (GINSBURG, J., dissenting). The respective merits of class actions and private arbitration as means of enforcing the law are questions constitutionally entrusted not to the courts to decide but to the policymakers in the political branches where those questions remain hotly contested. . . . This Court is not free to substitute its preferred economic policies for those chosen by the people's representatives. *That*, we had always understood, was *Lochner*'s sin.

* * *

[Justice THOMAS' concurring opinion is omitted.]

Justice GINSBURG, with whom Justice BREYER, Justice SOTOMAYOR, and Justice KAGAN join, dissenting.

The employees in these cases complain that their employers have underpaid them in violation of the wage and hours prescriptions of the Fair Labor Standards Act of 1938 and analogous state laws. Individually, their claims are small, scarcely of a size warranting the expense of seeking redress alone. But by joining together with others similarly circumstanced, employees can gain effective redress for wage underpayment commonly experienced. To block such concerted action, their employers required them to sign, as a condition of employment, arbitration agreements banning collective judicial and arbitral proceedings of any kind. The question presented: Does the Federal Arbitration Act permit employers to insist that their employees, whenever seeking redress for commonly experienced wage loss, go it alone, never mind the right secured to employees by the National Labor Relations Act "to engage in . . . concerted activities" for their "mutual aid or protection"? § 157. The answer should be a resounding "No."

In the NLRA and its forerunner, the Norris-LaGuardia Act (NLGA), 29 U. S. C. § 101 *et seq.*, Congress acted on an acute awareness: For workers striving to gain from their employers decent terms and conditions of employment, there is strength in numbers. A single employee, Congress understood, is disarmed in dealing with an employer. The Court today subordinates employee-protective labor legislation to the Arbitration Act. In so doing, the Court forgets the labor market imbalance that gave rise to the NLGA and the NLRA, and ignores the destructive consequences of diminishing the right of employees "to band together in confronting an employer." *NLRB v. City Disposal Systems, Inc.*, 465 U. S. 822, 835 (1984). Congressional correction of the Court's elevation of the FAA over workers' rights to act in concert is urgently in order.

To explain why the Court's decision is egregiously wrong, I first refer to the extreme imbalance once prevalent in our Nation's workplaces, and Congress' aim in the NLGA and the NLRA to place employers and employees on a more equal footing. I then explain why the Arbitration Act, sensibly read, does not shrink the NLRA's protective sphere.

I

It was once the dominant view of this Court that "[t]he right of a person to sell his labor upon such terms as he deems proper is . . . the same as the right of the purchaser of labor to prescribe [working] conditions." *Adair* v. *United States*, 208 U.S. 161, 174 (1908) (invalidating federal law prohibiting interstate railroad employers from discharging or discriminating against employees based on their membership in labor organizations). . . .

The NLGA and the NLRA operate on a different premise, that employees must have the capacity to act collectively in order to match their employers' clout in setting terms and conditions of employment. For decades, the Court's decisions have reflected that understanding.

A

The end of the 19th century and beginning of the 20th was a tumultuous era in the history of our Nation's labor relations. Under economic conditions then prevailing, workers often had to accept employment on whatever terms employers dictated. Aiming to secure better pay, shorter workdays, and safer workplaces, workers increasingly sought to band together to make their demands effective. Employers, in turn, engaged in a variety of tactics to hinder workers' efforts to act in concert for their mutual benefit. Notable among such devices was the "yel-low-dog contract." Such agreements, which employers required employees to sign as a condition of employment, typically commanded employees to abstain from joining labor unions. Many of the employer-designed agreements cast an even wider net, "proscrib[ing] all manner of concerted activities." Finkin, The Meaning and Contemporary Vitality of the Norris-LaGuardia Act, 93 Neb. L. Rev. 6, 16 (2014). . . .

Early legislative efforts to protect workers' rights to band together were unavailing. Courts, including this one, invalidated the legislation based on then-ascendant notions about employers' and employees' constitutional right to "liberty of contract." See *Coppage*, 236 U. S. [1, 26 (1915)]. . . .

In the 1930's, legislative efforts to safeguard vulnerable workers found more receptive audiences. As the Great Depression shifted political winds further in favor of worker-protective laws, Congress passed two statutes aimed at protecting employees' associational rights. First, in 1932, Congress passed the NLGA, which regulates the employer-employee relationship indirectly. Section 2 of the Act declares:

> Whereas . . . the individual unorganized worker is commonly helpless to exercise actual liberty of contract and to protect his freedom of labor, . . . it is necessary that he have full freedom of association, self-organization, and designation of representatives of his own choosing, . . . and that he shall be free from the interference, restraint, or coercion of employers . . . in the designation of such representatives or in self-organization or in other concerted activities for the purpose of collective bargaining or other mutual aid or protection.

29 U.S.C. § 102. Section 3 provides that federal courts shall not enforce "any . . . undertaking or promise in conflict with the public policy declared in [§ 2]." § 103. In adopting these provisions, Congress sought to render ineffective employer-imposed contracts proscribing employees' concerted activity of any and every kind. While banning court enforcement of contracts proscribing concerted action by employees, the NLGA did not directly prohibit coercive employer practices.

But Congress did so three years later, in 1935, when it enacted the NLRA. Relevant here, § 7 of the NLRA guarantees employees "the right to self-organization, to form, join, or assist labor organizations, to bargain collectively through represent-atives of their own choosing, *and to engage in other concerted activities for the purpose of collective bargaining or other mutual aid or protection*." 29 U.S.C. § 157 (emphasis added). Section 8(a)(1) safeguards those rights by making it an "unfair labor prac-tice" for an employer to "interfere with, restrain, or coerce employees in the exercise of the rights guaranteed in [§ 7]." § 158(a)(1). To oversee the Act's guarantees, the Act established the National Labor Relations Board (Board or NLRB), an inde-pendent regulatory agency empowered to administer "labor policy for the Nation." *San Diego Building Trades Council* v. *Garmon*, 359 U. S. 236, 242 (1959); see 29 U.S.C. § 160. . . .

B

Despite the NLRA's prohibitions, the employers in the cases now before the Court required their employees to sign contracts stipulating to submission of wage and hours claims to binding arbitration, and to do so only one-by-one.[2] When employees subsequently filed wage and hours claims in federal court and sought to invoke the collective-litigation procedures provided for in the FLSA and Federal Rules of Civil Procedure,[3] the employers moved to compel individual arbitration. The Arbitration Act, in their view, requires courts to enforce their take-it-or-leave-it arbitration agreements as written, including the collective-litigation abstinence demanded therein.

In resisting enforcement of the group-action foreclosures, the employees involved in this litigation do not urge that they must have access to a judicial forum. They argue only that the NLRA prohibits their employers from denying them the right to pursue work-related claims in concert in any forum. If they may be stopped by employer-dictated terms from pursuing collective procedures in court, they maintain, they must at least have access to similar procedures in an arbitral forum.

C

Although the NLRA safeguards, first and foremost, workers' rights to join unions and to engage in collective bargaining, the statute speaks more embracively. In addition to protecting employees' rights "to form, join, or assist labor organizations" and "to bargain collectively through representatives of their own choosing," the Act protects employees' rights "to engage in *other* concerted activities for the purpose of . . . mutual aid or protection." 29 U.S.C. § 157 (emphasis added). . . .

Suits to enforce workplace rights collectively fit comfortably under the umbrella "concerted activities for the purpose of . . . mutual aid or protection." 29 U.S.C. § 157. "Concerted" means "[p]lanned or accomplished together; combined." American Heritage Dictionary 381 (5th ed. 2011). "Mutual" means "reciprocal." *Id.*, at 1163. When employees meet the requirements for litigation of shared legal claims in joint, collective, and class proceedings, the litigation of their claims is undoubtedly "accomplished together." By joining hands in litigation, workers can spread the costs of litigation and reduce the risk of employer retaliation.

---

2. The Court's opinion opens with the question: "Should employees and employers be allowed to agree that any disputes between them will be resolved through one-on-one arbitration?" Were the "agreements" genuinely bilateral? Petitioner Epic Systems Corporation e-mailed its employees an arbitration agreement requiring resolution of wage and hours claims by individual arbitration. The agreement provided that if the employees "continue[d] to work at Epic," they would "be deemed to have accepted th[e] Agreement." Ernst & Young similarly e-mailed its employees an arbitration agreement, which stated that the employees' continued employment would indicate their assent to the agreement's terms. Epic's and Ernst & Young's employees thus faced a Hobson's choice: accept arbitration on their employer's terms or give up their jobs.

3. The FLSA establishes an opt-in collective-litigation procedure for employees seeking to recover unpaid wages and overtime pay. See 29 U.S.C. § 216(b). In particular, it authorizes "one or more employees" to maintain an action "in behalf of himself or themselves and other employees similarly situated." *Ibid.* "Similarly situated" employees may become parties to an FLSA collective action (and may share in the recovery) only if they file written notices of consent to be joined as parties. *Ibid.* The Federal Rules of Civil Procedure provide two collective-litigation procedures relevant here. First, Rule 20(a) permits individuals to join as plaintiffs in a single action if they assert claims arising out of the same transaction or occurrence and their claims involve common questions of law or fact. Second, Rule 23 establishes an opt-out class-action procedure, pursuant to which "[o]ne or more members of a class" may bring an action on behalf of the entire class if specified prerequisites are met.

Recognizing employees' right to engage in collective employment litigation and shielding that right from employer blockage are firmly rooted in the NLRA's design. Congress expressed its intent, when it enacted the NLRA, to "protec[t] the exercise by workers of full freedom of association," thereby remedying "[t]he inequality of bargaining power" workers faced. 29 U.S.C. § 151; see, *e.g., Eastex, Inc.* v. *NLRB*, 437 U.S. 556, 567 (1978) (the Act's policy is "to protect the right of workers to act together to better their working conditions" (internal quotation marks omitted)). . . . There can be no serious doubt that collective litigation is one way workers may associate with one another to improve their lot.

Since the Act's earliest days, the Board and federal courts have understood § 7's "concerted activities" clause to protect myriad ways in which employees may join together to advance their shared interests. For example, the Board and federal courts have affirmed that the Act shields employees from employer interference when they participate in concerted appeals to the media, *e.g., NLRB* v. *Peter Cailler Kohler Swiss Chocolates Co.*, 130 F. 2d 503, 505-506 (CA2 1942), legislative bodies, *e.g., Bethlehem Ship-building Corp.* v. *NLRB*, 114 F. 2d 930, 937 (CA1 1940), and government agencies, *e.g., Moss Planing Mill Co.*, 103 N. L. R. B. 414, 418-419, enf'd, 206 F. 2d 557 (CA4 1953). "The 74th Congress," this Court has noted, "knew well enough that labor's cause often is advanced on fronts other than collective bargaining and grievance settlement within the immediate employment context." *Eastex.*

Crucially important here, for over 75 years, the Board has held that the NLRA safeguards employees from employer interference when they pursue joint, collective, and class suits related to the terms and conditions of their employment. See, *e.g., Spandsco Oil and Royalty Co.*, 42 N. L. R. B. 942, 948-949 (1942) (three employees' joint filing of FLSA suit ranked as concerted activity protected by the NLRA); *Poultrymen's Service Corp.*, 41 N. L. R. B. 444, 460-463, and n. 28 (1942) (same with respect to employee's filing of FLSA suit on behalf of himself and others similarly situated), enf'd, 138 F. 2d 204 (CA3 1943). For decades, federal courts have endorsed the Board's view, comprehending that "the filing of a labor related civil action by a group of employees is ordinarily a concerted activity protected by § 7." *Leviton Mfg. Co.* v. *NLRB*, 486 F. 2d 686, 689 (CA1 1973); see, *e.g., Brady* v. *National Football League*, 644 F. 3d 661, 673 (CA8 2011) (similar). The Court pays scant heed to this longstanding line of decisions.[6]

D

In face of the NLRA's text, history, purposes, and longstanding construction, the Court nevertheless concludes that collective proceedings do not fall within the scope of § 7. None of the Court's reasons for diminishing § 7 should carry the day.

---

6. In 2012, the Board held that employer-imposed contracts barring group litigation in any forum— arbitral or judicial—are unlawful. *D. R. Horton*, 357 N.L.R.B. 2277. In so ruling, the Board simply applied its precedents recognizing that (1) employees have a § 7 right to engage in collective employment litigation and (2) employers cannot lawfully require employees to sign away their § 7 rights. It broke no new ground.

1

The Court relies principally on the *ejusdem generis* canon. . . . The Court concludes that § 7 should, therefore, be read to protect "things employees 'just do' for themselves." It is far from apparent why joining hands in litigation would not qualify as "things employees just do for themselves." In any event, there is no sound reason to employ the *ejusdem generis* canon to narrow § 7's protections in the manner the Court suggests.

The *ejusdem generis* canon may serve as a useful guide where it is doubtful Congress intended statutory words or phrases to have the broad scope their ordinary meaning conveys. Courts must take care, however, not to deploy the canon to undermine Congress' efforts to draft encompassing legislation. Nothing suggests that Congress envisioned a cramped construction of the NLRA. Quite the opposite, Congress expressed an embracive purpose in enacting the legislation, *i.e.*, to "protec[t] the exercise by workers of full freedom of association." 29 U.S.C. § 151.

2

In search of a statutory hook to support its application of the *ejusdem generis* canon, the Court turns to the NLRA's "structure." Citing a handful of provisions that touch upon unionization, collective bargaining, picketing, and strikes, the Court asserts that the NLRA "establish[es] a regulatory regime" governing each of the activities protected by § 7. . . . Observing that none of the NLRA's provisions explicitly regulates employees' resort to collective litigation, the Court insists that "it is hard to fathom why Congress would take such care to regulate all the other matters mentioned in [§ 7] yet remain mute about this matter alone—unless, of course, [§ 7] doesn't speak to class and collective action procedures in the first place."

This argument is conspicuously flawed. When Congress enacted the NLRA in 1935, the only § 7 activity Congress addressed with any specificity was employees' selection of collective-bargaining representatives. The Act did not offer "specific guidance" about employees' rights to "form, join, or assist labor organizations." Nor did it set forth "specific guidance" for any activity falling within § 7's "other concerted activities" clause. The only provision that touched upon an activity falling within that clause stated: "Nothing in this Act shall be construed so as to interfere with or impede or diminish in any way the right to strike." *Id.*, at 457. That provision hardly offered "specific guidance" regarding employees' right to strike.

Without much in the original Act to support its "structure" argument, the Court cites several provisions that Congress added later, in response to particular concerns. . . . It is difficult to comprehend why Congress' later inclusion of specific guidance regarding some of the activities protected by § 7 sheds any light on Congress' initial conception of § 7's scope.

But even if each of the provisions the Court cites had been included in the original Act, they still would provide little support for the Court's conclusion. For going on 80 years now, the Board and federal courts—including this one—have understood § 7 to protect numerous activities for which the Act provides no "specific" regulatory guidance.

3

In a related argument, the Court maintains that the NLRA does not "even whispe[r]" about the "rules [that] should govern the adjudication of class or collective actions in court or arbitration." The employees here involved, of course, do not look to the NLRA for the procedures enabling them to vindicate their employment rights in arbitral or judicial forums. They assert that the Act establishes their right to act in concert using existing, generally available procedures, and to do so free from employer interference. The FLSA and the Federal Rules on joinder and class actions provide the procedures pursuant to which the employees may ally to pursue shared legal claims. Their employers cannot lawfully cut off their access to those procedures, they urge, without according them access to similar procedures in arbitral forums.

To the employees' argument, the Court replies: If the employees "really take existing class and collective action rules as they find them, they surely take them subject to the limitations inherent in those rules—including the principle that parties may (as here) contract to depart from them in favor of individualized arbitration procedures." The freedom to depart asserted by the Court, as already underscored, is entirely one sided. Once again, the Court ignores the reality that sparked the NLRA's passage: Forced to face their employers without company, employees ordinarily are no match for the enterprise that hires them. Employees gain strength, however, if they can deal with their employers in numbers. That is the very reason why the NLRA secures against employer interference employees' right to act in concert for their "mutual aid or protection."

4

Further attempting to sow doubt about § 7's scope, the Court asserts that class and collective procedures were "hardly known when the NLRA was adopted in 1935." In particular, the Court notes, the FLSA's collective-litigation procedure postdated § 7 "by years" and Rule 23 "didn't create the modern class action until 1966."

First, one may ask, is there any reason to suppose that Congress intended to protect employees' right to act in concert using only those procedures and forums available in 1935? Congress framed § 7 in broad terms, "entrust[ing]" the Board with "responsibility to adapt the Act to changing patterns of industrial life." *NLRB v. J. Weingarten, Inc.*, 420 U.S. 251, 266 (1975). With fidelity to Congress' aim, the Board and federal courts have recognized that the NLRA shields employees from employer interference when they, *e.g.*, join together to file complaints with administrative agencies, even if those agencies did not exist in 1935. See, *e.g.*, *Wray Electric Contracting, Inc.*, 210 N.L.R.B. 757, 762 (1974) (the NLRA protects concerted filing of complaint with the Occupational Safety and Health Administration).

Moreover, the Court paints an ahistorical picture. As Judge Wood, writing for the Seventh Circuit, cogently explained, the FLSA's collective-litigation procedure and the modern class action were "not written on a clean slate." 823 F. 3d 1147, 1154 (2016). By 1935, permissive joinder was scarcely uncommon in courts of equity. See 7 C. Wright, A. Miller, & M. Kane, Federal Practice and Procedure § 1651 (3d ed. 2001). Nor were representative and class suits novelties. Indeed, their origins trace back to medieval times. See S. Yeazell, From Medieval Group Litigation to the

Modern Class Action 38 (1987). And beyond question, "[c]lass suits long have been a part of American jurisprudence." 7A Wright, *supra*, § 1751, at 12 (3d ed. 2005); see *Supreme Tribe of Ben-Hur* v. *Cauble*, 255 U. S. 356, 363 (1921). Early instances of joint proceedings include cases in which employees allied to sue an employer. *E.g., Gorley* v. *Louisville*, 65 S.W. 844 (Ky. 1901) (suit to recover wages brought by ten members of city police force on behalf of themselves and other officers); *Guiliano* v. *Daniel O'Connell's Sons*, 136 A. 677 (Conn. 1927) (suit by two employees to recover for injuries sustained while residing in housing provided by their employer). It takes no imagination, then, to comprehend that Congress, when it enacted the NLRA, likely meant to protect employees' joining together to engage in collective litigation.[7]

E

Because I would hold that employees' § 7 rights include the right to pursue collective litigation regarding their wages and hours, I would further hold that the employer-dictated collective-litigation stoppers, *i.e.*, "waivers," are unlawful. . . . Beyond genuine dispute, an employer "interfere[s] with" and "restrain[s]" employees in the exercise of their § 7 rights by mandating that they prospectively renounce those rights in individual employment agreements. The law could hardly be otherwise: Employees' rights to band together to meet their employers' superior strength would be worth precious little if employers could condition employment on workers signing away those rights. See *National Licorice Co.* v. *NLRB*, 309 U.S. 350, 364 (1940). Properly assessed, then, the "waivers" rank as unfair labor practices outlawed by the NLRA, and therefore unenforceable in court. . . .[9]

II

Today's decision rests largely on the Court's finding in the Arbitration Act "emphatic directions" to enforce arbitration agreements according to their terms, including collective-litigation prohibitions. Nothing in the FAA or this Court's case law, however, requires subordination of the NLRA's protections. Before addressing the interaction between the two laws, I briefly recall the FAA's history and the domain for which that Act was designed.

* * *

7. The Court additionally suggests that something must be amiss because the employees turn to the NLRA, rather than the FLSA, to resist enforcement of the collective-litigation waivers. But the employees' reliance on the NLRA is hardly a reason to "raise a judicial eyebrow." The NLRA's guiding purpose is to protect employees' rights to work together when addressing shared workplace grievances of whatever kind.

9. I would similarly hold that the NLGA renders the collective-litigation waivers unenforceable. That Act declares it the public policy of the United States that workers "shall be free from the interference, restraint, or coercion of employers" when they engage in "concerted activities" for their "mutual aid or protection." 29 U.S.C. § 102. Section 3 provides that federal courts shall not enforce any "promise in conflict with the [Act's] policy." § 103. Because employer-extracted collective-litigation waivers interfere with employees' ability to engage in "concerted activities" for their "mutual aid or protection," the arm-twisted waivers collide with the NLGA's stated policy; thus, no federal court should enforce them. See Finkin, The Meaning and Contemporary Vitality of the Norris-LaGuardia Act, 93 Neb. L. Rev. 6 (2014).

[Justice Ginsburg recounted the history of the Court's treatment of arbitration agreements under the FAA.]

B

. . . Pursuant to th[e FAA's] "saving clause," arbitration agreements and terms may be invalidated based on "generally applicable contract defenses, such as fraud, duress, or unconscionability."

Illegality is a traditional, generally applicable contract defense. See 5 R. Lord, Williston on Contracts § 12.1 (4th ed. 2009). . . . I would hold that the arbitration agreements' employer-dictated collective-litigation waivers are unlawful. By declining to enforce those adhesive waivers, courts would place them on the same footing as any other contract provision incompatible with controlling federal law. The FAA's saving clause can thus achieve harmonization of the FAA and the NLRA without undermining federal labor policy.

The Court urges that our case law—most forcibly, *AT&T Mobility LLC v. Concepcion*—rules out reconciliation of the NLRA and the FAA through the latter's saving clause. I disagree. Here [unlike in *Concepcion*], the Court is not asked to apply a generally applicable contract defense to generate a rule discriminating against arbitration. At issue is application of the ordinarily superseding rule that "illegal promises will not be enforced," to invalidate arbitration provisions at odds with the NLRA, a path-marking federal statute. That statute neither discriminates against arbitration on its face, nor by covert operation. It requires invalidation of *all* employer-imposed contractual provisions prospectively waiving employees' § 7 rights.

C

Even assuming that the FAA and the NLRA were inharmonious, the NLRA should control. Enacted later in time, the NLRA should qualify as "an implied repeal" of the FAA, to the extent of any genuine conflict. See *Posadas* v. *National City Bank*, 296 U. S. 497, 503 (1936). Moreover, the NLRA should prevail as the more pinpointed, subject-matter specific legislation, given that it speaks directly to group action by employees to improve the terms and conditions of their employment.

Citing statutory examples, the Court asserts that when Congress wants to override the FAA, it does so expressly. The statutes the Court cites, however, are of recent vintage. Each was enacted during the time this Court's decisions increasingly alerted Congress that it would be wise to leave not the slightest room for doubt if it wants to secure access to a judicial forum or to provide a green light for group litigation before an arbitrator or court. The Congress that drafted the NLRA in 1935 was scarcely on similar alert.

III

The inevitable result of today's decision will be the underenforcement of federal and state statutes designed to advance the well-being of vulnerable workers.

The probable impact on wage and hours claims of the kind asserted in the cases now before the Court is all too evident. Violations of minimum-wage and over-time laws are widespread. [See] A. Bernhardt et al., Broken Laws, Unprotected Workers: Violations of Employment and Labor Laws in America's Cities 11–16, 21–22 (2009).

One study estimated that in Chicago, Los Angeles, and New York City alone, low-wage workers lose nearly $3 billion in legally owed wages each year. *Id.*, at 6. The U.S. Department of Labor, state labor departments, and state attorneys general can uncover and obtain recoveries for some violations. Because of their limited resources, however, government agencies must rely on private parties to take a lead role in enfor-cing wage and hours laws. If employers can stave off collective employment litigation aimed at obtaining redress for wage and hours infractions, the enforcement gap is almost certain to widen. Expenses entailed in mounting individual claims will often far outweigh potential recoveries. . . .

Fear of retaliation may also deter potential claimants from seeking redress alone. . . . The upshot: Employers, aware that employees will be disinclined to pursue small-value claims when confined to proceeding one-by-one, will no doubt perceive that the cost-benefit balance of underpaying workers tips heavily in favor of skirting legal obligations. . . .

I note, finally, that individual arbitration of employee complaints can give rise to anomalous results. Arbitration agreements often include provisions requiring that outcomes be kept confidential or barring arbitrators from giving prior pro-ceedings precedential effect. As a result, arbitrators may render conflicting awards in cases involving similarly situated employees—even employees working for the same employer. Arbitrators may resolve differently such questions as whether certain jobs are exempt from overtime laws. With confidentiality and no-precedential-value provi-sions operative, irreconcilable answers would remain unchecked.

* * *

If these untoward consequences stemmed from legislative choices, I would be obliged to accede to them. But the edict that employees with wage and hours claims may seek relief only one-by-one does not come from Congress. It is the result of take-it-or-leave-it labor contracts harking back to the type called "yellow dog," and of the readiness of this Court to enforce those unbargained-for agreements. The FAA demands no such suppression of the right of workers to take concerted action for their "mutual aid or protection." . . . .

NOTES

1. *Predictable Outcome, Significant Broader Implications.* For those watching closely, the 5-4 outcome in *Epic Systems* was not surprising, at least once Justice Gorsuch ascended to the Court. Nor is one set of broader implications: As discussed in the dis-sent, the practical effect of *Concepcion* and this decision will be that many—perhaps most—employees will be subject to mandatory arbitration agreements that preclude joint, collective, and class treatment of their claims against their employers. This means that there will be fewer employment law claims litigated in court, and few collective or class actions in either judicial or arbitral fora. It seems hardly debatable that the ina-bility of employees to aggregate their claims will deter some—perhaps many—claims, particularly those for smaller damage amounts. And this will make enforcement of employee rights, especially for low wage workers, that much more challenging.

More unforeseen—but also very concerning for worker advocates—is Justice Gorsuch's seeming acceptance of a narrow view of concerted activity for mutual aid and protection. Whether one agrees with the Court's approach to interpreting the FAA or not, his assertion that concerted activity (under both the NLGA and NLRA) must be tied to union organizing or collectively bargaining is contrary to a significant body of Board and judicial case law. While Justice Ginsburg's dissent takes the majority opinion to task for this, it may be hard for you to appreciate just how ahistorical such a reading is unless you have already taken a Labor Law course. Still, recall what you learned about concerted activity in Chapter 7: Although the NLRA is often perceived as applying to unions and collective bargaining agreements, the right to concerted action applies to all covered workers, and its protection has included employee speech for mutual aid and protection in the workplace, either between employees or on behalf of other employees. *See* Chapter 7, pages 448-49. Where the majority's narrow reading might lead is an open question.

If there is a small bright spot for advocating labor rights in all of this, it is that the other holding in *D.R. Horton*—that, as drafted, the arbitration agreement and class action waiver violated the NLRA because a reasonable employee might understand it to require giving up her right to file unfair labor practice charges with the Board—was upheld by the Fifth Circuit and remains good law. The major effect of this ruling is likely to be employers amending their arbitration agreements to make clearer that worker rights to file with government agencies remain unaffected.

2. *Is There Really a Conflict Between the NLRA and the FAA?* Leaving aside the issue of the outer bounds of the right to concerted activity, which opinion has the more convincing argument with regard to the interaction between the FAA and the concerted action right under the NLGA and NLRA? If this right is to give way, it must be because the FAA so commands, and that is the thrust of the majority's opinion. But the FAA was passed before the NLGA and NLRA. Why would the earlier statute trump the later one? In the event of a conflict, wouldn't you expect exactly the opposite? Is the majority essentially treating the FAA as what has been called a "super-statute"? *See* William N. Eskridge, Jr. & John Ferejohn, *Super-Statutes*, 50 DUKE L.J. 1215, 1215-16 (2001). What would be the basis for doing so? It is true that the Court has emphasized the importance of a national policy favoring arbitration over a series of decisions, but it has similarly emphasized the importance of our national labor policy over dozens of cases. Further, the Court recently explicitly denied any "preference for arbitration." *See 14 Penn Plaza LLC v. Pyett*, 556 U.S. 247, 267 n.9 (2009); *see generally* Charles A. Sullivan & Timothy P. Glynn, Horton *Hatches the Egg: Concerted Action Includes Concerted Dispute Resolution*, 64 ALA. L. REV. 1013 (2013). *See also* Charles A. Sullivan & Timothy P. Glynn, *A Modest Opinion*, 19 EMPL. RTS & EMP. POL'Y J.103 (2015).

3. *Arbitration and Unions.* As the majority suggests, arbitration is a central feature of American labor relations, with almost every collective bargaining agreement incorporating an elaborate grievance mechanism, culminating in arbitration. But labor arbitration is the result of agreement between employers and the union as representative of the employees in the bargaining unit. Further, the union typically represents workers in any arbitration. Does it follow that because arbitration is viewed as pro-employee in this context it is necessarily pro-employee outside the unionized workplace?

4. *Comparing Costs, Comparing Access.* As discussed in Note 1 above, the inability of employees to join together to litigate or arbitrate in the wake *Epic Systems* is likely to deter claims. But it is worth drilling down a bit more on how arbitration works in practice, whether individual or joint (which is still possible *if* the arbitration clause allows it), and how it compares to litigation in court. Perhaps the first question is how arbitration will be financed. Unlike judges, arbitrators are private individuals rather than civil servants; the parties must pay for their services, which can easily cost more than a thousand dollars per day for each arbitrator. In contrast, a party need only pay a one-time filing fee to initiate a suit in federal court, and this may be waived on a demonstration of indigency.

Before you conclude that courts are more financially accessible than arbitration, however, consider the time and money that attorneys invest in preparing cases for trial. Many plaintiffs in employment cases do not pay out-of-pocket for legal representation, but as a consequence lawyers are extremely cautious about the cases they will pursue on contingency. It has been suggested that lawyers in private practice will not take on cases without a minimum of $75,000 in provable economic damages. Again, think about what types of employees are likely to have claims with this much money at stake. Would it surprise you to learn that an estimated 95 percent of employees who seek legal help are turned away? Does this change how you feel about arbitration? Of course, if arbitration is such a good idea, the employer and employee can always agree to arbitrate after a dispute has arisen—there is no need for an arbitration agreement as a condition of employment.

Even if aspects of arbitration are beneficial to some employees, that doesn't answer the question about who pays for it. If shifting part of the cost to the employee is prohibited, that must mean that the employer pays the full freight. Is that such a good idea? Won't arbitrators tend to be influenced by who is paying their fees?

5. *Government Suits.* Although the Supreme Court has supported private arbitration, so far it has drawn an important limit on the reach of its holdings as concerns public agencies. In *EEOC v. Waffle House*, 534 U.S. 279 (2002), the Court held that government agencies are not bound by a private agreement to arbitrate between an employer and employee. As a result, the EEOC or Department or Labor (and presumably analog state agencies) can take up a victim's cause by pursuing its own claim against the offending employer in court on behalf of the victim, even where that individual would be precluded from doing so on his or her own behalf. Indeed, *Waffle House* held that in so doing the EEOC could seek victim-specific relief including full monetary damages. *Id.* at 295-96 ("The agency may be seeking to vindicate a public interest, not simply provide make-whole relief for the employee, even when it pursues entirely victim-specific relief."). But before you conclude that this is a gaping loophole in the protection arbitration agreements afford employers, note that the EEOC prosecutes only a tiny fraction of discrimination charges lodged with it, and the Department of Labor can pursue only a similar tiny percentage of wage complaints. From an employer's risk management perspective, enforceable arbitration agreements still make good sense. And, of course, antidiscrimination claims are only a subset of potential employee suits.

6. *A Statutory Solution?* If one concludes that as a policy matter pre-dispute arbitration agreements of the kind at issue in *Concepcion* and *Epic Systems* are not desirable, the simplest (if at the moment politically infeasible) way to eliminate the problem is statutory amendment (as both opinions in the latter case suggest). Congress could amend the FAA to more broadly and explicitly exempt employment agreements.

Alternatively, Congress could amend the various federal antidiscrimination and minimum labor standards laws to preclude mandatory pre-dispute arbitration of claims arising under those statutes. Congress took this approach in the Dodd-Frank financial reform bill, which amended whistleblower protections under Sarbanes-Oxley. *See* 18 U.S.C.A. §1514A(e) (2018). Dodd-Frank also barred mandatory pre-dispute arbitration for the new whistleblower protections it created. *See* Chapter 4, page 262. Pre-dispute agreements would also seem to be invalid under the federal Employee Polygraph Protection Act. *See* 29 U.S.C.A. §2005(d) ("The rights and *procedures* provided by this chapter may not be waived by contract or otherwise.") (emphasis added).

7. *Limiting Issues Arbitrated.* Although arbitration increasingly seems to be generally favored by employers, it should be clear that it is unsuitable for some of the situations we have encountered. For example, a breach of a noncompetition agreement might result in truly irreparable injury if injunctive relief had to be postponed until the enforcement of an arbitration award. Accordingly, even contracts that provide for arbitration of disputes sometimes carve out certain issues. *See generally* Erin O'Hara O'Connor, Kenneth J. Martin, & Randall S. Thomas, *Customizing Employment Arbitration*, 98 Iowa L. Rev. 133 (2012) (empirical study of CEO employment contracts finding that, while half of the agreements provide for arbitration, almost half of those carve out disputes pertaining to the confidentiality, noncompetition, nonsolicitation, and nondisparagement clauses).

8. *Just Plain Contracts.* If there are few legal obstacles to employers obtaining worker consent to arbitration agreements, the remaining issues will largely be those of normal contract analysis: When will an employee be said to have agreed to arbitrate her disputes? In *Davis v. Nordstrom, Inc.*, 755 F.3d 1089 (9th Cir. 2014), the court overturned a decision that had held that the employee and employer did not enter into a valid arbitration agreement with respect to a post-*Concepcion* revision in the employer handbook that precluded employees from bringing most class action law suits. In reversing, the Ninth Circuit held that, under its reading of California law, (1) an employer seeking to terminate a unilateral contract (via a revision to a handbook or otherwise) must simply provide reasonable notice of the termination and refrain from interfering with vested rights, and (2) that employees need not be told expressly that continued employment constitutes acceptance. Having mastered the various tests for releases of substantive rights, are you surprised by the absence of a heightened "knowing and voluntary" standard for agreements to arbitrate in a case like *Nordstrom*? Nor have any courts required such agreements to comply with OWBPA where ADEA claims are concerned. *See, e.g., Rosenberg v. Merrill Lynch, Pierce, Fenner & Smith, Inc.*, 170 F.3d 1 (1st Cir. 1999). Since the federal discrimination laws afford plaintiffs the right to a jury, one could argue that a waiver or release of that right should be subject to the same tests that apply to the release of substantive claims. Although a few courts appear to scrutinize closely employee assent to arbitration agreements (*see, e.g., Alonso v. Huron Valley Ambulance*, 357 F. App'x 487 (6th Cir. 2010) (finding agreement unenforceable where employees were given only general information about employer's alternative dispute process which was provided one month after they began employment)), most simply apply normal contract analysis. Indeed, arguably that follows ineluctably from the language of §2 of the FAA.

9. *Contract Formation.* If "plain vanilla" contract law applies to arbitration, employers seeking to enforce an arbitration agreement must establish offer, acceptance, and consideration. As in *Nordstrom,* a number of employers have attempted to

impose arbitration on existing workers merely by unilaterally amending an employee handbook or providing an e-mail notification. The results in these situations have been mixed. *Compare Nordstrom* and *May v. Higbee Co.*, 372 F.3d 757, 764 (5th Cir. 2004) (assent to arbitration manifested by conduct where employee signed acknowledgment that she received copy of rules in which employer unambiguously notified employees that they were deemed to have agreed to arbitration by continuing their employment), *with Campbell v. Gen. Dynamics Gov't Sys. Corp.*, 407 F.3d 546, 556-58 (1st Cir. 2005) (no enforceable arbitration agreement where policy was distributed via hyperlink in e-mail notification and employee did not reply to message) and *Salazar v. Citadel Communs. Corp.*, 90 P.3d 466, 469-70 (N.M. 2004) (no enforceable arbitration agreement where policy was annexed to employee manual permitting employer to modify manual at will). Should the manner in which the employer establishes and communicates its arbitration policy matter in assessing contract enforceability? If most employees simply sign whatever documents the employer places before them in the application process, why is it any more objectionable to bind them to a handbook or e-mail arbitration policy?

10. *Consideration.* Normal contract analysis would not find any consideration problem in the usual mandatory agreement to arbitrate: After all, both sides are giving up something (the right to litigate in court) and gaining something (a different dispute resolution process), and, of course, the law "doesn't inquire into the adequacy of consideration." Plus, of course, the employee can be viewed as getting another benefit entirely for giving up her right to litigate: obtaining or continuing employment. Whether this analysis is too formalistic is another question. *See* Rachel Arnow-Richman, *Cubewrap Contracts: The Rise of Delayed Term, Standard Form Employment Agreements*, 49 ARIZ. L. REV. 637, 655 (2007) (arguing that employers who insist on post-hire arbitration "capitalize on preexisting [power] imbalances" between the parties by delaying "deal-breaking terms" of employment until the point where the worker already has a sunk investment in his or her new job and is unable to refuse).

However, a few courts have held that an arbitration agreement is "illusory" and consequently lacking consideration where the agreement does not treat employer and employee claims equally or where the employer retains significant discretion over the arbitration policy. *See, e.g., Gibson v. Neighborhood Health Clinics*, 121 F.3d 1126 (7th Cir. 1997) (no consideration where only the employee agreed to arbitrate); *Cheek v. United Healthcare of Mid-Atlantic, Inc.*, 835 A.2d 656, 661 (Md. 2003) (refusing to enforce arbitration clause in employment manual which reserved to employer permission to alter agreement "at its sole and absolute discretion . . . with or without notice"); *see also Saylor v. Ryan's Family Steak Houses*, 613 S.E.2d 914, 924 (W. Va. 2005) ("meager" promise to review employment application insufficient consideration to support applicant's promise to submit all disputes to arbitration).

Most courts, however, have rejected this argument, pointing out that contract law does not require equivalency of obligation with respect to specific terms but merely that "the contract as a whole is otherwise supported by consideration on both sides." *Walters v. AAA Waterproofing*, 85 P.3d 389, 392 (Wash. Ct. App. 2004); *see also Oblix v. Winiecki*, 374 F.3d 488, 491 (7th Cir. 2004) (that the employer "did not promise to arbitrate all of its potential claims is neither here nor there. [Plaintiff] does not deny that the arbitration clause is supported by consideration—her salary."). As we saw in Note 7 above, not committing to arbitration, or at least carving out some matters for the court, might be very important to some employers.

11. *Invalidating Doctrines.* If assent and consideration are established, *Concepcion* and *Epic Systems* suggest that an employee's only means of defeating an arbitration agreement is to invoke one of the traditional defenses to contract, such as fraud, duress, mistake, or unconscionability (although notice that Justice Thomas—in his concurrence in *Concepcion*—would not have read the FAA to permit any unconscionability attack, limiting the grounds for doing so to formation issues).

12. *Who Decides?* To this point, we have ignored one obvious question: who decides issues of unconscionability and other contractual defenses to arbitration clauses—a court or the arbitrator? As the cases you have read so far would suggest, issues of the validity of the arbitration agreement, including unconscionability, are generally decided by a court, under the theory that parties may not be compelled to use the arbitral forum absent an enforceable agreement. The Supreme Court reaffirmed that this is the general rule. *Granite Rock Co. v. International Brotherhood of Teamsters*, 561 U.S. 287 (2010). On the other hand, issues as to the scope of the arbitration clause, such as whether a particular type of dispute falls within the jurisdiction of the arbitrator, are generally decided by the arbitrator. The Supreme Court has made clear that this includes disputes over whether the agreement permits parties to bring class-based arbitration proceedings. *See Green Tree Financial Corp. v. Bazzle*, 539 U.S. 444 (2003). *Compare Stolt-Nielsen S. A. v. AnimalFeeds Int'l Corp.*, 559 U.S. 662 (2010) (overturning arbitral decision ordering class arbitration because it had no basis in the arbitration agreement) *with Oxford Health Plans LLC v. Sutter*, 133 S. Ct. 2064 (2013) (upholding arbitrator's order for class arbitration because the order was based on the agreement to arbitrate, whether or not it was a correct interpretation).

However, one Supreme Court arbitration case involving arbitration of an age discrimination claim blurs the distinction. In *Rent-A-Center West, Inc. v. Jackson*, 561 U.S. 63, 66 (2010), the employer's arbitration contract provided not only for arbitration of all employment disputes, but also that "[t]he Arbitrator, and not any federal, state, or local court or agency, shall have exclusive authority to resolve any dispute relating to . . . enforceability or formation of this Agreement, including . . . any claim that any part of this Agreement is void or voidable." The majority held that this committed any question as to unconscionability of the contract to the arbitrator. In light of *Rent-A-Center*, one would expect such delegation clauses to become increasingly common in employer-drafted contracts.

PROBLEM

13-7. You are in-house employment counsel for Cobalt Light Fixtures, a national company with employees all over the United States. The CEO would like to consider adopting an arbitration program as a means of reducing liability for employment disputes. She has asked you to make a recommendation and draft a sample contract. What would you counsel her about relative advantages and disadvantages to using arbitration? What features should your arbitration program have? Can you draft an agreement that would be enforceable in all states, including California? How would you recommend introducing it to the workforce?

---

2. Liquidated Damages Clauses

Smelkinson SYSCO v. Harrell
875 A.2d 188 (Md. 2002)

THIEME, J.

Appellant Smelkinson SYSCO, Inc. (SYSCO), asks us to enforce the stipulated damages provision of a Settlement Agreement and General Release that the company entered into with former employee James E. Harrell, appellee. The parties agreed, *inter alia*, that, if Harrell breached the agreement, SYSCO's damages would include the $185,000 the company paid to settle pending and future disputes with Harrell. [The trial court ruled that the clause was an unenforceable as a penalty.]

Harrell, a SYSCO truck driver for 13 years, filed race discrimination, labor complaints, and workers' compensation claims against the company. After consulting with counsel, Harrell and SYSCO settled those claims in a confidential "global" settlement covering all pending and potential claims involving Harrell and SYSCO. The parties executed a Settlement Agreement and General Release (the Settlement Agreement) dated July 2, 2001, and submitted it to the Workers' Compensation Commission for approval. The terms of that agreement became effective upon the Commission's August 31, 2001, approval of it as an "Agreement of Final Compromise and Settlement."

Under the Settlement Agreement, Harrell resigned his employment and promised never to seek re-employment with SYSCO. In addition, he covenanted that he would not "disparage" SYSCO and that he would "neither voluntarily aid nor voluntarily assist in any way third-party claims made or pursued against the Company." SYSCO, in turn, agreed not to challenge Harrell's unemployment compensation appeal and to pay Harrell a total of $185,000.[3]

At issue in this appeal is the parties' agreement regarding damages. With independent counsel advising him, Harrell agreed to the following stipulated damages provision in Paragraph 7 of the Settlement Agreement:

> Mr. Harrell agrees not to disparage the Company and the Company agrees not to disparage Mr. Harrell. . . . It is expressly understood that this paragraph is a *substantial and material provision* of the Agreement and *a breach of this paragraph will support a cause of action* for breach of contract and will entitle the aggrieved parties *to recover damages flowing from such breach specifically, including, but not limited to, the recovery of any payments made pursuant to paragraph numbers 1 and 2 above as well as payments made pursuant to the Agreement of Final Compromise and Settlement pending before the Maryland Workers' Compensation Commission.* It is expressly agreed that *the non-exclusive damages set forth in this paragraph in the event of a breach are not a penalty but are fair and reasonable in light of the difficulty of proving prejudice to the Company in the event of such a breach.* . . .

(Emphasis added.)

Shortly after executing the Settlement Agreement and accepting full payment under it, Harrell breached his promises not to disparage SYSCO and not to assist third-party claimants. In a letter dated December 11, 2001, Harrell wrote to Mike

---

3. Of that payment, $149,999 was allocated to the workers' compensation claims and the remaining $35,001 was allocated to Harrell's federal labor and discrimination claims.

Cutchember, a SYSCO shop steward, on behalf of John Womack, a SYSCO employee with whom Harrell worked. [The letter provided information about how Harrell was treated by supervisors that might be relevant to a claim of racial discrimination if it were brought by Womack against SYSCO.] The next day, on December 12, 2002, Womack initiated race discrimination charges against SYSCO at the Maryland Commission on Human Relations. Like Harrell, Womack complained that he was the victim of racial discrimination by J.B., a white female safety supervisor.

[This letter came to SYSCO's attention as part of Womack's suit. SYSCO then filed suit against Harrell for breach of contract and ultimately moved for summary judgment. The trial court found Harrell in breach of the non-disparagement clause and of another prohibiting him for "aiding and assisting third-party claims" against SYSCO. He was prospectively ordered to "perform each and every obligation" imposed upon him by the Settlement Agreement, but the court held the liquidated damages clause applied only to disparagement, and held it unenforceable because it "smacks directly of a penalty." The court found it "hard to see how a simple disparagement . . . could in any reasonable way be equated to a damage amount of $185,000." The case proceeded to trial, after which the court entered judgment for SYSCO, granting nominal damages only.]

I. Stipulated Damages

SYSCO challenges the trial court's decision not to enforce the parties' agreement that SYSCO could recover the $185,000 it paid to Harrell if Harrell breached his non-disparagement covenant. We find merit in SYSCO's challenge, even though for the reasons set forth below, we do not view the clause in question as a liquidated damages agreement.

A. *Liquidated Damages*[4]

The term "liquidated damages" means a "specific sum of money . . . expressly stipulated by the parties to a . . . contract as the amount of damages to be recovered by either party for a breach of the agreement by the other." *Traylor v. Grafton*, 332 A.2d 651 (Md. 1975). As a general rule, "a liquidated damage clause is within the substantive law of contracts, and—if not a 'penalty'—is an enforceable provision as a sum agreed upon by the parties to be paid in the event of a breach, enforceable as any other provision or valid promise in the contract."

---

4. The Law of Liquidated Damages is one of the most ancient concepts in the law. For example, one of the relics of Hammurabi's reign (1795–1750 BC) is the code, which provides: "If a man has knocked out the eye of a patrician, his eye shall be knocked out." Jewish law provided some interesting remedies with societal as well as private law consequences. *Exodus* 22:1 provides: "If a man shall steal an ox, or a sheep, and kill it, or sell it; he shall restore five oxen for an ox, and four sheep for a sheep."

After quite literally centuries of veneration of these concepts, like the camel's nose under the tent, once the concept of "penalty" crept into this area, the law of liquidated damages became *sui generis* within the law of contracts by overtly insulting the freedom of parties to structure their own agreement which is universally acknowledged to be at the heart of the law of contracts. Why should such clauses be treated differently than other contract provisions that may be equally unfair or one-sided?

. . . The burden of proving that a particular damage stipulation is not enforceable is "on the party seeking to invalidate" it. Maryland courts generally consider the following three factors as the defining characteristics of an enforceable liquidated damages clause:

(1) clear and unambiguous language providing for "a certain sum";
(2) stipulated damages that represent reasonable compensation for the damages anticipated from the breach, measured prospectively at the time of the contract rather than in hindsight at the time of the breach; and
(3) a "mandatory binding agreement[] before the fact which may not be altered to correspond to actual damages determined after the fact."

See Holloway v. Faw, Casson & Co., 572 A.2d 510 (Md. 1990). . . .

By including an agreed damages provision in the contract, contracting parties reduce the cost of contract breakdown by eliminating the expense of calculating damages and by reducing the likelihood of litigation. Either or both parties to a contract, therefore, commonly enjoy the right to terminate at some cost. . . .

The trial court, Harrell, and SYSCO premised their debate over the enforcement of Paragraph 7 on the conclusion that this is a liquidated damages provision. As a threshold matter, we point out that this characterization is not dictated by the parties' use of the label "liquidated damages." Although courts certainly consider "the nomenclature used by the parties," we are not bound by it when other language and circumstances support a different conclusion. For example, the parties' description of their damage agreement as liquidated damages "is not determinative in passing upon whether or not the payment of the designated sum is in fact a penalty." Instead, "the decisive element is the intention of the parties," which "is to be gleaned from the subject matter, the language of the contract and the circumstances surrounding its execution[,]" taken as a whole. We follow the same approach in determining whether a stipulated damages remedy is a liquidated damages clause.

Although the trial court focused on the second feature of a valid liquidated damage agreement, we shall set aside, for the moment, the question of whether the amount of stipulated damages in Paragraph 7 is reasonable. This is because we conclude that the agreement lacks both the first and third characteristics of a liquidated damages clause, in that it does not clearly identify a "certain sum" and does not create a "binding agreement before the fact that may not be altered to correspond to actual damages." By agreeing that the non-breaching party is "entitled . . . to recover *damages flowing from* such breach" (emphasis added), Harrell and SYSCO selected the same type of *post hoc* yardstick that traditionally has been used to measure actual or "unliquidated" damages. Instead of agreeing to either a pre-determined amount of damages, or to a formula for damage, in the event of a breach, the parties more broadly agreed that the recoverable damages "flowing from such breach" would include the settlement payments. Significantly, they also agreed that SYSCO's damages would . . . be "not limited to" that amount if the company also could show other actual damages from Harrell's breach. The parties' understanding that this agreement was not a mandatory and binding stipulation fixing the amount of damages at the $185,000 paid to Harrell is underscored by their explicit agreement that the stipulated "damages set forth in this paragraph in the event of a breach" are "*non-exclusive*." (Emphasis added.) Because Paragraph 7 does not contain a pre-determined "ceiling" on the amount of "damages flowing from" Harrell's breach of the *non-disparagement* covenant, we conclude that it is an unliquidated damage stipulation rather than a liquidated damages clause. . . .

B. Enforcement of Paragraph 7 Damages

It is debatable whether a stipulated damages clause such as the one before us is subject to the "reasonableness" or "penalty" standard that applies to a liquidated damages clause, or, instead, whether it is measured against a more deferent standard, such as unconscionability, that applies to other contractual terms. That question need not be answered to resolve this appeal, however. Assuming *arguendo* that this provision may not be enforced unless it is reasonable, we nevertheless conclude that it satisfies that test.

Determining whether a stipulated remedy is unreasonable "can be hard for the same reason the parties [find] it hard to calculate actual damages in the first place: what's the benchmark against which the stipulated damages will be compared to determine whether they are" reasonable? *Scavenger Sale Investors v. Bryant*, 288 F.3d 309, 311 (7th Cir. 2002). Moreover, as Judge Easterbrook observed in upholding the damages clause of a settlement agreement, "everything depends on which end of the telescope one looks through." *Id.*

Here, the language and circumstances surrounding the Settlement Agreement conclusively establish that both Harrell and SYSCO considered this stipulated damage remedy to be reasonable. They reasonably conceded that SYSCO would suffer harm to its reputation and/or additional labor and litigation expenses if Harrell continued to disparage the company for allegedly creating a hostile work environment in which long-term African-American union employees such as his co-worker Womack and himself were harassed, unfairly disciplined, not compensated for injuries, and retaliated against. In addition, Harrell reasonably acknowledged the difficulty SYSCO would have in proving a specific dollar figure for the "prejudice" "flowing from" his breach of the *non-disparagement* covenant. Thus, the record shows that Harrell understood that this settlement rested squarely on his assurances to SYSCO that this proof problem would not leave SYSCO out-of-pocket $185,000 with only a toothless remedy in the event he continued to disparage the company.

What SYSCO bought through the negotiated settlement, then, was immediate and long-term "peace" with Harrell, with the attendant right to expect that it would no longer have to expend money, effort, or goodwill in responding to his disparaging allegations. Indeed, the language in Paragraph 7 and the circumstances surrounding the execution of the Settlement Agreement leave no doubt that SYSCO and Harrell struck a bargain that was designed to prevent precisely what happened here—that SYSCO would pay Harrell $185,000 to drop all his allegations, claims, and agitations against the company, only to have Harrell later resume them. Without Harrell's assurance that he would not do so, SYSCO would not have agreed to pay Harrell $185,000 to settle his claims. Thus, Harrell's agreement that it is "fair and reasonable" for the "damages flowing from such breach" to include that settlement money was a negotiated cornerstone of this Settlement Agreement.

In this respect, Paragraph 7 fairly may be viewed as both a disincentive to Harrell *and* an assurance of performance to SYSCO. To the extent that it might arguably be characterized as exacting a "penalty for breach," we see nothing unreasonable about such a clearly understood and expressed *quid pro quo*. To the contrary, there are important reasons to enforce this remedy. . . .

In refusing to enforce Harrell's agreement regarding damages, the trial court effectively immunized Harrell from the consequences of deliberately breaching his obligations under the Settlement Agreement. We agree with SYSCO that, as a matter of policy and practice, if an employee is permitted to disregard the covenants upon which he settled, and then avoid the damage remedy that he agreed to, then "no employer should consider a settlement in these types of cases because it will likely be left without adequate redress in the event of a breach." . . .

As alternative grounds for this appeal, SYSCO complains that the trial court erred in refusing to let the jury decide the amount of its actual damages. . . . At trial and before this Court, however, SYSCO conceded that it did not offer any evidence that its pecuniary loss exceeded the $185,000 it paid in "peace money." To the contrary, counsel for SYSCO acknowledged the company's inability to prove such damages, observing that "this type of harm, which is reputational in nature, is hard, if not impossible, to quantify in dollar terms." Given this record, SYSCO is not entitled to a new jury trial on actual damages. . . .

NOTES

1. *Settlement Versus Initial Contract.* SYSCO involves a nondisparagement clause and a stipulated damages clause in a settlement agreement. But stipulated damages clauses, can be used in basic employment contracts. As we saw in Chapter 3, contracts for fixed-term or other secure employment arrangements, particularly with high-level employees, are often structured to allow parties to "breach" upon payment, either by providing severance to an employee terminated without cause or requiring forfeiture of deferred compensation to the employee who voluntarily terminates prematurely. See *Am. Consulting, Inc. v. Hannum Wagle & Cline Eng'g, Inc.*, 104 N.E.3d 573 (Ind. App. 2018). Nondisparagement clauses are becoming more common in an era of social media. As you consider the questions below, ask whether and when you might use either kind of clause in drafting the initial employment contract or in settling a matter after an employment dispute has arisen, or in both contexts.

2. *Nondisparagement versus Defamation.* One way of thinking about nondisparagement clauses is as a form of private ordering responding to the limits of tort law. Where an employee makes statements adverse to an employer's interests, an employer could pursue a defamation claim irrespective of whether the parties agreed to a nondisparagement clause. But, as we saw in the discussion of employee defamation claims in Chapter 5, the key to liability in this tort is the falsehood of the statement. Nondisparagement by virtue of a contract provision prevents the employee from saying or writing damaging things about the employer, even if they are true, not to mention avoiding other complexities of defamation law. *See Eichelkraut v. Camp*, 513 S.E.2d 267 (Ga. Ct. App. 1999) (defamation law not relevant to contract claim for disparagement). Nondisparagement clauses are related to nondisclosure agreements, which we considered in Chapters 7 and 8, but they can focus on more personal issues than NDAs usually address. The alleged contract at issue in the Stormy Daniels–Michael Cohen–Donald Trump dispute is described in the press as both an NDA and a nondisparagement agreement.

3. *Nondisparagement of Employees.* Employers are not the only ones who seek nondisparagement protection, and it is common for settlement agreements to have mutual covenants providing that neither side will disparage the other. This provides employees with the same advantages as employers in avoiding the proof hurdles associated with a defamation claim. A similar way of protecting the interests of the employee is for parties to agree to the content of any reference the employer will supply if contacted by prospective employers. While obviously useful for employees, this practice can also be beneficial to the employer in limiting the possibility of defamation claims by employees. See Chapter 5.

4. *The Public's Right to Know?* Since nondisparagement clauses prevent individuals from speaking the truth, there is an obvious tension between such clauses and the public's general interest in learning more about individuals and entities with whom they might deal. Such agreements have been criticized as private gag orders through with parties can hide criminal or other misconduct from the public eye. At the same time, they can result in backlash where such behavior ultimately comes to light. An earlier example was the Catholic Church's priest pedophilia scandals, which demonstrated that concealing serious wrongdoing can have devastating public relations effects as well as provide more ammunition to those injured by the employee wrongdoers. A current example is Harvey Weinstein and, more generally, the #MeToo movement, which has generated demands for declaring such agreements invalid as against public policy because they enable serial harassers to continue their predatory conduct. Again, recall discussion of such agreements in Chapter 7, pages 493-495.

Any such action would likely require legislative action since courts have not been inclined to strike down nondisparagement clauses on public policy grounds, even in situations where such an argument was especially plausible. For example, *Patlovich v. Rudd*, 949 F. Supp. 585 (N. D. Ill. 1996), rejected such an argument in enforcing a nondisparagement clause against a former employee physician who alleged that another doctor in the employer's practice had made a medical error and tried to conceal it from the patient. The court recognized a policy in favor of open communication between doctor and patients, but it held that it did not reach the former employee's alleged disclosure of the error and cover-up via hundreds of anonymous letters. Perhaps more pointedly, the court in *Giannecchini v. Hospital of St. Raphael*, 780 A.2d 1006 (Conn. Super. Ct. 2002), held a hospital in breach of the terms of a settlement agreement that promised a neutral reference to a former nurse who had been discharged for making serious medication errors. It did so despite recognizing that the settlement agreement, while benefiting both contracting parties, was "affirmatively disadvantageous" to future patients. *Id.* at 1010; *cf. Henley v. Cuyahoga County Bd. of Mental Retardation & Developmental Disabilities*, 141 F. App'x 437 (6th Cir. 2005) (rejecting First Amendment challenge to nondisparagement clause in agreement with public agency).

In the sexual harassment context, there is a lively debate about whether to ban NDAs in settlement agreements. The dispute pits those who worry about the down-the-road consequences of shielding misconduct from public view against those who feel that settlements benefitting current victims will be harder, and less generous, if confidentiality cannot be promised. Oddly enough, employment attorneys on both sides—that is, whether representing management or employees—tend to defend retaining such clauses. What do you make of that?

5. *Limiting Nondisparagement Clauses to Comply with Public Policy.* Most nondisparagement clauses are framed in terms of prohibiting employees from "voluntarily" disparaging the employer. The notion here is that employees are free to speak when they are subpoenaed or otherwise under legal compulsion. Thus, Harrell could have been subpoenaed in a suit by Womack if Womack learned of Harrell's information before the nondisparagement clause was signed. Further, employees may have a non-waivable right to report what they believe to be law violations to the authorities. Some nondisparagement clauses make this distinction clear, perhaps to avoid criticism that they are overbroad and therefore invalid. In some cases, there is a more concrete public policy than a generalized public right to know. We saw in Chapter 9 that the antidiscrimination laws protect employees from retaliation for, inter alia, participating in proceedings raising discrimination claims, and the Supreme Court has made clear recently that retaliation against employees but outside the employment context is also barred. *See Burlington Northern & Santa Fe Ry. v. White*, reproduced at page 679. Might a nondisparagement clause violate this provision by barring an employee from reporting a violation to the EEOC? *See EEOC v. Severn Trent Servs.*, 358 F.3d 438 (7th Cir. 2004) (finding "inadequately reasoned" a district court opinion enjoining the employer from enforcing a nondisparagement clause to prevent a witness from participating in an EEOC investigation). Should an employer's suit for breach of a nondisparagement clause be barred by the antiretaliation provisions (or more generally, the public policy tort) where the employee voluntarily discloses discrimination or other violations of public policy to an enforcement agency? What about contracts that purport to limit employees' right to collect bounties under the False Claims Act or Dodd Frank, discussed in Chapter 4? *See generally* Jennifer M. Pacella, *Silencing Whistleblowers by Contract*, 55 Am. Bus. L. J. 261 (2018); Richard Moberly, *Secrecy: Confidentiality and Whistleblowing*, 96 N.C.L. Rev. 751 (2018).

6. *Enforcing Unenforceable Clauses.* The pairing of a stipulated damages clause with a nondisparagement clause in the *SYSCO* settlement agreement likely reflects some careful planning on the employer's part. While nondisparagement clauses are increasingly standard in settling employment (and other disputes), they are very difficult to enforce by way of damages. This is because harm is often hard to prove and even harder to quantify. In *SYSCO* itself, the agreement allowed the employer to obtain damages in addition to the amount it paid Harrell, but the employer essentially conceded its inability to prove any pecuniary loss suffered as a result of disparagement. Could SYSCO have claimed the costs of defending Womack's suit as damages? Maybe not, because Womack might have gone forward without Harrell's supporting letter or because Harrell could have been subpoenaed by Womack in any event.

In this regard, nondisparagement clauses are similar to noncompetition clauses, which also pose proof of loss problems. It can be difficult for an employer to show, for instance, that a loss of business resulted from the competitive behavior of a particular employee. Also, in both contexts, the cat is typically out of the bag once the disparagement or competition takes place. For this reason, both clauses are typically enforced by injunctions, often sought in advance of a breach. Once a breach occurs, however, a stipulated damages clause might be the only way for an employer to obtain any monetary relief in such cases. The Stormy Daniels case offers a good example: Other than the stipulated damages clause, and assuming a valid contract in the first place, what remedy do Cohen and/or Trump have against Stephanie Clifford?

On the other hand, stipulated damages clauses create their own enforceability problems—the employee is frequently judgment proof. While the employer prevails in *SYSCO*, it is by no means clear that it will be able to enforce any judgment it gets against Harrell. But the mere possibility of enforcement may influence employee conduct, and that may be true even if the clause is invalid as a penalty. Some employers think the *in terrorem* effect of a possible large judgment hanging over the head of the employee is the best insurance of compliance, even if the validity of the clause is dubious. Is it appropriate for a lawyer to draft a clause that she knows to be unenforceable?

7. *Liquidated Damages Versus Penalties.* This is the second time you have encountered a case in which an employee defends against an employer's claim on grounds that the contract provision in question was an unenforceable liquidated damages clause. In *American Consulting Environmental Safety Services, Inc. v. Schuck*, reproduced at page 526 in Chapter 8, the court held that the defendant-employee was not required to reimburse her employer for training costs, concluding that the repayment amount stipulated in the parties' contract was disproportionate to the employer's actual loss. The rule limiting the enforceability of stipulated damages clause to those that are reasonable has been subject to criticism. Footnote 4 of *SYSCO* argues that freedom of contract is antithetical to court-imposed limitations on stipulated damages, and it seems to suggest that freedom of contract should prevail. The footnote is inartful, however, in its reference to the Code of Hammurabi, which is comparable to a statute that prescribes penalties for particular forms of misconduct. A closer analogy is *The Merchant of Venice*, where the parties agreed that damages for failure to repay a loan will be, literally, a pound of flesh. Is Judge Thieme really arguing that parties should be able to set whatever they wish (perhaps short of dismemberment) as stipulated damages? Perhaps it depends on who the parties are and the nature of the contract. Note that stipulated damages clauses are especially common in heavily lawyered commercial agreements between sophisticated parties. But in the employment context, they have most often been used in connection with noncompetition clauses, where the employees may or may not be high-level. Harrell certainly wasn't, and neither was Schuck. There is a lively academic literature on the merits of judicial policing of such clauses, focusing in particular on the economic case for and against intervention. *See, e.g., Lake River Corp. v. Carborundum Co.*, 769 F.2d 1284, 1288-89 (7th Cir. 1985); Seana Valentine Shiffrin, *Remedial Clauses: The Overprivatization of Private Law*, 67 HASTINGS L.J. 407 (2016).

8. *Judge Thieme's Fancy Footwork.* Whatever the commentators contend, the law has historically viewed liquidated damages clauses, unlike most other contractual terms, as subject to judicial policing. The RESTATEMENT (SECOND) OF CONTRACTS (ALI 1981) sets forth the conventional view in §356(1):

> Damages for breach by either party may be liquidated in the agreement but only at an amount that is reasonable in the light of the anticipated or actual loss caused by the breach and the difficulties of proof of loss. A term fixing unreasonably large liquidated damages is unenforceable on grounds of public policy as a penalty.

Is the law in Maryland significantly different? Are you persuaded by the court's analysis that the clause in question is *not* a liquidated damages clause? The court seems to view it as a minimum damages clause, but isn't that a variety of liquidated damages? Since Judge Thieme goes on to conclude that the clause is not a penalty, the issue is not important in this case—but note that he has cleverly set up the possibility that such clauses in the future are not reviewable for "reasonableness" but only for unconscionability, a much more difficult basis for challenge.

Judge Thieme's discussion of reasonableness is itself a paragon of confusion. He focuses heavily on what Harrell understood and agreed to, but why should consent matter if the whole point of the reasonableness doctrine is that parties are not permitted to agree to penalties? He speaks of SYSCO losing the benefit of its bargain, but the company might have used more reasonable means of protecting itself, for instance by drafting the agreement to permit it to rescind upon a breach the nondisparagement clause. Of course, true rescission would mean that, while the employer would recover the compensation paid, the employee would similarly regain the rights to assert the claims the settlement agreement was designed to extinguish. Perhaps that is precisely why the clause ought to be deemed unreasonable—it allows the employer to have its cake and eat it too. Finally, Judge Thieme appears concerned that, if the clause is not enforced, SYSCO will receive no damages from Harrell's breach. But that is simply a consequence of the fact that SYSCO cannot prove any loss; contract law does not permit damages unless actual harm is suffered.

The year after *SYSCO* was decided, the same court, without Judge Thieme sitting, handed down *Willard Packaging Co. v. Javier*, 899 A.2d 940, 955 (Md. Ct. Spec. App. 2006), which refused to enforce a $50,000 stipulated damages clause for a former employee's breach of a covenant not to compete, finding that "[n]o reasonable method was employed whatsoever in affixing the amount of stipulated damages in the case sub judice." The defendant had not been provided with any confidential information the employer had a legitimate interest in protecting, and the clause "was merely meant to penalize and punish Javier for taking a job with a competitor of Willard, rather than to compensate Willard for any loss, especially in light of the concession by Willard's officer that appellee was not possessed of any particular skill or talent, which, if practiced for a competitor, would likely result in damage to Willard." Other cases continue to see mixed results. *See Gwinnett Clinic, Ltd. v. Boaten*, 798 S.E.2d 110 (Ga. App. 2017) (refusing to enforce a clause in a physician's contract); *Kent State Univ. v. Ford*, 26 N.E.3d 868 (Ohio App. 2105) (enforcing a clause in a coach's contract).

9. *Representing Harrell.* Nondisparagement clauses are so routine that attorneys sometimes treat them as simply more boilerplate. *SYSCO* makes clear that attorneys representing employees must at least drive home to their clients the seriousness of the clause and the resultant consequences of breach, particularly when the agreement includes a damages stipulation. In hindsight, maybe Harrell should have been advised not to sign the settlement in the first place. If you were his lawyer, would you have tried to renegotiate, or would you have been concerned that doing so would jeopardize the deal? In other words, do you think the employer, if otherwise satisfied with the terms of settlement, would have been willing to go forward without the nondisparagement clause?

10. *Alternative Methods of Enforcing Settlement.* If the employer is worried about the possibility of breach and the dubious validity of a liquidated damage clause (or perhaps the uncollectibility of any resultant judgment), are there any other planning techniques available? Another possibility for an employer worried about disparagement is to structure the payout not as a lump sum but as a stream of payments whose continuance depends on the employee not breaching the nondisparagement clause).

PROBLEM

13-8. You are representing management in negotiating a settlement with the attorney for a former employee, an individual who is well liked by current employees and still socializes with them. He was employed in the Human Resources department for many years before his termination and had access to all relevant policies and their application by the corporation over that period of time. His lawyer indicated early in the negotiations that "there was a lot of dirty laundry" that would be relevant to the employee's age discrimination and state whistleblower claims. You are comfortable with all the terms of the proposed settlement, but you are very concerned about the ex-employee stirring up trouble and/or leaking sensitive information. Try drafting language to include in the final agreement that will address these concerns. Do you think your draft will be acceptable to the employee's attorney?

D. EMPLOYMENT PRACTICES LIABILITY INSURANCE

Individuals and businesses often transfer risk for financial losses they may incur by paying premiums to insurance carriers. In the employment context, employers have been required for about a century to carry workers' compensation insurance, but until relatively recently there was little market (and therefore little availability) for insurance for other employment-related liabilities. This was largely because the law posed few risks for employers, other than contractual claims by very highly placed employees, which were not the kind of loss normally contemplated by insurance in any event.

As statutory and decisional employment law began providing more meaningful remedies, some employers sought to recover both the costs of defending suits by workers and liabilities incurred when such suits were successful by making claims under traditional business coverage, General Liability ("GL") policies, or Director and Officer ("D&O") policies. These efforts were often a stretch. For example, the typical GL policy obligates the insurer to pay damages arising from property damage or personal injury caused by a covered occurrence. *See* Francis J. Mootz III, *Insurance Coverage of Employment Discrimination Claims*, 52 U. MIAMI L. REV. 1, 10-11 (1997). In most cases, the policy would seem not to cover an employee's suit, and GL policies often reinforced this with an explicit "employee exclusion" typically providing that the policy does not cover "bodily injury" to any "employee of the insured arising out of and in the course of employment by the insured." *See Am. Motorists Ins. Co. v. L-C-A Sales Co.*, 713 A.2d 1007 (N.J. 1998) (policy exclusion precluded coverage for employee's age discrimination claim). While GL policies have been found to reach a few employment-related claims, such as defamation (*see Meadowbrook v. Tower Insurance Co.*, 559 N.W.2d 411, 413 n.1 (Minn. 1997)), they provided, at best, very spotty coverage for employment-related risks.

As the threat of substantial liability increased, insurance carriers had two responses. The first was to strengthen the exclusions to lessen the risk of being held liable under traditional policies; and the second was to develop a new product: Employment Practices Liability Insurance ("EPLI") policies, which are specifically geared to employment-related practices. These policies typically cover liability arising out of the insured's employment-related offenses against its employees, including the costs of defending claims. They may also cover liability by agents of the employer (personal liability is a risk for some aspects of employment law but not for others). Risks covered include "wrongful termination, discrimination, sexual harassment, hostile work environment and in some cases, even wage and hour disputes. EPLI coverage is an essential coverage in today's litigious society." *See* http://www.epli.com/ (last visited June 7, 2018). This range of coverage, however, may be somewhat deceptive. Insurance companies are in the business of managing their own risks, and some policies are subject to significant exclusions. For example, EPLI policies usually exclude punitive damages from coverage. Further, policies may have significant deductibles to reduce the "moral hazard" that insurance creates.

There is an ongoing debate as to whether coverage of risks such as punitive damages and, indeed, insurance for any intentional employer conduct is against public policy. The argument to this effect is that shifting the loss to insurers blunts the employer incentives to comply with the law. *See generally* Richard A. Bales & Julie McGhghy, *Insuring Title VII Violations*, 27 S. ILL. U. L. J. 71 (2002). The contrary argument is that insurance actually increases compliance. Insurance companies seek to limit their risk not only through exclusions from coverage, but also by taking steps to require that the firms they cover are well positioned from a liability perspective. Thus, they deny coverage, or at least charge higher premiums, to higher risks, that is, firms that do not have policies and procedures in place to reduce potential liability. *See generally* Shauhin A. Talesh, *Insurance Companies As Corporate Regulators: The Good, the Bad, and the Ugly*, 66 DEPAUL L. REV. 463, 491 (2017) ("Insurers play a role in averting such risk and act as a regulatory intermediary because employers have an incentive to avoid discrimination; however, insurers do so in a way that focuses on avoiding litigation rather than fostering a discrimination-free work environment.").

PROBLEM

13-9. You are outside counsel for new law firm, High Tech, which expects to open its doors within the next week. The firm is comprised largely of former attorneys of a much larger firm, Hanover & Windsor. It has three partners, all of whom were partners at Hanover, and five associates, most of whom were Hanover associates. It also has about eight support staff, mostly paralegals and assistants. While the attorneys are all highly specialized in their field of expertise—patent law—they rely very heavily on you for advice on the business-oriented aspects of setting up a new business. And, because the firm's client base is still somewhat uncertain, it is determined to keep its expenses as low as possible for the first year.

You just received a phone call from Hi High, managing partner. He was meeting with an insurance agent about liability and malpractice insurance, and the agent pitched something called "EPLI" insurance against employment-related suits. The premium would be about $10,000 a year. High feels confident about his ability to assess risks for what he calls "normal" insurance, but he feels "out of my league" with this stuff.

He wants to know whether this is a good idea and what questions he should ask the agent before going forward. Advise him.

E. BANKRUPTCY AS RISK MANAGEMENT

While bankruptcy is a specialized field of study that can be, at most, mentioned here, it is a last-gasp risk management technique that some firms, particularly those in the airline industry, have successfully used to deal with financial problems caused in large part by collective bargaining agreements that impose higher costs on them than on their competitors. Another example is the automobile bankruptcies of GM and Chrysler. *See generally* Ralph Brubaker & Charles Jordan Tabb, *Bankruptcy Reorganizations and the Troubling Legacy of Chrysler and GM*, 2010 U. ILL. L. REV. 1375.

Outside the unionized setting, bankruptcy is less likely to be a tactic used by employers, but it nevertheless poses a threat to individual employment contracts. This reality means that the attorney representing employees negotiating such arrangements needs to worry not only about paper rights but also about the solvency of the company. This is an increasing concern as the length of the contract stretches into the future. Similarly, bankruptcy can also jeopardize pending employment claims. *See generally* Joanne Gelfand, *The Treatment of Employment Discrimination Claims in Bankruptcy: Priority Status, Stay Relief, Dischargeability, and Exemptions*, 56 MIAMI L. REV. 601 (2002). Finally, the financial health of the company can influence an employee's preference for lump-sum payments over more structured arrangements.

Table of Cases

Principal cases are indicated by italics.

Table of Secondary Authorities

Gowri Ramachandran, *Intersectionality as "Catch-22": Why Identity Performance Demands Are Neither Harmless nor Reasonable*, 69 Alb. L. Rev. 299 (2005), 380–381

Danielle J. Reid, Note, *Combating the Enemy Within: Regulating Employee Misappropriation of Business Information*, 71 Vand. L. Rev. 1033 (2018), 532

Lynn Rhinehart, *Workers at Risk: The Unfulfilled Promise of the Occupational Safety and Health Act*, 111 W. Va. L. Rev. 117 (2008), 843

Camille Gear Rich, *Performing Racial and Ethnic Identity: Discrimination by Proxy and the Future of Title VII*, 79 N.Y.U. L. Rev. 1134 (2004), 380

———, *Preempting Discrimination: Lessons from the Genetic Information Nondiscrimination Act*, 63 Vand. L. Rev. 439 (2010), 691

Russell Robinson, *Casting and Caste-ing: Reconciling Artistic Freedom and Antidiscrimination Norms*, 95 Calif. L. Rev. 1 (2007), 611

Brishen Rogers, *Employment Rights in the Platform Economy: Getting Back to Basics*, 10 Harv. L. & Pol'y. Rev 479 (2016), 34, 35

———, *Toward Third-Party Liability for Wage Theft*, 11 Berkeley J. Empl. & Lab. L. 1 (2010), 63, 818

Elizabeth Roseman, Comment, *A Phoenix from the Ashes?: Heightened Pleading Requirements in Disparate Impact Cases*, 36 Seton Hall L. Rev. 1043 (2006), 720

Lawrence D. Rosenthal, *The Emerging First Amendment Law of Managerial Prerogative*, 77 Fordham L. Rev. 33 (2008), 424

———, *Motions for Summary Judgment When Employers Offer Multiple Justifications for Adverse Employment Actions: Why the Exceptions Should Swallow the Rule*, 2002 Utah L. Rev. 335 (2002), 558

———, *Reading Too Much into What the Court Doesn't Write: How Some Federal Courts Have Limited Title VII's Participation Clause's Protections After* Clark County School District v. Breeden, 83 Wash. L. Rev. 345 (2008), 675

———, *To Report or Not to Report: The Case for Eliminating the Objectively Reasonable Requirement for Opposition Activities Under Title VII's Anti-Retaliation Provision*, 39 Ariz. St. L.J. 1127 (2007), 675

Mark Rothstein, Occupational Safety and Health Law (2018 ed.), 843

Nantiya Ruan, *Facilitating Wage Theft: How Courts Use Procedural Rules to Undermine Substantive Rights of Low-Wage Workers*, 63 Vand. L. Rev. 727 (2010), 818

———, *Same Law, Different Day: A Survey of the Last Thirty Years of Wage Litigation and Its Impact on Low-Wage Workers*, 30 Hofstra Lab. & Emp. L.J. 355 (2013), 63

Nantiya Ruan & Nancy Reichman, *Hours Equity Is the New Pay Equity*, 59 Vill. L. Rev. 35 (2014), 791

Paul H. Rubin & Peter Shedd, *Human Capital and Covenants Not to Compete*, 10 J. Legal Stud. 93 (1981), 485

Robert L. Rubin, *Accommodating Tort Law: Alternative Remedies for Workplace Injuries*, 69 Rutgers L. Rev. 1119 (2017), 876

———, *Our Nation's Forgotten Workers: The Unprotected Volunteers*, 9 U. Pa. J. Lab. & Emp. L. 147 (2006), 46

George Rutherglen, *Public Employee Speech in Remedial Perspective*, 24 J. L. & Politics 129 (2008), 408

Leticia M. Saucedo, *A New "U": Organizing Victims and Protecting Immigrant Workers*, 42 U. Rich. L. Rev. 891 (2008), 65

Todd D. Saveland, *FedEx's New "Employees": Their Disgruntled Independent Contractors*, 36 Transp. L.J. 95 (2009), 33

John Schmitt, *Why Does the Minimum Wage Have No Discernible Effect on Employment?*, Center for Economic and Policy Research (February 2013), 793

Naomi Schoenbaum, *The Case for Symmetry in Antidiscrimination Law*, 2017 Wis. L. Rev. 69 (2017), 555

Edward J. Schoen, *Completing Government Speech's Unfinished Business: Clipping* Garcetti's *Wings and Addressing Scholarship and Teaching*, 43 Hastings Const. L.Q. 537 (2016), 429

Vicki Schultz, *Life's Work*, 100 Colum. L. Rev. 1881 (2000), 776

———, *Reconceptualizing Sexual Harassment*, 107 Yale L.J. 1683 (1998), 652

———, *The Sanitized Workplace*, 112 Yale L.J. 2061 (2003), 662, 917

Stewart J. Schwab, *Life-Cycle Justice: Accommodating Just Cause and Employment At Will*, 92 Mich. L. Rev. 8 (1993), 114

Index